Personalize the study of human biology

Biology of Humans: Concepts, Applications, and Issues, **Third Edition** personalizes the study of human biology with a friendly writing style, stunning art, abundant applications, and tools that develop critical thinking skills.

Highlights of this Edition

The **Third Edition** features an expansion of the critical thinking elements and a significantly revised art program.

18a SPECIAL TOPIC

Autism Spectrum Disorders

Characterization and Prevalence
Symptoms
Communication
Social Skills
Motor Patterns and Behavior
Timing of Symptom Development
Diagnosis
Possible Causes
Treatment and Therapy
Fear That Vaccines Cause Autism

◀ **Abundant Applications**
See **pages W-2 – W-3** of this walkthrough.

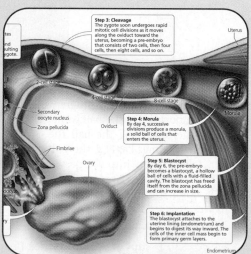

Step 3: Cleavage
The zygote soon undergoes rapid mitotic cell divisions as it moves along the oviduct toward the uterus, becoming a pre-embryo that consists of two cells, then four cells, then eight cells, and so on.

Uterus

2-cell stage

4-cell stage

8-cell stage

Secondary oocyte nucleus

Zona pellucida

Oviduct

Morula

Step 4: Morula
By day 4, successive divisions produce a morula, a solid ball of cells that enters the uterus.

Fimbriae

Ovary

Step 5: Blastocyst
By day 6, the pre-embryo becomes a blastocyst, a hollow ball of cells with a fluid-filled cavity. The blastocyst has freed itself from the zona pellucida and can increase in size.

Step 6: Implantation
The blastocyst attaches to the uterine lining (endometrium) and begins to digest its way inward. The cells of the inner cell mass begin to form primary germ layers.

Endometrium

▲ **Stunning Art**
See **page W-4** of this walkthrough.

what would you do?

For the past 50 years, some communities whose wate[r] fluoridated have added low doses of fluoride to the p[u] to reduce tooth decay. Nearly 98% of Americans have[,] tooth decay. Over 6 million teeth are removed each ye[ar] of fluoridation point out that the incidence of tooth de[cay] after the addition of fluoride to drinking water. Oppon[ents] tice argue that (1) fluoridation of the water supply is a [?] medication; (2) the dosage cannot be properly contro[lled] differences in people's body weight and the amount o[f] consume; and (3) excessive fluoride intake causes tee[th] brown and mottled. If you had to vote on fluoridation [of] water supply, what additional information would you [want] voting? How would you vote at present?

▲ **Stimulating Critical Thinking**
See **page W-5** of this walkthrough.

Special Topics Chapters ▶

Each of these eight short chapters builds on the "pure biology" presented in the immediately preceding chapter to cover personal health issues likely to interest and motivate students. This edition features two new Special Topics chapters on food safety and autism spectrum disorders. Other Special Topics chapters cover psychoactive drugs, infectious disease, nutrition and weight control, sexually transmitted diseases, stem cells, and cancer.

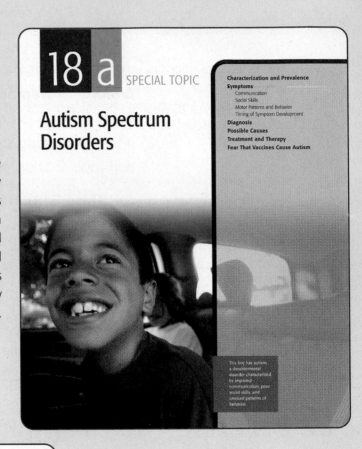

18 a SPECIAL TOPIC

Autism Spectrum Disorders

Characterization and Prevalence
Symptoms
    Communication
    Social Skills
    Motor Patterns and Behavior
    Timing of Symptom Development
Diagnosis
Possible Causes
Treatment and Therapy
Fear That Vaccines Cause Autism

This boy has autism, a developmental disorder characterized by impaired communication, poor social skills, and unusual patterns of behavior.

...To get a sense of how this "jumping" mode of transmission increases the speed at which a message travels, think of the different ways a ball can be moved down the court during a basketball game. When only seconds are left in the game, dribbling the ball the length of the court would take too much time. Passing the ball through a series of players is faster. Likewise, an impulse passed from one node to the next, as occurs in myelinated nerves, moves faster than one traveling uniformly along the full length of the axon, as occurs in unmyelinated nerves.

Writing Style

◀ The authors use **applications** and **analogies** throughout the text to anchor concepts to what students already know.

The authors also use ▶ **active learning** examples to demonstrate scientific concepts.

...Try to touch the tips of your two index fingers together above your head. You probably missed on the first attempt. However, the cerebellum makes the necessary corrections, and you will likely succeed on the next attempt. At the same time, the cerebellum calculates future positions of a body part during a movement. Then, just before that part reaches the intended position, the cerebellum sends messages to stop the movement at a specific point. Therefore, when you scratch an itch on your cheek, your hand stops before slapping your face!

Issue Essays

Three categories of boxed essays use the basic scientific content of the chapters to explore issues having broader impact on individual health, society, and the environment. These essays awaken student interest in lecture topics and provide information needed for informed in-class discussions.

Ethical Issues

These essays present balanced coverage of controversial ethical and social issues in the news today. Topics include anabolic steroid use, genetic testing, DNA fingerprinting, and scientific research on primates.

▲ Environmental Issues

These essays deal with ways in which human activities alter the environment and, conversely (sometimes simultaneously), ways in which the environment influences human health. Topics include radon gas, lead poisoning, noise pollution, and environmental estrogens.

▲ Health Issues

These essays provide current information on certain health problems that students, their families, or their friends might encounter. Topics include acne, traumatic brain injury, smoking and cardiovascular disease, skin cancer, and the common cold.

Questions to Consider ▶

These questions ask students to think about the ethical implications of certain behaviors, medical procedures, or legal issues.

Questions to Consider

- If you were the judge on the case of the United Farm Workers versus the EPA, what information would you use to decide whether to ban AZM?
- As a consumer, are you willing to pay more for foods if they are not sprayed with AZM?

Art reinforces key concepts

The stunning illustration program uses vibrant, three-dimensional figures to illuminate explanations in the text. Every figure has been touched in this edition to enhance readability.

Enlarged and Revised Art

Enlarged images and explanatory text throughout make the art program as instructive and functional as it is beautiful.

▼

▲ Voice Balloons

Multi-step art uses voice balloons to aid the reader in following complex processes.

◀ Micrographs

Micrographs often appear side-by-side with illustrations to aid interpretation and understanding and to give the actual view of a structure or process being studied.

Expanded critical thinking elements encourage students to ask "Why?"

Stop and think ▶

These periodic checks engage students in the learning process and promote active learning. Students are invited to pause, think about the concept explained, and apply that information to a new situation.

What would you do? ▶

These raise ethical questions about issues that society faces today. Students are able to see the relevance of information learned in a biology classroom to real-life problems or decisions that individuals, including themselves, must make. When the subject of these questions is controversial, the text presents examples of arguments from both sides, as well as evidence in support of competing arguments.

Q Look closely at the structure of the endocrine gland. How does it differ from the structure of an exocrine gland, such as an oil gland?

The hormone travels throughout the body.

The hormone diffuses into the bloodstream.

Capillary

Hormone

◀ Figure Questions

At least one figure in each chapter has a question that encourages students to examine the information in the figure critically. Answers are provided below the figure legend.

Becoming Information Literate

These end-of-chapter questions ask students to find and critically evaluate sources of information to answer questions or prepare a presentation on a human biology topic in the media today.

▼

Instructor Resource DVD makes class preparation easier than ever

▲ Editable PowerPoint® Slides

These presentation slides are embedded with links to *ABC News* videos and Human Biology Animations.

ABC News Videos

Twenty-eight videos, each 3-7 minutes in length, are included on the Instructor Resource DVD (IR-DVD). These videos show current events covering issues relevant to Human Biology—bringing the course material closer to students' every day lives.

Other tools included on the IR-DVD:

- An image library of all the art (a selection of which has customizable labels and stepped-out art), tables, and photos from the book
- PRS-enabled Clicker questions
- BLAST! Animations
- BioFlix™ and BioFlix PowerPoint slides
- PowerPoint slides for *Scientific American: Concepts and Current Issues in Biology*, Volumes 1-5
- *Interactive Physiology®* for Human Biology (IP for HB) Slides, worksheets, and answer sheets
- Interactive Quiz Show games for each unit
- Microsoft® Word files for the Instructor's Guide and Test Bank
- An all-electronic set of ready-to-print Transparency Masters of selected illustrations from the text
- Computerized test bank CD-ROM is packaged with the IR-DVD

beyond the classroom

The Human Biology Place
www.humanbiology.com

◀ RSS Feeds

ScienceDaily RSS feeds keep students up-to-date.

This open-access website offers a highly interactive way for students to get more involved in their studies with chapter overviews, Web Tutorials with animations and quizzes, book-specific self-tests and essay questions, crossword puzzles, and flashcards. *ScienceDaily* RSS feeds of summaries and links to human biology-related news stories are automatically updated six times a day. Accompanying *Becoming Information Literate* essay questions give students the opportunity to investigate and comment on current biology news.

▲ Multiple choice, True/False, and Essay Questions

Encourage students to assess their comprehension. Students can email results to their instructor.

Interactive Physiology® for Human Biology ▶

The *Interactive Physiology* for Human Biology (IP for HB) companion CD-ROM reinforces readings and lectures with a wealth of outstanding animations, engaging activities, helpful self-testing, and much more. This edition includes a new module on the Immune System along with assignable worksheets to help students gauge their progress and stay on track with their studies. IP for HB can be packaged at no additional charge with this book.

Teaching and Learning Solutions for Instructors and Students

For Instructors

Instructor's Guide
978-0-321-60281-7 | 0-321-60281-1
This resource provides tips for teaching non-majors by making the material relevant, interesting, and interactive.

Printed Test Bank
978-0-321-60282-4 | 0-321-60282-X
Includes over 1,000 multiple choice, fill-in-the-blank, short answer, and essay questions originally created and reviewed by a panel of educators. Microsoft® Word versions of the files are available on the Instructor Resource DVDs and for download from the Instructor's Resource Center.

Instructor Resource DVD
978-0-321-60284-8 | 0-321-60284-6
The Instructor Resource DVD provides a range of ready-to-use media supplements to help instructors teach the course, engage students, and accommodate different learning styles. For more information, see "Rich media tools" in this walkthrough.

The Human Biology Place
www.humanbiology.com
The Human Biology Place open-access student website offers a highly interactive way for students to get more involved in their studies with chapter overviews, Web Tutorials, book-specific self-tests and essay questions, crossword puzzles, and flashcards. For more information, see "Rich media tools" in this walkthrough.

Course Management Options

CourseCompass™
www.pearsonhighered.com/coursecompass
CourseCompass combines the strength of the content of the the Human Biology Place Website with state-of-the-art eLearning tools. CourseCompass is a nationally hosted, dynamic, interactive online course management system powered by Blackboard, the leading platform for Internet-based learning tools. This easy-to-use and customizable program enables professors to tailor content and functionality to meet individual course needs. The course includes all of the content found on the Instructor Resource DVD and the Human Biology Place website together with course management functionality.

WebCT
www.pearsonhighered.com/webct

BlackBoard
www.pearsonhighered.com/blackboard
WebCT and Blackboard combine the strength of the content of the The Human Biology Place Website with state-of-the-art eLearning tools. This course management system contains a range of preloaded content including everything found on the Human Biology Place website together with assessment activities and course management functionality.

For Students

Study Guide
978-0-13-507060-4 | 0-13-507060-0
This guide will help students grasp the key course concepts. It consists of learning objectives, key concepts, study tips, chapter summaries, critical thinking questions, short-answer questions, matching questions, labeling exercises, and fill-in-the-blank questions. A multiple choice "Practice Test" is included at the end of each chapter to help students assess their understanding.

The Human Biology Place
www.humanbiology.com
For more information, see "Rich media tools" in this walkthrough.

Scientific American Current Issues in Biology
Volume 1: 978-0-8053-7507-7 | 0-8053-7507-4
Volume 2: 978-0-8053-7108-6 | 0-8053-7108-7
Volume 3: 978-0-8053-7527-5 | 0-8053-7527-9
Volume 4: 978-0-8053-3566-8 | 0-8053-3566-8
Volume 5: 978-0-321-54187-1 | 0-321-54187-1
Volume 6: 978-0-321-59849-3 | 0-321-59849-0
Scientific American Current Issues in Biology gives your students the best of both worlds—accessible, dynamic, relevant articles from *Scientific American* magazine that present key issues in biology, paired with the authority, reliability, and clarity of Benjamin Cummings' non-majors biology texts. Articles include questions to help students check their comprehension and make connections to science and society.
Scientific American is available in Volumes 1–6. This resource is available at no additional charge when packaged with a new text.

Understanding Human Biology: Laboratory Exercises, Second Edition
978-0-13-179009-4 | 0-13-179009-9
This laboratory manual is designed specifically for the one-semester, non-majors, general biology lab courses with a human focus. The manual's approach infuses thinking and problem solving skills with the content areas. Activities and questions within an exercise build on previously learned information and encourage applying information from one section of the course to another.

Biological Explorations: A Human Approach, Sixth Edition by Stanley E. Gunstream
978-0-13-156072-7 | 0-13-156072-7
Compatible with any textbook, this manual provides 33 stimulating laboratory exercises for either human biology or introductory biology courses for non-majors in which the human organism is emphasized. The level of rigor, user-friendly language, and abundant illustrations make this manual ideal for students who have had little, if any, prior science laboratory experience.

BIOLOGY OF HUMANS

CONCEPTS, APPLICATIONS, AND ISSUES

JUDITH GOODENOUGH, BETTY McGUIRE

CUSTOM EDITION FOR TRITON COLLEGE
WITH CUSTOM APPENDICES

Taken from:

Biology of Humans: Concepts, Applications, and Issues, Third Edition
by Judith Goodenough and Betty McGuire

Essentials of Human Anatomy and Physiology, Ninth Edition
by Elaine N. Marieb

Learning Solutions

New York   Boston   San Francisco
London   Toronto   Sydney   Tokyo   Singapore   Madrid
Mexico City   Munich   Paris   Cape Town   Hong Kong   Montreal

Cover Art: Courtesy of Corbis.

Taken from:

Biology of Humans: Concepts, Applications, and Issues, Third Edition
by Judith Goodenough and Betty McGuire
Copyright © 2010 by Pearson Education, Inc.
Published by Benjamin Cummings
San Francisco, California 94111

Essentials of Human Anatomy & Physiology, Ninth Edition
by Elaine N. Marieb
Copyright © 2009 by Pearson Education, Inc.
Published by Benjamin Cummings

This special edition published in cooperation with Pearson Learning Solutions.

Printed in the United States of America

1 2 3 4 5 6 7 8 9 10 V3CR 14 13 12 11 10 09

2009140567

AK

www.pearsonhighered.com

ISBN 10: 0-558-49605-9
ISBN 13: 978-0-558-49605-0

Special-Interest Essays

Contents

Taken from:
Biology of Humans: Concepts, Applications, and Issues, Third Edition
by Judith Goodenough and Betty McGuire

PART I
THE ORGANIZATION OF THE BODY

SPECIAL TOPIC

SPECIAL TOPIC

21 a Cancer 469

PART VI
EVOLUTION AND ECOLOGY

22 Evolution and Our Heritage 482

23 Ecology, the Environment, and Us 505

24 Human Population, Limited Resources, and Pollution 522

Taken from: *Essentials of Human Anatomy & Physiology*, Ninth Edition by Elaine N. Marieb

Taken from: *Biology of Humans: Concepts, Applications, and Issues* Third Edition by Judith Goodenough and Betty McGuire

About the Authors

Judith Goodenough

Judith received her B.S. from Wagner College (Staten Island, NY), and her doctorate from New York University. She has 30 years of teaching experience at the University of Massachusetts, Amherst, specializing in introductory level courses. The insights into student concerns and problems—gained from more than 25 years of teaching Human Biology and 20 years of team-teaching The Biology of Social Issues—have helped shape this book. In 1986, Judith was honored with a "Distinguished Teaching Award." In addition to teaching, she has written articles in peer-reviewed journals, contributed chapters to several introductory biology texts, and written numerous laboratory manuals. With the author team of McGuire and Jakob, she is preparing *Perspectives on Animal Behavior*.

Judith Goodenough

Betty McGuire

Betty received her B.S. in Biology from Pennsylvania State University, where she also played varsity basketball. She went on to receive an M.S. and Ph.D. in Zoology from the University of Massachusetts, Amherst, and then spent two happy years as a postdoctoral researcher at the University of Illinois, Champaign-Urbana. Her field and laboratory research emphasize the social behavior and reproduction of small mammals. She has published numerous research papers, co-authored the text *Perspectives on Animal Behavior* as well as several introductory biology study guides, and served as an Associate Editor for *Mammalian Species*, a publication of the American Society of Mammalogists. Betty taught Human Biology, Introductory Biology, Vertebrate Biology, and Animal Behavior at Smith College. She now teaches Mammalogy and The Vertebrates: Structure, Function, and Evolution at Cornell University.

Betty McGuire

Preface

Humans are curious by nature. This book was written to stimulate that natural curiosity, inspiring an appreciation for the intricacy of human biology and the place of humans in the ecosphere. Once awakened, however, curiosity demands satisfaction in the form of solid information. Toward this end, we provide students with a conceptual framework for understanding how their bodies work and for dealing with issues relevant to human health in the modern world. All along, we sustain the student's interest and curiosity by continually illustrating the connections between biological concepts and issues of current social, ethical, and environmental concern. Our central belief is that the application of biological concepts to familiar experiences is the key to helping students see the excitement of science and understand its importance in their lives.

This edition builds on the strengths of clarity, liveliness, consistency, currency, and relevance that characterized the second edition. The writing is engaging, the explanations straightforward, and the pedagogical framework meticulously constructed. Great care has been taken to keep the level of coverage consistent throughout. All features—titles, outlines, headings, illustrations and legends, tables, vocabulary lists, summaries, questions, and so on—are designed to help students identify important facts and ideas, understand them, and appreciate why they matter.

As in the second edition, the text uses applications of scientific knowledge to engage students' interest, bring concepts to life, and illustrate the ethical and social relevance of human biology. This strategy is especially apparent in the Special Topics chapters and the dozens of Special-Interest Essays distributed throughout the other chapters.

Practical Goals and Special Features

The principal goal of this textbook is to give *a clear presentation of the fundamental concepts* of human anatomy, physiology, development, genetics, evolution, and ecology. The second goal is to *apply these concepts* in ways that will both interest and benefit students. The third goal is to help students *develop reasoning skills* so they can make use of their newly acquired knowledge in the situations they face in daily life. The fourth goal is to help students *evaluate the many sources of information* available to them and to select those that are reliable and accurate. The fifth goal is to give students an understanding of how the choices they make can *affect society and the planet, as well as their own quality of life.*

The entire book is written and structured with these five goals in mind. Thus, the chapters on organ systems explain how a healthy system functions, how that system might malfunction, steps to take to avoid a malfunction, and the ways in which medical science can help when systems are compromised or fail. Integrated discussions of topics that students are likely to encounter

in the media on an almost daily basis—smoking, food safety, contraception, STDs, cancer, antibiotic-resistant bacteria—help them see connections between classroom activities and the concerns of daily life. When students understand why a topic is relevant, they have a reason to want to learn about it.

Much of the material learned in human biology has a bearing on social and environmental issues that are important to us all. Connections between human biology topics and ethical, social, and environmental issues help students develop a global perspective on questions they once thought of as being strictly personal. This text will help instructors heighten students' awareness of how they impact the biosphere and will prepare them to be responsible citizens of their country and the world. Society is currently immersed in many pressing biological debates—concerning, for example, the cloning of human cells, stem cell research, genetically modified foods, gene therapy, organ transplants, the definition of death, and the prevention and treatment of HIV infections—and students need the tools to understand these issues and make informed decisions about them. The following special features are designed to support directly the book's goals.

Special Topic Chapters

The text contains eight **Special Topic** chapters: Chapter 2a, Food Safety; 8a, Drugs and the Mind; 13a, Infectious Disease; 15a, Nutrition and Weight Control; 17a, Sexually Transmitted Diseases and AIDS; 18a, Autism Spectrum Disorders; 19a, Stem Cells—A Repair Kit for the Body; and 21a, Cancer. Each of these short chapters builds on the "pure biology" presented in the immediately preceding chapter to cover issues likely to be of personal interest and therefore likely to motivate learning in students. The discussions they contain are more thoroughly developed than would be possible in a boxed essay. Even if instructors do not include these special topics in their reading assignments, we believe the issues are so pertinent to students that they will read the special chapters of their own volition, or at least refer to them occasionally as guides to a healthier lifestyle.

Much of the information offered in the text is practical: What can be done to prevent the spread of sexually transmitted diseases? How should food be selected, prepared, and stored to reduce the chances of foodborne illness? The body each of us is born with is a most intricate machine, but it does not come equipped with an owner's manual. In a sense, this book can be the students' owner's manual. Studying and applying the lessons to their individual lifestyles and health issues can help your students live longer, happier, and more productive lives.

Special-Interest Essays

Three categories of **Special-Interest Essays** use the basic scientific content of the chapters to explore issues having broader impact on individual health, society, and the environment.

Health Issue essays deal primarily with personal health topics. They provide current information on certain health problems that students, their families, or their friends might encounter. Examples of topics discussed in Health Issue essays are acne, osteoporosis, and treatments for the common cold.

Ethical Issue essays explore ethical and social issues related to the topics in a chapter. For example, they explore questions concerning such subjects as anabolic steroid use, gene testing, and the use of primates in research.

Finally, **Environmental Issue** essays deal with ways in which human activities alter the environment, or, conversely (sometimes simultaneously), ways in which the environment influences human health. Among the topics discussed in Environmental Issue essays are genetically modified foods, noise pollution, and environmental estrogens.

Certain essays within chapters raise ethical issues; to these essays we have added **Questions to Consider**. These questions ask students to think about the ethical implications of certain behaviors (such as taking anabolic steroids) or medical procedures (such as generating extra embryos as part of infertility treatments).

Stop and Think Questions

The **Stop and Think** questions scattered throughout each chapter are intended to promote active learning. They invite the student to pause in their reading in order to think about the information that was just presented and apply it to a new and interesting situation. These periodic checks allow the student to determine whether he or she has followed and understood the basic chapter content.

What Would You Do? Questions

The **What Would You Do?** questions, which are also placed throughout each chapter, challenge the student to form an opinion or to take a stand on a particular issue that society faces today, as well as to identify the criteria used in reaching that opinion or decision. These questions help students see the relevance of biology to real-life problems and foster the practice of thinking through such complicated issues as the fluoridation of water, the use of sperm sorting technology by parents to select the gender of their offspring, and strategies for slowing the growth of human populations. When the subject of one of these questions is controversial, the text presents examples of arguments from both sides, as well as evidence in support of competing arguments.

Enticing Illustration and Design Program

Users of previous editions—instructors and students alike—were unreservedly enthusiastic in praising the illustrations for their appeal and helpfulness. The visual program consists of simple but elegantly rendered illustrations that have been carefully designed for effective pedagogy. Their very beauty stimulates learning. This is particularly true of the many vibrant, three-dimensional anatomical figures, whose realistic style and appropriate depth and detail make them easy for students to interpret and use for review. Micrographs often appear side-by-side with illustrations to aid interpretation and understanding, and to give the actual view of a structure or process being studied.

Within each category of illustrations—from molecular models to depictions of human tissues and organs—the figures are consistent in plan and style throughout the text. Numerous key figures pull concepts together to present the "big picture." Reference figures help students locate particular structures within the body. Flowcharts walk students through a process one step at a time so they can visually follow the progress of a discussion after reading an explanation in the body of the text. Similarly, difficult concepts are reviewed using step-by-step figures that break the concepts down into simpler components. Finally, color is used in the visual program as an effective means of organizing information and maintaining consistency throughout the text.

Art Revisions

We have made several stylistic changes to the art in this edition in an effort to improve readability and to further streamline the art program for consistency and clarity. The most notable change is the use of larger, more legible type styles throughout. Also, we have modified the style of several recurring features, including the voice balloons, step text boxes, arrows, and flow chart elements for greater simplicity and functionality. In addition to refining the art styles, we have increased the size of figures and photographs wherever possible. All of the art in the book has been touched to apply the style modifications, and more than 60 percent of the figures have also been revised to be larger or otherwise made clearer and easier to follow.

Figure Questions

A new "figure question" now accompanies at least one figure in each chapter. This feature asks a question prompting students to pause and examine the information in the figure critically. Answers are provided below the figure legend.

New Design

This third edition of *Biology of Humans* incorporates a fresh, new text design. The new design was created with a goal of complementing the vibrancy of the illustrations, clarifying the organizational structure of the chapters, and increasing overall readability. Elements have been redesigned for more visual interest, and new photographs were selected for all chapter opening images and most Special-Interest Essay boxes.

Organization and Pedagogy

After an introductory chapter on the science of biology, the text begins with a discussion of the chemistry of life; proceeds through cells, tissues, organs, and organ systems; and ends with discussions of genetics, evolution, and ecology. As teachers ourselves, we understand the difficulty of covering all the topics in a human biology text in one semester. Instructors are inevitably forced to make difficult decisions concerning what to include and what to leave out. We also know there are many equally valid ways of organizing the material. For this reason, the chapters in this text are written so as not to depend heavily on material covered in earlier chapters. The independence of each chapter allows the instructor to tailor the use of this text to his or her particular course. At the same time, cross-references are given where they may be helpful to direct students to relevant discussions in other chapters.

The pedagogical features that provide a consistent framework for every chapter have been designed not only to help students understand the information presented in their human biology course, but to help them study more effectively. Some of the most important of these elements are described below.

Chapter Outlines

Each chapter begins with an **outline** constructed from the chapter's two major levels of headings. Because it identifies the chapter's important concepts and the relationships between them, this feature provides a conceptual framework on which students can mentally organize new information as they read. Special-Interest Essay boxes are also included in this outline.

Key Terms and Glossary

Because this text is intended for students who are not science majors, we have held the use of technical language to a minimum. Important terms are set in bold type where they are formally introduced, and are listed as key terms at the end of each chapter. New terms of lesser importance are set in italics. The **Recognizing Key Terms** list also provides chapter page numbers indicating where each term is defined. A **Glossary** at the end of the book contains definitions for all the key terms and many of the terms set in italics.

End-of-Chapter Questions

The questions provided at the end of each chapter are designed in several formats to encourage students to review and understand the relevant material instead of simply memorizing a few salient facts. Some, specifically the **Reviewing the Concepts**, are intended simply as content review; others—particularly those under the heading **Applying the Concepts**—require critical thinking and challenge the students to apply what they have learned to new situations. The third and newest type of end-of-chapter question, **Becoming Information Literate,** prompts students to explore and evaluate resources beyond the text, and can be used as a starting point for developing research papers or reports. Review questions that require a written answer are followed by the number of the page in the chapter containing the relevant discussion. Answers to the multiple choice and fill-in-the-blank questions are provided in an appendix, as are hints for answering the Applying the Concepts questions. These hints, which help students identify the information needed to answer each question, are intended to guide students in their thinking process instead of simply providing a quick answer.

Changes and Updates to the Third Edition

We have added new features to maintain the text as current and relevant, and to promote critical thinking.

New Special Topic Chapters
- Food Safety (Chapter 2a)
- Autism Spectrum Disorders (Chapter 18a)

New Critical Thinking Features

- **Becoming Information Literate** Information literacy—the ability to identify what information is needed, gather and organize that information, critically evaluate the sources, and present it appropriately—is necessary in every aspect of life. At the end of each chapter we provide an exercise to help students develop these skills.
- **Figure questions** This new art feature places questions above the figure that are designed to encourage the student to

think about the information presented in the figure. Answers are provided below the figure.
- **Questions to Consider** Many of the Special-Interest Essays explore controversial topics and raise ethical questions. These essays include Questions to Consider, designed to get students thinking about the relevance of the issues to their lives.

Chapter-by-Chapter Updates

All of the material in the book has been carefully reviewed, revised, and updated. The latest statistical information and medical advances have been incorporated throughout. The following is a list of some of the more significant changes in each chapter.

Chapter 1 An expanded explanation of the experimental process using real-world experiments includes a new figure showing a corresponding experimental design with four treatment groups. A new discussion of statistics and reading statistical graphs includes a new figure of a graph showing standard deviation.

Chapter 2 Two new Special-Interest Essays have been added on "Radon Gas" and "Toilet to Tap" water reclamation strategies. The essay on asbestos has been updated to include discussion of naturally occurring asbestos. New coverage of the use of radioactive pellets to treat prostate cancer is accompanied by a new figure of the procedure.

Chapter 3 A new discussion of microscopy covers the differences between light microscopes, SEM, and TEM. New discussion of how cell structure reflects cell function includes a new figure. A labeled micrograph has been added to the figure showing a generalized eukaryotic cell and its structures. New art and micrographs depict the two types of endoplasmic reticulum. A new figure shows the route by which vesicles move from rough endoplasmic reticulum to the Golgi complex. The cellular respiration summary figure has been completely redrawn to show the whole process and locate each step within the cell.

Chapter 4 The art and micrographs showing epithelial tissue, connective tissue, and muscle tissue have all been significantly enlarged to more clearly demonstrate the different structures. The figure showing the structure of the skin and hypodermis has been enlarged and improved for easier understanding. A new discussion of transdermal patches is accompanied by a new photograph and a new What Would You Do? question. A new Stop and Think question explores heat-related illness and sweat gland function.

Chapter 5 Coverage of the function and hormonal control of remodeling has been added to the discussion of bone remodeling. Art and micrographs showing bone structure have been enlarged for clarity. The figures of the vertebral column, rib cage, pectoral girdle, and pelvic girdle have all been enlarged.

Chapter 6 The Special-Interest Essay on anabolic steroid use has been updated and Questions to Consider have been added to it. The figure on sliding filament model has been revised to emphasize the cyclical nature of the process. The figure of a neuromuscular junction has been enlarged and improved. A new discussion of other functions of muscles, including heat generation, has been added. A new section on voluntary movement relates the discussion of motor units, muscle twitches, and summation to student experience. A new discussion of rigor mortis includes a new Stop and Think question. A new discussion of delayed onset muscle soreness has been added.

Chapter 7 An issue essay on pesticides and their effects on the nervous system has been updated and expanded to include Questions to Consider on the ban of AZM (azinphos methyl). The figure showing action potential has been revised to make the steps and accompanying text easier to follow. The figures of a synapse and of synaptic transmission have been revised to make structure and processes easier to distinguish.

Chapter 8 The nervous system overview figure has been revised to more clearly show the interrelationships of the nervous system components. A new Special-Interest Essay has been added on traumatic brain injury. The revised figure of a sagittal brain section uses a photograph of an actual brain section. The figure of the reflex response has been revised to clarify the path of the arc. The figure of the autonomic nervous system has been revised to more clearly indicate the location of synapses between nerves in both the sympathetic and parasympathetic systems.

Chapter 9 A revised figure of the visual overview process more clearly illustrates the steps. A new figure of a colorblindness test has been added. A new photograph of a cochlear implant has been added. The revised figure of dynamic and static equilibrium shows a cross-section of the semicircular canals. An enlarged figure of process of smell more clearly shows the structures involved. A new discussion of umami, the fifth primary taste, has been added.

Chapter 10 A new discussion of interactions among hormones explains antagonistic, synergistic, and permissive interactions. Increased emphasis has been placed on comparing the endocrine and nervous systems as systems involved in internal communication. The enlarged and revised figure of the endocrine system incorporates functions of each hormone and includes a close-up of the pituitary gland. A revised figure of the mode of action of water-soluble hormones shows the steps in more detail. A revised figure of oxytocin's stimulation of labor is used to illustrate discussion of positive feedback mechanisms. A new photograph showing Addison's disease has been added.

Chapter 11 A new discussion of the process and importance of blood donation has been added. The Special-Interest Essay on lead poisoning has been updated and now includes Questions to Consider on local government's roles and responsibilities for establishing lead-safe homes and workplaces.

Chapter 12 The chapter title has been changed to Cardiovascular and Lymphatic Systems to more clearly reflect the content. A new figure shows ranges for normal, low, and high blood pressure values. A new Special-Interest Essay has been added on the relationship between cardiovascular disease and cigarette smoking. An enlarged figure of the systemic and pulmonary circuits is easier to follow along with its text. The revised figure of balloon angioplasty shows placement of a stent. The figure of the lymphatic system has been revised to more clearly indicate the location of the tonsils and lymph nodes in the face.

Chapter 13 A new discussion of systemic lupus erythematosus includes a new photograph showing the butterfly rash characteris-

tic of the disease. A new Stop and Think question considers diarrhea as a protective response. Figures showing the various steps of the antibody-mediated and cell-mediated immune responses and clonal selection have all been enlarged and revised to be easier to follow. A new What Would You Do? question has been added on the HPV vaccine. Questions to Consider have been added to the organ transplant rejection essay.

Chapter 14 A new Special-Interest Essay on smoking and lung disease includes practical tips on how to quit smoking. A revised figure showing cilia lining the respiratory passageways now includes a photograph of damage to cilia caused by cigarette smoke. Photographs accompanying figures of the larynx and of changes in volume of thoracic cavity have been enlarged for clarity. A discussion of treatments for emphysema has been added. Discussion of lung cancer with an accompanying photograph of cancerous lungs has been newly added to the chapter.

Chapter 15 A new discussion of lactose intolerance has been added. Discussion of segmentation has been added to the section on muscularis. The figure showing the structure of the stomach and the micrograph of gastric pits have been enlarged for visibility. The figure showing chemical digestion in the small intestine has been revised to separate the processes of carbohydrate, fat, and protein digestion. A revised figure of the large intestine now shows cross sections of the cecum and the rectum.

Chapter 16 A new emphasis has been placed throughout on the fact that kidneys do more than just eliminate waste and that their many functions are critical to homeostasis. A new discussion of hyponatremia (water intoxication) has been added to the chapter opener. A more detailed description of the structure of the glomerular filter is accompanied by a new illustration and micrograph. Figures of renal corpuscle, glomeruler filtration, and water conservation in the loop of the nephron have been revised to use color coded arrows clarifying what substances are moving and in which direction. Information on the role of potassium in kidney function has been added. A new discussion on the possible use of kidneys from genetically modified pigs for transplantation into humans has been added. The figure showing the structure of a nephron has been enlarged and reorganized to enhance understanding. A new table lists the substances (and their amounts) reabsorbed by nephrons.

Chapter 17 Questions to Consider have been added to the environmental estrogens essay. Photographs of the contraceptive patch and vaginal contraceptive ring have been added to the figure showing methods of birth control. Information on new extended regimen contraceptive pills has been added.

Chapter 18 The fertilization figure has been revised to show more steps in the process. Modifications to figures showing early stages of development cross-sections and the formation of the nervous system make them easier to follow and interpret. Questions to Consider have been added to the assisted reproductive technology essay.

Chapter 19 The use of terminology has been adjusted for optimal precision and consistency in discussing the behavior of chromosomes during cell divisions. New micrographs have been added to the revised figure showing the stages of mitosis. The photograph of a karyotype has been enlarged for readability. Modifications to the figure showing the stages of meiosis make it easier to follow and understand. Color changes to the figure of nondisjunction clarify what is happening at each step.

Chapter 20 Revisions to the Punnett square figures throughout the chapter emphasize the alleles and the ratios to aid students in interpretation. The pedigree figure has been revised to include indication of generation numbers and clarification of shading. Questions to Consider have been added to the gene testing essay. The discussion of how breaks in chromosomes occur and lead to deletions or duplications has been expanded.

Chapter 21 The genetic code is now presented in a color-coded figure that is easier to reference and consistent with coloring of bases in figures throughout the chapter. Depictions of tRNA and ribosomes have been simplified throughout to aid interpretation and emphasize the fundamental concepts. Initiation, elongation, and termination have been divided into separate figures to better focus students' understanding of each process. Text discussion of the process of protein synthesis has been broken into numbered steps that correspond with the steps in initiation, elongation, and termination figures. Special-Interest Essays on genetically modified food and DNA fingerprinting have been updated, and Questions to Consider have been added to both. A new photograph shows a DNA microarray.

Chapter 22 A new description regarding how speciation occurs has been added. A new discussion of whale evolution as revealed by transitional fossils is accompanied by a new figure and photographs. A discussion of radiometric dating has been included. An updated section on primate diversity and phylogeny reflects the major change to Family *Hominidae*; figures showing human classifications have been updated accordingly. A new section comparing chimp and human skeletal anatomy is accompanied by a new figure. A discussion of paleoanthropology has been revised to highlight difficulties associated with reconstructing past human history. The Special-Interest Essay on primate research has been updated, and now includes Questions to Consider.

Chapter 23 An updated Special-Interest Essay on the loss of biodiversity is now included in this chapter along with new Questions to Consider. A revised and updated discussion of the importance of biodiversity is now included in this chapter. A revised food web figure now shows quaternary consumption. The sections on biogeochemical cycles now incorporate coverage of the negative impacts human activities have on each cycle, including discussion of freshwater shortages, global warming, acid rain, and eutrophication.

Chapter 24 An updated and expanded discussion of population growth includes an explanation of doubling time and a new Stop and Think question. The age structures figure has been updated with the latest estimates, and has been modified for easier interpretation. The concepts of ecological footprint, water footprint, and carbon footprint are now discussed. A new figure compares ecological footprints of different nations. Updated coverage of water shortages, water pollution, and global climate change is now included in this chapter. The ozone layer figure has been updated with the most recent statistics and new photographs. A new figure depicts the greenhouse effect. A new flowchart figure demonstrates relationships among human activities and different factors in global climate change. An updated Special-Interest Essay on air pollution is now in this chapter and accompanied by Questions to Consider.

Teaching and Learning Solutions for Instructors and Students

Biology of Humans third edition is supported by a full complement of carefully designed materials for both students and instructors.

For Instructors

Instructor Resource DVD
978-0-321-60284-8 | 0-321-60284-6
The Instructor Resource DVD provides a range of ready-to-use media supplements to help you teach the course, engage students, and accommodate different learning styles. Instructors can augment their lectures, show students the relevance of the subject matter, and increase student comprehension using the following tools:

- An image library of all the art, tables, and photographs from the book
- A selection of images with customizable labels and stepped-out art
- Editable PowerPoint® lecture presentation slides with embedded links to *ABC News* Videos and Human Biology Animations
- Active Lecture (Clicker) questions
- Human Biology Animations
- BLAST! Animations
- BioFlix™ and BioFlix PowerPoint slides
- 28 *ABC News* video clips
- PowerPoint slides for *Scientific American: Concepts and Current Issues in Biology,* Volumes 1–5
- *Interactive Physiology*® for human biology slides, worksheets, and answer sheets
- Interactive Quiz Show games
- Microsoft® Word files for the Instructor's Guide and Test Bank
- Computerized test bank
- An all-electronic set of ready-to-print Transparency Masters of selected illustrations from the text

Instructor's Guide
978-0-321-60281-7 | 0-321-60281-1
This resource provides tips for teaching non-majors by making the material relevant, interesting, and interactive. Each chapter includes:

- Lecture activity suggestions
- Answers to all the end of chapter Reviewing the Concepts questions
- Hints for answering the end of chapter Applying the Concepts questions
- Suggestions for class demonstrations and student activities
- Objectives that identify goals for students and instructors
- Resource listings

Test Bank
978-0-321-60282-4 | 0-321-60282-X
Over 1,000 multiple choice, fill-in-the-blank, short answer, and essay test questions originally created and reviewed by a panel of educators are included. The Test Bank features answers and section

references. Microsoft® Word versions of the files are available on the Instructor Resource DVD and for download from the Instructor's Resource Center.

Human Biology Place Companion Website
www.humanbiology.com
This open-access website offers a highly interactive way for students to get more involved in their studies with chapter overviews, animated Web Tutorials with accompanying quizzes, book-specific self-tests and essay questions, crossword puzzles, and flashcards. *ScienceDaily* RSS feeds of summaries and links to human biology-related news stories are updated six times a day. Accompanying Becoming Information Literate essay questions give students the opportunity to investigate and comment on current biology news.

The password-protected instructor portion of the site contains an image library, lecture presentations, clicker questions, instructor's guide, test bank, and other assets from the Instructor Resource DVD.

CourseCompass™
www.pearsonhighered.com/coursecompass
CourseCompass combines the strength of the content of the The Human Biology Place Web site with state-of-the-art eLearning tools. CourseCompass is a nationally hosted, dynamic, interactive online course management system powered by Blackboard, the leading platform for Internet-based learning tools. This easy-to-use and customizable program enables instructors to tailor content and functionality to meet individual course needs. The course includes all of the content found on the Human Biology Place Web site together with course management functionality.

WebCT Premium
978-0-321-60279-4 | 0-321-60279-X
This course management system contains a range of preloaded content such as testing and assessment question pools, chapter-level overviews and objectives, interactive web-based activities, animations, RSS feeds, flashcards, and exercises in Becoming Information Literate—all designed to help students master core course objectives. This course management system also includes access to chapter guides, a test bank, and animations.

BlackBoard Premium
978-0-321-60278-7 | 0-321-60278-1
This course management system contains a range of preloaded content such as testing and assessment question pools, chapter-level overviews and objectives, interactive web-based activities, animations, RSS feeds, flashcards, and exercises in Becoming Information Literate—all designed to help students master core course objectives. This course management system also includes access to chapter guides, a test bank, and animations.

For Students
Study Guide
978-0-13-507060-4 | 0-13-507060-0
This guide will help students grasp the key course concepts. It consists of learning objectives, key concepts, study tips, chapter summaries, critical-thinking questions, short-answer questions, labeling exercises, and fill-in-the-blank questions. A multiple choice "Practice Test" is included at the end of each chapter to help students assess their understanding.

Human Biology Place Companion Website
www.humanbiology.com
This open-access website offers a highly interactive way for students to get more involved in their studies with chapter overviews, animated Web Tutorials with accompanying quizzes, book-specific self-tests and essay questions, crossword puzzles, and flashcards. *ScienceDaily* RSS feeds of summaries and links to human biology-related news stories are updated six times a day. Accompanying Becoming Information Literate essay questions give students the opportunity to investigate and comment on current biology news.

Interactive Physiology® for Human Biology
The *Interactive Physiology* for Human Biology (IP for HB) companion CD-ROM reinforces readings and lectures with a wealth of outstanding animations, engaging activities, helpful self-testing, and much more. This edition includes a new module on the immune system along with assignable worksheets to help students gauge their progress and stay on track with their studies. IP for HB can be packaged at no additional charge with the book. Contact your Pearson sales representative for more information.

CourseCompass™ Student Access Kit
978-0-321-60288-6 | 0-321-60288-9

WebCT Student Access Kit
978-0-321-60287-9 | 0-321-60287-0

Blackboard Student Access Kit
978-0-321-60289-3 | 0-321-60289-7

Acknowledgments

It takes more than authors to get a book to the readers and many dedicated people have helped get this text to your hands.

The project was enthusiastically launched by Deirdre Espinoza, executive editor, who helped us plan this edition and assembled a team of professionals who brought our vision to reality.

We are especially thankful for the opportunity to work with Kari Hopperstead, our project editor. She kept our vision for this edition in mind through the entire project and was involved at every level. Kari was a source of ideas on how to improve quality and still keep to the schedule. Our developmental editor, Debbie Hardin, was a delight to work with. She looked at everything with a fresh eye and provided many great ideas for improvements in this edition.

Christianne Thillen copyedited the book with a detailed, accurate, and consistent touch. The text was further refined by our proofreader, Kim Mercer.

The art program is essential not only to the appearance of the book but also to its usefulness as an instrument for learning and teaching. Ideas for changes in art design developed by Deirdre, Kari, and Debbie, were ably carried out by our art coordinators, Victor Ayers and April Walsh, at Imagineering Media Services, Inc. Our photo researcher, Claire Maxwell, was diligent in her pursuit of striking and pedagogically important photographs.

The team at Pre-Press PMG was skillfully led by our production editor Jared Sterzer, and all aspects of the book's production were expertly overseen by our production supervisor at Benjamin Cummings, Caroline Ayres.

Nicole George-O'Brien, our supplements project editor, Alex Streczyn-Woods, our media producer, and Shannon Cutt, our assistant editor, developed an instructional package beyond compare.

Many thanks go out to all of the instructors who reviewed the book and provided us with the useful feedback that helped shape this new edition:

    Tamatha Barbeau, Francis Marion University
    Marilyn Bartels, Black Hawk College
    Susan Capasso, St. Vincent's College
    Charles Dick, Pasco Hernandez Community College
    Claudia Douglass, Central Michigan University
    Mary Louise Greely, Salve Regina University
    Kent Koerner, Indiana State University
    Julia Lee, Saint Joseph's University
    J. Mitchell Lockhart, Valdosta State University
    Roberta Meehan, Troy State University
    Qian Moss, Des Moines Area Community College, Ankeny
    Nick Nagle, Metropolitan State College of Denver
    Polly Phillips, Florida International University
    Susan Rohde, Triton College
    Kent Thomas, Wichita State University
    Wendy Vermillion, Columbus State Community College

From Judith Goodenough

I thank my family and friends who supported and encouraged me at every stage of this project. My husband, Steve, was a cheerleader and convinced me that I would complete this project. Without his witty quips, I would have lost my sanity. He reassures me that I'll always be his first wife. My daughters, Aimee and Heather, inspire me and continually remind me that the people you love should always come first. Aimee is a rehabilitation counselor for traumatic brain injured clients, and she contributed the essay in Chapter 8 *Brain Injury: A Silent Epidemic*. The willingness of my mother, Betty Levrat, to help in any way, allowed me to focus on writing.

Margaret Ludlam cheered me up and helped me cope when things got tense. Margaret's willingness to pick up the slack at UMass allowed me to take vacation days to work at home during the semester. Lee Estrin, one of "the group" of dear friends who have always provided moral support and advice, was always willing to visit for an "I need a break weekend," even when I couldn't actually stop working completely.

From Betty McGuire

I thank my husband, Willy Bemis, for support and encouragement throughout this edition, and my daughter Kate and son Owen, for (usually) waiting patiently for me to complete just one more sentence or paragraph. Dora, James, Kevin, and Cathy McGuire were endlessly encouraging and understanding, as they have been throughout my life. Lowell Getz, my long time friend and research colleague, waited with good humor as one after another of our papers took a back seat to a book chapter.

To Stephen, my husband,
best friend, personal hero,
and the funniest person I know.
To Aimee and Heather, my daughters,
who fill me with love, wonder, and amazement.
To Betty Levrat, my mother,
an excellent role model
and endless source of support and encouragement.
To "The Group," friends for nearly forty years,
who help me hold it all together.
—J. G.

In loving memory of James Patrick McGuire.
To Willy, Kate, and Owen Bemis,
and to Dora, Kevin, and Cathy McGuire.
—B. M.

1

Humans in the World of Biology

Humans are a small, but important, part of the diverse life on Earth.

The dugout canoe turns on the muddy river and approaches the slippery bank. A tribesman steps off into mud up to his knees and, watching his friend, who is pushing with a pole from the back, shoves the canoe as far as possible onto the bank and ties it to a tree.

The tribesman helps you and your fellow researcher to a grassy area just beyond the river, and you peer through the tangled, viney vegetation into the dark interior of the forest. Already you are soaked with sweat. Nevertheless, you remain eager to do what you came for—explore this part of the Amazon rain forest, searching for medicinal plants. You know that two chemicals from the rosy periwinkle of Madagascar are already being used to treat leukemia and Hodgkin's disease (Figure **1.1**). You also know that, like the rain forest of Madagascar, the Amazon rain forest is home to millions of plants, some of which yield medicines that are used by local people. The Amazon rain forest is being destroyed at an alarming rate. You want to learn the secrets of its plants before they disappear forever.

To learn those secrets, you need to talk to the native people about the plants they use for healing. You have spent months preparing—learning the language and the culture of the native people, cataloging the information already available on local plants and their uses, learning how to collect and preserve the plants, and gathering

FIGURE 1.1 The rosy periwinkle (*Catharanthus roseus*) is a source of two anticancer drugs.

tools and supplies. A physician helped prepare simple descriptions and photographs of diseases, which you will use to communicate with local healers. If these local healers recognize the symptoms you describe, they can show you the plants they use to treat them. Once the plants are collected, chemists and biologists in laboratories at home will study them to determine their medicinal value.

The rain forest is a fitting place to begin considering human biology. The forest's incredible diversity of life—the bewildering variety of plants, the brilliant colors of the flowers, the haunting songs of exotic birds—reminds us that humans are just a small part of life on Earth.

As we look around, we can see that life has many levels of organization: individual, population, community, ecosystem, and biosphere. Throughout most of this book, we focus on the human individual—how the individual human body functions and the biological principles that govern those functions. However, we also examine many of the larger health, social, and environmental issues that we must be aware of, because they can affect all of us. Our actions as individuals can affect the health of the rain forest. At the same time, the rain forest is a source of biological substances that may be used to improve the health of humans.

Basic Characteristics of All Living Things

As you continue exploring the rain forest, how do you determine if something unfamiliar to you is alive? In most cases, the question is easy to answer. Although the leaves around you have different shapes and sizes, a brief examination assures you that they are leaves, and the tree whose trunk you are exploring is clearly a tree—thus telling you that the tree specimen you are examining is indeed alive. But what about the gray material adhering to the trunk? Is it also alive?

Defining life might seem to be easy, but it is not. In fact, no single definition satisfies all life scientists. For example, if we say you can tell something is alive if it reproduces, someone is likely to note that a page with a wet ink spot can fall on top of another page and reproduce itself almost exactly. If we say you can tell something is alive if it grows, what should we conclude about crystals? They grow, but they are not alive. And so it goes.

No single definition applies to all forms of life, so we find that instead of defining life, we can only characterize it. That is, we can only list the traits associated with life. Most biologists agree that, in general, the following statements characterize life.

1. **Living things contain nucleic acids, proteins, carbohydrates, and lipids.** The same set of slightly more than 100 elements is present in various combinations in everything on Earth—living or nonliving. However, living things can combine certain of these elements to create molecules that are found in all living organisms. These include nucleic acids, proteins, carbohydrates, and lipids. The nucleic acid DNA (deoxyribonucleic acid) is especially important because DNA molecules can make copies of themselves, an ability that enables organisms to reproduce (Figure **1.2**). The molecules of life are discussed in Chapter 2.

2. **Living things are composed of cells. Cells** are the smallest units of life. Some organisms (called unicellular organisms) have only a single cell; others (multicellular organisms), such as humans, are composed of trillions of cells. All cells come from preexisting cells. Because cells can divide to form new

1. Living things contain nucleic acids, proteins, carbohydrates, and lipids.
This is a computer-generated model of the nucleic acid DNA, which carries genetic information.

2. Living things are composed of cells.
These are red blood cells (disks) and a white blood cell (sphere).

3. Living things grow and reproduce.
All organisms reproduce their own kind.

4. Living things use energy and raw materials.
This mother orangutan is sharing bananas with her offspring. This food will provide energy and raw materials for the maintenance, repair, and growth of their bodies.

5. Living things respond to their environment.
This chameleon sees and catches its prey.

6. Living things maintain homeostasis.
This person's body temperature will remain about 37°C (98.6° F) in spite of extreme environmental temperature.

7. Populations of living things evolve and have adaptive traits.
The orchid is adapted to live perched on branches of trees. It uses other plants for support so that it can receive enough sunlight to produce its own food by photosynthesis.

FIGURE 1.2 Characteristics of life

cells, reproduction, growth, and repair are possible. Cells are discussed in Chapter 3 and cell division in Chapter 19.

3. **Living things grow and reproduce.** Living things grow and ultimately generate new individuals that carry some of the genetic material of the parents. Some organisms, such as bacteria, reproduce simply by making new and virtually exact copies of themselves. Other organisms, including humans, reproduce by combining genetic material with another individual. Many organisms have stages of life. Humans progress from embryo to fetus, child, adolescent, and then adult. Reproduction and development are discussed in Chapters 17 and 18, respectively.

4. **Living things use energy and raw materials.** The term **metabolism** refers to all chemical reactions that occur within the cells of living things. Through metabolic activities, organisms extract energy from various nutrients and transform it to do many kinds of work. Metabolism maintains life and allows organisms to grow. Chemical reactions involved in the transformation of energy are discussed in Chapter 2.

5. **Living things respond to their environment.** A boxer weaves and ducks to avoid the blow of an opponent. A chameleon takes aim at and captures its prey. For a living thing to respond, it must first detect a stimulus and then have a way to react. As later chapters explain, your sensory organs detect stimuli. Your nervous system processes sensory input, and your skeletal and muscular systems enable you to respond. The skeletal and muscular systems are discussed in Chapters 5 and 6, respectively. The nervous system is discussed in Chapter 8, and sensory organs in Chapter 9.

6. **Living things maintain homeostasis. Homeostasis** is the relatively constant and self-correcting internal environment of a living organism. We generally find that life can exist only within certain limits and that living things tend to behave in ways that will keep their body systems functioning within those limits. For example, if you become too cold, you shiver (a metabolic response). Shivering produces heat that warms your body. Alternatively, if you become too hot, your sweat glands will be activated to cool you down. In addition to these and other physiological responses, the sensation of being hot or cold may motivate you to behave in ways that cool you down or warm you up. We discuss homeostasis in Chapter 4, where we make an initial survey of body systems.

7. **Populations of living things evolve and have adaptive traits.** Members of a population of reproducing organisms possessing beneficial genetic traits will survive and reproduce better than members of the population that lack these traits. As a result of this process, called *natural selection*, each of the amazing organisms you see around you has **adaptive traits**—that is, traits that help it survive and reproduce in its natural environment. For example, most plants in the rain forest have shallow root systems, because the topsoil in the Amazon is thin and nutrients are near the surface. As a result, tall trees have acquired, through evolution, supports like cathedral buttresses to hold them up, while vines climb over both roots and trees to reach the light. Many plants do not grow in the ground at all but live high above it in the canopy for greater exposure to sunlight, which provides energy to produce sugar. These plants, called epiphytes, are rooted on the surfaces of other plants. Rain forest animals also have

adaptations—the ability to fly or climb, for example—that enable them to reach the plants for food. Adaptive traits and evolution are discussed in Chapter 22.

stop and think

Scientists have discovered vents of water similar to geysers spouting on the surface of a small moon of Saturn called Enceladus. Locations near these vents may be the most likely place in the solar system to find extraterrestrial life. If samples of water from Enceladus were brought back to scientists on Earth, what characteristics of life could they look for to determine whether the samples contain anything that is or was once alive?

Classification by Evolutionary Relationship

At least 10 million species of organisms live on Earth. Organisms are unified because all species descended from the first cells. However, as organisms adapted to different environments through evolution, diversity among species arose.

Scientists organize, or classify, living organisms in a way that shows evolutionary relationships among them. This means, for the most part, that organisms with the greatest similarity are grouped together.

Several classification systems have been proposed over the years. One system recently favored by many biologists recognizes three domains. Two of the domains, Bacteria and Archaea, consist of the various kinds of prokaryotes—all very small, single-celled organisms that lack a nucleus or other internal compartments. All other organisms, including humans, belong to the third domain, Eukarya. Organisms in domain Eukarya have eukaryotic cells, which contain a nucleus and complex internal compartments called organelles. Domain Eukarya is subdivided into four kingdoms—protists, fungi, plants, and animals—as shown in Figure **1.3**. Within each kingdom, organisms are further categorized into groups whose members share characteristics that distinguish them from members of other groups in the kingdom. These groups in turn are subdivided into smaller groups to show successively closer relationships.

As humans, we belong to a subdivision of the animal kingdom called vertebrates (animals with a nerve cord protected by a backbone), and more specifically to the group called mammals. Two characteristics that make us mammals are that we have hair and that we feed our young milk produced by mammary glands. However, we are further defined as belonging to the primates, along with lemurs, monkeys, and apes, because we share a suite of features that includes forward-looking eyes and a particularly well-developed brain. Humans, monkeys, and apes also have opposable thumbs (a thumb that can touch the tips of the other four fingers). Smaller details, such as tooth structure and skeletal characteristics, serve to divide the primates into smaller subgroupings.

What most sets humans apart from all other living species? Human characteristics include a large brain size relative to body size and a two-legged gait. But nothing distinguishes humans more than culture. *Culture* may be regarded as a set of social influences that produce an integrated pattern of knowledge, belief, and behavior (Figure **1.4**). Other animals have social interactions, from various forms of cooperation and mating behavior to territoriality, competition, and social hierarchies. But social influences are much less pronounced in other animals than in corresponding human interactions. Consider, for example, our rituals—weddings,

Domain Bacteria	Domain Archaea	Domain Eukarya			
Unicellular prokaryotic organisms	Unicellular prokaryotic organisms; most live in extreme environments	Eukaryotic cells that contain a membrane-bound nucleus and internal compartments			
		Kingdoms			
		Protists	Fungi	Plants	Animals
		Protozoans, algae, diatoms	Molds, mushrooms	Mosses, ferns, seed plants	Invertebrates and vertebrates

FIGURE 1.3 One classification scheme showing three domains and four kingdoms of life

FIGURE 1.4 Social interactions are an important thread in the fabric of human life.

graduation, burial of the dead—and the way our lives are enriched with art, music, and dance.

Of course, there is not one human culture but many. If you were a scientist following native guides through the Amazon rain forest, you would quickly learn that their culture is different from ours. In fact, there are many different cultures within the rain forest. Separate groups of people in the same environment do not adapt to it in the same way. If you were to describe your culture to someone from a rain forest tribe, your description might elicit astonishment and even howls of laughter. However, you and your native guide would soon recognize that some things, especially love of children and the need to belong to a group, seem the same across cultures.

Levels of Biological Organization

As we study human biology, we learn that life can be organized on many levels (Figure **1.5**). Cells, the smallest unit of life, are themselves composed of molecules. A multicellular organism may

consist of different tissues, groups of similar cells that perform specific functions. Organs also may consist of different types of tissue that work together for a specific function. Two or more organs working together to perform specific functions form an organ system. Humans are described as having 11 organ systems, as we see in Chapter 4.

Life can also be organized at levels beyond the individual organism. A **population** is individuals of the same species (individuals that can interbreed) living in a distinct geographic area. Examples of a population include yellow-bellied marmots living in an alpine meadow or four-eyed butterfly fish living in a coral reef. A **community** is all living species that can potentially interact in a particular geographic area. Examples of a community include *all the species* that live and interact in an alpine meadow or all the species living in a coral reef.

An **ecosystem** includes all the living organisms in a community along with their physical environment. The size of the locality that defines the ecosystem varies with the interest of the person studying it. In other words, an ecosystem can be defined as the whole Earth, a particular forest, or even a single rotting log within a forest. Whatever its size, an ecosystem is viewed as being relatively self-contained.

The **biosphere** is that part of Earth where life is found. It encompasses all of Earth's living organisms and their habitats. In essence, the biosphere is the narrow zone in which the interplay of light, minerals, water, and gases produces environments where life can exist on Earth. The biosphere extends only about 11 km (7 mi) above sea level and the same distance below, to the deepest trenches of the sea. If Earth were the size of a basketball, the biosphere would have the depth of about one coat of paint. In this thin layer covering one small planet, we find all of the life we currently know of in the entire universe.

Scientific Method

It is not surprising that scientists are exploring the rain forest in search of any secrets it may reveal, including any plants that may have healing qualities (see the Environmental Issue essay, *Medicinal*

Molecule The chemical components of cells	
Cell The smallest unit of life	
Tissue A group of similar cells that perform the same function	
Organ A structure with two or more tissues working together to perform a function	
Organ systems At least two organs working together to perform a function	
Individual A single organism	
Population All individuals of the same species in an area	
Community All the species in an ecosystem that can interact	
Ecosystem A community and its physical environment	
Biosphere The part of the earth that supports life	

FIGURE 1.5 Levels of organization of life

Plants and the Shrinking Rain Forest). Humans are an irrepressibly curious species, constantly asking questions about the things they observe. **Science** is a systematic approach to answering those questions, a way of acquiring knowledge through carefully documented investigation and experimentation.

There is no such thing as *the* scientific method in the sense of a single, formalized set of steps to follow for doing an experiment. Instead, the **scientific method** is a way of learning about the natural world by applying certain rules of logic to the way information is gathered and conclusions are drawn. It often begins with an observation that raises a question. Next, a possible explanation is formulated to answer the question, but that explanation must be testable. Generally, the tentative explanation will lead to a prediction. If the prediction holds true when it is tested, the test results support the explanation. If the original explanation is not supported, an alternative explanation is generated and tested. For example, if you were a scientist looking for potentially useful compounds in the rain forest, you might proceed as follows:

1. **Make careful observations and ask a question about the observations.** If, while walking through the rain forest, you came across a patch of small trees—that you later identify as lemon ant trees—growing in a cluster, with no other trees or plants growing among them, you might record and describe that observation (Figure **1.6**). Considering the density of different plants that you see on most of the forest floor, the relative isolation of this group of plants strikes you as odd. You are aware that some of the chemicals that plants produce to protect themselves from damage by insects or other plants have been found to have medicinal value and wonder if this plant or the lemon ants living on it might also be producing a chemical with medicinal value. You make up your mind to discover why other plants don't grow alongside lemon ant trees. You begin your study of the situation by collecting information about the plant and its surroundings. This includes, among other things, measuring the area of the patch and counting the approximate number of each type of plant in it.

2. **Develop a testable hypothesis (possible explanation) as a possible answer to your question.** Now you start to

FIGURE 1.6 A patch of lemon ant trees, shown in the foreground, usually consists of only lemon ant trees. Other regions of the rain forest, as shown in the background, generally have a wide variety of organisms.

Medicinal Plants and the Shrinking Rain Forest

The healing powers of many plants have been known for centuries. Historically, such knowledge was gained by trial and error and passed along by word of mouth. For example, many cultures have long known that tea made from willow bark relieves pain and reduces fever. Scientists learned that willow bark contains salicylic acid. They isolated the compound and developed it into the drug we know today as aspirin. Similarly, digitalis, a heart medication, was discovered after a patient with an untreatable heart condition was seen to benefit from an herbal drink provided as a folk remedy. The potion contained purple foxglove, which, like willow bark, is frequently mentioned in ancient texts as a healing herb. Broccoli, a more familiar plant, contains the anticancer chemical sulforaphane.

More than 25% of the prescription medicines sold in the United States today contain chemicals that came from plants, and 70% of the newly developed drugs are from natural sources. Many more healing chemicals first discovered in plants used medicinally by native people are now routinely synthesized in laboratories (Table **1.A**). Unfortunately, scientists have not been able to synthesize the medicinal compounds for many plants.

Most plants that have proved to be medically useful are found in the tropics, regions where the human population is growing rapidly. Unfortunately, the forests in these regions are being cut to create living space and foster economic development. In Madagascar, home of the rosy periwinkle (Figure 1.1), which is the source of two cancer drugs, humans have destroyed 90% of the vegetation. Experts estimate that roughly nine-tenths of the original tropical rain forests of the world will have been destroyed by 2030. Considering that 155,000 of the known 250,000 plant species are from tropical rain forests, and that less than 2% of the known plant species have been tested for medicinal value, we have no way of knowing what potential new medicines are being destroyed.

TABLE 1.A Selected Medicinal Plants and Their Uses

Source Plant		Compound	Medicinal Use
Willow bark and meadowsweet		Salicylic acid (active ingredient in aspirin)	Pain relief, fever reduction
Foxglove		Digitalin	Treatment of heart conditions (increases intensity of heart contraction, slows heart rate)
Quinine tree		Quinine	Malaria preventive
Opium poppy		Morphine	Pain relief
Eucalyptus tree		Menthol	Decongestant
Rauvolfia root		Reserpine	Treatment of high blood pressure
Belladonna		Atropine	Dilates pupils for eye exams
Pacific yew		Taxol	Treatment of ovarian and breast cancer
Rosy periwinkle		Vincristine	Treatment of Hodgkin's disease (a type of cancer)
		Vinblastine	Treatment of leukemia

formulate ideas about why other plants do not grow within patches of lemon ant trees. This statement is your **hypothesis**—an explanation for your observation. A good hypothesis can be tested. If a hypothesis cannot be tested, it is not useful in a scientific investigation because it cannot be supported or refuted. For example, the local people call a patch of lemon ant trees a devil's garden because they believe that the trees are planted by an evil forest spirit. You cannot test the hypothesis that an evil spirit is to blame, so it cannot advance your scientific understanding of why other plants don't grow with lemon ant trees. So, you develop your own possible explanation: the lemon ant trees are producing a chemical that inhibits the growth of other plants within their midst. This hypothesis can be tested, and even if it is found to be incorrect, it can still be useful in developing alternative hypotheses. Note that a hypothesis cannot be *proven* true; it can only be proven untrue.

3. **Make a prediction based on your hypothesis and test it with a controlled experiment.** Now you must plan an experiment to test your hypotheses. Ideally, your experiment will be designed in such a way that there can be only one explanation for the results. In such an experiment, called a **controlled experiment**, the research subjects (in this case, Spanish cedar saplings) are randomly divided into two groups. One group is designated as the **control group** and the other one is designated as the **experimental group.** Both groups are treated in the same way except for the *one* factor, called the **variable**, whose effect the experiment is designed to reveal. You would predict that, if the lemon ant trees were secreting a chemical into the soil of the patch that inhibited growth of invading plants, then a sapling of a tree other than the lemon ant tree would grow well outside of the patch, but not inside the patch.

To test the hypothesis that lemon ant trees inhibit the growth of other plants you identify another tree, the Spanish cedar, that is common in the rain forest but is not usually found within a patch of lemon ant trees. You plant cedar saplings outside the patch of lemon ant trees (control group) and inside the patch (experimental group because this group is exposed to the hypothesized chemical from lemon ant trees). You find that the cedar saplings within the patch of lemon ant trees lose many of their leaves within 5 days.

Do these results support your hypothesis? They seem to . . . but, without intending to, you actually had two variables: the lemon ant trees and the lemon ants that call these trees home. Lemon ants are common within a patch of lemon ant trees, but they are rare outside a patch. Could the lemon ants be inhibiting the growth of other invading plants? In a scientific study, additional variables that have not been controlled for and may have affected the outcome are called *confounding variables*. When there are confounding variables, we cannot say for sure which variable or variables caused the effect. So you experiment again. This time, you control for the lemon ants.

You predict that if the ants were responsible, then preventing ants from reaching a different type of tree would allow the different tree to survive in the midst of lemon ant trees. Knowing that lemon ants almost never leave the patch of lemon ant trees, you randomly divide cedar saplings into four groups: (1) planted within the lemon ant tree patch with ants having access to them, (2) planted within the lemon ant tree patch with a sticky barrier preventing the ants from having access to them, (3) planted outside the lemon ant tree patch

with ants having access to them (though few lemon ants travel outside their own patch of trees), (4) planted outside the lemon ant tree patch with a sticky barrier preventing the ants from having access to them (Figure **1.7**). You measure the number of dead cedar leaves on the forest floor after 5 days.

stop and think

Predict the results of this experiment. Which group(s) of cedar saplings would suffer the most leaf damage if chemicals from the lemon ant trees inhibit the growth of other plants? Which group(s) of cedar saplings would suffer the most leaf damage if lemon ants are inhibiting the growth of other plants?

4. **Draw a conclusion based on the results of the experiment.** Next, you arrive at a **conclusion**, which is an interpretation of the data. The results of a scientific experiment are often summarized in a graph, such as the one shown in Figure **1.8**, which presents the results of the experiment we just described. When you read a graph, first look at the axes. The horizontal line, or x-axis, shows the independent variables—the variables altered by the researcher. In this case, the independent variables are the four treatment groups. The vertical line is the y-axis; it presents the dependent variable, that is, the variable that was changed by the independent variables. In your experiment, the dependent variable was the number of dead cedar leaves on the forest floor. Read the labels on the axes to see what the graph pertains to, and notice the scale to appreciate the extent of variation. This is a bar graph, and the height of the bar indicates the number of dead cedar leaves in each treatment. A bar graph is appropriate here because each treatment is a discrete category. (Variables that vary continuously, such as the change in factor *x* over time, would be better represented by a line graph.) Thus, the results of this experiment are that the number of dead leaves (a measure of damage to the cedar sapling) is greater in treatment 1 (sapling planted inside the patch of lemon ant trees with the ant permitted access to it) than in any other treatment group. We might have predicted that there would also be a greater number of dead leaves in treatment group 3 (sapling planted outside the patch of lemon ant trees with the ant permitted access to it), but few lemon ants leave the patch. A reasonable conclusion based on these results is that the lemon ants are inhibiting the growth of other plants, at least cedar trees, within the patch. Indeed, thanks to actual scientific research into this matter, we now know that lemon ants inject formic acid into the leaves of plants other than lemon ant trees. Once injected, the leaf dies within hours. Scientists suggest that lemon ants kill plants that invade a lemon ant tree patch to preserve and expand their habitat.

But what about your original hypothesis? Does the lemon ant tree itself also produce a chemical that inhibits the growth of other saplings? To answer this question, we compare the leaf damage to cedar saplings within the patch but with ants excluded (treatment 2) to leaf damage to cedar saplings outside the patch (treatments 3 and 4). The leaf damage to cedars within the patch is slightly greater. Scientists base conclusions on the **statistical significance** of the data, which is a measure of the possibility that the results were due to chance. A probability of less than 5% (written as $p < 0.05$) that the results are due to chance is generally acceptable. The lower the number, the more confidence we have in

Ants allowed access · Ants not allowed access

Within lemon ant tree patch

Outside of lemon ant tree patch

FIGURE 1.7 The experimental design used to test the hypothesis that lemon ants kill plants that invade the patch of lemon ant trees.

FIGURE 1.8 Leaf damage to cedar saplings planted within and outside of a patch of lemon ant trees. Lemon ants were excluded from two treatment areas—one inside and one outside the patch of lemon ant trees. These results indicate that lemon ants kill plants that invade a patch of lemon ant trees.

the accuracy of the results. The *standard error* reflects the degree of certainty of the results. In a graph, the standard error is shown as a vertical bar extending above and below the data point. If standard error bars overlap, the results are not statistically significant. Notice in Figure 1.8 that the standard error bars for treatment groups 2, 3, and 4 overlap. Thus, the differences in leaf damage in those treatment groups could be due to chance alone. Using leaf damage as a measure, we cannot conclude that a chemical from the lemon ant tree inhibits new plant growth. Thus, even successful experiments often lead to revised hypotheses and further experimentation (Figure **1.9**).

Another requirement of scientific inquiry is that experiments must be repeated and yield similar results. Other scientists following the same procedure should obtain a similar outcome. Note, however, that it can be very difficult to identify all the factors that might affect the outcome of an experiment. In our rain forest experiment, for example, over time the rainfall, amount of light, and soil characteristics might all influence the results. Each time an experiment is repeated, additional factors may be identified as important.

The testing and refinement of a hypothesis represents one level of the scientific process. As time passes, related hypotheses that have been confirmed repeatedly can be fit together to form a **theory**—a well-supported and wide-ranging explanation of some aspect of the physical universe. Because of its breadth, a theory cannot be tested by a single experiment but instead emerges from many observations, hypotheses, and experiments. Nevertheless,

a theory, like a hypothesis, leads to additional predictions and continued experimentation. Among the few explanations that have been tested thoroughly enough to be considered theories are the cell theory of life (which says all cells come from preexisting cells) and the theory of evolution by natural selection (which you learn about in Chapter 22).

Inductive and Deductive Reasoning

As you examined the lemon ant tree, asked questions about it, and devised experiments to answer those questions, you made use of two types of logical reasoning: inductive and deductive.

In **inductive reasoning**, facts are accumulated through observation until the sheer weight of the evidence allows some logical general statement to be made. An example is the way you collected as much information as you could about the lemon ant tree, other plants in the area, the soil, the light, and anything else that might have a bearing on your question. You then used those specific facts to draw the initial general conclusion that the lemon ant tree could be interfering with the growth of other plants in the area. You used inductive reasoning to develop a testable hypothesis.

Deductive reasoning, begins with a general statement that leads logically to one or more deductions, or conclusions. The process can usually be described as an "if-then" series of associations. *If* lemon ants are producing something that interferes with the growth of other plants, *then* there should be few plants other than

Q *How would you modify this diagram to indicate that testing alternative hypotheses is also part of the scientific process?*

FIGURE 1.9 The scientific process consists of observation, creating testable hypotheses, experimentation, drawing conclusions, revising hypotheses, and designing new experiments.

A *Add another arrow from "Observation" indicating Hypothesis 2. All the steps that are currently shown leading from "Hypothesis" would be repeated for Hypothesis 2.*

lemon ant trees in areas where lemon ants live; *then* other plants should grow in areas without lemon ants; and so on. You used deductive reasoning to make predictions that would support your hypothesis and to decide whether the results of your experiment supported or refuted the hypothesis.

Clinical Trials

Recall that the reason for your interest in chemicals from plants in the rain forest was the hope that some of them might yield drugs to treat human ailments. You interviewed several native healers, collected many species of plants they use for healing, and made extensive notes on how the plants are used and what maladies the plants are used to treat. Now, you will preserve the plants for the trip home, where their extracts will undergo extensive testing and possible development into pharmaceuticals.

Each plant you collected is used by native people to treat a particular illness, so the first step for researchers is to identify all the chemicals in the extract and determine which one is the active ingredient; that is, which chemical is effective in treatment of the illness. That chemical is then purified to be tested as a drug.

Before testing a new drug or treatment on humans, scientists must take steps to ensure that it will not do more harm than good (Table **1.1**). Usually a drug is tested first on animals such as laboratory rodents. Rats and mice are mammals, so some aspects of their physiology are similar to and can generalize to human physiology. The advantages of using rodents for testing drugs include that they are relatively inexpensive to use, have short life spans, and reproduce quickly. Research on animals also helps determine how the drug is handled by the body, which helps determine dosage. Most medical advances, including vaccinations,

TABLE 1.1	Tests Performed on a New Drug before It Is Approved by the Food and Drug Administration (FDA)
Tests on laboratory animals	
Is the drug safe for use on animals?	
Clinical trials	
Phase I	Is the drug safe for humans?
Phase II	Does the drug work for its intended purpose?
Phase III	How does the new drug compare with other available treatments?

chemotherapy, new surgical techniques, and organ transplants, began with animal studies. Strict rules safeguard the care and use of animals in research and testing.

If no ill effects are discovered in animals receiving the drug, then studies on humans, called *clinical trials*, may begin. In all phases of clinical testing, the studies are done on people who volunteer. In phase I of a clinical trial, the drug is screened for safety on fewer than 100 healthy people. At this stage, researchers hope to learn whether they can safely give the drug to humans, determine the effective dosage range, and identify side effects.

If the drug is found to be safe, it is tested further. In phase II of a clinical trial, a few hundred people with the target disease are given the drug to see if it works for its intended purpose. If it does, the new drug will be compared with alternative treatments in phase III trials. Thousands of participants are involved in phase III of a clinical trial. The Food and Drug Administration

(FDA) approves only those drugs or treatments that have passed all three phases of human-subjects testing.

Recall that a well-designed experiment has both an experimental group and a control group. Clinical studies are no different. In a drug trial, the experimental group receives the drug under consideration. The control group receives a **placebo**, an innocuous, nondrug substance made to look like the drug being tested. Study participants are randomly assigned to either the control group or the experimental group and do not know whether they are receiving the treatment or a placebo. When neither the researchers nor the study participants know which people are receiving treatment and which are receiving the placebo, the study is described as being *double-blind*. It is important that participants do not know whether they are receiving the placebo or the drug, because their expectations about the drug could affect the way they respond. Similarly, researchers should not know which people are in the experimental or control groups, because their expectations or desire for a particular result could affect their interpretation of the data.

Finally, it is extremely important, and legally required, that study participants give their **informed consent** before participating. An informed consent document lists all the possible harmful effects of the drug or treatment and must be signed before a person can take part in the study. To give informed consent, study participants must be mentally capable of understanding the treatment and risks, so they cannot be mentally impaired due to mental retardation, mental or other illness, or substance abuse.

Epidemiological Studies

Human health can also be studied without clinical trials. In an *epidemiological study*, researchers look at patterns that occur within large populations. For example, an epidemiological study to investigate the effects of air pollution on asthma (a condition in which airway constriction causes breathing problems) would look for a correlation of some kind between the variable of interest (air pollution) and its suspected effects (worsening of asthma). If the researchers' hypothesis is that air pollution aggravates asthma, they might predict and then look for evidence that the number of people admitted to hospitals for asthma-related problems increases with increased levels of air pollution.

Recent epidemiological studies have asked the question, "Does using a cell phone increase your risk of developing brain cancer?" Cell phones emit radiofrequency waves and are usually used by holding them to one's ear. A Danish study published in 2006[1] compared cancer rates of 426,000 cell phone users, some of whom had used cell phones for more than 20 years, with cancer rates of the general public, as recorded in the Danish national cancer registry. Researchers determined the amount of cell phone use by examining billing records, and people who had cancer before using a cell phone were excluded from the study. The cancer rates (in the brain, central nervous system, salivary gland, and the eye) among cell phone users was statistically the same as the cancer rates in the general population. Thus, this study does not demonstrate a link between cell phone use and cancer. Indeed, nearly all studies to date have failed to show such a link. Although these results are reassuring, additional research must be done. Cell phone use is a relatively new practice, and many cancers take years to develop. You can find current information on cell phones and cancer on the website of the American Cancer Society.

Critical Thinking to Evaluate Scientific Claims

Few of us perform controlled experiments in our everyday lives, but all of us must evaluate the likely validity of scientific claims. We encounter them in many forms—as advertisements, news stories, and anecdotes told by friends. We often must make decisions based on these claims, but how can we decide whether they are valid? Critical-thinking skills can help us analyze the information and make prudent decisions.

The key to becoming a critical thinker is to ask questions. The following list is not exhaustive, but it may help guide your thinking process.

1. **Is the information consistent with information from other sources?** The best way to answer this question is to gather as much information as possible, from a variety of sources. Do not passively accept a report as true. Do some research.

2. **How reliable is the source of the information?** Investigate the source of the information to determine whether that person or group has the necessary scientific expertise. Is there any reason to think the claim may be biased? Who stands to gain if you accept it as true? For example, the Food and Drug Administration (FDA) is probably a more reliable source of information on the effectiveness of a drug than is the drug company marketing the drug. If a claim is controversial, listen to both sides of the debate and be aware of who is arguing on each side.

3. **Was the information obtained through proper scientific procedures?** Information gathered through controlled experiments is more reliable than anecdotal evidence, which cannot be verified. For example, your friend might tell you that his muscles have gotten larger since he started using some special exercise equipment. But you cannot be sure unless measurements were taken before and after he began to use it. Even if your friend can prove his muscles are bigger with such measurements, there is no guarantee that exercising with this equipment will build *your* muscles.

[1] Joachim Schüz and others, "Cellular Telephone Use and Cancer Risk: Update of a Nationwide Danish Cohort," *Journal of the National Cancer Institute* 98, no. 23 (December 6, 2006): 1707–13.

4. **Were experimental results interpreted correctly?** Consider, for example, a headline advertising capsules containing fish oils: "Fish Oils Increase Longevity." It may be tempting to conclude from this headline that you will live longer if you take fish oil supplements, but in fact the headline is referring to an experiment in which *dietary* fish oil increased longevity in *rats*. Rats fed a diet high in fish oils lived longer than did rats on a diet low in fish oil. The claim that taking fish oil supplements will increase longevity is not a valid conclusion based on the experiment. First, the study was done on rats, not on humans. Not all aspects of rat physiology generalize to humans. For example, rats are more resistant to heart disease than are humans. Second, the amount of dietary fish oil, not the amount of fish oil from capsules that supplement dietary fish oil, was the variable in the study the headline refers to. Supplements of fish oil may not have the same effect as dietary fish oils. It could be that taking fish oil supplements would boost the amount of fish oil in your body to unhealthy levels.

5. **Are there other possible explanations for the results?** Suppose you learn that the fish oil headline is based on a study showing that people who eat fish at least three times a week live longer than those who eat fish less frequently. In this case, the data indicate that there is a correlation between fish in the diet and length of life. However, a correlation between two factors does not prove that one *caused* the other. Instead, the two factors may *both* be caused by a third factor. In this case, the difference in longevity may be due to other differences in the lifestyles of the two groups. For instance, people who eat fish may exercise more frequently or have less stressful jobs or live in areas with less pollution.

Throughout your life you will be asked to make many decisions about scientific issues. Some will affect your community and even beyond. For example, should we eliminate genetically modified food? Should stem cell research be permitted? Should we vaccinate the general public against smallpox? Should companies polluting the atmosphere be taxed at a higher rate? We will raise these and similar questions throughout this textbook. You will find others every day in the local and national news media.

Although you may never be one of the lawmakers deciding these issues, you are a voter who can help choose the lawmakers and voice your opinions to the lawmakers, who will decide. Scientists can provide facts that may be useful as we all struggle to answer the complex questions facing society, but they cannot provide simple answers. As scientific knowledge grows and our choices become increasingly complex, each of us must stay informed and review the issues critically.

highlighting the concepts

Basic Characteristics of All Living Things (pp. 2–4)
- Life cannot be defined, only characterized.
- Living things contain nucleic acids, proteins, carbohydrates, and lipids; are made of cells; grow and reproduce; metabolize; detect and respond to stimuli; and maintain homeostasis. Populations of living things evolve over long periods of time.

Classification by Evolutionary Relationship (pp. 4–5)
- Classifications of living organisms reflect the evolutionary relationships among them. One currently popular classification system recognizes three domains: Bacteria, Archaea, and Eukarya. Domain Eukarya consists of four kingdoms: protists, fungi, plants, and animals.
- Humans are classified as animals, vertebrates, mammals, and primates.
- Humans share traits with other species; but unlike most other animals, they also have many unique features, among the most important of which is culture.

Levels of Biological Organization (p. 5)
- Human biology can be studied at different levels. Within an individual, the levels of increasing complexity are molecules, cells, tissues, organs, and organ systems.
- Beyond the level of the individual are populations, communities, ecosystems, and the biosphere.

Scientific Method (pp. 5–11)
- The scientific method consists of observation, formulation of a question and a good hypothesis (a testable, possible explanation), experimentation (performed with controls), and drawing a conclusion, which may lead to further experimentation.
- As evidence mounts in support of related hypotheses, the hypotheses may be organized into a theory, which is a well-supported explanation of nature.
- Inductive reasoning uses a large number of specific observations to arrive at a general conclusion. Deductive reasoning, in contrast, uses "if-then" logic to progress from the general to the specific.
- There are strict rules concerning experiments on humans and other animals. Drugs are usually tested on animals before they are tested on humans. If no ill effects in animals are observed, the drug is then tested on humans. Phase I trials determine whether the drug is safe for humans, phase II whether it works for its intended purpose, and phase III whether it is more effective than existing treatments.
- The design of a human experiment often includes an experimental group that receives the treatment and a control group that receives a placebo. In what is known as a double-blind experiment, neither the study participants nor the researchers know who is receiving the real treatment.
- Study participants must sign an informed consent document indicating that they were made aware of the possible harmful consequences of the treatment.
- Epidemiological studies examine patterns within populations to find a correlation between a variable and its suspected effects.

Critical Thinking to Evaluate Scientific Claims (pp. 11–12)
- Critical thinking consists of asking questions, gathering information, and evaluating evidence and its source carefully before drawing conclusions.

recognizing key terms

cell *p. 2*
metabolism *p. 4*
homeostasis *p. 4*
adaptive trait *p. 4*
population *p. 5*
community *p. 5*

ecosystem *p. 5*
biosphere *p. 5*
science *p. 6*
scientific method *p. 6*
hypothesis *p. 8*
controlled experiment *p. 8*

control group *p. 8*
experimental group *p. 8*
variable *p. 8*
conclusion *p. 8*
statistical significance *p. 8*
theory *p. 9*

inductive reasoning *p. 9*
deductive reasoning *p. 9*
placebo *p. 11*
informed consent *p. 11*

reviewing the concepts

1. List seven traits that characterize life. *pp. 2–4*
2. Name two characteristics that classify humans as mammals. Name two that classify them as primates. *p. 4*
3. Distinguish between a population, a community, an ecosystem, and the biosphere. *p. 5*
4. What is a hypothesis? How does it differ from a theory? *pp. 6, 8–9*
5. Define a controlled experiment. *p. 8*
6. Differentiate between inductive and deductive reasoning. *pp. 9–10*
7. What is a placebo? *p. 11*
8. What is meant by a double-blind experiment? *p. 11*

9. Describe the procedure in an epidemiological study. *p. 11*
10. A theory is
    a. a testable explanation for an observation.
    b. a conclusion based on the results of an experiment.
    c. a wide-ranging explanation for natural events that has been extensively tested over time.
    d. the factor that is altered in a controlled experiment.
11. The maintenance of physical and chemical conditions inside the body within tolerable ranges is called _____.
12. A(n) _____ is a testable explanation for an observation.
13. A trait that increases the chance that an organism will survive and reproduce in its natural environment is described as being _____.

applying the concepts

1. Interpret the following graph to answer the questions.

Do you have access to a mobile phone?

Do you use a mobile phone that you share in the family?

Do you have a mobile phone of your own?

The percentage of Swedish children questioned who answered yes to three questions about cell phone use. (Söderqvist et al. 2007)[2]
    a. What percentage of these 7-year-old children have access to a cell phone?
    b. At a young age, these children share a cell phone with their family. At what age does sharing begin to decline?
    c. What percentage of 10-year-old children own their own cell phone?

2. A native you met in the rain forest told you that one of the plants you collected brings relief to people who are having difficulty breathing. You suspect that it might be a good treatment for asthma, a condition in which constriction of airways causes breathing problems. You are able to isolate a component of this plant as a drug. Tests on animals show that it is effective. Phase I and phase II of clinical trials on humans show that the drug can be given safely to humans. Design an experiment to test the hypothesis that this drug eases breathing during an asthma attack.

3. Find an article or advertisement that makes a scientific claim. Use your critical-thinking skills to evaluate the claim.

[2]F. Söderqvist, L. Hardell, M. Carlberg, and K. H. Mild, "Ownership and Use of Wireless Telephones: A Population-Based Study of Swedish Children Aged 7–14 Years," *BMH Public Health* 7 (2007):105–13 (fig. 1, p. 107).

becoming information literate

Humans have an impact on the world around us at every level of the organization of life: molecule, cell, tissue, organ systems, individual, population, community, ecosystem, and biosphere. Use reliable sources of information (books, newspapers, magazines, journals, the Internet) to identify at least one current issue or concern to humans at each level of life's organization. Provide a citation for each source you use.

Begin by planning a strategy for your search. Keep a log of each source you use and evaluate it for reliability and helpfulness.

2

Chemistry Comes to Life

Thanks to "green chemistry," the chemicals traditionally used in dry cleaning can be replaced with safer and more environmentally-friendly ones. Understanding basic chemical principles can also help in understanding how the human body is put together and how it works.

Sheyda was desperate to find a job to help with her increasing tuition costs. She scanned the newspaper and several online employment sites but didn't find anything. While out running errands, she dropped off a load of dry cleaning and noticed a "help wanted" sign at the counter. She spoke with the owner, and learned that the job was part-time and would allow her to continue to take classes.

It was a seemingly perfect fit, but Sheyda was reluctant to apply for the job. She had read that dry cleaning chemicals could be quite toxic, causing headaches, dizziness, and long-term effects on fertility. She knew that some of these chemicals were even believed to be cancer-causing agents. The owner explained that his business did not use traditional dry cleaning methods. Instead, he used a "wet cleaning" system of water and nontoxic detergents that was much safer for his employees and the environment. This new dry cleaning method, he explained, was developed using "green chemistry," a movement that encourages scientists and manufacturers to use and produce chemicals in a way that does less damage to the planet. The goal of green chemistry methods is to use fewer toxic chemicals and produce fewer hazardous waste by-products.

Sheyda went to a nearby Internet café and pulled out her laptop. She typed in "green chemistry" and soon found that the green chemistry movement is currently being used to develop such diverse products as plant-based fuel sources, a variety of pharmaceuticals, nonstick cookware, and biodegradable plastic-like material made from corn. Reassured that greener chemical processes were safer, she returned to the dry cleaners and applied for the job.

Green chemistry is increasingly important in the field of **chemistry,** a branch of science that is concerned with the composition and properties of substances, including the stuff our bodies are built from. Chemical concepts—such as the way atoms bond and the way molecules in our body join to form macro-molecules such as proteins and carbohydrates—contribute important insights into how our bodies work. This chapter reviews several of these fundamental concepts, laying a foundation for discussions throughout the rest of the book.

The Nature of Atoms

The world around you contains an amazing variety of physical substances: the grass or concrete you walk on, the water you drink, the air you breathe, and even this book that you are reading. All of these substances that make up our world are called matter. Fundamentally, **matter** is anything that takes up space and has mass. All forms of matter are made up of atoms.

Atoms are units of matter that cannot be broken down into simpler substances by ordinary chemical means. Each atom is composed of even smaller, subatomic particles, such as protons, neutrons, and electrons. These subatomic particles are characterized by their location within the atom, their electrical charge, and their mass.

Each atom has a nucleus at its center and a surrounding spherical "cloud" of electrons. As you can see in Figure **2.1**, the nucleus

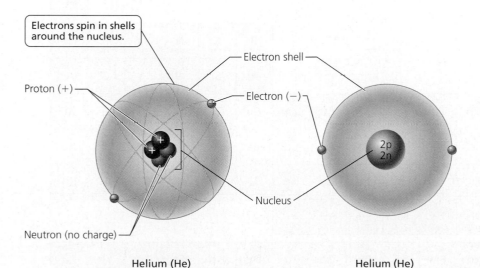

Electrons spin in shells around the nucleus.

Electron shell

Proton (+)

Electron (−)

Nucleus

Neutron (no charge)

Helium (He)

(a) A three-dimensional representation of an atom of helium, showing protons and neutrons in the nucleus and electrons occupying a region around the nucleus.

Helium (He)

(b) A two-dimensional representation of an atom of helium.

Oxygen (O)

(c) A two-dimensional representation of an atom of oxygen.

FIGURE 2.1 Atoms can be represented in different ways.

contains protons and neutrons. Electrons, on the other hand, move around the nucleus and occur at certain energy levels called shells. Note that shells are three-dimensional spaces, although they are often depicted in textbook figures as two-dimensional circles for convenience. The shell closest to the nucleus can hold up to 2 electrons. The next shell out can hold up to 8 electrons. Atoms with more than 10 electrons have additional shells. Electrons have different amounts of energy; those with the most energy are found furthest from the nucleus. The chemical properties of an atom are determined by the number of electrons in its outermost shell. As we will see, those atoms whose outermost shells are not full tend to interact with other atoms.

Neutrons, as their name implies, are neutral: they have no electrical charge. In contrast, protons have a positive charge and electrons have a negative charge. The negatively charged electrons stay near the nucleus because they are attracted to the positively charged protons in it. Most atoms have the same number of positively charged protons and negatively charged electrons. As a result, they are "neutral," having no net charge. Table **2.1** summarizes the basic characteristics of protons, neutrons, and electrons.

Elements

An **element** is a "pure" form of matter containing only one kind of atom. You are probably familiar with many elements, such as gold, silver, iron, and oxygen. Earth and everything on it or in its atmosphere is made up of a little more than 100 elements. Only about 20 elements are found in the human body, which consists mostly of carbon, oxygen, hydrogen, and nitrogen. Each element consists of atoms containing a certain number of protons in the nucleus. For example, all carbon atoms have 6 pro-

TABLE 2.1 Review of Subatomic Particles

Particle	Location	Charge	Mass
Proton	Nucleus	1 positive unit	1 atomic mass unit
Neutron	Nucleus	None	1 atomic mass unit
Electron	Outside the nucleus	1 negative unit	Negligible

tons. The number of protons in the atom's nucleus is called the *atomic number*.

The periodic table lists the elements and describes many of their characteristics. Figure **2.2** depicts the periodic table. Note that each element has a name and a one- or two-letter symbol. The symbol for the element carbon, for example, is C, and that for chlorine is Cl. (The abbreviations are not always as intuitive; for example, the abbreviation for gold is Au, based on the Latin name for the metal.) Besides an atomic number, each atom also has an atomic weight. Each proton and neutron has an approximate mass of 1 atomic mass unit, or amu. The mass of an electron is so small that it is usually considered zero. Because electrons have negligible mass, and protons and neutrons each have an atomic mass of 1, the *atomic weight* for any atom equals the number of protons plus the number of neutrons. Oxygen has an atomic weight of 16, indicating that it has 8 protons (we know this from its atomic number) and 8 neutrons in its nucleus.

FIGURE 2.2 The periodic table

Isotopes and Radioisotopes

All the atoms of a particular element contain the same number of protons; they can, however, have different numbers of neutrons. Such differences result in atoms of the same element having slightly different atomic weights. Atoms that have the same number of protons but differ in the number of neutrons are called **isotopes.** More than 300 isotopes occur naturally on Earth. The element carbon, for example, has 3 isotopes. All carbon atoms have 6 protons in the nucleus. Most carbon atoms also have 6 neutrons, but some have 7 or 8. The isotopes of carbon thus have atomic weights of 12, 13, and 14, respectively, depending on the number of neutrons in the nucleus. These isotopes are written ^{12}C (the most common form in nature), ^{13}C, and ^{14}C.

Radiation is energy moving through space. Examples include radio waves, light, heat, and the excess energy or particles given off by unstable isotopes as they break down. Some elements have both stable and unstable isotopes. Unstable, radiation-emitting isotopes are called **radioisotopes.** About 60 occur naturally, and many more have been made in laboratories.

Radiation can be dangerous or useful, depending on the context. When dangerous, it can damage the body directly or indirectly. Direct damage to a person absorbing harmful radiation may include a low white blood cell count, development of some cancers, and damage to organs and glands. Short-term, high-level exposure to radiation can cause skin burns (Figure **2.3**). In other cases, radiation may not produce any noticeable injury to the person who was exposed; but it may alter the hereditary material in the cells of his or her reproductive system, possibly causing defects in the individual's offspring. For an example of the harmful effects of radiation and how to protect yourself from radiation that occurs naturally in the environment, see the Environmental Issue essay, *Radon Gas: A Killer That Can Be Stopped*.

In stark contrast to the harmful effects of radiation are its medical uses. Medical professionals use radiation for diagnosis and therapy. Perhaps the most familiar diagnostic use of radiation is the x-ray. A less common diagnostic procedure is the use of small doses of radiation to generate visual images of internal body parts. Radioactive iodine, for example, is often used to identify disorders of the thyroid gland. This gland, located in the neck, normally accumulates the element iodine, which it uses to regulate growth and metabolism. Small doses of iodine-131 (^{131}I), a radioactive isotope, can be given to a patient suspected of having metabolic problems. The radioactive iodine is taken up by the patient's thyroid gland and detected by medical instruments, as shown in Figure **2.4**. The small amount of radioactive iodine used in imaging does not damage the thyroid gland or surrounding structures. However, larger doses can be used to kill thyroid cells when the gland is enlarged and overactive.

Radiation can also be used to kill cancer cells. Cancer cells divide more rapidly and have higher rates of metabolic activity than do most normal cells. For these reasons, cancer cells are more susceptible to the destructive effects of radiation. Still, when medical professionals aim an outside beam of radiation at a tumor to kill the cancer cells inside it, they must also take steps to shield the surrounding healthy tissue. Sometimes a radiation source is placed within the body to treat a cancer. For example, one treatment for prostate cancer (the prostate gland is an accessory reproductive gland in males) involves the placement of radioactive seeds (pellets) directly in the prostate gland (Figure **2.5**). Once in place, the seeds emit radiation that damages or kills nearby cancer cells. In most cases, the seeds are left in place, even though they stop emitting radiation within 1 year.

FIGURE 2.3 An example of direct damage caused by radiation. This individual survived the atomic explosion at Nagasaki, Japan, on August 9, 1945. Damage to the reproductive cells of people exposed to radiation has proved more difficult to recognize. Children of atomic bomb survivors are still being monitored.

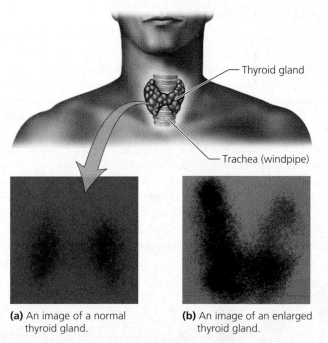

(a) An image of a normal thyroid gland.

(b) An image of an enlarged thyroid gland.

FIGURE 2.4 Radioactive iodine can be used to generate images of the thyroid gland. Such images may be used to diagnose metabolic disorders.

Prostate gland

Needle

Ultrasound probe

Needle releasing radioactive seeds

Prostate gland

FIGURE 2.5 Prostate cancer can be treated by the implantation of radioactive seeds in the prostate gland. A physician injects the seeds through needles, with guidance from an ultrasound probe placed in the rectum.

FIGURE 2.6 Logo for irradiated foods. This logo and words such as "Treated with radiation" must appear on food that has been irradiated.

Compounds and Chemical Bonds

Two or more elements may combine to form a new chemical substance called a **compound.** A compound's characteristics are usually different from those of its elements. Consider what happens when the element sodium (Na) combines with the element chlorine (Cl). Sodium is a silvery metal that explodes when it comes into contact with water. Chlorine is a deadly yellow gas. In combination, however, they form a crystalline solid called sodium chloride (NaCl)—plain table salt (Figure **2.7**).

The atoms (or, as we will soon see, ions) in a compound are held together by chemical bonds. There are two types of chemical bond: covalent and ionic. Recall that atoms have outer shells, which are the regions surrounding the nucleus where the electrons are most likely to be found. Figure **2.8** depicts the first two shells as concentric circles around the nucleus. As discussed earlier, a full innermost shell contains 2 electrons. A full second shell contains 8 electrons. Atoms with a total of more than 10 electrons have additional shells. When atoms form bonds, they lose, gain, or share the electrons in their outermost shell.

Covalent Bonds

A **covalent bond** forms when two or more atoms *share* electrons in their outer shells. Consider the compound methane (CH_4). Methane is formed by the sharing of electrons between one atom of carbon and four atoms of hydrogen. Notice in Figure **2.9a** that the outer shell of an isolated carbon atom contains only 4 electrons, even though it can hold as many as 8. Also note that hydrogen atoms only have 1 electron, although the first shell can hold up to 2 electrons. A carbon atom can fill its outer shell by joining with four atoms of hydrogen. At the same time, by forming a covalent bond

(a) The element sodium is a solid metal.

(b) Elemental sodium reacts explosively with water.

(c) The element chlorine is a yellow gas.

(d) When the elements sodium and chlorine join, they form table salt, a compound quite different from its elements.

FIGURE 2.7 The characteristics of compounds are usually different from those of their elements.

Radon Gas: A Killer That Can Be Stopped

Some lethal substances are obvious because you can see or smell them. Others are not obvious, even when surrounding you in your own home. Radon, a radioactive gas produced when uranium breaks down in rock, soil, or water, is among the silent killers. This invisible, odorless gas moves up through the soil, eventually seeping through cracks or holes in the foundations of buildings. Once inside a building, radon may accumulate, sometimes reaching

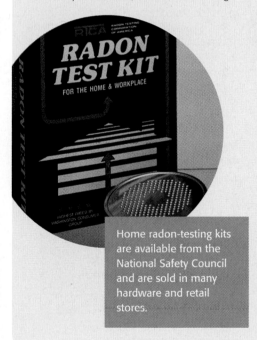

Home radon-testing kits are available from the National Safety Council and are sold in many hardware and retail stores.

what has been defined as harmful levels. The same techniques that help to make a building energy efficient also tend to limit the exchange of air from inside a building to outside; and, as a result, modern, energy-efficient buildings can accumulate radon.

Although radon can enter any type of building, the greatest exposure threat usually occurs in homes because people typically spend more time in their home than in their school or workplace. Most radon enters buildings as gas from the soil, but radon can also enter a home through well water. The greatest risk from radon in water occurs when it is released into the air during showers or other household uses of water. The Environmental Protection Agency (EPA) estimates that 1 in 15 homes in the United States has an unacceptable level of radon, defined as 4 or more picocuries of radon per liter of air (A picocurie is a measure of radioactivity that equals about 2.2 disintegrations of radioactive particles per minute; a picocurie is a trillionth of a curie.)

Each year in the United States, radon contributes to the death of about 21,000 people; this number exceeds deaths from drunk driving, drowning, and falls or fires in the home (Figure **2.A**). Radon kills by causing lung cancer. Smoking combined with exposure to radon is particularly risky: if 1000 people who smoked were exposed over a lifetime to 4 picocuries of radon per liter of air, 62 will likely get lung cancer as compared to 7 people in the same situation who have never smoked.

The EPA recommends that all homes be tested for radon. Residents can test for radon themselves using a do-it-yourself kit available at most hardware stores. Alternatively, residents can hire a certified radon professional to do the

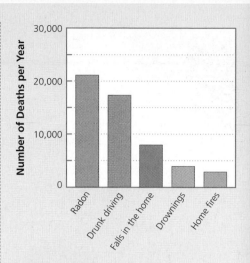

FIGURE 2.A Radon causes about 21,000 deaths from lung cancer each year. Here, the number of deaths from radon is shown in relation to numbers of deaths from other causes.
Sources: EPA's 2003 Assessment of Risks from Radon in Homes (EPA 402-R-03-003); Centers for Disease Control and Prevention's 1999–2001 National Center for Injury Prevention and Control Report; 2002 National Safety Council Reports.

testing. In either case, testing can last from a few days to several months, depending on how soon results are needed and whether a year-round average radon level is desired (the EPA publishes recommendations for testing). If testing reveals high levels of radon in a home, then a contractor trained to fix radon problems can install a venting system that pulls radon from beneath the house and releases it to the outside. New homes can be built with features to reduce radon levels; even so, testing should be performed to make sure that the construction techniques are effective.

Hydrogen atom (atomic number = 1)

Carbon atom (atomic number = 6)

Oxygen atom (atomic number = 8)

The shell closest to the nucleus can hold up to 2 electrons.

The next shell out can hold up to 8 electrons (the shell shown here has 6). Atoms with more than 10 electrons have additional shells.

FIGURE 2.8 Atoms of hydrogen, carbon, and oxygen. Each of the concentric circles around the nucleus represents a shell occupied by electrons.

Carbon atom   4 Hydrogen atoms   Methane (CH$_4$)

(a) The molecule methane (CH$_4$) is formed by the sharing of electrons between one carbon atom and four hydrogen atoms. Because in each case one pair of electrons is shared, the bonds formed are single covalent bonds.

Carbon atom   2 Oxygen atoms   Carbon dioxide (CO$_2$)

(b) The oxygen atoms in a molecule of carbon dioxide (CO$_2$) form double covalent bonds with the carbon atom. In double bonds, two pairs of electrons are shared.

Nitrogen atom   Nitrogen atom   Nitrogen gas (N$_2$)

(c) The nitrogen atoms in nitrogen gas (N$_2$) form a triple covalent bond in which three pairs of electrons are shared.

FIGURE 2.9 Covalent bonds form when electrons are shared between atoms. Shown here are examples of single, double, and triple covalent bonds. For each example, the structural formula is shown on the far right.

with the carbon atom, each hydrogen atom fills its first shell. We see, then, that the covalent bonds between the carbon atom and hydrogen atoms of methane result in filled outer shells for all five atoms involved.

A **molecule** is a chemical structure held together by covalent bonds. Recall that compounds are formed by two or more elements, so molecules that contain only one kind of atom are not considered compounds. For example, oxygen gas, formed by the joining of two oxygen atoms, is *not* a compound, but it *is* a molecule. Molecules are described by a formula that contains the symbols for all of the elements included in that molecule. If more than one atom of a given element is present in the molecule, a subscript is used to show the precise number of that kind of atom. For example, the molecular formula of sucrose (table sugar) is $C_{12}H_{22}O_{11}$, showing that one molecule of sucrose contains 12 atoms of carbon, 22 atoms of hydrogen, and 11 atoms of oxygen. Numbers placed in front of the molecular formula indicate more than one molecule. For example, three molecules of sucrose are described by the formula $3C_{12}H_{22}O_{11}$.

As shown in the methane molecule in Figure 2.9a, the bond between each of the four hydrogen atoms and the carbon atom consists of a single pair of electrons. A bond in which a single pair of electrons is shared is called a single bond; in this example, the methane molecule contains four single covalent bonds. Sometimes, however, two atoms share two or three pairs of electrons. These bonds are called double and triple covalent bonds, respectively. For example, carbon dioxide, CO_2, produced by chemical reactions inside our cells, has double covalent bonds between the carbon atom and each of two oxygen atoms (Figure 2.9b). And the nitrogen atoms in nitrogen gas, N_2, are joined by triple covalent bonds (Figure 2.9c).

Covalent bonds in molecules are sometimes depicted by a structural formula. Notice in the box at the right of Figure 2.9a that one straight line is drawn between the carbon atom and each hydrogen atom in the structural formula for the methane molecule. The single line indicates a single covalent bond resulting from a pair of shared electrons. In the box to the right of Figure 2.9b, the double lines between the carbon and oxygen atoms in the carbon dioxide molecule indicate a double covalent bond, or two pairs of shared electrons. In Figure 2.9c, three lines drawn between the two nitrogen atoms in gaseous nitrogen depict a triple covalent bond, or three pairs of shared electrons.

Ionic Bonds

We have all heard the phrase "opposites attract" in reference to human relationships—and it is no different for ions. An **ion** is an atom or group of atoms that carries either a positive (+) or a negative (−) electrical charge. Electrical charges result from the *transfer* (as opposed to sharing) of electrons between atoms. Recall that a neutral atom has the same number of positively charged protons and negatively charged electrons. An atom that loses an electron has one more proton than electrons and therefore has a positive charge. An atom that gains an electron has one more electron than protons and has a negative charge. Oppositely charged ions are attracted to one another. An **ionic bond** results from the mutual attraction of oppositely charged ions.

Ions form because of the tendency of atoms to attain a complete outermost shell. Consider, again, the atoms of sodium and chlorine that join to form sodium chloride. As shown in Figure **2.10**, an atom

of sodium has 1 electron in its outer shell. An atom of chlorine has 7 electrons in its outer shell. Sodium chloride is formed when the sodium atom transfers the single electron in its outer shell to the chlorine atom. The sodium atom now has a full outer shell. This comes about because the sodium atom loses its third shell, making the second shell its outermost shell. The sodium atom, having lost an electron, has one more proton than electrons and therefore now has a positive charge (Na^+). The chlorine atom, having gained an electron to fill its outer shell, has one more electron than protons and now has a negative charge (Cl^-). These oppositely charged ions are attracted to one another, and an ionic bond forms. Because they do not contain shared electrons, ionic bonds are weaker than covalent bonds.

The Role of Water in Life

Water is such a familiar part of our everyday lives that we often overlook its unusual qualities. Unique properties of water include its virtuosity as a dissolving agent, its high heat capacity, and its high heat of vaporization. As it turns out, water's unusual qualities can be traced to its polarity (tendency of its molecules to have positive and negative regions) and the hydrogen bonds between its molecules.

Polarity and Hydrogen Bonds

In covalently bonded molecules, electrons may be shared equally or unequally between atoms. When the sharing of electrons is unequal, different ends of the same molecule can have slight opposite charges. Unequal covalent bonds are called *polar*, and molecules with unevenly distributed charges are called polar molecules. In water (H_2O), for example, the electrons shared by oxygen and hydrogen spend more time near the oxygen atom than near the hydrogen atom. As a result, the oxygen atom has a slight negative charge; each hydrogen atom has a slight positive charge; and water

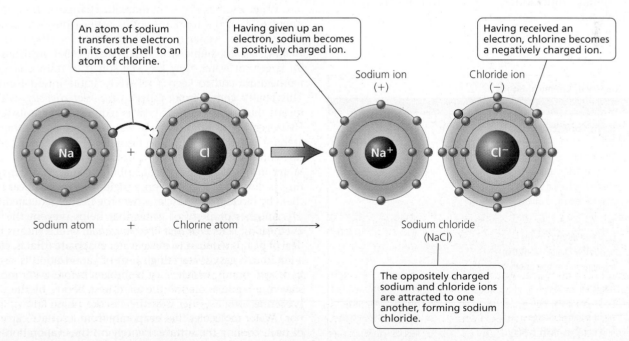

An atom of sodium transfers the electron in its outer shell to an atom of chlorine.

Having given up an electron, sodium becomes a positively charged ion.

Having received an electron, chlorine becomes a negatively charged ion.

Sodium ion (+)

Chloride ion (−)

Sodium atom + Chlorine atom ⟶ Sodium chloride (NaCl)

The oppositely charged sodium and chloride ions are attracted to one another, forming sodium chloride.

FIGURE 2.10 An ionic bond involves the transfer of electrons between atoms. Such a transfer creates oppositely charged ions that are attracted to one another.

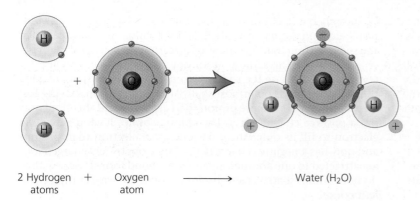

2 Hydrogen + Oxygen ⟶ Water (H_2O)
atoms atom

(a) Water is formed when an oxygen atom covalently bonds (shares electrons) with two hydrogen atoms. Due to unequal sharing of electrons, oxygen carries a slight negative charge and the hydrogen atoms carry a slight positive charge.

FIGURE 2.11 The hydrogen bonds of water

(b) The hydrogen atoms from one water molecule are attracted to the oxygen atoms of other water molecules. This relatively weak attraction (shown by dotted lines) is called a hydrogen bond.

molecules are polar (Figure **2.11a**). The hydrogen atoms of one water molecule are attracted to the oxygen atoms of other water molecules. The attraction between a slightly positively charged hydrogen atom and a slightly negatively charged atom nearby is called a **hydrogen bond.** In the case of water, the hydrogen bonding occurs between hydrogen and oxygen. However, sometimes hydrogen bonds form between hydrogen and atoms of other elements.

Hydrogen bonds are weaker than either ionic or covalent bonds. For this reason, they are generally illustrated by dotted lines rather than solid lines, as shown in Figure 2.11b. Even though individual hydrogen bonds are very weak, collectively they can be significant. Hydrogen bonds maintain the shape of proteins and our hereditary material, DNA, and they account for some of the unique physical properties of water.

Covalent bonds, ionic bonds, and hydrogen bonds are summarized in Table **2.2**.

TABLE 2.2 Review of Chemical Bonds			
Type	**Basis for Attraction**	**Strength**	**Example**
Covalent	Sharing of electrons between atoms; the sharing between atoms may be equal or unequal	Strongest	CH_4 (methane)
Ionic	Transfer of electrons between atoms creates oppositely charged ions that are attracted to one another	Strong	NaCl (table salt)
Hydrogen	Attraction between a hydrogen atom with a slight positive charge and another atom (often oxygen) with a slight negative charge	Weak	Between a hydrogen atom on one water molecule and an oxygen atom on another water molecule

Properties of Water

Life depends on the properties of water. Let's consider some of the ways that the polarity and hydrogen bonding of water give water the properties that make it so vital to life.

Due to the polarity of its molecules, water interacts with many substances. This interactivity makes it an excellent solvent, easily dissolving both polar and charged substances. Ionic compounds, such as NaCl, dissolve into independent ions in water. The sodium ions and chloride ions separate from one another in water because the sodium ions are attracted to the negative regions of water molecules and the chloride ions are attracted to the positive regions. Because of its excellence as a solvent, water serves as the body's main transport medium. As the liquid component of blood, it carries dissolved nutrients, gases, and wastes through the circulatory system. Metabolic wastes are excreted from the body in urine, another watery medium.

Water also helps prevent dramatic changes in body temperature. About 67% of the human body is water (thus, if a person weighs 68 kg (150 lb), water makes up about 45 kg (100 lb) of the body weight). Because humans, as well as many other organisms, are made up largely of water, they are well suited to resist changes in body temperature and to keep a relatively stable internal environment. This ability comes from water's *high heat capacity*, which simply means that a great deal of heat is required to raise its temperature. Hydrogen bonds hold multiple water molecules together, so a large amount of heat is required to break these bonds (a higher temperature corresponds to an increase in the movement of the molecules). Water in blood also helps redistribute heat within our bodies. Our fingers don't usually freeze on a frigid day because heat is carried to them by blood from muscles where the heat is generated.

Another property of water that helps prevent the body from overheating is its *high heat of vaporization*, which means that a great deal of heat is required to make water evaporate (that is, change from a liquid to a gas). Water's high heat of vaporization is also due to its hydrogen bonds, which must be broken before water molecules can leave the liquid and enter the air. (These bonds, by the way, remain broken as long as water is in the gaseous phase known as water vapor.) Water molecules that evaporate from a surface carry away a lot of heat, cooling the surface. We rely on the evaporation of water in sweat to cool the body surface and prevent overheating (Figure **2.12**). By the same token, water vapor in the air can inhibit the evaporation of sweat—which is why we tend to feel hotter on a humid day.

FIGURE 2.12 The evaporation of water in sweat cools the surface of this runner's body. Water has a high heat of vaporization, so when water molecules in sweat evaporate, they carry away a lot of heat.

stop and think

Sharp increases in body temperature can cause heat stroke, a condition that may damage the brain. Explain why heat stroke is more likely to occur on a hot, humid day than on an equally hot, dry day.

It is clear that water is essential for human life and for the lives of many other organisms we share the planet with. Despite our reliance on water, we continue to pollute both seawater and freshwater. Equally alarming is the global shortage of freshwater, caused largely by the burgeoning human population. For one community's creative response to the water shortage, see the Environmental Issue essay, *From Toilet to Tap: One Strategy for Confronting the Shortage of Freshwater.*

Acids and Bases

Sometimes a water molecule dissociates, or breaks up, forming a positively charged hydrogen ion (H^+) and a negatively charged hydroxide ion (OH^-):

$$H-O-H \rightleftharpoons H^+ + OH^-$$
$$\text{Water} \qquad \text{Hydrogen} \qquad \text{Hydroxide}$$
$$\text{ion} \qquad\quad \text{ion}$$

(Note that in equations describing chemical reactions, an arrow should be read as "yields.")

In any sample of water, the fraction of water molecules that are dissociated is extremely small, so water molecules are much more common in the human body than are H^+ and OH^-. In fact, the amount of H^+ in the body must be precisely regulated. Even slight changes in the concentration of H^+ can be disastrous, disrupting chemical reactions within cells. Substances called acids and bases influence the concentration of H^+ in solutions.

Acids and bases are defined by what happens when they are added to water. An **acid** is anything that releases hydrogen ions (H^+) when placed in water. A **base** is anything that releases hydroxide ions (OH^-) when placed in water. Hydrochloric acid (HCl),

for example, dissociates in water to produce hydrogen ions (H^+) and chloride ions (Cl^-). Because HCl increases the concentration of H^+ in solution, it is classified as an acid. Sodium hydroxide (NaOH), on the other hand, dissociates in water to produce sodium ions (Na^+) and hydroxide ions (OH^-). Because NaOH increases the concentration of OH^- in solution, it is classified as a base. The OH^- produced when NaOH dissociates reacts with H^+ to form water molecules and thus reduces the concentration of H^+ in solution. Therefore, acids increase the concentration of H^+ in solution, and bases decrease the concentration of H^+ in solution.

The pH Scale

We often want to know more than simply whether a substance is an acid or a base. For example, how strong an acid is battery acid? How strong a base is household ammonia? Questions like these can be answered by knowing the pH of these solutions and understanding the pH scale (Figure **2.13**). The **pH** of a solution is a measure of hydrogen ion concentration. The **pH scale** ranges from 0 to 14, with a

FIGURE 2.13 The pH scale and the pH of some body fluids and other familiar substances

From Toilet to Tap: One Strategy for Confronting the Shortage of Freshwater

We, like many organisms, depend on a steady supply of freshwater. Yet, experts tell us that our water supply is dwindling. The vast majority of Earth's water (97.4%) is in the oceans; this water is too salty for us to use for drinking, bathing, and even irrigation without first treating it. About 2% is locked away in glaciers and polar ice. This leaves 0.6% of Earth's water, in the form of freshwater, for humans and other organisms to use. The water available to humans is classified as surface water (rivers, lakes, reservoirs) and ground water (water in porous rock layers below the Earth's surface). Over the last century, we have damaged our supplies of freshwater by redirecting the flow of rivers, constructing dams, draining wetlands, and extracting groundwater at rates that exceed its replacement (as part of the water cycle, groundwater is naturally replaced when water that falls as precipitation seeps into the ground). Indeed, dams now intercept 35% of rivers as they flow to the sea; this value is up from 5% in 1950. Some estimates suggest that in the last 100 years, humans have destroyed half of all the wetlands in the world. These grim statistics highlight the impact that we have had on our water supply. If current activities and trends continue, this impact will worsen as the human population continues to grow.

Some communities in California have taken a unique approach to the problem. Like many western states, California has been experiencing

prolonged drought. At the same time, it has a steadily growing population, and it faces the threat of seawater moving into its groundwater. Orange County, in southern California, has responded to the impending water crisis by building the Groundwater Replenishment (GWR) System. Under construction since 2003, and receiving final approval to begin operations in early 2008, this new system accomplishes two very important things. First, it recharges the groundwater supply with treated wastewater rather than sending the wastewater out to sea. Second, it builds up the county's seawater intrusion barrier—a series of wells from which water is pumped to create an "underground water dam" that blocks seawater from entering the groundwater basin.

Here is how the new system works. Industrial and household sewage is treated at the Orange County Sanitation District, as it has been in the past. The sewage, or primary effluent, undergoes several treatments designed to break down organic material and to remove particulate matter. After these treatments, the water, called secondary effluent, would normally be discharged to the ocean. But under the new system, at this point, the treated wastewater enters the Advanced Water Purification Facility (AWPF). At the AWPF, the water undergoes a several-step purification process. These steps include (1) addition of sodium hypochlorite to disinfect the water; (2) microfiltration to remove any remaining suspended particles and microorganisms (bacteria will be removed, but some viruses may make it through the filters); (3) reverse osmosis, in which the water is forced under pressure through a semipermeable membrane to remove dissolved salts and metallic ions; and (4) addition of hydrogen peroxide followed by irradiation with ultraviolet light to remove any remaining organic contaminants. About half of the water exiting the AWPF is injected into Orange County's seawater intrusion barrier. The other half of the water exit-

The toilet-to-tap program replenishes groundwater supplies with reclaimed waste water.

ing the AWPF is piped to a giant percolation pond where it moves through gravel, sand, and clay into the groundwater supply, filtering naturally just as rainwater finds its way into groundwater. Eventually, this water will enter drinking well intakes. The project is controversial largely because of the graphic description of the water as going "from toilet to tap."

The end result of Orange County's Groundwater Replenishment System is water that meets or exceeds all existing standards for drinking water. While some may cringe at the thought of drinking water that has been recycled from sewage, it is a reality that many of us may have to get used to as global and regional water supplies continue to tighten.

Questions to Consider:

- Would you be hesitant to drink water that has been recycled from sewage, even if it met current drinking water standards? If yes, what is the reason for your hesitation?
- Do you think that human ingenuity will always be able to produce the technology needed to avoid major environmental crises, such as a global shortage of freshwater?

---

pH of 7 being neutral (the substance does not increase H^+ or OH^-), a pH of less than 7 being acidic, and a pH of greater than 7, basic.

Usually, the amount of H^+ in a solution is very small. For example, the concentration of H^+ in a solution with a pH of 6 is 1×10^{-6} (or 0.000001) moles per liter (a mole, here, is not a small furry animal with a star-shaped nose, but a unit of measurement that indicates a specific number of atoms, molecules, or ions). Similarly, the

concentration of H^+ in a solution with a pH of 5 is 1×10^{-5} (or 0.00001) moles per liter. Technically, pH is the negative logarithm of the concentration of H^+ in a solution. According to the pH scale, the lower the pH, the greater the acidity—or concentration of H^+—in a solution. Each reduction of pH by one unit represents a tenfold increase in the amount of H^+. So a solution with a pH of 5 is 10 times more acidic than a solution with a pH of 6.

TABLE 2.3 Review of the Characteristics of Acids and Bases

Characteristic	Acid	Base
Behavior in water	Releases H^+	Releases OH^-
pH	Less than 7	Greater than 7
Example	HCl (hydrochloric acid)	NaOH (sodium hydroxide)

And a solution with a pH of 4 is 100 times more acidic than one with a pH of 6. Some characteristics of acids and bases, including their values on the pH scale, are summarized in Table **2.3**.

Buffers

Most biological systems must keep their fluids within a narrow range of pH values. Substances called **buffers** keep pH values from changing dramatically. Buffers remove excess H^+ from solution when concentrations of H^+ increase. Buffers add H^+ when concentrations of H^+ decrease. For example, an important buffering system that keeps the pH of blood at about 7.4 is the carbonic acid–bicarbonate system. When carbon dioxide is added to water it forms carbonic acid (H_2CO_3), which dissociates into hydrogen ions and bicarbonate ions (HCO_3^-):

$$CO_2 + H_2O \rightleftharpoons H_2CO_3 \rightleftharpoons H^+ + HCO_3^-$$

Carbon dioxide   Water   Carbonic acid   Hydrogen ion   Bicarbonate ion

Carbonic acid and bicarbonate have a buffering action because when levels of H^+ decrease in the blood, carbonic acid dissociates, adding H^+ to solution. When levels of H^+ increase in the blood, the H^+ combines with bicarbonate and is removed from solution. Such action is essential because even slight changes in the pH of blood—say, a drop from 7.4 to 7.0 or an increase to 7.8—can cause death in a few minutes.

In the human body, almost all biochemical reactions occur around pH 7 and are maintained at that level by powerful buffering systems. An important exception occurs in the stomach, where hydrochloric acid (HCl) produces pH values from about 1 to 3. In the stomach, HCl kills bacteria swallowed with food or drink and promotes the initial breakdown of proteins. These activities require an acid stomach, and the stomach has several ways of protecting itself from the acid (discussed in Chapter 15). However, sometimes stomach acid backs up into the esophagus, and "heartburn" is the uncomfortable result. Taking an antacid can ease the discomfort of heartburn. Antacids consist of weak bases that temporarily relieve the pain of stomach acid in the esophagus by neutralizing some of the hydrochloric acid.

The critical link between pH and life is illustrated by the impact of acid rain on our environment and health. Acid rain is usually defined as rain with a pH lower than 5.6, the pH of natural precipitation. It is caused largely by the burning of fossil fuels in cars, factories, and power plants. The sulfur dioxide and nitrogen oxides produced by these activities react with water in the atmosphere to form sulfuric acid (H_2SO_4) and nitric acid (HNO_3). These acids fall to Earth as rain, snow, or fog, with pH values sometimes as low as 1.5.

The effects of acid rain on the environment have been devastating (Figure **2.14**). On land, acid rain has been linked to the decline of forests. Trees, for example, become stressed and more susceptible to disease when their nutrient uptake is disrupted by increased acidity in the soil. In aquatic environments, acid rain has been linked to the decrease and sometimes total elimination of populations of fish and amphibians. Embryos of spotted salamanders, for example, develop abnormally under somewhat acidic conditions and die when pH values are less than about 5. Acid rain is harmful to human health, as well. The pollutants that cause acid rain form fine particles of sulfate and nitrate that are easily inhaled. Once inside us, they cause irritation and respiratory illnesses such as asthma and bronchitis.

Because most acid rain is caused by human activity, it is within our power to reduce, if not eliminate, the problem. Power plants and automobile manufacturers have taken steps to reduce emissions of sulfur dioxide and nitrogen oxides, leading to significant progress in reducing acid rain.

(a) Acid rain has destroyed parts of our forests.

(b) In some areas, acid rain has reduced or eliminated populations of aquatic organisms. Acidic conditions have been shown, for example, to disrupt the development of spotted salamanders or to kill the embryos outright.

FIGURE 2.14 Effects of acid rain

Major Molecules of Life

Most of the molecules we have discussed so far have been small and simple. Many of the molecules of life, however, are enormous by comparison and have complex architecture. Some proteins, for example, are made up of thousands of atoms linked together in a chain that repeatedly coils and folds upon itself. Exceptionally large molecules, including many important biological molecules, are known as **macromolecules.**

Macromolecules that consist of many small, repeating molecular subunits linked in a chain are called **polymers.** The small molecular subunits that form the building blocks of the polymer are called **monomers.** We might think of a polymer as a pearl necklace, with each monomer representing a pearl. As we shall see, a protein is a polymer, or chain, of amino acid monomers linked together. And glycogen, the storage form of carbohydrates in animals, is a polymer of glucose monomers.

Polymers form through **dehydration synthesis** (sometimes called the condensation reaction). In this process, the reaction that bonds one monomer covalently to another releases a water molecule: one of the monomers donates OH, and the other donates H. The reverse process, called **hydrolysis,** which the body uses to break many polymers apart, requires the addition of water across the covalent bonds. The H from the water molecule attaches to one monomer and the OH attaches to the adjoining monomer, thus breaking the covalent bond between the two. Hydrolysis plays a critical role in digestion. Most foods consist of polymers too large to pass from our digestive tract into the bloodstream and on to our cells. Thus, the polymers are hydrolyzed into their component monomers. The monomers can then be absorbed into the bloodstream for transport throughout the body. Dehydration synthesis and hydrolysis are summarized in Figure **2.15.**

Carbohydrates

The **carbohydrates** known commonly as sugars and starches provide fuel (energy) for the human body. Carbohydrates are compounds made entirely of carbon, hydrogen, and oxygen, with each molecule having twice as many hydrogen atoms as oxygen atoms. Sugars and starches can be classified by size into monosaccharides, oligosaccharides, and polysaccharides. Some common carbohydrates are described in Table **2.4.**

Monosaccharides

Monosaccharides, also called simple sugars, are the smallest molecular units of carbohydrates. They contain from three to seven carbon atoms and, in fact, can be classified by the number of carbon atoms they contain. A sugar that contains five carbons is *pent*ose; one with six carbons is *hex*ose; and so on. Glucose, fructose, and galactose are examples of six-carbon sugars (Table 2.4). Monosaccharides can be depicted in several ways (Figure **2.16**).

Oligosaccharides

Oligosaccharides (*oligo* means "few") are chains of a few monosaccharides joined together by dehydration synthesis. **Disaccharides,** one type of oligosaccharide, are double sugars that form when two monosaccharides covalently bond to each other. The disaccharide sucrose (table sugar) consists of the monosaccharides glucose and fructose (Figure **2.17**). Two glucose molecules form the disaccharide maltose, an important ingredient of beer. Another disaccharide is lactose, the principal carbohydrate of milk and milk products. Lactose is formed by the joining of glucose and galactose.

Polysaccharides

Polysaccharides (*poly* means "many") are complex carbohydrates that form when monosaccharides (most commonly glucose) join together in long chains. Most polysaccharides store energy or provide structure. In plants, the storage polysaccharide is **starch;** in animals it is **glycogen,** a short-term energy source that can be broken down to release energy-laden glucose molecules. Humans store glycogen mainly in the cells of the liver and muscles (Figure **2.18a**).

Cellulose is a structural polysaccharide found in the cell walls of plants (Figure 2.18b). Humans lack the enzymes necessary to digest cellulose and, as a result, it passes unchanged through our digestive tract. (Enzymes are discussed later in this chapter.) Nevertheless, cellulose is an important form of dietary fiber (roughage) that helps fecal matter move through the large intestines. Including fiber in our diet may reduce the incidence of colon cancer.

(a) Polymers are formed by dehydration synthesis, in which a water molecule is removed and two monomers are joined.

(b) Polymers are broken down by hydrolysis, in which the addition of a water molecule disrupts the bonds between two monomers.

FIGURE 2.15 Formation and breaking apart of polymers

TABLE 2.4 Review of Some Common Carbohydrates

Carbohydrate	Molecular Formula	Source	Monomers
Monosaccharides			
Glucose	$C_6H_{12}O_6$	Blood, fruit, honey	
Fructose	$C_6H_{12}O_6$	Fruit, honey	
Galactose	$C_6H_{12}O_6$	From hydrolysis of lactose (milk sugar)	
Disaccharides			
Sucrose	$C_{12}H_{22}O_{11}$	Sugar cane, maple syrup	Glucose, fructose
Maltose	$C_{12}H_{22}O_{11}$	From hydrolysis of starch; ingredient in beer	Glucose
Lactose	$C_{12}H_{22}O_{11}$	Component of milk	Glucose, galactose
Polysaccharides			
Starch	*	Potatoes, corn, some grains	Glucose
Glycogen	*	Stored in muscle and liver cells	Glucose
Cellulose	*	Cell walls of plants	Glucose

*These complex carbohydrates consist of chains containing hundreds of glucose molecules joined to each other in long strings.

FIGURE 2.16 Monosaccharides are simple sugars, generally having a backbone of three to six carbon atoms. Many of these carbon atoms are also bonded to hydrogen (H) and a hydroxyl group (OH). In the fluid within our cells, the carbon backbone usually forms a ringlike structure. Here, three representations of the monosaccharide glucose ($C_6H_{12}O_6$) are shown.

FIGURE 2.17 Disaccharides are built from two monosaccharides. Here, a molecule of glucose and one of fructose combine to form sucrose.

(a) Glycogen is the storage polysaccharide in animals. Granules of glycogen are stored in cells of the liver.

(b) Cellulose is a structural polysaccharide found in the cell walls of plants.

FIGURE 2.18 Polysaccharides may function in storage (as in glycogen) or provide structure (as in cellulose).

Lipids

Lipids, such as fats, are compounds that do not dissolve in water. Lipids are nonpolar (having no electrical charges), while water is polar. Because of this difference, water shows no attraction for lipids and vice versa, so water and lipids do not mix. Three types of lipids that are important to human health are triglycerides, phospholipids, and steroids.

Triglycerides

Fats and oils are **triglycerides,** compounds made of one molecule of glycerol and three fatty acids. **Fatty acids** are chains of carbon atoms also bonded to hydrogens and having the acidic group COOH at one end. The fatty acids bond to glycerol through dehydration synthesis (Figure **2.19a**). Triglycerides are classified as saturated or unsaturated, depending on the presence or absence of double bonds between the carbon atoms in their fatty acids (Figure 2.19b). Saturated fatty acids have only single covalent bonds linking the carbon atoms. They are described as "saturated with hydrogen" because their carbon atoms are bonded to as many hydrogen atoms as possible. Saturated fats are made from saturated fatty acids. Butter, a saturated fat, is solid at room temperature because its fatty acids can pack closely together. Fatty acids with one or more double bond between carbon atoms are described as unsaturated—that is, not saturated with hydrogen—because they could bond to more hydrogen atoms if the double bonds between their carbon atoms were broken. The double bonds cause "kinks" in the fatty acids and prevent molecules of unsaturated fat from packing tightly into a solid. Thus, unsaturated fats, such as olive oil, are liquid at room temperature. Sometimes hydrogens are added to unsaturated fats to stabilize them, with the goal of lengthening their shelf life, or to solidify them. For example, hydrogens are added to vegetable oil to make margarine. These partially hydrogenated fats are called trans fats and are found in many packaged snacks, such as cookies and potato chips.

Fats and oils provide about twice the energy per gram that carbohydrates or proteins do. This high energy density makes fat an ideal way for the body to store energy for the long term. Our bulk would be much greater if most of our energy storage consisted of carbohydrates or proteins, given their relatively low energy yield compared with fat.

In preparation for long-term energy storage, excess triglycerides, carbohydrates, and proteins from the foods we consume are converted into small globules of fat that are deposited in the cells of adipose tissue. There, the fat remains until our body needs extra energy; at that time our cells break down the fat to release the energy needed to keep vital processes going. Besides long-term energy storage, fat serves a protective function in the body. Thin layers of fat surround major organs such as the kidneys, cushioning the organs against physical shock from falls or blows. Fat also serves as insulation and as a means of absorbing lipid-soluble vitamins from the intestines and transporting them to the cells that use them. Despite the importance of fats and oils to human health, in excess they can be dangerous, particularly to our circulatory system (discussed in Chapter 12).

Phospholipids

A **phospholipid** is made of a molecule of glycerol bonded to two fatty acids and a negatively charged phosphate group. Another small molecule of some kind—usually polar, called the variable group—is linked to the phosphate group. This general structure provides phospholipids with two regions having very different characteristics. As you will notice in Figure **2.20a**, the region made up of fatty acids is nonpolar; it is described as a **hydrophobic,** or "water-fearing," tail. The other, polar region consists of the **hydrophilic,** or "water-loving," head. The tails, being hydrophobic, do not mix with water. The heads, being hydrophilic, interact readily with water. The hydrophilic heads and hydrophobic tails of phospholipids are responsible for the structure of plasma (cell) membranes. In the membrane surrounding a cell, phospholipids are arranged in a double layer, called a bilayer (Figure 2.20b), with the hydrophilic heads of each layer facing away from each other. That way, each surface of the membrane consists of hydrophilic heads in contact with the watery solutions inside and outside the cell. The hydrophobic tails of the two layers point toward each other and help hold the membrane together.

Q *Would the triglyceride shown in part (b) be a solid or a liquid at room temperature? Why?*

(a) A fatty acid bonds to glycerol through dehydration synthesis.

(b) This triglyceride contains one unsaturated fatty acid (note the presence of a double bond between the carbon atoms) and two saturated fatty acids (note the absence of any double bonds between the carbon atoms).

FIGURE 2.19 Triglycerides are composed of a molecule of glycerol joined to three fatty acids.

A *The triglyceride would be a liquid at room temperature because the kink in the unsaturated fatty acid in part (b) would prevent close packing of adjacent molecules.*

Steroids

A **steroid** is a type of lipid made up of four carbon rings attached to molecules that vary from one steroid to the next. Cholesterol, one of the most familiar steroids, is a component of the plasma membrane and is also the foundation from which steroid hormones, such as estrogen and testosterone, are made. Cholesterol in our blood comes from two sources, our liver and our diet. A high level of cholesterol in the blood is considered a risk factor for heart disease (as described in Chapter 12). Cholesterol, estrogen, and testosterone are shown in Figure **2.21**.

Proteins

A **protein** is a polymer made of one or more chains of amino acids. In many proteins, the chains are twisted, turned, and folded to produce complicated structures. Thousands upon thousands of different proteins are found in the human body, contributing to structural support, transport, movement, and regulation of chemical reactions. Despite their great diversity in structure and function, all proteins are made from a set of only about 20 kinds of amino acids.

(a) A phospholipid consists of a variable group designated by the letter R, a phosphate, a glycerol, and two fatty acids. Because the variable group is often polar and the fatty acids nonpolar, phospholipids have a polar hydrophilic (water-loving) head and a nonpolar hydrophobic (water-fearing) tail.

(b) Within the phospholipid bilayer of the plasma membrane, the hydrophobic tails point inward and help hold the membrane together. The outward-pointing hydrophilic heads mix with the watery environments inside and outside the cell.

FIGURE 2.20 Structure of a phospholipid. Phospholipids are the main components of the plasma membrane encasing a cell and separating its internal and external watery environments.

FIGURE 2.21 The steroid cholesterol is a component of cell membranes, and it is the substance used to make steroid hormones such as estrogen and testosterone. All steroids have a structure consisting of four carbon rings. Steroids differ in the groups attached to these rings.

Amino acids

Amino acids are the building blocks of proteins. They consist of a central carbon atom bound to a hydrogen atom (H), an amino group (NH_2), an acidic carboxyl group (COOH), and a side chain, often designated by the letter R (Figure **2.22**). Amino acids differ from each other only in their side chains. Some amino acids, called nonessential amino acids, can be synthesized by our bodies. Other amino acids, called *essential amino acids*, cannot be synthesized by our bodies and must be obtained from the foods we eat.

The amino acids that form proteins are linked by bonds called peptide bonds, which are formed through dehydration synthesis. A peptide bond links the carboxyl group (COOH) of one amino acid to the amino group (NH_2) of the adjacent amino acid, as shown in Figure **2.23**. Chains containing only a few amino acids are called **peptides**. *Di*peptides contain two amino acids, *tri*peptides contain three amino acids, and so on. Chains containing 10 or more amino acids are called **polypeptides**. The term *protein* is used for polypeptides with at least 50 amino acids.

Protein structure

Proteins have four levels of structure: primary, secondary, tertiary, and quaternary (see Figure **2.24**). The **primary structure** of a protein is the particular sequence of amino acids. This sequence, determined by the genes, dictates a protein's structure and function. Even slight changes in primary structure can alter a protein's shape and ability to function. The inherited blood disorder sickle-cell anemia provides an example. This disease primarily affects populations in central Africa, but it also occurs in approximately 1 in 500 African Americans. It results from the substitution of one amino acid for another during synthesis of the protein hemoglobin, which carries oxygen in our red blood cells. This single substitution in a molecule that contains hundreds of amino acids creates a misshapen protein that then alters the shape of red blood cells. Death can result when the oddly shaped cells clog the tiny vessels of the brain and heart.

The **secondary structure** of proteins consists of patterns known as pleated sheets and helices, which are formed by certain kinds of bends and coils in the chain, as a result of hydrogen bonding. Alterations in the secondary structure of a protein normally found on the surface of nerve cells can transform the protein into an infectious agent known as a prion. Prions have been implicated in several diseases, including Creutzfeldt-Jakob disease in humans and "mad cow disease" in cattle (see Chapter 13a).

Primary structure is the specific sequence of amino acids. Each amino acid is depicted here as a bead within the polypeptide chain.

Secondary structure, such as the helix shown here, results from the bending and coiling of the chain of amino acids.

Tertiary structure is the three-dimensional shape of proteins.

Some proteins have two or more polypeptide chains, each chain forming a subunit. Quaternary structure results from the attractive forces between two or more subunits.

FIGURE 2.24 Levels of protein structure

Central carbon

Hydrogen atom

Amino group

Carboxyl group

Side chain

FIGURE 2.22 Structure of an amino acid. Amino acids differ from one another in the type of R group (side chain) they contain.

Amino acid glycine + Amino acid alanine

Dehydration synthesis

Peptide bond

Dipeptide glycylalanine + H_2O

FIGURE 2.23 Formation of a peptide bond between two amino acids through dehydration synthesis. The carboxyl group (COOH) of one amino acid bonds to the amino group (NH_2) of the adjacent amino acid, releasing water.

The **tertiary structure** is the overall three-dimensional shape of the protein. Hydrogen, ionic, and covalent bonds between different side chains may all contribute to tertiary structure. Changes in the environment of a protein, such as increased heat or changes in pH, can cause the molecule to unravel and lose its three-dimensional shape. This process is called **denaturation.** Even a minor change in the shape of a protein can result in loss of function.

Finally, some proteins consist of two or more polypeptide chains. Each chain, in this case, is called a subunit. **Quaternary structure** is the structure that results from the assembled subunits. The forces that hold the subunits in place are largely the attractions between oppositely charged side chains.

Enzymes

Life is possible because of enzymes. Without them, most chemical reactions within our cells would occur far too slowly to sustain life. **Enzymes** are substances—almost always proteins, but occasionally RNA molecules—that speed up chemical reactions without being consumed in the process. Typically, reactions with enzymes proceed 10,000 to 1,000,000 times faster than the same reactions without enzymes.

The basic process by which an enzyme speeds up a chemical reaction can be summarized by the following equation:

$$E + S \longrightarrow ES \longrightarrow E + P$$

| Enzyme | Substrate | Enzyme–substrate complex | Enzyme | Product |

The particular substance that an enzyme works on is called its substrate. For example, the enzyme sucrase speeds up the reaction in which sucrose is broken down into glucose and fructose. In this reaction, sucrose is the substrate, and glucose and fructose are products. Similarly, the enzyme maltase speeds up the breakdown of maltose (the substrate) into molecules of glucose (the product). From these examples you can see that an enzyme's name may resemble the name of its substrate. These particular examples are decomposition reactions, in which a substance is broken down into its component parts. Enzymes also increase the speed of many synthesis reactions.

During reactions promoted by enzymes, the substrate binds to a specific location, called the **active site,** on the enzyme, to form an **enzyme–substrate complex.** This binding orients the substrate molecules so they can react. The substrate is converted to one or more products that then leave the active site, allowing the enzyme to bind to another substrate molecule. The entire process occurs very rapidly. One estimate suggests that a typical enzyme can convert about 1000 molecules of substrate into product every second. Figure **2.25** summarizes the steps of enzymatic reactions.

Enzymes are very specific in their activity; each is capable of binding to and acting on only one or at most a few particular substrates. Maltase, for example, acts only on maltose and not on sucrose, a structurally similar compound. This specificity is due to the unique shape of each enzyme's active site. The enzyme's active site and the substrate fit together like pieces of a jigsaw puzzle.

Sometimes enzymes need *cofactors,* nonprotein substances that help them convert substrate to product. Some cofactors permanently reside at the enzyme's active site. Other cofactors bind to the active site at the same time as the substrate. Some cofactors are the organic (carbon-containing) substances we know as vitamins. Organic cofactors are called *coenzymes.* Other cofactors are inorganic (non-carbon-containing) substances such as zinc or iron.

Enzyme deficiencies sometimes occur and affect our health. Lactase deficiency is a relatively common example. Lactase is the

Step 1: The cycle begins when the active site of the enzyme is unoccupied and the substrate is present.

Step 2: The substrate binds to the active site of the enzyme, forming an enzyme–substrate complex.

Step 3: The substrate is converted to products that are released from the active site, and the cycle can begin again.

Substrate

Products

Enzyme Enzyme–substrate complex Enzyme

(a) A decomposition reaction involving an enzyme

Substrates Product

Enzyme Enzyme–substrate complex Enzyme

(b) A synthesis reaction involving an enzyme

FIGURE 2.25 The working cycle of an enzyme

enzyme needed to digest the lactose in milk products, breaking it down to its two component monosaccharides, glucose and galactose. Infants and young children usually produce adequate amounts of lactase, but many adults do not. For them, consumption of milk and milk products can lead to diarrhea, cramps, and bloating, caused by undigested lactose passing into the large intestine where it feeds resident bacteria. The bacteria, in turn, produce gas and lactic acid that irritate the bowels. The milk industry has responded to this problem (often called "lactose intolerance") by marketing lactose-reduced milk, and tablets and caplets that contain the enzyme lactase are also available.

Nucleic Acids and Nucleotides

In our discussion of protein structure we mentioned that genes determine the protein's primary structure, which is the sequence of amino acids. Genes, our units of inheritance, are segments of long polymers called **deoxyribonucleic acid (DNA).** DNA is one of the two types of nucleic acids.

Nucleotides

The two nucleic acids in our cells are DNA and **ribonucleic acid (RNA).** Both are polymers of smaller units called **nucleotides,** joined into chains through dehydration synthesis. Every nucleotide monomer consists of a five-carbon (pentose) sugar bonded to one of five nitrogen-containing bases and at least one phosphate group (Figure **2.26**). The five nitrogen-containing bases are adenine, guanine, cytosine, thymine, and uracil. The bases cytosine, thymine, and uracil have a single ring made of carbon and nitrogen atoms; adenine and guanine have two such rings. The sequence of bases in DNA and RNA determines the sequence of amino acids in a protein. DNA, as we said earlier, is the nucleic acid found in genes. RNA, in various forms, converts the genetic information found in DNA into proteins.

DNA and RNA

Key differences in the structures of RNA and DNA are summarized in Table **2.5**. RNA is a single strand of nucleotides. The five-carbon sugar in RNA is ribose. The nitrogen-containing bases in RNA are cytosine (C), adenine (A), guanine (G), and uracil (U; Figure **2.27**). In contrast, DNA is a double-stranded chain. Its two parallel strands, held together by hydrogen bonds between the nitrogen-containing bases, twist around one another to form a double helix. The five-carbon sugar in DNA is deoxyribose. The nitrogen-containing bases in DNA are adenine (A), thymine (T), cytosine (C), and guanine (G; Figure **2.28**).

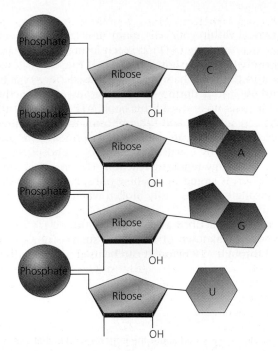

FIGURE 2.27 RNA is a single-stranded nucleic acid. It is formed by the linking together of nucleotides composed of the sugar ribose, a phosphate group, and the nitrogen-containing bases cytosine (C), adenine (A), guanine (G), and uracil (U).

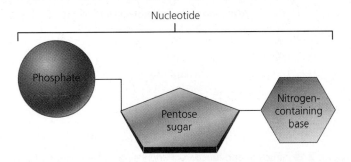

FIGURE 2.26 Structure of a nucleotide. Nucleotides consist of a five-carbon (pentose) sugar bonded to a phosphate molecule and one of five nitrogen-containing bases. Nucleotides are the building blocks of nucleic acids.

TABLE 2.5 Review of the Structural Differences between RNA and DNA

Characteristic	RNA	DNA
Sugar	Ribose	Deoxyribose
Bases	Adenine, guanine, cytosine, uracil	Adenine, guanine, cytosine, thymine
Number of strands	One	Two; twisted to form double helix

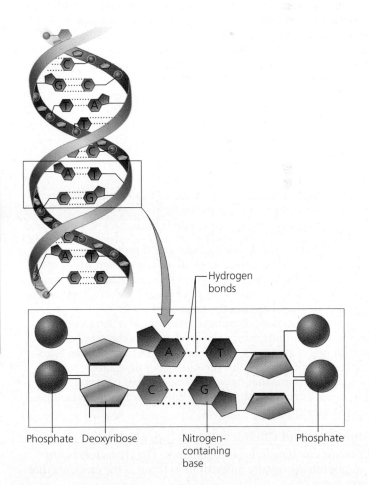

FIGURE 2.28 DNA is a nucleic acid in which two chains of nucleotides twist around one another to form a double helix. The two chains are held together by hydrogen bonds between the nitrogen-containing bases. Each nucleotide of DNA contains the pentose sugar deoxyribose, a phosphate group, and one of the following four nitrogen-containing bases: adenine (A), thymine (T), cytosine (C), and guanine (G).

ATP

At this moment within your cells, many molecules of the nucleotide **adenosine triphosphate (ATP)** are each losing a phosphate group. As the phosphate group is lost, energy that the molecule stored by holding on to the phosphate group is released. Your cells trap that energy and use it to perform work. It is because of this activity that you are able to sit up and read this book. ATP consists of the sugar ribose, the base adenine, and three phosphate groups, attached to the molecule by phosphate bonds. It is formed from adenosine diphosphate (ADP) by covalent bonding of a phosphate group to the ADP in an energy-requiring reaction. The energy absorbed during the reaction is stored in the new phosphate bond. This high-energy phosphate bond is easily broken when the cell requires energy (Figure **2.29**).

ATP is often described as the energy currency of cells. All energy from the breakdown of molecules such as glucose must be channeled through ATP before it can be used by the body.

FIGURE 2.29 Structure and function of adenosine triphosphate (ATP). This nucleotide consists of the sugar ribose, the base adenine, and three phosphate groups. The phosphate bonds of ATP are unstable. When cells need energy, the last phosphate bond is broken, yielding adenosine diphosphate (ADP), a phosphate molecule, and energy.

exploring further

In Chapter 2 we learned about the important roles that water plays in the human body. Recall that water serves as the body's main transport medium and helps to prevent dramatic changes in body temperature. Foodborne illnesses are caused by the ingestion of contaminated food or water, and they wreak havoc on the body's water balance. These illnesses are usually associated with severe diarrhea and vomiting, which rob the body of its water. In Chapter 2a we will consider the causes, treatments, and prevention of foodborne illness.

highlighting the concepts

The Nature of Atoms (pp. 15–17)

- Atoms consist of subatomic particles called protons, neutrons, and electrons. Protons have a positive charge. Neutrons have no charge. Both are found in the nucleus and have atomic masses equal to 1. Electrons have a negative charge, weigh almost nothing, and are found around the nucleus in shells.
- Each element is made of atoms containing a certain number of protons. The atomic number of an element is the number of protons in one of its atoms. The atomic weight for any atom equals the number of protons plus the number of neutrons.
- Isotopes are atoms that have the same number of protons but different numbers of neutrons. Some isotopes, called radioisotopes, emit radiation.

Compounds and Chemical Bonds (pp. 18–21)

- Elements combine to form compounds. The characteristics of compounds are usually different from those of the elements that form them.

- When atoms join to form compounds, chemical bonds form between them. Covalent bonds form when atoms share electrons. Atoms that have lost or gained electrons have an electric charge and are called ions. The attraction between oppositely charged ions is an ionic bond.

The Role of Water in Life (pp. 21–25)

- Sometimes the sharing of electrons in a covalent bond is unequal, resulting in a polar covalent bond and sometimes a polar molecule. Hydrogen bonds are weak attractive forces between the charged regions of polar molecules.
- Water is a polar molecule, and the polarity (the tendency to have positive and negative regions) results in hydrogen bonding. Both make water an important component of the human body. Water is an excellent solvent because of its polarity. Its hydrogen bonds give water a high heat capacity, which helps the body's internal temperature remain constant, and a high heat of vaporization, so that evaporation of perspiration from the body surface prevents overheating.

- Acids increase the concentration of H^+ in solution. Bases decrease the concentration of H^+ in solution. The strengths of acids and bases are measured on the pH scale. Biological fluids must remain within a narrow pH range. Buffers prevent dramatic changes in pH.

Major Molecules of Life (pp. 26–34)

- A polymer is a large molecule made of many smaller molecules, called monomers. Polymers form through dehydration synthesis (removal of a water molecule) and are broken apart by hydrolysis (addition of a water molecule).
- Carbohydrates are sugars and starches that provide fuel for the human body. Monosaccharides are the smallest monomers of carbohydrates. Oligosaccharides are chains of a few monosaccharides joined together by dehydration synthesis. Disaccharides consist of two monosaccharides and are one type of oligosaccharide. Polysaccharides are complex carbohydrates formed when large numbers of monosaccharides join through dehydration synthesis.
- Lipids, such as triglycerides, phospholipids, and steroids, are nonpolar molecules that do not dissolve in water. Triglycerides (fats and oils) are made of glycerol and three fatty acids and function in long-term energy storage. Phospholipids are important components of plasma membranes. Steroids include cholesterol, a component of the plasma membrane that also serves as the foundation for steroid hormones.
- Proteins are polymers made from a set of about 20 amino acids linked together through dehydration synthesis to form chains.

There are four levels of protein structure. Primary structure is the specific sequence of amino acids in a protein. Secondary structure results from the bending and coiling of the amino acid chain into pleated sheets or helices. Tertiary structure is the three-dimensional shape of the protein. Some proteins consist of two or more polypeptide chains, each comprising a subunit. Attractive forces between the subunits of these proteins produce quaternary structure.

- Enzymes are proteins, or sometimes RNA molecules, that speed up chemical reactions without being consumed in the process. The substrate binds to the enzyme at the active site, forming an enzyme–substrate complex, and is then converted to products that leave the active site.
- Deoxyribonucleic acid (DNA) and ribonucleic acid (RNA) are polymers of nucleotides. A nucleotide consists of a five-carbon sugar bonded to one of five nitrogen-containing bases and a phosphate group. Genes are stretches of DNA that determine the sequence of amino acids during protein synthesis. DNA is double stranded, its sugar component is deoxyribose, and its nitrogen-containing bases are adenine, guanine, cytosine, and thymine. RNA is a single-stranded molecule that also plays a major role in protein synthesis. The sugar in RNA is ribose, and the nitrogen-containing bases are adenine, guanine, cytosine, and uracil.
- Adenosine triphosphate (ATP), the energy currency of cells, is a nucleotide made of the sugar ribose, the base adenine, and three phosphate groups. When cells require energy, one of the high-energy phosphate bonds is broken and energy is released.

recognizing key terms

chemistry p. 15	pH p. 23	glycogen p. 26	secondary structure p. 31
matter p. 15	pH scale p. 23	cellulose p. 26	tertiary structure p. 32
atom p. 15	buffer p. 25	lipid p. 28	denaturation p. 32
element p. 16	macromolecule p. 26	triglyceride p. 28	quaternary structure p. 32
isotope p. 17	polymer p. 26	fatty acid p. 28	enzyme p. 32
radioisotope p. 17	monomer p. 26	phospholipid p. 28	active site p. 32
compound p. 18	dehydration synthesis p. 26	hydrophobic p. 28	enzyme–substrate complex p. 32
covalent bond p. 18	hydrolysis p. 26	hydrophilic p. 28	
molecule p. 20	carbohydrate p. 26	steroid p. 29	deoxyribonucleic acid (DNA) p. 32
ion p. 21	monosaccharide p. 26	protein p. 29	
ionic bond p. 21	oligosaccharide p. 26	amino acid p. 31	ribonucleic acid (RNA) p. 32
hydrogen bond p. 22	disaccharide p. 26	peptide p. 31	nucleotide p. 32
acid p. 23	polysaccharide p. 26	polypeptide p. 31	adenosine triphosphate (ATP) p. 34
base p. 23	starch p. 26	primary structure p. 31	

reviewing the concepts

1. What is an atom? p. 15
2. Compare protons, neutrons, and electrons with respect to their charge, mass, and location within an atom. p. 16
3. What is an isotope? p. 17
4. How is radiation used to diagnose or cure illness? p. 17
5. Describe covalent, ionic, and hydrogen bonds. Give an example of each. pp. 18–22
6. What characteristics of water make it a critical component of the body? pp. 22–23
7. Define acids and bases according to what happens when they are added to water. pp. 23–25

8. How are polymers formed and broken? Give three examples of polymers and their component monomers. pp. 26–27
9. Name two important energy-storage polysaccharides and one important structural polysaccharide. p. 26
10. Describe the structure of a phospholipid. What important roles do phospholipids play in the human body? pp. 28, 30
11. Describe the four levels of protein structure. pp. 31–32
12. Compare the structures of RNA and DNA. p. 33
13. Describe the structure and function of ATP. p. 34
14. Compare and contrast the ways in which proteins and nucleic acids are used in the body. pp. 29, 32–33

15. Hydrogen bonds
    a. are stronger than either ionic or covalent bonds.
    b. form between a slightly positively charged hydrogen atom and a slightly negatively charged atom nearby.
    c. maintain the shape of proteins and DNA.
    d. b and c
16. Water
    a. is a nonpolar molecule and therefore an excellent solvent.
    b. has a high heat capacity and therefore helps maintain a constant body temperature.
    c. has a low heat of vaporization and therefore helps prevent overheating of the body.
    d. makes up about 25% of the human body.
17. Carbohydrates
    a. consist of chains of amino acids.
    b. supply our cells with energy.
    c. contain glycerol.
    d. function as enzymes.
18. Triglycerides
    a. have one molecule of glycerol and three fatty acids.
    b. are poor sources of energy.
    c. are saturated when there are two or more double bonds linking carbon atoms.
    d. are major components of plasma membranes.

19. Enzymes
    a. speed up chemical reactions and are consumed in the process.
    b. are always proteins.
    c. are usually nonspecific and therefore capable of binding to many different substrates.
    d. have locations, known as active sites, to which the substrate binds.
20. Changes in temperature or pH can cause a protein to lose its three-dimensional shape and become nonfunctional. This process is called _____.
21. DNA and RNA are polymers of smaller units called _____.
22. The _____ structure of a protein is the precise sequence of amino acids.
23. _____ are arranged in a double layer (bilayer) that forms the plasma membrane of cells.
24. In plants, the storage polysaccharide is _____, and in animals it is _____.
25. Buffers prevent dramatic changes in _____.

applying the concepts

1. A friend eyes your lunch and begins to lecture you on the perils of high-fat foods. You decide to acknowledge the health risks of eating a high-fat diet but also to point out to her the important roles that lipids play in your body. What will you say?
2. Bill claims that eating fruits and vegetables is overrated because humans lack the enzyme needed to digest cellulose and thus cellulose passes unchanged through our digestive tract. Is Bill correct that we gain nothing from eating food that contains cellulose?
3. For years your mother has been telling you to drink several large glasses of water each day. Having just read this chapter, you now understand the critical roles that water plays in your body. You vow to admit during your next phone call home that she has been right all along. Explain why dehydration might be dangerous.
4. Dental x-rays are taken using small doses of radiation and are used to detect tooth decay, injuries to the roots of teeth, and problems with the bones supporting the teeth. A dental professional covers the patient with a lead apron that runs from the neck to the abdomen and then leaves the room to take the x-ray. Why are such precautions necessary?

becoming information literate

In Nutrition class, you and your fellow students are scheduled to debate the pros and cons of irradiating food. You have been assigned the position of supporting food irradiation. Use at least three reliable sources (books, scientific journals, Internet sites) to develop your arguments in favor of food irradiation and to gather information needed to refute potential arguments made by the opposing side. List the sources you used, and describe why you considered each source reliable.

Additional questions can be found online at the Human Biology Place, www.humanbiology.com.

2a SPECIAL TOPIC

Food Safety

Ingestion of food contaminated with chemicals or pathogens can cause foodborne illness.

Kate opened the box of dog biscuits and looked down to see Hudson's tail wagging wildly in anticipation of a treat. She had finally stopped worrying whenever she opened a new box of biscuits or a new can of food for her constant companion. All the news coverage about tainted pet food causing kidney failure in cats and dogs had really upset her. But she had begun to relax, reassured by how quickly the Food and Drug Administration (FDA) had reacted to reports of pet illnesses and deaths, and how quickly the agency had discovered the source of contamination. The FDA's investigation had shown that melamine, a compound used to make plastics, glues, cleaning products, and fertilizers, had been intentionally added to a key ingredient in many pet food recipes to give that ingredient the appearance of increased protein content. The investigation's findings had prompted major recalls of pet foods. Kate had carefully checked to make sure that the biscuits and cans in her cabinet were not among those that had been recalled. More recently she had read online that charges had been filed against the people and companies involved in the contamination. Because of the pet food scare, Kate had become aware of issues surrounding food safety. She had certainly become more careful when selecting, handling, and storing food, whether the food was for herself or for Hudson.

In this chapter, we examine some of the illnesses caused by consuming contaminated food or water. We also look at the agencies that protect our food supply, and what we can do as individuals to make sure that the food we eat and the water and beverages we drink are safe.

Foodborne Illnesses

Foodborne illnesses are the result of ingesting contaminated food or water. Disease-causing agents such as bacteria, viruses, prions (infectious proteins formed as a result of alterations in the secondary structure of a protein normally found on nerve cells), and parasitic protozoans (single-celled eukaryotic organisms) or worms can contaminate food; collectively, these agents are called pathogens. There are more than 250 different foodborne illnesses, including some caused by harmful chemicals such as those found in pesticides or that naturally occur in certain mushrooms or fish (Figure **2a.1**).

Foodborne illnesses caused by pathogens are described as infections, whereas those caused by chemicals or toxins are considered poisonings. The general public usually ignores this distinction and simply refers to all foodborne illnesses as "food poisoning." (Food allergies, described in Chapter 13, are also a type of foodborne illness.)

General Symptoms, Diagnosis, and Treatment

Despite their different causes and classifications, all foodborne illnesses have symptoms that first appear in the gastrointestinal (GI) tract. The GI tract is a long tube, specialized for the process-

(a) The death cap mushroom (*Amanita phalloides*), found in North America and many other parts of the world, contains toxins that can cause liver failure, kidney failure, and death within 2 weeks of ingestion. These toxins cannot be destroyed through cooking, drying, or freezing.

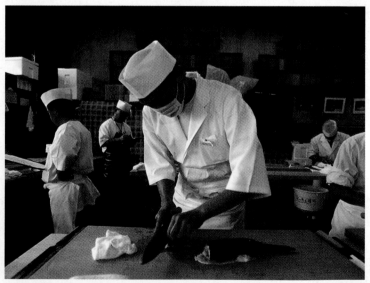

(b) Pufferfishes contain lethal amounts of tetrodotoxin in their skin and internal organs. If consumed, tetrodotoxin paralyzes muscles, eventually leading to death from asphyxiation (inability to breathe). Despite this danger, pufferfish is a highly prized dish in Japanese cuisine. Known as *fugu*, the dish is prepared by licensed chefs who carefully remove the most poisonous parts of the fish.

FIGURE 2a.1 Naturally occurring poisons can cause foodborne illness and death.

ing and absorption of food, that runs from the mouth and continues to the anus (see Chapter 15). These early symptoms may include nausea, vomiting, abdominal cramps, and diarrhea. Some pathogens do not move beyond the GI tract. Other pathogens, including some bacteria, produce toxins that are absorbed into the bloodstream, while still others directly invade other body tissues. For example, the bacterium *Clostridium botulinum,* found in improperly canned foods, produces a toxin that blocks communication between nerve and muscle cells, causing paralysis of muscles and making it difficult or impossible to breathe. Because new canning procedures have virtually eliminated the risk of botulism from commercially canned foods, foods canned improperly at home are the typical source of *C. botulinum* contamination (see Chapter 13a for discussion of how bacteria and viruses cause disease).

Many foodborne illnesses go undiagnosed and unreported to public health officials. Some ill people do not seek medical care, perhaps because they do not realize that they have a foodborne illness or because they can't afford to see a doctor. For those who seek medical attention, diagnostic tests may not be performed to confirm the particular illness and its causative agent; or if tests are performed, the results may not be communicated to public health officials. The latter situation can arise because each state decides which diseases should be monitored in that state, so some diseases are not reportable in the first place. Some estimates suggest that the actual number of cases of mild foodborne illnesses is 20 to almost 40 times the numbers reported. Even foodborne illnesses with very severe symptoms are underreported, though to a much lesser degree than those with milder symptoms. For example, the total number of cases of foodborne botulism in the United States each year is estimated to be twice the number of cases reported annually to the Centers for Disease Control and Prevention. In 1996 the Centers for Disease Control and Prevention, Food Safety and Inspection Service, Food and Drug Administration, and selected state health departments developed FoodNet, a collaborative monitoring system that collects data on pathogens commonly transmitted through food. This program tracks 7 bacterial and 2 parasitic foodborne illnesses, and it picks up illnesses in participating states that are diagnosed but not reported.

A diagnosis of foodborne illness requires a physical exam and additional research to obtain a detailed history of recently consumed foods and beverages. A stool sample may be collected for specific laboratory tests. When a bacterial illness is suspected, stool samples are cultured and the bacteria that grow on the culture medium are identified. If parasites are suspected, then the stool sample is also examined with a microscope, sometimes after the sample has been prepared with particular stains (chemicals) to make the parasite more visible. Because parasites often have several life stages, stool samples are examined for the presence of adults or younger stages, such as eggs or larvae. In the case of the protozoan parasite *Cryptosporidium parvum* (a major cause of waterborne diarrheal illness in the United States), trained laboratory personnel look for oocysts, the infectious early stage in the life history of this organism. During the oocyst stage, the parasite is enclosed in a protective capsule that makes it resistant to chlorine-based disinfectants. *Cryptosporidium parvum* is commonly transmitted through the swallowing of recreational water, such as that found in pools, hot tubs, and ponds. Tests for viruses are more complicated and usually involve testing the stool sample for the genetic markers that indicate presence of a specific virus. Patients may have a blood

sample collected for examination. The symptoms associated with diarrheal illness that warrant consultation with a health care professional are listed in Table **2a.1**.

Recall from Chapter 2 that water performs important functions in our body, such as serving as the main transport medium and helping to prevent dramatic changes in body temperature. The vomiting and diarrhea associated with foodborne illness, while functioning to expel the offending pathogens or toxins from the GI tract, rob the body of water it needs to function properly. Dehydration from diarrhea and vomiting can be deadly if not treated. Patients treated for foodborne illnesses are usually given clear, clean fluids to prevent dehydration. When foodborne illness is caused by bacteria, antibiotics may be prescribed as well. Antiparasitic drugs can be used to kill parasites.

Common Foodborne Infections

The most common foodborne infections in the United States are caused by the bacteria *Campylobacter jejuni, Salmonella,* and *Escherichia coli* O157:H7, along with a group of viruses known as caliciviruses. *Campylobacter jejuni* typically enters the body during the handling of raw poultry or the consumption of raw or undercooked poultry (chickens often carry the bacteria but show no signs of illness). The resulting illness is known as campylobacteriosis.

Species of bacteria within the genus *Salmonella* most often enter our bodies when we consume food contaminated with animal feces. The food, which is often—but not always—animal in origin (meat, milk, or eggs), usually looks and smells normal. The illness that results is salmonellosis.

Most strains of the bacterium *Escherichia coli* do not cause illness; in fact, *E. coli* live harmlessly in the intestines of most people. *Escherichia coli* O157:H7, however, is not harmless (the letters and numbers in its name refer to specific markers found on its surface that allow scientists to differentiate this bacterium from other strains of *E. coli*). This strain lives in the intestines of healthy farm animals such as cattle, goats, and sheep, and is most commonly passed to humans when they consume undercooked ground beef that contains the pathogen. *Escherichia coli* O157:H7 also occurs in animals at petting zoos, where it has been found on the animals' fur as well as on the ground, on railings, and in feed bins. Once a person is infected with *Escherichia coli* O157:H7, good hygiene is necessary to prevent its spread to others. If hand washing is inadequate, *Escherichia coli* O157:H7 in diarrhea can be

TABLE **2a.1** Symptoms Accompanying Diarrheal Illness for Which Consultation with a Health Care Provider Is Recommended
Symptom
Temperature over 101.5°F (measured orally)
Blood in stools
Prolonged vomiting (especially inability to keep liquids down)
Dizziness when standing up, dry mouth and throat, decreased urination (all indicate dehydration)
Diarrhea lasting more than 3 days

Source: Centers for Disease Control and Prevention

passed from person to person; family members and friends interacting with infected toddlers who are not proficient at toileting are especially at risk.

Finally, viral gastroenteritis, commonly called the stomach flu, is caused by many viruses, including a group known as caliciviruses. Individuals can become infected by consuming food or beverages contaminated with caliciviruses. Viral gastroenteritis is contagious and is spread by close contact with an infected person.

These four common foodborne illnesses—campylobacteriosis, salmonellosis, infection with *Escherichia coli* O157:H7, and viral gastroenteritis—have similar symptoms: diarrhea, nausea, vomiting, and abdominal cramps. Fever is present in some cases. *Campylobacter* and *Salmonella* infections that spread beyond the GI tract to the bloodstream are more serious, and infection with *Escherichia coli* O157:H7 occasionally causes kidney failure. All but caliciviruses can cause life-threatening illness. People most at risk include those whose immune system is compromised or incompletely developed, such as the very old, the very young, and those already suffering from a disease that reduces their immune function. However, even healthy people can die from foodborne illnesses if they are exposed to a very high dose of the pathogen, or if they do not receive proper treatment.

How Does Food Become Contaminated?

Food can become contaminated during any of the many steps that typically occur as it moves from "farm to fork" (Figure **2a.2**). At early stages, bacteria normally present in the intestines of food animals, such as cows or chickens, can contaminate carcasses at slaughterhouses and get into meat and poultry products. *Salmonella* can infect the ovaries and oviducts of chickens, which then produce eggs containing the bacterium. This route of infection, called the "transovarian" route, is thought to be the predominant way that eggs become contaminated. A less common route, called the "trans-shell" route, occurs when bacteria in the environment, such as those on nesting material or in shipping containers, penetrate the eggshell after the egg has been laid.

Oysters and other filter-feeding shellfish concentrate bacteria naturally found in seawater along with the bacteria dumped into our oceans in human sewage. Oysters also concentrate toxins and pollutants. Large individuals of some top predatory fish species in our oceans, such as king mackerel, act as bioconcentrators and store potentially dangerous levels of heavy metals (such as mercury) in their tissues (see Chapter 23). In freshwater and on land, parasitic worms, such as roundworms, tapeworms, and flukes, release eggs into the environment where they may be picked up by other animals including fish, pigs, and cattle. The eggs of the parasitic worms hatch into larvae in these animals, and the larvae can survive for some time after the animals have been killed for food.

Certain foods are more likely than others to be associated with foodborne illness. As evident from our discussion, raw foods originating from animals are most likely to be contaminated. In addition, foods that contain the products of many animals, such as ground beef, are especially dangerous because only one of the

Agricultural production　　　　　　**Natural production**

Harvesting → Storage and transport of raw food → Processing and manufacture → Storage and transport of processed and manufactured products → Wholesale and retail distribution → Food service sector

FIGURE 2a.2 A typical pattern of steps by which food moves from harvesting to consumption.

many contributing animals need contain the pathogen for the meat to be contaminated. To put this in perspective, it is estimated that a single hamburger patty may contain meat from hundreds of cattle, and a glass of milk may contain milk from hundreds of cows!

Contamination is not restricted to food from animals. Indeed, fresh fruits and vegetables can become contaminated with bacteria, viruses, and protozoan parasites when they are irrigated or washed with water containing animal (including human) waste. For example, fresh spinach contaminated with *E. coli* O157:H7 killed three people and sickened about 200 others in an outbreak that spanned 26 states in the fall of 2006. Washing fruits and vegetables may not protect against foodborne illness. Contaminated water can introduce pathogens to produce, and washing with clean water has been shown to decrease but not to completely eliminate contamination. Produce also may contain residues of pesticides, chemicals used to kill organisms that damage crops.

Food also can be contaminated during processing and preparation. People handling food with unwashed hands can introduce pathogens, and pathogens can be transferred from one food to another when utensils and cutting boards are used for different foods without being washed in between.

Methods of Combating Food Contamination

Once food is contaminated, the way it is handled becomes critical. Large numbers of bacteria are usually required to cause foodborne illness, so leaving contaminated food in conditions conducive to bacterial reproduction is particularly dangerous. Bacteria reproduce extremely rapidly, particularly under warm, moist conditions (temperatures between 40 and 140°F are considered the danger zone because they represent conditions under which bacteria are most likely to reproduce). In fact, a single bacterium reproducing by binary fission (dividing itself in half) can produce millions of new cells in only a few hours (see Chapter 13a).

Prompt refrigeration can slow reproduction by many bacteria, as can acidic conditions. Most microorganisms do not thrive at a pH of less than or equal to 5. To create such acidic conditions, vinegar (which is dilute acetic acid) is often added to foods like cucumbers and peppers during a process called pickling. High levels of salt or sugar can also be used to inhibit microbial growth in food; these solutes reduce the amount of water available to microorganisms. Fruits are typically preserved by adding sugar (to make jams and jellies), and meats and fish are often preserved with salt. Drying also reduces water available to microorganisms, and this method is used to preserve fruits, vegetables, meat, fish, eggs, and milk.

With few exceptions, parasites, bacteria, and viruses are killed by heat; the microorganisms die because very high temperatures cause their macromolecules, such as DNA and proteins, to lose their structure and function. In this way, heating contaminated food to sufficiently high temperatures can render it safe to eat. A food thermometer, placed in the thickest part of the food item, should reach at least 160°F to ensure that the food item is safe to eat. Toxins produced by bacteria vary in whether or not they are killed by heat. Prions are not destroyed by heat alone. However, research in the last few years has shown that the combination of high temperature (250–275°F) and short bursts of very high pressure, a technique used commercially to kill bacteria in food, also inactivates prions in processed meats, such as hot dogs. Prions also are inactivated by treatment with certain very strong chemicals, such as sodium hydroxide (a strong base) and household bleach, but such treatments cannot be applied to food.

Keeping Food Safe at International and National Levels

Our food supply today is global: Most of us consume food grown and processed in other countries as well as that produced nearer to home. It is not unusual, for example, for us to consume grapes and strawberries from Chile, salmon from Norway, and lamb from New Zealand. The nature of our food supply, along with the extreme mobility of people, make the regulation of food safety and the tracking of foodborne illnesses extremely challenging. To this end, several agencies regulate, monitor, and investigate the safety of our food.

International Oversight

The World Health Organization (WHO) is a United Nations agency whose primary mandate is to protect public health. One of its major tasks is to fight diseases, especially those that are communicable (able to be passed from one person to another). WHO functions regarding food safety include coordinating international efforts to effectively monitor and respond to outbreaks of foodborne illness and implementing international health regulations. These regulations relate to international travelers and the import/export of contaminated foods. WHO also sponsors research on foodborne illnesses and programs to prevent and treat these illnesses.

National Oversight

Several agencies within the United States are charged with overseeing food safety. The Food and Drug Administration (FDA) is responsible for the safety of about 80% of our food supply. More specifically, the FDA oversees all domestic and imported food except meat and poultry. In addition, the FDA oversees eggs (in the shell), bottled water, and wines containing less than 7% alcohol. The Bureau of Alcohol, Tobacco, and Firearms oversees all other alcoholic beverages. The Food Safety and Inspection Service (FSIS) oversees domestic and imported meat and poultry, including products that contain meat or poultry such as frozen foods. Processed egg products (such as liquid egg whites) are also overseen by the FSIS. The Environmental Protection Agency (EPA) regulates the use of pesticides in agriculture and establishes standards for safe public drinking water. The National Oceanic and Atmospheric Administration (NOAA) inspects fishing vessels and seafood processing plants. Finally, the Customs Service works with federal regulatory agencies to make sure the imported foods meet the regulations of the United States.

The Centers for Disease Control and Prevention (CDC) is not a regulatory agency, in the sense that it does not have the power to enforce federal rules. Nevertheless, it plays a critical role in keeping our food safe by working with state and local health officials to monitor the occurrence of foodborne illnesses (as well as other diseases). Another major function of the CDC is to investigate disease outbreaks. Working with local food safety officials, the CDC determines whether a cluster of similar cases suggests an outbreak of foodborne illness in a particular area. When an outbreak is suspected, the CDC begins an investigation to determine the particular pathogen involved and its source. Such investigations typically involve searching for more cases; characterizing the outbreak by time, place, and people involved; identifying the pathogen through laboratory tests performed on stool or blood samples; and determining through extensive interviews the source of the outbreak. The CDC also develops methods to prevent foodborne illnesses and continually assesses the effectiveness of prevention efforts. Because the CDC does not restrict its oversight activities to particular foods, it effectively oversees all foods. Table **2a.2** presents the major agencies concerned with food safety in the United States.

TABLE 2a.2 Major Agencies Involved with Food Safety in the United States

Agency	Oversight Responsibilities	Food Safety Role
Bureau of Alcohol, Tobacco, Firearms and Explosives (ATF)	Alcoholic beverages except wine beverages containing less than 7% alcohol	Enforces food safety laws governing production and distribution of alcoholic beverages; investigates cases of adulterated alcoholic products, sometimes with help from FDA
Centers for Disease Control and Prevention (CDC)	All foods	Investigates sources of foodborne disease outbreaks
		Maintains nationwide foodborne disease surveillance and techniques for rapid identification of foodborne pathogens
		Develops and advocates public health policies to prevent foodborne diseases
		Conducts research on foodborne illness and trains local and state food safety personnel
Customs Service	Imported foods	Works with federal regulatory agencies to ensure that all goods entering and exiting the U.S. do so according to U.S. laws and regulations
Environmental Protection Agency (EPA)	Drinking water	Establishes safe drinking water standards and assists states in monitoring public drinking water and finding ways to prevent contamination
		Regulates toxic substances and wastes to prevent entry into environment and food chain
		Determines safety of new pesticides and sets tolerances for pesticide residues in foods
Food and Drug Administration (FDA)	All domestic and imported food sold in interstate commerce, including shelled eggs, but not meat and poultry	Routinely inspects food production establishments and food warehouses and collects and analyzes samples for contamination
	Bottled water	Reviews safety of food and color additives and drugs for safety to animals that receive them and humans who eat food produced from these animals
	Wine beverages with less than 7% alcohol	Monitors safety of animal feeds used in food-producing animals
		Develops model codes and ordinances, guidelines, and interpretations for retail food establishments such as restaurants and grocery stores
		Establishes food-manufacturing production standards, such as plant sanitation and packaging requirements
		Works with foreign governments to ensure safety of certain imported food products
		Requests manufacturers to recall unsafe food products and monitors those recalls, taking appropriate enforcement actions
		Conducts research on food safety; educates industry and consumers on safe practices
Food Safety and Inspection Service (FSIS)	Domestic and imported meat and poultry and related processed products, such as stews, pizzas, and frozen foods	Inspects food animals for diseases before and after slaughter and inspects slaughterhouses, meatpacking, and food-processing plants; ensures that foreign suppliers meet U.S. standards
	Processed egg products such as liquid or dried egg whites	Collects and analyzes samples of food products for microbial and chemical contaminants and infectious or toxic agents
		Establishes standards for food additives and other ingredients in prepared and packaged meat and poultry products
		Sponsors research on meat and poultry safety and educates industry and consumers on safe food-handling practices
National Oceanic and Atmospheric Administration (NOAA)	Fish and seafood products	Inspects and certifies fishing vessels, seafood processing plants, and retail facilities for federal sanitation standards

Source: Modified from a table provided by the FDA, "Food Safety: A Team Approach"

Bioterrorism

So far in our discussion of food safety we have considered unintentional threats to food safety, such as pathogens accidentally entering our food or people mistakenly eating food that contains toxins. However, intentional threats to food safety also exist. For example, there is considerable concern that terrorists could introduce into food or water supplies biological, chemical, or radiological agents with the goal of generating fear, economic losses, and human casualties.

Bioterrorism is the use of biological agents (bacteria and their toxins, viruses, or parasites) to intimidate or attack societies or governments. The CDC classifies biological agents that could be used in terrorist attacks into three categories (A, B, and C) based on characteristics of the biological agent such as availability, ease of dissemination (distribution), severity of health effects produced, and degree of preparedness required by public health agencies to respond to an attack.

Biological agents in Category A are highest priority because they are easily disseminated or highly transmissible from person to person, produce high mortality rates, and require significant planning by public health agencies. Included in Category A is the toxin produced by the bacterium *Clostridium botulinum*. This toxin is the most poisonous substance known. Although the resulting illness (botulism) is not spread from person to person, the agent is placed in this category because of its extreme potency and lethality, and because it can so easily be produced and transported. We mentioned earlier in this chapter that the toxin might enter food unintentionally as a result of improper canning, but it could also *intentionally* be placed in food. It is unlikely to be placed in water because standard water treatment processes, such as chlorination, inactivate it.

Biological agents in Category B are moderately easy to disseminate, and they result in moderate rates of morbidity (sickness) and low rates of mortality. Included in Category B are several species of bacteria that could be intentionally added to food, including *Salmonella* and *Escherichia coli* O157:H7. The main threats to water safety also are included in Category B. These include the bacterium *Vibrio cholerae*, which causes the acute diarrheal illness cholera, and the single-celled parasite *Cryptosporidium parvum*, discussed earlier as a major cause of waterborne illness.

Biological agents in Category C include emerging pathogens that could be used in the future because they are easy to produce and disseminate, and they are associated with high rates of morbidity and mortality.

Personal Food Safety

Regardless of whether a risk is intentional or unintentional, systems are in place to limit exposure to contaminated food or water (refer again to Table 2a.2). While we may be uneasy about the many steps between the production of food and its arrival on our plate, each of us can do some things to make sure that the food we consume is as safe as possible.

Good personal food safety practices begin with a common-sense approach and the awareness that you should practice food safety from the moment you select an item in a market until you prepare it at home and store the leftovers.

Food Selection

Being informed and taking responsibility for your food selections will help you make better choices. When selecting any food, you should always look at "sell-by" dates and carefully examine the packaging for damage or tampering. Bacterial contamination and the possible growth of bacteria on food surfaces of fresh meat, poultry, seafood, or other food products rich in animal proteins is a very real concern. To limit bacterial growth, we rely primarily on cold temperatures in store display cases, rapid (and cool) transport of food from the store to a home refrigerator, and consistently cold temperatures in home refrigerators (always below 40°F).

Meat

A good rule of thumb when buying meat products is that whole cuts, such as steaks or roasts, are far less likely to carry bacterial contamination than are ground meat products. This is so because the surface area of the food serves as the site for bacterial contamination, and ground meat products have many times the surface area of an equivalent weight of steak. Recall, also, that meat from many individual animals goes into ground meat, raising the chances of pathogens being present in the first place.

Poultry

Because poultry is generally less expensive than other meats and seafood, it is an extremely popular choice of many consumers. However, fresh poultry is susceptible to bacterial contamination, particularly by *Salmonella*. Processors now deliver many fresh poultry items to markets pre-packaged in trays or strong bags that limit the contact and potential cross-contamination by bacteria from one item to another. That said, it is impossible to eliminate all risk, and you should not assume that the outside of the package does not harbor bacteria. When you select poultry from a market case, it is a good idea to place it apart from other foods—particularly vegetables or fruits that will be eaten raw—and to clean your hands before handling other food products. Always carry poultry products in bags separate from the rest of the groceries.

Seafood

Seafood selection when shopping poses some special concerns. For example, some seafood, such as fresh oysters, is traditionally eaten raw; so we cannot rely on high temperatures during cooking to kill pathogens or to destroy their toxins (Figure **2a.3**). Also, as noted

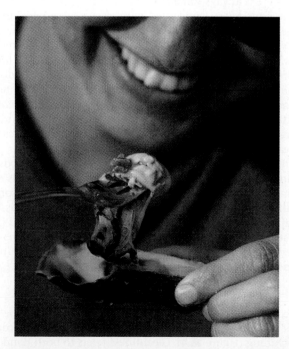

FIGURE 2a.3 Eating raw oysters poses certain risks because oysters are filter feeders that concentrate bacteria, toxins, and pollutants in their tissues.

earlier, oysters as filter feeders concentrate local microorganisms, toxins, and pollutants in their tissues. If you choose to eat raw oysters, then you should ask where the oysters came from. Even when you "know" their source, you must still be willing to accept the risk that this may not be the pristine natural environment you might assume it is. When you are selecting fresh fish, keep in mind that firmness, color, and odor are paramount. Reject any fish with a strong fishy odor. (Fresh saltwater fish smells like the sea.) You may also want to ask if the fish has been refreshed with any solutions in this display case. Such "refreshing" refers to washing the fish with a dilute bleach solution to eliminate bacterial contamination on the surface—not a very appetizing way to treat any food, and not even necessary if the fish has been handled carefully up to that point. (A quick sniff will often reveal the presence of bleach.)

A final concern when buying fresh fish—even fish that will be cooked to high enough temperatures to ensure safety from typical bacterial contamination—relates to the species of fish you are selecting. As mentioned earlier, large individuals of some top predator species concentrate and store potentially dangerous levels of mercury in their tissues. To avoid consuming dangerous levels of mercury, be aware of the current safety concerns related to individual species of fishes, and do not exceed the recommended weekly consumption rates for those species, especially if you are pregnant or nursing. Further information on mercury contamination is available at the FDA's Food Safety website (www.cfsan.fda.gov/seafood1.html) and information regarding the safety of locally caught fish can be found at the EPA's Fish Advisory website (www.epa.gov/waterscience/fish).

Produce

Shopping for fresh vegetables to be consumed raw has been greatly simplified in recent years. Pre-packed, pre-washed lettuce and salad mixes vie for our attention against whole lettuces and other vegetables. Should you buy the time-saving pre-packed versions, whose labels often promise they have been washed twice? From a food safety standpoint, there is no one clear answer. Bacterial contamination of fresh vegetables can happen at many points between farm and fork. Wash even these products that are packaged as ready to eat as thoroughly as possible before consumption, while recognizing that there is always some risk.

Some consumers, concerned with pesticide residues in fruits and vegetables, select certified organic foods, which are produced without synthetic pesticides and fertilizers. Each consumer will have to decide whether to accept conventionally produced foods or to pay somewhat more for foods produced organically. A deciding factor for many consumers is that foods that are certified to have been produced organically may be less harmful to natural environments than are foods produced using synthetic pesticides and fertilizers. Organically grown products are also often produced closer to home, leading to lower oil consumption during transport.

Similar concerns related to genetically modified foods (GM foods) and to foods that result from the cloning of animals ensure that many basic questions about food safety and the environment will continue far into the future (see Chapter 21 for a discussion of genetically modified food). As a responsible consumer, it is important to stay informed and to make conscientious decisions about your personal tolerance for food safety risks and the future of foods and the environment.

Food Handling and Storage

At home, good food safety practices for food handling can be sorted into four basic categories: (1) cleanliness; (2) separation; (3) cooking; and (4) chilling (Figure **2a.4**). Cleanliness refers to both hand wash-

Q *Explain the different effects that chilling and cooking have on bacteria in food. Also, is it best to thaw food in the refrigerator or on the counter in your kitchen?*

FIGURE 2a.4 This logo from the Be Food Safe program of the USDA and Partnership for Food Safety Education emphasizes the four basic ways to keep food safe at home.

A *Placing food in the refrigerator or freezer does not kill bacteria; it simply stops bacteria from increasing in number. Cooking food to an appropriate temperature kills bacteria. Food should always be thawed in the refrigerator because room temperatures allow bacteria to multiply on the surface of the food, even if the interior is still frozen.*

ing by the food preparer (and subsequently the food consumer) and cleanliness of surfaces that will come into contact with raw food, such as cutting boards, knives, and storage containers. Keeping the kitchen workplace clean is an obvious and basic way to improve food safety at home. Separation refers to keeping foods apart from one another and avoiding cross-contamination. For example, keeping fresh meat out of direct contact with cooked foods is an essential part of kitchen hygiene that can limit exposure to bacteria. Cooking refers to thoroughly cooking food products to temperatures that will kill most bacteria, which generally do not survive temperatures greater than 160°F. Proper and prompt chilling of both fresh and cooked foods helps to stop bacterial growth. Nevertheless, even refrigerated food is not safe to eat indefinitely (Table **2a.3**). Freezing to

TABLE 2a.3 Storage Times for Refrigerated Foods

Eggs		*Hot Dogs and Luncheon Meats*	
Fresh, in shell	3–5 weeks	Hot dogs	Unopened package, 2 weeks
Raw yolks, whites	2–4 days		Opened package, 1 week
Hard-cooked	1 week	Luncheon meats	Unopened package, 2 weeks
Liquid pasteurized eggs, egg substitutes	Unopened, 10 days		Opened package, 3–5 days
	Opened, 3 days	*Bacon and Sausage*	
Cooked egg dishes	3–4 days	Bacon	7 days
Mayonnaise, commercial, opened	2 months	Sausage, raw from meat or poultry	1–2 days
Deli and Vacuum-Packed Products		Smoked breakfast links, patties	7 days
Store-prepared (or homemade) egg, chicken, tuna, ham, and macaroni salads	3–5 days	Summer sausage labeled "Keep Refrigerated"	Unopened, 3 months
			Opened, 3 weeks
Pre-stuffed pork, lamb chops, and chicken breasts	1 day	Hard sausage (such as pepperoni)	2–3 weeks
Store-cooked dinners and entrees	3–4 days	*Cooked Meat, Poultry, and Fish Leftovers*	
Commercial brand vacuum-packed dinners with USDA seal, unopened	2 weeks	Pieces and cooked casseroles	3–4 days
		Gravy and broth, patties, and nuggets	1–2 days
Raw Hamburger, Ground and Stew Meat		Soups and stews	3–4 days
Ground beef, turkey, veal, pork, lamb	1–2 days	*Fresh Meat (Beef, Veal, Lamb, and Pork)*	
Stew meats	1–2 days	Steaks, chops, roasts	3–5 days
Ham, Corned Beef		Variety meats (tongue, kidneys, liver, heart, chitterlings)	1–2 days
Ham, canned, labeled "Keep Refrigerated"	Unopened, 6–9 months	*Fresh Poultry*	
	Opened, 3–5 days	Chicken or turkey, whole	1–2 days
Ham, fully cooked, whole	7 days	Chicken or turkey, parts	1–2 days
Ham, fully cooked, half	3–5 days	Giblets	1–2 days
Ham, fully cooked, slices	3–4 days	*Fresh Fish and Shellfish*	
Corned beef in pouch with pickling juices	5–7 days	Fresh fish and shellfish	1–2 days

Source: USDA Food Safety and Inspection Service, Fact Sheets: Safe Food Handling, www.fsis.usda.gov

0°F inactivates bacteria in food, but it does not kill them. Indeed, once the food is thawed, the bacteria will begin to reproduce at room temperature. When in doubt about the freshness of refrigerated food, throw it out.

In the end, personal food safety practices when shopping, preparing, and storing foods at home play a major role in ensuring that your food is safe. Keep these principles in mind when you plan, shop for, and prepare safer meals.

3

The Cell

The cells of the body cooperate like a well-coordinated team in which each member is suited to a particular role. At the same time, all cells have certain basic features in common.

The championship game was coming down to a thrilling conclusion. With only 5 minutes remaining in the fourth quarter, Rob Douglas kicked a stunning 47-yard field goal to bring Morinville within 6 points of arch rival Beaumont. Then, on the kickoff, Douglas put the ball deep into the end zone. The Beaumont offense made no headway against the rejuvenated Morinville defense, which forced them to punt on fourth down. This change of possession set up Morinville quarterback Joe Norton for a passing attack. After moving the ball for 30 yards and two first downs, he found Charlie Mendoza in the right corner of the end zone with just 15 seconds remaining. With the score tied, Douglas kicked the extra point to win the game for Morinville, 24 to 23. Mendoza's three touchdowns had sealed his place as Most Valuable Player in the championship game, but there was plenty of glory to go around for the whole team following Morinville's spectacular end of season victory.

As any coach knows, a team cannot function without the coordinated efforts of players in a wide range of specialized positions. By the same token, each player's body cannot contribute to the team's performance without the coordinated actions of a vast number of cell types. Our bodies contain more than 10 trillion cells that specialize in more than 100 different functions. To throw a pass, muscle cells contract in response to electrical signals from the brain. To dodge a tackle, cells of the adrenal glands release hormones such as norepinephrine that trigger near-instantaneous reactions. Meanwhile, kidney cells continuously remove wastes from the burning of cellular fuels. Neurons in the brain coordinate the perceptions and intellect of each player.

In this chapter we discover how cells work by examining the structures that all cells in the human body have in common. We begin with the plasma membrane, the outer boundary of a cell, and work inward. After examining the various organelles—small structures within cells that have specialized functions—we explore the ways that cells obtain the energy they need to do their work of running the body.

Eukaryotic Cells Compared with Prokaryotic Cells

The **cell theory** is a fundamental organizing principle of biology, guiding the way biologists think about and study living things. A theory, you may recall from Chapter 1, is a well-researched and well-supported explanation for some aspect of the physical universe. The cell theory states that (1) a cell is the smallest unit of life; (2) cells make up all living things, from unicellular to multicellular organisms; and (3) new cells can arise only from preexisting cells.

There are two basic types of cells—eukaryotic cells and prokaryotic cells. **Prokaryotic cells,** as shown in Figure **3.1**, are structurally simpler and typically smaller than eukaryotic cells. They are limited to bacteria and another group of microscopic organisms called archaea. You are probably already aware of bacteria, some of which inhabit your body. Many bacterial inhabitants are harmless, but others can cause illness (see Chapters 2a and 13a). Archaea may be less familiar to you. They include species that inhabit extreme environments such as the high-saline Great Salt Lake or the hot sulfur springs of Yellowstone National Park. Most prokaryotic cells are surrounded by a rigid cell wall.

The cells of plants, animals, and all other organisms except bacteria and archaea are eukaryotic. All the cells that make up your body, therefore, are eukaryotic. The difference between eukaryotic and prokaryotic cells relates to the presence or absence of membrane-bound organelles. An **organelle** or "little organ" is a component within a cell that carries out specific functions. Some organelles have membranes, others do not. Nonmembranous organelles such as ribosomes and cytoskeletal elements are found in both prokaryotic and eukaryotic cells. Unique to **eukaryotic cells**, however, are membrane-bound organelles such as mitochondria and endoplasmic reticulum (Figure **3.2**). Another of the membrane-bound organelles found in all typical eukaryotic cells is a well-defined nucleus containing DNA. Note that in prokaryotes, a membrane does not surround the DNA (refer, again, to Figure 3.1). Among eukaryotes, plant cells have cell walls, but animal cells do not. Table **3.1** reviews the major differences between eukaryotic and prokaryotic cells.

FIGURE 3.1 Prokaryotic cells, such as a bacterium, lack internal membrane-bound organelles.

Plasma membrane
DNA region (no nucleus)
Cytoplasm
Ribosome
Cell wall
1–10 μm

TABLE 3.1 Review of Features of Prokaryotic and Eukaryotic Cells

Feature	Prokaryotic Cells	Eukaryotic Cells
Organisms	Bacteria, archaea	Plants, animals, fungi, protists
Size	1–10 μm across	10–100 μm across
Membrane-bound organelles	Absent	Present
DNA form	Circular	Coiled, linear strands
DNA location	Cytoplasm	Nucleus
Internal membranes	Rare	Many
Cytoskeleton	Present	Present

Q *The nucleus is a membrane-bound organelle. Look closely at the other organelles in the cell and read their functions. Based on the structure and functions of the organelles shown, list those that you think are membrane-bound organelles and those that are nonmembranous organelles.*

Plasma membrane
• Regulates movement of materials into and out of cell

Cytoplasm
• The material surrounding the nucleus

Lysosome
• Digests substances brought into cell and destroys old parts of cells

Mitochondrion
• Provides cell with energy through the breakdown of glucose during cellular respiration

Nucleus
• Contains DNA and controls cellular activity

Nucleolus
• Produces components of ribosomes (RNA and proteins)

Ribosome
• Site where protein synthesis begins

Rough endoplasmic reticulum
• Studded with ribosomes and produces membrane

Smooth endoplasmic reticulum
• Detoxifies drugs and produces membrane

Golgi complex
• Sorts, modifies, and packages proteins

Microfilament
• Plays a role in muscle contraction and cell division

Centrioles
• May function in cell division

Microtubule
• Maintains cell shape and forms tracks on which vesicles move

10–100 μm

FIGURE 3.2 Eukaryotic cells, such as the generalized animal cell shown here, have internal membrane-bound organelles.

A *The membrane-bound organelles include the nucleus, rough endoplasmic reticulum, smooth endoplasmic reticulum, Golgi complex, mitochondrion, and lysosome. The nonmembranous organelles include ribosomes, microfilaments, centrioles, and microtubules.*

Cell Size and Microscopy

Most eukaryotic and prokaryotic cells are so small they are typically measured in micrometers (μm), which are equal to 1/1000 meters (m). (An obvious exception is the chicken egg.) The small size of cells is dictated by a physical relationship known as the **surface-to-volume ratio.** This relationship says that as a cell gets larger, its surface area increases much more slowly than its volume (Figure **3.3**). Nutrients enter a cell, and wastes leave a cell at its surface. Therefore, a large cell would have difficulty moving all the nutrients it needs and all the wastes it produces across its inadequate surface and would die. A small cell, on the other hand, has sufficient surface for the uptake and removal of substances and would survive.

Due to the small size of most cells, you need a microscope to see them. Throughout this book you will see micrographs, which are photographs obtained using a microscope (Figure **3.4**). Microscopic specimens can be imaged using beams of either light or electrons. Light microscopes, which are used in many classrooms, have the advantage that they are relatively inexpensive and simple to operate. Electron microscopes, though more complex and expensive, have the capacity to reveal finer details because the wavelength of an electron beam is smaller than the wavelengths of visible light. Whether using light or electrons, the beam can be either transmitted through a thinly sliced specimen or bounced off of the specimen's surface.

Figure 3.4a is a transmitted light micrograph through three striated muscle cells that have been stained with biological dyes to increase the contrast between different cellular components. The three nuclei visible in this picture are colored dark purple because the dye used has an affinity for acidic components in the cell such as DNA. Figure 3.4b is a transmitted electron micrograph that shows the structure of striated muscle cells in more detail than is possible using light to image the tissue. In this case, the contrast

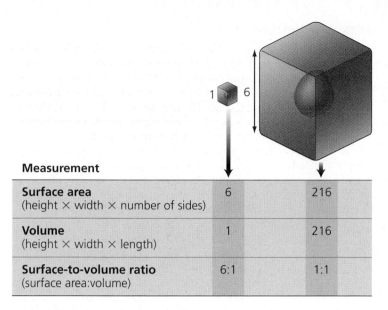

Measurement		
Surface area (height × width × number of sides)	6	216
Volume (height × width × length)	1	216
Surface-to-volume ratio (surface area:volume)	6:1	1:1

FIGURE 3.3 Cells must remain small in size because the ratio of surface area to volume decreases rapidly as cell size increases.

between different cellular components is produced by staining the tissue with heavy metals such as lead and uranium. Different components of the cells absorb different amounts of these heavy metals. Components that readily absorb the metals differentially block the electron beam from passing through the sample. Figure 3.4c is a scanning electron micrograph produced by bouncing an electron beam off the surface of several striated muscle cells. The beam is scanned across the surface of the sample, and electrons that bounce off the surface are collected by a detector. For every point that is scanned, the number of electrons reaching the detector is used to calculate the relative brightness of that spot on the sample. This information is used to construct the image. Images produced with electron beams are not in color. The pictures shown in Figures 3.4b and 3.4c have been colored to highlight certain features, an improvement made possible by computer-assisted processing of images. Other micrographs in the text have also been colored.

Cell Structure and Function

The structure of a cell exquisitely reflects its functions (Figure **3.5**). For example, few human cells are more specialized than sperm or eggs, the cells that carry genetic information and other materials

(a) Striated muscle cells viewed with a light microscope.

(b) Striated muscle cells viewed with a transmission electron microscope.

(c) Striated muscle cells viewed with a scanning electron microscope.

FIGURE 3.4 Micrographs are photographs taken through a microscope. Here, striated muscle cells have been photographed using three different types of microscope. Electron microscopes use beams of electrons to produce images with finer details than those viewed with light microscopes.

(a) A sperm is specialized to be highly mobile. In contrast, an egg is specialized to be large, immobile, and packed with material needed to initiate development.

(b) A mature red blood cell, devoid of most organelles, is specialized for carrying oxygen.

(c) A cardiac muscle cell is specialized for contraction and for propagating the signal for contraction.

FIGURE 3.5 A cell's structure reflects its specific function. These cell types from the human body illustrate the close tie between structure and function.

needed to make a new individual of the next generation. A sperm is specialized for swimming to the egg and fertilizing it. As such, a sperm is streamlined and equipped with a whiplike tail. In the head of the sperm is an enzyme-containing sac that spills open to release enzymes that digest a path through the layers of cells surrounding the egg. In contrast, the egg is immobile and much larger than a typical cell because it is literally packed with nutrients and other materials needed to initiate development. A mature red blood cell is another example of a cell whose structure reflects its function. As the red blood cell matures, it extrudes its nucleus and most organelles, leaving more space for hemoglobin, the protein that transports oxygen. A mature red blood cell is thus an exception to the rule that eukaryotic cells have a well-defined nucleus and other membrane-bound organelles. Consider, also, a cardiac muscle cell. This cell is specialized for contraction, and for propagating the signal for contraction from one muscle cell to the next. Thus it is filled with contractile proteins and joined to adjacent cells by specialized junctions that strengthen cardiac tissue and promote rapid conduction of impulses throughout the heart. In each of these cases, careful study of the cell's structure provides excellent clues to its function, and vice versa.

Plasma Membrane

We begin our examination of the cell at its outer surface—the **plasma membrane.** This remarkably thin outer covering controls the movement of substances both into and out of the cell. Because the concentrations of substances in a cell's interior are critically balanced, molecules and ions are not permitted to move randomly in and out.

Both prokaryotic and eukaryotic cells have a plasma membrane, but only eukaryotic cells also contain internal membranes that divide the cell into many compartments. Each compartment contains its own assortment of enzymes and is specialized for particular functions. In general, the principles described for the plasma membrane also apply to the membranes inside the cell.

Plasma Membrane Structure

The plasma membrane is made of lipids, proteins, and carbohydrates. Recall from Chapter 2 that phospholipids are the major components of the plasma membrane. These molecules, with their hydrophilic (water-loving) heads and hydrophobic (water-fearing) tails, form a double layer, called the phospholipid bilayer, at the surface of the cell (Figure **3.6**). The hydrophilic heads facing outside the cell interact with the **extracellular fluid** (also known as interstitial fluid), which is the watery solution outside cells. The hydrophilic heads facing inside the cell interact with the **cytoplasm,** which is the jellylike solution inside the cell. The cytoplasm includes all contents of the cell between the plasma membrane and the nucleus. Within the phospholipid bilayer, the hydrophobic tails point toward each other and hold the plasma membrane together.

Interspersed in the phospholipid bilayer are proteins, as seen in Figure 3.6. Some proteins are embedded in the membrane, and some of these span the bilayer completely. Other proteins are simply attached to the inner or outer surface of the membrane. In many cases, such surface proteins are attached to an exposed portion of an embedded protein. Molecules of cholesterol are also scattered throughout the bilayer.

As you can see in Figure 3.6, carbohydrates attach only to the outer surface of the plasma membrane. Most of these carbohydrates are attached to proteins, forming glycoproteins. We will see that glycoproteins often function in cell recognition. Other carbohydrates are attached to lipids, forming glycolipids.

The structure of the plasma membrane is often described as a **fluid mosaic.** The proteins are interspersed among the lipid molecules like tiles of different colors within a mosaic. Many of the proteins are able to move sideways through the bilayer to some degree, giving the membrane its fluid quality.

Plasma Membrane Functions

The plasma membrane performs several vital functions for the cell. First, by imposing a boundary between the cell's internal and external environment, the plasma membrane maintains the cell's structural integrity. Second, the structure of the plasma membrane

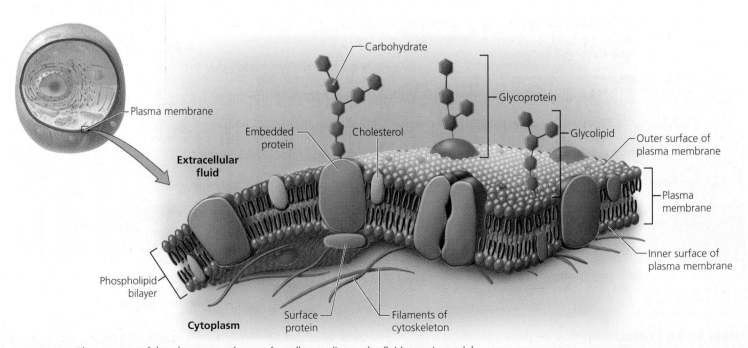

FIGURE 3.6 The structure of the plasma membrane of a cell according to the fluid mosaic model

regulates the movement of substances into and out of the cell, permitting entry to some substances but not others. For this reason, the membrane is often described as being **selectively permeable.** You will read more about the transport of materials across the plasma membrane in the next section of this chapter.

The plasma membrane also functions in cell–cell recognition. Cells distinguish one type of cell from another by recognizing molecules—often glycoproteins—on their surface. Membrane glycoproteins differ from one species of organism to another and among individuals of the same species. Even different cell types within an individual have different membrane glycoproteins. This variation allows the body to recognize foreign invaders such as bacteria. Your own body, for example, would recognize such invaders because the bacteria lack the surface molecules found on your cells. The bacteria, in turn, "read" the different surface molecules of your cells to settle preferentially on some kinds of cells but not others.

Another important function of the plasma membrane is communication between cells. Such communication relies on *receptors*, specialized proteins in the plasma membrane (or inside the cell) that bind particular substances that affect cell activities. For example, hormones secreted by one group of cells may bind to receptors in the plasma membranes of other cells. The receptors then relay a signal to proteins inside the cell, which transmit the message to other nearby molecules. Through a series of chemical reactions, the hormone's "message" ultimately initiates a response by the recipient cell, perhaps causing it to release a certain chemical.

Finally, the plasma membrane plays an important role in binding pairs or groups of cells together. **Cell adhesion molecules (CAMs)** extend from the plasma membranes of most cells and help attach the cells to one another, especially during the formation of tissues and organs in an embryo. Table **3.2** reviews the functions of the plasma membrane.

described as either active—requiring the cell to expend energy—or passive—requiring no energy expenditure by the cell.

Simple diffusion

Some materials cross the plasma membrane passively through **simple diffusion**, the random movement of a substance from a region of higher concentration to a region of lower concentration. *Concentration* is the number of molecules of a substance in a particular volume, while a **concentration gradient** is a difference in the relative number of molecules or ions of a given substance in two adjacent areas. The end result of simple diffusion is an equal distribution of the substance in the two areas; in other words, diffusion tends to eliminate the concentration gradient. Consider what happens when someone is cooking bacon in the kitchen. At first, the smell of bacon is localized in the kitchen. Soon, however, the smell permeates adjoining rooms, too, as odor molecules move from where they are more concentrated (the kitchen) to where they are less concentrated (other parts of the house). Eventually the odor molecules are equally distributed, but they still move randomly in all directions. Likewise, when a substance diffuses across a membrane from a region of higher concentration to a region of lower concentration, the movement of its molecules does not stop once the concentration has equalized. Instead, the molecules continue to move randomly back and forth across the membrane. The rate of movement in each direction, however, is now the same. Substances such as carbon dioxide and oxygen diffuse through the plasma membrane of our cells (Figure **3.7**).

Facilitated diffusion

Water-soluble substances are repelled by lipids and so cannot move through the phospholipid bilayer by simple diffusion. If they are to cross a cell membrane, their transport must be assisted,

Movement Across the Plasma Membrane

Recall that an important function of the plasma membrane is to control which substances move into and out of the cell. Substances cross the plasma membrane in several ways. These methods are

TABLE 3.2 Review of Plasma Membrane Functions
Maintain structural integrity of the cell
Regulate movement of substances into and out of the cell
Provide recognition between cells
Provide communication between cells
Stick cells together to form tissues and organs

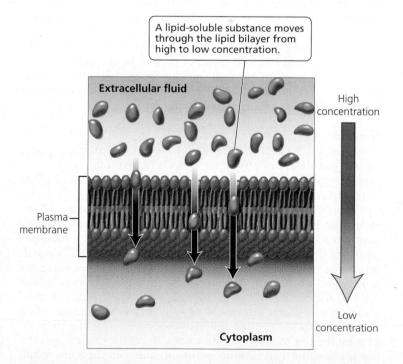

FIGURE 3.7 Simple diffusion is the random movement of a substance from a region of higher concentration to a region of lower concentration.

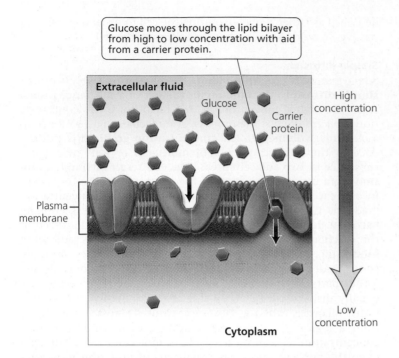

FIGURE 3.8 Facilitated diffusion is the movement through the plasma membrane of a substance from a region of higher concentration to a region of lower concentration with the aid of a membrane protein that acts as a channel or a carrier protein.

FIGURE 3.9 Osmosis is diffusion of water across a selectively permeable membrane. The drawings show what happens when a membranous bag through which water but not sugar can move is placed in solutions that are (a) hypertonic, (b) isotonic, or (c) hypotonic to the solution inside the bag. The width of the black arrows corresponds to the amount of water moving into and out of the bag. The photographs show what happens to red blood cells when placed in the three kinds of solutions. Red blood cells are normally shaped like flattened disks, as in part b.

or "facilitated," by certain proteins within the membrane. Some of these proteins, called carrier proteins, bind to a particular water-soluble substance. Such binding prompts a change in the protein's shape and has the effect of carrying the substance to the other side of the membrane. Other proteins form channels through which certain water-soluble substances can move. **Facilitated diffusion** is the movement of a substance from a region of higher concentration to a region of lower concentration with the aid of a membrane protein. Molecules of glucose, for example, enter fat cells by facilitated diffusion. In this example, a molecule of glucose in the extracellular fluid binds to a carrier protein in the plasma membrane, which helps to move the glucose molecule from outside to inside the fat cell (Figure **3.8**). Facilitated diffusion does not require energy and is thus a form of passive transport.

Osmosis
Osmosis is a type of diffusion in which water moves across a plasma membrane or any other selectively permeable membrane from a region of higher water concentration to a region of lower water concentration. The movement of water occurs in response to a concentration gradient of a dissolved substance (solute). Consider what happens when a substance such as table sugar (in this case, our solute) is dissolved in water (our solvent) in a membranous bag through which water, but not sugar, can move. Keep in mind that when solute concentration is low, water concentration is high; and when solute concentration is high, water concentration is low. If the membranous bag is placed into a **hypertonic solution**, meaning a solution whose solute concentration is higher than that inside the bag, more water moves out of the bag than in, causing the bag to shrivel (Figure **3.9a**). If, on the other hand, the bag is placed into an **isotonic solution**, one with the same solute (sugar) concentration as inside the bag, there is no net movement

of water in either direction, and the bag maintains its original shape (Figure 3.9b). When the bag is placed into a **hypotonic solution**, in which the concentration of solute is lower than that inside the bag, more water moves into the bag than out, causing the bag to swell and possibly burst (Figure 3.9c). Osmosis does not require energy and is thus a form of passive transport.

Red blood cells behave the same way the bag in our example does, as shown at the bottom of Figure 3.9. Red blood cells move through a fluid, called plasma. As the figure illustrates, the shape of red blood cells responds to different levels of solute concentration in the plasma.

Active transport
Active transport is a mechanism that moves substances across plasma membranes with the aid of a carrier protein and energy supplied by the cell (through the breakdown of ATP; see Chapter 2). So far in our discussion of movement across plasma membranes, we have described substances moving from regions of higher concentration to regions of lower concentration. However, in most cases

A substance moves through the lipid bilayer from low to high concentration with the aid of a carrier protein and energy.

FIGURE 3.10 Active transport is the movement of molecules across the plasma membrane, often from an area of lower concentration to one of higher concentration with help from a carrier protein and energy, usually in the form of ATP.

of active transport, substances are moved from regions of lower concentration to higher concentration, as shown in Figure **3.10**. This type of movement is described as going "against the concentration gradient" and occurs when cells need to concentrate certain substances. For example, the cells in our bodies contain higher concentrations of potassium ions (K^+) and lower concentrations of sodium ions (Na^+) than their surroundings. Through active transport, proteins in the plasma membrane help maintain these conditions, pumping potassium ions into the cell and sodium ions out of the cell. In this example, both potassium and sodium are moving from regions of lower concentration to regions of higher concentration.

Endocytosis

Most small molecules cross the plasma membrane by simple diffusion, facilitated diffusion, or active transport. Large molecules, single-celled organisms such as bacteria, and droplets of fluid containing dissolved substances enter cells through endocytosis (Figure **3.11**). In **endocytosis**, a region of the plasma membrane engulfs the substance to be ingested and then pinches off from the rest of the membrane, in this way enclosing the substance in a saclike structure called a **vesicle**. The vesicle then travels through the cytoplasm. Two types of endocytosis are phagocytosis ("cell eating") and pinocytosis ("cell drinking"). In **phagocytosis**, cells engulf large particles or bacteria (Figure 3.11a). In **pinocytosis**, they engulf droplets of fluid (Figure 3.11b), thus bringing all of the substances dissolved in the droplet into the cell.

Exocytosis

The process by which large molecules leave cells is **exocytosis**. In a cell that produces hormones, for example, the hormones are enclosed in membrane-bound vesicles that travel through the cell's

FIGURE 3.11 Endocytosis—phagocytosis or pinocytosis—occurs when a localized region of the plasma membrane surrounds a bacterium, large molecule, or fluid containing dissolved substances and then pinches inward to form a vesicle that moves into the cell.

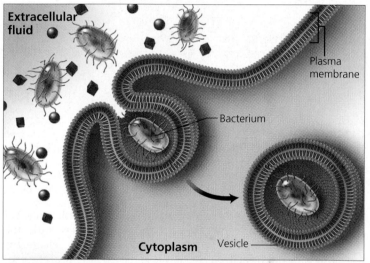

(a) Phagocytosis ("cell eating") occurs when cells engulf bacteria or other large particles.

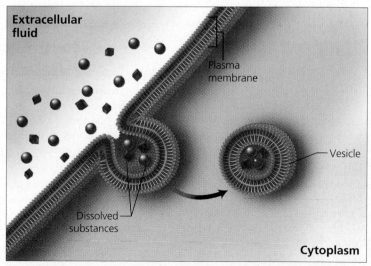

(b) Pinocytosis ("cell drinking") occurs when cells engulf droplets of extracellular fluid and the dissolved substances therein.

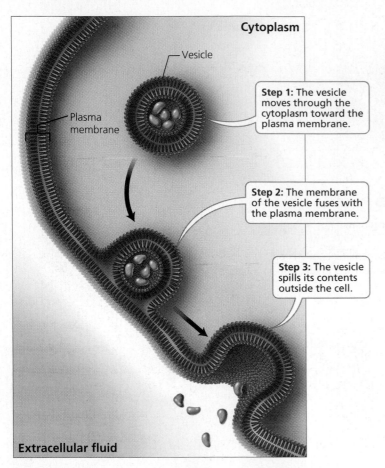

Cytoplasm

Vesicle

Plasma membrane

Step 1: The vesicle moves through the cytoplasm toward the plasma membrane.

Step 2: The membrane of the vesicle fuses with the plasma membrane.

Step 3: The vesicle spills its contents outside the cell.

Extracellular fluid

FIGURE 3.12 Cells package large molecules in membrane-bound vesicles, which then spill their contents by exocytosis.

TABLE 3.3 Review of Mechanisms of Transport Across the Plasma Membrane

Mechanism	Description
Simple diffusion	Random movement from region of higher concentration to region of lower concentration
Facilitated diffusion	Movement from region of higher concentration to region of lower concentration with the aid of a carrier or channel protein
Osmosis	Movement of water from region of higher water concentration (lower solute concentration) to region of lower water concentration (higher solute concentration)
Active transport	Movement often from region of lower concentration to region of higher concentration with the aid of a carrier protein and energy usually from ATP
Endocytosis	Process by which materials are engulfed by plasma membrane and drawn into cell in a vesicle
Exocytosis	Process by which a membrane-bound vesicle from inside the cell fuses with the plasma membrane and spills contents outside of cell

cytoplasm toward the plasma membrane. When the vesicle reaches the plasma membrane, the vesicle membrane fuses with the plasma membrane and then the vesicle opens up to release the hormone outside the cell. Nerve cells also release chemicals by exocytosis. Exocytosis is shown in Figure **3.12**.

Table **3.3** reviews the ways in which substances move across the plasma membrane.

stop and think

People with kidney disorders may need dialysis to remove waste products from their blood. The blood is passed through a long, coiled tube submerged in a tank filled with dialyzing fluid. The tubing is porous, allowing small molecules to diffuse out of the blood into the dialyzing fluid. Urea is a waste product that must be removed from the blood. Glucose molecules, on the other hand, should remain in the blood. To achieve these goals, what should the concentrations of urea and glucose be like in the dialyzing fluid?

Organelles

Inside the eukaryotic cell, the primary role of membranes is to create separate compartments where specific chemical processes critical to the life of the cell are carried out. The membrane-bound organelles distributed in the cells' cytoplasm have different functions—just like the different offices within a large company, some of which are responsible for production, some for purchasing, and others for shipping. The compartmentalization allows segregated combinations of molecules to carry out specific tasks (see Figure 3.2). Some organelles give directions for manufacturing cell products. Others make or modify the products or transport them. Still other organelles process energy or break down substances for use or disposal. Nonmembranous organelles also perform specific functions for the cell.

Nucleus

The cell **nucleus** contains almost all of the cell's genetic information (Figure **3.13**). The DNA within the nucleus controls cellular structure and function because it contains a code for the production of proteins. All our cells contain the same genetic information. The characteristics of a particular cell—what makes it a muscle cell or a liver cell—are determined largely by the specific directions it receives from its nucleus.

A double membrane called the **nuclear envelope** surrounds the nucleus and separates it from the cytoplasm, as shown in Figure 3.13. Communication between the nucleus and cytoplasm occurs through openings in the envelope called **nuclear pores**. The traffic of selected materials across the nuclear envelope allows the contents of the cytoplasm to influence the nucleus, and vice versa.

Genetic information within the nucleus is organized into **chromosomes**, threadlike structures made of DNA and associated proteins. The number of chromosomes varies from one species to another. For example, humans have 46 chromosomes (23 pairs), house mice have 40 chromosomes, and domestic dogs have 78. Individual chromosomes are visible with a light microscope during cell division, when they shorten and condense (Figure **3.14a**). At all other times, however, the chromosomes are extended and

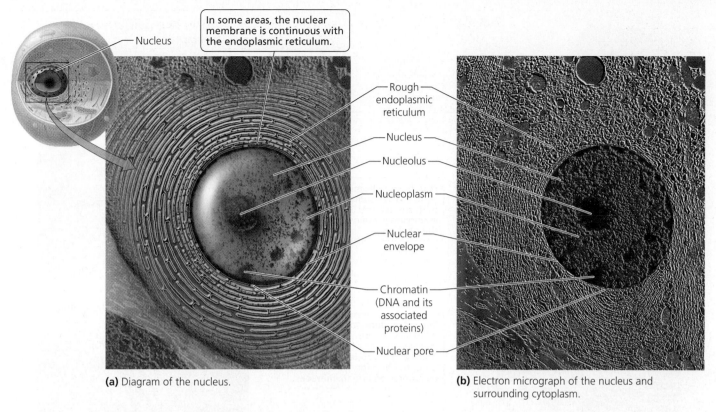

In some areas, the nuclear membrane is continuous with the endoplasmic reticulum.

Nucleus

Rough endoplasmic reticulum

Nucleus

Nucleolus

Nucleoplasm

Nuclear envelope

Chromatin (DNA and its associated proteins)

Nuclear pore

(a) Diagram of the nucleus.

(b) Electron micrograph of the nucleus and surrounding cytoplasm.

FIGURE 3.13 The nucleus contains almost all the genetic information of a cell.

(a) Individual chromosomes are visible during cell division, when they shorten and condense.

(b) At all other times, the genetic material is dispersed and called chromatin.

Nucleus

Chromatin

FIGURE 3.14 Chromosomes are composed of DNA and associated proteins.

not readily visible. In this dispersed state, the genetic material is called *chromatin* (Figure 3.14b). The chromatin and other contents of the nucleus constitute the *nucleoplasm*. We will discuss chromosomes and cell division in Chapter 19.

The **nucleolus**, a specialized region within the nucleus (see Figure 3.13), forms and disassembles during the course of the cell cycle (see Chapter 19). It is not surrounded by a membrane but is simply a region where DNA has gathered to produce a type of RNA called ribosomal RNA (rRNA). Ribosomal RNA is a component of **ribosomes**, which are sites where protein synthesis begins. Ribosomes may be suspended in the cytoplasm (free ribosomes) or attached to the endoplasmic reticulum (bound ribosomes).

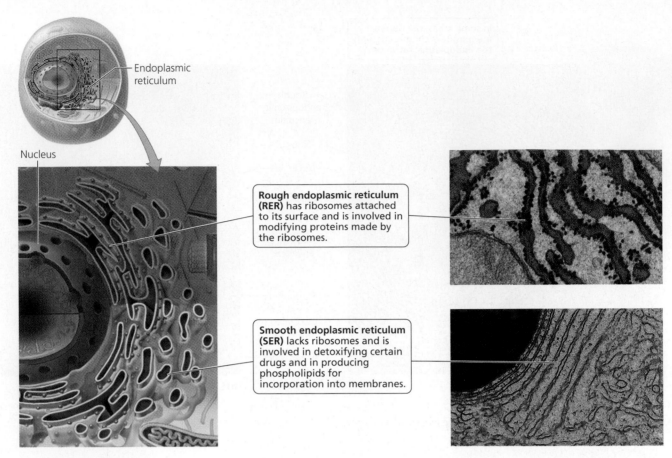

Nucleus

Endoplasmic reticulum

Rough endoplasmic reticulum (RER) has ribosomes attached to its surface and is involved in modifying proteins made by the ribosomes.

Smooth endoplasmic reticulum (SER) lacks ribosomes and is involved in detoxifying certain drugs and in producing phospholipids for incorporation into membranes.

FIGURE 3.15 The endoplasmic reticulum (ER) is continuous with the nuclear membrane and consists of two regions: rough ER and smooth ER.

Endoplasmic Reticulum

The **endoplasmic reticulum (ER)** is part of an extensive network of channels connected to the nuclear envelope and certain organelles (Figure **3.15**). In some regions, the ER is studded with ribosomes and because of this is called **rough endoplasmic reticulum (RER).** The amino acid chains made by the attached ribosomes are threaded through the RER's membrane to its internal spaces. There the chains are processed and modified, enclosed in vesicles formed from the RER membrane, and transferred to the Golgi complex (discussed later) for additional processing and packaging. Proteins made by ribosomes bound to ER will be incorporated into membranes or eventually secreted by the cell. Proteins produced by free ribosomes will remain in the cell.

Smooth endoplasmic reticulum (SER) lacks ribosomes. The SER (particularly in liver cells) detoxifies alcohol and other drugs such as phenobarbital. Typically, enzymes of SER modify the drugs to make them more water soluble and easier to eliminate from the body. Another function of SER is the production of phospholipids. These phospholipids, along with proteins from the RER, are used to make the RER membrane. Because the RER membrane is continually used to form vesicles for shipping, it must be replenished constantly.

Golgi Complex

Resembling a stack of dinner plates, the **Golgi complex** consists of a series of interconnected, flattened membranous sacs. This organelle is the cell's protein processing and packaging center (Figure **3.16**).

Protein-filled vesicles from the RER arrive at the "receiving side" of the Golgi complex, fuse with its membrane, and empty their contents inside. The Golgi complex then chemically modifies many of the proteins as they move, by way of vesicles, from one membranous disk in the stack to the next. When the processing is finished, the Golgi complex sorts the proteins, much as a postal worker sorts letters, and sends them to their various destinations. Some of the proteins emerging from the "shipping side" are packaged in vesicles and sent to the plasma membrane for export from the cell or to become membrane proteins. Other proteins are packaged in lysosomes. Figure **3.17** summarizes the movement of protein-filled vesicles from the rough endoplasmic reticulum to the Golgi complex for processing and eventual release.

Lysosomes

How does the cell break down worn-out parts or digest large objects that it takes in by phagocytosis? If it simply released digestive enzymes into its cytoplasm, for example, it would soon destroy itself. Instead, intracellular digestion occurs mainly within lysosomes. **Lysosomes** are roughly spherical organelles consisting of a single membrane packed with about 40 different digestive enzymes. The enzymes and membranes of lysosomes are made by the RER and then sent to the Golgi complex for additional processing. Eventually, enzyme-filled lysosomes bud and then pinch off from the Golgi complex (see Figure 3.17) and begin their diverse roles in digestion within the cell. These roles include destroying foreign invaders, such as bacteria, and breaking down worn-out organelles.

(a) Diagram of the Golgi complex. This organelle serves as the site for protein processing and packaging within the cell.

(b) Electron micrograph showing the Golgi complex and its associated vesicles.

FIGURE 3.16 The Golgi complex

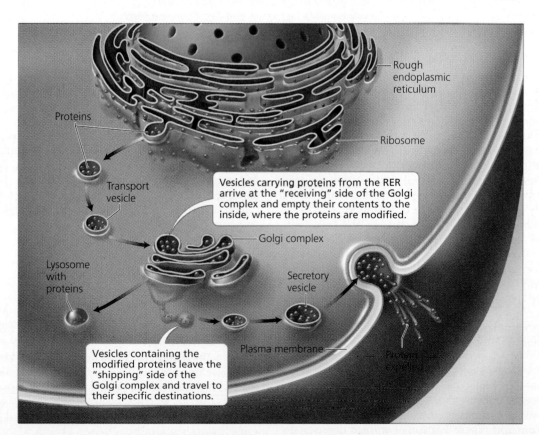

FIGURE 3.17 The route by which protein-filled vesicles from the rough endoplasmic reticulum travel to the Golgi complex for processing and eventual release

Nucleus

Step 1: Cell engulfs bacterium through phagocytosis.

Bacterium

Rough ER

Transport vesicle

Step 2: Lysosome fuses with vesicle containing bacterium.

Vesicle containing bacterium

Golgi complex

Damaged organelle

Lysosome

Step 3: Lysosomal enzymes break the bacterium down into smaller molecules that diffuse into cytoplasm.

Digestion

Step 1: Lysosome engulfs a damaged organelle.

Step 4: Some indigestible substances leave the cell by exocytosis.

Step 2: Lysosomal enzymes break down the organelle into smaller molecules that will return to the cytoplasm for reuse.

Step 5: Other indigestible substances remain in the cell.

FIGURE 3.18 Lysosome formation and function in intracellular digestion. Lysosomes, released from the Golgi complex, digest a bacterium engulfed by the cell (see pathway on right). Lysosomes also digest obsolete parts of the cell itself (see pathway on left).

Consider, for example, what happens when a cell engulfs a bacterium. You can follow this process in Figure **3.18** (see pathway on right). During the process of phagocytosis (Step 1), a vesicle encircles the bacterium. A lysosome released from the Golgi complex then fuses with the vesicle (Step 2), and the lysosome's digestive enzymes break the bacterium down into smaller molecules. These molecules diffuse out of the vesicle into the cytoplasm, where they can be used by the cell (Step 3). Indigestible residues may be expelled from the cell by exocytosis (Step 4), or they may be stored indefinitely in vesicles inside the cell (Step 5).

Lysosomes also break down obsolete parts of the cell itself. Worn-out organelles and macromolecules are broken down into smaller components that can be reused (see Figure 3.18, pathway on left). For example, an organelle called a mitochondrion (discussed later) lasts only about 10 days in a typical liver cell before being destroyed by lysosomes. After worn-out mitochondria are destroyed, their component monomers, such as amino acids, are returned to the cytoplasm for reuse. Such "housecleaning" keeps the cell functioning properly and promotes the recycling of essential materials.

The absence of a single kind of lysosomal enzyme can have devastating consequences. Molecules that would normally be broken down by the missing enzyme start to collect in the lysosomes and cause them to swell. Ultimately, the accumulating molecules interfere with cell function. These lysosomal storage diseases are inherited and progress with age.

Tay-Sachs disease is a lysosomal storage disease caused by the absence of the lysosomal enzyme hexosaminidase (Hex A), which breaks down lipids in nerve cells. When Hex A is missing, the lysosomes swell with undigested lipids. Infants with Tay-Sachs disease appear normal at birth but begin to deteriorate by about 6 months of age as abnormal amounts of lipid accumulate in the nervous system. By the age of 4 or 5, Tay-Sachs causes paralysis and death. At present there is no cure for this disease. However, there is a blood test to detect individuals who carry the gene for Tay-Sachs. Called carriers, these individuals do not have the disease but could pass the gene to their offspring.

what would you do?

Imagine that you and your spouse want to start a family, but both of you are carriers of Tay-Sachs disease and could pass the gene to your children. The possible outcomes for any child you might conceive are as follows: the child may not have the gene for Tay-Sachs and may be healthy, may have the disease and die in early childhood, or may be a carrier as you are. Your parents urge adoption. Your spouse prefers not to adopt but to use prenatal screening to check if your fetus has the disease. What would you do?

Certain environmental factors cause disease by interfering with lysosomes. In the Environmental Issue essay, *Asbestos: The Deadly Miracle Material*, we describe the impact of asbestos on lysosomes and health.

Mitochondria

Most cellular activities require energy. Energy is needed to transport certain substances across the plasma membrane and to fuel many of the chemical reactions that occur in the cytoplasm. Specialized cells such as muscle cells and nerve cells require energy to perform their particular activities. The energy needed by cells is provided by **mitochondria** (singular, mitochondrion), the organelles within which most of cellular respiration occurs. Cellular respiration, discussed later in the chapter, is a four-phase process in which oxygen and an organic fuel such as glucose are consumed and energy in the form of ATP is released. The first phase takes place in the cytoplasm. The remaining three phases occur in the mitochondria.

The number of mitochondria varies considerably from cell to cell and is roughly correlated with a cell's demand for energy. Most cells contain several hundred to thousands of mitochondria. Like the nucleus, but unlike other organelles, mitochondria are bounded by a double membrane (Figure **3.19**). The inner and outer membranes create two separate compartments that serve as sites for some of the reactions in cellular respiration. The infoldings of the inner membrane of a mitochondrion are called *cristae*, and these are the sites of the last phase of cellular respiration. Finally, mitochondria contain ribosomes and a small percentage of a cell's total DNA (the rest being found in the nucleus, as noted earlier). Mitochondria contain ribosomes and DNA because they are likely descendants of once free-living bacteria that invaded or were engulfed by ancient cells (see Chapter 22). Table **3.4** reviews the functions of organelles.

Mitochondrion

Outer membrane

Inner membrane

Cristae

(a) Diagram of a mitochondrion showing the double membrane that creates two compartments.

(b) Electron micrograph of a mitochondrion.

FIGURE 3.19 Mitochondria are sites of energy conversion in the cell.

TABLE 3.4 Review of Major Organelles and Their Functions

Organelle	Function
Nucleus	Contains almost all the genetic information and influences cellular structure and function
Rough endoplasmic reticulum (RER)	Studded with ribosomes (sites where the synthesis of proteins begins); produces membrane
Smooth endoplasmic reticulum (SER)	Detoxifies drugs; produces membrane
Golgi complex	Sorts, modifies, and packages products of RER
Lysosomes	Digest substances imported from outside the cell; destroy old or defective cell parts
Mitochondria	Provide cell with energy through the breakdown of glucose during cellular respiration

Cytoskeleton

Traversing the cytoplasm of the cell is a complex network of fibers called the **cytoskeleton**. The fibers are divided into three types: microtubules are the thickest; microfilaments are the thinnest; and intermediate filaments are the diverse group in between. Microtubules and microfilaments are seen to disassemble and reassemble, whereas intermediate filaments tend to be more permanent.

Microtubules are straight, hollow rods made of the protein tubulin. Some microtubules near the plasma membrane maintain cell shape. Microtubules also form tracks along which organelles or vesicles travel (Figure **3.20**). For example, secretory vesicles (membrane-bound vesicles containing material to be released from the cell) that have budded from the Golgi complex make their way to the plasma membrane by moving along a microtubule track. Finally, microtubules play a role in the separation of chromosomes during cell division. A microtubule-organizing center, located near the nucleus, contains a pair of **centrioles**, each composed of nine sets of triplet (three) microtubules arranged in a ring (Figure **3.21**). Centrioles may function in cell division and in the formation of cilia and flagella.

Microtubules serve as the working parts of two types of cell extensions called cilia (singular, cilium) and flagella (singular, flagellum). **Cilia** are numerous, short extensions on a cell, resembling hairs that move with the back-and-forth motion of oars. They are found, for example, on the surfaces of cells lining the

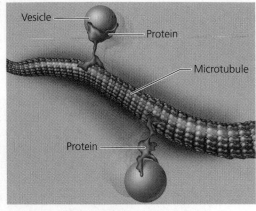

(a) Vesicles carried by proteins travel along a microtubule.

(b) A micrograph showing the microtubule component of the cytoskeleton for several cells. The round area in the center of each cell is the nucleus.

FIGURE 3.20 Microtubules serve as tracks along which organelles or vesicles move.

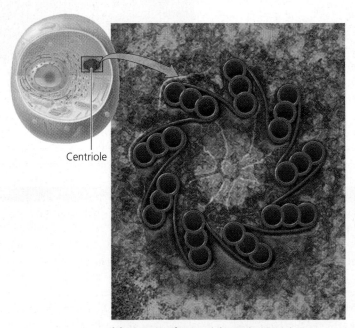

(a) Diagram of a centriole. Each centriole is composed of nine sets of triplet microtubules arranged in a ring.

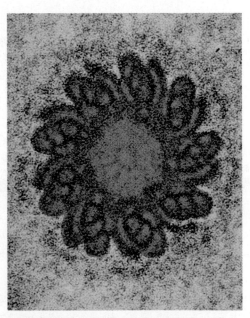

(b) Electron micrograph showing the microtubules of a centriole

FIGURE 3.21 Centrioles may play a role in cell division.

Asbestos: The Deadly Miracle Material

During the first three-quarters of the twentieth century, more than 30 million tons of asbestos were used for various purposes in the United States, including simple insulation in homes and office buildings. About half a million people are estimated to have died from diseases brought on by exposure to asbestos. What is asbestos? Why do we use it? And why do we sometimes die from it?

Asbestos is a fibrous silicate mineral, found in many forms in nature, that is strong, flexible, and resistant to heat and corrosion (Figure **3.A**). Because of these properties, asbestos was used widely in construction—as an insulator on ceilings and pipes, for example, or to soundproof and fireproof the walls of schools.

The very properties that make asbestos an ideal building material—its fibrous nature and durability—also can make it deadly. For example, when fibers of asbestos insulation are dislodged, small, light particles become suspended in the air and can be inhaled into the lungs. There is some evidence that the different forms of asbestos differ in the time they persist in lung tissue. Nevertheless, particles of at least one form appear resistant to degradation and remain in the lungs for life (Figure **3.B**).

Inhalation of asbestos particles can cause lung cancer and mesothelioma, a form of cancer specific to the lining of the lungs and chest cavity (pleura) and the lining of the abdomen (peritoneum). Asbestosis, a third condition, is the most common disease caused by exposure to asbestos. It results from the dangerous interaction between asbestos and lysosomes. Cells responsible for cleaning the respiratory passages engulf small particles of asbestos inhaled into the lungs; lysosomes inside the cleaning cells then fuse with the vesicles containing the asbestos particles. Unfortunately, the lysosomal enzymes cannot break down the asbestos particles. Instead, the particles destabilize the membranes of the lysosomes, causing massive release of enzymes, and the enzymes destroy the cells of the respiratory tract. Irreversible scarring of lung tissue is the

FIGURE 3.A The deadly miracle material asbestos. The qualities of asbestos that make it so useful for construction—strength, durability, and flexibility—also make it hazardous to our health. Particles of asbestos released into the air may be inhaled into the lungs, where they cause asbestosis (scarring of lung tissue).

result, eventually interfering with the exchange of gases in the lungs. People with asbestos-damaged lungs experience chronic coughing and shortness of breath. These symptoms become more severe over time and may cause death from impaired respiratory function.

At present, there is no effective treatment for asbestosis. The focus, therefore, has been on prevention. In the United States, the use of asbestos for insulation and fireproofing, or for any new purposes, is banned. However, asbestos is still present in many buildings constructed before the ban went into effect. This point was made painfully clear when asbestos was detected in the debris and dust at the site where the World Trade Center towers collapsed on September 11, 2001. Asbestos had been used as a fire retardant in parts of the towers. The destruction and collapse of the towers released asbestos particles into the air, where they could be inhaled by people at and near the World Trade Center site. The potential threat from asbestos is not short term; even in April of 2006, a search for human remains (bone fragments) on top of a building near the World Trade Center was halted due to asbestos in the debris. This building was damaged during the collapse of the south tower of the World Trade Center, and workers were in the midst of searching and clearing it before its scheduled dismantling.

What can be done about the asbestos already present in our schools and workplaces? It is

Asbestos fibers

FIGURE 3.B Asbestos fibers in lung tissue. The destruction of lung tissue characteristic of asbestosis results from the release of lysosomal enzymes inside the cells responsible for cleaning the respiratory tract.

generally recommended and often required that exposed asbestos be removed, enclosed by other building materials, or covered with a sealant. Experts should determine which method is best in any given situation. Moreover, the sealing or removal of asbestos must be done by experts, because the greatest risk of asbestos exposure occurs when asbestos is handled improperly. Workers at risk of exposure to asbestos—plumbers, electricians, insulation workers, and carpenters, to name a few—should insist upon frequent testing of the air in their workplace, as was done at the World Trade Center site and in surrounding neighborhoods. Workers at Ground Zero were instructed to wear respirators and other protective equipment. So far, monitoring of workers involved in the rescue, recovery, and cleanup effort has revealed that many are experiencing persistent respiratory symptoms, and some show reduced ability to move air in and out of their lungs. There also has been an increased incidence of sarcoidosis, another potentially fatal lung-scarring disease, among Ground Zero workers. It is too early to know if any of these health effects can be specifically attributed to asbestos. However, many doctors believe that the effects are generally related to the dust, ash, and smoke inhaled by the workers in the aftermath of the attacks on September 11, 2001.

Naturally occurring asbestos can also be dangerous, as discovered by the residents of Libby, Montana. Mining for vermiculite, a mineral used in building insulation and as a soil conditioner, provided jobs to the people of Libby going as far back as 1919. This was especially so beginning in the 1960s, when mining efforts went into high gear. But in addition to jobs, the mining had a secondary and very negative consequence: years of exposure to a naturally occurring form of asbestos that had contaminated the vermiculite. Workers were exposed to dust containing asbestos in the mine, and they carried it home on their clothing. Many residents also spread the contaminated vermiculite in their yards to condition the soil. The mine closed in 1990, but the ensuing investigation and cleanup (including the removal of soil around homes) by the Environmental Protection Agency (EPA) did not start until 1999. Screening of town residents in 2001 indicated that about 25% showed abnormalities associated with exposure to asbestos. The incidence of mesothelioma was 1000 times the national average. Because asbestosis can take 20 or 30 years to develop, the number of residents who will suffer from this disease is difficult to estimate now, but it will likely be high. The EPA reportedly considers the situation in Libby to be the worst case of industrial poisoning of a whole community in the history of America. In March 2008, the mining company agreed to reimburse the federal government $250 million for the investigation and cleanup—but this scarcely begins to address the loss of life, health, and property in Libby, Montana.

Proper protective equipment, such as a respirator, can safeguard those exposed to asbestos in the workplace.

respiratory tract (Figure **3.22a**), where they sweep debris trapped in mucus away from the lungs. Smoking destroys these cilia and hampers cleaning of respiratory surfaces. A **flagellum** resembles a whip and moves in an undulating manner. Flagella are much longer than cilia. The only cell with a flagellum in humans is the sperm cell (Figure 3.22b).

Cilia and flagella differ in length, number per cell, and pattern of movement. Nevertheless, they have a similar arrangement of microtubules, called a 9 + 2 pattern (Figure 3.22c), at their core. This arrangement consists of nine pairs of microtubules arranged in a ring with two microtubules at the center. The microtubules of a cilium or flagellum are anchored to the cell by a *basal body*. Like the centrioles described earlier, basal bodies contain nine triplets of microtubules arranged in a ring. Loss of ciliary and flagellar function appears to be caused by the absence of armlike structures that normally link the nine pairs of microtubules in the 9 + 2 pattern. Immotile cilia syndrome is a genetic disorder characterized by severe loss of function in cilia and flagella throughout the body. People with immotile cilia syndrome experience chronic respiratory problems, and men with the syndrome may be sterile because of immotile sperm.

Microfilaments are solid rods made of the protein actin. These fibers are best known for their role in muscle contraction, where they slide past thicker filaments made of the protein myosin. Finally, microfilaments play a role in cell division, forming a band that contracts and pinches the cell in two.

Intermediate filaments are a diverse group of ropelike fibers helping to maintain cell shape and anchoring certain organelles in place. Their protein composition varies from one type of cell to another.

(a) Cilia on cells lining the respiratory tract

(b) Sperm cells in a fallopian tube

(c) Several cilia in cross section showing the 9 + 2 pattern of microtubules. Flagella (not shown) have a similar arrangement of microtubules.

FIGURE 3.22 Microtubules are responsible for the movement of cilia and flagella.

Cellular Respiration and Fermentation in the Generation of ATP

Living requires work, and work requires energy. Logic tells us, therefore, that living requires energy.

We get our energy from the food we eat. Our digestive system (discussed in Chapter 15) breaks down complex macromolecules such as carbohydrates, proteins, and fats into their simpler components, such as glucose, amino acids, and fatty acids. These simpler molecules are then absorbed into the bloodstream and carried to our cells, where some of the energy stored in the molecules' chemical bonds is used to make ATP, the energy-rich molecule that our cells use to do their work. (Some energy is also given off as heat.) Although carbohydrates, proteins, and fats are all sources of cellular energy, we will focus on carbohydrates. Cells have two ways of breaking glucose molecules apart for energy: cellular respiration and fermentation. Cellular respiration requires oxygen; fermentation does not.

All the chemical reactions that take place in a cell constitute its **metabolism**. These chemical reactions are organized into metabolic pathways. Each pathway consists of a series of steps in which a starting molecule is modified, eventually resulting in a particular product. Specific enzymes speed up each step of the pathway. Cellular respiration and fermentation are examples of *catabolic pathways*, pathways in which complex molecules, such as carbohydrates, are broken down into simpler compounds, releasing energy. *Anabolic pathways*, on the other hand, build complex molecules from simpler ones and consume energy in the process.

Cellular Respiration

Cellular respiration is the oxygen-requiring pathway in which glucose is broken down by cells. It is an elaborate series of chemical reactions whose final products are carbon dioxide, water, and energy. In a laboratory beaker, glucose and oxygen can be combined to produce those products in a single step. However, under those circumstances, the glucose burns, and all the energy is lost as heat. The process used by cells, in which glucose is broken down in a series of steps, enables the cells to obtain much of the energy in a usable form—specifically, as a high-energy chemical bond in ATP. Recall from Chapter 2 that ATP is formed from ADP (adenosine diphosphate) and inorganic phosphate (P*i*) in a process that requires energy.

Cellular respiration has four phases: (1) glycolysis, (2) the transition reaction, (3) the citric acid cycle, and (4) the electron transport chain. All four phases occur continuously within cells. Glycolysis takes place in the cytoplasm of the cell. The transition reaction, the citric acid cycle, and the electron transport chain take place in mitochondria. You will see that some of these phases consist of a series of reactions in which the **products** from one reaction become the **substrates** (raw materials) for the next reaction. You will also see that the transfer of electrons from one atom or molecule to another is a key feature of the process our cells use to capture energy from fuel. As the electrons are passed along a chain of intermediate compounds, their energy is used to make ATP.

Glycolysis

The first phase of cellular respiration, called **glycolysis** (*glyco*, sugar; *lysis*, splitting), begins with glucose, a six-carbon sugar,

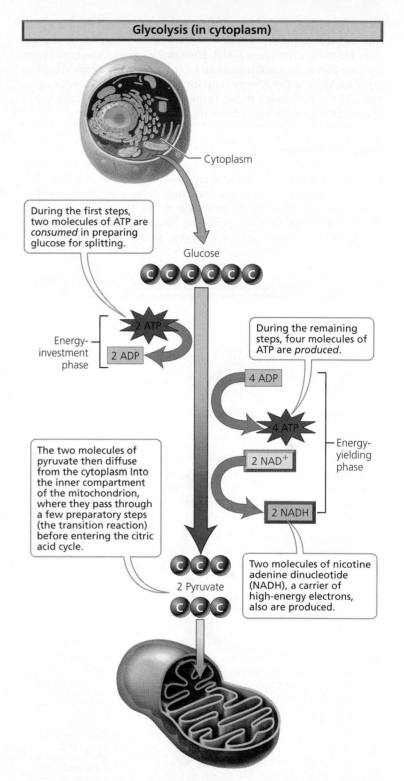

Glycolysis (in cytoplasm)

Cytoplasm

During the first steps, two molecules of ATP are *consumed* in preparing glucose for splitting.

Glucose

Energy-investment phase

2 ATP

2 ADP

During the remaining steps, four molecules of ATP are *produced*.

4 ADP

4 ATP

2 NAD⁺

Energy-yielding phase

2 NADH

The two molecules of pyruvate then diffuse from the cytoplasm into the inner compartment of the mitochondrion, where they pass through a few preparatory steps (the transition reaction) before entering the citric acid cycle.

2 Pyruvate

Two molecules of nicotine adenine dinucleotide (NADH), a carrier of high-energy electrons, also are produced.

FIGURE 3.23 Glycolysis is a several-step sequence of reactions in the cytoplasm. Glucose, a six-carbon sugar, is split into 2 three-carbon molecules of pyruvate.

being split into 2 three-carbon sugars. These three-carbon sugars are then converted into two molecules of **pyruvate** (Figure **3.23**), another three-carbon compound. Glycolysis occurs in several steps, each requiring a different, specific enzyme. During the first steps, two molecules of ATP are consumed because energy is needed to prepare glucose for splitting. During the remaining steps, four molecules of ATP are produced, for a net gain of two

ATP. Glycolysis also produces two molecules of nicotine adenine dinucleotide (NADH), which are generated when electrons are donated to the coenzyme NAD^+. Glycolysis does not require oxygen and releases only a small amount of the chemical energy stored in glucose. Most of the energy remains in the two molecules of pyruvate. These molecules move from the cytoplasm into the inner compartment of the mitochondrion.

Transition reaction

Once inside the inner compartment of the mitochondrion, pyruvate reacts with a substance called coenzyme A (CoA) in a reaction called the transition reaction. The transition reaction results in the removal of one carbon (in the form of carbon dioxide, CO_2) from each pyruvate (Figure **3.24**). The resulting two-carbon molecule, called an acetyl group, then binds to CoA

to form acetyl CoA. A molecule of NADH is also produced from each pyruvate.

Citric acid cycle

Still in the inner compartment of the mitochondrion, acetyl CoA reacts with a four-carbon compound in the first of a cyclic series of eight chemical reactions known as the **citric acid cycle**, named after the first product (citric acid, or citrate) formed along its route (Figure **3.25**). The cycle is also called the Krebs cycle—after the scientist Hans Krebs, who described many of the reactions. Rather than considering each of the chemical reactions in the citric acid cycle, we will simply say that it completes the loss of electrons from glucose and yields two molecules of ATP (one from each acetyl CoA that enters the cycle) and several molecules of NADH and $FADH_2$ (flavin adenine dinucleotide). NADH and $FADH_2$ are carriers of high-energy electrons. The NADH and $FADH_2$ produced in glycolysis, in the transition reaction, and in the citric acid cycle enter the electron transport chain, the final phase of cellular respiration. The citric acid cycle also produces CO_2 as waste.

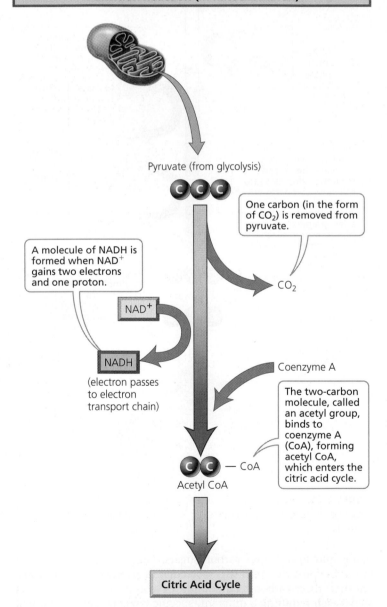

FIGURE 3.24 The transition reaction takes place inside the mitochondrion and is the link between glycolysis and the citric acid cycle.

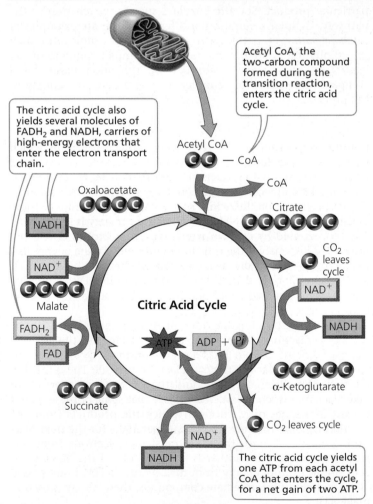

FIGURE 3.25 The citric acid cycle is a cyclic series of eight chemical reactions that occurs inside the mitochondrion and yields two molecules of ATP and several molecules of NADH and $FADH_2$ per molecule of glucose.

Electron transport chain

During the final phase of cellular respiration, the molecules of NADH and FADH$_2$ produced by earlier phases pass their electrons to a series of carrier proteins embedded in the inner membrane of the mitochondrion. These proteins are known as the **electron transport chain** (Figure **3.26**). (Recall that the inner membrane of the mitochondrion is highly folded, providing space for thousands of sets of carrier proteins.) During the transfer of electrons from one protein to the next, energy is released and used to make ATP. Eventually, the electrons are passed to oxygen, the final electron acceptor, which then combines with two hydrogen ions to form water. Oxygen has a critical role in cellular respiration. When oxygen is absent, electrons accumulate in the carrier proteins, halting the citric acid cycle and cellular respiration. But when oxygen is present, and accepts the electrons, respiration continues. The electron transport chain produces 32 molecules of ATP per molecule of glucose.

Altogether, cellular respiration generally produces 36 molecules of ATP per molecule of glucose: 2 ATP from glycolysis, 2 ATP from the citric acid cycle, and 32 ATP from the electron transport chain. The results of cellular respiration are summarized in Figure **3.27**. Basic descriptions of each phase can be found in Table **3.5**.

Fermentation

As noted earlier, cellular respiration depends on oxygen as the final electron acceptor in the electron transport chain. Without oxygen, the transport chain comes to a halt, blocking the citric acid cycle and stopping cellular respiration. Is there a way for cells to harvest energy when molecules of oxygen are scarce? The answer is yes, and the pathway is fermentation.

Fermentation is the breakdown of glucose without oxygen. It begins with glycolysis, which as you recall occurs in the cytoplasm and does not require oxygen. From one molecule of glucose, glycolysis produces two molecules each of pyruvate, the electron carrier NADH, and ATP. The remaining fermentation reactions also take place in the cytoplasm, transferring electrons from NADH to pyruvate or a derivative of pyruvate. This transfer of electrons is critical because it regenerates NAD$^+$, which is essential for the production of ATP through glycolysis. Recall that in cellular respiration, oxygen is the final electron acceptor in the electron transport chain, whereas in fermentation it is pyruvate or a pyruvate derivative.

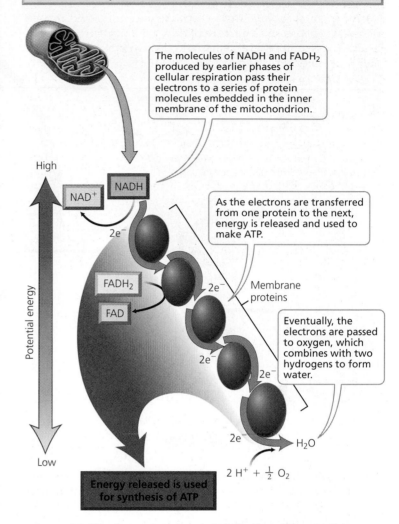

Electron Transport Chain (inner membrane of mitochondrion)

The molecules of NADH and FADH$_2$ produced by earlier phases of cellular respiration pass their electrons to a series of protein molecules embedded in the inner membrane of the mitochondrion.

As the electrons are transferred from one protein to the next, energy is released and used to make ATP.

Membrane proteins

Eventually, the electrons are passed to oxygen, which combines with two hydrogens to form water.

High

Low

Potential energy

NAD$^+$ NADH

2e$^-$

FADH$_2$ 2e$^-$

FAD

2e$^-$

2e$^-$

2e$^-$ H$_2$O

2 H$^+$ + $\frac{1}{2}$ O$_2$

Energy released is used for synthesis of ATP

FIGURE 3.26 The electron transport chain is the final phase of cellular respiration. This phase yields 32 ATP per molecule of glucose.

TABLE 3.5 Review of Cellular Respiration

Phase	Location	Description	Main Products
Glycolysis	Cytoplasm	Several-step process by which glucose is split into 2 pyruvate	2 pyruvate 2 ATP 2 NADH
Transition reaction	Mitochondria	One CO$_2$ is removed from each pyruvate; the resulting molecules bind to CoA, forming 2 acetyl CoA	2 acetyl CoA 2 NADH
Citric acid cycle	Mitochondria	Cyclic series of eight chemical reactions by which acetyl CoA is broken down	2 ATP 2 FADH$_2$ 6 NADH
Electron transport chain	Mitochondria	Electrons from NADH and FADH$_2$ are passed from one protein to the next, releasing energy for ATP synthesis	32 ATP H$_2$O

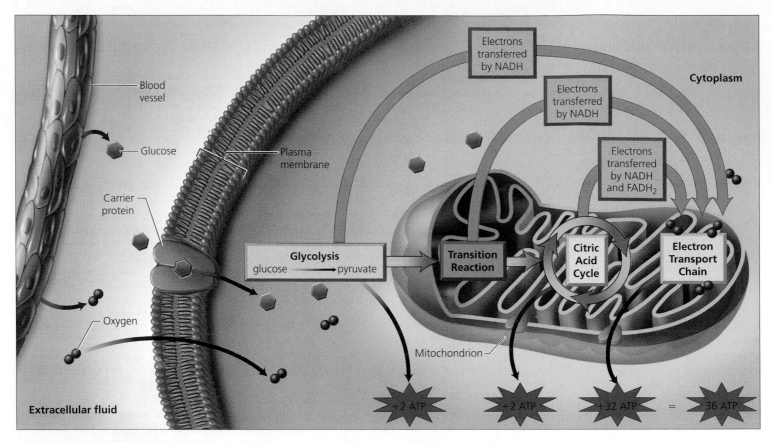

FIGURE 3.27 Summary of cellular respiration. Cellular respiration produces 36 ATP per molecule of glucose (2 ATP from glycolysis, 2 ATP from the citric acid cycle, and 32 ATP from the electron transport chain).

Fermentation therefore nets only 2 molecules of ATP compared with the 36 molecules of ATP produced by cellular respiration (refer, again, to Figure 3.27). In short, fermentation is a very inefficient way for cells to harvest energy.

Different types of fermentation found in different organisms differ in the waste products formed from pyruvate. The fermentation that takes place in the human body is **lactic acid fermentation**, in which NADH passes electrons directly to pyruvate to produce lactate or lactic acid as a waste product (Figure **3.28**). During strenuous exercise, the oxygen supply in our muscle cells runs low. Under these conditions, the cells increase lactic acid fermentation to ensure the continued production of ATP. The muscle pain we often experience after intense exercise is caused partly by the accumulation of lactic acid due to fermentation. In time, the soreness disappears as the lactic acid moves into the bloodstream and is carried to the liver, where it is converted back to pyruvate.

FIGURE 3.28 Lactic acid fermentation. Fermentation occurs in the cytoplasm, does not require oxygen, and yields only two molecules of ATP per molecule of glucose. The symbol Pi stands for inorganic phosphate (PO_4^{-2}).

Eukaryotic Cells Compared with Prokaryotic Cells (p. 47)

- There are two main types of cell. Prokaryotic cells, unique to bacteria and archaea, lack membrane-bound organelles. Eukaryotic cells, found in all other organisms, have membrane-bound organelles.

Cell Size and Microscopy (pp. 48–49)

- As a cell grows, its volume increases more than its surface area; therefore, a cell that is too large will encounter problems due to inadequate surface area. For that reason, most cells are very small.
- Because most cells are very small, they can be seen only with a microscope. Whereas light microscopes use beams of light to image specimens, electron microscopes use beams of electrons. Electron microscopes can reveal finer details because the wavelength of an electron beam is smaller than the wavelengths of visible light.

Cell Structure and Function (pp. 49–50)

- All eukaryotic cells have certain features in common, including a plasma membrane and membrane-bound organelles. Structural differences between eukaryotic cells often reflect differences in function. For example, a sperm has a tail and streamlined shape so that it can swim to the egg. The egg, in contrast, is large, immobile, and packed with materials needed to initiate development.

Plasma Membrane (pp. 50–54)

- The plasma membrane is made of phospholipids arranged in a bilayer with proteins and molecules of cholesterol interspersed throughout and carbohydrates attached to the outer surface. The structure of the plasma membrane is often described as a fluid mosaic.
- The plasma membrane maintains the cell's integrity, regulates movement of substances into and out of the cell, functions in cell–cell recognition, promotes communication between cells, and binds cells together to form tissues and organs.
- Substances cross the plasma membrane in several ways. Some cross by random movement from higher to lower concentration (simple diffusion); others need help from a carrier or channel protein (facilitated diffusion). Water also moves across the plasma membrane from higher to lower concentration (osmosis). Substances being concentrated by cells cross the plasma membrane from lower to higher concentration with the help of ATP and a carrier protein (active transport). Finally, cells may engulf outside materials by surrounding them with plasma membrane (endocytosis) or may release substances to the external environment by fusing internal vesicles with the plasma membrane and spilling their contents to the outside (exocytosis).

Organelles (pp. 54–59)

- Within a eukaryotic cell, membranes delineate specialized compartments within which specific processes occur. The nucleus contains almost all the genetic information and thus holds the code for the cell's structure and many of its functions. The nucleolus is a region within the nucleus that makes ribosomal RNA. Ribosomes are the sites where protein synthesis begins. Endoplasmic reticulum (ER) functions in membrane production and may be studded with ribosomes (rough endoplasmic reticulum, RER) or free of ribosomes (smooth endoplasmic reticulum, SER). The Golgi complex sorts, modifies, and packages products of the RER. Lysosomes digest bacteria engulfed by cells and break down old or defective components within cells. Mitochondria process energy for cells.

Cytoskeleton (pp. 60–62)

- The cytoskeleton, a complex network of fibers throughout the cytoplasm of the cell, consists of three categories of fibers, all made of proteins: microtubules, microfilaments, and intermediate filaments. Microtubules are hollow rods of tubulin that function in cell movement (cilia and flagella), support, and the movement within cells of chromosomes, organelles, and vesicles. Microfilaments are rods of actin that function in muscle contraction and cell division. Intermediate filaments, which are different kinds of ropelike fibers, maintain cell shape and anchor organelles.

Cellular Respiration and Fermentation in the Generation of ATP (pp. 63–66)

- Cells require energy to work. We get this energy from the food we eat. Carbohydrates, fats, and proteins that we consume are each broken down by our digestive system into smaller units such as simple sugars, fatty acids, and amino acids. These simpler substances are absorbed into the bloodstream and carried to our cells, where the energy stored in the substances' chemical bonds is transferred for the cell's use to the chemical bonds of ATP. (Some energy is also given off as heat.)
- Cells use two catabolic pathways—cellular respiration and fermentation—to break down the carbohydrate glucose and store its energy as ATP. Cellular respiration requires oxygen and usually yields 36 molecules of ATP per molecule of glucose.
- Cellular respiration has four phases—glycolysis, the transition reaction, the citric acid cycle, and the electron transport chain—all occurring continuously within cells. Glycolysis occurs in the cytoplasm and splits glucose into pyruvate while producing NADH (a carrier of high-energy electrons) and a net gain of 2 ATP. The molecules of pyruvate move from the cytoplasm into the inner compartment of the mitochondrion, where they pass through a few preparatory steps, known as the transition reaction, before entering the citric acid cycle. The citric acid cycle is an eight-step cycle that completes the breakdown of glucose into carbon dioxide. The citric acid cycle also yields 2 ATP and carriers of high-energy electrons (NADH and $FADH_2$). In the electron transport chain, the carriers of high-energy electrons produced during glycolysis, the transition reaction, and the citric acid cycle pass their electrons to a series of proteins embedded in the inner membrane of the mitochondrion; oxygen is the final electron acceptor. Energy released during the transfer of electrons yields 32 ATP.
- Fermentation is the breakdown of glucose without oxygen. It occurs in the cytoplasm and begins with glycolysis, the splitting of glucose into pyruvate. The remaining chemical reactions involve the transfer of electrons from NADH to pyruvate or a derivative of pyruvate. Compared with cellular respiration, fermentation is an inefficient way for cells to harvest energy because it yields only 2 ATP as compared with the 36 ATP of cellular respiration.

cell theory *p. 47*
prokaryotic cell *p. 47*
organelle *p. 47*
eukaryotic cell *p. 47*
surface-to-volume ratio *p. 48*
plasma membrane *p. 50*
extracellular fluid *p. 50*
cytoplasm *p. 50*
fluid mosaic *p. 50*
selectively permeable *p. 51*
cell adhesion molecule (CAM)
  p. 51
simple diffusion *p. 51*
concentration gradient *p. 51*
facilitated diffusion *p. 52*

osmosis *p. 52*
hypertonic solution *p. 52*
isotonic solution *p. 52*
hypotonic solution *p. 52*
active transport *p. 52*
endocytosis *p. 53*
vesicle *p. 53*
phagocytosis *p. 53*
pinocytosis *p. 53*
exocytosis *p. 53*
nucleus *p. 54*
nuclear envelope *p. 54*
nuclear pore *p. 54*
chromosome *p. 54*
nucleolus *p. 55*

ribosome *p. 55*
endoplasmic reticulum
  (ER) *p. 56*
rough endoplasmic reticulum
  (RER) *p. 56*
smooth endoplasmic reticulum
  (SER) *p. 56*
Golgi complex *p. 56*
lysosome *p. 56*
mitochondrion *p. 59*
cytoskeleton *p. 60*
microtubule *p. 60*
centriole *p. 60*
cilia *p. 60*
flagellum *p. 62*

microfilament *p. 62*
intermediate filament *p. 62*
metabolism *p. 63*
cellular respiration *p. 63*
product *p. 63*
substrate *p. 63*
glycolysis *p. 63*
pyruvate *p. 63*
citric acid cycle *p. 64*
electron transport
  chain *p. 65*
fermentation *p. 65*
lactic acid fermentation *p. 66*

1. How do prokaryotic and eukaryotic cells differ? *p. 47*
2. Describe the structure of the plasma membrane. *p. 50*
3. List five functions of the plasma membrane. *pp. 50–51*
4. What is the difference between simple and facilitated diffusion? Give an example of each. *pp. 51–52*
5. Describe and differentiate endocytosis and exocytosis. *p. 53–54*
6. Where are chromosomes found in the cell?? *pp. 54–55*
7. List two functions of lysosomes. *pp. 56, 58*
8. What are lysosomal storage diseases? *p. 58*
9. Name the three types of fibers that make up the cytoskeleton. Describe their structures and functions. *pp. 60, 62*
10. What is the basic function of cellular respiration? *p. 63*
11. How do cellular respiration and fermentation differ with respect to the number of ATP molecules produced and the requirement for oxygen? *p. 65–66*
12. Prokaryotic cells
    a. have internal membrane-bound organelles.
    b. are usually larger than eukaryotic cells.
    c. lack internal membrane-enclosed organelles.
    d. have linear strands of DNA within a nucleus.
13. The plasma membrane
    a. is selectively permeable.
    b. contains lipids that function in cell–cell recognition.
    c. has cell adhesion molecules that prevent cells from sticking together.
    d. is made of nucleic acids.
14. Facilitated diffusion is
    a. the random movement of a substance from a region of higher concentration to a region of lower concentration.
    b. the movement of water across the plasma membrane.
    c. the movement of molecules across the plasma membrane against a concentration gradient with the aid of a carrier protein and energy supplied by the cell.
    d. the movement of a substance from a region of higher concentration to a region of lower concentration with the aid of a membrane protein.

15. Almost all the genetic information of a cell is found in the
    a. endoplasmic reticulum.
    b. Golgi complex.
    c. nucleus.
    d. mitochondria.
16. Ribosomes
    a. are found on smooth endoplasmic reticulum.
    b. are sites where protein synthesis begins.
    c. process and modify proteins.
    d. break down foreign invaders and old organelles.
17. Mitochondria
    a. process energy for cells.
    b. lack ribosomes and DNA.
    c. are bounded by a single membrane.
    d. function in cell digestion.
18. Microtubules
    a. are found in eukaryotic cilia and flagella.
    b. are made of the protein actin.
    c. play a role in muscle contraction.
    d. pinch a cell in two during cell division.
19. Glycolysis
    a. occurs in the mitochondria.
    b. requires oxygen.
    c. splits glucose into pyruvate.
    d. nets 32 molecules of ATP per molecule of glucose.
20. _____ is the jellylike solution within a cell that contains everything between the nucleus and the plasma membrane.
21. _____ is called "cell drinking."
22. The _____ is a specialized region within the nucleus that is involved in the production of rRNA.
23. _____ is the final electron acceptor in the electron transport chain.
24. Our muscle cells may switch from cellular respiration to _____ when oxygen is low.

applying the concepts

1. Given what you know about the composition of the plasma membrane, would you expect an anesthetic to be soluble or insoluble in lipids? Explain your answer.
2. Would you expect to find more mitochondria in muscle cells or bone cells? Explain your answer.
3. During cell division, the nucleus and cytoplasm of a cell split into two cells. Cancer is characterized by uncontrolled cell division and is often treated with chemotherapy. Some drugs used in chemotherapy halt cell division by affecting the cytoskeleton. Which of the cytoskeletal elements (microtubules, microfilaments, intermediate filaments) might be affected?

becoming information literate

Using at least three reliable sources, prepare a brochure on Tay-Sachs disease. Be sure to include the following sections: (1) Symptoms; (2) Causes; (3) Transmission; (4) Diagnosis (before and after birth); (5) Treatment, if any; and (6) Prognosis. List each source you considered and explain why you chose the sources you used.

Additional questions can be found online at the Human Biology Place, www. humanbiology. com.

4

Body Organization and Homeostasis

Cells are arranged in tissues, and tissues, in turn, form organs. The skin, our largest organ, helps protect underlying tissues and helps to regulate body temperature.

The children greeted Jenna happily when they got home from the beach, where they had been with her younger brother, Mark (their favorite uncle). But Jenna could see that Mark wasn't feeling well. She was sure he had followed her child-care instructions to the letter: restoring the sun block on Allison and Andrew's shoulders every time they came out of the water, keeping hats on their heads when the sun was strong, giving them frequent sips of water, and reminding them to lie down occasionally under the umbrella. She was equally sure that he hadn't bothered to take the same precautions himself. He never let himself get dehydrated or overheated when training with the track team at his college; but while chasing over the sand after his niece and nephew, he probably never noticed that he was hot and perspiring, and the thought of taking a drink of water, wearing a hat, or resting in the shade probably didn't cross his mind. An important function of the skin is regulation of body temperature. As body temperature rises, as it might in the scorching heat of the sun, the brain signals the skin's sweat glands to increase their activity. Evaporation of perspiration lowers body temperature. But, if the water lost in perspiration is not replaced, water balance between the cells and the blood is upset, affecting nearly every cell in the body. In addition, the loss of salts in perspiration can upset blood chemistry, disturbing metabolic reactions. No wonder Matt was complaining of a headache now and looking rather green around the gills. The human body does a fairly good job of adjusting to function optimally under a wide range of conditions, but it does need a little assistance from the owner.

This chapter describes the body's organization at four levels: cells, tissues, organs, and organ systems. It looks at the functions of the skin as an organ system and discusses how all the body's systems interact to maintain relatively constant internal conditions, when they can, at every organizational level.

From Cells to Organ Systems

Think for a moment about the multitude of functions taking place in your body at this very instant. Your heart is beating. Your lungs are taking in oxygen and eliminating carbon dioxide. Your eyes are forming an image of these words, and your brain is thinking about them. Your body can carry out these functions and more because its cells are specialized to perform specific tasks. But cell specialization is only the beginning. Specialized cells are organized into tissues, organs, and organ systems.

Tissues

A **tissue** is a group of cells of similar type that work together to serve a common function. Human tissues come in four primary types: epithelial tissue, connective tissue, muscle tissue, and nervous tissue. **Epithelial tissue** covers body surfaces, lines body cavities and organs, and forms glands. **Connective tissue** serves as a storage site for fat, plays an important role in immunity, and provides the body and its organs with protection and support. **Muscle tissue** is responsible for body movement and for movement of substances through the body. **Nervous tissue** conducts nerve impulses from one part of the body to another. As you read this chapter, you learn more about each of these types of tissue.

Epithelial tissue

All epithelial tissues share two characteristics: a free surface and a basement membrane. The free surface may be specialized for protection, secretion, or absorption. The **basement membrane** is a noncellular layer that binds the epithelial cells to underlying connective tissue and helps the epithelial tissue resist stretching.

The three basic shapes of epithelial cells are suited to their functions. **Squamous** (skwa'-mus) **epithelium** is made up of flattened, or scale-like, cells. These cells form linings—in the blood vessels or lungs, for instance—where their flattened shape allows oxygen and carbon dioxide to diffuse across the lining easily. In blood vessels, the smooth surface of the blood vessel lining reduces friction. **Cuboidal epithelium** is made up of cube-shaped cells. Cuboidal cells are found in many glands and in the lining of kidney tubules, where they provide some protection and are specialized for secretion and absorption. **Columnar epithelium**, consisting of elongated, column-shaped cells, is specialized for absorption and secretion. The small intestine is lined with columnar cells. These, like many examples of columnar cells, have numerous small, fingerlike folds on their exposed surfaces, greatly increasing the surface area for absorption. The goblet cells of this lining produce mucus to ease the passage of food and protect the cells of the lining.

Squamous, cuboidal, and columnar epithelium can be either simple (a single layer of cells) or stratified (multiple layers of cells). Stratified epithelium often serves a protective role, because its multiple layers provide additional thickness that makes it more difficult for molecules to pass through. Table **4.1** and Figure **4.1** summarize the types of epithelial tissue.

A **gland** is epithelial tissue that secretes a product. **Exocrine glands** secrete their products into ducts leading to body surfaces, cavities, or organs. Examples of exocrine glands include the glands that produce digestive enzymes, milk glands, and the oil and sweat glands of the skin. **Endocrine glands** (covered in more depth in Chapter 10) lack ducts and secrete their products, hormones, into spaces just outside the cells. Ultimately, hormones diffuse into the bloodstream and are carried throughout the body.

Connective tissue

Connective tissue has many forms and functions. Sometimes described as the body's glue, its most common role is to bind (tendons and ligaments) and support the other tissues (cartilage and bone). However, certain connective tissues specialize in transport (blood) and energy storage (adipose tissue). Connective tissue is the most abundant and widely distributed tissue in the body.

SIMPLE EPITHELIUM

Simple squamous
- One layer of flattened cells
- Located in air sacs of lungs, heart and blood vessel linings
- Allows exchange of nutrients, gases, and wastes

Simple cuboidal
- One layer of cube-shaped cells
- Located in linings of kidney tubules and glands
- Functions in absorption and secretion

Simple columnar
- One layer of tall, slender cells
- Located in lining of gut and respiratory tract
- Functions in absorption and secretion

STRATIFIED EPITHELIUM

Stratified squamous
- Several layers of flattened cells
- Located on surface of skin, lining of mouth, esophagus, and vagina
- Provides protection against abrasion, infection, and drying out

Stratified cuboidal
- Usually two layers of cube-shaped cells
- Located in ducts of mammary glands, sweat glands, and salivary glands
- Functions in protection

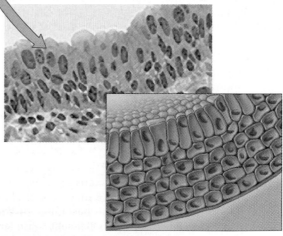

Stratified columnar
- Several layers of tall, slender cells
- Rare, located in urethra (tube through which urine leaves the body)
- Functions in protection and secretion

FIGURE 4.1 Types of epithelial tissue. These are named for the shape of the cell and the number of cell layers.

All connective tissues contain cells embedded in an extracellular **matrix**. This matrix consists of protein fibers and a noncellular material called ground substance. The **ground substance** may be solid (as in bone), fluid (as in blood), or gelatinous (as in cartilage). It is secreted by the connective tissue cells themselves or by other cells nearby. Whereas all other types of tissue consist primarily of cells, connective tissue is made up mostly of its matrix. The cells are distributed in the matrix much like pieces of fruit suspended in a gelatin dessert.

The connective-tissue matrix contains three types of protein fibers in proportions that depend on the type of connective tissue. **Collagen fibers** are strong and ropelike and can withstand pulling because of their great tensile strength. **Elastic fibers** contain random coils and can stretch and recoil like a spring. They are common in structures where great elasticity is needed, including the skin, lungs, and blood vessels. **Reticular fibers** are thin strands of collagen[1] that branch extensively, forming interconnecting networks suitable for supporting soft tissues (for example, they support the liver and spleen).

[1]Reticular fibers have the same subunits as collagen fibers, but they are assembled into a slightly different kind of structure.

All three types of protein fibers—collagen, elastic, and reticular—are produced by cells called **fibroblasts** in the connective tissue. Fibroblasts also repair tears in body tissues. For example, when skin is cut, fibroblasts move to the area of the wound and produce collagen fibers that help close the wound, cover the damage, and provide a surface upon which the outer layer of skin can grow back.

Table **4.2** and Figure **4.2** group the many types of connective tissue into two broad categories—connective tissue proper (loose and dense connective tissue) and specialized connective tissue (cartilage, bone, and blood)—and summarize the characteristics of each type. The characteristics of any specific connective tissue are determined more by its matrix than by its cells.

Connective Tissue Proper Loose and dense connective tissues differ in the ratio of cells to extracellular fibers. **Loose connective tissue** contains many cells but has fewer and more loosely woven fibers than are seen in the matrix of dense connective tissue (Figure 4.2). One type of loose connective tissue, **areolar** (ah-re'-o-lar) **connective tissue**, functions as a universal packing material between other tissues. Its many cells are embedded in a gelatinous matrix that is soft

TABLE 4.1 Review of Epithelial Tissue

Shape	Number of Layers	Example Locations	Functions
Squamous (flat, scale-like cells)	Simple (single layer)	Lining of heart and blood vessels, air sacs of lungs	Allows passage of materials by diffusion
	Stratified (more than one layer)	Linings of mouth, esophagus, and vagina; outer layer of skin	Protects underlying areas
Cuboidal (cube-shaped cells)	Simple	Kidney tubules, secretory portion of glands and their ducts	Secretes; absorbs
	Stratified	Ducts of sweat glands, mammary glands, and salivary glands	Protects underlying areas
Columnar	Simple	Most of digestive tract (stomach to anus), air tubes of lungs (bronchi), excretory ducts of some glands, uterus	Absorbs; secretes mucus, enzymes, and other substances
	Stratified	Rare; urethra, junction of esophagus and stomach	Protects underlying areas, secretes

TABLE 4.2 Review of Connective Tissue

Type	Example Locations	Functions
Connective tissue proper		
Loose, areolar	Between muscles, surrounding glands, wrapping small blood vessels and nerves	Wraps and cushions organs
Loose, adipose (fat)	Under skin, around kidneys and heart	Stores energy, insulates, cushions organs
Dense	Tendons, ligaments	Attaches bone to bone (ligaments) or bone to muscle (tendons)
Specialized connective tissue		
Cartilage (semisolid)	Nose (tip); rings in respiratory air tubules; external ear	Provides support and protection (by enclosing) and serves as lever for muscles to act on
Bone (solid)	Skeleton	Provides support and protection (by enclosing), and levers for muscles to act on
Blood (fluid)	Within blood vessels	Transports oxygen and carbon dioxide, nutrients, hormones, and wastes; helps fight infections

CONNECTIVE TISSUE PROPER

Areolar connective tissue
• Widely distributed; found under skin, around organs, between muscles
• Wraps and cushions organs

Adipose (fat) tissue
• Found under skin, around kidneys and heart
• Functions in energy storage and insulation; cushioning for organs

Dense connective tissue
• Found in tendons and ligaments
• Forms strong bands that attach bone to muscle or bone to bone

SPECIALIZED CONNECTIVE TISSUE

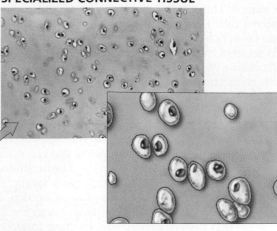

Cartilage
• Found in rings of respiratory air tubes, external ear, tip of nose
• Provides flexible support; cushions

Bone
• Found in the skeleton
• Functions in support, protection (by enclosing organs), and movement

Blood
• Found within blood vessels
• Transports nutrients, gases, hormones, wastes; fights infections

FIGURE 4.2 Types of connective tissue

and easily shaped. Areolar connective tissue is found, for example, between muscles, where it permits one muscle to move freely over another. It also anchors the skin to underlying tissues and organs.

The second type of loose connective tissue is **adipose tissue**, which contains cells that are specialized for fat storage. Most of the body's long-term energy stores are fat. Fat also serves as insulation and, around certain organs, as a shock absorber.

Dense connective tissue forms strong bands because of its large amounts of tightly woven fibers. It is found in ligaments (structures that join bone to bone), tendons (structures that join muscle to bone), and the dermis (layer of skin below the epidermis).

Specialized Connective Tissue Specialized connective tissue, as shown in Figure 4.2, comes in three types: cartilage, bone, and blood. **Cartilage** is tough but flexible. It serves as cushioning between certain bones and helps maintain the structure of certain body parts, including the ears and the nose. The cells in cartilage (chondrocytes) sit within spaces in the matrix called lacunae. The protein fibers and somewhat gelatinous ground substance of cartilage are responsible for the tissue's resilience and strength. Cartilage lacks blood vessels and nerves, so nutrients reach cartilage cells by diffusion from nearby capillaries. Because this process is fairly slow, cartilage heals more slowly than bone, which is a tissue with a rich blood supply.

The human body has three types of cartilage:

- *Hyaline cartilage,* the most abundant, provides support and flexibility. It contains numerous cartilage cells in a matrix of collagen fibers and a bluish white, gel-like ground substance. Known commonly as gristle, hyaline cartilage is found at the ends of long bones (look carefully at your next drumstick), where it allows one bone to slide easily over another. It also forms part of the nose, ribs, larynx, and trachea.
- *Elastic cartilage* is more flexible than hyaline cartilage because of the large amounts of wavy elastic fibers in its matrix. Elastic cartilage is found in the external ear, where it provides strength and elasticity.
- *Fibrocartilage* contains fewer cells than either hyaline or elastic cartilage. Like hyaline cartilage, its matrix contains collagen fibers. Fibrocartilage forms a cushioning layer in the knee joint as well as the outer part of the shock-absorbing disks between the vertebrae of the spine. It is made to withstand pressure.

Bone, in combination with cartilage and other components of joints, makes up the skeletal system. To many people's surprise, bone is a living, actively metabolizing tissue with a good blood supply that promotes prompt healing. Bone has many functions: protection and support for internal structures; movement, in conjunction with muscles; storage of lipids (in yellow marrow), calcium, and phosphorus; and production of blood cells (in red marrow). The matrix secreted by bone cells is hardened by calcium, enabling bones to provide rigid support. Collagen fibers in bone also lend it strength. You will read more about the structure and function of bones in Chapter 5.

Blood is a specialized connective tissue consisting of a liquid matrix, called *plasma*, in which so-called formed elements (cells and cell fragments called platelets) are suspended (Figure 4.2). The "fibers" in blood are soluble proteins, visible only when the blood clots. An important function of blood is to transport various substances, many of which are dissolved in the plasma. One kind of formed element, the *red blood cell*, transports oxygen to cells and also carries some of the carbon dioxide away from cells. The other two kinds of formed elements are *white blood cells*, which help fight infection, and *platelets*, which help with clotting. Both white blood cells and platelets help protect the body. You will read more about blood in Chapter 11.

Muscle tissue

Muscle tissue is composed of muscle cells (called muscle fibers) that contract when stimulated. As shown in Figure **4.3**, there are three types of muscle tissue: skeletal, cardiac, and smooth. Their characteristics are summarized in Table **4.3**. You will read more about muscle tissue in Chapters 6 and 12.

- **Skeletal muscle tissue** is so named because it is usually attached to bones. When skeletal muscle tissue contracts, therefore, it usually moves a part of the body. Because skeletal muscle is under conscious control, it is described as *voluntary muscle*. Skeletal muscle cells are long, cylinder-shaped cells, each containing several nuclei. In addition, skeletal muscle cells have striations, which are alternating light and dark bands visible under a light microscope. The striations are caused by the orderly arrangement of the contractile proteins actin and myosin, which interact to cause muscle contraction.
- **Cardiac muscle tissue** is found only in the walls of the heart, where its contractions are responsible for pumping blood to the rest of the body. Cardiac muscle contractions are not under conscious control; we cannot *make* them contract by thinking about them. Thus, cardiac muscle is considered *involuntary muscle*. Cardiac muscle cells resemble branching cylinders and have striations and typically only one nucleus. Special junctions at the plasma membranes of these cells strengthen cardiac tissue and promote rapid conduction of impulses throughout the heart.
- **Smooth muscle tissue** is involuntary and is found in the walls of blood vessels and airways, where its contraction reduces the flow of blood or air. Smooth muscle is also found in the walls

TABLE 4.3 Review of Muscle Tissue

Type	Description	Example Locations	Functions
Skeletal	Long, cylindrical cells; multiple nuclei per cell; obvious striations	Muscles attached to bones	Provides voluntary movement
Cardiac	Branching, striated cells; one nucleus; specialized junctions between cells	Wall of heart	Contracts and propels blood through the circulatory system
Smooth	Cells taper at each end; single nucleus; arranged in sheets; no striations	Walls of digestive system, blood vessels, and tubules of urinary system	Propels substances or objects through internal passageways

Skeletal muscle
- Long cylindrical striated cells with many nuclei
- Voluntary contraction
- Most are found attached to the skeleton
- Responsible for voluntary movement

Cardiac muscle
- Branching striated cells, one nucleus
- Involuntary contraction
- Found in wall of heart
- Pumps blood through the body

Smooth muscle
- Cells tapered at each end, one nucleus
- Involuntary contraction
- Found in walls of hollow internal organs, such as the intestines, and tubes, such as blood vessels
- Contractions in digestive system move food along
- When arranged in circle, controls diameter of tube

FIGURE 4.3 Types of muscle tissue

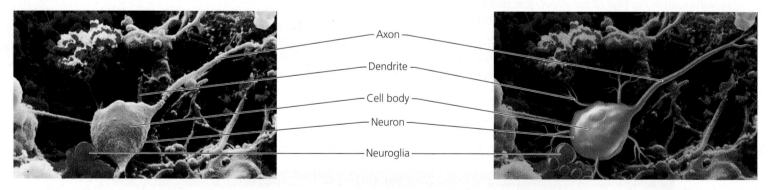

FIGURE 4.4 Neurons and neuroglia

of organs such as the stomach, intestines, and bladder, where it aids in mixing and propelling food through the digestive tract and in eliminating wastes. The cells of smooth muscle tissue taper at each end, contain a single nucleus, and lack striations.

Nervous tissue

The final major type of tissue, nervous tissue, makes up the nervous system: brain, spinal cord, and nerves. Nervous tissue consists of two general cell types, neurons and accessory cells called neuroglia (Figure **4.4**). **Neurons** generate and conduct nerve impulses, which they conduct to other neurons, muscle cells, or glands. Although neurons come in many shapes and sizes, most have three parts—the cell body, dendrites, and an axon. The cell body houses the nucleus and most organelles. Dendrites are highly branched processes that provide a large surface area for the reception of signals from other neurons. A neuron generally has one axon, a long extension that usually conducts impulses away from the cell body. Far more numerous than neurons, the **neuroglia** (or more simply, glial cells) support, insulate, and protect neurons. They increase the rate at which impulses are conducted by neurons and provide neurons with nutrients from nearby blood vessels. Recent studies indicate that glial cells communicate with one another and with neurons. You will read more about nervous tissue in Chapters 7 and 8.

Cell Junctions

In many tissues, especially epithelial tissue, the cell membranes have structures for forming attachments between adjoining cells. There are three kinds of junctions between cells: tight junctions, adhesion junctions, and gap junctions. Each type of junction suits the function of the tissue. In **tight junctions** (Figure **4.5a**), the membranes of neighboring cells are attached so securely that they form a leakproof seal. Tight junctions are found in the linings of the urinary tract and intestines, where secure seals between cells prevent urine or digestive juices from passing through the epithelium. Less rigid than tight junctions, **adhesion junctions** (also called desmosomes; Figure 4.5b) resemble rivets holding adjacent tissue layers together. The plasma membranes of adjacent cells do not actually touch but are instead bound together by intercellular filaments attached to a thickening in the membrane. Thus, the cells are connected but can still slide slightly relative to one another. Adhesion junctions are common in tissues that must withstand stretching, such as the skin and heart muscle. **Gap junctions** (Figure 4.5c) connect the cytoplasm of adjacent cells through small holes, allowing certain small molecules and ions to flow directly from one cell into the next. In heart and smooth muscle cells, gap junctions help synchronize electrical activity and thus contraction.

(a) Tight junction
- Creates an impermeable junction that prevents the exchange of materials between cells
- Found between epithelial cells of the digestive tract, where they prevent digestive enzymes and microorganisms from entering the blood

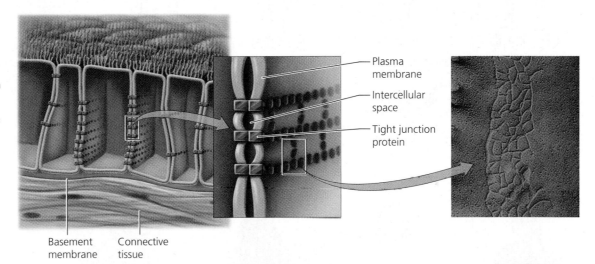

(b) Adhesion junction
- Holds cells together despite stretching
- Found in tissues that are often stretched, such as the skin and the opening of the uterus

(c) Gap junction
- Allows cells to communicate by allowing small molecules and ions to pass from cell to cell
- Found in epithelia in which the movement of ions coordinates functions, such as the beating of cilia; found in excitable tissue such as heart and smooth muscle

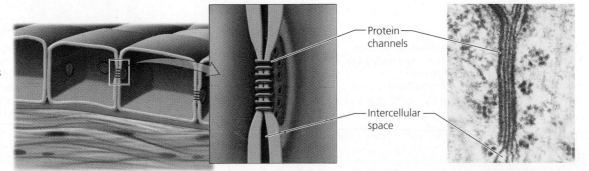

FIGURE 4.5 Specialized cell junctions

Integumentary system
- Protects underlying tissues
- Provides skin sensation
- Helps regulate body temperature
- Synthesizes vitamin D

Skeletal system
- Attachment for muscles
- Protects organs
- Stores calcium and phosphorus
- Produces blood cells

Muscular system
- Moves body and maintains posture
- Internal transport of fluids
- Generation of heat

Nervous system
- Regulates and integrates body functions via neurons

Endocrine system
- Regulates and integrates body functions via hormones

Cardiovascular system
- Transports nutrients, respiratory gases, wastes, and heat
- Transports immune cells and antibodies
- Transports hormones
- Regulates pH

Lymphatic system
- Returns tissue fluids to bloodstream
- Protects against infection and disease

Respiratory system
- Exchanges respiratory gases with the environment

Digestive system
- Physical and chemical breakdown of food
- Absorbs, processes, stores food

Urinary system
- Maintains constant internal environment through the excretion of nitrogenous waste

Reproductive system
- Produces and secretes hormones
- Produces and releases egg and sperm cells
- Houses embryo/fetus (females only)

FIGURE 4.6 Major organ systems of the human body

Organs and Organ Systems

An **organ** is a structure composed of two or more different tissues that work together to perform a specific function. Organs themselves do not usually function as independent units but instead form part of an **organ system**—a group of organs with a common function. For example, organs such as the trachea, bronchi, and lungs constitute the respiratory system. The common function of these organs is to bring oxygen into the body and remove carbon dioxide. The human body includes the 11 major organ systems, as described and illustrated in Figure **4.6**.

Body Cavities Lined with Membranes

Most of our organs are suspended in internal body cavities (Figure **4.7**). These cavities have two important functions. First, they help protect the vital organs from being damaged when we walk or jump. Second, they allow organs to slide past one another

FIGURE 4.7 Body cavities. The internal organs are suspended in body cavities that protect the organs and allow organs to slide past one another as the body moves. *Ventral* means "toward the abdomen," and *dorsal* means "toward the back."

and change shape. Sliding and changing shape are important when the lungs fill with air, the stomach fills with food, the urinary bladder fills with urine, or our bodies bend or stretch.

There are two main body cavities—the ventral and dorsal cavities—each of which is further subdivided. The ventral (toward the abdomen) cavity is divided into the *thoracic* (chest) *cavity* and the *abdominal cavity*. The thoracic cavity is subdivided again into the pleural cavities, which house the lungs, and the pericardial cavity, which holds the heart. The abdominal cavity contains the digestive system, the urinary system, and the reproductive system. A muscle sheet called the diaphragm separates the thoracic and abdominal cavities. The dorsal (toward the back) cavity is subdivided into the *cranial cavity*, which encloses the brain, and the *spinal cavity*, which houses the spinal cord.

Body cavities and organ surfaces are covered with membranes—sheets of epithelium supported by connective tissue. Membranes form physical barriers that protect underlying tissues. The body has four types of membrane.

1. **Mucous membranes** line passageways that open to the exterior of the body, such as those of the respiratory, digestive, reproductive, and urinary systems. Some mucous membranes, including the mucous membrane of the small intestine, are specialized for absorption. Others, those of the respiratory system, for instance, secrete mucus that traps bacteria and viruses that could cause illness.

2. **Serous membranes** line the thoracic and abdominal cavities and the organs within them. They secrete a fluid that lubricates the organs within these cavities.

3. **Synovial membranes** line the cavities of freely movable joints, such as the knee. These membranes secrete a fluid that lubricates the joint, easing movement.

4. **Cutaneous membrane**, or skin, covers the outside of the body. Unlike other membranes, it is thick, relatively waterproof, and relatively dry.

We will consider the structure and function of the skin in the next section. Details about the structure and functions of the other organ systems are presented in subsequent chapters.

Skin: An Organ System

We have all been told that "beauty is only skin deep," but our skin does much more than just make us attractive. The skin and its derivatives—hair, nails, sweat glands, and oil glands—are sometimes called the **integumentary system** (an *integument* is an outer covering). It is considered an organ system because the skin and its derivatives function together to provide many services for the body.

Skin Functions

A major function of our skin is protection. It serves as a physical barrier that shields the contents of the body from invasion by foreign bacteria and other harmful particles, from ultraviolet (UV) radiation, and from physical and chemical insult. Besides offering this somewhat passive form of protection, skin contains cells called *macrophages* that have a more active way of fighting infection, as we will see in Chapter 13.

The skin has many other functions, as well. For example, because its outermost layer of cells contains the water-resistant protein keratin, the skin plays a vital role in preventing excessive water loss from underlying tissues. It plays a role in temperature regulation, too. Although we perspire (imperceptively) through our skin almost constantly, during times of strenuous exercise or high environmental temperatures our sweat glands become active and increase their output of perspiration dramatically. The evaporation of this perspiration from the skin's surface helps rid the body of excess heat. Later we will see how changes in the flow of blood to the skin help regulate body temperature. The skin even functions in the production of vitamin D. Modified cholesterol molecules in the skin's outer layer are converted to vitamin D by UV radiation. The vitamin D then travels in the bloodstream to the liver and kidneys, where it is chemically modified to assume its role in stimulating the absorption of calcium and phosphorus from the food we eat.

In addition, the skin contains structures for detecting temperature, touch, pressure, and pain stimuli. These receptors—components of the nervous system—help keep us informed about conditions in our external environment. Keep these many functions of the integumentary system in mind as you read on about the structure of the skin and its derivatives.

Skin Layers

On most parts of your body, the skin is less than 5 mm (less than a quarter of an inch) thick, yet it is one of your largest organs. It represents about one-twelfth of your body weight and has a surface area of 1.5 to 2 m^2 (1.8 to 2.4 yd^2).

The skin has two principal layers, as shown in Figure **4.8**. The thin, outer layer, the **epidermis**, forms a protective barrier against environmental hazards. The inner layer, the **dermis**, contains blood vessels, nerves, sweat and oil glands, and hair follicles. Beneath the skin is a layer of loose connective tissue called the *hypodermis* or *subcutaneous layer*, which anchors the skin to the tissues of other organ systems that lie beneath.

The epidermis

The outermost layer of skin, the epidermis, is itself composed of several layers of epithelial cells. The outer surface of epidermis, the part you can touch, is made up of dead skin cells. Thus, when we look at another person, most of what we see on the person's surface is dead. These dead cells are constantly being shed, at a rate of about 30,000 to 40,000 each minute. In fact, much of the dust in any room consists of dead skin cells. When you go swimming or soak in the bathtub for a long time, the dead cells on your skin's surface absorb water and swell, causing the skin to wrinkle. This is particularly noticeable where the layer of dead cells is thickest, such as on the palms of the hands and soles of the feet.

The skin does not get thinner as the dead cells are shed, because they are continuously replaced from below. The deepest layer of epidermis contains rapidly dividing cells. As new cells are produced in this layer, older cells are pushed toward the surface. On their way, they flatten and die because they no longer receive nourishment from the dermis. Along this death route, keratin—a tough, fibrous protein—gradually replaces the cytoplasmic contents of the cells. It is keratin that gives the epidermis its protective properties. About 2 weeks to a month pass from the time a new cell is formed to the time it is shed.

FIGURE 4.8 Structures of the skin and underlying hypodermis

Drugs that must be continuously administered are often given across the skin (transdermally) using a drug-containing patch that adheres to the skin (Figure **4.9**). Although the epidermis is a water-resistant protective barrier, lipid-soluble materials are able to cross the lipid cell membranes of the cells of the epidermis. Thus, if you dissolve a drug in a lipid solvent, it can cross the epidermis, diffuse into the underlying connective tissue, and be absorbed into the blood. Today, transdermal drug administration is commonly used to provide hormones for birth control or the treatment of menopausal symptoms, nicotine to ease the urge to smoke while trying to quit, and anti-emetics to stop nausea from motion sickness.

what would you do?

To speed up the movement of a drug from a transdermal patch to the patient's blood supply, the patch is prepared with a higher concentration of the drug than would be found in a pill. In transdermal patches that deliver hormones for birth control, the blood levels of hormones may also be higher than would result with birth control pills. During the last few years, several young women using a transdermal patch for birth control have had heart attacks or strokes; some have died. There are warning labels with contraceptive patches informing women of these increased risks. Do you think that women or their families should be able to sue the patch manufacturer for their losses?

The dermis

Over most parts of the body, the dermis is a much thicker layer than the epidermis. The dermis lies just beneath the epidermis and consists primarily of connective tissue. In addition, it contains blood vessels, hair follicles, oil glands, the ducts of sweat glands, sensory structures, and nerve endings. Unlike the epidermis, the dermis does not wear away. This durability explains why tattoos—designs created when tiny droplets of ink are injected

into the dermal layer—are permanent (Figure **4.10**). Because the dermis is laced with nerves and sensory receptors, getting a tattoo hurts. In the past, the only way to remove a tattoo was by surgical means, such as "shaving" (abrading) of the skin. Today, laser treatments that destroy the pigments of the tattoo can often be used for tattoo removal.

Blood vessels are present in the dermis but not in the epidermis. Nutrients reach the epidermis by passing out of dermal blood vessels and diffusing through tissue fluid into the layer above. Such tissue fluid is probably quite familiar to you. Where skin is traumatized by, for example, a burn or an ill-fitting shoe rubbing against your heel, this fluid accumulates between the epidermis and dermis, separating the layers and forming blisters.

stop and think

Burns—tissue damage caused by heat, radiation, electric shock, or chemicals—can be classified according to how deep the damage penetrates. First-degree burns are confined to the upper layers of epidermis, where they cause reddening and slight swelling. In second-degree burns, damage extends through the epidermis into the upper regions of the dermis. Blistering, pain, and swelling occur. Third-degree burns extend through the epidermis and dermis into underlying tissues. Severe burns, particularly if they cover large portions of the body, are life threatening. Given your knowledge of skin functions, what would you predict the immediate medical concerns to be when a patient has third-degree burns?

The lower layer of the dermis consists of dense connective tissue containing collagen and elastic fibers, a combination that allows the skin to stretch and then return to its original shape. Unfortunately, the skin's elasticity has limits. Pregnancy or substantial weight gain may exceed the skin's ability to return completely to its earlier size after stretching; instead, the dermis tears, and stretch marks appear. The resilience of our skin also decreases as we age. The most pronounced effects begin in the late forties, when collagen fibers begin to stiffen and decrease in number and elastic fibers thicken and lose elasticity. These changes, combined with reductions in moisture and the amount of fat in the hypodermis, lead to wrinkles and sagging skin.

FIGURE 4.9 A transdermal patch continuously delivers a drug across the skin. Here, a cigarette smoker uses a nicotine patch to help quit smoking.

FIGURE 4.10 Tattoos—designs created when droplets of ink are injected into the dermis—are essentially permanent because, unlike the epidermis, the dermis is not shed.

FIGURE 4.11 Before and after Botox injections

Certain wrinkles, such as frown lines, are caused by the contraction of facial muscles. A controversial and popular treatment for these wrinkles is to inject Botox, the toxin from the bacterium that causes botulism. When Botox is injected into facial muscles, they become temporarily paralyzed. The muscle contractions that form the wrinkles cannot occur, and the skin smoothes out. The muscles regain the ability to contract over the next several months, however, and the injection has to be repeated (Figure **4.11**).

The hypodermis

The **hypodermis**, a layer of loose connective tissue just below the epidermis and dermis, is not usually considered part of the skin. It does, however, share some of the skin's functions, including cushioning blows and helping to prevent extreme changes in body temperature, because it contains about half of the body's fat stores. In infants and toddlers, this layer of fat that lies under the skin—often called baby fat—covers the entire body, but as we mature, some of the fat stores are redistributed. In women, subcutaneous fat tends to accumulate in the breasts, hips, and thighs. In both sexes, it has a tendency to accumulate in the abdominal hypodermis, contributing to the all-too-familiar potbelly, and in the sides of the lower back, forming "love handles."

Liposuction, a procedure for vacuuming fat from the hypodermis, is a way to reshape the body. The physician makes a small incision in the skin above the area of unwanted fat, inserts a fine tube, and moves the tube back and forth to loosen the fat cells, which are then sucked into a container. Liposuction is not a way of losing a lot of weight, because only a small amount of fat—not more than a few pounds—can be removed. However, it is a way of sculpting the body and removing bulges. Furthermore, because liposuction removes the cells that store the fat, fat does not usually return to those areas. The procedure is generally safe, but it is not risk free. In some patients, it has produced blood clots that traveled to the lungs, causing death. People who are considering liposuction should choose their doctor carefully.

what would you do?

Many social issues are connected to liposuction. One is the procedure's increasing popularity among teenagers. What does this trend say about the value we place on physical beauty? Should there be age restrictions on liposuction? If you decided to have liposuction, what criteria would you use to choose a physician?

Skin Color

Two interacting factors produce skin color: (1) the quantity and distribution of pigment and (2) blood flow. The pigment, called **melanin**, is produced by cells called **melanocytes** at the base of the epidermis. These cells, with their spiderlike extensions, produce two kinds of melanin: a yellow-to-red form and the more common black-to-brown form. The melanin is then taken up by surrounding epidermal cells, thus coloring the entire epidermis.

All people have about the same number of melanocytes. Differences in skin color are due to differences in the form of melanin produced and the size and number of pigment granules. A person's genetic makeup determines the combination of the yellowish red or the brown form of melanin produced.

Albinism is an inherited condition in which an individual's melanocytes are incapable of producing melanin. It occurs in about 1 in 10,000 people and is not specific to a particular race. Individuals with this condition, known as albinos, lack pigment in their eyes, hair, and skin (Figure **4.12a**). The eyes and skin of albinos have a pinkish color because the underlying blood supply shows through. Vitiligo, in contrast, is a condition in which melanocytes disappear

(b)

(a)

FIGURE 4.12 Conditions caused by abnormalities in melanocytes. (a) Albinism, a genetic condition in which an individual's melanocytes cannot produce melanin, occurs throughout the world. Here, an Angolan mother holds her albino child. (b) Vitiligo is a condition in which melanocytes disappear from areas of the skin, leaving white patches.

Fun in the Sun? Sunlight and Skin Cancer

It's a sunny day, and the beach is packed with people. Some jump in the surf; some build sand castles, and others lie on blankets or towels. It is hardly a scene we would equate with disfigurement and death. Nonetheless, that is a connection we should make, because skin cancers are increasing at an alarming rate, largely due to our enjoyment of the sun.

The ultraviolet (UV) radiation of sunlight causes the melanocytes of the skin to increase their production of the pigment melanin. The melanin, taken up by surrounding epidermis, absorbs UV radiation before the radiation can travel any deeper into the body and damage the genetic information of the cells.

Unfortunately, this protective buildup of melanin is not instantaneous. Sunburn—damage to skin accompanied by reddening and peeling—is a typical sequel to the first day at the beach. Excessive exposure to sun destroys the cells at the surface of the skin, causing blood vessels in the dermis to dilate, which turns the skin red. The large-scale destruction of epidermis provokes an increased production of new cells. These push the burned cells off the skin surface, and the skin peels—sometimes in small strands, but in severe cases, in large sheets.

In skin cancer, the genetic material in skin cells is altered by UV radiation so that the cells grow and divide uncontrollably, forming a tumor. Some experts fear that the rates of skin cancer will increase dramatically if the ozone layer, which blocks some of the UV radiation before it reaches Earth, continues to become thinner (the ozone layer is discussed in Chapter 24). Three types of skin cancer are caused by overexposure to the sun (Figure **4.A**):

- Basal cell carcinoma arises in the rapidly dividing cells of the deepest layer of epidermis. It is the most common type of skin cancer.
- Squamous cell carcinoma arises in the newly formed skin cells as they flatten and move toward the skin surface. It is the second most common form of skin cancer.
- Melanoma is the least common and most dangerous type of skin cancer. It arises in melanocytes, the pigment-producing cells of the skin. Unlike basal or squamous cell carcinomas, melanomas, when left untreated, often metastasize (spread rapidly) throughout the body, first infiltrating the lymph nodes and later the vital organs. The survival rate in persons whose melanoma is found before it has metastasized is about 90% but drops to about 14% if the cancerous cells have spread throughout the body.

You can catch melanomas at an early stage if you carefully examine your skin while applying the ABCD mnemonic of the American Cancer Society:

A—stands for asymmetry. Most melanomas are irregular in shape.

B—stands for border. Melanomas often have a diffuse, unclear border.

C—stands for color. Melanomas usually have a mottled appearance and contain colors such as brown, black, red, white, and blue.

D—stands for diameter. Growths with a diameter of more than 5 mm (about 0.2 in.) are threatening.

Most skin cancers are treated either by excision, along with nearby tissue, or by radiation. Sometimes laser surgery, cryosurgery (freezing), or electrodesiccation (drying by electric current) are used to destroy cancerous cells. Many skin cancers occur on the face, and disfigurement caused by removal of large chunks of the nose or ears may necessitate reconstructive surgery.

The best way to avoid getting skin cancer is to avoid prolonged exposure to the sun. If you must be out in the sun, wear a hat, long sleeves, and sunglasses. Use a sunscreen and avoid exposure between 10:00 A.M. and 3:00 P.M., when the UV rays are the strongest. Use sunscreen even when it is overcast, because UV rays can penetrate the clouds. Sunscreens should have a sun protection factor (SPF) of at least 15. Apply your sunscreen about 45 minutes before going out into the sun, allowing time for it to be absorbed by the skin so that it is less likely to wash away with perspiration. Reapply it after swimming.

Always remember that sunscreens are not foolproof. Most block the higher-energy portion of the sun's UV radiation, known as UV-B, while providing only limited protection against the lower-energy portion, called UV-A. Whereas UV-B causes skin to burn, recent research suggests that exposure to UV-A weakens the body's immune system, possibly impairing its ability to

(a) Basal cell carcinoma

(b) Squamous cell carcinoma

(c) Melanoma

FIGURE 4.A Three skin cancers

CONTINUED ON PAGE 84

fight melanoma. Ironically, by providing protection from sunburn, sunscreens have had the potentially devastating effect of enabling people to spend more time in the sun, possibly increasing their risk of developing melanoma.

Sunblocks such as zinc oxide, the white ointment used by lifeguards and others who spend long hours in the sun, differ from

sunscreens in that they totally deflect ultraviolet rays. For this reason, sunblocks are recommended for particularly sensitive or already burned areas of the face, such as the nose and lips.

Avoid tanning salons. For many years, tanning salons claimed to use "safe" wavelengths of UV radiation because they did not

use skin-reddening UV-B. But these "safe" wavelengths are actually UV-A. Given the apparent link between UV-A and increased risk of melanoma, the potential danger of these "safe" wavelengths is now obvious.

---

either partially or completely from certain areas of the skin, leaving white patches in their wake (Figure 4.12b).

Circulation influences skin color in non-albinos, as well. When well-oxygenated blood flows through vessels in the dermis, the skin has a pinkish or reddish tint that is most easily seen in light-skinned people. Intense embarrassment can increase the blood flow, causing the rosy color to heighten, particularly in the face and neck. This response, known as blushing, is impossible to stop. Other intense emotions may cause color to disappear temporarily from the skin. A sudden fright, for example, can cause a rapid drop in blood supply, making a person pale. Skin color may also change in response to changing levels of oxygen in the blood. Compared to well-oxygenated blood, which is ruby red, poorly oxygenated blood is a much deeper red that gives the skin a bluish appearance. Poor oxygenation is why the lips appear blue in extremely cold conditions. When it is cold, your body shunts blood away from the skin to the body's core, which conserves heat and keeps vital organs warm. This shunting reduces the oxygen supply to the blood in the small vessels near the surface of the skin. The oxygen-poor blood seen through the thin skin of the lips makes them look blue. When you do not get enough sleep, the amount of oxygen in your blood may be slightly lower than usual, causing the color to darken. In some people, the darker color of blood is visible through the thin skin under their eyes as dark circles.

Tanning is a change in skin color from exposure to the sun. Melanocytes respond to the UV radiation in sunlight by increasing the production of melanin. This is a protective response, because melanin absorbs some UV radiation, preventing it from reaching the lower epidermis and the dermis. The skin requires some UV radiation for the production of vitamin D, but too much can be harmful. See the Health Issue essay, *Fun in the Sun? Sunlight and Skin Cancer.*

Hair, Nails, and Glands

Many seemingly diverse structures are derived from the epidermis: hair, nails, oil glands, sweat glands, and teeth. We will now consider the first four of these in view of their structure and roles in everyday life. (Teeth are discussed in Chapter 15.)

Hair

Hair usually grows all over the body, except on a few areas such as the lips, palms of the hands, and soles of the feet. Although hair is not essential for our survival, its presence or absence in certain places can have a strong psychological impact. Indeed,

the strong emotional response of some individuals to the growth or loss of hair seems surprising when we learn that hair is essentially nothing more than dead cells filled with keratin and packed into a column.

What functions do these dead cells serve? An important one is protection. Hair on the scalp protects the head from UV radiation. Hair in the nostrils and external ear canals keeps particles and bugs from entering. Likewise, eyebrows and eyelashes help keep unwanted particles and glare (and perspiration and rain) out of the eyes. Hair also has a sensory role: receptors associated with hair follicles are sensitive to touch.

A hair consists of a shaft and a root (see Figure 4.8). The shaft projects above the surface of the skin, and the root extends below the surface into the dermis or hypodermis, where it is embedded in a structure called the hair follicle. Nerve endings surround the follicle and are so sensitive to touch that we are aware of even slight movements of the hair shaft. (Try to move just one hair without feeling it.) Each hair is also supplied with an oil gland that opens onto the follicle and supplies the hair with an oily secretion that makes it soft and pliant. In the dermis, a tiny smooth muscle called the arrector pili is attached to the hair follicle. Contraction of this muscle—which pulls on the follicle, causing the hair to stand up—is associated with fear and with cold. The tiny mound of flesh that forms at the base of the erect hair is sometimes called a goose bump.

A strand of hair, as we said earlier, is made up of dead, keratinized cells. The cuticle, or outermost layer of the strand, consists of a single layer of thin, flat, scale-like cells that are packed with keratin. Exposure to the elements and abrasion can cause the cuticle to wear off at the hair's tip, making the underlying cortex frizz and thus producing dreaded split ends.

Nails

Nails protect the sensitive tips of fingers and toes. Although the nail itself is dead and lacks sensory receptors, it is embedded in tissue so sensitive that we detect even the slightest pressure of an object on the nail. In this way, nails serve as sensory "antennas." They also help us manipulate objects, as when we undo a tight knot in a shoelace.

Like hair, nails are modified skin tissue hardened by the protein keratin. Nails differ from hair, however, in that they grow continuously (a hair stops growing after 2 to 6 years) but much more slowly.

Glands

Three types of glands—oil, sweat, and wax—are found in the skin. Although all three types develop from epidermal cells, they differ in their locations, structures, and functions.

Acne: The Misery, the Myths, and the Medications

Acne and adolescence go hand in hand. In fact, about four out of five teenagers have acne, a skin condition that will probably annoy, if not distress, them well into their twenties and possibly beyond. What is acne, and what causes it? Is it really brought on by the chocolate, potato chips, and sodas so prevalent in the teenage diet? Why do males usually experience more severe acne than females do? Can acne be treated?

Simple acne is a condition that affects hair follicles associated with oil glands. During the teenage years, oil glands increase in size and produce larger amounts of oily sebum. These changes are prompted by increasing levels of "male" hormones called androgens in the blood of both males and females; the androgens are secreted by the testes, ovaries, and adrenal glands. The changes thus induced in the activity and structure of oil glands set the stage for acne. It should come as no surprise, then, that acne occurs most often on areas of the body where oil glands are largest and most numerous: the face, chest, upper back, and shoulders.

Acne is the inflammation that results when sebum and dead cells clog the duct where the oil gland opens onto the hair follicle (Figure **4.B**). A follicle obstructed by sebum and cells is called a whitehead. Sometimes the sebum in plugged follicles mixes with the skin pigment melanin, forming a blackhead. Thus, melanin, not dirt or bacteria, lends the dark color to these blemishes. The next stage of acne is pimple formation, beginning with the formation of a red, raised bump, often with a white dot of pus at the center. The bump occurs when obstructed follicles rupture and spew their contents into the surrounding epidermis. Such ruptures may occur naturally by the general buildup of sebum and cells or may be induced by squeezing the area. The sebum, dead cells, and bacteria that thrive on them then cause a small infection—a pimple or pustule—that will usually heal within a week or two without leaving a scar.

Eating nuts, chocolate, pizza, potato chips, or any of the other "staples" of the teenage diet does not cause acne. Also, acne is not caused by poor hygiene. Follicles plug from below, so dirt or oil on the skin surface is not responsible. (Most doctors do, however, recommend washing the face two or three times a day with hot water to help open plugged follicles.)

Treatments for acne fall into two main categories: topical (those applied to the skin) and oral (those taken by mouth). Most topical medicines must be used for several weeks before improvements are noticed. One topical preparation is a 5% solution of benzoyl peroxide sometimes sold over the counter. Applied once or twice a day as a cream after the affected area has been washed, benzoyl peroxide kills bacteria living in the follicles. Another topical option, tretinoin (retinoic acid, Retin-A), available only by prescription, is a derivative of vitamin A that helps thin the epidermis, reduce the stickiness of dead cells, and increase the rate at which the cells are sloughed off. These actions help keep follicles clear and speed the removal of existing whiteheads and blackheads.

Severe cases of acne may call for oral, or systemic, medicines—such as tetracycline or minocycline—that work by inhibiting the bacteria in the follicle. Isotretinoin (Accutane), another prescription-only derivative of vitamin A, is probably the most effective treatment for severe acne. This drug works by poisoning the oil glands, causing them to shrink and reduce their output of sebum. Some of the shrinkage is permanent, making Accutane different from other treatments in that it suppresses acne even after the treatment has stopped.

(a) A normal follicle
Note the tiny hair and cells of the oil gland.

(b) A follicle with sebum
The canal becomes clogged with sebum, dead cells, and bacteria.

(c) A whitehead
Sebum, cells, and bacteria accumulate in the follicle.

(d) A blackhead
Sebum in the clogged follicle oxidizes and mixes with melanin.

(e) An inflamed pimple
The follicle wall ruptures, releasing the contents of a whitehead or blackhead into the surrounding epidermis.

FIGURE 4.B The stages of acne

Oil (sebaceous) **glands** are found virtually all over the body except on the palms of the hands and soles of the feet. They secrete sebum, an oily substance made of fats, cholesterol, proteins, and salts. The secretory part of these glands is located in the dermis, as shown in Figure 4.8. Sebum lubricates hair and skin and contains substances that inhibit growth of certain bacteria. Sometimes, however, the duct of an oil gland becomes blocked, causing sebum to accumulate and disrupt the gland's proper function. Then, bacteria can invade the gland and hair follicle, resulting in a condition called acne. See the Health Issue essay, *Acne: The Misery, the Myths, and the Medications*.

As their name implies, **sweat glands** produce sweat, which is largely water plus some salts, lactic acid, vitamin C, and metabolic wastes such as urea. Although some wastes are eliminated through sweating, the principal function of sweat is to help regulate body temperature by evaporating from the skin surface. Wax glands are modified sweat glands found in the external ear canal. As their name implies, they produce wax, which protects the ear by trapping small particles.

Homeostasis

To remain healthy, the organ systems of the body must constantly adjust their functioning in response to changes in the internal and external environment. We have already learned that the body's organ systems are interdependent, working together to provide the basic needs of all cells—water, nutrients, oxygen, and a normal body temperature. Just as city dwellers breathe the same air and drink the same city water, the cells of the body are surrounded by the same extracellular fluid. Changes in the makeup of that fluid will affect every cell.

One advantage of our body's multicellular, multi-organ-system organization is its ability to provide a controlled environment for the cells. Although conditions outside the body sometimes vary dramatically, our organ systems interact to maintain relatively stable conditions within. This ability to maintain a relatively stable internal environment despite changes in the surroundings is called **homeostasis** (meaning "to stay the same"). But, conditions within the body never stay the same. As internal conditions at any level vary, the body's processes must shift to counteract the variation. Homeostatic mechanisms do not maintain absolute internal constancy, but they do dampen fluctuations around a set point to keep internal conditions within a certain range. Thus, homeostasis is not a static state but a dynamic one.

Illness can result if homeostasis fails. We see this in diabetes, a condition in which either the pancreas does not produce enough of the hormone insulin or the body cells are unable to use insulin. Normally, as a meal is digested and nutrients are absorbed into the bloodstream, the rising level of glucose in the blood stimulates the pancreas to release insulin. The general effect of insulin is to lower the blood level of glucose, returning it to a more desirable value. Without insulin, blood glucose can rise to a point that causes damage to the eyes, kidney, nerves, and blood vessels. A healthy diet, exercise, medication, and sometimes insulin injections can help people with diabetes regulate their blood glucose level.

Homeostasis depends on communication within the body. The nervous and endocrine systems are the two primary means of communication. The nervous system can bring about quick responses to changes in internal and external conditions. The endocrine system produces hormones, which bring about slower and longer-lasting responses to change.

stop and think

When you exercise, your breathing rate, blood pressure, and heart rate increase. Is this a violation of homeostasis?

Negative Feedback Mechanisms

Homeostasis is maintained primarily through **negative feedback mechanisms**—corrective measures that slow or reverse a variation from the normal value of a factor, such as blood glucose level or body temperature, and return the factor to its normal value. When the normal value is reached, the corrective measures cease; the normal value is the feedback that turns off the response. (In contrast, a positive feedback mechanism causes a change that promotes continued change in the same direction. Positive feedback mechanisms are described in Chapter 10.)

Homeostatic mechanisms have three components (Figure **4.13**):

1. A *receptor* detects change in the internal or external environment. A receptor, in this context, is a sensor that monitors the environment. When the receptor detects a change in some factor or event—some variable—it sends that information to the control center, the second of the three components.

2. A *control center* determines the factor's set point—the level or range that is normal for the factor in question. The control center integrates information coming from all the pertinent receptors and selects an appropriate response. In most of the body's homeostatic systems, the control center is located in the brain.

3. An *effector*, often a muscle or gland, carries out the selected response.

Consider how a negative feedback mechanism controls the temperature in your home during the frigid winter months. A thermostat in the heating system serves as both the temperature-sensing receptor and the control center. If it senses that the temperature inside your home has fallen below a certain programmed set point, the thermostat turns on the heating system (the effector). When the thermostat senses that the internal temperature has returned to the set point, it turns the heating system off. Thus, the temperature fluctuates around the set point but remains within a certain range. Now, let's apply these principles to see how homeostatic mechanisms regulate body temperature.

Hypothalamus and Body Temperature

The body's temperature control center is located in a region of the brain called the hypothalamus. Its set point is approximately 37°C (98.6°F), although it differs slightly from one person to the next. Body temperature must not vary too far from this mark, because even small temperature changes have dramatic effects on metabolism. Temperature is sensed at the body's outer surface by skin receptors and deep inside the body by receptors that sense the temperature of the blood. The hypothalamus receives input from both types of receptor. If the input indicates that body temperature is below the set point, the brain initiates mechanisms to increase heat production and conserve heat. When the input indicates that body temperature is above the set point, the brain initiates mechanisms that promote heat loss.

Q *Stable blood calcium levels are important to many physiological processes. Calcitonin is a hormone from the thyroid gland that lowers blood calcium levels. Parathyroid hormone from the parathyroid glands is a hormone that raises blood calcium levels. Describe a negative feedback relationship involving these hormones as effectors that would maintain homeostasis by keeping blood calcium levels stable.*

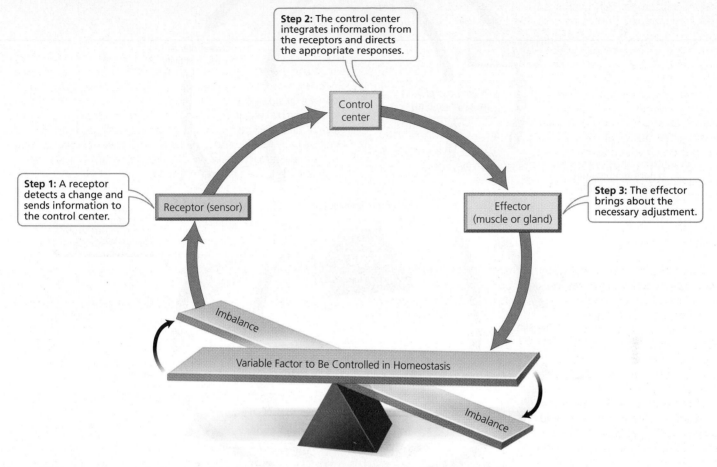

Step 2: The control center integrates information from the receptors and directs the appropriate responses.

Step 1: A receptor detects a change and sends information to the control center.

Receptor (sensor)

Control center

Effector (muscle or gland)

Step 3: The effector brings about the necessary adjustment.

Imbalance

Variable Factor to Be Controlled in Homeostasis

Imbalance

FIGURE 4.13 The components of a homeostatic control system maintained by negative feedback mechanisms

A *An elevation in blood calcium level would be sensed by receptors. In response, a control center in the brain would stimulate the thyroid gland to increase production of calcitonin, which lowers blood calcium level. If the calcium level dropped too low, receptors would signal the control center in the brain. In response, the control center would stimulate the parathyroid glands to increase production of parathyroid hormone, which would raise blood calcium levels.*

Let's consider what happens when we find ourselves in an environment where the temperature is above our set point, say 38°C (100.4°F). Thermoreceptors in the skin detect heat and activate nerve cells that send a message to the hypothalamus, which then sends nerve impulses to the sweat glands to increase their secretions. As the secretions (perspiration) evaporate and body temperature drops below 37°C (98.6°F), the signals from the brain to the sweat glands are discontinued. In this homeostatic system, the thermoreceptors in the skin are the receptors, the hypothalamus is the control center, and the sweat glands are the effectors. The system is a negative feedback mechanism because it produces an effect (cooling of the skin) that is relayed (feeds back) to the control center, shutting off the corrective mechanism when the desired change has been produced.

Other mechanisms the brain may activate to lower body temperature include dilation of blood vessels in the dermis and relaxation of the arrector pili muscles attached to the hair follicles. The former response releases more heat to the surrounding air and explains the flushed appearance we get during strenuous exercise. The latter keeps damp, cooling hair lying close to the skin. The brain may also initiate behavioral responses to a high body temperature, such as seeking shade or removing a sweatshirt.

stop and think

As people age, the activity of their sweat glands declines. How does this explain why public authorities are less concerned about children than they are about the elderly developing a heat-related illness during a heat wave?

Now let's consider what happens when body temperature drops below the set point. Subtle drops in body temperature are detected largely by thermoreceptors in the skin, which send a message to the

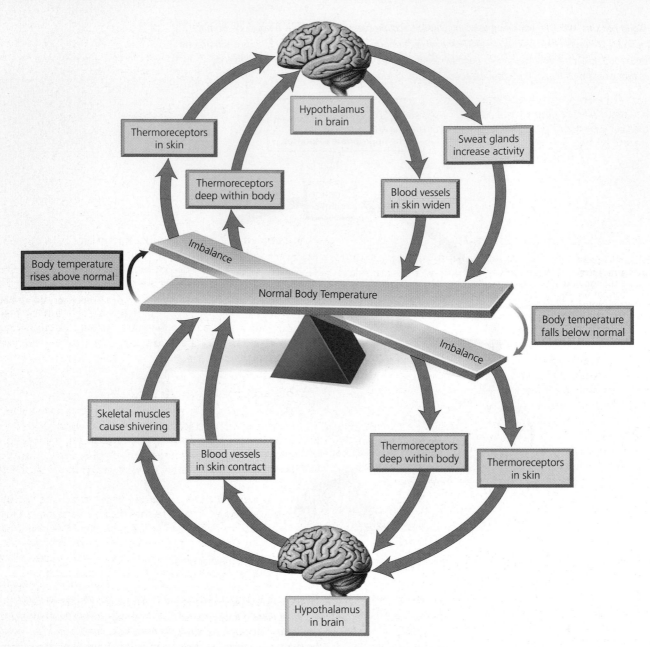

FIGURE 4.14 Homeostatic regulation of body temperature by negative feedback mechanisms. In this homeostatic control system, thermoreceptors are the sensors, the hypothalamus is the control center, and sweat glands, blood vessels in the skin, and skeletal muscles are the effectors.

hypothalamus in the brain. The brain then sends nerve impulses to sweat glands, ordering a decrease in their activity, as well as messages to vessels in the dermis, telling them to constrict. This constriction reduces blood flow to the extremities, conserving heat for the internal organs and giving credence to the saying, "cold hands, warm heart." Another response to decreasing body temperature is contraction of arrector pili muscles, causing hairs to stand on end and thereby trapping an insulating layer of air near the body. This response, known as piloerection, is less effective in humans than in more heavily furred animals. The body also responds to cooling by increasing metabolic activity to generate heat and by the repeated contraction of skeletal muscles, known as shivering. Finally, behavioral responses, such as folding one's arms across one's chest, may be called upon to help combat a drop in body temperature. See Figure **4.14** for a summary of body temperature regulation.

Sometimes the mechanisms for lowering higher-than-normal temperatures fail, resulting in potentially deadly *hyperthermia*—abnormally elevated body temperature. Some marathon runners have died as a result of elevated core temperatures, as have people sitting in a hot tub heated to too high a temperature (say, up around 114°F). In both situations, perspiration could bring no relief; its evaporation would be prevented by high humidity in the case of the runners or by the surrounding water in the case of the hot-tubbers. Commonly called heat stroke, hyperthermia is marked by confusion and dizziness. If the core temperature reaches about 42°C (107°F), the heartbeat becomes irregular, oxygen levels in the blood drop, the liver ceases to function, and unconsciousness and death soon follow. Few people can survive core temperatures of 43°C (110°F).

If the body's temperature drops too far—to 35°C (95°F) or below—a condition called *hypothermia* results, disrupting nervous system function and temperature-regulating mechanisms. People suffering from hypothermia usually become giddy and confused at first. When their temperature drops to 33°C (91.4°F), they lose consciousness. Finally, at a body temperature of 30°C (86°F), blood vessels are completely constricted and temperature-regulating mechanisms are fully shut down. Death soon follows. Hypothermia can be treated if detected early enough. In severe cases, dialysis machines may be used to artificially warm the blood and pump it back into the body.

stop and think

Frostbite is damage to tissues exposed to cold temperatures. Given what you know about the body's response to cold temperature, why are fingers and toes particularly susceptible to frostbite?

highlighting the concepts

From Cells to Organ Systems (pp. 71–79)

- Tissues are groups of cells that work together to perform a common function. There are four main types of tissue in the human body: epithelial (covers body surfaces, forms glands, and lines internal cavities and organs), connective (acts as storage site for fat, plays a role in immunity and in transport, and provides protection and support), muscle (generates movement), and nervous tissue (coordinates body activities through initiation and transmission of nerve impulses).
- All connective tissues contain cells in an extracellular matrix composed of protein fibers and ground substance. The types of connective tissue are connective tissue proper (loose and dense connective tissue) and specialized connective tissue (cartilage, bone, and blood).
- Blood consists of formed elements (red blood cells, white blood cells, and platelets) suspended in a liquid matrix (plasma). The protein fibers are normally dissolved in the plasma and play a role in blood clotting. Red blood cells transport oxygen and carbon dioxide; white blood cells aid in fighting infections; and platelets function in blood clotting.
- Muscle tissue is composed of muscle fibers that contract when stimulated, generating a mechanical force. There are three types of muscle tissue: skeletal, cardiac, and smooth. Skeletal muscle tissue is usually attached to bone, is voluntary, has cross-striations visible under a microscope, and has several nuclei in each cell. Cardiac muscle tissue is found in the walls of the heart, is involuntary, has cross-striations, and usually contains only one nucleus in each cell. Smooth muscle tissue is in the walls of blood vessels, airways, and organs. It is involuntary and lacks striations. A smooth muscle cell tapers at each end and has a single nucleus.
- Nervous tissue consists of cells called neurons and accessory cells called neuroglia. Neurons convert stimuli into nerve impulses that they conduct to glands, muscles, or other neurons. Neuroglia increase the rate at which impulses are conducted by neurons and provide neurons with nutrients from nearby blood vessels. Neuroglial cells can communicate with one another and with neurons.
- Three types of specialized junctions hold tissues together. Tight junctions prevent the passage of materials through the boundaries where cells meet. Adhesion junctions link cells by intercellular filaments attached to thickenings in the plasma membrane. Gap junctions have small pores that allow physical and chemical communication between cells.
- An organ is a structure that is composed of two or more different tissues and has a specialized function.
- Two or more organs that participate in a common function are collectively called an organ system. The human body has 11 major organ systems.

- Internal organs are located in body cavities. There are two main body cavities: (1) the dorsal cavity, which is subdivided into the cranial cavity, where the brain is located, and the spinal cavity, where the spinal cord is located; (2) the ventral cavity, which is subdivided into the thoracic (chest) cavity and the abdominal cavity. The thoracic cavity is further divided into the pleural cavities, which contain the lungs, and the pericardial cavity, which contains the heart. Membranes line body cavities and spaces within organs.

Skin: An Organ System (pp. 79–86)

- The integumentary system includes the skin and its derivatives, such as hair, nails, and sweat and oil glands. It protects underlying tissues from abrasion and dehydration; regulates body temperature; synthesizes vitamin D; detects stimuli associated with touch, temperature, and pain; and initiates body defense mechanisms.
- The skin has two layers. The outermost layer, or epidermis, is composed of epithelial cells that die and wear away. The dermis, just below, is a much thicker, nondividing layer composed of connective tissue and containing nerves, blood vessels, and glands. Below the dermis is the hypodermis, a layer of loose connective tissue that anchors the skin to underlying tissues.
- The epidermis is a renewing barrier. Cells produced in the deepest layer are pushed toward the skin surface, flattening and dying as they move away from the blood supply of the dermis and replace their cytoplasmic contents with keratin.
- Skin color is partially determined by melanin, a pigment released by melanocytes at the base of the epidermis and taken up by neighboring cells on their way to the surface. Blood flow and blood oxygen content also influence skin color.
- Hair is a derivative of skin. The primary function of hair is protection.
- Nails are modified skin tissue hardened by keratin. They protect the tips of our fingers and toes and help us grasp and manipulate small objects.
- Oil and sweat glands are derivatives of skin. Sebum, the oily substance secreted by oil glands, lubricates the skin and hair, prevents desiccation, and inhibits the growth of certain bacteria.

Homeostasis (pp. 86–89)

- Homeostasis is the relative internal constancy maintained at all levels of body organization. It is a dynamic state, with small fluctuations occurring around a set point, and is sustained primarily through negative feedback mechanisms.
- Homeostatic mechanisms consist of receptors, a control center, and effectors.

recognizing key terms

tissue *p. 71*
epithelial tissue *p. 71*
connective tissue *p. 71*
muscle tissue *p. 71*
nervous tissue *p. 71*
basement membrane *p. 71*
squamous epithelium *p. 71*
cuboidal epithelium *p. 71*
columnar epithelium *p. 71*
gland *p. 71*
exocrine gland *p. 71*
endocrine gland *p. 71*
matrix *p. 73*

ground substance *p. 73*
collagen fibers *p. 73*
elastic fibers *p. 73*
reticular fibers *p. 73*
fibroblast *p. 73*
loose connective tissue *p. 73*
areolar connective tissue *p. 73*
adipose tissue *p. 75*
dense connective tissue *p. 75*
cartilage *p. 75*
bone *p. 75*
blood *p. 75*
skeletal muscle tissue *p. 75*

cardiac muscle tissue *p. 75*
smooth muscle tissue *p. 75*
neurons *p. 76*
neuroglia *p. 77*
tight junction *p. 77*
adhesion junction *p. 77*
gap junction *p. 77*
organ *p. 79*
organ system *p. 79*
mucous membrane *p. 79*
serous membrane *p. 79*
synovial membrane *p. 79*

cutaneous membrane *p. 79*
integumentary system *p. 79*
epidermis *p. 80*
dermis *p. 80*
hypodermis *p. 82*
melanin *p. 82*
melanocyte *p. 82*
oil gland *p. 86*
sweat gland *p. 86*
homeostasis *p. 86*
negative feedback mechanism
p. 86

reviewing the concepts

1. What are the four types of tissue found in the human body? *p. 71*
2. Contrast the organization of epithelial and connective tissues. How are differences in the matrix of different types of connective tissue related to their functions? *pp. 71, 73–75*
3. Why does bone heal more rapidly than cartilage? *p. 75*
4. What type of tissue is blood? *p. 75*
5. Contrast skeletal, cardiac, and smooth muscle with respect to structure and function. *pp. 75–76*
6. What types of cells are found in nervous tissue? What are their functions? *pp. 76–77*
7. List the functions of the integumentary system. *pp. 79–80*
8. Describe the roles of pigments and blood flow in determining skin color. *pp. 82, 84*
9. What causes goose bumps? *p. 84*
10. What are oil glands? *p. 86*
11. Describe the functions of the sweat glands. *p. 86*
12. What is homeostasis? *p. 86*
13. Describe the body's homeostatic mechanisms for raising and lowering core body temperature. *pp. 86–89*

14. The four basic tissue types in the body are
    a. simple, cuboidal, squamous, columnar.
    b. neural, epithelial, muscle, connective.
    c. blood, nerves, bone, cartilage.
    d. fat, cartilage, muscle, neural.
15. The lining of the intestine is composed primarily of _____ cells.
    a. epithelial
    b. muscle
    c. connective tissue
    d. nerve
16. Cells that form disks that cushion the vertebrae are
    a. bone.
    b. muscle.
    c. epithelium.
    d. cartilage.
17. The mineral that makes bone hard is _____.
18. The maintenance of body processes within a relatively constant range is called _____.

applying the concepts

1. Thor, a ski champion at his college, tore the cartilage in his knee in a ski accident. He asked the doctor if he would be ready to compete in a month. Why would you expect the doctor's answer to be "No"?
2. Hannah has the flu. As her fever rises, she gets the chills. She shivers and covers herself in extra blankets. She takes some acetaminophen and her fever breaks. As her body temperature returns to normal, she throws off the blankets, looks flushed, and perspires. Use the mechanisms of body temperature control to explain what is happening as Hannah's fever rises and falls.
3. Ehlers-Danlos syndrome (EDS) is a group of disorders caused by defects in genes that disrupt the production of collagen, which is a chief component of connective tissue. Explain why symptoms of EDS include joints that extend beyond their normal range and stretchy, saggy skin.

becoming information literate

Prepare a brochure or other presentation explaining ways to avoid skin cancer. Use at least three reliable sources (books, journals, websites). List each source you considered, and explain why you chose the three sources you used.

5

The Skeletal System

The 206 bones of the human body provide support against gravity and protect internal organs. The joints, places where bones meet, determine the type of movement that is possible.

Aimee was excited to be on a vacation with her sister and friends in Colorado. She'd never gone snowboarding outside of Vermont before, and the mountains there were just hills compared to the Rockies. The first day on the mountain, Aimee stepped off the chairlift and took in the view. She watched the tall form of her sister gliding down the trail ahead of her, then took a deep breath and headed down the slope. The weather was perfect, the snow was fresh powder, and her ride seemed to last forever.

Although Aimee wasn't thinking about her skeletal system as she sped down the mountain, she had taken precautions to protect it. She's experienced enough to fall back on her elbows instead of her hands if she loses her balance, but she was wearing wrist guards as a precaution anyway. Her sister had sprained her wrist on a trail last year, so Aimee knew how common it is for a snowboarder to hurt her wrist by instinctively stretching out a hand to break the fall. Indeed, emergency personnel have named this mechanism FOOSH (for Fall Onto Out Stretched Hand). Aimee also knew that it would be easy to get a concussion if she fell and hit her head. Her skull protects her brain at all times, but in case of the extra trauma of a high-speed fall, she wore a helmet while snowboarding.

Aimee could whoosh down the mountain largely due to the structure of her bones, which support her against gravity, and her joints, which allow her to shift position to maintain her balance.

In reading about the structure and properties of bone in this chapter, you may be surprised to learn that bone is a dynamic, living tissue and to discover the number of functions our skeletal system performs. In considering how bones grow, we will learn a few of the reasons why Aimee is shorter than her sister.

Bone Functions

The **skeleton** is a framework of bones and cartilage that performs the following functions for the body:

1. **Support.** It provides a rigid framework that supports soft tissues. The leg bones and backbone hold our bodies upright, and the pelvic girdle supports the abdominal organs.
2. **Movement.** It provides places of attachment for muscles. Contraction of muscles allows bones to move at joints.
3. **Protection.** It shields our internal organs, such as the heart and lungs, which are enclosed within the chest cavity, and the brain, which lies within the skull.
4. **Storage of minerals.** It stores minerals, particularly calcium and phosphorus, that can be released to the rest of the body when needed.
5. **Storage of fat.** It stores energy-rich fat in yellow bone marrow (the soft tissue within some bones). The fat can be metabolized when the energy is needed.
6. **Blood cell production.** It produces blood cells in the red marrow of certain bones.

Bone Structure

The 206 bones of the human body come in a range of sizes and a variety of shapes. Most bones contain both compact tissue and spongy tissue in proportions that depend on the bone's size and shape.

Compact bone is very dense, with few internal spaces (Figure **5.1**). It forms most of the shaft of long bones, such as those of the arms and legs. Compact bone is what you see when you look at the outside of any bone. In the body, compact bone (except for the joint surfaces) is covered by a glovelike membrane, the **periosteum**, that nourishes the bone. The periosteum contains blood vessels and nerves as well as cells that function in bone growth and repair. The blood vessels pass through the periosteum and extend into the underlying bone. When a bone is bruised or fractured, most of the pain results from injury to the periosteum.

Spongy bone is a latticework of tiny beams and thin plates of bone with open areas between. This internal network braces the bone from within. Spongy bone is largely found in small, flat bones, such as most of the bones of the skull, and in the heads (enlarged ends) and near the ends of the shafts of long bones (refer to Figure 5.1). Some of the spongy bone in adults (for example, in the ribs, pelvis, backbone, skull, sternum, and long-bone ends) is filled with **red marrow**, where blood cells form. The cavity in the shaft of adult long bones is filled with **yellow marrow**, a fatty tissue used for energy storage.

Bone as a Living Tissue

Compact bone is highly organized living tissue containing a microscopic, repeating structural unit called an **osteon** (shown in Figure 5.1). Each osteon consists of mature bone cells, called **osteocytes** (*osteo*, bone; *cyte*, cell), arranged in concentric rings around a central canal. Each osteocyte lies within a tiny cavity called a **lacuna** in the hardened matrix. Tiny canals connect nearby lacunae and eventually connect with the central canal. Similarly, the osteocytes have projections that extend through the tiny canals to touch neighboring cells. Nutrients, oxygen, and wastes pass from cell to cell, traveling to or from the blood vessels in the central canal.

As noted, bone is a living tissue. But its most noticeable characteristics result from its nonliving component, the solid matrix. Secreted by the osteocytes, the matrix makes bone both hard and resilient. The hardness of the matrix comes from mineral salts, primarily calcium and phosphorus. The resilience comes from strands of the strong, elastic protein collagen that are woven throughout the matrix. Without the calcium and phosphorus salts, bone would be rubbery and flexible like a garden hose. Without the collagen, bone would be brittle and crumbly like chalk. In some disorders, bones do bend, causing bowlegs. An example is rickets, in which the amount of calcium salts in the bones is greatly reduced.

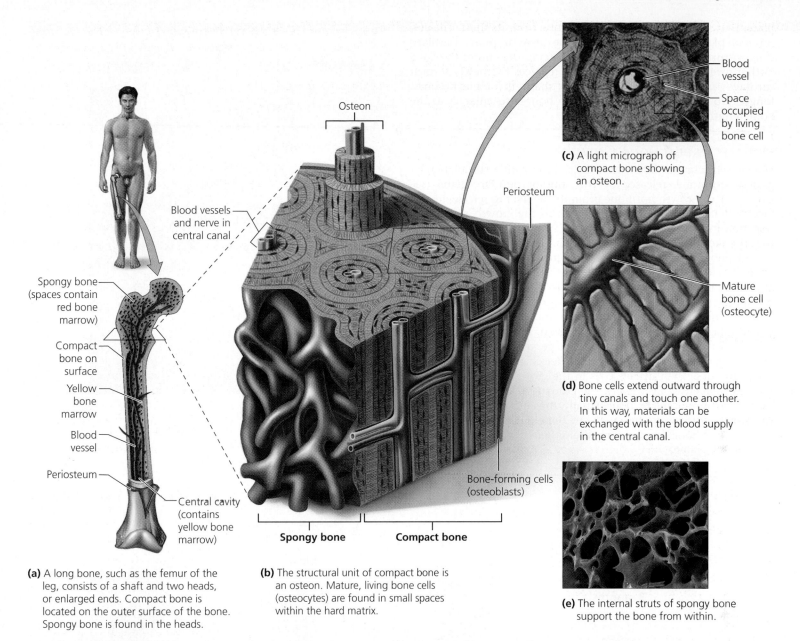

Osteon

Blood vessels
and nerve in
central canal

Spongy bone
(spaces contain
red bone
marrow)

Compact
bone on
surface

Yellow
bone
marrow

Blood
vessel

Periosteum

Central cavity
(contains
yellow bone
marrow)

Periosteum

Spongy bone

Compact bone

Bone-forming cells
(osteoblasts)

Blood
vessel

Space
occupied
by living
bone cell

(c) A light micrograph of
compact bone showing
an osteon.

Mature
bone cell
(osteocyte)

(d) Bone cells extend outward through
tiny canals and touch one another.
In this way, materials can be
exchanged with the blood supply
in the central canal.

(a) A long bone, such as the femur of the
leg, consists of a shaft and two heads,
or enlarged ends. Compact bone is
located on the outer surface of the bone.
Spongy bone is found in the heads.

(b) The structural unit of compact bone is
an osteon. Mature, living bone cells
(osteocytes) are found in small spaces
within the hard matrix.

(e) The internal struts of spongy bone
support the bone from within.

FIGURE 5.1 The structure of bone

stop and think

Strontium-90 is a radioactive substance that enters the atmosphere after
atomic explosions. Humans may ingest it in milk from cows that grazed
on contaminated grass. The strontium-90 can then replace calcium in bone,
killing nearby cells or altering their genetic information. Explain why exposure
to strontium-90 can lead not just to bone cancer but also to disruption of
blood cell formation.

Cartilage Model

During human embryonic development, most of the skeleton is
first formed of cartilage, a strong yet flexible connective tissue
(Figure **5.2**). Unlike mature bone cells, which cannot divide
because they are enclosed in a solid matrix, cartilage cells are able
to divide and multiply quickly. Thus, the cartilage model can grow
as rapidly as the fetus does. Beginning in the third month and
continuing through prenatal development, the cartilage is gradually replaced by bone.

The transformation from cartilage to a mature long bone,
such as an arm or leg bone, begins with the formation of a collar
of bone around the shaft of the cartilaginous model. The collar is
produced by bone-forming cells called **osteoblasts** (*osteo*, bone;
blast, beginning or bud). Osteoblasts produce the matrix of bone
around the shaft by secreting collagen (as well as other organic
materials) and then depositing calcium salts on it. The bony collar
supports the shaft as the cartilage within it breaks down, leaving
the marrow cavity. Blood vessels then carry osteoblasts into the
bone cavity, which in turn fill the cavity with spongy bone. Unlike cartilage, osteoblasts cannot undergo cell division. Once osteoblasts form the matrix around themselves, they are called
osteocytes, which, as we have seen, are mature bone cells and the
principal cells in bone tissue.

Near the time of birth, bone growth centers form in the ends
of long bones, and spongy bone begins to fill them. Two kinds of
structures made of cartilage will remain. One is a cap of cartilage
over each end of the bone, where one bone rubs against another
in a joint. The second is a plate of cartilage, called an epiphyseal

plate, that separates each end of the bone from its shaft. The epiphyseal plate is commonly called the **growth plate**. Cartilage cells within the growth plate divide, forcing the end of the bone farther away from the shaft. As bone replaces the newly formed cartilage in the region closer to the shaft, the bone becomes longer. Note that the diameter of the bone also enlarges as the bone lengthens (Figure **5.3**).

Hormones and Bone Growth

During childhood, bone growth is powerfully stimulated by growth hormone, released by the anterior pituitary gland (see Chapter 10). Growth hormone prompts the liver to release growth factors that produce a surge of growth in the growth plate. Thyroid hormones modify the activity of growth hormone to ensure that the skeleton grows with the proper proportions.

At puberty, many children experience a growth spurt during which the length of pant legs seems to shrink almost weekly. These dramatic changes are orchestrated by the increasing levels of sex hormones (testosterone and estrogen) produced during puberty. Initially the sex hormones stimulate the cartilage cells of the growth plates into a frenzy of cell division. But this growth generally stops toward the end of the teenage years (about age 18 in females and 21 in males) because of later changes initiated by the sex hormones. The cartilage cells in the growth plates start dividing less frequently. Eventually, the growth plates become thinner as cartilage is replaced by bone. Finally, the ends of the bone where the growth plates were fuse with the bone in the shaft. Note that even though bones can no longer lengthen at this stage, they can continue to widen.

Q *It is recommended that young adult women consume 1100 to 1300 mg of calcium each day, but that requirement doubles during pregnancy. Explain why.*

FIGURE 5.2 The fetal skeleton is first made of cartilage and gradually replaced by bone. This image shows the cartilaginous model of the skeleton of a 16-week-old human fetus. The darker areas of this skeleton are regions that have already been replaced with bone.

A *Calcium is needed for replacing the cartilage with bone in the skeleton of the fetus.*

FIGURE 5.3 Steps of bone formation in long and short bones, from an embryo into childhood

We have considered the mechanism by which long bones grow and the role of growth hormone in that process. Why would it be ineffective for a short, middle-aged person to be treated with growth hormone to stimulate growth?

The Role of Fibroblasts and Osteoblasts in Repairing Bone Fractures

Despite their great strength, bones occasionally break. Fortunately, bone tissue can heal. When a bone breaks, the first thing that happens is bleeding from blood vessels in the bone and periosteum, followed by formation of a clot (hematoma) at the break (Figure **5.4**). Within a few days, connective tissue cells called fibroblasts grow inward from the periosteum and invade the clot. The fibroblasts secrete collagen fibers that form a mass called a *callus*, which links the broken surfaces of the bone. Some of the fibroblasts then transform into cartilage-producing cells that secrete cartilage into the callus.

Next, osteoblasts from the periosteum invade the callus and begin to transform the newly deposited cartilage into new bone material, changing it into a bony callus. During this transformation, the bony callus becomes thicker than the undamaged part of the bone and protrudes from it. In time, however, the extra material will be broken down, and the healed part of the bone returns to normal size.

Bone Remodeling

Even after reaching our full height, we continue to undergo a lifelong process of bone deposition and absorption called **remodeling**. Bone remodeling keeps bones strong by repairing tiny cracks in bones, such as might occur if you jump from a high place. We have seen that bone is deposited by osteoblasts. Another kind of bone cell, called an **osteoclast**, breaks down bone, releasing calcium and other minerals that are reabsorbed by the body. Thus, bone remodeling is also a mechanism for regulating blood calcium levels, which is important because calcium plays a role in the functioning of nerves and muscles as well as blood clotting.

Two hormones, calcitonin and parathyroid hormone, play an important part in both the control of bone remodeling and the regulation of blood levels of calcium. When blood levels of calcium are high, as might occur after a meal, the hormone **calcitonin**, which is released from the thyroid gland, removes calcium from the blood and causes it to be stored in bone. Calcitonin brings about these effects by stimulating the activities of osteoblasts while inhibiting those of osteoclasts. In contrast, when blood calcium levels are low, **parathyroid hormone (PTH)**, which is released by the parathyroid glands found embedded in the tissues of the thyroid gland, causes calcium to be released from bone and reabsorbed into the blood. PTH accomplishes this by stimulating the activities of osteoclasts. The interplay of these two hormones keeps blood calcium levels fairly steady. (The regulation of blood calcium levels is discussed in more detail in Chapter 10.)

In women, estrogen also plays a role in bone remodeling. It promotes the absorption of calcium from the digestive system, stimulates bone formation, and impairs the ability of osteoclasts to break down bone.

During bone remodeling, new bone forms along the lines of stress on the bone. Bone forms in response to stress and gets absorbed when it is not stressed. Weight-bearing exercise, such as walking or jogging, thickens the layer of compact bone tissue, leading to a stronger bone. Bones that are used frequently may actually change shape. For example, continual practice may enlarge the knuckles of pianists and the big toes of ballet dancers. On the other hand, a few weeks without stress can cause a bone to lose nearly a third of its mass. This is a concern for astronauts living in the weightless environment of space as well as for the person right here on Earth who is using crutches with a leg in a cast.

If the breakdown process occurs faster than the deposition of new tissue, a bone becomes weak and easy to break. This imbalance occurs in **osteoporosis**, a condition in which there is a progressive loss in bone density. (See the Health Issue essay, *Osteoporosis: Fragility and Aging.*) Now that we are familiar with

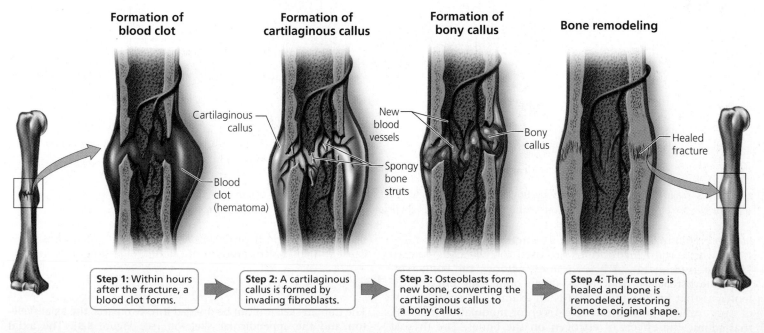

FIGURE 5.4 The progress of healing in a bone

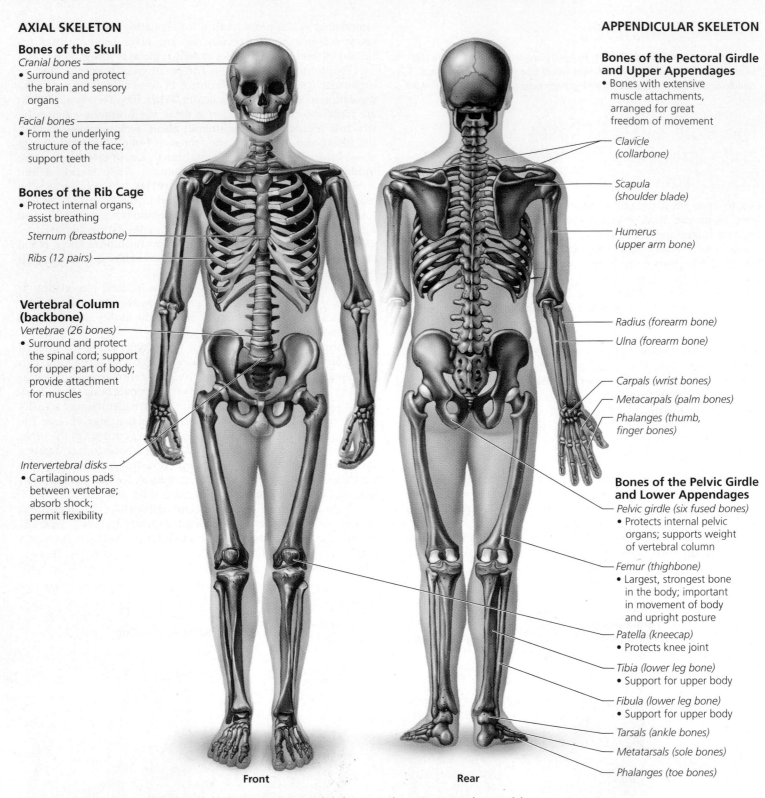

AXIAL SKELETON

Bones of the Skull
Cranial bones
- Surround and protect the brain and sensory organs

Facial bones
- Form the underlying structure of the face; support teeth

Bones of the Rib Cage
- Protect internal organs, assist breathing

Sternum (breastbone)

Ribs (12 pairs)

Vertebral Column (backbone)
Vertebrae (26 bones)
- Surround and protect the spinal cord; support for upper part of body; provide attachment for muscles

Intervertebral disks
- Cartilaginous pads between vertebrae; absorb shock; permit flexibility

APPENDICULAR SKELETON

Bones of the Pectoral Girdle and Upper Appendages
- Bones with extensive muscle attachments, arranged for great freedom of movement

Clavicle (collarbone)

Scapula (shoulder blade)

Humerus (upper arm bone)

Radius (forearm bone)

Ulna (forearm bone)

Carpals (wrist bones)

Metacarpals (palm bones)

Phalanges (thumb, finger bones)

Bones of the Pelvic Girdle and Lower Appendages
Pelvic girdle (six fused bones)
- Protects internal pelvic organs; supports weight of vertebral column

Femur (thighbone)
- Largest, strongest bone in the body; important in movement of body and upright posture

Patella (kneecap)
- Protects knee joint

Tibia (lower leg bone)
- Support for upper body

Fibula (lower leg bone)
- Support for upper body

Tarsals (ankle bones)

Metatarsals (sole bones)

Phalanges (toe bones)

Front

Rear

FIGURE 5.5 Major bones of the human body. Bones of the axial skeleton are shown in orange; bones of the appendicular skeleton are shown in light brown. Cartilage is shown in light purple.

factors regulating bone growth and remodeling, we can understand why certain medications are used to treat osteoporosis. The bisphosphonates, such as Fosamax, Actonel, and Boniva, inhibit the osteoclasts that break down bone, but not the osteoblasts that build bone. Evista is an example of another class of drug, called selective estrogen receptor modulators (SERMs), that mimic the effects of estrogen on the bones. The thyroid hormone calcitonin can also be used to treat osteoporosis, because it increases the amount of calcium deposited in bones.

Axial Skeleton

The human skeleton can be divided into two parts: the axial skeleton and the appendicular skeleton (see Figure **5.5**). The **axial**

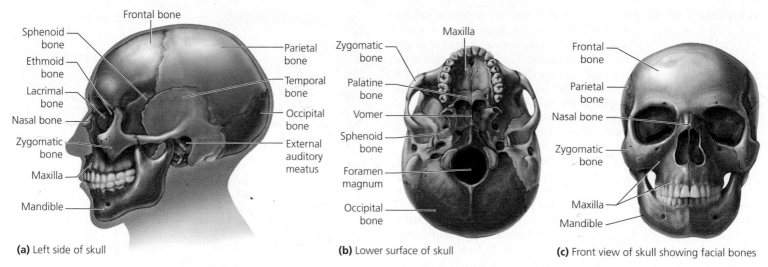

(a) Left side of skull

(b) Lower surface of skull

(c) Front view of skull showing facial bones

FIGURE 5.6 Major bones of the skull and face

skeleton (shown here in orange) includes the skull, the vertebral column (backbone), and the bones of the chest region (sternum and rib cage). The **appendicular skeleton** (shown in light brown) includes the pectoral girdle (shoulders), the pelvic girdle (pelvis), and the limbs (arms and legs).

In general, the axial skeleton protects and supports our internal organs. We will focus on only the major bones of the 80 that make up this portion of the skeleton, beginning with the bones of the skull.

Skull

The *skull* is the most complex bony structure in the body (Figure **5.6**). Its principal divisions are the cranium and the face. Several bones of the skull contain air spaces called *sinuses*, which make the head lighter in weight and serve as resonating chambers for the voice, as discussed in Chapter 14.

The cranial bones

The *cranium* protects the brain, houses the structures of hearing, and provides attachment sites for the muscles of the head and neck. It is formed from eight (or sometimes more) flat bones. The single *frontal bone* forms the forehead and the front of the brain case. Behind it, extending from either side of the midline, the two *parietal bones* form the top and sides of the skull. The *occipital bone* lies at the back of the head and surrounds the *foramen magnum*, the opening through which the spinal cord passes.

Before and shortly after birth, the bones of the cranium are connected by membranous areas called the *fontanels*, often referred to as soft spots. During birth, the fontanels allow the skull to be compressed, easing the passage of the head through the birth canal. The fontanels also accommodate the rapid enlargement of the brain during fetal growth and infancy (Figure **5.7**). They are replaced by bone by the age of 2 years.

The cranium also contains the *temporal bones*, part of which form what we think of as our temples. The *sphenoid bone*, with its bow-tie shape, forms the cranium's floor. The *ethmoid bone*, the smallest bone in the cranium, separates the cranial cavity from the nasal cavity. The olfactory nerves from the nasal cavity, which are responsible for our sense of smell, communicate with the brain through tiny holes in the ethmoid.

Facial bones

The 14 bones of the face (Figure 5.6c) support several sensory structures and serve as attachments for most facial muscles.

The *nasal bones* form the bridge of the nose. They are paired and fused at the midline. Inside the nose, a partition called the *nasal septum* (composed of the *vomer* and part of the ethmoid bone) divides the left and right chambers of the nasal cavity.

Cheekbones are formed largely from the paired *zygomatic bones*. Flat areas of these bones form part of the bottom of the eye sockets. Each zygomatic bone has an extension that joins with an extension from the temporal bone to form the *zygomatic arch* (the "cheekbone").

The smallest facial bones are the two *lacrimal bones*, located at the inner corners of the eyes, near the nose. A duct passes through each lacrimal bone and drains tears from the eyes into the nasal chambers; this connection explains why our nose runs when we cry.

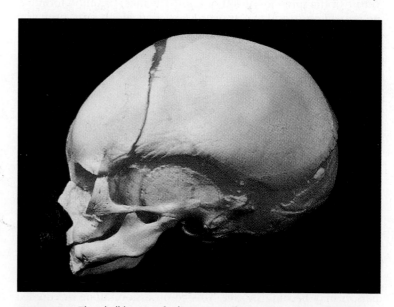

FIGURE 5.7 The skull bones of a human newborn are not fused but are instead connected by fibrous connective tissue. These "soft spots" allow the skull bones to move during the birth process, easing the passage of the skull through the birth canal. By 2 years of age, the child's soft spots have been replaced by bone.

The jaw is formed by two pairs of bones, the maxillae and the pair that forms the mandible. The *maxillae* form the upper jaw. Most of the other facial bones are joined to them, giving the upper jaw an important role in facial structure. The maxillae also form part of the hard palate, or roof of the mouth, the rest of which is formed by the two *palatine bones* that lie behind. When the maxillae fail to fuse to one another at the midline of the face below the nasal septum, the mouth cavity and nasal cavity do not fully separate, and a cleft palate results. This condition is easily corrected by surgery.

The lower jaw, called the *mandible*, is also formed from two bones connected at the midline. The mandible is connected to the skull at the temporal bone, forming a hinge called the *temporomandibular joint.* (Joints are discussed later in this chapter.) This joint allows the mouth to open and close. Emotional stress causes some people to clench or grind their teeth, sometimes unconsciously. This clenching can cause physical stress on the temporomandibular joint, causing headaches, toothaches, or even earaches. The condition is known as temporomandibular joint (or TMJ) syndrome.

Vertebral Column

The **vertebral column**, known more familiarly as the backbone or spine, is a series of bones through which the spinal cord passes as it descends down the back (Figure **5.8**). Each of these bones is called a **vertebra**. The vertebrae (plural of vertebra) are classified according to where they lie along the vertebral column. The vertebral column includes 26 vertebrae, organized as follows:

- 7 *cervical* (neck) vertebrae (C1–C7)
- 12 *thoracic* (chest) vertebrae (T1–T12)
- 5 *lumbar* (lower back) vertebrae (L1–L5)
- 1 *sacrum* (formed by the fusion of five *sacral vertebrae*)
- 1 *coccyx* (or tailbone, formed by fusion of four vertebrae)

Scoliosis, which means "twisted disease," is an abnormal curvature of the spine to the left or right. The most common form has no known cause and affects over 1.5 million adolescents, primarily females. It usually begins during, and progresses through, the adolescent growth spurt. Treatment, if needed, may consist of a brace or surgery to straighten the spine.

The fusion of the sacral vertebrae into a single sacrum gives additional strength to the backbone in the region where the sacrum joins the pelvic girdle. This reinforcement is necessary because of the great stress placed on the sacrum by the weight of the vertebral column and the powerful movements of the leg. The coccyx, on the other hand, serves no function and is regarded as a vestigial tail (*vestigial* means "an evolutionary relic") whose bones may have joined as a side effect of growth without movement. (The upper part of the coccyx, however, is supplied with nerves and can be extremely painful when injured.)

Above the sacrum, the vertebrae are separated from one another by **intervertebral disks**, pads of fibrocartilage that help cushion the bones of the vertebral column. The smooth, lubricated surfaces of these disks help give the column flexibility. As the intervertebral disks become compressed over the years, the person may become shorter. This compression, alone or coupled with osteoporosis, can have a pronounced effect on an aging person's height.

Excessive pressure on the disks, as might occur during improper lifting, can cause various problems. The term *slipped disk* is a misnomer, because a disk doesn't actually move out of place.

FIGURE 5.8 A side view of the vertebral column

Cervical vertebrae (7)

Thoracic vertebrae (12)

Lumbar vertebrae (5)

Sacrum (5 fused)

Coccyx (4 fused)

Intervertebral disks

Instead, it bulges. If a disk bulges inward, it can press against the spinal cord, interfering with muscle control and perception of incoming stimuli. On the other hand, a disk that presses outward against a spinal nerve branching from the spinal cord can be a source of great pain. The sciatic nerve, a large nerve that extends down the back of the leg, is one of the nerves most frequently affected in this way. Sciatica, the resulting inflammation, can be cripplingly painful.

Lower back pain is a particularly mysterious human ailment that accounts for more missed workdays than does any medical problem besides colds. The source of the pain is notoriously difficult to pinpoint. A person with a slipped disk in the region may or may not have pain, whereas a person whose back looks perfectly normal may complain of terrible pain. Part of the diagnostic problem seems to be that the pain may originate solely from muscle rather than bone, and muscles do not show up on x-rays. Some cases may occur because of weak abdominal muscles that cannot counteract the pull of the powerful back muscles and therefore cause the vertebrae to misalign.

Rib Cage

Twelve pairs of ribs attach at the back of the rib cage to the thoracic vertebrae (Figure **5.9**). At the front, the upper 10 pairs of ribs are attached by cartilage either directly or indirectly to the *sternum* (breastbone). Their flexibility permits the ribs to take some blows without breaking and to move during breathing. The last two pairs of ribs do not attach to the sternum and are called floating ribs (although they *are* attached at the back to the thoracic vertebrae).

Appendicular Skeleton

The appendicular skeleton consists of the pectoral and pelvic girdles and the attached limbs. A *girdle* is a skeletal structure that supports the arms, in the case of the **pectoral girdle**, or the legs, in the case of the **pelvic girdle**. The pectoral girdle connects the arms to the rib cage. The pelvic girdle connects the legs to the vertebral column, enabling the body to move from one place to another.

Pectoral Girdle

The pectoral girdle is composed of the *scapulae* (shoulder blades) and the *clavicles* (collarbones; Figure **5.10**). The clavicles are more curved in males than in females (one way to tell the sex of a skeleton), and each forms a relatively rigid bridge between a scapula and the sternum. One corner of the roughly triangular scapula has a socket into which fits one end of the *humerus*, the upper arm bone. The other end of the humerus joins, at the elbow, the *radius* and *ulna*—the bones of the lower arm, or forearm. The elbow is formed by the extension of the ulna past the junction with the humerus. The radius and ulna meet the eight *carpals* at the wrist, and these join with the five *metacarpals*, which are the bones of the hand. Each finger includes three *phalanges*, and the thumb includes two.

The carpal tunnel is a narrow opening through the carpal bones that form the wrist, and through it passes a nerve that controls sensations in the fingers and in some of the muscles in the hand. *Tendons*, bands of connective tissue that attach muscles to bones, also pass through the carpal tunnel. Repetitive motion in the hand or wrist can cause these tendons to become inflamed and press against the nerve, resulting in numbness or tingling in the hand and pain that may affect the wrist, hand, and fingers. This condition, known as carpal tunnel syndrome, has been experienced by barbers, cab drivers, and pianists. It is increasingly common as people spend more time operating computer keyboards and playing video games. The computer industry has responded by redesigning the keyboards and games. Employers have responded, too, by providing adjustable workstations and rest and exercise periods.

what would you do?

People who have developed carpal tunnel syndrome after endless hours of using keyboards and video game controllers are bringing a rash of lawsuits against computer manufacturers and video game designers. If you developed carpal tunnel syndrome from using a keyboard or video game, would you sue the manufacturer? What criteria would you use to decide?

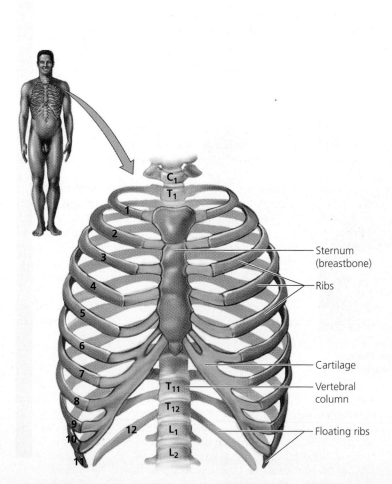

FIGURE 5.9 The bones of the rib cage. Cartilage is shown in light purple.

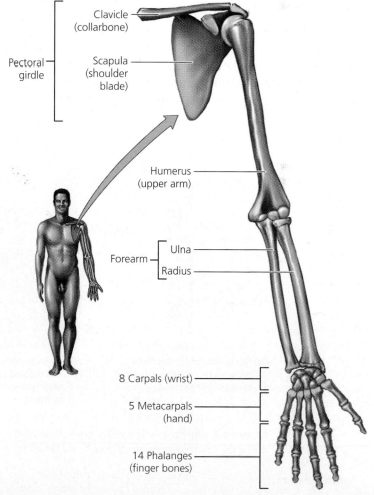

FIGURE 5.10 The pectoral girdle and arm

Osteoporosis: Fragility and Aging

About 20 million Americans, most of them elderly white women, suffer from osteoporosis—a decrease in bone density that occurs when the destruction of bone outpaces the formation of new bone during bone remodeling. The net destruction causes bones to become thin, brittle, and susceptible to fracture. A fall, blow, or lifting action that would not bruise a person with healthy bones could easily cause a bone to fracture in a person with severe osteoporosis.

Osteoporosis is sometimes very apparent. The afflicted person becomes hunched and shorter as the vertebrae lose mass and compress (Figure **5.A**). It can be startling to encounter a middle-aged or elderly person you haven't seen in a while and find that you suddenly tower above them!

As we have seen, bone remodeling occurs throughout life. Until we reach about age 35, bone is formed faster than it is broken down. Our bones are strongest and densest during our mid-thirties, after which they begin to lose density. Peak bone density is influenced by several factors, including sex, race, nutrition (dietary levels of calcium and vitamin D), exercise (we have seen the importance of weight-bearing exercise), and overall health. In men, bone mass is generally 30% higher than in women. The bones of African Americans are generally 10% denser than those of Caucasians and Asians.

Women are at greater risk for developing osteoporosis than are men. This difference is not just because women have less bone mass at peak but also because their rate of bone loss is accelerated for several years after menopause (the time in a woman's life when she stops producing mature eggs or menstruating). The acceleration occurs because menopause is followed by a sharp decline in the hormone estrogen, and estrogen stimulates bone formation and is important in the absorption of calcium from the intestines.

Other factors have been implicated in the onset of osteoporosis. For example, height is important. Short people are at greater risk, perhaps because they generally start with less bone mass. People with a good supply of body fat are less at risk because fat can be converted to estrogen. Heavy drinkers are at higher risk, because alcohol interferes with estrogen function.

Smoking is also bad for bones, because it can reduce estrogen levels. We have already noted that people who do not take in enough calcium, or who cannot absorb it because of insufficient vitamin D, have thinner bones because calcium is necessary for bone growth. (Calcium-rich foods include milk products as well as broccoli, spinach, shrimp, and soybean products.) Certain drugs, such as caffeine (a diuretic), tetracycline, and cortisone, can promote osteoporosis. Finally, as mentioned earlier, sedentary people have thinner bones than do active people.

The degree to which our bones will become weakened as we age depends largely on how dense they were at their peak. We can expect osteoporosis and other afflictions associated with aging to become more common as life expectancy increases. Thus, it would seem prudent for each of us to start an early program of prevention. Eat a diet rich in calcium and vitamin D. As adults, we need 1100 to 1300 mg of calcium each day; so eat 3 to 4 servings of foods rich in calcium and vitamin D. Engage in regular weight-bearing exercise, such as walking or jogging, for 30 minutes every day. Avoid drinking alcohol and caffeinated beverages, and don't smoke cigarettes.

Pressure

Vertebra
Disk
Fractures

Pressure

(a) Normal bending can place pressure on vertebrae that can cause small fractures.

(b) Osteoporosis can be seen in this colored x-ray image of vertebrae as the pink regions in the bones.

(c) A loss of height and a stooped posture result as the weakened bones of the vertebrae become compressed.

FIGURE 5.A Osteoporosis is a loss of bone density that occurs when bone destruction outpaces bone deposition during the continuous process of bone remodeling. The bones become brittle and are easily fractured.

Pelvic Girdle

The pelvic girdle is much more rigid than the pectoral girdle (as you know if you have ever tried to shrug your hips). The two *pelvic bones* that make up the pelvic girdle (Figure **5.11**) attach in back to the sacrum. The pelvic bones curve down and around to the front, where they join to a cartilage disk at the *pubic symphysis*. The male and female hips are easily distinguishable because the opening in the female is wider to facilitate childbirth.

The *femur*, or thighbone, rotates within a socket in the pelvis. At the knee, the femur joins the *tibia* (the shinbone). The *fibula* is a smaller bone running down the side of the tibia. The junction where the tibia joins the femur is covered by a *patella* (kneecap). At the ankle, the lower leg bones meet the *tarsals*, or ankle bones. These are connected to the *metatarsals*, or foot bones, which in turn are connected to the toe bones, called phalanges (as with finger bones).

Joints

Joints are the places where bones meet. They can be classified as fibrous, cartilaginous, or synovial, depending on their components and structure. Some joints allow no movement; others permit slight movement; and still others are freely movable.

Fibrous joints are held together by fibrous connective tissue. They have no joint cavity, and most fibrous joints do not permit movement. For example, the joints between the skull bones of an adult, called **sutures**, are considered to be immovable because the bones are interlocked and held together tightly by fibrous connective tissue (Figure **5.12**). In fact, the sutures can actually move ever so slightly. This ability is fortunate, because the movements serve as a shock absorber when you hit your head.

Cartilage, which is rather rigid, holds bones together in *cartilaginous joints*. Some cartilaginous joints are immovable, and others allow slight movement. We find cartilaginous joints between vertebrae; in the attachment of ribs to the sternum; and in the pubic symphysis, the joint between the two pelvic bones. In a pregnant woman, hormones loosen the cartilage of the pubic symphysis, allowing the pelvis to widen to ease childbirth.

Synovial Joints

Most of the joints of the body are freely movable **synovial joints**. Because of these joints, muscles can maneuver the body into thousands of positions. All synovial joints share certain common features. One is that the surfaces that move past one another in the joints have a thin layer of *cartilage*. The cartilage reduces friction, so the bones slide over one another without grating and grinding. In addition, synovial joints are surrounded by a two-layered joint capsule. The inner layer of the capsule, the *synovial membrane*, secretes viscous, clear fluid (synovial fluid) into the space, or *joint cavity*, between the two bones. The synovial fluid lubricates and cushions the joint. The outer layer of the capsule is continuous with the covering membranes of the bones forming the joint. The entire synovial joint is reinforced with **ligaments**, strong straps of connective tissue that hold the bones together, support the joint, and direct the movement of the bones.

- Pelvic bones
- Pelvis
- Pubic symphysis
- Femur (upper leg)
- Patella (kneecap)
- Tibia
- Fibula
- Lower leg
- 7 Tarsals (ankle)
- 5 Metatarsals (foot)
- 14 Phalanges (toe bones)

FIGURE 5.11 The pelvic girdle and leg

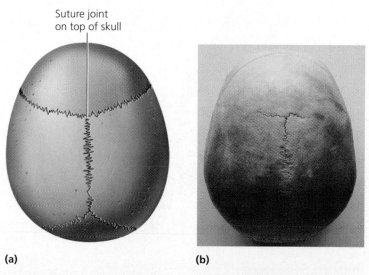

Suture joint on top of skull

(a)   **(b)**

FIGURE 5.12 The bones of the skull are joined by suture joints. (a) Top view of the skull. (b) Photograph of suture joints in an adult skull.

All synovial joints share these features but may differ in the type and range of motion they permit (Figure **5.13**). As the name implies, hinge joints, such as at the knee and elbow, resemble a hinge on a door in that they permit motion in only one plane. A ball-and-socket joint, such as the shoulder and hip, allows movement in all planes: the ball at the head of one bone fits into a socket on another bone. Notice that you can swing your arm around in a complete circle. Some of the ways that body parts move at synovial joints are shown in Figure **5.14**.

A **bursa** is a fluid-filled sac that cushions certain joints and reduces friction between tendons and ligaments.

A layer of **cartilage** on the articulating surfaces of the bones reduces friction as the bones move.

The **joint cavity** is filled with synovial fluid, which serves as a shock absorber and lubricant.

Femur

Fat pad

The **synovial membrane** forms the inner surface of the joint cavity and secretes synovial fluid.

Tibia

(a) Synovial joints, such as the knee shown here, permit a great range of movement.

Quadriceps tendon

Femur

Posterior cruciate ligament

Lateral collateral ligament

Anterior cruciate ligament

Medial collateral ligament

Patellar ligament

Fibula

Patella (kneecap)

Tibia

(b) Ligaments hold bones together, support the joint, and direct the movement of the bones.

FIGURE 5.13 The knee is a synovial joint.

Flexion
Motion that *decreases* the angle between the bones of the joint, bringing the bones closer together

Extension
Motion that *increases* the angle between the bones of the joint

Adduction
Movement of a body part *toward* the body midline

Abduction
Movement of a body part *away from* the body midline

Imaginary cone of movement

Rotation
Movement of a body part around it own axis

Circumduction
Movement of a body part in a wide circle so that the motion describes a cone

Humerus

Radius

Ulna

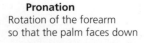

Supination
Rotation of the forearm so that the palm faces up

Pronation
Rotation of the forearm so that the palm faces down

FIGURE 5.14 Types of movement at synovial joints

Damage to Joints

Damage to a ligament is called a *sprain* and may range from slight, caused by overstretching, to serious, caused by tearing of the ligament. A torn ligament results in swelling and enough pain to inhibit movement. Sometimes, because ligaments are covered with a concentration of pain receptors that are very sensitive to stretching and swelling, the injury is not as severe as the pain would suggest. As with most musculoskeletal swelling, the initial treatment is likely to be an ice pack to reduce the swelling. Ice constricts underlying blood vessels and reduces bleeding. Bleeding would be stopped by the next day. Then, heat would be applied to dilate blood vessels, allowing blood to carry in the nutrients, oxygen, and anti-inflammatory chemicals that assist healing. Like tendons, ligaments have few blood vessels and therefore heal slowly.

A common knee injury among athletes, especially gymnasts and football and soccer players, is a tear in the *anterior cruciate ligament* (ACL; Figure **5.15**). Why is this ligament so vulnerable? When the knee is bent, the ACL acts as a restraining wire that restricts front-to-back twisting movement between the thighbone (femur) and the shinbone (tibia). An external blow to a bent knee—as may occur during a tackle or a hard landing—can stretch the ACL. If the force applied to the two bones is greater than the strength of the ligament, the ACL can tear.

In synovial joints and certain other locations where movement might cause friction between moving parts, the body has its own "ball bearings" in the form of fluid-filled sacs called **bursae** (singular, *bursa*; meaning "pouch or purse"). Bursae are lined with synovial membranes. They are found in places where skin rubs over bone as the joint moves and between tendons and bones, muscles and bones, and ligaments and bones.

Joint injury or repeated pressure can cause bursae to become inflamed and swell with excess fluid, a condition called bursitis (–*itis* means "an inflammation"). For example, the repetitive movement of throwing a baseball or swinging a tennis racket may cause bursitis in the elbow. Bursitis is characterized by intense pain that becomes worse when the joint is moved and that cannot be relieved by resting in any position. Nonetheless, bursitis is not serious and usually subsides on its own within a week or two. In severe cases, a physician may drain some of the excess fluid to remove the pressure.

Arthritis

Arthritis is a general term referring to joint inflammation. Some of the more than 100 kinds of arthritis are far more serious than others. *Osteoarthritis* is a degeneration of the surfaces of a joint, caused by wear and tear. Eventually the slippery cartilage at the ends of the affected bones begins to disintegrate until the bones themselves come into contact and grind against each other, causing intense pain and stiffness. Any joint surface that undergoes friction is bound to wear down, but osteoarthritis is most likely to occur in weight-bearing joints, such as the hip, knee, and spine. It is also occasionally seen in the finger joints or wrist.

Prevention is always better than treatment. One tip for preventing osteoarthritis is to control your weight to avoid overburdening your knees and hips. Another tip is to exercise. Lifting weights will strengthen the muscles that help support your joints. Stretching will give you a greater range of movement.

A far more threatening form of arthritis (and, unfortunately, one of the most common) is *rheumatoid arthritis*. Rheumatoid arthritis

FIGURE 5.15 A common sports injury is a tear in the anterior cruciate ligament of the knee.

FIGURE 5.16 Replacement prosthesis of the hip

is marked by inflammation of the synovial membrane. The resulting accumulation of synovial fluid in the joint causes swelling, pain, and stiffness. Eventually, the constant irritation can destroy the cartilage, which may then be replaced by fibrous connective tissue that further impedes joint movement.

Rheumatoid arthritis differs from other types of arthritis in that it is apparently an autoimmune disease. That is, the body mistakenly attacks its own synovial membranes just as it would some invasive foreign matter. Rheumatoid arthritis can vary in severity over time, but it is a permanent condition. It normally affects the joints of the fingers, wrist, knees, neck, ankles, and hips. Sometimes the only effective treatment is to replace the damaged joint with an artificial one (Figure **5.16**).

Bone Functions (p. 92)

- The skeleton is a framework of bone and cartilage that supports and protects the internal organs and has a role in movement. It also serves as a storage site for minerals (calcium and phosphorus) and fat. Blood cells are produced in the red marrow of certain bones.

Bone Structure (p. 92)

- Compact bone is dense bone tissue found on the outside of all bones. It is covered by the periosteum, a membrane that nourishes the bone cells. Spongy bone is a latticework of tiny, bony beams found in flat bones and near the knobby ends, or heads, of long bones.
- The shaft of an adult long bone has a cavity filled with fatty yellow marrow. The spongy bone of certain bones in adults is filled with red marrow.

Bone as a Living Tissue (pp. 92–94)

- The structural unit of bone, called an osteon, consists of a central canal surrounded by concentric circles made of bone cells (osteocytes) in a hard matrix. Cellular extensions of the osteocytes touch one another through tiny canals in the matrix, allowing exchange of materials between cells and the central canal. Bone matrix is hardened by calcium and phosphorous salts and strengthened by strands of collagen.
- In an embryo, most of the skeleton forms first as cartilage that is gradually replaced by bone. In the replacement process, osteoblasts form a bony collar around the shaft of the cartilaginous model. Next, cartilage within the shaft begins to break down and is replaced by bone, after which the cartilage in the heads (epiphyses) is replaced. Epiphyseal growth plates of cartilage remain and allow bones to grow in length until the person is fully grown.
- Bone growth is stimulated by growth hormone from the anterior pituitary gland. Sex hormones (estrogen and testosterone) initially stimulate growth, but later they cause the growth plates to disappear, and bones cease to lengthen.

The Role of Fibroblasts and Osteoblasts in Repairing Bone Fractures (p. 95)

- In bone-fracture repair, blood clot formation is followed by a cartilaginous callus that links the broken ends and is gradually replaced by bone.

Bone Remodeling (pp. 95–96)

- Bone is constantly being remodeled. Osteoblasts deposit new bone in response to stress, and osteoclasts break bone down when it is not stressed.

Axial Skeleton (pp. 96–98)

- The skeleton is described as consisting of two parts. One part, the axial skeleton, protects and supports internal organs; it includes the skull, backbone, rib cage, and sternum.

Appendicular Skeleton (pp. 99, 101)

- The other part, the appendicular skeleton, allows you to move from place to place; it includes the shoulders, pelvis, arms, and legs.

Joints (pp. 101–103)

- Joints, the places where bones meet, are classified by composition and degree of movement they allow. Some joints, such as the sutures between the skull bones, are considered to be immoveable.
- Synovial joints are freely movable. They have cartilage on the adjoining bone surfaces, are surrounded by a synovial cavity filled with synovial fluid, and are held together by ligaments.
- Damage to a ligament is called a sprain, which is often less serious than the pain.
- Arthritis is inflammation of a joint. Osteoarthritis occurs when the surface of a joint degenerates because of use. Rheumatoid arthritis is an autoimmune disease.

skeleton *p. 92*
compact bone *p. 92*
periosteum *p. 92*
spongy bone *p. 92*
red marrow *p. 92*
yellow marrow *p. 92*
osteon *p. 92*
osteocyte *p. 92*

lacuna *p. 92*
osteoblast *p. 93*
growth plate *p. 94*
remodeling *p. 95*
osteoclast *p. 95*
calcitonin *p. 95*
parathyroid hormone (PTH)
 p. 95

osteoporosis *p. 95*
axial skeleton *p. 96*
appendicular skeleton *p. 97*
vertebral column *p. 98*
vertebra *p. 98*
intervertebral disk *p. 98*
pectoral girdle *p. 99*
pelvic girdle *p. 99*

joint *p. 101*
sutures *p. 101*
synovial joint *p. 101*
ligament *p. 101*
bursae *p. 103*
arthritis *p. 103*

1. List six functions of the skeleton. *p. 92*
2. Compare compact and spongy bone. *p. 92*
3. Describe the structure of a long bone. Where are the yellow and red marrow found in adults? *p. 92*
4. Describe the structure of an osteon, and explain the function of osteocytes and the central canal. *p. 92*
5. Describe the formation of bone in a fetus. Explain how bone growth continues after birth. *pp. 93–94*
6. Explain how a bone heals after it has been fractured. *p. 95*
7. What is bone remodeling? Explain the role of osteoblasts and osteoclasts. How does stress on the bones affect remodeling? *pp. 95–96*

8. Describe the axial and appendicular parts of the skeleton. *pp. 96–99, 101*
9. Describe a synovial joint. *pp. 101–102*
10. The functional units of compact bone are called
    a. osteoblasts.
    b. striations.
    c. osteons.
    d. osteocytes.
11. Which of the following persons would be expected to have the *densest* bones?
    a. an elderly woman whose favorite pastime is knitting
    b. a 16-year-old female who swims regularly
    c. a 33-year-old male who loves to drink milk and plays basketball regularly
    d. a 50-year-old male workaholic with a desk job

12. The skull, vertebral column, sternum, and rib cage constitute the _____ skeleton.
13. Bone is hardened by the minerals _____ and _____.
14. The cells that form bone are called _____.
15. A _____ is the overstretching or tear in a ligament that may cause pain after the injury.

applying the concepts

1. Edith is a 64-year-old woman who has been confined to a wheelchair since she was 35 because of a car accident that left her legs paralyzed. Her leg bones are very thin and weak. Why?
2. Hannah and Becca are fraternal twins. They are both athletic. Hannah is a swimmer, and Becca is a runner. Which sister would have the densest bones?

3. A forensic scientist is examining skeletal remains that include a femur (thighbone) and a tibia (lower leg bone). By measuring the length of the bones, she determines that these leg bones could have belonged to a tall child or a short adult. What should the scientist look for to determine whether the bones were from a child or short adult?

becoming information literate

Mihoko is a 43-year-old woman with osteoporosis. It is uncommon for someone so young to have osteoporosis. Use reliable references to develop a plan for diagnosing the cause(s) of Mihoko's osteoporosis.

Develop a list of hypotheses for the cause. For each hypothesis, formulate a list of information you would need to know to test each hypothesis. What questions would you ask Mihoko? What medical tests would you want to perform? List each source you considered and explain why you chose the sources you used.

Additional questions can be found online at the Human Biology Place, www.humanbiology.com.

6

The Muscular System

We have about 700 skeletal muscles that are usually attached to bones. Our muscles contract to move our body parts, so we can make our impact on the world.

While hiking on the mountain trail, Michael felt exhilarated by the fresh breeze, the scent of pine needles, and the warm sun. He had been walking for about an hour, his mind finally freed of worries. Between the demands of his job, his courses at the community college, and the stress of a recent breakup with Heather, he hadn't had a decent night's sleep for weeks. This hike, he thought to himself, was the first real exercise he had had since the Heather debacle. The only problem at the moment was that he was getting uncomfortably thirsty because he had forgotten his water bottle. Deciding to head home, he changed direction and suddenly felt a sharp pain in his left calf. It felt as if the whole muscle had locked up in a severe cramp that prevented him from taking another step. He knew that he now had to stretch his leg gradually to work out the cramp. What he didn't realize was that the cramp was caused by the very problems that had just been passing through his mind: his fatigue (from insomnia), lack of regular exercise, and dehydration.

Fortunately, gentle stretching relieved the pain in a matter of minutes, and after a brief rest Michael was able to walk home.

In this chapter, we will explore muscle structure and the mechanism of contraction and learn why muscle contraction rarely results in a cramp. Then, we will see how nerves control contractions and study the energy sources that fuel muscle activity.

Function and Characteristics of Muscles

There are three kinds of muscles—*skeletal, cardiac,* and *smooth.* Each has distinct qualities and functions, but they all have four traits in common.

1. **Muscles are excitable.** They respond to stimuli.
2. **Muscles are contractile.** They have the ability to shorten (contract).
3. **Muscles are extensible.** They have the ability to stretch.
4. **Muscles are elastic.** They can return to their original length after being shortened or stretched.

This chapter focuses on skeletal muscle, the kind of muscle we usually think of when muscles are mentioned. Smooth and cardiac muscles are discussed in Chapters 4 and 12, respectively. Skeletal muscles allow you to smile with pleasure and scowl in anger. They allow you to move, some of us more gracefully than others. And they allow you to remain erect, maintaining your posture despite the pull of gravity. Besides these obvious functions of skeletal muscle, those forming the abdominal wall and the floor of the pelvic cavity support internal organs. Contraction of muscles also pushes against veins and lymphatic vessels, moving blood and lymph along. Importantly, contraction of skeletal muscles generates heat, which warms our bodies above most of the environmental temperatures we experience. If we get too warm, other mechanisms come into play to cool our bodies, as described in Chapter 4. Unlike cardiac and smooth muscle, skeletal muscle is under voluntary control—meaning we can contract it when we want to.

Skeletal Muscles Working in Pairs

Most muscles work in pairs or groups. Muscles that must contract at the same time to cause a certain movement are called *synergistic muscles.* Most muscles, however, are arranged in *antagonistic pairs* (Figure **6.1**), which produce a movement when one of the pair contracts and the other relaxes. When a muscle in an antagonistic

Origin of muscle: attachment of muscle to less moveable bone

The biceps contracts and pulls the forearm up, flexing the arm.

The relaxed triceps is stretched.

Insertion of muscle: attachment of muscle to more moveable bone

(a) Flexion

The triceps contracts and pulls the forearm down, extending the arm.

The relaxed biceps is stretched.

(b) Extension

FIGURE 6.1 Antagonistic action of the triceps and biceps muscles during flexion and extension. The origins and insertions of the muscles are shown.

Triceps brachii
• Straightens arm at elbow

Pectoralis major
• Flexes and rotates arm

Serratus anterior
• Helps raise arm, draws shoulder blade forward; useful in pushing

External oblique
• Assists in lateral twisting of body, compresses abdomen

Rectus abdominis
• Compresses abdomen and chest, bends backbone

Adductor longus
• Rotates thigh laterally, flexes thigh, draws thigh toward body

Sartorius
• Bends lower leg at knee, bends and rotates thigh at hip

Quadriceps femoris
• Flexes thigh at hips, extends leg at knee

Tibialis anterior
• Flexes foot toward knee

Biceps brachii
• Bends forearm at elbow, rotates hand

Deltoid
• Raises arm

Trapezius
• Raises, turns, and lowers the shoulder; turns head

Latissimus dorsi
• Rotates and draws arm backwards (toward the body); helps in climbing

Gluteus maximus
• Extends and rotates thigh when walking or climbing

Hamstring group
• Draws thigh backward, bends knee

Gastrocnemius
• Bends lower leg at knee, extends foot away from knee

(a) Front view   **(b)** Back view

FIGURE 6.2 Some major muscles of the body

pair contracts, it shortens and pulls on one of the bones that meet at a given joint, causing movement of the bone in one direction. Any time an antagonistic muscle contracts and pulls on a bone, its partner, which has an opposing action, must relax. For the bone to then move back to its former position, the first muscle must relax and the other muscle in the pair must contract, thus pulling the bone in the opposite direction. The biceps muscle (the muscle people like to show off), located on the top of the upper arm, co-operates in this way with the triceps muscle (the one we feel when we do push-ups), on the back of the arm. Contracting the biceps causes the arm to flex and bend at the elbow, but contracting the triceps causes the arm to extend and straighten at the elbow.

Most of the major muscles we use for locomotion, manipulation, and other voluntary movements are attached to bones. Each end of the muscle is attached to a bone by a **tendon**, which is a band of connective tissue. A muscle is often attached to two bones on opposite sides of a joint. The muscle's **origin** is the end attached to the bone that remains relatively stationary during a movement. The muscle's **insertion** is the end attached to the bone that moves. Thus, the bones act as levers in working with skeletal muscles to produce movement. The body has more than 600 skeletal muscles. The major ones—those most prominent in giving shape to the body—are shown in Figure **6.2**.

In the preceding description, we said that a contracting muscle pulls a bone. In actuality, the contraction of a muscle pulls on the tendon that connects that muscle to a bone. Excessive stress on a tendon can cause it to become inflamed, a condition called *tendinitis*. Most tendinitis is probably due to overuse, misuse (as when lifting improperly), or age. Unfortunately, tendons heal slowly because they are poorly supplied with blood vessels. The most effective treatment is rest: if it hurts, do not use it.

The terms *muscle pull*, *muscle strain*, and *muscle tear* are used almost interchangeably to describe damage to a muscle or its tendons caused by overstretching. This common sports injury may also include damage to small blood vessels in the muscle, causing bleeding and pain. Treatment includes applying ice to the injured area to reduce swelling and keeping the muscle stretched.

Contraction of Muscles

Skeletal muscle cells can be several centimeters long, which is enormously long compared to most of the body's other cells. Muscle cells in the thigh can be 30 cm (1 ft) in length. The fine structure of these cells provides numerous clues to the mechanism responsible for muscle contraction.

Skeletal muscle is also called **striated** (striped) **muscle**, because under the microscope, the muscle cells are seen to have pronounced bands that look like stripes (Figure **6.3**). The striations are caused by the orderly arrangement of many elongated **myofibrils**, which are specialized bundles of proteins within the muscle cell. Each myofibril contains two types of the long protein filaments called **myofilaments**: the thicker **myosin filaments** and a greater number of the thinner **actin filaments**. The bundles of myofilaments make up about 80% of the cell volume.

Along its length, each myofibril has tens of thousands of contractile units called **sarcomeres**. The ends of each sarcomere are marked by dark bands of protein, called *Z lines*. Within each sarcomere, the actin and myosin filaments are arranged in a specific manner. One end of each actin filament is attached to a Z line. Myosin filaments lie in the middle of the sarcomere, their ends partially overlapping with surrounding actin filaments. The degree of overlap increases when the muscle contracts.

Sliding Filament Model

According to the **sliding filament model** of muscle contraction, a muscle contracts when the actin filaments slide along the myosin filaments, increasing the degree of overlap between actin and myosin and thus shortening the sarcomere. When many sarcomeres shorten, the muscle as a whole contracts.

To understand the sliding of the actin and myosin filaments, let's look at their molecular structures. A thin, actin myofilament is made up of two chains of spherical actin molecules resembling two strings of beads twisted around each other to form a helix. A thick,

(a) A section of a skeletal muscle

Skeletal muscle consists of many bundles of muscle cells.

A muscle cell consists of many myofibrils.

A bundle of muscle cells is called a fascicle.

The striped (striated) appearance of a skeletal muscle cell is due to the regular arrangement of myofilaments.

(b) A light micrograph of a longitudinal view of skeletal muscle cells

Z line

One sarcomere

(c) A diagram and electron micrograph of a myofibril

Z line One sarcomere Z line

Actin

Myosin

(d) A sarcomere, the contractile unit of a skeletal muscle, contains actin and myosin myofilaments.

FIGURE 6.3 The structure of a skeletal muscle

myosin filament is composed of myosin molecules shaped like two-headed golf clubs. In a myosin filament, the "shafts" of several hundred myosin molecules lie along the filament's length, and the "heads" protrude along each end of the bundle in a spiral pattern.

(a) Sarcomere relaxed

(b) Sarcomere contracted

FIGURE 6.4 Each myofibril is packed with actin filaments and myosin filaments. When a muscle contracts, actin filaments slide past myosin filaments. Movements of the heads of myosin filaments pull actin filaments toward the center of a sarcomere.

The club-shaped *myosin heads* are the key to the movement of actin filaments and, therefore, to muscle contraction (Figure **6.4**).

The sliding filament model holds that muscle contraction results from the following cycle of interactions between myosin and actin (Figure **6.5**):

- **Resting sarcomere.** At the start of each cycle, the myosin heads have already split a molecule of adenosine triphosphate (ATP) to adenosine diphosphate (ADP) and inorganic phosphate (P_i). The energy released from splitting the ATP causes the myosin heads to swivel in a way that extends them toward the Z lines at the ends of the sarcomere. This step is analogous to cocking a pistol so it is poised and ready to fire.
- **Step 1: Cross-bridge attachment.** The myosin heads attach themselves to the nearest actin filament. When the myosin head is bound to an actin molecule, it acts as a bridge between the thick and thin filaments. For this reason, myosin heads are also called **cross-bridges**.
- **Step 2: Bending of myosin head (the power stroke).** Binding to actin causes the myosin heads to swing forcefully back to their bent positions. The actin filaments, still bound to the myosin heads, are therefore pulled toward the midline of the sarcomere. This so-called power stroke is analogous to pulling the trigger on a pistol. The ADP and inorganic phosphate then pop off of the myosin head.
- **Step 3: Cross-bridge detachment.** New ATP molecules now bind to the myosin heads, causing the myosin heads to disengage from the actin.

- **Step 4: Myosin reactivation.** The myosin heads split the ATP into ADP and P_i and store the energy, causing the contraction cycle to begin again.

This cycle of events is repeated hundreds of times in a second.

Calcium Ions and Regulatory Proteins

Muscle contractions are controlled by the availability of calcium ions. How? Muscle cells contain the proteins **troponin** and **tropomyosin**, which together form a troponin–tropomyosin complex (Figure **6.6**). During muscle *relaxation*, the actin–myosin-binding sites where the myosin heads would otherwise attach to the actin filaments are covered over by the troponin–tropomyosin complex. Contraction occurs when calcium ions enter the sarcomere and bind to troponin, causing it to change shape. This change causes tropomyosin to shift position, which pulls the tropomyosin molecule away from the myosin-binding sites on the actin. The exposed binding sites enable actin to bind to myosin.

Where do the calcium ions come from? Calcium ions are stored in the **sarcoplasmic reticulum**, an elaborate form of smooth endoplasmic reticulum found in muscle cells. The sarcoplasmic reticulum can be pictured as a sleeve of thick lace surrounding each myofibril in a muscle cell. (Recall that a myofibril is a bundle of actin and myosin.) Also scattered through the cell are a number of **transverse tubules** (T tubules), which are tiny, cylindrical inpocketings of the muscle cell's plasma membrane. The T tubules carry signals from motor neurons deep into the muscle cell to virtually every sarcomere.

As we have seen, it takes an ATP molecule to break the cross-bridges so that new ones may be formed. This dependency explains why muscles become stiff within a few hours after death, through a phenomenon known as *rigor mortis*. Soon after death, calcium ions begin to leak out of the sarcoplasmic reticulum, initiating muscle contraction. Muscle contraction will occur as long as ATP is present. However, after a person dies, ATP is no longer being produced and the supply runs out. Without ATP, cross-bridges cannot be broken, and within 3–4 hours after death the muscles becomes stiff. The muscles' proteins actin and myosin gradually break down, allowing the muscles to relax again after 2–3 days.

stop and think

How would the degree of rigor mortis help a forensic scientist determine the approximate time of death of a corpse?

Role of Nerves

The stimulus that ultimately leads to the release of calcium ions, and therefore to muscle contraction, is a nerve impulse from a motor neuron (described in Chapter 7). The junction between the tip of a motor neuron and a skeletal muscle cell is called a **neuromuscular junction**. When a nerve impulse reaches a neuromuscular junction, it causes the release of the chemical acetylcholine (a neurotransmitter) from small packets in the tip of the motor neuron. Acetylcholine then diffuses across a small gap onto the surface of the muscle cell, where it binds to special receptors on the muscle cell membrane. Acetylcholine causes changes in the membrane's permeability, thus creating an electrochemical message similar to a nerve impulse. The message travels along the muscle cell's plasma membrane, into the T tubules, and then to

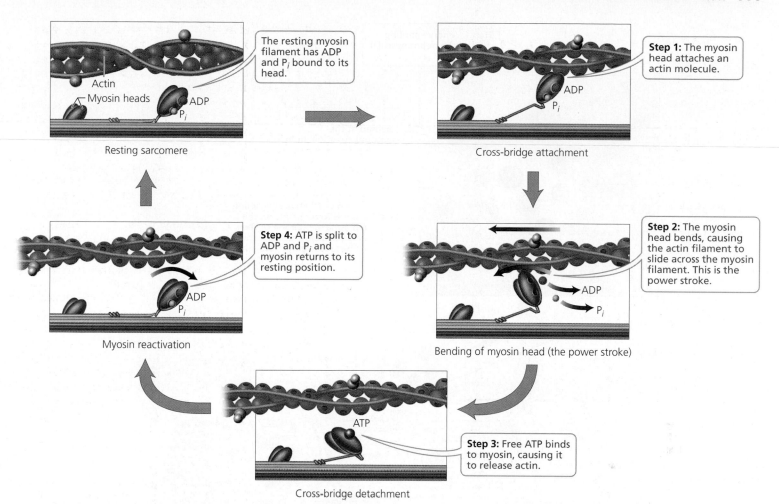

The resting myosin filament has ADP and P_i bound to its head.

Actin

Myosin heads — ADP P_i

Resting sarcomere

Step 1: The myosin head attaches an actin molecule.

ADP P_i

Cross-bridge attachment

Step 4: ATP is split to ADP and P_i and myosin returns to its resting position.

ADP P_i

Myosin reactivation

Step 2: The myosin head bends, causing the actin filament to slide across the myosin filament. This is the power stroke.

ADP P_i

Bending of myosin head (the power stroke)

ATP

Step 3: Free ATP binds to myosin, causing it to release actin.

Cross-bridge detachment

FIGURE 6.5 Sliding filament model of muscle contraction. (The regulatory proteins on the actin are described in the text.)

the sarcoplasmic reticulum, causing channels there to open and release calcium ions. The calcium ions then combine with troponin, the myosin-binding sites on actin are exposed, and the muscle contracts. This is the chain of events that must happen in order for you to absentmindedly scratch your head, and it happens a lot faster than it takes to describe.

When the nerve impulse stops, membrane pumps quickly clear the sarcomere of calcium ions, and the troponin–tropomyosin complexes move to where they again block the binding sites, causing the muscle to relax. The contraction of *other* muscles then stretches the sarcomere back to its original length (Figure **6.7**).

Muscular Dystrophy

We have seen that calcium ions must enter the cell for muscle contraction to occur. However, if too many calcium ions enter the cell, those ions can destroy proteins within the cell, causing it to die. If this cell death occurs on a large scale, muscles become increasingly damaged and weak. That is, in fact, what happens in *muscular dystrophy,* which is a general term for a group of inherited conditions. One of the most common forms, Duchenne muscular dystrophy, is caused by a defective gene for production of the protein dystrophin. The lack of dystrophin allows excess calcium ions to enter the muscle cell and rise to levels that destroy other important proteins and kill the cell. Dead muscle cells are replaced by fat and connective tissue, so the skeletal muscles become progressively

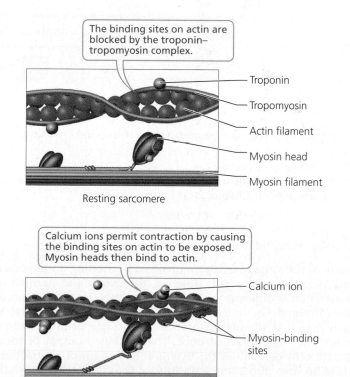

The binding sites on actin are blocked by the troponin–tropomyosin complex.

Troponin

Tropomyosin

Actin filament

Myosin head

Myosin filament

Resting sarcomere

Calcium ions permit contraction by causing the binding sites on actin to be exposed. Myosin heads then bind to actin.

Calcium ion

Myosin-binding sites

Cross-bridge formation

FIGURE 6.6 Calcium ions initiate muscle contraction.

Step 1: A nerve impulse reaches the neuromuscular junction.

Step 2: Acetylcholine is released at the neuromuscular junction.

Step 3: When acetylcholine binds to receptors on the plasma membrane of the muscle cell, an electrochemical message is generated.

Step 4: The electrochemical message spreads through T tubules, causing the release of calcium ions from the sarcoplasmic reticulum.

Motor neuron

Axon terminal

Synaptic vesicle

Synaptic cleft

Acetylcholine

Neuromuscular junction

Electrical impulse

Plasma membrane

T tubule

Sacroplasmic reticulum

Myofibril

Calcium ions

FIGURE 6.7 The connection between a motor neuron and a muscle cell is called a neuromuscular junction.

weaker. (The mode of inheritance of Duchenne muscular dystrophy is described in Chapter 20.)

Voluntary Movement

Many of the same muscles are involved in strolling on the beach and kicking a soccer ball. However, the extent and strength of contraction is different in these two activities. How is this possible? Although an individual muscle cell contracts completely each time it is stimulated to do so, only some of the cells in a whole muscle contract at once. The combined output of these muscle cells determines the extent and strength of contraction. There are two important ways to vary the contraction of whole muscles: (1) changing the number of muscle cells contracting at a given moment and (2) changing the force of contraction in individual muscle cells by altering the frequency of stimulation. Let's see how this works.

Motor Units and Recruitment

As described earlier, skeletal muscles are stimulated to contract by motor neurons. Each motor neuron that brings an impulse from the brain to a muscle makes contact with a number of different muscle cells in that muscle. A motor neuron and all the muscle cells it stimulates are called a **motor unit** (Figure **6.8**). All the muscle cells in a given motor unit contract together. On average there are 150 muscle cells in a motor unit, but this number is quite variable. Muscles responsible for precise, finely controlled movements, such as those of the fingers or eyes, have small numbers of muscle cells in each motor unit. In contrast, muscles for less precise movements, such as those of the hip or calf, have many

FIGURE 6.8 A motor unit includes a motor neuron and the muscle cells it stimulates.

muscle cells in a motor unit. A single motor neuron in a motor unit in a tiny eye muscle may control only three muscle cells, making its action highly localized, whereas a single motor neuron in a motor unit in a calf muscle may control thousands of muscle cells.

The nervous system increases the strength of a muscle contraction by increasing the number of motor units being stimulated, through a process called **recruitment.** The muscle cells of a given motor unit are generally spread throughout the muscle. Thus, if a single motor unit is stimulated, the entire muscle contracts, but only weakly. Although several of the same muscles are used to lift a table as are used to lift a fork, the number of motor units summoned in those muscles is greater when lifting the table.

Our movements tend to be smooth and graceful rather than jerky because the nervous system carefully choreographs the stimulation of different motor units, timing it so that they are not all active simultaneously or for the same amount of time. Although an individual muscle cell is either contracted or relaxed at any given instant, the muscle as a whole can consist of thousands of muscle cells, and usually only some of those cells are contracted at the same time. Even when a muscle is relaxed, some of its motor units are active (but not the same units all the time). As a result, the muscle is usually firm and solid, even when it is not being used. This state of intermediate contraction of a whole skeletal muscle is called *muscle tone.* A muscle that lacks muscle tone is limp.

Muscle Twitches, Summation, and Tetanus

If a whole skeletal muscle is artificially stimulated briefly in the laboratory, some of the muscle cells will contract, causing a **muscle twitch** (Figure **6.9a**). The interval between the reception of

FIGURE 6.9 Muscle contraction shown graphically: (a) muscle twitch, (b) summation, (c) tetanus

the stimulus and the time when contraction begins is called the latent period. The contraction phase is quite short and is followed by a longer relaxation phase as the muscle returns to its resting state. Muscle twitches are too brief to be part of normal movements (but they can generate heat to maintain body temperature when we shiver).

Most movements, including strolling along the beach, require sustained contraction of muscles. Sustained contractions begin when the frequency of stimulation increases. If a second stimulus is given before the muscle is fully relaxed, the second twitch will be stronger than the first. This phenomenon is described as **summation**, because the second contraction is added to the first (Figure 6.9b). Summation occurs because an increasing number of muscle cells are stimulated to contract.

When stimuli arrive even more frequently, the contraction becomes increasingly stronger as each new muscle twitch is added. If the stimuli occur so frequently that there is no time for any relaxation before the next stimulus arrives, the muscle goes into a sustained, powerful contraction called **tetanus** (Figure 6.9c). Tetanus cannot continue indefinitely. Eventually, the muscle will become unable to produce enough ATP to fuel contraction, and lactic acid will accumulate (as discussed below). As a result, the muscle will stop contracting despite continued stimulation, a condition called *fatigue*.

Energy for Muscle Contraction

A single contracting muscle cell can require as much as 600 trillion ATP molecules per second simply to form and break the cross-bridges producing the contraction. When we consider that even small muscles contain thousands of muscle cells, it is clear that muscle contraction requires an enormous store of energy. So where does all the ATP come from?

Our muscles have various sources of ATP and typically use them in a certain sequence, depending on the duration and intensity of exercise. These sources include (1) ATP stored in muscle cells, (2) creatine phosphate stored in muscle cells, (3) anaerobic (without oxygen) metabolic pathways within cells, and (4) aerobic (with oxygen) respiration within cells (Figure **6.10**). (Recall that cell respiration was discussed in Chapter 3.)

A resting muscle stores some ATP, but this reserve is used up quickly. During vigorous exercise, the ATP reserves in the active muscles are depleted in about 6 seconds. Earlier, when the muscles were resting, energy was transferred to another high-energy compound, called creatine phosphate, that is stored in muscle tissue. Creatine phosphate has a high-energy bond connecting the creatine and the phosphate parts of the molecule. A resting muscle contains about six times as much stored creatine phosphate as stored ATP and can release its energy when needed to convert ADP to ATP. This energy supports the next 10 seconds of exercise.

$$\text{Creatine phosphate} \xrightarrow{\quad ADP \quad ATP \quad} \text{Creatine}$$

Activities such as diving, weight lifting, and sprinting, which require a short burst of intense activity, are powered entirely by ATP and creatine phosphate reserves.

Once the supply of creatine phosphate is diminished, ATP must be generated from either anaerobic metabolic pathways or aerobic respiratory pathways. The primary fuel for either pathway is glucose, and the glucose that fuels muscle contraction comes mainly from glycogen, which—as you learned in Chapter 2—is stored in muscle (and liver) cells and consists of a large chain of glucose molecules. When an active muscle cell runs short of ATP and creatine phosphate, enzymes begin converting glycogen to glucose. About 1.5% of a muscle cell's total weight is glycogen. Even so, long-term activity, as in an endurance sport, may deplete

Q *Which energy source would fuel walking up a single flight of stairs?*

6 seconds	10 seconds	30–40 seconds	End of exercise		After prolonged exercise
ATP stored in muscles	ATP formed from creatine phosphate and ADP	ATP generated from glycogen stored in muscles and broken down to form glucose			Oxygen debt paid back
		Oxygen limited • Glucose oxidized to lactic acid	Oxygen present • Heart beats faster to deliver oxygen more quickly • Myoglobin releases oxygen		Breathe heavily to deliver oxygen • Lactic acid used to produce ATP • Creatine phosphate restored • Oxygen restored to myoglobin • Glycogen reserves restored

FIGURE 6.10 Energy sources for muscle contraction

a muscle's glycogen reserves. The accompanying feeling of overwhelming fatigue is known to runners as "hitting the wall," to cyclists as "bonking," and to boxers as becoming "arm weary."

The cardiovascular system can supply enough oxygen for aerobic respiratory pathways to power *low* levels of activity, even if continued for a prolonged time. However, anaerobic pathways produce ATP 2.5 times faster than do aerobic pathways. Therefore, during strenuous activity lasting 30 or 40 seconds, anaerobic pathways supply the ATP that fuels muscle contraction. Indeed, burst-like activities such as used in tennis or soccer rely nearly completely on anaerobic pathways of ATP production. In anaerobic respiratory pathways, the pyruvic acid produced in glycolysis is converted to lactic acid.

$$\text{Glycogen} \longrightarrow \text{Glucose} \xrightarrow[\text{No oxygen required}]{\overset{\text{ADP} \quad \text{ATP}}{\curvearrowright}} \text{Pyruvic acid} \longrightarrow \text{Lactic acid}$$

During more prolonged muscular activity, the body gradually switches back to aerobic pathways for producing ATP. The necessary oxygen can come from either of two sources. One is the oxygen bound to hemoglobin in the blood supply. As activity continues, the heart rate increases, and blood is pumped more quickly; moreover, it is shunted to the neediest tissues. Another oxygen source is *myoglobin*, an oxygen-binding pigment within muscle cells. Aerobic pathways produce more than 90% of the ATP required for intense activity lasting more than 10 minutes. These pathways also produce nearly 100% of the ATP that powers a truly prolonged intense activity, such as running a marathon.

$$\text{Glycogen} \longrightarrow \text{Glucose} \xrightarrow[\text{Oxygen required}]{\overset{\text{ADP} \quad \text{ATP}}{\curvearrowright}} \text{Carbon dioxide} + \text{Water}$$

After prolonged exercise, a person continues to breathe heavily for several minutes. Taking in extra oxygen in this way relieves the **oxygen debt** that was created by the muscles' using more ATP than was provided by aerobic metabolism. Most of the oxygen is used to generate ATP to convert lactic acid back to glucose. In addition, the oxygen that was released by myoglobin is replaced, and glycogen and creatine phosphate reserves are restored.

Slow-Twitch and Fast-Twitch Muscle Cells

There are two general types of skeletal muscle cells: slow-twitch and fast-twitch (Figure **6.11**). **Slow-twitch muscle cells** contract slowly when stimulated, but with enormous endurance. These cells are dark and reddish because they are packed with the oxygen-binding pigment myoglobin and because they are richly supplied with blood vessels. Slow-twitch cells also contain abundant mitochondria, the organelles in which aerobic production of ATP occurs. Because they

Q *Which type of muscle cell is best suited for cross-country skiing? Which type of muscle fiber is best suited for weight lifting?*

Slow-twitch muscle cells:
- Designed for endurance
- Contract slowly
- Strong, sustained contraction
- Steady supply of energy
  - Many mitochondria (structures for aerobic production of ATP)
  - Many capillaries
  - Packed with the oxygen-binding pigment myoglobin

Fast-twitch muscle cells:
- Designed for rapid, powerful response
- Contract rapidly
- Short, powerful contraction because there is more actin and myosin than in slow-twitch muscle cell
- Depend more heavily on anaerobic metabolic pathways to generate ATP, so fatigue rapidly

FIGURE 6.11 Slow- and fast-twitch muscle cells

A *Slow-twitch muscle cells for cross-country skiing; fast-twitch muscle cells for weight lifting.*

can produce ATP aerobically for a long time, slow-twitch cells are specialized to deliver prolonged, strong contractions.

In contrast, **fast-twitch muscle cells** contract rapidly and powerfully, but with far less endurance. Fast-twitch cells have a form of an enzyme that can split ATP bound to myosin more quickly than the same enzyme in slow-twitch cells. Because they can make and break cross-bridge attachments more quickly, fast-twitch cells can contract more rapidly. In addition, compared with their slow-twitch cousins, fast-twitch cells have a wider diameter because they are packed with more actin and myosin. This feature adds to their power. However, fast-twitch cells, rich in glycogen deposits, depend more heavily on anaerobic means of producing ATP. As a result, fast-twitch cells tire more quickly than slow-twitch cells.

The two kinds of cells are distributed unequally throughout the human body. The abdominal muscles do not need to contract rapidly, but they need to be able to contract steadily to hold our paunch in at the beach and to balance the powerful, slow-twitch back muscles so that we can stand upright. Fast-twitch cells are more common in the legs and arms, because our limbs may be called on to move quickly.

People vary in the relative amounts of slow- and fast-twitch muscle cells they possess. Whereas the leg muscles of endurance athletes, such as marathoners, are made up of about 80% slow-twitch cells, those of sprinters are about 60% fast-twitch cells. To some extent these differences are genetic, so if you are a "fast-twitch person," you can build a certain level of endurance, but only to a degree. Endurance runners, on the other hand, dread those times when, at the end of a long race, some well-trained competitor, genetically endowed with lots of fast-twitch cells, sprints past them at the finish line.

Building Muscle

Exercise can greatly influence the further development of muscle. (The hormone testosterone also builds muscle; see the Ethical Issue essay, *Building Muscle Fair and Square?*.) Different kinds of exercise produce different results. In *aerobic exercise*, such as walking, jogging, or swimming, enough oxygen is delivered to the muscles to keep them going for long periods. This kind of exercise fosters the development of new blood vessels that service the muscles and development of more mitochondria to facilitate energy usage. Aerobic exercise also increases muscle coordination, improves digestive tract movement, and increases the strength of the skeleton by exerting force on the bones. It brings cardiovascular and respiratory system improvements that help muscles to function more efficiently. For example, it enlarges the heart so that each stroke pumps more blood.

Aerobic exercises, however, generally do not increase muscle size. Muscular development—the kind that helps you look good on the beach—comes mostly from *resistance exercise*, which can be developed by lifting heavy weights. To build muscle tone and mass, you have to make your muscles exert more than 75% of their maximum force. These exercises can be very brief. Only a few minutes of exercise every other day for a year are needed to build 50% more muscle and improve tone and strength. The bulk results from the existing muscle cells increasing in diameter, although some researchers suggest that heavy exercise splits or tears the muscle cells and that each of the parts then regrows to a larger size.

Nautilus and other muscle-building machines available at many gyms automatically adjust the resistance they offer to muscles during an exercise (Figure **6.12**). This is a valuable feature because muscles are weaker at some parts of their range of motion than at others. The design of the exercise machine makes the lifting easier where

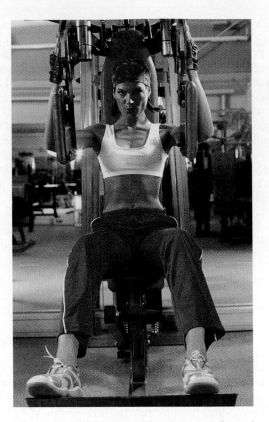

FIGURE 6.12 Muscles get larger when they are repeatedly made to exert more than 75% of their maximum force.

the muscle is weaker and more difficult in the range the muscle can handle. "Free weights," such as barbells and dumbbells, require more training to use safely than does an exercise machine.

One difficulty with building muscle is that you have to keep at it. If you train in the spring only to look good at the beach, you have an uphill battle because all the mass of muscle you built last year began to disappear 2 weeks after the training stopped.

Exercise has many health benefits in addition to those to the heart and blood vessels and an increase in strength. Exercise improves your mood. If you are having a stressful day, go for a walk or work out at the gym to calm down. Exercise even reduces depression and anxiety and improves the quality of sleep. Weight-bearing exercise strengths bones. Are you concerned about your weight? Add exercise to your weight-loss program to burn calories faster.

Begin a fitness program slowly. If you have a medical condition, first seek medical advice. Warm up by walking and gently stretching to improve blood flow to your muscles. Increase the length of time you exercise gradually as you build stamina. While you are cooling down after exercise, walk and stretch as you did before exercise.

A day or two after intense exercise, muscles sometimes become tender and weak. This phenomenon, known as *delayed onset muscle soreness* (DOMS), is especially common following exercises that force a muscle to lengthen while it is contracting. For example, DOMS is more likely to occur after you run downhill than after you run on level ground. Other activities that cause a muscle to lengthen while it is contracting include walking down stairs, climbing down a mountain, skiing, and horseback riding. The cause of DOMS isn't known for certain, but researchers suggest that microscopic muscle damage or an inflammatory response in the muscle may be to blame.

what would you do?

The International Olympics Committee and the World Anti-Doping Agency are concerned about the future possibility of creating genetically modified athletes. Gene therapy techniques (see Chapter 21) may soon be developed for inserting genes into people to improve their athletic performance. For example, researchers exploring muscle deterioration have developed gene therapy that repairs and rebuilds muscles in old mice. Clinical trials of the technique are now under way on humans who have muscular dystrophy. If you were a competitive athlete, would you use gene therapy to repair damaged muscle tissue? Would you use gene therapy to build muscle tissue and enhance your performance? Do you think any of these uses of gene therapy should be illegal?

Building Muscle Fair and Square? Anabolic Steroid Abuse

In recent years allegations and confessions of anabolic steroid use have rocked professional sports. Accusations of steroid use in Major League baseball began in 1998 with the home run competition between Sammy Sosa and Mark McGwire and haven't quieted yet. Steroid use is not restricted to baseball; it extends to other sports, including football, wrestling, track, and cycling. Almost all international athletic committees prohibit steroid use. Indeed, more than a few medals have had to be returned when evidence of illegal steroid use was discovered.

The prevalence of steroid use in professional sports is a reflection of the growing problem of steroid use in general, particularly among young adults. A 2007 confidential survey of high school students funded by the National Institute on Drug Abuse revealed that 1.6% of eighth-grade students, 1.8% of tenth-grade students, and 2.7% of seniors had used steroids. Of the students who admitted steroid use, 57% said that steroid use by professional athletes influenced their decision.

What are anabolic steroids, and why are so many young people using them? Anabolic steroids are a class of drugs related to the steroid hormone testosterone. These synthetic hormones mimic testosterone's ability to stimulate the body to build muscle, often leading to a dramatic increase in strength. The steroids promote these improvements by stimulating protein formation in muscle cells and by reducing the amount of rest needed between workouts.

If steroids simply mimic a hormone we naturally produce, why is there so much concern about their use? Anabolic steroids have more than 70 possible unwanted side effects that can range in severity from acne to liver cancer. Most common and most serious are the damage to the liver, cardiovascular system, and reproductive system. Cardiovascular problems, including heart attacks and strokes, may not show up for years;

but effects on the reproductive system are more immediate. The testicles of male steroid users often become smaller, and the user may become sterile and impotent (unable to achieve an erection). These effects occur because anabolic steroids inhibit natural testosterone production. Female steroid abusers develop irreversible masculine traits such as a deeper voice, growth of body hair, loss of scalp hair, smaller breasts, and an enlarged clitoris (during embryological development, the clitoris develops from the same structure that develops into the penis in a male). Among the other risks are injuries resulting from the intended effect of the drug—increased muscle strength—because that increase is not accompanied by a corresponding increase in the strength of tendons and ligaments. Injuries to tendons and ligaments may take a long time to heal.

Steroid use can have psychological effects, too. For instance, it may promote aggression and a feeling of invincibility, often referred to as "'roid rage." Users may also develop severe depression. In addition, steroids are addictive. Although anabolic steroids are available only by prescription, school-age children report that it is not difficult to obtain them without a prescription. Because most steroids are obtained illegally through the black market or from foreign countries, their purity and quality are questionable at best.

Steroid use is controlled by the Food and Drug Administration (FDA), banned from professional athletics, and stigmatized in the media. We might ask, then, why is steroid use still so attractive to young people? Among high school and college athletes, the reason for steroid use is clear: it gives the user a distinct competitive edge. Of the high school students surveyed, 65% said they used anabolic steroids to reach athletic goals. These students are not denying the possible health risks. Fifty-seven percent of the users admitted that they would use steroids even if they *knew* for certain that use would shorten their lives.

Another reason for steroid use is the perception that they provide an easy route to the body image so prized by society. Nearly one-third of high school males who use steroids admit that they use the drugs to acquire a muscular, well-built look. Young women who use

steroids also confess that they are seeking a well-sculpted body.

Some athletes at both the college and professional level skirt the legal issues connected with steroid use by taking a drug called androstenedione that is legally available without a prescription. The liver converts this drug to testosterone. Although there are no laws prohibiting the use of androstenedione, the National Football League, the National Collegiate Athletic Association, and the International Olympic Committee have banned its use among their athletes. The long-term effects are largely unknown; but in the short term, androstenedione increases blood cholesterol levels, thereby increasing the risk of heart disease. It is also thought to increase the risk of prostate cancer.

Questions to Consider:

- **If you were coaching a high school football team and knew that some of your players were using anabolic steroids, would you ignore their actions?**
- **If you were the owner of a professional baseball team, and suspected that one of your all-star players was using anabolic steroids, what would you do?**

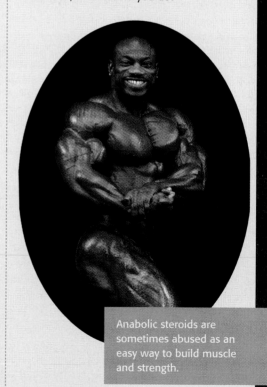

Anabolic steroids are sometimes abused as an easy way to build muscle and strength.

Function and Characteristics of Muscles (p. 107)

- There are three types of muscle: skeletal, smooth, and cardiac. All types of muscle cells are excitable, contractile, extensible, and elastic.

Skeletal Muscles Working in Pairs (pp. 107–109)

- Many of the skeletal muscles of the body are arranged in antagonistic pairs so that the action of one opposes the action of the other. One member of such a pair usually causes flexion (bending at the joint) and the other, extension (straightening at the joint).
- Muscles are attached to bones by tendons. The muscle origin is the end attached to the bone that is more stationary during the muscle's movement, and the insertion is the end attached to the bone that moves.

Contraction of Muscles (pp. 109–112)

- A muscle cell is packed with myofibrils, which are composed of myofilaments (the contractile proteins actin and myosin).
- A muscle contracts when myosin heads in some of its cells bind to actin, swivel, and thereby pull the actin toward the midlines of sarcomeres, causing the actin and myosin filaments to slide past one another and increasing their degree of overlap.
- Contraction is controlled by the availability of calcium ions. Calcium ions interact with two proteins on the actin filament—troponin and tropomyosin—that determine whether myosin can bind to actin. Calcium ions are stored in the sarcoplasmic reticulum of muscle cells and released when a motor nerve sends an impulse.
- Motor nerves contact muscle cells at neuromuscular junctions. When the nerve impulse reaches a neuromuscular junction, acetylcholine is released and causes a change in the permeability of the muscle cell's membrane that, in turn, causes calcium ions to be released from the sarcoplasmic reticulum.

Voluntary Movement (pp. 112–114)

- The extent and strength of contraction can be changed by altering the number of muscle cells contracting or by altering the strength of contraction of individual cells.
- A motor neuron and all the muscle cells it stimulates are collectively called a motor unit.
- The response of a muscle cell to a single brief stimulus in the laboratory is called a twitch. If a second stimulus arrives before the muscle has relaxed, the second contraction builds upon the first. This phenomenon is known as summation. Frequent stimuli cause a sustained contraction, called tetanus. Most body movements require muscle cells in tetanus.

Energy for Muscle Contraction (pp. 114–115)

- Each time an attachment between myosin and actin forms and is broken, two ATP molecules are used. The sources of ATP are (1) stored ATP, (2) creatine phosphate, (3) anaerobic metabolic pathways, and (4) aerobic respiration.

Slow-Twitch and Fast-Twitch Muscle Cells (pp. 115–116)

- Slow-twitch muscle cells contract slowly but with enormous endurance. Fast-twitch muscle cells contract rapidly and powerfully but with less endurance.

Building Muscle (p. 116)

- Resistance exercise will increase muscle size. Forcing muscles to exert more than 75% of their maximal strength adds myofilaments to existing muscle cells and increases the cell diameter.

tendon   *p. 109*
origin   *p. 109*
insertion   *p. 109*
striated muscle   *p. 109*
myofibril   *p. 109*
myofilament   *p. 109*

myosin filament   *p. 109*
actin filament   *p. 109*
sarcomere   *p. 109*
sliding filament model   *p. 109*
cross-bridge   *p. 110*
troponin   *p. 110*

tropomyosin   *p. 110*
sarcoplasmic reticulum   *p. 110*
transverse tubules   *p. 110*
neuromuscular junction   *p. 110*
motor unit   *p. 112*
recruitment   *p. 113*

muscle twitch   *p. 113*
summation   *p. 114*
tetanus   *p. 114*
oxygen debt   *p. 115*
slow-twitch muscle cells   *p. 115*
fast-twitch muscle cells   *p. 115*

1. Why are most skeletal muscles arranged in antagonistic pairs? Give an example illustrating the roles of each member of an antagonistic pair of muscles.   *pp. 107–108*
2. Describe a skeletal muscle, including descriptions of muscle cells, myofibrils, and myofilaments.   *p. 109*
3. What is the sliding filament model of muscle contraction?   *pp. 109–110*
4. What causes actin to move during muscle contraction? *p. 110*
5. Explain the roles of troponin, tropomyosin, and calcium ions in regulating muscle contraction.   *p. 110*
6. Explain how muscle contraction results from the events that occur when an impulse from a motor nerve cell reaches a neuromuscular junction and calcium ions are released from the sarcoplasmic reticulum.   *p. 110–111*

7. Define a motor unit. What are the consequences of the differences in sizes of motor units?   *pp. 112–113*
8. Define muscle twitch, summation, and tetanus.   *pp. 113–114*
9. List the sources of ATP for muscle contraction, and explain when each source is typically called on.   *pp. 114–115*
10. Characterize the difference in function between slow- and fast-twitch muscle cells.   *pp. 115–116*
11. What type of exercise can build muscles?   *p. 116*
12. A single motor neuron and all the muscle cells it stimulates is called a
    a. sarcoplasmic reticulum.
    b. neuromuscular junction.
    c. motor unit.
    d. summation.

13. In a muscle, energy is stored in the form of
    a. creatine phosphate.
    b. ADP.
    c. myosin.
    d. glucose.

14. A muscle cell contracts when _____ filaments and _____ filaments slide past one another.
15. The contractile unit of a muscle is called a/an _____.

applying the concepts

1. Hakeem is a 22-year-old who ate some of his Aunt Sophie's canned tomatoes for dinner last night. This morning, his speech is slurred and he is having trouble standing and walking, so his brother rushes him to the emergency room. The doctor tells Hakeem that he probably has botulism, a type of food poisoning produced by a bacterium that can grow in improperly sealed canned goods. The botulinum toxin prevents the release of acetylcholine at neuromuscular junctions. Explain how Hakeem's symptoms are related to this effect.
2. A new injury called "BlackBerry thumb" is becoming increasingly common because people send e-mails on their handheld devices and text messages on their cell phones. BlackBerry thumb is a form of tendinitis. What would cause BlackBerry thumb? What would the symptoms be? How would you treat it?
3. You are the CEO of a drug company. A research scientist approaches you with a plan to develop a new muscle-relaxing drug. The scientist explains that the drug works by flooding the muscle cell with calcium ions. Would you finance the development of this drug? Why or why not?
4. Chickens are ground-dwelling birds. They run to escape from predators, and they can fly only short distances. How do these activities explain the distribution of "white" and "dark" meat on a chicken? (Meat is skeletal muscle.)

becoming information literate

Use at least three reliable sources (books, journals, websites) to design an exercise program for yourself. Begin by deciding on your fitness goals. Next, plan a logical progression of activity that considers the type of activities you enjoy. List each source you considered, and explain why you chose the three sources you used.

Additional questions can be found online at the Human Biology Place, www.humanbiology.com.

7

Neurons: The Matter of the Mind

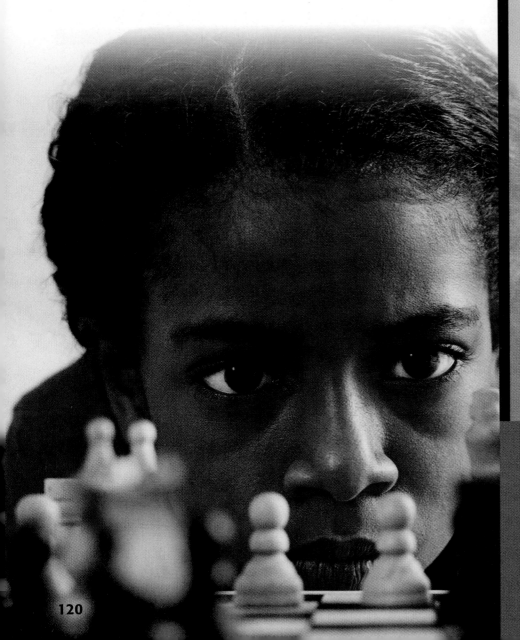

The brain cells we use to plot and plan our way to victory in a chess match have the same design and mode of functioning as the cells that tell our muscles to contract or that carry information from our sensory organs to our brain. They are neurons, the basic functional units of the nervous system.

A melia, age 12, has won every junior chess tournament in her state. She remembers every chess game she has ever played, categorizing them by opening, general strategy, and closing moves. Her IQ is extremely high, but competitive chess demands all her ability. Today she is taking part in a chess club exhibition, playing 15 games simultaneously with a 5-minute time limit for each game. Walking from board to board, she looks briefly at the chess pieces, makes her move, and presses the timer button on the clock. As she walks, she mentally retraces the moves in a difficult match she played 2 weeks ago. An hour passes, and after winning all 15 games and giving a brief interview to a television reporter, Amelia goes home to finish her calculus assignment.

Amelia is gifted almost beyond measure, yet her brain functions with the same biological materials we all possess. In this chapter, we begin exploring the brain and other parts of the nervous system, starting with the cells they are built from. We discover the special features that allow these cells to communicate with one another. We then proceed, in Chapter 8, "The Nervous System," to explore the larger divisions of the brain and spinal cord and identify their functions.

Cells of the Nervous System

The *nervous system* integrates and coordinates all the body's varied activities. Its two primary divisions, which are the subject of Chapter 8, are (1) the central nervous system, consisting of the brain and spinal cord; and (2) the peripheral system, consisting of all the nervous tissue in the body outside the brain and spinal cord. Both these major divisions of the nervous system are composed of two types of specialized cells. **Neurons** (nerve cells) are excitable cells that generate and transmit messages. Outnumbering the neurons by about 10 to 1, **neuroglial cells** (also called glial cells) support and protect neurons.

Neuroglial Cells

The nervous system has several types of glial cells, each with different jobs to do. Some glial cells provide structural support for the neurons of the brain and spinal cord. Glial cells also provide a steady supply of chemicals, called nerve growth factors, that stimulate nerve growth. Without nerve growth factors, neurons die. Other glial cells form insulating sheaths around axons that, as described shortly, are the long projections extending from certain neurons. This sheath, called the myelin sheath, has several important functions that are also described shortly. Scientists now know that glial cells can communicate with one another and with neurons.

Neurons

The basic unit of the nervous system is the neuron, or nerve cell. Neurons, which are responsible for an amazing variety of functions, can be grouped into the three general categories depicted in Figure **7.1**.

- **Sensory** (or afferent) **neurons** conduct information *toward* the brain and spinal cord. These neurons generally extend from sensory receptors, which are structures specialized to gather information about the conditions within and around our bodies.
- **Motor** (or efferent) **neurons** carry information *away from* the brain and spinal cord to an **effector**—either a muscle, which will contract, or a gland, which will secrete its product, as a response to information from a sensory or interneuron.
- Association neurons, commonly called **interneurons**, are located between sensory and motor neurons. They are found only within the brain and spinal cord, where they integrate and interpret the sensory signals, thereby "deciding" on the

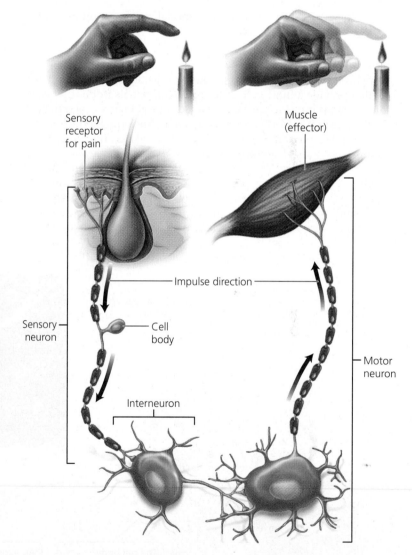

FIGURE 7.1 Neurons may be sensory neurons, interneurons, or motor neurons. This diagram traces the pathway of an impulse from a sensory receptor to an interneuron and from there to a motor neuron and its effector. Sensory receptors detect changes in the external or internal environment. An interneuron usually receives input from many sensory neurons, integrates that information, and if the input is appropriate, stimulates a motor neuron. The motor neuron then causes a muscle or a gland (an effector) to respond.

appropriate response. Interneurons are by far the most numerous nerve cells in the body; they account for more than 99% of the body's neurons.

We can appreciate the specific roles of each type of neuron by considering the symptoms of a progressive disease called *amyotrophic lateral sclerosis (ALS),* also known as Lou Gehrig's disease. In ALS, motor neurons throughout the brain and spinal cord die and stop sending messages to skeletal muscles. Without stimulation from motor neurons, the muscles gradually weaken, and the person loses control over arms, legs, and body. The cause of death is respiratory failure, because the muscles that control breathing (the diaphragm and rib muscles) eventually die. Sensory neurons and interneurons are not affected by ALS, so awareness and reasoning do not deteriorate.

Structure of Neurons

The shape of a typical neuron is specialized for communicating with other cells (Figure **7.2**).

Axons and Dendrites

A neuron has many short, branching projections called **dendrites**, which provide a huge surface for receiving signals from other cells. Such signals travel toward an enlarged central region called the cell body, which has all the normal organelles, including a nucleus, for maintaining the cell. When a neuron responds to an incoming signal, it transmits its message along the **axon**, a single long extension of the neuron. The axon carries messages away from the cell body either to another neuron or to an effector, which can be a muscle or a gland. In some cases, the axon allows the neuron to communicate over very long distances. For example, a motor neuron that allows you to wiggle your big toe has its cell body in the

spinal cord and its axon runs all the way to the muscles of your toe. The end of the axon has many branches specialized to release a chemical, called a neurotransmitter, that alters the activity of the effector. The axon is the *sending* portion of the neuron, whereas the dendrites and cell body are typically the *receiving* portions.

To appreciate the dimensions of a neuron, imagine a "typical" motor neuron, one that carries a message from the spinal cord to a muscle. Now picture the cell body of this neuron as being the size of a tennis ball. At that scale, the axon of this neuron would be about 1 mile (1.6 km) long and only about one-half inch (1.3 cm) in diameter. At the same scale, the dendrites—the shorter but more numerous projections of the neuron—would fill an average-sized living room.

A **nerve** is a bundle of parallel axons, dendrites, or both arising from many neurons. Each nerve is covered with connective tissue and, depending on the type of neurons it contains, can be classified as sensory, motor, or mixed (a mixed nerve is made up of both sensory and motor neurons).

Myelin Sheath

Most of the axons outside the brain and spinal cord, and some of those within, have an insulating outer layer called a **myelin sheath** (Figure **7.3**), which increases the rate of conduction of a nerve impulse and helps its repair. The myelin sheath is composed of the plasma membranes of glial cells. Outside of the brain and spinal cord, for example, glial cells known as **Schwann cells** form neurons' myelin sheaths. A Schwann cell plasma membrane wraps around the axon many times to provide a covering that looks somewhat like a jelly roll. This covering, the myelin sheath, serves as a kind of living electrical tape, insulating individual axons and preventing messages from short-circuiting between neurons. The myelin sheath is kept alive by the Schwann cell's nucleus and cytoplasm, which are squeezed to the periphery as the sheath forms.

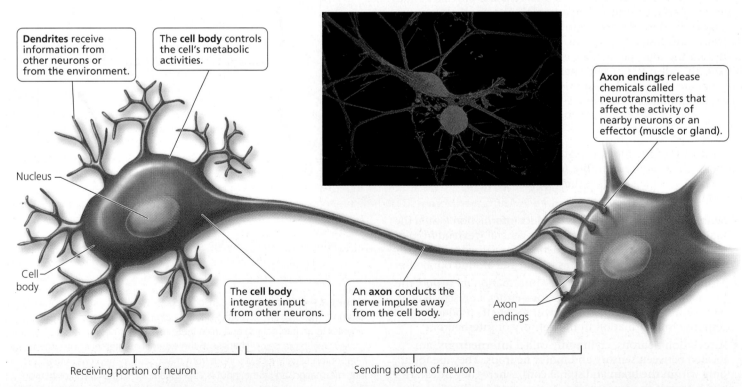

Dendrites receive information from other neurons or from the environment.

The **cell body** controls the cell's metabolic activities.

Axon endings release chemicals called neurotransmitters that affect the activity of nearby neurons or an effector (muscle or gland).

Nucleus

Cell body

The **cell body** integrates input from other neurons.

An **axon** conducts the nerve impulse away from the cell body.

Axon endings

Receiving portion of neuron

Sending portion of neuron

FIGURE 7.2 The structure of a neuron

Q *Long axons are myelinated, but short axons may not be. Why?*

(a)

(b)

(c) Myelin sheath surrounding cut end of axon

FIGURE 7.3 The myelin sheath. (a) An axon protected by a myelin sheath. The Schwann cells that form the myelin sheath are separated by nodes of Ranvier—areas of exposed axon that allow for saltatory conduction. (b) The myelin sheath forms from multiple wrappings of Schwann cell plasma membranes. (c) An electron micrograph of the cut end of a myelinated axon.

A *Saltatory conduction, which increases the speed of conduction, is possible only on myelinated axons. The increased speed is important when nerve impulses must travel long distances.*

A single Schwann cell encloses only a small portion, about 1 mm long, of an axon. The gaps between adjacent Schwann cells, where the axon is exposed to the extracellular environment, are called *nodes of Ranvier*. Their presence is crucial to how rapidly a neuron transmits messages. With the myelin sheath in place, a nerve impulse "jumps" successively from one node of Ranvier to the next in a type of transmission called **saltatory conduction** (*saltare*, to jump), which is up to 100 times faster than signal conduction would be on an unmyelinated axon of the same diameter. Not surprisingly, the axons responsible for conducting signals over long distances are typically myelinated.

To get a sense of how this "jumping" mode of transmission increases the speed at which a message travels, think of the different ways a ball can be moved down the court during a basketball game. When only seconds are left in the game, dribbling the ball the length of the court would take too much time. Passing the ball through a series of players is faster. Likewise, an impulse passed from one node to the next, as occurs in myelinated nerves, moves faster than one traveling uniformly along the full length of the axon, as occurs in unmyelinated nerves.

The myelin sheath also plays a role in helping to repair a neuron when a nerve is cut or crushed. When a neuron in the peripheral nervous system is cut, the part of the axon that has been separated from the cell body can no longer receive life-sustaining materials from the rest of the cell and begins to degenerate within a few minutes. Once such degeneration occurs, the Schwann cells that wrapped the axon begin to remove all the axon fragments from inside the myelin sheath. Finally, the cut end of the axon begins "sprouting" from the cell body and regrows along the previous path, guided by the remaining myelin sheath.

The importance of the myelin sheath becomes dramatically clear in people with *multiple sclerosis*, a disease in which the myelin sheaths in the brain and spinal cord are progressively destroyed. The damaged regions of myelin become hardened scars called scleroses (hence the name of the disease) that interfere with the transmission of nerve impulses. Short-circuiting between normally unconnected conduction paths delays or blocks the signals going from one brain region to another. Depending on the part of the nervous system affected, the result can be paralysis or the loss of sensation, including loss of vision.

Nerve Impulses

The neuron membrane is specialized for communication. A nerve's message, which is called a nerve impulse or an action potential, is an electrochemical signal caused by sodium ions (Na^+) and potassium ions (K^+) crossing the neuron's membrane to enter and leave the cell.

Plasma Membrane of a Neuron

Like most living membranes, the plasma membrane of a neuron is selectively permeable; it allows some substances through but not others. The membrane contains many pores, called **ion channels**, that ions are able to pass through without using cellular energy (Figure **7.4**). Each ion channel is designed to allow only certain ions

to pass through. For example, sodium channels allow the passage of only sodium ions, and potassium channels allow the passage of only potassium ions. In this way, ion channels function as molecular sieves. Some channels are permanently open. Others are regulated by a "gate"—a protein that changes shape in response to changing conditions, either opening the channel, which allows ions to pass through, or closing it, which prevents ions from crossing the membrane.

The cell membrane also contains **sodium-potassium pumps**, which are special proteins in the cell membrane that actively transport sodium and potassium ions across the membrane. These pumps use cellular energy in the form of ATP to move the ions against their concentration gradients. Each pump ejects sodium ions (Na^+) from within the cell while bringing in potassium ions (K^+; see Figure 7.4).

Cross section

Axon membrane

Neuron plasma membrane

Extracellular fluid

Cytoplasm

Continually open ion channels

"Gated" ion channels

Sodium-potassium pump

Ion channels
Ion channels can be open continuously or opened and closed by a molecular gate

Sodium-potassium pump
The sodium-potassium pump uses cellular energy (ATP) to pump sodium ions out of the cell and potassium ions into the cell

FIGURE 7.4 The plasma membrane of a neuron provides two general ways for ions to enter or leave the cell: (1) diffusion through a channel or (2) active transport by the sodium-potassium pump.

Pesticides and the Nervous System

Many of us are exposed each day to substances that can harm our nervous system. The exposure may occur because of our job, our lifestyle, the foods we eat, or the medications we use. The death of neurons can lead to irreversible loss of function. Some damage may take years to become apparent, but other effects are immediate.

Pesticides are chemicals for killing organisms that would otherwise damage crops and property. The use of pesticides increases crop production, preserves produce, and keeps our public lawns and gardens beautiful. Pesticides also reduce infestations of insects, rats, and mice that might cause diseases. However, the misuse and overuse of pesticides can cause illness and even death. For example, the organophosphate insecticides Malathion, Parathion, and Diazinon are poisons that kill insects by excessively boosting the activity at certain synapses in the insect's body. They work by inhibiting acetylcholinesterase, the enzyme that breaks down the neurotransmitter acetylcholine. As a result, acetylcholine accumulates in the synapses and has a continuous effect.

Because they have the same effect in the human body, these insecticides accidentally poison approximately 500,000 people around the world each year, primarily farm workers. One symptom of pesticide poisoning is muscle spasms (continuous involuntary contractions).

The spasms occur because acetylcholine is the neurotransmitter that triggers contraction of voluntary muscles, such as those in the arms or legs. Death can occur if spasms occur in the muscles responsible for breathing.

Deciding whether to use pesticides usually requires balancing economic benefits with health risks. Currently, such a balancing act is occurring regarding the use of an organophosphate pesticide AZM (azinphos methyl). In 2001, the Environmental Protection Agency (EPA) banned the use of AZM on two dozen crops. However, it allowed continued use on orchard fruits (apples, pears, and cherries), berries, and nuts until 2010. The EPA's reason for the delayed ban is to allow development of cost-effective alternatives to AZM. In 2006, the ban on use of AZM was delayed another two years.

The courts will soon decide whether the potential health risks of AZM outweigh the potential economic benefits of continuing to use it. The EPA argues that the cost of quickly switching to other pesticides would be staggering. It could cost apple growers tens of millions of dollars. Furthermore, some other countries do not allow import of apples with residues from the alternative pesticides. On the other hand, the United Farm Workers argue that thousands of workers become seriously ill each year from exposure to AZM. Environmental groups point out that AZM is usually sprayed on crops from planes, allowing AZM to contaminate neighboring communities, rivers, and lakes.

Certain pesticides disrupt communication between neurons and muscles, which can be fatal.

Questions to Consider

- If you were the judge on the case of the United Farm Workers versus the EPA, what information would you use to decide whether to ban AZM?
- As a consumer, are you willing to pay more for foods if they are not sprayed with AZM?

Resting Potential

It will be easier to understand the movement of ions during an action potential if we first consider a neuron that is not transmitting an action potential—that is, a neuron in its resting state. As we will see, however, *resting* is hardly the word to describe what is going on at this stage. The membrane of a resting neuron maintains a difference in the electrical charges near the two membrane surfaces (the surface facing inside the cell and the surface facing outside the cell), keeping the inside surface more negative than the outside one. This charge difference across the membrane, called the **resting potential**, results from the unequal distribution of ions across the membrane.

In a resting neuron, sodium and potassium ions are unequally distributed across the plasma membrane. There are more sodium ions outside the membrane than inside. Furthermore, there are more potassium ions inside than outside. Potassium ions tend to leak out because they are more concentrated inside the axon. (Recall from Chapter 3 that substances tend to move from an area of higher concentration to one of lower concentration.) To a lesser extent, sodium ions leak in. However, sodium-potassium pumps maintain the resting potential of a neuron by pumping out sodium ions while moving potassium ions back in. The cell also contains some negatively charged ions that are too large to pass through the membrane.

The result of this unequal distribution of ions is that the inner surface of a resting neuron's membrane is typically about 70 mV (millivolts) more negative than the outer surface. This voltage is the resting potential, and it is about 5% of the strength of a size AA flashlight battery.

Although the neuron's sodium-potassium pumps consume a lot of energy to maintain the resting potential, the energy is not wasted. The resting potential allows the neuron to respond more quickly than it could if the membrane were electrically neutral in its resting state. This situation is somewhat analogous to keeping your car's battery charged so that the car will start as soon as you turn the key.

Resting Neuron
Plasma membrane is charged, with the inside negative relative to the outside.

Action Potential
The charge difference across the membrane reverses and then is restored.

Step 1: The loss of the charge difference across the membrane (depolarization) occurs as sodium ions (Na$^+$) enter the axon.

Na$^+$ flows inward

Step 2: The return of the membrane potential to near its resting value (repolarization) occurs as potassium (K$^+$) ions leave the axon.

K$^+$ flows outward

Restoration of Original Ion Distribution
The sodium-potassium pump restores the original distribution of ions.

Sodium-potassium pump active here

Na-K pump restores the original ion distribution

FIGURE 7.5 The resting state and the propagation of an action potential along an axon. The sequential opening and closing of sodium-channel gates and potassium-channel gates produces the action potential.

Action Potential

Now we are ready to consider what happens when a neuron is stimulated—that is, when it receives some kind of excitatory signal. The **action potential**, or nerve impulse, resulting from such stimulation can be described briefly as a sudden reversal in the charge difference across the membrane, followed by the restoration of the original charge difference. Let's take a closer look at these two parts of a nerve impulse.

1. **Sodium ions (Na⁺) enter the axon.** An excitatory stimulus causes the gates on sodium channels to open. Sodium ions then enter the neuron, and their positive charge begins to reduce the negative charge within. Reduction of the charge difference across the membrane is called *depolarization*. The action potential begins when membrane depolarization reaches a certain value called the **threshold**. When the threshold is reached, the gates on more sodium channels open. Enough sodium ions enter through the open gates to create a net positive charge in that region (about +30 mV), as shown in Figure **7.5**.

2. **Potassium (K⁺) ions leave the axon.** About halfway through the action potential, the gates on potassium channels open. Potassium ions now leave the cell. The exodus of potassium ions with their positive charge causes the interior of the neuron to become negative once again relative to the outside. The outward flow of potassium ions returns the membrane potential to close to its resting value. Restoration of the charge difference across the membrane is called *repolarization*.

As noted, at the end of an action potential, the charge distribution across the membrane returns to the resting potential. However, there are slightly more sodium ions and slightly fewer potassium ions inside the cell than before. This alteration is corrected by the sodium-potassium pump, which restores the original distribution of sodium and potassium ions. The action of the sodium-potassium pump is slow. Therefore, it does not contribute directly to the events of the action potential.

To summarize, the action potential is a reversal of the charge difference across the membrane caused by the inward flow of sodium ions, followed immediately by restoration of the original charge difference caused by the outward flow of potassium ions (Figure **7.6**). These changes occur sequentially along the axon, like a wave rippling away from the cell body.

The action potential is described as a *wave* of changes that travels down the neuron's plasma membrane because the events just described do not occur simultaneously along the entire length of the axon. Instead, as sodium ions enter the cell at one location along the membrane, and the charge inside the membrane becomes less negative in that region of the cell, the change in charge causes the opening of the sodium channel gates in an adjacent part of the membrane. Due to this sequential opening of gates, the change in charge travels down the length of the axon. Once started, action potentials do not diminish—just like the last domino in a falling row falls with the same energy as the first. Moreover, the intensity of the nerve impulse does not vary with the strength of the stimulus that triggered it. If an action potential occurs at all, it is always of the same intensity as any other action potential. This "all-or-nothing" aspect of nerve cell conduction is similar to the firing of a gun in that the force of the bullet is not changed by how hard you pull the trigger.

Immediately after an action potential occurs, the neuron cannot be stimulated again for a brief instant called the **refractory period.** During the refractory period, the sodium channels are

FIGURE 7.6 A graphic representation of an action potential. Voltage across the membrane can be measured by electrodes placed inside and outside the axon. The graph shows the changes in voltage that accompany an action potential.

closed and cannot be reopened. Consequently, a new action potential cannot yet be generated. Because of the refractory period, a prolonged stimulus that is above threshold can cause only a series of discrete nerve impulses, not a single, larger, sustained impulse. For this reason, increasing the strength of a stimulus will increase the frequency of impulses. For example, the frequency of nerve impulses increases with the heat of an object touched. However, the frequency can increase only to a point. The inability of the sodium gates to open during the refractory period is also the reason that the nerve impulses cannot reverse and go backward toward the cell body.

stop and think

"Red tides" in the ocean are caused by proliferation of dinoflagellates. These single-celled marine algae contain a chemical called saxitoxin (STX), extremely small concentrations of which prevent sodium channels in mammalian neurons from opening. The clams, scallops, and mussels that consume the dinoflagellates are insensitive to the toxin, but the STX accumulates in their tissues. What effect would you expect STX to have on nerve transmission in humans who accidentally consume tainted shellfish?

Synaptic Transmission

When a nerve impulse reaches the end of an axon, in almost all cases the message must be relayed to the adjacent cell across a small gap that the impulse cannot jump across. To transmit the message to the adjacent cell requires a brief change of the medium of communication from an electrochemical signal to a chemical signal. Therefore, when an action potential reaches the end of the axon, a chemical is released from the axon's tip. That chemical, called a **neurotransmitter,** diffuses across the gap and conveys the message to the adjacent cell.

The junction between a neuron and another cell is called a **synapse.** The structure of a synapse between two neurons is shown in Figure **7.7**. The gap between the cells is called the *synaptic cleft*. Recall that the axon branches near the end of its length. Each branch ends with a small bulblike swelling called a *synaptic knob*. The neuron sending the message is the *presynaptic neuron* (meaning "before the synapse"). The neuron receiving the message is the *postsynaptic neuron* ("after the synapse").

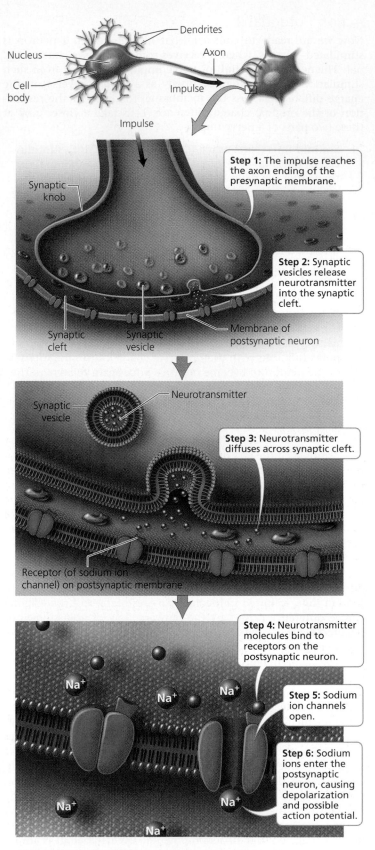

Dendrites

Nucleus

Axon

Cell body

Impulse

Impulse

Step 1: The impulse reaches the axon ending of the presynaptic membrane.

Synaptic knob

Step 2: Synaptic vesicles release neurotransmitter into the synaptic cleft.

Synaptic cleft

Synaptic vesicle

Membrane of postsynaptic neuron

Synaptic vesicle

Neurotransmitter

Step 3: Neurotransmitter diffuses across synaptic cleft.

Receptor (of sodium ion channel) on postsynaptic membrane

Step 4: Neurotransmitter molecules bind to receptors on the postsynaptic neuron.

Step 5: Sodium ion channels open.

Na⁺ Na⁺ Na⁺

Step 6: Sodium ions enter the postsynaptic neuron, causing depolarization and possible action potential.

Na⁺ Na⁺

Na⁺

FIGURE 7.8 Transmission across an excitatory synapse

Plasma membrane of an axon ending of a sending (presynaptic) neuron

Synaptic knob

Synaptic vesicle

Synaptic cleft

Plasma membrane of a receiving (postsynaptic) neuron

Ion channel

Receptor for neurotransmitter

(a)

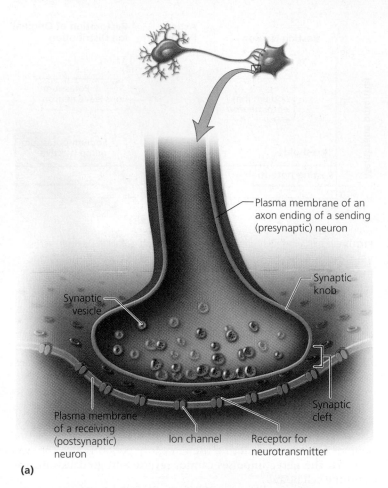

Axon of presynaptic neuron

Synaptic vesicles

(b)

FIGURE 7.7 Structure of a synapse. (a) The synaptic knob at the end of the axon on the presynaptic neuron is separated from the dendrite or cell body of the postsynaptic neuron by a small gap called a synaptic cleft. Within the synaptic knob are small sacs, called synaptic vesicles, filled with neurotransmitter molecules. (b) An electron micrograph of a synapse.

Axon Myelin sheath Receiving cell body Excitatory synapse Inhibitory synapse

FIGURE 7.9 A neuron may have as many as 10,000 synapses at which it receives input from other neurons. Some synapses have an excitatory effect on the membrane of the postsynaptic neuron and increase the likelihood that the neuron will fire. Other synapses have an inhibitory effect and reduce the likelihood that the postsynaptic neuron will fire. The net effect of all the synapses determines whether an action potential is generated in the postsynaptic neuron. (The shape of the synaptic knobs shown in this electron micrograph is distorted as a result of the preparation process.)

Release of the Neurotransmitter and the Opening of Ion Channels

Let's consider the events that occur in the synapse as the message is sent from one neuron to the next (Figure **7.8**).

1. **The nerve impulse reaches the axon ending of the presynaptic neuron.**
2. **Synaptic knobs release packets of neurotransmitter.** Within the synaptic knobs of the presynaptic neuron, the neurotransmitter is contained in tiny sacs called *synaptic vesicles*. When a nerve impulse reaches the synaptic knob, the gates of calcium ion channels in the membrane there open. Calcium ions move into the knob, causing the membranes of the synaptic vesicles to fuse with the plasma membrane at the synaptic knob and to dump the enclosed neurotransmitter into the synaptic cleft.
3. **Neurotransmitter diffuses across the synaptic cleft.**
4. **Neurotransmitter binds with receptors on the membrane of the postsynaptic neuron.** A receptor is a protein that recognizes a particular neurotransmitter, much as a lock "recognizes" a key. The only cells a neurotransmitter can stimulate are cells that have receptors specific for that particular neurotransmitter. Thus, only certain neurons can be affected by a given neurotransmitter.
5. **When a neurotransmitter binds to its receptor, an ion channel is opened.** The binding of the neurotransmitter to a receptor causes the opening of an ion channel in the postsynaptic neuron. The response that is triggered as a result depends on the type of ion channel the receptor opens. It is the receptor that determines which ion channels will open and what the effect of a given neurotransmitter will be.

An *excitatory synapse* is one where the binding of the neurotransmitter to the receptor opens sodium channels, allowing sodium ions to enter and increasing the likelihood that an action potential will begin in the postsynaptic cell. In contrast, an *inhibitory synapse* is one where the binding of the neurotransmitter opens different ion channels, which decreases the likelihood that an action potential will be generated in the postsynaptic neuron. In this case, the cell's interior becomes more negatively charged than usual. As a result, the cell will require larger than usual amounts of an excitatory neurotransmitter in order to reach threshold.

Summation of Input from Excitatory and Inhibitory Synapses

A neuron may have as many as 10,000 synapses with other neurons at the same time (Figure **7.9**). Some of these synapses will have excitatory effects on the postsynaptic membrane. Others will have inhibitory effects. The **summation** (combined effects) of excitatory and inhibitory effects on a neuron at any given moment determines whether an action potential is generated. This integration of input from large numbers of different kinds of synapses gives the nervous system fine control over neuronal responses, just as having both an accelerator and a brake gives you finer control over the movement of a car.

Removal of Neurotransmitter

After being released into a synapse, neurotransmitters are quickly removed so their effects are temporary. If they were not removed, they would continue to excite or inhibit the postsynaptic membrane indefinitely. Depending on the neurotransmitter, disposal is accomplished in one of two ways. First, enzymes can deactivate a neurotransmitter. For example, the enzyme acetylcholinesterase removes the neurotransmitter **acetylcholine** from synapses where it has been released. Second, the neurotransmitter may be actively pumped back into the presynaptic knob. (See the Ethical Issue essay, *Pesticides and the Nervous System*.)

Roles of Different Neurotransmitters

As we have seen, neurotransmitters are the chemical means of communication within the nervous system. There are dozens of neurotransmitters, carrying messages among neurons and between neurons and muscles or glands. The activities of neurotransmitters produce our thoughts and feelings and enable us to interact appropriately with the world around us. Some neurotransmitters produce different effects on different types of cells.

Acetylcholine and norepinephrine are neurotransmitters that act in both the peripheral and the central nervous systems. Both have either excitatory or inhibitory effects, depending on where they are released. As we see in Chapter 8, most internal organs receive input from neurons that release acetylcholine *and* from neurons that release norepinephrine. Norepinephrine stimulates most organs but inhibits certain others. Whatever the effect of norepinephrine on any particular organ, acetylcholine will have the opposite effect.

Acetylcholine is also the neurotransmitter released at every neuromuscular junction (the junction of a motor neuron and a skeletal muscle cell), where it triggers contraction of voluntary (skeletal) muscles. We can see how important the nerve activation of muscle is whenever the interaction of nerve and muscle is interrupted. An example of such interruption is *myasthenia gravis*, an autoimmune disease in which the body's defense mechanisms attack the acetylcholine receptors at neuromuscular junctions. With any repeated movement, the amount of acetylcholine released with each nerve impulse decreases after the neurons have fired a few times in succession. The low number of acetylcholine receptors in people with myasthenia gravis makes such people extremely sensitive to even the slightest decline in acetylcholine availability. As a result, a person with myasthenia gravis has little muscle strength, and their repeated movements become feeble quite rapidly. Drugs that inhibit acetylcholinesterase are prescribed to prevent the breakdown of acetylcholine, elevating the level of acetylcholine in the neuromuscular junction.

About 50 neurotransmitters are used by the central nervous system for communication between the neurons in our brains. Why so many? One reason seems to be that different neurotransmitters are involved with different behavioral systems. Norepinephrine, for instance, is important in the regulation of mood, in the pleasure system of the brain, and in arousal. Norepinephrine is thought to produce an energizing "good" feeling. It is also thought to be essential in hunger, thirst, and the sex drive. Serotonin is thought to promote a generalized feeling of well-being. Dopamine helps regulate emotions. It is also used in pathways that control complex movements.

A change in the level of a neurotransmitter affects the behaviors controlled by neurons that communicate using that neurotransmitter. Neurotransmitter levels may change as a result of taking certain drugs (see Chapter 8a). Changes in neurotransmitter levels also cause certain diseases.

Alzheimer's disease and acetylcholine

Alzheimer's disease is progressive and results in loss of memory, particularly for recent events, followed by sometimes severe personality changes (Figure **7.10**). In Alzheimer's disease, the parts of the brain

FIGURE 7.10 Former President Ronald Reagan died in June 2004 at the age of 93. He had Alzheimer's disease since at least 1994. His wife, Nancy Reagan, described Alzheimer's disease as "the long good-bye" because it robs people of their memories long before it takes their lives.

important in memory and intellectual functioning (hippocampus and cerebral cortex; see Chapter 8) lose large numbers of neurons. Some of the neurons in these regions use the neurotransmitter acetylcholine, which may decrease in level by as much as 90% in a person with Alzheimer's and possibly explains the loss of memory and mental capacity. In addition, a brain affected by Alzheimer's disease is pocked with clusters of proteins, some between the neurons (amyloid plaques) and others within the neurons (neurofibrillary tangles). The amyloid plaques and neurofibrillary tangles are the prime suspects for the cause of the death of acetylcholine-producing neurons.

In hypothesizing that the loss of acetylcholine is responsible for some of the Alzheimer's symptoms, researchers and physicians have attempted to treat Alzheimer's disease with drugs meant to raise or at least maintain acetylcholine levels. Although such drugs (Aricept, Exelon, and Reminyl) do improve the memory and intellectual ability of some people with Alzheimer's, they do not help in all cases. Moreover, any improvement is rapidly lost when a person stops taking the drugs.

Depression, serotonin, dopamine, and norepinephrine

We all describe ourselves as feeling depressed at times. However, more than 19 million Americans experience depression that lasts for weeks, months, or years and interferes with their ability to function in daily life. This condition is considered *clinical depression*, and it can affect anyone. It is thought to be related in some way to insufficient levels of the neurotransmitter serotonin as well as of dopamine and norepinephrine. Signs of depression can include a loss of interest and pleasure in the activities and hobbies that were previously pleasurable; anxiety; sleep problems; decreased energy; and feelings of sadness, hopelessness, worthlessness, and guilt. Depression takes the joy out of life and complicates certain medical conditions such as heart disease, cancer, diabetes, epilepsy, and osteoporosis.

Many depressed people exhibit suicidal behavior or actually commit suicide (currently, the third-ranking cause of death for teenagers). Studies comparing the brains of people who committed suicide with those of people who died of other causes reveal structural and chemical differences. The brains of people who took their own lives indicate a problem in the production and activity of serotonin.

Depression can be treated successfully. Unfortunately, few of the millions of people suffering from depression recognize the symptoms and seek help. Antidepressant drugs affect the functioning of the neurotransmitters responsible for the problem: norepinephrine and serotonin. Older medications affected both neurotransmitters simultaneously. Newer ones, including Prozac, Zoloft, and Paxil, specifically affect serotonin functioning, increasing the level of serotonin in the synapse by reducing its rate of removal. Other antidepressants (such as Welbutrin) increase norepinephrine and dopamine functioning by reducing their rates of removal from the synapse.

what would you do?

Few people would question the justifiability of providing drugs that elevate neurotransmitter function to someone who is depressed or suicidal in order to help the person live a normal life. However, researchers believe that the levels of key neurotransmitters also affect personality traits, such as shyness or impulsiveness. If so, we may someday be able to design our own personalities. Should minor personality problems be treated with drugs? Should a personality "flaw" like shyness or impulsiveness be treated? What do you think?

Parkinson's disease and dopamine

Parkinson's disease is a progressive disorder that results from the death of dopamine-producing neurons deep in the brain's movement control center (Figure **7.11**). A person with Parkinson's disease moves slowly, usually with a shuffling gait and a hunched posture, and may suffer from involuntary muscle contractions that further interfere with intended movements. The contractions may cause tremors (involuntary rhythmic shaking) of the hands or head, because of muscles alternately contracting and relaxing; or they may cause muscle rigidity, because of muscles contracting continuously. This muscle rigidity may cause sudden "freezing" in the middle of a movement.

As the dopamine-producing neurons in the brain's movement control center die, dopamine levels begin to fall. Initially, the symptoms are subtle and are often written off as part of the aging process. By the time the Parkinson's diagnosis is apparent, 80% of the neurons in this small area of the brain may already have died.

Attempts to treat Parkinson's disease have focused on replacing dopamine or helping the brain get by with the remaining

FIGURE 7.11 Actor Michael J. Fox and former heavyweight champion Muhammad Ali have Parkinson's disease, a progressive debilitating disease characterized by slowed movements, tremors, and muscle rigidity. The symptoms result from insufficient amounts of the neurotransmitter dopamine, caused by the death of dopamine-making nerve cells in a movement control center of the brain. The Michael J. Fox Foundation for Parkinson's Research (www.michaeljfox.org) funds research on the early diagnosis and treatment of Parkinson's disease.

dopamine. Unfortunately, swallowing pills containing dopamine does not help, because dopamine is prevented from reaching the brain by the blood–brain barrier you will read about in Chapter 8. Instead, patients are given other substances that *can* reach the brain. The most common and effective treatment combines two drugs: L-dopa, an amino acid that the brain converts to dopamine, and carbidopa, which prevents dopamine from forming outside of the brain and causing undesirable side effects. However, this treatment does not stop the steady loss of dopamine-producing neurons, so it loses effectiveness as the disease progresses. Some patients are treated with drugs that enhance their levels of dopamine by inhibiting the enzyme that breaks down dopamine.

highlighting the concepts

Cells of the Nervous System (pp. 121–122)

- The nervous system has two types of specialized cells: neurons (nerve cells) and neuroglial cells.
- Neuroglial cells outnumber neurons. They provide structural support for neurons, supply nerve growth factors, and form myelin sheaths around certain axons.
- There are three general categories of neurons. Sensory (or afferent) neurons conduct information from the sensory receptors toward the central nervous system. Motor (or efferent) neurons conduct information away from the central nervous system to an effector. Association neurons (interneurons) are positioned between sensory and motor neurons and are located in the central nervous system.

Structure of Neurons (pp. 122–123)

- Neurons are specialized for communicating with other cells. A "typical" neuron has a cell body containing the organelles that maintain the cell. Many branching fibers called dendrites conduct messages *toward* the cell body. A single long axon conducts impulses *away* from the cell body.
- An axon may be enclosed in an insulating layer called a myelin sheath. Neuroglia called Schwann cells form the myelin sheath by wrapping their plasma membranes repeatedly around the axon. The myelin sheath greatly increases the rate at which impulses are conducted along an axon; it also plays a role in the regeneration of cut axons in the peripheral nervous system.

Nerve Impulses (pp. 124–127)

- The message conducted by a neuron, called a nerve impulse or action potential, is caused by sodium ions (Na^+) and potassium ions (K^+) crossing the neuron's plasma membrane to enter and leave the cell.
- Ion channels in the plasma membrane are small pores through which ions move without the use of cellular energy. Ion channels are usually specific to one or a few types of ions.
- The sodium-potassium pump uses cellular energy in the form of ATP to pump sodium ions out of the cell and potassium ions into the cell against their concentration gradients.
- In the resting state, a neuron has an electrical potential difference, called the resting potential, across its plasma membrane. The resting potential is generated by an unequal distribution of charges across the membrane that makes the neuron more negative inside than outside; there are many negatively charged proteins inside the cell. Sodium ions are in greater concentration outside the neuron, and potassium ions are in greater concentration inside.
- The action potential begins when a region of the membrane suddenly becomes permeable to sodium ions. If enough sodium ions enter to reach threshold, an action potential is generated. The gates on sodium channels open, and many sodium ions enter the cell, making its interior in that region of the membrane temporarily positive (depolarization). Potassium ions then leave the cell, making that region inside once again more negative than the outside (repolarization). The same events are repeated all along the axon in a wave of depolarization and repolarization called an action potential.
- At the end of an action potential, the sodium-potassium pump moves sodium ions out of the neuron and potassium ions into the neuron, restoring the original ion distribution.
- Once initiated, an action potential sweeps to the end of the axon without diminishing in strength.
- During the brief refractory period immediately following an action potential, the neuron cannot be stimulated.

Synaptic Transmission (pp. 127–131)

- The point where one neuron meets another is called a synapse. The neuron sending the message (the presynaptic neuron) and the neuron receiving the message (the postsynaptic neuron) are separated by a small gap called the synaptic cleft.
- The arrival of a nerve impulse at the axon's end causes calcium ions to enter the presynaptic cell there. These ions cause synaptic vesicles that store neurotransmitters to fuse with the plasma membrane of the presynaptic neuron and release their contents into the synaptic cleft. The neurotransmitter then diffuses across the gap and binds to receptors on the membrane of the postsynaptic neuron.
- If the synapse is excitatory, sodium ions enter the postsynaptic cell and increase the likelihood that it will generate a nerve impulse. If the synapse is inhibitory, the charge difference across the membrane of the receiving neuron is increased, reducing the likelihood that the postsynaptic neuron will generate a nerve impulse.
- Postsynaptic cells integrate excitatory and inhibitory input from many cells. If threshold is reached, an action potential is generated in the postsynaptic cell.
- The neurotransmitter is quickly removed from the synapse either by enzymatic breakdown or by transport back into the presynaptic neuron.
- Acetylcholine, epinephrine, and norepinephrine are neurotransmitters used in both the peripheral and central nervous systems.
- Many neurotransmitters are found in the brain. Different ones are active in different behavioral systems. Disturbances in brain chemistry affect mood and behavior.

recognizing key terms

reviewing the concepts

1. List the three types of neurons, and give their general functions. *p. 121*
2. What are the functions of neuroglial cells? *p. 121*
3. Draw a typical neuron and label the following: cell body, nucleus, dendrites, and axon. *p. 122*
4. Explain how a myelin sheath is formed. What are the functions of the myelin sheath? *pp. 122–123*
5. Describe the distribution of sodium ions and potassium ions during a neuron's resting state. Explain how the movements of these ions affect the charge difference across the membrane. *p. 125*
6. Why is the resting potential important? *p. 125*
7. What happens to sodium ions at the beginning of an action potential? *p. 127*
8. Describe the events that bring about the restoration of the charge difference across the membrane (repolarization). *p. 127*
9. How is the original ion distribution of sodium and potassium ions restored? *p. 127*
10. What is the refractory period? *p. 127*
11. Draw a synapse between two neurons. Label the following: presynaptic neuron, postsynaptic neuron, synaptic cleft, synaptic vesicles, neurotransmitter molecules, and receptors. *pp. 127–129*
12. How do the events at an excitatory synapse differ from those at an inhibitory synapse? *p. 129*
13. How is the action of a neurotransmitter terminated? *pp. 129–130*

14. Choose the *incorrect* statement:
    a. Neurotransmitters diffuse across the myelin sheath.
    b. An inhibitory neurotransmitter makes it less likely that an action potential will be generated in the postsynaptic (after the synapse) neuron.
    c. Neurotransmitters are stored in synaptic vesicles.
    d. Most interneurons are found in the central nervous system.

15. In botulism, a type of food poisoning, the poison produced by bacteria in the spoiled food prevents the person's synaptic vesicles from fusing with the neuron's membrane. You would expect that this effect would
    a. cause excessive destruction of neurotransmitter in the synaptic cleft.
    b. destroy myelin.
    c. prevent the message of the presynaptic cell from reaching the postsynaptic cell.
    d. cause neurotransmitter to clog the synaptic cleft.

16. In a resting neuron
    a. potassium ions are more concentrated outside the membrane than inside.
    b. the inside is more negative than the outside.
    c. sodium ions are more concentrated inside than outside.
    d. action potentials are being generated.

17. You are a neurophysiologist trying to identify the function of a particular nerve cell. You notice that this nerve cell fires immediately before a person's pinky finger bends. You correctly conclude that this axon
    a. may be part of a sensory neuron carrying information from the finger toward the brain.
    b. may be part of a motor neuron carrying information from the brain toward the pinky.
    c. is without a doubt part of an interneuron.
    d. is dead.

18. The synaptic cleft
    a. is a chemical that allows two neurons to communicate with one another.
    b. is a gap between two neurons.
    c. is a gap between two Schwann cells forming the myelin sheath.
    d. allows saltatory conduction.

19. The _____ is an insulating layer formed by Schwann cells that increases the rate of an action potential.

20. The _____ uses cellular energy to move sodium ions out of the axon and potassium ions into the axon.

21. Parkinson's disease is caused by the loss of neurons that produce the neurotransmitter _____.

applying the concepts

1. Indira has taken the sedative Valium, a drug that has a molecular shape similar to that of the neurotransmitter GABA (an inhibitory neurotransmitter). When Valium binds to GABA receptors, it causes the same effects as the binding of GABA itself. Based on this information, explain why Valium has a calming effect on the nervous system.

2. A nerve gas (diisopropyl fluorophosphate) that was once used in chemical warfare blocks the action of acetylcholinesterase, the enzyme that breaks down acetylcholine in the synapse. What effects would you expect this gas to have at the synapses that use acetylcholine?

3. Mohammed has a kidney condition that raises the level of potassium ions in the extracellular fluid that bathes cells. What effect would you expect this condition to have on his ability to generate nerve impulses (action potentials)?

4. Kerry is experiencing a weakness in her legs. A physician tells her that she has Guillain-Barré syndrome, which is a progressive but reversible condition in which the myelin sheath is lost from parts of the nervous system. Explain why the loss of myelin would cause weakness in Kerry's legs.

5. Ouabain is a drug that causes a neuron to lose its resting potential. What effect would ouabain have on the ability of a neuron to generate action potentials?

becoming information literate

Attention deficit/hyperactivity disorder (ADHD) is caused by a neurotransmitter imbalance. Write a short article for the health section of a local newspaper describing the symptoms, causes, and treatment of ADHD. Use at least three reliable sources (books, journals, or websites). List each source you considered, and explain why you chose the three sources you used.

Additional questions can be found online at the Human Biology Place, www.humanbiology.com.

8

The Nervous System

Gasp! Gulp. The nervous system works in concert with other systems in the body to interpret and respond to events and objects in the world around us.

John's fingers trembled as he rang Tegan's doorbell. How would their first date go? Would he know the right things to say? To do? Would she like the movie he had selected? His mind was racing. In the theater, he could hardly taste the popcorn they were sharing. He barely felt the ice from his cola when he spilled it on his lap.

Eventually his nervousness subsided, and he got caught up in the film. His pulse raced as the aliens attacked with missiles, guns, and chainsaws. He dodged in his seat as smashed cars and shattered glass appeared to fly off the screen. He laughed at the crisp one-liners.

On the way home, Tegan smiled and thanked him for a lovely evening. She said she had really enjoyed the witty script and amazing special effects. Could they see another film next week, he asked nervously? "Of course," she said, "perhaps the new Brad Pitt film at the Cineplex downtown." Awkwardly, they kissed goodnight.

Although they were probably not aware of it, John and Tegan's night at the movies was sponsored by their nervous systems. Emotion, foresight, language, reflexes, reasoning, and awareness of sensory stimuli all depend on the actions of billions of neurons in the brain, spinal cord, and peripheral nerves. How can this array of cellular wires and switches control such a wide range of human responses?

In this chapter, we explore the organization of the nervous system and the structures responsible for its many functions. We also discuss some disorders of the brain and spinal cord and their effects on the human body and mind.

Organization of the Nervous System

If you were to view the nervous system apart from the rest of the body, you would see a dense mass of neural tissue where the head should be, with a cord of neural tissue extending downward from it where the middle of the back should be. These structures are the brain and spinal cord, respectively, and they constitute the **central nervous system** (**CNS**; Figure **8.1**), which integrates and coordinates all voluntary and involuntary nervous functions. Connected to the brain and spinal cord are many communication "cables"—the nerves that carry messages to and from the CNS. The nerves branch extensively, forming a vast network. Some of their cell bodies are grouped together in small clusters called **ganglia** (singular, *ganglion*). The nerves and ganglia are located outside of the CNS and make up the **peripheral nervous system (PNS).** The PNS keeps the CNS in continuous contact with almost every part of the body.

The peripheral nervous system can be further subdivided on the basis of function into the somatic nervous system and the autonomic nervous system. The **somatic nervous system** consists of nerves that carry information to and from the CNS, resulting in sensations and voluntary movement. The **autonomic nervous system,** on the other hand, governs the involuntary, subconscious activities that keep the body functioning properly. The autonomic nervous system has two parts that generally produce opposite effects on the muscles or glands they control. One, the **sympathetic nervous system,** is in charge during stressful or emergency conditions. The other, the **parasympathetic nervous system,** adjusts bodily function so that energy is conserved during nonstressful times.

Although we have described the nervous system as having different parts and divisions, remember that all the parts function as a coordinated whole. Imagine for a moment that you are meditating in the park; your eyes are closed, and you are resting. While you are relaxing, the parasympathetic nervous system is ensuring that your life-sustaining bodily activities continue. Suddenly, someone grasps your hand. Sensory receptors in the skin (which are part of the somatic nervous system) respond to the pressure and warmth of the hand by sending messages over sensory nerves to the spinal cord. Neurons within the spinal cord relay the messages to the brain. The brain integrates incoming sensory information and "decides" on an appropriate response. For example, the brain may generate messages that cause your eyes to open. If the sight of the person holding your hand produces strong emotion, the sympathetic nervous system may speed up your heartbeat and perhaps even your breathing.

The Central Nervous System

The central nervous system includes the brain and spinal cord, which are made up of many closely packed neurons. Neurons are very fragile, and most cannot divide and produce new cells. Therefore, with few exceptions, a neuron that is damaged or dies cannot be replaced.

Protection of the Central Nervous System

The brain and spinal cord are protected by bony cases (the skull and vertebral column), membranes (the meninges), and a fluid cushion (cerebrospinal fluid).

The meninges

The **meninges** are three protective connective tissue coverings of the brain and spinal cord (Figure **8.2**). The outermost layer, the dura mater, is tough and leathery. Beneath the dura mater is the arachnoid (Latin, meaning "like a cobweb"). The arachnoid is anchored to the next-lower layer of meninges by thin, threadlike extensions that resemble a spider's web (hence the name of the layer). The innermost layer, the pia mater, is molded around the brain. Fitting like a leotard, the pia mater dips into every irregularity on the brain's surface.

Meningitis is an inflammation of the meninges. All cases of meningitis must be taken seriously because the infection can spread to the underlying nervous tissue and cause encephalitis (inflammation of the brain), which can be deadly. Many types of bacteria and certain viruses can cause meningitis. If bacteria are the cause, the person is treated with antibiotics. If a virus is the cause, treatment includes medicines to alleviate pain and fever while the body's immune system fights the virus.

Freshmen college students housed in dormitories are at increased risk of getting bacterial meningitis because of their close living quarters. Part of the reason is the means by which the bacteria are

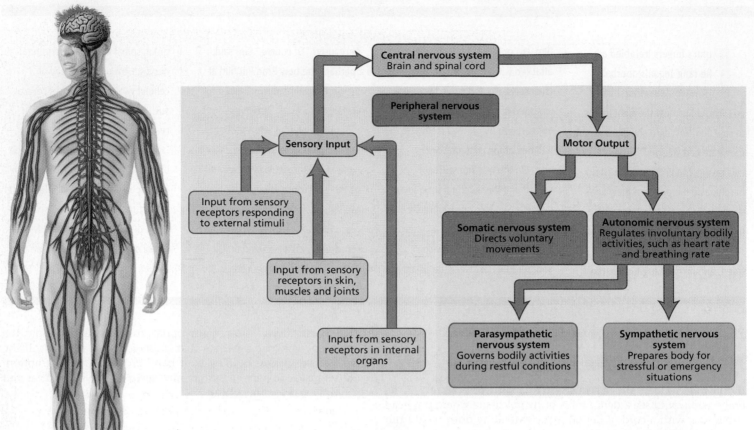

FIGURE 8.1 An overview of the nervous system. The various parts of the human nervous system have special functions but work together as an integrated whole.

spread. People can carry the bacteria in their throat without having any symptoms of illness and can spread the infection through coughing, sneezing, or intimate kissing. Upperclassmen are less susceptible, perhaps because they have built up immune defenses against the bacteria. Vaccines are available against most, but not all, forms of meningitis. Some colleges are now requiring that incoming freshmen be vaccinated against some of the most common forms of meningitis.

Cerebrospinal fluid

The **cerebrospinal fluid** fills the space between layers of the meninges as well as the internal cavities of the brain, called *ventricles,* and the cavity within the spinal cord, called the *central canal.* This fluid is formed in the ventricles and circulates from them through the central canal. Eventually, cerebrospinal fluid is reabsorbed into the blood.

Cerebrospinal fluid has several important functions:

- **Shock absorption.** Just as an air bag protects the driver of a car by preventing impact with the steering wheel, the cerebrospinal fluid protects the brain by cushioning its impact with the skull during blows or other head trauma.

- **Support.** Because the brain floats in the cerebrospinal fluid, it is not crushed under its own weight.

The bones of the skull and vertebral column are hard cases that protect the brain and spinal cord.

The meninges are three membranes that protect the brain and spinal cord.

Ventricles of the brain

Cerebrospinal fluid cushions the brain and spinal cord.

FIGURE 8.2 The central nervous system is protected by the meninges, the cerebrospinal fluid, and the bones of the skull and vertebral column.

Brain Injury: A Silent Epidemic

Most of us take our brain for granted. We assume that this fragile control center is safe from harm, safely guarded by the thick bones of our skulls and cushioned by cerebrospinal fluid. The truth is that the brain is more vulnerable than we may think, and injuries to this vital organ are frighteningly common. Brain injury has been termed a "silent epidemic." It is silent because a brain injured person doesn't have visible physical symptoms. It is an epidemic because it is so common. One in every 220 people in the United States is suffering from a brain injury. A brain injury occurs every 16 seconds; a death from head injury occurs every 12 minutes.

Brain injuries are categorized as either acquired or traumatic. Acquired brain injury (ABI) is caused by a disruption in oxygen flow to the brain. Examples of ABIs include strokes and aneurysms, heart attacks, brain tumors, anoxia, meningitis, seizure disorders, and substance abuse. There is a strong correlation between substance abuse and acquired brain injury because alcohol and other substances are neurotoxins that cause damage to the brain with repeated use. Furthermore, substance abuse is associated with poor nutrition, which can cause dehydration and ultimately wastes brain cells.

Traumatic brain injury, or TBI, is caused by an external force. There are two types of TBI:

open and closed. An open head injury is when the scalp is cut through and the skull is broken, damaging the brain underneath. A closed head injury happens when the head suddenly changes motion, forcing the brain to follow the movement, like when a car stops very suddenly. The brain is soft and jellylike, and it sits snugly within the skull. Sudden movement of the head can cause it to ricochet within the skull, damaging the millions of nerve fibers that run from one part of the brain to another. Also, the inside of the skull has many ridges and sharp edges that can cut or bruise the brain. Common causes of TBI include motor vehicle accidents, firearms, brawls, slip-and-fall accidents, and accidents related to sports such as skiing. Substance abuse is also associated with TBI, as the impairment caused by alcohol and drugs can lead to vehicular accidents and increase risk of falls and physical altercations. You can protect yourself against TBI by wearing a helmet when biking, skiing, or doing any other sport where a fall is likely. Since motor vehicle accidents cause nearly half of all head injuries, please buckle up!

TBI is getting a lot of attention recently because nearly two-thirds of injured U.S. soldiers sent from Iraq to Walter Reed Medical Center have been diagnosed with traumatic brain injury. That percentage, thought to be higher than in any other past U.S. conflict, is said to be due to improved armor that allows soldiers to survive injuries that previously would have been fatal.

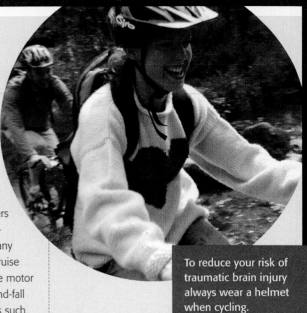

To reduce your risk of traumatic brain injury always wear a helmet when cycling.

Also, compared to other wars, fewer firearms and more improvised explosive devices (IEDs) are being used in combat; the intense vibrations from these explosives cause the brain to move within the soldiers' skulls.

Regardless of cause, no two brain injuries are the same. The symptoms are diverse and vary widely due to severity and location of injury as well as the individual's functioning before the accident. Symptoms frequently include cognitive and emotional limitations, including difficulties with memory, attention, and reasoning; depression; anxiety; and impulse control and anger management issues. Physical impairments are common and can range from weakness on one side of the body to paralysis.

- **Nourishment and waste removal.** The cerebrospinal fluid delivers nutrients and chemical messengers and removes waste products.

The brain is, indeed, protected by the skull, meninges, and cerebrospinal fluid. Nonetheless, 7 million brain injuries occur annually in the United States. We discuss brain injury further in the Health Issue essay, *Brain Injury: A Silent Epidemic.*

The blood–brain barrier

The CNS is also protected by the **blood–brain barrier,** a mechanism that selects the substances permitted to enter the cerebrospinal fluid from the blood. This barrier is formed by the tight junctions between the cells of the capillary walls that supply blood to the brain and spinal cord. Because the cells are held together much more tightly than are cells in capillaries in the rest of the body, substances in the blood are forced to pass through the cells of the capillaries instead of between the cells. Thus, the mem-

branes of the capillary cells filter and adjust the composition of the filtrate by selecting the substances that can leave the blood. The plasma membranes of the capillary walls are largely lipid. So, lipid-soluble substances, including oxygen and carbon dioxide, can pass through easily. Certain drugs, including caffeine and alcohol, are lipid soluble, explaining why they can have a rapid effect on the brain. However, the blood–brain barrier prevents many potentially life-saving, infection-fighting, or tumor-suppressing drugs that are not lipid soluble from reaching brain tissue, which frustrates physicians.

Brain: Command Center

In a sense, your brain is more "you" than is any other part of your body, because it holds your emotions and the keys to your personality. Yet, if you were to look at your brain, you might not recognize it as yourself. The brain is the consistency of soft cheese and weighs less than 1600 g (3 lb), which is probably less than 3% of your

Q *How do the left and right cerebral hemispheres communicate with one another?*

Cerebrum
- Contains sensory areas for skin senses, vision, hearing, olfaction
- Motor areas for voluntary control of movement
- Association areas for interpreting sensations, language, thinking, decision making, self-awareness, creativity, and storage of memories

Corpus callosum
- Allows left and right cerebral hemispheres to communicate with one another

Thalamus
- Processes all sensory information (except olfaction)
- Relays information to appropriate higher brain centers

Hypothalamus
- Controls heart rate, blood pressure, breathing rate, body temperature, food intake
- Is a center for emotions
- Serves as "master biological clock"

Brainstem

Midbrain
- Relays information between the cerebellum or spinal cord and the cerebrum
- Integrates sensory input

Pons
- A bridge between higher and lower brain centers

Medulla oblongata
- Contains autonomic centers for heart rate and digestive activities
- Relays sensory information to thalamus

Cerebellum
- Coordinates sensory–motor voluntary movement
- Stores memory of learned motor patterns

FIGURE 8.3 A section through the brain from front to back, indicating the functions of selected structures

A *The corpus callosum*

body weight. Nevertheless, it is the origin of your secret thoughts and desires; it remembers your most embarrassing moment; and it keeps all your body systems functioning harmoniously while your conscious mind concentrates on other activities. Let's look at how its many circuits are organized to perform these amazing feats.

Cerebrum

The **cerebrum** is the largest and most prominent part of the brain (Figure **8.3**). It is, quite literally, your "thinking cap." Accounting for 83% of the total brain weight, the cerebrum gives you most of your human characteristics.

The many ridges and grooves on the surface of the cerebrum make it appear wrinkled. Some furrows are deeper than others. The deepest indentation is in the center and runs from front to back. This groove, called the longitudinal fissure, separates the cerebrum into two hemispheres (Figure **8.4**). Each hemisphere receives sensory information from and directs the movements of the opposite side of the body. In addition, the hemispheres process information in slightly different ways and are, therefore, specialized for slightly different mental functions.

The thin outer layer of each hemisphere is called the **cerebral cortex**. (*Cortex* means "bark or rind.") The cerebral cortex consists of billions of neuroglial cells, nerve cell bodies, and unmyelinated axons and is described as **gray matter.** Although the cerebral cortex

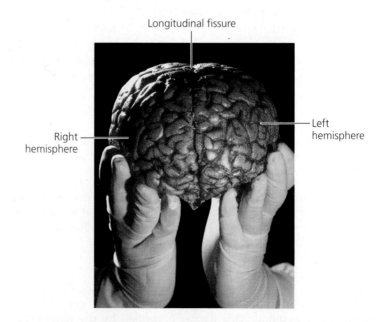

Longitudinal fissure

Right hemisphere

Left hemisphere

FIGURE 8.4 A photograph of the human brain from the front, showing the left and right cerebral hemispheres

is only about 2.5 mm (about 1/8 in.) thick, it is highly folded. These folds, or convolutions, triple the surface area of the cortex.

The **corpus callosum** is a band of white matter that allows communication between the cerebral hemispheres.

Gray matter consists of interneurons, cell bodies, and unmyelinated axons that integrate information.

White matter consists of myelinated axons that allow communication over long distances.

FIGURE 8.5 A cross section through the brain, showing the gray matter (the cerebral cortex), white matter, and corpus callosum

Beneath the cortex is the cerebral **white matter,** which appears white because it consists primarily of myelinated axons. Recall from Chapter 7 that myelin sheaths increase the rate of conduction along axons and are, therefore, found on axons that conduct information over long distances. The axons of the cerebral white matter allow various regions of the brain to communicate with one another and with the spinal cord. A very important band of white matter, called the *corpus callosum,* connects the two cerebral hemispheres so they can communicate with one another (Figure **8.5**).

Other grooves on the surface of the brain mark the boundaries of four lobes on each hemisphere: the *frontal, parietal, temporal,* and *occipital lobes* (Figure **8.6**). Each of these lobes has its own specializations. Although the assignment of a specific function to a particular region of the cerebral cortex is imprecise, it is generally agreed that there are three types of functional areas: sensory, motor, and association.

Sensory Areas   Our awareness of sensations depends on the sensory areas of the cerebral cortex. The various sensory receptors of the body send information to the cortex, where each sense is processed in a different region. If you stand on a street corner watching a parade go by, you hear the band play because information from your ears is sent to the auditory area in the temporal

FIGURE 8.6 The cerebral cortex. (a) The cerebral cortex has four lobes. Some of the functions associated with each lobe are indicated. (b) These PET scans of the brain show regions of increased blood flow during different mental activities. The increased flow of blood shows which region becomes active when the cerebrum is engaged in hearing words, seeing words, speaking words, and reading words. Notice the relation between active regions of the cerebral cortex during these tasks and the cortical areas for various language skills shown in part (a).

lobe. You see the flags wave because information from your eyes is sent to the visual area in the occipital lobe. When you catch a whiff of popcorn, information is sent from the olfactory (smell) receptors in your nose to the olfactory area in the temporal lobe of the cortex. As you eat that popcorn, you know it is too salty because information from the taste receptors is sent to gustatory areas in the parietal lobe.

Still watching the parade, you know that you are standing in the hot sun and that your belt is too tight because information from touch, pain, and temperature receptors in the skin and from receptors in the joints and skeletal muscles is sent to the **primary somatosensory area**. This region forms a band in the parietal lobes that stretches over the cortex from ear to ear (Figure **8.7**). Sensations from different parts of the body are represented in different regions of the primary somatosensory area (of the hemisphere on the opposite side of the body). The greater the degree of sensitivity, the greater the area of cortex devoted to that body part. Thus, your most sensitive body parts, such as the tongue, hands, face, and genitals, have more of the cortex devoted to them than do less sensitive areas, such as the forearm.

Motor Areas If you decide to join the parade, the **primary motor area** (Figure 8.7) of the cerebral cortex will send messages to your skeletal muscles. This motor area controls voluntary movement. It also forms a band in the frontal lobe that stretches over the cortex, just anterior to the primary somatosensory area. The motor area is organized in a manner similar to the somatosensory area. Each point on its surface corresponds to the movement of a different part of the body. The parts of the body we have finer control over, such as the tongue and fingers, have greater representation on the motor cortex than do regions with less dexterity, such as the trunk of the body.

Just in front of the motor cortex is the *premotor cortex*. It coordinates learned motor skills that are patterned or repetitive, such as typing or playing a musical instrument. The premotor cortex coordinates the movement of several muscle groups at the same time. When a pattern of movement is repeated many times, the proper pattern of stimulation is stored in the premotor cortex. For example, as a guitar player practices playing a particular song many times, the pattern of stimulation needed to play that song is stored in the premotor cortex. Then, each time the song is played,

Q *Our lips are more sensitive than is the skin on our forearm. We also have greater motor control of our lips than we do of our forearm. How is this difference in sensitivity and motor control represented on the cerebral cortex?*

FIGURE 8.7 The primary motor and the primary somatosensory regions of the cerebral cortex are organized in such a way that each location on their surface corresponds to a particular part of the body. The general arrangement is similar in the two regions.

A *Areas with greater sensitivity and motor control have a proportionally larger area of representation on the cortex than do areas with less sensitivity and motor control, such as the forearm.*

the premotor cortex will stimulate the primary cortex in the pattern needed to play that song, without requiring the musician to think about where on the strings the fingers should be placed.

Association Areas Next to each primary sensory area is an association area. These communicate with the sensory and motor areas, and with other parts of the brain, to analyze and act on sensory input. In particular, each sensory association area communicates with the general interpretation area, to recognize what the sensory receptors are sensing. The general interpretation area assigns meaning to sensory information by integrating the input from sensory association areas with stored sensory memories. For example, on a dark night your eyes may detect a small, moving object. If the object then rubs against your legs and purrs, your general interpretation area will assist you in recognizing it as the neighbor's friendly cat. However, if the object turns away from you and raises its tail, you will recognize it as a skunk.

Once the sensory input has been interpreted, the information is sent to the most complicated of all association areas, the **prefrontal cortex**. This most anterior part of the frontal lobe predicts the consequences of various possible responses to the information it receives and decides which response will be best for you in your current situation. The prefrontal cortex enables us to reason, plan for the long term, and think about abstract concepts. It also plays a key role in determining our personality.

Thalamus

The cerebral hemispheres sit comfortably over the **thalamus** (see Figure 8.3). The thalamus is often described as the gateway to the cerebral cortex because all messages *to* the cerebral cortex must pass *through* the thalamus first. The thalamus functions in sensory experience, motor activity, stimulation of the cerebral cortex, and memory. Sensory input from every sense except smell and from all parts of the body is delivered to the thalamus. The thalamus sorts the information by function and relays it to appropriate regions of the cortex for processing. Some regions of the thalamus also integrate information from different sources rather than just relaying it. At the thalamic level of processing, you have a general impression of whether the sensation is pleasant or unpleasant. If you step on a tack, for instance, you may experience pain by the time the messages reach the thalamus; however, you will not know where you hurt until after the message is directed to the cerebral cortex.

Hypothalamus

Below the thalamus is the **hypothalamus** (*hypo,* under), a small region of the brain that is largely responsible for homeostasis—the body's maintenance of a stable environment for its cells (discussed in Chapter 4). The hypothalamus, shown in Figure 8.3, coordinates the activities of the nervous and endocrine (hormonal) systems through its influence on the pituitary gland. The hypothalamus also influences blood pressure, heart rate, digestive activity, breathing rate, and many other vital physiological processes. It keeps body temperature near the set point, and it regulates hunger and thirst and therefore the intake of food. Moreover, because the hypothalamus receives input from the cerebral cortex, it can make your heart beat faster when you so much as see or think of something exciting or dangerous—a rattlesnake about to strike, for instance.

The hypothalamus is part of the limbic system (discussed later in this chapter), so it is also part of the circuitry for emotions. Specific regions of the hypothalamus play a role in the sex drive and in the perception of pain, pleasure, fear, and anger.

The hypothalamus also contains an area called the *suprachiasmatic nucleus,* often described as the body's "master biological clock." Day after day, many of the physiological processes within the body, affecting many physical abilities and even a person's mental sharpness, fluctuate so predictably that the variations are called biological rhythms and are described as being controlled by biological clocks. The suprachiasmatic nucleus synchronizes all these biological clocks and sets the timing for all the body's biological rhythms. Note that these fluctuations do not negate the concept of homeostasis; they simply remind us that the body's optimal internal state is not always the same. Instead, homeostasis is often rhythmic, so physiological processes fluctuate in a predictable manner.

Cerebellum

The **cerebellum** (see Figure 8.3) is the part of the brain responsible for sensory–motor coordination. It acts as an automatic pilot that produces smooth, well-timed voluntary movements and controls equilibrium and posture. Sensory information concerning the position of joints and the degree of tension in muscles and tendons is sent to the cerebellum from all parts of the body. By integrating this information with input from the eyes and the equilibrium receptors in the ears, the cerebellum knows the body's position and direction of movement at any given instant.

The coordination of sensory input and motor output by the cerebellum involves two important processes: comparison and prediction. During every move you make, the cerebellum continuously compares the actual position of each part of the body with where it *ought* to be at that moment (in relation to the intended movement) and makes the necessary corrections. Try to touch the tips of your two index fingers together above your head. You probably missed on the first attempt. However, the cerebellum makes the necessary corrections, and you will likely succeed on the next attempt. At the same time, the cerebellum calculates future positions of a body part during a movement. Then, just before that part reaches the intended position, the cerebellum sends messages to stop the movement at a specific point. Therefore, when you scratch an itch on your cheek, your hand stops before slapping your face!

Brain stem

The brain stem consists of the medulla oblongata, the midbrain, and the pons. The **medulla oblongata** is often called simply the medulla (see Figure 8.3). This marvelous inch of nervous tissue contains reflex centers for some of life's most vital physiological functions—including the pace of the basic breathing rhythm, the force and rate of heart contraction, and blood pressure. The medulla connects the spinal cord to the rest of the brain. Therefore, all sensory information going to the upper regions of the brain and all motor messages leaving the brain are carried by nerve pathways running through the medulla.

stop and think

Why would a brain tumor that destroyed the functioning of nerve cells in the medulla lead to death more quickly than a tumor of the same size on the cerebral cortex?

The **midbrain** processes information about sights and sounds and controls simple reflex responses to these stimuli. For example, when you hear an unexpected loud sound, your reflexive response is to turn your head and direct your eyes toward the source of the sound.

The **pons**, which means "bridge," connects lower portions of the CNS with higher brain structures. More specifically, it connects the spinal cord and cerebellum with the cerebrum, thalamus, and hypothalamus. In addition, the pons has a region that assists the medulla in regulating respiration.

Limbic system

The **limbic system** is a collective term for a group of structures that help to produce emotions and memory (Figure **8.8**). The limbic system is defined on the basis of function rather than anatomy, and it includes parts of several brain regions and the neural pathways that connect them.

The limbic system is our emotional brain. It allows us to experience countless emotions, including rage, pain, fear, sorrow, joy, and sexual pleasure. Emotions are important because they motivate behavior that will increase the chance of survival. Fear, for example, may have evolved to focus the mind on the threats in the environment so it can prepare the body to face them.

Connections between the cerebrum and the limbic system allow us to have *feelings* about *thoughts*. As a result, you may become excited at the thought of winning the lottery. Such connections also allow us to have thoughts about feelings, thus keeping us from responding to emotions, such as rage, in ways that would be unwise. The limbic system includes the hypothalamus, as Figure 8.8 shows. In addition, it is connected to lower brain centers, such as the medulla, that control the activity of internal organs. Therefore, we also have "gut" responses to emotions.

You wouldn't be you without your memories, and the limbic system plays a role in forming them. Memory, the storage and retrieval of information, takes place in two stages. The first is **short-term memory,** which holds a small amount of information for a few seconds or minutes, as when you look up a phone number and remember it only long enough to place the call. The

second stage, **long-term memory**, stores seemingly limitless amounts of information for hours, days, or years. Not all short-term memories get consolidated into long-term memories, but when they do, the **hippocampus** plays an essential role. The amygdala, another part of the limbic system that functions in long-term memory, has widespread connections to sensory areas as well as to emotion centers. It associates memories gathered through different senses and links them to emotional states.

The olfactory bulb transmits information about odors from the nose to the limbic system. Thus, the limbic system is a center where emotions, memory, and our sense of smell meet. As a result, we often have emotional responses to odors. The association between odor and emotion is the basis of aromatherapy as well as the perfume and scented candle industries. The interaction of emotion, sense of smell, and memory explains why odors can bring back memories. For example, the smell of cinnamon rolls may be pleasant because it reminds you of your grandmother baking special treats.

Reticular Activating System

The **reticular activating system (RAS)** is an extensive network of neurons that runs through the medulla and projects to the cerebral cortex (shown in Figure 8.8 in green). The RAS functions as a net, or filter, for sensory input. Our brain is constantly flooded with tremendous amounts of sensory information, about 100 million impulses each second, most of them trivial. The RAS filters out repetitive, familiar stimuli—the sound of street traffic, paper rustling, the coughing of the person next to you, or the pressure of clothing. However, infrequent or important stimuli pass through the RAS to the cerebral cortex and, therefore, reach our consciousness. Because of the RAS, you can fall asleep with the television on but wake up when someone whispers your name.

In addition, the RAS is an activating center. Unless inhibited by other brain regions, the RAS activates the cerebral cortex, keeping it alert and "awake." Consciousness occurs only while the RAS stimulates the cerebral cortex. When sleep centers in other regions of the brain inhibit activity in the RAS, we sleep. In essence, then, the cerebrum "sleeps" whenever it is not stimulated by the RAS. Sensory input to the RAS results in stimulation of the cerebral cortex and an increase in consciousness, which explains why it is usually easier to sleep in a dark, quiet room than in an airport terminal. Conscious activity in the cerebral cortex can also stimulate the RAS, which in turn will stimulate the cerebral cortex. Therefore, thinking about a problem may keep you awake all night.

Cerebrum

Thalamus

Hypothalamus

Hippocampus

Amygdala

Olfactory bulb

FIGURE 8.8 The limbic system and reticular activating system. The diagram shows the limbic system in purple as a three-dimensional structure within the brain, viewed from the left side. The reticular activating system is shown in green. Note the upward arrows.

stop and think

When a boxer is hit very hard in the jaw, his head—containing his medulla and RAS—is twisted sharply. Why might this twisting result in a knockout, in which the boxer loses consciousness?

Spinal Cord: Message Transmission and Reflex Center

The other major component of the central nervous system besides the brain is the spinal cord. The **spinal cord** is a tube of neural tissue that is continuous with the medulla at the base of the brain and extends about 45 cm (17 in.) to just below the last rib. For most of its length, the spinal cord is about the diameter of your little finger. It becomes slightly thicker in two regions, just below the neck and at the end of the cord, because of the large group of nerves connecting these regions of the cord with the arms and legs. The central canal, filled with cerebrospinal fluid, runs the length of the spinal cord.

The spinal cord is encased in and protected by the stacked bones of the vertebral column (Figure **8.9**). Pairs of spinal nerves (considered part of the peripheral nervous system) extend from the spinal cord through openings between the vertebrae to serve different parts of the body. The vertebrae are separated by disks of cartilage that act as cushions.

The spinal cord has two functions: (1) to transmit messages to and from the brain and (2) to serve as a reflex center. The transmission of messages is performed primarily by white matter, found toward the outer surface of the spinal cord. White matter in the spinal cord consists of myelinated axons grouped into tracts. Ascending tracts carry sensory information up to the brain. Descending tracts carry motor information from the brain to a nerve leaving the spinal cord.

The second function of the spinal cord is to serve as a reflex center. A reflex is an automatic response to a stimulus, prewired in a circuit of neurons called a **reflex arc**. The circuit consists of a receptor, a sensory neuron (which brings information from the receptors toward the CNS), usually at least one interneuron, a motor neuron (which brings information from the CNS toward an effector), and an effector (a muscle or a gland). The gray matter, which is located in the central region of the spinal cord, houses the interneurons and the cell bodies of motor neurons involved in reflexes.

Spinal reflexes are essentially "decisions" made by the spinal cord. They are beneficial when a speedy reaction is important to a person's safety. Consider, for example, the withdrawal reflex. When you step on a piece of broken glass, impulses speed toward the spinal cord over sensory nerves (Figure **8.10**). Within the gray matter of the spinal cord, the sensory neuron synapses with an interneuron. The interneuron, in turn, synapses with a motor neuron that sends a message to the appropriate muscle to contract and lift your foot off the glass.

While the spinal reflexes were removing the foot from the glass, pain messages from the cut foot were sent to the brain through ascending tracts in the spinal cord. However, it takes longer to get a message to the brain than it does to get one to the spinal cord, because the distance and number of synapses to be crossed are greater. Therefore, by the time pain messages reach the brain, you have already withdrawn your foot. Nonetheless, once the sensory information reaches the conscious brain, decisions can be made about how to care for the wound.

The Peripheral Nervous System

The nerves and ganglia of the PNS carry information between the CNS and the rest of the body. The PNS consists of spinal nerves and cranial nerves.

The body has 31 pairs of **spinal nerves**, each of which originates in the spinal cord and services a specific region of the body.

Back view

View from left side

Top view

Spinal cord

Meninges (protective coverings)

Nerve

Vertebra

Intervertebral disk

(c) A micrograph of a cross section of the spinal cord. The white matter transmits messages to and from the brain. The gray matter (shaped like a butterfly) functions as a reflex center.

Connective tissue surrounding one nerve

Blood supply

Axons within a connective tissue sheath

One axon

(d) The anatomy of a nerve

(a) Spinal nerves conduct sensory and motor information between the central nervous system and a specific region of the body.

(b) Pairs of spinal nerves leave through openings between the vertebrae.

FIGURE 8.9 The spinal cord is a column of neural tissue that runs from the base of the brain to just below the last rib. It is protected by the bones of the vertebral column.

Step 1: A stimulus initiates a pain sensation.

Step 2: Sensory messages are carried to the spinal cord by a sensory neuron.

Step 3: Interneurons in the spinal cord integrate information from sensory neurons and stimulate the appropriate motor neurons.

Step 4: Motor neurons stimulate the appropriate muscles.

Step 5: Leg muscles contract, causing them to lift the foot off the glass.

FIGURE 8.10 A reflex arc consists of a sensory receptor, a sensory neuron, usually at least one interneuron, a motor neuron, and an effector.

White matter

Gray matter

Dorsal root

Dorsal-root ganglion

Ventral root

Pair of spinal nerves

(a) View from front of body

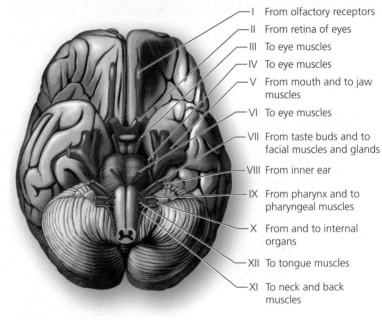

I   From olfactory receptors

II   From retina of eyes

III   To eye muscles

IV   To eye muscles

V   From mouth and to jaw muscles

VI   To eye muscles

VII   From taste buds and to facial muscles and glands

VIII   From inner ear

IX   From pharynx and to pharyngeal muscles

X   From and to internal organs

XII   To tongue muscles

XI   To neck and back muscles

(b) View of underside of brain

FIGURE 8.11 (a) Spinal and (b) cranial nerves. The 12 pairs of cranial nerves can be seen in this view of the underside of the brain. Most cranial nerves service structures within the head, but some service organs lower in the body. The descriptions indicate whether the neuron carries sensory information (toward the brain) or motor information (away from the brain).

One member of each pair serves a part of the right side of the body, and the other serves the corresponding part of the left side. (Figure **8.11a**). All spinal nerves carry both sensory and motor fibers. Fibers from the sensory neurons enter the spinal cord from the dorsal, or posterior, side, grouped into a bundle called the *dorsal root*. The cell bodies of these sensory neurons are located in a ganglion in the dorsal root. The axons of motor neurons leave the ventral (front side) of the spinal cord in a bundle called the *ventral root*. The cell bodies of motor neurons are located in the gray matter of the spinal cord. The dorsal and ventral roots join to form a single spinal nerve, which passes through the opening between the vertebrae.

The 12 pairs of **cranial nerves** (Figure 8.11b) arise from the brain and service the structures of the head and certain body parts, including the heart and diaphragm. Some cranial nerves carry only sensory fibers, others carry only motor fibers, and others carry both types of fibers.

Somatic Nervous System

The peripheral nervous system is subdivided into the somatic nervous system and the autonomic nervous system. The somatic nervous system carries sensory messages that tell us about the world around us and within us, and it controls movement. Sensory messages carried by somatic nerves result in conscious sensations, including light, sound, and touch. The somatic nervous system also controls our voluntary movements, allowing us to smile, stamp a foot, sing a lullaby, or frown as we sign a check.

Autonomic Nervous System

As part of the body's system of homeostasis, the autonomic nervous system automatically adjusts the functioning of our body organs so that the proper internal conditions are maintained and the body is able to meet the demands of the world around it. The somatic nervous system sends information about conditions within the body to the autonomic nervous system. The autonomic nervous system then makes the appropriate adjustments. Its activities alter digestive activity, open or close blood vessels to shunt blood to areas that need it most, and alter heart rate and breathing rate.

Recall that the autonomic nervous system consists of two branches: the sympathetic and the parasympathetic nervous systems. The sympathetic nervous system gears the body to face an emergency or stressful situation, such as fear, rage, or vigorous exercise. Thus, the sympathetic nervous system prepares the body for fight or flight. In contrast, the parasympathetic nervous system adjusts body function so that energy is conserved during relaxation.

Both the parasympathetic and the sympathetic nervous systems send nerve fibers to most, but not all, internal organs (Figure **8.12**). When both systems send nerves to a given organ,

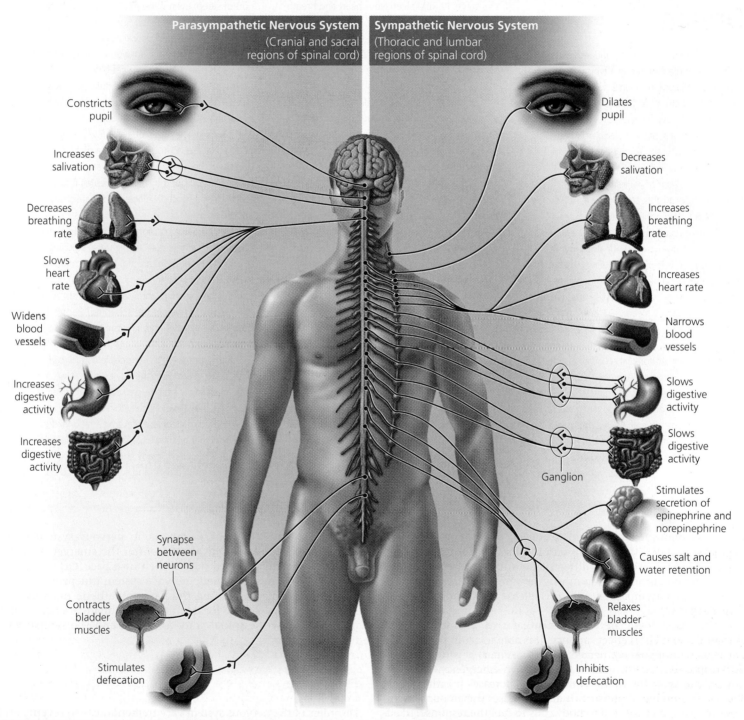

FIGURE 8.12 Structure and function of the autonomic nervous system. Most organs are innervated by fibers from both the sympathetic and the parasympathetic nervous systems. When this dual innervation occurs, the two branches of the autonomic nervous system have opposite effects on the activity level of that organ. A chain of ganglia links the pathways of the sympathetic nervous system, which therefore usually acts as a unit, with all its effects occurring together. In contrast, the ganglia of the parasympathetic nervous system are each near the organ they service, so parasympathetic effects are more localized.

To Sleep, Perchance to Dream

Not all sleep is the same. Indeed, each hour and a half during a typical night's sleep, you will cycle through a sequence of sleep stages. If the natural sleep pattern is disturbed, you may not feel well rested, even if you have "slept" for 8 hours. Stage 1 sleep occurs while you "drift off to sleep." During this period of transition from wakefulness to sleep, you become less aware of your surroundings, slowly tuning out lights and low-level noises (Figure **8.A**). Within the next few minutes, stage 2 sleep usually occurs. During stage 2 sleep, you are unaware of your surroundings. Muscle tension is lower than during wakefulness, and breathing and heart rate also decrease. More than half the night's sleeping time is spent in periods of stage 2 sleep.

Soon after entering stage 2, you sink even deeper into sleep—stages 3 and 4—and become increasingly difficult to awaken. After about 20 minutes of stage 4 sleep, you usually switch back to stage 3 followed by stage 2. Then, you begin an interval of paradoxical sleep, so named because the type of brain waves that occur are similar to those seen during alert mental activity. It would therefore seem that the brain is quite active at this time, and yet it is more difficult to

awaken a person in paradoxical sleep than at any other stage. Paradoxical sleep is also called rapid eye movement (REM) sleep, because your eyes move rapidly behind closed eyelids during this stage. In REM sleep, your heart and breathing rate can be quite variable, but almost every skeletal muscle in your body, except for those of eyes and ears, is virtually paralyzed. This paralysis may keep us from hurting ourselves or others by acting out our dreams.

REM is the stage when dreams that have a storylike progression of events are apt to occur. About 80% of the people who are awakened during REM sleep and asked what was going on say they were dreaming. Only about 20% report that they were dreaming if awakened during other stages of sleep. Moreover, the dreams that occur outside of REM sleep are more likely to be a thought, an image, or an emotion than a story.

The function of REM sleep is not well understood, but it appears to be important for survival. Sleep researchers believe that REM sleep facilitates learning and memory consolidation. Other ideas are that REM is important for CNS development and for the maintenance of normal physiology.

The first bout of REM sleep usually occurs about 90 minutes after falling asleep and lasts about 10 minutes. The REM period of each successive cycle is a little longer. By morning, the interval of REM sleep may be about an hour long. As the bouts of REM lengthen, stages 3 and 4 are lost. So the second half of a night's

sleep is not identical to the first half: there is much more REM in the second half. This is why taking several short catnaps does not provide the same quality of sleep as a single longer period of sleep, even if the total number of hours of sleep is identical.

How much sleep do we need to stay healthy? There's no set answer to this question. You need less sleep as you get older. A newborn sleeps 18 hours a day, young adults generally sleep 7 to 8 hours, and elderly people usually need only 4.5 to 6.5 hours. Sleep requirements also vary between individuals. A few people need as little as 3 hours of sleep a night. Others don't feel their best unless they get 10 hours or more. So, you need as much sleep as it takes to feel well and function efficiently the next day—and no more.

Unfortunately, millions of Americans cheat on sleep. Students pull "all-nighters" studying for exams. Many of them are holding down jobs as well. Parents juggle jobs and family. Workers cope with long shifts and long commutes. And when does *fun* fit into the schedule? People this busy may not have enough time for a good night's sleep.

After insufficient sleep, people usually can manage to get through the day as long as what they are doing is simple—walking, seeing, hearing. However, they have difficulty thinking clearly about complicated matters and reaching a rational decision. Their attention span is short, and their ability to learn is affected. Sleepy students often sit through class in a daze and sometimes nod off.

---

they have opposite, or antagonistic, effects on its function. If one system stimulates, the other system inhibits. The antagonistic effects are brought about by different neurotransmitters. Whereas sympathetic neurons release mostly norepinephrine at their target organs, parasympathetic neurons release acetylcholine at their target organs.

The sympathetic nervous system acts as a unified whole, bringing about all its effects at once. It is able to act in this way because its neurons are connected through a chain of ganglia. A unified response is exactly what is needed in an emergency. To meet a threat, the sympathetic nervous system increases breathing rate, heart rate, and blood pressure. It also increases the amount of glucose and oxygen delivered to body cells to fuel the response. In addition, it stimulates the adrenal glands to release two hormones, epinephrine and norepinephrine, into the bloodstream. These hormones back up and prolong the other effects of sympathetic stimulation. Lastly, the sympathetic nervous system inhibits digestive activity, because digesting the previous meal is hardly a priority during a crisis.

The effects of the parasympathetic nervous system occur more independently of one another. After the emergency, organ systems return to a relaxed state at their own pace. Organs can respond to the parasympathetic nervous system independently because the ganglia containing the parasympathetic neurons that stimulate each organ are located near the individual organs—not in a chain near the spinal cord, as they are in the sympathetic nervous system.

Disorders of the Nervous System

Disorders of the nervous system vary tremendously in severity and impact on the body. Some disorders, such as a mild headache, are often more of a nuisance than a health problem. Others, such as insufficient sleep, can cause more problems than a person might expect (see the Health Issue essay, *To Sleep, Perchance to Dream*). Still other disorders, such as stroke, coma, and spinal cord injury, can have devastating effects on a person's well-being.

Sleep deprivation can be hazardous to health. Drowsiness is a major cause of industrial accidents and traffic fatalities. In a national poll, 20% of American drivers reported having fallen asleep at the wheel within the past year. Driving on Friday night is a greater risk than on Monday night, because so many drivers have been sleep deprived all week.

Ironically, because of the pressures of life, sleep does not always come easily—even when your body is sleep deprived. Tens of millions of Americans will lie awake tonight suffering from insomnia. This sleep disorder occurs in different patterns—difficulty falling asleep, waking up during the night, or waking up earlier than desired.

Here are some suggestions for what to do if you occasionally have trouble sleeping. Establish a regular bedtime and a regular waking time, but do not remain in bed if you cannot sleep. Relax before bedtime: read a book, watch television, take a warm shower—whatever helps you unwind. For at least 6 hours before bedtime, avoid caffeinated beverages, such as coffee, tea, and cola. Also, avoid drinking alcohol for 2 hours before bedtime. Establish a regular pattern of exer- cise, because mild exercise promotes sleep and reduces stress. However, do not exercise too close to bedtime. Lastly, avoid using sleeping pills, even those sold over the counter in the drugstore. At best, they decrease the amount of time it takes to fall asleep by only 10 to 20 minutes and lengthen the night's sleep by only 20 to 40 minutes. Sleeping pills decrease the user's REM sleep, and the REM sleep that does occur is not normal. Furthermore, people quickly become less sensitive to the effects of sleeping pills and as a result tend to increase the dosage to a dangerous level.

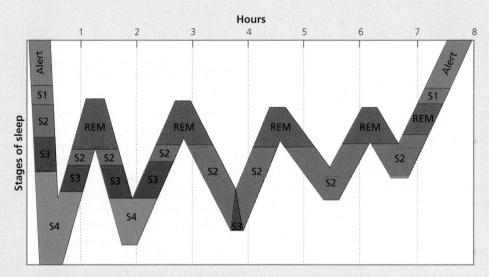

FIGURE 8.A During a good night's sleep, a person generally cycles through a sequence of sleep stages every 90 minutes.

Headaches

Excessive exercise may make your muscles hurt. However, thinking too much cannot cause a headache. The brain has no pain receptors, so a headache is not a brainache. Headaches can occur for almost any reason: they can be caused by stress or by relaxation, by hunger or by eating the wrong food, or by too much or too little sleep. The most common type of headache is a *tension headache,* affecting some 60% to 80% of people who suffer from frequent headaches. In response to stress, most of us unconsciously contract the muscles of our head, face, and neck. Therefore, the pain of a tension headache is usually a dull, steady ache, often described as feeling like a tight band around the head. *Migraine headaches* are usually confined to one side of the head, often centered behind one eye. A migraine headache typically causes a throbbing pain that increases with each beat of the heart. It is sometimes called a sick headache because it may cause nausea and vomiting. Some migraine sufferers experience an aura, a group of sensory symptoms, different for differ- ent people, that occurs just before an attack. The aura may include visual disturbances (a blind spot, zigzag lines, flashing lights), auditory hallucinations, or numbness. Though the causes of migraine are not entirely understood, some researchers believe that migraines are set off by an imbalance in the brain's chemistry. Specifically, the level of one of the brain's chemical neurotransmitters, serotonin, is low. With too little serotonin, pain messages flood the brain.

what would you do?

In an experimental pain treatment for severe headaches, a tiny electrode is implanted in the skin and placed near the nerve responsible for the pain. The device, powered by a battery implanted near the collarbone, delivers continuous electric pulses intended to block the pain signals in the nerve and stop the pain. If you suffered from severely painful headaches, would you opt for this treatment? What criteria would you use to decide?

Strokes

A *stroke,* also called a cerebrovascular accident, is the death of nerve cells caused by an interruption of blood flow to a region of the brain. Neurons have a high demand for both oxygen and glucose. Therefore, when the blood supply to a portion of the brain is shut off, the affected neurons begin to die within minutes. The extent and location of the mental or physical impairment caused by a stroke depend on the region of the brain involved. If the left side of the brain is affected, the person may lose sensations in or the ability to move parts of the right side of his or her body because motor nerve pathways cross from one side of the brain to the other in the lower brain. Because the language centers are usually in the left hemisphere, the person may also have difficulty speaking. When the stroke damages the right rear of the brain, some people show what is called the neglect syndrome and behave as if the left side of things, even their own bodies, does not exist. The person may comb only the hair on the right side of the head or eat only the food on the right side of the plate.

Common causes of strokes include blood clots blocking a vessel, hemorrhage from the rupture of a blood vessel in one of the meninges, or the formation of fatty deposits that block a vessel. High blood pressure, heart disease, diabetes, smoking, obesity, and excessive alcohol intake increase the risk of stroke.

Coma

Although a comatose person seems to be asleep—with eyes closed and no recognizable speech—a coma is not deep sleep. A person in a *coma* is totally unresponsive to all sensory input and cannot be awakened. Although the cerebral cortex is most directly responsible for consciousness, damage to the cerebrum is rarely the cause of coma. Instead, coma is caused by trauma to neurons in regions of the brain responsible for stimulating the cerebrum, particularly those in the reticular activating system or thalamus. Coma can be caused by mechanical shock—as might be caused by a blow to the head—tumors, infections, drug overdose, or failure of the liver or kidney.

Spinal Cord Injury

The spinal cord is the pathway that allows the brain to communicate with the rest of the body. Therefore, damage to the spinal cord can impair sensation and motor control below the site of injury. The extent and location of the injury will determine how long these symptoms persist, as well as the degree of permanent damage. Depending on which nerve tracts are damaged, injury may result in paralysis, loss of sensation, or both. If the cord is completely severed, there is a complete loss of sensation and voluntary movement below the level of the cut.

Restoring the ability to function to people with spinal cord injuries is an active area of research. Some researchers are trying to reestablish neural connections by stimulating nerve growth through treatments with nerve growth factors. Others are exploring the potential use of stem cells for treatment (discussed in Chapter 19a). Stem cells retain the ability to develop into nerve cells, and they have been used successfully by researchers to restore some movement in laboratory mice with spinal cord injuries. Another approach to restoring the ability to move is to use computers to electronically stimulate specific muscles and muscle groups. The stimulation is delivered through wires that are either implanted under the skin or woven into the fabric of tight-fitting clothing. A small computer, usually worn at the wrist, directs the stimulation to the appropriate muscles. This technology has helped some people with a spinal cord injury to walk again. It has also helped some people by stimulating the diaphragm, a muscle important in breathing.

exploring further

In Chapter 7, we learned that neurons communicate with one another using chemicals called neurotransmitters. Neurotransmitter molecules fit into receptors on the membrane of the receiving neuron and cause ion channels to open, either exciting or inhibiting the receiving neuron. Different neurotransmitters play roles in different behavioral systems.

In this chapter, we learned that different parts of the nervous system are specialized for different functions. The limbic system of the brain is a "pleasure center." The sympathetic nervous system prepares the body for emergency situations.

Next, in Chapter 8a, Special Topic: Drugs and the Mind, we will consider psychoactive drugs—those that affect a person's mental state. We will see that psychoactive drugs work by increasing or decreasing the effects of specific neurotransmitters and therefore affecting specific regions of the brain.

highlighting the concepts

Organization of the Nervous System (p. 135)

- The nervous system is divided into the central nervous system (CNS), which includes the brain and spinal cord; and the peripheral nervous system (PNS), which includes all the neural tissue outside the CNS. The peripheral nervous system can be further subdivided into the somatic nervous system and the autonomic nervous system.

The Central Nervous System (pp. 135–143)

- The brain and the spinal cord are protected by the bony cases of the skull and vertebral column, by membranes (the meninges), and by a fluid cushion (cerebrospinal fluid).
- The meninges are three protective layers of connective tissue that cover the brain and spinal cord. Bacteria and viruses can cause inflammation of the meninges, resulting in the condition called meningitis.
- The cerebrospinal fluid, located between layers of the meninges, serves as a shock absorber for the brain, supports the brain, and provides nourishment to and removes waste from the brain.
- The blood–brain barrier is a filter that allows only certain substances to enter the cerebrospinal fluid from the blood, thus protecting the brain and spinal cord from many potentially damaging substances.
- The brain serves as the body's central command center, coordinating and regulating the body's other systems.
- The cerebrum is the thinking, conscious part of the brain. It consists of two hemispheres. Each hemisphere receives sensory

impressions from and directs the movements of the opposite side of the body. The cerebrum has an outer layer of gray matter called the cerebral cortex and an underlying layer of white matter consisting of myelinated nerve tracts that allow communication between various regions of the brain.

- The cerebral cortex has three types of functional areas: sensory, motor, and association. Our awareness of sensation depends on the sensory areas of the cerebral cortex. Motor areas of the brain control the movement of different parts of the body. Association areas communicate with the sensory and motor areas to analyze and act on sensory input.
- The thalamus is an important relay station for all sensory experience except smell. It also plays a role in motor activity, stimulation of the cerebral cortex, and memory.
- The hypothalamus is essential in maintaining a stable environment within the body. It regulates many vital physiological functions, such as blood pressure, heart rate, breathing rate, digestion, and body temperature. The hypothalamus also coordinates the activities of the nervous and endocrine systems through its connection to the pituitary gland. As part of the limbic system, the hypothalamus is a center for emotions. It also serves as a "master biological clock."
- The primary function of the cerebellum is sensory–motor coordination. It integrates information from the motor cortex and sensory pathways to produce smooth movements.
- The medulla oblongata regulates breathing, heart rate, and blood pressure. It also serves as a pathway for all sensory messages to higher brain centers and for motor messages leaving the brain.
- The pons connects lower portions of the CNS with higher brain structures. It connects the spinal cord and cerebellum to the cerebrum, thalamus, and hypothalamus.
- The limbic system, which includes several brain structures, is largely responsible for emotions. The hippocampus, which is part of the limbic system, is essential to converting short-term memory to long-term memory.
- The reticular activating system is a complex network of neurons that filters sensory input and keeps the cerebral cortex in an alert state.
- The spinal cord is a cable of nerve tissue extending from the medulla to approximately the bottom of the rib cage. The spinal cord has two functions: to conduct messages between the brain and the body and to serve as a reflex center.

The Peripheral Nervous System (pp. 143–146)

- The PNS consists of spinal nerves, each originating in the spinal cord and serving a specific region of the body, and cranial nerves, each arising from the brain and serving the structures of the head and certain body parts such as the heart and diaphragm.
- The PNS is divided into the somatic nervous system, which governs conscious sensations and voluntary movements, and the autonomic nervous system, which helps regulate our unconscious, involuntary internal activities.
- The autonomic nervous system can be divided into the sympathetic and parasympathetic nervous systems, two branches with antagonistic actions. The sympathetic nervous system gears the body to face stressful or emergency situations. The parasympathetic nervous system adjusts body functioning so that energy is conserved during restful times.

Disorders of the Nervous System (pp. 146–148)

- Headaches can range from relatively mild (tension headaches) to severe (migraine).
- A stroke is caused by an interruption of blood flow leading to the death of nerve cells. The effects depend on the region of the brain affected.
- Coma, a condition in which a person is totally unresponsive to sensory input, can be caused by a blow to the head, tumors, infections, drugs, or failure of the liver or kidney.
- Because the spinal cord contains the pathways of communication between the brain and the rest of the body, damage to the spinal cord impairs functioning below the site of injury.

recognizing key terms

central nervous system *p. 135*	parasympathetic nervous system *p. 135*	primary somatosensory area *p. 140*	limbic system *p. 142*
ganglia *p. 135*	meninges *p. 135*	primary motor area *p. 140*	short-term memory *p. 142*
peripheral nervous system *p. 135*	cerebrospinal fluid *p. 136*	prefrontal cortex *p. 141*	long-term memory *p. 142*
somatic nervous system *p. 135*	blood–brain barrier *p. 137*	thalamus *p. 141*	hippocampus *p. 142*
autonomic nervous system *p. 135*	cerebrum *p. 138*	hypothalamus *p. 141*	reticular activating system *p. 142*
sympathetic nervous system *p. 135*	cerebral cortex *p. 138*	cerebellum *p. 141*	spinal cord *p. 142*
	gray matter *p. 138*	medulla oblongata *p. 141*	reflex arc *p. 143*
	white matter *p. 139*	midbrain *p. 141*	spinal nerves *p. 143*
		pons *p. 141*	cranial nerves *p. 144*

reviewing the concepts

1. Distinguish between the central nervous system and the peripheral nervous system. List two components of each. *p. 135*
2. Describe three features that protect the brain and spinal cord. *pp. 135–137*
3. What are the functions of cerebrospinal fluid? *pp. 136–137*
4. What forms gray matter? What is its function? What forms white matter? What is its function? *pp. 138–139*
5. Describe the three types of functional areas of the cerebral cortex. *pp. 139–141*

6. In what way are the organizations of the primary somatosensory area and that of the primary motor area of the cerebral cortex similar? In what way do these areas differ? *p. 140*
7. List five functions of the hypothalamus. *p. 141*
8. What is the function of the cerebellum? *p. 141*
9. Which functional system of the brain is responsible for emotions? *p. 142*
10. Describe the two functions of the reticular activating system. *p. 142*
11. List the two functions of the spinal cord and relate each function to the structure of the spinal cord. *pp. 142–143*
12. You are cooking dinner and carelessly touch the hot burner on the stove. You remove your hand before you are even aware of the pain. Using the anatomy of a spinal reflex arc, explain how you could react before you were aware of the pain. *p. 143*
13. What are the two divisions of the peripheral nervous system? What type of response does each control? *pp. 143–144*
14. Compare and contrast the functions of the sympathetic and parasympathetic nervous systems. *pp. 144–146*
15. List some effects of sympathetic stimulation, and explain how these prepare the body for an emergency. *pp. 145–146*
16. You are watching a football game with your friends. A wide receiver makes an incredible catch and then runs 20 yards, skillfully dodging defensive players to make a touchdown. Your friend Joe says, "Amazing! How *does* he do that?" The receiver's outstanding sensory–motor coordination is largely due to the actions of his
    a. cerebellum.
    b. medulla.
    c. reticular activating system.
    d. hypothalamus.
17. As you sit here studying, you are unlikely to be aware of the pressure of your clothes against your body and the rustling of paper as other students turn pages. The part of the brain that "decides" that these are unimportant stimuli is the
    a. reticular activating system.
    b. cerebellum.
    c. hypothalamus.
    d. medulla.
18. Belinda was riding a bicycle without a helmet and was struck by a car. She hit the back of her head very hard in the fall. The physician is quite concerned because the medulla is located at the base of the skull. She explains to Belinda's parents that injury to the medulla could result in
    a. the loss of coordination so that the child may never regain the motor skills needed to ride a bicycle.
    b. the loss of speech.
    c. amnesia (the loss of memory).
    d. death because many life-support systems are controlled here.
19. The neural center that regulates body temperature is the _____.
20. The region of the brain that regulates basic physiological processes such as breathing and heart rate is the _____.
21. The branch of the nervous system that prepares the body to respond to emergency situations is the _____.
22. The brain region responsible for intelligence and thinking is the _____.

applying the concepts

1. Joe and Henry were both in car accidents, and both suffered spinal cord damage. Joe's injury was in the lower back, and Henry's was in the neck region. The degree of injury to the spinal cord is similar in both Joe and Henry. Would the resulting problems be equal in severity? Explain. Describe some of the difficulties that you might expect Joe and Henry to have.
2. When you have a cold, you might take a decongestant to help you breathe. Some decongestants contain pseudoephedrine, which mimics the effects of the sympathetic nervous system. What side effects might you expect? Would you expect this medication to make you drowsy?
3. When you have dental work done, the dentist often administers a local anesthetic in the gums near the region that requires drilling. You are usually advised not to eat anything until the anesthetic wears off. This advice is given out of concern for your tongue, not your teeth. Why?
4. After Jorge's car accident he could remember events that took place before the accident, but he would quickly forget a conversation or a television show he just watched. What part of the brain was injured in the accident?

becoming information literate

When a person has a head injury, physicians may induce a coma by administering a high dose of barbiturates or sedative drugs. The intent of medically induced coma is to allow the brain to rest. It prevents additional injury by reducing blood flow, which reduces swelling. There are success stories. However, there are also risks—pneumonia or a blood clot in the lung—that could be fatal.

Use at least three reliable sources (books, journals, or websites) to gather information that would help you decide whether you would want someone you loved, who had sustained a severe head injury, to be placed in a medically induced coma. Explain why you made your decision. List each source you considered and explain why you chose the three sources you used.

Additional questions can be found online at the Human Biology Place, www.humanbiology.com.

8a

SPECIAL TOPIC

Drugs and the Mind

Sleeping pills and other sedatives can cause dependence. Withdrawal symptoms include insomnia and anxiety.

Maddie had decided to keep her wedding small and was excited to be planning it herself. Even so, she was beginning to feel overwhelmed by all the details. After weeks of lying awake nights thinking through a long mental checklist of errands to be run and decisions to be made, she realized that what she needed more than anything was a decent night's sleep. Her doctor consented to prescribe a mild sedative that helped her get more rest and feel calmer in the days leading up to the celebration.

The wedding went as smoothly and happily as she had dreamed. But a few weeks later, when she was beginning to feel settled in her new life, Maddie stopped taking the sleeping pills and was distressed to find that her sleeplessness and anxiety flared up worse than ever. Alarmed, she consulted her doctor. Apparently, her nervous system had developed a dependency on the drug, even in the limited period during which she had taken it. She and her doctor made a plan to decrease her dependency on the drug that included substituting the original sedative for a similar one and gradually reducing her use of it. If that didn't work, she might have to seek more specialized treatment.

In this chapter, we will consider how drugs affect the nervous system and alter our state of mind. We will see why the use of some drugs leads to a need to continue using the drug. Then we will take a look at some of the more common mind-altering drugs.

Psychoactive Drugs and Communication between Neurons

A drug that alters one's mood or emotional state is often described as a psychoactive drug. The mind-altering effects of these drugs result from their ability to cross the blood–brain barrier, a membranous structure that prevents most substances from reaching the brain. The drugs then interfere with the communication between nerve cells. As you learned in Chapter 7, neurons communicate with one another using neurotransmitters. Neurotransmitters are released by one neuron, diffuse across a small gap between neurons, and bind to specific receptors on another neuron, triggering changes in the activity of the second neuron. Under normal conditions, the action of the neurotransmitter is stopped almost immediately after its message is conveyed because the neurotransmitter is either broken down by enzymes, is reabsorbed into the cell that released it, or simply diffuses away.

A psychoactive drug may alter this communication between neurons in any of several ways (Figure **8a.1**). A drug may stimulate the release of a neurotransmitter and enhance the response of the receiving neuron. It may inhibit the release of a neurotransmitter and thus dampen the response of the receiving neuron. Or it may increase and prolong the effect of a neurotransmitter by delaying its removal from the gap between neurons. If the drug is chemically similar to the natural neurotransmitter, the drug may bind to the receptor and affect the activity of the receiving neuron in the same manner as the neurotransmitter, increasing its effect. Alternatively, its binding to the receptor may prevent the neurotransmitter from acting at all.

One of the problems with using psychoactive drugs is that the user may develop some level of psychological or physical dependence on the drug. Before we consider the drugs themselves, let's consider the concepts of tolerance and dependence.

Drug Dependence

Tolerance is a progressive decrease in the effectiveness of a drug in a given person. As tolerance to a particular drug develops, a person must take larger or more frequent doses to produce the same effect. Tolerance develops partly because the body naturally steps up its production of enzymes that break down the drug, disabling it from having a continued effect, and partly because of changes in the nerve cells themselves that make them less responsive to the drug. *Cross-tolerance* occurs when tolerance to one drug results in a lessened response to another, usually similar drug. If a person abuses codeine, for instance, tolerance develops not only for codeine but also for other drugs that have similar effects on the nervous system, such as morphine and heroin.

A loose definition of *dependence* might be, "It is what causes a person to continue using a drug." More precisely, dependence is the state in which the drug is necessary for physical or psychological well-being. A person who is physically dependent on a drug experiences physical withdrawal symptoms when the drug use is stopped.

Certain drugs encourage users to continue using them because the drugs stimulate the "pleasure" centers in the limbic system of the brain (see Chapter 8). Just as an animal with electrodes implanted in the pleasure center will quickly learn to press a lever to stimulate this brain region to the point of exhaustion, an animal will learn to press a lever to self-administer a dose of a drug that stimulates the pleasure center. Drugs that stimulate the pleasure center include cocaine, amphetamine, morphine, and nicotine.

In the following discussions of psychoactive drugs, we will consider their habit-forming potential as well as possible health risks associated with their use.

Alcohol

In every alcoholic drink, the alcohol is ethanol. Ethanol is produced as a by-product of fermentation, when yeast cells break down sugar to release energy for their own use. The taste of the beverage is determined by the source of the sugar, which comes from the fruit or vegetable that is fermented. For example, grapes are fermented to make wine, grain (barley, oats, rice, wheat, or malt) to make beer, and malt to make scotch.

The effects of alcohol on a person's behavior depend on the blood alcohol level, which is measured as the number of grams of alcohol in 100 ml of blood. One gram of alcohol in 100 ml of blood is a blood alcohol level of 1%. The blood alcohol level in a person depends on several factors, including how much alcohol is consumed; how rapidly it is consumed (over what period of time); and its rate of absorption, distribution, and metabolism.

(a) The natural sequence of events: molecules of neurotransmitter released by one neuron diffuse across a gap and fit into receptors on the membrane of a receiving neuron, causing a response.

(b) A psychoactive drug may increase the number of neurotransmitter molecules released, increasing the response of the receiving neuron.

(c) A psychoactive drug may decrease the number of neurotransmitter molecules released, decreasing the response of the receiving neuron.

(d) A psychoactive drug may fit into the receptors for a neurotransmitter, causing a similar response by the receiving neuron.

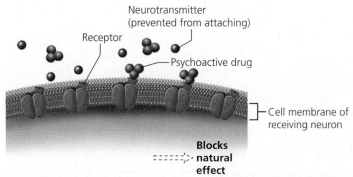

(e) A psychoactive drug may fit into the receptors for a neurotransmitter and prevent the neurotransmitter from entering the receptor, blocking the natural response by the receiving neuron.

FIGURE 8a.1 Psychoactive drugs alter a person's mental state by affecting communication between neurons.

TABLE 8a.1 The Alcoholic Content of Selected Beverages	
Alcoholic Beverage	**Percent Alcohol (Ethanol)**
Light beer	4.5
Most beer	~5
Flavored malt beverages (coolers)	5
Ice beer	5.5–5.9
Dark beer (stout, porter, bock)	6–7
Malt liquor	8
French and German wines	8.5–10
American wine (most)	12–14
Sherry and port	18–21
Distilled liquor (vodka, gin, scotch, whiskey, rum, brandy, cognac)	Most 40% (80 proof); some 45% (90 proof) or 50% (100 proof)

A "drink" can mean different things to different people. For some it is a can of beer, for others a glass of wine, and for others scotch on the rocks. The amount of pure ethanol in the beverage varies tremendously (Table **8a.1**). Natural fermentation, the process used to make beer and wine, cannot yield more than 15% alcohol, because the alcohol kills the yeast cells producing it. In contrast, liquor (distilled spirits) is produced by distillation, a process that concentrates the alcohol. The alcohol content of distilled spirits is measured as "proof." One degree of proof equals 0.5% alcohol. Most distilled spirits (vodka, gin, scotch, whiskey, rum, brandy, and cognac) are 80 proof, which means they contain 40% alcohol. But some brands are 90 proof (45% alcohol) or even 100 proof (50%). So, a small 3-oz[1] martini, which contains only distilled spirits and therefore about 1.2 oz of alcohol, is actually more intoxicating than a larger 8-oz mug of beer, which contains about 0.4 oz of alcohol.

The differences in the alcohol content of beverages are reflected in the standard amounts in which they are served as drinks. Generally, the standard drink contains 0.5 oz of pure ethanol. A standard drink is one bottle or can of beer; a glass of wine; or a jigger (1.5 oz) of 80 proof distilled spirits, such as gin, whisky, vodka, or scotch (alone or in combination with another beverage) (Figure **8a.2**).

Absorption

The intoxicating effects of alcohol begin when it is absorbed from the digestive system into the blood and is delivered to the brain. As a rule, the absorption rate of alcohol depends on the concentration of alcohol in the drink: the higher the concentration, the faster the rate of absorption. So wine, beer, or distilled spirits diluted with a mixer will be absorbed more slowly than pure liquor. The choice of mixer also influences the rate of absorption. Carbonated beverages increase the absorption rate because of the pressure of the gas bubbles.

Although very few substances are absorbed across the walls of the stomach, about 20% of the alcohol consumed is absorbed there. The remaining alcohol is absorbed through the intestines. Because alcohol can be absorbed from the stomach, a person begins to feel the effects of a drink quickly, usually within about

[1]In this chapter, the term *oz* (ounce) refers to a fluid ounce, which is equal to about 29 ml.

Type of drink	Serving size	Caloric content
6 oz Mixer Fruit juice	1 glass	35–105 calories
8 oz Mixer Carbonated beverage	1 glass	~70–120 calories
1.5 oz Distilled spirits (80 proof gin, whiskey, vodka, scotch)	1 jigger	~100 calories
5 oz Wine (12% alcohol)	1 glass	110–200 calories
12 oz Most beer	1 bottle or can	140–150 calories

FIGURE 8a.2 A standard drink contains 0.5 oz of alcohol. Different types of alcoholic beverages vary in their alcohol content, so the size of a standard drink varies with its alcoholic content.

15 minutes. The presence of food in the stomach slows alcohol absorption because it dilutes the alcohol, covers some of the stomach lining through which alcohol would be absorbed, and slows the rate at which the alcohol passes into the intestines.

Distribution to All Body Tissues

Ethanol is a small molecule that is soluble in both fat and water, so it is distributed to all body tissues. Therefore, overall body size affects one's blood alcohol level and the degree of intoxication. A large person would have a lower blood alcohol level and as a result be less intoxicated than would a small person after they both consumed the same amount of alcohol (Figure **8a.3**).

Rate of Elimination

Ninety-five percent of the alcohol that enters the body is metabolized (broken down) before it is eliminated. Most of that metabolism occurs in the liver, which converts alcohol to carbon dioxide and water. The rate of metabolism is slow, about one-third of an ounce of pure ethanol per hour.

In practical terms, it takes slightly more than an hour for the liver to break down the alcohol contained in one standard drink—a can of beer or a glass of wine. Because alcohol cannot be stored anywhere in the body, it continues to circulate in the bloodstream until it is metabolized. Therefore, if more alcohol is consumed in an hour than is metabolized, both the blood alcohol level and the degree of intoxication increase along with consumption (Figure **8a.4**).

There is no way to increase the rate of alcohol metabolism by the liver and, therefore, no way to sober up quickly. The caffeine in a cup of coffee may slightly counter the drowsiness caused by alcohol, but it does not reduce the level of intoxication. Furthermore, because muscles do not metabolize alcohol, exercise does not help, either. Walking around the block will not make a person sober, nor will a cold shower.

If a man and a woman consume the same amount of alcohol, the woman will usually feel the effects before the man does. Part of the reason for this difference is that women are usually smaller than men. In addition, on average, a woman's body contains a higher percentage of fat than a man's does. Alcohol dissolves in fat more slowly than in water. As a result, the alcohol is diluted more slowly in a woman's body, and the effects are prolonged. But there's more to the story; the difference also has to do with differences in metabolism between men and women. Although the liver is the primary

Q *If a 140-lb man has 3 beers over a 2-hour interval, in what range is his blood alcohol level? If a 180-lb man has 3 beers over a 2-hour interval, in what range is his blood alcohol level?*

Number of standard drinks over a 2-hour interval

Driving may be impaired
Blood alcohol level (BAC) to .05%

Driving is risky and may be illegal
BAC .05%–.07%

Driving is dangerous and illegal
BAC .08% or higher

FIGURE 8a.3 Alcohol consumption can impair driving. The blood level of alcohol depends on both the number of drinks consumed and body size. After they consume the same amount of alcohol, a small person has a higher blood alcohol level than a large person does. The blood level of alcohol determines the effect on the nervous system.

A *Probably over .05%; Probably under .05%*

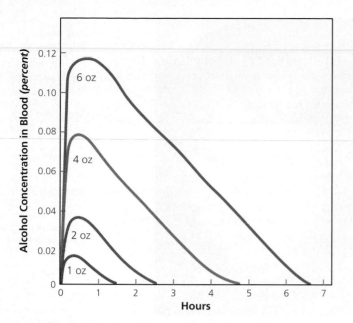

FIGURE 8a.4 Blood alcohol levels in an average man at hourly intervals after drinking 1, 2, 4, or 6 oz of alcohol. Alcohol remains in the blood and has mind-altering effects until it is broken down in the liver. The liver breaks down alcohol at a slow, constant rate of about one-third ounce of pure ethanol an hour. Therefore, it takes slightly more than an hour to metabolize the alcohol in one standard drink.

Source: Reproduced with permission from *The Encyclopedia Britannica*, © 2004 by Encyclopedia Britannica, Inc.

site for alcohol metabolism, some alcohol is broken down by an enzyme found in the stomach lining. Alcohol that is metabolized in the stomach never enters the bloodstream and cannot cause intoxication. Women have less of this enzyme in their stomach linings than do men. Consequently, a woman absorbs about 30% more of the alcohol in a drink than a man does. When weight differences between an average man and woman are also taken into account, 2 oz of liquor can have approximately the same effect on an average woman as 4 oz would have on an average man.

A small amount of alcohol, about 5%, is eliminated from the body unchanged through the lungs or in the urine. Alcohol eliminated from the lungs is the basis of the breathalyzer test that may be administered by law enforcement officers who want an on-the-spot sobriety check.

Health-Related Effects

Because alcohol has a negative effect on virtually every organ of the body, people do not have to be alcoholics for alcohol to impair their health. In this section we look at some ways that alcohol affects the body.

Nervous system

Many people believe that alcohol is a stimulant, but it is actually a depressant. In other words, it slows down the activity of all the neurons of the brain, beginning with the higher cortical, or "thinking," centers. Alcohol often is mistakenly thought to be a stimulant because it depresses the inhibitory neurons first, allowing the excitatory ones to take over. As alcohol removes the "brakes" from the brain, normal restraints on behavior may be lost. Release from inhibitory controls also tends to reduce anxiety and often creates a sense of well-being. However, discrimination, control of fine movements, memory, and concentration are gradually lost as well.

The brain centers for balance and coordination are affected next, causing a staggering gait. Numbed nerve cells send slower messages, resulting in slower reflexes. Eventually, the brain regions responsible for consciousness are inhibited, causing a person to pass out. Still higher concentrations of alcohol can cause coma and death from respiratory failure.

Liver

Excessive alcohol consumption damages the liver, an organ that performs many vital functions in the body. Severe damage to the liver is a serious threat to life. Alcohol is metabolized in the liver before fats are, which allows fats to accumulate in liver cells. Four or five drinks daily for several weeks are enough to cause fat accumulation to begin. At this early stage, however, the liver cells are not yet harmed; and with abstinence, they can be restored to normal. With continued drinking, the accumulating fat causes liver cells to enlarge, sometimes so much that the cells rupture or form cysts. The accumulated fat in liver cells also reduces blood flow through the liver, causing inflammation known as alcoholic hepatitis. Signs of alcoholic hepatitis include fever and tenderness in the upper abdominal region. Gradually, fibrous scar tissue may form, a condition known as cirrhosis, which further impedes blood flow and impairs liver functioning. Cirrhosis can lead to intestinal bleeding, kidney failure, fluid accumulation, and eventually death, if drinking continues. Indeed, cirrhosis of the liver, the ninth leading cause of death in the United States, is most often caused by alcohol abuse.

Cancer

A person who drinks heavily is at least twice as likely to develop cancer of the mouth, tongue, or esophagus than is a nondrinker. Evidence also exists that the combined risk of cancer from both drinking and smoking cigarettes is greater than the sum of the risks caused by either drinking or smoking alone.

Heart and blood vessels

Here's the good news: *Moderate* amounts of alcohol can be good for the heart. Teetotalers are more likely to suffer heart attacks than are persons who drink moderately, say a drink a day. One reason may be that the relaxing effect of alcohol helps to relieve stress. But alcohol also seems to raise the levels of the "good" form of a cholesterol-carrying particle—HDL—in the blood (discussed in Chapters 12 and 15a). This form of cholesterol reduces the likelihood that fats in the blood will be deposited in the walls of blood vessels, clog the vessels, and reduce the blood supply to vital organs such as the heart or brain. In addition, moderate amounts of alcohol reduce the likelihood that blood clots will form when they should not. Such clots can cause a heart attack by blocking blood vessels that nourish the heart muscle. Thus, persons who imbibe moderately generally live longer than nondrinkers.

When alcohol is consumed in more than moderate quantities, however, it damages the heart and blood vessels. It weakens the heart muscle itself, reducing the heart's ability to pump blood. It also promotes the deposit of fat in the blood vessels, making the heart work harder to pump blood through them. Consuming more than moderate quantities of alcohol may also elevate blood pressure substantially. Together, these effects—damage to heart muscle, blood vessels clogged with fatty materials, and high blood pressure—can enlarge the heart to twice its normal size (Figure **8a.5**).

Injuries due to accidents

Accidents—at home or on the road—are more likely to happen when a person has been drinking. The effect of alcohol is not all-or-none. Impairment *begins* with a single drink. A blood alcohol level of only 0.04% to 0.05%, which can result from as few as one or two drinks, decreases peripheral vision, decreases the light sensitivity of the eye by 30% (equivalent to wearing sunglasses at

FIGURE 8a.5 The alcoholic's heart, on the right, is nearly twice the normal size.

- Small head circumference
- Low nasal bridge
- Vertical skin folds in the inner eyelid
- Small midface
- Short nose
- Indistinct depression in area under nose
- Thin upper lip

FIGURE 8a.6 Characteristic facial features of children with fetal alcohol syndrome

night), slows recovery from headlight glare, and reduces reaction time by as much as 25%. At the same time, alcohol impairs the ability to concentrate and to judge distances and speed. Considering that a single mile of city driving requires a driver to make roughly 300 split-second decisions, such impairments can mean the difference between life and death.

Effects on fetal development

Alcohol moves freely from a drinking mother's blood to the fetus. Soon the blood alcohol level of the fetus is the same as the mother's. If a pregnant woman consumes even one or two drinks a day, she increases the chance that her baby will be of lower than normal birth weight, and low birth weight is associated with complications after birth. Heavy drinking during pregnancy increases the risk of miscarriage and stillbirth.

Fetal alcohol syndrome (FAS) is a pattern of growth abnormalities and birth defects common among children of women who drink during pregnancy. These include mental retardation, growth deficiency, and characteristic facial features (Figure **8a.6**), although all the characteristics of FAS are not always present in any one infant. After Down syndrome and spina bifida, alcohol is the third leading cause of birth defects associated with mental retardation. Of these three leading causes, alcohol use is the only one that is wholly preventable.

FAS may be caused by chronic alcohol abuse throughout pregnancy or by binge drinking at critical times during fetal development. The fetus is particularly sensitive to chemicals, such as alcohol, during the first 3 months of pregnancy, when most organ systems are forming. The best advice for pregnant women is to avoid alcohol consumption entirely, because it is not clear what amount of alcohol—if any—is safe during pregnancy.

Alcoholism

Alcohol is a legal drug, and alcoholism is America's number one drug problem. Alcoholics can be young or old, rich or poor, and of any race, economic status, or profession. Because there is no such thing as a typical alcoholic, alcoholism can be difficult to identify.

Different alcoholics have different drinking patterns. Some binge, and some chronically overindulge. But what they all share is a loss of control over their drinking. When an alcoholic takes the first sip of alcohol, he or she cannot predict how much or how long the drinking episode will continue.

Marijuana

Marijuana is the most widely used illegal drug in the United States today. It consists of the leaves, flowers, and stems of the Indian hemp plant, *Cannabis sativa*. The principal psychoactive ingredient (the component that produces mind-altering effects) is delta-9-tetrahydrocannabinol, or THC.

The effects of marijuana depend on the concentration of THC and on the amount consumed. In small to moderate doses, THC produces feelings of well-being and euphoria. In large doses, THC can cause hallucinations and paranoia. Anxiety may even reach panic proportions at very high doses.

Marijuana is not addicting in the sense of producing severe, unpleasant withdrawal symptoms. Nonetheless, a withdrawal syndrome has been identified. It includes symptoms such as restlessness, irritability, mild agitation, insomnia, nausea, and cramping. Withdrawal symptoms are not common and, if they do occur, are usually relatively mild and short-lived.

THC Receptors in the Brain

Researchers are just beginning to understand how marijuana affects the brain. When THC binds to certain receptors on nerve cells, it triggers a cascade of events that ultimately lead to the "high" that the user experiences (Figure **8a.7**).[2] After discovering the receptors, researchers quickly set about looking for the neurotransmitter that normally binds to them, reasoning that the receptors did not evolve millions of years ago just in case someone would someday decide to smoke marijuana. The researchers sorted through thousands of chemicals in pig brains to find one that would bind to THC receptors. The first one to be identified was a hitherto unknown chemical messenger they named *anandamide*, after the Sanskrit word meaning "internal bliss" (*ananda*). Anandamide functions as the brain's own THC. Its normal functions probably include the regulation of mood, memory, pain, appetite, and movement. In addition

[2]A slightly different type of THC receptor is found primarily on cells of the immune system.

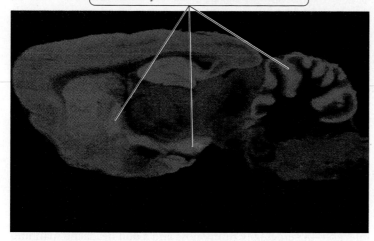

Marijuana receptors are most highly concentrated in regions involved in thinking and memory and in motor control areas.

FIGURE 8a.7 The areas with marijuana receptors appear yellow in this photograph showing a section of a rat's brain.

to mimicking anandamide, THC seems to stimulate the release of dopamine in the reward pathways of the brain.

Health-Related Effects of Long-Term Use

Marijuana is usually smoked. It should not be surprising, then, that the most clearly harmful effects of marijuana are on the respiratory system. However, the damage, it seems, is done by the residual materials in the smoke and not by the THC itself. Compared to the daily consumption of cigarettes by tobacco smokers, marijuana smokers smoke fewer joints (marijuana cigarettes) per day. However, compared with a regular cigarette, a joint has 50% more tar, which contains cancer-causing chemicals. Also, marijuana smoke is usually inhaled more deeply and held within the lungs longer. As a result, three times as much tar is deposited in the airways, and five times as much carbon monoxide is inhaled than with a normal cigarette. Carbon monoxide prevents red blood cells from carrying needed oxygen to the cells of the body. The end result of prolonged smoking of marijuana is marked trauma to the respiratory system. Similar to cigarette smoke, marijuana smoke inflames air passages and reduces breathing capacity.

Another known effect of smoking marijuana is that it makes the heart beat faster, sometimes double its normal rate. In some people, marijuana also increases blood pressure. Either change increases the heart's workload and could pose a threat to people with preexisting cardiovascular problems, such as high blood pressure or atherosclerosis (fatty deposits in the arteries). Thus, although the risk is small, marijuana increases one's risk of immediate heart attack.

Some studies have shown that THC can interfere with reproductive functions in both males and females. At least some of these disturbances may result from the structural similarity between THC and the sex hormone estrogen. Males who smoke marijuana often have lower levels of the sex hormone testosterone and produce fewer sperm than do nonusers. Testosterone and sperm levels return to normal when THC is cleared from the body.

The effects of marijuana on the female reproductive system are not clear. Although we know that THC interferes with ovulation in female monkeys, we know less about what it may do to human females. Some doctors, however, report menstrual problems and reproductive irregularities in women who smoke marijuana.

Legalization of Medical Marijuana

In response to public pressure to permit the use of marijuana for medicinal purposes, several years ago the Office of National Drug Control Policy funded a study by the Institute of Medicine (IOM), a branch of the National Academy of Sciences. The study team carefully evaluated what was known and what was not known about the medicinal use of marijuana—its helpful and harmful effects, its potential for abuse, and the likelihood that its use will lead to the use of other drugs.[3]

The study concluded that the THC in marijuana can relieve some symptoms of certain medical problems. It is an effective antinausea drug for patients undergoing chemotherapy. It can also stimulate the appetite and combat the weight loss (wasting syndrome) that afflicts some people with AIDS. In addition, marijuana can relieve pain and so may help some patients with multiple sclerosis or phantom limb pain (pain that seems to originate in an amputated limb). Pressure within the eye is also reduced by marijuana. Thus, marijuana is often described as an effective treatment for glaucoma, a condition in which the pressure within the eyeball increases to the point where it can cause blindness. However, the study team found that this effect is short-lived and requires high doses. Thus, other existing therapies for glaucoma are better than marijuana.

One interesting conclusion of the IOM team is that marijuana's future as medicine does not involve smoking it. The team decided that the risks of smoking marijuana outweigh the benefits. Crude marijuana contains some 400 chemicals that when burned may release 2000 chemicals, some of which are known carcinogens. The researchers therefore recommend developing other means of delivering this drug to its targets in the body. Possibilities include inhalers, nasal sprays or gels, rectal suppositories, or a pill that could be placed under the tongue and from there absorbed directly into the blood.

The team also concluded that there are no convincing data to support the notion that legalization of marijuana will lead to an increase in its nonmedical use or to general drug abuse. Will medical use of THC lead to addiction? Probably not. As noted earlier, few long-term marijuana users show withdrawal symptoms when they discontinue use, but some do.

Stimulants

Stimulants are drugs that excite the central nervous system (CNS; see Chapter 8). Here we'll look at three types of stimulants: cocaine, the amphetamines, and nicotine.

Cocaine

Cocaine is extracted from the leaves of the coca plant (*Erythroxylon coca*), which grows naturally in the mountainous regions of South America. When cocaine powder extracted from the plant is inhaled into the nasal cavity ("snorted"), it reaches the brain within a few seconds and produces an effect almost as intense as when a solution of cocaine is injected. Smoking the drug is an even more effective delivery route. Forms of cocaine that can be smoked—specifically, freebase and crack—are obtained by further extraction and purification of the coca plant.

[3]Janet E. Joy, Stanley J. Watson, Jr., and John A. Benson, Jr., eds., *Marijuana and Medicine: Assessing the Scientific Base* (Washington, DC: National Academy Press, 1999); Alison Mack and Janet Joy for the Institute of Medicine, *Marijuana as Medicine? The Science Beyond the Controversy* (Washington, DC: National Academy Press, 1999).

When ingested in one of these ways, cocaine brings about a rush of intense pleasure, a sense of self-confidence and power, mental alertness, and increased physical vigor. It does so by increasing the levels of two "feel-good" neurotransmitters: dopamine and norepinephrine (Figure **8a.8**). The euphoria is caused primarily by cocaine's effect on dopamine, a neurotransmitter used by nerve cells in the pleasure centers of the brain. Normally, dopamine is almost immediately reabsorbed into the nerve cell that released it, and its effect soon ceases. Cocaine, however, interferes with the reuptake of dopamine, thus increasing and prolonging dopamine's effect. Cocaine also increases the effects of another neurotransmitter, norepinephrine. Norepinephrine stimulates the effects of the sympathetic nervous system, the part of the nervous system that prepares the body to face an emergency. Thus, cocaine also triggers the responses that ready the body for stress: increased heart rate and blood pressure, narrowing of certain blood vessels, dilation of pupils, a rise in body temperature, and a reduction of appetite.

The effects of cocaine are short-lived, lasting from 2 to 90 minutes depending on how the cocaine enters the body. When the high wears off, it is generally followed by a "crash," a period of deep depression, anxiety, and extreme fatigue. These uncomfortable feelings often produce a craving for more cocaine. The higher the high, the harder the crash, and therefore, the more intense the craving for more of the drug. Crack, which is estimated to be about 75% pure cocaine compared with the 10% to 35% purity of street cocaine, causes higher highs and lower crashes and therefore is extremely addicting.

Cardiovascular risks

Cocaine may cause heart attack or stroke, emergencies in which an interruption of blood flow deprives heart cells or brain neurons of oxygen and nutrients. One way that cocaine blocks blood flow is by constricting arteries. Thus, one way it produces heart attack is by causing spasms in the arteries supplying the heart. Blood flow to the heart can also be disturbed by irregularities in heartbeat. By disabling the nerves that regulate heartbeat, cocaine

can cause disturbed heartbeat rhythms that result in chest pain and heart palpitations (that uncomfortable feeling of being aware of your heart beating). Cocaine use may even cause the heart to stop beating. In addition, cocaine increases blood pressure, which may cause a blood vessel to burst.

Respiratory risks

Stimulation of the CNS is always followed by depression. As the stimulatory effects of cocaine wear off, the respiratory centers in the brain that are responsible for breathing become depressed, or inhibited. Breathing may become shallow and slow and may stop completely. In short, cocaine use can cause respiratory failure that can lead to death.

Damage to the respiratory system as a result of cocaine use depends largely on how the drug is taken. If it is snorted, cocaine causes damage to the nerves, lining, and blood vessels of the nose. It can dry out the nose's delicate mucous membranes so that they crack and bleed almost continuously. Symptoms of a sinus infection—a perpetually runny nose and a dull headache spanning the bridge of the nose—are common. What is more alarming, the partition between the two nasal cavities may disintegrate. Because cocaine is a painkiller, considerable damage to the nose may occur before being discovered.

Smoking crack, on the other hand, damages the lungs and airways. The chronic irritation leads to bronchitis and may also cause lung damage from reduced oxygen flow into the lungs or blood flow through the lungs.

Amphetamines

Amphetamines are synthetically produced stimulants that closely resemble dopamine and norepinephrine (the same neurotransmitters whose levels are increased by cocaine). There are many forms of amphetamine, including dextroamphetamine and methamphetamine, also known as crystal meth. Methamphetamine is illegally sold as a powder that can be injected, snorted, swallowed, or smoked. All amphetamines are stimulants of the CNS. Like cocaine, when active, amphetamines make the user feel good—exhilarated, energetic, talkative, and confident. They suppress appetite and the need for sleep. Amphetamines are active for longer periods than cocaine—hours as opposed to minutes.

Amphetamines can be swallowed in a pill or injected intravenously. One crystalline form of methamphetamine is smoked to produce effects similar to those of crack cocaine. Methamphetamine can produce hazardous effects, including blood vessel spasm, blood clot formation, insufficient blood flow to the heart, and accumulation of fluid in the lungs.

Amphetamines bring about their physical and psychological effects by causing the release of certain neurotransmitters, such as norepinephrine and especially dopamine. As a result, the drugs elevate blood pressure, increase heart rate, and open up airways in the lungs (refer to Figure 8.12).

Tolerance to amphetamines develops (accompanied by simultaneous tolerance to cocaine) along with both physical and psychological dependence. Withdrawal symptoms include extreme fatigue, depression, and increased appetite. Also, the pleasurable feelings caused by amphetamine use can lead to a compulsion to overuse the drug.

Amphetamines cross the placenta and can affect the developing fetus. Compared to nonusers, women who use amphetamines during pregnancy are more likely to give birth prematurely and to have a low-birth-weight baby.

LSD and "ecstasy" (MDMA) act in brain regions where neurons communicate using serotonin.

Heroin acts in brain regions where neurons communicate using endorphins.

Cocaine and amphetamine act in brain regions where neurons communicate using dopamine and norepinephrine.

FIGURE 8a.8 The effects of certain drugs on the brain

Nicotine

Nicotine, the psychoactive ingredient in tobacco products, is a stimulant that activates acetylcholine receptors. In the peripheral nervous system, activation of acetylcholine receptors increases heart rate and blood pressure. In the central nervous system, activation of acetylcholine receptors, which facilitates the release of dopamine and serotonin, creates pleasurable feelings of relaxation. It is nicotine that causes smokers to become "hooked" on cigarettes, ensuring continued exposure to the other injurious substances in the smoke (Figure **8a.9**).

Although smoking can be relaxing, nicotine is actually a stimulant of the brain and heart and blood vessels. Under the influence of nicotine, the heart beats as many as 33 more beats per minute. At the same time, the blood vessels constrict, so the heart is not only beating faster, but it is forcing blood through a less receptive circulatory system. The result is an increase in blood pressure. Nicotine also affects the platelets in the blood (these are described in Chapter 11 as cell fragments containing chemicals that initiate clotting). Nicotine causes the platelets to become sticky, increasing the likelihood of abnormal clots forming that may lead to heart attacks or strokes. A heart attack is the death of heart muscle cells, and a stroke is the death of nerve cells in the brain. Either can be caused by blockage of a blood vessel by a clot.

Nicotine is powerfully addictive. Ninety-five percent of smokers are physiologically dependent on it. Nicotine causes dopamine to be released in the brain's reward center, causing a pleasurable feeling. Drugs that stimulate the brain's reward center, such as nicotine, cocaine, and heroin, are highly addictive. Thus, smokers experience withdrawal symptoms when they try to quit. When a smoker tries to quit, nerve cells become hyperactive, causing withdrawal symptoms that include irritability, anxiety, headache, nausea, constipation or diarrhea, craving for tobacco, and insomnia. Most smokers continue smoking to avoid these unpleasant symptoms. Those who quit find that most of the withdrawal symptoms begin to lessen after a week without nicotine, but some may continue for weeks or even months. Certain symptoms, such as drowsiness, difficulty concentrating, and craving for a cigarette, seem to worsen about 2 weeks after quitting. Consequently, many smokers return to their habit and resume their exposure to nicotine and the other harmful substances in smoke.

Hallucinogens

The drugs that are classified as hallucinogenic are grouped together because of their similar effects, despite having very different structures. These effects include visual, auditory, or other distortions of sensation as well as vivid, unusual changes in thought and emotions.

The psychedelic drugs include some natural and some synthetic compounds. There are about six natural psychedelic drugs, the best known being mescaline, which comes from peyote cactus, and psilocybin, which is found in certain mushrooms. There are also synthetic drugs, including LSD (lysergic acid diethylamide) and MDMA,[4] which is popularly known as ecstasy.

These drugs are thought to act by augmenting the action of the neurotransmitters serotonin, norepinephrine, or acetylcholine. For example, LSD, psilocybin, DMT (dimethyltryptamine), and bufotenin bind to the serotonin receptors in the brain, thereby mimicking the natural effects of serotonin. Ecstasy both binds to serotonin receptors and promotes the release of serotonin and

[4]3,4-methylenedioxymethamphetamine

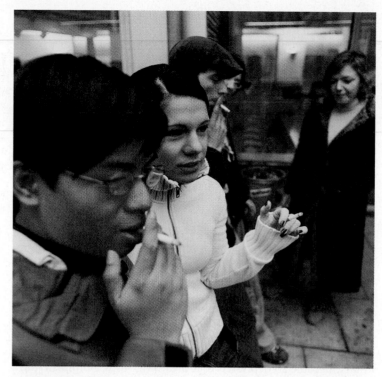

FIGURE 8a.9 Nicotine in cigarette smoke is a stimulant to the central nervous system and the cardiovascular system. It is also the chemical in cigarette smoke that causes smokers to become addicted to cigarettes.

dopamine. Mescaline, on the other hand, is structurally similar to norepinephrine and binds to norepinephrine receptors.

The normal physiological reactions to psychedelic drugs are not especially harmful, but the distortions of reality the drugs produce may lead to behavior that is quite dangerous. "Bad trip" is the term most often used to describe an unpleasant reaction to a psychedelic drug. The symptoms may include paranoia, panic, depression, and confusion. The trip usually ends within 24 hours, when drug levels decrease. Brief recurrences of the sensory or emotional alterations produced by the drug are called flashbacks. Almost any aspect of the drug experience may be relived during a flashback. Most flashbacks are fleeting and merely annoying, but sometimes they can be frightening.

Tolerance for psychedelic drugs develops quickly. Furthermore, cross-tolerance among these drugs is the rule; that is, a person who has become tolerant of one psychedelic drug will be tolerant to others as well. Craving and withdrawal reactions are unknown, however, and laboratory animals offered LSD will not take it voluntarily.

Ecstasy deserves additional consideration because its use is growing rapidly. It is sometimes called the "love drug" or "hug drug" because of users who say it puts them at peace with themselves and at ease with others. Also a stimulant, ecstasy causes increases in heart rate, blood pressure, and body temperature—sometimes to dangerous levels. People using ecstasy feel energetic enough to dance all night, sometimes suffering dehydration and heat stroke—which occasionally lead to death—as a result. (Deaths are rare, however.) The release of serotonin from neurons causes a euphoric high, but the temporary depletion of serotonin in the days following ecstasy use can bring depression and anxiety. Ecstasy can also cause nausea, vomiting, and dizziness. Another danger is that ecstasy pills may contain drugs other than ecstasy. Among the drugs commonly found in these pills are the cough suppressant dextromethorphan, caffeine, ephedrine, and pseudoephedrine. Even the poison strychnine has been found.

Phencyclidine, or PCP, and ketamine are classified as psychedelic anesthetics. That is, they cause hallucinations and alter physical sensations. Unlike other psychedelic drugs, they do not work by raising serotonin levels.

Ketamine is gaining popularity as a "club drug." It can be snorted as a powder or swallowed as pills. Its effects range from a dreamy feeling to hallucinations to a deep, paralyzing, out-of-body experience. High doses can cause seizures and coma.

Sedatives

Sedatives are drugs that depress the CNS. They belong to the drug class known as benzodiazepines, two prescription examples of which are Xanax and Ativan. Like alcohol, the depressant drugs affect inhibitory neurons first. As a result, low doses initially relieve anxiety and cause mild euphoria. Higher doses also inhibit excitatory neurons, and sleep follows.

The effects of different depressants are additive, so if you drink alcohol (a CNS depressant, as described earlier) and take a sedative, the depressant effects will be greatly intensified. Combining depressant drugs can easily lead to overdose. The respiratory system can, in fact, become so depressed that breathing stops. Administering a CNS stimulant—amphetamine, for example—cannot reverse an overdose of depressants. Although the drugs may have antagonistic (meaning opposite) effects, they work by binding to different receptors or by affecting different regions of the brain. Thus, taking a stimulant and a depressant at the same time is like simultaneously stepping on the brake and the accelerator of a car. Hitting the accelerator does not remove the brake. To stop an overdose, it would be necessary to remove the drug from its receptors. A stimulant may temporarily arouse the person, but when it wears off, the stimulation becomes depression. This rebound depression, added to the residual depression caused by the sedative, could be fatal.

Continued use of sedatives leads to tolerance as well as both psychological and physical dependence. Cross-tolerance also develops, so tolerance to one sedative reduces the response to other sedatives. Tolerance develops because the liver produces more of the enzymes that break down the drug and, to some extent, because the nerve cells become less sensitive to its effects. As tolerance develops, overdose becomes a greater risk. Increased doses are required for the drug's sedating effect, but the neurons in the breathing center are still sensitive to a lethal dose.

A dangerous depressant that has gained popularity in recent decades is GHB (gamma-hydroxybutyrate). It is a clear liquid that is administered by being mixed with a beverage. This fast-acting sedative has been called a "date rape" drug because men have used it to make women vulnerable to sexual assault. The most common negative effects of GHB are dizziness, nausea, vomiting, confusion, and sometimes blackouts. Overdoses can be fatal because GHB inhibits the respiratory system.

Opiates

The opiates are natural or synthetic drugs that affect the body in ways similar to morphine, the major pain-relieving agent in opium. These and related drugs have two faces. On one hand, they have a high potential for abuse because tolerance and physical dependence occur. On the other hand, they are medically important because they alleviate severe pain.

Morphine and codeine, which come from the opium poppy, were among the first opiates used. Heroin is a synthetic derivative of morphine that is more than twice as powerful. Heroin is usually injected intravenously, but there are now forms that can be smoked or inhaled into the nasal cavity. Regardless of how it enters the body, heroin reaches the brain very quickly, producing a feeling that is usually described in ecstatic or sexual terms.

The opiates, including heroin, exert their effects by binding the receptors for the body's endogenous (natural, internally produced) opiates: compounds called endorphins, enkephalins, and dynomorphins. These are neurotransmitters whose functions include roles in the perception of pain and fear.

Heroin and other commonly abused opiates have effects similar to those of morphine: euphoria, pain suppression, and reduction of anxiety. They also slow the breathing rate. An overdose may cause the user to fall into a coma or stop breathing. Overdose is always a potential problem with opiates bought on the street for illegal use. The buyer has no idea of the strength of the drug. Street supplies are often diluted with sugar. If a heroin addict who is accustomed to a diluted drug injects heroin that is much more potent than he or she is used to, death due to overdose often occurs. Extremely constricted pupils in an unconscious person are a sign of heroin overdose.

Many of the problems associated with heroin use arise because heroin addicts often suffer from a general disregard for good health practices. Other problems are associated with the injections themselves. Frequent intravenous injection of any drug is associated with certain ailments. Because of the constant puncturing, veins can become inflamed. In addition, shared needles may spread disease-causing organisms, including the viruses that cause AIDS and hepatitis and the bacterium that causes syphilis.

9

Sensory Systems

We generally rely on our own senses—sight, hearing, taste, touch, and so on—for identifying the resources and conditions our bodies require and for recognizing danger. When extra-sensitive olfaction is needed, however, we sometimes borrow the smell receptors of a dog.

Lani, a trained and certified Labrador retriever, is being used by a mold-testing company. Her job is to sniff through buildings in search of hidden mold that may be growing behind deceptively clean-looking drywall or beneath solid floors. She has been trained to recognize the odors of 18 genera of undesirable molds.

When she senses one, she sits and points her nose toward its source. Lani works faster and is easier to transport and deploy than any electronic mold-detecting device, and follow-up laboratory analyses show that she is extremely accurate. Like dogs who sniff out bombs, drugs, accident victims, or evidence of arson, she provides her human

partners with information about the environment that their own senses are not able to perceive.

Although most humans cannot sniff out mold hidden under floorboards, our senses are nevertheless quite impressive and do a good job of telling us about our surroundings. In this chapter, we explore the human body's general senses (such

as touch, pressure, vibration, temperature, and pain) and our special senses (vision, hearing, balance, smell, and taste). We look closely at vision, hearing, and balance, examining how light, sound, and body position are reported by the intricate structures of the eye and ear. We also explore the relationship between smell and taste.

Sensory Receptors

Information about the external world and about the internal world of our bodies comes to us through our **sensory receptors**, structures that are specialized to detect and respond to changes in the environment, known as **stimuli**, by generating electrochemical messages. If a stimulus is strong enough, these messages eventually become nerve impulses (action potentials) that are then conducted to the brain.

Sensation is an awareness of a stimulus. Whether a sensation is experienced as sight, sound, or something else depends on which part of the brain receives the nerve impulses. For example, photoreceptors respond best to light, but they can also respond to pressure. Regardless of the stimulus, nerve impulses from photoreceptors go to the visual cortex of the brain, and we see light. This is why, if you press gently on your closed eyelids, you will have the sensation of seeing spots of light. The pressure stimulates photoreceptors, which send nerve impulses to the visual cortex, and you sense light.

We use the word *perception* to describe the conscious awareness of sensations. Perception occurs when the cerebral cortex integrates sensory input (Figure **9.1**). For example, light reflected from a banana strikes the eye, stimulating some of the photoreceptors. The brain interprets the pattern of input from the photoreceptors, and we perceive a banana.

As we've seen, each type of sensory receptor responds best to one form of stimulus. The response of a sensory receptor is an electrochemical message (a change in the charge difference across plasma membrane) that varies in magnitude with the strength of the stimulus. For instance, the louder a sound, the larger the change in the charge difference across the membrane—up to a point. When the change reaches a critical level, called threshold level, an action potential (nerve impulse) is generated. Most types of sensory receptors gradually stop responding when they are continuously stimulated. This phenomenon is called **sensory adaptation.** As receptors adapt in this way, we become less aware of the stimulus. For example, the musty smell of an antique store may be obvious to a person who just walked in, but the salesclerk working in the store no longer notices it. Some receptors, such as those for pressure and touch, adapt quickly. For this reason, we quickly become unaware of the feeling of our clothing against our skin. (Adaptation can also occur in the central nervous system. The reticular activating system in the brain filters stimuli, as discussed in Chapter 8.) Other receptors

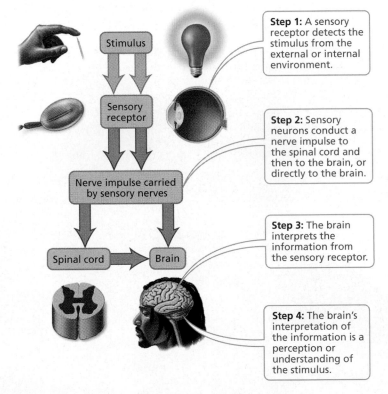

Step 1: A sensory receptor detects the stimulus from the external or internal environment.

Step 2: Sensory neurons conduct a nerve impulse to the spinal cord and then to the brain, or directly to the brain.

Step 3: The brain interprets the information from the sensory receptor.

Step 4: The brain's interpretation of the information is a perception or understanding of the stimulus.

FIGURE 9.1 An overview of the steps involved in sensation and perception

adapt more slowly or not at all. For instance, the receptors in muscles and joints that report on the position of body parts never adapt. Their continuous input is essential for coordinated movement and balance.

Classes of Receptors

Receptors are classified according to the stimulus they respond to. Several classes of receptors are traditionally recognized:

1. **Mechanoreceptors** are responsible for the sensations we describe as touch, pressure, hearing, and equilibrium. In

addition, the body has mechanoreceptors that detect changes in blood pressure and others that indicate the body's position. Mechanoreceptors respond to distortions in the receptor itself or in nearby cells.

2. **Thermoreceptors** detect changes in temperature.

3. **Photoreceptors** detect changes in light intensity.

4. **Chemoreceptors** respond to chemicals. We describe the input from the chemoreceptors of the mouth as taste (gustation) and those from the nose as smell (olfaction). Other chemoreceptors monitor levels of specific substances such as carbon dioxide, oxygen, or glucose in our body fluids.

5. **Pain receptors** (or nociceptors) respond to very strong stimuli that usually result from physical or chemical damage to tissues. Pain receptors are sometimes classed with the chemoreceptors because they often respond to chemicals liberated by damaged tissue. These receptors are occasionally classed with the mechanoreceptors because they are stimulated by physical changes, such as swelling, in the damaged tissue.

We can sense stimuli both outside of our bodies and within them. Receptors located near the body surface respond to stimuli in the environment. We are usually aware of these stimuli. Other receptors are inside the body and monitor conditions there. Although we often are unaware of the activity of internal receptors, they play a vital role in maintaining homeostasis. In fact, they are key components of the feedback loops that regulate blood pressure, blood chemistry, and breathing rate. Internal receptors also cause us to feel pain, hunger, or thirst, thereby prompting us to attend to our body's needs.

The **general senses**—touch, pressure, vibration, temperature, body and limb position, and pain—arise from receptors in the skin, muscles, joints, bones, and internal organs. Although we are not usually aware of the general senses, they are important because they provide information about body position and help keep internal body conditions within the limits optimal for health. The **special senses** are vision, hearing, the sense of balance or equilibrium, smell, and taste. These are what usually come to mind when we think of "the senses," largely because we are so dependent on them for perceiving and understanding the world. The receptors of the special senses are located in the head. Most of them reside within specific structures.

The General Senses

The receptors for general senses are distributed throughout the body. Some monitor conditions within the body; others provide information about the world around us. Some of the receptors are free nerve endings; in other cases the nerve endings are encapsulated. *Free nerve endings,* the tips of dendrites of sensory neurons, are not protected by an accessory structure. In contrast, an *encapsulated nerve ending* is one in which a connective tissue capsule encloses and protects the tips of the dendrites of sensory neurons (Figure **9.2**).

Touch, Pressure, and Vibration

As noted earlier, mechanoreceptors respond to touch and pressure—to any stimulus that stretches, compresses, or twists the receptor membrane. Throughout life, we actively use touch as a way of

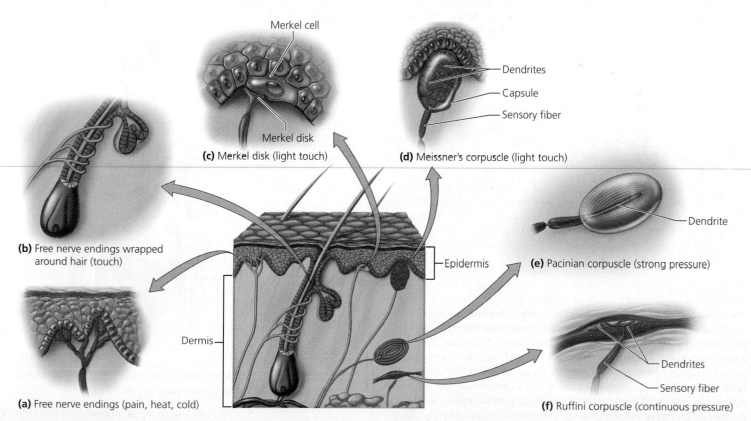

(c) Merkel disk (light touch)

(d) Meissner's corpuscle (light touch)

(b) Free nerve endings wrapped around hair (touch)

(e) Pacinian corpuscle (strong pressure)

(a) Free nerve endings (pain, heat, cold)

(f) Ruffini corpuscle (continuous pressure)

FIGURE 9.2 General sense receptors of the skin allow us to feel touch, pressure, temperature, and pain.

learning about the world and of communicating with one another. The messages we get from pressure can be equally important. Some pressure receptors inform us of the need to loosen our belt after a big meal. Other pressure receptors monitor internal conditions, including blood pressure.

Light touch, as when the cat's tail brushes your legs, is detected by several types of receptors. For example, free nerve endings wrapped around the base of the fine hairs on the skin detect any bending of those hairs. Free nerve endings and the special cells they end on (Merkel cells) form *Merkel disks*. When compressed, Merkel cells stimulate the free nerve endings in the associated Merkel disks to tell us that something has touched us. Merkel disks are found on both the hairy and hairless parts of the skin. *Meissner's corpuscles* are encapsulated nerve endings that tell us exactly where we have been touched. They are common on the hairless, very sensitive areas of skin, such as the lips, nipples, and fingertips.

The sensation of pressure generally lasts longer than does touch and is felt over a larger area. *Pacinian corpuscles*, which consist of onionlike layers of tissue surrounding a nerve ending, respond when pressure is first applied and therefore are important in sensing vibration. They are scattered in the deeper layers of skin and the underlying tissue. *Ruffini corpuscles* are encapsulated endings that respond to continuous pressure.

Temperature Change

Thermoreceptors respond to changes in temperature. In humans, thermoreceptors are specialized free nerve endings found just below the surface of the skin. One kind responds to cold and another responds to warmth. They are widely distributed throughout the body but are especially numerous around the lips and mouth. You may have noticed that the sensation of hot or cold fades rapidly. This fading occurs because thermoreceptors are very active when temperature is changing but adapt rapidly when temperature is stable. As a result, the water in a hot tub may feel scalding at first, but very soon it feels comfortably warm.

Body and Limb Position

Whether you are at rest or in motion, the brain "knows" the location of all your body parts. It continuously scans the signals from muscles and joints to check body alignment and coordinate balance and movement. **Muscle spindles**—specialized muscle fibers wrapped in sensory nerve endings—monitor the length of a skeletal muscle. **Golgi tendon organs**—highly branched nerve fibers located in tendons (connective tissue bands that connect muscles to bones)—measure the degree of muscle tension. The brain combines information from muscle spindles and Golgi tendon organs with information from the inner ear (as we see shortly) to coordinate our movements.

Pain

The receptors for pain are free nerve endings found in almost every tissue of the body. When tissue is damaged, cells release chemicals that alert the free nerve endings of the injury. The stimulated sensory neurons then carry the message to the brain, where it is interpreted as pain. Aspirin and ibuprofen reduce pain by interfering with the production of one of the released chemicals. Any stimulus strong enough to damage tissues, including heat, cold, touch, and pressure, can cause pain.

Many of our internal organs also have pain receptors. However, pain originating in an internal organ is sometimes perceived as pain in an uninjured region of the skin (Figure **9.3**). This phenomenon is called **referred pain**. For example, the pain of a heart attack is often experienced as pain in the left arm. This pain probably occurs because sensory neurons from the internal organ and those from a particular region of the skin communicate with the same neurons in the spinal cord. Because the message is delivered to the brain by the same neurons, the brain interprets the input as coming from the skin.

Pain is an important mechanism that warns the body and protects it from further injury. For example, pain usually prevents a person with a broken leg from causing additional damage by moving the limb. Nonetheless, few of us appreciate the value of pain while we are experiencing it. Furthermore, pain that persists long after the warning is needed can be debilitating.

Vision

Humans are very visual creatures. We may not see detail as well as an eagle or movement as well as an insect, but we see far better than most other mammals and depend on vision in most of the activities that make up our daily lives.

Wall of the Eyeball

The human eyeball is an irregular sphere about 25 mm (1 in.) in diameter. As shown in Figure **9.4**, the wall of the eyeball consists of three layers: the sclera and cornea; the choroid, ciliary body, and iris; and the retina. The outermost layer is a tough, fibrous covering with two distinct regions: the sclera and the cornea. The **sclera**,

Q *If you had pain caused by a kidney stone, where would you experience the pain?*

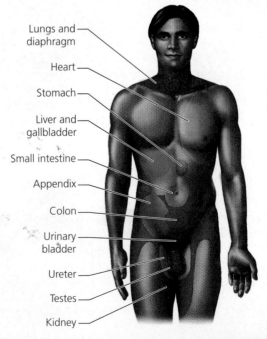

Lungs and diaphragm
Heart
Stomach
Liver and gallbladder
Small intestine
Appendix
Colon
Urinary bladder
Ureter
Testes
Kidney

FIGURE 9.3 Referred pain. Pain from certain internal organs is sensed as originating in particular regions of the skin.

A *The lower body trunk and inner thigh.*

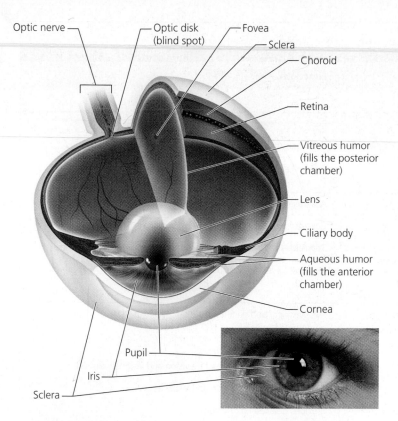

Optic nerve — Optic disk (blind spot) — Fovea — Sclera — Choroid — Retina — Vitreous humor (fills the posterior chamber) — Lens — Ciliary body — Aqueous humor (fills the anterior chamber) — Cornea — Pupil — Iris — Sclera

FIGURE 9.4 Structure of the human eye. Light enters the eye through the transparent cornea and then passes through the pupil. The lens focuses light on the light-sensitive retina, which contains the rods and cones.

often called the white of the eye, protects and shapes the eyeball and serves as an attachment site for the muscles that move the eye. In the front and center of the eye, the transparent **cornea** bulges slightly outward and provides the window through which light enters the eye.

The middle layer of the eye has three distinct regions—the choroid, the ciliary body, and the iris. The **choroid** is a layer containing many blood vessels that supply nutrients and oxygen to the tissues of the eye. The choroid layer also contains the brown pigment melanin, which absorbs light reflected from the light-sensitive layer inside the eye (the retina). This absorption of light results in sharper vision by helping to prevent excessive reflection of light within the eye.

Toward the front of the eye, the choroid becomes the **ciliary body**—a ring of tissue, primarily muscle—that encircles the **lens**, which focuses light on the retina. The ciliary body holds the lens in place and controls its shape, which is important for focusing light on the light-sensitive layer of the eye.

The part of the choroid layer in front of the ciliary body is the iris. The **iris**, the colored portion of the eye that can be seen through the cornea, regulates the amount of light that enters the eye. The iris is shaped like a flat doughnut. The doughnut hole—the opening in the center of the iris through which light enters the eye—is called the **pupil.**

The iris contains smooth muscle fibers that automatically adjust the size of the pupil to admit the appropriate amount of light. The pupil becomes larger (dilates) in dim light and smaller (constricts) in bright light. Pupil size is also affected by emotions. The pupils dilate when you are frightened or when you are very interested in something. They constrict when you are bored. Can-

dlelight creates a romantic setting partly because its dimness dilates the pupils, making the lovers appear more attentive and interested.

The innermost layer of the eye, the **retina**, contains almost a quarter-billion photoreceptors, the structures that respond to light by generating electrical signals. The retina contains two types of photoreceptors: rods and cones. The structure and function of rods and cones are discussed in more detail later in the chapter. The photoreceptors are most concentrated in a small region in the center of the retina called the **fovea**. Therefore, when we want to see fine details of an object, the light reflected from the object must be focused on the fovea. However, the fovea is only the size of the head of a pin. Consequently, at any given moment, only about a thousandth of our visual field is in sharp focus. Eye movements bring different parts of the visual field to the fovea. The **optic nerve** carries the message from the eye to the brain, where the message is interpreted. The region where the optic nerve leaves the retina has no photoreceptors. As a result, we cannot see an image that strikes this area. This area is called the **blind spot.** To find your blind spot, cover your left eye and focus on the X with your right eye. You should see the circle in your peripheral vision. Place this book in front of you and slowly move your head toward it. As your head moves, the image of the circle becomes focused on different regions of the retina. When the circle disappears, its image is focused on the blind spot.

You are not usually aware of your blind spot because involuntary eye movements constantly move the position of the image on the retina, allowing the brain to "fill in" the missing parts as the visual information is processed by the brain. Table **9.1** summarizes the structures of the eye and their functions.

Fluid-Filled Chambers

The ciliary body and lens divide the interior of the eyeball into two fluid-filled cavities, or chambers (see Figure 9.4). The posterior chamber, located at the back of the eye between the lens and the retina, is filled with a jellylike fluid called **vitreous humor.** This fluid helps keep the eyeball from collapsing and holds the thin retina against the wall of the eye. The anterior chamber, located at the front of the eye between the cornea and the lens, is filled with a fluid called **aqueous humor.** This clear fluid supplies nutrients and oxygen to the cornea and lens and carries away their metabolic wastes. In addition, the aqueous humor creates pressure within the eye, helping to maintain the shape of the eyeball. Unlike the vitreous humor, which is produced during embryonic development and is never replaced, aqueous humor is replaced bit by bit about every 90 minutes. It is continuously produced from the capillaries of the ciliary body, circulates through the anterior chamber, and drains into the blood through a network of channels that surround the eye.

If the drainage of aqueous humor is blocked, the pressure within the eye may increase to dangerous levels. This condition, called *glaucoma,* is the second most common cause of blindness (after cataracts, which are discussed shortly). The accumulating aqueous humor pushes the lens partially into the posterior cavity of the eye, increasing the pressure there and compressing the retina and optic nerve. This pressure, in turn, collapses the tiny blood vessels

TABLE 9.1 A Review of the Structures of the Eye and Their Functions

Structure	Description	Function
Outer layer		
Sclera	Outer layer of the eye	Protects the eyeball
Cornea	Transparent dome of tissue forming the outer layer at the front of the eye	Refracts light, focusing it on the retina
Middle layer		
Choroid	Pigmented layer containing blood vessels	Absorbs stray light; delivers nutrients and oxygen to tissues of eye
Ciliary body	Encircles lens; contains the ciliary muscles	Controls shape of lens; secretes aqueous humor
Iris	Colored part of the eye	Regulates the amount of light entering the eye through the pupil
Pupil	Opening at the center of the iris	Opening for incoming light
Inner layer		
Retina	Layer of tissue that contains the photoreceptors (rods and cones); also contains bipolar and ganglion cells involved in retinal processing	Receives light and generates neural messages
Rods	Photoreceptor	Responsible for black-and-white vision and vision in dim light
Cones	Photoreceptor	Responsible for color vision and visual acuity
Fovea	Small pit in the retina that has a high concentration of cones	Provides detailed color vision
Other structures of the eye		
Lens	Transparent, semispherical body of tissue behind the iris and pupil	Fine focusing of light onto retina
Aqueous humor	Clear fluid found between the cornea and the lens	Refracts light and helps maintain shape of the eyeball
Vitreous humor	Gelatinous substance found within the chamber behind the lens	Refracts light and helps maintain shape of the eyeball
Optic nerve	Group of axons from the eye to the brain	Transmits impulses from the retina to the brain

that nourish the photoreceptors and the fibers of the optic nerve. Deprived of nutrients and oxygen, the photoreceptors and nerve fibers begin to die, and vision fades. Unfortunately, glaucoma is progressive but painless, making detection difficult. Late signs include blurred vision, headaches, and seeing halos around objects. Many people do not realize they have a problem until some vision has been lost.

Focusing and Sharp Vision

Sharp, clear vision requires that the light rays entering the eye converge so that their focal point, the point where they are "in focus," is on the retina. The structures of the eye accomplish this focusing by bending the light rays to the necessary degree.

Most bending of light occurs as the light passes through the curved surface of the cornea. Because of the way that the curved cornea bends the light rays, the image created on the retina is upside down and backward. The cornea has a fixed shape, so it always bends light to the same degree and cannot make the adjustments needed to focus on objects at varying distances.

The lens, on the other hand, is elastic and can change shape to focus on both near and distant objects. Picture the lens as an underinflated round balloon. If you pull on the sides of such a bal-

loon, it flattens. When you release its sides, the balloon assumes its usual, rounder shape. Similar pulling and releasing changes the shape of the lens. Figure **9.5** shows that a rounder, thicker lens bends light to a greater degree, enabling the eye to focus on objects that are near. Changing the shape of the lens to change the bending of light is called **accommodation.**

These changes in lens shape are controlled by the ciliary muscle, which is attached to the lens by ligaments. Because the ciliary muscle is circular, its diameter becomes smaller when it contracts, much like pursed lips do. This contraction relaxes the tension on the ligaments, freeing the lens to assume the rounded shape needed to focus on nearby objects. Relaxation of the ciliary muscle increases the diameter of the ciliary muscle, increasing the tension on the ligaments and the lens. Consequently, the lens flattens and focuses light from more distant objects on the retina. As we age, the lens becomes less elastic and does not round up to focus on nearby objects as easily. This is why we hold the newspaper farther away as we become older.

Cataracts

A **cataract** is a cloudiness or opaqueness in the lens, usually a result of aging. Typically, the lens takes on a yellowish hue that blocks light on its way to the retina. In the beginning, cataracts may cause

FIGURE 9.5 The lens changes shape so the eye can view objects at different distances.

a person to see the world through a haze that can limit activities and cause automobile accidents, early retirement, and dangerous falls. As the lens becomes increasingly opaque, the fog thickens. Indeed, cataracts are the leading cause of blindness worldwide. Cataracts can be treated by surgically removing the clouded lens and replacing it with an artificial lens.

Cataracts are the most common eye problem affecting men and women older than 50. However, there are some things that everyone can do to minimize the risk of developing cataracts. Wear sunglasses in bright sunlight because exposure to ultraviolet radiation and bright light can cause cataracts. Cigarette smoke also causes cataracts, so minimize your exposure.

Focusing problems

The three most common visual problems that occur in individuals of all ages are all problems in focusing. These include farsightedness, nearsightedness, and astigmatism. With each of these focusing problems, normal vision can usually be restored with corrective lenses (Table **9.2**). Roughly 60% of Americans are farsighted. In *farsightedness,* distant objects are seen more clearly than nearby ones because the eyeball is too short or the lens is too thin, causing images of nearer objects to be focused behind the retina. Although distant objects can be seen clearly, the lens cannot become round enough to bend the light sufficiently to focus on nearby objects. Corrective lenses that are thicker in the middle than at the edges (convex) cause the light rays to converge a bit before they enter

the eye. The lens can then focus the image on the retina. Other solutions to vision problems are discussed in the Health Issue essay, *Correcting Vision Problems.*

About 30% of the American population is nearsighted; that is, they can see nearby objects more clearly than those far away. *Nearsightedness* (myopia) occurs when the eyeball is elongated or when the lens is too thick. This condition causes the image to focus in front of the retina. Nearsighted people see nearby objects clearly because the lens becomes round enough to focus the image on the retina. However, the lens simply cannot flatten enough to bring the focused image of distant objects to the retina, and so those objects appear blurred. Lenses that are thinner in the middle than at the edges (concave) can correct nearsightedness. These lenses cause the light rays to diverge only slightly before entering the eye.

Although genetics undoubtedly plays a role in the development of nearsightedness, frequent close work, such as reading or working at a computer, is also a cause. When you do a lot of close work, the frequent contractions of the ciliary muscles that change the shape of the lens increase the pressure within the eye. This pressure can cause the eye to stretch and elongate, resulting in nearsightedness. Eye specialists recommend that you look up from the page or away from the computer screen at frequent intervals—particularly if nearsightedness runs in your family.

Irregularities in the curvature of the cornea or lens will cause distortion of the image because they cause the light rays to converge unevenly. This condition is called *astigmatism.* Vision can

TABLE 9.2 Focusing Problems of the Eye

Problem	Description	Cause	Correction
Farsightedness	See distant objects more clearly than nearby objects	Eyeball too short or lens too thin; lens cannot become round enough	Convex lens; increases corneal curvature
Nearsightedness	See nearby objects more clearly than distant objects	Eyeball too long or lens too thick; lens cannot flatten enough	Concave lens; decreases corneal curvature
Astigmatism	Visual image is distorted	Irregularities in curvature of cornea or lens	Lenses that correct for the asymmetrical bending of light

(a) Normal eye
- Close and distant objects seen clearly
- Image focuses on retina

(b) Farsightedness
- Distant objects seen clearly
- Close objects out of focus
- Short eyeball causes image to focus behind retina

Convex lens
- Causes light rays to converge so that the image focuses on the retina

(c) Nearsightedness (myopia)
- Close objects seen clearly
- Distant objects out of focus
- Long eyeball causes image to focus in front of retina

Concave lens
- Causes light rays to diverge so that the image focuses on the retina

(d) Astigmatism
- Image blurred
- Irregular curvature of cornea or lens causes light rays to focus unevenly

Uneven lens
- Focuses entire image on retina

FIGURE 9.6 Focusing problems such as farsightedness, nearsightedness, and astigmatism are caused when the image of an object is not focused on the retina. These vision problems can be corrected with the use of specific lenses.

almost always be restored to normal by corrective lenses that compensate for the asymmetrical bending of light rays (Figure **9.6**).

Light and Pigment Molecules

The eye contains a whopping 70% of all the sensory receptors in the body. The function of the eye's receptors, both rods and cones,

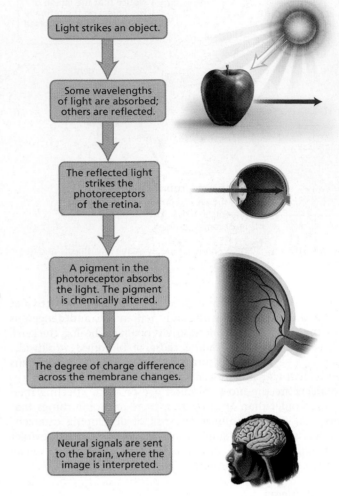

FIGURE 9.7 An overview of the visual process

is to respond to light by sending neural messages to the brain, where they are translated into images of our surroundings.

So how does vision work? First, light waves in the visible spectrum (the spectrum of wavelengths our eyes can detect) strike an object (Figure **9.7**). At least some wavelengths are reflected off the object to the eye, where they are focused by the cornea and lens onto the retina and absorbed by photopigment molecules in the photoreceptors. When light strikes a photopigment, it causes the photopigment molecule's components to split apart. This change causes a series of reactions that reduce the photoreceptor's release of inhibitory neurotransmitter. The neurotransmitter normally inhibits the cells involved in processing the information (discussed shortly); and so, by leading to reduced neurotransmitter levels, light increases the activity of these processing cells. The optic nerve carries these nerve signals from the retina to the thalamus of the brain, where some processing of the information occurs. The information is then sent to the visual cortex, located at the back of the brain, where a perception of the world outside takes shape.

The processing of electrical signals from the rods and cones begins before the signals leave the retina. The messages are first sent to bipolar cells in the retina. These cells are rare examples of neurons that have only two processes, an axon and a single dendrite, extending from opposite sides of the cell body.

(a) Light enters the left eye and strikes the retina.

(b) When light is focused on the retina, it passes through the ganglion cell layer and bipolar cell layer before reaching the rods and cones. In response to light, the rods and cones generate electrical signals that are sent to bipolar cells and then to ganglion cells. These cells begin the processing of visual information.

(c) The axons of the ganglion cells leave the eye at the blind spot, carrying nerve impulses to the brain (viewed from below) by means of the optic nerve.

FIGURE 9.8 Neural pathways of the retina convert light to nerve signals.

Bipolar neurons direct the information to interneurons called ganglion cells (Figure **9.8**). Together, bipolar cells and ganglion cells convert the input from the retina into patterns, such as edges and spots.

Rods: Vision in Dim Light

The **rods** are more numerous than the cones and are the photoreceptors responsible for black-and-white vision (Figure **9.9**). Rods are exceedingly sensitive to light and are capable of responding to light measuring one 10-billionth of a watt—the equivalent of a match burning 50 mi (80.5 km) away on a clear, pitch-dark night! (Of course, the ideal environmental conditions necessary to actually *see* a burning match at such a distance are impossible to attain.) The rods allow us to see in dimly lit rooms and in pale moonlight. By detecting changes in light intensity across the visual field, rods contribute to the perception of movements.

The pigment in rods, called **rhodopsin**, is packaged in membrane-bound disks that are stacked like coins in the outer segment of the rod. Light strikes a rod, splits the rhodopsin, and triggers events that reduce the permeability of the plasma membrane to sodium ions. This reaction eventually leads to changes in the activity of bipolar cells and ganglion cells. In the dark, rhodopsin is resynthesized. The reason you have difficulty seeing when you first walk into a dark room from a brightly lit area is that the rhodopsin in your photoreceptors has been split. As rhodopsin is resynthesized, your vision becomes sharper.

Cones: Color Vision

The **cones** are the photoreceptors responsible for color vision. Unlike the rods, the cones produce sharp images, because each cone usually sends information to only one bipolar cell for processing.

What makes you see red? Red, or any other color, is determined by wavelengths of light. White light, such as that emitted by an ordinary lightbulb or the sun, consists of all wavelengths. (Rainbows are created when the various wavelengths of white light are separated as they pass through tiny droplets of water in the air.) When light strikes an object, some of the wavelengths may be absorbed and others reflected; we see the wavelengths that are reflected. Thus, an apple looks red because it reflects mostly red light and absorbs most of the other wavelengths.

We see color because we have three types of cones, called blue, green, and red. The cones are named for the wavelengths they absorb best, not for their color. When light is absorbed, the cone is stimulated. Actually, each type of cone absorbs a range of wavelengths, and the ranges overlap quite a bit. As a result, colored light stimulates each type of cone to a different extent. For instance, when we look at a bowl of fruit, light reflected by a red apple stimulates red cones, light reflected by a ripe yellow banana stimulates both red and green cones, and light reflected from blueberries stimulates both blue and green cones. The brain then interprets color according to how strongly each type of cone is stimulated.

stop and think

Most bipolar cells receive input from several rods but from only one cone in the fovea. How might this difference explain why rods permit us to see at lower light intensities than do cones? How might it explain why the sharpest images are formed when the object is focused on the fovea?

Correcting Vision Problems

Although most people wear glasses to correct vision problems, 24 million Americans use contact lenses instead. The contact lens sits on the cornea over a layer of tears. The outer surface of the lens is the corrective surface, and the inner surface fits snugly on the cornea. There are two types of contact lenses. Rigid gas-permeable lenses are made of slightly flexible plastic. These lenses are tough and durable, but some people find that they irritate the eyes. Soft lenses are made of a more malleable plastic. Although soft lenses are gentler on the eyes, they are more easily scratched and damaged.

Some soft contact lenses are made to be disposed of after a single use, but those that are reused must be cleaned and disinfected regularly using special solutions. Infections, caused by bacteria, fungi, or *Acanthamoeba* (a type of amoeba), can develop behind the lens. Tears leave deposits of protein, fats, and calcium that help infectious organisms adhere to the contact lens. At best, these deposits are difficult to remove. The more infrequently the lenses are cleaned, the more difficult it becomes to remove the deposits and the more likely infection becomes. Extended-wear contact lenses of both types have been developed, some of which can be left in place for a month or more. Initially, eye specialists thought that less frequent insertion and removal of lenses would reduce trauma to the cornea. However, a serious safety concern with contact lenses that are left in overnight or for extended periods of time is ulcerative keratitis, a condition in which the cells of the cornea may be rubbed away by the contact lens, sometimes leading to infection and scarring. If not promptly treated, ulcerative keratitis can lead to blindness. Another problem with leaving contact lenses in overnight seems to be a reduced oxygen supply to the cornea, which causes it to swell.

Many people who are tired of depending on glasses or contact lenses have opted to undergo laser eye surgery. This procedure is popularly known as LASIK, which stands for laser-assisted in situ keratomileusis. LASIK permanently changes the shape of the cornea. The procedure involves cutting a flap in the cornea, using pulses from a computer-controlled laser to reshape the middle layer of the cornea, and then replacing the flap. This treatment is used to correct for nearsightedness, farsightedness, and astigmatism.

Another procedure for reshaping the cornea is LASEK (laser-assisted subepithelial keratomileusis). It differs from LASIK in that the surgeon creates a flap in the epithelium only, instead of in the entire cornea, eliminating some of the complications caused by the deeper corneal flaps. LASEK is used mostly for people who are poor candidates for LASIK because their corneas are thin or flat. In yet another procedure, photorefractive keratectomy (PRK), a surgeon uses short bursts of a laser beam to shave a microscopic layer of cells off the corneal surface and flatten it. A computer calculates and controls the laser exposure.

Contact lenses, thin disks of plastic that float on the eye, correct the same visual problems that eyeglasses correct.

The shape of the cornea can also be altered using a surgical procedure that does not involve lasers. A surgeon can place corneal ring segments, two tiny crescent-shaped pieces of plastic, in the cornea to flatten it. This 15-minute procedure reduces nearsightedness. The ring segments are intended to be permanent but can be removed if necessary.

Lastly, a procedure called orthokeratology uses special hard contact lenses to produce long-lasting, but not permanent, changes in the cornea. At first, the lenses are worn for 8 hours a day. After the cornea has been reshaped for clearest vision, the lenses need only be worn a few hours every few days. If their use is discontinued, the cornea gradually returns to its natural shape.

Color blindness is a condition in which certain colors cannot be distinguished from each other. Most people who are color blind see some colors, but they tend to confuse certain colors with others. Thus, a standard test for color blindness is to show the individual a color plate with dots of two colors (Figure **9.10**). Dots of one color indicate a number. A person who is color blind cannot distinguish the number. A lack, or a reduced number, of one of the types of cones causes the confusion. A person who lacks red cones sees deep reds as black. In contrast, a person who lacks green cones sees deep reds but cannot distinguish between reds, oranges, and yellows. Absence of blue cones is extremely rare.

People who are color blind generally function normally in everyday life. They compensate for the inability to distinguish certain colors by using other cues, such as intensity, shape, or position. Ironically, red and green—the universal traffic colors for stop and go—are the most commonly confused colors. However, it is usually possible to pick out the brightest of the lights in a traffic signal, and all traffic signals are arranged the same way—red on top and green on the bottom. Schoolchildren are regularly tested for color blindness so that both students and teachers are aware of the condition. Color blindness may cause difficulty with class work, such as reading maps or graphs that are presented in color. If a teacher is aware of the condition,

FIGURE 9.9 Rods and cones, the photoreceptors in the retina, are named for their shapes. Their function is to generate neural messages in response to light. The outer portion of each photoreceptor is packed with membrane-bound disks that contain pigment molecules.

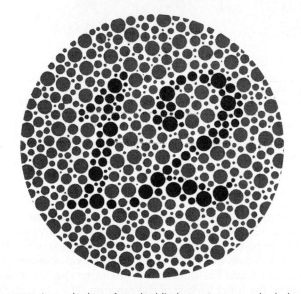

FIGURE 9.10 A standard test for color blindness. A person who lacks one of the three types of cones would not be able to distinguish the number 12 in the center of this circle.

steps can be taken to avoid frustration and confusion for the student.

Hearing

From a social perspective, hearing is perhaps the most important of our senses because speech plays such an important role in the communication that binds society. Hearing can also make us aware of things in the external world that we cannot see—telling us of a car approaching from behind as we jog, for instance. Hearing can also add to our understanding of events that we *can* see, as when a mother determines by the sound of the cry whether her baby is hungry or in pain. And hearing can enrich the quality of our lives, as when we listen to music or hear waves crashing on the shore.

In every instance, what we hear are sound waves produced by vibration. Vibrating objects, such as guitar strings, the surface of

(a) Sound is caused by a vibrating object that causes pressure waves in the air (or water).

(b) The amplitude (height) of the wave determines the loudness of the sound. Loudness increases with amplitude.

(c) The frequency (cycles per second) of the waves determines the pitch of the sound. Pitch goes up as frequency increases.

FIGURE 9.11 A sound wave and the effects of amplitude (height) and frequency (cycles per second)

the stereo speaker, or vocal cords, move rapidly back and forth. The vibrations push repeatedly against the surrounding air, creating sound waves, as shown in Figure **9.11**. The loudness of sound is determined by the amplitude of the sound wave, represented graphically as the distance between the top of peaks and the bottom of troughs. The pitch is determined by the frequency, the number of cycles (repetitions of the wave) per second. The more cycles there are, the higher the pitch.

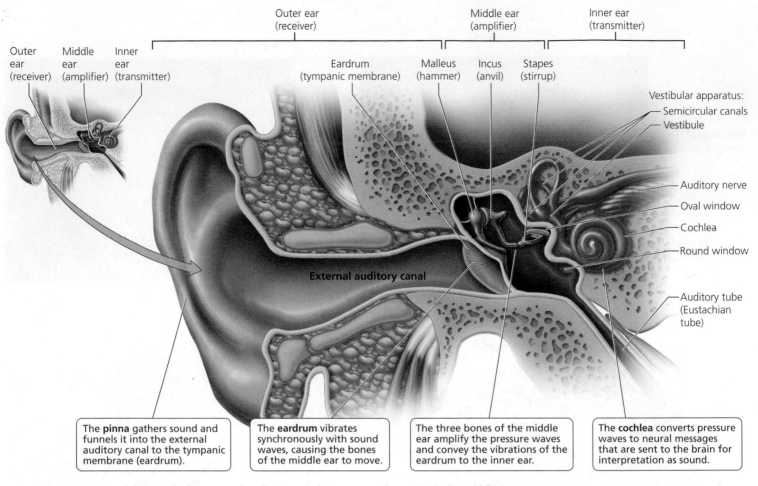

Outer ear
(receiver)

Middle ear
(amplifier)

Inner ear
(transmitter)

Outer
ear
(receiver)

Middle
ear
(amplifier)

Inner
ear
(transmitter)

Eardrum
(tympanic membrane)

Malleus
(hammer)

Incus
(anvil)

Stapes
(stirrup)

Vestibular apparatus:
Semicircular canals
Vestibule

Auditory nerve

Oval window

Cochlea

Round window

External auditory canal

Auditory tube
(Eustachian
tube)

The **pinna** gathers sound and funnels it into the external auditory canal to the tympanic membrane (eardrum).

The **eardrum** vibrates synchronously with sound waves, causing the bones of the middle ear to move.

The three bones of the middle ear amplify the pressure waves and convey the vibrations of the eardrum to the inner ear.

The **cochlea** converts pressure waves to neural messages that are sent to the brain for interpretation as sound.

FIGURE 9.12 Structure of the ear. The human ear has three parts: the outer ear (the receiver), the middle ear (the amplifier), and the inner ear (the transmitter).

Form and Function of the Ear

The ear has three main parts—the outer ear, the middle ear, and the inner ear—as shown in Figure **9.12**. The **outer ear** functions as a receiver. The part of the outer ear visible on the head consists of a fleshy funnel called the **pinna.** The pinna gathers the sound and channels it into the **external auditory canal,** which leads from the pinna to the eardrum. The pinna also accentuates the frequencies of the most important speech sounds, making speech easier to pick out from background noise. The pinnas' shape and placement at either side of the head help us determine the direction a sound comes from.

The tissue that separates the outer ear from the middle ear is the eardrum, or **tympanic membrane.** It is as thin as a sheet of paper and as taut as the head of a tambourine. When sound waves strike the eardrum, it vibrates at the same frequency as the sound waves and transfers these vibrations to the middle ear.

stop and think

As we age, the tissues of the eardrum thicken and become less flexible. How do these changes partially explain why sensitivity to high-frequency sounds is usually lost as we grow older?

The **middle ear** serves as an amplifier. It consists of an air-filled cavity within a bone of the skull and is spanned by the three smallest bones of the body: the **malleus** (hammer), **incus** (anvil), and **stapes** (stirrup)—named to indicate their respective shapes. Together, these bones function as a system of levers to convey the airborne sound waves from the eardrum to the **oval window,** a sheet of tissue that forms the threshold of the inner ear. The malleus is attached to the inner surface of the eardrum. Therefore, the vibrations of the eardrum in response to sound cause the malleus to rock back and forth. The rocking of the malleus, in turn, causes the incus and then the stapes to move. The base of the stapes fits into the oval window.

The force of the eardrum's vibrations is amplified 22 times in the middle ear. The magnification of force is necessary to transfer the vibrations to the fluid of the inner ear. The amplification occurs because the eardrum is larger than the oval window. This size difference concentrates the pressure against the oval window.

The air pressure must be nearly equal on both sides of the eardrum for the eardrum to vibrate properly. If the pressure is not equal, the eardrum will bulge inward or outward and will be held in that position, causing pain and difficulty hearing. For instance, when a person ascends quickly to a high altitude, the atmospheric pressure is lower than the pressure in the middle ear, and the eardrum bulges outward. Unequal pressure usually is alleviated by the **auditory tube** (also known as the Eustachian tube), a canal that connects the middle ear cavity with the upper region of the throat. Most of the time, the auditory tube is closed and flattened. However, swallowing or yawning opens it briefly, allowing the

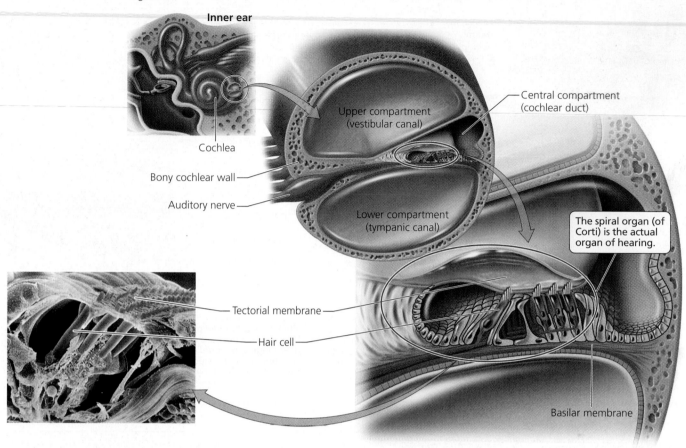

Right ear

Inner ear

Upper compartment (vestibular canal)

Central compartment (cochlear duct)

Cochlea

Bony cochlear wall

Auditory nerve

Lower compartment (tympanic canal)

The spiral organ (of Corti) is the actual organ of hearing.

Tectorial membrane

Hair cell

Basilar membrane

FIGURE 9.13 The cochlea houses the spiral organ (of Corti). The spiral organ consists of the hair cells and the overhanging gelatinous tectorial membrane. The spiral organ rests on the basilar membrane. The hairs are the receptors for hearing. In the micrograph, the hair cells are colored pink and their "hairs" are colored yellow.

pressure in the middle ear cavity to equalize with the air pressure outside the ear. The sensation of pressure suddenly equalizing is described as the ear "popping." It can occur whenever the pressure on the external eardrum changes quickly, as when you ride up or down in an elevator, take off or land in an airplane, or go scuba diving.

The **inner ear** is a transmitter. It generates neural messages in response to pressure waves caused by sound waves, and it sends the messages to the brain for interpretation. The inner ear contains two sensory organs, only one of which, the **cochlea** (kok'-le-ah), is concerned with hearing. The other sensory organ, the vestibular apparatus, is concerned with sensations of body position and movement and will be discussed in the next section.

The cochlea is about the size of a pea, and it can be considered the true seat of hearing. It is a bony tube about 35 mm (1.4 in.) long that is coiled about two-and-a-half times and looks somewhat like the shell of a snail, as you can see in Figure **9.13**. (*Cochlea* is from the Latin for "snail.") The wider end of the tube, where the snail's head would be, has two membrane-covered openings. The upper opening is the oval window, into which the stapes fits. The lower opening, called the **round window**, serves to relieve the pressure created by the movements of the oval window.

The internal structure of the cochlea is easier to understand if we imagine the cochlea uncoiled so that it forms a long straight tube. We would then see that two membranes divide the interior of the cochlea into three longitudinal compartments, each filled with fluid. The central compartment (the cochlear duct) ends

blindly, like the finger on a glove, and does not extend completely to the end of the cochlea's internal tube. As a result, the upper and lower compartments (the vestibular canal and the tympanic canal) are connected at the end of the tube nearest to the tip of the coil. The **basilar membrane** is the floor of the central compartment. The **spiral organ** (of Corti), the portion of the cochlea most directly responsible for the sense of hearing, is supported on the basilar membrane (Figure **9.14**). The spiral organ consists of the **hair cells** and the overhanging **tectorial membrane**. Each hair cell has about 100 "hairs," slender projections from its upper surface that project into the tectorial membrane. The hair cells are arranged on the basilar membrane in rows that resemble miniature picket fences.

When the stapes moves to and fro against the oval window, it sets up corresponding movements—pressure waves—in the fluid of the inner ear (Figure 9.14). Those pressure waves are then transmitted from the fluid of the cochlea's upper compartment to the fluid of the lower compartment, because the compartments are continuous. The movements of the fluid cause the basilar membrane to swing up and down; this swinging, in turn, causes the projections on the hair cells to be pressed against the tectorial membrane. The bending of the hairs ultimately alters the rate of nerve impulses in the auditory (cochlear) nerve, which arises within the cochlea and carries sound information to the brain. The structures of the ear and their functions are summarized in Table **9.3**.

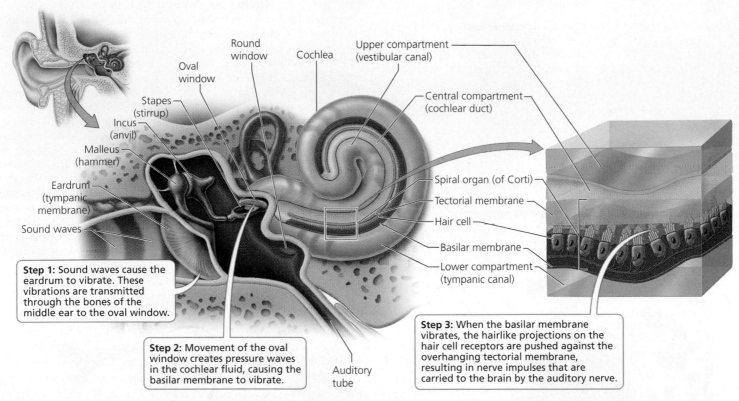

Round window

Oval window

Cochlea

Upper compartment (vestibular canal)

Stapes (stirrup)

Incus (anvil)

Malleus (hammer)

Eardrum (tympanic membrane)

Sound waves

Central compartment (cochlear duct)

Spiral organ (of Corti)

Tectorial membrane

Hair cell

Basilar membrane

Lower compartment (tympanic canal)

Auditory tube

Step 1: Sound waves cause the eardrum to vibrate. These vibrations are transmitted through the bones of the middle ear to the oval window.

Step 2: Movement of the oval window creates pressure waves in the cochlear fluid, causing the basilar membrane to vibrate.

Step 3: When the basilar membrane vibrates, the hairlike projections on the hair cell receptors are pushed against the overhanging tectorial membrane, resulting in nerve impulses that are carried to the brain by the auditory nerve.

FIGURE 9.14 The sequence of events from sound vibration to a nerve impulse begins when sound enters the external auditory canal.

TABLE 9.3 Review of the Structures of the Ear and Their Functions

Structure	Description	Function
Outer ear		
Pinna	Fleshy, funnel-shaped part of the ear protruding from the side of the head	Collects and directs sound waves
External auditory canal	Canal between pinna and tympanic membrane	Directs sound to the middle ear
Middle ear		
Eardrum (tympanic membrane)	Membrane spanning the end of the external auditory canal	Vibrates in response to sound waves
Malleus (hammer), incus (anvil), and stapes (stirrup)	Three tiny bones of the middle ear	Amplify the vibrations of the tympanic membrane and transmit vibrations to inner ear
Auditory tube (Eustachian tube)	A tube that connects the middle ear with the throat	Allows equalization of pressure in middle ear with external air pressure
Inner ear		
Cochlea	Fluid-filled, bony, snail-shaped chamber	Houses spiral organ (of Corti) and has openings called oval window and round window
Spiral organ (of Corti)	Contains hair cells	The organ of hearing
Oval window	Membrane between the middle and inner ear that the stapes presses against	Transmits the movements of the stapes to the fluid in the inner ear
Round window	Membrane at the end of the lower canal in cochlea	Relieves pressure created by the movements of the oval window
Vestibular apparatus	Fluid-filled chambers and canals	Monitors position and movement of the head
Vestibule (utricle and saccule)	Two fluid-filled chambers	Maintains static equilibrium (body and head stationary, information on position of head)
Semicircular canals	Three fluid-filled chambers oriented at right angles to one another	Maintain dynamic equilibrium (body or head moving)

Loudness and Pitch of Sound

The louder the sound, the greater the pressure changes in the fluid of the inner ear and, therefore, the stronger the bending of the basilar membrane. Because hair cells have different thresholds of stimulation, more vigorous vibrations in the basilar membrane stimulate more hair cells. In addition, each hair cell bends more with more vigorous vibrations of the basilar membrane, which increases the number of nerve impulses. The brain interprets the increased number of impulses as louder sound.

How does the ear determine the pitch of a sound? Different regions of the basilar membrane vibrate in response to sounds of different pitch. In a sense, the cochlea is like a spiral piano keyboard. The basilar membrane varies in width and flexibility along its length. Near the oval window, the basilar membrane is narrow and stiff. Like the shorter strings on a piano, this region vibrates maximally in response to high-frequency sound, such as a whistle. At the tip of the tube in the cochlea, the basilar membrane is wider and floppier. Low-frequency sounds, such as a bass drum, cause maximum vibrations in this region of the basilar membrane. Thus, sounds of different pitches activate hair cells at different places along the basilar membrane. The brain then interprets input from hair cells in different regions as sounds of different pitch.

Hearing Loss

An estimated 28 million Americans have some degree of hearing loss, and 2 million of them are completely deaf. Hearing loss that is severe enough to interfere with social and job-related communication is among the most common chronic neural impairments in the United States.

There are two types of hearing loss: *conductive loss* and *sensorineural loss*. Conductive loss results when an obstruction anywhere along the route prevents sounds from being conducted through the external auditory canal to the eardrum and over the bones of the middle ear to the inner ear. The external auditory canal can become clogged with wax or other foreign matter. In this case, inserting cotton-tipped swabs usually aggravates the situation by further clogging the canal and should therefore be avoided. Other possible causes for conductive hearing loss are thickening of the eardrum, which might occur with chronic infection, or perforation of the eardrum, which might occur as a result of trauma. Excess fluid in the middle ear, which often occurs with middle ear infections, can prevent movement of the eardrum and cause temporary conductive hearing loss. In *otosclerosis*, conductive hearing loss is caused by fusion of the bones of the middle ear. The fused bones can no longer transmit sound, and the only way that sound can be transmitted to the inner ear is through the bones of the skull, which is much less efficient. Otosclerosis is routinely corrected by surgery.

Sensorineural deafness is caused by damage to the hair cells or to the nerve supply of the inner ear. A common cause is gradual loss of hair cells throughout life. Some of the loss is simply due to aging. After age 20, the loss of hair cells causes us to lose about 1 Hz of our total perceptive range of 20,000 Hz every day. However, much of the damage to hair cells is caused by exposure to loud noise (see the Environmental Issue essay, *Noise Pollution*). Neural damage can also be caused by infections, including mumps, rubella (German measles), syphilis, and meningitis. In addition, drugs such as those used for treating tuberculosis and certain cancers can cause neural damage.

One of the first signs of sensorineural damage is the inability to hear high-frequency sounds. Because consonants, which are needed to decipher most words, have higher frequencies than do vowels, speech becomes difficult to understand. So beware if you find yourself asking, "Could you repeat that?"

The most effective way to deal with hearing loss is with a hearing aid. The basic job of a hearing aid is to amplify sound. One type of hearing aid presents amplified sound to the eardrum. Another type uses a vibrator or stimulator placed in the bone of the skull behind the ear. Sound is then conducted through the bones of the skull to the inner ear.

Hearing aids often are unable to help profoundly deaf people, but cochlear implants can pierce the silence for some of them. A cochlear implant does not amplify sounds like a hearing aid does; instead, it compensates for parts of the inner ear that are not functioning properly. A cochlear implant consists of an array of electrodes that transforms sound into electrical signals that are delivered to the nerve cells near the cochlea. The implant is surgically inserted into the cochlea through the round window (Figure **9.15**). A cochlear implant allows some people who were severely hearing impaired or totally deaf to converse with someone in person or on the phone. By providing exposure to sounds during the time when language is developing, cochlear implants also help deaf children learn to speak well.

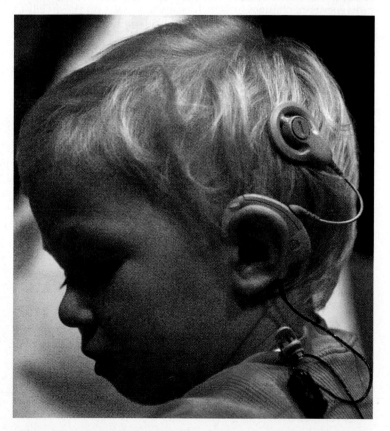

FIGURE 9.15 A cochlear implant. Unlike a hearing aid, which amplifies sounds, a cochlear implant is an array of electrodes that is surgically inserted into the cochlea. It transforms sound into neural impulses that are sent to the cochlea.

Ear Infections

An external ear infection is an infection in the ear canal. *Swimmer's ear*, the most common such infection, is precipitated by water trapped in the canal, which creates an environment favorable for bacterial growth. The first symptom of swimmer's ear is itching, usually followed by pain that can become intense and constant. Chewing food or touching the earlobe sharpens the pain. The usual treatment consists of antibiotic ear drops, heat, and pain medication. To prevent swimmer's ear, always be sure to drain any remaining water from the ear canal after swimming or bathing—if necessary, by shaking the head.

Middle ear infections usually result from infections of the nose and throat that work their way through the auditory tubes connecting the throat and middle ear. At least half of all children get an ear infection at some time; some children get four or five ear infections a year. Middle ear infections are more common in children than in adults because the auditory tubes curve and tilt downward in adults. In children, the tubes are nearly horizontal, allowing infectious organisms to travel through them more easily. The signs of a middle ear infection are a stabbing earache, impaired hearing, and a feeling of fullness in the ear, often accompanied by fever. A middle ear infection usually is treated with an antibiotic.

Balance and the Vestibular Apparatus of the Inner Ear

The **vestibular apparatus**, a fluid-filled maze of chambers and canals within the inner ear, is responsible for monitoring the position and movement of the head. The receptors in the vestibular apparatus are hair cells similar to those in the cochlea. Head movements or changes in velocity cause the hairs on these cells to bend, sending messages to the brain. The brain uses this input to maintain balance.

The vestibular apparatus consists of the semicircular canals and the vestibule. The **semicircular canals** are three canals in each ear that contain sensory receptors and help us stay balanced as we move. They monitor any sudden movements of the head, including those caused by acceleration and deceleration, to help us maintain our equilibrium when the body or head is moving (see "dynamic equilibrium" in Figure **9.16**). At the base of each semicircular canal is an enlarged region called the *ampulla*. Within the ampulla is a tuft of hair cells. The hairlike projections from these cells are embedded in a pointed "cap" of stiff, pliable, gelatinous material called the *cupula*. When you move your head, fluid in the canal lags a little behind, causing the cupula to bend the hair cells and stimulate them.

The three semicircular canals in each ear are oriented at right angles to one another. Head movements cause the fluid in the canals to move in the direction opposite the direction of movement, in the same way that sudden acceleration slams passengers back against the car seat. Whereas nodding your head to say yes will cause the fluid in the canals parallel to the sides of the head to swirl, shaking it from side to side to say no will cause fluid in the canals parallel to the horizon to move. Tilting your head to look under the bed will cause fluid in the canals that are parallel to your face to move back and forth. Even the most complex movement can be analyzed in terms of motion in three planes.

The **vestibule**, the other part of the vestibular apparatus, is important for static equilibrium—the maintenance of balance when we are not moving. The vestibule consists of the utricle and the saccule, two fluid-filled cavities that literally let us know which end is up (Figure 9.16). These cavities tell the brain the position of the head with respect to gravity when the body is not moving. They also respond to acceleration and deceleration, but not to rotational changes as the semicircular canals do. Both the utricle and the saccule contain hair cells overlaid with a gelatinous material in which small chalklike granules of calcium carbonate are embedded. These granules, called *otoliths*, make the gelatin heavier than the surrounding material and thus make it slide over the hair cells whenever the head is moved. The movement of the gelatin stimulates the hair cells, which send messages to the brain, and the brain interprets the messages to determine the position of the head relative to gravity.

The utricle and saccule sense different types of movement. The utricle senses the forward tilting of the head, as well as forward motion, because its hair cells are on the floor of the chamber and oriented vertically when the head is upright. In contrast, the hair cells of the saccule are on the wall of the chamber, oriented horizontally when the head is upright. They respond when you move vertically, as when you jump up and down.

Motion sickness—that dreadful feeling of dizziness and nausea that sometimes causes vomiting—is thought to be caused by a mismatch between sensory input from the vestibular apparatus and sensory input from the eyes. For example, you may be one of the many people who get carsick from reading in the car. When looking down at a book, your eyes tell your brain that your body is stationary. However, as the car changes speed, turns, and hits bumps in the road, your vestibular system is detecting motion. Similarly, seasickness results when the vestibular apparatus tells the brain that your head is rocking back and forth, but the deck under your feet looks level. The brain is somehow confused by the conflicting information, and the result is motion sickness. Staring at the horizon, so you can see that you are moving, can sometimes relieve the feeling. Over-the-counter drugs to prevent motion sickness, such as Dramamine, work by inhibiting the messages from the vestibular apparatus.

Smell and Taste

Smell is perhaps the least appreciated of our senses. You could easily get along without it, but life would not be as interesting. For one thing, about 80% of what we usually think of as the flavor of a food is really detected by our sense of smell. This relationship explains why food often tastes bland when the nose is congested.

You have millions of **olfactory (smell) receptors**, located not in the nostrils but in a small patch of tissue the size of a postage stamp in the roof of each nasal cavity. These receptors are sensory neurons that branch into long olfactory hairs that project outward from the lining of the nasal cavity and are covered by a coat of mucus, which keeps them moist and is a solvent for odorous molecules. The hairs move, gently swirling the mucus. Olfactory receptors, by the way, are one of the few kinds of neuron known to be replaced during life—about every 60 days.

Odor molecules are carried into the nasal cavity in air, dissolve in the mucus, and bind to receptor sites on the hairs of the olfactory receptor cells, thereby stimulating the cells. If threshold is reached, the message is carried to the two olfactory bulbs of the brain. The olfactory bulbs process the information from the olfactory receptors and pass it on to the limbic system and to

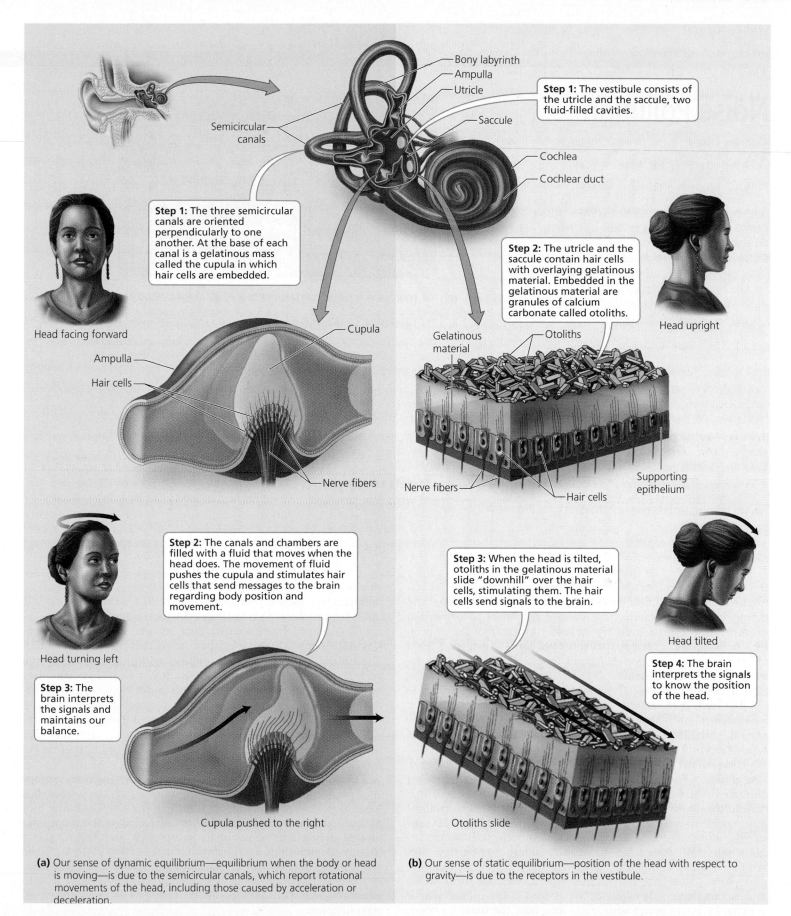

Bony labyrinth
Ampulla
Utricle

Step 1: The vestibule consists of the utricle and the saccule, two fluid-filled cavities.

Semicircular canals

Saccule

Cochlea

Cochlear duct

Step 1: The three semicircular canals are oriented perpendicularly to one another. At the base of each canal is a gelatinous mass called the cupula in which hair cells are embedded.

Step 2: The utricle and the saccule contain hair cells with overlaying gelatinous material. Embedded in the gelatinous material are granules of calcium carbonate called otoliths.

Head upright

Head facing forward

Cupula

Gelatinous material

Otoliths

Ampulla

Hair cells

Nerve fibers

Nerve fibers

Hair cells

Supporting epithelium

Step 2: The canals and chambers are filled with a fluid that moves when the head does. The movement of fluid pushes the cupula and stimulates hair cells that send messages to the brain regarding body position and movement.

Step 3: When the head is tilted, otoliths in the gelatinous material slide "downhill" over the hair cells, stimulating them. The hair cells send signals to the brain.

Head turning left

Step 3: The brain interprets the signals and maintains our balance.

Head tilted

Step 4: The brain interprets the signals to know the position of the head.

Cupula pushed to the right

Otoliths slide

(a) Our sense of dynamic equilibrium—equilibrium when the body or head is moving—is due to the semicircular canals, which report rotational movements of the head, including those caused by acceleration or deceleration.

(b) Our sense of static equilibrium—position of the head with respect to gravity—is due to the receptors in the vestibule.

FIGURE 9.16 Dynamic and static equilibrium

Noise Pollution

It is difficult to escape the din of modern life—noise from airports, city streets, loud appliances, stereos. Noise pollution threatens your hearing and your health. Exposure to excessive noise is to blame for the hearing loss of one-third of all hearing-impaired people. Loud noise damages the hairs on the hair cells of the inner ear. When the hairs are exposed to too much noise, they wear down, lose their flexibility, and can fuse together (Figure **9.A**). Unfortunately, there is no way to undo the damage; you cannot grow spare parts for your ears.

The loudness of noise is measured in decibels (dB). The decibel scale is logarithmic. An increase of 10 dB generally makes a given sound twice as loud. The decibel ratings and effects of some familiar sounds are given in Table **9.A**. Most people judge sounds over 60 dB to be intrusive, over 80 dB to be annoying, and over 100 dB to be extremely bothersome. The federal Occupational Safety and Health Administration (OSHA) has set 85 dB as the safety limit for 8 hours of exposure. The threshold for physical pain is 140 dB.

FIGURE 9.A The hair cells of the inner ear can be permanently damaged by loud noise. The micrograph on the left shows a portion of the spiral organ (of Corti) from a normal guinea pig, showing the characteristic three rows of outer hair cells and a single inner row. The micrograph on the right shows the spiral organ (of Corti) from a guinea pig that had been exposed to loud (120 dB) sound. Note that scars have replaced some injured cells. On most of the hair cells that have survived, the hairs are no longer in an orderly pattern.

Hearing can be damaged by exposure to noise that is loud enough to make conversation difficult. The louder a sound, the shorter the exposure time necessary to damage the ear. Even a brief, explosively loud sound is capable of damaging hair cells. More commonly, however, hearing loss results from prolonged exposure to volumes over 85 dB. Your ears can endure sound at 90 dB for about 8 hours. For every 5 dB above that, it takes half as long for damage to begin. Thus, sound at 95 dB will damage your ears in only 4 hours. At 110 dB, the average rock concert or stereo headset at full blast can damage your ears in as little as

---

the cerebral cortex (see Chapter 8), where it is interpreted. As you might recall, the limbic system is a center for emotions and memory. Thus, we rarely have neutral responses to odors. For example, the perfume industry makes a fortune from the association between scents and sexuality. Odors can also trigger a flood of long-forgotten memories. If your first kiss was near a blooming lilac bush, for instance, a simple sniff of lilac may take you back in time and place.

We have about 1000 types of olfactory receptors, with which we can distinguish about 10,000 odors. Each receptor responds to several odors. Thus, the brain relies on input from more than one type of receptor to identify an odor (Figure **9.17**).

There are at least five primary tastes: sweet, salty, sour, bitter, and umami (oo-ma'-mee; savory flavor). These five tastes are enough to answer the important question about food or drink: Should we swallow it or spit it out? We are prompted to swallow if it tastes sweet, because sweetness implies a rich source of calories and thus energy. Salty tastes also prompt swallowing, because salts will replace those lost in perspiration. Sourness may pose a dilemma. Sour is the taste of unripe fruit that would have more food value later on. As fruit ripens, starches break down into sugars that create a sweet taste and mask the sourness. So it is often better to reject sour fruits and wait for them to ripen. However, some sour fruits, such as oranges, lemons, and tomatoes, are rich sources of vitamin C, an essential vitamin. Bitter is

easy. We generally reject foods that taste bitter. Bitterness usually indicates that food is poisonous or spoiled. We swallow food if it tastes umami, because it indicates the food is high in protein.

The less widely known fifth taste, umami, is savory or brothy. Umami is derived from a Japanese word that means "delicious." The umami taste occurs when amino acids, especially glutamic acid, small proteins, and nucleotides (DNA and RNA) stimulate umami receptors. The brain interprets input from umami receptors, perhaps with simultaneous input from other receptors as the taste umami. To experience the flavor umami, boil a cup of water with a tablespoon of dried shitake mushrooms. Let it cool and take a sip. Other umami foods include chicken broth, beef broth, and parmesan cheese.

Children have about 10,000 **taste buds**, the structures responsible for our sense of taste. Most taste buds are on the tongue, but some are scattered on the inner surface of the cheeks, on the roof of the mouth, and in the throat. Most taste buds on the tongue are located in papillae, those small bumps that give the tongue a slightly rough feeling. Each papilla contains 100 to 200 taste buds. The cells of a taste bud are completely replaced about every 10 days, so you need not worry about permanently losing your sense of taste when you burn your mouth eating overly hot pizza, as almost always happens.

A taste bud is the meeting point between chemicals dissolved in saliva and the sensory neurons that will convey information about

30 minutes. If sounds seem muffled to you or if your ears are ringing after you leave a noisy area, you probably sustained some damage to your ears.

Hearing loss is expected in the elderly, but a surprising number of young people also have impaired hearing. The culprit is most likely noise—probably in the form of music. How can you protect yourself? Don't listen to loud music. Keep it tuned low enough that you can still hear other sounds. If you are listening with earphones, no one else should be able to hear the sound from them. When you cannot avoid loud noise, as when you are mowing the lawn, vacuuming, or attending a rock concert, wear earplugs to protect your hearing. You can buy them at most drugstores, sporting goods stores, and music stores.

TABLE 9.A Effects of Noise Pollution

Sound Source	Loudness (dB)	Effect from Prolonged Exposure
Jet plane at takeoff	150	Eardrum rupture
Deck of aircraft carrier	140	Very painful; traumatic injury
Rock-and-roll band (at maximum volume)	130	Irreversible damage
Jet plane at 152 m (500 ft)	110	Loss of hearing
Subway; lawn mower	100	
Electric blender	90	Annoying
Freight train at 15 m (50 ft)	80	
Traffic noise	70	Intrusive
Normal conversation	65	
Chirping bird	60	
Quiet neighborhood (daytime)	50	
Soft background music	40	Quiet
Library	30	
Whisper	20	Very quiet
Breathing; rustling leaves	10	
	0	Threshold of hearing

FIGURE 9.17 Our sense of smell resides in a small patch of tissue in the roof of each nasal cavity. Within each cavity are some 5 million olfactory receptors.

them to the brain. Each taste bud is a lemon-shaped structure containing about 40 modified epithelial cells. Some of these cells are the taste cells that respond to chemicals; others are supporting cells (Figure **9.18**). The taste cells have long *taste hairs* that project into a pore at the tip of the taste bud. These taste hairs bear the receptors for certain chemicals found in food. When dissolved in saliva, food molecules enter the pore and stimulate the taste hairs. Although taste cells are not neurons, they generate electrical signals that are then sent to sensory nerve cells wrapped around the taste cell.

Each taste bud responds to all five basic tastes but is usually more sensitive to one or two of them than to the others. Because of the way the taste buds are distributed, different regions of the tongue have *slightly* different sensitivity to these tastes. In general, the tip of the tongue is most sensitive to sweet tastes, the back to bitter, and the sides to sour. Sensitivity to salty tastes is fairly evenly distributed on the tongue. Sensitivity to umami is thought to be distributed throughout the tongue, but it certainly exists at the back of the tongue.

Papilla

Umami (and throughout)

Bitter

Sour

Salty

Sweet

(a) The taste receptors on different parts of the tongue respond more strongly to certain tastes than to others.

(b) The papillae of the tongue contain most of the taste buds.

Supporting cell

Taste cell

Taste pore

Taste hairs

Sensory nerves

(c) A taste bud (shown here) is composed of taste cells and supporting cells.

(d) A micrograph of a taste bud

FIGURE 9.18 Taste buds

highlighting the concepts

Sensory Receptors (p. 162)

- Changes in external and internal environments stimulate sensory receptors, which in turn generate electrochemical messages that are converted to nerve impulses that are conducted to the brain.

Classes of Receptors (pp. 162–163)

- There are five types of sensory receptors. Mechanoreceptors are responsible for touch, pressure, hearing, equilibrium, blood pressure, and body position. Thermoreceptors detect changes in temperature. Photoreceptors detect light. Chemoreceptors monitor chemical levels within the body and detect smells and tastes. Pain receptors respond to strong stimuli that cause physical or chemical damage to tissues.
- Some sensory receptors are located near the body surface and respond to environmental changes. Other sensory receptors are located inside the body and monitor internal conditions.

The General Senses (pp. 163–164)

- Touch, pressure, and vibration are monitored by mechanoreceptors: Merkel's disks, Meissner's corpuscles, Pacinian corpuscles, and Ruffini corpuscles.
- Internal and external temperature is monitored by thermoreceptors, which are widely distributed throughout the body.
- Body and limb position is sensed by the mechanoreceptors called muscle spindles and Golgi tendon organs. Muscle spindles are specialized muscle fibers with sensory nerve endings wrapped around them, and Golgi tendon organs are highly branched nerve fibers in tendons.
- Pain receptors, located in almost every tissue of the body, respond to any strong stimulus that results in physical or chemical damage to tissues.

Vision (pp. 164–171)

- The wall of the eye has three layers. The sclera and the cornea make up the outer layer. The choroid, ciliary body, and iris make up the middle layer. The retina, which contains the photoreceptors (rods and cones), is the innermost layer.
- The cornea and the lens work together to focus images on the retina. A normal lens can accommodate (change in shape) to focus on near or distant objects.
- When pigment molecules in the rods or cones (photoreceptors) absorb light, a chemical change occurs in the pigment molecule. The resulting change in the permeability of the membrane of the photoreceptor generates a neural message that is carried by the optic nerve to the brain.
- Color vision depends on the cones. The three types of cones are named for the color of light they absorb best—green, red, or blue—and allow us to see colors.

Hearing (pp. 171–176)

- The ear is divided into three regions: the outer ear, the middle ear, and the inner ear. The outer ear, which functions as a receiver, consists of the pinna and the external auditory canal. The middle ear, which serves as an amplifier, consists of the tympanic membrane (eardrum), three small bones (malleus, incus, and stapes), and the auditory tube. The inner ear is a transmitter and consists of the cochlea and vestibular apparatus.
- Hearing is the sensing of sound waves caused by vibration. Sound enters the outer ear and vibrates the eardrum. These vibrations move the malleus, which moves the incus and the stapes. The stapes conveys these vibrations to the inner ear by means of the oval window.
- Pressure on either side of the eardrum is regulated by the auditory tube.
- The cochlea is a coiled tube enclosed in bone. Its interior is divided into three longitudinal tubes. The middle tube contains the spiral organ (of Corti), which is lined with hair cells and is the portion of the cochlea most responsible for hearing. Sensory hair cells extend from the basilar membrane, which forms the floor of the spiral organ. Vibrations in the oval window cause fluid in the cochlea to move. Movement of the fluid causes the basilar membrane to vibrate and push hair cells into the overlying tectorial membrane, bending hair cells and initiating nerve impulses.

Balance and the Vestibular Apparatus of the Inner Ear (pp. 176–177)

- Balance is controlled by the vestibular apparatus, which consists of the semicircular canals and the vestibule. The semicircular canals monitor sudden movements of the head. The vestibule is made of two components, the saccule and the utricle, which tell the brain the position of the head with respect to gravity.

Smell and Taste (pp. 176, 178–180)

- Olfactory receptors are located in the nasal cavity. They are lined with cilia and coated with mucus. Odorous molecules dissolve in the mucus and bind to the receptors' hairs, stimulating the receptors. Information is passed to the olfactory bulbs and then to the limbic system and the cerebral cortex.
- Taste buds are responsible for our sense of taste. They are on the tongue, inside the cheeks, on the roof of the mouth, and in the throat. They sense the five primary tastes of sweet, salty, sour, bitter, and umami.

recognizing key terms

sensory receptors *p. 162*	sclera *p. 164*	cataract *p. 166*	oval window *p. 172*
stimulus *p. 162*	cornea *p. 165*	rods *p. 169*	auditory tube *p. 172*
sensory adaptation *p. 162*	choroid *p. 165*	rhodopsin *p. 169*	inner ear *p. 173*
mechanoreceptor *p. 162*	ciliary body *p. 165*	cones *p. 169*	cochlea *p. 173*
thermoreceptor *p. 163*	lens *p. 165*	outer ear *p. 172*	round window *p. 173*
photoreceptor *p. 163*	iris *p. 165*	pinna *p. 172*	basilar membrane *p. 173*
chemoreceptor *p. 163*	pupil *p. 165*	external auditory	spiral organ *p. 173*
pain receptor *p. 163*	retina *p. 165*	canal *p. 172*	hair cells *p. 173*
general senses *p. 163*	fovea *p. 165*	tympanic membrane	tectorial membrane *p. 173*
special senses *p. 163*	optic nerve *p. 165*	*p. 172*	vestibular apparatus *p. 176*
muscle spindle *p. 164*	blind spot *p. 165*	middle ear *p. 172*	semicircular canal *p. 176*
Golgi tendon organ	vitreous humor *p. 165*	malleus *p. 172*	vestibule *p. 176*
p. 164	aqueous humor *p. 165*	incus *p. 172*	olfactory receptor *p. 176*
referred pain *p. 164*	accommodation *p. 166*	stapes *p. 172*	taste buds *p. 178*

reviewing the concepts

1. Define sensory adaptation, and give an example. *p. 162*
2. What are the five classes of receptors? Which would give rise to the general senses? Which would give rise to special senses? *pp. 162–164*
3. When stimulated, what do Merkel disks tell us? *pp. 163–164*
4. What are the functions of the two distinct regions of the outer layer of the eye? *pp. 164–165*
5. How is light focused on the retina? *p. 166*
6. How is light converted to a neural message? *p. 168*
7. How are sound waves produced? How are loudness and pitch determined? *p. 171*
8. What is the function of the eardrum (tympanic membrane)? *p. 172*
9. Why is it necessary for the force of the vibrations to be amplified in the middle ear? How is amplification accomplished? *p. 172*
10. What are the effects of unequal air pressure on either side of the eardrum? How does the auditory tube help regulate air pressure? *pp. 172–173*

11. How does the basilar membrane respond to pitch? *p. 175*
12. What are the two types of hearing loss? Explain how they differ. *p. 175*
13. What are the two structures for equilibrium in the inner ear? Explain the structure of each and how it detects body position and motion. *p. 176*
14. What is believed to cause motion sickness? How can it be counteracted? *p. 176*
15. Where are the olfactory receptors located? Explain their structure as it is related to their function. *p. 176*
16. What are the structures responsible for taste? Where are they found? *pp. 178, 180*
17. What are the five primary tastes? *p. 178*
18. Describe the structure of a taste bud. *pp. 178, 180*
19. Pacinian corpuscles sense
    a. pressure.
    b. light touch.
    c. warmth.
    d. pain.
20. The spiral organ (of Corti) is important in sensing
    a. body movement.
    b. sound.
    c. light.
    d. degree of muscle contraction.
21. The greatest concentration of cones is found in the
    a. sclera.
    b. lens.
    c. ciliary body.
    d. fovea.
22. Noah is a 4-year-old boy who has a middle ear infection. The cause of the infection could be
    a. bacteria that spread to the ear from a sore throat.
    b. excessive wax buildup in the ear canal.
    c. water that was trapped in the ear after bathing.
    d. noise pollution.
23. The blind spot of the eye is
    a. located in the cornea.
    b. the region where the optic nerve leaves the eye.
    c. the region of the eye where rods outnumber cones.
    d. the region where the ciliary muscle attaches.
24. The receptors responsible for color vision are the _____.
25. The _____ of the eye changes shape to focus.
26. The snail-shaped structure concerned with hearing is the _____.
27. The semicircular canals help us_____.

applying the concepts

1. Molly needs glasses for driving but not for reading. What is the name for her visual problem? Describe the shape of the lens she needs to correct her vision.
2. Sarah has a viral infection that is causing vertigo (dizziness). In which part of the ear is the infection?
3. You are at a baseball game. After watching the ball fly into the stands for a home run, you turn to your friend sitting next to you to ask for some peanuts. What changes in your eyes for your friend's face to come into focus?

becoming information literate

1. Computer visual syndrome (CVS) is a visual problem common among people who spend long hours in front of a computer. Use at least three reliable sources (books, journals, websites) to identify the causes, symptoms, treatment, and ways to avoid CVS. Cite your sources, and explain why you chose them.
2. Imagine that you are interested in gourmet cooking. Use at least three reliable sources (books, journals, websites) to learn more about the fifth taste, umami. It is not only a taste; it also enhances the other flavors of foods. What natural sources of umami might you add to a dish to enhance its flavor? What beverages might you serve with it to create a true taste delight? Cite your sources, and explain why you chose them.

Additional questions can be found online at the Human Biology Place, www.humanbiology.com.

10

The Endocrine System

The endocrine system produces hormones, substances often described as the chemical messengers of the body. The messages they carry are varied but vital, and include effects on body height, level of alertness, energy production, and fluid balance.

Basketball was Kazuo's passion. He was only 5 feet 4 inches tall, but what he lacked in size he made up for in speed, skill, and desire. Although most of the guards he played against were 6 feet or taller, he had done well, averaging eight points and eight assists per game.

In a particularly grueling game against the Tigers, Kazuo was pitted against Conklin, a 6-foot-3-inch all-conference point guard. Kazuo had been outmatched and out-played all night, thanks to Conklin's height advantage. With the score tied and only 6 seconds left to play, Kazuo suddenly managed to reach around Conklin's back and knock the ball away. He felt a huge surge of energy as he dove for the ball, got back on his feet, and raced down the court toward his team's basket, with Conklin hot on his heels. With Conklin nearly rim high and hanging in midair above him, Kazuo drove his pivot foot into the floor, sprang to the left, switched the ball to his left hand, and deftly spun the ball off the backboard and through the hoop. The ending buzzer rang just as he hit the floor, exhausted and exhilarated at the same time.

Kazuo's late-in-the-game surge of energy came in the form of epi-nephrine, a hormone released from his adrenal glands. In this chapter, you learn about the adrenals and other endocrine glands and the hor-mones they secrete. You also learn that organs communicate with each other and with other tissues by means of hormones. These hormones initiate both long-term changes, such as Kazuo's growth and development, and short-term changes, such as Kazuo's winning surge of energy. By the end of the chapter, you will understand that proper body functioning depends on this system of internal com-munication. The endocrine system complements our body's other, more rapid system of internal communication, the nervous system (Chapters 7 and 8). Because the nervous and endocrine systems share the common function of regulating and coordinating the activities of all body systems, some consider these two systems to be one—and some call it the neuro-endocrine system.

Functions and Mechanisms of Hormones

Our bodies contain two types of glands: exocrine glands (see Chapter 4) and endocrine glands. **Endocrine glands** (Figure **10.1**) are made of secretory cells that release their products, called hor-mones. Hormones move from the cells that produced them to the fluid just outside the cells, where they diffuse directly into the bloodstream. The **endocrine system** consists of endocrine glands and of organs that contain some endocrine tissue; these organs have other functions besides hormone secretion (Figure **10.2**). The major endocrine glands are the pituitary gland, thyroid gland, parathyroid glands, adrenal glands, and pineal gland. Organs with some endocrine tissue include the hypothalamus, thymus, pan-creas, ovaries, testes, heart, and placenta. Organs of the digestive and urinary systems, such as the stomach, small intestine, and kidneys, also have endocrine tissue.

Our discussion focuses on the major endocrine glands. As we describe individual glands, keep in mind that the main function of the endocrine system—like that of the nervous system—is to regu-late and coordinate other body systems and thereby maintain home-ostasis. Recall also that whereas the nervous system is our rapid system of internal communication, the endocrine system is our more leisurely system, often coordinating and regulating longer-term processes such as growth, development, and reproduction.

We also examine three organs with endocrine tissue: hypothala-mus, thymus, and pancreas. The other organs containing endocrine tissue are discussed in the chapters that cover the organs' other func-tions. For example, the kidneys are discussed in Chapter 16 on the urinary system, and the ovaries and testes are discussed in Chap-ter 17 on the reproductive systems.

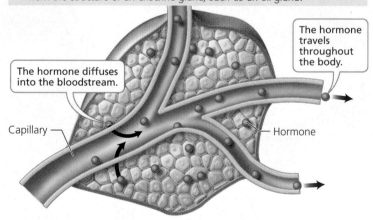

Q *Look closely at the structure of the endocrine gland. How does it differ from the structure of an exocrine gland, such as an oil gland?*

The hormone diffuses into the bloodstream.

The hormone travels throughout the body.

Capillary

Hormone

FIGURE 10.1 An endocrine gland. Endocrine glands release their products, called hormones, into the fluid just outside cells. The hormones then diffuse into the bloodstream to be transported throughout the body.

A *Endocrine glands lack ducts. Rather than secreting their products into ducts that open to a surface, endocrine glands secrete hormones to the fluid just outside their cells, and from there the hormone moves into the bloodstream.*

Hormones as Chemical Messengers

Hormones are the chemical messengers of the endocrine system. They are released in very small amounts by the cells of endocrine glands and tissues and enter the bloodstream to travel throughout

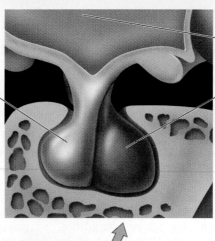

Hypothalamus

Posterior lobe of pituitary gland
Antidiuretic hormone (ADH)
• Promotes water reabsorption by the kidneys
Oxytocin (OT)
• Stimulates milk ejection from the breasts
• Stimulates uterine contractions during childbirth

Anterior lobe of pituitary gland
Growth hormone (GH)
• Stimulates growth
• Stimulates breakdown of fat
Prolactin (PRL)
• Stimulates breasts to produce milk
Thyroid-stimulating hormone (TSH)
• Stimulates synthesis and release of thyroid hormones
Adrenocorticotropic hormone (ACTH)
• Stimulates synthesis and release of hormones from adrenal glands
Follicle-stimulating hormone (FSH)
• Stimulates gamete production
• Stimulates secretion of estrogen by ovaries
Luteinizing hormone (LH)
• Causes ovulation and stimulates ovaries to secrete estrogen and progesterone
• Stimulates testes to synthesize and secrete testosterone

Pineal gland
Melatonin
• Reduces jet lag and promotes sleep

Parathyroid glands (two of four)
Parathyroid hormone (PTH)
• Increases blood levels of calcium

Thymus gland
Thymopoietin, thymosin
• Promote maturation of white blood cells

Heart

Adrenal gland (one on each kidney)
Adrenal cortex
Glucocorticoids (cortisol, corticosterone, cortisone)
• Stimulate glucose synthesis and conservation
• Inhibit the inflammatory response
Mineralocorticoids (aldosterone)
• Increase sodium reabsorption by kidneys
• Increase potassium excretion by kidneys
Gonadocorticoids (androgens, estrogens)
• Insignificant effects in adulthood, relative to secretion by gonads
Adrenal medulla
Epinephrine
• Fight-or-flight response to stress
Norepinephrine
• Fight-or-flight response to stress

Kidney

Thyroid gland
Thyroid hormone (TH)
• Regulates metabolism and heat production
• Promotes development and function of nervous, muscular, skeletal, and reproductive systems
Calcitonin (CT)
• Decreases blood levels of calcium and phosphate

Stomach

Pancreas
Glucagon
• Increases blood glucose level
Insulin
• Decreases blood glucose level

Small intestine

Testis (one of a pair)
Androgens (testosterone)
• Develop male secondary sex characteristics

Uterus (contains the placenta when pregnant)

Ovary (one of a pair)
Estrogens and progesterone
• Develop female secondary sex characteristics

FIGURE 10.2 The endocrine system. The endocrine system is made up of endocrine glands and of organs that contain some endocrine tissue. Here, the hormones and their functions are listed under the endocrine gland or organ that produces them. (Note that hormones secreted by organs for which hormone secretion is a secondary function—the heart, stomach, small intestine, kidneys, testes, ovaries, and uterus with placenta—are discussed in chapters that cover the organs' other functions.)

the body. Although hormones come into contact with virtually all cells, most affect only a particular type of cell, called a **target cell.** Target cells have *receptors*, protein molecules that recognize and bind to specific hormones. Once a hormone binds to its specific receptor, this hormone–receptor complex begins to exert its effects on the cell. Because cells other than target cells lack the correct receptors, they are unaffected by the hormone.

The mechanisms by which hormones influence target cells depend on the chemical makeup of the hormone. Hormones are classified as being either lipid soluble or water soluble. **Lipid-soluble hormones** include **steroid hormones,** a group of closely related hormones derived from cholesterol. The ovaries, testes, and adrenal glands are the main organs that secrete steroid hormones. Lipid-soluble hormones move easily through any cell's plasma membrane because it is a lipid bilayer (see Figure **10.3**). Once inside a target cell, a steroid hormone combines with receptor molecules in the cytoplasm (only target cells have the proper receptors for a given hormone). This hormone–receptor complex then moves into the nucleus of the cell, where it attaches to DNA and activates certain genes. Ultimately, such activation leads the target cell to synthesize specific proteins. (The precise steps involved in protein synthesis are described in Chapter 21.) These proteins may include enzymes that stimulate or inhibit particular metabolic pathways.

Water-soluble hormones, such as protein or peptide hormones, cannot pass through the lipid bilayer of the plasma membrane and therefore cannot enter target cells themselves. Instead, the hormone—which in this situation is called the **first messenger**—binds to a receptor on the plasma membrane of the target cell. This binding activates a molecule—called the second messenger—in the cytoplasm. **Second messengers** are molecules within the cell that influence the activity of enzymes, and ultimately the activity of the cell, to produce the effect of the hormone. Cyclic adenosine monophosphate (cAMP) is a common second messenger (illustrated in Figure **10.4**). As an example of how cAMP functions in its role as a second messenger, we consider the effects of the water-soluble hormone epinephrine on a liver cell. Binding of epinephrine to a receptor on the plasma membrane of a liver cell (the target cell) prompts the conversion of ATP to cAMP within the cell. Cyclic adenosine monophosphate then activates an enzyme within the cell (a protein kinase), which in turn activates another enzyme, and so on. The end result of this enzyme cascade is the activation of an enzyme that catalyzes the breakdown of glycogen to glucose within the liver cell. Thus, whereas lipid-soluble hormones stimulate the synthesis of proteins by a cell, water-soluble hormones like epinephrine activate proteins that are already present in the cell.

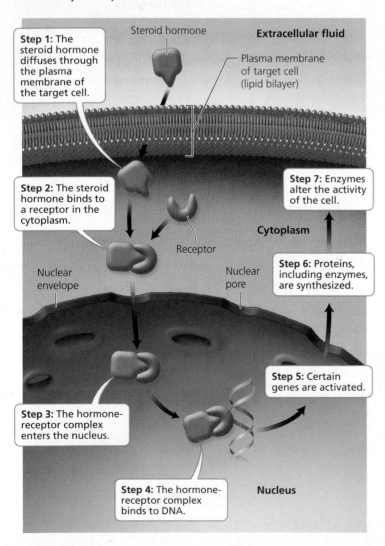

FIGURE 10.3 Mode of action of lipid-soluble (steroid) hormones

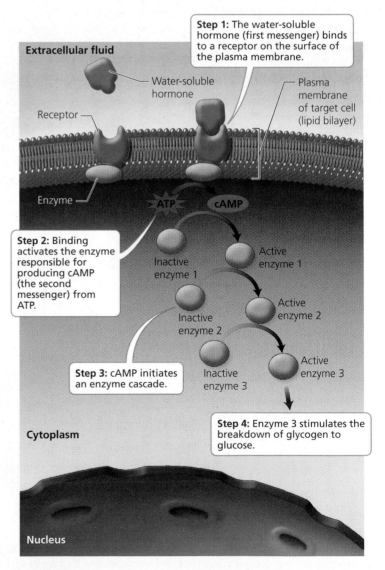

FIGURE 10.4 Mode of action of some water-soluble hormones: the second messenger system of cAMP

Feedback Mechanisms and Secretion of Hormones

Now that we have seen how hormones work at the cellular level, let's turn our attention to the factors that stimulate and regulate the release of hormones from endocrine glands. Stimuli that cause endocrine glands to manufacture and release hormones include other hormones, signals from the nervous system, and changes in the levels of certain ions (such as calcium, Ca^{2+}) or nutrients (such as glucose) in the blood.

Recall from Chapter 4 that homeostasis keeps the body's internal environment relatively constant. Such constancy most often is achieved through **negative feedback mechanisms**, which, as we also saw in Chapter 4, are homeostatic mechanisms in which the outcome of a process feeds back to the system, shutting the process down. Negative feedback mechanisms regulate the secretion of some hormones. Typically, a gland releases a hormone, and then rising blood levels of that hormone inhibit its further release. In an alternative form of negative feedback, some endocrine glands are sensitive to the particular condition they regulate rather than to the level of the hormone they produce. For example, the pancreas secretes the hormone insulin in response to high levels of glucose in the blood. Insulin prompts the liver to store glucose, which in turn causes the blood level of glucose to decline. The pancreas senses the low glucose in the blood and stops secreting insulin.

Secretion of hormones is sometimes regulated by **positive feedback mechanisms**, in which the outcome of a process feeds back to the system and stimulates the process to continue. For example, during childbirth, the pituitary gland releases the hormone oxytocin (OT), which stimulates the uterus to contract. Uterine contractions then stimulate release of more oxytocin, which stimulates even more contractions (Figure **10.5**). The feedback is described as positive because it acts to stimulate, rather than to inhibit, the release of oxytocin. Eventually, some change breaks the positive feedback cycle. In the case of childbirth, expulsion of the baby and placenta terminates the feedback cycle. When we discuss the various glands and their hormones in the sections that follow, we also describe the feedback mechanisms by which they are regulated.

Sometimes the nervous system overrides the controls of the endocrine system. During times of severe stress, for example, the nervous system overrides the mechanism controlling the release of the hormone insulin. Recall that the level of insulin in the blood is controlled by a negative feedback system. Because of this negative feedback system, levels of glucose in the blood are normally maintained within a relatively narrow range. However, under conditions of severe stress, such as those associated with strong emotional reactions, heavy bleeding, or starvation, the nervous system permits levels of blood glucose to rise much higher than normal. This response gives cells access to the large amounts of energy they need for coping with the stressful situation.

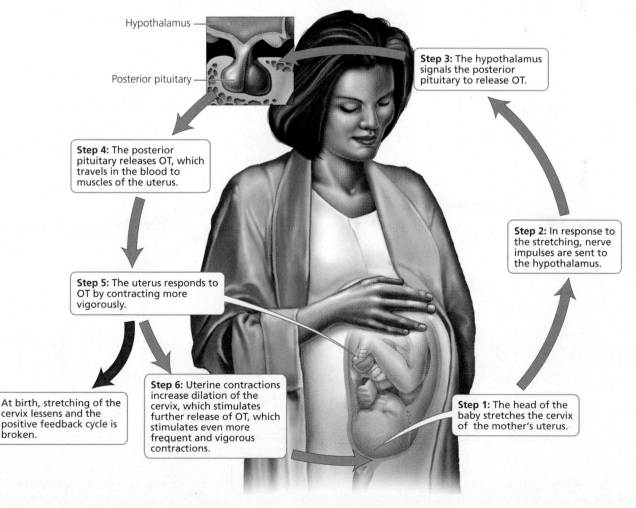

Hypothalamus

Posterior pituitary

Step 3: The hypothalamus signals the posterior pituitary to release OT.

Step 4: The posterior pituitary releases OT, which travels in the blood to muscles of the uterus.

Step 2: In response to the stretching, nerve impulses are sent to the hypothalamus.

Step 5: The uterus responds to OT by contracting more vigorously.

At birth, stretching of the cervix lessens and the positive feedback cycle is broken.

Step 6: Uterine contractions increase dilation of the cervix, which stimulates further release of OT, which stimulates even more frequent and vigorous contractions.

Step 1: The head of the baby stretches the cervix of the mother's uterus.

FIGURE 10.5 The positive feedback cycle by which OT stimulates uterine contractions during childbirth

Interactions between Hormones

Interactions between hormones may be antagonistic, synergistic, or permissive. When the effect of one hormone opposes that of another hormone, the interaction is described as *antagonistic*. For an example of an antagonistic interaction, consider glucagon and insulin, two hormones secreted by the pancreas. Whereas glucagon increases the level of glucose in the blood, insulin decreases the level of glucose in the blood. During *synergistic* interactions, the response of a tissue to a combination of two hormones is much greater than its response to either individual hormone. For example, epinephrine (from the adrenal glands) and glucagon both prompt the liver to release glucose to the blood. When the two hormones act together, the amount of glucose released by the liver is greater than the combined amount released by each hormone acting alone. During *permissive* interactions, one hormone must be present for another hormone to exert its effects. For example, thyroid hormone must be present for the hormone aldosterone to stimulate reabsorption of sodium within the tubules of the kidneys.

Next we look at the individual endocrine glands, describing the location and general structure, hormones, and hormonal effects of each. We also consider disorders associated with each gland and its hormones.

Pituitary Gland

The **pituitary gland** is the size of a pea and is suspended from the base of the brain by a short stalk (see Figure 10.2). The stalk connects the pituitary gland to the **hypothalamus**, the area of the brain that regulates physiological responses like body temperature, sleeping, and water balance. The pituitary gland consists of two lobes, the anterior lobe and the posterior lobe. These lobes differ in size and in their relationship with the hypothalamus; the two lobes release different hormones.

The anterior lobe is the larger one. A network of capillaries runs from the base of the hypothalamus through the stalk of the pituitary. The capillaries connect to veins that lead into more capillaries in the anterior lobe of the pituitary gland (Figure **10.6**). This circulatory connection allows hormones of the hypothalamus to control the secretion of hormones from the anterior lobe of the pituitary. Nerve cells in the hypothalamus synthesize and secrete hormones that travel by way of the bloodstream to the anterior lobe, where they stimulate or inhibit hormone secretion. Substances produced by the hypothalamus that stimulate hormone secretion by the anterior pituitary are called **releasing hormones**. Those that inhibit hormone secretion by the anterior pituitary are called **inhibiting hormones**.

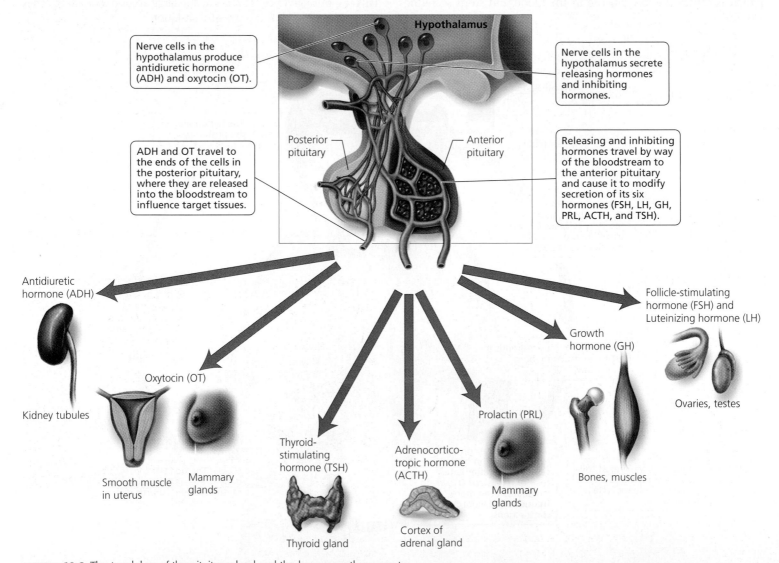

FIGURE 10.6 The two lobes of the pituitary gland and the hormones they secrete

The anterior pituitary responds to releasing and inhibiting hormones from the hypothalamus by modifying its own synthesis and secretion of six hormones. These hormones are growth hormone (GH), prolactin (PRL), thyroid-stimulating hormone (TSH), adrenocorticotropic hormone (ACTH), follicle-stimulating hormone (FSH), and luteinizing hormone (LH).

The posterior lobe of the pituitary is very small, just larger than the head of a pin. It consists of neural tissue that releases hormones. In contrast to the *circulatory* connection between the hypothalamus and the anterior lobe, the connection between the hypothalamus and the posterior lobe is a *neural* one. As shown in Figure 10.6, nerve cells from the hypothalamus project directly into the posterior lobe. Oxytocin (OT) and antidiuretic hormone (ADH) are produced by the hypothalamus and move along the axons of nerve cells to the posterior pituitary, where they are stored and released.

Anterior Lobe

As noted, the anterior lobe of the pituitary produces and secretes six major hormones. We begin with **growth hormone (GH)**, the primary function of which is to stimulate growth through increases in cell size and rates of cell division. The target cells of GH are quite diverse. Cells of bone, muscle, and cartilage are most susceptible to GH, but cells of other tissues are affected as well. Growth hormone also plays a role in glucose conservation by making fats more available as a source of fuel.

Two hormones of the hypothalamus regulate the synthesis and release of GH. Growth hormone-releasing hormone (GHRH) stimulates the release of GH. Growth hormone-inhibiting hormone (GHIH) inhibits the release of GH. Through the actions of these two hormones, levels of GH in the body are normally maintained within an appropriate range. However, excesses or deficiencies of the hormone can dramatically affect growth. For example, abnormally high production of GH in childhood, when the bones are still capable of growing in length, results in *gigantism,* a condition characterized by rapid growth and eventual attainment of heights up to 8 or 9 feet (Figure **10.7**). Increased production of GH in adulthood, when the bones can thicken but not lengthen, causes acromegaly (literally, "enlarged extremities"). *Acromegaly* is characterized by enlargement of the tongue and a gradual thickening of the bones of the hands, feet, and face (Figure **10.8**). Both conditions are associated with

decreased life expectancy. The excesses of GH that cause such conditions as gigantism and acromegaly may be caused by a tumor of the anterior pituitary. Tumors can be treated with surgery, radiation, or drugs that reduce GH secretion and tumor size. Insufficient production of GH in childhood results in *pituitary dwarfism.* Typically, pituitary dwarfs are sterile and attain a maximum height of

FIGURE 10.7 Robert Wadlow, a pituitary giant, was born in 1918 at a normal size but developed a pituitary tumor as a young child. The tumor caused increased production of GH. Robert never stopped growing until his death at 22 years of age, by which time he had reached a height of 8 feet 11 inches.

(a) Age 9   **(b)** Age 16   **(c)** Age 33   **(d)** Age 52

FIGURE 10.8 Acromegaly. Excess secretion of GH in adulthood, when the bones can thicken but not lengthen, causes acromegaly, a gradual thickening of the bones of the hands, feet, and face. The disorder was not apparent in this female at ages 9 or 16, but it became apparent by age 33. The symptoms were even more obvious at age 52.

about 4 feet (Figure **10.9**). Administering GH in childhood can treat pituitary dwarfism but not other forms of dwarfism.

In the past, the use of GH for the treatment of medical conditions (such as pituitary dwarfism) was extremely limited because GH was scarce, given that the hormone had to be extracted from the pituitary glands of cadavers. Beginning in the late 1970s, however, GH could be made in the laboratory. With this greater availability came research on its potential uses in the treatment of aging in adults and below-average height in children. Many aspects of normal aging, such as thinning of the skin, decreased muscle mass, and increased body fat, appear to be reversed by the administration of GH. For children who are of below-average height, administration of GH appears to add a few inches of adult height. Negative side effects of taking GH include fluid accumulation and increased blood pressure.

what would you do?

A recent review of studies in which children of below-average height were administered GH concluded that such therapy could yield an additional 2 inches of adult height. Opponents of this use of GH believe it is wrong to give a powerful and potentially harmful hormone to children who are basically healthy. Rather than administering GH to such children, opponents suggest working to increase societal acceptance of persons who are short. Opponents also point out that GH therapy has negative side effects and is expensive (the average yearly cost of GH therapy is $20,000, and some children remain on therapy for 10 or more years). Do you think that GH should be used to "treat" below-average height in children? What would you do if you were the parent of a healthy child who was destined to be very short? What if your child were a pituitary dwarf; would you approve the use of GH then?

FIGURE 10.9 Pituitary dwarfism is caused by insufficient GH in childhood.

Prolactin (PRL), another hormone secreted by the anterior lobe of the pituitary gland, stimulates the mammary glands to produce milk. (Oxytocin, a hormone secreted from the posterior pituitary, causes the ducts of the mammary glands to eject milk, as discussed later in the chapter.) PRL interferes with female sex hormones, which explains why most mothers fail to have regular menstrual cycles while nursing their newborn. (Lactation should not, however, be relied upon as a method for birth control, because the suppression of female hormones and ovulation lessens as mothers breast-feed their growing infants less frequently.)

Growth of a pituitary tumor may cause excess secretion of PRL, which may cause infertility in females, along with production of milk when birth has not occurred. In males, PRL appears to be involved in the production of mature sperm in the testes, but its precise role is not yet clear. Nevertheless, production of too much PRL, as might occur with a pituitary tumor, can cause sterility and impotence in men. Some hormones from the hypothalamus stimulate and others inhibit production and secretion of PRL.

The remaining hormones produced by the anterior lobe of the pituitary gland influence other endocrine glands. A hormone produced by one endocrine gland or organ that influences another endocrine gland is called a **tropic hormone.** Two such hormones secreted by the anterior lobe of the pituitary are thyroid-stimulating hormone and adrenocorticotropic hormone. **Thyroid-stimulating hormone (TSH)** acts on the thyroid gland in the neck to stimulate synthesis and release of thyroid hormones. **Adrenocorticotropic hormone (ACTH)**, also called corticotropin, controls the synthesis and secretion of glucocorticoid hormones from the outer portion (cortex) of the adrenal glands (see Figure 10.2).

Two other tropic hormones secreted by the anterior lobe of the pituitary gland influence the gonads (ovaries in the female and testes in the male). **Follicle-stimulating hormone (FSH)** promotes development of egg cells and secretion of the hormone estrogen from the ovaries in females. **Luteinizing hormone (LH)** causes ovulation, the release of a future egg cell by the ovary in females. LH also stimulates the ovaries to secrete estrogen and progesterone. These two hormones prepare the uterus for implantation of a fertilized ovum and the breasts for production of milk. In males, FSH promotes maturation of sperm, while LH stimulates cells within the testes to produce and secrete the hormone testosterone.

Posterior Lobe

The posterior pituitary does not produce any hormones of its own. However, neurons of the hypothalamus manufacture antidiuretic hormone and oxytocin. These hormones travel down the nerve cells into the posterior pituitary, where they are stored and released.

The main function of **antidiuretic hormone (ADH)** is to conserve body water by decreasing urine output. ADH accomplishes this task by prompting the kidneys to remove water from the fluid destined to become urine. The water is then returned to the blood. Alcohol temporarily inhibits secretion of ADH, causing increased urination following alcohol consumption. The increased output of urine causes dehydration and the resultant headache and dry mouth typical of many hangovers. ADH is also called vasopressin. This name comes from its role in constricting blood vessels and raising blood pressure, particularly during times of severe blood loss.

A deficiency of ADH may result from damage to either the posterior pituitary or the area of the hypothalamus responsible for the hormone's manufacture. Such a deficiency results in *diabetes insipidus,* a condition characterized by excessive urine production and resultant dehydration. Mild cases may not require treatment. Severe cases may cause extreme fluid loss, and death through dehydration can result. Treatment usually includes administration of synthetic ADH in a nasal spray. Diabetes insipidus (*diabetes,* overflow; *insipidus,* tasteless) should not be confused with *diabetes mellitus* (*mel,* honey). The latter is a condition in which large amounts of glucose are lost in the urine as a result of an insulin deficiency. Both conditions, however, are characterized by increased production of urine. (We discuss diabetes mellitus later, when we discuss the hormones of the pancreas.)

Oxytocin (OT) is the second hormone produced in the hypothalamus and released by the posterior pituitary. The name *oxytocin* (*oxy,* quick; *tokos,* childbirth) reveals one of its two main functions, stimulating the uterine contractions of childbirth. As described earlier, the control of OT during labor is an example of a positive feedback mechanism (see Figure 10.5). Pitocin is a synthetic form of OT sometimes administered to induce and speed labor.

The second major function of oxytocin is to stimulate milk ejection from the mammary glands. Milk ejection occurs in response to the sucking stimulus of an infant (Figure **10.10**). Recall that prolactin secreted by the anterior pituitary stimulates the mammary glands to produce, but not to eject, milk. Men also secrete OT, and there is some evidence that this hormone facilitates the transport of sperm in the male reproductive tract.

Thyroid Gland

The **thyroid gland** is a shield-shaped, deep red structure in the front of the neck, as shown in Figure 10.11a. (The color stems from its prodigious blood supply.) Within the thyroid are small, spherical chambers called follicles (Figure 10.11b). Cells line the walls of the follicles and produce thyroglobulin, the substance from which thyroxine (T_4) and triiodothyronine (T_3) are made. These two very similar hormones have different numbers of iodine molecules; as indicated by their abbreviations, thyroxine has four iodine molecules and triiodothyronine has three. Thyroxine is usually produced in greater quantity than triiodothyronine, and most thyroxine is eventually converted to triiodothyronine. Because these two hormones are so similar, we will simply refer to

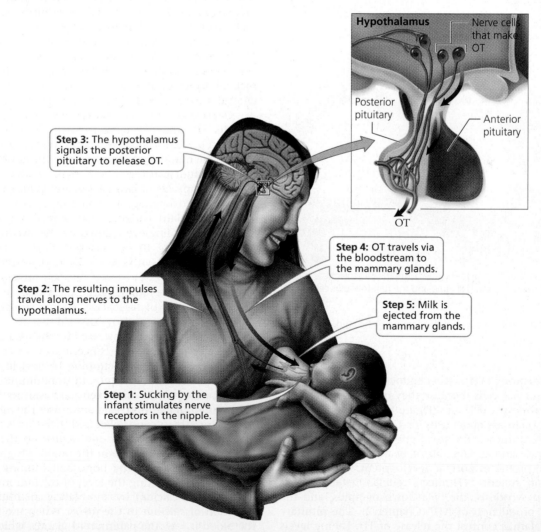

FIGURE 10.10 The steps by which OT stimulates milk ejection from the mammary glands

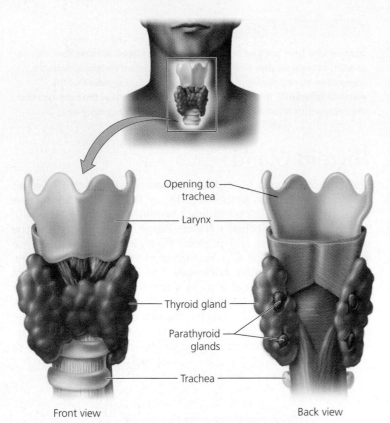

Opening to trachea

Larynx

Thyroid gland

Parathyroid glands

Trachea

Front view

Back view

(a) The thyroid gland lies over the trachea, just below the larynx.

Follicular cells

Follicle

Parafollicular cell

Capillary

(b) Diagram showing structure of thyroid tissue. Note the follicular cells that produce the precursor to thyroid hormone and the parafollicular cells that produce calcitonin.

FIGURE 10.11 Location and structure of the thyroid gland and parathyroid glands

them as **thyroid hormone (TH).** Other endocrine cells in the thyroid, called parafollicular cells (because they occur near the follicles), secrete the hormone calcitonin (Figure 10.11b).

Nearly all body cells are target cells for TH. Therefore, it is not surprising that the hormone has broad effects. TH regulates the body's metabolic rate and production of heat. It also maintains blood pressure and promotes normal development and functioning of several organ systems. TH affects cellular metabolism by stimulating protein synthesis, the breakdown of lipids, and the use of glucose for production of ATP (Chapter 2). The pituitary gland and hypothalamus control the release of TH. Falling levels of TH in the blood prompt the hypothalamus to secrete a releasing

hormone. The releasing hormone stimulates the anterior pituitary to secrete TSH, which, in turn, causes the thyroid to release more TH.

Iodine is needed for production of TH. A diet deficient in iodine can produce a *simple goiter,* that is, an enlarged thyroid gland (Figure **10.12a**). When intake of iodine is inadequate, the level of TH is low, and the low level of TH in turn triggers secretion of TSH. TSH stimulates the thyroid gland to increase production of thyroglobulin. The lack of iodine prevents formation of TH from the accumulating thyroglobulin. In response to continued low levels of TH, the pituitary continues to release increasing amounts of TSH, which cause the thyroid to enlarge in a futile effort to filter more iodine from the blood. In the past, goiters were quite common, especially in parts of the Midwestern United States (dubbed the Goiter Belt), where iodine-poor soil and little access to iodine-rich shellfish led to diets deficient in iodine. The incidence of goiter in the United States dramatically decreased once iodine was added to most table salt beginning in the 1920s. Simple goiter can be treated by iodine supplements or administration of TH.

Undersecretion of TH during fetal development or infancy causes *cretinism,* a condition characterized by dwarfism and delayed mental and sexual development (Figure 10.12b). If a pregnant woman produces sufficient TH, many of the symptoms of cretinism do not appear until after birth, when the deficient infant begins to rely solely on its own malfunctioning thyroid gland to supply the needed hormones. Oral doses of TH can prevent cretinism, so most infants in industrialized nations are now tested for proper thyroid function shortly after birth. In the United States, such testing reveals that incomplete development of the thyroid gland occurs in about 1 in every 3,000 births. Undersecretion of TH in adulthood causes *myxedema,* a condition in which fluid accumulates in facial tissues. Other symptoms of TH undersecretion include decreases in alertness, body temperature, and heart rate. Oral administration of TH can prevent and treat these symptoms.

Oversecretion of TH causes *Graves' disease,* an autoimmune disorder in which a person's own immune system produces Y-shaped proteins called antibodies (discussed in Chapter 13) that in this case mimic the action of TSH. The antibodies stimulate the thyroid gland, causing it to enlarge and overproduce its hormones. Symptoms of Graves' disease include increased metabolic rate and heart rate, accompanied by sweating, nervousness, and weight loss. Many patients with Graves' disease also have *exophthalmos,* protruding eyes caused by the swelling of tissues in the eye orbits (Figure 10.12c). Graves' disease may be treated with drugs that block synthesis of thyroid hormones. Alternatively, thyroid tissue may be reduced through surgery or the administration of radioactive iodine. Because the thyroid gland accumulates iodine, ingestion of radioactive iodine (usually administered in capsules) selectively destroys thyroid tissue.

The **calcitonin (CT)** secreted by the parafollicular cells of the thyroid helps regulate the concentration of calcium in the blood to ensure the proper functioning of muscle cells and neurons. Calcium ions bind to the protein troponin, leading to changes in other muscle proteins and eventually causing muscle contraction (Chapter 6). In addition, calcium causes the release of neurotransmitters into the synaptic cleft and therefore is critical in the transmission of messages from one neuron to the next (Chapter 7). When the level of calcium in the blood is high, CT stimulates the absorption of calcium by bone and inhibits the breakdown of bone, thereby lowering the level of calcium in the blood. CT also lowers blood calcium by stimulating an initial increase in the excretion of calcium in the urine. When the level of calcium in the blood is low, the parathyroid glands, which we discuss next, are prompted to release their hormone.

(a) Simple goiter   **(b)** Cretinism

(c) Exophthalmos

FIGURE 10.12 Disorders of the thyroid gland

Parathyroid Glands

The **parathyroid glands** are four small, round masses at the back of the thyroid gland (Figure 10.11a, back view). These glands secrete **parathyroid hormone (PTH)**, also called *parathormone*. As mentioned earlier, CT from the thyroid gland lowers the level of calcium in the blood. In contrast, PTH increases levels of calcium in the blood (see Chapter 5). Low levels of calcium in the blood stimulate the parathyroid glands to secrete PTH, which causes calcium to move from bone and urine into the blood. PTH exerts its effects by stimulating (1) bone-destroying cells called osteoclasts that release calcium from bone into the blood, (2) the removal of calcium from the urine and its return to the blood, and (3) the rate at which calcium is absorbed into the blood from the gastrointestinal tract. PTH also inhibits bone-forming cells called osteoblasts and thereby reduces the rate at which calcium is deposited in bone. The feedback system by which CT and PTH together regulate levels of calcium in the blood is summarized in Figure **10.13**.

Surgery on the neck or thyroid gland may damage the parathyroid glands. The resultant decrease in PTH causes decreased blood calcium that in turn produces nervousness and irritability (low calcium is associated with hyperexcitability of the membranes of neurons) and muscle spasms (recall that calcium is also important in muscle contraction). In severe cases, death may result from spasms of the larynx and paralysis of the respiratory system. PTH is difficult to purify, so deficiencies are not usually treated by

When levels of calcium are high, the thyroid gland releases CT, and calcium is taken up by the bones.

CT

Thyroid gland secretes CT

Bones take up calcium

High blood calcium

Blood calcium decreases

Homeostasis
Normal blood calcium

Blood calcium increases

Low blood calcium

Parathyroid glands release PTH

PTH

Intestines absorb calcium

Kidneys reabsorb calcium

Bones release calcium

When levels of calcium are low, the parathyroid glands release PTH. In response, calcium is released by bones, reabsorbed by kidneys, and absorbed by the intestines.

FIGURE 10.13 Regulation of calcium levels in the blood by CT from the thyroid gland (top) and by PTH from the parathyroid glands (bottom)

administering the hormone. Instead, calcium is given either in tablet form or through increased dietary intake.

A tumor of the parathyroid gland can cause excess secretion of PTH. Oversecretion of PTH pulls calcium from bone tissue, causing increased blood calcium and weakened bones. High levels of calcium in the blood may lead to kidney stones, calcium deposits in other soft tissue, and decreased activity of the nervous system.

Adrenal Glands

The body's two **adrenal glands** (*ad*, upon; *renal*, kidney), each about the size of an almond, are located at the tops of the kidneys. Each adrenal gland has an outer and an inner region. The outer region of the gland, the **adrenal cortex**, secretes more than 20 different lipid-soluble (steroid) hormones, generally divided into three groups: the gonadocorticoids, mineralocorticoids, and glucocorticoids (Figure **10.14**). The inner region, called the **adrenal medulla**, secretes two water-soluble hormones, epinephrine (also known as adrenaline) and norepinephrine (also known as noradrenaline).

Adrenal Cortex

The **gonadocorticoids** are male and female sex hormones known as **androgens** and **estrogens.** In both males and females, the adrenal cortex secretes both androgens and estrogens. However, in normal adult males, androgen secretion by the testes far surpasses that by the adrenal cortex. Thus, the effects of adrenal androgens in adult males are probably insignificant. In females, the ovaries and placenta also produce estrogen, although during menopause, the ovaries decrease secretion of estrogen and eventually stop secreting it. The gonadocorticoids from the adrenal cortex may somewhat alleviate the effects of decreased ovarian estrogen in menopausal women. One option for menopausal women suffering from estrogen deficiency is hormone therapy. The advantages and disadvantages of this therapy are considered in the Health Issue essay, *Is It Hot in Here, or Is It Me? Hormone Therapy and Menopause.*

The **mineralocorticoids** secreted by the adrenal cortex affect mineral homeostasis and water balance. The primary mineralocorticoid is **aldosterone,** a hormone that acts on cells of the kidneys to increase reabsorption of sodium ions (Na^+) into the blood. This reabsorption prevents depletion of Na^+ and increases water retention. Aldosterone also acts on kidney cells to promote the excretion of potassium ions (K^+) in urine. *Addison's disease* is a disorder caused by the undersecretion of aldosterone and the glucocorticoid cortisol (see the following discussion). This disease appears to be an autoimmune disorder in which the body's own immune system perceives cells of the adrenal cortex as foreign and destroys them. The resulting deficiency of adrenal hormones causes weight loss, fatigue, electrolyte imbalance, poor appetite, and poor resistance to stress. A peculiar bronzing of the skin also is associated with Addison's disease (Figure **10.15**). Recall that the pituitary gland secretes ACTH, which stimulates the cortex of the adrenal glands to secrete its hormones. Thus, Addison's disease can also be caused by inadequate secretion of ACTH by the pituitary. Regardless of its cause, Addison's disease can be treated with hormone tablets.

stop and think

High blood pressure can signal abnormal aldosterone secretion. Would high blood pressure be associated with the undersecretion or oversecretion of aldosterone?

The **glucocorticoids** are hormones secreted by the adrenal cortex that affect glucose levels. Glucocorticoids act on the liver to promote the conversion of fat and protein to intermediate substances that are ultimately converted into glucose. The glucocorticoids also act on adipose tissue to prompt the breakdown of fats to

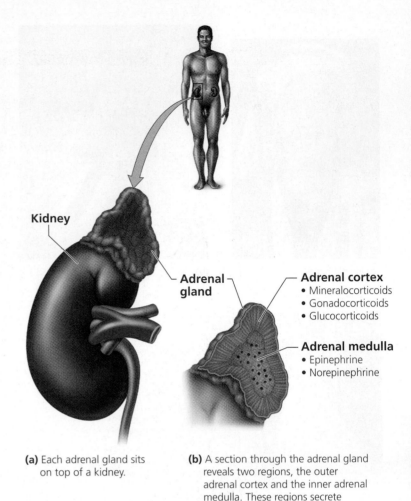

Kidney

Adrenal gland

Adrenal cortex
• Mineralocorticoids
• Gonadocorticoids
• Glucocorticoids

Adrenal medulla
• Epinephrine
• Norepinephrine

(a) Each adrenal gland sits on top of a kidney.

(b) A section through the adrenal gland reveals two regions, the outer adrenal cortex and the inner adrenal medulla. These regions secrete different hormones.

FIGURE 10.14 Location and structure of an adrenal gland

FIGURE 10.15 John F. Kennedy suffered from Addison's disease, which is caused by undersecretion of cortisone and aldosterone from the adrenal cortex. JFK's complexion showed the peculiar bronzing of the skin characteristic of Addison's disease.

Is It Hot in Here, or Is It Me? Hormone Therapy and Menopause

Many endocrine disorders are characterized by little or no secretion of certain hormones. Cretinism, for example, is caused by the undersecretion of thyroid hormone during fetal development or infancy. In other cases, hormone secretion declines as part of the normal aging process. Estrogen, a hormone produced primarily by the ovaries, is secreted in decreasing amounts beginning when women are about age 30. This decrease eventually leads into menopause, the termination of ovulation and menstruation. Menopause usually occurs when women are between 45 and 55 years of age. Undersecretion of hormones, whether caused by malfunctioning glands or normal aging, often is treated with hormone replacement therapy (HRT). In HRT, the deficient hormone is replaced using injections, pills, patches, or creams. Today, HRT is commonly called hormone therapy.

Hormone therapy has had many successes, but it is not without controversy, particularly when it is used to treat normal declines in hormone levels. As mentioned, levels of ovarian hormones decline as women age; menopause is the ultimate result. Some women face a host of uncomfortable symptoms in conjunction with the eventual end of ovulation and menstruation. Such symptoms include hot flashes, night sweats, vaginal dryness, stress incontinence (involuntary loss of small amounts of urine when laughing, coughing, or sneezing), heightened mood swings, and memory loss. Symptoms may last only a few months or a few years. Declining estrogen levels also have been linked to increased risk of osteoporosis (increased bone loss leading to increased risk of fracture; see Chapter 5). For many years doctors administered ovarian hormones to millions of women at or past menopause to treat these effects. For women who naturally entered menopause, doctors prescribed estrogen and progestin (a form of progesterone). This combination was used because of the increased risk of uterine cancer associated with using estrogen alone. For women who entered menopause because their uterus had been surgically removed (this surgical procedure is known as a hysterectomy), doctors prescribed estrogen alone.

In recent years, there has been a significant research effort to evaluate the benefits and risks of hormone therapy for the treatment of menopause. Both estrogen therapy and the combination estrogen and progestin therapy have some benefits; they relieve hot flashes and night sweats, and slow the loss of bone. Hormone therapy involving estrogen plus progestin also seems to reduce the risk of colorectal cancer. There are also risks associated with these therapies. Both therapies are associated with increased risk of blood clots and stroke. Therapy involving estrogen plus progestin is also associated with increased risk of heart attack and breast cancer.

In view of the risks of hormone therapies, many physicians are now urging women to consider other ways available to stave off osteoporosis. These physicians urge women to avoid smoking, to eat a diet rich in calcium and vitamin D, and to exercise regularly. Nonhormonal drugs may be better and safer for preventing bone fractures. Some alternative practitioners advise getting estrogen from dietary sources such as yams and soybeans. These foods are certainly weaker sources than prescription estrogen and may reduce the risks.

---

fatty acids that are released into the bloodstream, where they are available for use by the body's cells. Glucocorticoids further conserve glucose by inhibiting its uptake by muscle and fat tissue.

Glucocorticoids also inhibit the inflammatory response; such inhibition can be beneficial when the body is faced with the swelling and intense irritation associated with skin rashes such as that caused by poison ivy. One way glucocorticoids inhibit inflammation is by slowing the movement of white blood cells to the site of injury. Another way is by reducing the likelihood that other cells will release chemicals that promote inflammation. Unfortunately, these activities of glucocorticoids inhibit wound healing. Steroid creams containing synthetic glucocorticoids are therefore intended to be applied only to the surface of the skin and to be used for superficial rashes only. These creams should not be applied to open wounds. Some examples of glucocorticoids are cortisol, corticosterone, and cortisone.

Cushing's syndrome results from prolonged exposure to high levels of the glucocorticoid cortisol. Body fat is redistributed, and fluid accumulates in the face (Figure **10.16**). Additional symptoms include fatigue, high blood pressure, and elevated glucose levels.

(a) Patient diagnosed with Cushing's syndrome

(b) Same patient after treatment

FIGURE 10.16 Cushing's syndrome. Prolonged exposure to cortisol causes fluid to accumulate in the face. Most often, Cushing's syndrome is caused by the administration of cortisol for allergies or inflammation.

A tumor on either the adrenal cortex or the anterior pituitary may cause the oversecretion of cortisol that leads to Cushing's syndrome. (Recall that the anterior pituitary secretes ACTH, which stimulates the release of hormones from the adrenal cortex.) Tumors are treated with radiation, drugs, or surgery. Cushing's syndrome also may result from glucocorticoid hormone treatment for asthma, lupus, or rheumatoid arthritis. Treatment in medically induced cases of Cushing's syndrome typically entails a gradual reduction of the glucocorticoid dose, ideally to the lowest level necessary to control the existing disorder without prompting adverse affects.

Adrenal Medulla

As introduced earlier, the adrenal medulla produces **epinephrine** and **norepinephrine**. These hormones are critical in the **fight-or-flight response**, the reaction by the body's sympathetic nervous system to emergencies (Chapter 8). Imagine that you are walking home alone late at night and a stranger suddenly steps toward you from the bushes. Impulses received by your hypothalamus are sent by neurons to your adrenal medulla. These impulses cause cells in your adrenal medulla to increase output of epinephrine and norepinephrine. In response to these hormones, your heart rate, respiratory rate, and blood glucose levels rise. Blood vessels associated with the digestive tract constrict because digestion is not of prime importance during times of extreme stress. Vessels associated with skeletal and cardiac muscles dilate, allowing more

blood, glucose, and oxygen to reach them. These substances also reach your brain in greater amounts, leading to the increased mental alertness needed for fleeing or fighting.

In contrast to the near instantaneous response of the sympathetic nervous system to a perceived threat, the hormonal response takes about 30 seconds to mount. This is because epinephrine and norepinephrine must be released by the adrenal medulla, travel in the bloodstream to all cells, bind to receptors on their target cells, and initiate changes in those cells. Even after the danger has passed, we feel the changes brought on by these hormones for a few additional minutes. Epinephrine and norepinephrine thus augment and prolong the response of the sympathetic nervous system to stress. The more leisurely onset and conclusion of the effects of epinephrine and norepinephrine highlight the differences between neural and hormonal systems of internal communication. We explore further how our bodies react to stress in the Health Issue essay, *Hormones and Our Response to Stress*.

Pancreas

The **pancreas** is located in the abdomen just behind the stomach (Figure **10.17**); it contains both endocrine and exocrine cells; the role of the exocrine cells of the pancreas in digestion will be discussed in Chapter 15. The endocrine cells occur in small clusters called **pancreatic islets** (or islets of Langerhans). These clusters contain three types of hormone-producing cells. One type produces

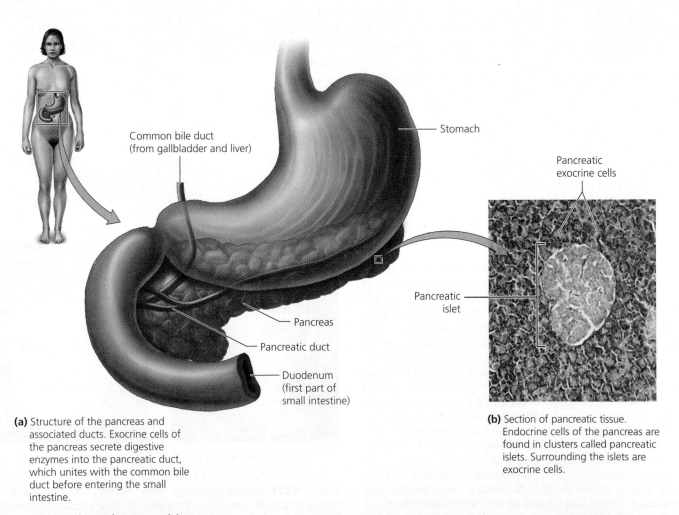

Common bile duct
(from gallbladder and liver)

Stomach

Pancreatic
exocrine cells

Pancreatic
islet

Pancreas

Pancreatic duct

Duodenum
(first part of
small intestine)

(a) Structure of the pancreas and associated ducts. Exocrine cells of the pancreas secrete digestive enzymes into the pancreatic duct, which unites with the common bile duct before entering the small intestine.

(b) Section of pancreatic tissue. Endocrine cells of the pancreas are found in clusters called pancreatic islets. Surrounding the islets are exocrine cells.

FIGURE 10.17 Location and structure of the pancreas

the hormone glucagon; a second produces the hormone insulin; and a third produces the hormone somatostatin. Somatostatin is also secreted by the digestive tract, where it inhibits secretions of the stomach and small intestine, and by the hypothalamus, where it inhibits secretion of growth hormone. The somatostatin secreted by the pancreas may regulate the secretion of glucagon and insulin. However, the precise function of pancreatic somatostatin is not well understood, so we focus on glucagon and insulin.

Between meals, as the level of blood sugar declines, the pancreas secretes glucagon. **Glucagon** increases the level of blood sugar. It does so by prompting cells of the liver to increase conversion of glycogen (the storage polysaccharide in animals) to glucose (a simple sugar, or monosaccharide). Glucagon also stimulates the liver to form glucose from lactic acid and amino acids. The liver releases the resultant glucose molecules into the bloodstream, causing a rise in blood sugar level.

After a meal, as the level of blood sugar rises with the absorption of sugars from the digestive tract, the pancreas secretes insulin. In contrast to glucagon, **insulin** decreases glucose in the blood; insulin and glucagon thus have opposite or antagonistic effects. Insulin decreases blood glucose in several ways. First, insulin stimulates transport of glucose into muscle cells, white blood cells, and connective tissue cells. Second, insulin inhibits the breakdown of glycogen to glucose. Third, insulin prevents conversion of amino and fatty acids to glucose. As a result of these actions, insulin promotes protein synthesis, fat storage, and the use of glucose for energy. Figure **10.18** summarizes the regulation of glucose in the blood by insulin and glucagon.

Insulin has dramatic effects on health. More than 120 million people worldwide, over 15 million of them in the United States, suffer from *diabetes mellitus,* a group of metabolic disorders characterized by an abnormally high level of glucose in the blood. There are several types of diabetes mellitus; we focus on type 1 and type 2 diabetes mellitus. *Type 1 diabetes mellitus* used to be known as insulin-dependent diabetes. It also was called juvenile-onset diabetes, because it usually develops in people younger than 25 years of age. In this autoimmune disorder, which represents about 5% to 10% of all diagnosed cases of diabetes, a person's own immune system attacks the cells of the pancreas responsible for insulin production. Symptoms include nausea, vomiting, thirst, and excessive urine production. Treatment involves daily, sometimes multiple, injections of insulin or the use of an insulin pump (a relatively small device that delivers the insulin at an infusion site, often on the abdomen). Exercise and careful monitoring of diet and blood glucose levels also are essential.

Type 2 diabetes mellitus used to be known as non-insulin-dependent diabetes. It was formerly called adult-onset diabetes as well, because it usually develops after age 40, although it recently has begun showing up in younger people. Type 2 diabetes, which accounts for between 90% and 95% of diabetes cases, is characterized by decreased sensitivity to insulin (a condition called insulin resistance). Many people with type 2 diabetes are overweight. Research suggests that type 2 diabetes results from an interaction between obesity, insulin resistance, and failure of the insulin-producing cells of the pancreas to fully compensate for the decreased sensitivity to insulin. The link between these factors may be certain fatty acids released by adipose tissue. These fatty acids induce insulin resistance in cells and impair the function of insulin-producing cells of the pancreas. Treatment typically involves dietary restrictions, exercise (which increases the sensitivity of body cells to insulin), and weight loss. Oral medications that increase insulin sensitivity or production also may be given. About 40% of people with type 2 diabetes need insulin injections. (This

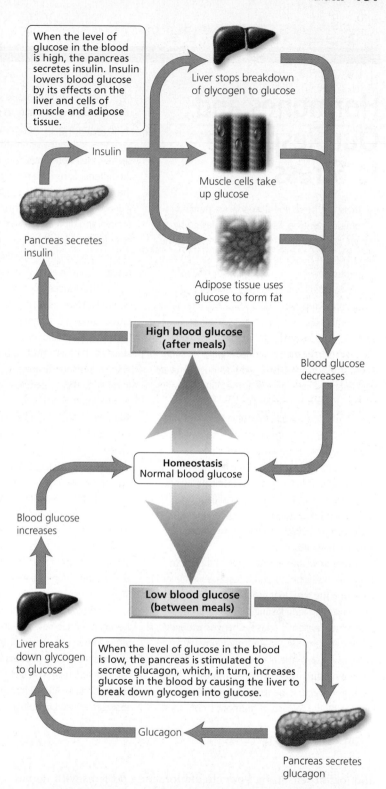

FIGURE 10.18 Regulation of glucose level in the blood by insulin (top) and glucagon (bottom), both of which are secreted by the pancreas

was one reason for dropping the name non-insulin-dependent diabetes.)

Diabetes has serious complications. Diabetics are at increased risk for blindness, kidney disease, heart disease, high blood pressure, and atherosclerosis (buildup of fatty deposits in the arteries). Many diabetics suffer from gum disease and from damage to their nervous system that may include impotence

Hormones and Our Response to Stress

Stress can be defined broadly as mental or physical tension. Rarely does a day go by that we are not subjected to stress. Awaiting the start of an exam, some personal performance, or an interview can be stressful. Our bodies usually can deal with everyday stresses and maintain the relative constancy of our internal environment. Sometimes, however, stress is extreme in its intensity and duration, and our coping mechanisms prove inadequate. At such times, stress triggers the hypothalamus to initiate the general adaptation syndrome (GAS), a series of physiological adjustments made by our bodies in response to extreme stress.

The GAS has three phases: alarm, resistance, and exhaustion. The alarm phase is popularly known as the fight-or-flight response. Recall that the fight-or-flight response is initiated by epinephrine from the adrenal medulla. The response immediately funnels huge amounts of glucose and oxygen to the organs most critical in responding to danger.

Sometimes the adjustments of the alarm phase are sufficient to end or escape whatever is causing the stress. At other times, stress is so intense and long lasting that the individual enters the resistance phase. Changes wrought by the resistance phase are more long term than are those of the alarm phase. Also, rather than being stimulated by nerve impulses from the hypothalamus, the resistance phase is initiated by the release of hormones from the

hypothalamus. The released hormones stimulate the anterior pituitary to secrete several more hormones. In turn, some of these newly secreted hormones stimulate other glands to secrete their hormones. Glucocorticoids from the adrenal cortex are the main hormones of the resistance phase. Two primary effects of glucocorticoids are to mobilize the body's protein and fat reserves and to conserve glucose for use by cells of the nervous system. The hormones of the resistance phase also result in conservation of body fluids.

The resistance phase is sustained by the body's fat reserves. This phase may last for weeks or months, but it cannot go on indefinitely. Sooner or later, lipid reserves are exhausted and structural proteins must be broken down to meet energy demands. Eventually, organs are unable to meet the heavy demands of the resistance phase, and they begin to fail. This is the exhaustion phase. Without immediate attention, death may result from collapse of one or more organ systems.

Stress, especially when it is prolonged and uncontrollable, can dramatically affect our health. It depresses wound healing, increases our susceptibility to infections, and leads to disorders such as hypertension, irritable bowel syndrome, and asthma. Some studies have shown that stress puts people at greater risk for developing chronic diseases. Overall, prolonged stress appears to shorten the life span.

Given the connection between stress and health, it is important to reduce some of the stress in our lives. Commonly used means to alleviate the effects of stress include regular exercise and relaxation techniques. A specialized relaxation technique is biofeedback, a procedure that can be used to help a person recognize the

symptoms of stress and learn how to control them. During a stress biofeedback session, a health care professional connects a patient to a machine that monitors one or more physiological indicators of stress, such as heart rate or muscle tension (Figure **10.A**). The health care worker then discusses a stressful situation with the patient. The machine gives off signals when the conversation makes the patient exhibit physiological symptoms that indicate experience of stress. For example, increased tension in muscles might elicit a clicking sound from the machine. The patient can use the clicking sound as a signal of stress, and then practice decreasing the muscle tension that prompted the clicks through deep breathing and relaxation. Eventually, patients are able to recognize and cope with signs of stress without the help of the machine.

FIGURE 10.A Biofeedback is one way that people can learn to recognize the symptoms of stress and how to cope with them.

and loss of sensation. Poor circulation and problems with nerves in the lower legs may make amputation of the lower limbs necessary. Indeed, more than half of lower limb amputations in the United States are done in people with diabetes. Given these serious complications, it is important to diagnose and treat diabetes early and, of course, to prevent it when possible (type 2 diabetes can be prevented or delayed; type 1 diabetes cannot be actively prevented at this time). The risk factors for type 2 diabetes include obesity, high blood pressure, having a parent or sibling with diabetes, and a history of gestational diabetes (a form of diabetes mellitus that develops in some women during pregnancy). The risk factors for type 1 diabetes are not so clearly

defined, although development of this disease has genetic, autoimmune, and environmental components.

Too much insulin sometimes results from a tumor of the pancreas. More typically, however, a diabetic person mistakenly injects too much insulin. The result is depressed levels of glucose in the blood. Initial symptoms of low blood glucose include anxiety, sweating, hunger, weakness, and disorientation. Because brain cells fail to function properly when starved of glucose, the initial symptoms may be followed by convulsions and unconsciousness. The consequences associated with severe depletion of blood glucose are known collectively as *insulin shock*. Insulin shock can prove fatal unless blood sugar levels are raised.

Thymus Gland

The **thymus gland** lies just behind the breastbone, on top of the heart (see Figure 10.2). It is more prominent in infants and children than in adults because it decreases in size as we age. The hormones it secretes, such as **thymopoietin** and **thymosin**, promote the maturation of white blood cells called T lymphocytes. Precursor cells from the bone marrow travel by way of the bloodstream to the thymus gland where they mature into T lymphocytes, also known as T cells, to become part of the body's defense mechanisms (Chapter 13).

Pineal Gland

The **pineal gland** is a tiny gland at the center of the brain (Figure **10.19**). Its secretory cells produce the hormone **melatonin**. Levels of circulating melatonin are greater at night than during daylight hours, because of input the pineal gland receives from visual pathways. Neurons of the retina, stimulated by light entering the eye, send impulses to the hypothalamus and ultimately the pineal gland, where they inhibit secretion of melatonin.

Research in the past few decades has suggested diverse roles for melatonin. Melatonin may inhibit production of the pigment melanin by melanocytes of the skin, as it does in some nonhuman animals. Melatonin may also influence daily rhythms. Sleep and, for some people, seasonal changes in mood appear to be influenced by melatonin. Melatonin also may slow the aging process. The possible links between melatonin and sleep, daily rhythms, and aging have led to widespread over-the-counter purchasing of melatonin, a situation described as "melatonin mania." We examine the promise and possible risks of taking melatonin in the Health Issue essay, *Melatonin: Miracle Supplement or Potent Drug Misused by Millions?*

One disorder associated with too much melatonin is *seasonal affective disorder (SAD)*. This form of depression is associated with winter, when short day length and a decreased exposure to light results in overproduction of melatonin. Too much melatonin causes symptoms such as lethargy, long periods of sleep, low spirits, and a craving for carbohydrates. The symptoms usually appear around October and end about April in the Northern Hemisphere. Three-quarters of persons who suffer from SAD are female. Treatment of SAD often includes repeated exposure to very bright light for about an hour each day. The intense light inhibits melatonin production.

Locally Acting Chemical Messengers

Now that we have surveyed the endocrine glands and their hormones, let's consider another group of chemical messengers—those that act locally. Once secreted by a cell, these **local signaling molecules** act near the site of their release, on adjacent target cells, within seconds or milliseconds. Communication via local signaling molecules occurs much more rapidly than the communication carried out by hormones, which travel to distant sites within the body (recall that the flight-or-fight response may take 30 seconds to initiate physiological changes). Neurotransmitters, discussed in Chapter 7, are examples of chemicals that rapidly convey messages from one cell (a neuron) to a neighboring cell (often another neuron). Prostaglandins, growth factors, and nitric oxide (NO) are other examples of local signaling molecules.

Prostaglandins are lipid molecules continually released by the plasma membranes of most cells. Different types of cells secrete different prostaglandins. At least 16 different prostaglandin molecules function within the human body. These molecules have remarkably diverse effects, influencing blood clotting, regulation of body temperature, diameter of airways to the lungs, and the body's inflammatory response. Prostaglandins also affect the reproductive system. Menstrual cramps are thought to be caused by prostaglandins released by cells of the uterine lining. These prostaglandins act on the smooth muscle of the uterus, causing muscle contractions and cramping. Anti-inflammatory drugs, such as aspirin and ibuprofen, inhibit the synthesis of prostaglandins and thus may lessen the discomfort of menstrual cramps. Prostaglandins also are found in semen. Once in the female reproductive tract, prostaglandins in semen cause the smooth muscles of the uterus to contract, perhaps helping the sperm continue their journey.

Other chemical messenger molecules, called **growth factors**, are peptides or proteins that, when present in the fluid outside target cells, stimulate those cells to grow, develop, and multiply. For example, one growth factor causes precursor cells in the bone marrow to proliferate and differentiate into particular white blood cells. Another growth factor prompts endothelial cells to proliferate and organize into tubes that eventually form blood vessels (see Chapter 12).

The gas **nitric oxide (NO)** functions in the cellular communication that leads to the dilation of blood vessels. Basically, endothelial cells of the inner lining of blood vessels make and release NO, which signals the smooth muscles in the surrounding (middle) layer to relax, allowing the vessel to dilate. NO aids in peristalsis, the rhythmic waves of smooth muscle contraction and relaxation that push food along the digestive tract. NO also functions as a neurotransmitter, carrying messages from one neuron to the next. Histamine, another local signaling molecule, is discussed in Chapter 13.

Pineal gland   Cerebrum   Hypothalamus

Skull

Pituitary gland

FIGURE 10.19 The pineal gland. Located near the center of the brain, the pineal gland secretes the hormone melatonin.

Melatonin: Miracle Supplement or Potent Drug Misused by Millions?

Melatonin, a hormone secreted by the pineal gland, has often been billed as a wonder drug. There are claims that melatonin can reduce jet lag, cure insomnia, boost immunity, and slow the aging process. In addition, melatonin is apparently well tolerated. But which, if any, of these claims are well supported by scientific evidence? And even if melatonin can be helpful under certain circumstances, should this potent hormone be sold as an over-the-counter dietary supplement to self-prescribing consumers?

The claim that melatonin helps to alleviate jet lag is well supported by scientific evidence. Studies have shown that melatonin taken by mouth on the day of travel and continued for several days has the following effects in about half the people who take it to fight jet lag: (1) reduced fatigue during the day; (2) reduced time to fall asleep at night; and (3) more rapid development of a normal sleep pattern. Such benefits are usually most evident during eastward travel that crosses more than four time zones. For people who are not traveling, but who toss and turn and watch the clock on the nightstand at home, there is some evidence that melatonin can bring sleep. Research, beginning in the 1980s and continuing today, has shown that melatonin reduces the time it takes to fall asleep and may lengthen the time that people stay asleep. Although most agree that melatonin

can be an effective sleep aid, scientists debate the precise mechanism by which melatonin produces its soporific effect.

What about the claims that melatonin can be used to boost immunity? Recall that the thymus gland, responsible for the production of infection-fighting white blood cells called T lymphocytes, is largest in infants and young children and shrinks as we age. Old mice also show shrinkage of the thymus. Such shrinkage can be reversed in geriatric mice by injections of melatonin. Indeed, the immune systems of injected animals showed signs of revitalization. Human trials on the potential immune-enhancing effects of melatonin in cancer patients are now under way. Although some promising results have been reported, there is insufficient evidence at present to support the claim that melatonin effectively boosts the human immune system.

Melatonin may slow aging through its effective scavenging of free radicals, molecular fragments that contain an unpaired electron. Free radicals have been implicated in many chronic diseases of old age, such as cancer and heart disease. Substances, such as melatonin, that destroy free radicals are called antioxidants. Free radicals are normally generated by some cells of the body for the purpose of destroying bacteria and old cells. Environmental agents such as drugs, toxins, and radiation also generate free radicals. What evidence is there to support melatonin as an effective antioxidant? Although numerous studies with other animals have supported the antioxidant properties of melatonin, well-designed studies with humans are lacking.

Should consumers hoping to cure jet lag or insomnia or to boost immunity and slow aging be gobbling down melatonin pills and lozenges purchased at health food stores? At present, melatonin is sold as a dietary supplement in the United States and thus is not subject to intense

Scientific evidence supports the claim that melatonin reduces jet lag.

scrutiny by the Food and Drug Administration. This lack of intense scrutiny raises questions about the strength and purity of the final marketed product. Additionally, researchers are still investigating the benefits of melatonin. For these reasons, some people in the medical profession caution consumers to wait until melatonin is further scrutinized and the research results are in. Others argue, however, that melatonin is probably safe for most people but that certain groups should avoid it until additional information is available. For example, pregnant and nursing women should avoid melatonin (the effects of high doses on fetuses or infants are unknown), as should children (who normally produce melatonin in large amounts). People with autoimmune disorders or cancers of the immune system should also avoid melatonin, because it may stimulate the immune system and worsen these conditions. Finally, people taking other medications should consult their physician before taking melatonin. Such consultation should help people avoid dangerous drug interactions.

Functions and Mechanisms of Hormones (pp. 184–188)

- Endocrine glands lack ducts and release their products, hormones, into the spaces just outside cells. The hormones then diffuse into the bloodstream. Endocrine glands and organs that contain some endocrine tissue constitute the endocrine system, which regulates and coordinates other organ systems and helps maintain homeostasis.
- Hormones, the chemical messengers of the endocrine system, contact virtually all cells within the body. However, hormones affect only target cells, those cells with receptors that recognize and bind specific hormones.
- Steroid hormones are lipid soluble. Steroids cross through the plasma membrane of target cells into the cytoplasm, where they combine with a receptor molecule, forming a hormone–receptor complex that moves into the nucleus of the cell. There the complex directs synthesis of specific proteins, including enzymes that stimulate or inhibit particular metabolic pathways.
- Water-soluble hormones, many of which are peptides and proteins, cannot pass through the lipid bilayer of the plasma membrane. Thus, they exert their effects indirectly by activating second messenger systems. The hormone, considered the first messenger, binds to a receptor on the plasma membrane. This event activates a molecule in the cytoplasm, considered the second messenger, which carries the hormone's message inside the cell, changing the activity of enzymes and chemical reactions. Thus, whereas lipid-soluble hormones prompt the synthesis of proteins, water-soluble hormones activate existing proteins.
- Endocrine glands are stimulated to manufacture and release hormones by chemical changes in the blood, hormones released by other endocrine glands, and messages from the nervous system. Hormone secretion is usually regulated by negative feedback mechanisms but sometimes by positive feedback mechanisms. The interactions between hormones may be antagonistic, synergistic, or permissive.

Pituitary Gland (pp. 188–191)

- The pituitary gland has an anterior lobe and a posterior lobe. The anterior lobe is influenced by the hypothalamus through a circulatory connection. Nerve cells in the hypothalamus release hormones that travel by way of the bloodstream to the anterior lobe, where they stimulate or inhibit release of hormones. The anterior pituitary releases six hormones (growth hormone, GH; prolactin, PRL; thyroid-stimulating hormone, TSH; adrenocorticotropic hormone, ACTH; follicle-stimulating hormone, FSH; and luteinizing hormone, LH). Four (TSH, ACTH, FSH, LH) of the six hormones are tropic hormones, meaning they influence other endocrine glands.
- In contrast to the circulatory connection between the hypothalamus and the anterior lobe of the pituitary gland, the connection between the hypothalamus and the posterior lobe is neural. Nerve cells in the hypothalamus make oxytocin (OT) and antidiuretic hormone (ADH); these two hormones travel down the axons of the nerve cells to the posterior lobe, where they are stored and released.

Thyroid Gland (pp. 191–192)

- The thyroid gland, at the front of the neck, produces thyroid hormone (TH) and calcitonin (CT). Thyroid hormone—which includes two very similar hormones, thyroxine (T_4) and triiodothyronine (T_3)—has broad effects, including regulating metabolic rate, heat production, and blood pressure. CT maintains low levels of calcium in the bloodstream.

Parathyroid Gland (p. 193)

- The parathyroid glands, four small masses of tissue at the back of the thyroid gland, secrete parathyroid hormone (PTH, or parathormone), an antagonist to CT. As such, PTH is responsible for raising blood levels of calcium by stimulating the movement of calcium from bone and urine to the blood.

Adrenal Glands (pp. 194–196)

- Each of two adrenal glands sits on top of a kidney and has two regions. The adrenal cortex (outer region) secretes gonadocorticoids, mineralocorticoids, and glucocorticoids. The adrenal medulla (inner region) produces epinephrine (adrenaline) and norepinephrine (noradrenaline) that initiate the fight-or-flight response.

Pancreas (pp. 196–198)

- The pancreas secretes the hormones glucagon (increases glucose in the blood) and insulin (decreases glucose in the blood). Type 1 diabetes mellitus is a disorder in which a person's own immune system attacks the insulin-producing cells of the pancreas, causing insulin deficiency. Type 2 diabetes mellitus is characterized by a decreased sensitivity to insulin that usually develops in middle age.

Thymus Gland (p. 199)

- The thymus gland lies on top of the heart and plays an important role in immunity. Its hormones influence the maturation of white blood cells called T lymphocytes.

Pineal Gland (p. 199)

- The pineal gland, at the center of the brain, secretes the hormone melatonin. Melatonin appears to be responsible for establishing biological rhythms and triggering sleep.

Locally Acting Chemical Messengers (p. 199)

- Some local chemical messengers convey information between adjacent cells, evoking rapid responses in target cells. Examples of local signaling molecules include neurotransmitters, prostaglandins, growth factors, and nitric oxide.

recognizing key terms

endocrine gland   *p. 184*
endocrine system   *p. 184*
hormone   *p. 184*
target cell   *p. 186*
lipid-soluble hormone   *p. 186*
steroid hormone   *p. 186*
water-soluble hormone
   p. 186
first messenger   *p. 186*
second messenger   *p. 186*
negative feedback mechanism
   p. 187
positive feedback mechanism
   p. 187
pituitary gland   *p. 188*
hypothalamus   *p. 188*
releasing hormone   *p. 188*

inhibiting hormone   *p. 188*
growth hormone (GH)
   p. 189
prolactin (PRL)   *p. 190*
tropic hormone   *p. 190*
thyroid-stimulating hormone
   (TSH)   *p. 190*
adrenocorticotropic hormone
   (ACTH)   *p. 190*
follicle-stimulating hormone
   (FSH)   *p. 190*
luteinizing hormone (LH)
   p. 190
antidiuretic hormone (ADH)
   p. 190
oxytocin (OT)   *p. 191*
thyroid gland   *p. 191*

thyroid hormone (TH)   *p. 192*
calcitonin (CT)   *p. 192*
parathyroid glands   *p. 193*
parathyroid hormone (PTH)
   p. 193
adrenal glands   *p. 194*
adrenal cortex   *p. 194*
adrenal medulla   *p. 194*
gonadocorticoids   *p. 194*
androgen   *p. 194*
estrogen   *p. 194*
mineralocorticoids
   p. 194
aldosterone   *p. 194*
glucocorticoids   *p. 194*
epinephrine   *p. 196*
norepinephrine   *p. 196*

fight-or-flight response
   p. 196
pancreas   *p. 196*
pancreatic islets
   p. 196
glucagon   *p. 197*
insulin   *p. 197*
thymus gland   *p. 199*
thymopoietin   *p. 199*
thymosin   *p. 199*
pineal gland   *p. 199*
melatonin   *p. 199*
local signaling molecules
   p. 199
prostaglandin   *p. 199*
growth factor   *p. 199*
nitric oxide (NO)   *p. 199*

reviewing the concepts

1. Given that hormones contact virtually all cells in the body, why are only certain cells affected by a particular hormone? *p. 186*
2. How do lipid-soluble (steroid) and water-soluble hormones differ in their mechanisms of action? *p. 186*
3. Compare negative and positive feedback mechanisms with regard to regulation of hormone secretion. Provide an example of each. *p. 187*
4. How do the anterior and posterior lobes of the pituitary gland differ in size and relationship with the hypothalamus? *pp. 188–189*
5. List the hormones secreted by the anterior lobe of the pituitary and their functions. *pp. 189–190*
6. List the hormones released by the posterior lobe of the pituitary and their functions. *pp. 190–191*
7. What are the effects of thyroid hormone? *p. 192*
8. Describe the feedback system by which calcitonin and parathyroid hormone regulate levels of calcium in the blood. *pp. 192–193*
9. What are the major functions of the glucocorticoids, mineralocorticoids, and gonadocorticoids secreted by the adrenal cortex? *p. 194*
10. What is the fight-or-flight response? Which hormones are critical in initiating this response? *p. 196*
11. What hormones are secreted by the pancreas? What are their functions? *pp. 196–197*
12. Explain the differences between type 1 and type 2 diabetes mellitus. *pp. 197–198*
13. What is the basic function of hormones secreted by the thymus gland? *p. 199*
14. What roles might melatonin play in the body? *pp. 199–200*
15. How do local signaling molecules differ from true hormones? *p. 199*
16. Which of the following does *not* characterize the anterior lobe of the pituitary gland?
    a. releases oxytocin and antidiuretic hormone
    b. circulatory connection to the hypothalamus

    c. larger of the two lobes
    d. secretes growth hormone and prolactin

17. A diet deficient in iodine may produce
    a. cretinism.
    b. Graves' disease.
    c. Cushing's syndrome.
    d. goiter.
18. Which of the following does *not* characterize the adrenal medulla?
    a. inner region of the adrenal gland
    b. secretes epinephrine and norepinephrine
    c. secretes glucocorticoids
    d. secretes hormones involved in fight-or-flight response
19. Type 1 diabetes
    a. is more common than type 2 diabetes.
    b. usually develops after age 40.
    c. is an autoimmune disorder.
    d. is characterized by decreased sensitivity to insulin.
20. Overproduction of melatonin by the pineal gland may cause
    a. seasonal affective disorder.
    b. diabetes insipidus.
    c. acromegaly.
    d. Addison's disease.
21. _____ hormones combine with receptor molecules in the cytoplasm of target cells, whereas _____ hormones bind to receptors on the surface of target cells and activate second messengers.
22. Oversecretion of growth hormone in childhood causes _____. Oversecretion in adulthood causes _____.
23. The hormone _____ lowers blood levels of calcium, whereas the hormone _____ increases blood levels of calcium.
24. In males, androgens are produced by the testes and the _____.
25. The hormone _____ lowers glucose in the blood, whereas the hormone _____ increases glucose in the blood.

applying the concepts

1. Mary has an itchy rash on the surface of her skin, and Rick has cut his finger on glass. Would either person benefit from applying a steroid cream containing cortisone? Why? Why not?
2. Matt is a thin 20-year-old. He is weak, disoriented, and sweating profusely. His friend brings him to the emergency room of the local hospital and explains that Matt is diabetic. Which type of diabetes does Matt likely have? What might explain his current condition? What might be done to help him?
3. It is winter in Massachusetts, and Theresa has felt "down" and lethargic since the fall. She has trouble getting out of bed in the morning, and once up, she craves carbohydrates. What might explain Theresa's symptoms? What might alleviate them, and why?
4. Velma tells her friend Carlos that he produces the female hormone estrogen. Is she correct? If yes, where is the estrogen produced in Carlos? Where is it produced in Velma?

becoming information literate

Recall that insulin, a hormone secreted by the pancreas, decreases the level of glucose in the blood. Recall also that diabetes mellitus, a condition that afflicts more than 15 million people in the United States, is a group of metabolic disorders characterized by abnormally high levels of blood glucose. Two major forms of diabetes mellitus are type 1 and type 2 diabetes mellitus.

Prepare a brochure in which you describe the symptoms, causes, and treatments of type 1 and type 2 diabetes mellitus. Use at least three reliable sources (books, journals, or websites). List each source you considered, and explain why you chose the three sources you used.

Additional questions can be found online at the Human Biology Place, www.humanbiology.com.

11

Blood

Blood, which brings oxygen and nutrients to each of our cells and carries waste away, is at all times a sensitive indicator of our well-being. A checkup at the doctor's office frequently includes the drawing of blood samples for various kinds of analyses.

lberto settled Mrs. Daniels into a chair in the nurse's station and prepared to draw a specimen of blood from the woman's arm. Before palpating the inside of her elbow and selecting a vein, he glanced again at the laboratory order form to double-check the kind and number of blood tests Dr. Mejia had ordered. In the four long rows of boxes on the form, only the ones pertaining to a cholesterol profile had checks inside them. There were at least 80 other choices on the form—levels of plasma proteins, the various blood cells, glucose, electrolytes, minerals, waste products, enzymes, cardiac risk factors, thyroid hormones, insulin, and on and on—all ways in which blood could be examined to provide information about specific organs and the overall health of the body. Alberto drew the blood, carefully labeled the tube, showed Mrs. Daniels how to keep pressure on the puncture site until any bleeding had stopped, and promptly took the specimen to the lab.

You probably know that blood is a critical life-sustaining fluid. We encounter many of the reasons it is so vital in this chapter as we consider the functions and composition of blood. In addition, we discuss blood type and why it is so important. Finally, we consider how blood forms clots to prevent blood loss from a wound.

Functions of Blood

Blood is sometimes referred to as the river of life. The comparison is apt because, like many a river, blood serves as a transportation system. It carries vital materials to all the cells of the body and carries away the wastes that cells produce. But blood does more than passively move its cargo. Its white blood cells help protect us against disease-causing organisms, and its clotting mechanisms help protect us from excessive blood loss when a vessel is damaged. In addition, buffers in the blood help regulate the acid–base balance of body fluids. Blood also helps regulate body temperature by absorbing heat produced in metabolically active regions and distributing it to cooler regions and to the skin, where the heat is dissipated. So the diverse functions of blood can be grouped into three categories: transportation, protection, and regulation.

Composition of Blood

Blood *is* thicker than water. The reason for the difference is that blood contains cells suspended in its watery fluid. In fact, a single drop of blood contains more than 250 million blood cells. You may recall from Chapter 4 that blood is classified as a connective tissue because it contains cellular elements suspended in a matrix. The liquid matrix is called plasma, and the cellular elements are collectively called the formed elements (Figure **11.1**).

Whole blood

Plasma is a medium for transporting materials in the blood.

The formed elements consist of the red blood cells, white blood cells, and platelets.

55%

45%

Platelets are cell fragments essential to blood clotting.

White blood cells defend the body against disease.

Red blood cells transport oxygen.

FIGURE 11.1 Blood can be separated into its major components when it is placed in a test tube with a substance that prevents coagulation and then spun in a centrifuge. Whole blood consists of a straw-colored liquid, called plasma, in which cellular elements, called formed elements, are suspended. After separation, the uppermost layer in the test tube consists of plasma. The formed elements are found in two layers below the plasma. Just below the plasma is a thin layer consisting of platelets and white blood cells (leukocytes). The red blood cells (erythrocytes) are packed at the bottom of the test tube.

Plasma

Plasma is a straw-colored liquid that makes up about 55% of blood. Plasma serves as the medium in which materials are transported by the blood. Almost every substance that is transported by the blood is dissolved in the plasma. These include nutrients (such as simple sugars, amino acids, lipids, and vitamins), ions (such as sodium, potassium, and chloride), dissolved gases (including carbon dioxide, nitrogen, and a small amount of oxygen), and every hormone. In addition to transporting materials to the cells, the plasma carries away cellular wastes. For example, urea from protein breakdown and uric acid from nucleic acid breakdown are carried to the kidneys, where they can be removed from the body. Blood also transports carbon dioxide from the cells where it is produced to the lungs for release. Indeed, if wastes were not removed the cells would die.

Despite the amount and variety of substances transported by the blood, most of the dissolved substances (solutes) in the blood are **plasma proteins**, which make up 7% to 8% of plasma. Plasma proteins help balance water flow between the blood and the cells. You may recall from Chapter 3 that water moves by osmosis across biological membranes from an area of lesser solute concentration to an area of greater solute concentration. Without the plasma proteins, water would be drawn out of the blood by the proteins in cells. As a result, fluid would accumulate in the tissues, causing swelling.

Most of the 50 or so types of plasma proteins fall into one of three general categories: albumins, globulins, and clotting proteins. The albumins make up more than half of the plasma proteins. They are most important in the blood's water-balancing ability. The globulins have a variety of functions. Some globulins transport lipids, including fats and some cholesterol, as well as fat-soluble vitamins. Other globulins are antibodies, which provide protection against many diseases. An example of the third category of plasma protein, the clotting proteins, is fibrinogen, whose role we discuss later in the chapter.

Formed Elements

Among the substances transported by the plasma are the **formed elements**—platelets, white blood cells, and red blood cells. These cell fragments and cells perform some of the key functions of the blood. Descriptions and functions of the formed elements of the blood are summarized in Table **11.1**.

Red bone marrow, a porous connective tissue that fills the cavities within many bones, is the birthplace and nursery for the formed elements. Its spongelike framework supports fat cells, but in addition it supports the undifferentiated cells called blood **stem cells** that divide and give rise to all the formed elements (Figure **11.2**).

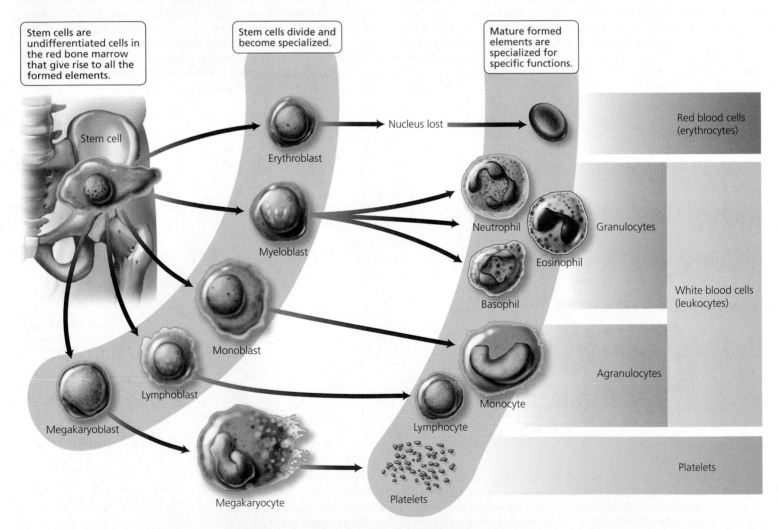

FIGURE 11.2 All formed elements originate in the red bone marrow from an undifferentiated cell called a stem cell. Stem cells divide and differentiate, giving rise to the various types of blood cells.

TABLE 11.1 The Formed Elements of Blood

Type of Formed Element	Cell Function	Description	No. of Cells/mm³	Life Span
Platelets	Play role in blood clotting	Fragments of a megakaryocyte; small, purple-stained granules in cytoplasm	250,000–500,000	5–10 days

White Blood Cells (WBCs; leukocytes)

Granulocytes

Neutrophils	Consume bacteria by phagocytosis	Multilobed nucleus, clear-staining cytoplasm, inconspicuous granules	3000–7000	6–72 hours
Eosinophils	Consume antibody–antigen complex by phagocytosis; attack parasitic worms	Large, pink-staining granules in cytoplasm, bilobed nucleus	100–400	8–12 days
Basophils	Release histamine, which attracts white blood cells to the site of inflammation and widens blood vessels	Large, purple-staining cytoplasmic granules; bilobed nucleus	20–50	3–72 hours

Agranulocytes

Monocytes	Give rise to macrophages, which consume bacteria, dead cells, and cell parts by phagocytosis	Gray-blue cytoplasm with no granules; U-shaped nucleus	100–700	Several months
Lymphocytes	Attack damaged or diseased cells, or disease-causing organisms; produce antibodies	Round nucleus that almost fills the cell	1500–3000	Many years

Red Blood Cells (RBCs; erythrocytes)	Transport oxygen and carbon dioxide	Biconcave disk, no nucleus	4–6 million	About 120 days

Platelets

Platelets, sometimes called thrombocytes (*thromb,* clot; *cyte,* cell), are essential to blood clotting. They are actually fragments of larger cells called megakaryocytes and are formed in the red bone marrow when megakaryocytes break apart. The fragments are released into the blood at the astounding rate of about 200 billion a day. They then mature during the course of a week, after which they circulate in the blood for about 5 to 10 days. Platelets contain several substances important in stopping the loss of blood through damaged blood vessels. This vital function of platelets is considered later in the chapter.

White Blood Cells and Defense against Disease

White blood cells (WBCs), or **leukocytes** (*leuk–,* white; *–cyte,* cell), perform certain mundane housekeeping duties—such as removing wastes, toxins, and damaged or abnormal cells—but they also serve as warriors in the body's fight against disease (see Chapters 13). Although leukocytes represent less than 1% of whole blood, we simply could not live without them. We would succumb to the microbes that surround us. Because the number of white blood cells increases when the body responds to microbes, white blood cell counts are often used as an index of infection.

Like the other formed elements, white blood cells are produced in the red bone marrow.[1] Unlike platelets and red blood cells, however, white blood cells are nucleated. Moreover, although they circulate in the bloodstream, they are not confined there. By squeezing between neighboring cells that form the walls of blood vessels, white blood cells can leave the circulatory system and move to a site of infection, tissue damage, or inflammation (Figure **11.3**). Having slipped out of the capillary into the fluid bathing the cells, white blood cells roam through the tissue spaces. Chemicals released by invading microbes or damaged cells attract the white blood cells and cause them to gather in areas of tissue damage or infection. Certain types of white blood cells may then engulf the "offender" in a process called **phagocytosis** (*phago–,* to eat; *–cyt–,* cell; see Chapter 3). Our consideration of white blood cells in this chapter is brief; Chapter 13 contains a more detailed discussion of their many tactics for defending our bodies.

There are two groups of white blood cells. **Granulocytes** have granules in their cytoplasm. The granules are actually sacs containing chemicals that are used as weapons to destroy invading pathogens, especially bacteria. **Agranulocytes** lack cytoplasmic granules or have very small granules. These two groups include a total of five types of white blood cells.

Granulocytes

All white blood cells are colorless, and thus they are often stained so that they are visible under a microscope. Depending on the color of the granules after they have been stained for microscopic study, the granulocytes are classified as neutrophils, eosinophils, or basophils. Neutrophils have small granules that don't stain with either acidic red stain eosin or with a basic blue stain. The granules in eosinophils pick up a pink color from the stain eosin. Basophils have purple-staining granules (see Table 11.1).

- **Neutrophils**, the most abundant of all white blood cells, are the blood cell soldiers on the front lines. Arriving at the site of infection before the other types of white blood cells, neutrophils immediately begin to engulf microbes by phagocytosis, thus curbing the spread of the infection. After engulfing a dozen or so bacteria, a neutrophil dies. But even in death it helps the body's defense by releasing chemicals that attract more neutrophils to the scene. Dead neutrophils, along with bacteria and cellular debris, make up pus, the yellowish liquid we usually associate with infection.

- **Eosinophils** contain substances that are important in the body's defense against parasitic worms, such as tapeworms and hookworms. They also lessen the severity of allergies by engulfing antibody–antigen complexes and inactivating inflammatory chemicals.

- **Basophils** release histamine, a chemical that attracts other white blood cells to the site of infection and causes blood vessels to dilate (widen), thereby increasing blood flow to the affected area. They also play a role in some allergic reactions.

Agranulocytes

The agranulocytes, which lack visible granules in the cytoplasm, are classified as monocytes or lymphocytes.

- **Monocytes**, the largest of all formed elements, leave the bloodstream and enter various tissues, where they develop into macrophages. Macrophages are phagocytic cells that engulf invading microbes, dead cells, and cellular debris.

- **Lymphocytes** are classified into two types: B lymphocytes and T lymphocytes. The *B lymphocytes* give rise to plasma cells, which, in turn, produce antibodies. *Antibodies* are proteins that recognize specific molecules—called *antigens*—on the surface of invading microbes or other foreign cells. After recognizing the foreign cell by its antigens, the antibodies help prevent it from harming the body. There are several types of *T lymphocytes,* specialized white blood cells that play roles in the body's defense mechanisms. We will discuss lymphocytes further in Chapter 13.

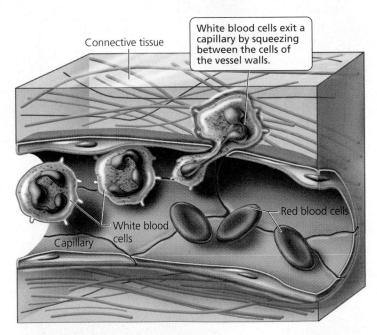

Connective tissue

White blood cells exit a capillary by squeezing between the cells of the vessel walls.

Red blood cells

White blood cells

Capillary

FIGURE 11.3 White blood cells can squeeze between the cells that form the wall of a capillary. They then enter the fluid surrounding body cells and, attracted by chemicals released by microbes or damaged cells, gather at the site of infection or injury.

[1]One type, the lymphocytes, also may be produced in the lymph nodes and other lymphoid tissues.

Red Blood Cells and Transport of Oxygen

Red blood cells (RBCs), also called **erythrocytes** (*erythro–*, red; *–cyt–*, cell), pick up oxygen in the lungs and ferry it to all the cells of the body. Red blood cells also carry about 23% of the blood's total carbon dioxide, a metabolic waste product. They are by far the most numerous cells in the blood. Indeed, they number 4–6 million/mm³ of blood and constitute approximately 45% of the total blood volume.

Red blood cells and hemoglobin

The shape of red blood cells, as shown in Figure **11.4**, is marvelously suited to their function of picking up and transporting oxygen. Red blood cells are quite small, and each is shaped like a biconcave disk—a flattened disk indented on each side. This shape maximizes the surface area of the cell. Because of the greater surface area, oxygen can enter the red blood cell more rapidly than if the disk did not have an indent. A red blood cell is unusually flexible and thus able to squeeze through capillaries (the smallest blood vessels, those in which gas exchange occurs), even those with a diameter much smaller than red blood cells. Each red blood cell is packed with **hemoglobin**, the oxygen-binding pigment that is responsible for the cells' red color. As a red blood cell matures in the red bone marrow, it loses its nucleus and most organelles. Thus, it is scarcely more than a sack of hemoglobin molecules. Each red blood cell is packed with approximately 280 million molecules of hemoglobin. As can be seen in Figure **11.5**, each hemoglobin molecule is made up of four subunits. Each subunit consists of a polypeptide chain and a heme group. The heme group includes an iron ion that actually binds to the oxygen. Therefore, each hemoglobin molecule can carry up to four molecules of oxygen. The compound formed when hemoglobin binds with oxygen is called, logically enough, *oxyhemoglobin*. Body cells use the oxygen to boost the amount of energy extracted from food molecules in cellular respiration. As oxygen is used, carbon dioxide is produced. Most of the carbon dioxide travels to the lungs dissolved in plasma, but some of it binds to hemoglobin (at a site other than that where the iron atom binds oxygen).

As wonderfully adapted as it is for carrying oxygen, the hemoglobin molecule binds 200 times more readily to carbon monoxide, a product of the incomplete combustion of any carbon-containing fuel. In other words, if concentrations of carbon monoxide and oxygen were identical in inhaled air, for every 1 molecule of hemoglobin that binds to oxygen molecules, 200 molecules of hemoglobin would bind to carbon monoxide molecules. This is the reason carbon monoxide can be deadly. When carbon monoxide binds to the oxygen-binding sites on hemoglobin, it blocks oxygen from binding to it, preventing the blood from carrying life-giving oxygen to the cells. Carbon monoxide is a particularly insidious poison because it is odorless and tasteless. Its primary source is automobile exhaust, but it can also come from indoor sources, including improperly vented heaters and leaky chimneys. Thus, indoor carbon monoxide detectors can save lives.

Life cycle of red blood cells

The creation of a red blood cell, which takes about 6 days, entails many changes in the cell's activities and structure. First, the very immature cell becomes a factory for hemoglobin molecules. And as noted earlier, after the cell is packed with hemoglobin, its nucleus is pushed out. Then a structural metamorphosis occurs, culminating in a mature red blood cell with a typical biconcave shape. Once this change in shape takes place, the cell leaves the bone marrow and

FIGURE 11.4 Red blood cells serve to ferry oxygen from the lungs to the needy tissues. Each red blood cell is packed with the oxygen-binding pigment hemoglobin. A red blood cell is a small disk that is indented on both sides. This design maximizes the surface area for gas exchange.

Each hemoglobin molecule consists of four polypeptide chains (globins).

Each polypeptide chain contains a heme group with an iron atom that binds to oxygen.

Oxygen molecules bind to hemoglobin

Oxygen molecules released

Each hemoglobin molecule can carry up to four molecules of oxygen.

FIGURE 11.5 The structure of hemoglobin, the pigment in red blood cells that transports oxygen from the lungs to the cells enters the bloodstream. Red marrow produces roughly 2 million red blood cells a second, throughout the life of an individual, for a cumulative total of more than half a ton in a lifetime.

A red blood cell lives for only about 120 days. During that time, it travels through approximately 100 km (62 mi) of blood vessels, being bent, bumped, and squeezed along the way. Its life span is probably limited by the lack of a nucleus that would otherwise maintain it and direct needed repairs. Without a nucleus, for instance, protein synthesis needed to replace key enzymes cannot take place, so the cell becomes increasingly rigid and fragile.

The liver and spleen are the "graveyards" where worn-out red blood cells are removed from circulation. The old, inflexible red blood cells tend to become stuck in the tiny circulatory channels of these organs. Macrophages then engulf and destroy the dying cells. The demolished cells release their hemoglobin, which the liver degrades into its protein (globin) component and heme. The protein is digested to amino acids, which can be used to make other proteins. The iron from the heme is salvaged and sent to the red marrow for recycling.

The remaining part of the heme is degraded to a yellow pigment, called *bilirubin,* which is excreted by the liver in bile. Bile is released into the small intestine, where it assists in the digestion of fats. It is then carried along the digestive system to the large intestine with undigested food and becomes a component of feces. The color of feces is partly due to bilirubin that has been broken down by intestinal bacteria.

Products formed by the chemical breakdown of heme also create the yellowish tinge in a bruise that is healing. A bruise, or black-and-blue mark, results when tiny blood vessels or capillaries are ruptured and blood leaks into the surrounding tissue. As the tissues use up the oxygen, the blood becomes darker and, viewed through the overlying tissue, looks black or blue. Gradually, the red blood cells degenerate, releasing hemoglobin. The breakdown products of hemoglobin then make the bruise appear yellowish.

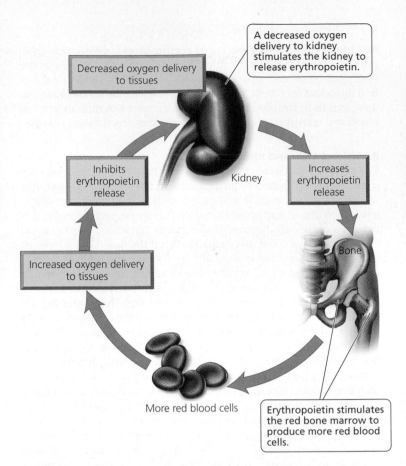

FIGURE 11.6 The production of red blood cells is regulated by a negative feedback relationship between the oxygen-carrying capacity of the blood and the production of erythropoietin.

stop and think

Hepatitis is an inflammation of the liver that can be caused by certain viruses or exposure to certain drugs. It impairs the liver's ability to handle bilirubin properly. A symptom of hepatitis is jaundice, a condition in which the skin develops a yellow tone. Why does hepatitis cause jaundice?

A negative feedback mechanism regulates red blood cell production according to the needs of the body, especially the need for oxygen (Figure **11.6**). Most of the time, red blood cell production matches red blood cell destruction. However, there are circumstances—blood loss, for instance—that trigger a homeostatic mechanism that speeds up the rate of red blood cell production. This mechanism is initiated by a decrease in the oxygen supply to the body's cells. Certain cells in the kidney sense the reduced oxygen, and they respond by producing the hormone **erythropoietin.** Erythropoietin then travels to the red marrow, where it steps up both the division rate of stem cells and the maturation rate of immature red blood cells. When maximally stimulated by erythropoietin, the red marrow can increase red blood cell production tenfold—to 20 million cells per second! The resulting increase in red blood cell numbers is soon adequate to meet the oxygen needs of body cells. The increased oxygen-carrying capacity of the blood then inhibits erythropoietin production.

Blood Cell Disorders

Disorders of red and white blood cells have many different causes. The problems associated with each disorder depend on the type of blood cells affected, because red and white blood cells have different functions.

Disorders of Red Blood Cells

Anemia, a condition in which the blood's ability to carry oxygen is reduced, can result from too little hemoglobin, too few red blood cells, or both. The symptoms of anemia include fatigue, headaches, dizziness, paleness, and breathlessness. In addition, an anemic person's heart often beats faster to compensate for the blood's decreased ability to carry oxygen. The accelerated pumping can cause heart palpitations—the uncomfortable awareness of one's own heartbeat. Although anemia is not usually life threatening, it can affect the quality of life because lack of energy and low levels of productive activity often go hand in hand.

Worldwide, the most common cause of anemia is an insufficiency of iron in the body, which leads to inadequate hemoglobin production. *Iron-deficiency anemia* can be caused by a diet that contains too little iron, by an inability to absorb iron from the digestive system, or from blood loss, such as might occur because of menstrual flow or peptic ulcers. Treatment for iron-deficiency anemia includes dealing with the cause of the iron depletion, as well as restoring iron levels to normal by eating foods that are rich in

Lead Poisoning

What do children in old buildings in America today have in common with the ancient upper-class Romans? Lead poisoning. Today, some children are poisoned by the lead in paint chips that they unintentionally ingest as aging paint peels (or, in very young children, when they chew or bite objects that have been treated with lead paint). Centuries ago, Romans were poisoned by lead in their eating and drinking vessels.

The types of cells that are most sensitive to lead are nerve cells and the bone marrow cells that give rise to red blood cells. The best-known effects of lead on human health are probably those on the nervous system—mental retardation, lowered IQs, reading disabilities, irritability, hyperactivity, and even death. However, the effects of lead on the blood, including anemia and changes in blood enzymes, can also be devastating. Indeed, a blood test is the only way to positively diagnose lead poisoning.

Lead launches a two-pronged attack on the blood's ability to carry oxygen. First, it interferes with the absorption of iron from the digestive system. Second, it inhibits one of the essential enzymes leading to hemoglobin synthesis.

As our example of ancient Romans suggests, lead has been a common pollutant for centuries, encountered in a surprising number of substances. The major causes of lead poisoning in the United States are as follows:

1. **House paint** Although lead has not been added to house paint for years, this remains the most prevalent cause of poisoning. Young children tend to put almost anything they find into their mouths, and lead-containing paint chips are no exception. Although most cases of lead poisoning occur in children of poor families living in big cities, lead poisoning can also affect the affluent and those living in the country or suburbs. The entire family—adults, children, and even pets—can be exposed to lead during the renovation of old homes. For example, lead dust is created as lead paint is sanded from surfaces. That dust can then be inhaled and absorbed into the bloodstream.

2. **Drinking water** One out of every five Americans drinks tap water containing excess levels of lead, according to Environmental Protection Agency estimates. Most of these people are unaware that their drinking water is contaminated with lead because the water still tastes and smells normal. Lead leaches into the water from sources within the homes— copper pipes that contain lead solder, lead connectors in the plumbing, or fancy faucets made of brass or bronze. The leaching process is hastened by heat, acidity, and soft water.

3. **Air and soil pollution** The primary source of lead in the atmosphere has been leaded gasoline. As early as the 1920s, tetraethyl lead was added to motor fuel because it slowed combustion and therefore reduced engine knock and wear. Tiny particles of lead are released into the atmosphere when leaded fuel is burned. Thus, as the use of leaded motor fuel increased, so did the concentration of atmospheric lead. (Leaded gasoline is no longer sold in the United States for use in automobiles, although it is permissible in farm equipment, race cars, and other off-road vehicles.)

4. **Lead solder on food cans** The lead in the solder used to seal the seams in food and beverage cans can leach into the contents, especially if the contents are acidic foods such as tomatoes or citrus juices. Although the use of lead solder on food cans has been banned in the United States, it is still found on some imported food cans.

5. **Lead-containing dishware** China, ceramic, and earthenware dishes may be coated with lead-containing glaze. When the glazes are not properly fired, lead can leach into the food or beverage contained in the dish. Lead is most likely to leach into foods or beverages that are hot or acidic. Thus, it is probably best to avoid daily use of a ceramic mug for coffee or tea. Wine should not be stored in lead crystal decanters, and if a wine bottle is sealed with a lead foil capsule, clean the rim of the bottle before removing the cork.

6. **Fruits and vegetables grown on lead-contaminated soil** Soil can be contaminated by lead from the atmosphere or by leakage from lead-containing solid wastes, such as lead batteries in automobiles that are dumped into landfills. Important sources of atmospheric lead are the combustion of lead motor fuel, the smelting of ores and other industrial processes, and the incineration of refuse. Fruits and vegetables can then incorporate the lead or be coated in lead dust. When the contaminated food is eaten, the lead is absorbed into the bloodstream.

Although it is true that blood levels of lead are at an all-time low in the United States, the lead problem has not been eliminated. In 2008 the Environmental Protection Agency (EPA) proposed tightening the federal limits for lead in the air. An important problem now is deciding who should be financially responsible for keeping us safe. China's safety standards are not as high as those in the United States. Recently, the paint on children's toys imported from China contained lead. Some people blame the companies that imported the toys. In turn, some of those companies blame the failure of federal agencies to protect us.

Questions to Consider

In 2008 San Diego, California, wrestled with establishing lead-safe apartments and workplaces. The city has about 310,000 buildings built before 1979 that contain lead paint, and the average cost of lead reduction is $704 for each housing unit.

- Who do you think should bear the financial responsibility of removing lead paint from old apartment buildings? The residents? The landlords? The city? The federal government?

- Do you think the residents of buildings with lead paint should be compensated for any lead-related health problems they experience? If so, who do you think should pay— the landlords? The original contractors? The government?

Children often put objects into their mouths. They may unintentionally ingest lead paint chips if the object has been treated with lead.

iron—such as meat, leafy green vegetables, and fortified cereals—or by taking pills that contain iron.

Blood loss will obviously lower red blood cell counts, but so will any condition that causes the destruction of red blood cells at an amount that exceeds the production of red blood cells. For example, in hemolytic anemias, red blood cells are ruptured because of infections, defects in the membranes of red blood cells, transfusion of mismatched blood, or hemoglobin abnormalities. *Sickle-cell anemia* is an example of a hemolytic anemia caused by abnormal hemoglobins. This abnormal hemoglobin (hemoglobin S) causes the red blood cells to become deformed to a crescent (or sickle) shape when the blood's oxygen content is low. The misshapen cells are fragile and rupture easily, clogging small blood vessels and promoting clot formation. These events prevent oxygen-laden blood from reaching the tissues and can cause episodes of extreme pain.

Red blood cell numbers also drop when the production of red blood cells is halted or impaired, as occurs in *pernicious anemia*. The production of red blood cells depends on a supply of vitamin B_{12}. The small intestine absorbs vitamin B_{12} from the diet with the aid of a chemical called intrinsic factor, which is produced by the stomach lining. People with pernicious anemia do not produce intrinsic factor and are therefore unable to absorb vitamin B_{12}. They are treated with injections of B_{12}. Lead poisoning can also cause anemia. (See the Environmental Issue essay, *Lead Poisoning.*)

what would you do?

Blood doping is a practice that boosts red blood cell numbers and, therefore, the blood's ability to carry oxygen. In one method, blood is drawn from the body and stored, prompting the body temporarily to boost its production of red blood cells. The stored blood is then returned to the body. Some athletes who compete in aerobic events, such as swimming or cycling, have used blood doping to increase their endurance and speed. Although blood doping is considered unethical and is prohibited in Olympic competition, it is difficult to detect. One sign is an exceptionally high number of red blood cells; another is the presence in the urine of a hormone (erythropoietin) that stimulates red blood cell production; but tests can detect only about 50% of the athletes who practice blood doping. Considering the large percentage of blood-doped athletes who will escape detection even if they are tested, do you think that those who are caught should be punished?

Disorders of White Blood Cells

Infectious mononucleosis ("mono") is a viral disease of the lymphocytes. It is caused by the Epstein-Barr virus, which is common in humans but usually asymptomatic. In mononucleosis, the infection causes an increase in lymphocytes that have an atypical appearance. Because mono often is spread from person to person by oral contact, it is sometimes called the kissing disease; however, it can also be spread by sharing eating utensils or drinking glasses. Mono is most common among teenagers and young adults, particularly those living in dormitories. It often strikes at stressful times, such as during final exams, when immune resistance is low.

The initial symptoms of mono are similar to those of influenza: fever, chills, headache, sore throat, and an overwhelming sense of being ill. Within a few days, the lymph node (commonly called "glands") in the neck, armpits, and groin become painfully swollen. There is no treatment, so mono must simply run its course. The major symptoms generally subside within a few weeks, but fatigue may linger for several months or longer.

Leukemia is a cancer of the white blood cells that causes their uncontrolled multiplication, so that their number increases greatly. These cancerous cells—all descendants of a single abnormal cell—remain immature and are therefore unable to defend the body against infectious organisms. Because they divide more rapidly than do normal cells, the abnormal cells "take over" the bone marrow, preventing the development of all normal blood cells, including red blood cells, white blood cells, and platelets.

Symptoms of leukemia generally result either from the insufficient number of normal blood components or from the invasion of organs by abnormal white blood cells. The increased number of white blood cells crowds out the other formed elements. Insufficient numbers of platelets lead to inadequate clotting, which causes gum bleeding and frequent bruising. Reduced levels of red blood cells lead to anemia, which in turn causes chronic fatigue, breathlessness, and pallor. Because their white blood cells do not function properly, leukemia patients may suffer from repeated respiratory or throat infections, herpes, or skin infections. Also, bone tenderness may be experienced because the immature white blood cells pack the red marrow. Headaches, another symptom of leukemia, may be caused by anemia or by the effects of abnormal white blood cells in the brain.

Treatment of leukemia usually includes radiation therapy and chemotherapy to kill the rapidly dividing cells. In addition, transfusions of red blood cells and platelets may be given to alleviate anemia and prevent excessive bleeding. Today, many patients with acute leukemia are cured with bone marrow transplants. Someone, most often a family member whose tissue type closely matches that of the patient, must be located and agree to serve as a donor. Then the bone marrow in the leukemia patient must be destroyed by irradiation and drugs. Next, the donor's bone marrow is given to the patient intravenously, just like a blood transfusion. The marrow cells find their way to the patient's marrow and begin to grow. Treatment with stem cells from umbilical cord blood seems to be as effective as bone marrow transplant in helping some patients with leukemia go into remission (the signs and symptoms of leukemia go away). Stem cells from umbilical cord blood are discussed in Chapter 19a, Special Topic: *Stem Cells—A Repair Kit for the Body.*

Blood Types

Human blood is classified into different **blood types**, depending on the presence or absence of certain molecules, mostly proteins, on the surface of a person's red blood cells. Each of your body cells is labeled as "self" (that is, as belonging to your body) by proteins on its surface. If a cell that lacks these self markers enters the body, the body's defense system recognizes that the foreign cell is "nonself" and does not belong. The foreign cell will have different proteins on its surface. To the body's defense system, these proteins are antigens, identifying the cell as foreign and marking it for destruction. As was mentioned earlier, one way the body attacks the foreign cell is by producing proteins called antibodies that specifically target the antigen on the foreign cell's surface. Let's consider the role of antigens and antibodies in blood types and transfusions.

ABO Blood Types

When asked about your blood type, you are probably used to responding by indicating one of the types in the ABO series: A, B, AB, or O. Red blood cells with only the antigen A on their surface

Q *What blood type will agglutinate to each serum when mixed separately with sera containing anti-A, anti-B, and anti-Rh antibodies?*

(a) Agglutination relationship among blood types

(b) Micrographs showing no agglutination (top) and agglutination (bottom)

(c) Diagrams of antigens and antibodies with no agglutination and with agglutination

FIGURE 11.7 Blood is typed by mixing it with serum known to contain antibodies specific for a certain antigen. If blood containing that antigen is mixed with the serum, the blood will agglutinate (clump). Thus, one drop of blood is mixed with serum containing anti-A and another drop with serum containing anti-B. A third drop of blood is mixed with serum containing antibodies to Rh. Agglutination in response to an antibody reveals the presence of the antigen.

A AB+

are type A. When only the B antigen is on the red blood cell surface, the blood is type B. Blood with both A and B antigens on the red blood cell surface is designated type AB. When neither A nor B antigens are present, the blood is type O.

Normally, a person's plasma contains antibodies against those antigens that are not on his or her own red blood cells. Thus, individuals with type A blood have antibodies against the B antigen (anti-B antibodies[2]), and those with type B blood have antibodies against A (anti-A antibodies). Because individuals with type AB blood have both antigens on their red blood cells, they have neither antibody. Those with type O blood have neither antigen, so they have both anti-A and anti-B antibodies in their plasma.

In a typical test for blood type, technicians mix a drop of a person's blood with a solution containing anti-A antibodies and mix another drop of the blood with a solution containing anti-B antibodies. If clumping occurs in one of the mixtures, it means the antigen corresponding to the antibody in that mixture is present (Figure **11.7**).

Similarly, when a person is given a blood transfusion with donor blood containing foreign antigens, the antibodies in the recipient's blood will cause the donor's cells to clump, or **agglutinate.** This clumping of the donor's cells is damaging and perhaps even fatal. The clumped cells can get stuck in small blood vessels and block blood flow to body cells. Or they may break open, releasing their cargo of hemoglobin. The hemoglobin then clogs the filtering system in the kidneys, causing death.

It is important to be sure that the blood types of a donor and recipient are compatible, which means that the recipient's blood does not contain antibodies to antigens on the red blood cells of the donor. The plasma of the donor's blood may contain antibodies against antigens on the recipient's red blood cells, but these will be diluted as they enter the recipient's circulation. Therefore, the donor's antibodies are not a major problem. The questions to ask in this case are (1) what, if any, antigens are on the donor's cells and (2) what, if any, antibodies are in the recipient's blood. For example, if a person with blood type A is given a transfusion of blood type B or of type AB, the naturally occurring anti-B antibodies in the recipient's blood will cause the donor's red blood cells to clump because they have the B antigen. The transfusion relationships among blood types in the ABO series are shown in Table **11.2.**

Rh Factor

The A and B antigens are not the only important antigens found on the surface of red blood cells. The presence or absence of an **Rh factor** is also an important component of blood type. The name Rh comes from the beginning of the name of the rhesus monkey, in which an Rh antigen was first discovered. People who have the Rh antigens on their red blood cells are considered Rh-positive (Rh[+]). When Rh antigens are missing from the red blood cell surface, the individual is considered Rh-negative (Rh[−]).

An Rh-negative person will not form anti-Rh antibodies unless he or she has been exposed to the Rh antigen. For this reason, an Rh-negative individual should be given only Rh-negative blood in a transfusion. If he or she is mistakenly given Rh-positive blood, it will stimulate the production of anti-Rh antibodies. A transfusion reaction will not occur after the first such transfusion, because it takes time for the body to start making anti-Rh antibodies. After a

[2]It is not certain why these antibodies form without exposure to red blood cells bearing the foreign antigen. It may be that either the bacteria that invade our bodies or the foods we eat contain a small amount of A and B antigens, enough to stimulate antibody production.

TABLE 11.2 Transfusion Relationships among Blood Types

Blood Types	Antigens on Red Blood Cells	Antibodies in Plasma	Blood Types (RBCs) That Can Be Received in Transfusions	Incidence of Blood Type in United States
A	A	Anti-B	A, O	Caucasian, 40% African American, 27% Asian, 28% Native American, 8%
B	B	Anti-A	B, O	Caucasian, 10% African American, 20% Asian, 27% Native American, 1%
AB	A and B	None	A, B, AB, O	Caucasian, 5% African American, 4% Asian, 5% Native American, 0%
O	None	Anti-A, Anti-B	O	Caucasian, 45% African American, 49% Asian, 40% Native American, 91%

second transfusion of Rh-positive blood, however, the antibodies in the recipient's plasma will react with the antigens on the red blood cells of the donated blood. This reaction may lead to the death of the patient.

The Rh factor can also have medical importance for pregnancies in which the mother is Rh-negative and the fetus is Rh-positive, a situation that may occur if the father is Rh-positive (see Chapter 20; Figure **11.8**). Ordinarily, the maternal and fetal blood supplies do not mix during pregnancy. However, as a result of blood vessel damage, some mixing may occur during a miscarriage or delivery. If the baby's red blood cells, which bear Rh antigens, accidentally pass into the mother's bloodstream, she will produce anti-Rh antibodies. There are usually no ill effects associated with the first introduction of the Rh antigen. However, if antibodies are present in the maternal blood from a previous pregnancy with an Rh-positive child or from a transfusion of Rh-positive blood, the anti-Rh antibodies may pass into the blood of the fetus during a subsequent pregnancy. This transfer can occur because anti-Rh antibodies, unlike red blood cells, can cross the placenta (a structure that forms during pregnancy to allow the exchange of selected substances between the maternal and fetal circulatory systems). These anti-Rh antibodies may destroy the fetus's red blood cells. As a result, the child may be stillborn or very anemic at birth. This condition is called *hemolytic disease of the newborn.*

The incidence of hemolytic disease of the newborn has decreased in recent years due to the development of a means of destroying any Rh-positive fetal cells in an Rh-negative mother's blood supply before they can stimulate the mother's cells to produce her own anti-Rh antibodies. The Rh-positive cells are killed by injecting RhoGAM, a serum containing antibodies against the Rh antigens, at about the seventh month of pregnancy and shortly after delivery if the baby is Rh-positive. Rh antigens are thus prevented from being "set" in the memory of the mother's immune system. The injected antibodies disappear after a few months. Therefore, no antibodies linger to affect the fetus in a subsequent pregnancy.

Blood Donation

We have seen that blood is indeed a life-saving fluid, and someone in the United States or Canada needs donated blood every two seconds. If you are a healthy person at least 17 years old (16 years in some states), weigh at least 110 lbs, and are willing to spend 10 to 20 minutes, you may be eligible to give the gift of life. When you donate you may feel a slight twinge as the needle is inserted, but the procedure is generally painless. Each donation is a pint of blood. The donated plasma is replaced within hours, and the cells are replaced within weeks. The donated blood can be separated into its components: red blood cells to increase the oxygen-carrying capacity of the recipient's blood, platelets to help the recipient's blood clot, and plasma to help the recipient control bleeding.

An Rh⁺ man and an Rh⁻ woman could have an Rh⁺ baby.

Rh⁺ red blood cells

First pregnancy: At birth some of the Rh⁺ blood of the fetus may enter the mother's circulation.

Anti–Rh antibodies

After delivery: The mother forms anti-Rh antibodies over the next few months.

Second pregnancy with an Rh⁺ fetus: anti-Rh antibodies may pass into the fetus's blood, causing its blood cells to burst.

FIGURE 11.8 Rh incompatibility can result when an Rh-negative (Rh⁻) woman is pregnant with an Rh-positive (Rh⁺) baby if the woman has been previously exposed to Rh⁺ blood.

Blood Clotting

When a blood vessel is cut, several responses are triggered to stop the bleeding. To understand the process of clotting, imagine how you might respond if the garden hose you are using springs a leak. Your initial response might be to squeeze the hose in hopes of stopping the water flow. Likewise, the body's immediate response to blood vessel injury is for the vessel to constrict (squeeze shut).

The next response is to plug the hole (Figure **11.9**). Your thumb might do the job on your garden hose; in an injured blood vessel, platelets form a plug that seals the leak. The *platelet plug* is formed when platelets cling to cables of collagen, a protein fiber on the torn blood vessel surface. When the platelets attach to collagen, they swell, form many cellular extensions, and stick together. Platelets also produce a chemical that attracts other platelets to the wound and makes them stick together even more. Aspirin prevents the formation of this chemical and, therefore, inhibits clot formation. For this reason, a daily dose of aspirin is sometimes prescribed to prevent the formation of blood clots that could block blood vessels nourishing heart tissue and thus cause the death of heart cells (a heart attack). It is also why aspirin can cause excessive bleeding.

The next stage in stopping blood loss through a damaged blood vessel is the formation of the clot itself. There are more than 30 steps in the process of clot formation, but here we will describe only the key events. Clot formation begins when clotting factors are released from injured tissue and from platelets. At the site of the wound, the clotting factors convert an inactive blood protein to **prothrombin activator**,[3] which then converts **prothrombin**, a plasma protein produced by the liver, to an active form, **thrombin**. Thrombin then causes a remarkable change in another plasma protein produced by the liver, **fibrinogen**. The altered fibrinogen forms long strands of **fibrin**, a protein that makes a web that traps blood cells and forms a clot. The clot is a barrier that prevents additional blood loss through the wound in the vessel.

[3]Prothrombin activator is an enzyme called prothrombinase.

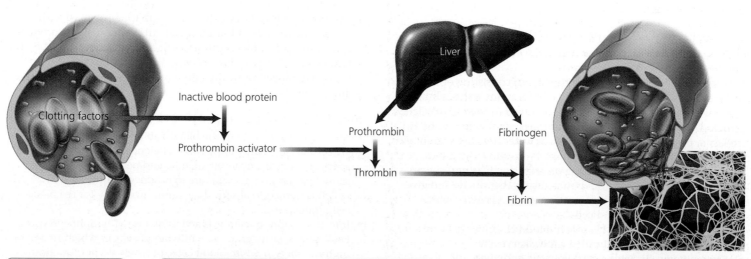

Clotting factors

Inactive blood protein

Prothrombin activator

Liver

Prothrombin

Fibrinogen

Thrombin

Fibrin

Step 1: Injured cells in the walls of the vessels and platelets release clotting factors.

Step 2: Clotting factors convert an inactive blood protein to prothrombin activator.

Step 3: Prothrombin activator converts prothrombin to thrombin.

Step 4: Thrombin converts fibrinogen to fibrin.

Step 5: The fibrin network traps red blood cells and platelets, forming a blood clot.

FIGURE 11.9 Selected steps in the blood-clotting process

If even one of the many factors needed for clotting is lacking, the process can be slowed or completely blocked. Vitamin K is needed for the liver to synthesize prothrombin and three other clotting factors. Thus, without vitamin K, clotting does not occur. We have two sources of vitamin K. One is our diet. Vitamin K is found in leafy green vegetables, tomatoes, and vegetable oils. The second source is bacteria living in our intestines and producing vitamin K, some of which we absorb for our own use. Vitamin K is used rapidly by body tissues, so both sources are needed for proper blood clotting. Antibiotic treatment for serious bacterial infections can kill gastrointestinal bacteria and lead to a vitamin K deficiency in as few as 2 days.

Hemophilia is an inherited condition in which the affected person bleeds excessively owing to a fault in one of the genes involved in producing clotting factors. As noted earlier, there are many steps in the clotting process, and so there are many clotting factors. Although a loss of any of the clotting factors could cause hemophilia, the two most common types of hemophilia are caused by insufficient amounts of clotting factors VIII or IX. Because of the way hemophilia is inherited, the condition usually occurs in males (see Chapter 20). Symptoms appear when the affected child first becomes physically active. Crawling, for instance, causes bruises on the elbows and knees, and cuts tend to bleed longer than is nor-

mal. Excessive internal bleeding can damage nerves or, when it occurs in joints, permanently cripple the hemophiliac.

Treatment for hemophilia involves restoring the missing clotting factor. Bleeding episodes can be controlled with repeated transfusions of fresh plasma or with injections of concentrated clotting factor. Concentrated clotting factor is made by combining the plasma donations of many people. In fact, each injection requires 2000 to 5000 individual donations. Fortunately, two of the clotting factors (factors VIII and IX) are now being manufactured using recombinant DNA technology.

The failure of blood to clot can shorten the life of a person with hemophilia. But in people without hemophilia, the formation of unnecessary blood clots can have much more immediate health consequences because clots can disrupt blood flow. A blood clot lodged in an unbroken blood vessel is called a *thrombus*. A blood clot that drifts through the circulatory system is called an *embolus*. Emboli can drift through the circulatory system until they become stuck in a narrow vessel. When the tiny vessels that nourish the heart or brain become clogged with a clot, the consequences can be severe—a stroke or heart attack, which can be disabling or even fatal. After a wound has healed, clots are normally dissolved by an enzyme called **plasmin**, which is formed from an inactive protein, *plasminogen*. Plasmin dissolves clots by digesting the fibrin strands that form the framework of the clot.

highlighting the concepts

Functions of Blood (p. 205)

- Blood transports vital material to cells and carries wastes away from cells. White blood cells defend against disease. Blood clotting prevents excessive blood loss. Blood also helps regulate body temperature.

Composition of Blood (pp. 205–210)

- Blood is a type of connective tissue that contains formed elements in a liquid (plasma) matrix.
- Plasma is the liquid portion of the blood, consisting of water and certain dissolved components, mostly proteins. (The substances transported by the blood are also dissolved in the plasma. These include nutrients, ions, gases, hormones, and waste products.) Plasma proteins aid in the balance of water flow between blood and cells. These proteins are grouped into three categories: albumins, globulins, or clotting proteins (such as fibrinogen).
- Blood stem cells are undifferentiated cells that divide and give rise to all of the formed elements—namely, platelets, white blood cells, and red blood cells.
- Platelets play an important role in blood clotting. They are fragments of a larger cell called a megakaryocyte.
- White blood cells (leukocytes) help the body fight off disease and help remove wastes, toxins, and damaged cells.
- There are five types of leukocytes: neutrophils, eosinophils, basophils, monocytes, and lymphocytes. Neutrophils are the most abundant and immediately phagocytize foreign microbes. Eosinophils help the body defend against parasitic worms and

play a role in allergic reactions. Basophils can increase the flow of blood by releasing histamines. Monocytes are the largest leukocytes and, after maturing into macrophages, actively fight chronic infections. Lymphocytes take part in body defense responses.

- Red blood cells (erythrocytes) are flexible cells packed with hemoglobin, an oxygen-binding pigment. Red blood cell production is controlled by erythropoietin, a hormone produced by the kidney in response to low oxygen. Worn and dead red blood cells are removed from circulation and broken down in the liver and spleen.

Blood Cell Disorders (pp. 210–212)

- Anemia is a reduction in the blood's ability to carry oxygen. There are several forms, including iron-deficiency anemia; hemolytic anemias, such as sickle-cell anemia; and pernicious anemia, caused by the stomach's failure to produce intrinsic factor, which is needed to absorb the vitamin necessary for red blood cell production.
- Infectious mononucleosis is a viral disease of lymphocytes. Leukemia is a cancer of the white blood cells in which there are high numbers of white blood cells, but they do not function properly to defend against infectious agents.

Blood Types (pp. 212–215)

- Blood types are determined by the presence of certain proteins (antigens) on the surface of red blood cells: the ABO and Rh groups. The plasma contains antibodies against A and B antigens if the antigens are not present on the red blood cells. Antibodies to Rh antigens are formed only after exposure to Rh-positive blood. If blood containing foreign antigens is introduced during a transfusion, a reaction between the antibodies and antigens can cause red blood cells to clump and clog the recipient's bloodstream, which can lead to death.

- Rh incompatibility becomes important to an Rh-negative woman who has been previously exposed to Rh-positive blood and who is pregnant with an Rh-positive fetus. Antibodies to the Rh antigens can cross the placenta and destroy the red blood cells of the fetus; this condition is called hemolytic disease of the newborn.

Blood Clotting (pp. 215–216)

- The prevention of blood loss involves three mechanisms: blood vessel constriction, platelet plug formation, and clotting. Clotting is initiated when platelets and damaged tissue release clotting factors that lead to the production of a chemical called prothrombin activator, which converts the blood protein prothrombin to thrombin. Thrombin then converts the blood protein fibrinogen to fibrin. Strands of fibrin make a mesh that traps red blood cells and forms the clot. Hemophiliacs are missing an important clotting factor and, therefore, bleed excessively.

recognizing key terms

plasma *p. 206*
plasma protein *p. 206*
formed elements *p. 206*
stem cell *p. 206*
platelet *p. 208*
white blood cell *p. 208*
leukocyte *p. 208*

phagocytosis *p. 208*
granulocyte *p. 208*
agranulocyte *p. 208*
neutrophil *p. 208*
eosinophil *p. 208*
basophil *p. 208*
monocyte *p. 208*

lymphocyte *p. 208*
red blood cell *p. 209*
erythrocyte *p. 209*
hemoglobin *p. 209*
erythropoietin *p. 210*
blood type *p. 212*
agglutinate *p. 213*

Rh factor *p. 213*
prothrombin activator *p. 215*
prothrombin *p. 215*
thrombin *p. 215*
fibrinogen *p. 215*
fibrin *p. 215*
plasmin *p. 216*

reviewing the concepts

1. What is plasma? What are its functions? *p. 206*
2. What are the three categories of plasma proteins? *p. 206*
3. List the three types of formed elements, and describe the function of each. *pp. 206–210*
4. Compare the size, structure, and numbers of leukocytes with the size, structure, and numbers of erythrocytes. *pp. 207–209*
5. Leukocytes function in defending the body against foreign invaders. List the five types of white blood cells, and describe the role each plays in body defense. *p. 208*
6. Describe the characteristics of red blood cells that make them specialized for delivering oxygen to the tissues. *p. 209*
7. Describe the function of hemoglobin. *p. 209*
8. Where are red blood cells produced? How is the production of red blood cells controlled? *pp. 209–210*
9. Describe what happens to worn or damaged red blood cells and their hemoglobin. *p. 210*
10. Why would pernicious anemia be treated with regular injections of vitamin B_{12} instead of by dietary supplements of this vitamin? *p. 212*
11. What determines a person's blood type? *pp. 212–214*
12. What happens if a person is given a blood transfusion with blood of an incompatible type? *pp. 212–214*
13. What blood type(s) can a person with type B blood receive? Explain. *pp. 212–214*
14. What is hemolytic disease of the newborn? What causes it? *p. 214*
15. After a blood vessel is cut, what mechanisms prevent excessive blood loss? *p. 215*

16. Describe the steps involved in blood clotting. *pp. 215–216*
17. What is the difference between the blood clotting that occurs after an injury and the clumping that occurs after a mismatched transfusion? *pp. 213, 215–216*
18. Type B blood contains which antibodies?
    a. A
    b. B
    c. both A and B
    d. neither A nor B
19. An important function of white blood cells is
    a. blood clotting.
    b. transportation of oxygen.
    c. fighting infection.
    d. maintaining blood pressure.
20. A condition in which the oxygen-carrying capacity of the blood is low is
    a. infection.
    b. anemia.
    c. leukemia.
    d. a kidney problem.
21. The primary function of red blood cells is to _____.
22. _____ is a protein in red blood cells that transports oxygen.
23. The protein that forms a net that traps red blood cells and platelets and forms blood clots is _____.

1. Erin has leukemia, and her white blood cell count is elevated. Why does Erin have an elevated risk of infection?
2. José is a runner for his college track team from New York City. The championship meet is in Denver, which is called the Mile-High City because of its elevation above sea level. There is less oxygen available for breathing as elevation increases. Because this meet is so important, José plans to arrive in Denver several weeks before the meet. Why? Would you expect José's red blood cell count to be higher or lower than normal when he returns home to New York City, which is at sea level?
3. Indira is a 25-year-old woman who has uterine polyps that cause heavy vaginal bleeding. She complains that she tires easily with physical activity and always feels fatigued. The doctor orders

that a blood test be done to determine what percentage of her blood is red blood cells. Why? Would you expect the percentage to be higher or lower than normal? The doctor suggests that she take iron supplements. Why?
4. Raul is in a car accident and is taken to the emergency room. He has type AB blood. Which blood types can he receive?
5. Elizabeth has type Rh-negative blood. She is pregnant for the second time. What information would the doctor want to know about the first and second children to know whether to expect a problem with this pregnancy?
6. Sarala was given an antibiotic that caused her platelet count to fall. What symptoms would be expected?

The umbilical cord is a lifeline for a growing fetus that connects the fetus to the mother through the placenta. Within the umbilical blood (and blood from the placenta) are blood stem cells that retain the ability to develop into red blood cells, white blood cells, and platelets. There is a growing interest in collecting umbilical cord blood when a baby is born and storing it for future use.

Use at least three reliable sources (books, journals, websites) to answer the following questions. Cite your sources, and explain why you chose them.

1. What are potential uses for stem cells from umbilical cord blood?
2. What are advantages of using umbilical cord blood over a bone marrow transplant as a source of stem cells?
3. Based on what you have learned about umbilical cord blood, do you think that there should be umbilical cord blood banks? Why? If so, do you think that use of the cord blood should be restricted to the family whose infant donated the blood, or should it be made available to anyone?

Additional questions can be found online at the Human Biology Place, www.humanbiology.com.

12

The Cardiovascular and Lymphatic Systems

Cardiovascular System
Blood Vessels
Arteries
Capillaries
Veins
Heart
Two Circuits of Blood Flow
Coronary Circulation
Cardiac Cycle
Internal Conduction System
Electrocardiogram
Blood Pressure
Cardiovascular Disease
High Blood Pressure
Atherosclerosis
Coronary Artery Disease
Heart Attack
Lymphatic System

Health Issue
Cardiovascular Disease and Cigarette Smoking

Health Issue
The Cardiovascular Benefits of Exercise

The cardiovascular system consists of a pump, the heart, and a loop of blood vessels. All the organs of the body require a continuous supply of blood to deliver oxygen and nutrients, and to remove waste. This blood supply is particularly important for the heart—the hardest working muscle in the body. If the blood vessels of the heart become clogged, steps must be taken to restore adequate blood flow.

It was past midnight, and Mya, a 38-year-old air traffic controller, had come to the emergency room because of severe pains in her chest. It was frustrating to her that she had continued to have these symptoms night after night and occasionally during the day for the past week. She was lucky that she did not have to wait for treatment. The doctor gave her supplemental oxygen, ordered some blood tests, and decided to call in a heart specialist.

The specialist performed more tests, including a coronary angiogram (a procedure to examine blood flow through blood vessels) and afterward informed Mya that an important coronary artery was almost completely blocked. The reason for her chest pain—he called it angina—was that the blocked artery was not allowing enough oxygen to be delivered to her heart. He recommended a coronary angioplasty, a procedure that uses a balloon

to stretch open the blockage in the artery and restore the supply of oxygen to the heart muscle; a stent is then inserted into the artery, to keep it from becoming blocked again.

Mya had the angioplasty done. Afterward, during her several-month period of cardiac rehabilitation, she was given a diet and exercise plan that would help reduce the future possibility of heart problems.

In this chapter, you learn about the structure and function of the

heart blood vessels. You also see why Mya was right to be concerned about her chest pains. An understanding of how the heart functions may help you better care for your own and take steps to maintain its health. The chapter also examines the network of vessels and other structures that make up the lymphatic system. Together, the heart and blood vessels and the lymphatic system constitute the circulatory system.

Cardiovascular System

The **cardiovascular system** consists of the **heart**—a muscular pump that contracts rhythmically and provides the force that moves the blood—and the blood vessels—a system of tubules through which blood flows (Figure **12.1**). The blood delivers a continuous supply of oxygen and nutrients to the cells of the body and carries away metabolic waste products so that they cannot poison the cells.

Why is the cardiovascular system so critical to survival? It is the body's transportation network, similar in some ways to the highways within a country. Our bodies are too large and complex for diffusion alone to distribute materials efficiently. The cardiovascular system provides a means for distributing vital chemicals from one part of the body to another quickly enough to sustain life. The cardiovascular system is more than just a passive system of pipelines, however. The heart rate and the diameter of certain blood vessels are continually being adjusted in prompt response to the body's changing needs.

Blood Vessels

Once every minute, or about 1440 times each day, the blood moves through a life-sustaining circuit. The circuit of blood vessels is extensive. Indeed, if all the vessels in an average adult's body were placed end to end, they would stretch about 100,000 km (60,000 mi), long enough to circle the Earth's equator more than twice!

The blood vessels do not form a single long tube. Instead, they are arranged in branching networks. With each circuit through the body, blood is carried away from the heart in *arteries,* which branch to give rise to narrower vessels called *arterioles.* Arterioles lead into networks of microscopic vessels called *capillaries,* which allow the exchange of materials between the blood and body cells. The capillaries eventually merge to form *venules,* which in turn join to form larger tubes called *veins.* The venules and veins return the blood to the heart.

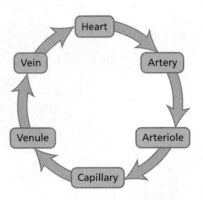

All blood vessels share some common features, but each type also has its own traits and is marvelously adapted for its specific function (Figure **12.2**). The hollow interior of a blood vessel, through which the blood flows, is called the *lumen.* The inner lining that comes into contact with the blood flowing through the lumen is composed of simple squamous epithelium (the flattened, tight-fitting cells we encountered in Chapter 4). This lining, called the endothelium, provides a smooth surface that minimizes friction so that the blood flows easily. The lumen and endothelium are characteristic of all blood vessels.

Arteries

Arteries are muscular tubes that transport blood *away* from the heart, delivering it rapidly to the body tissues. As noted, the innermost layer of an arterial wall is the endothelium. Immediately outside the endothelium is a middle layer that contains elastic fibers and circular layers of smooth muscle (Figure 12.3). The elastic fibers allow an artery to stretch and then return to its original shape. The smooth muscle enables the artery to contract. The outer layer of an arterial wall is a sheath of connective tissue that contains elastic fibers and collagen. This layer adds strength to the arterial wall and anchors the artery to surrounding tissue.

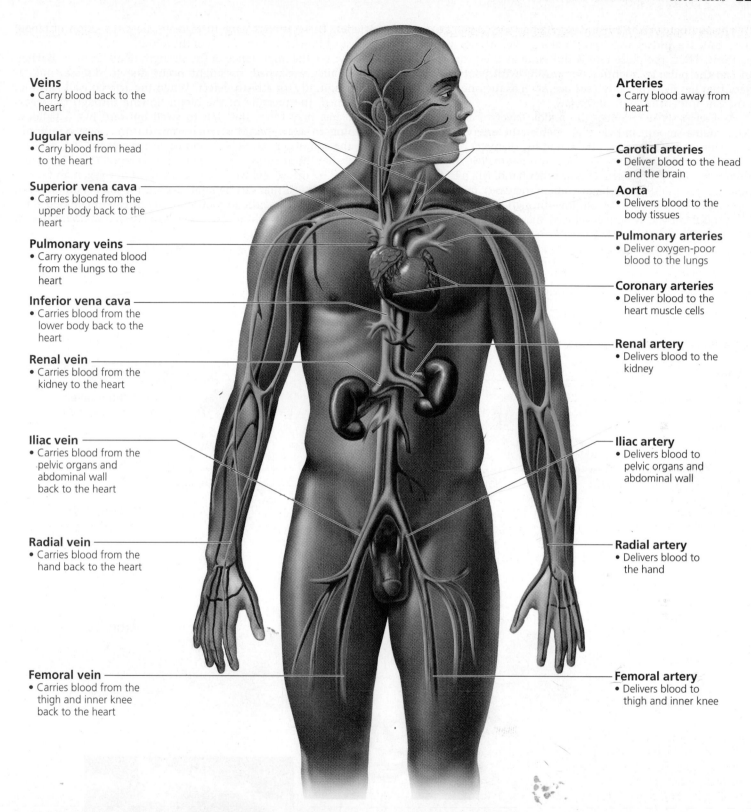

Veins
- Carry blood back to the heart

Jugular veins
- Carry blood from head to the heart

Superior vena cava
- Carries blood from the upper body back to the heart

Pulmonary veins
- Carry oxygenated blood from the lungs to the heart

Inferior vena cava
- Carries blood from the lower body back to the heart

Renal vein
- Carries blood from the kidney to the heart

Iliac vein
- Carries blood from the pelvic organs and abdominal wall back to the heart

Radial vein
- Carries blood from the hand back to the heart

Femoral vein
- Carries blood from the thigh and inner knee back to the heart

Arteries
- Carry blood away from heart

Carotid arteries
- Deliver blood to the head and the brain

Aorta
- Delivers blood to the body tissues

Pulmonary arteries
- Deliver oxygen-poor blood to the lungs

Coronary arteries
- Deliver blood to the heart muscle cells

Renal artery
- Delivers blood to the kidney

Iliac artery
- Delivers blood to pelvic organs and abdominal wall

Radial artery
- Delivers blood to the hand

Femoral artery
- Delivers blood to thigh and inner knee

FIGURE 12.1 A diagrammatic view of the cardiovascular system (heart and blood vessels). Throughout this chapter, red indicates blood that is high in oxygen. Blue indicates blood that is low in oxygen.

The elastic fibers in the middle layer of an artery have two important functions: (1) They help the artery tolerate the pressure shock caused by blood surging into it when the heart contracts; and (2) they help maintain a relatively even pressure within the artery, despite large changes in the volume of blood passing through it. Consider, for instance, what happens when the heart contracts and sends blood into the **aorta**, the body's main artery. Each beat of the heart causes 70 ml (about one-fourth cup) of blood to pound against the wall of the aorta like a tidal wave. A rigid pipe could not withstand the repeated pressure surges, but the elastic walls of the artery stretch with each wave of blood and return to their original size when the surge has moved past; this results in a continuous stream of blood rather than intermittent waves.

The alternate expansion and recoil of arteries create a pressure wave, called a **pulse**, that moves along the arteries with each heartbeat. Thus, the pulse rate is the same as the heart rate. You can feel the pulse by slightly compressing with your fingers any artery that lies near the body's surface, such as the one at the wrist or the one under the angle of the jaw.

As previously mentioned, the middle layer of an artery wall also contains smooth muscle that enables the artery to contract. When this circular muscle contracts and the diameter of the lumen becomes narrower, a process called *vasoconstriction,* blood flow through the artery is reduced. On the other hand, when the smooth muscle relaxes and the arterial lumen increases in diameter, a process called *vasodilation,* blood flow through the artery increases. The smooth muscle is best developed in small- to medium-sized

arteries. These arteries serve to regulate the distribution of blood, adjusting flow to suit the needs of the body.

We see the importance of the strength of an artery wall when it becomes weakened, as might occur due to disease, inflammation, injury, or a birth defect. When the arterial wall becomes weakened, the pressure of the blood flowing through the weakened area may cause the wall to swell outward like a balloon, forming an *aneurysm*. Most aneurysms do not cause symptoms, but the condition can be threatening just the same. The primary risk is that the aneurysm will burst, causing blood loss. The tissues serviced by that vessel will then be deprived of oxygen and nutrients, a situation that can be fatal. Even if the aneurysm does not rupture, it can cause the formation of life-threatening blood clots. A clot can break free from the site of formation and float through

FIGURE 12.2 The structure of blood vessels

the circulatory system until it lodges in a small vessel, where it can block blood flow and cause tissue death beyond that point. In some cases, an aneurysm can be repaired surgically. The risk of blood clots and aneurysms is exacerbated by the nicotine in tobacco products. (See the Health Issue essay, *Cardiovascular Disease and Cigarette Smoking*.)

The smallest arteries, called **arterioles**, are barely visible to the unaided eye. Their walls have the same three layers found in arteries; but the middle layer is primarily smooth muscle with only a few elastic fibers, and the outer layer is much thinner.

Arterioles have two extremely important regulatory roles. First, they are the prime controllers of blood pressure, which is the pressure of blood against the vessel walls (discussed later in this chapter). When the muscle in arteriole walls contracts, blood pressure increases. The greater the number of arterioles contracted, the higher the blood pressure. Relaxation of arteriole walls lowers blood pressure. Second, they serve as gatekeepers to the capillary networks. A capillary network can be open or closed, depending on whether the smooth muscle in the walls of the arteriole leading to it allows blood through. In this way, arterioles can regulate the amount of blood sent to cells based on those cell's immediate needs. Arterioles are constantly responding to input from hormones, the nervous system, and local conditions, modifying blood pressure and flow to meet the body's changing needs.

Capillaries

Capillaries are microscopic blood vessels that connect arterioles and venules. The capillaries are well suited to their primary function: the exchange of materials between the blood and the body cells (Figure **12.3**). Capillary walls are only one cell layer thick, and so substances move easily between the blood and the fluid surrounding the cells outside the capillary. The plasma membrane of the capillary's endothelial cells is an effective and selective barrier that determines which substances can cross. Some substances that cross the capillary walls do not pass *through* the endothelial cells. Instead, these substances filter through small slits *between* adjacent endothelial cells. The slits between the cells are just large enough for some fluids and small dissolved molecules to pass through.

The design of the capillary networks allows blood flow through capillaries to be adjusted to deliver the necessary amount of oxygen and nutrients to meet the needs of particular regions of the body. The network of capillaries servicing a particular area is called a **capillary bed** (Figure **12.4**). The number of capillaries in a bed generally ranges from 10 to 100, depending on the type of tissue. A ring of smooth muscle called a **precapillary sphincter** surrounds the capillary where it branches off the arteriole and regulates blood flow into it.

The precapillary sphincters act as valves that open and close the capillary beds. Contraction of the precapillary sphincter squeezes the opening to the capillary shut. For instance, while you are resting on the beach after finishing a picnic lunch, the capillary beds servicing the digestive organs will be open, and nutrients from the food will be absorbed. If you dive into the water and start swimming, the capillary beds of the digestive organs will close down, and those in the skeletal muscles will open.

Collectively, the capillaries provide a tremendous surface area for the rapid exchange of materials between body and blood. Capillary beds bring capillaries very close to nearly every cell. Your fingernails provide windows that allow you to appreciate the

(a) Substances are exchanged between the blood and tissue fluid across the plasma membrane of the capillary or through slits between capillary cells.

(b) At the arterial end of a capillary, blood pressure forces fluid out of the capillary to the fluid surrounding tissue cells. At the venous end, fluid is drawn back into the capillary by osmotic pressure.

(c) Capillaries are so narrow that red blood cells must travel through them in single file.

FIGURE 12.3 Capillaries are the sites where materials are exchanged between the blood and the body cells.

efficiency with which capillary networks reach all parts of the body. You may have noticed that the tissue beneath a fingernail normally has a pink tinge. The color results from blood flowing through numerous capillaries there. Gentle pressure on the nail causes the tissue to turn white as the blood is pushed from those capillaries.

A capillary is so narrow that red blood cells must squeeze through single file. Despite their size, there are so many capillaries that their *combined* cross-sectional area is enormous, much greater

(a)

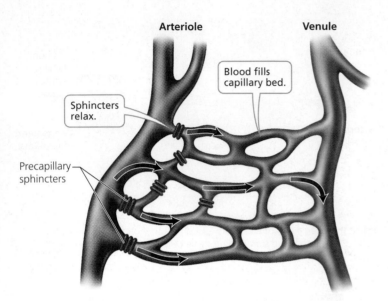

Arteriole

Venule

Blood fills capillary bed.

Sphincters relax.

Precapillary sphincters

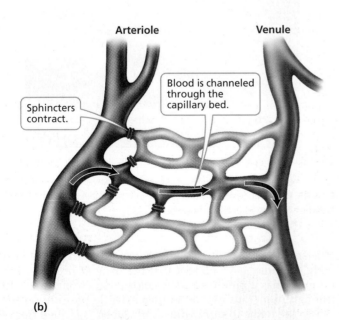

Arteriole

Venule

Sphincters contract.

Blood is channeled through the capillary bed.

(b)

FIGURE 12.4 (a) A capillary bed is a network of capillaries. (b) The entrance to each capillary (the arterial side) is guarded by a ring of muscle called a precapillary sphincter. Blood flow through a capillary bed is regulated according to the body's metabolic needs.

than that of the arteries or veins. Because of the large cross-sectional area of the capillaries, the blood flows much more slowly through them than through the arteries or veins. The slower rate of flow in the capillaries provides more time for the exchange of materials (Figure **12.5**).

Veins

After the capillary bed, capillaries merge to form the smallest kind of vein, a **venule.** Venules then join to form larger veins. **Veins** are blood vessels that return the blood to the heart.

Although veins share some structural features with arteries, there are also some important differences. The walls of veins have the same three layers found in arterial walls, but the walls of veins are thinner and the lumens of veins are larger than those of arteries of equal size (see Figure 12.2). The thin walls and large lumens allow veins to hold a large volume of blood. Indeed, veins serve as blood reservoirs, holding up to 65% of the body's total blood supply.

The same amount of blood that is pumped out of the heart must be conducted back to the heart, but it must be moved through the veins without assistance from the high pressure generated by the heart's contractions. In the head and neck, of course, gravity helps move blood toward the heart. But how is it possible to move blood against the force of gravity—from the foot back to the heart, for instance (unless, by chance, your foot was in your mouth)?

Three mechanisms move blood from lower parts of the body toward the heart:

1. **Valves in veins prevent backflow of blood.** Veins often contain valves that act as one-way turnstiles, allowing blood to move toward the heart but preventing it from flowing backward. These valves are pockets of connective tissue projecting from the lining of the vein, as shown in Figure **12.6a**.

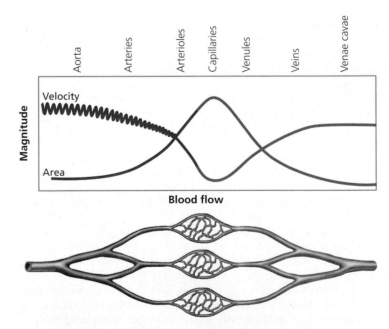

FIGURE 12.5 The capillaries are so numerous that their total cross-sectional area is much greater than that of arteries or veins. Thus, blood pressure drops and blood flows more slowly as it passes through a capillary bed. The slower rate of flow allows time for the exchange of materials between the blood and the tissues.

Valve
closed

Muscle contraction
squeezes the vein,
pushing blood
through the open
valve toward the
heart.

Valve
open

Skeletal muscles
relax, and blood
fills the valves
and closes them.

Valve
closed

(a)

(b)   **Relaxed calf
muscles**

**Contracted calf
muscles**

FIGURE 12.6 (a) A micrograph of a vein showing a valve. (b) Pocketlike valves on the inner surface of veins
assist the return of blood to the heart against gravity by preventing backflow.

A simple experiment can demonstrate the effectiveness of venous valves. Allow your hand to hang by your side until the veins on the back of your hand become distended. Place two fingertips from the other hand at the end of one of the distended veins nearest to the knuckles. Then, leaving one fingertip pressed on the end of the vein, move the other toward the wrist, pressing firmly and squeezing the blood from the vein. Lift the fingertip near the knuckle and notice that blood immediately fills the vein. Repeat the procedure, but this time lift the fingertip near the wrist. You will see the vein remains flattened, because the valves prevent the backward flow of blood.

2. **Contraction of skeletal muscle squeezes veins.** Virtually every time a skeletal muscle contracts, it squeezes nearby veins. This pressure pushes blood past the valves toward the heart. The mechanism propelling the blood is similar to the one that causes toothpaste to squirt out of the uncapped end of the tube regardless of where the tube is squeezed; valves in veins ensure that blood flows in only one direction. When skeletal muscles relax, any blood that moves backward fills the valves. As the valves fill with blood, they extend further into the lumen of the vein, closing the vein and preventing the flow of blood from reversing direction (Figure 12.6b). Thus, the skeletal muscles are always squeezing the veins and driving blood toward the heart.

3. **Breathing causes pressure changes that move blood toward the heart.** The thoracic (chest) cavity increases in size when we inhale (see Chapter 14). The expansion reduces pressure within the thoracic cavity and at the same time increases pressure in the abdominal cavity. Blood naturally moves toward regions of lower pressure. Thus, the reduced pressure in the thoracic cavity that comes with each breath

pulls blood back toward the heart. In addition, the increased pressure in the abdominal cavity squeezes veins, also forcing blood back toward the heart.

Heart

The heart is about the size of a fist, but it is an incredible muscular pump that generates the force needed to circulate blood. It beats about 72 times a minute, every hour of every day—although this rate varies with age, physical fitness, and current physical exertion. To appreciate the work done by the heart, alternately clench and relax a fist 70 times a minute. How many minutes does it take before the muscles of your hand are too tired to continue? In contrast, the healthy heart does not fatigue. It beats more than 100,000 times each day, which adds up to about 2 billion beats over a lifetime. The volume of blood pumped by the heart is equally remarkable. It pumps slightly less than 5 liters (10 pt) of blood a minute through its chambers, which adds up to more than 9400 liters (2500 gal) per day.

The heart has three layers, each one contributing to the heart's ability to function as a pump. The wall of the heart, called the **myocardium**, is mostly cardiac muscle tissue. The myocardium's contractions are responsible for the heart's incredible pumping action. The **endocardium** is a thin lining in the cavities of the heart. By reducing friction, the endocardium's smooth surface lessens the resistance to blood flow through the heart. The **pericardium** is a thick, fibrous sac that holds the heart in the center of the chest (thoracic) cavity and slides over the surface of the heart without hampering its movements, even when they are vigorous.

Although the heart appears to be a single structure, it actually has two halves, with the right and left halves functioning as two separate pumps. As we will see shortly, the right side of the heart pumps blood to the lungs, where it picks up oxygen. The left side pumps the blood to the body cells. The two pumps are physically separated by a partition called a **septum.** Each half of the heart consists of two chambers: an upper chamber, called an **atrium** (plural, atria), and a lower chamber, called a **ventricle** (Figure **12.7**). The two atria function as receiving chambers for the blood returning to the heart. The two ventricles function as the main pumps of the heart. Contraction of the ventricles forces blood out of the heart under

Q *When the ventricles contract, which valves would open and which valves would close?*

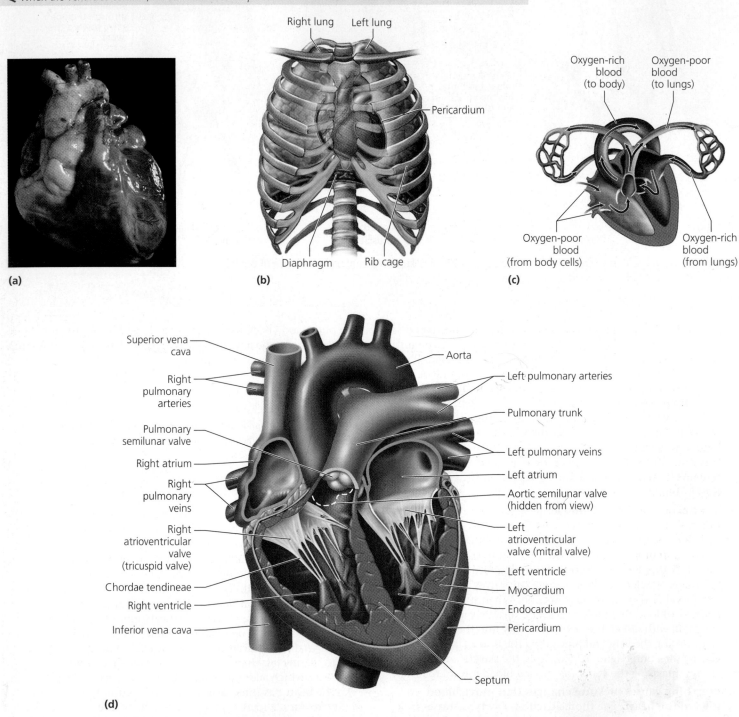

FIGURE 12.7 (a) The human heart. (b) The heart is located in the thoracic (chest) cavity. (c) Blood flows through the heart from the atria to the ventricles. (d) This diagram of a human heart shows the four chambers, the major vessels connecting to the heart, and the two pairs of heart valves.

A *The semilunar valves would open and the AV valves would close.*

Cardiovascular Disease and Cigarette Smoking

When we think about the hazards of tobacco smoke, lung cancer generally leaps to mind. But the increased risk of cardiovascular (heart and blood vessel) disease is even more significant. Each year, cardiovascular disease kills many more people than does lung cancer, and smokers have a twofold to threefold increase in the risk of heart disease (Figure **12.A**). The American Heart Association estimates that about 25% of all fatal heart attacks are caused by cigarette smoke. This translates to roughly 200,000 heart attacks a year in the United States that could have been prevented by not smoking.

Nicotine and carbon monoxide in cigarette smoke stress the heart and blood vessels in many ways. Nicotine makes the heart beat faster and constricts blood vessels, raising blood pressure. In addition, nicotine makes platelets, the cell fragments responsible for blood clotting, stick together, increasing the risk of forming abnormal blood clots. The resulting clots may break loose from the site where they form and travel through the bloodstream until they lodge in a small vessel and block the blood flow. These blockages may result in a heart attack or stroke.

The amount of carbon monoxide in cigarette smoke is 1600 ppm (parts per million), which greatly exceeds the 10 ppm considered dangerous in industry. Furthermore, carbon monoxide from smoking a cigarette lingers in the bloodstream for up to 6 hours. You may recall from Chapter 11 that carbon monoxide is a poison that prevents red blood cells from transporting oxygen. In fact, carbon monoxide from smoking a cigarette lowers the oxygen-carrying capacity of the blood by about 12%, reducing oxygen delivery to every part of the body, including the brain and heart. Thus, the heart must work harder to deliver oxygen to the cells. The diminished oxygen supply to the brain can impair judgment, vision, and attentiveness to sounds. For these reasons, smoking can be hazardous for drivers.

A less immediate but no less important way that smoking leads to cardiovascular disease is by increasing atherosclerosis, a condition in which lipid deposits, primarily composed of cholesterol, form in the walls of blood vessels and restrict the flow of blood. Smoking influences atherosclerosis in two ways. One is by decreasing the levels of protective cholesterol-transport particles, called HDLs, that carry cholesterol to the liver, perhaps even removing cholesterol from cells, so that it can be eliminated from the body. With fewer HDLs, more cholesterol begins to clog the arteries. A second way that smoking promotes cholesterol deposits is by raising blood pressure. The elevated blood pressure causes rapid, turbulent blood flow that damages the walls of the arteries, making them more susceptible to cholesterol deposit. The cholesterol deposits cause inflammation, which leads to atherosclerosis. The narrowing of blood vessels caused by atherosclerosis leads to starvation of tissue downstream and an increase in blood pressure. When atherosclerotic deposits form in the arteries that supply blood to the heart, as they often do, the blood supply to the heart may be reduced or shut down completely, causing heart cells to die.

The cardiovascular system benefits from quitting smoking within five years. In regard to heart disease, 61% of the full benefit of quitting smoking is gained within 5 years. And, 42% of the full benefit of reduced risk of stroke is gained within 5 years.

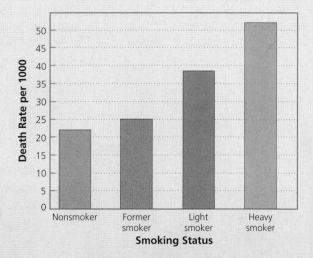

FIGURE 12.A Death rates due to heart disease among nonsmokers and smokers. Notice that the death rate from heart disease increases with the number of cigarettes smoked per day. People who smoke over a pack per day (heavy smokers) have more than twice the risk of death due to heart disease than do people who have never smoked. In any case, a smoker who successfully quits is much less likely to die of heart disease than if the smoking habit continues.

great pressure. When we think about the work of the heart, we are in fact thinking about the work of the ventricles. It should not be surprising, then, that the ventricles are much larger chambers than the atria and have thicker, more muscular walls.

Two pairs of valves ensure that the blood flows in only one direction through the heart. The first pair is the **atrioventricular (AV) valves,** each leading from an atrium to a ventricle, as shown in Figure **12.8**. The AV valves are connective tissue flaps, called cusps, anchored to the wall of the ventricle by strings of connective tissue called the *chordae tendineae*—the heartstrings. These strings prevent the AV valves from flapping back into the atria under the pressure developed when the ventricles contract. The AV valve on the right side of the heart has three flaps and is called the *tricuspid valve*. The AV valve on the left side of the heart has two flaps and is called the *bicuspid,* or *mitral, valve.*

Each of the second pair of valves, the **semilunar valves,** is located between a ventricle and its connecting artery—either the aorta or the pulmonary artery. The cusps of the semilunar valves are small pockets of tissue attached to the inner wall of the respective artery. When the pressure in the arteries becomes greater than the pressure in the ventricles, these valves fill with blood in a manner similar to a parachute filling with air. In this way, the semilunar valves prevent the backflow of blood into the ventricles from the aorta or pulmonary artery.

Two Circuits of Blood Flow

As we mentioned, the left and right sides of the heart function as two separate pumps, each circulating the blood through a different route, as shown in Figure **12.9**. Note that in both circuits the blood moves through the arteries, arterioles, capillaries, and venules before returning to the heart via the veins. The right side of the heart pumps blood through the **pulmonary circuit,** which transports blood to and from the lungs. The left side of the heart pumps blood through the **systemic circuit,** which transports blood to and from body tissues. This arrangement prevents oxygenated blood (blood rich in oxygen) from mixing with blood that is low in oxygen.

The pulmonary circuit begins in the right atrium, as veins return oxygen-poor blood from the systemic circuit. (You can trace the flow of blood through the heart in the pulmonary and systemic circuits in Figure 12.9 as you read the following description.) The blood then moves from the right atrium to the right ventricle. Contraction of the right ventricle pumps poorly oxygenated blood to the lungs through the pulmonary trunk (main pulmonary artery), which divides to form the left and right *pulmonary arteries*. In the lungs, oxygen diffuses into the blood, and carbon dioxide diffuses out. The now oxygen-rich blood is delivered to the left atrium through four *pulmonary veins,* two from each lung. (Note that the pulmonary circulation is an *exception* to the general rule that arteries carry oxygen-rich blood and veins carry oxygen-poor blood. Exactly the opposite is true of vessels in the pulmonary circulation.) The pathway of blood pumped through the pulmonary circuit by the right side of the heart is

Right atrium $\longrightarrow$ AV valve (tricuspid) $\longrightarrow$
Right ventricle $\longrightarrow$ Pulmonary semilunar valve $\longrightarrow$
Pulmonary trunk $\longrightarrow$ Pulmonary arteries $\longrightarrow$ Lungs $\longrightarrow$
Pulmonary veins $\longrightarrow$ Left atrium

The systemic circuit begins when oxygen-rich blood enters the left atrium (see Figure 12.9). Blood then flows to the left ventricle. When the left ventricle contracts, oxygenated blood is pushed through the largest artery in the body, the aorta. The aorta arches over the top of the heart and gives rise to the smaller arteries that eventually feed the capillary beds of the body tissues. The venous system collects the oxygen-depleted blood and eventually culminates in veins that return the blood to the right atrium. These veins are the *superior vena cava,* which delivers blood from regions above the heart, and the *inferior vena cava,* which returns blood from regions below the heart. Thus, the pathway of blood through the systemic circuit pumped by the left side of the heart is

Left atrium $\longrightarrow$ AV (bicuspid or mitral) valve $\longrightarrow$
Left ventricle $\longrightarrow$ Aortic semilunar valve $\longrightarrow$ Aorta $\longrightarrow$
Body tissues $\longrightarrow$ Inferior vena cava or superior
vena cava $\longrightarrow$ Right atrium

The familiar sounds of the heart, which are often described as "lub-dup," are associated with the closing of the valves. The first heart sound ("lub") is produced by the turbulent blood flow when

Atrioventricular (AV) valves are located between each atrium and ventricle.

Semilunar valves are located between each ventricle and its artery.

FIGURE 12.8 The valves of the heart keep blood flowing in one direction.

the AV valves snap shut as the ventricles begin to contract. The higher-pitched second heart sound ("dup") is produced by the turbulent blood flow when closure of the semilunar valves and the beginning of ventricular relaxation occur.

Heart murmurs, which are swooshing heart sounds other than lub-dup, are created by disturbed blood flow. Although heart murmurs are sometimes heard in normal, healthy people, they can also indicate a heart problem. For instance, malfunctioning valves often disturb blood flow through the heart, causing the swishing or gurgling sounds of heart murmurs. Several conditions can cause valves to malfunction. In some cases, thickening of the valves narrows the opening and impedes blood flow. In other cases, the valves do not close properly and, therefore, allow the backflow of blood. In either case, the heart is strained because it must work harder to move the blood.

Coronary Circulation

Cells of the heart muscle themselves obtain little nourishment from blood flowing through the heart's chambers. Instead, an extensive network of vessels, known as the **coronary circulation**, services the tissues of the heart. The first two arteries that branch off the aorta are the **coronary arteries** (Figure **12.10**). These arteries give rise to numerous branches, ensuring that the heart receives a rich supply of oxygen and nutrients. After passing through the capillary beds that nourish the heart tissue, blood enters cardiac veins and eventually flows into the right atrium.

(a)

(b)

FIGURE 12.9 Circuits of blood flow. The right side of the heart pumps blood through the pulmonary circuit, which carries blood to and from the lungs. The left side of the heart pumps blood through the systemic circuit, which conducts blood to and from the body tissues.

FIGURE 12.10 Coronary circulation. (a) The coronary vessels deliver a rich supply of oxygen and nutrients to the heart muscle cells and remove the metabolic wastes. (b) This cast of the coronary blood vessels reveals the complexity of the coronary circuit.

Cardiac Cycle

Although the two sides of the heart pump blood through different circuits, they work in tandem. The two atria contract simultaneously, and then the two ventricles contract simultaneously.

We see, then, that a heartbeat is not a single event. Each beat involves contraction, which is called **systole** (*sis*-to-lee) and relaxation, which is called **diastole** (di-*as*-to-lee). All the events associated with the flow of blood through the heart chambers during a single heartbeat are collectively called the **cardiac cycle**, as illustrated in Figure **12.11**. First, all chambers relax (diastole) and blood passes through the atria and enters the ventricles. When the ventricles are about 70% filled, the atria contract (atrial systole) and push their contents into the ventricles. The atria then relax (atrial diastole) and the ventricles begin their contraction phase (ventricular systole). Upon completion of this contraction, the whole heart again relaxes. If we were to add the contraction time of the heart during a day and compare it with the relaxation time during a day, the heart's workday might turn out to be equivalent to yours. In 24 hours, the heart spends a total of about 8 hours working (contracting) and 16 hours relaxing. However, unlike your workday, the heart's day is divided into repeating cycles of work and relaxation.

Internal Conduction System

If a human heart is removed, as in a transplant operation, and placed in a dish, it will continue to beat, keeping a lonely and useless rhythm until its tissues die. In fact, if a few cardiac muscle cells are grown in the laboratory, they, too, will beat on their own, each twitch a reminder of the critical role the intact organ plays. Clearly, then, the heart muscle does not require outside stimulation to beat. Instead, the tendency is intrinsic, within the heart muscle itself.

Another remarkable observation has been made of heart muscle cells grown in a laboratory dish. Although isolated heart cells twitch independently of each other, if two cells should touch, they will begin beating in unison. This, too, is an inherent property of the cells, but it is partly due to the type of connections between heart muscle cells. The cell membranes of adjacent cardiac muscle cells interweave with one another at specialized junctions called intercalated disks. Cell junctions in the *intercalated disks* mechanically and electrically couple the connected cells. Adjacent cells are held together so tightly that they do not rip apart during contraction but instead transmit the pull of contraction from one cell to the next. At the same time, the junctions permit electrical communication between adjacent cells, allowing the electrical events responsible for contraction to spread rapidly over the heart by passing from cell to cell. Yet even though heart cells contract automatically, they still need some outside control to contract at the proper rate.

The tempo of the heartbeat is set by a cluster of specialized cardiac muscle cells, called the **sinoatrial (SA) node**, located in the right atrium near the junction of the superior vena cava (Figure **12.12**). Because the SA node sends out the impulses that initiate each heartbeat, it is often referred to as the **pacemaker**.

Early diastole
Atria and ventricles are relaxed and fill passively

Ventricular systole
Both ventricles contract
• The right ventricle forces blood into the pulmonary trunk
• The left ventricle forces blood into the aorta

Later diastole
Ventricles are still relaxing and filling passively

Atrial systole
Both atria contract and force blood into ventricles

FIGURE 12.11 The cardiac cycle—all of the events associated with the flow of blood through the heart during each heartbeat. The atria contract together and the ventricles contract together. Red indicates blood high in oxygen. Blue indicates blood low in oxygen.

SA node

AV node

Bundle of
conducting
muscle cells

Purkinje
fibers

SA node   AV node

SA node initiation

• **Atria contract**

• **Signal reaches
AV node**

• **Signal conducted to
Purkinje fibers**

• **Atria fully contracted**

Ventricles contract

FIGURE 12.12 The conduction system of the heart consists of specialized cardiac muscle cells that speed electrical signals through the heart. The sinoatrial (SA) node serves as the heart's internal pacemaker that determines the heart rate. Electrical signals from the SA node spread through the walls of the atria, causing them to contract. The signals then stimulate the atrioventricular (AV) node, which in turn sends the signals along the AV bundle to its forks and finally to the many Purkinje fibers that penetrate the ventricular walls. The Purkinje fibers distribute the signals to the walls of the ventricles, causing them to contract. Electrical activity is indicated by the color green in the bottom row of drawings.

About 70 to 80 times a minute, the SA node sends out an electrical signal that spreads through the muscle cells of the atria, causing them to contract. The signal reaches another cluster of specialized muscle cells called the **atrioventricular (AV) node**, located in the partition between the two atria, and stimulates it. The AV node then relays the stimulus by means of a bundle of specialized muscle fibers, called the *atrioventricular bundle,* that runs along the wall between the ventricles. The bundle forks into right and left branches and then divides into many other specialized cardiac muscle cells, called *Purkinje fibers,* that penetrate the walls of the ventricles. The rapid spread of the impulse through the ventricles ensures that they contract smoothly.

When the heart's conduction system is faulty, cells may begin to contract independently. Such cellular independence can result in rapid, irregular contractions of the ventricles, called *ventricular*

fibrillation, which render the ventricles useless as pumps and stop circulation. With the brain no longer receiving the blood it needs to function, death will occur unless an effective heartbeat is restored quickly. A method for stopping ventricular fibrillation is to subject the heart to an electric shock; in many cases, the SA node will once again begin to function normally. Although costly, an implantable defibrillator (a device that electrically shocks the heart) can provide a life-saving "jump start" when needed.

Problems with the conduction system of the heart can sometimes be treated with an artificial pacemaker, a small device implanted just below the skin that monitors the heart rate and rhythm and responds to abnormalities if they occur. For instance, if the heart rate becomes too slow, the pacemaker will send an electrical stimulus to the heart through an electrode.

The pace or rhythm of the heartbeat changes constantly in response to activity or excitement. The autonomic nervous system and certain hormones make the necessary adjustments so that the heart rate suits the body's needs. During times of stress, the sympathetic nervous system increases the rate and force of heart contractions. As part of this response, the adrenal medulla produces the hormone epinephrine, which can prolong the sympathetic nervous system's effects. In contrast, when restful conditions prevail, the parasympathetic nervous system dampens heart activity, in keeping with the body's more modest metabolic needs.

Electrocardiogram

The electrical events that spread through the heart with each heartbeat actually travel throughout the body, because body fluids are good conductors. Electrodes placed on the body surface can detect these electrical events, transmitting them so that they cause deflections (movements) in the tracing made by a recording device. An **electrocardiogram** (**ECG** or **EKG**) is an image of the electrical activities of the heart, generated by such a recording device.

A typical ECG consists of three distinguishable deflection waves, as shown in Figure **12.13**). The first wave, called the P wave, accompanies the spread of the electrical signal over the atria and the atrial contraction that follows. The next wave, the QRS wave, reflects the spread of the electrical signal over the ventricles and ventricular contraction. The third wave, the T wave, represents the return of the ventricles to the electrical state that preceded contraction (ventricular repolarization). Because the pattern and timing of these waves are remarkably consistent in a healthy heart, abnormal patterns can indicate heart problems.

Blood Pressure

We hear a lot about blood pressure, usually when someone worries about having a high blood pressure reading or brags about having a low one. **Blood pressure** is the force exerted by the blood against the walls of the blood vessels. When the ventricles contract, they push blood into the arteries under great pressure. This pressure is the driving force that moves blood through the body, but it also pushes outward against vessel walls. Ideally, a person's blood pressure should be great enough to circulate the blood but not so great that it stresses the blood vessels and the heart, as we see later in the chapter. Many factors influence blood pressure, including gender, age, time of day, physical activity, stress, and lifestyle.

Blood pressure in the arteries varies predictably during each heartbeat. It is highest during the contraction of the ventricles (ventricular systole), when blood is being forced into the arteries. In a typical, healthy adult, the optimal **systolic pressure**, the highest

(a)

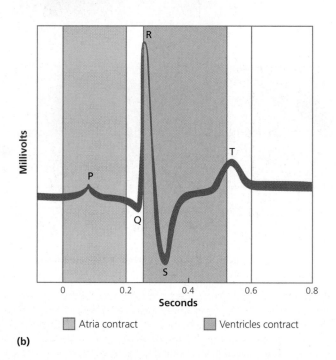

(b)

FIGURE 12.13 (a) A person having an electrocardiogram (ECG) recorded. (b) The electrical activity that accompanies each heartbeat can be visualized in an ECG tracing. The P wave is generated as the electrical signals from the SA node spread across the atria and cause them to contract. The QRS wave represents the spread of the signal through the ventricles and ventricular contraction. The T wave occurs as the ventricles recover and return to the electrical state that preceded contraction.

pressure in the artery during each heartbeat, is 110–120 mm of mercury (mm Hg).[1] Blood pressure is lowest when the ventricles are relaxing (diastole). In a healthy adult, the optimal lowest pressure, or **diastolic pressure**, is 70–80 mm Hg. A person's blood pressure is usually expressed as two values—the systolic followed by the diastolic. For instance, optimal adult blood pressure is said to be less than 120/80. (Do you know what your blood pressure is?)

Blood pressure is measured with a device called a *sphygmomanometer* (sfig-mo-mah-nom'-e-ter), which consists of an

[1]Pressure is measured as the height to which that pressure could push a column of mercury (Hg).

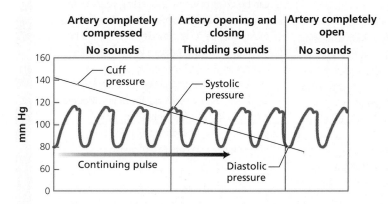

FIGURE 12.14 Blood pressure is measured with a sphygmomanometer, which consists of an inflatable cuff and a means of measuring the pressure within the cuff. The cuff is placed around the upper arm and inflated so that it compresses the brachial artery. The pressure in the cuff is slowly released, and as it descends it reaches a point where blood is able to spurt through the constricted artery only at the moments of highest blood pressure. This pressure, at which "tapping" sounds are first heard, is the systolic pressure, the blood pressure when the heart is contracting. As the pressure in the cuff continues to drop, a point is reached where the sounds disappear. The blood is now flowing continuously through the brachial artery. The pressure in the cuff when the sounds first disappear is the diastolic pressure, the blood pressure when the heart is relaxing.

inflatable cuff that wraps around the upper arm and is attached to a device that can measure the pressure within the cuff. Figure **12.14** shows how a manually operated sphygmomanometer uses the easily measured pressure of the air pumped into the cuff to measure the blood pressure in the brachial artery (which runs along the inner surface of the arm).

Cardiovascular Disease

Cardiovascular disease is the single biggest killer of men and women in the United States. It affects slightly more men than women be-cause, until menopause, women receive some natural protection from cardiovascular disease through the action of the sex hormone estrogen. Ironically, although slightly fewer women than men have heart attacks, women who do have heart attacks are twice as likely to die within the following weeks as are men. Because heart attacks are commonly thought of as a male problem, women and their physicians often fail to recognize the symptoms, thus delaying treatments that could be lifesaving. (See the Health Issue essay, *The Cardiovascular Benefits of Exercise.*)

High Blood Pressure

High blood pressure, or *hypertension,* is often called the silent killer. It is *silent* because it does not produce any telltale symptoms. It is a *killer* because it can cause fatal problems, usually involving the heart, brain, blood vessels, or kidneys. Hypertension damages the heart in a number of ways, primarily by causing the heart to work harder to keep the blood moving. In response, the heart muscle thickens, and the heart enlarges. The enlarged heart works less efficiently and has difficulty keeping up with the body's needs. At the same time, the increased workload increases the heart's need for oxygen and nutrients. If these cannot be delivered rapidly enough, a heart attack can result.

High blood pressure can also damage the kidneys, reducing the blood flow through them. In response, the kidneys make matters worse by secreting renin, a chemical that leads to further increases in blood pressure in an ever-escalating cycle.

Although about 90% of the cases of hypertension have no *known* cause, many contributing factors have been identified. When a cause can be identified, the kidneys are sometimes to blame. If kidneys have an impaired ability to handle sodium, the resulting fluid retention increases blood pressure by increasing blood volume. In other cases of hypertension, the sympathetic nervous system reacts too strongly to stress, constricting the blood vessels and increasing heart rate. Thus, more blood per minute is pumped through vessels that provide a greater resistance to flow.

Most physicians agree that a blood pressure of 160/90 is high and should be treated (see Figure **12.15**). But uncertainty clouds

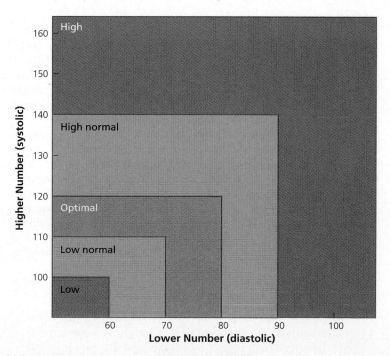

FIGURE 12.15 Values of blood pressure in adults

The Cardiovascular Benefits of Exercise

What would you say if you were told there is a simple way to reduce your risk of heart attack, stroke, diabetes, and cancer while controlling your weight, strengthening your bones, relieving anxiety and tension, and improving your memory? "Impossible!" you might say. "What's the catch?" There is none. This key to life is regular aerobic exercise that uses large muscle groups rhythmically and continuously and elevates heart rate and breathing rate for at least 15 to 20 minutes.

Although exercise has many beneficial effects on the body, here we will consider only the benefits to the cardiovascular system. Exercise benefits the heart by making it a more efficient pump, thus reducing its workload. A well-exercised heart beats more slowly than the heart of a sedentary person—during both exercise and rest. The lower heart rate gives the heart more time to rest between beats. Yet at the same time, the well-exercised heart pumps more blood with each beat.

Exercise also increases the oxygen supply to the heart muscle by widening the coronary arteries, thereby increasing blood flow to the heart. Moreover, because the capillary beds within the heart muscle become more extensive with regular exercise, oxygen and nutrients can be delivered to the heart cells and wastes can be removed more quickly.

Furthermore, exercise helps to ensure continuous blood flow to the heart. One way it accomplishes this benefit is by increasing the body's ability to dissolve blood clots that can lead to heart attacks or strokes. Exercise stimulates the release of a natural enzyme that prevents blood clotting and remains effective for as long as $1\frac{1}{2}$ hours after you stop exercising. Besides this, exercise stimulates the development of collateral circulation, that is, additional blood vessels that provide alternative pathways for blood flow. As a result, blood flows continuously through the heart, even if one vessel becomes blocked.

Exercise affects the blood in ways that allow more oxygen to be delivered to the cells. The amount of hemoglobin, the oxygen-binding protein in red blood cells, increases. In addition, the blood volume and the numbers of red blood cells increase.

Exercise lowers the risk of coronary artery disease by lowering blood pressure and by shifting the balance of lipids in the blood. High-density lipoproteins (HDLs), which are the "good" form of cholesterol-carrying particles that remove cholesterol from the arterial walls, increase with exercise.

To reap cardiovascular benefits, you must exercise hard enough, long enough, and often enough. The exercise must be vigorous enough to elevate your heart rate to the so-called target zone, which is between 70% and 85% of your maximal attainable heart rate. The target zone can be determined by subtracting your age in years from 222 beats per minute. The exercise must continue for at least 20 minutes and be performed at least 3 days a week, with no more than 2 days between sessions.

Doing *something* active on a regular basis can improve your quality of life. Moderate activity helps you feel better emotionally and physically. The difference has been likened to traveling first class instead of coach.

---

the treatment issue when the person's diastolic pressure is between 80 and 89, the higher end of normal. Although drug treatment may help in borderline cases, it usually must be continued for life. A diagnosis of high blood pressure may influence other aspects of a person's life, such as life insurance premiums. So, sometimes, only lifestyle changes are recommended for high normal values of blood pressure.

When the diagnosis of hypertension is clear, one or more of various kinds of drugs can be prescribed, each type combating a different mechanism that contributes to high blood pressure. The diuretics, for instance, decrease blood volume by increasing the excretion of sodium and fluids, thereby reducing blood pressure by reducing blood volume. Other drugs cause the blood vessels to dilate (become wider), reducing hypertension in instances where is it caused by overly constricted vessels.

A number of changes in lifestyle are recommended to treat or prevent hypertension.

1. **Control weight.** Maintaining normal body weight can help control blood pressure. Many overweight people with high blood pressure benefit from shedding just a few extra pounds. The best way to lose weight is to eat a moderate, balanced diet; reduce fat intake; and increase physical activity.

2. **Exercise regularly.** Aerobic exercise, such as brisk walking, jogging, swimming, or cycling, performed for at least 20 minutes at least three times a week, helps lower blood pressure and keep it low.

3. **Do not smoke.** Cigarette smoke contains nicotine, a drug that increases heart rate and constricts blood vessels; both of those effects increase blood pressure.

4. **Limit dietary salt.** Some people with hypertension can lower their blood pressure by lowering the amount of salt in their diet. Salt can affect fluid retention and, therefore, blood volume.

Atherosclerosis

Atherosclerosis (*ather-*, yellow, fatty deposit; *sclerosis*, a hardening) is a buildup of fatty substances in the walls of arteries, fueled by an inflammatory response. In some cases, the deposits narrow the artery (Figure **12.16**). Such narrowing causes problems because it reduces blood flow through the vessel, choking off the vital supply of oxygen and nutrients to the tissues served by that vessel. But contrary to the beliefs held just a few years ago, atherosclerosis is more than just a plumbing problem, akin to a clog in a passive pipeline.

Lumen narrowed

Blood clot

(a) A normal artery

(b) An artery partially obstructed with plaque

(c) An artery completely obstructed with plaque and a blood clot

FIGURE 12.16 Atherosclerosis, a low-level inflammatory response in the wall of an artery, is associated with the formation of fat-filled plaques. Plaque can obstruct blood flow through the artery, thus depriving the cells that would be fed life-sustaining blood by the artery. Plaque can also rupture, causing a blood clot to form. The clot may then completely clog the vessel and cause the death of tissue downstream.

The inflammatory response thought to cause atherosclerosis is the same process that wards off infection when you scrape your knee (discussed in Chapter 13). In this case, it begins with an injury to the wall of an artery. The injury may be caused by some kind of bloodborne irritant (such as the chemicals inhaled in cigarette smoke), by cholesterol deposits in the artery lining, or by infection. Perhaps the excessively rapid or turbulent blood flow caused by high blood pressure can also produce such arterial damage. The damaged cells begin to pick up low-density lipoproteins (LDLs), the so-called bad form of cholesterol. This accumulation of LDLs is most likely to occur when the LDL concentration in the blood is high. The LDLs undergo chemical changes that stimulate the cells of the arterial lining to enlist the body's defense responses: inflammatory chemicals and defense cells. Growth factors produced by defense cells stimulate smooth muscle cells in the arterial wall to divide, thereby thickening the wall. Other defense cells engulf LDLs, become enlarged, and form fatty streaks on the arterial lining. As these defense cells continue to scavenge lipids, the fatty streak increases in size and forms plaque, a bumpy, fatty layer in the artery wall. The plaque can bulge into the artery channel, blocking the blood flow, or it can expand outward into the artery wall. Although the plaque has a fibrous cap that initially keeps pieces from breaking away, the fat-filled cells secrete inflammatory substances that weaken the cap. A small break in the cap can allow the plaque to rupture, which triggers the formation of a blood clot. In any case, restriction of the blood flow can starve and kill the cells lying downstream. Such an occurrence in the heart (leading to a heart attack) or brain (leading to a stroke) can be fatal. Because plaques do not necessarily bulge into the artery and cause symptoms of atherosclerosis before they rupture, heart attacks often occur in patients without previous symptoms.

There are several approaches to treating atherosclerosis. A healthy lifestyle promotes healthy arteries, so control your weight, engage in regular aerobic exercise, and eat a heart-healthy diet (see Chapter 15a). Medications to treat atherosclerosis include drugs to lower blood pressure, drugs to reduce blood cholesterol levels, and drugs to prevent unwanted blood clot formation. Some physicians recommend a daily dose of a low-strength aspirin, because aspirin reduces the risk of blood clot formation.

stop and think

C-reactive protein (CRP) is an inflammatory chemical released by injured cells in the artery lining. Why might CRP prove to be a better predictor of atherosclerosis than blood cholesterol level?

Coronary Artery Disease

Coronary artery disease is a condition in which the fatty deposits associated with atherosclerosis form within coronary arteries, the arteries that nourish the heart muscle. Coronary artery disease is the underlying cause of the vast majority of heart attacks.

A temporary shortage of oxygen to the heart is accompanied by angina pectoris—chest pain, usually experienced in the center of the chest or slightly to the left. The name *angina* comes from the Latin word *angere*, meaning "to strangle." The name is apt, since the pain of angina is often described as suffocating, viselike, or choking. Typically, the pain begins during physical exertion or emotional stress, when the demands on the heart are increased and the blood flow to the heart muscle can no longer meet the needs. The pain stops after a period of rest. Angina serves as a warning that part of the heart is receiving insufficient blood through the coronary arteries, but it does not cause permanent damage to the heart. The warning should be taken seriously, however, because each year up to 15% of those people who have angina later die from a heart attack.

Although coronary artery disease is usually diagnosed from the symptoms of angina and a physical examination, a procedure called *coronary angiography* may be used to spot areas in the coronary arteries that have become narrowed by atherosclerosis. In this procedure, a contrast dye that is visible in x-rays is released in the heart, allowing the coronary vessels to be seen on film. A catheter (a slender, flexible tube) is inserted into an artery in the arm or leg and then threaded through the blood vessels until it reaches the heart. The dye is then squirted into the openings of the coronary arteries, and its movement through the arteries is recorded in a series of high-speed x-rays.

Coronary artery disease can be treated with medicines or with surgery. Among the medicines commonly used are some that dilate

FIGURE 12.17 Balloon angioplasty opens a partially blocked artery.

(widen) blood vessels, such as nitroglycerin. Certain other drugs specifically dilate only the coronary arteries. Wider blood vessels make it easier for the heart to pump blood through the circuit. When the coronary arteries dilate, more blood is delivered to the heart muscle. Also used are drugs that dampen the heart's response to stimulation from the sympathetic nervous system, thus decreasing its need for oxygen.

Two surgical operations for treating coronary artery disease are balloon angioplasty and coronary artery bypass. In *angioplasty,* the channel of an artery narrowed by soft, fatty plaque is widened by inflating a tough, plastic balloon inside the artery (Figure **12.17**). First the tiny, uninflated balloon is attached to the end of a catheter and inserted through an artery in the arm or upper thigh. It is then pushed to the blocked spot in a coronary artery; high-speed x-rays are used to track its progress. After it reaches the blockage, the balloon is inflated under pressure, stretching the artery and pressing the soft plaque against the wall to widen the lumen.

After angioplasty, physicians commonly insert a metal-mesh tube called a stent into the treated arteries. The stent prevents the arteries from collapsing and keeps loose pieces of plaque from being swept into the bloodstream. Although stents boost the percentage of arteries that stay open, they sometimes trigger an inflammatory response, and some arteries become clogged again, even with a stent in place. One kind of stent slowly releases sirolimus, a drug that blocks cell division, preventing scar tissue from forming and blocking the artery again.

A *coronary bypass* is a procedure in which a segment of a leg vein is removed and grafted so that it provides an alternate pathway that bypasses a point of obstruction between the aorta and a coronary artery (Figure **12.18**).

FIGURE 12.18 In coronary bypass surgery, a section of a leg vein is removed. One end of the vein is attached to the heart's main artery, the aorta, and the other to a coronary artery, bypassing the obstructed region. The grafted vein provides a pathway through which blood can reach the previously deprived region of heart muscle.

Heart Attack

In a heart attack, technically known as a *myocardial infarction,* a part of the heart muscle dies because of an insufficient blood supply. (*Myocardial* refers to heart muscle; *infarct* refers to dead tissue.) Heart muscle cells begin to die if they are cut off from their essential blood supply for more than 2 hours. Depending on the extent of damage, the effects of a heart attack can spread quickly

stop and think

In a coronary bypass operation, why is it important for the surgeon to insert the grafted vein in the correct orientation? What would happen if the piece of vein were inserted backward?

throughout the body: as a result of a heart attack, the brain receives insufficient oxygen; the lungs fill with fluid; and the kidneys fail. Within a short time, white blood cells swarm in to remove the damaged heart tissue. Then—if the individual survives—over the next 8 weeks or so, scar tissue replaces the dead cardiac muscle (Figure **12.19**). Because scar tissue cannot contract, part of the heart permanently loses its pumping ability.

Heart attacks can be caused in many ways. The most common type of heart attack is a coronary thrombosis, which means the attack is caused by a blood clot blocking a coronary artery. Coronary thrombosis is unlikely to happen unless the artery already contains plaques of atherosclerosis, as occurs in coronary artery disease. In some instances, the blood clot is formed elsewhere in the body but is swept along in the bloodstream until it lodges in a coronary artery. In other instances of heart attacks, the blockage is temporary, caused by constriction of a coronary artery, called a coronary artery spasm.

Chest pain is a common indication that a heart attack is in progress, especially in men. Unlike angina, the pain is not necessarily brought on by activity, and it doesn't go away with rest. In some cases, the victim feels a severe, crushing pain that begins in the center of the chest and often spreads down the inside of one or both arms (most commonly the left one) as well as up to the neck and shoulders. Although the pain is usually severe enough to cause the victim to stop whatever he or she is doing, it is not always so strong that it is recognized as a sign of heart attack. A heart attack may also cause nausea and dizziness, which can prompt the victim to interpret the symptoms as an upset stomach. Oddly, persons who experience severe pain may be the lucky ones, because they are more likely to realize they are having a heart attack and seek immediate help. Doubt about the cause of the symptoms is unfortunate because it often delays treatment, and treatment within the first few hours after a heart attack can make the difference between life and death.

If a large enough section of heart muscle is damaged by a heart attack, the heart may not be able to continue pumping blood to the lungs and the rest of the body at an adequate rate. A condition in which the heart is no longer an efficient pump is known as *heart*

failure. Symptoms of heart failure include shortness of breath, fatigue, weakness, and fluid accumulation in the lungs or limbs. Although the heart can never be restored to its former health, the symptoms of heart failure can be treated with drugs. For instance, digitalis can increase the strength of heart contractions, and diuretics reduce fluid accumulation, thus lessening the heart's workload. Other drugs relax constricted arteries, thereby reducing resistance to blood flow and lowering the blood pressure. Together, these drugs help a weakened heart pump more efficiently.

Sometimes, drugs and bypass surgery cannot halt progressive heart failure. In this case, heart transplant surgery may provide hope for some patients, but generally only for those younger than 80 years of age. First, a donor heart must be found whose tissue is an acceptable match with that of the recipient. During transplant surgery, a heart-lung machine takes over the circulation while the weakened heart is removed, and the new heart is sewn in place. The patient is then treated with drugs that lessen the chances of organ rejection (discussed in Chapter 13).

Lymphatic System

The **lymphatic system** consists of **lymph**, which is a fluid identical to interstitial fluid (the fluid that bathes all the cells of the body); of **lymphatic vessels** through which the lymph flows; and of various lymphoid tissues and organs scattered throughout the body.

The functions of the lymphatic system are as diverse as they are essential to life:

1. **Return excess interstitial fluid to the bloodstream.** The lymphatic system maintains blood volume by returning excess interstitial fluid to the bloodstream. Only 85% to 90% of the fluid that leaves the blood capillaries and bathes the body tissues as interstitial fluid is reabsorbed by the capillaries. The rest of that fluid (as much as 3 liters a day) is absorbed by the lymphatic system and then returned to the circulatory system. This job is important. If the surplus interstitial fluid were not drained, it would cause the tissue to swell; the volume of blood would drop to potentially fatal levels; and the blood would become too viscous (thick) for the heart to pump.

    A dramatic example of the importance of returning fluid to the blood is provided by *elephantiasis,* a condition in which parasitic worms block lymphatic vessels (Figure **12.20**). The blockage can cause a substantial buildup of fluid in the affected body region, followed by the growth of connective tissue. Elephantiasis is so named because it results in massive swelling and the darkening and thickening of the skin in the affected region, making the region resemble the skin of an elephant. Elephantiasis is a tropical disease that is transmitted by mosquitoes.

2. **Transport products of fat digestion from the small intestine to the bloodstream.** The products of fat digestion are too large to be absorbed into the capillaries in the small intestine. Instead, these products enter a lymphatic vessel, called a lacteal, and travel in the lymphatic system to be returned to the blood circulatory system.

3. **Help defend against disease-causing organisms.** The lymphatic system helps protect against disease and cancer. We will learn more about its role in body defense in Chapter 13.

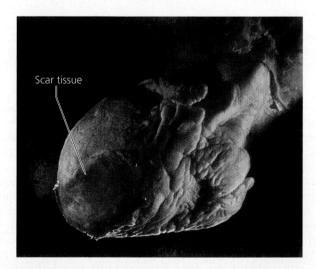

Scar tissue

FIGURE 12.19 The ravages of a prior heart attack are visible as scar tissue at the bottom of this lifeless heart. Scar tissue replaced cardiac muscle when the blood supply to the heart muscle was shut down. Because scar tissue cannot contract, that part of the life-sustaining pump becomes ineffective.

FIGURE 12.20 The leg of a person with elephantiasis. In this condition, parasitic worms plug lymphatic vessels and prevent the return of fluid from the tissues to the circulatory system.

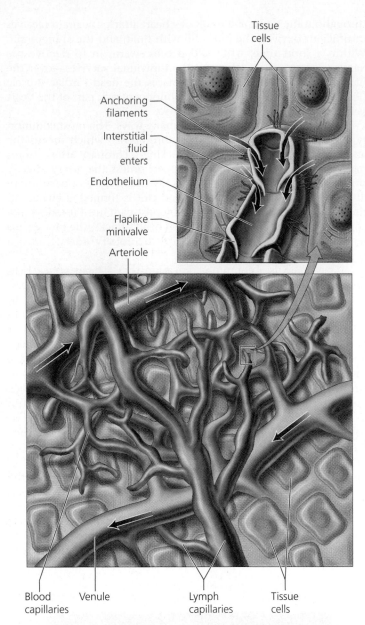

FIGURE 12.21 The lymphatic capillaries are microscopic, blind-ended tubules through which surplus tissue fluid enters the lymphatic system to be returned to the bloodstream.

The structure of the lymphatic vessels is central to their ability to absorb the interstitial fluid not carried away by capillaries. The extra fluid enters a branching network of microscopic tubules, called *lymphatic capillaries,* that penetrate between the cells and the capillaries in almost every tissue of the body (except teeth, bones, bone marrow, and the central nervous system; Figure **12.21**). The lymphatic capillaries differ from the blood capillaries in two ways. First, unlike blood capillaries, which form continuous networks, lymphatic capillaries end blindly, like the fingers of a glove. In essence, lymphatic capillaries serve as drainage tubes. Fluid enters at the "fingertips" and moves through the system in only one direction. Second, lymphatic capillaries are much more permeable than blood capillaries, a feature that is crucial to their ability to absorb the digestive products of fats as well as excess interstitial fluid. The lymphatic capillaries drain into larger lymphatic vessels, which merge into progressively larger tubes with thicker walls. Lymph is eventually returned to the blood through one of two large ducts that join with the large veins at the base of the neck.

With no pump to drive it, lymph flows slowly through the lymphatic vessels, propelled by the same forces that move blood through the veins. That is, the contractions of nearby skeletal muscles compress the lymphatic vessels, pushing the lymph along. One-way valves similar to those in veins prevent backflow. And as with the flow of blood back to the heart from the lower part of the body, pressure changes in the thorax (chest cavity) that accompany breathing also help pull the lymph upward from the lower body. Gravity assists the flow from the upper body.

The lymphatic vessels are studded with **lymph nodes,** small bean-shaped structures that cleanse the lymph as it slowly filters through. The lymph nodes contain macrophages and lymphocytes, white blood cells that play an essential role in the body's defense system. Macrophages engulf bacteria, cancer cells, and other debris, clearing them from the lymph. Lymphocytes serve as the surveillance squad of the immune system. They are continuously on the lookout for specific disease-causing invaders,

as we will see in Chapter 13. When lymphocytes detect bacteria or viruses, the lymphocytes are stimulated to divide. The increased number of lymphocytes causes the lymph nodes to swell. Thus, swollen and painful lymph nodes (commonly called "glands") are a symptom of infection.

Besides the lymph nodes, there are several other *lymphoid organs* (Figure **12.22**). Among these are the *tonsils,* which form a ring around the entrance to the throat, where they help protect against disease organisms that are inhaled or swallowed. The **thymus gland,** located in the chest, is another lymphoid organ. It plays its part during early childhood by helping the maturation of certain lymphocytes that protect us from specific disease-causing organisms. On the left side of the abdominal region is the largest lymphoid organ, the **spleen.** Besides containing a reservoir of lymphocytes, the spleen clears the blood of old and damaged

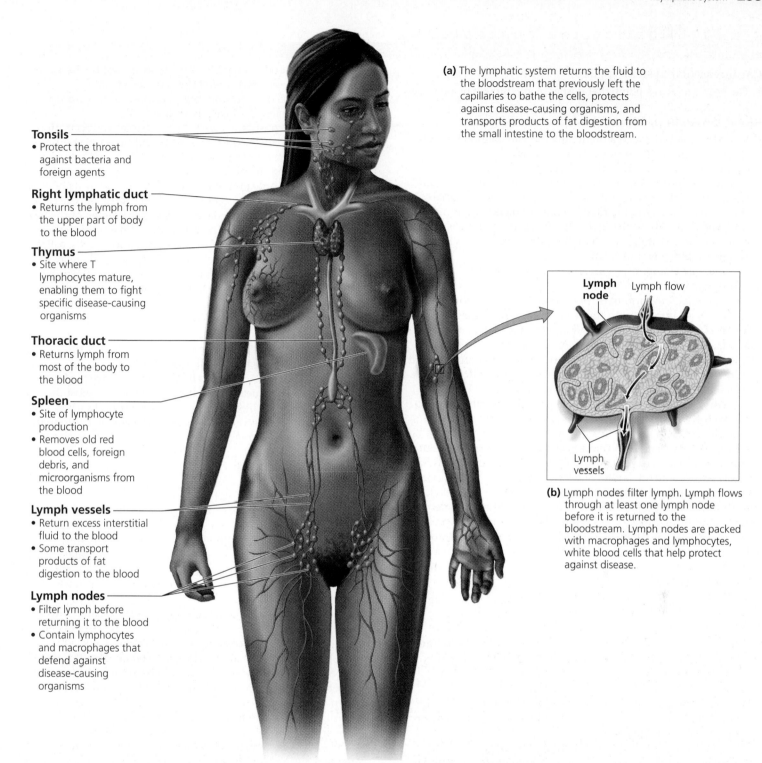

(a) The lymphatic system returns the fluid to the bloodstream that previously left the capillaries to bathe the cells, protects against disease-causing organisms, and transports products of fat digestion from the small intestine to the bloodstream.

Tonsils
• Protect the throat against bacteria and foreign agents

Right lymphatic duct
• Returns the lymph from the upper part of body to the blood

Thymus
• Site where T lymphocytes mature, enabling them to fight specific disease-causing organisms

Thoracic duct
• Returns lymph from most of the body to the blood

Spleen
• Site of lymphocyte production
• Removes old red blood cells, foreign debris, and microorganisms from the blood

Lymph vessels
• Return excess interstitial fluid to the blood
• Some transport products of fat digestion to the blood

Lymph nodes
• Filter lymph before returning it to the blood
• Contain lymphocytes and macrophages that defend against disease-causing organisms

Lymph node   Lymph flow

Lymph vessels

(b) Lymph nodes filter lymph. Lymph flows through at least one lymph node before it is returned to the bloodstream. Lymph nodes are packed with macrophages and lymphocytes, white blood cells that help protect against disease.

FIGURE 12.22 The lymphatic system is a system of lymphatic vessels containing a clear fluid, called lymph, and various lymphatic tissues and organs located throughout the body. Green indicates lymphatic vessels and nodes.

red blood cells and platelets. Finally, isolated clusters of lymph nodules along the small intestine, known as *Peyer's patches*, keep bacteria from breaching the intestinal wall. The *red bone marrow*, where white blood cells and other formed elements are produced, is a lymphoid organ found in the ends of long bones, ribs, sternum, and vertebrae.

stop and think

Cancer cells that break loose from their original site in a process called metastasis have easy access to the highly permeable lymphatic capillaries. The lymphatic vessels then provide a route by which the cancer cells may spread to nearly every part of the body. Why are the lymph nodes often examined to determine whether cancer has spread? Why are the lymph nodes near the original cancer site often removed?

highlighting the concepts

Cardiovascular System (p. 220)

- The heart serves as a pump that pushes blood through blood vessels.

Blood Vessels (pp. 220–225)

- Blood circulates through a branching network of blood vessels in a path that travels from the heart to arteries to arterioles to capillaries to venules to veins and then back to the heart.
- Arteries are elastic, muscular tubes that carry blood away from the heart. By stretching and then returning to their original shape, they withstand the high pressure of blood as it is pumped from the heart. These changes help maintain a relatively even blood pressure within the arteries despite large changes in the volume of blood within them.
- The pressure change along an artery as it expands and returns to its original size is called a pulse.
- Arteries branch to form narrower tubules called arterioles. Arterioles are important in the regulation of blood pressure, and they regulate blood flow through capillary beds.
- The exchange of materials between the blood and tissues takes place across the thin walls of capillaries. Capillaries are arranged in highly branched networks that provide a tremendous surface area for the exchange. Each network of capillaries is called a capillary bed. Rings of muscle called precapillary sphincters determine whether blood flows into a capillary bed or is channeled through it.
- Capillaries merge to form venules; and these, in turn, merge to form veins, which conduct blood back to the heart. Blood is returned to the heart against gravity by nearby skeletal muscles that contract and push the blood along within the veins. Valves within the veins prevent blood from flowing backward when the skeletal muscles are relaxed. Pressure differences generated by breathing also help draw blood toward the heart from the lower torso.

Heart (pp. 225–233)

- Every minute, the heart beats about 72 times and moves slightly less than 5 liters (10 pt) of blood through its chambers.
- Most of the wall of the heart is composed of cardiac muscle and is called the myocardium. The endocardium is a thin inner lining. The heart is enclosed in a fibrous sac called the pericardium, which allows the heart to beat while still confining it near the midline of the thoracic cavity.
- The right and left halves of the heart function as two separate pumps. Each side consists of two chambers: an upper chamber called the atrium and a lower chamber called the ventricle. The smaller, thin-walled atria function primarily as receiving chambers that accept blood returning to the heart and pump it a short distance to the ventricles. When the larger, thick-walled ventricles contract, they push blood through the arteries to all parts of the body.
- Blood circulates in one direction through the heart due to the action of two pairs of valves. The atrioventricular (AV) valves are located between each atrium and ventricle. The semilunar valves are located between each ventricle and its connecting artery. The heart sounds, lub-dup, are caused by blood turbulence associated with the closing of the heart valves.
- The right side of the heart pumps blood to the lungs through a loop of vessels called the pulmonary circuit. The left side of the heart pumps blood to all parts of the body except the lungs through a loop of vessels called the systemic circuit.
- The heart has its own network of vessels, called the coronary circuit, that services the heart tissue itself.
- Each heartbeat consists of contraction (systole) and relaxation (diastole). The atria contract in unison, and then the ventricles do the same. The events associated with each heartbeat are collectively called the cardiac cycle.
- The rhythmic contraction of the heart is produced by its internal conduction system. A cluster of specialized cardiac muscle cells, called the sinoatrial (SA) node, usually sets the tempo of the heartbeat and is therefore called the pacemaker. When the electrical signal reaches another cluster of specialized muscle cells, called the atrioventricular (AV) node, the stimulus is quickly relayed along the atrioventricular bundle that runs through the wall between the two ventricles and then fans out into the ventricular walls through the Purkinje fibers.
- The rate of heartbeat changes constantly to suit the body's level of activity.
- An electrocardiogram (ECG or EKG) is a recording of the electrical events associated with each heartbeat.
- Blood pressure, the force created by the heart to drive the blood around the body, is measured as the force of blood against the walls of blood vessels. The blood pressure in an artery peaks when a ventricle contracts. This is called the systolic pressure. In contrast, the lowest blood pressure of each cardiac cycle, the diastolic pressure, occurs while the heart is relaxing between contractions. Blood pressure is measured with a device called a sphygmomanometer.

Cardiovascular Disease (pp. 233–237)

- Cardiovascular diseases are those that affect the heart and blood vessels.
- Hypertension (high blood pressure) is called a silent killer because it does not always produce symptoms and can have fatal consequences, involving the heart, brain, blood vessels, or kidneys. As a result of hypertension, the heart enlarges, but it works less efficiently.
- Atherosclerosis is an inflammatory response associated with a buildup of fatty deposits within artery walls. The fatty material is covered with a fibrous cap and is called plaque. The plaque can bulge into the artery channel, restricting blood flow. Plaque that does not bulge into the artery may still be vulnerable to rupture, triggering blood clot formation that can block blood flow.
- When the vessel affected by atherosclerosis is a coronary artery that supplies blood to heart tissues, the condition is known as coronary artery disease. A temporary reduction in blood supplied to the heart is accompanied by chest pain, called angina pectoris. Angina is a warning of a heart problem, but it does not cause permanent damage to the heart.
- A heart attack (myocardial infarction) is the death of a region of heart muscle. In a surviving patient, the dead cells are gradually replaced by scar tissue. A heart attack may be caused by blocked blood flow in a coronary artery due to a blood clot or atherosclerosis. Another cause of a heart attack is a coronary artery spasm.
- In heart failure, the heart becomes an inefficient pump.

Lymphatic System (pp. 237–239)

- The lymphatic system consists of lymph, lymphatic vessels, lymphoid tissue, and lymphoid organs.

- Three vital functions of the lymphatic system are to return interstitial fluid to the bloodstream, to transport products of fat digestion from the digestive system to the bloodstream, and to defend the body against disease-causing organisms or abnormal cells.
- Tissue fluid enters lymphatic capillaries—microscopic tubules that end blindly and are more permeable than blood capillaries. The fluid, then called lymph, is moved along larger lymphatic vessels by contraction of nearby skeletal muscles. The lymphatic vessels have valves to prevent the backflow of lymph.
- Lymph nodes filter lymph and contain cells that actively defend against disease-causing organisms.
- Lymphoid organs include the red bone marrow, lymph nodes, tonsils, thymus gland, spleen, and Peyer's patches of the small intestine.

recognizing key terms

cardiovascular system p. 220
heart p. 220
artery p. 220
aorta p. 221
pulse p. 222
arteriole p. 223
capillary p. 223
capillary bed p. 223
precapillary sphincter p. 223
venule p. 224
vein p. 224

myocardium p. 225
endocardium p. 225
pericardium p. 225
septum p. 226
atrium p. 226
ventricle p. 226
atrioventricular (AV) valve p. 228
semilunar valves p. 228
pulmonary circuit p. 228
systemic circuit p. 228

coronary circulation p. 229
coronary arteries p. 229
systole p. 230
diastole p. 230
cardiac cycle p. 230
sinoatrial (SA) node p. 230
pacemaker p. 230
atrioventricular (AV) node p. 231
electrocardiogram (ECG or EKG) p. 232

blood pressure p. 232
systolic pressure p. 232
diastolic pressure p. 232
lymphatic system p. 237
lymph p. 237
lymphatic vessel p. 237
lymph nodes p. 238
thymus gland p. 238
spleen p. 238

reviewing the concepts

1. Trace the flow of blood from the heart and back to it by naming, in order, the general types of vessels through which the blood flows. p. 220
2. What is a pulse? p. 222
3. What is an aneurysm? Why is it dangerous? pp. 222–223
4. What are two important functions of arterioles? p. 223
5. What determines whether blood flows through any particular capillary bed? p. 223
6. Compare the structure of arteries, capillaries, and veins. Explain how the structure is suited to the function of each type of vessel. pp. 220–225
7. Explain how blood is returned to the heart from the lower torso against the force of gravity. pp. 224–225
8. Describe the structure of the heart valves. Explain how they function. p. 228
9. Describe the structure of the heart. Explain how it functions as two separate pumps. pp. 225–229
10. Trace the path of blood from the left ventricle to the left atrium, naming each major vessel associated with the heart and the heart chambers in the correct sequence. pp. 228–229
11. Describe the cardiac cycle. p. 230
12. Explain how clusters or bundles of specialized cardiac muscle cells coordinate the contraction associated with each heartbeat. pp. 230–232
13. What is hypertension? In what ways does it damage the body? p. 233
14. What is atherosclerosis? Why is it harmful? How does it develop? pp. 234–235
15. Explain the relationships between coronary artery disease, angina pectoris, and heart attack. pp. 235–237
16. What is a heart attack? What are the common causes? pp. 236–237
17. List three important functions of the lymphatic system. p. 237
18. Compare the structure of lymphatic capillaries with the structure of blood capillaries. How does the structure of lymphatic capillaries allow them to absorb tissue fluid? p. 238

19. What is the function of lymph nodes? p. 238
20. The semilunar valves prevent the backflow of blood from the
    a. arteries to the ventricles.
    b. veins to the atria.
    c. ventricles to the atria.
    d. arteries to the atria.
21. If you cut all the nerves to the heart but kept the heart alive,
    a. the heart would stop beating.
    b. the heart would continue beating.
    c. only systole would occur.
    d. only diastole would occur.

For questions 22 and 23, imagine that you have been miniaturized and are riding through the circulatory system using a red blood cell as a life raft.

22. You are in the big toe traveling toward the heart. The last vessel you pass through before entering the heart is the
    a. aorta.
    b. inferior vena cava.
    c. coronary artery.
    d. pulmonary vein.
23. You are nearly deafened by the first heart sound, which is caused by
    a. the opening of the atrioventricular valves.
    b. the closing of the atrioventricular valves.
    c. the opening of the semilunar valves.
    d. the closing of the semilunar valves.

24. The _____ is a cluster of specialized heart muscle cells that determines the heart rate by initiating each cardiac cycle.
25. A weakened area on an artery wall that can balloon outward is called _____.
26. Oxygen and nutrients move through the walls of _____ to reach the body cells.

applying the concepts

1. Ying is a 75-year-old woman who broke her hip and had difficulty walking for several weeks. She passed the time watching television. After her hip healed, she suddenly had a heart attack while food shopping. The doctor said that the heart attack was caused by a blood clot in a leg vein that was swept away with the flow of blood. Explain the connection between these events.

2. Amelia is a friend of yours. When you call her to ask about dinner plans, she tells you that she is not feeling well. She aches all over and has swollen "glands" in her neck. You explain that these are not really glands, because they do not secrete anything. What are they? Why are they swollen?

3. Nicotine, a substance in cigarette smoke, causes vasoconstriction (narrowing of certain blood vessels) and increases heart rate. Explain how these effects lead to high blood pressure. Explain why cigarette smokers are more likely to die of cardiovascular diseases than are nonsmokers.

4. Abnormally short (or long) chordae tendineae of the mitral (bicuspid) valve can cause a condition known as mitral valve prolapse, in which the mitral valves do not close properly. Why would mitral valve prolapse cause the heart to produce abnormal heart sounds?

becoming information literate

Use at least three reliable sources (books, journals, websites) to plan a program for yourself to increase your cardiovascular fitness. Begin by deciding which aspects of your lifestyle you might change to improve cardiovascular fitness. Examples might include but are not limited to weight loss, change in diet, increased physical activity, and stress reduction. Next, plan a logical progression of changes that considers the type of activities and the foods that you enjoy. List each source you considered, and explain why you chose the three sources you used.

Additional questions can be found online at the Human Biology Place, www.humanbiology.com.

13

Body Defense Mechanisms

Fever, one of the body's defense mechanisms, helps us fight bacterial infections.

Esha was eating dinner with her family when she started to feel slightly nauseated. "Feeling like this on top of my headache is all I need," she moaned. Her mother, placing her palm on Esha's forehead, said, "You have a fever. Let's get you into bed." On the way up the stairs, Esha felt weak, as if her muscles were protesting even this slight exertion. She briefly wondered if she might have the flu. The next day her symptoms worsened and a rash appeared on her arm. It was clearly time for a visit to the doctor. Fortunately, the family physician was well aware that Colorado had been experiencing an increase in cases of West Nile virus that summer. She ordered diagnostic tests, which determined that Esha had indeed contracted the disease. The virus had entered Esha's body by way of a bite from a mosquito that had previously fed on the blood of an infected bird. Esha's symptoms disappeared within a couple of days, as is usually the case with West Nile virus patients who exhibit symptoms. (Most do not show symptoms.) In the worst cases, the brain becomes inflamed and the result may be death, particularly in people 60 years of age or older.

In this chapter, we study how the body reacts to an invasion such as the West Nile virus and many other organisms and substances that it perceives as threats. We see that there are three lines of defense. We also learn that the body can acquire long-lasting resistance to a microbe by becoming ill or by being immunized. Finally, we consider some potential problems caused by the immune system.

The Body's Defense System

Your body generally defends you against anything that it does not recognize as being part of or belonging inside you. Common targets of your defense system include organisms that cause disease or infection and body cells that have turned cancerous.

The bacteria, viruses, protozoans, fungi, parasitic worms, and prions (infectious proteins) that cause disease are called **pathogens** (discussed further in Chapter 13a). Note that this term does not apply to most of the microorganisms we encounter. Many bacteria, for example, are actually beneficial. They flavor our cheese, help rid the planet of corpses through decomposition, and help keep other, potentially harmful bacteria in check within our bodies. Indeed, certain bacteria are essential because they decompose dead material, thereby recycling nutrients to support new life.

Cancerous cells also threaten our well-being. A cancer cell was once a normal body cell; but because of changes in its genes, it can no longer regulate its cell division. If left unchecked, these renegade cells can multiply until they take over the body, upsetting its balance, choking its pathways, and ultimately causing great pain and sometimes death.

Three Lines of Defense

The body has three strategies for defending against foreign organisms and molecules or cancer cells:

1. **Keep the foreign organisms or molecules out of the body in the first place.** This is accomplished by the first line of defense—*chemical and physical surface barriers.*

2. **Attack *any* foreign organism or molecule or cancer cell inside the body.** The second line of defense consists of *internal cellular and chemical defenses* that become active if the surface barriers are penetrated.

3. **Destroy a *specific* type of foreign organism or molecule or cancer cell inside the body.** The third line of defense is the *immune response*, which destroys *specific* targets, usually disease-causing organisms, and remembers those targets so that a quick response can be mounted if that target enters the body again.

Thus, the first and second lines of defense consist of nonspecific mechanisms that are effective against *any* foreign organisms or substances. The third line of defense, the immune response, is a specific mechanism of defense. The three lines of defense against pathogens are summarized in Figure **13.1**.

First Line of Defense: Physical and Chemical Barriers

The skin and mucous membranes that form the first line of defense are physical barriers that help keep foreign substances from entering the body (Figure **13.2**). In addition, they produce several protective chemicals.

Physical barriers

Like a suit of armor, unbroken skin helps shield the body from pathogens by providing a barrier to foreign substances. A layer of dead cells forms the tough outer layer of skin. These cells are filled with the fibrous protein keratin, which waterproofs the skin and makes it resistant to the disruptive toxins (poisons) and enzymes

FIGURE 13.1 The body's three lines of defense against pathogens

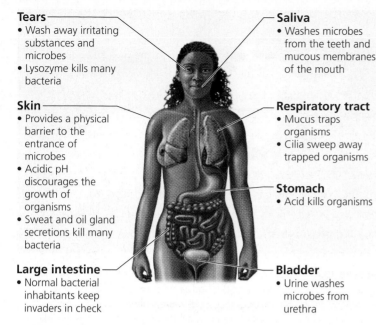

Tears
- Wash away irritating substances and microbes
- Lysozyme kills many bacteria

Skin
- Provides a physical barrier to the entrance of microbes
- Acidic pH discourages the growth of organisms
- Sweat and oil gland secretions kill many bacteria

Large intestine
- Normal bacterial inhabitants keep invaders in check

Saliva
- Washes microbes from the teeth and mucous membranes of the mouth

Respiratory tract
- Mucus traps organisms
- Cilia sweep away trapped organisms

Stomach
- Acid kills organisms

Bladder
- Urine washes microbes from urethra

FIGURE 13.2 The body's first line of defense consists of physical and chemical barriers that serve as nonspecific defenses against *any* threats to our well-being. Collectively, they prevent many invading organisms and substances from entering the body, or confine them to a local region, kill them, remove them, or slow their growth.

of most would-be invaders. Some of the strength of this barrier results from the tight connections binding the cells together. What is more, the dead cells are continuously shed and replaced, at the rate of about a million cells every 40 minutes. As dead cells flake off, they take with them any microbes that have somehow managed to latch on. Another physical barrier, the mucous membranes lining the digestive and respiratory passages, produces sticky mucus that traps many microbes and prevents them from fully entering the body. The cells of the mucous membranes of the upper respiratory airways have cilia—short, hairlike structures that beat constantly. This beating moves the contaminated mucus to the throat. We eliminate the mucus in the throat by swallowing, coughing, or sneezing.

Chemical barriers

The skin also provides chemical protection against invaders. Sweat and oil produced by glands in the skin wash away microbes.

Moreover, the acidity of the secretions slows bacterial growth, and the oils contain chemicals that kill some bacteria.

Other chemical barriers include the lining of the stomach, which produces hydrochloric acid and protein-digesting enzymes that destroy many pathogens. Beneficial bacteria in a woman's vagina create an acidic environment that discourages the growth of some pathogens. The acidity of urine slows bacterial growth. (Urine also works as a physical barrier, flushing microbes from the lower urinary tract.) Saliva and tears contain an enzyme called *lysozyme* that kills some bacteria by disrupting their cell walls.

stop and think

Harmful bacteria within the digestive system often cause diarrhea. How might this be a protective response of the body?

Second Line of Defense: Defensive Cells and Proteins, Inflammation, and Fever

The second line of defense consists of nonspecific internal defenses against any pathogen that breaks through the physical and chemical barriers and enters the body. This second line of defense includes defensive cells and proteins, inflammation, and fever (see Table **13.1**).

Defensive cells

Specialized "scavenger" cells called **phagocytes** (*phage*, to eat; *cyte*, cell) engulf pathogens, damaged tissue, or dead cells by the process of phagocytosis (Chapter 3). This class of white blood cells serves not only as the front-line soldiers in the body's internal defense system but also as janitors that clean up debris. When a phagocyte encounters a foreign particle, cytoplasmic extensions flow from the phagocytic cell, bind to the particle, and pull it inside the cell. Once inside the cell, the particle is enclosed within a membrane-bound vesicle and quickly destroyed by digestive enzymes.

The body has several types of phagocytes. One type, *neutrophils*, arrives at the site of attack before the other types of white blood cells and immediately begins to consume the pathogens, especially bacteria, by phagocytosis. Other white blood cells (monocytes) leave the vessels of the circulatory system and enter the tissue fluids, where they develop into large

TABLE 13.1 The Second Line of Defense—Nonspecific Internal Defenses

Defense	Example	Function
Defensive cells	Phagocytic cells such as neutrophils and macrophages	Engulf invading organisms
	Eosinophils	Kill parasites
	Natural killer cells	Kill many invading organisms and cancer cells
Defensive proteins	Interferons	Slow the spread of viruses in the body
	Complement system	Stimulates histamine release; promotes phagocytosis; kills bacteria; enhances inflammation
Inflammation	Widening of blood vessels and increased capillary permeability, leading to redness, heat, swelling, and pain	Brings in defensive cells and speeds healing
Fever	Abnormally high body temperature	Slows the growth of bacteria; speeds up body defenses

FIGURE 13.3 A macrophage ingesting a bacterium (the rod-shaped structure). The bacterium will be pulled inside the cell within a membrane-bound vesicle and quickly killed.

FIGURE 13.4 Natural killer cells (shown in orange) attacking a leukemia cell (shown in red). NK cells patrol the body, bumping and touching other cells as they go. When NK cells contact a cell with an altered cell surface, such as a cancer cell or a virus-infected cell, a series of events is immediately initiated. The NK cell attaches to the target cell and releases proteins that create pores in the target cell, making the membrane leaky and causing the cell to burst.

macrophages (*macro*, big; *phage*, to eat). Macrophages have hearty and less discriminating appetites than neutrophils do, and they attack and consume virtually anything that is not recognized as belonging in the body—including viruses, bacteria, and damaged tissue (Figure **13.3**).

A second type of white blood cell, *eosinophils*, attacks pathogens that are too large to be consumed by phagocytosis, such as parasitic worms. Eosinophils get close to the parasite and discharge enzymes that destroy the organism. Macrophages then remove the debris.

Natural killer cells

A third type of white blood cell, called **natural killer (NK) cells**, roams the body in search of abnormal cells and quickly orchestrates their death. In a sense, NK cells function as the body's police walking a beat. They are not seeking a specific villain. Instead, they respond to any suspicious character, including a cell whose cell membrane has been altered by the addition of proteins that are unfamiliar to the NK cell. The prime targets of NK cells are cancerous cells and cells infected with viruses. Cancerous cells routinely form but are quickly destroyed by NK cells and prevented from spreading (Figure **13.4**).

As soon as it touches a cell with an abnormal surface, the NK cell attaches to the abnormal cell and delivers a "kiss of death" in the form of proteins that create many pores in the target cell. The pores make the target cell "leaky," so that it can no longer maintain a constant internal environment and eventually bursts.

Defensive proteins

The second line of defense also includes defensive proteins. We will discuss two types of defensive proteins: interferons, which slow viral reproduction, and the complement system, which assists other defensive mechanisms.

Interferons A cell that has been infected with a virus can do little to help itself. But cells infected with a virus can help cells that are not yet infected. Before certain virally infected cells die, they secrete small proteins called **interferons** that act to slow the spread of viruses already in the body. As the name implies, interferons interfere with viral activity.

Interferons mount a two-pronged attack. First, they help rid the body of virus-infected cells by attracting macrophages and NK cells that destroy the infected cells immediately. Second, interferons protect cells that are not yet infected with the virus. When released, an interferon diffuses to neighboring cells and stimulates them to produce proteins that prevent viruses from replicating in those cells. Because viruses cause disease by replicating inside body cells, preventing replication curbs the disease. Interferon helps protect uninfected cells from *all* strains of viruses, not just the one responsible for the initial infection.

Pharmaceutical preparations of interferon have been shown to be effective against certain cancers and viral infections. Interferons inhibit cell division of cancer cells. For instance, interferon is often successful in combating a rare form of leukemia (hairy cell leukemia) and Kaposi's sarcoma, a form of cancer that often occurs in people with AIDS. Interferon has also been approved for treating the hepatitis C virus, which can cause cirrhosis of the liver and liver cancer; the human papillomavirus (HPV), which causes genital warts and cervical cancer; and the herpes virus, which causes genital herpes.

Complement System The **complement system**, or simply *complement*, is a group of at least 20 proteins whose activities enhance, or complement, the body's other defense mechanisms. Until these proteins are activated by infection, they circulate in the blood in an inactive state. Once activated, these proteins enhance both nonspecific and specific defense mechanisms. The effects of complement include the following:

- **Destruction of pathogen** Complement can act *directly*, by punching holes in a target cell's membrane (Figure **13.5**), so that the cell is no longer able to maintain a constant internal environment. Just as when NK cells secrete proteins that

Step 1: Activated complement proteins form holes in the cell wall and membrane of the bacterium.

Step 2: The bacterium can no longer maintain a constant internal environment. Water enters the cell.

Step 3: The bacterium bursts.

Intact bacterium

Pores in membrane caused by complement

Bacterium bursting

FIGURE 13.5 Complement has a direct destructive effect on pathogens.

make a target cell's membrane leaky, water enters the cell, causing it to burst.

- **Enhancement of phagocytosis** Complement enhances phagocytosis in two ways. First, complement proteins attract macrophages and neutrophils to the site of infection to remove the foreign cells. Second, one of the complement proteins binds to the surface of the microbe, making it easier for macrophages and neutrophils to "get a grip" on the intruder and devour it.

- **Stimulation of inflammation** Complement also causes blood vessels to widen and become more permeable. These changes provide increased blood flow to the area and increased access for white blood cells.

Inflammation

When body tissues are injured or damaged, a series of events called the **inflammatory response** or reaction occurs. This response destroys invaders and helps repair and restore damaged tissue. The four cardinal signs of inflammation that occur at the site of a wound are redness, heat (or warmth), swelling, and pain. These signs announce that certain cells and chemicals have combined efforts to contain infection, clean up the damaged area, and heal the wound. Let's consider the causes of the cardinal signs and how they are related to the benefits of inflammation.

- **Redness** Redness occurs because blood vessels dilate (widen) in the damaged area, causing blood flow in this area to increase. The dilation is caused by **histamine**, a substance that is also released during allergic reactions (discussed later in the chapter). Histamine is released by small, mobile connective tissue cells called **mast cells** in response to chemicals from damaged cells.

The increased blood flow to the site of injury delivers phagocytes, blood-clotting proteins, and defensive proteins, including complement and antibodies. At the same time, the increased blood flow washes away dead cells and toxins produced by the invading microbes.

- **Heat** The increased blood flow also elevates the temperature in the area of injury. The elevated temperature increases the metabolic rate of the body cells in the region and speeds healing. Heat also increases the activities of phagocytic cells and other defensive cells.

- **Swelling** The injured area swells because histamine also makes capillaries more permeable, or leakier, than usual. Fluid seeps into the tissues from the bloodstream, bringing with it many beneficial substances. Blood-clotting factors enter the injured area and begin to wall off the region, thereby helping to protect surrounding areas from injury and preventing excessive loss of blood. The seepage also increases the oxygen and nutrient supply to the cells. If the injured area is a joint, swelling can hamper movement, an effect that might seem to be an inconvenience, but it permits the injured joint to rest and recover.

- **Pain** There are several causes for the pain in an inflamed area. For example, the excessive fluid that has leaked into the tissue presses on nerves and contributes to the sensation of pain. Some soreness might be caused by bacterial toxins, which can kill body cells. Injured cells also release pain-causing

Foreign object

Skin

Mast cells

Blood vessel

Histamine

Injured tissue releases chemical signals.

Blood vessels widen

Redness: Blood flow carries defensive cells and chemicals to damaged tissue and removes toxins.

Heat: Increases the metabolic rate of cells in the injured area to speed healing.

Capillaries become more permeable

Swelling: Fluid containing defensive chemicals, blood-clotting factors, oxygen, nutrients, and defensive cells seeps into the injured area.

Pain: Hampers movement, allowing the injured area to heal.

Bacteria

Complement

Complement destroys bacteria.

Phagocytes engulf bacteria.

Clot formation prevents loss of blood.

FIGURE 13.6 The inflammatory response is a general response to tissue injury or invasion by foreign microbes. It serves to defend against pathogens and to clear the injured area of pathogens and dead body cells, allowing repair and healing to occur. The four cardinal signs of inflammation are redness, heat, swelling, and pain.

chemicals, such as prostaglandins. Pain usually causes a person to protect the area to avoid additional injury.

Because of the wider blood vessels and increased capillary permeability that bring about the inflammatory response, phagocytes begin to swarm to the injured site, attracted by chemicals released when tissue is damaged. Within minutes, the neutrophils squeeze through capillary walls into the fluid around cells and begin engulfing pathogens, toxins, and dead body cells. Soon macrophages arrive and continue the body's counterattack for the long term. Macrophages are also important in cleaning debris, such as dead body cells, from the damaged area. As the recovery from infection continues, dead cells, including microbes, body tissue cells, and phagocytes, may begin to ooze from the wound as pus (Figure **13.6**).

Fever

A *fever* is an abnormally high body temperature (Figure **13.7**). Fevers are caused by *pyrogens* (*pyro*, fire; *gen*, producer), chemicals that raise the "thermostat" in the brain (the hypothalamus) to a higher set

FIGURE 13.7 Although a fever might make us feel uncomfortable, it can help the body fight disease.

point. Bacteria release toxins that sometimes act as pyrogens. It is interesting to note, however, that the body produces its own pyrogens as part of its defensive strategy. Regardless of the source, pyrogens have the same effect on the hypothalamus, raising the set point so that physiological responses, such as shivering, are initiated to raise body temperature (as discussed in Chapter 4). Thus, we have the chills while the fever is rising. When the set point is lowered, the fever breaks and physiological responses such as perspiring reduce the body temperature until it reaches the new set point.

A mild or moderate fever helps the body fight bacterial infections by slowing the growth of bacteria and stimulating body defense responses. Bacterial growth is slowed because a mild fever causes the liver and spleen to remove iron from the blood, and many bacteria require iron to reproduce. Fever also increases the metabolic rate of body cells; the higher rate speeds up defensive responses and repair processes. On the other hand, a very high fever (over 105°F, or 40.6°C) is dangerous. It can inactivate enzymes needed for biochemical reactions within body cells.

Third Line of Defense: Immune Response

When the body's first and second lines of defense fail to stop a pathogen, the body's specific defenses respond and target the particular pathogen, cancer cell, or foreign molecule that has entered the body. The third line of defense, the **immune system**, provides the specific responses and memory. The organs of the lymphatic system (see Chapter 12) are important components of the immune system because they produce the various cells responsible for immunity. The immune system is not an organ system in an anatomical sense. Instead, the immune system is defined by its *function:* recognizing and destroying specific pathogens or foreign molecules. The body's specific defenses working together are called an *immune response.*

There are several important characteristics of an immune response. First, an immune response is directed at a particular pathogen. For example, the immune system of a child infected with measles recognizes the measles virus as a foreign substance (not belonging in the body) and then acts to immobilize, neutralize, or destroy it. An effective immune system will enable the child to recover from the illness. Second, the immune system has memory. If the same child is again exposed to the same pathogen years later, the immune system remembers the pathogen and attacks it so quickly and vigorously that she will not become ill with measles a second time.

Distinguishing Self from Nonself

To defend against a foreign organism or molecule, the body must be able distinguish it from a body cell and recognize it as foreign. This ability depends on the fact that each cell in your body has special molecules embedded in the plasma membrane that label the cell as *self*. These molecules serve as flags declaring the cell as a "friend." The molecules are called **MHC markers**, named for the major histocompatibility complex genes that code for them. The self labels on your cells are different from those of any other person (except an identical twin) as well as from those of other organisms, including pathogens. The immune system uses these labels to distinguish between what is part of your body and what is not (Figure **13.8**). It doesn't attack cells that are recognized as self.

A nonself substance or organism that triggers an immune response is called an **antigen**. Because an antigen is not recognized as belonging in the body, the immune system directs an attack against it. Typically, antigens are large molecules, such as proteins, polysaccharides, or nucleic acids. Often, antigens are found on the

A self (MHC) marker labels the body's cells as self or "friend."

An antigen is a molecule, often on the surface of a pathogen, that the immune system recognizes as a specific "foe."

FIGURE 13.8 All nucleated cells in the body have molecular MHC markers on their surface that label them as self. Foreign substances, including potential disease-causing organisms, have molecules on their surfaces that are not recognized as belonging in the body. Foreign molecules that are capable of triggering an immune response are called antigens.

surface of an invader—embedded in the plasma membrane of an unwelcome bacterial cell, for instance, or part of the protein coat of a virus. However, pieces of invaders and chemicals secreted by invaders, such as bacterial toxins, can also serve as antigens. Each antigen is recognized by its shape.

Certain white blood cells, called lymphocytes, are responsible for both the specificity and the memory of the immune response. There are two principal types of lymphocytes: **B lymphocytes,** or more simply *B cells*, and **T lymphocytes,** or *T cells*. Both types form in the bone marrow, but they mature in different organs of the body. It is thought that B cells mature in the bone marrow. The T cells, on the other hand, mature in the thymus gland, which overlies the heart.

As the T lymphocytes mature, they develop the ability to distinguish between cells that belong in the body and those that do not. The T cells must be able to recognize the specific MHC self markers of that person and *not* respond vigorously to cells bearing that MHC self marker. If T cells do respond to cells with those self markers, they are destroyed. Once they are mature, T lymphocytes circulate through the body, bumping into other cells and checking to be sure those cells have the correct self (MHC) marker. Cells with proper MHC markers are passed by.

In addition, both T and B lymphocytes, as they mature, are programmed to recognize one particular type of antigen. This recognition is the basis of the specificity of the immune response. Each lymphocyte develops its own particular receptors—molecules having a unique shape—on its surface. Thousands of *identical* receptor molecules pepper the surface of each lymphocyte, and they are unlike the receptor molecules on other lymphocytes. When an antigen fits into a lymphocyte's receptors, much like a key into a lock, the body's defenses target that particular antigen. Due to the tremendous diversity of receptor molecules, each type occurring on a different lymphocyte, a few of the billions of lymphocytes in your body are able to respond to each of the thousands of different antigens that you will be exposed to in your lifetime.

When an antigen is detected, B cells and T cells bearing receptors able to respond to that particular invader are stimulated to divide repeatedly, forming two lines of cells. One line of descendant cells is made up of **effector cells**, which carry out the attack on the enemy. Effector cells generally live for only a few days. Thus, after the invader has been eliminated from the body, the number of effector cells declines. The other line of descendant cells is composed of **memory cells**, long-lived cells that "remember" that particular invader and mount a rapid, intense response to it if it should ever appear again. The quick response of memory cells is the mechanism that prevents you from getting ill from the same pathogen twice.

Antibody-Mediated Responses and Cell-Mediated Responses

An analogy can be made between the body's immune defenses and a nation's military defense system. The military has scouts who look for invaders. If an invader is found, the scout alerts the commander of the military forces and provides an exact description of the villain. The scout must also provide the appropriate password so that the commander knows he or she is not a spy planting misinformation. The body also has scouts, called macrophages, that are part of the nonspecific defenses. Macrophages roam the tissues, looking for any invader. The cells that act as the immune system's commander are a subset of T cells called helper T cells. When properly alerted, helper T cells call out the body's specific defensive forces, and the immune responses begin.

A nation's military may have two (or more) branches. For example, it may consist of an army and a navy. Specialized to respond in slightly different ways to enemy invasion, each branch is armed with certain types of weapons. Either branch can be activated to combat a particular threat, say little green people with purple hair. The navy may be called into action if the enemy is encountered at sea, whereas the army will come to the defense if the enemy is on land.

The body, similarly, has two types of specific defenses. These specific defenses recognize the same antigens and destroy the same invaders, but they do so in different ways.

- *Antibody-mediated immune responses* defend primarily against antigens found traveling freely in intercellular and other body fluids—for example, toxins or extracellular pathogens

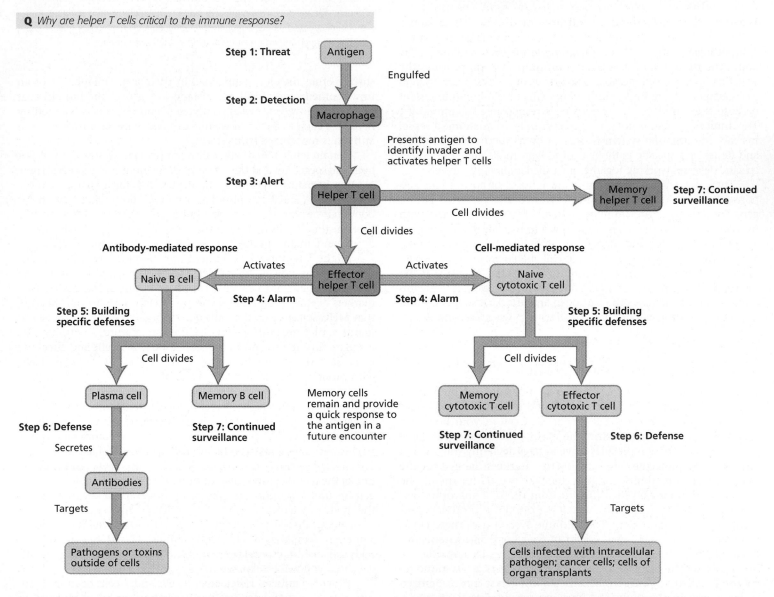

Q *Why are helper T cells critical to the immune response?*

FIGURE 13.9 An overview of the immune response

A *Helper T cells activate both naive cytotoxic T cells and naive B cells. Thus, helper T cells turn on both the cell-mediated and the antibody-mediated immune responses.*

such as bacteria or free viruses. The warriors of this branch of immune defense are the effector B cells (also called plasma cells), and their weapons are Y-shaped proteins called *antibodies*, which neutralize and remove potential threats from the body. Antibodies are programmed to recognize and bind to the antigen posing the threat; they help eliminate the antigen from the body. We discuss how this works in greater detail later in the chapter.

- *Cell-mediated immune responses* protect against cellular pathogens or abnormal cells, including body cells that have become infected with viruses or other pathogens and cancer cells. The lymphocytes responsible for cell-mediated immune responses are a type of T cell called cytotoxic T cell (discussed at greater length later in the chapter). Once activated, cytotoxic T cells quickly destroy the cellular pathogen, infected body cells, or cancerous cells by causing them to burst.

Now that the various defenders have been introduced, let's see how they work together to produce your body's highly effective immune response. Table **13.2** below summarizes the functions of the cells participating in the immune response, and Table **13.3** on page 253 summarizes the steps in the immune response.

Steps of Immune Response

Although the cell-mediated immune response and the antibody-mediated immune response use different mechanisms to defend against pathogens or foreign molecules (nonself), the general steps in these responses are the same (Figure **13.9**).

Step 1: Threat The immune response begins when a molecule or organism (an antigen) lacking the self (MHC) marker manages to evade the first two lines of defense and enters the body (Figure **13.10**).

Step 2: Detection Recall that macrophages are phagocytic cells that roam the body, engulfing any foreign material or organisms they may encounter. Within the macrophage, the engulfed material is digested into smaller pieces.

Step 3: Alert The macrophage then alerts the immune system's commander, a helper T cell, that an antigen is present. The macrophage accomplishes this task by transporting some of the digested pieces to its own surface, where they bind to the MHC self markers on the macrophage membrane. The self marker acts as a secret password that identifies the macrophage as a "friend." On the other hand, the antigen bound to the self markers function as a kind of wanted poster, telling the lymphocytes that there is an invader and revealing

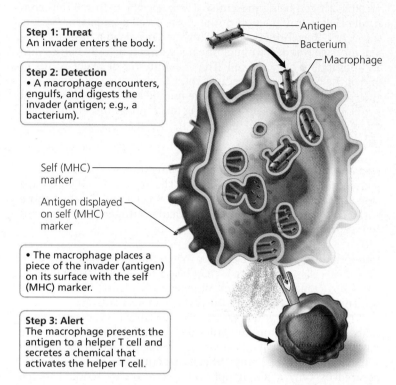

Step 1: Threat
An invader enters the body.

Step 2: Detection
• A macrophage encounters, engulfs, and digests the invader (antigen; e.g., a bacterium).

• The macrophage places a piece of the invader (antigen) on its surface with the self (MHC) marker.

Step 3: Alert
The macrophage presents the antigen to a helper T cell and secretes a chemical that activates the helper T cell.

Antigen
Bacterium
Macrophage
Self (MHC) marker
Antigen displayed on self (MHC) marker

FIGURE 13.10 A macrophage is an important antigen-presenting cell. It presents the antigen, which is attached to a self (MHC) marker, to a helper T cell, and activates the helper T cell.

TABLE 13.2 Cells Involved in the Immune Response

Cell	Functions	Cell	Functions
Macrophage	**An antigen-presenting cell** • Engulfs and digests pathogen or invader • Places a piece of digested antigen on its plasma membrane • Presents the antigen to a helper T cell • Activates the helper T cell	Suppressor T cell	**The "off" switch for both lines of immune responses** Suppresses the activity of the B cells and T cells after the foreign cell or molecule has been successfully destroyed
T Cells		*B Cells*	**Involved in antibody-mediated responses** When activated by helper T cell, it divides to form plasma cells and memory cells
Helper T cell	**The "on" switch for both lines of immune response** • After activation by macrophage, it divides, forming effector helper T cells and memory helper T cells • Helper T cells activate B cells and T cells	Plasma cell	**Effector in antibody-mediated response** Secretes antibodies specific to extracellular antigens, such as toxins, bacteria, and free viruses
Cytotoxic T cell (effector T cell)	**Responsible for cell-mediated immune responses** • When activated by helper T cells, it divides to form effector cytotoxic T cells and memory cytotoxic T cells • Destroys cellular targets, such as infected body cells, bacteria, and cancer cells	*Memory Cells*	**Responsible for memory of immune system** • Generated by B cells or any type of T cell during an immune response • Enable quick and efficient response on subsequent exposures of the antigen • May live for years

how the invader can be identified. The displayed antigens trigger the immune response. Thus, the macrophage is an important type of **antigen-presenting cell (APC).** (B cells and dendritic cells—cells with long extensions found in lymph nodes—are two other kinds of antigen-presenting cells.)

The macrophage presents the antigen to a **helper T cell**, the kind of T cell that serves as the main switch for the entire immune response. However, the macrophage must alert the *right* kind of helper T cell—a helper T cell bearing receptors that recognize the specific antigen being presented. These specific helper T cells constitute only a tiny fraction of the entire T cell population. Finding the right helper T cell is like looking for a needle in a haystack. The macrophage wanders through the body until it literally bumps into an appropriate helper T cell. The encounter most likely occurs in one of the lymph nodes, because these bean-shaped structures, discussed in Chapter 12, contain huge numbers of lymphocytes of all kinds. When the antigen-presenting macrophage meets the appropriate helper T cell and binds to it, the macrophage secretes a chemical that activates the helper T cell.

Step 4: Alarm Within hours, an activated helper T cell begins to secrete its own chemical messages. The helper T cell's message calls into active duty the appropriate B cells and T cells—those with the ability to bind to the particular antigen that triggered the response.

Step 5: Building Specific Defenses When the appropriate "naive"[1] B cells or T cells are activated, they begin to divide repeatedly. The result is a clone (a population of genetically identical cells) that is specialized to protect against the particular target antigen.

The process by which this highly specialized clone is produced, called **clonal selection**, underlies the entire immune response. We have seen that each lymphocyte is equipped to recognize an antigen of a specific shape. Any antigen that enters the body will be recognized by only a few lymphocytes at most. By binding to the receptors on a lymphocyte's surface, an antigen *selects* a lymphocyte that was preprogrammed during its maturation with receptors able to recognize that particular antigen. That particular lymphocyte is then stimulated to divide and produces a clone of millions of identical cells able to recognize that same antigen (Figure **13.11**).

The following analogy may be helpful for understanding clonal selection. Consider a small bakery with only sample cookies on display. A customer chooses a particular cookie and places an order for many cookies of that type. The cookies are then prepared especially for that person. The sample cookies do not take a lot of space, so a wide selection can be on display for other customers to select. The baker does not waste energy making cookies that have not been specifically requested. Your body prepares samples of many kinds of lymphocytes; a given lymphocyte responds to only one antigen. When an antigen selects the appropriate lymphocyte, the body produces many additional copies of the lymphocyte chosen by that particular antigen.

stop and think

A primary target of HIV, the human immunodeficiency virus that leads to AIDS, is the helper T cell. Why does the virus's preference for the helper T cell impair the immune system more than if another type of lymphocyte were targeted?

[1]A "naive" cell is one that has been preprogrammed to respond to a particular antigen but has not been previously activated to respond.

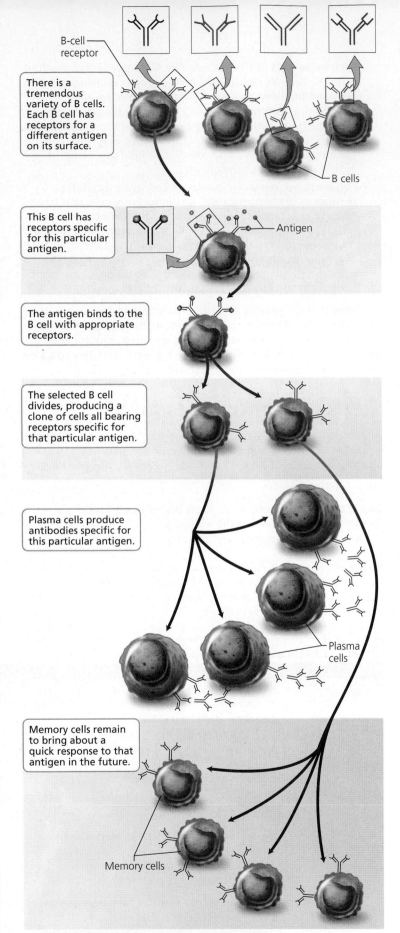

There is a tremendous variety of B cells. Each B cell has receptors for a different antigen on its surface.

B-cell receptor

B cells

This B cell has receptors specific for this particular antigen.

Antigen

The antigen binds to the B cell with appropriate receptors.

The selected B cell divides, producing a clone of cells all bearing receptors specific for that particular antigen.

Plasma cells produce antibodies specific for this particular antigen.

Plasma cells

Memory cells remain to bring about a quick response to that antigen in the future.

Memory cells

FIGURE 13.11 Clonal selection is the process by which an immune response to a specific antigen becomes amplified. This figure shows clonal selection of B cells, but a similar process occurs with T cells.

We have already mentioned that two types of cells are produced in step 5: memory cells and effector cells. Before turning to the role of memory cells, let's look more closely at exactly *how* the effector cells protect us.

Step 6: Defense—The Antibody-Mediated Response In the **antibody-mediated immune response**, activated B cells divide. The effector cells they produce through clonal selection, which are called **plasma cells**, secrete antibodies into the bloodstream to defend against antigens free in the blood or bound to a cell surface (Figure **13.12**). **Antibodies** are Y-shaped proteins that recognize a specific antigen by its shape. Each antibody is specific for one particular antigen. The specificity results from the shape of the proteins that form the tips of the Y (Figure **13.13**). Because of their shapes, the antibody and antigen fit together like a lock and a key.

Antigen on surface of a bacterial cell

Antigen on surface of a virus particle

Site on antibody that binds specifically with the viral antigen

The site on antibody that binds specifically with the bacterial antigen

FIGURE 13.13 An antibody is a Y-shaped protein designed to recognize an antigen having a specific shape. The recognition of a specific antigen occurs due to the shape of the tips of the Y in the antibody molecule.

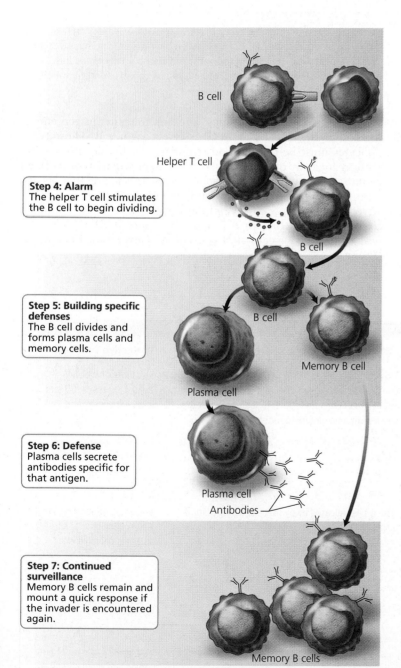

B cell

Helper T cell

Step 4: Alarm
The helper T cell stimulates the B cell to begin dividing.

B cell

Step 5: Building specific defenses
The B cell divides and forms plasma cells and memory cells.

B cell

Memory B cell

Plasma cell

Step 6: Defense
Plasma cells secrete antibodies specific for that antigen.

Plasma cell
Antibodies

Step 7: Continued surveillance
Memory B cells remain and mount a quick response if the invader is encountered again.

Memory B cells

FIGURE 13.12 Antibody-mediated immune response

TABLE 13.3 Steps in the Immune Response

Step 1: Threat	Foreign cell or molecule enters the body
Step 2: Detection	Macrophage detects foreign cell or molecule and engulfs it
Step 3: Alert	• Macrophage puts antigen from the pathogen on its surface and finds the helper T cell with correct receptors for that antigen • Macrophage presents antigen to the helper T cell • Macrophage alerts the helper T cell that there is an invader that "looks like" the antigen • Macrophage activates the helper T cell
Step 4: Alarm	Helper T cell activates both lines of defense to fight that specific antigen
Step 5: Building specific defenses (clonal selection)	• Antibody-mediated defense—B cells are activated and divide to form plasma cells that secrete antibodies specific to the antigen • Cell-mediated defense—T cells divide to form cytotoxic T cells that attack cells with the specific antigen
Step 6: Defense	• Antibody-mediated defense—antibodies specific to antigen eliminate the antigen • Cell-mediated defense—cytotoxic T cells cause cells with the antigen to burst
Step 7: Continued surveillance	Memory cells formed when helper T cells, cytotoxic T cells, and B cells were activated remain to provide swift response if the antigen is detected again
Step 8: Withdrawal of forces	Once the antigen has been destroyed, suppressor T cells shut down the immune response to that antigen

Each antibody can bind to two identical antigens, one at the tip of each arm on the Y.

Antibodies can bind only to antigens that are free in body fluids or attached to the surface of a cell. Their main targets are toxins and extracellular microbes, including bacteria, fungi, and protozoans. Antibodies help defend against these pathogens in several ways that can be remembered with the acronym PLAN.

- **P**recipitation: The antigen–antibody binding causes antigens to clump together and precipitate (settle out of solution), enhancing phagocytosis by making the antigens easier for phagocytic cells to capture and engulf.
- **L**ysis (bursting): Certain antibodies activate the complement system, which then pokes holes through the membrane of the target cell and causes it to burst.
- **A**ttraction of phagocytes: Antibodies also attract phagocytic cells to the area. Phagocytes then engulf and destroy the foreign material.
- **N**eutralization: Antibodies bind to toxins and viruses, neutralizing them and preventing them from causing harm.

There are five classes of antibodies, each with a special role to play in protecting against invaders. Antibodies are also called **immunoglobulins** (Ig), and each class is designated with a letter: IgG, IgA, IgM, IgD, and IgE. As you can see in Table **13.4**, the antibodies of some classes exist as single Y-shaped molecules (monomers), in one class they exist as two attached molecules (dimers), and in one class they exist as five attached molecules (pentamers) radiating outward like the spokes of a wheel.

Step 6: Defense—The Cell-Mediated Response The **cytotoxic T cells** are the effector T cells responsible for the **cell-mediated immune response**, which destroys antigen-bearing cells. Each cytotoxic T cell is programmed to recognize a particular antigen

bound to MHC markers on the surface of a cellular pathogen, an infected or cancerous body cell, or on cells of a tissue or organ transplant. A cytotoxic T cell becomes activated to destroy a target cell when two events occur simultaneously, as shown in Figure **13.14**. First, the cytotoxic T cell must encounter an antigen-presenting cell, such as a macrophage. Second, a helper T cell must release a chemical to activate the cytotoxic T cell. When activated, the cytotoxic T cell divides, producing memory cells and effector cytotoxic T cells.

An effector cytotoxic T cell releases chemicals called **perforins**, which cause holes to form in the target cell membrane. The holes are large enough to allow some of the cell's contents to leave the cell so that the cell disintegrates. The cytotoxic T cell then detaches from the target cell and seeks another cell having the same type of antigen.

stop and think

Rejection of an organ transplant occurs when the recipient's immune system attacks and destroys the cells of the transplanted organ. Why would this attack occur? Which branch of the immune system would be most involved?

Step 7: Continued Surveillance The first time an antigen enters the body, only a few lymphocytes can recognize it. Those lymphocytes must be located and stimulated to divide in order to produce an army of lymphocytes ready to eliminate that particular antigen. As a result, the primary response, the one that occurs during the body's first encounter with a particular antigen, is relatively slow. A lapse of several days occurs before the antibody concentration begins to rise, and the concentration does not peak until 1 to 2 weeks after the initial exposure to the antigen (Figure **13.15**).

TABLE 13.4 Classes of Antibodies

Class	Structure	Location	Characteristics	Protective Functions
IgG	Monomer	Blood, lymph, and intestines	Most abundant of all antibodies in body; involved in primary and secondary immune responses; can pass through placenta from mother to fetus and provides passive immune protection to fetus and newborn	Enhances phagocytosis; neutralizes toxins; triggers complement system
IgA	Dimer or monomer	Present in tears, saliva, and mucus as well in secretions of gastrointestinal system and excretory systems; present in breast milk	Levels decrease during stress, raising susceptibility to infection	Prevents pathogens from attaching to epithelial cells of surface lining
IgM	Pentamer	Attached to B cell, where it acts as a receptor for antigens; free in blood and lymph	First Ig class released by plasma cell during primary response	Powerful agglutinating agent (10 antigen-binding sites); activates complement
IgD	Monomer	Surface of many B cells; blood and lymph	Life span of about 3 days	Thought to be involved in recognition of antigen and in activating B cells
IgE	Monomer	Secreted by plasma cells in skin, mucous membranes of gastrointestinal and respiratory systems	Become bound to surface of mast cells and basophils	Involved in allergic reactions by triggering release of histamine and other chemicals from mast cells or basophils

Step 4: Alarm
The helper T cell stimulates a naive or memory cytotoxic T cell to begin dividing.

Step 5: Building specific defenses
The cytotoxic T cell divides and forms effector cytotoxic T cells and memory cytotoxic T cells.

Step 6: Defense
Effector cytotoxic cells cause the target cell to burst and die. In this case, the target cell is a cell infected with a virus that triggered the response.

Step 7: Continued surveillance
Memory cytotoxic T cells remain and mount a quick response if the invader is encountered again.

Antigen

Virus

Helper T cell

Cytotoxic T cell

Memory cytotoxic T cell

Effector cytotoxic T cell

Target cell

Perforin

T cell membrane

Target cell membrane

Perforin assembling into pores

Memory cytotoxic T cells

FIGURE 13.14 Cell-mediated immune response

Following subsequent exposure to the antigen, the *secondary response* is strong and swift. Recall that when naive B cells and T cells were stimulated to divide, not only did they produce effector cells that actively defended against the invader, but they also produced memory cells. These memory B cells, memory cytotoxic T cells, and memory helper T cells live for years or even decades. As a result, the number of lymphocytes programmed to respond to that particular antigen is much greater than it was before the

FIGURE 13.15 The primary and secondary immune responses. In the primary response, which occurs after the first exposure to an antigen, there is a delay of several days before the concentration of circulating antibodies begins to increase. It takes 1 to 2 weeks for the antibody concentration to peak because the few lymphocytes programmed to recognize that particular antigen must be located and activated. (The T cells show a similar pattern of response.) The secondary response following a subsequent exposure to an antigen is swifter and stronger than the primary response. The difference is due to the long-lived memory cells produced during the primary response; these are a larger pool of lymphocytes programmed to respond to that particular antigen.

first exposure. When the antigen is encountered again, each of those memory cells divides and produces new effector cells and memory cells specific for that antigen. Therefore, the number of effector cells rises quickly during the secondary response, and within 2 or 3 days reaches a higher peak than it did during the primary response.

Step 8: Withdrawal of Forces As the immune system begins to conquer the invading organism and the level of antigens declines, another type of T cell, the **suppressor T cell**, releases chemicals that dampen the activity of both B cells and T cells. Suppressor T cells turn off the immune response when the antigen no longer poses a threat. This may be a mechanism that prevents the immune system from overreacting and harming healthy body cells.

Active and Passive Immunity

There are two types of immunity: In **active immunity** the body actively defends itself by producing memory B cells and T cells following exposure to an antigen. Active immunity happens naturally whenever a person gets an infection. Fortunately, active immunity can also develop through *vaccination* (also known as immunization), a procedure that introduces a harmless form of an antigen into the body to stimulate immune responses against that antigen. Today, some vaccines, such as the vaccine for hepatitis B, are prepared using bacteria that are genetically modified to produce a protein from the pathogen. Since only the protein (antigen) is injected, rather than the actual virus, the vaccine can't cause disease. In some kinds of vaccination—whooping cough and typhoid fever, for instance—the microbe is killed before the vaccine is prepared. Other vaccines must be made from live organisms in order to be effective. In these cases, the microbes are first weakened so that they can no longer cause disease. The microbes are weakened by transferring them repeatedly in tissue culture, which allows unpredictable mutations to occur. Still other vaccines, including the one against smallpox, are prepared from microbes that cause related but milder diseases.

Because it leads to the production of memory cells, active immunity—occurring naturally or via vaccination—is relatively long-lived. The first dose of a vaccine causes the primary immune response, and antibodies and some memory cells are generated. In certain cases, especially when inactivated antigens are used in the vaccine, the immune system may "forget" its encounter with the antigen after a time. A booster is administered periodically to make sure the immune system does not forget. The booster results in a secondary immune response and enough memory cells to provide for a quick response should a potent form of that pathogen ever be encountered.

Vaccinations have saved millions of lives. In fact, they have been so effective in preventing diseases such as whooping cough and tetanus that many people mistakenly think those diseases have been eliminated. However, most of the diseases that vaccines prevent still exist, so vaccinations are still important. Children should be immunized (given vaccines) on a recommended schedule, as shown in Table **13.5**.

Although adverse reactions to vaccines are possible, the risk of being harmed by a vaccine is much lower than the risk associated with the disease that it prevents. For example, a severe paralytic illness called Guillain-Barré syndrome may develop in one or two people out of a million receiving the influenza (flu) vaccine. But the flu kills tens of thousands of unvaccinated people each year. In most cases, a reaction to a vaccine is mild: warmth, redness, and tenderness at the site of injection.

Passive immunity is protection that results when a person receives antibodies produced by another person or animal. For instance, some antibodies produced by a pregnant woman can cross the placenta and give the growing fetus some immunity.

These maternal antibodies remain in the infant's body for as long 3 months after birth, at which point the infant is old enough to produce its own antibodies. Antibodies in breast milk also provide passive immunity to nursing infants, especially against pathogens that might enter through the intestinal lining. The mother's antibodies are a temporary yet critical blanket of protection, because most of the pathogens that would otherwise threaten the health of a newborn have already been encountered by the mother's immune system.

People can acquire passive immunity medically by being injected with antibodies produced in another person or animal. In this case, passive immunity is a good news–bad news situation. The good news is that the effects are immediate. Gamma globulin, for example, is a preparation of antibodies used to protect people who have been exposed to diseases such as hepatitis B or who are already infected with the microbes that cause tetanus, measles, or diphtheria. Gamma globulin is often given to travelers before they visit a country where viral hepatitis is common. The bad news is that the protection is short-lived. The borrowed antibodies circulate for 3 to 5 weeks before being destroyed in the recipient's body. Because the recipient's immune system was not stimulated to produce memory cells, protection disappears with the antibodies.

stop and think

The viruses that cause influenza (the flu) mutate rapidly, so the antigens in the protein coat continually change. Why does this characteristic make it difficult to develop a flu vaccine that will be effective for several consecutive years?

what would you do?

There is now a vaccine against the human papillomavirus, a sexually transmitted virus that is also the most important cause of cervical cancer. Health officials recommend the vaccine for girls 11 or 12 years of age, but it can be given to girls as young as 9 years and to women as old as 26 years. Some social conservatives fear that use of this vaccine will encourage vaccinated teenagers to be sexually active. If you were (or are) a parent, would you have your daughter vaccinated? Why or why not?

Monoclonal Antibodies

Suppose you wanted to determine whether a particular antigen was present in a solution, tissue, or even somewhere in the body. An antibody specific for that antigen would be just the tool you would need. Because of its specificity, any such antibody would go directly to the target antigen. If a label (such as a radioactive tag or a molecule that fluoresces) were attached to the antibody, the antibody could reveal the location of the antigen. You can see that for a test of this kind, it is desirable to have a supply of identical antibodies that react with a specific antigen. Groups of identical antibodies that bind to one specific antigen are called **monoclonal antibodies**.

Monoclonal antibodies have many uses. Home pregnancy tests contain monoclonal antibodies produced to react with a hormone (human chorionic gonadotropin; see Chapter 18)

TABLE 13.5 Childhood Immunization Schedule Recommended by CDC, 2008

Vaccine	Age (months)	Age (years)
Hepatitis B	Birth–18	
Rotavirus	2, 4, 6	
Diphtheria, tetanus, pertussis (DtaP)	2, 4, 6, 15–18	4–6, 11–12
Haemophilus influenzae, type B	2, 4, 6, 12–15	
Pneumococcal	2, 4, 6, 12–15	
Inactivated poliovirus	2, 4, 6–18	4–6
Measles, mumps, rubella (MMR)	12–15	4–6
Varicella (chicken pox)	12–15	4–6
Hepatitis A	12–23	
Meningococcal		11–12
Human papillomavirus (HPV)		11–12 (years)

secreted by membranes associated with the developing embryo. Monoclonal antibodies have also proved useful in screening for certain diseases, including Legionnaire's disease, hepatitis, certain sexually transmitted diseases, and certain cancers, including those of the lung and prostate. Some monoclonal antibodies are also used in cancer treatment. The radioactive material or chemical treatment to combat the cancer is attached to a monoclonal antibody that targets the tumor cells but has little effect on healthy cells.

Problems of the Immune System

The immune system protects us against myriad threats from agents not recognized as belonging in the body. However, sometimes the defenses are misguided. In autoimmune disease, the body's own cells are attacked. Allergies result when the immune system protects us against substances that are not harmful. Tissue rejection following organ transplant is also caused by the immune system (see the Health Issue essay, *Rejection of Organ Transplants*).

Autoimmune Disorders

Autoimmune disorders occur when the immune system fails to distinguish between self and nonself and attacks the tissues or organs of the body. If the immune system can be called the body's military defense, then autoimmune disease is the equivalent of "friendly fire."

As we have seen, during their development, lymphocytes are programmed to attack a specific foreign antigen while still tolerating self antigens. Lymphocytes that do not learn to make this distinction are usually destroyed. Unfortunately, some lymphocytes that are primed to attack self antigens escape destruction. These cells are like time bombs ready to attack the body's own cells at the first provocation. For example, if these renegade lymphocytes are activated by a virus or bacterium, they may direct their attack against healthy body cells as well as the invading organism.

Autoimmune disorders are often classified as organ-specific or non-organ-specific. As the name implies, organ-specific autoimmune disorders are directed against a single organ. Organ-specific autoimmune disorders are usually caused by T cells that have gone awry. The thyroid gland, for example, is attacked in *Hashimoto's thyroiditis*. In contrast, non-organ-specific autoimmune disorders are generally caused by antibodies produced by B cells gone awry

Rejection of Organ Transplants

Each year, tens of thousands of people receive a gift of life in the form of a transplanted kidney, heart, lungs, liver, or pancreas. Although these transplants seem almost commonplace today, they have been performed for only about 30 years. Before organ transplants could be successful, physicians had to learn how to prevent the effector T cells of the immune system from attacking and killing the transplanted tissue because it lacked appropriate self markers. When transplanted tissue is killed by the host's immune system, we say that the transplant has been rejected.

The success of a transplant depends on the similarity between the host and transplanted tissues. The most successful transplants are those in which tissue is taken from one part of a person's body and transplanted to another part. In cases of severe burns, for example, healthy skin from elsewhere on the body can replace badly burned areas of skin.

Another way to increase the likelihood that a transplant will be accepted is to use cells from the person's body to grow the transplant in a laboratory. Today, it is possible to grow some organs, urinary bladders for instance, in the laboratory. Cells are taken from the defective organ and grown in tissue culture. When there are enough cells, they are placed on a 3-D model of the organ. Then the cell-covered mold is incubated until the new organ is formed. We discuss laboratory-grown organs in more detail in Chapter 19a.

Because identical twins are nearly genetically identical, their cells have the same self markers, and organs can be transplanted from one twin to another with little fear of tissue rejection. But few of us have an identical twin. The next best source for tissue for a transplant, and the most common, is a person whose cell surface markers closely match those of the host. Usually the transplanted tissue comes from a person who has recently died. The donor is usually brain-dead, but his or her heart is kept beating by life-support equipment. Some organs—primarily kidneys—can be harvested from someone who has died and whose heart has stopped beating. In some cases, living people can donate organs; one of two healthy kidneys can be donated to a needy recipient, as can sections of liver.

The odds in favor of a successful transplant are always improving, and so the waiting list of patients in need of an organ from a suitable donor has outpaced the supply. Some researchers believe that in the future, organs from nonhuman animals may fill the gap between the supply of organs and the demand. So far, however, attempts to transplant animal organs into people have failed. The biggest obstacle is hyperacute rejection. Within minutes to hours after transplant, the animal organ dies because its blood supply is choked off by the human immune system.

Other dangers may remain, even if the rejection problem is solved. Animals carry infectious agents that are harmless to their hosts but that might "jump species" and then gain the ability to spread from the transplant recipient to another person. If that were possible, we would have to ask whether it is ethical to expose a third party to risk.

Questions to Consider

- If you are a tissue match for someone who needs a kidney or a bone marrow transplant, how would you decide whether to be a donor?
- Do you think that family members who are a tissue match should be obligated to donate a kidney or bone marrow?
- Do you think that people should be able to buy a kidney or bone marrow from a suitable donor?

and tend to have effects throughout the body. In *systemic lupus erythematosus*, for instance, connective tissue is attacked. Since connective tissue can be found throughout the body, almost any organ can be affected. Lupus can cause skin lesions or rashes, especially a butterfly-shaped rash centered on the nose and spreading to both cheeks (Figure **13.16**). It may affect the heart (pericarditis), joints (arthritis), kidneys (nephritis), or nervous system (seizures).

A number of autoimmune disorders occur because portions of disease-causing organisms resemble proteins found on normal body cells. If the immune system mistakes the body's antigens for the foreign antigens, it may attack them. For instance, the body's attack on certain streptococcal bacteria that cause a sore throat may result in the production of antibodies that target not only the streptococcal bacteria but also similar molecules that are found in the valves of the heart and joints. The result is an autoimmune disorder known as *rheumatic fever*.

Treatment of autoimmune disorders is usually two pronged. First, any deficiencies caused by the disorder are corrected. Second, drugs are administered to depress the immune system.

Allergies

An **allergy** is an overreaction by the immune system to an antigen, in this case called an *allergen*. The immune response in an allergy is considered an overreaction because the allergen itself usually is not harmful to the body (Table **13.6**). The most common allergy is hay fever—which, by the way, is not caused by hay and does not cause a fever. *Hay fever* is more correctly known as *allergic rhinitis* (*rhino*, nose; *–itis*, inflammation of). The symptoms of hay fever—sneezing and nasal congestion—occur when an allergen is inhaled, triggering an immune response in the respiratory system. Mucous membranes of the eyes may also respond, causing red, watery eyes. Common causes of hay fever include pollen, mold spores, animal dander, and the feces of dust mites—microscopic creatures that are found throughout your home (Figure **13.17**). The same allergens, however,

FIGURE 13.16 In autoimmune diseases, the body's lymphocytes attack the body's own cells. One example is lupus erythematosus, in which lymphocytes attack connective tissue throughout the body. The butterfly rash shown here is characteristic of lupus.

Pollen grains

Dust mite

FIGURE 13.17 Common causes of allergies are pollen grains and the feces of dust mites, such as the mite shown here.

TABLE 13.6 Common Allergies

Type of Allergic Response	Common Causes	Location of Reactive Mast Cells	Symptoms
Hay fever (allergic rhinitis)	Pollen, mold spores, animal dander (bits of skin and hair), feces of dust mites	Lining of nasal cavity	Sneezing, nasal congestion
Asthma	Pollen, mold spores, animal dander	Airways of lower respiratory tract	Difficulty breathing
Food allergy	Chicken, eggs, fish, milk, nuts (especially peanuts), shellfish, soybeans, and wheat	Lining of digestive system	Nausea, vomiting, abdominal cramps, and diarrhea
Hives	Foods (especially shellfish, strawberries, chocolate, nuts, and tomatoes); insect bites; certain drugs (especially penicillin and aspirin); chemicals such as food additives, dyes, and cosmetics	Skin	Patches of skin become red and swollen
Anaphylactic shock	Insect stings (especially from bees, wasps, hornets, yellow jackets, fire ants); medicines (especially penicillin and tetracycline); certain foods (especially eggs, seafood, nuts, and grains)	Throughout the body	Widening of blood vessels, causing blood to pool in capillaries and resulting in dizziness, nausea, diarrhea, unconsciousness, and sometimes death

can trigger asthma. During an asthma attack, the small airways in the lung (bronchioles) constrict, making breathing difficult. In food allergies, the immune response occurs in the digestive system and may cause nausea, vomiting, abdominal cramps, and diarrhea. Food allergies can also cause hives, a skin condition in which patches of skin temporarily become red and swollen.

An immediate allergic response begins when a person is exposed to an allergen and a primary immune response is launched (Figure **13.18**). Soon, plasma cells churn out the antibody IgE, which binds to either basophils or mast cells. In subsequent exposures to that allergen, the allergen binds to IgE antibodies on the surface of basophils or mast cells and causes granules within the cells to release their contents: histamine.

Histamine then causes the swelling, redness, and other symptoms of an allergic response. The blood vessels widen, slowing blood flow and causing redness. At the same time, the blood vessels become leaky, allowing fluid to flow from the vessels into spaces between tissue cells, swelling the tissues. Histamine also causes the release of large amounts of mucus, so the nose begins to run. In addition, histamine can cause smooth muscles of internal organs to contract. Thus, if the allergen is in the respiratory system, histamine can trigger an asthma attack by causing the air tubules to contract. If the allergen moves from the area where it entered the body, these effects can be widespread. The result can be anaphylactic shock.

Anaphylactic shock is an extreme allergic reaction that occurs within minutes after exposure to the substance a person is allergic to. It can cause pooling of blood in capillaries, which leads to dizziness, nausea, and sometimes unconsciousness as well as extreme difficulty in breathing. Anaphylactic shock can be fatal, but most people survive. Allergies that are common triggers of anaphylactic shock include certain foods; medicines, including antibiotics such as penicillin; and insect stings, especially stings from bees, wasps, yellow jackets, and hornets.

People with allergies often know which substances cause their problems. When the culprits are not known, doctors can identify them using a crude but effective technique in which small amounts of suspected allergens are injected into the skin. If the person is allergic to one of the suspected allergens, a red welt will form at the site of injection.

If you know you have an allergy, the simplest way to avoid the miseries of an allergic reaction is to avoid exposure to the substances that cause problems. During pollen season, spend as much time as possible indoors, using an air conditioner to filter pollen out of the incoming air. Unfortunately, spores from molds growing in air conditioners and humidifiers are also common triggers of allergies. Some common allergy-causing foods, for instance, strawberries or shellfish, may be easy to avoid. Others, such as peanut oil, can show up in some unlikely dishes, including stew, chili, baked goods, or meat patties.

Certain drugs may reduce allergy symptoms. As their name implies, antihistamines block the effects of histamine. Antihistamines are most effective if they are taken before the allergic reaction begins. Unfortunately, allergies tend to become less susceptible to antihistamines over time, and most antihistamines cause drowsiness, which can impair performance on the job or in school and can make driving a car extremely hazardous.

Some allergies can be treated by gradually desensitizing the person to the offending allergens. Allergy shots containing gradually increasing amounts of a known allergen are injected into the person's bloodstream. During this treatment, the allergen causes the production of another class of antibodies—IgG. Afterward, when the allergen enters the body, IgG antibodies bind to it and prevent it from binding to IgE antibodies on mast cells and triggering an allergic reaction.

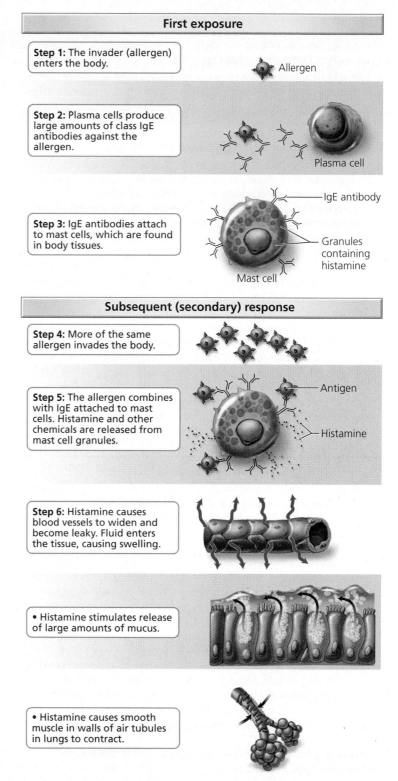

First exposure

Step 1: The invader (allergen) enters the body.

Allergen

Step 2: Plasma cells produce large amounts of class IgE antibodies against the allergen.

Plasma cell

Step 3: IgE antibodies attach to mast cells, which are found in body tissues.

IgE antibody

Granules containing histamine

Mast cell

Subsequent (secondary) response

Step 4: More of the same allergen invades the body.

Step 5: The allergen combines with IgE attached to mast cells. Histamine and other chemicals are released from mast cell granules.

Antigen

Histamine

Step 6: Histamine causes blood vessels to widen and become leaky. Fluid enters the tissue, causing swelling.

• Histamine stimulates release of large amounts of mucus.

• Histamine causes smooth muscle in walls of air tubules in lungs to contract.

FIGURE 13.18 Steps in an allergic reaction

exploring further

In this chapter, we have considered the ways that our bodies protect us from foreign agents that could cause us harm. In the next chapter, we learn more about the pathogens that can make us ill. We consider the mechanisms by which they cause harm and the ways they are transmitted.

The Body's Defense System (p. 244)

- The targets of the body's defense system include anything that is not recognized as belonging in the body, such as disease-causing organisms and cancerous cells. These foreign agents are called pathogens.

Three Lines of Defense (pp. 244–249)

- The first line of defense is nonspecific physical barriers, such as skin and mucous membranes, and chemical barriers, such as sweat, oil, tears, and saliva, all of which prevent entry of pathogens.
- The second line of defense includes defensive cells and proteins, inflammation, and fever. Defensive cells include phagocytes, eosinophils, and natural killer cells. Two types of defensive proteins are antiviral interferons and complement, which cause cells to burst.
- The inflammatory response occurs as a result of tissue injury or invasion by foreign microbes. It begins when mast cells in the injured area release histamine, which increases blood flow by dilating blood vessels to the region and by increasing the permeability of capillaries there. Increased blood flow causes redness and warmth in the region. Fluid leaking from the capillaries causes swelling.
- Fever, an abnormally high body temperature, helps the body fight invading microbes by enhancing several body defense mechanisms and slowing the growth of many pathogens.
- The third line of defense, the immune system, has responses to specific target pathogens. The immune system has memory.

Distinguishing Self from Nonself (pp. 249–250)

- All body cells are labeled with proteins called major histocompatibility complex (MHC) proteins, which serve as self markers. Cells that lack self markers (MHC) are considered nonself and are attacked. A nonself substance or organism triggers an immune response and is called an antigen.
- Lymphocytes are white blood cells that are responsible for immune responses. Both B lymphocytes (B cells) and T lymphocytes (T cells) develop in the bone marrow. The B cells are thought to mature in the bone marrow, but the T cells mature in the thymus gland. During maturation, B cells and T cells develop receptors on their surfaces that allow each of those cells to recognize an antigen of a different shape.
- When an antigen is detected, B cells and T cells with receptors that respond to that antigen divide repeatedly, forming effector cells that destroy the antigen and forming memory cells that remain in the body over years or even decades to provide a quick response on subsequent exposure to that antigen.

Antibody-Mediated Responses and Cell-Mediated Responses (pp. 250–251)

- The antibody-mediated immune response and the cell-mediated immune response simultaneously defend against the same antigen.

Steps of Immune Response (pp. 251–255)

- Macrophages are phagocytic cells that engulf any foreign material or organism they encounter. After engulfing the material, the macrophage places a part of the destroyed substance on its own surface to serve as an antigen that alerts lymphocytes to the presence of an invader and reveals what the invader looks like. Macrophages also have molecular (MHC) markers on their membranes that identify them as belonging in the body, that is, as self.
- A macrophage then presents the antigen to a helper T cell, which serves as the main switch to the entire immune response. When this encounter occurs, the macrophage secretes a chemical that activates the helper T cell. The helper T cell, in turn, secretes a chemical that activates the appropriate B cells and T cells (those specific for the antigen that the macrophage engulfed).
- B cells are responsible for antibody-mediated immune responses, which defend against antigens that are free in body fluids, including bacteria, free virus particles, and toxins. When called into action by a helper T cell, a B cell divides repeatedly, forming two lines of descendant cells: effector cells that transform into plasma cells and memory B cells. Plasma cells secrete Y-shaped proteins called antibodies into the bloodstream. Antibodies bind to the particular antigen and inactivate it or help remove it from the body.
- Cytotoxic T cells are responsible for cell-mediated immune responses, which are effective against cellular threats, including infected body cells and cancer cells. When a T cell is activated, it divides, forming two lines of descendant cells: effector cells, called cytotoxic T cells, and memory T cells. Cytotoxic T cells secrete perforins that poke holes in the foreign or infected cell, causing it to burst and die.
- After the first encounter with a particular antigen, the primary response is initiated, which may take several weeks to become effective against the antigen. However, because of memory cells, a subsequent exposure to the same antigen triggers a quicker response, called a secondary response.
- Suppressor T cells dampen the activity of B cells and T cells when antigen levels begin to fall.

Active and Passive Immunity (p. 255–256)

- In active immunity, the body actively participates in forming memory cells to defend against a particular antigen. Active immunity may occur when an antigen infects the body, or it may occur through vaccination, a procedure that introduces a harmless form of an antigen into the body.
- Passive immunity results when a person receives antibodies that were produced by another person or animal. Passive immunity is short-lived.

Monoclonal Antibodies (pp. 256–257)

- Monoclonal antibodies are identical antibodies that bind to a specific antigen. They are useful in research and in the diagnosis and treatment of diseases.

Problems of the Immune System (pp. 257–259)

- Autoimmune disorders occur when the immune system mistakenly attacks the body's own cells.
- An allergy is a strong immune response against an antigen (called an allergen). An allergy occurs when the allergen binds to IgE antibodies on the surface of mast cells or basophils, causing them to release histamine. Histamine, in turn, causes the redness, swelling, itching, and other symptoms of an allergic response.

recognizing key terms

pathogen *p. 244*
phagocyte *p. 245*
macrophage *p. 246*
natural killer (NK) cells
 p. 246
interferon *p. 246*
complement system *p. 246*
inflammatory response
 p. 247
histamine *p. 247*

mast cell *p. 247*
immune system *p. 249*
MHC marker *p. 249*
antigen *p. 249*
B lymphocyte *p. 249*
T lymphocyte *p. 249*
effector cell *p. 250*
memory cell *p. 250*
antigen-presenting cell (APC)
 p. 252

helper T cell *p. 252*
clonal selection *p. 252*
antibody-mediated immune
 response *p. 253*
plasma cell *p. 253*
antibody *p. 253*
immunoglobulin *p. 254*
cytotoxic T cell *p. 254*
cell-mediated immune
 response *p. 254*

perforins *p. 254*
suppressor T cells *p. 255*
active immunity *p. 255*
passive immunity *p. 256*
monoclonal antibody *p. 256*
autoimmune disorders *p. 257*
allergy *p. 258*

reviewing the concepts

1. Explain the difference between nonspecific and specific defense mechanisms. *p. 244*
2. List seven types of nonspecific defense mechanisms. Explain how each type helps protect us against disease. *pp. 244–249*
3. How does a natural killer cell kill its target cell? *p. 246*
4. What are interferons? What type of cell produces them? How do they help protect the body? *p. 246*
5. What is the complement system? Explain how it acts directly and indirectly to protect the body against disease. *pp. 246–247*
6. Signs of inflammation include redness, warmth, swelling, and pain. What causes each of these symptoms? How does inflammation help defend against infection? *pp. 247–248*
7. What does an antigen-presenting cell do? How do other cells recognize the antigen-presenting cell as a "friend"? *pp. 251–252*
8. What cells are responsible for antibody-mediated immune responses? What are the targets of antibody-mediated immune responses? *pp. 253–254*
9. Describe an antibody. How do antibodies inactivate or eliminate antigens from the body? *pp. 253–254*
10. What is responsible for cell-mediated immune responses? What are the targets of cell-mediated immune responses? *p. 254*
11. How does a natural killer cell differ from a cytotoxic T cell? *pp. 246, 254*
12. Why does a secondary response occur more quickly than the primary response? *pp. 254–255*
13. Differentiate between active and passive immunity. *pp. 255–256*
14. What are monoclonal antibodies? What are some medical uses for them? *pp. 256–257*
15. What is an autoimmune disorder? *pp. 257–258*
16. What is an allergy? What causes the symptoms? *pp. 258–259*
17. Indicate the *correct* statement.
    a. An antibody is specific to one particular antigen.
    b. Antibodies are held within the cell that produces them.
    c. Antibodies are produced by macrophages.
    d. Antibodies can be effective against viruses that are inside the host cell.
18. An antigen is a
    a. cell that produces antibodies.
    b. receptor on the surface of a lymphocyte that recognizes invaders.
    c. memory cell that causes a quick response to an invader when it is encountered a second time.
    d. large molecule on the surface of an invader that triggers an immune response.
19. Indicate the choice with the *incorrect* pairing of cell type and function.
    a. Helper T cell—serves as "main switch" that activates both the cell-mediated immune responses and the antibody-mediated immune responses
    b. Cytotoxic T cells—present antigen to the helper T cell
    c. Macrophage—roams the body looking for invaders, which are engulfed and digested when they are found
    d. Suppressor T cells—shut off the immune response when the invader has been removed
20. When the doctors say they are looking for a suitable donor for a kidney transplant, they are looking for someone
    a. whose tissues have self markers similar to those of the recipient.
    b. who lacks antibodies to the recipient's tissues.
    c. who has suppressor T cells that will suppress the immune response against the donor kidney.
    d. who lacks macrophages.
21. The piece of the antigen displayed on the surface of a macrophage
    a. stimulates the suppressor T cells to begin dividing.
    b. attracts other invaders to the cell, causing them to accumulate and making it easier to kill the invaders.
    c. informs the other cells in the immune system of the exact nature of the antigen they should be looking for (what the antigen "looks like").
    d. has no function in the immune response.
22. A cell that kills any unrecognized cell in the body and is part of the nonspecific body defenses is a(n) _____.
23. _____ is a chemical released by mast cells and basophils that produces most of the symptoms of an allergy.
24. Antibodies are produced by _____.
25. _____ are important antigen-presenting cells.

applying the concepts

1. After being exposed to the hepatitis B virus, Barbara goes to the doctor and asks to be vaccinated against it. Instead, the doctor gives her an injection of gamma globulin (a preparation of antibodies). Why wasn't she given the vaccine?
2. More than 100 viruses can cause the common cold. How does this fact explain why you can catch a cold from Raymond immediately after recovering from a cold you caught from Jessica?
3. HIV is a virus that kills helper T cells. This virus is not the direct cause of death in people who are infected with it. Instead, people die of diseases caused by organisms that are common in the environment. Explain why HIV-infected persons are susceptible to these diseases.
4. Ira found a deer tick attached to the back of his leg. He knows that deer ticks can transmit the bacterium that causes Lyme disease and that untreated Lyme disease can cause arthritis and fatigue. He immediately went to the doctor to get tested, which would involve drawing blood to look for antibodies to the bacterium. The doctor refused to test Ira for Lyme disease. Why?
5. Rashon has leukemia, a cancer in which the number of white blood cells increases dramatically. The doctors decide that a bone marrow transfer might help by replacing defective bone stem cells with healthy ones. His girlfriend offered to be a donor, but the doctors chose his brother instead. Why? Why was Rashon given drugs to suppress his immune system after the transplant?

becoming information literate

1. Vaccination has reduced or eliminated many diseases that were killers, including diphtheria, typhoid, polio, smallpox. The Centers for Disease Control (CDC) has a recommended schedule for childhood immunization. Yet some parents don't have their children vaccinated.

   If you were or are a parent, would you have your child vaccinated according to the recommended schedule? Write a few paragraphs that include the benefits and potential risks of vaccination. Explain how and why you made your decision.

   Use at least three reliable sources (books, journals, or websites) to gather information that would help you decide. List each source you considered, and explain why you chose the three sources you used.
2. AIDS is an immune deficiency disease that is occurring in epidemic proportions in Africa. Write a few paragraphs describing the African AIDS crisis and strategies for relieving the crisis.

   Use at least three reliable sources (books, journals, or websites) to gather information. List each source you considered, and explain why you chose the three sources you used.

Additional questions can be found online at The Human Biology Place, www.humanbiology.com.

13 a SPECIAL TOPIC

Infectious Disease

Vaccinations have helped eliminate certain infectious diseases.

263

Dani was thrilled to be chosen as a resident of her university's international dormitory, campus housing shared by students from around the world. She loved getting to know people from other countries and learning about their cultures, and she enjoyed sharing her experiences with them.

Unfortunately, during Dani's second semester in the dorm, a minor drawback became apparent. Some of the students came from countries where children are not habitually immunized against childhood diseases. One student developed measles a few days after returning from winter break, and three others in the same dormitory became infected before anyone realized what was happening. By the time the staff had been mobilized into action, a total of 10 students (including some who had been vaccinated when they were younger but who apparently had not received timely booster vaccines) had fallen ill. The sick ones had to stay in the health center or were hospitalized, the dorm rooms they had been sleeping in were quarantined, and any unimmunized students who had not come down with measles were removed from the building for a short time. No one became seriously ill, and in a few weeks dorm life was back to normal—except that everyone had a new appreciation for the challenges of disease control in the modern world.

More serious infectious diseases than measles have left their marks on humanity—and indeed, they are still a major concern today. In the past, the plague, cholera, and diphtheria decimated human populations. Today, tuberculosis (a lung disease) is making a comeback. HIV, the human immunodeficiency virus, has caused the deaths of millions of people worldwide.

In this chapter, we discuss the most important categories of pathogens, the disease-causing organisms introduced in the previous chapter. We explore how they cause harm, how they are transmitted from person to person, and how they are studied so that steps may be taken to hold them in check.

Pathogens

As indicated in the previous chapter, pathogens are disease-causing organisms. There are different types of pathogens and a wide range of differences within each type. As a result, each pathogen has specific effects on the body, and some pathogens are a greater menace than others. In this chapter, we look at bacteria, viruses, protozoans, fungi, parasitic worms, and prions. We consider the general means by which these different types of pathogen attack the body and cause symptoms. Keep in mind, however, as we do so, that some of the symptoms are caused not by the pathogen itself but by the immune responses our body uses to protect us (Chapter 13).

Virulence is the relative ability of a pathogen to cause disease. Some factors contributing to this ability are how easily the pathogen invades tissues and the degree and type of damage it does to body cells. An organism that always causes disease—the typhoid bacterium, for instance—is highly virulent. On the other hand, the yeast *Candida albicans,* which *sometimes* causes disease, is moderately virulent.

Bacteria

Bacterial cells differ greatly from the cells that make up our bodies. Recall from Chapter 3 that our bodies are made up of eukaryotic cells that contain a nucleus and membrane-bound organelles. Bacteria, in contrast, are prokaryotes, which means they lack a nucleus and other membrane-bound organelles. Nearly all bacteria have a semirigid cell wall composed of a strong mesh of peptidoglycan, a type of polymer consisting of sugars and amino acids. The cell wall endows most types of bacteria with one of three common shapes: a sphere (a spherical bacterium is called a coccus) that can occur singly, in pairs, or in chains; a rod (bacillus) that usually occurs singly; or a spiral or corkscrew shape (spirilla) (Figure **13a.1**).

Spherical bacteria are called cocci.

Rod-shaped bacteria are called bacilli.

Spiral-shaped bacteria are called spirilla.

(a)

(b)

(c)

FIGURE 13a.1 Bacteria have three basic shapes: (a) round (coccus), (b) rod-shaped (bacillus), and (c) corkscrew-shaped (spirilla). All bacteria are prokaryotic cells, meaning they lack a nucleus and membrane-bound organelles.

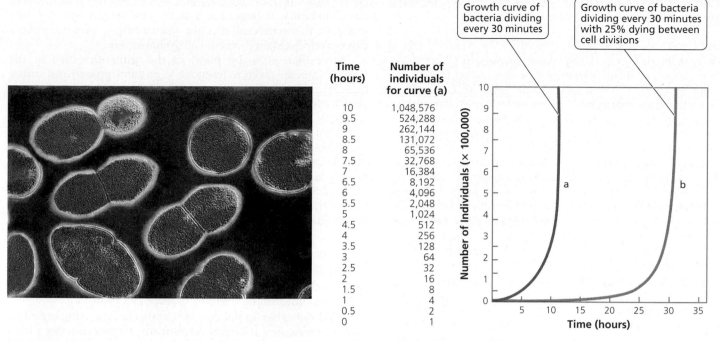

Time (hours)	Number of individuals for curve (a)
10	1,048,576
9.5	524,288
9	262,144
8.5	131,072
8	65,536
7.5	32,768
7	16,384
6.5	8,192
6	4,096
5.5	2,048
5	1,024
4.5	512
4	256
3.5	128
3	64
2.5	32
2	16
1.5	8
1	4
0.5	2
0	1

FIGURE 13a.2 Bacteria reproduce by binary fission; they copy their genetic information and pinch in half. This is one reason they reproduce very rapidly.

Bacteria can reproduce rapidly. This rapid growth rate is a matter of concern because the greater the number of bacteria, the greater harm they can potentially do. Rapid reproduction is possible because bacteria reproduce asexually in a type of cell division called *binary fission* (Figure **13a.2**), in which the bacterial genetic material (DNA) is copied, the cell is pinched in half, and each new cell contains a complete copy of the original genetic material. Under ideal conditions, certain bacteria can divide every 20 minutes. Thus, if every descendant lived, a single bacterium could result in a massive infection of trillions of bacteria within 24 hours. If a percentage of the descendant bacteria die before dividing, the population of bacteria will begin to grow more slowly than does a population in which all descendants survive, but the populations will eventually have the same growth rate.

Bacteria have defenses or other adaptive mechanisms that affect their virulence. Some bacteria have long, whiplike structures called flagella that allow them to move and spread through tissues to new areas where they can cause infection. Bacteria may also have filaments, called pili, that help them attach to the cells they are attacking. Outside the bacterial cell, there is often a capsule that provides a means of adhering to a surface and prevents scavenger cells of the immune system (phagocytes; see Chapter 13) from engulfing them.

Bacterial enzymes and toxins

Destructive enzymes and toxins (poisons) are among the offensive mechanisms certain bacteria use to spread and to attack. Some of these bacteria secrete enzymes that directly damage tissue and cause lesions, allowing the bacteria to push through tissues like a bulldozer. An example is *Clostridium,* the bacterium that causes gas gangrene, a condition in which tissue dies because its blood supply is shut off. The bacterium secretes an enzyme that dissolves the material holding muscle cells together, permitting the bacteria to spread with ease. When this bacterium digests muscle cells for energy, a gas is produced that presses against blood vessels and

shuts off the blood supply. In addition, *Clostridium* causes anemia by secreting an enzyme that bursts red blood cells.

Most bacteria, however, do their damage by releasing toxins (poisons) into the bloodstream or the surrounding tissues. If the toxins enter the bloodstream, they can be carried throughout the body and disturb body functions.

The disease symptoms depend on which body tissues are affected by the toxin. Thus, the bacteria that cause various types of food poisoning have different effects. *Staphylococcus* is often found contaminating poultry, meat and meat products, and creamy foods such as pudding or salad dressing. These bacteria multiply when food is undercooked or unrefrigerated. The toxins they produce stimulate cells in the immune system to release chemicals that result in inflammation, vomiting, and diarrhea. Another type of food poisoning is caused by *Salmonella,* often encountered in undercooked contaminated chicken or eggs. In this case, the toxin causes changes in the permeability of intestinal cells, leading to diarrhea and vomiting. One type of *Escherichia coli* (*E. coli*) food poisoning is often caused by contaminated meat, particularly ground meat. Besides vomiting and diarrhea, *E. coli* toxin can cause kidney failure in children and the elderly. The toxin that causes botulism, a type of food poisoning often brought on by eating improperly canned food, is one of the most toxic substances known. Produced by the bacterium *Clostridium botulinum,* it interferes with nerve functioning, especially motor nerves that cause muscle contraction. Death occurs because muscle paralysis prevents breathing. If enough of it is consumed, this toxin is almost always fatal.

Beneficial bacteria

Many bacteria are beneficial. For instance, certain bacteria are important in food production, especially of dairy products such as cheese and yogurt. Other bacteria are important in the environment, serving as decomposers or driving the cycling of nitrogen, carbon, and phosphorus between organisms and the environment (see Chapter 23). Yet other bacteria are important in genetic engineering (see Chapter 21). Some bacteria are normal residents in the body that keep potentially harmful microorganisms in check.

Antibiotics

Fortunately, bacteria can be killed. As we learned in Chapter 13, the human body has its own array of defenses against foreign invaders. But when the body needs outside help, we can call on *antibiotics*, chemicals that inhibit the growth of microorganisms. Antibiotics work to reduce the number of bacteria or slow the growth rate of the population, allowing time for body defenses to conquer the bacteria. Some antibiotics kill bacteria directly by preventing the synthesis of bacterial cell walls, causing them to burst. Recall that our body cells lack cell walls (see Chapter 3). Thus, our cells are unaffected by antibiotics that target cell walls. Some antibiotics block protein synthesis by bacteria but do so without interfering with cell protein synthesis in human body cells. This selective action is possible because the structure of ribosomes, the organelles on which proteins are synthesized, is slightly different in bacteria and humans.

When antibiotics were introduced during the 1940s, they were considered to be miracle drugs. For the first time, there was a cure for devastating bacterial diseases such as pneumonia, bacterial meningitis, tuberculosis, and cholera. Today, there are more than 160 antibiotics. These lifesaving drugs have become so commonplace that we take them for granted.

Unfortunately, antibiotics are losing their power. Infections that were once easy to cure with antibiotics can now turn deadly as bacteria gain resistance to the drugs. Several bacterial species capable of causing life-threatening illnesses have produced strains that are resistant to every antibiotic available today.[1]

Contradictory as it may seem, the use of antibiotics can actually increase antibiotic resistance in a strain of bacteria. When a strain of bacteria is exposed to an antibiotic, the bacteria that are susceptible die. The more resistant bacteria may survive and multiply. If the bacteria are exposed to the antibiotic again, the selection process is repeated. With each exposure to the drug, the resistant bacteria gain a stronger foothold. Making matters worse, antibiotics kill beneficial bacteria along with the harmful ones. Normally, the beneficial bacterial strains help keep the harmful strains in check. Loss of the "good" bacteria can allow the harmful ones to dominate.

The overuse and misuse of antibiotics are largely to blame for the resistance problem. An example of overuse is when physicians prescribe antibiotics for illnesses that are viral, such as a cold or flu. This is overuse; antibiotics have no effect on viruses, so they are unnecessary for treating such illnesses. Patients misuse antibiotics when they stop taking their medicine as soon as they feel better instead of completing the full course of treatment. By stopping too early, they may be leaving the bacteria with greater resistance alive. Hospitals use antibiotics heavily, so it is not surprising that they are breeding grounds for antibiotic-resistant bacteria. The resistant bacteria survive, outgrow susceptible strains, and spread from person to person. Indeed, most infections by antibiotic-resistant bacteria occur in hospitals. An example is *Staphylococcus aureus,* which can cause many types of infections, including blood poisoning, pneumonia, skin infections, heart infections, and nervous system infections. The strain of *S. aureus* called MRSA (**m**ethicillin-**r**esistant *Staphylococcus **a**ureus*), is actually resistant to many antibiotics. For many years, MRSA existed only in hospitals; but it is now found in the community at large. For a time, vancomycin was the only antibiotic that remained effective against MRSA. Unfortunately, a vancomycin-resistant *S. aureus* (VRSA) has arisen.

More than 40% (by mass) of the antibiotics used in the United States are given to livestock to promote growth and ensure health. Farmers also spray crops with antibiotics to control or prevent bacterial infections in the crops. These practices also contribute to antibiotic resistance.

What can you do to slow the spread of drug-resistant bacteria? Use antibiotics responsibly. Do not insist on a prescription for antibiotics against your doctor's advice. Take antibiotics exactly as prescribed, and be sure to complete the recommended treatment. Also, reduce your risk of getting an infection that might require antibiotic treatment by washing your hands frequently, rinsing fruits and vegetables before eating them, and cooking meat thoroughly.

Viruses

Viruses are responsible for many human illnesses. Some viral diseases, such as the common cold, are usually not very serious. Other viral diseases, such as yellow fever, can be deadly.

Most biologists do not consider a virus to be a living organism because, on its own, it cannot perform any life processes (see Chapter 1 for a review on the basic characteristics of life). To copy itself, a virus must enter a host cell. The virus exploits the host cell's nutrients and metabolic machinery to make copies of itself that then infect other host cells.

Viruses are much smaller than bacteria. A virus consists of a strand or strands of genetic material, either DNA or RNA, surrounded by a coat of protein, called a capsid (Figure **13a.3**). The genetic material carries the instructions for making new viral proteins. Some of these proteins become structural parts of the new viruses. Some of them serve as enzymes that help carry out biochemical functions important to the virus. Some are regulatory proteins, such as the proteins that trigger specific viral genes to become active under certain sets of conditions or the proteins that convert the host cell into a virus-producing factory.

Some viruses have an envelope, an outer membranous layer studded with glycoproteins. In some viruses, the envelope is actually a bit of plasma membrane from the previous host cell that became wrapped around the virus as it left the host cell. The envelope of certain other viruses—those in the herpes family, for instance—comes from a previous host cell's nuclear membrane. In any case, the virus produces the glycoproteins on the envelope. Some glycoproteins are important for attachment of the virus to the host cell.

A virus can replicate (make copies of itself) only when its genetic material is inside a host cell. Figure 13a.3 illustrates the general steps in the replication of viruses that infect animal cells:

1. **Attachment.** The virus gains entry by binding to a receptor (a protein or other molecule of a certain configuration) on the host cell surface. Such binding is possible because the viral surface has molecules of a specific shape (glycoproteins or capsids) that fit the host's receptors. The host cell receptors play a role in normal cell functioning. However, a molecule on the surface of the virus has a shape that is similar to the chemical that would normally bind to the receptor. Viruses generally attack only certain kinds of cells in certain species, because a particular virus can infect only cells bearing a receptor the virus can bind to. For example, the virus that causes the common cold infects only cells in the respiratory system, and the virus that causes hepatitis infects only liver cells.

[1]Bacteria resistant to all antibiotics available today include some strains of *Staphylococcus aureus* (skin infection, pneumonia), *Mycobacterium tuberculosis* (tuberculosis), *Enterococcus faecalis* (intestinal infections), and *Pseudomonas aeruginosa* (many types of infections).

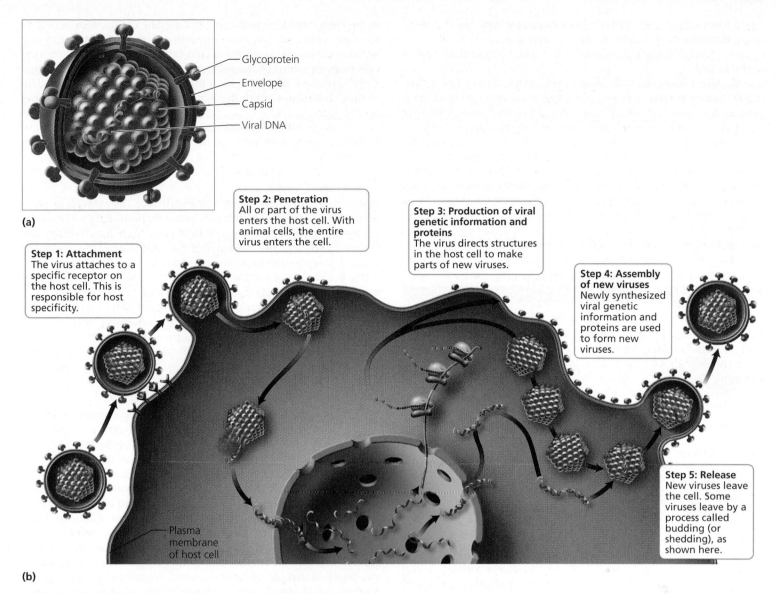

(a)

Glycoprotein
Envelope
Capsid
Viral DNA

Step 1: Attachment
The virus attaches to a specific receptor on the host cell. This is responsible for host specificity.

Step 2: Penetration
All or part of the virus enters the host cell. With animal cells, the entire virus enters the cell.

Step 3: Production of viral genetic information and proteins
The virus directs structures in the host cell to make parts of new viruses.

Step 4: Assembly of new viruses
Newly synthesized viral genetic information and proteins are used to form new viruses.

Step 5: Release
New viruses leave the cell. Some viruses leave by a process called budding (or shedding), as shown here.

Plasma membrane of host cell

(b)

FIGURE 13a.3 (a) The structure of a typical virus. A coat, called a capsid, made of protein surrounds a core of genetic information made of DNA or RNA. Some viruses have an outer membranous layer, called the envelope, from which glycoproteins project. (b) Steps in viral replication.

2. **Penetration.** After a virus has bound to a receptor on a host cell, the entire virus enters the host cell, often by phagocytosis by the host cell. Once inside, the virus loses its capsid, leaving only its genetic material intact.

3. **Production of viral genetic information and proteins.** Viral genes then direct the host cell machinery to make thousands of copies of viral DNA or RNA. Next, viral genes direct the synthesis of viral proteins, including coat proteins and enzymes.

4. **Assembly of new viruses.** Copies of the viral DNA (or RNA) and viral proteins then assemble to form new viruses.

5. **Release.** Some viruses leave the cell through *budding,* or shedding. In this process, the newly formed viruses push through the host cell's plasma membrane and become wrapped in this membrane, which forms an envelope. Budding need not kill the host cell. Other virus types do not acquire an envelope, but rather cause the host cell membrane to rupture, releasing the newly formed viruses and killing the host cell.

Viruses can cause disease in several ways, as summarized in Table **13a.1**. Some viruses cause disease when they kill the host cells, or cause the cells to malfunction. The host cell dies when viruses leave it so rapidly that it lyses (bursts). In such cases, disease symptoms will depend on which cells are killed. However, if viruses are shed slowly, the host cell may remain alive and continue to produce new viruses. Slow shedding causes *persistent infections* that can last a long time. Some viruses can produce *latent infections,* in which the viral genes remain in the host cell for an extended period without harming the cell. At any time, however, the virus can begin replicating and cause cell death as new viruses are released.

An example of a virus that can act in all of these ways is the herpes simplex virus that causes fever blisters ("cold sores") on the mouth. The virus is spread by contact (discussed shortly) and enters the epithelial cells of the mouth, where it actively replicates. Rapid shedding kills the host cells, causing fever blisters. Slow shedding may not cause outward signs of infection, but the virus can still be transmitted. When the blisters are gone, the virus remains in a latent form within nerve cells without causing symptoms. However, stress can activate the virus. It then follows nerves to the skin and begins actively replicating, causing new blisters in the same region of the mouth.

Certain viruses can also cause cancer. Some do this when they insert themselves into the host chromosome near a cancer-causing gene and, in so doing, alter the functioning of that gene. Still other viruses bring cancer-causing genes with them into the host cell.

Unfortunately, viruses are not as easy to destroy as bacteria. One reason is the difficulty of attacking viruses inside their host cells without killing the host cell itself. Most attempts to develop antiviral drugs have failed for this reason. Nonetheless, some drugs are now available to slow viral growth, and others are being developed. Most of the antiviral drugs available today, including those against the

herpes virus and HIV, work by blocking one of the steps necessary for viral replication. As mentioned in Chapter 13, interferons are proteins produced by virus-infected cells that protect neighboring cells from all strains of viruses. Interferons are not as useful as originally hoped, but they have been used for certain viral infections, including hepatitis C and the human papillomavirus that causes genital warts.

Because of these obstacles to treatment, the best way to fight viral infections is to prevent them with vaccines (discussed in Chapter 13).

Protozoans

Protozoans are single-celled eukaryotic organisms with a well-defined nucleus. They can cause disease by producing toxins or by releasing enzymes that prevent host cells from functioning normally. Protozoans are responsible for many diseases, including malaria, sleeping sickness, amebic dysentery, and giardiasis. Giardiasis is a diarrheal disease that can last for weeks. There are frequent outbreaks of giardiasis in the United States, most of them resulting from water supplies contaminated with human or animal feces. Even clear and seemingly clean lakes and streams in the wilderness can contain *Giardia* (Figure **13a.4**). Fortunately, drugs are available to treat protozoan infections. Some of these drugs work by preventing protozoans from synthesizing proteins.

Fungi

Like the protozoans, fungi are also eukaryotic organisms with a well-defined nucleus in their cells. Some fungi exist as single cells. Others are organized into simple multicellular forms, with not much difference among the cells. There are more than 100,000 species of fungi, but fewer than 0.1% cause human ailments. Fungi obtain food by infiltrating the bodies of other organisms—dead or alive—secreting enzymes to digest the food, and absorbing the resulting nutrients. If the fungus is growing in or on a human, body cells of the human are digested, causing disease symptoms. Some fungi cause serious lung infections, such as histoplasmosis and coccidioidomycosis. Other, less-threatening fungal infections occur on the skin and include athlete's foot and ringworm. Most fungal infections can be cured. Fungal cell membranes have a slightly different composition from those of human cells. As a result, the membrane is a point of vulnerability. Some antifungal drugs work by altering the permeability of the fungal cell membrane. Others

TABLE 13a.1 Possible Effects of Animal Virus on Cells

Lytic infection	Rapid release of new viruses from infected cell causes cell death. Symptoms of the disease depend on which cells are killed.
Persistent infection	Slow release of new viruses causes cell to remain alive and continue to produce new viruses for a prolonged period of time.
Latent infection Primary infection Latent period Secondary infection	Delay between infection and symptoms. Virus is present in the cell without harming the cell. Symptoms begin when the virus begins actively replicating, and new viruses exiting the host cell can cause cell death.
Transformation to cancerous cell	Certain viruses insert their genetic information into host cell chromosomes. Some carry oncogenes (cancer-causing genes) that are active in the host cell. Some disrupt the functioning of the host cell's genes that regulate cell division, causing the cell to become cancerous.

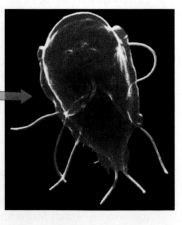

FIGURE 13a.4 *Giardia* is a protozoan that is commonly found in lakes and streams used as sources of drinking water, even those in pristine areas. It causes severe diarrhea that lasts for weeks and can be especially dangerous for children.

interfere with membrane synthesis by fungal cells. Fungal infections of the skin, hair, and nails can be combated with a drug that prevents the fungal cells from dividing.

Parasitic Worms

Parasitic worms are multicellular animals that benefit from a close, prolonged relationship with their hosts while harming, but usually not killing, their hosts. They include flukes, tapeworms, and roundworms, such as hookworms and pinworms. They can cause illness by releasing toxins into the bloodstream, feeding off blood, or competing for food with the host. Parasitic worms cause many serious human diseases, including ascariasis, schistosomiasis, and trichinosis.

Ascariasis is caused by a large roundworm, *Ascaris,* that is about the size of an earthworm. People become infected with *Ascaris* when they consume food or drink contaminated with *Ascaris* eggs. The eggs develop into larvae (immature worms) in the person's intestine. The larvae then penetrate the intestinal wall, enter the bloodstream, and travel to the lungs. After developing further, the worms are coughed up and swallowed, thus returning to the intestine. Within 2 to 3 months, they mature into male and female worms, which live for about 2 years. During those years, female worms can produce more than 200,000 eggs a day.

As much as 25% of the world population is infected with *Ascaris,* particularly in tropical regions. Up to 50% of the children in some parts of the United States (mostly rural areas in the Southeast) are infected. Many people with ascariasis have no symptoms. However, the worms can cause lung damage and severe malnutrition. When many worms are present, they can block or perforate the intestines, leading to death.

Prions

Prions (pree'-ons) are infectious particles of proteins—or, more simply, infectious proteins. They are misfolded versions of a harmless protein normally found on the surface of nerve cells. If a prion is present, it somehow causes the host protein to change its shape to the abnormal form. Prions cause a group of diseases called transmissible spongiform encephalopathies (TSEs), which are associated with degeneration of the brain. The misshapen proteins clump together and accumulate in the nerve tissue of the brain. These clumps of prions may damage the plasma membrane or interfere with molecular traffic. Spongelike holes develop in the brain, causing death.

Transmissible spongiform encephalopathies are progressive and fatal. Prions cannot be destroyed by heat, ultraviolet light, or most chemical agents. Currently, there is no treatment for any disease they cause. Several of the TSEs are animal infections, notably mad cow disease, scrapie in sheep, and chronic wasting disease (CWD), which is spreading through herds of deer and elk in the United States (Figure **13a.5**). Mad cow disease severely damaged the British beef industry in the 1990s. The U.S. and Canadian governments responded quickly when the first cases of mad cow disease appeared in these countries in 2003. In 2006, cases of atypical mad cow disease in Texas and in Alabama appeared to be a different strain, similar to cases in France, Italy, and Japan. As of 2008, there were two cases of atypical mad cow disease in Canada. This strain of prion appears spontaneously, and some researchers fear that it may be spread from cow to cow.

Prions also cause a human neurological disorder called Creutzfeldt-Jakob disease (CJD). Indeed, the prion responsible for mad cow disease is thought to cause one form of CJD. The incubation period for CJD can be months to decades. Symptoms include

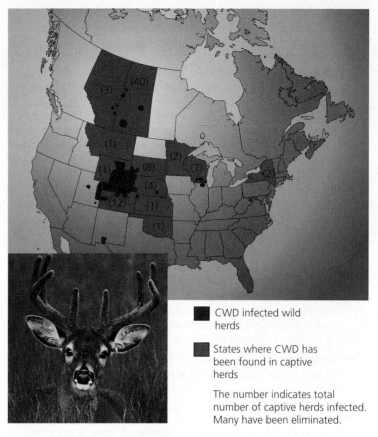

- ■ CWD infected wild herds
- ■ States where CWD has been found in captive herds

The number indicates total number of captive herds infected. Many have been eliminated.

FIGURE 13a.5 Chronic wasting disease (CWD), which is caused by a prion, is spreading through herds of deer and elk in the United States.

sensory and psychiatric problems. Once the symptoms begin, death usually occurs within a year.

How does an animal become infected with prions? In the case of mad cow disease, it appears that cattle become infected when they eat prions in contaminated food. For example, prions have been passed along in the protein supplements fed to cattle to increase their growth and milk production. Those protein supplements had been prepared from the carcasses of animals considered unfit for human consumption, a practice banned in the United States in 1997. A broader ruling prohibiting the use of any high-risk animal parts in *any* animal feed goes into effect in 2009. Any protein supplements prepared from animals infected with mad cow disease would have contained prions. The prions pass through the intestinal wall, enter the lymphatic system, and are then transported by nerves to the brain and spinal cord. In contrast, CWD can apparently be spread by animal-to-animal contact, including contact with body fluids such as urine or feces from infected animals. Scientists also think that the prions responsible for CWD may remain in the soil or water for years. As a result, healthy animals may become infected from living in a region previously occupied by diseased animals. Humans can become infected with prions by eating contaminated substances, through tissue transplant, or through contaminated surgical instruments.

Spread of a Disease

Obviously, you catch a disease when the pathogen enters your body. But how do diseases travel from person to person or enter the body in the first place? The answer to this question varies with the type of pathogen.

- **Direct contact** One means of transmission is direct contact of an infected person with an uninfected person, as might occur when shaking hands, hugging and kissing, or being sexually intimate. For example, sexually transmitted diseases (STDs) including chlamydia, gonorrhea, syphilis, genital herpes, and HPV are spread when a susceptible body surface touches an infected body surface (see Chapter 17a). The organisms that cause STDs generally cannot remain alive outside the body for very long, so direct intimate contact is necessary. A few disease-causing organisms—HIV and the bacterium that causes syphilis, for instance—can spread across the placenta from a pregnant woman to her growing fetus.

- **Indirect contact** Indirect contact, the transfer from one person to another without their touching, can spread other diseases. Most respiratory infections, including the common cold, are spread by indirect contact (see Chapter 14). When an infected person coughs or sneezes, airborne droplets of moisture full of pathogens are carried through the air (Figure **13a.6**). The infected droplets may be inhaled or land on nearby surfaces. When another person touches an affected surface, the organisms are transmitted. In this way, droplet infection spreads pathogens on contaminated inanimate objects, including doorknobs, drinking glasses, and eating utensils.

- **Contaminated food or water** Certain diseases are transmitted in contaminated food or water. You have read that spoiled food can cause food poisoning. Other diseases transmitted by food or water include hepatitis A, an inflammation of the liver caused by a certain virus. *Legionella,* the bacterium that causes a severe respiratory infection known as Legionnaires' disease, is a common inhabitant of the water in condensers of large air conditioners and cooling towers. The disease-causing bacteria are spread through tiny airborne water droplets. Coliform bacteria come from the intestines of humans and are, therefore, an indicator of fecal contamination of water. Their numbers are monitored in drinking and swimming water. To be safe, drinking water should not have any coliform bacteria.

- **Animal vectors** Another means of transmission is by *vector,* an animal that carries a disease from one host to another. The most common vector-borne disease in the United States is Lyme disease. It is caused by a bacterium transmitted by the deer tick (the vector), an insect that is about the size of the head of a pin (Figure **13a.7**). The tick larva picks up the infectious agent when it bites and sucks blood from an infected animal. When the tick subsequently feeds on a human or other mammalian host, the bacteria gradually move from the tick's gut to its salivary glands and then are passed to its victim. The incubation period, during which there are no symptoms, can be as long as 6 to 8 weeks. Early symptoms include a headache, backache, chills, and fever. Often, a rash resembling a bull's eye develops, with an intense red center and border. Over a period of weeks, the circle increases in diameter. Weeks to months later, unless the disease is treated promptly, pain, swelling, and arthritis may develop. Cardiovascular and nervous system problems may follow the arthritis.

  Mosquitoes transmit the West Nile virus, which can cause both meningitis (inflammation of the meninges, the protective coverings of the central nervous system) and encephalitis (brain inflammation; Figure **13a.8**). The first reported cases of

❄ Actual size

FIGURE 13a.7 A tiny tick, the deer tick, is a vector that transmits the bacterium responsible for Lyme disease. One characteristic sign of Lyme disease is a red bull's-eye rash surrounding the tick bite. The rash gradually increases in diameter.

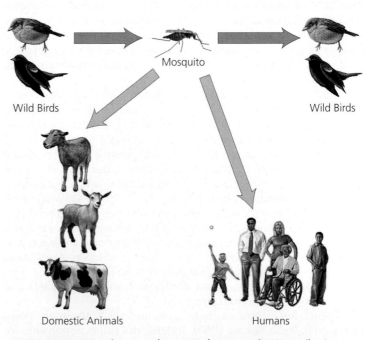

FIGURE 13a.8 Mosquitoes are the vector that transmits West Nile virus.

FIGURE 13a.6 Pathogens can be spread through the air in droplets of moisture when an infected person sneezes or coughs.

West Nile virus in North America were in New York City in 1999. Since then, the disease has spread to nearly every state. The virus can infect certain vertebrates, including humans, horses, birds, and occasionally dogs and cats. Testing mosquitoes and dead birds, especially crows and starlings, for the virus is one way to track its spread. Because the symptoms are similar to those of the flu—fever, headache, and muscle and joint pain—many people who become infected are unaware of it; and most people under the age of 50 have few symptoms or none at all. However, older people have weaker immune systems. If they become infected, they are more likely to develop meningitis or encephalitis, either of which can cause brain damage, paralysis, or death.

You can protect yourself from West Nile virus by avoiding wet and humid places that harbor mosquitoes. If you must enter an area where mosquitoes are likely to be, wear light-colored clothing that covers your body and use insect repellent.

Infectious Diseases as a Continued Threat

An epidemic is a large-scale outbreak of an infectious disease. The most notorious epidemics—bubonic plague, cholera, diphtheria, and smallpox—have happened in the distant past, although new outbreaks may occur sporadically. However, outbreaks of serious new diseases continue to present problems. We discuss some of these modern-day plagues in this chapter and elsewhere in the text (see Table **13a.2**).

Emerging Diseases and Reemerging Diseases

An *emerging disease* is a disease with clinically distinct symptoms whose incidence has increased, particularly over the last two decades. Between 1940 and 2004, a total of 335 infectious diseases appeared in the human population for the first time. Among these diseases are HIV, Ebola virus, and SARS. Other diseases have reemerged that were thought to have been conquered. A *reemerging disease* is a disease that has reappeared after a decline in incidence (Figure **13a.9**). For example, due to new drug-resistant strains of

TABLE 13a.2 Examples of Modern-Day Infectious Threats

Disease	Cause	Discussion
Meningitis	Bacterium or virus	Chapter 8
West Nile disease	Virus	Chapter 13a
Lyme disease	Bacterium	Chapter 13a
Transmissile spongiform encephalolopathies (TSEs; e.g., mad cow disease, chronic wasting disease, Creutzfeldt-Jakob disease)	Prion	Chapter 13a
Hantavirus pulmonary syndrome	Virus	Chapter 13a
Avian flu	Virus	Chapter 13a
Tuberculosis	Bacterium	Chapter 14
Severe acute respiratory syndrome (SARS)	Virus	Chapter 13a
Influenza	Virus	Chapter 14
Hepatitis C	Virus	Chapter 15
Chlamydia	Bacterium	Chapter 17a
Gonorrhea	Bacterium	Chapter 17a
Genital herpes	Virus	Chapter 17a
Genital warts	Virus	Chapter 17a
HIV/AIDS	Virus	Chapter 17a

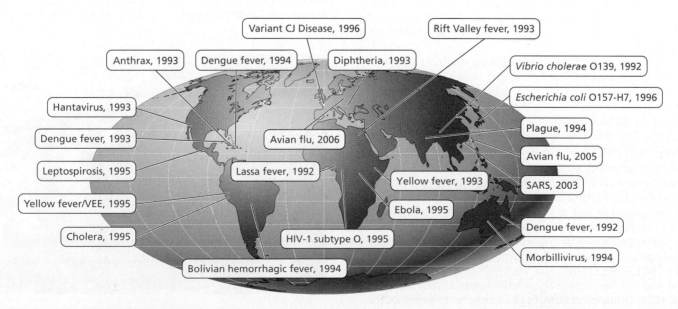

FIGURE 13a.9 Recent emerging or reemerging diseases

bacteria, tuberculosis is once again a global problem. We consider three factors that play important roles in the emergence and reemergence of disease.

1. **Development of new organisms that can infect humans and of drug-resistant organisms.** Most of the time, a pathogen infects only one type or a few types of organism. Mutations are changes in genetic information that occur randomly. Some mutations allow the pathogen to "jump species" from its original host and infect another type of organism. For example, the H5N1 influenza virus that causes a particularly dangerous form of bird flu can jump from birds to humans by direct contact with infected birds or their droppings. Recall that a virus can penetrate a cell only if the virus has the appropriate molecule on its surface—one that will fit into a receptor on the host cell. Mutations—spontaneous, random changes in genetic information—have altered surface proteins on the H5N1 influenza virus so that it can now also infect humans. Another mechanism that could allow an animal virus to infect humans is mixing of genetic information of an animal virus and a human virus, which might occur if both viruses infected the same cell.

    Pathogens can also undergo changes in their response to drugs. We have seen that certain bacteria have acquired resistance to antibiotics, for example. As a result, some diseases that were once easily cured by antibiotics are now much more difficult to treat. Improper antibiotic treatment during the reemergence of tuberculosis (TB) has led to antibiotic-resistant strains of TB that, in turn, make TB more difficult to treat. In the United States, incidences of TB reached an all-time low in 2007; but globally it is still a leading cause of death.

    In some parts of the world, multi-drug-resistant tuberculosis accounts for more than 10% of the new cases of tuberculosis a year. This drug resistance develops because many patients stop taking the prescribed antibiotic before completing 6 to 12 months of treatment. The reasons for stopping treatment range from forgetfulness to poverty. Not completing the antibiotic regimen allows the more resistant bacteria that withstood the initial drug onslaught to reproduce, creating strains of bacteria that are difficult or impossible to kill. The resistant bacteria then grow unchecked, and the patient suffers a relapse. When another course of antibiotics is prescribed, the patient may again stop taking it too soon. In this way, resistance to several drugs has developed in tuberculosis bacteria.

    Infections with multi-drug-resistant strains of *Mycobacterium tuberculosis,* the bacterium that causes TB, are increasing at an alarming rate. The World Health Organization coined a new term to describe drug resistance in a new strain of the tuberculosis bacterium—XDR, which stands for *extensively drug resistant.* The new XDR strain causes a tuberculosis infection that is nearly impossible to treat.

2. **Environmental change.** Changes in local climate—the annual amount of rainfall and the average temperature—can affect the distribution of organisms and change the size of the geographical region where certain organisms can live. For example, El Niño is a warming of the Pacific Ocean that occurs in cycles of 3 to 7 years. The warmer water causes atmospheric changes that, in turn, cause climate changes. The 1991–1992 El Niño and the 1997–1998 El Niño caused wet and mild winters in the Southwestern United States. Scientists think these climate changes were responsible for outbreaks of the hantavirus in the Southwest in 1993 and 1999. In each of these episodes, the change in climate led to a population explosion of adult rodents. Rodents, especially the deer mouse and the cotton rat, carry the hantavirus. The virus is transmitted to people when they inhale air contaminated by virus shed in the rodents' urine, feces, and saliva. The hantavirus causes a severe respiratory illness similar to influenza. It can result in respiratory failure and, in some cases, death.

3. **Population growth.** Another important factor in the emergence or reemergence of diseases is the increase of the human population in association with the development and growth of cities. Swelling human populations in cities cause people to move out of the city into surrounding areas, creating suburbs. If the surrounding areas were previously undeveloped, the move brings more people into contact with animals and insects that might carry infectious organisms. Indeed, wild animals serve as reservoirs for more than a hundred species of pathogens that can affect humans. The development of suburbs also destroys populations of predators, such as foxes and bobcats. In some regions of New York, the loss of predators has led to an increase in numbers of tick-carrying mice and an increase in the incidence of Lyme disease.

    Population density and mobility also enable infectious diseases to spread more easily today than in the past. Densely populated cities allow diseases to begin spreading quickly, and air travel enables them to spread over great distances, as we saw during the outbreak of SARS in 2003 (Figure **13a.10**). In two separate instances in 2007, air travelers with drug-resistant tuberculosis flew across the Atlantic Ocean, arousing health alerts by public health officials.

Global Trends in Emerging Infectious Diseases

Emerging infectious diseases are a concern because of economic costs and public health issues. These diseases are not evenly distributed throughout the world (Figure **13a.11**). The most important factors determining where new infectious disease will emerge are (1) the rate of human population growth and the density of the human population and (2) the number of species of wild mammals. Most pathogens responsible for emerging infectious diseases are spread to humans by animals—wildlife, pets and livestock, and vectors. As we have seen, the development of drug resistance in some pathogens has also led to emergent infectious diseases.

FIGURE 13a.10 Air travel is one reason that new diseases can spread rapidly.

Q *Look at the map showing the relative risk of an emerging disease caused by a vector-borne pathogen. What is the climate in the red and yellow regions? Why is the risk of a vector-borne disease greater in these parts of the world?*

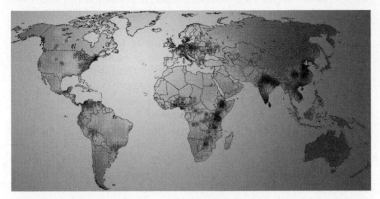

Pathogens Spread from Wild Animals to Humans

Pathogens Spread from Animal Pets and Livestock to Humans

Drug-resistant Pathogens

Vector-borne Pathogens

FIGURE 13a.11 The relative risk of an emerging infectious disease varies throughout the world. The risk of an emerging disease is greatest in areas with a fast-growing, dense human population and areas with the greatest numbers of wild mammals. Green represents the lowest risk and red represents the highest risk.

A *The risk is greatest in tropical regions of the world, where common vectors are plentiful.*

Epidemiology

Epidemiology is the study of patterns of disease, including rate of occurrence, distribution, and control. Most diseases can be described as having one of the following four patterns:

- *Sporadic diseases* occur only occasionally at unpredictable intervals. They affect a few people within a restricted area. Typhoid fever, an intestinal infection, is a sporadic disease in the United States. It is contracted by consuming food or water infected with the bacterium *Salmonella typhi*.

- Endemic diseases are always present in a population and pose little threat. The common cold provides an example.

- An epidemic disease occurs suddenly and spreads rapidly to many people. Outbreaks of smallpox and cholera are examples of epidemics.

- A *pandemic* is a global outbreak of disease. HIV/AIDS is considered to be a pandemic. There is concern that avian flu caused by the H5N1 virus may become pandemic.

Epidemiologists are "disease detectives" who try to determine why a disease is triggered at a particular time and place. The first step in answering this question is to verify that there is indeed a disease outbreak, defined as more than the expected number of cases of individuals with similar symptoms in a given area. Next, epidemiologists try to identify the cause of the disease; whether it can be transmitted to other people; and, if it can be, how the disease is transmitted. To identify the cause of an infectious disease, epidemiologists try to isolate the same infectious agent from all people showing symptoms of the condition. They also try to identify factors—including age, sex, race, personal habits, and geographic location—shared by people with symptoms of the condition. These factors might provide a clue as to whether the condition can be transmitted and how. Information about whether the incidence of the disease changes with seasons can also be important in determining the means of transmission. For example, the incidence of West Nile disease increases in the summer because mosquitoes, which are prevalent during warmer months, transmit the virus responsible for the disease. On the other hand, influenza, which is spread by droplet infection, is more common in the winter, when people are indoors and in closer contact with each other. Intestinal pathogens are usually spread in food or water, so epidemiologists look for similarities in the food and drink consumed among affected people and for the locations where consumption occurred.

As an example of how epidemiologists track a disease, we consider how the cause of SARS, the first new infectious disease of the millennium, was determined and controlled within a few months during 2003. SARS, a type of pneumonia characterized by a high fever, was first reported in China in February 2003. A Chinese physician who cared for patients with pneumonia developed symptoms himself. Nonetheless, he traveled to Hong Kong and stayed in a hotel while visiting relatives. The next day, he was admitted to the hospital and died of respiratory failure a week or so later. Shortly afterward, people displaying the symptoms that have come to be associated with SARS appeared in Hong Kong, Singapore, Vietnam, Canada, and the United States.

By questioning these early victims, epidemiologists determined that the factor they all had in common was contact with the Chinese physician. Some patients were guests in the same hotel, and others were close family members. This pattern of occurrence is typical of a disease caused by an infectious agent. Therefore, measures for limiting the spread of the infectious agent were put in place. These included quarantining thousands of people, restricting travel, and even checking the body temperature of people in airports. The idea was that this would identify infected individuals, who could then be prevented from traveling and further spreading the disease. Although SARS affected more than 8000 people in 30 countries and caused more than 800 deaths in the months that followed, the restrictive measures were eventually successful in limiting its spread.

Other scientists determined that the cause of SARS was a specific type of virus called a coronavirus. It was identified as the cause of SARS because it could be isolated from all SARS patients tested. We now know that SARS is transmitted from person to person in droplets of moisture spread into the air when an infected person coughs, and that it can cause infection after 24 hours on a dry surface.

14

The Respiratory System

In goes the "good" air and out goes the "bad" air: your respiratory system brings in oxygen-laden air and removes carbon dioxide from the body. A healthy respiratory system enhances the quality of life.

Helvi was both hopeful and upset. She had spent the past 2 hours surfing the web to learn more about emphysema and chronic bronchitis because she was anxious about her favorite aunt, Ilta. Helvi's mother had sent an e-mail earlier in the day describing Ilta's trip to the doctor, the tests, the prognosis, and the new lifestyle that Ilta was going to have to embrace. Helvi couldn't help feeling angry and disappointed that Ilta had not quit smoking 30 years ago when Helvi's mother did. Instead, Ilta had continued smoking in spite of constant coughing, shortness of breath, general poor health, and other family members' pleas to stop. During her web search of authoritative sites, Helvi learned that one couldn't state with 100% accuracy that Ilta's lung diseases arose from smoking, but she learned that 80% to 90% of patients with lung disease were smokers. Her web search also yielded some hope that there are treatments to alleviate the symptoms, permitting some short-term relief, but the fact remains that there is no cure. She gathered her strength for the painful call to her aunt.

In this chapter, we learn why the respiratory system is so essential to life and why damage to it is debilitating. We follow the course of inhaled air to the lungs and describe the mechanics of breathing. We then consider the transport of oxygen and carbon dioxide between the lungs and the cells and examine the control of respiration. Finally, we discuss several disorders of the respiratory system.

Structures of the Respiratory System

Without oxygen, we would die within a few minutes. Why? To stay alive, our cells need energy, and oxygen plays an essential role in extracting energy from food molecules (see Chapter 3). We store the extracted energy by producing a molecule called ATP (adenosine triphosphate), which then releases the energy as needed to do the work of the cell. Our cells can make a little ATP without oxygen, but it is not enough to supply the body's energy needs. Cells can make 18 times more ATP if oxygen is present.

The same chemical reactions that require oxygen for the production of ATP produce carbon dioxide as a by-product. In solution—for example, in water or blood—carbon dioxide forms carbonic acid, which can be harmful to cells.

The function of the **respiratory system** is to provide the body with oxygen and to dispose of carbon dioxide, an exchange that also regulates the acidity of body fluids. Four processes play a part in respiration (Figure **14.1**).

- **Breathing (also called ventilating):** bringing oxygen-rich air into the lungs and moving air laden with carbon dioxide out of the lungs.
- **External respiration:** the exchange of oxygen and carbon dioxide between the lungs and the blood. Oxygen moves from the lungs into the blood, and carbon dioxide moves from the blood into the lungs.

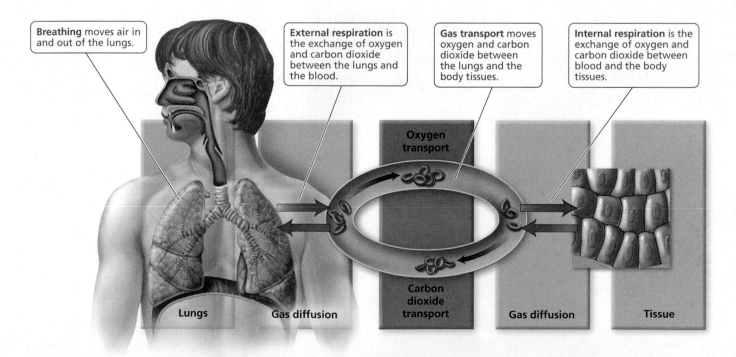

Breathing moves air in and out of the lungs.

External respiration is the exchange of oxygen and carbon dioxide between the lungs and the blood.

Gas transport moves oxygen and carbon dioxide between the lungs and the body tissues.

Internal respiration is the exchange of oxygen and carbon dioxide between blood and the body tissues.

Oxygen transport

Carbon dioxide transport

Lungs   Gas diffusion   Gas diffusion   Tissue

FIGURE 14.1 An overview of respiration

- **Gas transport:** transport of oxygen from the lungs to the cells and of carbon dioxide from the cells to the lungs.

- **Internal respiration:** the exchange of oxygen and carbon dioxide between the blood and tissue cells. Oxygen moves from the blood to the cells, where it is used in cellular respiration to produce ATP and carbon dioxide. Carbon dioxide produced by the cells moves into the blood.

We begin our exploration of how humans obtain oxygen and dispose of carbon dioxide by following the path of air from the nose to the lungs. The structures the air passes along the way are identified and described in Figure **14.2** and Table **14.1**. The path the air travels is summarized in Figure **14.3**. The respiratory system is generally divided into upper and lower regions. The nose (nasal cavities) and pharynx make up the *upper respiratory system*. The *lower respiratory system* consists of the larynx, epiglottis, trachea, bronchi, bronchioles, and lungs.

Nose

However large someone's nose might seem from the outside, the inside is not as roomy as you might imagine. One reason is that a thin partition of cartilage and bone called the *nasal septum* divides the inside of the nose into two **nasal cavities.** In addition, much of the space within the nasal cavities is taken up by three convoluted, shelflike bones. These bones increase the surface area inside the nasal cavities and divide each cavity into three narrow passageways through which the air flows. Moist mucous membrane covers the entire inner surface of the nasal cavities.

We all know what a nose looks like, but what does a nose do? Your nose has three important functions: (1) filtration and cleansing, (2) conditioning the air that is inhaled, and (3) olfaction (smell).

Filtration and cleansing

The nose helps clear particles from the air that moves through its passages. Considering that each of us inhales about 150,000 bacteria

Q *Trace the path of oxygen from air entering the nose to the structures in the lungs where oxygen enters the blood supply.*

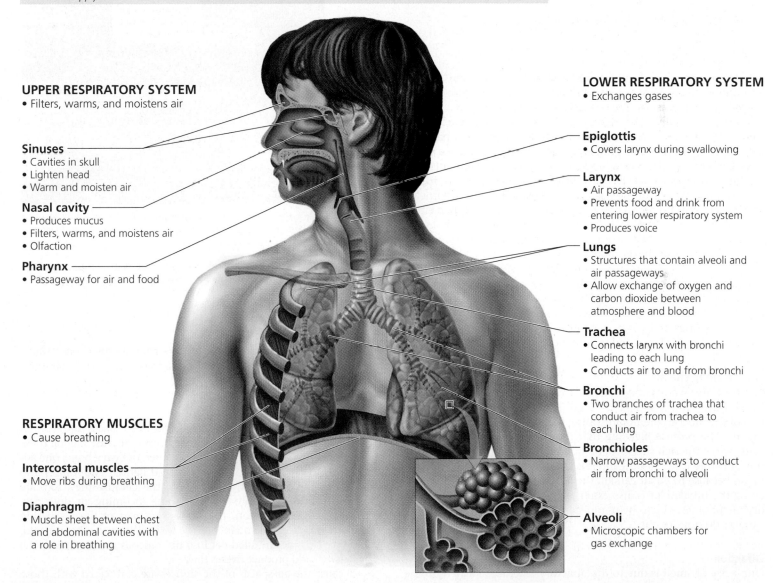

UPPER RESPIRATORY SYSTEM
- Filters, warms, and moistens air

Sinuses
- Cavities in skull
- Lighten head
- Warm and moisten air

Nasal cavity
- Produces mucus
- Filters, warms, and moistens air
- Olfaction

Pharynx
- Passageway for air and food

RESPIRATORY MUSCLES
- Cause breathing

Intercostal muscles
- Move ribs during breathing

Diaphragm
- Muscle sheet between chest and abdominal cavities with a role in breathing

LOWER RESPIRATORY SYSTEM
- Exchanges gases

Epiglottis
- Covers larynx during swallowing

Larynx
- Air passageway
- Prevents food and drink from entering lower respiratory system
- Produces voice

Lungs
- Structures that contain alveoli and air passageways
- Allow exchange of oxygen and carbon dioxide between atmosphere and blood

Trachea
- Connects larynx with bronchi leading to each lung
- Conducts air to and from bronchi

Bronchi
- Two branches of trachea that conduct air from trachea to each lung

Bronchioles
- Narrow passageways to conduct air from bronchi to alveoli

Alveoli
- Microscopic chambers for gas exchange

FIGURE 14.2 The respiratory system

A *Nasal cavity, pharynx, trachea, bronchi, bronchioles, alveoli*

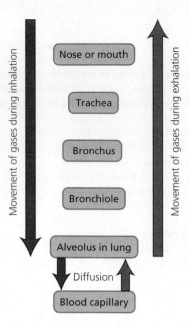

FIGURE 14.3 The path of air during inhalation and exhalation

(a) The cilia are yellow in this color-enhanced electron micrograph. The cells without cilia secrete mucus.

(b) Cigarette smoke first paralyzes and then destroys the cilia. As a result, hazardous materials can accumulate on the surfaces of the air passageways.

FIGURE 14.4 The respiratory passageways are lined with clumps of short hairlike structures, called cilia, interspersed between mucus-secreting cells.

along with a great deal of pollen and dust each day, filtering the air is an important job. Most pollen and dust particles are removed from the air we inhale before they reach the lungs.

The nose and air tubules (described below) clean inhaled air in a variety of ways. Hairs inside the nose filter out the largest particles. In addition, certain cells in the membrane lining the surface of the nasal cavities and air tubules produce mucus, a sticky substance that catches dust particles. Cilia, tiny projections extending from the membranous lining, then sweep the mucus, trapped dirt particles, and bacteria toward the throat. The trapped particles can then either be swallowed and subsequently destroyed by digestive enzymes or coughed up (Figure **14.4**). Particles that do not become trapped in the nasal cavities or the air tubules are deposited in the lungs. Many of the particles deposited in the lungs are engulfed and removed by macrophages, large irregularly shaped cells that wander across the surfaces of the lungs. However, if too many particles are inhaled or if the mechanisms for removing them fail, the particles may accumulate in the lungs and cover some of the surfaces for gas exchange, reducing their efficiency and setting the stage for infection.

Conditioning the air

The nose also warms and moistens the inhaled air before it reaches the delicate lung tissues. The blood in the extensive capillary system of the mucous membrane lining the nasal cavity warms incoming air. The profuse bleeding that follows a punch to the nose is evidence of the rich supply of blood in these membranes. Warming the air before it reaches the lungs is extremely important in cold climates because frigid air can kill the delicate cells of the lung. Moistening the inhaled air is also essential because oxygen cannot cross dry membranes. Mucus helps moisten the incoming air so that lung surfaces do not dry out.

Olfaction

Our sense of smell is due to the olfactory receptors located on the mucous membranes high in the nasal cavities behind the nose. The sense of smell is discussed in Chapter 9.

stop and think

Very cold temperatures can slow the action of the cilia in the nasal cavities. Why does the loss of ciliary action sometimes cause a runny nose on a very cold day?

Sinuses

Connected to the nasal cavities are large air-filled spaces in the bones of the face. These spaces are called the **sinuses**. Because having these air spaces means less of the head is composed of heavy bone, one advantage of the sinuses is to make the head lighter. The sinuses also help warm and moisten the air we breathe because they, too, are lined with mucous membranes and some incoming air does pass through them. In addition, the sinuses are part of the resonating chamber that affects the quality of the voice. When you have a cold, your voice becomes muffled because the mucous membranes of the sinuses swell and produce excess fluid.

Because the air spaces of the sinuses are connected with those of the nasal cavities, any excess mucus and fluids drain from the sinuses into the nasal cavities. However, when the mucous membranes of the sinuses become inflamed, as they do in *sinusitis* (*–itis,* inflammation of), the swelling can block the connection between the nasal cavities and the sinuses, preventing the sinuses from draining the mucous fluid they produce. The pressure caused by the accumulation of fluids in the sinuses causes pain over one or both eyes or in the cheeks or jaws; this condition is usually called a sinus headache. Sinusitis may be caused by the virus responsible for a cold or by a subsequent bacterial infection. Decongestant nasal sprays reduce the swelling in the tubes that connect the sinuses with the nasal cavity, allowing the sinuses to drain more easily—but such sprays should be used only as directed, because they can lead to dependency.

TABLE 14.1 Review of Structures of the Respiratory System

Structure	Description	Function
Upper respiratory system		
Nasal cavity	Cavity within the nose, divided into right and left halves by nasal septum; has three shelflike bones	Filters and conditions (moistens and warms incoming air); olfaction (sense of smell)
Sinuses	Large, air-filled spaces in the bones of the face	Lessen the weight of the head; warm and moisten inhaled air
Pharynx (throat)	Chamber connecting nasal cavities to esophagus and larynx	Common passageway for air, food, and drink
Lower respiratory system		
Larynx	Cartilaginous, boxlike structure between the pharynx and trachea that contains the vocal cords and the glottis	Allows air but not other materials passage to the lower respiratory system; source of the voice
Epiglottis	Flap of tissue reinforced with cartilage	Covers the glottis during swallowing
Trachea	Tube reinforced with C-shaped rings of cartilage that leads from the larynx to the bronchi	The main airway; conducts air from larynx to bronchi
Bronchi (primary)	Two large branches of the trachea reinforced with cartilage	Conduct air from trachea to each lung
Bronchioles	Narrow passageways leading from bronchi to alveoli	Conduct air to alveoli; adjust airflow in lungs
Lungs	Two lobed, elastic structures within the thoracic (chest) cavity containing surfaces for gas exchange	Exchange oxygen and carbon dioxide between blood and air
Alveoli	Microscopic sacs within lungs, bordered by extensive capillary network	Provide immense, internal surface area for gas exchange

Pharynx

The **pharynx,** commonly called the throat, is the space behind the nose and mouth. It is a passageway for air, food, and drink. Small, narrow passages, called the *auditory* (Eustachian) *tubes,* connect the upper region of the pharynx with the middle ear. These passages help equalize the air pressure in the middle ear with that of the pharynx.

Larynx

After moving through the pharynx, the air next passes through the **larynx,** which is commonly called the voice box or Adam's apple. The larynx is a boxlike structure composed primarily of cartilage (Figure **14.5**).

The larynx has two main functions. It is a traffic director for materials passing through the structures in the neck, allowing air,

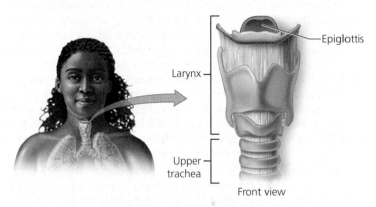

Front view

(a) The epiglottis is open during breathing but covers the opening to the larynx during swallowing to prevent food or drink from entering the trachea.

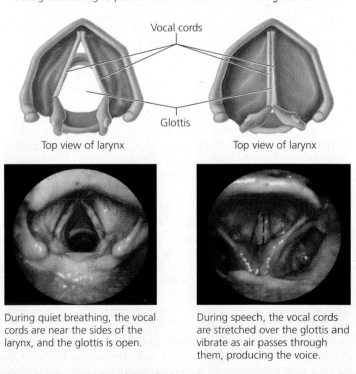

Top view of larynx Top view of larynx

During quiet breathing, the vocal cords are near the sides of the larynx, and the glottis is open.

During speech, the vocal cords are stretched over the glottis and vibrate as air passes through them, producing the voice.

(b) The vocal cords are the folds of connective tissue above the opening of the larynx (the glottis) that produce the voice.

FIGURE 14.5 The larynx, commonly called the voice box or Adam's apple, is an adjustable entryway to the trachea and the source of the voice.

but not other materials, to enter the lower respiratory system. The larynx is also the source of the voice. Let's consider these two functions in more detail.

1. **A selective entrance to the lower respiratory system.** The larynx provides a selective opening to the trachea (windpipe) and lower respiratory system: it can be opened to allow air to pass into the lungs and closed to prevent other matter, such as food, from entering the lungs. Because the esophagus (the tube leading to the stomach) is behind the larynx, food and drink must pass over the opening to the larynx to reach the digestive system. If solid material such as food were to enter the lower respiratory system, it could lodge in one of the tubes conducting air to the lungs and prevent air flow. Fluid entering the lungs is equally dangerous because it can cover the respiratory surfaces, decreasing the area available for gas exchange. Normally, foreign material is prevented from entering the lower respiratory system during swallowing because the larynx rises and causes a flap of cartilage called the **epiglottis** to move downward and form a lid over the **glottis**, the opening in the larynx through which air passes. You can feel the larynx moving if you put your fingers on your Adam's apple while swallowing. Because of this movement, you cannot breathe and swallow at the same time. (Try it!)

    If food or drink accidentally enters the trachea, we usually cough and expel it. However, if food lodges in the trachea, it may block air flow. The **Heimlich maneuver** can be used to remove the blockage and restore air flow (Figure **14.6**).

2. **Production of voice.** The voice is generated in the larynx by the vibration of the **vocal cords**, two thick strands of tissue stretched over the opening of the glottis (see Figure 14.5). When you speak, muscles stretch the vocal cords across the air passageway, narrowing the opening of the glottis. Air passing between the stretched vocal cords causes them to vibrate and produce a sound, just as the edges of the neck of an inflated balloon vibrate and make noise if you stretch the balloon's neck while allowing air to escape. The vibrations of the vocal cords set up sound waves in the air spaces of the nose, mouth, and pharynx. This resonation is largely responsible for the tonal quality of your voice.

    The pitch of the voice depends on the tension of the vocal cords. When the cords are stretched, becoming thinner and tighter, the pitch of the sound when they vibrate is higher. You can demonstrate the relationship between thickness and pitch for yourself by plucking a rubber band stretched between your thumb and forefinger. The more the rubber band is stretched, the higher the pitch of the twang.

    When you suffer from *laryngitis,* an inflammation of the larynx, the vocal cords become swollen and thick. As a result, they cannot vibrate freely, and the voice becomes deeper and huskier. When the vocal cords are very inflamed, a person can hardly speak at all because the cords cannot vibrate in that condition.

Trachea

The **trachea**, or windpipe, is a tube that conducts air between the outside of the body and the lungs. It is held open by rings of cartilage that give it the general appearance of a vacuum cleaner hose. These rings of cartilage are C-shaped; the open ends of the rings face the side of the trachea next to the esophagus, which allows the esophagus to expand and compress the trachea when a large mass of food is swallowed. You can feel these rings of cartilage in your neck, just below the larynx.

A person who is choking cannot speak or breathe and needs immediate help. The **Heimlich maneuver** is a procedure intended to force a large burst of air out of the lungs and dislodge the object blocking air flow.

Step 1: Stand behind the choking person with arms around the waist.

Step 2: Make a fist and place the thumb of the fist beneath the victim's rib cage about midway between the navel (belly button) and the breastbone.

Step 3: Grasp the fist with your other hand and deliver a rapid "bear hug" up and under the rib cage with the clenched fist. Be careful not to press on the ribs or the breastbone because doing so could cause serious injury.

— Blocking object

Step 4: Repeat until the object is dislodged.

FIGURE 14.6 The Heimlich maneuver can be performed on a choking person who is standing or sitting. If a choking victim is lying on the ground, the same lifesaving pressure changes can be generated by pushing inward and upward on the upper part of the victim's abdomen. If you begin to choke and there is no one to perform the Heimlich maneuver on you, it may be possible to dislodge the obstruction in your trachea by throwing your upper abdominal region against a table, chair, or other stationary object.

The support rings are necessary in the trachea and its branches to prevent these airways from collapsing during each breath when the rapid flow of air into the lungs creates a drop in pressure. Air (or fluid) passing rapidly over a surface causes a lower pressure, experienced as a "pull," on that surface. Maybe you have noticed that when you get into the shower and turn on the water, the shower curtain is drawn in toward you. The curtain moves inward because the moving water lowers the air pressure, just as the rapid movement of air through the respiratory tubules does. If the trachea were not supported open by cartilage rings, the rapid flow of air during breathing would cause it to collapse or flatten.

Bronchial Tree

The trachea divides into two air tubes called primary **bronchi**; each bronchus (singular) conducts air from the trachea to one of the lungs. The bronchi branch repeatedly within the lungs, forming progressively smaller air tubes. The smallest bronchi divide to form yet smaller tubules called **bronchioles**, which finally terminate in *alveoli*, sacs with surfaces specialized for gas exchange (discussed shortly).

The repeated branching of air tubules in the lung is reminiscent of a branching tree. In fact, the resemblance is so close that the system of air tubules is often called the **bronchial tree** (Figure **14.7**). All the bronchi are held open by cartilage, just as occurs in the trachea. However, the amount of cartilage decreases with the diameter of the tube. The bronchioles have no cartilage, but their walls contain smooth muscle, which is controlled by the autonomic nervous system so that airflow can be adjusted to suit metabolic needs (see Chapter 8).

Although the contraction of the muscle in bronchial walls is usually closely attuned to the body's needs, sometimes the bronchial muscles go into spasms that severely obstruct the flow of air. Such is the case with *asthma*, a chronic condition characterized by recurring attacks of wheezing and difficulty breathing. The difficult breathing is worsened by persistent inflammation of the airways. An allergy to substances such as pollen, dog or cat dander (skin particles), and the feces of tiny mites in household dust often trigger asthma attacks. However, a cold or respiratory infection, certain drugs, inhaling irritating substances, vigorous exercise, and psychological stress can also cause an attack. Some attacks start for no apparent reason. Certain inhalants prescribed to treat asthma attacks work by relaxing the bronchial muscles. Other inhalants contain steroids that reduce the inflammation of the air tubules that occurs in asthma.

FIGURE 14.7 A resin cast of the bronchial tree of the lungs. In the body, this branching system of air tubules is hollow and serves as a passageway for the movement of air between the atmosphere and the alveoli, where gas exchange takes place.

Alveoli

Each bronchiole ends either with an enlargement called an alveolus (plural, *alveoli*) or, more commonly, with a grapelike cluster of alveoli. Each **alveolus** is a thin-walled, rounded chamber surrounded by a dense network of capillaries (Figure **14.8**). Oxygen diffuses from the alveoli into the blood, which delivers the oxygen to cells. Carbon dioxide produced by the cells diffuses from the blood into the alveolar air to be exhaled.

Most of the lung tissue is composed of alveoli, making the structure of the lung much more like foam rubber than like a balloon, the image sometimes used to describe a lung. The surface area inside a simple, hollow balloon the same size as our lungs would be roughly 0.01 m^2 (about 0.2 yd^2). However, each of our lungs contains approximately 300 million alveoli, whose total surface area is about 70 to 80 m^2 (about 84 to 96 yd^2). In other words, the alveoli increase the surface area of the lung about 8500 times.

For the alveoli to function properly as a surface for gas exchange, they must be kept open. Phospholipid molecules called **surfactant**,

(a) Each alveolus is a small air-filled sac. In this section, some of the alveoli have been cut open and you can see into them.

(b) Much of the surface of each alveolus is covered with capillaries. The interface provides a vast surface area for the exchange of gases between the alveoli and the blood.

FIGURE 14.8 Alveoli in the lungs create a huge surface area where oxygen and carbon dioxide are exchanged between the lungs and the blood. Oxygen diffuses from the alveoli into the blood, and carbon dioxide diffuses from the blood to the alveoli.

which coat the alveoli, act to keep them open. Moist membranes, such as those of the alveolar walls, are attracted to one another because of an attraction between water molecules called surface tension. If this attraction were not disrupted by surfactant, it would pull the alveolar walls together, collapsing the air chambers.

Surfactant production usually begins during the eighth month of fetal life, so enough surfactant is present to keep the alveoli open when the newborn takes his or her first breath. Unfortunately, some premature babies have not yet produced enough surfactant to overcome the attractions between the alveolar walls. As a result, their alveoli collapse after each breath. This condition, called *respiratory distress syndrome* (RDS), makes breathing difficult for the premature newborn. Some newborns with RDS die as a result. However, many are saved by the use of mechanical respirators and artificial surfactant to keep them alive until their lungs mature.

stop and think

Pneumonia is a lung infection that results in an accumulation of fluid and dead white blood cells in the alveoli. Why might this result in lower blood levels of oxygen?

Mechanism of Breathing

Air moves between the atmosphere and the lungs in response to pressure gradients. It moves into the lungs when the pressure in the atmosphere is greater than the pressure in the lungs, and it moves out when the pressure in the lungs is greater than the pressure in the atmosphere.

The pressure changes in the lungs are created by changes in the volume of the thoracic cavity, a relationship explained by the characteristics of the *pleural membrane*. Each lung is enclosed in a double-layered sac of pleural membrane. One layer of membrane adheres to the wall of the thoracic cavity; the other adheres to the lung. Fluid between the layers of membrane lubricates the membrane layers and holds them together by surface tension. As a result, a change in the volume of the thoracic cavity causes a similar change in the volume of the lungs. Let's consider how the changes in the size of the thoracic cavity are brought about.

Inhalation

Air moves into the lungs when the size of the thoracic cavity increases; this increase causes the pressure in the lungs to drop below atmospheric pressure. The increase is due to the contraction of both the **diaphragm**, a broad sheet of muscle that separates the abdominal and thoracic cavities, and the muscles of the rib cage, called the **intercostal muscles** (*costa,* rib; Figure **14.9a**). The air pressure in the lungs decreases, and air rushes into the lungs. This process is called inhalation, or **inspiration.** The intercostals lie between the ribs, so that when those muscles contract, they pull the rib cage upward and outward. By placing your hands on your rib cage while you inhale, you can feel the rib cage move up and out. Raising the rib cage increases the size of the thoracic cavity from the front to the back. Meanwhile, the contraction of the diaphragm lengthens the thoracic cavity from top to bottom. This lengthening occurs because the diaphragm is dome-shaped when relaxed, and it flattens when contracted, as shown in Figure 14.9a.

Exhalation

The process of breathing out, called exhalation or **expiration**, is usually passive. In other words, it doesn't require work but occurs when the muscles of the rib cage and the diaphragm relax. The lungs

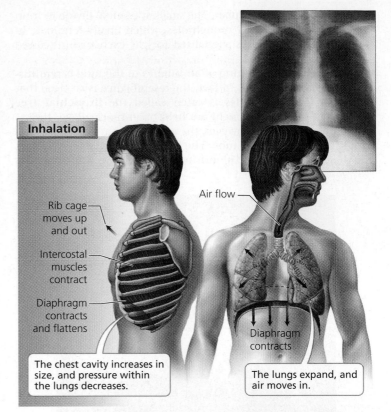

Inhalation

Rib cage moves up and out

Intercostal muscles contract

Diaphragm contracts and flattens

Air flow

Diaphragm contracts

The chest cavity increases in size, and pressure within the lungs decreases.

The lungs expand, and air moves in.

(a)

Exhalation

Rib cage moves down and inward

Intercostal muscles relax

Diaphragm relaxes and moves upward

Air flow

Diaphragm relaxes

The chest cavity decreases in size, and pressure within the lungs increases.

The lungs recoil, and air moves out.

(b)

FIGURE 14.9 Changes in the volume of the thoracic cavity bring about inhalation and exhalation. The x-rays show the actual changes in lung volume during inhalation and exhalation.

are elastic; that is, after stretching they return to their former size. When the elastic tissues of the lung recoil, the rib cage falls back to its former lower position and the diaphragm bulges into the thoracic cavity (Figure 14.9b). The pressure within the lungs increases as the volume of the lungs decreases. When the pressure within the lungs exceeds atmospheric pressure, air moves out.

If it is necessary to exhale more air than usual, as in heavy breathing or coughing, other muscles assist the process. For example, there is another layer of muscles between the ribs. When the rib muscles in this layer contract, they pull the rib cage even further down and inward, increasing the pressure on the lungs. In addition, the muscles of the abdomen can be contracted. Abdominal contractions push the organs in the abdomen against the diaphragm, which causes it to bulge even further into the thorax.

stop and think

In Victorian times, a woman often wore a corset containing whalebone that formed a band around her waist and lower chest. Corsets were laced tightly to create a wasplike waistline, and women who wore them frequently fainted. What is the most likely cause of these fainting spells?

The Volume of Air Moved Into or Out of the Lungs during Breathing

The volume of air moved during each breath varies from person to person, depending largely on the person's sex, age, and height. During quiet breathing, about 500 ml, or roughly 1 pint, of air moves in and out with each breath. The amount of air inhaled or exhaled during a normal breath is called the **tidal volume** (Figure **14.10**).

If, after inhaling normally, you were to inhale until you could not take in any more air, you would probably bring another 1900 to 3300 ml of air into your lungs. This volume of air is nearly 4 to 7 times the volume moved during quiet breathing. The additional volume of air that can be brought into the lungs after normal inhalation is called the **inspiratory reserve volume.**

After you have exhaled normally, you can still force about 1000 ml of additional air from the lungs. This additional volume of air that can be expelled from the lungs after the tidal volume is called the **expiratory reserve volume.** Decreases in expiratory reserve volume are characteristic of obstructive lung diseases such as bronchitis and asthma. New York City firefighters and other rescue workers at the scene of the collapse of the World Trade Center on September 11, 2001, experienced a significant decrease in expiratory reserve volume in the year following the disaster. The decline in lung function among rescue workers, presumably due to the inhalation of toxic dust, was equivalent to that expected from 12 years of aging. Those who were on the scene when the towers fell, or shortly afterward, suffered the most damage.

If you were to take the deepest breath possible and exhale until you could not force any more air from your lungs, you would be demonstrating your **vital capacity**, the maximum amount of air that can be moved into and out of the lungs during forceful breathing. The vital capacity, therefore, equals the sum of the tidal volume, the inspiratory reserve, and the expiratory reserve. Although average values for college-age people are about 4800 ml in men and 3400 ml in women, the values can vary tremendously depending on a person's health and fitness. One illness that affects vital capacity is pneumonia. It causes fluid to accumulate within the alveoli, taking up space that would normally be occupied by air.

The lungs can never be completely emptied, even with the most forceful expiration. The amount of air that remains in the lungs after exhaling as much air as possible, called the **residual**

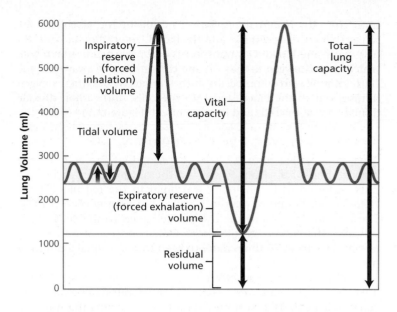

Tidal volume (~500 ml)	Amount of air inhaled or exhaled during an ordinary breath
Inspiratory reserve volume (~1900–3300 ml)	Amount of air that can be inhaled in addition to a normal breath
Expiratory reserve volume (~1000 ml)	Amount of air that can be exhaled in addition to a normal breath
Vital capacity (~3400–4800 ml)	Maximum amount of air that can be inhaled or exhaled in a single forced breath
Residual volume (~1100–1200 ml)	Amount of air remaining in the lungs after maximum exhalation
Total lung capacity (4500–6000 ml)	Total amount of air in the lungs after maximal inhalation (vital capacity + residual volume)

FIGURE 14.10 A spirometer is used to measure the volumes of air in the lungs.

volume, is roughly 1100 to 1200 ml of air. As we will see later in the chapter, emphysema is a lung condition in which the alveolar walls break down, creating larger air spaces that are more difficult to empty. Thus, the residual volume increases. This residual air is lower in oxygen than is inhaled air, so a person with emphysema feels short of breath.

Because some air is always left in the lungs, the vital capacity is not a measure of the total amount of air that the lungs can hold. The **total lung capacity**, the total volume of air contained in the lungs after the deepest possible breath, is calculated by adding the residual volume to the vital capacity. This volume is approximately 6000 ml in men and 4500 ml in women.

Transport of Gases between the Lungs and the Cells

We have seen that breathing brings air into the lungs and expels air from the lungs. Recall that three other processes then play roles in delivering the oxygen to the cells and disposing of carbon dioxide from the cells. External respiration occurs in the alveoli of the lungs; there oxygen diffuses into the blood, and carbon dioxide diffuses from the blood. Gas transport is accomplished by the blood, which carries oxygen to the cells and carbon dioxide away from the cells. Internal respiration occurs in the various tissues; there oxygen diffuses out of the blood and into the cells, and carbon dioxide diffuses out of the cells and into the blood (Figure **14.11**).

Oxygen Transport and Hemoglobin

Oxygen is carried from the alveoli throughout the body by the blood. Almost all—about 98.5%—of the oxygen that reaches the cells is bound to hemoglobin, a protein in the red blood cells. Hemoglobin bound to oxygen is called **oxyhemoglobin** (HbO_2). The remaining 1.5% of the oxygen delivered to the cells is dissolved in the plasma. Whole blood, which consists of cells as well as plasma, carries 70 times more oxygen than an equal amount of plasma alone.

Hemoglobin picks up oxygen at the lungs and releases it at the cells. But what determines whether hemoglobin will bind to oxygen or release it? The most important factor deciding this question is the partial pressure of oxygen, which is directly related to its concentration. In a mixture of gases, each gas contributes only part of the total pressure of the whole mixture of gases. The pressure exerted by one of the gases in a mixture is called its partial pressure.

Recall from Chapter 3 that substances always diffuse from regions of higher concentration or pressure to regions of lower concentration or pressure. In the alveoli of the lungs, where the concentration of oxygen is high, hemoglobin in the red blood cells in nearby capillaries picks up oxygen. The oxygen is then released near the cells, where the oxygen concentration is low.

Carbon Dioxide Transport and Bicarbonate Ions

The carbon dioxide produced by cells as they use oxygen is removed by the blood. Carbon dioxide transport occurs in three principal ways:

1. **Dissolved in blood plasma.** Between 7% and 10% of the carbon dioxide is transported dissolved in the plasma as molecular carbon dioxide.

2. **Carried by hemoglobin.** Hemoglobin molecules in red blood cells carry slightly more than 20% of the transported carbon dioxide. When carbon dioxide combines with hemoglobin, it forms a compound called **carbaminohemoglobin.**

3. **As a bicarbonate ion.** By far the most important means of transporting carbon dioxide is as bicarbonate ions dissolved in the plasma. About 70% of the carbon dioxide is transported this way. Carbon dioxide (CO_2) produced by cells diffuses into the blood and into the red blood cells. In both the plasma and the red blood cells, it reacts with water (H_2O) and forms carbonic acid (H_2CO_3). Carbonic acid quickly dissociates to form hydrogen ions (H^+) and bicarbonate ions (HCO_3^-). The process of bicarbonate ion

O_2 = oxygen
CO_2 = carbon dioxide

Blood flow

Capillary network on surface of alveolus

Body cell

O_2 diffuses into body cells

CO_2 diffuses into blood

Blood

Internal Respiration: Gas exchange in capillary beds throughout body tissues

CO_2 diffuses from blood plasma into alveolus

O_2 binds to hemoglobin in red blood cell

Alveolus

Red blood cell

Capillary

External Respiration: Gas exchange in lungs

FIGURE 14.11 In the lungs, oxygen diffuses from the alveoli into the blood. Oxygen is carried to the cells in red blood cells. At the cells, oxygen diffuses from the blood to the body cells, which use the oxygen and produce carbon dioxide in the process. Carbon dioxide diffuses into the blood and is carried back to the lungs, where it diffuses from the blood into an alveolus and is exhaled.

formation in the capillaries of the tissues is represented by the following formula:

$$CO_2 + H_2O \xrightarrow{\text{Carbonic anhydrase}} H_2CO_3 \longrightarrow HCO_3^- + H^+$$

Carbon Water   Carbonic   Bicarbonate Hydrogen
dioxide   acid   ion   ion

Although these reactions occur in the plasma as well as in red blood cells, they occur hundreds of times faster in red blood cells. The higher rate of reaction is caused by the enzyme **carbonic anhydrase** that is found within red blood cells but not in the plasma. The hydrogen ions produced by the reaction combine with hemoglobin. In this way, hemoglobin acts as a buffer, and the acidity of the blood changes only slightly as it passes through the tissues. The bicarbonate ions diffuse out of the red blood cells into the plasma and are transported to the lungs.

In the lungs, the process is reversed. When the blood reaches the capillaries of the lungs, carbon dioxide diffuses from the blood into the alveoli because the concentration (partial pressure) of carbon dioxide is comparatively low in the alveoli. Because the concentration of carbon dioxide in the blood is higher than in the alveoli, the chemical reactions we have just described reverse direction. The bicarbonate ions rejoin the hydrogen ions to form carbonic acid. In the presence of carbonic anhydrase within the red blood cells, carbonic acid is converted to carbon dioxide and water. The carbon dioxide then leaves the red blood cells, diffuses into the alveolar air, and is exhaled. The reactions in the lungs are summarized below.

$$HCO_3^- + H^+ \xrightarrow{\text{Carbonic anhydrase}} H_2CO_3 \longrightarrow CO_2 + H_2O$$

Bicarbonate Hydrogen   Carbonic   Carbon Water
ion   ion   acid   dioxide

Besides being the form in which carbon dioxide is transported by the blood, bicarbonate ions are an important part of the body's *acid–base buffering system.* They help neutralize acids in the blood. If the blood becomes too acidic, the excess hydrogen ions are removed by combining with bicarbonate ions to form carbonic acid. The carbonic acid then forms carbon dioxide and water, which are exhaled. (Bicarbonate ions and the acid–base balance of the blood are also discussed in Chapter 2.)

stop and think

Carbon monoxide is a poisonous gas that binds to hemoglobin much more readily than does oxygen, and it binds in the same site as oxygen. Thus, when carbon monoxide is bound to hemoglobin, oxygen cannot bind. Why is carbon monoxide poisoning potentially fatal?

Respiratory Centers in the Brain

Breathing rate influences the amount of oxygen that can be delivered to cells and the amount of carbon dioxide that can be removed from the body. Neural and chemical controls adjust breathing rate to meet the body's needs.

Basic Breathing Pattern

As you sit there reading your text, your breathing is probably rather rhythmic, with about 12 to 15 breaths a minute. The basic rhythm is controlled by a breathing (respiratory) center located in the medulla of the brain (Figure **14.12**). Within the breathing center are an inspiratory area and an expiratory area.

During quiet breathing, when you are calm and breathing normally, the inspiratory area shows rhythmic bouts of neural activity. While the inspiratory neurons are active, impulses that stimulate contraction are sent to the muscles involved in inhalation (the diaphragm and the intercostals). As we have seen, contraction of the diaphragm and the intercostals causes the size of the thoracic cavity

NEURAL CONTROLS

Cerebral cortex
• Conscious control of breathing

Medulla oblongata
• Breathing center

CHEMICAL CONTROLS

Medulla oblongata
• Chemoreceptors respond to rising blood level of carbon dioxide (increased acidity, H$^+$) and lowered blood level of oxygen

Carotid bodies
• Chemoreceptors respond to lowered blood level of oxygen

Aortic bodies
• Chemoreceptors respond to rising blood level of carbon dioxide and lowered blood level of oxygen

Lungs

Heart

Intercostal muscles

Diaphragm

FIGURE 14.12 Neural and chemical controls of breathing

to increase, thus moving air into the lungs. After about 2 seconds of inhalation, the activity of the neurons in the inspiratory center ceases for about 3 seconds. When inspiratory neurons cease activity, the diaphragm and intercostals relax, and passive exhalation occurs. During heavy breathing, such as might occur during exercise, the expiratory center causes contraction of other intercostal muscles and abdominal muscles, quickly pushing air out of the lungs.

Most of the time we breathe without giving it a thought. However, we can voluntarily alter our pattern of breathing through impulses originating in the cerebral cortex (the "conscious" part of the brain). We control breathing when we speak or sigh, and we can voluntarily pant like a dog. Holding our breath while swimming underwater is obviously a good idea. At certain other times, holding our breath can protect us from inhaling smoke or irritating gases.

During forced breathing, as might occur during strenuous exercise, stretch receptors in the walls of the bronchi and bronchioles throughout the lungs prevent the overinflation of the lungs. When a deep breath greatly expands the lungs and stretches these receptors, they send impulses over the vagus nerve that inhibit the breathing center, permitting exhalation. As the lungs deflate, the stretch receptors are no longer stimulated.

Chemoreceptors

The purpose of breathing is to control the blood levels of carbon dioxide and oxygen. We now consider how the levels of these gases control the breathing rate, which in turn influences the levels of the gases (Figure **14.13**).

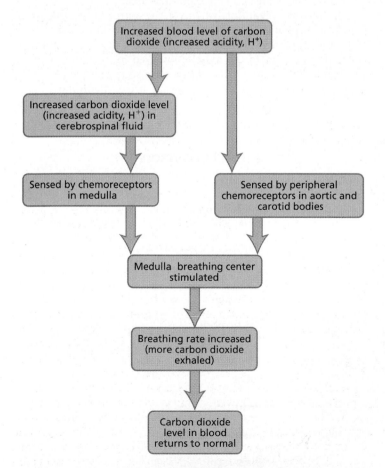

FIGURE 14.13 The role of carbon dioxide in controlling the breathing rate

Carbon dioxide

The most important chemical influencing breathing rate is carbon dioxide. The mechanism by which carbon dioxide regulates breathing depends on the hydrogen ions produced when carbon dioxide goes into solution and forms carbonic acid:

$$CO_2 + H_2O \longrightarrow H_2CO_3 \longrightarrow H^+ + HCO_3^-$$

Carbon dioxide   Water   Carbonic acid   Hydrogen ion   Bicarbonate ion

Three groups of chemoreceptors respond to the changing levels of hydrogen ions in the blood (Figure 14.12). Central chemoreceptors are located in a region of the brain called the medulla, near the breathing center. Peripheral chemoreceptors are located in the aortic bodies and the carotid bodies, small structures associated with the main blood vessel leaving the heart and going to the body as well as with the main blood vessels to the head. The chemoreceptors in the aortic bodies and carotid bodies also respond when the blood level of oxygen is low.

The chemoreceptors in the medulla are near its surface, where they are bathed in cerebrospinal fluid. Carbon dioxide diffuses from the blood into the cerebrospinal fluid, where it raises the hydrogen ion concentration by forming carbonic acid. When the rising hydrogen ion concentration stimulates the chemoreceptors in the medulla, breathing rate is increased and more carbon dioxide is exhaled, causing a decrease in the blood level of carbon dioxide.

Oxygen

Because oxygen, not carbon dioxide, is essential to survival, it may be somewhat surprising to learn that oxygen does not influence the breathing rate unless its blood level falls dangerously low. Only then do oxygen-sensitive chemoreceptors in the aortic bodies and carotid bodies send a message that the blood oxygen level is at a critical point, initiating a last-minute call to the medulla to increase the breathing rate and raise oxygen levels. If the oxygen level falls much more, the neurons in the inspiratory area die from a lack of oxygen and do not respond well to impulses from the chemoreceptors. As a result, the inspiratory area begins to send fewer impulses to the muscles of inspiration, the breathing rate decreases, and breathing may even cease completely.

Respiratory Disorders

Even in a restful day, you move more than 86,000 liters of air into and out of your lungs. The inhaled air may contain disease-causing organisms or noxious chemicals and particles. The respiratory system clears most of these materials out before they can cause harm. However, some of the disease-causing organisms, including viruses and bacteria, and other harmful substances remain and cause problems.

Common Cold

Any one of more than 200 viruses can cause a cold. Not surprisingly, some 30 million Americans have a cold at this moment. (The "common cold" is indeed common.) Because there are so many cold-causing viruses, you can, and usually do, get several colds a year, each from a different virus. Most people get their first cold before they are a year old.

Typically, a cold begins with a runny nose, possibly a sore throat, and sneezing. In the beginning, the nasal discharge is thin and watery, but it becomes thicker as it fills the nasal cavity. Almost any part of the respiratory system can be affected. Sneezing and a stuffy nose indicate that the infection is in the upper respiratory system. When the pharynx is affected, a sore throat results. The infection may spread to the bronchi, causing a cough, or to the larynx, making your voice hoarse.

As miserable as you feel with a cold, you can take comfort from knowing that your suffering will not last forever (see the Health Issue essay, *Surviving a Common Cold*). A cold is self-limiting, lasting only 1 to 2 weeks. Furthermore, colds are seldom fatal, except occasionally among the very young or very old or in those people already seriously ill with another malady.

Colds are spread when the causative virus is transmitted from an infected person. The viruses are plentiful in nasal secretions. However, transmission of the virus is not usually the result of direct inhalation of infected droplets from a cough or sneeze. It is more likely to be the result of handling an object that is contaminated with the virus. Cold viruses may remain alive on the skin or on an object for several hours, waiting for an unsuspecting person to touch them and contaminate his or her fingers. Subsequently, when the virus-laden fingers are touched to the mucous membranes of the nose, the transfer is completed. The best ways to prevent a cold are to wash your hands frequently and avoid being around people who have colds.

Flu

Flu is an abbreviation of *influenza,* another viral disease. The kinds of viruses that cause the flu are few compared to the number of different viruses that can cause a cold. In fact, the viruses that cause the flu in humans are all variants of three major types—A, B, and C (but there are hundreds of variants of these three basic types). Influenza of the A type is often more serious than B in that it is more frequently accompanied by severe complications, and it more frequently results in death. Influenza C causes a mild illness with cold symptoms.

Symptoms of the flu are similar to those of a cold, but they appear more suddenly and are more severe. (Though the onset of the flu may seem sudden, actually, by the time flu symptoms emerge, the disease has been incubating for several days.) A typical flu begins with chills and a high fever, about 103°F (39°C) in adults and perhaps higher in children. Many flu victims experience aches and pains in the muscles, especially in the back. Other common symptoms include a headache, sore throat, dry cough, weakness, pain and burning in the eyes, and sensitivity to light. When the flu hits, you usually feel sick enough to go to bed. The flu generally lasts for 7 to 10 days, but an additional week or more may pass before you are completely back on your feet.

The flu is often complicated by secondary infections, which set in when other disease-causing organisms take advantage of the body's weakened state. The most common complication is pneumonia, an inflammation of the lungs (described next). Possible secondary infections caused by bacteria include bronchitis, sinusitis, and ear infections.

One way to prevent the flu is by getting a flu shot—a vaccine made from the strains of viruses that scientists anticipate will cause the next outbreaks of the illness. Flu shots are only about 60% to 70% effective because the viruses they target mutate rapidly, causing new strains to appear. The new strains are not recognized by the immune system defenses that were programmed by the latest vaccine. Because each flu season brings new strains of flu viruses, the effectiveness of the vaccine lasts only as long as that season's most prevalent strains. As a result, new vaccines must be developed continually to protect us, and flu shots must be repeated each year.

Pneumonia

Pneumonia is an inflammation of the lungs that causes fluid to accumulate in the alveoli, thus reducing gas exchange. It also causes swelling and narrowing of the bronchioles, making breathing difficult. Pneumonia is usually caused by infection with bacteria or viruses, but fungi and protozoans can also cause it. Many cases of pneumonia develop after a common cold or influenza. Radiation, chemicals, and allergies can also bring it on.

Symptoms of pneumonia often begin suddenly. They include fever and chills, chest pain, cough, and shortness of breath. The severity of pneumonia varies from mild to life threatening. Treatment depends on the cause of the illness.

Strep Throat

Strep throat, a sore throat caused by *Streptococcus* bacteria, is a problem mainly in children 5 to 15 years old. The soreness is usually accompanied by swollen glands (lymph nodes) and a fever.

Although the pain of strep throat may be so mild that a doctor is never consulted, ignoring a strep infection can have serious consequences. If untreated, the *Streptococcus* bacteria can spread to other parts of the body and cause rheumatic fever or kidney problems. The main symptoms of rheumatic fever are swollen, painful joints and a characteristic rash. About 60% of rheumatic fever sufferers develop disease of the heart valves. Another possible consequence of a streptococcal infection is kidney disease (glomerulonephritis). The kidney damage is due to a reaction from the body's own protective mechanisms. The body produces antibodies that destroy the bacteria; but if these antibodies persist after the bacteria have been killed, they can cause the kidneys to become inflamed. The inflamed kidneys may be unable to filter the blood, and blood may leak into the urine.

Symptoms of strep throat include a sore throat and two of three of the following: fever of 101°F (38.33°C), white or yellow coating on tonsils, or swollen glands in the neck. Because many viruses can cause sore throats that look like strep infections, the only way to identify strep throat is to test for the causative organism. If *Streptococcus* bacteria are found, an antibiotic, usually penicillin, is prescribed to prevent rheumatic fever and kidney disease.

Tuberculosis

Tuberculosis (TB) is caused by a rod-shaped bacterium, *Mycobacterium tuberculosis*. It is spread when the cough of an infected person sends bacteria-laden droplets into the air and the bacteria are inhaled into the lungs of an uninfected person. Because the bacteria are inhaled, the lungs are usually the first sites attacked; but the bacteria can spread to any part of the body, especially to the brain, kidneys, or bone.

As a defense against the bacteria, the body forms fibrous connective tissue casings, called tubercles, that encapsulate the bacteria (hence, the name of the disease). Although the formation of tubercles slows the spread of the disease, it does not actually kill the bacteria. The immune system destroys at least some of the walled-off bacteria and may, in fact, kill them all. But pockets of bacteria may persist undetected for many years. Later, if the immune system becomes weakened, the disease may progress to the secondary stage as pockets of bacteria become reactivated and multiply. Furthermore, bacteria may escape from the tubercles and be carried by the bloodstream to other parts of the body. Whenever the patient becomes weak, ill, or poorly nourished, bacteria can become active and multiply, causing the disease to flare up.

Surviving a Common Cold

The only thing more common than the cold is advice on how to treat it. Here we will examine the validity of some frequently suggested treatments for a cold.

1. **Take large doses of vitamin C?** Vitamin C will not prevent a cold unless you are malnourished or under extreme physical stress. Nonetheless, some people who take vitamin C may experience less severe or shorter colds than do people who do not take vitamin C.

2. **Suck on a zinc lozenge?** Some evidence exists that zinc slows viral replication, prevents cold viruses from adhering to nasal membranes, and boosts the immune system. But it is not clear whether zinc lozenges can alleviate cold symptoms. Some people who begin taking zinc within the first day or two of the onset of symptoms and continue taking a lozenge every two or three hours for several days do experience some relief from cold symptoms.

3. **Take echinacea?** Commonly known as the purple coneflower, echinacea has been used for centuries by cold sufferers. However, scientific studies examining whether the herbal medication is effective in preventing or treating the common cold have produced conflicting results.

4. **Take an antibiotic?** Antibiotics are *not* effective against viruses and cannot cure a cold. However, a doctor may prescribe antibiotics to control secondary bacterial infections—such as a middle ear infection, bronchitis, or sinusitis—that may accompany a cold. Unnecessary use of an antibiotic may cause side effects such as diarrhea and can lead to the development of bacterial resistance to the drug. The rise of strains of bacteria that are resistant to antibiotics is likely to be a major threat to public health in the coming years, as discussed in Chapter 13a.

5. **Go to bed?** Bed rest enables the body to muster its resources and fight secondary infections. Staying at home with a cold is also socially responsible, because it helps prevent the spread of the virus. But if you are too busy to spend a few days in bed because of a cold, you probably are not hurting yourself. Bed rest will not cure your cold or shorten its duration.

6. **Have some chicken soup?** Grandmothers have long prescribed chicken soup to treat a cold, and doctors finally agree that the advice has some merit. You should always consume plenty of fluids when you have a cold. They help loosen secretions in the respiratory tract and thus reduce congestion. As a result, the patient can breathe more freely, and the amount of time the cold viruses are in contact with the cells lining the respiratory system is reduced. Hot fluids, such as chicken soup, are more effective than cold ones for increasing the flow of nasal mucus.

Although a cold cannot be cured, there are ways to make it more bearable. Some ways to relieve the misery of a cold are as follows.

For Nasal Congestion

The congestion is caused when the mucous membranes of the nasal cavities become swollen and produce increased amounts of mucus because of viral infection. The best ways to relieve the congestion are to drink plenty of extra fluids and to inhale moist air from a hot bath, shower, or vaporizer.

By constricting small blood vessels in the nose, decongestants may reduce the accumulation of fluid causing nasal congestion. Unfortunately, if taken orally, decongestants constrict small blood vessels throughout the body; in the process, they raise blood pressure. Other possible side effects of oral decongestants include nervousness, sleeplessness, and dryness of the mouth. Therefore, if you must use a decongestant, it is wise to choose one in the form of nose sprays or drops. Use these at the recommended dosage and only for a few days.

Although antihistamines are present in many cold remedies, there is no evidence that they are effective in reducing nasal congestion caused by colds. Furthermore, antihistamines may cause blurred vision, retention of urine, and dizziness. Drowsiness is a major side effect, so if you do take an antihistamine, avoid driving or other hazardous activities.

For Coughs

Coughing is a protective reflex controlled by a cough center in the brain. Besides clearing the respiratory tubules of foreign material, coughing loosens and removes phlegm and mucus. Therefore, it is not always a good idea to suppress a cough. On the other hand, if a cough persists for more than a week, you should see a physician.

The safest and cheapest cough remedies are substances such as hard candy or honey, which coat and soothe the throat, and drinking extra fluids, which loosens the mucus and helps relieve some irritation.

Cough medications fall into two general classes: suppressants and expectorants. Cough suppressants work by reducing the activity of the brain's cough center. These are helpful in easing dry, hacking coughs. The most effective nonprescription cough suppressant is dextromethorphan. Codeine also suppresses coughs, but it is available only by prescription. A cough that brings up sputum is performing a useful function and should not be suppressed. Instead, removal of the irritating substances should be assisted with an expectorant, which increases the flow of respiratory tract secretions.

For Fever and Pain Relief

The most common medicines for relief of fever and pain are aspirin, acetaminophen, and ibuprofen. Children and teenagers should not take aspirin because it is linked to Reye's syndrome, a deadly disease that affects all body organs. Keep in mind that fever can be a good thing. The additional body heat slows the growth and reproduction (or replication) of many disease-causing organisms (discussed in Chapter 13). Unless the fever is very high (above 102°F, 40°C, in an adult), you may want to let it run its course.

The initial symptoms of tuberculosis, if they occur, are similar to those of the flu. In the secondary stage, the patient usually develops a fever, loses weight, and feels tired. If the infection is in the lungs, as is usual, it causes a dry cough that eventually produces pus-filled and blood-streaked phlegm. If the immune system is weak or if the disease is untreated, TB progresses to a second stage. In this stage the bacteria multiply rapidly and destroy the cells of the affected organ. The second stage of TB can be fatal, especially if it is caused by a multi-drug-resistant strain of bacteria; and resistant strains are becoming increasingly common (discussed in Chapter 13a).

what would you do?

DOTS (Directly Observed Therapy, short course) is the World Health Organization's recommended treatment for tuberculosis. DOTS, which mandates that someone witness the TB patient swallowing medication each day, is in place in most major cities in the United States. The treatment ranges from 6 months to 2 years (the latter, if a multi-drug-resistant strain is present). Patients' failure to complete TB treatment is what has led to the drug-resistant strains of the TB bacterium. Is DOTS a fair balance of protection of the public with personal rights? What do you think?

(a) Normal alveoli

(b) Emphysema causes breakdown of alveolar walls.

FIGURE 14.14 A comparison of (a) normal alveoli and (b) alveoli in an individual with emphysema. Notice that in emphysema, the alveolar walls rupture and there is a decrease in the surface area for gas exchange, an increase in the dead air space, and a thickening of the alveolar walls.

Bronchitis

Viruses, bacteria, or chemical irritation may cause the mucous membrane of the bronchi to become inflamed—a condition called *bronchitis*. The inflammation results in the production of excess mucus, which triggers a deep cough that produces greenish yellow phlegm.

There are two types of bronchitis: acute and chronic. Acute bronchitis, which often follows a cold, is usually caused by the cold virus itself, but it may be caused by bacteria that take advantage of the body's lowered resistance and invade the trachea and bronchi. An antibiotic will hasten recovery if the cause is bacterial.

When a cough that brings up phlegm is present for at least 3 months in each of 2 consecutive years, the condition is called chronic bronchitis, a more serious problem that is usually associated with cigarette smoking or air pollution. Some people with chronic bronchitis may lack an enzyme that normally protects the air passageways from such irritants. As the disease progresses, breathing becomes increasingly difficult, partly because the linings of the air tubules thicken, narrowing the passageway for air. Contraction of the muscles in bronchiole walls and excessive secretion of mucus further obstruct the air tubules.

Chronic bronchitis can have serious consequences. The degenerative changes in the lining of the air tubules make removal of mucus more difficult. As a result, the patient is more likely to develop lung infections such as pneumonia, which can be fatal, and degenerative changes—such as emphysema—in the lungs.

Emphysema

Emphysema is a common consequence of smoking, although this condition can have other causes as well. In *emphysema*, the walls of the alveoli break down and merge, thereby making the alveoli fewer

and larger (Figure **14.14**). This change has two major effects: a reduction in the surface area available for gas exchange and an increase in the volume of residual, or "dead," air in the lungs. Exhalation, you may recall, is a passive process that depends on the elasticity of lung tissue. In emphysema, the lungs lose that elasticity, and air becomes trapped inside them. As the dead air space increases, adequate ventilation requires more forceful inhalation. Forcing the air in causes more alveolar walls to rupture, further increasing the dead air space. Lung size gradually increases as the residual volume of air becomes greater, giving a person with emphysema a characteristic barrel chest; but gas exchange continues to become more difficult because surface area is reduced, despite the increase in lung size. To get an idea of what poor lung ventilation caused by increased dead air space feels like, take a deep breath, then exhale only slightly, and repeat this process several times. Notice how quickly you feel an oxygen shortage if you continue taking very shallow breaths that keep the lungs almost completely filled with air.

Shortness of breath, the main symptom of emphysema, is a result of both the decreased alveolar surface area and the increased dead air space. As the disease progresses, gas exchange becomes even more difficult because the alveolar walls thicken with fibrous connective tissue. The oxygen that does reach the alveoli has difficulty crossing the connective tissue to enter the blood. Thus, a person with emphysema constantly gasps for air.

Emphysema can be treated, but it cannot be cured. Cigarette smoking is the most common cause for emphysema, so the first step in treatment is usually to quit smoking. Medicines to widen the respiratory air tubules can be prescribed to make airflow to and from the lungs easier. In addition, supplemental oxygen may be administered to increase the amount of oxygen reaching the patient's body cells, which will relieve some of the symptoms of emphysema.

Cigarette Smoking and Lung Disease

Smoking is the greatest single preventable cause of disease, disability, and death in our society. In fact, every cigarette pack and cigarette advertisement in the United States must bear a warning from the Surgeon General stating the dangers of tobacco smoke. Yet tobacco, which causes bodily harm when used exactly as intended, is legal to sell to anyone at least 18 years old.

Because the objective of smoking is to bring smoke into the lungs, we can expect some of its most damaging effects to be seen there. The damage to the respiratory system of smokers is gradual and progressive. It begins as the smoke hampers the actions of two of the lungs' cleansing mechanisms—cilia and macrophages. Even the first few puffs from a cigarette slow the movement of the cilia, making them less effective in sweeping debris from the air passageways. Smoking an entire cigarette prevents the cilia from moving for an hour or longer. With continued smoking, the nicotine and sulfur dioxide in the smoke paralyze the cilia, and the cyanide destroys the ciliated cells.

Cigarette smoke causes a smoker's lungs to be chronically inflamed. The inflammation summons macrophages, the wandering cells that engulf foreign debris, to the lungs for the purpose of cleaning the lung surfaces. But, just as smoke paralyzes the cilia, it also paralyzes the macrophages, further hampering the cleansing efforts. As the cilia and macrophages become less effective, greater quantities of tar and disease-causing organisms remain within the respiratory system. As a result, cigarette smokers spend more time sick in bed and lose more workdays each year than do nonsmokers.

At the same time that the cilia and macrophages are being slowed, the smoke stimulates the mucus-secreting cells in the linings of the respiratory passageways. Consequently, the smaller airways become plugged with mucus, making breathing more difficult. At this point, if not before, "smoker's cough" begins. Coughing is a protective reflex, and initially the smoker coughs simply because smoke irritates air passageways. However, as smoking continues and the cilia become less and less able to remove mucus and debris, the only way to remove the material from the passageways is to cough. The cough is generally worse in the morning, when the body attempts to clear away the mucus that accumulated overnight.

Gradually, the inflammation and congestion within the lungs, along with the constant irritation from smoke, lead to chronic bronchitis, a disease characterized by a persistent deep cough that brings up mucus. The air passageways become narrow due to the thickening of their linings caused by repeated infection, accumulation of mucus, and contraction of the smooth muscle in their walls. Airflow is restricted, resulting in breathlessness and wheezing.

Emphysema, in which the walls of alveoli are destroyed, is often the next stage in the progressive damage to the lungs. Airways and alveolar walls lose elasticity as tar causes body defense cells to secrete destructive enzymes. Consequently, the lung tissues can no longer absorb the increase in pressure that accompanies a cough, and the delicate alveolar walls break like soap bubbles. With more and more alveoli destroyed, the surface area for gas exchange is reduced, so less oxygen is delivered to the body. Besides all these negative effects on the respiratory system, smoking is the single major cause of lung cancer, and it causes other cancers as well. In fact, smoking is responsible for 30% of all cancer deaths.

The health benefits if you quit smoking are enormous. Much of the damage caused by smoke is reversible once you quit. For example, the risk of lung cancer drops, though it never falls as low as the level for people who have never smoked (Figure **14.A**).

Lung Cancer

Between 85% and 90% of all cases of lung cancer are caused by smoking and are, therefore, preventable. Lung cancer usually has no symptoms until it is quite advanced. Therefore, it is not usually detected in time for a cure.

The progression to lung cancer begins with chronic inflammation of the lungs and is marked by changes in the cells of the airway linings. These cell changes are often caused by inhaled carcinogens, including those found in tobacco smoke (more chemicals found in tobacco smoke—and the respiratory problems they cause—are discussed in the Health Issue essay, *Cigarette Smoking and Lung Disease*.)

In a nonsmoker, the lining of the air passageways has a basement membrane underlying basal cells and a single layer of ciliated columnar cells. In a smoker, one of the first signs of damage is an increase in the number of layers of basal cells. Next, the ciliated columnar cells die and disappear. The nuclei of the basal cells then begin to change as mutations accumulate, and the cells become disorganized. This is the beginning of cancer. Eventually, the uncontrolled cell division forms a tumor (Figure **14.15**). When cancer cells break through the basement membrane, they can spread to other parts of the lung and to the rest of the body through a process called metastasis (see Chapter 21a).

FIGURE 14.15 Lung cancer. The tumor is the light-colored solid mass shown in the upper region of the lung.

If you are a smoker who would like to break the habit, here are some suggestions from the Centers for Disease Control and Prevention:

1. **Prepare. Set a date to quit.** Throw away all cigarettes and ashtrays in your home, car, and workplace. Do not allow other people to smoke inside your home. If this is not the first time you are trying to quit, review the actions that helped your efforts in the past and those that did not help.

2. **Do not have even a puff of any kind of cigarette.** Low tar, low nicotine cigarettes do not help you quit.

3. **Enlist support and encouragement from your family, friends, and health care provider.**

4. **Make a list of the reasons you want to quit.** Do you want to gain control of your life? Do you want better health? Do you want to protect your family and friends from the smoke from your cigarette? Focusing on why you want to quit increases motivation to quit.

5. **Learn new skills and behaviors.** Distract yourself from smoking by walking, talking, or keeping busy with a task. Change your routine to avoid behaviors or places that you associate with smoking. Find ways to reduce your stress; you could try taking a hot bath, exercising, or reading a book.

6. **Recognize that quitting will be difficult.** You are addicted to nicotine. There are medications to help you quit. Most of these medications provide nicotine in a form other than smoking: gum, patch, inhaler, or nasal spray.

7. **Be prepared to face difficult situations.** Try to avoid drinking alcohol, because drinking lowers the likelihood of success. Try to avoid places where people will be smoking, because the smoke will increase your cravings. Be aware that you are likely to gain weight. Many people gain weight when they quit smoking, but the gain is usually less than 10 pounds. Do not let weight gain discourage your attempt to quit smoking.

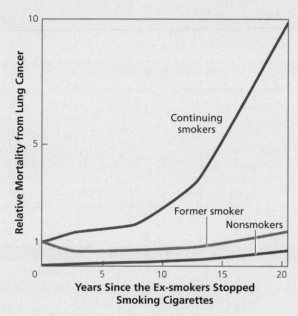

FIGURE 14.A Comparison of lung cancer deaths among lifetime nonsmokers, ex-smokers, and continuing smokers. Quitting results in dramatic reduction of a smoker's risk of death due to lung cancer.

highlighting the concepts

Structures of the Respiratory System (pp. 276–282)

- The role of the respiratory system is to exchange oxygen and carbon dioxide between the air and the blood. The oxygen that we breathe is needed to maximize the number of energy-storing ATP molecules formed from food energy. Exhaling carbon dioxide, a waste product formed by the same reactions, helps regulate the acid–base balance of body fluids.
- The first structure that inhaled air usually passes through is the nose, which serves to clean, warm, and moisten the incoming air.
- The sinuses are air-filled spaces in the facial bones that also help warm and moisten the air.
- After leaving the nose, the inhaled air passes through the pharynx, or throat, and then the larynx, or voice box. Movements of the larynx during swallowing prevent food from entering the airways and lungs.
- The air passageways include the trachea, which branches to form bronchi, which branch various times in the lungs and eventually form progressively smaller branching tubules called bronchioles. The bronchioles terminate at the lungs' gas-exchange surfaces, the alveoli. Each alveolus is a thin-walled air sac encased in a capillary network.

Mechanism of Breathing (pp. 282–283)

- Pressure changes within the lungs, caused by changes in the size of the thoracic cavity, move air into and out of the lungs. Inspiration occurs when the size of the thoracic cavity increases, causing the pressure in the lungs to drop below atmospheric pressure. Expiration occurs when the size of the thoracic cavity decreases and pressure in the lungs rises above atmospheric pressure.

Transport of Gases between the Lungs and the Cells (pp. 283–285)

- Oxygen and carbon dioxide are exchanged between the alveolar air and the capillary blood by diffusion along their concentration (partial pressure) gradients. Oxygen diffuses from the alveoli into the blood, where it binds to hemoglobin within the red blood cells and is delivered to the body cells. A small amount of carbon dioxide is carried to the lungs dissolved in the blood plasma or bound to hemoglobin. Most, however, is transported to the lungs as bicarbonate ions.

carbon dioxide dissolves in plasma. Extremely low levels of oxygen also increase breathing rate.

Respiratory Centers in the Brain (pp. 285–286)

- The basic rhythm of breathing is controlled by the inspiratory area within the medulla of the brain. The neurons within this center undergo spontaneous bouts of activity. When they are active, messages are sent, causing contraction of the diaphragm and the muscles of the rib cage. As a result, the thoracic cavity increases in size and air is drawn into the lungs. When the inspiratory neurons are inactive, the diaphragm and rib cage muscles relax, and exhalation occurs passively. Also in the medulla is an expiratory area that causes forceful exhalation during heavy breathing.
- The most powerful stimulant to breathing is an increased number of hydrogen ions in the blood, formed from carbonic acid when

Respiratory Disorders (pp. 286–291)

- The common cold and the flu are caused by viruses. Pneumonia is an inflammation of the lungs (caused by bacteria or viruses) that causes fluid to fill the alveoli and narrows bronchioles. Strep throat is a sore throat caused by *Streptococcus* bacteria. Acute bronchitis is caused by either bacteria or a virus. Chronic bronchitis is a persistent irritation of the bronchi. Emphysema is a breakdown of the alveolar walls and thus a reduction in the gas-exchange surfaces. Chronic bronchitis and emphysema are usually caused by smoking or air pollution. The primary cause of lung cancer is cigarette smoking.

recognizing key terms

respiratory system *p. 276*	vocal cords *p. 280*	intercostal muscles *p. 282*	vital capacity *p. 283*
nasal cavities *p. 277*	trachea *p. 280*	inspiration *p. 282*	residual volume *p. 283*
sinuses *p. 278*	bronchi (sing. bronchus) *p. 280*	expiration *p. 282*	total lung capacity *p. 283*
pharynx *p. 279*	bronchioles *p. 281*	tidal volume *p. 283*	oxyhemoglobin *p. 284*
larynx *p. 279*	bronchial tree *p. 281*	inspiratory reserve	carbaminohemoglobin *p. 284*
epiglottis *p. 280*	alveolus (pl. alveoli) *p. 281*	volume *p. 283*	carbonic anhydrase *p. 285*
glottis *p. 280*	surfactant *p. 281*	expiratory reserve	
Heimlich maneuver *p. 280*	diaphragm *p. 282*	volume *p. 283*	

reviewing the concepts

1. Why must we breathe oxygen? *p. 276*
2. Trace the path of air from the nose to the lungs. *pp. 277–278*
3. How are most particles and disease-causing organisms removed from the inhaled air before it reaches the lungs? *p. 278*
4. Explain why food does not usually enter the lower respiratory system when you swallow. *p. 280*
5. How is human speech produced? *p. 280*
6. What is the function of the cartilage rings in the trachea? What would happen to the trachea without these rings? *p. 280*
7. What is the bronchial tree? *p. 281*
8. How are the pressure changes in the thoracic cavity that are responsible for breathing created? *pp. 282–283*
9. Which is a larger volume of air: tidal volume or vital capacity? Explain. *p. 283*
10. How is most oxygen transported to the body cells? *pp. 283–284*
11. How is most carbon dioxide transported from the cells to the lungs? *pp. 284–285*
12. What region of the brain causes the basic breathing rhythm? *p. 285*
13. Explain how blood carbon dioxide levels regulate the breathing rate. *p. 286*
14. What are the causes of the shortness of breath experienced by people with emphysema? *p. 289*
15. Choose the *correct* statement.
    a. During quiet breathing, expiration does not usually involve the contraction of muscles.
    b. Expiration occurs when the diaphragm and the rib muscles contract.
    c. Expiration occurs as the chest (thoracic) cavity enlarges.
    d. The larynx acts like a suction pump to pull air into the lungs.

16. You should be able to hold your breath longer than normal after you hyperventilate (breathe rapidly for a while) because hyperventilating
    a. decreases your blood oxygen levels.
    b. decreases blood carbon dioxide levels.
    c. increases blood oxygen levels.
    d. increases blood carbon dioxide levels.
17. The structure specialized to produce the sound of your voice is the
    a. trachea.
    b. larynx.
    c. bronchiole.
    d. epiglottis.
18. In a healthy person, most of the particles that are inhaled into the respiratory system
    a. are trapped in the mucus and moved by cilia to the pharynx (toward the digestive system).
    b. pass through the alveoli into the circulatory system, where they are engulfed by white blood cells.
    c. are caught on the vocal cords.
    d. are trapped in the sinuses.
19. In emphysema
    a. the number of alveoli is reduced.
    b. cartilage rings in the trachea break down.
    c. the diaphragm is paralyzed.
    d. the epiglottis becomes less mobile.
    e. the pharynx is constricted.
20. The _____ is the flap that covers the trachea to prevent food from entering during swallowing.
21. The enzyme in red blood cells that reversibly converts carbonic acid to bicarbonate ions and hydrogen ions is _____.

applying the concepts

1. Tatyana is a young woman with iron-deficiency anemia, so her blood does not carry enough oxygen. Would you expect this condition to affect her breathing rate or tidal volume? Why or why not?

2. Cigarette smoke destroys the cilia in the respiratory system. Explain why the loss of these cilia is a reason that cigarette smokers tend to lose more workdays because of illness than do nonsmokers.

3. Rosa has a 4-year-old son, Juan, who threatens to hold his breath until she gives him a candy bar. Should she be worried about Juan holding his breath? Why?

4. Vincent is having an asthma attack. During an asthma attack the bronchioles constrict (get narrower in diameter). Does Vincent have more difficulty inhaling or exhaling? Why?

becoming information literate

Use at least three reliable sources (books, journals, or websites) to answer the following questions. List each source you considered, and explain why you chose the three sources you used.

1. The incidence of childhood asthma has increased steadily during the last few decades. What hypotheses have been proposed (at least three) to explain this increase in asthma? What evidence supports each hypothesis?

2. Studies have shown that secondhand cigarette smoke can pose health risks to nonsmokers nearby. Many state and local governments have laws preventing smoking in public places so that nonsmokers are not exposed to secondhand smoke. Present at least two arguments for and two against laws that ban smoking in public places. Then take a stand for or against such laws and defend your position.

3. Many of the first responders to the site of the collapse of the World Trade Center on September 11, 2001, have developed respiratory problems. Describe some of these respiratory problems. What is being done to treat these problems? Is there financial assistance for the affected people to help pay for their treatment?

Additional questions can be found online at The Human Biology Place, www.humanbiology.com.

15

The Digestive System

The Gastrointestinal Tract

Specialized Compartments for Food Processing
- Mouth
- Pharynx
- Esophagus
- Stomach
- Small Intestine
- Accessory Organs: Pancreas, Liver, and Gallbladder
- Large Intestine

Nerves and Hormones in Digestion

Health Issue

Heartburn and Peptic Ulcers—Those Burning Sensations

The digestive system breaks food into its component subunits that are small enough to absorb. The subunits are then used for energy or as building blocks to make new molecules.

As Balamani was reading his human biology textbook, he was startled by a discussion of gastroesophageal reflux: the symptoms being described matched his own! He often experienced heartburn—an occasional backing up of stomach content—when he could feel a burning sensation behind his breast bone, and once in a while his stomach hurt. Antacids didn't seem to help. He had assumed that the symptoms were due to the drastic changes in his diet since his move from India to the United States and that they would go away after a while. The textbook, however, said that "acid reflux" is caused by a problem at the base of the esophagus where it empties into the stomach.

The next day Balamani consulted his doctor, who gave him several instructions for dealing with his condition: elevate the head of his bed to allow gravity to work for his esophagus (keeping fluids down), cut back on fatty foods, cut out acidic beverages like orange juice and caffeinated beverages like coffee, reduce the size of meals while increasing their frequency, and by all means pay fewer visits to fast-food restaurants. Within a few weeks, Balamani was feeling much better.

We learn in this chapter that food usually travels in one direction through the digestive system, unless there is a problem such as gastroesophageal reflux. We see how the digestive system is organized for breaking down food molecules and making them available for use as a source of energy or as raw material for the growth and repair of cells. Food is digested and nutrients and water are absorbed in specialized compartments along a long tube, the GI tract. Undigested materials are then eliminated from the body.

The Gastrointestinal Tract

There is some truth to the saying, "You are what you eat." Rest assured, however, that no matter how many hamburgers you eat, you will never become one. Instead, the hamburger becomes *you*. This transformation is largely due to the activities of the digestive system. Like an assembly line in reverse, the digestive system takes the food we eat and breaks the complex organic molecules into their chemical subunits. The subunits are molecules small enough to be absorbed into the bloodstream and delivered to body cells, where they either provide fuel for growth and repair of the body or they provide energy for daily activities. Imagine that you just ate a cheeseburger on a bun. The starch in the bun may fuel a jump for joy; the protein in the beef may be used to build muscle; and the fat in the cheese may become myelin sheaths that insulate nerve fibers. The digestive system breaks food into molecules small enough to be absorbed and delivered to the cells that use them. Table **15.1** identifies the structures of the digestive system and describes their roles in both mechanical and chemical digestion. You can refer to the table as you read about each of the digestive structures below.

The **digestive system** consists of a long, hollow tube, called the **gastrointestinal (GI) tract**, into which various accessory glands release their secretions (Figure **15.1**). The GI tract begins at the mouth and continues to the esophagus, stomach, small intestine, and large intestine. The hollow area of the tube through which food and fluids travel is called the *lumen*. Along most of its length, the walls of the GI tract have four basic layers.

- **Mucosa.** The innermost layer of the GI tract is the moist, mucus-secreting layer called the **mucosa.** The mucus helps lubricate the lumen, allowing food to slide through easily. Mucus also helps protect the cells in the lining of the GI

TABLE 15.1 Review of Structures of the Digestive System

Structure	Description/Functions	Mechanical Digestion	Chemical Digestion
Mouth	Receives food; contains teeth and tongue; tongue manipulates food and monitors quality	Teeth tear and crush food into smaller pieces	Digestion of carbohydrates begins
Pharynx	Area that both food and air pass through	None	None
Esophagus	Tube that transports food from mouth to stomach	None	None
Stomach	J-shaped muscular sac for food storage	Churning of stomach mixes food with gastric juice, creating liquid chyme	Protein digestion begins
Small intestine	Long tube where digestion is completed and nutrients are absorbed	Segmental contractions mix food with intestinal enzymes, pancreatic enzymes, and bile	Carbohydrate, protein, and fat digestion completed
Large intestine	Final tubular region of GI tract; absorbs water and ions; houses bacteria; forms and expels feces	None	Some digestion is carried out by bacteria
Anus	Terminal outlet of digestive tract	None	None

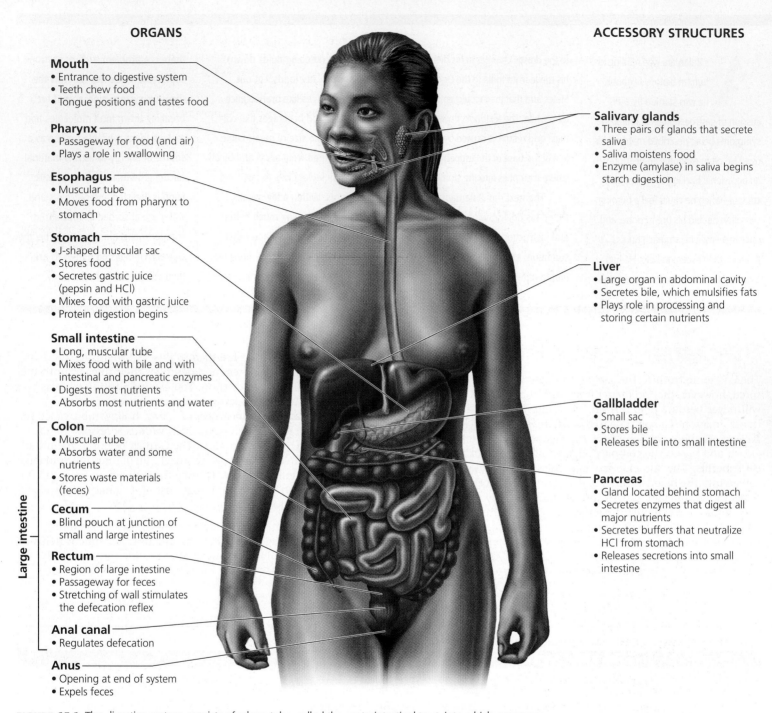

ORGANS

Mouth
- Entrance to digestive system
- Teeth chew food
- Tongue positions and tastes food

Pharynx
- Passageway for food (and air)
- Plays a role in swallowing

Esophagus
- Muscular tube
- Moves food from pharynx to stomach

Stomach
- J-shaped muscular sac
- Stores food
- Secretes gastric juice (pepsin and HCl)
- Mixes food with gastric juice
- Protein digestion begins

Small intestine
- Long, muscular tube
- Mixes food with bile and with intestinal and pancreatic enzymes
- Digests most nutrients
- Absorbs most nutrients and water

Large intestine

Colon
- Muscular tube
- Absorbs water and some nutrients
- Stores waste materials (feces)

Cecum
- Blind pouch at junction of small and large intestines

Rectum
- Region of large intestine
- Passageway for feces
- Stretching of wall stimulates the defecation reflex

Anal canal
- Regulates defecation

Anus
- Opening at end of system
- Expels feces

ACCESSORY STRUCTURES

Salivary glands
- Three pairs of glands that secrete saliva
- Saliva moistens food
- Enzyme (amylase) in saliva begins starch digestion

Liver
- Large organ in abdominal cavity
- Secretes bile, which emulsifies fats
- Plays role in processing and storing certain nutrients

Gallbladder
- Small sac
- Stores bile
- Releases bile into small intestine

Pancreas
- Gland located behind stomach
- Secretes enzymes that digest all major nutrients
- Secretes buffers that neutralize HCl from stomach
- Releases secretions into small intestine

FIGURE 15.1 The digestive system consists of a long tube, called the gastrointestinal tract, into which accessory structures release their secretions.

tract from rough substances in the food and from digestive enzymes. In some regions of the digestive system, cells in the mucosa also secrete digestive enzymes. In addition, the mucosae in some parts of the digestive tract are highly folded, which increases the surface area for absorption.

- **Submucosa.** The next layer, the **submucosa**, consists of connective tissue containing blood vessels, lymph vessels, and nerves. The blood supply maintains the cells of the digestive system and, in some regions, picks up and transports the products of digestion. The nerves are important in coordinating the contractions of the next layer.

- **Muscularis.** The next layer, the **muscularis**, is responsible for movement of materials through the GI tract and for mixing ingested materials with digestive secretions. In most sections of the GI tract, the muscularis is a double layer of smooth muscle. (The stomach, as you will read later, is an exception; it has three layers of muscle.) In the inner, "circular" layer of muscle, the muscle cells encircle the tube, causing a constriction when they contract. In the outer, longitudinal layer, the muscle cells are arranged parallel to the GI tract. Longitudinal muscles shorten the GI tract when they contract. The muscle layers churn the food until it is

Lumen

Blood vessels

Lymphatic vessel

Nerve

The **mucosa** is a mucous membrane that lines the GI tract and secretes mucus that lubricates and protects the GI tract.

The **submucosa** is a layer of connective tissue that contains blood vessels, lymph vessels, and nerves.

The **muscularis** is made up of two layers of smooth muscle—one circular and one longitudinal.

The **serosa** is a connective tissue covering that secretes a fluid to lubricate the outside of the GI tract.

FIGURE 15.2 Along most of its length, the wall of the GI tract has four basic layers: the mucosa, the submucosa, the muscularis, and the serosa.

liquefied, mix the resulting liquid with enzymes, and propel the food along the GI tract in a process called peristalsis, which is discussed later in this chapter. Local muscle contractions in random regions of the GI tract, especially in the small intestine, are called segmental contractions. Segmental contractions mix intestinal contents—food and digestive juices (fluids containing enzymes and other fluids that aid in digestion). Segmental contractions also assist absorption of digested food by moving intestinal contents over the intestinal wall.

• **Serosa.** The **serosa,** a thin layer of epithelial tissue supported by connective tissue, wraps around the GI tract. It secretes a fluid that lubricates the outside of the GI tract to reduce friction with contacting surfaces of the intestine and other abdominal organs. (Figure **15.2**).

Regions of the GI tract are specialized to process food in particular ways. One aspect of that processing is *mechanical digestion,* the physical breaking of food into smaller pieces, and another is *chemical digestion,* the breaking of chemical bonds so that complex molecules are taken apart into smaller subunits. Chemical digestion produces molecules that can be absorbed into the bloodstream and used by the cells. Next we trace the path food travels along the GI tract to see how it is processed and absorbed.

Specialized Compartments for Food Processing

As food moves along the GI tract, it passes through the mouth, pharynx, esophagus, stomach, small intestine, and large intestine. The salivary glands, liver, and pancreas add secretions along the way. Most nutrients are absorbed from the small intestine. Additional water is absorbed in the large intestine. Undigested and indigestible materials pass out the anus.

Mouth

The entryway to the digestive system and the first stop on food's journey through it is the *mouth,* also called the oral cavity. The roof of the mouth is called the *palate.* The region of the palate closest to the front of the mouth, the hard palate, is reinforced with bone. Toward the back of the mouth is the soft palate, which consists only of muscle and prevents food from entering the nose during swallowing. The mouth serves several functions: (1) it begins mechanical and, to some extent, chemical digestion; (2) it monitors food quality; and (3) it moistens and manipulates food so that it can be swallowed. The teeth, salivary glands, and tongue all contribute to these functions.

Teeth and mechanical digestion

As we chew, our teeth break solid foods into smaller fragments that are easier to swallow and digest. The sharp, chisel-like incisors in the front of the mouth (see Figure **15.3a**) slice the food as we bite into it.

Incisors (8)

Canines (4)

Premolars (8)

Molars (12)

Upper jaw   Lower jaw

(a) The teeth slice, tear, and grind food until it can be swallowed.

Enamel

Dentin

Pulp cavity (contains blood vessels and nerves)

Gum (gingiva)

Root canal

Cementum

Bone

Crown

Root

(b) The structure of the human tooth is suited for its function of breaking food into smaller pieces.

FIGURE 15.3 Adult human teeth

At the same time, the pointed canines to the sides of the incisors tear the food. Then the food is ground, crushed, and pulverized by the premolars and molars, which lie along the sides of the mouth.

Teeth are alive. In the center of each tooth is the pulp, which contains the tooth's life-support systems—blood vessels that nourish the tooth and nerves that sense heat, cold, pressure, and pain (Figure 15.3b). Surrounding the pulp is a hard, bonelike substance, called dentin. The crown of the tooth (the part visible above the gum line) is covered with enamel, a nonliving material that is hardened with calcium salts. The root of the tooth (the part below the gum line) is covered with a calcified, yet living and sensitive connective tissue called cementum. The roots of the teeth fit into sockets in the jawbone. Blood vessels and nerves reach the pulp through a tiny tunnel through the root, called the root canal.

Tooth decay is caused by acid produced by bacteria living in the mouth (Figure **15.4**). When you eat, food particles become trapped between the teeth, in the small spaces where the teeth meet the gums, and in the hollows of molars. Bacteria in the mouth are nourished by the sugar in these food particles. As bacteria digest the sugar, acid is produced that erodes the enamel and causes a cavity to form. Blood vessels in the pulp widen in response to this erosion, allowing greater numbers of white bloods cells to reach the area and fight infection. The widened blood vessels may press on nerves, causing a toothache. When the enamel has been penetrated, bacteria can invade the softer dentin beneath. If a dentist does not fill the cavity, the bacteria can infect the pulp. *Plaque,* an invisible film of bacteria, mucus, and food particles, promotes tooth decay because it holds the acid against the enamel. Daily brushing and flossing helps remove plaque, reducing the chance of tooth decay.

Gum disease, which affects two of three middle-aged people in the United States, is a major cause of tooth loss in adults. *Gingivitis* (*gingiv–*, the gums; *–itis,* inflammation of), an early stage of gum disease, occurs when plaque that has formed along the gum line causes the gums to become inflamed and swollen. The swollen gums can bleed and do not fit as tightly around the teeth as they should. The pocket that forms between the tooth and the gum traps additional plaque. The bacteria in the plaque can then attack the bone and soft tissues around the tooth, a condition called *periodontitis* (*peri–*, around; *dont,* teeth; *–itis,* inflammation of). As the tooth's bony socket and the tissues that hold the tooth in place are eroded, the tooth becomes loose.

what would you do?

For the past 50 years, some communities whose water is not naturally fluoridated have added low doses of fluoride to the public water supply to reduce tooth decay. Nearly 98% of Americans have, or have had, tooth decay. Over 6 million teeth are removed each year. Proponents of fluoridation point out that the incidence of tooth decay has declined after the addition of fluoride to drinking water. Opponents of the practice argue that (1) fluoridation of the water supply is a form of forced medication; (2) the dosage cannot be properly controlled because of differences in people's body weight and the amount of water people consume; and (3) excessive fluoride intake causes teeth to become brown and mottled. If you had to vote on fluoridation of your public water supply, what additional information would you want before voting? How would you vote at present?

Salivary glands and chemical digestion

Three pairs of salivary glands—the sublingual (below the tongue), submandibular (below the jaw), and parotid (in front of the ears)—release their secretions, collectively called **saliva**, into the mouth (Figure **15.5**). As we chew, food is mixed with saliva. Water in saliva moistens food, and mucus binds food particles together, making it easier for the food to pass through the GI tract.

Saliva also contains an enzyme, called **salivary amylase**, that begins to chemically digest starches into shorter chains of sugar.

Enamel —
Dentin —
Pulp —

Step 1: Tooth decay is caused by acid produced when bacteria living on the tooth surface break down sugars in food particles adhered to teeth.

Step 2: The acid erodes the tooth's enamel, causing a cavity to form.

Step 3: The body responds by widening blood vessels in the pulp, to increase delivery of white blood cells to fight the infection. When widened blood vessels press on nerves within the pulp, a toothache results.

Step 4: Bacteria can then infect the softer dentin beneath the enamel and later the pulp at the heart of the tooth.

A dental cavity can be seen as an orange area in this artificially colored x-ray of teeth.

Bacteria break down sugars.

Acid erodes enamel.

Blood vessels widen, pressing on nerves in the pulp.

Bacteria invade dentin and pulp.

FIGURE 15.4 The development of a dental cavity

You will notice the result of salivary amylase activity if you chew a piece of bread for several minutes: The bread will begin to taste sweet. Try it.

Tongue: Taste and food manipulation

The tongue is a large skeletal muscle studded with taste buds. Our ability to control the position and movement of the tongue is critical to both speech and the manipulation of food within the mouth. Once food molecules are dissolved in saliva, the chemicals in the food can stimulate receptors in taste buds located primarily on the tongue. Information from the taste buds, along with input from the olfactory receptors in the nose, helps us to monitor the

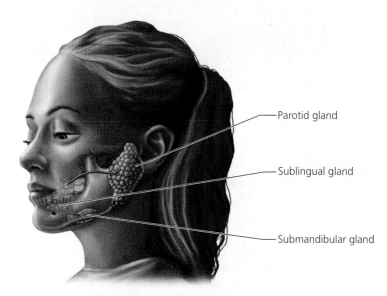

FIGURE 15.5 Three pairs of salivary glands release their secretions into the mouth. These secretions, collectively called saliva, make food easier to swallow, dissolve substances so they can be tasted, and begin the chemical digestion of starch.

quality of food. For instance, spoiled or poisonous food usually tastes and smells bad, so we can spit it out before swallowing. The tongue moves food to position it for crushing and grinding by the teeth, to mix it with saliva, and to shape it into a small, soft mass, called a *bolus*, that is easily swallowed. The tongue also initiates swallowing by pushing the bolus to the back of the mouth.

Pharynx

The **pharynx**, which is the passageway commonly called the throat, is shared by the respiratory and digestive systems. When we swallow, food is pushed from the mouth, through the pharynx, and into the **esophagus**, the tube that connects the pharynx to the stomach.

Swallowing consists of a voluntary component followed by an involuntary one. When a person begins to swallow, the tongue pushes the bolus of softened and moistened food into the pharynx (Figure **15.6**). Once food is in the pharynx, it is too late to change one's mind about swallowing. Sensory receptors in the wall of the pharynx detect the presence of food and stimulate the involuntary swallowing reflex. Reflex movements of the soft palate prevent food from entering the nasal cavities. Other involuntary muscle contractions push the larynx (the voice box, commonly called the Adam's apple) upward. As we learned in Chapter 14, the movement of the larynx causes a cartilaginous flap called the *epiglottis* to move, covering the opening to the airways of the respiratory system (the glottis). The movement of the epiglottis prevents food from entering the airways. Instead, food is pushed into the esophagus.

Esophagus

The esophagus is a muscular tube that conducts food from the pharynx to the stomach. Food is moved along the esophagus and all the rest of the GI tract by rhythmic waves of muscle contraction called **peristalsis**. In the esophagus, small intestine, and large intestine, peristalsis is produced by the two layers of muscle in the muscularis. The muscles of the inner layer circle the tube, causing a constriction when they contract. The muscles in the outer layer run lengthwise, causing a shortening of the region where they contract.

Soft palate

Bolus

Hard palate

The tongue pushes food bolus toward the pharynx.

Tongue

Pharynx

Epiglottis

Trachea

The esophagus is closed.

(a) Voluntary phase

Reflex movement of the soft palate prevents food from entering the nasal cavity.

Muscles contract, forcing the bolus into the esophagus.

The epiglottis closes the opening to the respiratory system, preventing food from entering.

A muscle ring at the top of the esophagus relaxes, opening the esophagus. Food is pushed into esophagus.

(b) Involuntary phase

FIGURE 15.6 Swallowing consists of (a) voluntary and (b) involuntary phases.

FIGURE 15.7 Peristalsis is a wave of muscle contraction that pushes food along the esophagus and the entire remaining GI tract. When circular muscles contract, the tube is narrowed and food is pushed forward. The longitudinal muscles in front of the bolus contract, shortening that region.

The presence of food stretches the walls in one region of the tube, and this triggers the contraction of circular muscles in the region of the tube immediately behind the food mass. When these circular muscles contract, that region of the tube pinches inward, pushing food forward. The food then stretches the next adjacent region of the tube, again stimulating contraction of circular muscles behind it. At the same time, longitudinal muscles in front of the food contract, shortening this region and widening its walls to receive the food. We see, then, that gravity is not important in moving food along the digestive tract. It is possible, therefore, to swallow while standing on your head or in the weightless conditions of outer space (Figure **15.7**).

Stomach

The **stomach** is a muscular sac that is well designed to carry out its three important functions: (1) storing food and regulating the release of food to the small intestine, (2) liquefying food, and (3) carrying out the initial chemical digestion of proteins. The structure of the stomach is shown in Figure **15.8**.

Storage of food and regulation of the release of food to the small intestine

Like any good storage compartment, the stomach is expandable and has openings that can close to seal the contents within as well as open for filling and emptying. When empty, the stomach is a small, J-shaped sac that can hold only about 50 ml (a quarter of a cup) without stretching. However, the wall of the empty stomach has folds that can spread out, allowing the stomach to expand as it fills. When fully expanded, as after a large meal, the stomach can hold several liters of food.

Bands of circular muscle called sphincters guard the openings at each end of the stomach and regulate the release of food to the small intestine. Contraction of a sphincter closes the opening, and relaxation of a sphincter allows material to pass through.

Liquefaction of food

Food is generally stored and processed within the stomach for 2 to 6 hours. The stomach wall has three layers of smooth muscle, each oriented in a different direction. The coordinated contractions of these layers twist, knead, and compress the stomach contents, phys-

(a) The stomach wall has three layers of smooth muscle, each oriented in a different direction, that allow the stomach to churn and mix food with digestive secretions.

(b) Gastric glands in the wall of the stomach produce gastric juice, a mixture of hydrochloric acid and pepsin.

(c) The holes seen in this electron micrograph are the gastric pits, openings in the stomach wall through which gastric glands release their secretions.

FIGURE 15.8 The structure of the stomach is well suited to its functions of churning food with digestive secretions, storing food, and beginning protein digestion.

ically breaking food into smaller pieces. This additional mechanical digestion occurs as the food is churned and mixed with secretions produced by the glands of the stomach until it is a soupy mixture called **chyme.**

Initial chemical digestion of proteins

Chemical digestion in the stomach is limited to the initial breakdown of proteins. The lining of the stomach has millions of gastric pits, within which are **gastric glands** containing several types of secretory cells. Certain secretory cells produce hydrochloric acid (HCl), which kills most of the bacteria swallowed with food or drink. Hydrochloric acid also breaks down the connective tissue of meat and activates pepsinogen, which is secreted by other cells in the gastric glands. Once activated by HCl, pepsinogen becomes **pepsin,** a protein-digesting enzyme. When the mixture of pepsin and HCl, called *gastric juice,* is released into the stomach, the pepsin begins the chemical digestion of the protein in food. Still other cells within the gastric glands secrete mucus, which helps protect the stomach wall from the action of gastric juice. Although not related to the digestive function of the stomach, a very important material secreted by the gastric glands is *intrinsic factor,* a protein necessary for the absorption of vitamin B_{12} from the small intestine.

The stomach wall is composed of the same materials that gastric juice is able to attack, so various protections are in place to keep the stomach from digesting itself. One, mentioned previously, is the presence of mucus. Mucus forms a thick, protective coat that prevents gastric juice from reaching the cells of the stomach wall. The alkalinity of mucus helps to neutralize the HCl. Another protection is that pepsin is produced in an inactive form (pepsinogen) that cannot digest the cells that produce it. In addition, neural and hormonal reflexes regulate the production of gastric juice so that little is released unless food is present to absorb and dilute it. Finally, if the stomach lining is damaged, it is quickly repaired. The high rate of cell division in the stomach lining replaces a half million cells every minute. As a result, you have a new stomach lining every 3 days!

Very little absorption of food and other ingested materials occurs in the stomach because food simply has not been broken down into molecules small enough to be absorbed. Notable exceptions are alcohol and aspirin. The absorption of alcohol from the stomach is the reason its effects can be felt very quickly, especially if there is no food present to dilute it. The absorption of aspirin can cause bleeding of the wall of the stomach, which is the reason aspirin should be avoided by people who have stomach ulcers (see the Health Issue essay, *Heartburn and Peptic Ulcers—Those Burning Sensations*).

Small Intestine

The next region of the digestive tract, the **small intestine,** has two major functions: chemical digestion and absorption. As food moves along this twisted tube, it passes through three specialized regions: the duodenum, the jejunum, and the ileum. Chyme from the stomach enters the **duodenum,** the first region of the small intestine, in squirts, so that only a small amount enters the small intestine at one time. Digestive juices also enter the duodenum from the pancreas and liver. However, most chemical digestion and absorption occur in the *jejunum* and the *ileum.*

Chemical digestion within the small intestine

Within the small intestine, a battery of enzymes completes the chemical digestion of virtually all the carbohydrates, proteins, fats, and nucleic acids in food. Although both the small intestine and the pancreas contribute enzymes, most of the digestion that occurs in the small intestine is actually performed by pancreatic enzymes (Table **15.2**).

Fats present a special digestive challenge because they are insoluble in water. You have observed this when the oil (a fat) quickly separates from the vinegar (a water solution) in your salad dressing. In water, droplets of fat tend to coalesce into large globules. This poses a problem for digestion because lipase, the enzyme that chemically breaks down fats, is soluble in water and not in fats. As a result, lipase can work only at the surface of a fat globule. Large fat globules have less combined surface area than do smaller droplets, so their digestion by lipase proceeds more slowly.

Bile, a mixture of water, ions, cholesterol, bile pigments, and bile salts, plays an important role in the digestion of fats. The bile salts emulsify fats; that is, they keep fats separated into small

TABLE 15.2 Major Digestive Enzymes			
Site of Production	**Enzyme**	**Site of Action**	**Substrate and Products**
Salivary glands	Salivary amylase	Mouth	Polysaccharides into shorter molecules
Stomach	Pepsin	Stomach	Proteins into protein fragments (polypeptides)
Pancreas	Trypsin	Small intestine	Proteins and polypeptides into smaller fragments
	Chymotrypsin	Small intestine	Proteins and polypeptides into smaller fragments
	Amylase	Small intestine	Polysaccharides into disaccharides
	Carboxypeptidase	Small intestine	Polypeptides into amino acids
	Lipase	Small intestine	Triglycerides (fats) into fatty acids and glycerol
	Nucleases (deoxyribonuclease and ribonuclease)	Small intestine	DNA or RNA into nucleotides
Small intestine	Maltase	Small intestine	Maltose into glucose units
	Sucrase	Small intestine	Sucrose into glucose and fructose
	Lactase	Small intestine	Lactose into glucose and galactose
	Aminopeptidase	Small intestine	Peptides into amino acids

droplets that disperse in liquid. This separation exposes a larger combined surface area to lipase, making the digestion and absorption of fats faster and more complete. Bile is produced by the liver, is stored in the gallbladder, and acts in the small intestine.

We have more to say about the pancreas, liver, and gallbladder shortly.

Structure of the small intestine

The small intestine, the primary site of absorption in the digestive system, is extremely effective at its task because it is long and has several structural specializations that vastly increase its surface area (Figure **15.9**). First, the entire lining of the small intestine is pleated, like an accordion, into circular folds. These circular folds increase the surface area for absorption and cause chyme to flow through the small intestine in a spiral pattern. The spiral flow helps mix the chyme with digestive enzymes and increases its contact with the absorptive surfaces. Covering the entire lining surface are tiny 1-mm projections called **villi** (singular, villus). The villi give the lining a velvety appearance and, like the pile on a bath towel, increase the absorptive surface. Indeed, the villi increase the surface area of the small intestine tenfold. In addition, the absorptive epithelial cells covering the surface of each villus contain thousands of microscopic projections, called *microvilli*, that increase the surface area of the small intestine by another 20 times. The microvilli form a fuzzy surface, known as a *brush border*. The circular folds, villi, and microvilli create a surface area of 300 to 600 m²—greater than the size of a tennis court!

The core of each villus is penetrated by a network of capillaries and a **lacteal**, which is a lymphatic vessel. As substances are absorbed from the small intestine, they cross only two cell layers: the epithelial cells of the villi and the wall of either a capillary or a lacteal. Most materials enter the epithelial cells by active transport, facilitated diffusion, or simple diffusion (Figure **15.10**; see Chapter 3). Monosaccharides, amino acids, water, ions, vitamins, and minerals diffuse across the capillary wall into the bloodstream and are delivered to body cells. The products of fat digestion, glycerol and fatty acids, combine with bile salts in the small intestine, creating particles called *micelles* (pronounced my-*cells*). When a micelle contacts an epithelial cell of a villus, the products of fat digestion easily diffuse into the cell. Within an epithelial cell, the glycerol and fatty acids are reassembled into triglycerides, mixed with cholesterol and phospholipids, and coated with special proteins, thus becoming part of a complex known as a *chylomicron*. The protein coating makes the fat soluble in water, allowing it to be transported throughout the body. The chylomicrons leave the epithelial cell by exocytosis (see

---

Q *List three structural adaptations of the small intestine that increase its surface area for absorption of digested nutrients.*

FIGURE 15.9 The small intestine is specialized for the absorption of nutrients by structural modifications that increase its surface area. (a) Its wall contains accordion-like pleats called circular folds. (b) This electron micrograph shows the intestinal villi, the numerous fingerlike projections on the intestinal lining (the mucosa in part c). (d) The surface of each villus bristles with thousands of microscopic projections (of cell membranes) called microvilli. In the center of each villus, a network of blood capillaries, which carries away absorbed products of protein and carbohydrate digestion as well as ions and water, surrounds a lacteal (a small vessel of the lymphatic system) that carries away the absorbed products of fat digestion. (e) An electron micrograph of the microvilli that cover each villus.

A *Circular folds, villi, and microvilli.*

(a)

Circular folds

(b)

Villi

Intestinal gland

Blood vessels

Lymphatic vessel

Mucosa

Submucosa

(c)

Lacteal (lymphatic vessel)

Capillary

Microvilli

Villus

Mucus-secreting cell

Absorbing cell

(d)

(e)

(a) Carbohydrate digestion

(b) Protein digestion

(c) Fat digestion

FIGURE 15.10 The small intestine is the primary site for chemical digestion and absorption. The digestive products, such as monosaccharides, amino acids, fatty acids, and glycerol, enter absorptive epithelial cells of villi by active transport, facilitated diffusion, or diffusion. Monosaccharides and amino acids, along with water, ions, and vitamins, then enter the capillaries within the villus and are carried to body cells by the bloodstream. The products of fat digestion diffuse into the lacteal within the villus.

Chapter 3). Chylomicrons are too large to pass through capillary walls. However, they easily diffuse into the more porous lacteal and enter the lymphatic system, which carries them to the bloodstream.

Accessory Organs: Pancreas, Liver, and Gallbladder

The pancreas, liver, and gallbladder are not part of the GI tract. However, they play vital roles in digestion by releasing their secretions into the small intestine. The functions of the secretions of the accessory organs are summarized in Table **15.3**.

Pancreas

The **pancreas** is an accessory organ that lies behind the stomach, extending toward the person's left from the small intestine. Pancreatic juice drains from the pancreas into the pancreatic duct, which fuses with the common bile duct from the liver just before

TABLE 15.3 Review of Accessory Structures of the Digestive System

Structure	Secretions/Functions	Site of Action of Chemical Secretions
Salivary glands (sublingual, submandibular, parotid)	Secrete saliva, a liquid that moistens food and contains an enzyme (amylase) for digesting carbohydrates	Mouth
Pancreas	Digestive secretions include bicarbonate ions that neutralize acidic chyme and enzymes that digest carbohydrates, proteins, fats, and nucleic acids	Small intestine
Liver	Digestive function is to produce bile, a liquid that emulsifies fats, making chemical digestion easier and facilitating absorption	Small intestine
Gallbladder	Stores bile and releases it into small intestine	Small intestine

The liver produces bile, which is stored in the gallbladder before being released into the small intestine.

The pancreas produces several digestive enzymes that act in the small intestine

FIGURE 15.11 The pancreas, liver, and gallbladder are accessory organs of the digestive system.

entering the duodenum of the small intestine (Figure **15.11**). In addition to enzymes, pancreatic juice contains water and ions, including bicarbonate ions that are important in neutralizing the acid in chyme when it emerges from the stomach. Neutralization is essential for optimal enzyme activity in the small intestine.

Collectively, the pancreatic enzymes and intestinal enzymes break nutrients into their component building blocks: proteins to amino acids, carbohydrates to monosaccharides, and triglycerides (a type of lipid) to fatty acids and glycerol.

Heartburn and Peptic Ulcers— Those Burning Sensations

Heartburn is a burning sensation behind the breastbone that occurs when acidic gastric juice backs up into the esophagus. At least 30% of all Americans suffer from heartburn on a monthly basis and 10% on a daily basis. Heartburn occurs when the pressure of the stomach contents overwhelms the sphincter at the lower end of the esophagus. In some people, this sphincter is weak and unable to keep stomach contents out of the esophagus. A person with a normal esophageal sphincter will experience heartburn when the stomach contents exert a greater pressure than usual against the sphincter, as might occur after a large meal, during pregnancy, when lying down, or when constipated. Acidic foods, such as tomatoes and citrus fruits, and spicy, fatty, or caffeine-containing products can aggravate the problem by causing the sphincter to relax and open. Tight clothing also worsens heartburn, because it compresses the stomach, increasing the pressure against the sphincter.

There are several treatments for heartburn. Antacids will provide temporary relief. Unfortunately, long-term use of certain antacids can have undesirable side effects. The fizzing bicarbonate types are high in sodium and should be avoided by people with high blood pressure. Others are high in calcium, which might promote the formation of kidney stones and stimulate the production of stomach acid. Newer medications, such as Tagamet, Zantac, Pepcid, Axid, Prilosec, and Nexium, decrease the production of stomach acid, which as we have seen is required at normal levels.

People who have chronic heartburn—at least one attack per week—have an increased risk of developing cancer of the esophagus. The risk increases with the frequency of attacks and the number of years of experiencing heartburn. Those who have one attack per week have a risk eight times higher than normal. Esophageal cancer is particularly aggressive and has become more common in recent years. It is detected using a test called endoscopy, in which a thin, lighted tube is snaked down the throat. A more recently developed means of detecting potentially harmful changes in the esophagus is the PillCam ESO. The patient swallows a camera that is about the size of a vitamin pill. As the camera moves through the esophagus, it takes thousands of pictures and sends them to a small recording device worn by the patient.

At some point in their lives, nearly 13% of Americans experience a failure of the mechanisms that protect the stomach and duodenum from their acidic contents, so that the lining of some region in the GI tract becomes eroded. The resulting sore resembles a canker sore of the mouth and is called a peptic ulcer (Figure **15.A**). Although a peptic ulcer may form in the esophagus or the stomach, the most common site is the duodenum of the small intestine. Ulcers are usually between 10 and 25 mm (0.33 and 1 in.) in diameter and may occur singly or in multiple locations.

The symptoms of an ulcer are variable. A common symptom is abdominal pain, which can be quite severe. Vomiting, loss of appetite, bloating, indigestion, and heartburn are other common symptoms. However, some people with ulcers, especially those who are taking nonsteroidal anti-inflammatory drugs (NSAIDs), have no pain. Unfortunately, the degree of pain is a poor indicator of the severity of ulceration. Often, people with no symptoms are unaware of their ulcers until serious complications develop. Gastric juice can erode the lining of the GI tract until it bleeds. In some cases, the ulcer can eat a hole completely through the wall of the GI tract (a condition called perforated ulcer). Recurrent ulcers can cause scar tissue to form, which may narrow or block the lower end of the stomach or duodenum.

Although acidic gastric juice is the direct cause of peptic ulcers, factors that interfere with the mechanisms that normally protect the lining of the GI tract from the acid are considered to be the real causes. For example, NSAIDs, which include aspirin, ibuprofen, and naproxen, can cause ulcers because they slow the production of chemicals called prostaglandins, which normally help protect the lining of the GI tract from damage by acid.

The leading cause of peptic ulcers, however, is an infection with the bacterium *Helicobacter pylori*. More than 80% of persons with ulcers in the stomach or duodenum are infected with *H. pylori*. This bacterium produces an alkaline compound that neutralizes the stomach acid. These corkscrew-shaped bacteria live in the layer of mucus that protects the lining of the GI tract. Here, the bacteria attract body defense cells—specifically, macrophages and neutrophils—that cause inflammation leading to ulcer formation. Toxic chemicals produced by the bacteria also contribute to ulcers.

H. pylori infections may last for years. These bacteria affect more than a billion people throughout the world and approximately 50% of the people in the United States who are over 60 years of age. For some reason, however, only about 10% to 15% of those who are infected actually develop peptic ulcers. Besides ulcers, an *H. pylori* infection is a risk factor for esophageal and stomach cancer. However, it may soon be possible to vaccinate children against this bacterium, thereby reducing the risk of both peptic ulcers and stomach cancer.

Gastric ulcer

Duodenal ulcer

FIGURE 15.A A peptic ulcer is an open sore that forms when gastric juice erodes the lining of the esophagus, stomach, or, most commonly, the duodenum. The ulcer shown in this stomach wall is bleeding. The most common symptom is abdominal pain that occurs when the stomach is empty.

Liver

The nutrient-laden blood from the capillaries in the villi travels through the hepatic portal vein to the **liver**, the largest internal organ in the body, which has a variety of metabolic and regulatory roles. A portal system consists of the blood vessels that link two capillary beds. The hepatic portal system delivers blood from a capillary bed in the small intestine to a second capillary bed in the liver (Figure **15.12**).

We have already seen that the liver's primary role in digestion is to produce bile. One of its other roles is to control the glucose level of the blood, either removing excess glucose and storing it as glycogen or breaking down glycogen to raise blood glucose levels. Thus, the liver keeps the glucose levels of the blood within the proper range. The liver also packages lipids with protein carrier molecules to form lipoproteins, which transport lipids in the blood. After the liver adjusts the blood composition, the blood is returned to the general circulation through the hepatic veins. In addition, the liver stores iron and vitamins A, D, E, K, B_{12}, and folate.

The liver also removes poisonous substances, including lead, mercury, and pesticides, from the blood and in some cases breaks them down into less harmful chemicals. What's more, the liver converts the breakdown products of amino acids into urea, which can then be excreted by the kidney. These are but a few of the approximately 500 functions of the liver.

Considering the liver's many vital functions, it is no surprise that diseases of the liver can be serious and life threatening. Cirrhosis is a condition in which the liver becomes fatty and gradually deteriorates, its cells eventually being replaced by scar tissue. Because cirrhosis is sometimes caused by prolonged, excessive alcohol use, it is discussed in Chapter 8a.

Hepatitis is inflammation of the liver. It is most commonly caused by one of six viruses, designated as A, B, C, D, E, and G. Al-

though all the hepatitis viruses attack the liver and destroy liver cells, there are differences in their means of transmission and their symptoms, as well as their severity. All forms of hepatitis do have one symptom in common: healthy liver cells remove bilirubin, a yellowish pigment produced by the breakdown of red blood cells, from the bloodstream and use it to make bile. Liver cells injured by hepatitis viruses stop filtering bilirubin from the blood. The accumulating bilirubin is deposited in the skin and the whites of the eyes, giving them a yellowish tint. This condition, called jaundice, is characteristic of any disease that damages the liver.

Currently, about 4 million people in the United States have hepatitis C, and most of them have no idea that they are infected. For years, the disease has spread silently because it has no outward warning signs or very mild symptoms—vague fatigue, or flu-like muscle and joint pain. It is spread primarily through contaminated blood. Hundreds of thousands of intravenous drug users have been infected by sharing contaminated needles. Hepatitis C can also be spread through contaminated needles used in body piercing or tattooing. Before there was a way to test for the virus, many people became infected when they received transfusions with contaminated blood.

Gallbladder

After it is produced by the liver, bile is stored, modified, and concentrated in a muscular, pear-shaped sac called the **gallbladder.** When chyme enters the small intestine, a hormone causes the gallbladder to contract, squirting bile through the common bile duct into the duodenum of the small intestine.

Bile is rich in cholesterol. Sometimes, if the balance of dissolved substances in bile becomes upset, a tiny crystalline particle precipitates out of solution. Cholesterol and other substances can then build up around the particle to form a *gallstone* (Figure **15.13**). Many people develop several gallstones, which can cause problems if they block the flow of bile and may necessitate surgical removal of the gallbladder.

Q *Where are the two capillary beds in the hepatic portal system? What does the liver do in this system?*

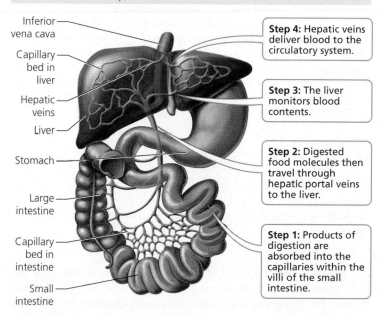

Inferior vena cava

Capillary bed in liver

Hepatic veins

Liver

Stomach

Large intestine

Capillary bed in intestine

Small intestine

Step 4: Hepatic veins deliver blood to the circulatory system.

Step 3: The liver monitors blood contents.

Step 2: Digested food molecules then travel through hepatic portal veins to the liver.

Step 1: Products of digestion are absorbed into the capillaries within the villi of the small intestine.

FIGURE 15.12 A portal system transports blood from one capillary bed to another. In the hepatic portal system the hepatic portal vein carries blood from the capillary network of the villi of the small intestine to the capillary beds of the liver. The liver monitors blood content and processes nutrients before they are delivered to the bloodstream.

A *The small intestine and the liver. The liver monitors and adjusts blood content.*

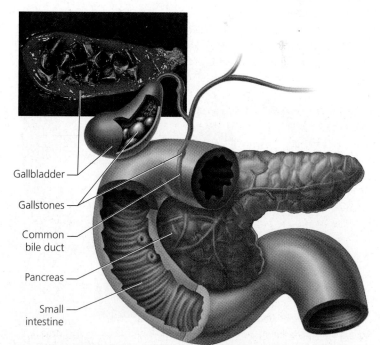

Gallbladder

Gallstones

Common bile duct

Pancreas

Small intestine

FIGURE 15.13 Gallstones consist primarily of cholesterol that has precipitated from bile during storage in the gallbladder. A gallstone can intermittently or continuously block the ducts that drain bile into the small intestine. The photograph shows a gallbladder and several gallstones.

Large Intestine

Now that we have discussed the accessory organs that assist digestion and absorption in the small intestine, we go back to following the movement of ingested substances through the GI tract. The material that was not absorbed in the small intestine moves into the final major structure of the digestive system, the **large intestine**. The principal functions of the large intestine are (1) to absorb most of the water remaining in the indigestible food residue, thereby adjusting the consistency of the waste material, or feces; (2) to store the feces; and (3) to eliminate them from the body. The large intestine is home to many types of bacteria, some of which produce vitamins that may be absorbed for use by the body.

Regions of the large intestine

The large intestine has four regions: the cecum, colon, rectum, and anal canal, as shown in Figure **15.14**. The **cecum** is a pouch that hangs below the junction of the small and large intestines. Extending from the cecum is another slender, wormlike pouch, called the **appendix**. The appendix has no digestive function. Some scientists believe the appendix plays a role in the immune system, which protects the body against disease.

Each year, about 1 in 500 people develops *appendicitis,* inflammation of the appendix. Appendicitis is usually caused by an infection that arises in the appendix after it becomes blocked by a piece of hardened stool from the cecum, food, or a tumor. After the blockage occurs, bacteria that are normally present in the appendix can multiply and cause an infection. At first, appendicitis is usually experienced as vague bloating, indigestion, and a mild pain in the region of the navel (bellybutton). As the condition worsens, the pain becomes more severe and is localized in the region of the appendix, the lower right abdomen. The pain is typically accompanied by fever, nausea, and vomiting. When appendicitis is diagnosed, anti-

biotics are administered and the infected appendix is surgically removed. Untreated infection in the appendix usually causes the appendix to rupture, allowing its infected contents to spill into the abdominal cavity. Spillage from the appendix generally leads to infection and inflammation throughout the abdomen (a condition called peritonitis), which is potentially fatal.

The largest region of the large intestine, the **colon,** is composed of the ascending colon on the right side of the abdomen, the transverse colon across the top of the abdominal cavity, and the descending colon on the left side (see Figure 15.14). Although much of the water that is originally in chyme is absorbed in the small intestine, the material entering the colon is still quite liquid. The colon absorbs 90% of the remaining water and sodium and potassium ions. The material left in the large intestine after passing through the colon is called feces and consists primarily of undigested food, sloughed-off epithelial cells, water, and millions of bacteria. The brown color of feces comes from bile pigments.

The bacteria in the colon are not normally disease causing and, in fact, are beneficial. Intestinal bacteria produce several vitamins that we are unable to produce on our own, including vitamin K and some of the B vitamins. Some of these vitamins are then absorbed from the colon for our own use. There are roughly 50 species of bacteria, including the well-known *Escherichia coli* (*E. coli*) that live in the healthy colon. Bacteria are nourished by undigested food and by material that we are unable to digest, including certain components of plant cells. When the intestinal bacteria use the undigested and indigestible food for their own nutrition, their metabolic processes liberate gas that sometimes has a foul odor. Although most of the gas is absorbed through the intestinal walls, the remaining gas can produce some embarrassing moments when released as flatus.

People who are *lactose intolerant* lack the enzyme lactase, which is normally produced by and acts in the small intestine. Lactase breaks down lactose, the primary sugar in milk, into its component monosaccharides. Without lactase, then, lactose moves intact into the colon, where it provides a nutritional bonanza for the bacteria living there. As a result, when people who are lactose intolerant consume milk products, the intestinal bacteria ferment the lactose and produce the gases carbon dioxide and methane that, in turn, produces bloating, gas, and abdominal discomfort. Although lactose intolerance is common in adults, it is not dangerous. Problems can usually be avoided by swallowing capsules or tablets of lactase or by modifying the diet to avoid dairy products.

FIGURE 15.14 The large intestine consists of the cecum, colon, rectum, and anal canal. It absorbs water from undigested material, forming the feces, and houses bacteria.

stop and think

Certain foods—beans, for instance—are notorious for producing intestinal gas. Beans contain large amounts of certain short-chain carbohydrates that our bodies are unable to digest. How is the nutritional content of beans related to flatulence?

Periodic peristaltic contractions move material through the large intestine, but these contractions are slower than the contractions in the small intestine. Slower contractions allow for adequate water absorption as material moves through the large intestine. Eventually, the feces are pushed into the **rectum**, stretching the rectal wall and initiating the *defecation reflex*. Nerve impulses from the stretch receptors in the rectal wall travel to the spinal cord, which sends motor impulses back to the rectal wall, stimulating muscles there to contract and propel the feces into the **anal canal.** Two rings of muscles, called sphincters, must relax to allow *defecation,* the expulsion of feces. The internal sphincter relaxes automatically as part of the defecation reflex. The external sphincter is under voluntary control, allowing the person to decide whether to defecate. Conscious contraction of the abdominal muscles can increase abdominal pressure and help expel the feces.

Disorders of the colon

The water absorption that occurs in the colon adjusts the consistency of feces. When material passes through the colon too rapidly, as might occur when colon contractions are stimulated by toxins from microorganisms or by excess food or alcoholic drink, too little water is absorbed. As a result, the feces are very liquid. This condition, which results in frequent loose stools, is called *diarrhea.* Persistent diarrhea can be dangerous, especially in an infant or young child, because it can lead to dehydration. Diarrhea is a major cause of death worldwide.

On the other hand, if material passes through the colon too slowly, too much water is absorbed, resulting in infrequent, hard stools—a condition called *constipation.* People who are constipated may need to strain during bowel movements. Straining increases pressure within veins in the rectum and anus, causing them to stretch and enlarge. The wall of the large intestine also experiences great pressure during a strained bowel movement. Then, like the inner tube of an old tire, the weaker spots in the intestinal wall can begin to bulge outward, forming small outpouchings called diverticula (singular, diverticulum; Figure **15.15**). Diverticula are very common in people older than age 50. When diverticula do not cause problems or symptoms, the condition is called *diverticulosis.* But if the diverticula become infected with bacteria and inflamed, the condition is then called *diverticulitis,* which can cause abrupt, cramping abdominal pain, a change in bowel habits, fever, and rectal bleeding. Diverticulitis can be treated by changing the diet (increasing fiber, avoiding nuts), taking drugs that reduce muscle spasms, or having surgery.

Large intestine   Diverticulum

FIGURE 15.15 A diverticulum is a small pouch that forms in the wall of the large intestine and is usually caused by repeated straining during bowel movements. A high-fiber diet results in softer, bulkier stools that are easier to pass, thus making it less likely that diverticula will form.

Cancers of the colon or rectum are common and can be deadly. *Colorectal cancer* is the second leading cause of cancer deaths. Early detection and treatment cut the risk of death dramatically.

Colorectal cancer begins with a small, noncancerous growth called a polyp. If the polyp continues to grow, genetic mutations accumulate in them that can transform a cell into a cancerous tumor. Polyps may take as long as 10 years to grow and turn cancerous, generally allowing plenty of time for detection. Sometimes polyps bleed, so one sign of colorectal polyps and perhaps cancer is blood in the stool. However, the blood is not usually visible and must be detected with a diagnostic test. Because many polyps do not bleed, screening methods that allow a direct view of the wall of the rectum and colon are generally more effective. A long, flexible fiber-optic tube is threaded through the first third of the colon in a procedure known as a sigmoidoscopy, or through the entire colon in a procedure called a colonoscopy. If a polyp is detected, it can be removed and biopsied to determine whether it is cancerous (see Chapter 21a).

Nerves and Hormones in Digestion

As we have seen, ingested material moves along the GI tract, stopping for specific kinds of treatment along the way. For digestion to occur, enzymes must be present in the right place at the right time. However, because the body is composed of many of the same substances found in food, digestive enzymes should not be released until food is present (otherwise the enzymes might start digesting the digestive system). Both nerves and hormones play a role in orchestrating the release of digestive secretions, timing the release of each to the presence of food at each stop.

Food spends little time in the mouth; so to be effective, saliva must be secreted quickly. Because nervous stimulation is faster than hormonal stimulation, it is not surprising to learn that the nervous system controls salivation. Some saliva is released before food even enters the mouth, which may begin to "water" simply at the *thought* of food—and certainly begins at the sight or smell of food. The major trigger for salivation, however, is the presence of food in the mouth—its flavor and pressure. Salivary juices continue to flow for some time after the food is swallowed, helping to rinse out the mouth.

While food is still being chewed, neural reflexes stimulate the stomach lining to begin secreting gastric juice and mucus. Distention of the stomach by swallowed food, along with the presence of partially digested proteins, stimulates cells in the stomach lining to release the hormone *gastrin.* Gastrin enters the bloodstream and circulates throughout the body and back to the stomach, where it increases the production of gastric juice.

The presence of acidic chyme in the small intestine, which triggers local nerve reflexes, is the most important stimulus for the release of enzymes from both the small intestine and the pancreas, as well as bile from the gallbladder. Acid chyme also causes the small intestine to release several hormones that, in turn, are responsible for the release of digestive enzymes and bile. For instance, one hormone, *vasoactive intestinal peptide,* is released from the small intestine into the bloodstream and is carried back to the small intestine, where it causes the release of intestinal juices. At the same time, the small intestine releases a second hormone, *secretin,* which stimulates the release of sodium bicarbonate from the pancreas into the small intestine to help neutralize the acidity of chyme. A third hormone from the small intestine is *cholecystokinin,* which causes the pancreas to release its digestive enzymes and causes the gallbladder to contract and release bile. The neural and hormonal controls of the digestive system are summarized in Tables **15.4** and **15.5,** respectively.

exploring further

In this chapter, we have seen how the digestive system is organized to break down food molecules for energy or building materials. In the next chapter, we learn about your body's use of specific nutrients and consider how what you eat affects your health.

TABLE 15.4 Examples of Neural Controls on Digestive Activity

Stimulus	Effect
Sight of food, thought of food, presence of food in mouth	Release of saliva from salivary glands
Chewing food	Release of gastric juice (enzymes from stomach and HCl) and mucus from cells of stomach lining
Presence of acidic chyme in small intestine	Release of enzymes from small intestine and pancreas into the small intestine; release of bile from gallbladder into small intestine; increased motility in small intestine

TABLE 15.5 Examples of Hormonal Control on Digestive Activity

Hormone	Stimulus	Origin	Target	Effects
Gastrin	Distention of stomach by food; presence of partially digested proteins in stomach	Stomach	Stomach	Release of gastric juice (enzymes from stomach and HCl)
Vasoactive intestinal peptide	Presence of acidic chyme in small intestine	Small intestine	Small intestine	Release of enzymes from small intestine
Secretin	Presence of acidic chyme in small intestine	Small intestine	Pancreas	Release of sodium bicarbonate from pancreas into small intestine to neutralize acidic chyme
Cholecystokinin	Arrival of chyme-containing lipids	Small intestine	Pancreas Gall bladder	Release of enzymes from pancreas Contraction of gallbladder and release of bile

highlighting the concepts

The Gastrointestinal Tract (pp. 295–297)
- The digestive system consists of a long tube called the gastrointestinal (GI) tract, which starts at the mouth and continues through the pharynx, esophagus, stomach, small intestine, large intestine. The digestive system also includes several accessory organs (salivary glands, pancreas, liver, and gallbladder).
- The GI tract has four layers. Moving from the inside out, they are the mucosa, submucosa, muscularis, and serosa.

Specialized Compartments for Food Processing (pp. 297–307)
- The mouth serves several functions. Teeth tear and grind food, making it easier to swallow. The salivary glands produce salivary amylase, which is released into the mouth to begin the chemical breakdown of starches. Taste buds help monitor the quality of food. Finally, the tongue manipulates food so that it can be swallowed.
- The pharynx is shared by the digestive and respiratory systems. Food swallowed moves from the mouth through the pharynx and into the esophagus.

- The esophagus is a tube that leads to the stomach. When we swallow, food is pushed from the mouth, and waves of muscle contraction called peristalsis push the food along the esophagus.
- The stomach stores food and regulates its release to the small intestine, liquefies it by mixing it with gastric juice, begins the chemical digestion of proteins, and regulates the release of chyme into the small intestine. Gastric juice consists of hydrochloric acid (HCl) and pepsin, a protein-splitting enzyme. Pepsin is produced in an inactive form, called pepsinogen, that is activated by HCl.
- The small intestine is the primary site of digestion and absorption, where enzymes produced by the small intestine and pancreas work to chemically digest carbohydrates, proteins, and fats into their component subunits.
- Bile emulsifies fat (breaks it into tiny droplets) in the small intestine, thereby increasing the combined surface area of fat droplets. Bile's action makes fat digestion by water-soluble lipase faster and more complete.
- The small intestine's surface area for absorption is increased by circular folds in its lining, fingerlike projections called villi, and microscopic projections covering the villi, called microvilli.

- Products of digestion are absorbed into the epithelial cells of villi by active transport, facilitated diffusion, or simple diffusion. Most materials, including monosaccharides, amino acids, water, and ions, then enter the capillary blood network in the center of each villus. However, fatty acids and glycerol are resynthesized into triglycerides, combined with cholesterol and phospholipids, and covered in protein, forming droplets called chylomicrons. The chylomicrons diffuse into a lymphatic vessel called a lacteal in the core of each villus. They are then delivered to the bloodstream by way of lymphatic vessels.
- The pancreas, liver, and gallbladder are accessory organs that aid in digestion and absorption within the small intestine. The pancreas secretes enzymes to digest most nutrients. The liver produces bile, which is then stored in the gallbladder.
- The large intestine consists of the cecum, colon, rectum, and anal canal. The large intestine absorbs water, ions, and vitamins. It is home to millions of beneficial bacteria that live on undigested material that has passed from the small intestine. The bacteria produce several vitamins, some of which we then absorb for our own use.
- Material left in the large intestine after passing through the colon is called feces. Feces consist of undigested or indigestible material, bacteria, sloughed-off cells, and water. Defecation is the discharge of feces from the rectum through the anus.

Nerves and Hormones in Digestion (pp. 307–308)

- Neural and hormonal mechanisms regulate the release of digestive secretions. Neural reflexes trigger the release of saliva, initiate the secretion of some gastric juice, and are the most important factors regulating the release of intestinal secretions. Gastrin, vasoactive intestinal peptide, secretin, and cholecystokinin are hormones that regulate digestive activities.

recognizing key terms

digestive system *p. 295*	salivary amylase *p. 298*	small intestine *p. 301*	large intestine *p. 306*
gastrointestinal (GI) tract *p. 295*	pharynx *p. 299*	duodenum *p. 301*	cecum *p. 306*
mucosa *p. 295*	esophagus *p. 299*	bile *p. 301*	appendix *p. 306*
submucosa *p. 296*	peristalsis *p. 299*	villi (sing. villus) *p. 302*	colon *p. 306*
muscularis *p. 296*	stomach *p. 300*	lacteal *p. 302*	rectum *p. 306*
serosa *p. 297*	chyme *p. 301*	pancreas *p. 303*	anal canal *p. 306*
saliva *p. 298*	gastric glands *p. 301*	liver *p. 305*	
	pepsin *p. 301*	gallbladder *p. 305*	

reviewing the concepts

1. List the structures of the GI tract, in the order that food passes through them. *p. 295*
2. Describe how food is processed in the mouth. What are the functions of the teeth and tongue? *pp. 297–298*
3. Describe the structures of a tooth that are involved in tooth decay. What causes tooth decay? *p. 298*
4. What are the three primary functions of the stomach? What are the functions of gastric juice? *pp. 300–301*
5. Why are so few substances absorbed from the stomach? *p. 301*
6. How does bile assist in the digestion and absorption of fats? *pp. 301–302*
7. Where are carbohydrates digested? Proteins? Fats? *pp. 301–302*
8. Describe the structural features that increase the surface area for absorption in the small intestine. *p. 302*
9. Which structures produce the digestive enzymes that act in the small intestine? *pp. 303, 305*
10. What are the functions of the large intestine? *p. 306*
11. Describe the neural or hormonal mechanisms that regulate the release of digestive juices from each structure involved in digestion. *pp. 307–308*
12. The villi in the wall of the small intestine function to _____.
    a. increase the surface area for absorption.
    b. help mix the food with digestive enzymes.
    c. secrete bile.
    d. secrete digestive enzymes.
13. It is possible to swallow while standing on one's hands because
    a. valves in the digestive system keep food from moving backward.
    b. peristalsis pushes food along the digestive tract in the right direction.
    c. bacteria clog the digestive tube and prevent food from moving in the wrong direction.
    d. of a wave of muscle contraction called emulsification.
14. The most important function of the stomach is
    a. absorption of nutrients.
    b. chemical digestion.
    c. mucus secretion.
    d. storage of food.
15. You go out with your friends to celebrate your birthday and share a sausage pizza. The digestion of the oil *begins* in the
    a. mouth.
    b. esophagus.
    c. stomach.
    d. small intestine.
16. _____ is a liquid mixture of food and gastric juices found in the stomach.
17. The _____ is the organ that produces bile.
18. Saliva contains an enzyme that begins the chemical digestion of _____.
19. _____ is a hormone produced by the small intestine that causes the gallbladder to contract and release bile.

applying the concepts

1. Barbara is a 20-year-old woman with cystic fibrosis, a genetic disease in which abnormally thick mucus is produced. The thick mucus sometimes blocks the pancreatic duct that allows pancreatic juice to enter the small intestine. Explain why cystic fibrosis has caused Barbara to be malnourished.

2. Dehydration occurs when too much body fluid is lost. It can be a serious, even fatal, condition. Doctors worry about dehydration if a person, especially an infant, has severe diarrhea lasting several days. Why?

3. A 35-year-old man sporting a tattoo visits the dermatologist to have the tattoo removed. Noticing that the patient's skin has a yellowish tint, the dermatologist strongly recommends that the patient visit a physician. Why? What is the dermatologist concerned about?

4. You spend the day with your Aunt Sally on her 55th birthday. She has a salad for lunch and suffers no ill effects. However, she indulges in fried chicken and French fries for dinner. A few hours later, she is rushed to the emergency room with a severe pain on the right side of her abdomen. She reports that she has had bouts of pain over the last month or so. What do you think is Aunt Sally's problem? Why isn't the pain continuous?

becoming information literate

The PillCam is a small camera that is swallowed by the patient and takes pictures of the GI tract as it moves through the body. Write a short article for the Health section of a local newspaper, describing the PillCam in more detail and answering the following questions in easily understood words. How does a PillCam differ from a traditional endoscope? What conditions and diseases can be diagnosed using the PillCam? Compared with endoscopy, what are the advantages and disadvantages of the PillCam?

Use at least three reliable sources (books, journals, or websites). List each source you considered, and explain why you chose the three sources you used.

Additional questions can be found online at The Human Biology Place, www.humanbiology.com.

15a

SPECIAL TOPIC

Nutrition and Weight Control

Eating a balanced diet and maintaining a healthy weight are important ways of safeguarding one's health.

Amber was excited about spending the weekend with her former college roommate. She hadn't seen Dana for more than a year and looked forward to some long talks and laughter-filled reminiscences. Secretly, Amber had to admit, she also couldn't wait to show off her newly slimmed figure. "It's so good to see you!" Dana exclaimed, followed immediately by, "Wow, you've really lost weight! You look great."

Amber couldn't help but blush with pride. "It's nothing—just one of those low-carbohydrate diets." An hour later, though, after they'd been talking a while, Amber admitted that although she had lost more than 20 pounds, she wasn't feeling as well as she'd expected. She was frequently constipated, and she had developed intense cravings for fruit and any kind of bread product. Dana remembered taking some nutrition courses in college that had stressed

the importance of a balanced diet. She pointed out that the lack of fiber was probably causing Amber's constipation. She also warned that the next phase of her weight-loss program could be even more difficult if she wanted to keep the weight off, because she would have to focus on nutritional balance while restricting carbohydrates. Amber nodded and told Dana that she was going to make an appointment with a nutritionist when she returned home.

They toasted her commitment, enjoyed the dinner Dana had prepared, and spent the evening discussing the fun and perils of their lives since graduating from college.

In this chapter, we consider carbohydrates as well as the other nutrients in a balanced diet—proteins, fats, vitamins, minerals, and water. We see how the body uses these nutrients and examine ways to combine the foods we eat to promote health and fitness.

Planning a Healthy Diet

Planning a healthy diet requires more than simply eating certain foods to avoid deficiencies of particular nutrients. Choosing the right balance of foods can help improve health and reduce the risk of serious chronic diseases, such as heart disease, cancer, and diabetes.

MyPyramid is a food guide released by the U.S. Department of Agriculture (USDA) in 2005 to help any person plan a well-balanced diet (Figure **15a.1**). The easy-to-use website www.MyPyramid.gov personalizes the nutritional information, guiding each user to one of 12 pyramid-shaped diagrams that summarize the eating pattern considered optimal for someone of his or her age, gender, and level of activity. MyPyramid follows the recommendations in the USDA's Dietary Guide for Americans 2005. This guide promotes a healthy lifestyle that includes wise decisions about food and physical activity. All 12 pyramids share certain features. The human figure shown running up the steps on the side of the pyramid reminds us that daily physical activity is a key to healthy living. There are 12 different pyramids because a healthy dietary plan needs to allow for individual differences in the number of calories each person requires. Each food group is color coded, corresponding to colored bands on the pyramid that remind us to eat a variety of foods. The width of each band suggests what proportion of our daily diets should come from that food group. The bands are wider at the bottom, suggesting that most of the food we eat in each food group should be nutrient dense and contain few "empty" calories (a concept we explain later in this chapter). The pyramid's slogan, "Steps to a Healthier You," reminds us that improvements in diet should happen gradually. Besides being personalized, MyPyramid differs from the old food pyramid by specifying quantities to be consumed in cups or ounces instead of in servings. The 2005 Dietary Guide also allows discretionary calories. These are calories from any food group that are allowable after you have met your basic nutrient needs. The flexibility represented by discretionary calories allows you to consume *some* foods and drinks that contain added fats, added sugar, or alcohol.

The 2005 Dietary Guide makes three general recommendations for a healthy lifestyle: (1) choose food wisely, (2) stay within your calorie needs, and (3) engage in physical activity. MyPyramid can help you plan a nutritionally balanced diet to satisfy the first recommendation. The remainder of this chapter explains some of the biology the dietary guidelines are based on.

Nutrients

What does the body do with the food you eat? Food provides fuel, building blocks, molecules needed to carry out chemical processes in the body, and water.

- Food is needed as an energy source for all cellular activities. (Energy is measured in a unit called a calorie, which is the amount needed to raise the temperature of 1 g of water 1°C. In discussions of biochemical reactions, gains and losses of energy are usually reported in kilocalories. A kilocalorie is 1000 calories of energy. In nonscientific discussions, however, the kilo is dropped, and kilocalories are referred to simply as "calories." We will follow this tradition because it is the way most nutritional values are reported to the public.[1])

- Building blocks are needed for cell division, maintenance, and repair.

- Molecules, such as vitamins, are needed to coordinate life's processes.

- Water is necessary for maintaining the proper cellular environment and for certain cellular reactions.

The digestive system breaks complex molecules of carbohydrates, proteins, fats, and nucleic acids into their component subunits. Most cells of the body, especially those of the liver, are able to use these subunits as building blocks by joining them together and sometimes by converting one type of molecule into another.

---

[1]In technical writing, kilocalories are written as Calories.

Q *You are following a diet of 2000 calories a day. If you eat a cup of cereal for breakfast and a turkey sandwich for lunch, how many cups of spaghetti can you eat for dinner?*

GRAINS	VEGETABLES	FRUITS	MILK	MEAT & BEANS
Make half your grains whole	Vary your veggies	Focus on fruits	Get your calcium-rich foods	Go lean with protein
Eat at least 3 oz. of whole-grain cereals, breads, crackers, rice, or pasta every day	Eat more dark-green veggies like broccoli, spinach, and other dark leafy greens	Eat a variety of fruit	Go low-fat or fat-free when you choose milk, yogurt, and other milk products	Choose low-fat or lean meats and poultry
1 oz. is about 1 slice of bread, about 1 cup of breakfast cereal, or 1/2 cup of cooked rice, cereal, or pasta	Eat more orange vegetables like carrots and sweet potatoes	Choose fresh, frozen, canned, or dried fruit	If you don't or can't consume milk, choose lactose-free products or other calcium sources such as fortified foods and beverages	Bake it, broil it, or grill it
	Eat more dry beans and peas like pinto beans, kidney beans, and lentils	Go easy on fruit juices		Vary your protein routine—choose more fish, beans, peas, nuts, and seeds
Eat 6 oz. every day	Eat 2.5 cups every day	Eat 2 cups every day	Eat 3 cups every day	Eat 5.5 oz. every day

Find your balance between food and physical activity

- Be sure to stay within your daily calorie needs.
- Be physically active for at least 30 minutes most days of the week.
- About 60 minutes a day of physical activities may be needed to prevent weight gain.
- For sustaining weight loss, at least 60 to 90 minutes a day of physical activities may be required.
- Children and teenagers should be physically active for 60 minutes every day, or most days.

Know the limits on fats, sugars, and salt (sodium)

- Make most of your fat sources from fish, nuts, and vegetables oils.
- Limit solid fats like butter, stick margarine, shortening, and lard, as well as foods that contain them.
- Check the Nutrition Facts label to keep saturated fats, *trans* fats, and sodium low.
- Choose food and beverages low in added sugars. Added sugars contribute calories with few, if any, nutrients.

FIGURE 15a.1 The food guide pyramid helps you plan a well-balanced diet, even if you are not an expert nutritionist. The amounts specified in this figure are for a diet totaling 2000 calories per day.

A *1-1/2 cups*

Your body, however, cannot synthesize all of the required kinds of amino and fatty acids, at least not in quantities sufficient to meet bodily needs. These substances that the body cannot synthesize are called essential amino acids and essential fatty acids. *Essential* means that the substances must be included in the diet because the body cannot produce them.

A nutrient is a substance in food that provides energy; becomes part of a structure; or performs a function in growth, maintenance, or repair. Three nutrients—fats (lipids), carbohydrates, and proteins—can provide energy (Table **15a.1**). Although proteins are included in this list, they are usually used to build cell structures or regulatory molecules, such as enzymes or certain hormones.

TABLE 15a.1 Energy-Containing Nutrients

Nutrient	Good Sources	Functions	Recommendations
Fats (lipids)	Milk, cheese, meat, vegetable oils, nuts	Provides 9 calories per gram; component of cell membranes; component of nerve sheaths; insulates body; forms protective cushions around vital body organs	• Limit all fats in the diet, to reduce obesity. • Balance the types of fats in the diet. • Minimize saturated fats and *trans* fats. • Make most dietary fats monounsaturated or polyunsaturated.
Carbohydrates	Cereal, bread, pasta, vegetables, fruits, sweets	Provides 4 calories per gram; primary fuel for all cells	• Make most of the carbohydrate calories in the diet complex carbohydrates, especially fruits, vegetables, and whole grains. • Avoid carbohydrates with a high glycemic response. • Increase dietary fiber.
Protein and amino acids	Meat, poultry, fish, legumes, nuts	Provides 4 calories per gram; important component of all cells; structural proteins including muscle fibers; regulatory proteins including enzymes and certain hormones	• Choose lean, low-fat, or fat-free sources of protein. • Combine plant sources of protein that contain complementary amino acids.

Vitamins, minerals, water, and fiber do not provide energy, but they are essential to cellular functioning, as we'll see later.

Lipids

Lipid is the more technical name for what we have been calling fat. There are several types of lipids. They include fats, oils, and cholesterol. Even so, 95% of the lipids found in food are triglycerides—the fats that we commonly think of when we hear the term *fat*. A triglyceride is a molecule made from three fatty acids (hence, *tri–*) attached to a molecule of glycerol (hence, *–glyceride*). The fatty acids in the triglyceride give the molecule its characteristics.

An important way that fatty acids can differ is in their degree of saturation, or the extent to which each carbon in the fatty acid is bonded to as many hydrogen atoms as possible. Recall from Chapter 2 that a saturated fatty acid contains all the hydrogen it can hold. A polyunsaturated fatty acid can hold four or more additional hydrogens, and a monounsaturated fatty acid can hold two more hydrogens. In general, saturated fats are solid at room temperature, and they usually come from animal sources. In contrast, unsaturated fats are liquid at room temperature. Oils are unsaturated fats. The oils in our diet usually come from plant sources.

We have a biological need for lipids. Certain lipids, including cholesterol, are essential components of all cell membranes; some are used in the construction of myelin sheaths that insulate nerve fibers. Lipids are also needed for the absorption of the fat-soluble vitamins A, D, E, and K. These vitamins are absorbed from the intestines along with the products of fat digestion. Lipids then carry these vitamins in the bloodstream to the cells that use them. Glands in our skin produce oils that keep the skin soft and prevent dryness. Cholesterol is the structural basis of the steroid hormones, including the sex hormones.

The daily need for dietary fat is a mere tablespoon, yet the average American adult consumes 6 to 8 tablespoons of fat (78 to 196 g) a day, which can quickly add inches to the waistline. Obesity is associated with health problems such as high blood pressure and increased risk of diabetes. In addition, the high consumption of fat is related to certain cancers, including cancer of the colon, prostate gland, lungs, and perhaps the breast.

The blood level of cholesterol, which is partly influenced by the amount and kinds of fat in the diet, affects the risk of developing atherosclerosis, a condition in which fatty deposits form in the walls of blood vessels. The deposits promote an inflammatory response in the artery wall, thereby increasing the risk of heart attack and stroke (see Chapter 12). The risk of atherosclerosis increases with the blood level of cholesterol. In general, blood cholesterol levels under 200 mg/dl[2] are recommended for adults. The bad news is that the average blood cholesterol level for a middle-aged adult in the United States is 215 mg/dl. The good news is that people who lower their blood cholesterol levels can slow, or even reverse, atherosclerosis and, therefore, their risk of heart attack.

Blood cholesterol comes from one of two sources: the diet or the liver. Of the two, cholesterol production by the liver is more significant because most of the cholesterol in blood comes from the liver and not from the food we eat. Diet is still important, and, surprisingly, saturated fat in the diet raises blood levels of cholesterol more than dietary cholesterol does. Moreover, different people's bodies handle cholesterol differently depending on their genetic makeup (as well as the amount of cholesterol consumed in a meal). As a result, there is not a clear relationship between dietary and blood cholesterol.

Total blood cholesterol provides only a partial picture of a person's risk of atherosclerosis. Before cholesterol can be transported in the blood or lymph, it is combined with protein and triglycerides to form a lipoprotein, which makes it soluble in water. Low-density lipoproteins (LDLs) are considered to be a damaging, or bad, form of cholesterol. Although LDLs bring cholesterol to the cells that need it to sustain life, they also deposit cholesterol in artery walls. In contrast, high-density lipoproteins (HDLs) carry cholesterol from the cells, perhaps even from the artery walls, to the liver for elimination. Because HDLs are protective against heart disease, they are considered to be a good form of cholesterol.

Because of the different roles the two kinds of lipoproteins play in transporting cholesterol, the proportion of HDLs and LDLs in the blood is considered a more important indicator of risk than is the

[2]dl = deciliter (100 milliliters).

total blood cholesterol (HDL+LDL) level alone. The ratio of total cholesterol to HDLs should not be greater than 4:1. HDL levels higher than 60 mg/dl are considered to reduce the risk of heart disease.

The types of fat in the diet can influence blood cholesterol level and, more importantly, the ratios of LDLs and HDLs. Saturated fats and *trans* fats are bad for the heart. Saturated fat consistently boosts blood levels of harmful LDL cholesterol, both by directly stimulating the liver to step up its production of LDLs and by slowing the rate at which LDLs are cleared from the bloodstream. Foods high in saturated fat include meat (especially red meat), butter, cheese, whole milk, and other dairy products. *Trans* fatty acids are formed when hydrogens are added to unsaturated fats (oils) in such a way as to stabilize them or to solidify them, as when margarine is formed from vegetable oil. *Trans* fats are also found in many packaged foods (Figure **15a.2**). *Trans* fatty acids may behave like saturated fatty acids and raise LDL levels. In addition, they lower good HDLs.

But not all fats are bad. Monounsaturated fats and polyunsaturated fats, such as omega-3 fatty acids and omega-6 fatty acids,[3] are good fats; they lower total blood cholesterol and LDLs. Monounsaturated fats are found in olive, canola, and peanut oils and in nuts. Omega-3 fatty acids are found in the oils of certain fish,

such as Atlantic mackerel, lake trout, herring, tuna, and salmon. The most important omega-6 fatty acid is linoleic acid, an essential fatty acid found in corn and safflower oils (Figure **15a.3**).

Carbohydrates

Carbohydrates in the diet come primarily from plant sources and include sugars, starches, and roughage (dietary fiber). The basic unit of a carbohydrate molecule is a monosaccharide. Sugars are simple carbohydrates, meaning they are generally monosaccharides or disaccharides (two monosaccharides linked together). Sugars taste sweet and are naturally present in whole foods such as fruit and milk. In whole foods, sugars are present with other nutrients, including vitamins and minerals. However, refined sugars have been removed from their plant sources and concentrated, so they are no longer mixed with other nutrients. The calories from refined sugars are therefore described as "empty." They provide energy but have no other nutritive value. Refined sugars are found in candies, cookies, cakes, and pies.

Starches and fiber are complex carbohydrates, which means they are polysaccharides. Plants store energy in starches—long, sometimes branched chains of hundreds or thousands of linked molecules of the monosaccharide glucose. Common sources of starches include wheat, rice, oats, corn, potatoes, and legumes. Fiber is the indigestible part of edible plants. Complex carbohydrates are usually accompanied by other nutrients; but even complex carbohydrates are not all healthful, because they differ in the way they affect blood glucose.

The most important function of carbohydrates is to provide fuel for the body. Recall that the digestive system breaks down all carbohydrates (except fiber) to simple sugars, primarily glucose, which is absorbed into the bloodstream. Glucose is the carbohydrate that cells use for fuel most of the time. A measure called the glycemic response describes how quickly a serving of food is converted to blood sugar and how much the level of blood sugar is affected. The glycemic index is a numerical ranking of carbohydrates based on their glycemic response. The scale of the glycemic index ranges from 0 to 100, with pure glucose serving as a reference point

> Saturated fats and *trans* fats raise the risk of atherosclerosis and heart disease.

Saturated fats   Trans fats

> Most of the fat in the diet should be monounsaturated, polyunsaturated, or omega-3.

Monounsaturated fats   Polyunsaturated fats   Omega-3 fats

FIGURE 15a.2 Types of dietary fats. The total fat content of the diet should be moderate. The types of fats in the diet can influence the risk of heart attack and stroke.

> Simple carbohydrates are empty calories, because they provide only energy.

> Complex carbohydrates provide energy along with other nutrients.

FIGURE 15a.3 Types of carbohydrates. Simple carbohydrates, especially refined sugars, should be minimized in the diet. Most of the carbohydrates in the diet should be complex carbohydrates.

[3]The number in omega-3 and omega-6 refers to the location of the first double bond in the carbon chain of the fatty acid.

of 100. Sugar and starchy foods such as white bread, potatoes, and white rice have a high value on the glycemic index because they cause the blood sugar level to rise sharply. Foods with a low value on the glycemic index, including whole fruit, whole-grain foods, brown rice, and barley, cause a more modest and gradual increase in blood sugar. Generally, foods with a low value on the glycemic index are high in fiber.

The glycemic response is important because it influences how the body reacts to different foods. After you eat a carbohydrate with a high glycemic index value, your blood sugar rises. As discussed in Chapter 10, a rise in blood glucose level causes the pancreas to release more of the hormone insulin, which lowers blood glucose (thus inducing hunger) by converting excess glucose to fat. In short, in a healthy person, consumption of a high glycemic food is followed by fat formation and by increased hunger. In people with diabetes mellitus, rising blood sugar levels due to high-glycemic foods may cause medical problems, because these people are unable to produce or to use insulin (see Chapter 10).

Nutritionists recommend that you limit your intake of simple carbohydrates, especially refined sugars, and instead choose sources of carbohydrates that contain more than just calories. For example, fruits, vegetables, grains, and milk are food groups that have low glycemic index values and supply many other nutrients besides carbohydrates.

Dietary fiber is found in all plants that are eaten for food, including fruits, vegetables, dried beans, and whole grains. Fiber is a form of carbohydrate that humans cannot digest into its component monosaccharides. Because only monosaccharides can be absorbed from the small intestine, dietary fiber is passed along to the large intestine. Some of the fiber is digested by the bacteria living in the large intestine, and the remaining fiber gives bulk to feces.

Although fiber cannot be digested or absorbed, it is still an important part of a healthful diet. Fiber is good for the heart and blood vessels, because it lowers LDLs but does not lower the beneficial HDLs. Intestinal disorders such as constipation and hemorrhoids improve when the amount of fiber in the diet is increased (discussed in Chapter 15). Fiber can absorb an amazing amount of water, thereby softening stools and making them easier to pass.

Proteins

A protein consists of one or more chains of amino acids. Human proteins contain 20 different kinds of amino acids. The protein in the food you eat is digested into its component amino acids, which are then absorbed into the bloodstream and delivered to the cells, creating a pool of available amino acids. Your cells then draw the amino acids needed to build proteins in your body from

those available in the pool. In addition, the body is able to synthesize 11 of the amino acids from nitrogen and molecules derived from carbohydrates, fats, or other amino acids. The 9 remaining amino acids that the body cannot synthesize—called essential amino acids—must be supplied by the diet.

When your body makes a protein, the amino acids are strung together in a specific order, depending on which protein is being made. If a particular amino acid is needed for a certain protein but is not available, then that protein cannot be synthesized. Consider this analogy: A sign maker with a bag containing only 1 copy of the letter *R* and 100 copies of the other 25 letters in the alphabet could make only one NO PARKING sign. There is simply no way to substitute for the limiting letter, *R*. The same principle applies to protein synthesis; if a needed amino acid is lacking, protein production stops or the body breaks down existing proteins to get that amino acid.

In short, the pool of amino acids available for protein synthesis must always contain sufficient amounts of all the essential amino acids. Dietary proteins described as complete proteins contain ample amounts of all the essential amino acids. Animal proteins are generally complete. Plant proteins are generally incomplete proteins and are low in one or more of the essential amino acids. Eating certain combinations of incomplete proteins from two or more plant sources can ensure that the pool of amino acids available for protein synthesis will contain ample amounts of all the essential amino acids (Figure **15a.4**). Such combinations are called complementary proteins because if the combinations are correct, they supply enough of all the essential amino acids (Figure **15a.5**). A vegetarian must be sure to consume complementary proteins.

Complete proteins contain all the essential amino acids and usually come from animal sources.

Incomplete proteins lack one or more of the essential amino acids and usually come from plant sources.

FIGURE 15a.4 Types of protein in the diet

Nuts and seeds

- Hummus (chickpeas and sesame seeds)
- Tofu and cashew stir-fry

- Trail mix (roasted soybeans and nuts)
- Tahini (sesame seeds) and peanut sauce

Legumes

- Rice and beans
- Black-eyed peas and corn bread
- Bean burrito in corn tortilla

- Peanut butter on bread
- Rice and tofu
- Rice and lentils

Grains

FIGURE 15a.5 Complementary proteins are combinations of two or more incomplete proteins that together supply all the essential amino acids.

TABLE 15a.2 Vitamins

Vitamin	Good Sources	Function	Effects of Deficiency	Effect of Excess
Fat-soluble vitamins				
A	Liver, egg yolk, fat-containing and fortified dairy products; formed from beta-carotene (found in deep yellow and deep green leafy vegetables)	Components of rhodopsin, the eye pigment responsible for black-and-white vision; maintains epithelia; cell differentiation	Night blindness; dry, scaly skin; dry hair; skin sores; increased respiratory, urogenital, and digestive infections; xerophthalmia (the leading cause of preventable blindness worldwide); most common vitamin deficiency in world	Drowsiness; headache; dry, coarse, scaly skin; hair loss; itching; brittle nails; abdominal and bone pain
D	Fortified milk, fish liver oil, egg yolk; formed in skin when exposed to ultraviolet light	Increases absorption of calcium; enhances bone growth and calcification	Bone deformities in children; rickets, bone softening in adults	Calcium deposits in soft tissues, kidney damage, vomiting, diarrhea, weight loss
E	Whole grains, dark green vegetables, vegetable oils, nuts, seeds	May inhibit effects of free radicals; helps maintain cell membranes; prevents oxidation of vitamins A and C in gut	Rare; possible anemia and nerve damage	Muscle weakness, fatigue, nausea
K	Primary source from bacteria in large intestine; leafy green vegetables, cabbage, cauliflower	Important in forming proteins involved in blood clotting	Easy bruising, abnormal blood clotting, severe bleeding	Liver damage and anemia
Water-soluble vitamins				
C (ascorbic acid)	Citrus fruits, cantaloupe, strawberries, tomatoes, broccoli, cabbage, green pepper	Collagen synthesis; may inhibit free radicals; improves iron absorption	Scurvy, poor wound healing, impaired immunity	Diarrhea, kidney stones; may alter results of certain diagnostic lab tests
Thiamin (B_1)	Pork, legumes, whole grains, leafy green vegetables	Coenzyme in energy metabolism; nerve function	Water retention in tissues, nerve changes leading to poor coordination, heart failure, beriberi	None known
Riboflavin (B_2)	Dairy products such as milk; whole grains, meat, liver, egg whites, leafy green vegetables	Coenzyme used in energy metabolism	Skin lesions	None known
Niacin (B_3)	Nuts, green leafy vegetables, potatoes; can be formed from tryptophan found in meats	Coenzyme used in energy metabolism	Contributes to pellagra (damage to skin, gut, nervous system)	Flushing of skin on face, neck, and hands; possible liver damage
B_6	Meat, poultry, fish, spinach, potatoes, tomatoes	Coenzyme used in amino acid metabolism	Nervous, skin, and muscular disorders; anemia	Numbness in feet, poor coordination
Pantothenic acid	Widely distributed in foods, animal products, and whole grains	Coenzyme in energy metabolism	Fatigue, numbness and tingling of hands and feet, headaches, nausea	Diarrhea, water retention
Folic acid (folate)	Dark green vegetables, orange juice, nuts, legumes, grain products	Coenzyme in nucleic acid and amino acid metabolism	Anemia (megaloblastic and pernicious), gastrointestinal disturbances, nervous system damage, inflamed tongue, neural tube defects	High doses mask vitamin B_{12} deficiency
B_{12}	Poultry, fish, red meat, dairy products except butter	Coenzyme in nucleic acid metabolism	Anemia (megaloblastic and pernicious), impaired nerve function	None known
Biotin	Legumes, egg yolk; widely distributed in foods; bacteria of large intestine	Coenzyme used in energy metabolism	Scaly skin (dermatitis), sore tongue, anemia	None known

Sources of animal protein usually contain a lot of fat, whereas plant protein sources usually contain less fat and are good sources of carbohydrates, too. The tendency in the United States to make meat the focal point of every meal is the main reason that the typical diet here contains excess fat. For a healthier diet, **choose lean, low-fat, or fat-free sources of protein.** Eating a variety of plant proteins will supply all the essential amino acids and will help reduce the percentage of fat calories in the diet as well as boost the percentage of calories from complex carbohydrates. When choosing among animal sources of protein, reduce the amount of fatty red meat in favor of chicken (with the fatty skin removed) or fish.

Vitamins

A vitamin (*vita*, life) is an organic (carbon-containing) compound that, although essential for health and growth, is needed only in minute quantities—milligrams or micrograms. All the vitamins you need in a day would fill only an eighth of a teaspoon. These tiny amounts are sufficient because vitamins are not broken down or destroyed during use. Most function as coenzymes, which are nonprotein molecules necessary for certain enzymes to function. Enzymes and coenzymes are continuously recycled and, therefore, can be used repeatedly by the body.

There are two categories of vitamins: water-soluble vitamins, which dissolve in water, and fat-soluble vitamins, which are stored in fat. Of the 13 vitamins known to be needed by humans, 9 are water soluble (C and the various B vitamins) and 4 are fat soluble (A, D, E, and K). Table **15a.2** lists the vitamins, their functions, good sources for them, and the problems associated with deficiencies or excesses.

Except for vitamin D, our cells cannot make vitamins, so we must obtain them in our food. A varied, balanced diet is the best way to ensure an adequate supply of all vitamins. No one food contains every vitamin, but most contain some. Vitamins are often more easily available for absorption when the foods containing them are cooked. Cooked carrots, for instance, are a better source of vitamin A than are raw carrots. However, water-soluble vitamins are likely to be lost if the vegetables containing them are cooked by being boiled in water. Steaming those vegetables is a better way to preserve their vitamin content.

Certain vitamins have to be consumed in adequate amounts every day. Folic acid, one of the B vitamins that is particularly abundant in dark leafy greens, plays a role in preventing birth defects, such as spina bifida, that involve the brain and spinal cord. It now seems that folic acid, along with vitamins B_6 and B_{12}, may also help prevent heart disease. Five daily servings of fruits and vegetables should provide enough of these vitamins to protect the heart. Antioxidant vitamins, including vitamin C, vitamin E, and beta-carotene, protect against cell damage due to oxidation. Some researchers believe that antioxidants slow the aging process and protect against cancer, atherosclerosis, and macular degeneration (the leading cause of irreversible blindness in people over age 65). These, too, should be ingested every day. Spinach, collard greens, and carrots are good sources of antioxidant vitamins.

Minerals

The minerals needed in our diet are inorganic substances essential to a wide range of life processes. We need fairly large amounts, although not what would be described as "megadoses," of seven minerals: calcium, phosphorus, potassium, sulfur, sodium, chloride, and magnesium. In addition, we need trace amounts of about a dozen others. Table **15a.3** lists selected minerals, their functions, good sources for them, and the problems associated with deficiencies or excesses.

We can obtain the necessary minerals from the foods we eat, as long as we prepare them in ways that do not reduce their mineral content. Like certain vitamins, many minerals are water soluble and can be lost during food preparation.

Sodium, a component of table salt, is essential to health, but most Americans consume too much of it. High salt intake causes high blood pressure in some people. The Dietary Recommendations for Americans advises that salt intake should not exceed 2400 mg (slightly more than 1 teaspoon) a day. Processed foods are especially high in salt, which is added to preserve food and enhance the taste. Salt is found in nearly every processed food product, including canned vegetables, cheese, bread, and processed meats. To reduce your salt intake, use salt sparingly when cooking fresh food, and read the labels on prepared food.

Water

Water is perhaps the most important nutrient; it transports materials through our bodies, lubricates and cushions organs, helps in temperature regulation, and provides a medium for many vital chemical reactions. We can live without food for about 8 weeks, but without water for only about 3 days. Nutritionists recommend that we consume eight 8-ounce glasses (2 quarts) of water a day. Water in fruits and vegetables makes up about half of that requirement for the average adult. The rest of the requirement does not have to be consumed as plain water, but it should not come from carbonated sweet drinks, caffeinated beverages, or alcoholic beverages. Carbonation interferes with water absorption, and sugar adds empty calories. Caffeine and alcohol increase water loss in urine.

Food Labels

Grocery stores generally offer several choices for essentially the same product. Food labels and the knowledge you now have about nutrients can help you make healthy choices.

Figure **15a.6** shows a food label from a box of baked whole wheat crackers. It provides some useful general pointers for reading

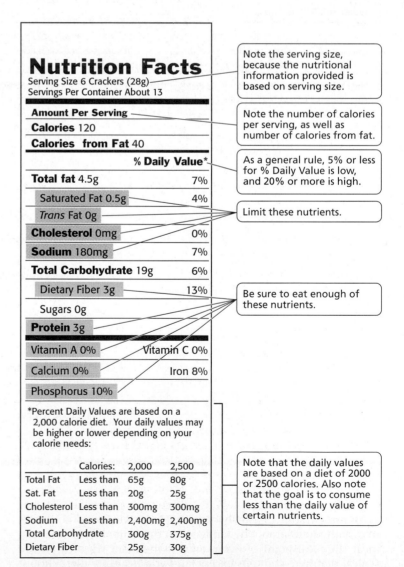

FIGURE 15a.6 Tips for reading food labels

TABLE 15a.3 Selected Minerals

Mineral	Good Sources	Function	Effects of Deficiency	Effects of Excess
Major minerals				
Calcium	Milk, cheese, dark green vegetables, legumes	Hardness of bones, tooth formation, blood clotting, nerve and muscle action	Stunted growth, loss of bone mass, osteoporosis, convulsions	Impaired absorption of other minerals; kidney stones
Phosphorus	Milk, cheese, red meat, poultry, whole grains	Bone and tooth formation; components of nucleic acids, ATP, and phospholipids; acid–base balance	Weakness, demineralized bone	Impaired absorption of some minerals
Magnesium	Whole grains, green leafy vegetables, milk, dairy products, nuts, legumes	Component of enzymes	Muscle cramps, neurologic disturbances	Neurologic disturbances
Potassium	Available in many foods including meats, fruits, vegetables, and whole grains	Body water balance, nerve function, muscle function, role in protein synthesis	Muscle weakness	Muscle weakness, paralysis, heart failure
Sulfur	Protein-containing foods including meat, legumes, milk, and eggs	Component of body proteins	None known	None known
Sodium	Table salt	Body water balance, nerve function	Muscle cramps, reduced appetite	High blood pressure in susceptible people
Chloride	Table salt, processed foods	Formation of hydrochloric acid in stomach, role in acid–base balance	Muscle cramps, reduced appetite, poor growth	High blood pressure in susceptible people
Trace minerals				
Iron	Meat, liver, shellfish, egg yolk, whole grains, green leafy vegetables, nuts, dried fruit	Component of hemoglobin, myoglobin, and cytochrome (transport chain enzyme)	Iron-deficiency anemia, weakness, impaired immune function	Liver damage, heart failure, shock
Iodine	Marine fish and shellfish, iodized salt, dairy products	Thyroid hormone function	Enlarged thyroid	Enlarged thyroid
Fluoride	Treated drinking water, tea, seafood	Bone and tooth maintenance	Tooth decay	Digestive upsets, mottling of teeth, deformed skeleton
Copper	Nuts, legumes, seafood, drinking water	Synthesis of melanin, hemoglobin, and transport chain components; collagen synthesis; immune function	Rare; anemia, changes in blood vessels	Nausea, liver damage
Zinc	Seafood, whole grains, legumes, nuts, meats	Component of digestive enzymes; required for normal growth, wound healing, and sperm production	Difficulty in walking; slurred speech, scaly skin, impaired immune function	Nausea, vomiting, diarrhea, impaired immune function
Manganese	Nuts, legumes, whole grains, leafy green vegetables	Role in synthesis of fatty acids, cholesterol, urea, and hemoglobin; normal neural function	None known	Nerve damage

food labels. First, note the serving size described on the label, and remember that the amount you actually eat, whether larger or smaller than what is described on the label, will be what determines the number of calories and amount of nutrients you consume.

Next, notice the number of calories reported per serving and the number of calories from fat. In the example shown in the figure, 40 of the 120 calories in a serving, or nearly 34% of the calories, come from fat. Dietary guidelines recommend that you consume less than 30% of your total calories as fat. However, if you crave these crackers, you can make up for the amount of fat

in them, to some extent, by eating low-fat food at another time during the day. Also note the amount of saturated fat and *trans* fat reported on the label, because these kinds of fat should be minimized in your diet.

In considering the percent daily values of various nutrients reported on the label, keep two things in mind. First, these values are based on a 2000-calorie diet. Your own diet may require more or fewer calories. Second, as becomes clear from the daily values provided at the bottom of the label, you should be attempting to keep dietary fat and sodium consumption *below* those amounts.

Food labels can also help you increase your intake of nutrients that are important to consume. Be sure to get enough vitamin A, vitamin C, calcium, iron, and phosphorus. The daily values reported for carbohydrates and dietary fiber will also help you consume enough of those substances.

Energy Balance

The body requires energy for maintenance of basic body functions, for physical activity, and for processing the food that is eaten. The energy that is needed strictly for maintenance is called the basal metabolic rate (BMR); it is the minimum energy needed to keep an awake, resting body alive, and it generally represents between 60% and 75% of the body's energy needs. A male usually has a higher metabolic rate than does a female because a male's body has more muscle and less fat than a female's. Muscles use more energy than fat does. So, while a man and a woman of equal size sit on the couch and watch television together, he burns 10% to 20% more calories than she does. As you age, muscle mass and metabolic rate both decline. Together, these factors reduce caloric needs. If other adjustments in lifestyle are not made to compensate, these metabolic changes can add extra pounds each year after age 35. Besides gender and age, a person's BMR is influenced by age, health, food intake, and genetics.

The second largest use of energy is physical activity. Exercise is an excellent way to burn calories. It not only boosts your energy needs during the activity but also speeds up metabolic rate for a while afterward. The calories you habitually use in exercise are added to those needed to maintain your BMR when you determine your calorie needs.

Exercise helps keep the body in good working order. The Dietary Guide for Americans 2005 encourages adults to engage in at least 30 minutes of moderate-intensity physical activity on most days of the week. Aerobic exercise reduces the risk of diseases of the heart and blood vessels and lowers blood pressure (discussed in Chapter 12). Weight-bearing exercise reduces the risk of osteoporosis, a loss of bone density (discussed in Chapter 5). In general, regular physical exercise reduces stress and the risk of certain chronic diseases, including diabetes. Regular exercise also manages body weight, helping to prevent the unhealthy weight gain that can occur in adulthood.

Obesity

Although *overweight* and *obese* are both terms used to describe people who have excess body weight, they do not have exactly the same meaning. An obese person is overweight because of excess fat. An athletic person who because of well-developed muscle weighs more than the weight listed as desirable on height–weight tables is not obese. However, most people who are overweight have too much body fat. *Overweight* and *obese* generally refer to ranges of weight that are considered to be unhealthy.

The Body Mass Index (BMI) is a number that provides a reliable indicator of body fat because it evaluates your weight in relation to your height (Figure **15a.7**). A BMI greater than 30 is generally considered unhealthy and an indication of obesity. However, just as it is possible for a very muscular person to have a BMI above 30 and not be considered obese, it is possible for a person in the healthy weight range to have too much fat and little muscle. The Centers for Disease Control and Prevention estimates that 64% of Americans are overweight and that almost 31% are obese. The number of

FIGURE 15a.7 The Body Mass Index (BMI) evaluates body weight relative to height. A BMI over 30 is usually considered to be unhealthy and a sign of obesity.

obese people in the United States has been steadily rising since 1985 (Figure **15a.8**).

Although most dieters are motivated to slim down for cosmetic reasons, more important reasons are the health risks associated with obesity. For instance, obesity leads to disease of the heart and blood vessels. Even individuals who are just slightly overweight are at increased risk of having a heart attack. Obesity also raises total cholesterol levels in the blood while lowering levels of the beneficial HDL cholesterol. In addition, it increases the risk of high blood pressure, which can lead to death from heart attack, stroke, or kidney disease. Obesity has harmful effects besides those on the heart and blood vessels. It can induce diabetes, which results in elevated blood glucose levels; it is a major cause of gallstones; and it can worsen degenerative joint diseases.

Weight-Loss Programs

Successful weight-loss programs generally have three components: (1) a reduction in the number of calories consumed, without departing from the recommended nutritional guidelines; (2) an increase in energy expenditure; and (3) behavior modification. Gradual changes in eating habits are most likely to lead to permanent lifestyle changes.

To determine the number of calories needed each day to maintain a desirable weight, a person must take activity level and age into account. A pound of fat contains approximately 3500 calories, so to lose 1 pound a week, a person should reduce calorie consumption by 500 calories a day (500 calories × 7 days = 3500 calories), or increase calorie use by 500 calories a day, or any equivalent combination. The

Obesity Trends* among U.S. Adults
1991–2006

| ☐ No Data | ■ <10% | ■ 10%–14% | ■ 15%–19% | ■ 20%–24% | ■ 25%–29% | ■ ≥30% |

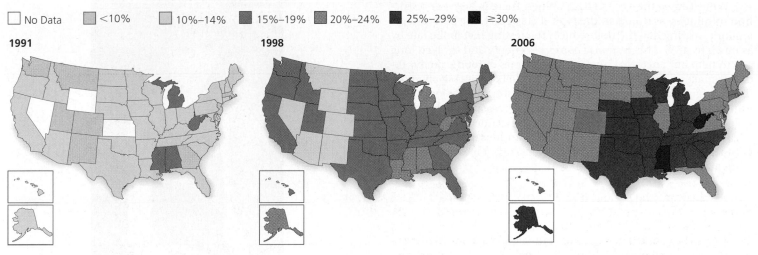

1991   **1998**   **2006**

(*BMI ≥ 30, or ∼ 30 lb overweight for 5'4" woman)

FIGURE 15a.8 Obesity trends among adults in the United States. Obesity is defined as a high amount of body fat relative to total body weight. There has been an alarming increase in the number of obese people over the last decade. (Centers for Disease Control and Prevention)

(a) 1986   **(b)** 1988   **(c)** 2008

FIGURE 15a.9 Typical dieters change their energy balance temporarily, and, when old habits are resumed, the weight is regained. The cycle is then repeated. The yo-yo effect makes weight loss more difficult with successive diets. The popular talk show host Oprah Winfrey has been candid about her struggle with fluctuating weight.

lowest daily caloric intake recommended is 1200 calories for an adult female and 1500 calories for an adult male, unless they are in a medically supervised program.

The easiest way to reduce calorie intake while continuing to eat healthily is to cut back on fatty foods, especially those containing saturated fat, because fat contains more than twice as many calories as an equivalent weight of carbohydrate or protein. In addition, it is easier for the body to store the unused fat from foods as body fat than as protein or carbohydrate. Indeed, most of us do end up wearing the fat we eat.

Another recommended way of reducing calories is to avoid sugar. As we have seen, foods that taste sweet are packed with sugar and, therefore, calories. Recall that sugar is a high-glycemic carbohydrate.

A third healthful diet tip is to increase the amount of fiber in the diet. High-fiber foods, such as fruits and vegetables, tend to be low in calories and fat but also high in vitamins and minerals. Because fiber is bulky, these foods are also filling.

Approximately 60% to 90% of dieters who lose weight will later regain all the weight they lost (Figure **15a.9**). Often, the weight is regained because the weight loss was achieved by drastically cutting back calories, which can be unhealthy and is very difficult to sustain for long periods. As old eating habits return, so do the pounds. When the determination to shed some pounds returns, the diet begins again. This process is commonly known as "the yo-yo effect."

What causes the yo-yo effect? When there is a severe restriction in calories, as occurs in the typical crash diet, the body adopts a calorie-sparing defense that reduces the resting metabolic rate by as much as 45%. This response conserves energy and evolved long ago to help our ancestors survive during times of food scarcity. Today, it makes weight loss from successive diets progressively more difficult. Furthermore, with each diet, a person usually loses both lean and fat tissue, especially if increased exercise is not part of the weight-loss program. When the weight is regained, most of it is fat. Fat is less metabolically active than lean muscle tissue, so the person's metabolic rate drops even lower. Thus, repeated crash dieting may be a "no-lose situation."

Eating Disorders

Obesity can be considered an eating disorder associated with overeating. The obese and overweight would be wise to follow a nutritionally sound weight-loss program. It is important to remember, however, that dieting can be taken too far. Most people with the eating disorders anorexia nervosa and bulimia nervosa began their descent into these disorders by dieting. Anorexia nervosa is a deliberate self-starvation. A person whose body weight is 85% or less than expected for his or her height and weight is considered to be anorexic. In contrast, bulimia nervosa is marked by binge eating large quantities of food and then purging by self-induced vomiting, enemas, laxatives, diuretics, or excessive exercise.

The changes in eating habits associated with these eating disorders are thought to be the result of psychological, social, and physiological factors. Both disorders are associated with a preoccupation with body size and shape. Anxious depression also seems to play a role.

The behavior patterns associated with anorexia nervosa and bulimia differ, but both result in a severe deficit in calories and nutrients. A person with anorexia nervosa eats very little food and, therefore, consumes few calories. But *anorexia*, which means "lack of appetite," is misnamed. Although people with anorexia nervosa deny feeling hunger, their refusal to eat stems from an intense fear of becoming fat—not from lack of appetite. Excessive exercise is also typical in anorexia nervosa. No matter how much weight is lost, it is never enough, because an anorexic person has a distorted body image. He or she perceives the body as fat even when emaciated (Figure **15a.10**). In contrast, a person with bulimia eats a huge amount of food at one time but then eliminates it from the body. During a bulimic binge, which may last as long as 8 hours, as many as 20,000 calories may be consumed. Each binge is followed by attempts to purge the body of the calories, usually by self-induced vomiting or by laxatives.

Eating disorders have many negative effects on the body. Negative health effects of bulimia include esophageal injuries, tooth decay, and gum disease resulting from frequent vomiting, as well as dehydration, constipation, and electrolyte imbalance. One major side effect of anorexia nervosa is a severe decrease in bone health. Although the excessive exercise engaged in by most anorexic people may have a slight strengthening effect on bones, many other factors work to weaken the bones. For example, amenorrhea (cessation of menstruation), malnutrition, and low body

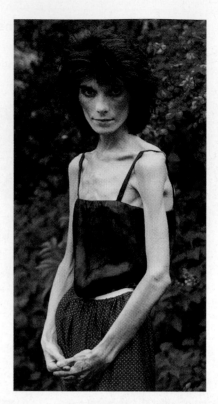

FIGURE 15a.10 Anorexia is a form of self-starvation. No matter how emaciated the person becomes, the individual still perceives the body as being fat.

weight, particularly low body fat, are all consequences of anorexia nervosa, and they can contribute to poor bone health.

The effects of anorexia nervosa are not so different from those of starvation. In the early phase of the illness, an anorexic person typically chooses a diet that is low in energy-dense foods but rather high in proteins and other essential nutrients. Dietary protein, combined with the high activity levels characteristic of a person with anorexia nervosa, has a nitrogen-sparing effect. As a result, the initial weight loss is almost entirely due to loss of fat tissue. However, when fat reserves are exhausted and refusal of food becomes more severe, the body begins to break down its own proteins to use as an energy source. The primary sources of these proteins are skeletal and heart muscle; therefore, skeletal and heart muscle mass decreases. At the same time, water loss is accelerated, especially from within the body cells. This water loss leads to disturbances in metabolism and electrolyte balance.

Without treatment, up to 20% of people with serious eating disorders die. Even with treatment, 2% to 3% die. Heart problems are the most common cause of death in people with anorexia nervosa. Starvation, dehydration, and electrolyte disturbances cause the heartbeat to slow (bradycardia) and blood pressure to fall (hypotension). A potential cause of death associated with either anorexia nervosa or bulimia is hypoglycemia, an abnormally low blood glucose level. Because the brain depends entirely on glucose for its metabolism, hypoglycemia can cause unconsciousness and death.

Help for people with anorexia nervosa and bulimia nervosa is available. Treatment usually involves the family and centers on psychotherapy to help the person develop a healthier body image.

16

The Urinary System

Proper fluid balance is critical to homeostasis. We challenge the balance of fluids in our bodies through diet and exercise. In the face of such challenges, our kidneys help to achieve the correct balance by filtering the blood and regulating its volume and solute concentration.

323

Graciella had just finished running her first marathon, and she was exhausted, hot, and thirsty. She had been careful about the amount of fluids she drank before and during the race, and knew that she had to remain careful in the minutes after the race. Indeed, in preparing for her first marathon she had done more than the many months of intense physical training. She also had researched how the body maintains the proper balance of fluids and electrolytes, such as sodium, potassium, chloride, and calcium.

Graciella knew that dehydration could be deadly. Through her research she learned that the body's thirst center is in the hypothalamus, and that this center issues the message to drink when levels of sodium in the blood rise or when blood volume and pressure fall. Drinking water when dehydrated can help to restore fluid balance, but drinking too much water can be fatal because it can cause *hyponatremia*, an abnormally low concentration of sodium in the blood. Hyponatremia (also called water intoxication) is associated with excessive water

consumption during high-endurance sporting events when sodium and water are lost through sweat. Drinking excess amounts of water at such times replenishes water, but not sodium. The excess water dilutes sodium in the blood, prevents the kidneys from being able to maintain proper fluid balance, and causes cells of the body to swell. This is particularly dangerous to the brain, which cannot expand because it is surrounded by the skull. Symptoms of hyponatremia include nausea, headache, confusion, and in severe cases, seizures. Sports drinks that

contain electrolytes may help to replace those lost in sweat and thereby aid in preventing hyponatremia. Reassured that she was well informed about how to avoid dramatic challenges to her body's fluid balance, Graciella began thinking about her next marathon.

In this chapter we focus on the urinary system and maintenance of fluid balance in the body. Specifically, we consider the critical roles that kidneys play in maintaining homeostasis by removing wastes from the body and regulating the volume, solute concentration, and pH of blood.

Eliminating Waste

Excretion is the elimination of wastes and excess substances from the body. Metabolic wastes include carbon dioxide, water, heat, salts, and nitrogen-containing molecules such as ammonia, urea, uric acid, and creatinine. Kidneys and other organs that eliminate metabolic wastes help to maintain homeostasis.

The organs that eliminate wastes and excess essential ions—such as hydrogen (H^+), sodium (Na^+), potassium (K^+), and chloride (Cl^-)—are shown in Figure **16.1**. Lungs and skin eliminate heat, water, and carbon dioxide (as the gas CO_2 from the lungs and as bicarbonate ions, HCO_3^- from the skin). Skin also excretes salts and small amounts of urea and uric acid. Minor amounts of other substances, such as alcohol, are also eliminated from the skin and lungs. (Alcohol excretion by the lungs forms the basis of the Breathalyzer test.) Organs of our gastrointestinal tract eliminate solid wastes and

some metabolic wastes. Defecation is the elimination of feces from the digestive tract. Feces contain undigested food, bacteria, water, bile pigments, and sloughed-off epithelial cells (see Chapter 15).

Our focus in this chapter is the kidneys, which are the organs of the urinary system that form urine. **Urine**, a yellowish fluid, is a mix of water and solutes. Through urine, the body excretes water, HCO_3^-, inorganic salts, H^+, urea, uric acid, and creatinine. Ammonia is formed in the liver during the breakdown of amino acids. Because ammonia is toxic, the liver converts it to urea, a less harmful waste. Uric acid is formed during the recycling of nitrogen-containing bases of nucleotides (see Chapter 2). In excess, uric acid may form crystals in the synovial fluid of joints (particularly in the big toe), causing the painful condition called gout. Creatinine is generated in skeletal muscle from the breakdown of creatine phosphate, a compound that serves as an alternative energy source for muscle contraction.

Integumentary system (skin)

HCO_3^-
Heat
Water
Urea, uric acid
Salt

Respiratory system

O_2
CO_2
Water
Heat

Digestive system

Food, water

Elimination of feces

Urinary system

Elimination of nitrogen-containing wastes, water, salts, and excess ions

FIGURE 16.1 Organs from several systems eliminate wastes of different kinds from the body. The kidneys, organs of the urinary system, play a major role in the excretion of nitrogen-containing wastes, water, salts, and excess ions.

Components of the Urinary System

The **urinary system** consists of two kidneys, two ureters, one urinary bladder, and one urethra (Figure **16.2**). The main function of this system is to regulate the volume, pressure, and composition of the blood. The **kidneys** are the organs of the urinary system that accomplish this task by regulating the amount of water and dissolved substances that are removed from and returned to the blood. Substances not returned to the blood form urine.

Urine from the kidneys travels down muscular tubes called **ureters** to the urinary bladder. Each ureter is 25 to 30 cm in length. Peristaltic (wavelike) contractions begin where the ureters leave the kidneys and travel down the ureters, pushing urine toward the urinary bladder. Depending on the rate of urine formation, up to five peristaltic waves occur per minute. Each ureter enters the urinary bladder through a slit-like opening. The **urinary bladder** is a muscular, expandable organ that temporarily stores urine until it is excreted from the body. Urine leaves the body through the **urethra**, a tube that transports urine from the urinary bladder to the outside of the body through an external opening. The female urethra transports only urine. The male urethra, however, carries urine and reproductive fluids (but not simultaneously). The reproductive function of the male urethra is discussed in Chapter 17.

Kidneys and Homeostasis

Our kidneys are reddish brown in color and shaped like kidney beans. Each one is about the size of a fist. They are located just above the waist, sandwiched between the parietal peritoneum (the membrane that lines the abdominal cavity) and the muscles of the dorsal body wall. The slightly indented, or concave, border of each kidney faces the midline of the body. Perched on top of each kidney is an adrenal gland.

The kidneys are covered and supported by several layers of connective tissue (Figure **16.3**). The outermost layer is a tough, fibrous layer that anchors each kidney and its adrenal gland to the abdominal wall and surrounding tissues. Beneath this layer is a protective cushion of fat (the middle connective tissue layer, also called the *adipose capsule*). The innermost layer covering the kidneys is a layer of collagen fibers that protects the kidneys from trauma.

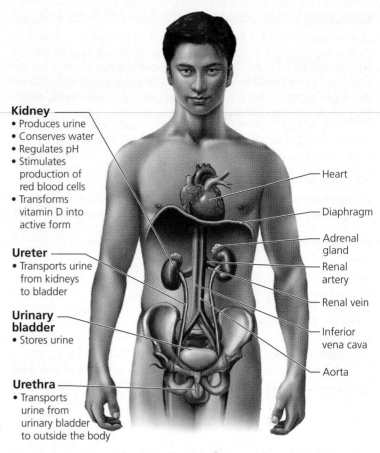

Kidney
- Produces urine
- Conserves water
- Regulates pH
- Stimulates production of red blood cells
- Transforms vitamin D into active form

Ureter
- Transports urine from kidneys to bladder

Urinary bladder
- Stores urine

Urethra
- Transports urine from urinary bladder to outside the body

Heart

Diaphragm

Adrenal gland

Renal artery

Renal vein

Inferior vena cava

Aorta

FIGURE 16.2 Organs of the urinary system (labeled on the left side) and their relation to major blood vessels (identified on the right side)

Adrenal gland

Renal artery

Renal vein

Ureter

Outermost connective tissue layer

Innermost connective tissue layer

Adipose capsule

(a) Blood vessels and protective layers around kidneys

Renal cortex

Renal medulla

Renal pyramid (of renal medulla)

Renal column (extension of renal cortex)

Renal pelvis

(b) Internal kidney structure

Nephron

Collecting duct

(c) Nephrons

FIGURE 16.3 Structure of the kidney

Structure of the Kidneys

One ureter leaves each kidney at a notch in the concave border, as shown in Figure 16.3. This notch is also the area where blood vessels enter and exit the kidney. The renal arteries branch off the aorta and carry blood to the kidneys. The renal veins carry filtered blood away from the kidneys to the inferior vena cava, which transports the blood to the heart.

Each kidney has three regions: an outer region, the **renal cortex;** a region enclosed by the cortex, the **renal medulla;** and an inner chamber, the **renal pelvis** (see Figure 16.3). The renal cortex begins at the outer border of the kidney, and portions of it, called renal columns, extend inward between the pyramid-shaped subdivisions *(renal pyramids)* of the renal medulla. The narrow end of each renal pyramid joins a cuplike extension of the renal pelvis. As we will soon see, urine produced by the kidneys eventually drains into the renal pelvis and out the ureter to the urinary bladder.

Nephrons

Nephrons are the microscopic functional units of the kidneys and are responsible for the formation of urine. Each kidney contains 1 million to 2 million nephrons.

Structure of nephrons

A nephron has two basic parts: the renal corpuscle and the renal tubule, as shown in Figure **16.4**. The **renal corpuscle** is the portion of the nephron where fluid is filtered from the blood. It consists of a tuft of capillaries, the **glomerulus;** and a surrounding cuplike structure, the **glomerular capsule** (sometimes called *Bowman's capsule*). Within the glomerular capsule is a space that is continuous with the lumen of the renal tubule. Blood enters a glomerulus by an afferent (incoming) arteriole. Inside the glomerular capillaries, water and small solutes move from the blood into the space within the glomerular capsule and then into the renal tubule, where they are considered filtrate (a fluid similar to blood plasma but typically lacking proteins). The blood then leaves the glomerulus by an efferent (outgoing) arteriole. The **renal tubule** is the site where substances are removed from and added to the filtrate. This tubule has three sections: the *proximal convoluted tubule,* the *loop of the nephron* (sometimes called the *loop of Henle*), and the *distal convoluted tubule.* The **proximal convoluted tubule**, its name reflecting its location nearest the glomerular capsule, has cells with many tiny projections called microvilli. Microvilli allow the efficient removal (reabsorption) of useful substances from the filtrate, which are eventually returned to the blood (see below). **The loop of the nephron** resembles a hairpin turn, with a descending limb and an ascending limb. Next comes the **distal convoluted tubule**, its name reflecting this section's more distant location from the glomerular capsule. The loop of the nephron and the distal convoluted tubule have cells with few or no microvilli. The distal convoluted tubules of many nephrons empty into a single **collecting duct;** many collecting ducts eventually drain into the renal pelvis. The renal pelvis is connected to the ureter. Urine exits the kidney by way of the ureter and moves into the urinary bladder.

(a) Location of nephrons within a sectioned kidney. These nephrons extend from the renal cortex into the renal medulla.

(b) A nephron and its blood supply

(c) Simplified view of a nephron, showing the basic structural components but not the associated capillaries

FIGURE 16.4 Structure of the nephron

Urinalysis: What Your Urine Says about You

The kidneys are our body's filtering system, so the urine they produce contains substances that originate from almost all of our different organs. A detailed analysis of the urine, therefore, tells us not only how the organs of the urinary tract are functioning but also about the general health of our other organ systems. In other words, a complete urinalysis including measures of volume, microorganisms, and the physical and chemical properties of urine provides an overview of a person's basic health.

Healthy urine exiting the body typically contains no microorganisms. The presence of bacteria in a properly collected urine sample usually signals infection of the urinary system. Bacteria found in a sample may be cultured to determine their identity, which can help in diagnosing the infection. Urine also may be screened for fungi or protozoans that cause inflammation within the urinary tract.

Sometimes a urine sample is contaminated because of improper collection. For example, if the perineal area has not been cleaned and the collection cup or urine is allowed to contact that area, bacteria may be introduced. (In males, this is the area between the anus and scrotum; in females, it is between the anus and vulva.) It is therefore important to be careful when collecting a urine sample.

The following physical characteristics are routinely checked in urine analyses: color, turbidity (cloudiness), pH, and specific gravity, or density, of urine (the ratio of its weight to the weight of an equal volume of distilled water). The color of urine comes from urochrome, a yellow pigment produced as a waste product by the liver during the breakdown of hemoglobin in red blood cells. The urochrome travels in the bloodstream from the liver to the kidneys, where it is filtered from the blood and excreted with urine. The color of urine varies somewhat according to diet. Beets and blackberries, for example, lend urine a red color, and asparagus causes a green tinge. The color of urine also varies with concentration. More concentrated urine, such as that collected first thing in the morning, is darker than more dilute urine. An abnormal color of urine—particularly red, when followed by microscopic confirmation of the presence of red blood cells—can indicate kidney stones and trauma to urinary organs. Because menstrual blood can contaminate urine samples, women should always inform their doctor if they are menstruating at the time of urine collection.

Freshly voided urine is usually transparent. Cloudy, or turbid, urine may indicate a urinary tract infection, particularly if white blood cells are detected. Healthy urine has a pH of about 6, although considerable variation may occur in response to diet. High-protein diets produce acidic urine, and vegetarian diets produce alkaline urine. An alkaline pH also is associated with some bacterial infections. The specific gravity is a measure of the concentration of solutes in urine and therefore of the concentrating ability of the nephrons within our kidneys. When urine becomes highly concentrated for long periods, substances such as calcium and uric acid may precipitate out and form kidney stones.

Quantitative chemical tests are run to assess the levels of specific chemical constituents of urine. The major constituent is water, making up about 95% of the total volume. The remaining 5% consists of solutes from outside sources (such as drugs) or from the metabolic activities of our cells. Tests run on urine specimens look for certain abnormal constituents of urine (such as glucose, red blood cells, or white blood cells) and for normal constituents present in abnormal amounts (such as higher-than-normal amounts of protein, and increases or decreases in calcium, potassium, or sodium).

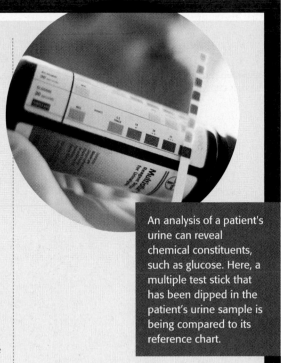

An analysis of a patient's urine can reveal chemical constituents, such as glucose. Here, a multiple test stick that has been dipped in the patient's urine sample is being compared to its reference chart.

Although daily urine volume varies considerably, most people expel between 1000 and 2000 ml (about 1 to 2 qt) of urine each day. Factors such as diet, fluid intake, temperature, and blood volume and pressure influence urine volume. For example, high blood volume and pressure cause decreased reabsorption of water in the renal tubules of nephrons, resulting in increased urine output. Thus, in conjunction with other tests, an analysis showing high urine volume may indicate high blood pressure. Typically, volume is not measured at the time of providing a routine urine sample. It is only when a problem with the urinary tract is suspected that people are asked to monitor their urine output over a 24-hour period. Such monitoring may reveal polyuria, which is excessive urine production (well over 2 liters or 2.1 qt per day), or oliguria, an inadequate urine production (less than 500 ml, or 0.53 qt per day). Failure to produce any urine is an extreme health crisis called anuria. Causes of anuria include renal failure and complete urinary tract obstruction by kidney stones or tumors.

About 80% of the nephrons in our kidneys are confined almost entirely to the renal cortex; they have short loops that dip only a short distance into the renal medulla. The remaining 20% have long loops that extend from the cortex deep into the renal medulla. Once in the medulla, the loops of these nephrons turn abruptly upward, back into the cortex, where they lead into distal convoluted tubules. As we will see, the nephrons whose loops extend deep into the medulla play an important role in water conservation.

Functions of nephrons

The kidneys are crucial for maintaining homeostasis. For one thing, they filter wastes and excess materials from the blood. Indeed, over

Glomerulus

Glomerular capsule

Space within the glomerular capsule

Proximal convoluted tubule

Filtrate

Capillary wall

Path of filtrate
Path of blood
Movement of water and small solutes

Afferent (incoming) arteriole

Efferent (outgoing) arteriole

(a) The renal corpuscle consists of the glomerular capsule and a ball of capillaries called the glomerulus.

Capillary
Fenestration (pore)
Capillary endothelium
Basement membrane
Extensions of epithelial cells of glomerular capsule
Filtration slit
Filtrate in space within glomerular capsule

(b) Diagram of the glomerular filter showing how water and small solutes in the blood move first through the pores in the endothelium of the capillary, then through the basement membrane, and finally through slits in the inner lining of the glomerular capsule.

(c) Micrograph of the glomerular filter

FIGURE 16.5 The renal corpuscle is the site of glomerular filtration.

the course of one day, two healthy kidneys filter all the blood in the body 30 times! They also assist the respiratory system in the regulation of blood pH. Finally, the kidneys maintain fluid balance by regulating the volume and composition of blood and urine.

To understand what occurs in the kidneys, we must examine the work of nephrons. Nephrons perform three functions: (1) glomerular filtration, (2) tubular reabsorption, and (3) tubular secretion.

We can compare these functions to the steps you might take during a selective cleaning of small items from your bedroom closet. First, you might remove almost all of the small items—the valuable along with the unwanted. This activity is analogous to glomerular filtration, which removes from the blood all materials small enough to

fit through the pores of the kidney's filter (see below). The next step in cleaning your closet might be to look through the various items you have removed and put back "the good stuff," the items worth saving. Returning valuable materials to the closet is analogous to tubular reabsorption, which returns useful materials to the blood. The final step in cleaning the closet might be to once again scan what you have in your closet and to selectively remove items, such as those in excess. This last step is analogous to tubular secretion, in which wastes and excess materials are removed from the blood and added to the filtrate that will eventually leave the body as urine. Secretion also removes from the blood substances not naturally found in the body, such as pesticides and certain drugs. Here are the three steps in more detail.

Microvilli of the cells lining the tubule greatly increase the surface area for reabsorption.

Lumen of tubule

Microvilli

Proximal convoluted tubule

Nucleus of a cell lining proximal convoluted tubule

Capillary

(a) Micrograph showing a cross section through a proximal convoluted tubule

(b) Diagram showing a cross section through a proximal convoluted tubule. Substances move from the filtrate through the cells of the proximal convoluted tubule and into the surrounding fluid. Eventually, the substances move into the capillaries nearby.

FIGURE 16.6 The proximal convoluted tubule is the site of tubular reabsorption.

1. **Glomerular filtration** occurs as blood pressure forces water and small solutes from the blood in the glomerulus to the space inside the glomerular capsule (Figure **16.5**). Reaching the space inside the glomerular capsule requires passing sequentially through the following three layers: (1) the single layer of endothelial cells that forms the walls of the capillaries; (2) the basement membrane just outside the capillary walls; and (3) the epithelial lining of the glomerular capsule.

   Water and small solutes in the blood first move through the walls of the glomerular capillaries. The capillary walls consist of a single layer of endothelial cells; the walls of these capillaries are fenestrated, meaning they have many pores. The pores allow some substances to move out of the capillaries, but prevent red blood cells from doing so. Next, the filtered substances cross the basement membrane, a layer of protein fibers in a glycoprotein matrix. This layer of extracellular material, secreted by the cell layers on either side (i.e., the cells of the capillaries and those of the lining of the glomerular capsule), restricts the passage of large proteins. Finally, the filtered substances pass through slits in the inner lining of the glomerular capsule; these slits occur in between extensions of the epithelial cells of the capsule (refer, again, to Figure 16.5). These substances are known collectively as glomerular filtrate. The concentrations of the molecules dissolved in the glomerular filtrate are approximately the same as in the blood plasma.

   Several things can change the rate of filtration by the glomerulus. An increase in the diameter of afferent (incoming) arterioles brings more blood into the glomerulus and produces higher pressure in the glomerular capillaries. Higher pressure results in higher filtration rates (more filtrate produced by the kidneys each minute). A reduction in the diameter of efferent (outgoing) arterioles also produces higher pressure in glomerular capillaries and higher filtration rates. General (systemic) increases in blood pressure can also produce higher filtration rates.

2. **Tubular reabsorption** is the process that removes useful materials from the filtrate and returns them to the blood. This process occurs in the renal tubule, primarily in the proximal convoluted tubule. The characteristics of the cells lining the proximal convoluted tubule make it an ideal location for reabsorption (Figure **16.6**). As mentioned, these epithelial cells have numerous microvilli (projections of the plasma membrane) that reach into the lumen of the tubule. Similar in function to the microvilli in the small intestine, these microvilli dramatically increase the surface area for the reabsorption of materials. Reabsorption returns water, essential ions, and nutrients to the blood (see Table **16.1**). Remarkably, as the glomerular filtrate passes through the renal tubule, about 99% of it is returned to the blood in the surrounding capillaries. Thus, only about 1% of the glomerular filtrate is eventually excreted as urine. Put another way, of the approximately 180 liters (48 gal) of filtrate that enter the glomerular capsule each day, between 178 and 179 liters (47 gal) are returned to the blood by reabsorption. The remaining 1 to 2 liters (about 0.5 to 1 gal) are excreted as urine. Imagine how much water and food we would have to consume if we did not have reabsorption to offset the losses from glomerular filtration! Some wastes are not reabsorbed at all, and will eventually be excreted; others, such as urea, are partially reabsorbed. We will see that antidiuretic hormone (ADH), manufactured by the hypothalamus and released by the posterior pituitary gland, regulates the amount of water reabsorbed in parts of the renal tubule.

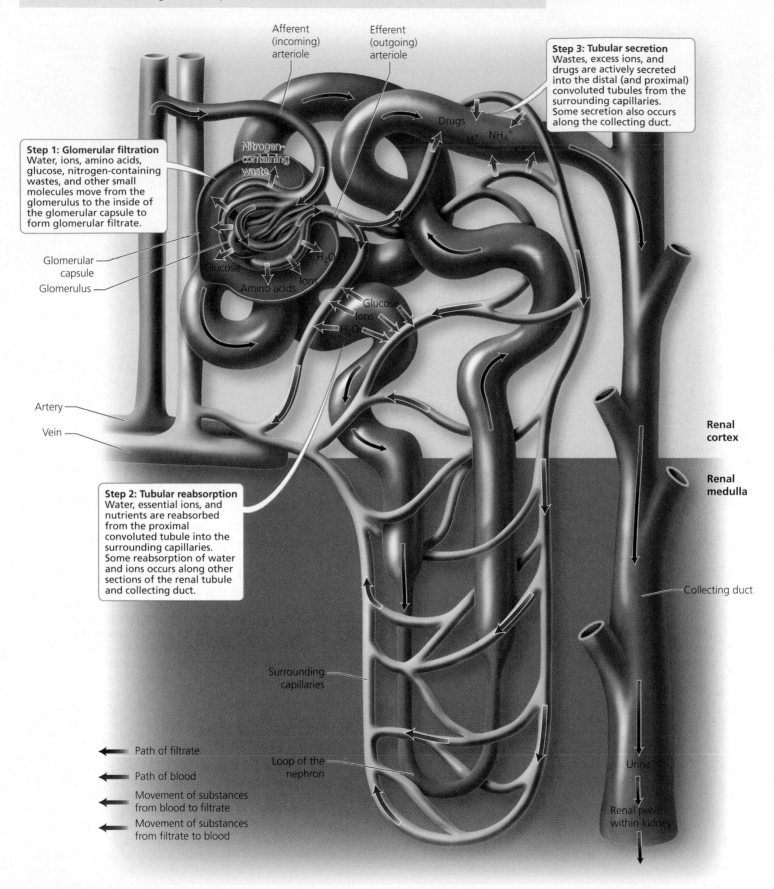

Afferent (incoming) arteriole

Efferent (outgoing) arteriole

Step 3: Tubular secretion
Wastes, excess ions, and drugs are actively secreted into the distal (and proximal) convoluted tubules from the surrounding capillaries. Some secretion also occurs along the collecting duct.

Drugs

H^+ NH_4^+

Step 1: Glomerular filtration
Water, ions, amino acids, glucose, nitrogen-containing wastes, and other small molecules move from the glomerulus to the inside of the glomerular capsule to form glomerular filtrate.

Nitrogen-containing waste

Glucose

H_2O

Amino acids

Ions

Glucose

Ions

H_2O

Glomerular capsule

Glomerulus

Artery

Vein

Renal cortex

Renal medulla

Step 2: Tubular reabsorption
Water, essential ions, and nutrients are reabsorbed from the proximal convoluted tubule into the surrounding capillaries. Some reabsorption of water and ions occurs along other sections of the renal tubule and collecting duct.

Collecting duct

Surrounding capillaries

◄ Path of filtrate

◄ Path of blood

◄ Movement of substances from blood to filtrate

◄ Movement of substances from filtrate to blood

Loop of the nephron

Urine

Renal pelvis within kidney

FIGURE 16.7 Overview of glomerular filtration, tubular reabsorption, and tubular secretion along the nephron

A *The walls of glomerular capillaries have pores that allow many substances (but not red blood cells) to move out of the capillaries.*

3. **Tubular secretion** removes additional wastes and excess ions from the blood. For example, hydrogen ions (H^+), potassium ions (K^+), and ammonium ions (NH_4^+) in the blood are actively transported into the renal tubule, where they become part of the filtrate to be excreted. Tubular secretion also removes foreign substances from the blood, including pesticides and drugs such as penicillin, cocaine, and marijuana. These substances are added to the filtered fluid that will become urine. Tubular secretion occurs along the proximal and distal convoluted tubules and collecting duct.

The regions of the nephron and their roles in filtration, reabsorption, and secretion are shown in Figure **16.7** and reviewed in Table **16.2**. When reviewing these, keep in mind the directions that substances move in each of the three processes: (1) during glomerular filtration, substances move from the blood into the nephron to form filtrate; (2) during tubular reabsorption, useful substances move from the filtrate within the nephron back into the blood; (3) during tubular secretion, drugs and substances in excess move from the blood into the filtrate.

By the end of glomerular filtration, tubular reabsorption, and tubular secretion, blood leaving the kidneys contains most of the water, nutrients, and essential ions that it contained upon entering the kidneys. Wastes and excess materials have been removed, leaving the blood cleansed. This purified blood now moves from the capillaries surrounding the nephron into small veins that eventually join the renal vein.

The final filtrate, now called urine, contains all of the materials that were filtered from the blood and not reabsorbed, plus substances that were secreted from the blood. Urine empties from the distal convoluted tubules into collecting ducts. There, more water may be reabsorbed, and some additional removal of excess substances, such as hydrogen and potassium ions, also occurs. From the collecting ducts, urine moves into the renal pelvis and leaves each kidney through a ureter. It then travels down the ureters to the urinary bladder, which stores the urine until it is eliminated from the body through the urethra. The precise composition of urine can be examined in a medical laboratory. See the Health Issue essay, *Urinalysis: What Your Urine Says About You.*

Acid–Base Balance

In addition to removing wastes and regulating the volume and solute concentration of blood plasma, the kidneys help regulate the pH of blood. Recall from Chapters 2 and 14 that blood pH must be regulated precisely for proper functioning of the body. This precise regulation is achieved through the actions of the kidneys, through buffer systems in the blood, and through respiration. Buffer systems regulate pH by picking up hydrogen ions (H^+) when their concentrations are high and releasing hydrogen ions when their concentrations are low. Chapter 2 described the importance of carbonic acid as such a buffer in the blood. The role of the kidneys in maintaining pH is twofold. First, by secreting hydrogen ions into the urine, the kidneys remove excess hydrogen ions from the blood, thereby increasing blood pH. Second, the kidneys help sustain the carbonic acid buffer system by returning bicarbonate to the blood. Because of their role in regulating blood pH, the kidneys ultimately influence breathing rate. Recall from Chapter 14 that chemoreceptors in the medulla of the brain respond to changes in the pH of blood (and cerebrospinal fluid) by adjusting breathing rate.

Water Conservation

Our kidneys enable us to conserve water through the production of concentrated urine. Because of their role in water conservation, the kidneys participate in the maintenance of cardiac output and blood

TABLE 16.1 Reabsorption by Nephrons of Some Substances

Substance	Amount filtered per day (in liters or grams)	% Reabsorbed (removed from filtrate and returned to blood)
Water	180 L	99%
Glucose	180 g	100%
Urea	52 g	50%
Creatinine	1.6 g	0%
Sodium ions (Na^+)	620 g	99%
Potassium ions (K^+)	30 g	93%
Bicarbonate (HCO_3^-)	275 g	100%

TABLE 16.2 Review of Nephron Regions and their Roles

Region of Nephron	Roles*
Renal corpuscle (glomerular capsule and glomerulus)	Filters the blood, removing water, glucose, amino acids, ions, nitrogen-containing wastes, and other small molecules
Proximal convoluted tubule	Reabsorbs water, glucose, amino acids, some urea, Na^+, Cl^-, and HCO_3^- Secretes drugs, H^+, NH_4^+
Loop of the nephron	Reabsorbs water, Na^+, Cl^-, and K^+
Distal convoluted tubule	Reabsorbs water, Na^+, Cl^-, and HCO_3^- Secretes drugs, H^+, K^+, and NH_4^+

NOTE: *Major reabsorbed or secreted substances are listed here.

pressure. Production of concentrated urine is performed by the 20% of our nephrons with long loops that dip deep into the renal medulla. The special ability of these nephrons to concentrate urine derives from an increasing concentration of solutes in the interstitial fluid (the fluid that fills the spaces between cells) from the cortex to the medulla of the kidneys. The most important of these solutes are sodium chloride (NaCl) and urea. Let's explore this mechanism for urine concentration by tracing the path of the filtrate as it flows through these long loops (Figure **16.8**).

The solute concentration of the filtrate passing from the glomerular capsule to the proximal tubule is about the same as that of blood. As the filtrate moves through the proximal convoluted tubule, large amounts of water *and* salt are reabsorbed (recall from our earlier discussion of reabsorption that nutrients are also reabsorbed at this time). This reabsorption produces dramatic reductions in the volume of filtrate but little change in its solute concentration (because both water and salt are reabsorbed). However, when the filtrate enters the descending limb of the loop of the nephron, major changes in solute concentration begin (Figure 16.8). This path takes it from the cortex to the medulla.

Along the descending limb, water leaves the filtrate by osmosis (a special type of diffusion described in Chapter 3). The departure of water creates an increase in the concentration of solutes, including sodium chloride, within the filtrate. The concentration of salt in the filtrate peaks at the curve of the loop, setting the stage for the next step in the process of urine concentration. Now the filtrate moves up the ascending limb of the loop. As it does so, large amounts of sodium chloride are actively transported out of the filtrate into the interstitial fluid of the medulla. Water, however, remains in the filtrate because the ascending limb is not permeable to water. When the filtrate reaches the distal convoluted tubule in the cortex, it is quite dilute. In fact, the filtrate is hypotonic to body fluids. (Recall from Chapter 3 that *hypotonic* means having a lower solute concentration than another fluid. *Hypertonic* means

having a greater solute concentration than another fluid. *Isotonic* means having the same solute concentration as another fluid.) The filtrate then moves into a collecting duct and begins to descend once again toward the medulla. This pathway is one of increasing salt concentration in the interstitial fluid because of all the salt that was transported out of the filtrate as it ascended the loop. Collecting ducts are permeable to water but not to salt (antidiuretic hormone

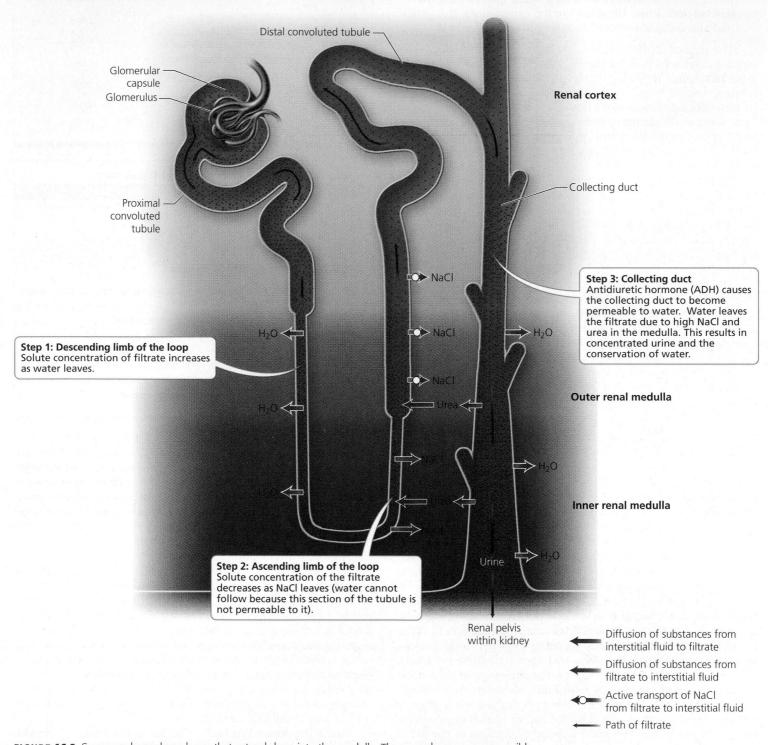

Step 1: Descending limb of the loop
Solute concentration of filtrate increases as water leaves.

Step 2: Ascending limb of the loop
Solute concentration of the filtrate decreases as NaCl leaves (water cannot follow because this section of the tubule is not permeable to it).

Step 3: Collecting duct
Antidiuretic hormone (ADH) causes the collecting duct to become permeable to water. Water leaves the filtrate due to high NaCl and urea in the medulla. This results in concentrated urine and the conservation of water.

Distal convoluted tubule

Glomerular capsule
Glomerulus

Proximal convoluted tubule

Renal cortex

Collecting duct

Outer renal medulla

Inner renal medulla

Renal pelvis within kidney

Urine

Diffusion of substances from interstitial fluid to filtrate

Diffusion of substances from filtrate to interstitial fluid

Active transport of NaCl from filtrate to interstitial fluid

Path of filtrate

FIGURE 16.8 Some nephrons have loops that extend deep into the medulla. These nephrons are responsible for water conservation. The steps by which these nephrons concentrate urine and conserve water are shown here. Stippling indicates solute concentration of the filtrate within the nephron and collecting duct. The color gradient behind the nephron and collecting duct indicates solute concentration in the interstitial fluid of different regions of the kidney (renal cortex, and outer and inner renal medulla; darker is more concentrated).

increases the permeability of the collecting duct to water; see below). Thus, as the filtrate encounters increasing concentrations of salt in the fluid of the inner medulla, water leaves the filtrate by osmosis. With this departure of large amounts of water, urea is now concentrated in the filtrate. In the lower regions of the collecting duct, some of the urea moves into the interstitial fluid of the medulla. This leakage of urea contributes to the high solute concentration of the inner medulla and thus aids in concentrating the filtrate. The remaining urea is excreted.

At its most concentrated, urine is hypertonic to blood and interstitial fluid from any other part of the body except the inner medulla, where it is isotonic. Together, the loop of the nephron and collecting duct maintain extraordinarily high solute concentrations in the interstitial fluid of the kidneys, making possible the concentration of urine and conservation of water by the kidneys.

Hormones and Kidney Function

Our health depends on our keeping the salt and water levels in our body near certain optimum values. This, as we have seen, is an important job of the kidneys. It is also a challenging job, because our activities produce constant fluctuations in those levels. For example, on a hot day or after exercise, we may lose body water and salts through perspiration. In contrast, eating a tub of salted popcorn at the movies can boost our salt intake. The kidneys must deal with these challenges and adjust the concentration of solutes in the urine and in the blood to keep water and salt levels in our body relatively constant.

Three hormones—ADH, aldosterone, and atrial natriuretic peptide—play important roles in adjusting kidney function to meet the body's needs (Table **16.3**). **Antidiuretic hormone (ADH)** is manufactured by the hypothalamus and then travels to the posterior pituitary for storage and release. This hormone regulates the amount of water reabsorbed by the collecting ducts. The hypothalamus responds to changes in the concentration of water in the blood by increasing or decreasing secretion of ADH. Decreases in the concentration of water in the blood stimulate increased secretion of ADH, as shown in Figure **16.9**. Higher levels of ADH in the bloodstream then increase the permeability to water of the collecting ducts of nephrons, resulting in more water being reabsorbed from the filtrate. The movement of increased amounts of water from the filtrate back into the blood results in increased blood volume and pressure and production of small amounts of concentrated urine.

FIGURE 16.9 The pathway by which ADH influences kidney function and blood volume and blood pressure

Just the opposite occurs when the concentration of water in the blood increases. In this case, the release of ADH is inhibited, thereby reducing water reabsorption from the filtrate. Reduced water reabsorption causes reduced blood volume and pressure and the production of large amounts of dilute urine. Alcohol, too, inhibits the secretion of ADH, causing reduced water reabsorption by the kidneys and production of large amounts of dilute urine. Thus, it makes little sense to try to quench your thirst and restore body fluids by drinking an alcoholic beverage on a hot day. Substances such as alcohol that promote urine production are called **diuretics.** *Diabetes insipidus,* a disease characterized by excretion of large amounts of dilute urine, is caused by a deficiency of ADH (see Chapter 10).

Aldosterone is released by the adrenal cortex. It increases reabsorption of sodium by the distal convoluted tubules and collecting ducts. Aldosterone accomplishes this task by stimulating the synthesis of sodium ion pumps and sodium channels in cell membranes along the distal convoluted tubules and collecting ducts; at these locations, sodium ions are reabsorbed, usually in exchange for potassium ions. Sodium reabsorption is important because water

---

TABLE 16.3 Review of Some Hormones that Influence Kidney Function

Hormone	Effect on Water and Solute Reabsorption in Nephron	Effect on Blood Volume and Pressure	Urine Produced
Antidiuretic hormone (ADH)	Increases permeability to water of collecting ducts, resulting in more water moving from filtrate to blood	Increases	Concentrated
Aldosterone	Increases reabsorption of Na^+ by distal convoluted tubules and collecting ducts, resulting in more water following Na^+ as it moves from filtrate to blood	Increases	Concentrated
Atrial natriuretic peptide (ANP)	Decreases reabsorption of Na^+ by distal convoluted tubules and collecting ducts, resulting in more Na^+ and water remaining in filtrate	Decreases	Dilute

follows sodium. As more sodium is transported out of the nephron into the capillaries, increased amounts of water go with it, resulting in increased blood volume and pressure and the production of small amounts of concentrated urine. Caffeine, a familiar chemical found in coffee, tea, and many soft drinks, has just the opposite effect. Caffeine decreases the blood's reabsorption of sodium, thus decreasing the amount of water moving out of tubules back into the bloodstream. Ingestion of caffeine causes decreased blood volume and pressure and large amounts of dilute urine. Because caffeine, like alcohol, increases urine output, it is considered a diuretic, too.

What stimulates the release of aldosterone? Ultimately, it is the blood pressure in the afferent (incoming) arteriole carrying blood to the glomerulus. The blood pressure in this arteriole is monitored by a part of the nephron called the **juxtaglomerular apparatus**, a group of cells located where the distal convoluted tubule contacts the afferent arteriole (Figure **16.10**). When the blood pressure in the afferent arteriole drops, so does the glomerular filtration rate. In turn, this drop in filtration rate reduces the volume of filtrate within nephrons. Cells within the juxtaglomerular apparatus respond by releasing the enzyme renin. **Renin** converts angiotensinogen, a protein produced by the liver, into another protein, *angiotensin I*. Angiotensin I is then converted by yet another enzyme into angiotensin II. *Angiotensin II* is the active form of the protein that stimulates the adrenal gland to release aldosterone. Aldosterone increases reabsorption of sodium and water by the distal convoluted tubules and collecting ducts of nephrons, resulting in increased blood volume and pressure. These changes increase the filtration rate within the glomerulus, resulting in an increased volume of filtrate within the nephron.

stop and think

Estrogens are sex hormones, found in significantly greater amounts in females, that are chemically similar to aldosterone. As a result, the effects of estrogens on the distal convoluted tubules and collecting ducts of the kidneys are similar to those of aldosterone. How might this similarity explain the water retention experienced by many women as their estrogen levels rise during the menstrual cycle?

A final hormone that influences kidney function is **atrial natriuretic peptide (ANP)**, released by cells in the right atrium of the heart. The cells release ANP in response to stretching of the heart caused by increased blood volume and pressure. Atrial natriuretic peptide decreases water and Na^+ reabsorption by the kidneys, causing declines in blood volume and pressure and the production of large amounts of dilute urine. ANP also influences kidney function by inhibiting secretion of aldosterone and renin.

Red Blood Cells and Vitamin D

The kidneys have two additional functions that are important to homeostasis but are not directly related to the urinary system. First, the kidneys release **erythropoietin**, a hormone that travels to the red bone marrow, where it stimulates production of red blood cells. Second, the kidneys have an effect on vitamin D. Vitamin D is a substance provided by certain foods in our diet or produced by the skin in response to sunlight. The kidneys transform vitamin D into its active form, calcitriol, which promotes the absorption and use of calcium and phosphorus by the body.

Dialysis and Transplant Surgery

Renal failure is a decrease or complete cessation of glomerular filtration. In other words, the kidneys stop working. The failure can be acute or chronic. *Acute renal failure* is an abrupt, complete—or nearly complete—cessation of kidney function. It typically develops over a few hours or days and is characterized by little output of urine. Causes of acute renal failure include nephrons damaged by severe inflammation, certain drugs, and poison. Acute renal failure also may be caused by low blood volume due to profuse bleeding or obstruction of urine flow by kidney stones (see the Health Issue essay, *Kidney Stones and Their Shocking Treatment*). *Chronic renal failure,* on the other hand, is a progressive and often irreversible decline in the rate of glomerular filtration over a period of months or years. Kidney disease may destroy nephrons and cause a progressive decline of this type. Nephrons lost to kidney disease cannot be replaced. *Polycystic*

(a) The juxtaglomerular apparatus (within the square) is a section of the nephron where the distal convoluted tubule contacts the afferent arteriole. The nearby renal corpuscle is shown in ghosted view to reveal its components, the glomerular capsule and the glomerulus.

(b) Close-up view of the juxtaglomerular apparatus

FIGURE 16.10 The juxtaglomerular apparatus

Health Issue

Kidney Stones and Their Shocking Treatment

Kidney stones are small, hard crystals that form in the kidneys when substances such as calcium or uric acid precipitate out of urine because of higher-than-normal concentrations. In most cases, dehydration is the reason for these higher-than-normal concentrations of stone-forming substances. Most people's urine also contains substances that prevent the formation of crystals, but these substances may not function in people with a history of kidney stones.

Kidney stones often begin as extremely tiny grains in the renal pelvis. They grow larger over a period of years as additional material is deposited on them (Figure **16.A**). Some stones may attain diameters of 25 mm (1 in.). Before reaching anything near that size, however, many stones are flushed out of the kidneys and down the ureters to the bladder, and from there they are expelled with urine out the urethra. These tiny stones rarely cause problems, and people may not even be aware of their passing. However, somewhat larger stones may cause considerable pain during their journey through the urinary tract. The sharp edges of large stones may gouge into the walls of the ureters and urethra. The pain comes in waves, and each wave may cause the person to double over. Nausea, vomiting, and chills accompany the pain, and blood may appear in the urine. Even more serious problems arise when large stones become lodged in the kidneys or ureters, blocking the flow of urine. The high internal pressure that results from the obstruction can damage the nephrons and impair kidney function.

Kidney stones usually are diagnosed with x-rays of the kidneys, ureters, and bladder. Blood and urine tests also are performed to determine what might be causing the problem. Today, a large stone in a kidney may be surgically removed through an incision in the back that extends into the kidney. To locate a stone lodged in a ureter, doctors may pass a small fiber-optic instrument through the urethra and bladder and then use another instrument to remove the stones without making an incision. Certain stones can be dissolved with drugs. Another option is extra-corporeal shock wave lithotripsy, a relatively painless technique in which high-energy shock waves are created outside the body and then directed at the stones within. During the procedure, the patient lies in a water bath or on a soft cushion. The shock waves pulverize the stones into tiny pieces that can be passed painlessly in the urine. This technique also does not require an incision, and recovery is rapid. Nevertheless, recent data suggest that lithotripsy may increase the risk of developing diabetes and hypertension later in life. Because the pancreas is in the "blast path" of the shock waves, it may be damaged during treatment for kidney stones, resulting in diabetes. Hypertension may be caused by scarring of the kidneys from the shock waves; it is possible that such scarring influences production of renin, the protein produced by the kidneys that influences blood pressure.

A simple way to prevent the formation of kidney stones is to drink about 2.5 liters (2.6 quarts) of water over the course of a typical day. Drinking this amount of liquid helps to dilute the urine and flushes any existing stones from the urinary tract. For people who are prone to developing certain types of kidney stones, dietary changes may be recommended. Finally, people with a history of developing kidney stones usually can take specific medications to prevent formation of new stones once the old ones have been removed.

Kidney stones

(a) An x-ray showing several kidney stones in the left kidney

(b) This kidney stone, 8 mm in length, was removed through surgery.

FIGURE 16.A Kidney stones

kidney disease, for example, is an inherited and progressive condition in which fluid-filled cysts and tiny holes form throughout kidney tissue. Few symptoms are apparent at the beginning of chronic renal failure because the remaining nephrons enlarge and take over for those that have been destroyed. With time, however, the loss of nephrons becomes so severe that symptoms of decreased glomerular filtration rate appear. For example, increased levels of nitrogen-containing wastes are found in the blood. By end-stage renal failure, about 90% of the nephrons have been lost, making necessary a kidney transplant or the use of an artificial kidney machine.

Renal failure, whether acute or chronic, has many consequences. These include (1) acidosis, a decrease in blood pH caused

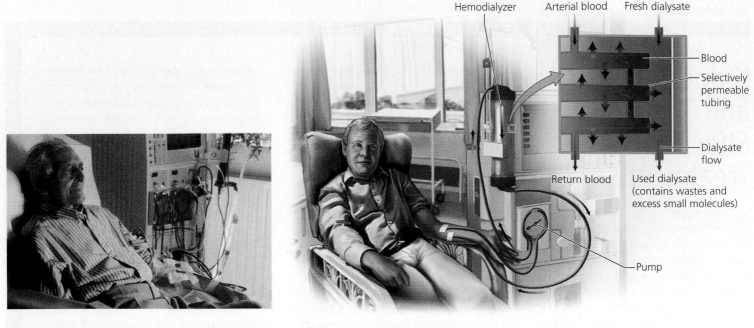

Hemodialyzer   Arterial blood   Fresh dialysate

Blood

Selectively permeable tubing

Dialysate flow

Return blood   Used dialysate (contains wastes and excess small molecules)

Pump

FIGURE 16.11 An artificial kidney machine can be used to cleanse the blood when the kidneys fail.

by the inability of the kidneys to excrete hydrogen ions; (2) anemia, low numbers of red blood cells caused by the failure of damaged kidneys to release erythropoietin; (3) edema, the buildup of fluid in the tissues because of water and salt retention; (4) hypertension, an increase in blood pressure caused by failure of the renin-angiotensin system and salt and water retention; and (5) accumulation of nitrogen-containing wastes in the blood. In short, failure of the kidneys severely disrupts homeostasis. Untreated kidney failure will lead to death within a few days.

Dialysis

A common way of coping with failure or severe impairment of the kidneys is **hemodialysis**, the use of artificial devices to cleanse the blood of wastes and excess fluid. Often this is done with an artificial kidney machine (Figure **16.11**). A tube is inserted into an artery of the patient's arm. Blood flows through the tube and into the kidney machine. The machine pumps the blood into a large canister (called the hemodialyzer), where it is filtered and then returned to the patient's body. Within the hemodialyzer, the blood flows through tubing made of a selectively permeable membrane and immersed in a dialysis solution called the dialysate. The selectively permeable membrane of the tubing permits wastes and excess small molecules to move from the blood into the dialysate. At the same time, the membrane prevents passage into the dialysate of blood cells and most proteins because they are too large. Nutrients are sometimes provided in the dialysate for absorption into the blood. The composition of the dialysate is precisely controlled to maintain proper concentration gradients between the dialysate and the blood. Once the blood has completed the circuit through the tubing, it is returned, free of wastes, to a vein in the arm. Patients requiring hemodialysis typically undergo the procedure about three times a week at a dialysis clinic. Each session lasts about 4 hours. Side effects associated with hemodialysis include low blood pressure, fatigue, leg cramps, nausea, and headaches;

these can result from the removal of too much fluid or too rapid removal of fluid during hemodialysis.

Another option for removing wastes from the blood is continuous ambulatory peritoneal dialysis (CAPD), a procedure that is normally performed by the patient at home. In this procedure the peritoneum, one of the body's own selectively permeable membranes, is used as the dialyzing membrane (Figure **16.12**). The peritoneum lines the abdominal cavity and covers the internal organs. Dialyzing fluid held in a plastic container suspended over the patient flows down a tube inserted into the abdomen. As the fluid bathes the peritoneum, wastes move from the blood vessels that line the abdomen across the peritoneum and into the solution. The solution is then returned to the plastic container and discarded. Typically, fluid is passed into the abdomen, left for a few hours, and then removed and replaced with new fluid. CAPD requires about three or four fluid changes each day. However, the patient is free to move around between fluid changes while the dialysis proceeds internally, which tends to be less disruptive than traditional hemodialysis.

Because CAPD is performed daily over long periods of time, it is gentler in its waste removal than hemodialysis, resulting in a steadier physical condition in the patient. CAPD is also less costly than hemodialysis. However, CAPD requires that the patient perform several daily changes of dialysis fluid, and each change requires hooking up a new container of dialysate. Thus, CAPD provides more opportunities for bacteria to move down the tube and into the abdomen, where they may cause peritonitis (inflammation of the peritoneum). Even the most meticulous patients suffer at least one episode of peritonitis a year, and every episode requires hospitalization and treatment with an antibiotic. Eventually, the peritoneum may become so scarred from bouts of peritonitis that CAPD is no longer possible.

In some cases of acute renal failure, dialysis may be needed for a short time, until kidney function returns. Patients with chronic renal failure, however, will need dialysis for the rest of their lives, unless they receive a kidney transplant.

FIGURE 16.12 CAPD uses the peritoneum (the membrane that lines the abdominal cavity and covers the organs within) as the dialyzing membrane.

Kidney Transplant Surgery

The ultimate hope for many people whose kidneys fail is to receive a healthy kidney from another person. The kidney was one of the first organs to be successfully transplanted. The availability of dialysis was a crucial part of this success, because dialysis keeps people alive until a suitable donor organ can be found. Progress in liver and heart transplantation has been slower due to the difficulty of providing temporary mechanical replacements for those organs.

What makes a suitable donor organ? The main obstacle to successful acceptance of a transplanted organ is the rejection of foreign tissue by the patient's own immune system (see Chapter 13). The most suitable kidney would come from a patient's identical twin. In fact, the first successful transplant occurred in 1955 between identical twins. A kidney from a close relative, such as a parent or sibling, would be the next best choice. Removal of a healthy kidney is a safe operation, and a healthy donor who gives a kidney away can get along fine with the remaining kidney (of course, all surgeries involve risks, and in the United States about 3 in 10,000 people die from kidney donation). About 90% of kidneys donated by close relatives are still functioning 2 years after transplantation. However, most donated kidneys come from individuals who are unrelated to the patient but who agreed before their death (usually a sudden death in an accident) to donate their organs. About 75% of kidneys donated from unrelated individuals, matched as closely as possible to the patient's tissue and blood type, are still functioning 2 years after transplantation. Even if a transplant fails after a few years, successful second and third transplants may extend a patient's life.

In most situations, the kidneys of the patient needing a transplant are not removed, because survival post surgery is higher when the recipient's own kidneys are left in place. The donor kidney is simply transplanted into a protected area within the pelvis (Figure 16.13). The ureter of the donated kidney is attached to the recipient's bladder, and blood vessels of the donated kidney are attached to the recipient's vessels. The recipient's own kidneys would be removed if they were infected or if they were causing problems such as high blood pressure.

The high success rate of kidney transplants is linked to the use of drugs that suppress the recipient's immune system. Typically,

FIGURE 16.13 During a kidney transplant, the donor organ is located in a safe region within the pelvis and its ureter is attached to the recipient's bladder. Blood vessels from the transplanted kidney are attached to the recipient's vessels. Typically, the recipient's own kidneys are left in place.

transplant recipients must take two or more of these medications for the rest of their lives. Recently, a team of researchers developed a way to perform kidney transplants without the recipients' needing to permanently remain on immune-suppressing drugs. The suppressing drugs were given to recipients after transplant surgery. Then, the recipients received several radiation treatments, which were directed at reducing the number of cells in their immune system capable of attacking the new organ. Finally, the recipients received blood stem cells from the person who donated the transplanted kidney. These new stem cells moved to the recipient's bone marrow and generated new blood cells and immune cells. In essence, each recipient now had a hybrid immune system—a mix of his or her own cells and those of the donor. The hybrid immune systems did not recognize the transplanted kidneys as foreign, and recipients were gradually weaned off the immune-suppressing medications.

what would you do?

The constant shortage of donor organs has led some people to suggest a change in the laws regarding organ donation. Currently, a person must give permission to use his or her organs after death. If a potential donor is incapable of giving such permission, then medical personnel may consult close relatives. In recent years, people concerned about organ shortages have suggested changing the laws so that people would have to provide written proof that they did *not* want their organs made available for transplantation after death. In other words, without anything in writing, the law would presume that people have no objection to organ donation. Many healthy people probably have no objections to organ donation, but simply do not think about death and the future use of their organs. On the other hand, some might worry that doctors and nurses may let certain people die because other people needed their organs. If you were given the responsibility of deciding whether to change the laws regarding organ donation, what would you do?

FIGURE 16.14 Before transplantation, donor kidneys must be kept in a cool salt solution under sterile conditions. Even under such conditions, kidneys will deteriorate after about 1 or 2 days.

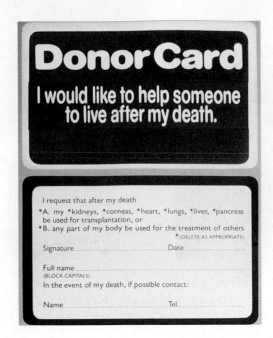

FIGURE 16.15 An organ donor card available through www.organdonor.gov. In addition to carrying this card, it is important to let family members know of your decision to donate your organs or tissues. Your intent to donate also can be indicated on your driver's license.

Despite major advances in kidney transplantation, there is still room for improvement. For example, donor kidneys can be kept alive and healthy for only about 24 to 48 hours (Figure **16.14**). This short window of opportunity necessitates rapid location of a recipient, shipment of the donor kidney, and transplantation. Perhaps most important, kidneys available for transplantation are always in short supply. The total number of candidates on the waiting list for organs in the United States is updated minute by minute. At 3:21 P.M. on May 25, 2008, that number totaled 99,472. The vast majority of these candidates—76,073—were waiting for kidneys. Many patients wait for months or years for a new kidney. Perhaps you have considered carrying an organ donor card that says you wish to donate organs or tissues at the time of your death (Figure **16.15**). If you haven't already signed an organ donor card, you might want to reconsider it after you have finished reading this chapter: Your kidney could save someone else's life—or perhaps someone else's kidney could save you.

In the future, kidneys for transplantation may come from sources other than humans. For example, scientists are investigating the possibility of using kidneys from genetically modified pigs for transplantation into humans. The DNA of these pigs is modified to make the molecules on the surface of their cells unlikely to trigger rejection when transplanted into humans. Transplanting organs from other animals into humans raises ethical issues and poses several concerns, including the transmission of infectious microbes from the pig organ to the human recipient (see Chapter 13).

Urination

Urination is the process by which the urinary bladder is emptied. This process includes both involuntary and voluntary actions and is summarized in Figure **16.16**. The kidneys produce urine around the clock. The urine trickles into the ureters and down to the urinary bladder, where it is temporarily stored. When at least 200 ml (0.42 pt) of urine have accumulated, stretch receptors in the wall of the bladder send impulses along sensory neurons to the lower part of the spinal cord. From there, impulses are sent along motor neurons back to the bladder, where they cause a smooth muscle in the wall of the bladder, called the *detrusor muscle,* to contract. The impulses also cause the *internal urethral sphincter,* a thickening of smooth muscle located at the junction of the bladder and urethra, to relax. Upon arrival of sensory impulses in the lower spinal cord, information also travels up to the brain and initiates a desire to urinate. If the circumstances are appropriate, the brain permits voluntary relaxation of the *external urethral sphincter,* a small band of skeletal muscle farther down the urethra. When the external sphincter relaxes, urine exits the body. If the circumstances are not appropriate for urination, the brain does not permit the external sphincter to relax, and the bladder continues to store the urine until a better time. With normal functioning, urine will exit the body later, when the person consciously allows the external sphincter to relax.

Thus, although urination is a reflex—a relatively rapid response to a stimulus that is mediated by the nervous system—it can nevertheless be started and stopped voluntarily because of the conscious control exerted by the brain over the external urethral sphincter. However, not everyone can control his or her external urethral sphincter. Lack of voluntary control over urination is called *urinary incontinence.* Incontinence is the norm for infants and children younger than 2 or 3 years of age, because nervous connections to the external urethral sphincter are incompletely developed. As a result, infants and young children void whenever their bladder fills with enough urine to activate its stretch receptors (Figure **16.17**). Toilet training occurs when toddlers learn to bring urination under

conscious control. This step is made possible by the development of complete neural connections to the external sphincter.

Damage to the external sphincter may cause incontinence in adults. In men, such damage may occur during surgery on the prostate gland. The prostate gland surrounds the male urethra just below the urinary bladder and contributes substances to semen (see Chapter 17). Incontinence also may occur because of bladder muscles that contract before the bladder is full. This condition is often described as an overactive or spastic bladder. Infection of the urinary system (see below) can also cause incontinence, in any age group.

Mild incontinence, especially the kind called stress incontinence, is common in adults. *Stress incontinence* is characterized by the escape of small amounts of urine when sudden increases in abdominal pressure force urine past the external sphincter. Laughing, sneezing, or coughing may cause these sudden increases in pressure. Stress incontinence is more common in women, particularly late in pregnancy when the enlarging uterus puts pressure on the bladder, and after childbirth. Giving birth may stretch or damage the external sphincter, making it less effective in controlling the flow of urine. Such damage can be minimized or repaired by exercises designed to strengthen the external sphincter and muscles along the floor of the pelvic cavity.

Urinary retention is the failure to expel urine from the bladder to a normal degree. This condition may result from a lack of the sensation that one must urinate, as might occur temporarily after general anesthesia. It may also result from contraction or obstruction of the

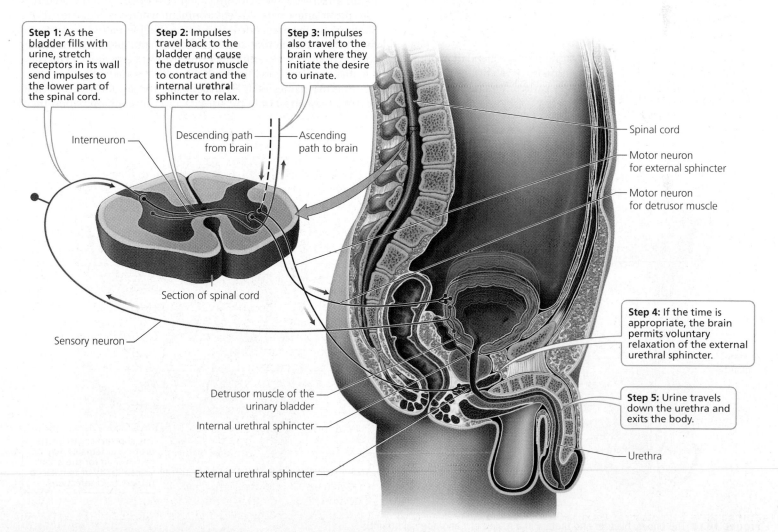

FIGURE 16.16 The steps involved in urination

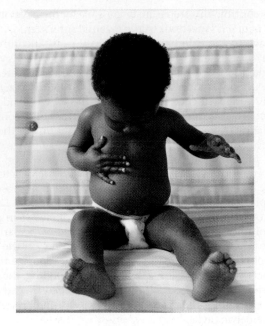

FIGURE 16.17 Conscious control over urination is usually acquired by the age of 3, when neural connections to the external urethral sphincter are fully developed. Before that age, urination occurs as an involuntary reflex.

urethra. For example, enlargement of the prostate gland in men may obstruct the urethra. Immediate treatment for retention usually involves the use of a tube called a urinary catheter to drain urine from the bladder.

Urinary Tract Infections

Presence of microorganisms in the organs of the urinary system can cause a **urinary tract infection (UTI)**. Most bacteria enter the urinary system by moving up the urethra from outside the body. Bacteria called *Escherichia coli* normally inhabit the colon and can cause UTIs if they enter the urethra. Sometimes, microorganisms called *Chlamydia* and *Mycoplasma* cause UTIs. In contrast to *E. coli,* these bacteria are sexually transmitted (see Chapter 17a). Some bacteria arrive at the kidneys by way of the bloodstream.

The urethras of males and females differ in length, as shown in Figure **16.18**. The urethra in females is 3 to 4 cm (1.5 in.) long and lies in front of the vagina. The urethra in males is about 20 cm (8 in.) long and opens to the outside at the tip of the penis. Urinary tract infections are more common in females than in males, perhaps because of their shorter urethras. In females, the bacteria need to travel only a short distance from the external urethral orifice (opening) through the urethra to the bladder. In addition, the external urethral orifice is closer to the anus in females than it is in males. Thus, improper wiping after defecation can easily carry fecal bacteria to the female urethra. (Proper wiping is front to back.) Bacteria also may enter the urethra during sexual intercourse. Women are advised to urinate soon after sex to flush bacteria from the lower urinary tract.

To avoid UTIs, men and women alike are advised to drink plenty of water each day and to urinate frequently throughout the day. Other tips to prevent UTIs include avoiding wet or tight clothing and nylon underwear. Such clothing allows the opening of the urethra to stay moist and creates an environment where bacteria can thrive. Showers are recommended over baths. Bubble baths, in particular, may irritate the urethra and increase susceptibility to UTIs. Finally, some physicians recommend drinking cranberry juice. This juice acidifies the urine and inhibits the growth of some bacteria.

Specific names of UTIs depend on the location of infection. Bacteria may infect only the urethra and cause inflammation there,

Urinary bladder

Internal urethral sphincter

Rectum

External urethral sphincter

Urethra

Testis

Prostate gland

Penis

Uterus

Vagina

The shorter length of the urethra in females may be responsible for the greater susceptibility of females to urinary tract infections.

FIGURE 16.18 The urinary bladder and urethra in a male (left) and a female (right)

a type of infection called *urethritis*. Sometimes, however, the bacteria travel farther into the urinary system. These bacteria may cause *cystitis,* infection of the urinary bladder. Bacteria may also be introduced into the bladder when a catheter is used. Although the insertion of a catheter does pose a risk of infection, use of these devices can be lifesaving. Sometimes bacteria do not stop at the bladder and move through the ureters and into the kidneys. An infection of the kidneys is called *pyelonephritis*.

Symptoms of urinary tract infections include fever, blood in the urine, and painful and frequent urination. Bed wetting may be a symptom in young children. In addition, there may be lower abdominal pain (if the bladder is involved) or back pain (if the kidneys are involved). Physicians usually diagnose such infections by having the urine checked for bacteria and blood cells. People who have recurrent UTIs may wish to purchase nonprescription dipsticks to check for infection. The dipstick is held in the stream of the first morning urine and changes color when it detects nitrite, a compound made by the bacteria. These dipsticks can detect about 90% of UTIs.

Urinary tract infections are treated with antibiotics. Infections of the lower urinary tract (the urethra and bladder) should be treated immediately and the prescribed antibiotics taken for their full term. These steps are critical to prevent the spread of infection to the kidneys, where very serious damage can occur.

highlighting the concepts

Eliminating Waste (p. 324)

- Several organs from different body systems remove waste from our bodies. Lungs and skin eliminate carbon dioxide, heat, and water. The skin also excretes salt and small amounts of urea and uric acid. Organs of the digestive system eliminate solid wastes (feces), and those of the urinary system excrete nitrogen-containing wastes, water, carbon dioxide, inorganic salts, and hydrogen ions.

Components of the Urinary System (p. 325)

- Two kidneys, two ureters, the urinary bladder, and the urethra make up the urinary system. The main function of this system is to regulate the volume, pressure, and composition of the blood. The kidneys filter excess materials and wastes from the blood and produce urine. Urine travels down the ureters to the urinary bladder, where it is stored until excreted from the body through the urethra. The male urethra transports reproductive fluid in addition to urine (but not at the same time). The female urethra transports only urine.

Kidneys and Homeostasis (pp. 325–334)

- The kidneys are located just above the waist against the back wall of the abdominal cavity. Each kidney has an outer portion (the renal cortex), an inner region (the renal medulla), and an inner chamber (the renal pelvis).
- Properly functioning kidneys are critical to maintaining homeostasis. These organs filter wastes and excess materials from the blood, help regulate blood pH, and maintain fluid balance by regulating the volume and composition of blood and urine.
- Nephrons are tiny tubules responsible for the formation of urine. There are two basic parts to a nephron: (1) the renal corpuscle, which consists of a tuft of capillaries called the glomerulus and a surrounding cuplike structure called the glomerular capsule; and (2) the renal tubule. The renal tubule has three sections: the proximal convoluted tubule, the loop of the nephron, and the distal convoluted tubule. The distal convoluted tubules of several nephrons empty into a single collecting duct. Urine in collecting ducts moves into a large chamber within the kidneys called the renal pelvis. From the renal pelvis, urine leaves the kidneys by traveling down the ureters to the urinary bladder.
- Glomerular filtration is the process by which only certain substances are allowed to pass out of the blood and into the nephron. High pressure within glomerular capillaries forces water and small solutes in the blood across a filter into the space within the glomerular capsule. Large proteins and blood cells normally cannot cross the filter.
- From the glomerular capsule, the filtrate—consisting of water, ions, and small molecules filtered from the blood—moves into the renal tubule of the nephron. As it passes through the renal tubule, about 99% of it is returned to the blood in a process known as tubular reabsorption. Almost all the water, ions, and nutrients in the filtrate are returned to the blood. Wastes are either partially reabsorbed or not reabsorbed at all. Most reabsorption occurs in the proximal convoluted tubule.
- During tubular secretion, drugs and any wastes or excess essential ions that may have escaped glomerular filtration are removed from the blood in the capillaries surrounding nephrons and added to the filtered fluid that will become urine. This process occurs primarily along the proximal and distal convoluted tubules and collecting ducts.
- The kidneys work with the lungs and buffer systems to regulate pH. Specifically, tubular reabsorption returns bicarbonate to the blood (for use in buffering), and tubular secretion removes excess hydrogen ions from the blood.
- Most nephrons have short loops that are restricted almost entirely to the renal cortex. About 20% of the nephrons have long loops that extend deep into the renal medulla. These nephrons are responsible for the extreme water-conserving ability of the kidneys because they maintain high solute concentrations in the interstitial fluid within the kidneys. Maintenance of this gradient between the interstitial fluid and the filtrate enables large amounts of water to move out of collecting ducts by osmosis for conservation by the body, and leads to the production of concentrated urine.
- Several hormones influence kidney function. Antidiuretic hormone (ADH) is produced by the hypothalamus and released by the posterior lobe of the pituitary gland. ADH increases water reabsorption in the collecting ducts of nephrons. Aldosterone is secreted by the adrenal cortex. Aldosterone increases sodium reabsorption by the distal convoluted tubules and collecting ducts. Because water follows sodium, aldosterone increases water reabsorption by nephrons. Atrial natriuretic peptide (ANP) is a hormone released by cells of the right atrium of the heart. ANP causes decreased water and sodium reabsorption by the kidneys, which causes a decrease in blood pressure and volume.
- The kidneys release the hormone erythropoietin, which is necessary for red blood cell production. The kidneys also convert vitamin D into its active form that promotes the body's absorption of calcium and phosphorus.

Dialysis and Transplant Surgery (pp. 334–338)

- Renal failure is a decrease or complete cessation of glomerular filtration. Failure of the kidneys severely disrupts homeostasis.

Conditions such as acidosis, anemia, edema, hypertension, and a toxic buildup of nitrogen-containing wastes in the blood may result when the kidneys stop working.

- Treatments for renal failure include hemodialysis (using artificial devices to cleanse the blood), continuous ambulatory peritoneal dialysis (using the patient's own peritoneum as the dialyzing membrane), and kidney transplantation.

Urination (pp. 338–340)

- Urination, the process by which the urinary bladder is emptied, entails both involuntary and voluntary actions. Moderate filling of the bladder stimulates stretch receptors in its wall that send impulses along sensory neurons to the lower spinal cord. From the spinal cord, impulses move along motor neurons back to the bladder, where they cause the muscular wall of the bladder to contract. The impulses also cause the internal urethral sphincter, a thickening of smooth muscle at the junction of the bladder and urethra, to relax. These actions push stored urine into the urethra. If conditions are appropriate, the brain then permits voluntary relaxation of the external urethral sphincter, a band of skeletal muscle farther down the urethra, causing urine to exit the body.

Urinary Tract Infections (pp. 340–341)

- Urinary tract infections (UTIs) are more common in females than in males, possibly because bacteria can more readily move from outside the body up the shorter urethra of females to the bladder. Infections may occur in the urethra, bladder, and kidneys, with infections of the kidneys being the most serious.

recognizing key terms

excretion *p. 324*
urine *p. 324*
urinary system *p. 325*
kidney *p. 325*
ureter *p. 325*
urinary bladder *p. 325*
urethra *p. 325*
renal cortex *p. 326*
renal medulla *p. 326*
renal pelvis *p. 326*

nephron *p. 326*
renal corpuscle *p. 326*
glomerulus *p. 326*
glomerular capsule *p. 326*
renal tubule *p. 326*
proximal convoluted
    tubule *p. 326*
loop of the nephron *p. 326*
distal convoluted
    tubule *p. 326*

collecting duct *p. 326*
glomerular filtration *p. 329*
tubular reabsorption *p. 329*
tubular secretion *p. 331*
antidiuretic hormone
    (ADH) *p. 333*
diuretic *p. 333*
aldosterone *p. 333*
juxtaglomerular apparatus
    p. 334

renin *p. 334*
atrial natriuretic peptide
    (ANP) *p. 334*
erythropoietin *p. 334*
renal failure *p. 334*
hemodialysis *p. 336*
urination *p. 338*
urinary tract infection
    (UTI) *p. 340*

reviewing the concepts

1. Name four nitrogen-containing wastes produced by humans. Describe the processes that generate them, and name the organs primarily responsible for excreting them. *p. 324*
2. List the components of the urinary system and their functions. *p. 325*
3. Describe the ways in which kidneys maintain homeostasis. *p. 325*
4. Explain glomerular filtration, tubular reabsorption, and tubular secretion by nephrons. Where in the nephron does each process occur? *pp. 328–331*
5. How do nephrons contribute to the regulation of blood pH? *p. 331*
6. How do the kidneys conserve water, and why is this important? *pp. 331–333*
7. Identify three hormones that play a significant role in kidney function, and explain how each hormone works to help the kidney meet the body's needs on a daily basis. *pp. 333–334*
8. Does the solute concentration in interstitial fluid increase, decrease, or stay the same from the renal cortex to the renal medulla? Please explain. *pp. 331–333*
9. Describe the process and mechanisms involved in urination. *pp. 338–340*
10. How do the urethras of males and females differ? What are the clinical implications of these differences? *pp. 340–341*

11. Glomerular filtration
    a. occurs at the renal corpuscle.
    b. returns useful substances to the blood.
    c. occurs along the renal tubule.
    d. is the last step of three in cleansing the blood.
12. Which of the following substances would normally *not* pass through the glomerular filter?
    a. water
    b. ions
    c. red blood cells
    d. glucose
13. Which of the following would *not* be helpful to someone suffering from hyponatremia?
    a. administering hypotonic fluids
    b. administering a diuretic
    c. administering an intravenous saline solution
    d. drinking a sodium-containing sports drink
14. Which of the following would raise blood pH?
    a. reabsorption of H^+
    b. secretion of HCO_3^-
    c. secretion of H^+
    d. reabsorption of glucose

15. Tubular reabsorption
    a. allows only certain substances to pass from the blood into the nephron.
    b. returns useful substances from the filtrate to the blood.
    c. removes wastes and excess essential ions that escaped filtration from the blood.
    d. occurs at the renal corpuscle.

16. _____ is the region of the nephron that monitors the pressure of blood entering the glomerulus, and it ultimately influences the release of aldosterone.
17. _____ is the use of artificial devices to cleanse the blood.
18. The _____ urethral sphincter is made of _____ muscle and is involuntary. The _____ urethral sphincter is made of _____ muscle and allows voluntary control over urination.

applying the concepts

1. Rachel has noticed that since she gave birth, a small amount of urine escapes whenever she sneezes. What condition might Rachel have? What would explain this condition, and what can she do to improve it?
2. Miguel has noticed that after he drinks coffee or beer, his urine output increases. Why does this happen? Is the same mechanism involved in each situation?
3. Li has polycystic disease, an inherited and progressive condition that is destroying her kidneys. What will be the health consequences of her chronic renal failure? What are her options for restoring kidney function? What are the advantages and disadvantages of each option?
4. Varian has proteinuria, a condition in which an abnormal amount of protein is present in his urine. His physician suspects that hypertension caused the proteinuria. Which region of the nephron did hypertension likely damage to produce proteinuria? How might proteinuria be diagnosed?

becoming information literate

Write a paper on some of the major changes that occur in the urinary system across the life span. Include in your paper the general changes to kidney function caused by age-related declines in number of nephrons, rates of glomerular filtration, and sensitivity of nephrons to ADH. Keep a log of the sources (books, journal articles, websites) that you look at during your search for information. Next to each source, indicate whether you found it helpful and accurate.

Additional questions can be found online at The Human Biology Place, www.humanbiology.com.

17

Reproductive Systems

This beautiful baby girl seems comfortable in her new surroundings, although they can hardly be as sheltering and secure as her mother's uterus.

For two years Tim and Andrea had attempted to get Andrea pregnant, listening to everything from advice they read in medical columns to ideas suggested by old wives' tales. Nothing worked. Finally, they went to a highly recommended fertility clinic for help. After they had undergone many tests and examinations, and answered many questions about their medical history, Dr. Perry told them that Tim was likely to be the source of the problem. He explained that Tim had "poor—performing sperm—slow swimmers and too few of them." He went on to explain that these problems with Tim's sperm were probably caused by varicoceles, enlargements of the veins that drain blood from the testes. The varicoceles create a slightly warmer environment for sperm, resulting in a reduced sperm count and a high percentage of deformed sperm. Tim had surgery to correct the problem, and 18 months later, Andrea gave birth to their beautiful baby girl.

In this chapter, we gain an understanding of why Tim and Andrea had difficulty conceiving a child. We look at the structures of the reproductive systems and how they function. We also consider the sex hormones and the ways in which they regulate reproductive processes.

Gonads

In both males and females, the **gonads**—testes or ovaries—are the most important structures in the reproductive system. The gonads serve two important functions: (1) they produce the **gametes**, meaning the eggs and sperm—the cells that will fuse and develop into a new individual; and (2) they produce the sex hormones. The male gonads are the **testes**, and the gametes they produce are the **sperm**. The testes also produce the sex hormone **testosterone**. The **ovaries** are the female gonads. The gametes they produce are the **eggs**. The sex hormones they produce are **estrogen** and **progesterone**.

Male and Female Reproductive Roles

Males and females make an equal genetic contribution to the next generation by contributing one copy of each chromosome to their offspring. However, they have different "reproductive strategies" to help ensure that their DNA (packaged in their chromosomes) is passed along to a new generation. A male's strategy is to produce millions of sperm, deliver them to the female reproductive system, and hope that one sperm reaches an egg. In contrast, a female usually produces only one egg approximately once a month. If sperm delivery is appropriately timed with egg production, a sperm and egg may fuse in a process called **fertilization.** If conditions are right, the cell created by fertilization, called a zygote, will develop into a new individual (see Chapter 18). A male's role in the reproductive process ends with delivery of sperm, but a female's role continues after egg production; she nourishes and protects the offspring until birth. The egg is packed with nutrients to provide for early development, and the woman's uterus serves as a nourishing, protective environment for the developing offspring.

The development of eggs and sperm involves two types of cell division. The first is *mitosis,* a process in which a cell with 23 pairs of chromosomes replicates its chromosomes and divides into two identical cells, each with 23 pairs of chromosomes. The alterations in genetic content occur during the second type of cell division, called *meiosis,* which begins with a cell that has two copies of each of the 23 kinds of chromosome (called a *diploid* cell) and ends with up to four cells that each contain only one of each kind of chromosome (called *haploid* cells). Meiosis entails two rounds of cell division. (The details of mitosis and meiosis are described in Chapter 19.)

Each cell in your body contains 23 pairs of chromosomes (for a total of 46 chromosomes). One member of each pair came from your father's sperm; the other member of each pair came from your mother's egg. Each of the 23 kinds of chromosome contains a different portion of the instructions for making and maintaining your body, and two of each kind are necessary for health and normal development. It is important, therefore, that only one member of each pair be present in a gamete.

Form and Function of the Male Reproductive System

The male reproductive system consists of the testes, a system of ducts through which the sperm travel, the penis, and various accessory glands. Accessory glands produce secretions that help protect and nourish the sperm as well as provide a transport medium that aids the delivery of sperm to the outside of the male's body. The structure of the male reproductive system is summarized in Table **17.1**.

TABLE 17.1 Review of Male Reproductive System

Structure	Function
Testes	Produce sperm and testosterone
Epididymis	Location of sperm storage and maturation
Vas deferens	Conducts sperm from epididymis to urethra
Urethra	Tube through which sperm or urine leaves the body
Prostate gland	Produces secretions that make sperm mobile and that counteract the acidity of the female reproductive tract
Seminal vesicles	Produce secretions that make up most of the volume of semen
Bulbourethral glands	Produce secretions just before ejaculation; may lubricate; may rinse urine from urethra
Penis	Delivers sperm to female reproductive tract

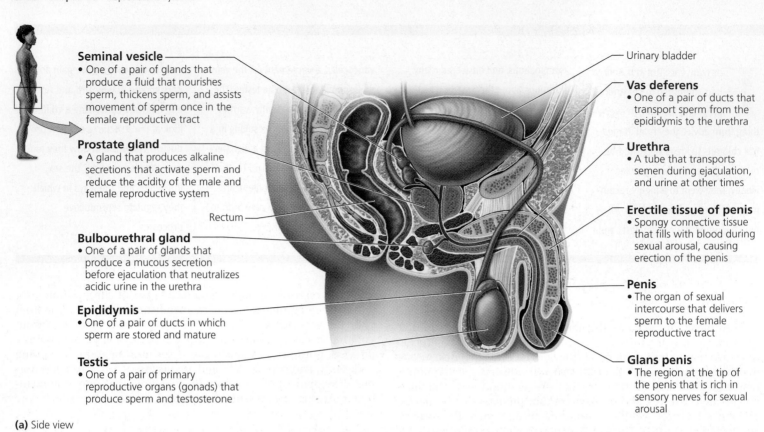

Seminal vesicle
• One of a pair of glands that produce a fluid that nourishes sperm, thickens sperm, and assists movement of sperm once in the female reproductive tract

Prostate gland
• A gland that produces alkaline secretions that activate sperm and reduce the acidity of the male and female reproductive system

Rectum

Bulbourethral gland
• One of a pair of glands that produce a mucous secretion before ejaculation that neutralizes acidic urine in the urethra

Epididymis
• One of a pair of ducts in which sperm are stored and mature

Testis
• One of a pair of primary reproductive organs (gonads) that produce sperm and testosterone

Urinary bladder

Vas deferens
• One of a pair of ducts that transport sperm from the epididymis to the urethra

Urethra
• A tube that transports semen during ejaculation, and urine at other times

Erectile tissue of penis
• Spongy connective tissue that fills with blood during sexual arousal, causing erection of the penis

Penis
• The organ of sexual intercourse that delivers sperm to the female reproductive tract

Glans penis
• The region at the tip of the penis that is rich in sensory nerves for sexual arousal

(a) Side view

Urinary bladder
Ureter
Vas deferens
Seminal vesicle
Prostate
Bulbourethral gland
Erectile tissue of penis
Urethra
Testis
Glans penis
Epididymis
Uncoiled seminiferous tubules

Blood vessels

Cross section of penis

(b) Rear view

FIGURE 17.1 The male reproductive system

Testes

The male reproductive system has two testes (singular, testis; Figure **17.1**). Each is located externally to the body in a sac of skin called the **scrotum.** The temperature in the scrotum is several degrees cooler than within the abdominal cavity. The lower temperature is important in the production of healthy sperm.

Reflexes in the scrotum help keep the temperature within the testes fairly stable. Cooling of the scrotum, such as might occur when a male jumps into frigid water, triggers contraction of a muscle that pulls the testes closer to the warmth of the body. In a hot shower, however, the muscle relaxes, and the testes hang low, away from the heat of the body. The skin of the scrotum is also amply supplied with sweat glands that help cool the testes.

Beginning at puberty (the transition to sexual maturity), which usually occurs during the teenage years, a healthy male produces more than 100 million sperm each day. The microscopic

Vas deferens Epididymis Coiled seminiferous tubule

Wall of seminiferous tubule

Tails of sperm

Testis

Uncoiled seminiferous tubule

FIGURE 17.2 The internal structure of the testis and epididymis

sites of sperm production are the **seminiferous tubules** (Figure **17.2**). We will consider the development of sperm in more detail later in this chapter.

The *interstitial cells* are located between the seminiferous tubules of the testis. They produce the steroid sex hormones, collectively called *androgens*. The most important androgen is *testosterone,* which is needed for sperm production and the maintenance of male reproductive structures.

Testicular cancer is the most common form of cancer among men between the ages of 15 and 35 years, although it affects only 1% of all men. Testicular cancer is more likely to occur in men whose testes did not descend into the scrotum or descended after 6 years of age. Because this cancer does not usually cause pain, it is important for every man to examine his testes each month to feel for a lump or a change in consistency. The cure rate for tumors caught in the early stages is nearly 100%.

Duct System

Sperm produced in the seminiferous tubules next enter a highly coiled tubule called the **epididymis**, where the sperm mature and are stored (see Figure 17.1). Sperm that enter the epididymis look mature, but they cannot yet function as mature sperm. During their stay in the epididymis, the sperm become capable of fertilizing an egg and of moving on their own, although they do not yet do so.

The tube that conducts sperm from the epididymis to the urethra is called the **vas deferens.** Some sperm may be stored in the part of the vas deferens closest to the epididymis. When a man reaches sexual climax, rhythmic waves of muscle contraction propel the sperm along the vas deferens.

The *urethra* conducts urine (from the urinary bladder) or sperm (from the vas deferens) out of the body through the *penis,* the male organ of sexual intercourse and urination. Sperm and urine do not pass through the urethra at the same time. A circular muscle contracts and pinches off the connection to the urinary bladder during sexual excitement.

Accessory Glands

Semen, the fluid released through the urethra at sexual climax, contains sperm and is composed of the secretions of the accessory glands: the prostate gland, the paired seminal vesicles, and paired bulbourethral glands. Very little of the volume of semen is made up of sperm.

About the size of a walnut, the **prostate gland** surrounds the upper portion of the urethra, just beneath the urinary bladder. Prostate secretions are slightly alkaline and serve both to activate the sperm, making them fully capable of moving, and to counteract the acidity of the female reproductive tract.

The prostate often begins enlarging when a man reaches middle age. The enlarged prostate may squeeze the urethra and restrict urine flow, making urination difficult. This benign enlargement of the prostate gland that accompanies aging is not related to prostate cancer.

Prostate cancer is an important cause of cancer deaths among men. Unlike testicular cancer, prostate cancer usually affects older men. There are two ways of detecting prostate cancer: a rectal exam and a blood test. Most physicians recommend that both tests be used in the diagnosis. During a rectal exam for prostate cancer, a physician inserts a gloved finger into the rectum and feels the prostate through the rectum's wall (see Figure 17.1). A cancerous prostate is firm or may contain a hard lump. The blood test for prostate cancer measures the amount of a protein called prostate-specific antigen (PSA). Because this protein is produced only by the prostate gland, the amount of PSA in the blood reflects the size of the prostate. As a tumor within the prostate grows, the blood level of PSA usually rises.

The secretions of the **seminal vesicles** contain citric acid, fructose, amino acids, and prostaglandins.[1] Fructose is a sugar that provides energy for the sperm's long journey to the egg. Some of the amino acids thicken the semen. This thickening helps keep the sperm within the vagina and protects the sperm from contacting the acidic environment of the vagina. The prostaglandins serve to cut the viscosity of female cervical mucus (which could otherwise slow the movement of sperm) and to cause uterine contractions that assist the movement of sperm.

The **bulbourethral glands** release a clear, slippery liquid immediately before ejaculation. This fluid may serve to rinse the slightly acidic urine remnants from the urethra before the sperm pass through.

[1]Prostaglandins are chemicals secreted by one cell that alter the activity of nearby cells.

Penis

The **penis** is a cylindrical organ whose role in reproduction is to deliver the sperm to the female reproductive system. The tip of the penis is enlarged, forming a smooth, rounded head known as the *glans penis,* which has many sensory nerve endings and is important in sexual arousal. When a male is born, a cuff of skin called the *foreskin* covers the glans penis. The foreskin can be pulled back to expose the glans penis. The surgical removal of the foreskin is called circumcision.

The transfer of sperm to the female reproductive system during sexual intercourse usually requires the penis to be erect. An erection consists of increases in the length, width, and firmness of the penis, due to changes in the blood supply to the organ. Within the penis are three columns of spongy *erectile tissue,* which is a loose network of connective tissue with many empty spaces (see Figure 17.1). During sexual arousal, the arterioles that pipe blood into the spongy tissue dilate (widen), and the spongy tissue fills with blood, causing the penis to become larger. At the same time, the expanding spongy tissue squeezes shut the veins that drain the blood from the penis. As a result, the blood flows into the penis faster than it can leave, causing the spongy tissue to fill with blood and press against a connective tissue casing. This makes the penis firm, larger, and erect.

Erectile dysfunction (ED, also called impotence) is a male's inability to achieve or maintain an erection (and thus to have sexual intercourse). It is not unusual for a man to experience ED at some point in his life. This condition has some psychological causes, including worry, stress, a quarrel with the partner, and depression. However, it also has many physical causes. Nerve damage, which often accompanies chronic alcoholism and sometimes diabetes, can be responsible. Because an erection depends on adequate blood supply, fatty deposits in the arteries serving the penis (as in atherosclerosis) can also cause ED. Medications—especially certain drugs used to treat high blood pressure, antihistamines, antinausea and antiseizure drugs, antidepressants, sedatives, and tranquilizers—may cause the problem. Cigarette smoking, heavy alcohol consumption, or marijuana use can also cause ED.

The first step in treating ED is to eliminate the cause of the problem, if possible. Should impotency continue, drugs for erectile dysfunction—Viagra, Levitra, Cialis—may be prescribed. These drugs can help a man achieve and maintain an erection when he is sexually aroused. They work by prolonging the effect of nitric oxide, a chemical that is released when the man becomes sexually aroused and that causes the widening of the arterioles in the penis. As the arterioles widen, blood flow increases, and an erection results.

stop and think

Why is it that Viagra, Levitra, or Cialis cannot cause an erection in a man who is not sexually aroused?

Sperm Development

The sequence of events within the seminiferous tubules that leads to the development of sperm is called *spermatogenesis.* This process reduces the number of chromosomes in the resulting gametes to one member of each pair and changes the sperm cells' shape and functioning to make the sperm efficient chromosome-delivery vehicles.

The process of spermatogenesis (Figure **17.3**) begins in the outermost layer of each seminiferous tubule, where undifferentiated diploid cells called *spermatogonia* (singular, spermatogonium) develop. Each spermatogonium divides by mitosis to produce two new diploid spermatogonia. One of these spermatogonia pushes

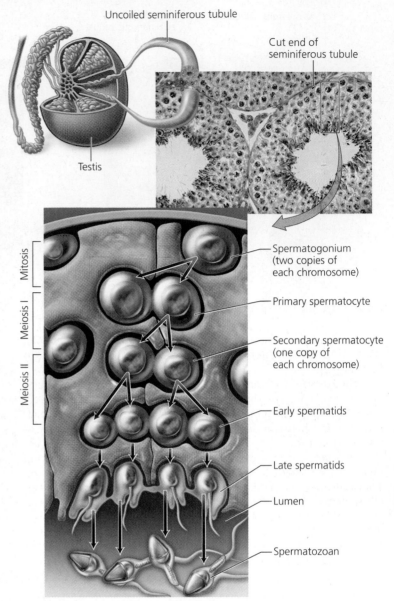

FIGURE 17.3 The stages of spermatogenesis in the wall of a seminiferous tubule. As the cells that will become sperm develop, they are pushed from the outer wall of the tubule to the lumen, or central canal.

deeper into the wall of the tubule, where it will enlarge to form a *primary spermatocyte,* which is also a diploid cell. Primary spermatocytes undergo the two divisions of meiosis to form *secondary spermatocytes* (after meiosis I), which mature into *spermatids* (after meiosis II). Although the spermatids are haploid and have the correct set of chromosomes for joining with the egg during fertilization, numerous structural changes must still occur to create cells capable of swimming to the egg and fertilizing it. These changes convert spermatids to streamlined *spermatozoa,* or sperm.

The mature sperm cell has three distinct regions: the head, the midpiece, and the tail (Figure **17.4**). The head of the sperm is a flattened oval that contains little else besides the 23 densely packed chromosomes (remember that the sperm is haploid). Positioned like a ski cap on the head of the sperm is the **acrosome**, a membranous sac containing enzymes. A few hours after the sperm have been deposited in the female reproductive system, the membranes of the acrosomes break down. The enzymes then spill out

The whiplike movements of the **tail** propel the sperm.

The **midpiece** contains mitochondria that will provide metabolic energy to fuel the trip to the egg.

The **head** contains the father's chromosomes, his genetic contribution to the next generation.

The **acrosome**, a sac that covers the head of the sperm, contains enzymes that will assist in fertilization.

FIGURE 17.4 The structure of a mature sperm (spermatozoan)

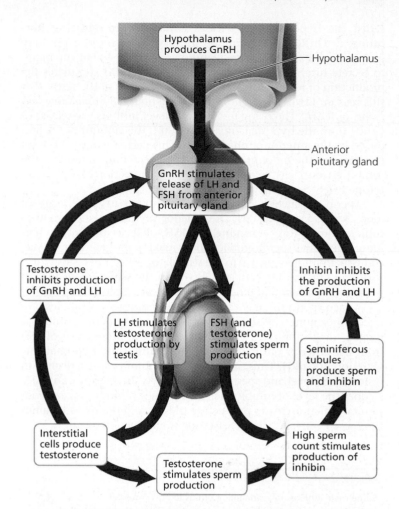

Hypothalamus produces GnRH

Hypothalamus

Anterior pituitary gland

GnRH stimulates release of LH and FSH from anterior pituitary gland

Testosterone inhibits production of GnRH and LH

Inhibin inhibits the production of GnRH and LH

LH stimulates testosterone production by testis

FSH (and testosterone) stimulates sperm production

Seminiferous tubules produce sperm and inhibin

Interstitial cells produce testosterone

Testosterone stimulates sperm production

High sperm count stimulates production of inhibin

FIGURE 17.5 The feedback relationships among the hypothalamus, anterior pituitary, and testes control the production of both sperm and testosterone.

and digest through the layers of cells surrounding the egg, assisting fertilization. Within the midpiece, mitochondria are arranged in a spiral. Remember that the mitochondria are the powerhouses of the cell. They provide energy in the form of ATP to fuel the movements of the tail. The tail contains contractile filaments. The whiplike movements of the tail propel the sperm during its long journey through the female reproductive system.

Hormones

Testosterone, secreted by the interstitial cells of the testes, is important for sperm production as well as the development of male characteristics. At puberty, testosterone turns boys into men (literally). It is responsible for the growth spurt that occurs when a male reaches puberty, stimulating the growth of the long bones of the arms and legs. It also makes the male reproductive organs, including the testes and penis, larger. In addition, testosterone is responsible for the development and maintenance of the male secondary sex characteristics, which are features associated with "masculinity" but not directly related to reproductive functioning. For example, the growth of muscles and the skeleton tends to result in wide shoulders and narrow hips. Pubic hair develops, as does hair under the arms. A beard appears, perhaps accompanied by hair on the chest. Meanwhile, the voice box enlarges and the vocal cords thicken, causing a deepening of the male voice. And, importantly, testosterone is responsible for sex drive.

The level of testosterone in the body remains relatively steady because its production is regulated by a negative feedback loop (see Chapter 10) involving hormones from the hypothalamus, the anterior pituitary gland, and the testes. The hormones that regulate male reproductive processes are summarized in Figure **17.5** and Table **17.2**. Testosterone levels rise when a region of the brain

TABLE 17.2	Hormones Important in Regulating Male Reproductive Processes	
Hormone	**Source**	**Effects**
Testosterone	Interstitial cells in testes	Sperm production; development and maintenance of male reproductive structures, male secondary sex characteristics; sex drive
Gonadotropin-releasing hormone (GnRH)	Hypothalamus (in brain)	Stimulates the anterior pituitary gland to release LH
Luteinizing hormone (LH)	Anterior pituitary gland (in brain)	Stimulates interstitial cells of testis to produce testosterone
Follicle-stimulating hormone (FSH)	Anterior pituitary gland (in brain)	Enhances sperm formation
Inhibin	Seminiferous tubules in testes	Inhibits FSH secretion by anterior pituitary gland, causing a decrease in sperm production and testosterone production

called the hypothalamus releases **gonadotropin-releasing hormone,** or **GnRH.** This hormone stimulates the anterior pituitary gland, a pea-sized endocrine gland on the underside of the brain, to secrete **luteinizing hormone (LH).** In turn, LH stimulates the production of testosterone by the interstitial cells of the testis. (For this reason, LH is sometimes called *interstitial cell–stimulating hormone,* or *ICSH.*) The rising testosterone level inhibits the release of GnRH from the hypothalamus. As a result, the amount of LH produced by the anterior pituitary drops. This decrease in the LH level then lowers the amount of testosterone secretion, removing the inhibition on the hypothalamus. These interactions keep testosterone levels constant.

Sperm production is regulated by another negative feedback loop. Besides secreting LH, the anterior pituitary gland produces **follicle-stimulating hormone,** or **FSH.** Follicle-stimulating hormone stimulates sperm production by making the cells that will become sperm more sensitive to the stimulatory effects of testosterone. FSH works by causing certain cells within the seminiferous tubules to secrete a protein that binds and concentrates testosterone.

When sperm numbers are high, the seminiferous tubules produce a hormone called *inhibin* in addition to sperm. Inhibin is named for its ability to *inhibit,* or lessen, the production of FSH from the anterior pituitary. It also may inhibit the hypothalamic secretion of GnRH. Thus, rising levels of inhibin cause a decline in testosterone level and sperm production. As the sperm count falls, so does the level of inhibin. Released from inhibition, the anterior pituitary then increases production of FSH, and the hypothalamus produces GnRH, which increases sperm production again.

stop and think

Some male athletes take anabolic steroids to build muscles. A side effect of steroid abuse is a reduction in testis size. Considering that the anabolic steroids mimic the effect of testosterone, how can the shrinking testis size be explained?

Form and Function of the Female Reproductive System

The female reproductive system consists of the ovaries, the oviducts, the uterus, the vagina, and the external genitalia. Its structure is shown in Figure **17.6**, and its functions are summarized in Table **17.3**.

Ovaries

Each ovary is about twice the size of an almond. There is an ovary on each side of the uterus. The ovaries have two important functions: (1) to produce eggs in a process called *oogenesis* and (2) to produce the hormones estrogen and progesterone. These two functions are intimately related and occur in cycles, as we will see.

Oviducts

Two **oviducts,** also known as fallopian tubes or uterine tubes, extend from the uterus to the ovaries—although they do not attach to the ovaries. They transport the immature egg, called an *oocyte,* from the ovary to the uterus. The end of each oviduct nearest the ovary is open and funnel shaped. Its many ciliated, fingerlike projections drape over the ovary but are rarely in direct contact with it. Shortly before the egg is released from the ovary, the projections

from the tubes begin to wave. The currents they create, and those caused by the cilia lining the tubes, help draw the oocyte into the oviduct. If fertilization occurs, it usually takes place in the oviduct, near the ovary. The resulting zygote begins its development into an embryo in the oviduct. The beating cilia and the rhythmic, muscular contractions of the oviduct sweep the egg or the early embryo along the oviduct toward the uterus.

Uterus

The **uterus** is a hollow, muscular organ that before pregnancy is about the size and shape of an inverted pear. The uterus receives and nourishes the developing baby (first called an embryo, but after 8 weeks called a fetus). During pregnancy, as the fetus grows, the uterus expands to about 60 times its original size. After childbirth, the uterus never quite returns to its prepregnancy size.

The wall of the uterus has two main layers: a muscular layer and a lining called the **endometrium** (*endo–,* within; *metr–,* uterus; *–ium,* region). The smooth muscle of the uterine wall contracts rhythmically in waves during childbirth and forces the infant out. The thickness of the endometrium varies over a cycle of approximately 1 month (this cycle is discussed later in this chapter). If an embryo forms, it implants (embeds) in the endometrium, which provides nourishment during early pregnancy. If an embryo does not form, the endometrium completes its cycle by being lost as menstrual flow.

If an embryo implants in an area other than the uterus, the condition is described as an ectopic pregnancy (*ect–,* outside). The most common type of ectopic pregnancy is a tubal pregnancy, in which the embryo implants in an oviduct. A tubal pregnancy cannot be carried to term. It must be surgically terminated because it endangers the mother's life. If the embryo is permitted to continue growing, it will eventually rupture the oviduct, and the rupture can cause the mother to bleed to death internally.

The narrow neck of the uterus, called the **cervix,** projects into the **vagina,** a muscular tube that opens to the outside of the body. The vagina receives the penis during sexual intercourse. Sperm that are deposited in the vagina can enter the uterus through an opening in the cervix and then swim to the oviduct to meet the egg. The vagina is also the birth canal. The infant is pushed through the cervix and then the vagina on its way to greet the world.

External Genitalia

The female reproductive structures that lie outside the vagina are collectively known as the external genitalia or the **vulva.** Two hair-covered folds of skin surround the vaginal opening. The *labia*

TABLE 17.3 Review of Female Reproductive System

Structure	Function
Ovary	Produces eggs and the hormones estrogen and progesterone
Oviducts	Transport ovulated egg (or embryo if fertilization occurred) from ovary to uterus; the usual site of fertilization
Uterus	Receives and nourishes embryo
Vagina	Receives penis during intercourse; serves as birth canal
Clitoris	Contributes to sexual arousal
Breasts	Produce milk

Uterus
- A pear-shaped organ that houses and nourishes the developing baby (the embryo and later the fetus) until birth

Uterine wall
- Muscle layers that stretch to accommodate the developing baby; contract during childbirth to deliver the baby

Endometrium
- The lining of the uterus that is built up and lost each month as menstrual flow; the usual site of implantation

Cervix
- The opening of the uterus that extends into the vagina

Rectum

Vagina
- A muscular tube that receives the penis during sexual intercourse; the birth canal

Oviduct
- One of two ciliated tubes that conduct the egg (or embryo if fertilization occurred) toward the uterus; the usual site of fertilization

Ovary
- One of two glands that produce eggs and sex hormones (estrogen and progesterone)

Urinary bladder

Urethra in side view

Clitoris
- A small organ that is rich in sensory nerves for sexual arousal

Labium minora
- One of the two inner skin folds that are part of the external genitalia

Labium majora
- One of the two outer skin folds that are part of the external genitalia

(a) Side view

Ovary

Oviduct

Uterus

Uterine wall

Endometrium

Cervix

Vagina

(b) Rear view

Mons veneris

Clitoris

Opening to urethra

Opening to vagina

Labium minora

Labium majora

Anus

(c) External genitalia

FIGURE 17.6 The female reproductive system

majora ("big lips") enclose two thinner skin folds, the *labia minora* ("little lips"). The anterior portions of the labia minora form a hood over the *clitoris*. Like the penis, the clitoris has many nerve endings sensitive to touch. During tactile stimulation, the erectile tissue in the clitoris becomes swollen with blood and contributes to a woman's sexual arousal.

Breasts

The *breasts*, or mammary glands, are present in both sexes, but they produce milk to nourish a newborn only in females. Inside

the female breast are 15 to 25 groups of milk-secreting glands. A milk duct drains each group through the nipple. Interspersed around the glands and ducts is fibrous connective tissue that supports the breast. Most of the breast consists of fatty tissue (Figure **17.7**). Breast cancer is the second leading cause of cancer deaths among women (see the Health Issue essay, *Breast Cancer*).

Ovarian Cycle

The changes in the ovary that produce the egg occur in a cycle about 1 month long called the **ovarian cycle**. Although the ovaries

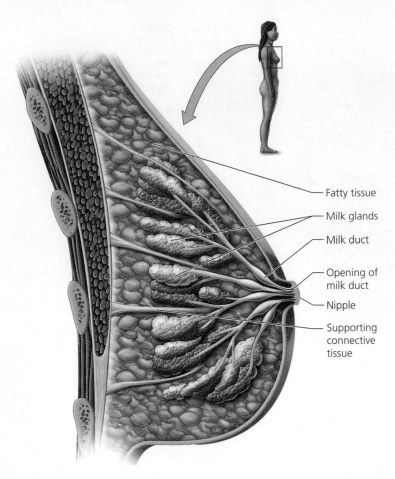

FIGURE 17.7 Breast structure

Labels: Fatty tissue · Milk glands · Milk duct · Opening of milk duct · Nipple · Supporting connective tissue

The inner layer of follicle cells directly surrounds the primary oocyte. The outer layer forms a balloonlike sphere enclosing the fluid and the oocyte. This structure grows rapidly.

- **Formation of a mature follicle.** Within about 10 to 14 days after its development began, the follicle assumes its mature form, called a secondary or Graafian follicle. The primary oocyte then completes the first meiotic division, which it prepared for years earlier. When the primary oocyte divides, it forms two cells of unequal size: a large cell that contains most of the cytoplasm and nutrients, called a *secondary oocyte,* and a tiny cell, called the first *polar body.* The polar body is essentially a garbage bag for one set of chromosomes. It has very few cellular constituents and plays no further role in reproduction. The secondary oocyte is a much larger cell packed with nutrients that will nourish the embryo until it reaches the uterus.

- **Ovulation.** About 12 hours after the secondary oocyte has formed, the mature follicle pops, like a blister, releasing the oocyte mass, which is about the size of the head of a pin. The release of the oocyte from the ovary is called **ovulation.** If a sperm penetrates the secondary oocyte, meiosis advances to completion: the replicate chromosomes are separated. This time, too, the cytoplasm divides unequally. One of the resulting sets of chromosomes goes into a small cell, called the second polar body, and the other set goes into a large cell, the mature *ovum,* or egg. If fertilization does not occur, the egg does not complete meiosis.

- **Formation of the corpus luteum.** The cells that made up the outer sphere of the mature Graafian follicle remain in the ovary, and luteinizing hormone (LH) transforms them into an endocrine structure called the **corpus luteum** (meaning "yellow body"). The corpus luteum secretes both estrogen and progesterone. Unless pregnancy occurs, the corpus luteum degenerates. If pregnancy occurs, the corpus luteum

do not produce mature eggs until a female reaches puberty, the preparations for egg production begin before she is born. Recall that the egg is a haploid cell formed by meiosis, the type of cell division that forms gametes. During fetal development, *oogonia,* which are diploid cells in the ovaries, enlarge and begin to store nutrients. Some begin meiosis by making a copy of their chromosomes (but the copies of each chromosome remain attached to one another). The cells that prepare for meiosis are called *primary oocytes.* (They are immature eggs.) A single layer of flattened cells, called follicle cells, surrounds each primary oocyte. The entire structure is called a primary **follicle.**

Long before her birth, all of a woman's potential eggs have formed. In fact, she may have formed as many as 2 million primary follicles. Only about 700,000 remain when she is born, and the number continues to decrease after birth. The eggs remain in this immature state until she reaches puberty, usually at 10 to 14 years of age. By the time of puberty, a female's lifetime supply of potential eggs has dwindled to between 200,000 and 400,000. Only 400 to 500 of these eggs will ever mature.

Beginning at puberty, some primary follicles, usually one each month, resume their development (Figure **17.8**). The follicle's outer cells begin dividing, forming layers of cells and secreting a fluid that contains estrogen. The ovarian cycle that converts a primary follicle into an egg each month consists of the following steps:

- **Follicle maturation.** The follicle cells continue dividing, and fluid begins to accumulate between them. As the fluid accumulates, the wall of follicle cells splits into two layers.

TABLE 17.4 Hormones Involved in Regulating Female Reproductive Processes

Hormone	Source	Effects
Estrogen	Ovaries (follicle cells and corpus luteum)	Maturation of the egg; development and maintenance of female reproductive structures, secondary sex characteristics; thickens endometrium of uterus in preparation for implantation of embryo; cell division in breast tissue
Progesterone	Ovaries (corpus luteum)	Further prepares uterus for implantation of embryo; maintains endometrium
Follicle-stimulating hormone (FSH)	Anterior pituitary gland (in brain)	Stimulates development of a follicle in the ovary
Luteinizing hormone (LH)	Anterior pituitary gland (in brain)	Triggers ovulation; causes formation of the corpus luteum

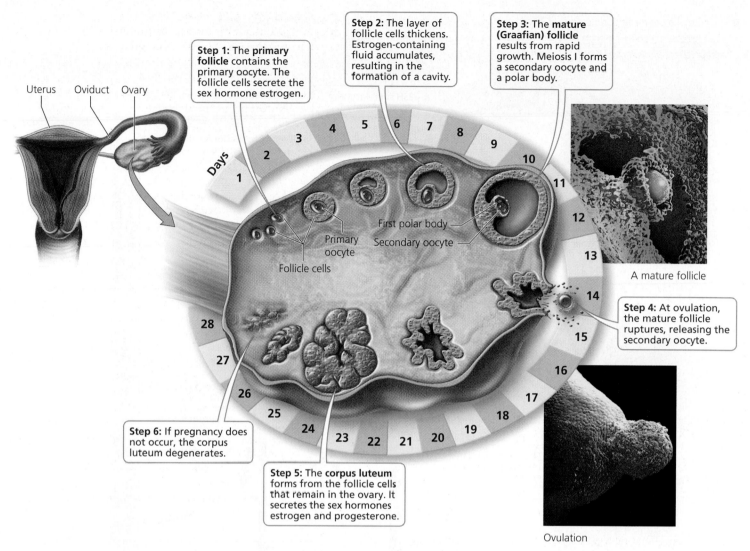

Step 1: The **primary follicle** contains the primary oocyte. The follicle cells secrete the sex hormone estrogen.

Step 2: The layer of follicle cells thickens. Estrogen-containing fluid accumulates, resulting in the formation of a cavity.

Step 3: The **mature (Graafian) follicle** results from rapid growth. Meiosis I forms a secondary oocyte and a polar body.

Step 4: At ovulation, the mature follicle ruptures, releasing the secondary oocyte.

Step 5: The **corpus luteum** forms from the follicle cells that remain in the ovary. It secretes the sex hormones estrogen and progesterone.

Step 6: If pregnancy does not occur, the corpus luteum degenerates.

Uterus   Oviduct   Ovary

Days

Primary oocyte

Follicle cells

First polar body

Secondary oocyte

A mature follicle

Ovulation

FIGURE 17.8 The ovarian cycle. A follicle does not move around the ovary during its development, as depicted here. The steps indicate the sequence of events that occur in a single place in the ovary during the approximately 28-day cycle.

will be maintained by a hormone from the embryo called human chorionic gonadotropin, as we will see later in this chapter.

Coordination of the Ovarian and Uterine Cycles

Because of the events we have been describing, a woman's fertility is cyclic. At approximately monthly intervals, an egg matures and is released from an ovary. Simultaneously, the uterus is readied to receive and nurture the young embryo. These two processes must be coordinated. If fertilization does not occur, the uterine provisions are discarded as menstrual flow. The ovaries and uterus will prepare for fertilization again during the next cycle. The events in the ovary, known as the ovarian cycle, must be closely coordinated with those in the uterus, known as the **uterine cycle** (or the *menstrual cycle*). The length of the uterine cycle may vary from cycle to cycle and from woman to woman. The timing of events within a uterine cycle will vary with the cycle's length. We will describe the events as they might occur in a 28-day cycle.

A female's fertility is governed by hormones (Table **17.4**). Events in both the uterus and the ovary are coordinated by interactions between hormones from the anterior pituitary gland and from the

ovary (Figure **17.9**). The anterior pituitary gland produces follicle-stimulating hormone (FSH) and luteinizing hormone (LH). As in the male, the release of these hormones is regulated by a hormone from the hypothalamus called GnRH. In the female, FSH and LH cause the ovary to release its hormones, estrogen and progesterone. Progesterone and estrogen (except at a very high level) exert negative feedback on the anterior pituitary, which causes the levels of FSH and LH to decline. As a result, the levels of estrogen and progesterone decline, reducing the inhibition on the anterior pituitary gland—and so, the hormones cycle.

Menstruation

Traditionally, the first day of menstrual flow is considered day 1 of the uterine cycle because it is the most easily recognized event in the cycle. The bleeding usually lasts an average of 5 days. During menstruation, the ovarian hormones, estrogen and progesterone, are at their lowest levels, allowing the anterior pituitary gland to produce its hormones, especially FSH. In turn, FSH causes a new egg follicle in the ovary to develop and produce estrogen. (Hence its name, follicle-stimulating hormone.) Thus, even as the uterus loses the endometrial lining it prepared during the previous cycle in

Q *Couples who are trying to conceive a child can purchase kits to help them predict when ovulation will occur, so that intercourse can be timed to increase the chance of becoming pregnant. Which hormone would be the best predictor of ovulation? Why?*

FIGURE 17.9 The ovarian and uterine cycles are coordinated by the interplay of hormones from the anterior pituitary gland and the ovary. The timing of events shown is for a 28-day cycle.

A *LH, because the surge in LH levels triggers ovulation.*

which no egg was fertilized, the egg that will be released in the next cycle is developing.

Endometrium thickens

As the egg follicle develops, it produces an increasing amount of estrogen. Estrogen causes the cells in the endometrial lining of the uterus to divide. These cells store nutrients to nourish a future embryo during its early stages of development. In addition, estrogen inhibits the release of FSH through a negative feedback cycle (see Chapter 10). When the egg and follicle are nearly mature, the

estrogen level rises rapidly and causes a sudden and spectacular release of LH (and FSH) from the anterior pituitary gland.[2]

Ovulation and formation of corpus luteum (in ovary)

The LH surge causes several important events. It causes the egg to undergo its first meiotic division. Next, LH triggers ovulation, and the egg bursts out of the ovary to begin its journey along the

[2]Above a critical level, estrogen exerts a positive feedback on the brain and anterior pituitary gland.

TABLE 17.5 Ovarian and Uterine Cycles

Ovarian Cycle		Uterine Cycle	
Approximate Timing in 28-Day Cycle	Events	Approximate Timing in 28-Day Cycle	Events
Days 1–13	Follicle develops, caused by FSH Follicle cells produce estrogen	Day 1	Onset of menstrual flow (breakdown of endometrium)
Day 14	Ovulation is triggered by LH surge	Day 6	Endometrium begins to get thicker
Days 15–21	Corpus luteum forms and secretes estrogen and progesterone	Days 15–23	Endometrium is further prepared for implantation of the embryo by estrogen and progesterone
Days 22–28	Corpus luteum degenerates, causing estrogen and progesterone level to decline	Days 24–28	Endometrium begins to degenerate owing to declining maintenance by progesterone

oviduct. Continued secretion of LH then transforms the remaining follicle cells into the corpus luteum. The corpus luteum continues the estrogen secretion begun by the follicle cells and, importantly, also secretes progesterone.

Endometrium further prepared for implantation

Together, estrogen and progesterone make the endometrial lining of the uterus a hospitable place for the embryo. The blood supply to the endometrium increases. Uterine glands develop and then secrete a mucous material that can nourish the young embryo when it arrives in the uterus.

The rising estrogen and progesterone levels inhibit pituitary secretion of FSH and LH. As FSH levels decline, the development of new follicles is inhibited.

Corpus luteum degenerates

If fertilization does not occur, the corpus luteum will degenerate within about 2 weeks (14 days plus or minus 2 days, regardless of the length of the menstrual cycle). The degeneration of the corpus luteum results in falling levels of estrogen and progesterone.

Menstruation begins again

Progesterone is essential to the maintenance of the endometrium. As progesterone levels drop because of the degeneration of the corpus luteum, the blood vessels nourishing the endometrial cells collapse. The cells of the endometrium then die and are sloughed off, along with mucus and blood, as menstrual flow. No longer inhibited by estrogen and progesterone, FSH and LH levels begin to climb. Thus, the cycle begins again (Table **17.5**).

If the egg is fertilized, a hormone from the embryo, called *human chorionic gonadotropin* (*HCG*), maintains the corpus luteum. If implantation occurs, HCG will prevent the degeneration of the corpus luteum, keeping estrogen and progesterone levels high enough to prevent endometrial shedding. HCG is detectable in the mother's blood within 7 to 9 days after fertilization and in her urine less than 2 weeks after fertilization. Between the second and third month of development, the placenta has developed sufficiently to take over the production of estrogen and progesterone during the rest of the pregnancy. The corpus luteum then degenerates.

We have seen that reproductive processes in males and females are controlled by the interplay of hormones. Unfortunately, we humans have polluted our environment with chemicals that can interfere with the normal effects of reproductive hormones (see Environmental Issue, *Environmental Estrogens*).

Menopause

A woman's fertility usually peaks when she is in her twenties and then gradually declines. By the time she reaches 45 to 55 years of age, few of the potential eggs prepared before birth remain in the ovaries. Those that do remain become increasingly less responsive to FSH and LH, the hormones that cause egg development and ovulation. The ovaries, therefore, gradually stop producing eggs, and the levels of estrogen and progesterone fall. During this time, menstrual cycles become increasingly irregular. Eventually ovulation and menstruation stop completely, at a stage in a woman's life called **menopause.**

The drop in estrogen levels has some physiological effects that can range in severity from annoying to life threatening. At one end of the scale is the loss of a layer of fat that was formerly promoted by estrogen. This loss results in a reduction in breast size and the appearance of wrinkles. Estrogen also plays an important role in regulating a woman's body thermostat. So, as estrogen levels fall, many women experience hot flashes—waves of warmth spreading upward from the trunk to the face. In addition, the absence of estrogen can cause vaginal dryness that can make sexual intercourse painful. Furthermore, without estrogen, the male hormones produced by the adrenal gland predominate and can cause facial hair to grow.

More serious problems associated with the estrogen deficit that accompanies menopause include an increased risk of diseases of the heart and blood vessels. Estrogen offers some protection against atherosclerosis, a condition in which fatty deposits clog the arteries. Thus, after menopause, this protective effect on the heart is lost. Another serious problem stems from the role estrogen plays in the body's ability to absorb calcium from the digestive system and to deposit it in bone. Without calcium, bone becomes weak and porous—a condition known as osteoporosis (discussed in Chapter 5). See the Health Issue essay in Chapter 10, *Is It Hot in Here, or Is It Me?* for a discussion on hormone replacement therapy and menopause.

Disorders of the Female Reproductive System

Premenstrual syndrome (*PMS*) is a collection of symptoms that appear in some women 7 to 10 days before their period begins. These symptoms include depression, irritability, fatigue, and headaches.

Breast Cancer

Breast cancer usually begins with abnormal growth of the cells lining the milk ducts of the breast, but it sometimes begins in the milk glands themselves. Some types of breast cancer aggressively invade surrounding tissues. Typically, cancerous cells begin to spread when the tumor is about 20 mm (about 3/4 in.) in diameter. At this point, they break through the membranes of the ducts or glands where they initially formed and move into the connective tissue of the breast. They may then move into the lymphatic vessels or blood vessels permeating the breast or into both; the vessels may transport the cells throughout the body.

Detecting Breast Cancer

Early detection is a woman's best defense against breast cancer. A monthly breast self-exam (BSE) is helpful in detecting a lump early (Figure **17.A**). If a woman begins doing regular breast self-exams in early adulthood, she becomes familiar with the consistency of her breast tissue. With this experience, it is easy to notice changes that might be signs of breast cancer.

Mammograms, which are x-rays of breast tissue, can also help detect early breast cancer because they can reveal a tumor too small to be felt as a lump. A tumor large enough to be felt contains a billion or more cells—a few of which may already have spread from the tumor to other tissues of the body. After cancer cells spread, the woman's chance of survival decreases dramatically. An added benefit of mammograms is that they can detect tumors that are small enough to be removed by a type of surgery called lumpectomy, which removes the lump but spares the breast. At later stages of breast cancer, the entire breast may have to be removed in a type of surgery called mastectomy.

Risk Factors

Many of the factors that increase a woman's risk of breast cancer cannot be altered. One of these is the genes she inherited from her parents. At least two known genes increase a woman's risk of breast cancer. Although only 5% to 10% of all breast cancers are related to these genes, the unlucky women who inherit either of them have an 85% chance of developing breast cancer at some point in life.

Exposure to estrogen is a common thread running through the tapestry of risk factors associated with breast cancer. During each menstrual cycle, estrogen stimulates breast cells to begin dividing in preparation for milk production, in case the egg is fertilized. Excessive estrogen exposure, therefore, may be a factor that pushes cell division to a rate characteristic of cancer.

One factor that influences estrogen levels is the number of times a woman ovulates during her lifetime, because estrogen is produced by both the maturing ovarian follicle and the corpus luteum. The number of times a woman ovulates is, in turn, affected by factors such as the following.

1. **Age when menstruation begins.** Ovulation usually occurs in each menstrual cycle. Thus, the younger a woman is when menstruation begins, the more opportunities there are for ovulation and the greater her exposure to estrogen.

2. **Menopause after age 55.** The older a woman is at menopause, the more menstrual cycles she is likely to have experienced. Estrogen levels are low and ovulation ceases after menopause.

3. **Childlessness and late age at first pregnancy.** Ovulation does not occur during pregnancy. Thus, pregnancy gives the ovaries a rest. Furthermore, the hormonal patterns of pregnancy appear to transform breast tissue in a way that protects against cancer. As a result, delaying pregnancy until after age 30 or remaining childless increases a woman's risk of developing breast cancer later in life.

4. **Breast-feeding.** Nursing may guard against breast cancer by blocking ovulation or by causing physiological changes that leave the breast tissue more resistant to cancer-producing chemicals in the environment. Women who breast-feed their infants have a 20% lower risk of developing breast cancer at a young age—before they reach

---

Some researchers suggest that a progesterone deficiency is to blame for the symptoms of PMS. Progesterone has a calming effect on the brain. It also decreases fluid retention. As progesterone levels plummet in the days just before menstruation, the nervous system may be stimulated and fluids may be retained. Fluid retention causes an uncomfortable, bloated feeling.

Treatments for PMS are varied. For women whose symptoms are severe, drugs that elevate the levels of serotonin—a neurotransmitter in the brain (Chapter 7)—are administered. Some women with milder symptoms are helped by changes in diet. Caffeine, alcohol, fat, and sodium should be avoided. On the other hand, foods high in calcium, potassium, manganese, and magnesium should be increased. Aerobic exercise for at least half an hour a day stimulates the release of enkephalins and endorphins (brain chemicals that produce pleasure), which may provide some relief.

Prostaglandins, chemicals used in communication between cells in many parts of the body, are the primary cause of *menstrual cramps*. Endometrial cells produce prostaglandins that, among other things, make the smooth muscle cells of the uterus contract, causing cramps. High levels of prostaglandins can cause sustained contractions, called muscle spasms, of the uterus. These muscle spasms may cut down blood flow—and therefore, the oxygen supply to the uterine muscles—and result in pain.

Endometriosis is a condition in which tissue from the lining of the uterus is found outside the uterine cavity—commonly in the oviducts, on the ovaries, or on the outside surface of the uterus, the bladder, or the rectum. In these cases, the endometrial tissue has moved out the open ends of the oviducts to the abdominal cavity. Endometrial tissue, wherever it is, grows and breaks down with the hormonal changes that occur during each menstrual cycle. These cyclic changes can cause extreme pain. Moreover, women with endometriosis often have difficulty becoming pregnant because endometrial tissue may block the oviduct or coat the ovary.

Step 1: Stand in front of the mirror and look at each breast to see if there is a lump, a depression, a difference in texture, or any other change in appearance.

Step 2: Get to know how your breasts look. Be especially alert for any changes in the nipples' appearance.

Step 3: Raise both arms and check for any swelling or dimpling in the skin of your breasts.

Step 4: Lie down with a pillow under your shoulder and put your arm behind your head. Perform a manual breast examination. With the nipple as the center, divide your breast into imaginary quadrants.

Step 5: With the pads of the fingers, make firm circular movements over each quadrant, feeling for unusual lumps or areas of tenderness. When you reach the upper, outer quadrant of your breast, continue toward your armpit. Press down in all directions.

Step 6: Feel your nipple for any change in size and shape. Squeeze your nipple to see if there is any discharge. Repeat from step 4 on the other breast.

FIGURE 17.A A monthly breast self-exam can help a woman find lumps in her breast before they have spread to surrounding tissue. It also makes a woman familiar with the consistency of her breast tissue and therefore able to detect changes in consistency that might indicate cancer.

menopause—than do women who bottle-feed their infants.

5. **Exercise.** Even moderate exercise can suppress ovulation (and thus estrogen levels) in adolescents and women in their twenties (but, unfortunately, exercise is not as likely to suppress ovulation in older women).

Other factors may also influence estrogen levels. For instance, obese women have higher estrogen levels than do thin ones because estrogen is produced in fat cells as well as by the ovaries. Indeed, obesity—especially if the fat is carried above the waist—translates to a threefold elevated risk of breast cancer.

Stages of the Human Sexual Response

In both men and women, sexual arousal and sexual intercourse involve two basic physiological changes: certain tissues fill with blood (vasocongestion) and certain muscles undergo sustained or rhythmic contractions (myotonia). However, men and women differ in which tissues fill with blood and which muscles contract. The sequence of events that accompanies sexual arousal and intercourse is called the sexual response cycle. Let's consider the four stages of the human response cycle in men and in women.

1. **Excitement.** During the excitement phase of the sexual response cycle, sexual arousal increases. This stage occurs during foreplay, the activities that precede sexual intercourse, and prepares the penis and vagina for intercourse. In a male, blood fills the spongy tissue of the penis, which becomes erect, as described earlier. In a female, blood flow to the breasts, nipples, labia, and clitoris causes these structures to swell. Partly due to an increase in blood flow, the vaginal walls seep fluid that serves as a lubricant, which makes the insertion of the penis easier. In both men and women, muscle contraction can cause the erection of nipples and tension in the arms and legs. Breathing rate and heart rate increase.

2. **Plateau.** During the plateau stage, sexual arousal is maintained at a high level. The changes that began during the first phase will continue through the plateau stage until orgasm. In men, increased blood flow causes the testes to enlarge, and muscle contraction pulls them closer to the body. In women, increased blood flow causes the outer third of the vagina to enlarge and the clitoris to retract under the clitoral hood. In both men and women, breathing rate and heart rate continue to increase. Muscle spasms may begin in the hands, feet, and face.

3. **Orgasm.** The peak of the sexual response cycle, orgasm, is brief but usually intensely pleasurable. In both sexes, orgasm is characterized by muscle contractions of the reproductive structures.

Environmental Estrogens

According to the International Union of Pure and Applied Chemistry (IUPAC), certain pollutants are causing gender changes in certain animals, including alligators, polar bears, seals, and some fish. Some of these pollutants, such as the pesticide DDT and bisphenol A (a breakdown product of plastics), mimic the effects of estrogen. Others, such as certain PCBs (polychlorinated biphenyls) that were once used in coolants and plastics, block the effects of natural estrogens. Some pollutants bind to receptors for androgens and can feminize a male by blocking the action of natural androgens. There are at least 45 environmental contaminants reported to cause changes in reproductive systems.

PCBs may be found in freshwater fish and some farmed salmon. Farm animals given steroids to boost growth convert the steroids to estrogen-like substances that are passed to humans when they eat the tainted meat. Certain pesticides also break down to estrogenic compounds that can be consumed by humans.

Environmental estrogens may also leach into foods stored in certain plastic containers.

There is already evidence that chemicals with estrogenic properties, consumed as contaminants in food, can accumulate in humans. For example, seal and beluga whale blubber, which are loaded with DDT and PCBs, are a common component of the diet of the Inuit, a native people living in northern Quebec. The breast milk of Inuit women who eat blubber is four to seven times higher in estrogenic pesticides than is the breast milk of women in Quebec who do not eat blubber.

Sex hormones choreograph so many biological activities—development, anatomy, physiology, and behavior—that environmental estrogens can play havoc with human reproduction in myriad ways. Some researchers argue that synthetic estrogenic chemicals cause cancers of the reproductive system, such as breast cancer and testicular cancer, as well as a variety of noncancerous effects, including the development of female characteristics in males, decreased sperm counts, higher probability of endometriosis in women, and weakened immune systems. Although evidence of effects on other animal species is mounting, studies of effects on humans remain contradictory.

The developing fetus is probably the most sensitive of all biological entities, and as its organ systems take shape, the proper balance of sex hormones is critical. Too much estrogen at the wrong time can cause a genetically male fetus to have the physical appearance of a female, including feminized sex organs, or to exhibit female behaviors later in life.

It is clear that we have polluted our environment with chemicals that have the potential of altering reproductive anatomy, physiology, and behavior. It is also clear that this pollution is already affecting various animal species. What is not clear is how great a threat these chemicals are to humans, or how we humans will decide to cope with this kind of self-induced problem.

Questions to Consider

IUPAC recommends research and monitoring of environmental estrogens. Implementing these recommendations would be costly.

1. As a taxpayer, are you willing to pay for these precautions?
2. Would you vote for a political candidate who supported their implementation?

In men, ejaculation occurs during orgasm. Ejaculation takes place in two stages. In the first stage, contractions of glands and ducts in the reproductive system force sperm and the secretions of the accessory glands to the urethra. During the second stage of ejaculation, the urethra contracts and semen is forcefully expelled from the penis. Orgasm in women involves rhythmic muscle contractions in the vagina and uterus. Some women experience orgasm rarely or not at all, and others can experience orgasm repeatedly. The absence of orgasm does not affect a woman's ability to become pregnant.

4. **Resolution.** During the resolution stage, the body slowly returns to its normal level of functioning. Resolution usually takes longer in women than it does in men. Many women are capable of becoming aroused again during the resolution phase, but men usually experience an interval during the resolution stage when it is impossible for them to achieve another erection or orgasm.

Birth Control

Sexual activity carries with it the risk of both unwanted pregnancy and the possibility of contracting a sexually transmitted disease (STD; many STDs are discussed in Chapter 17a). The method couples use (if any) to avoid pregnancy influences the chances of

contracting STDs. For this reason, as we discuss various means of contraception, we will also consider whether they reduce the risk of spreading sexually transmitted infections.

Abstinence

Abstinence—not having intercourse at all—is the most reliable way to avoid both pregnancy and the spread of STDs. However, abstinence is not always used as a means of contraception.

Sterilization

Well before the end of their reproductive life spans, most people have had all the children they want. Other than abstinence, *sterilization* is the most effective way to ensure that pregnancy does not occur. However, unlike abstinence, sterilization offers no protection against STDs.

Sterilization in men usually involves an operation called a *vasectomy,* in which the vas deferens on each side is cut to prevent sperm from leaving the man's body. The procedure usually takes about 20 minutes and can be performed in a physician's office under local anesthesia. The physician makes small openings in the scrotum through which each vas deferens can be pulled and cut; a small segment is removed, and at least one end is sealed shut. Because sperm make up only about 1% of the semen, the volume of semen the man ejaculates is not noticeably reduced. His interest in sex is not lessened, because testosterone, which is responsible for the sex drive, is still released from the interstitial cells of the testis and carried around the body in the blood.

The most common method of female sterilization, *tubal ligation,* involves blocking the oviducts to prevent the egg and sperm from meeting. Commonly, the tubes are cut and the ends seared shut or mechanically blocked with clips or rings. Tubal ligation is frequently done using a procedure called *laparoscopy,* in which two small incisions are made in the abdominal cavity and the operation is visualized through a telescopic lens inserted through one of them. Laparoscopy is generally performed in a hospital under general anesthesia. Because the abdominal cavity is opened, the risk of infection is greater after tubal ligation than it is after a vasectomy. A woman continues to menstruate after a tubal ligation, because the ovarian hormones continue to be produced in a cyclic manner.

A newer method of sterilization for women does not require an incision. Instead, a small wire coil is inserted into the oviducts through the vagina, cervix, and uterus. During the next 3 months, scar tissue forms around the coil and blocks the passage of sperm.

Sterilization should be considered permanent even though it is sometimes possible to reverse the procedure. At best, the reversal procedure is expensive and requires that the surgeon have special training in microsurgical techniques. Even then, success is not guaranteed.

Hormonal Contraception

Hormonal contraception is currently available only to females. There are two basic types: the methods that combine estrogen and progesterone and the progesterone-only means of contraception.

Combination estrogen and progesterone contraception

Several forms of birth control combine synthetic forms of estrogen and progesterone. Each of these methods works by mimicking the effects of natural hormones that would ordinarily be produced by the ovaries. Among these effects is the suppression of the release of FSH and LH from the anterior pituitary gland. Without these pituitary hormones, the egg does not mature and is not released from the ovary.

When most people speak about "the pill," they are referring to the combination birth control pill, so named because it contains synthetic forms of both estrogen and progesterone. A hormone-containing "combination" birth control pill is taken daily for 3 weeks, followed by a week of daily pills without hormones.

Over the past few years, additional methods of combined hormonal contraception have been developed. There is a vaginal ring (NuvaRing) and a skin patch (Ortho Evra), each of which slowly releases hormones for the 3 weeks it is in place (Figures **17.10a** and 17.10b). When a woman uses the birth control pill, the vaginal ring, or the patch, she menstruates during the week in which hormones are not administered. Women who have difficulty remembering to take a pill each day may prefer these newer options. In addition, there are regimens of hormonal contraception (Seasonale and Seasonique) in which estrogen and progesterone pills are taken for 84 days, followed by a week of placebo pills or low-dose estrogen pills. A woman who is using Seasonale or Seasonique menstruates only four times a year, while taking the placebo pills. Lybrel is a regimen of pills that are taken continuously for one year, so that a woman menstruates only once a year.

For most healthy, nonsmoking women younger than 35 years of age, combination hormonal methods are extremely safe means of contraception. Nonetheless, a small number of hormonal contraceptive users do die each year from a complication, so the possibility of such complications should be recognized. The risk increases

(a) Hormone-containing skin patch

(b) Vaginal contraceptive ring

(c) Intrauterine device (IUD)

(d) Diaphragm and spermicidal cream or jelly

(e) Male latex condom

(f) Female polyurethane condom

FIGURE 17.10 Selected methods of birth control

with age and with cigarette smoking. Hormonal contraception and cigarette smoking can both increase blood pressure and the risk of abnormal blood clot formation. Together, they have a greater effect than either does alone. Problems with the circulatory system are the most important of the serious (sometimes fatal) complications of pill use. Most pill-associated deaths are caused by heart attack or stroke that results when the blood supply to the heart or a region of the brain is blocked. Hormonal contraception also increases the risk of abnormal blood clot formation.

Women who use combination hormonal contraceptives have a greater risk of catching certain STDs from an infected partner than do women who use other forms of birth control or no birth control at all. One way the pill increases the likelihood of transmission of these diseases is by making the vaginal environment more alkaline, a condition that favors the growth of bacteria that cause gonorrhea and chlamydia. Another reason that women on the pill have a greater risk of getting STDs is that it makes the user's cervix more vulnerable to disease-causing organisms.

Progesterone-only contraception

The most popular form of progesterone-only contraception is an injection (Depo-Provera) given every 3 months. Progesterone injections are an extremely effective means of contraception. There is also a progesterone-only pill (POP; also called the mini-pill). As when using the combined birth control pill, a woman must take the minipill faithfully every day. POPs are generally less effective than the combined pill. A progesterone-releasing in-trauterine device (IUD; discussed shortly) is also available. A prog-esterone-containing implant, Implanon, was approved by the Food and Drug Administration in mid-2006. It is a slender, flexible silicone rod about the size of a matchstick. An Implanon rod, when inserted under the skin in a woman's upper arm, is barely visible and provides extremely effective protection for three years as the progesterone slowly diffuses out of the capsules.

Progesterone-only contraceptives can prevent pregnancy in several ways. All types may prevent ovulation, but they vary in their ability to do so. They all cause thickening of cervical mucus, which hampers the passage of sperm to reach the egg. In addition, because estrogen is not used in this contraceptive, the en-dometrium is not prepared properly for the implantation of an embryo should fertilization occur. An important drawback is that, as with all hormonal contraceptives, progesterone-only contracep-tives provide no protection against sexually transmitted diseases.

what would you do?

Clinical trials are under way to test the safety and effectiveness of various forms of hormonal birth control implants designed to be used by males. The hormones reduce sperm levels enough to make a man infertile, and sperm production resumes within a few months without the hormones. The implants do not protect against STDs. If you were a male in a long-term relationship, would you volunteer for this study? If you were the female in this relationship, would you want your partner to participate in the study? What criteria would you use to decide?

Intrauterine Devices

An *intrauterine device (IUD)* is a small device that is inserted into the uterus by a physician to prevent pregnancy (Figure 17.10c). It can be left in place for several years and should be removed by a physician. An IUD is highly effective in preventing pregnancy. It can interfere with both fertilization and implantation. However, IUDs offer no protection against the spread of sexually transmit-ted diseases. In the future, there may be a male equivalent of an IUD, called an Intra Vas Device, which is a plug inserted into the vas deferens to block the passage of sperm.

A risk associated with using an IUD is pelvic inflammatory disease, which is a general term for any bacterial infection of the pelvic organs. The risk is greatest in the weeks following IUD inser-tion, because disease-causing organisms, usually sexually transmit-ted organisms, can enter the uterus from the vagina at this time. The risk of pelvic infection due to an IUD is low—less than 1%. However, if it does occur, it can lead to sterility or ectopic pregnancy.

Barrier Methods

Barrier methods of contraception include the diaphragm, cervical cap, contraceptive sponge, and male and female condoms. Meth-ods in this category work, as their name suggests, by creating a barrier between the egg and sperm.

A *diaphragm* is a dome-shaped, soft rubber cup containing a flexible ring. It is inserted into the vagina before intercourse so that it covers the cervix, preventing sperm from passing through (Figure 17.10d). A *cervical cap* is smaller than a diaphragm and fits

snugly over the cervix. Before the diaphragm or cervical cap is in-serted, spermicidal cream or jelly should be added to the inner surface. Because a diaphragm covers the cervix and the top of the vagina, it offers some, though limited, protection to the woman against important STDs, including chlamydia and gonorrhea. By protecting the cervix from the virus that causes genital warts, many types of which cause cervical cancer, it also lessens the risk of cervical cancer. A cervical cap, being smaller, offers no protec-tion against STDs.

Unlike a diaphragm or cervical cap, a contraceptive sponge or condom can be purchased without a prescription. A *contraceptive sponge* is a small sponge that contains a spermicide. One side of the sponge has an indentation that the cervix fits into. The other side has a strap that makes removal easier. To activate the spermicide, the sponge must be thoroughly moistened before use. It is then inserted and offers protection against pregnancy for the next 24 hours.

The *male condom* is a thin sheath of latex, polyurethane, or natural membranes ("skin") that is rolled onto an erect penis, where it fits like a glove (Figure 17.10e). The sperm are trapped within the condom and cannot enter the vagina. The effectiveness of condoms in preventing pregnancy depends largely on how con-sistently they are used.

Other than complete abstinence from sexual activity, the la-tex condom is the best means of preventing the spread of STDs available today. The skin condoms may offer greater sensitivity; but they do allow some microorganisms, particularly viruses, to pass through. Latex has no pores, so microorganisms cannot pass through it. Health advisors highly recommend that people who might be exposed to STDs use a latex condom for disease protec-tion, even if they are already using another means of birth control to prevent pregnancy. Keep in mind, however, that a condom can prevent disease transmission only between the body surfaces it separates. Diseases can still be spread by contact between other, unprotected body surfaces that are vulnerable to infection.

The *female condom* is a loose sac of polyurethane, a clear plas-tic that resembles the type used in a food-storage bag. At each end of the sac is a flexible ring that helps hold the device in place (Figure 17.10f). The female condom does reduce the risk of spreading sexually transmitted infections. Female condoms offer a barrier against STDs and prevent pregnancy for women who can-not count on their male partner to use condoms.

stop and think

A latex condom provides an impenetrable barrier to disease-causing organisms. Yet, studies indicate that women who use a diaphragm or vaginal sponge routinely have lower rates of STDs than do women who rely on their male partners to use a condom. What might explain this seemingly illogical difference?

Spermicidal Preparations

Spermicidal preparations consist of a sperm-killing chemical (nonoxynol-9) in some form of carrier, such as foam, cream, jelly, film, or tablet. When spermicide is used without any other means of contraception, foams are the most effective option because they act immediately and disperse more evenly than other preparations. The sperm-killing effect of any spermicide lasts for about 1 hour after the product has been activated. Laboratory tests have shown that nonoxynol-9 kills the organisms responsible for many STDs. However, this chemical also damages the cells lining the vagina, and this damage could increase a woman's susceptibility to STDs.

Fertility Awareness

Fertility awareness, which also goes by the names of *natural family planning* and the *rhythm method,* is a way to reduce the risk of pregnancy by avoiding intercourse on all days on which sperm and egg might meet. This sounds easier than it is. Sperm can live in the female reproductive tract for 2 to 5 days, but the lower value is most likely. An egg lives only 12 to 24 hours after ovulation. Consequently, there are only 4 days in each cycle during which fertilization might occur. But which 4 days? Therein lies the problem. It is difficult enough to pinpoint when ovulation occurs, much less predict it several days in advance. The situation is not entirely hopeless, however. There are several ways for a woman to track her menstrual cycle: the calendar, body temperature, and cervical mucus. All of these methods require training to be used effectively.

Emergency Contraception

Emergency contraception, or the so-called morning-after pill, is a means of contraception that can actually be used in the *first few days* after unprotected intercourse. Doctors have prescribed birth control pills and inserted IUDs as emergency contraception for decades, but only recently have two pills specifically marketed for this use become available in the United States. One type (Preven) combines estrogen and progesterone. The second type (Plan B) contains only progesterone. With either type, the first dose should be taken within 3 to 5 days of unprotected intercourse and the second 12 hours later. Scientists do not fully understand the precise mechanisms of action; possible explanations for the pill's efficacy include inhibition or delay of ovulation, prevention of fertilization, thickening of cervical mucus, and alteration of the endometrium, making it an inhospitable place for implantation of the young embryo. Plan B can be purchased over the counter in a pharmacy by women 18 years of age or older.

exploring further

In this chapter, we have seen how the male and female reproductive systems function to produce offspring. Unfortunately, during sexual intimacy, the vulnerable surfaces of certain parts of the reproductive system come into contact, potentially allowing sexually transmitted organisms to spread. We explore this topic further in the next chapter.

highlighting the concepts

Gonads (p. 345)

- The gonads (testes and ovaries) are the reproductive structures that produce the gametes (sperm and eggs), as well as sex hormones. Male testes produce the sex hormone testosterone. Female ovaries produce the sex hormones estrogen and progesterone. A sperm and egg fuse at fertilization, producing a cell called a zygote that under the right circumstances will develop into a new individual.

Male and Female Reproductive Roles (p. 345)

- A male produces a large number of sperm and delivers them to the female reproductive system. A female usually produces only one nutrient-filled egg during each approximately month-long interval. The female also nourishes and protects the developing baby (the embryo and later the fetus) in her uterus.

Form and Function of the Male Reproductive System (pp. 345–350)

- The male reproductive system is composed of the testes, a series of ducts (the epididymis, vas deferens, and urethra), accessory glands (the prostate, seminal vesicles, and bulbourethral glands), and the penis.
- The testes are located outside the body cavity in a sac called the scrotum, which helps regulate the temperature of the testes to ensure proper sperm development.
- Within the seminiferous tubules of the testes, the production of gametes, called spermatogenesis, is a continuous process. Sperm are haploid gametes produced by meiosis.
- After leaving the seminiferous tubules, sperm mature and are stored in the epididymis. At ejaculation, sperm travel through the vas deferens and the urethra to leave the body.
- Semen is the fluid released when a man ejaculates. Most of the semen consists of the secretions of the accessory glands.
- The penis transfers sperm to the female during sexual intercourse. Erectile dysfunction is the inability to achieve or maintain an erection. There are several options for treatment.

- Each sperm has three distinct regions. The head of the sperm contains the male's genetic contribution to the next generation. The midpiece is packed with mitochondria, which produce ATP to power movement. The whiplike tail propels the sperm to the egg.
- In males, the hormone testosterone is produced by the interstitial cells, which are located within the testes between the seminiferous tubules.
- Male reproductive processes are regulated by an interplay of hormones from the anterior pituitary gland in the brain (LH and FSH), from the hypothalamus (GnRH), and from the testes (testosterone and inhibin).

Form and Function of the Female Reproductive System (pp. 350–355)

- The female reproductive system consists of the ovaries, oviducts, uterus, vagina, and external genitalia.
- The ovaries produce eggs and the sex hormones estrogen and progesterone.
- The oviducts transport the immature egg, zygote, and then the early embryo to the uterus. Fertilization usually occurs in the oviduct.
- The uterus supports the growth of the developing baby (embryo and then fetus). The embryo implants in the lining of the uterus, the endometrium, which provides nourishment during development. The muscular wall of the uterus allows the uterus to stretch as the fetus grows, and contractions of the muscle force the baby out of the uterus during childbirth. The cervix is the opening of the uterus.
- The female breasts produce milk to nourish the baby after childbirth.
- The events of the ovarian cycle lead to the release of an egg. A female is born with a finite number of primary follicles. A primary follicle is a primary oocyte (an immature egg) surrounded by a single layer of follicle cells. The primary oocytes will remain in this state until puberty, when (usually) one each month will resume development and be ovulated as a secondary oocyte.

- Hormones from the pituitary gland (FSH and LH) and from the ovary (estrogen and progesterone) regulate the ovarian cycle (which prepares an egg for fertilization) and the uterine or menstrual cycle (which prepares the endometrium of the uterus for implantation of the embryo). However, if the egg is fertilized, the young embryo produces human chorionic gonadotropin (HCG), which maintains the corpus luteum. HCG is the hormone that pregnancy tests detect.
- At menopause, which usually occurs between the ages of 45 and 55, menstruation and ovulation stop. As a result, the levels of estrogen and progesterone drop. Menopause has many psychological and physiological effects on a woman's body.

Disorders of the Female Reproductive System (pp. 355–356)

- Premenstrual syndrome (PMS), a collection of symptoms that occur in some women several days before their period begins, may be caused by low levels of progesterone or of the brain chemical serotonin. Menstrual cramps are caused by prostaglandins, which make muscles contract.
- Endometriosis is a condition in which endometrial tissue is found outside the uterus.

Stages of the Human Sexual Response (pp. 357–358)

- The human sexual response is the sequence of events that occur during sexual intercourse. This cycle consists of four phases: excitement (increased arousal), plateau (continued arousal), orgasm (climax), and resolution (return to a normal level of functioning).

Birth Control (pp. 358–361)

- Abstinence (refraining from intercourse) and sterilization (vasectomy or tubal ligation) are the most effective ways to prevent pregnancy. Hormonal contraception (combined estrogen plus progesterone or progesterone-only methods) interferes with the regulation of reproductive processes. An intrauterine device interferes with fertilization and implantation. Barrier methods of contraception (the diaphragm, cervical cap, contraceptive sponge, and male or female condom) prevent the union of sperm and egg. Spermicidal preparations kill sperm. Natural family planning (the rhythm method) consists of abstinence at times when fertilization could occur.
- Morning-after pills are emergency contraception that can reduce the risk of an unwanted pregnancy resulting from unprotected intercourse.

recognizing key terms

gonad *p. 345*	scrotum *p. 346*	gonadotropin-releasing	vagina *p. 350*
gamete *p. 345*	seminiferous tubule *p. 347*	hormone (GnRH) *p. 350*	vulva *p. 350*
testes *p. 345*	epididymis *p. 347*	luteinizing hormone (LH)	ovarian cycle *p. 351*
sperm *p. 345*	vas deferens *p. 347*	*p. 350*	follicle *p. 352*
testosterone *p. 345*	semen *p. 347*	follicle-stimulating hormone	ovulation *p. 352*
ovary *p. 345*	prostate gland *p. 347*	(FSH) *p. 350*	corpus luteum *p. 352*
egg *p. 345*	seminal vesicles *p. 347*	oviduct *p. 350*	uterine cycle (menstrual cycle)
estrogen *p. 345*	bulbourethral gland *p. 347*	uterus *p. 350*	*p. 353*
progesterone *p. 345*	penis *p. 348*	endometrium *p. 350*	menopause *p. 355*
fertilization *p. 345*	acrosome *p. 348*	cervix *p. 350*	

reviewing the concepts

1. Name the male and female gonads. What are the functions of these organs? *p. 345*
2. How is the temperature maintained in the testes? Why is temperature control important? *p. 346*
3. Trace the path of sperm from their site of production to their release from the body, naming each tube the sperm pass through. *p. 347*
4. Name the male accessory glands and give their functions. *p. 347*
5. What is the function of the penis in reproduction? Describe the process by which the penis becomes erect. *p. 348*
6. Name and describe the functions of the three regions of a sperm cell. *pp. 348–349*
7. List the hormones from the hypothalamus, the anterior pituitary gland, and the testes that are important in the control of sperm production. Explain the interactions between these hormones. *pp. 349–350*

8. What are the two main layers in the wall of the uterus? *p. 350*
9. List the major structures of the female reproductive system and give their functions. *p. 350*
10. What is an ectopic pregnancy? Why is it dangerous to the mother's health? *p. 350*
11. Describe the structure of female breasts. What is their function? *p. 351*
12. Describe the ovarian cycle. Include in your description primary oocytes, primary follicles, mature Graafian follicles, and the corpus luteum. *pp. 351–353*
13. Describe the interplay of hormones from the anterior pituitary and from the ovaries that is responsible for the menstrual cycle. *pp. 353–355*
14. What is menopause? Why does menopause lower estrogen levels? What are some effects of lowered estrogen levels? *p. 355*

15. What are the stages of the human sexual response?
    pp. 357–358
16. Describe a vasectomy and a tubal ligation.   *pp. 358–359*
17. How does the combination birth control pill reduce the chances of pregnancy?   *p. 359*
18. What health risks are associated with use of the birth control pill?   *pp. 359–360*
19. How do progesterone-only means of contraception reduce the risk of pregnancy?   *pp. 359–360*
20. What is an IUD?   *p. 360*
21. How do the diaphragm, male condom, and female condom prevent pregnancy?   *p. 360*
22. The interstitial cells
    a. are found in the seminal vesicles.
    b. produce a secretion that makes up most of the volume of semen.
    c. secrete testosterone.
    d. store sperm.
23. Choose the *incorrect* statement about semen.
    a. It helps lubricate passageways in the male reproductive system, so sperm travel through them more easily.
    b. Sperm cells make up most of the volume of semen.
    c. It helps reduce the acidity of the female reproductive system, thereby increasing sperm survival.
    d. It contains nourishment for the sperm.

24. After sperm are released in the female reproductive system, they can move to the egg and fertilize it. Which is the correct order of structures through which the *sperm* will pass?
    a. Vagina, cervix, body of uterus, oviduct
    b. Ovary, cervix, body of uterus, oviduct
    c. Endometrium, cervix, oviduct, ovary
    d. Ovary, oviduct, endometrium, cervix
25. Which is the *correct pairing* of a structure with its function?
    a. Endometrium; the usual site of fertilization
    b. Corpus luteum; production of estrogen and progesterone
    c. Epididymis; production of testosterone
    d. Seminal vesicles; store sperm while they mature
26. The controversial pill Mifepristone (formerly called RU486) works to terminate a pregnancy by preventing progesterone from acting. This effect would cause an abortion because progesterone is needed to
    a. trigger ovulation.
    b. cause the formation of the corpus luteum.
    c. maintain the endometrium.
    d. increase the levels of LH.
27. Sperm are stored and mature in the _____.
28. Fertilization usually occurs in the _____.

applying the concepts

1. You are a health care provider in a family planning clinic. Your first client is a woman who is 22 years old and in excellent health. She is about to marry her high school sweetheart. She and her fiancé have never had sexual intercourse with anyone else. They want a very effective means of contraception because they would like to wait until he finishes graduate school to start a family. She does not smoke. Which means of birth control would you recommend for this client? Why?
2. Endometriosis, a condition in which endometrial tissue implants on pelvic organs outside the uterus, causes pain in the pelvic area. Why would the pain be greatest around the time of menstruation?

3. Doctors in fertility clinics sometimes use FSH as a fertility drug to treat women who are having difficulty conceiving a child. Women who use FSH as a fertility drug are more likely than women who conceive naturally to have several babies at once. Why would FSH increase the incidence of multiple births?
4. A male friend of yours and his wife would like to have a baby. They are having difficulty conceiving a child. The doctor told him that the reason for this difficulty is a low sperm count. Since further tests are costly and would take time to complete, the doctor told your friend that as a first step, he might try wearing loose clothing and switching to boxer shorts, rather than his customary tight briefs. Why do you think the doctor made this suggestion?

becoming information literate

Use at least three reliable sources (journals, newspaper, websites) to answer the following questions. Explain why you chose those sources.

1. Three extended-use hormonal contraceptives are available for women: Lybrel (used for one year) Seasonale, and Seasonique (both used for 90 days). How do these contraceptives prevent pregnancy? Are they safe? What are the pros and cons of using them?

2. There is contradictory evidence that environmental estrogens are affecting human reproductive systems. What are some effects that some researchers attribute to environmental estrogen? Discuss the evidence for and against a link between environmental estrogens and at least one of these effects.

Additional questions can be found online at The Human Biology Place, www.humanbiology.com.

Sexually Transmitted Diseases and AIDS

STDs can be dangerous and highly infectious. You would be wise to learn about modes of transmission, signs and symptoms, and how to protect yourself from contracting STDs.

Betu was one of only 20 young adults chosen to be a peer educator by Health Services at his college. His father was the one who suggested he apply, admitting that parents find giving the "birds and the bees" talk as awkward as young adults do hearing it. Betu was looking forward to the 40 hours of training he would get on sexuality and communication skills. Besides meeting with formal groups of students, he was anxious to be a reliable source of information for his friends. He knew how common sexually transmitted diseases are, especially on college campuses, and knew he could help peers make responsible decisions.

At his first training session, Betu was not surprised to learn that the highest rates of STDs are among adolescents and young adults (aged 14–26) because they are the most sexually active segment of the population. He was surprised to learn, however, that 26% of female adolescents 14 to 19 years old have at least one STD, and 15% have more than one STD. Furthermore, 20.1% of females who had only one lifetime sexual partner (so far) had contracted at least one STD. And, 50% or more of female adolescents with three or more partners had an STD. The most common STD was genital infections with the human papillomavirus (HPV). With his new knowledge, Betu knew he could make a difference by talking with teens and young adults.

In this chapter we discuss sexually transmitted diseases (STDs), diseases that are transmitted by sexual contact. We first describe three STDs that are caused by bacteria: chlamydia, gonorrhea, and syphilis. Then we describe three STDs that are caused by viruses: genital herpes, genital warts, and HIV/AIDS. HIV is discussed in this chapter because sexual contact is the most common means of transmission, although the virus can be transmitted in other ways as well.

Long-Lasting Effects of STDs

Sexually transmitted diseases (STDs) take a serious toll on humanity, both in their direct effects on the infected individuals and because of the cost to society in general. Thirteen million infections occur each year in the United States. Two-thirds of the U.S. residents infected are younger than 25. The cost of treating their infections is in the millions of dollars.

We should also mention another trait of STDs: they are sexist. They affect women more severely than men, causing sterility more often in women than in men, ectopic pregnancy (a pregnancy in which the embryo begins development outside the uterus), and cervical cancer.

One reason STDs are so rampant is that people are often unaware of being infected. Many cases of STDs lack symptoms. Indeed, the prevalence of asymptomatic cases has led to use of the term *sexually transmitted infection* (STI) rather than sexually transmitted *disease*. Also, the symptoms of some STDs, such as syphilis, disappear without treatment, leading the person to believe—mistakenly—that he or she is cured.

STDs Caused by Bacteria

We consider three STDs that are caused by bacteria: chlamydia, gonorrhea, and syphilis.

Chlamydia and Gonorrhea

Chlamydia, the most frequently reported infectious disease in the United States, is caused by a very small bacterium *(Chlamydia trachomatis)* that cannot grow outside a human cell. One of the oldest known sexually transmitted diseases, gonorrhea, is caused by the bacterium *Neisseria gonorrhoeae.*

Chlamydial infections are rapidly becoming epidemic because they are highly contagious and because they do not necessarily cause noticeable symptoms that would prompt the infected person to seek treatment (Figure **17a.1**). In fact, most people who have chlamydia do not have symptoms, and many people learn that they have it only because a responsible partner diagnosed with the infection informs them. Any symptoms that do develop may take weeks or months to appear. In the meantime, even without outward signs of infection, the disease can be passed along to others.

Chlamydia and gonorrhea primarily infect the mucous membranes of the genital or urinary tract, throat, or anus. The bacteria that cause these STDs cannot survive long if exposed to air, so they are generally transferred by direct contact between an infected mucous membrane and an uninfected one during sexual intimacy. The bacteria can infect the cells of mucous membranes, including those of the urethra, vagina, cervix, oviducts, throat, anus, and eyes. The most common sites of infection are the mucous membranes of the urethra or the reproductive structures, because these are most

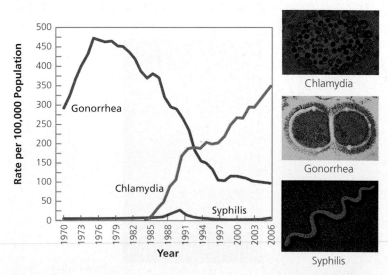

Chlamydia

Gonorrhea

Syphilis

FIGURE 17a.1 The relative rates of chlamydia, gonorrhea, and syphilis from 1984 to 2006. The bacteria that cause these STDs are shown at the right.

likely to be in contact during sexual intimacy. Chlamydia and gonorrhea can also spread to the lining of the anus during anal intercourse or to the throat during oral sex. Furthermore, they can infect the eyes if an eye is touched by a finger that has just touched an infected area. In the case of infants, eye infection can occur as the baby passes through an infected vagina or cervix during the birth process.

The most common symptoms of chlamydia or gonorrhea are those of urinary tract infection. Inflammation of the urethra causes a burning sensation during urination, itching or burning around the opening of the urethra, and a discharge from the urethra (Figure **17a.2**). In males, the most common site of chlamydial infection is the urethra, because this is the mucous membrane most likely to be exposed to the bacteria during sexual intimacy.

In women, chlamydia and gonorrhea are more likely to affect the pelvic organs than the urethra, because the vagina and cervix are a woman's primary sites of contact during sexual intimacy. The general term for an infection of the pelvic organs is *pelvic inflammatory disease* (PID). The symptoms of PID—abdominal pain or tenderness, lower-back pain, pain during intercourse, abnormal vaginal bleeding or discharge, fever, or chills—can come on gradually or suddenly and vary in intensity from mild to severe.

Pelvic inflammatory disease can be caused by a number of organisms, but the most common culprits are the sexually transmitted bacteria that cause chlamydia and gonorrhea. The bacteria ascend from the vagina through the cervix to the uterus. There, they may infect the endometrium and then spread to the wall of the uterus and to the oviducts. Near the ovary, the oviduct opens to the abdominal cavity, allowing the infection to spread into the abdominal cavity. The infection can be curbed by treatment with antibiotics, which kill the bacteria. Unfortunately, pelvic infections are less likely to produce symptoms than are urinary tract infections, and the untreated infection may permanently damage a female's reproductive system.

Because a man is more likely to experience noticeable symptoms of chlamydia and gonorrhea, men are more likely to seek diagnosis and treatment before the infections have caused lasting damage. However, undiagnosed chlamydia and gonorrhea can have long-term reproductive consequences for both men and women, so it is important that a man who is diagnosed with chlamydia or gonorrhea inform everyone he has been sexually intimate with. If left untreated, chlamydia and gonorrhea can cause scar tissue to form in the tubes through which gametes travel. If the vas deferens or oviducts are completely blocked by scar tissue,

the man or woman becomes sterile. Sterility is more likely to occur in women than in men, because women are less likely to have symptoms that prompt treatment. In a woman, partial blockage of the oviduct may allow the tiny sperm to reach the egg and fertilize it, but the blockage will not allow the much larger embryo to move past the scar tissue to reach the uterus (Figure **17a.3**). The embryo may then implant in the oviduct, resulting in an ectopic pregnancy that places the woman's life in danger.

Chlamydia and gonorrhea are of special concern to pregnant women. Newborns can be infected with either chlamydia or gonorrhea as they pass through an infected cervix or vagina at birth. Chlamydial or gonorrheal infections picked up during birth can affect the mucous membrane of the eye (the conjunctiva), the throat, vagina, rectum, or lungs. These infections are sometimes fatal to an infant. Chlamydial infections during pregnancy place the fetus at risk as well. Specifically, chlamydia can cause the protective membranes around the fetus to rupture early, which can kill the fetus.

Diagnosis of chlamydia and gonorrhea can now be done in a physician's office with quick, accurate tests. Urine tests detect the DNA of *Chlamydia* or the gonococcal bacterium. Gonorrhea can also be diagnosed by observing the bacterium in a smear of cells taken from the infected area or grown in a laboratory. Both chlamydia and gonorrhea can be cured with antibiotics. Some strains of the gonococcal bacteria are now drug resistant. Therefore, every patient undergoing treatment for gonorrhea must be retested for the bacterium when the antibiotic regimen has been completed to make sure the infection is cured.

Syphilis

Syphilis rates decreased steadily during the 1990s, reaching their lowest point in 2000. Since then, the frequency of syphilis has risen slightly, primarily among men who have sex with men.

FIGURE 17a.2 A yellowish white discharge from the urethra caused by gonorrhea

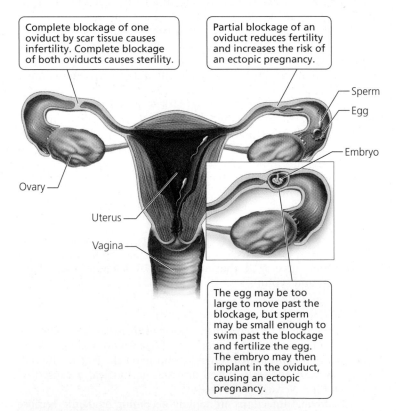

Complete blockage of one oviduct by scar tissue causes infertility. Complete blockage of both oviducts causes sterility.

Partial blockage of an oviduct reduces fertility and increases the risk of an ectopic pregnancy.

Sperm

Egg

Embryo

Ovary

Uterus

Vagina

The egg may be too large to move past the blockage, but sperm may be small enough to swim past the blockage and fertilize the egg. The embryo may then implant in the oviduct, causing an ectopic pregnancy.

FIGURE 17a.3 Chlamydia and gonorrhea can cause pelvic inflammatory disease, which can cause scar tissue to form in the oviducts.

Syphilis is caused by a corkscrew-shaped bacterium (a spirochete) called *Treponema pallidum*. As terrible as these bacteria are, they are extremely delicate and cannot survive drying or even minor temperature changes. A person can contract syphilis only by direct contact with an infected sexual partner. The bacteria can invade any mucous membrane or enter through a break in the skin. The bacteria can also cross the placenta and infect the growing fetus if a pregnant woman is infected.

If untreated, syphilis progresses through three stages. The first stage is characterized by a painless bump, called a chancre (shang'-ker), that forms at the site of contact, usually (but not always) the genitals, and normally appears within 2 to 8 weeks of the initial contact (Figure **17a.4**). The chancre appears as a hard, reddish brown bump with raised edges that make it resemble a crater. Unfortunately, a chancre is not always noticed, because it can form in places that are difficult to see and because it may be mistaken for something else. The chancre lasts for one to a few weeks. During that time it ulcerates, becomes crusty, and disappears. The disease, however, has not disappeared.

During the primary stage of syphilis, diagnosis is made by identifying the bacterium in the discharge from a chancre. At this

Step 1: The first stage of syphilis is characterized by a chancre, a hard, painless, crater-shaped bump at the place in the body where the bacteria entered, usually the genitals.

Step 2: A reddish-brown rash covers the entire body, including the palms of the hands and the soles of the feet.

Step 3: Lesions, called gummas, shown here on the hand, are characteristic of the third stage of syphilis. These lesions can also form on the blood vessels, the central nervous system, and the bones.

FIGURE 17a.4 Untreated syphilis goes through three stages.

stage, syphilis can be treated and cured with an antibiotic such as penicillin.

If syphilis is not detected and treated in the first stage, it can progress to the second stage, which is characterized by a reddish brown rash covering the entire body, including the palms of the hands and soles of the feet. The rash usually appears within a few weeks to a few months after the disappearance of the chancre. The infected person may confuse the rash with an ordinary skin rash, such as might be caused by an allergy or German measles. The rash does not hurt or itch. Each bump eventually breaks open, oozes fluid, and becomes crusty. The ooze contains millions of bacteria. Therefore, the secondary stage is the most contagious stage of syphilis.

Secondary syphilis usually has symptoms besides the rash, and these may produce the first pain associated with the disease. At first, there may be flu-like symptoms, including a slight temperature, chills, a sore throat, and gastrointestinal upset. In addition, warty growths may appear in the genital area. Patches of hair may fall out from the head, eyebrows, and eyelashes.

Syphilis in this stage is diagnosed by a blood test to detect antibodies for *Treponema* bacteria. Second-stage syphilis *can* be cured with antibiotics such as penicillin, but the disease becomes increasingly difficult to treat as it progresses. Again, the symptoms go away whether or not they are treated. However, in some people, the symptoms recur periodically. Other people may have no outward signs of syphilis for years.

The third stage brings the drama to a grisly conclusion. At this stage, lesions called gummas may appear on the skin or certain internal organs. Gummas often form on the aorta, the major artery that delivers blood from the heart to the rest of the body. As a result, the artery wall may be weakened and may burst, causing the person to bleed to death internally. The bacteria that cause syphilis can also infect the nervous system, damaging the brain and spinal cord, so that the person may have difficulty walking, become paralyzed, or become insane. The disease may also cause blindness by affecting the optic nerve, the iris, and other parts of the eye.

In its third stage, syphilis is very difficult to treat. Treatment requires massive doses of antibiotics over a prolonged period. The damage that has already been done to the body cannot be repaired.

Characteristics of bacterial STDs (their symptoms, diagnosis, treatment, and effects) are summarized in Table **17a.1**.

STDs Caused by Viruses

Unlike STDs caused by bacteria, viral STDs cannot be cured with antibiotics. One can treat the symptoms, but one can never be certain that the virus has been eliminated. Therefore, it is always important to take precautions not to pass the virus on to others.

Genital Herpes

Genital herpes is caused by herpes simplex viruses (HSVs). There are actually two types of HSV. They cause similar sores but tend to be active in different parts of the body. Type 1 (HSV-1) is most commonly found above the waist, where it causes fever blisters, or cold sores. Type 2 (HSV-2) is more likely to be found below the waist, where it causes genital herpes on the genitals, buttocks, or thighs. As a result of oral–genital sex with an infected person, however, HSV-1 can cause sores on the genitals, and HSV-2 can cause cold sores (Figure **17a.5**).

Herpes simplex viruses are quite contagious and can be spread by direct contact with viruses that are being shed from an infected surface or that are in the fluid on the blisters. Mucous membranes

(a) Oral herpes: Cold sores (also called fever blisters) are most often caused by HSV-1.

(b) Genital herpes, shown here on the external genitalia of a female, is usually caused by HSV-2.

(c) Genital herpes, shown here on the penis of a male, is usually caused by HSV-2.

FIGURE 17a.5 Herpes simplex viruses cause blisters to form at the site of infection.

are most susceptible. Skin is a good barrier, unless there is a cut, abrasion, or burn; acne; eczema; or other break.

The first hints of genital herpes infection begin about 2 to 20 days (an average of 6 days) after the initial contact. The initial bout may be severe, often accompanied by fever, aching muscles, and swollen glands in the groin. Soon blisters appear, accompanied by local swelling, itching, and possibly burning, especially if the blisters get wet during urination. The blisters form at the site of contact and last about 2 days before they ulcerate, leaving small, painful sores. At this point individuals infected with genital herpes are at an increased risk of acquiring an HIV infection as well, if they are exposed to the HIV virus.

During dormant periods, the virus retreats to ganglia (clusters of nerve cells) near the spinal cord. Then, at times of emotional or physical stress, the virus may be reactivated and blisters may re-form.

Most people with herpes apparently never develop symptoms, or the symptoms are so mild that they go unnoticed. Nonetheless, these asymptomatic individuals can unwittingly transmit the virus. In fact, *most* cases of genital herpes are transmitted by partners who never had symptoms or whose symptoms were atypical and undiagnosed! If they had known, they would likely have avoided unprotected sexual contact.

Genital herpes is most contagious when active sores are present, so sexual contact should be avoided during an outbreak. Unprotected contact should be avoided at all times, because genital herpes can also be spread when there are no symptoms.

Most women with herpes have successful pregnancies and normal deliveries. In some cases, however, the infection spreads to the fetus as it is growing in the uterus and can cause miscarriage or stillbirth. HSV can also be transmitted to the newborn during

vaginal delivery, especially if active sores are present. To avoid exposing the baby to HSV, physicians often recommend delivery by cesarean section (surgical removal from the uterus) if the mother has active sores.

Clinicians diagnose herpes by examining the sores or by testing the fluid from sores for the presence of the virus. It is also possible to identify the DNA of the herpes virus in the material wiped off when the genital area is gently swabbed. Blood tests can also detect antibodies to the herpes viruses. However, such blood tests may not be useful during an initial attack, because the antibodies may not show up for several months.

Although there is no cure for HSV, there are three antiviral drugs—Zovirax, Famvir, and Valtrex—that help ease symptoms during the initial outbreak and reduce the frequency of recurrences. Unfortunately, strains of HSV that are resistant to antiviral drugs are beginning to crop up.

HPV and Genital Warts

Genital warts may be caused by any of several human papillomaviruses (HPVs). These are not the same viruses that cause warts on the hands and feet. Although chlamydia holds the title of being the most common of all STDs in the United States, HPV is the most common of the viral STDs. Roughly 50% of sexually active people will acquire an infection with HPV at some point in their lives. The body's defense mechanisms usually eliminate HPV without the virus causing serious health problems.

Most people with genital HPV are not aware of the infection, because they don't have any symptoms. However, HPV can be spread by genital contact with an infected person, even when there are no symptoms. Recall from Chapter 13a that viruses replicate in a host cell, and new viruses can be released from the cell slowly, without causing symptoms. The newly released viruses can cause genital HPV on uninfected areas of the same person or on another person if genital contact is made.

There are many strains of HPV. Genital infections with some strains of HPV are considered low-risk infections; these cause genital warts. The warts can be flat or raised and can occur singly or in groups. Without treatment, they often grow in size. Although warts can form in a visible location (Figure **17a.6**), they often form in locations where they are not likely to be discovered—the vagina, cervix, or anus. Genital warts are usually diagnosed on the basis of their appearance. However, flat warts are not usually visible unless they are painted with a vinegar-like solution. In women, a Pap test,

FIGURE 17a.6 Genital warts on the penis

TABLE 17a.1 Overview of Bacterial STDs

Disease	Symptoms	Diagnosis and Treatment	Effects
Chlamydia	First symptoms occur 7–21 days after contact Up to 75% of women and 50% of men show no symptoms *Women*: Vaginal discharge Vaginal bleeding between periods Pain during urination and intercourse Abdominal pain accompanied by fever and nausea *Men*: Urethral discharge Pain during urination	*Diagnosis:* Urine test for chlamydial DNA *Treatment:* Antibiotics	Long-term reproductive consequences such as sterility Infection can pass to infant during childbirth Can cause rupture of the protective membrane surrounding the fetus
Gonorrhea	First symptoms occur 2–21 days after contact About 30%–40% of men and women show no symptoms *Women*: Vaginal discharge Pain during urination and bowel movement Cramps and pain in lower abdomen More pain than usual during menstruation *Men*: Thick yellow or white discharge from penis Inflammation of the urethra Pain during urination and bowel movements	*Diagnosis:* Examination of penile discharge or cervical secretions Urine test for DNA of the bacterium that causes gonorrhea Cell culture *Treatment:* Antibiotics	Can cause long-term reproductive consequences such as sterility Infection can pass to infant during childbirth Can cause heart trouble, arthritis, and blindness
Syphilis	*Stage 1*: Occurs 2–8 weeks after contact Chancre forms at site of contact Lymph nodes in groin area swell *Stage 2*: Occurs 6 weeks to 6 months after contact Reddish brown rash appears anywhere on the body Flu-like symptoms present Ulcers or warty growth may appear Patches of hair may be lost *Stage 3*: Lesions appear on skin and internal organs May affect nervous system Blindness Brain damage	*Diagnosis:* Identification of the bacterium from a chancre Blood test to detect antibodies to the bacterium that causes syphilis *Treatment:* Large doses of antibiotics over a prolonged period of time	Infection can pass to fetus during pregnancy Can cause heart disease, brain damage, blindness, and death

which looks for precancerous cells on the cervix, is also helpful. A Pap test is a painless test in which the cervix is gently swabbed to collect cells that are then examined for abnormalities under a microscope.

Treatments for genital warts are intended to kill the cells that contain the virus. Methods for removing genital warts include (1) freezing (cold cautery), (2) burning with an electrical instrument (hot cautery), (3) laser (high-intensity light), (4) surgery, and (5) podophyllin (a chemical that is painted onto the warts and washed off after the prescribed time period, before it burns the skin). Also available are creams that the patient applies to shrink genital warts. The creams work by boosting the body's

defense mechanisms against the virus. These treatments may destroy visible warts; but HPV may remain nearby in normal-looking tissue and can cause new warts to form weeks or months after old ones have been destroyed.

Other strains of HPV cause high-risk genital infections, which can persist for long periods of time and are closely linked to both cervical cancer in women and penile cancer in men. HPV is thought to be responsible for one-third of all cases of penile cancers in the United States, and it can be isolated in 90% of women with cervical cancer. HPV can also cause anal cancer.

Women should have Pap tests regularly, and those who have ever had HPV should have a Pap test at least once a year. There is

TABLE 17a.2 Overview of Viral STDs

Disease	Symptoms	Diagnosis and Treatment	Effects
Genital herpes	First symptoms appear 2–20 days after contact Many people have no symptoms Flu-like symptoms present Small, painful blisters that can leave painful ulcers appear Blisters go away but the virus remains Symptoms recur periodically	*Diagnosis*: Examination of blisters Laboratory test on the fluid from the sore to detect the presence of the virus Blood test for antibodies *Treatment*: Antiviral drugs can ease symptoms	Cannot be cured Recurrences of blisters Infection can pass to fetus, causing miscarriage or stillbirth Can cause brain damage in newborns
HPV genital infection	First symptoms appear 1–6 months after exposure; presence of symptoms depends on type of HPV Small warts appear on sex organs May cause itching, burning, irritation, discharge, bleeding	*Diagnosis*: Appearance of growth In women, Pap test may help *Treatment*: For removal: freezing, burning, laser surgery	Formation of additional warts Closely associated with cervical cancer and penile cancer Infection can pass to infant during childbirth

now a vaccine that is effective against four HPVs, including two strains that are responsible for most cases of cervical cancer. Health advisors recommend that girls be vaccinated when they are 10 to 12 years old. There is no equivalent vaccine available for men.

The characteristics of genital herpes and genital HPV, both caused by viruses, are summarized in Table **17a.2**.

HIV/AIDS

In the past several decades, acquired immune deficiency syndrome, or AIDS, has left its mark on many aspects of society, including medicine, science, law, economics, and education. The name of the condition is apt, because the symptoms are those associated with a damaged immune system. Unlike many other immune deficiencies, however, AIDS is not inherited but acquired. A syndrome is a set of symptoms that tend to occur together, and people with AIDS experience a devastating set of symptoms.

We now know that a virus, the human immunodeficiency virus (HIV), causes AIDS. However, as we will learn shortly, AIDS is actually the final stage in an HIV infection during which the immune system is slowly weakened. A primary target of HIV is helper T cells, which serve as the main switch for the entire immune response (see Chapter 13). Once HIV enters a helper T cell, the T cell stops functioning well, although this cessation of function is not immediately apparent. HIV will eventually kill the infected helper T cell. The infection and eventual death of helper T cells cripple the immune system, giving disease-causing organisms that routinely surround us the opportunity to cause infection. These are the opportunistic infections that characterize AIDS and, in time, cause death.

Global Epidemic

According to the World Health Organization (WHO), at the end of 2007, from 30.6 to 36.1 million people globally were living with an HIV infection. Africa is currently the area hardest hit by HIV: more than 22.5 million people there were living with HIV/AIDS in 2007.

Form of HIV

The genetic material in HIV is RNA. The RNA, along with several virus-specified enzymes, is encased in a protein coat. The RNA and protein coat constitute the core of the virus (Figure **17a.7**).

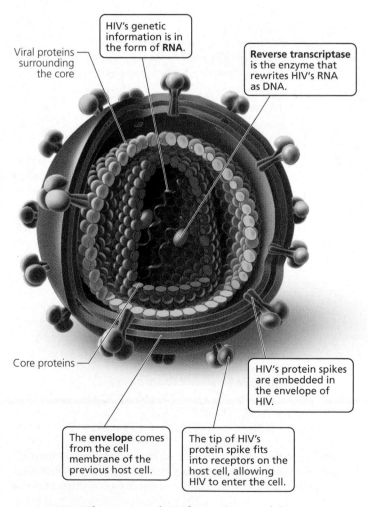

Viral proteins surrounding the core

HIV's genetic information is in the form of **RNA**.

Reverse transcriptase is the enzyme that rewrites HIV's RNA as DNA.

Core proteins

HIV's protein spikes are embedded in the envelope of HIV.

The **envelope** comes from the cell membrane of the previous host cell.

The tip of HIV's protein spike fits into receptors on the host cell, allowing HIV to enter the cell.

FIGURE 17a.7 The structure of HIV (human immunodeficiency virus)

Surrounding the protein coat is an outer covering, or envelope, consisting of spikes of protein embedded in a lipid membrane. The lipid membrane is actually a piece of plasma membrane stolen from the previous host cell and altered for use by the virus. The protein spikes of the viral envelope are responsible for binding the virus to the host cell.

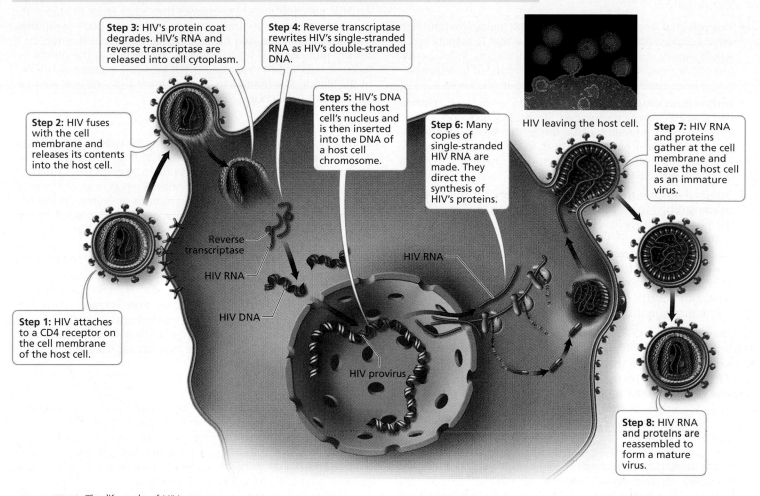

Q *Why is the insertion of HIV DNA into the host cell chromosome so important to HIV's replication?*

Step 3: HIV's protein coat degrades. HIV's RNA and reverse transcriptase are released into cell cytoplasm.

Step 4: Reverse transcriptase rewrites HIV's single-stranded RNA as HIV's double-stranded DNA.

Step 5: HIV's DNA enters the host cell's nucleus and is then inserted into the DNA of a host cell chromosome.

Step 2: HIV fuses with the cell membrane and releases its contents into the host cell.

Step 6: Many copies of single-stranded HIV RNA are made. They direct the synthesis of HIV's proteins.

HIV leaving the host cell.

Step 7: HIV RNA and proteins gather at the cell membrane and leave the host cell as an immature virus.

Step 1: HIV attaches to a CD4 receptor on the cell membrane of the host cell.

Reverse transcriptase

HIV RNA

HIV DNA

HIV RNA

HIV provirus

Step 8: HIV RNA and proteins are reassembled to form a mature virus.

FIGURE 17a.8 The life cycle of HIV

A If HIV DNA does not insert into the host cell chromosome, it cannot produce HIV RNA or HIV-specified proteins.

Replication of HIV

HIV binds to an uninfected cell when the spherical region at the end of a protein spike fits into a receptor on the host cell surface—like a key in a lock. The host cell receptor is a surface protein called CD4. Helper T cells are the predominant cell types with these CD4 receptors and are therefore the most common targets of HIV. When an HIV spike is properly docked in a CD4 receptor, the contents of the virus enter the host cell (Figure **17a.8**).

Once within the host cell, the RNA of HIV undergoes a process called reverse transcription. During this process, the viral RNA is rewritten as double-stranded DNA. Because going from RNA to DNA is the reverse of the usual genetic information transfer, viruses that work this way are known as retroviruses (*retro–*, backward). The backward copying of genetic information from RNA into DNA is performed by an enzyme called reverse transcriptase, which is inserted into the host cell along with viral RNA.

The newly formed viral DNA, which contains all the instructions necessary for producing thousands of new viruses, is then spliced into the host DNA. Once HIV's DNA is integrated into the host cell chromosome, that DNA is called the HIV provirus. After they have been incorporated into the host cell DNA, the host cell treats the HIV genes as it would its own. Each time the cell reproduces, the viral DNA is copied along with the cell's DNA. When HIV is transmitted to another person, it is usually in the form of a latent—that is, inactive—HIV provirus when the infected cell enters the other person's body.

The HIV genes can reside in a helper T cell chromosome for years, until the cell is activated to respond to some foreign antigen, such as another kind of virus, a fungus, or a parasite. At this point, the virus begins making copies of itself instead of allowing the cell to fight the invader. The viral genome is activated and turns the cell into a virus factory. Some of the newly produced HIV RNA will become genetic material for new viruses, and some will be used to produce virus-specified proteins. The viral components gather at the cell membrane and bud off from the host cell. The HIV RNA and proteins then self-assemble into new, mature viruses, which move through the bloodstream to infect new cells.

Transmission of HIV

HIV is found in bodily fluids—blood, semen, vaginal secretions, breast milk, saliva, tears, urine, cerebrospinal fluid, and amniotic fluid. However, HIV is not easily transmitted. Only the first four of the bodily fluids listed contain HIV concentrations high enough to cause infection in another person.

HIV *cannot* be transmitted by casual contact. The major modes of transmission are:

- **Unprotected sexual activity.** HIV can be transmitted through unprotected sexual activity of any kind—that is, activity in which skin or mucous membranes of the vagina, vulva, penis, mouth, or anus of the partners are not separated by a barrier (i.e., a latex condom) that the virus cannot penetrate.

- **Intravenous drug use.** Contact with infected blood is another way that HIV can be transmitted. Since 1985, all blood donated to blood banks is tested for HIV; this testing has essentially eliminated the risk of getting HIV from a blood transfusion. However, intravenous drug users who share needles *do* have an increased risk of HIV infection.

- **Infected mother to child before or during birth.** HIV can be transmitted from an infected mother to her child across the placenta during fetal development or in breast milk during nursing. An HIV-infected woman who is not treated for HIV during pregnancy and does not breast-feed her infant has about a 25% chance of spreading HIV to her newborn. However, if the mother is treated with drugs that slow replication of HIV (antiretroviral drugs), she has less than a 2% chance of transmitting the virus to her newborn.

Sites of HIV Infection

HIV can infect any cell that has a CD4 receptor. The most important of these cells is the helper T cell, which turns on the entire immune response (see Chapter 13). The hallmark of an HIV infection is a progressive decline in helper T cell numbers. This loss is devastating because it leaves the body increasingly defenseless against other infections.

HIV can also infect the brain, killing nerve cells. When the brain is infected, the symptoms can include forgetfulness, impaired speech, inability to concentrate, depression, seizures, and personality changes. Roughly 60% of people with AIDS have signs of dementia.

Stages of HIV Infection

An HIV infection usually progresses through a series of stages: the initial infection, an asymptomatic stage, initial disease symptoms, early immune failure, and AIDS. The progress of an HIV infection is usually monitored by following both the decline in the number of helper T cells and the increase in viral load (the number of HIV free in the blood). The changes in T cell number and viral load are summarized in Figure **17a.9**.

Initial infection

During the initial stages of infection, the virus actively replicates, and the circulating level of HIV rises. The body's immune system produces antibodies against the virus in an attempt to eliminate it. Antibodies can usually be detected within 8 weeks or so, but in some cases they are not detected for many months or even years. An HIV test looks for the presence of antibodies to HIV in the blood. If antibodies are found, the person is said to be HIV positive (HIV+).

Many people have no symptoms when they first become infected; others experience some mild disease symptoms during the initial infection. Early symptoms might include enlarged lymph nodes throughout the body, fatigue, and fever. If the brain becomes infected, the initial symptoms may include headaches, fever, and difficulty concentrating, remembering, or solving problems. This initial stage is particularly dangerous, because even though many people are unaware they are infected at this point, they are particularly contagious.

Asymptomatic stage

Weeks to months after the initial stage of infection, the person usually feels well again, often for several years. This is the period of asymptomatic infection. During this stage, the immune system mounts a defense strong enough to control, but not conquer, the infection. The rate of helper T cell production increases. For a while, helper T cell production matches destruction.

During the asymptomatic stage, HIV is far from idle. It is "hiding out" in certain lymphatic organs, including the spleen, tonsils,

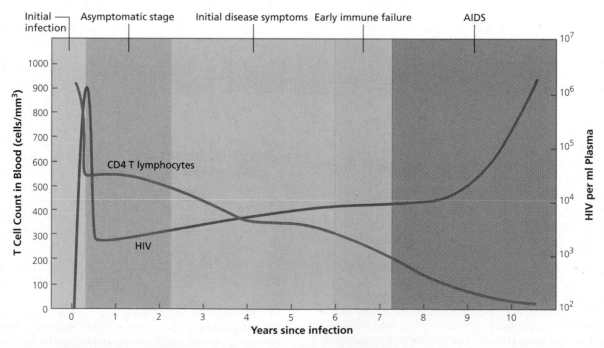

FIGURE 17a.9 An HIV infection can be monitored by following the decline in the number of T cells and the rise in viral load (number of viruses in the bloodstream).

and adenoids, but most importantly in the lymph nodes, where it replicates. Consequently, the spaces between cells in the lymph nodes become packed with virus particles. Most helper T cells reside in the lymph nodes, and many of them have the DNA form of HIV genes incorporated into their own chromosomes. Because helper T cells frequently circulate through the lymph nodes, this is an opportune place for HIV to encounter healthy T cells. Thus, millions of T cells become infected as they move through the lymph nodes on their way to other parts of the body.

Initial disease symptoms

Eventually, the immune system begins to falter as the virus gains the upper hand. As helper T cell numbers gradually drop, symptoms set in again. The initial disease symptoms fall into three classes.

1. *Wasting syndrome* is characterized by an otherwise unexplained loss in body weight of more than 10%, often accompanied by diarrhea. The weight loss is similar to that experienced by a cancer patient.

2. *Swollen lymph nodes* occur in the neck, armpits, and groin. These structures may remain swollen until later stages of HIV infection.

3. *Neurological symptoms* may appear, either because HIV has spread to the brain or because other organisms have caused a brain infection. Among the neurological symptoms are dementia, weakness, and paralysis caused by spinal cord damage. Other symptoms include pain, burning, or a tingling sensation, usually in hands or feet, caused by peripheral nerve damage.

Early immune failure

As T cell numbers continue their gradual decline, the body becomes increasingly vulnerable to infection. Early signs of immune failure include thrush (a fungal infection in the mouth) and shingles (a painful rash caused by the same virus that causes chickenpox).

AIDS

AIDS is the final stage of an HIV infection. The time from HIV infection to diagnosis of AIDS can be 10 or more years, depending on the number of other infections the person is exposed to and the health of the immune system before infection with HIV. Now, although the body has fought long and hard, it is beginning to lose the battle. The immune system is crippled, making the person vulnerable to certain characteristic fungal, protozoan, bacterial, and viral infections, as well as cancers.

A diagnosis of AIDS is made when an HIV$^+$ person develops one of the following conditions: (1) a helper T cell count below $200/mm^3$ of blood; (2) one of 26 opportunistic infections, the most common of which are *Pneumocystis carinii* pneumonia and Kaposi's sarcoma, a cancer of connective tissue that primarily affects the skin; (3) a greater than 10% loss of body weight (wasting syndrome); or (4) dementia.

Treatments

Death in a person with AIDS is usually caused by one of the opportunistic infections. Thus, treating opportunistic infections, or preventing their onset, can improve the quality of life and extend the length of life for people with AIDS. Treatment for HIV infection is also aimed at slowing the progress of the infection, both before and after the diagnosis of AIDS. The current prevailing strategy is to slow the rate at which HIV can make new copies of itself. At present, there are five classes of drugs that slow viral replication: reverse transcriptase inhibitors, protease inhibitors, fusion inhibitors, HIV entry inhibitors, and inhibitors of HIV DNA integration into the host cell

chromosome. Each class of drug prevents HIV from replicating by blocking a different step in the virus replication cycle.

The original class of antiviral drugs used to slow the progression of an HIV infection consisted of drugs that act on reverse transcriptase (AZT, ddI, ddC). As discussed earlier, reverse transcriptase is the enzyme necessary for converting the RNA of HIV to DNA that can then be inserted into the DNA of the host cell chromosome.

A second class of antiviral drugs consists of protease inhibitors. Recall that after the HIV genetic information has been inserted into the DNA of the host cell, it can begin producing proteins needed to form new copies of HIV. The proteins initially produced are too big to be used and must be cut to the proper size by an enzyme called a protease. Protease inhibitors block the action of this enzyme, preventing a necessary step in the preparation of proteins for the assembly of new viruses.

A treatment called highly active antiretroviral therapy (HAART), also known as a drug cocktail, consists of combinations of drugs. Typically, the cocktail contains two inhibitors of reverse transcriptase and a protease inhibitor. The idea behind this drug combination is that a protease inhibitor will slow the rate of formation of new viruses. If HIV becomes resistant to inhibitors of reverse transcriptase, the protease inhibitor will prevent the assembly of HIV components into new viruses. Thus, the development of resistance to the other drugs will be minimized. Combination drug treatments are prolonging the lives of HIV-positive individuals. HAART can reduce the viral load to undetectable levels, but the treatment is not a cure. If treatment is stopped, HIV can leave the latent state and begin actively replicating again.

There are newer classes of antiviral drugs. Fusion inhibitors block the proteins on the surface of HIV that bind to the CD4 receptor on host cells, thereby blocking HIV from entering the host cell. Integrase inhibitors prevent HIV DNA from inserting itself into the host chromosome. Other drugs prevent HIV from entering cells, and still others prevent HIV DNA from being inserted into the host cell chromosome.

A variety of other approaches to combating an HIV infection are under active investigation. Clearly, though, the best way to fight the devastation caused by HIV is to prevent it from establishing the initial infection. Currently, the best way to do this is to avoid high-risk behaviors such as unprotected sex or intravenous drug use. Theoretically, prevention of HIV infection could also be accomplished by developing a vaccine similar to those for other viral infections such as smallpox and measles. Recall from Chapter 13 that vaccines work by causing a person's body to produce antibodies against the organisms that cause a disease, without actually causing the disease. Unfortunately, HIV has several characteristics that have thwarted efforts to develop a vaccine:

- The mutation rate in HIV is very high, especially for the proteins in its outer coat, which are the proteins that an antibody would have to recognize.

- There are two types of HIV and many strains of each type. Antibodies would have to recognize the exact strain entering the body.

- An HIV infection is latent when its genetic material has become incorporated into the host DNA (as a provirus). Antibodies cannot attack the virus while it is hidden within the host cell.

- HIV can pass directly from the interior of an infected cell to the interior of an adjacent uninfected cell. Antibodies can attack viruses outside the cell only; they cannot prevent the virus from spreading by this means of transmission.

18

Development throughout Life

Human development begins with fertilization and continues until death. This couple is viewing ultrasound images of their fetus, who is a few months into a life that may last 70 to 80 years.

"Hey, want to see a picture of my baby?" Maritza held up a black-and-white image that seemed to show what a tiny Martian alien would look like on the radar screen of a star cruiser. Her coworkers hadn't even known she was pregnant (though some now claimed they had suspected it). She told them that because she was under treatment for hypertension and had miscarriages in the past, she'd waited to make the announcement. Her family physician had sent her to an obstetrician who specialized in complicated pregnancies, and the obstetrician had done an ultrasound examination of her developing baby at 6 weeks and again at 20 weeks, to see if its development was proceeding normally. Her friends peered through the "snow" on the photographed ultrasound image as Maritza pointed to the baby's head (the largest and most easily recognizable feature); the chambers of the heart, which she had been able to see beating during the procedure; and the edge of the placenta, which according to the doctor was exactly where it belonged. Various measurements of the developing baby had confirmed its age and indicated a normal rate of growth. Relieved that her baby had been given a clean bill of health so far, Maritza was ready to share her excitement with everyone she knew.

Development is the process of growth and change that a living organism experiences throughout its life. Maritza's baby is still in the earliest stages of its development. Maritza, though a fully grown adult, has many decades of health and new stages in her own life to look forward to. In this chapter, we describe the major milestones of human development, from conception to the transition into old age.

Periods of Development in Human Life

A newborn enters the world outside his mother's womb and rests (Figure **18.1**). How did this tiny human develop? Consider that he—like you—began as a fertilized egg, no bigger than the period at the end of this sentence. The miracle of human development begins with **fertilization**, the union of a sperm and an egg, and the early stages take place within the female reproductive system (see Chapter 17). Birth occurs about 266 days after fertilization, marking the transition to development outside the mother's body.

The period of development before birth is the prenatal period. The period after birth is the postnatal period. Relative to prenatal development, postnatal development is a lengthy process, taking from 20 to 25 years to reach adulthood. Bodily changes do not cease once adulthood is reached, however. Our bodies continue to change throughout our lives as part of the growth and aging process.

Prenatal Period

We start our discussion of human development at the moment it all begins—when sperm meets egg. In this section, which presents the major events of prenatal development, we consider what normally happens and what can happen when things go wrong. The major events that occur during prenatal development are summarized by developmental period in Table **18.1**.

The human prenatal period is divided into three periods: (1) the **pre-embryonic period**, from fertilization through the second week (during which the developing human is called a **pre-embryo**); (2) the **embryonic period**, from week 3 through week 8 (during which the developing human is called an **embryo**); and (3) the **fetal period**, from week 9 until birth (during which the developing human is called a **fetus**). *Gestation* refers to the time a pre-embryo,

FIGURE 18.1 A newborn and his mother. Birth is the transition from prenatal to postnatal development.

TABLE 18.1 Review of Major Events during Prenatal Development

Period	Major Events
Pre-embryonic (fertilization–week 2)	Fertilization Cleavage Formation and implantation of the blastocyst Beginning of formation of extraembryonic membranes and placenta
Embryonic (week 3–week 8)	Gastrulation Formation of tissues, organs, and organ systems
Fetal (week 9–birth)	Continued differentiation and growth of tissues and organs Increase in length as measured from head to rump Increase in weight

(a) A zygote

(b) A blastocyst implanting into the wall of the uterus

(c) An embryo about 7 weeks old

(d) A fetus about 5 months old

FIGURE 18.2 The developing human

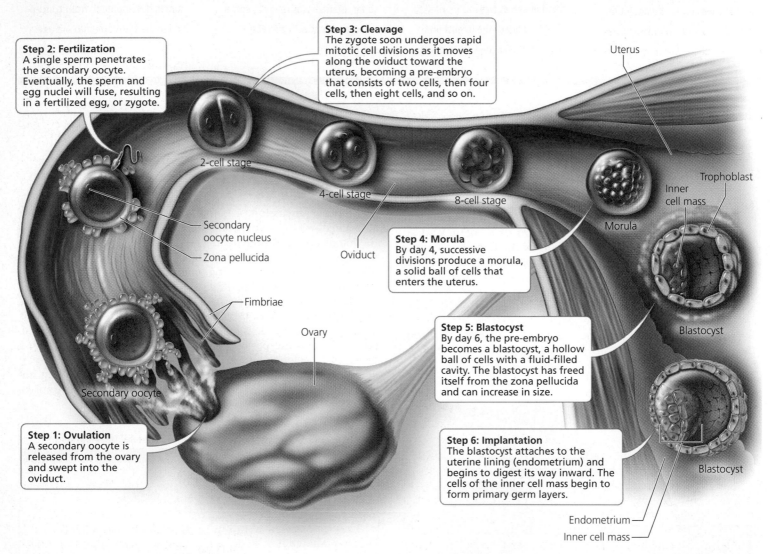

Step 1: Ovulation
A secondary oocyte is released from the ovary and swept into the oviduct.

Step 2: Fertilization
A single sperm penetrates the secondary oocyte. Eventually, the sperm and egg nuclei will fuse, resulting in a fertilized egg, or zygote.

Step 3: Cleavage
The zygote soon undergoes rapid mitotic cell divisions as it moves along the oviduct toward the uterus, becoming a pre-embryo that consists of two cells, then four cells, then eight cells, and so on.

Step 4: Morula
By day 4, successive divisions produce a morula, a solid ball of cells that enters the uterus.

Step 5: Blastocyst
By day 6, the pre-embryo becomes a blastocyst, a hollow ball of cells with a fluid-filled cavity. The blastocyst has freed itself from the zona pellucida and can increase in size.

Step 6: Implantation
The blastocyst attaches to the uterine lining (endometrium) and begins to digest its way inward. The cells of the inner cell mass begin to form primary germ layers.

Secondary oocyte nucleus
Zona pellucida
2-cell stage
4-cell stage
Oviduct
8-cell stage
Fimbriae
Ovary
Secondary oocyte
Uterus
Morula
Inner cell mass
Trophoblast
Blastocyst
Blastocyst
Endometrium
Inner cell mass

FIGURE 18.3 Early stages in the reproductive process

embryo, or fetus is carried in the female reproductive tract. Several stages of prenatal human development are shown in Figure **18.2**.

Pre-embryonic Period

The pre-embryonic period begins with fertilization, the union between the nucleus of an egg and the nucleus of a sperm. Fertilization takes about 24 hours and usually occurs in a widened portion of the

oviduct, not far from the ovary, as shown in Figure **18.3**. Fertilization is a beautifully orchestrated performance by egg and sperm, aided by the actions of the oviducts and uterus.

Fertilization

At ovulation, the ovary releases the egg, still a secondary oocyte (see Chapter 17). The egg is swept into the oviduct by fingerlike

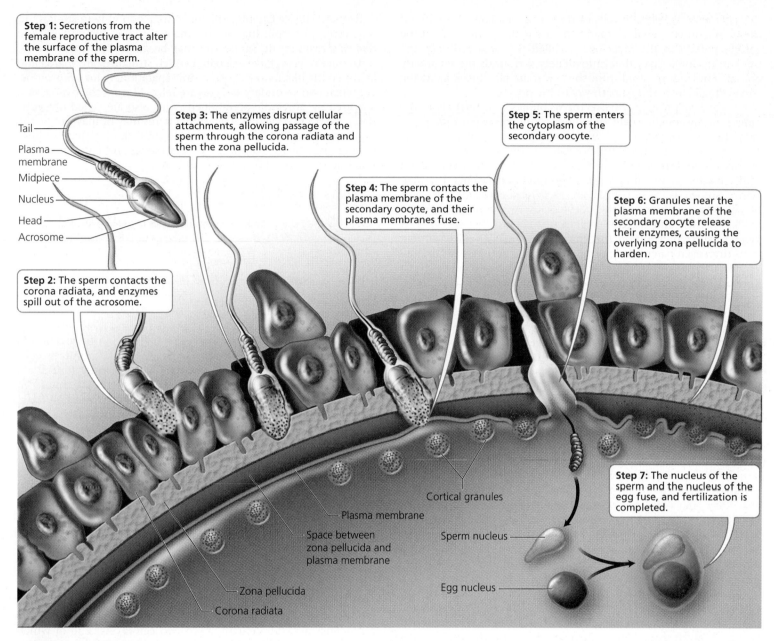

Step 1: Secretions from the female reproductive tract alter the surface of the plasma membrane of the sperm.

Step 3: The enzymes disrupt cellular attachments, allowing passage of the sperm through the corona radiata and then the zona pellucida.

Step 5: The sperm enters the cytoplasm of the secondary oocyte.

Step 4: The sperm contacts the plasma membrane of the secondary oocyte, and their plasma membranes fuse.

Step 6: Granules near the plasma membrane of the secondary oocyte release their enzymes, causing the overlying zona pellucida to harden.

Tail

Plasma membrane

Midpiece

Nucleus

Head

Acrosome

Step 2: The sperm contacts the corona radiata, and enzymes spill out of the acrosome.

Step 7: The nucleus of the sperm and the nucleus of the egg fuse, and fertilization is completed.

Cortical granules

Plasma membrane

Sperm nucleus

Space between zona pellucida and plasma membrane

Zona pellucida

Egg nucleus

Corona radiata

FIGURE 18.4 Fertilization

projections called fimbriae (singular, *fimbria;* see Figure 18.3). Cilia and waves of peristalsis move the oocyte slowly along the oviduct toward the uterus (*peristalsis* is a general term for the rhythmic waves of contraction and relaxation of smooth muscles in the walls of tubular organs, such as oviducts or digestive organs, that push the contents through the tubes).

The trip made by sperm is a considerably more competitive and precarious venture than the movements of the typically lone oocyte. During sexual intercourse, from 200 million to 600 million sperm are deposited in the vagina and on the cervix, the neck of the uterus that extends into the vagina. Many sperm become trapped at the boundary of the vagina and cervix. Indeed, less than 1% of deposited sperm actually enter the uterus. Sperm that escape entrapment use their whiplike tails (recall from Chapters 3 and 17 that each sperm has a flagellum) to move into the uterus and eventually the oviduct. Along the way, the sperm are aided by small uterine contractions stimulated by chemicals (prostaglandins) in the semen. Of the vast number of sperm originally deposited in the fe-

male reproductive tract, only about 200 reach the site of fertilization in the widened portion of the oviduct.

Typically, an egg lives only 12 to 24 hours after its release from the ovary. Most eggs are fertilized within 12 hours after their release. In addition, most sperm survive no more than 2 days in the female reproductive tract, though some may survive 5 days.

Two critical processes must precede fertilization (Figure **18.4**). First, secretions from the uterus or oviducts must alter the surface of the acrosome, the enzyme-containing cap on the head of a sperm. Alteration of the acrosome requires about 6 to 7 hours and appears to involve the removal of cholesterol and possibly other substances from the surface of the sperm. These changes destabilize the sperm's plasma membrane. The second process occurs when sperm with unstable membranes contact the *corona radiata,* a layer of cells surrounding the secondary oocyte. Once such contact occurs, perforations develop in the sperm's weakened plasma membrane and outer acrosomal membrane. Enzymes (shown as green dots in Figure 18.4) then spill out of the acrosome and digest the attachments between cells of the corona radiata. Digestion of these attachments enables sperm to pass between the cells of the corona radiata to the layer below called the *zona pellucida,* the thick noncellular layer that immediately surrounds the secondary oocyte. Enzymes released from the acrosome also break apart the zona pellucida, creating a pathway to the oocyte.

Several sperm may arrive at the secondary oocyte at about the same time, although usually only one sperm crosses the zona pellucida and reaches the plasma membrane of the secondary oocyte. The plasma membrane of the successful sperm and that of the secondary oocyte fuse, and the sperm enters the egg cytoplasm. Fusion of the plasma membranes triggers two important events. First, enzymes (shown as red dots in Figure 18.4) released by granules near the plasma membrane of the oocyte cause the zona pellucida to quickly harden and thereby prevent passage of other sperm. This block to entry by additional sperm ensures equal genetic contributions from each parent and prevents abnormal numbers of chromosomes in the resulting embryo, which would make it incapable of normal development. Second, the oocyte undergoes its second meiotic division (Chapter 17) and is now considered an ovum. The nucleus of the sperm (located in the sperm's head) and the nucleus of the ovum fuse (Figure 18.4). The remaining parts of the sperm (midpiece and tail) degenerate. The fertilized ovum is called a **zygote.** Just visible to the unaided eye, the zygote contains genetic material from both the mother (23 chromosomes) and father (23 chromosomes).

Cleavage

About 1 day after fertilization, the zygote undergoes **cleavage,** a rapid series of mitotic cell divisions. During cleavage, the single-celled zygote becomes a pre-embryo, first consisting of two cells, then four cells, then eight cells, and so on. Cleavage occurs as the pre-embryo moves along the oviduct toward the uterus (see Figure 18.3). The cleaving pre-embryo becomes a solid ball of cells by about day 3. By day 4, the pre-embryo is a *morula,* a solid ball of 12 or more cells produced by successive divisions of the zygote. These early cell divisions do not result in an overall increase in size; such increases are prevented by the tight-fitting zona pellucida that still covers the morula. Instead, the cells within the ball become progressively smaller as divisions occur.

Sometimes during an early stage of cleavage, the mass of cells splits, and two pre-embryos are formed. *Identical twins,* also called monozygotic twins ("from one zygote"), develop in this way. Such twins are always the same gender and have nearly identical genetic material (see Chapter 18a for a discussion of twin studies). In rare cases, the splitting of the pre-embryo is incomplete and *conjoined twins* result. Such twins may be surgically separated after birth once doctors have evaluated which structures are shared and analyzed the likelihood of successful separation. *Fraternal twins* occur when two secondary oocytes are released from the ovaries and fertilized by different sperm. Such twins also are called dizygotic twins ("from two zygotes"). Fraternal twins may or may not be the same gender and are no more genetically similar than siblings who are not twins. Identical twins (separate and conjoined) and fraternal twins are shown in Figure **18.5**.

stop and think

Given what you know about the events necessary to produce identical and fraternal twins, how might a set of triplets form in which two are identical and one fraternal?

The morula enters the uterus about 5 days after fertilization. As cell division continues, a cavity begins to form at the morula's center. Cells lining the cavity flatten and compact as the zona pellucida still prevents increases in overall size. Fluid from the uterine cavity passes through the zona pellucida and accumulates within the forming cavity, and the morula is converted into a **blastocyst,** a ball of cells with an inner fluid-filled cavity. As shown in Figure 18.3, the blastocyst is made up of two parts: an inner cell mass and a trophoblast. The **inner cell mass** (see above) is a group of cells that will become both the embryo proper and some of the extraembryonic membranes that will extend from or surround the embryo. The **trophoblast** is a thin layer of cells that will give rise to the extraembryonic membrane that is the embryo's contribution to the placenta. The **placenta** is the organ that delivers oxygen and nutrients to the embryo and carries carbon dioxide and other wastes away. Before the blastocyst becomes implanted in the uterine wall and the placenta develops, the blastocyst floats freely in the uterus. Increases in overall size of the blastocyst become possible when it frees itself from the degenerating zona pellucida.

Implantation

The blastocyst attaches to the endometrium (the lining of the uterus) about 6 days after fertilization. The trophoblast rapidly proliferates and differentiates into two cell layers, one of which begins to invade the endometrium. During this process, called

(a) Identical twins result when a single fertilized egg splits in two very early in development.

(b) Rarely, the splitting is incomplete and conjoined twins result.

(c) Fraternal twins result from the fertilization of two oocytes by different sperm.

FIGURE 18.5 Twins

Making Babies, but Not the Old-Fashioned Way

Some couples desperately want a child, but they cannot conceive one. The inability to become pregnant or to cause a pregnancy is called infertility. Couples are considered infertile if conception does not occur after 1 year of unprotected sexual intercourse. Infertility is not uncommon, striking about one in six American couples. In some of these couples, the woman is infertile. Hormonal imbalances may disrupt ovulation or implantation, or scarring from disease may block the oviducts and prevent passage of gametes. In women older than 40, aging eggs may be the problem. Some women are actually sterile (they can never conceive and carry a child) because they have had their uterus (and sometimes their ovaries) removed for medical reasons. In other couples, it is the man who is infertile. Male infertility often is caused by production of few or sluggish sperm or sperm with structural abnormalities. Some men are sterile (they can never cause a pregnancy) as a result of conditions such as cryptorchidism (failure of the testes to descend from the abdomen to the scrotum) or Klinefelter syndrome, a chromosomal disorder. Also, in a strange twist of fate, otherwise compatible couples may be incompatible at the cellular level. Women, for example, are sometimes allergic to their partner's sperm and produce antibodies that kill the sperm before they are able to fertilize an egg. Finally, in many of the most frustrating cases, the cause of infertility is unknown.

Can anything be done to help those who are infertile? For roughly half of the couples seeking help the answer is yes, although the road to reproduction may be long, expensive, and filled with emotional ups and downs. The procedures to treat infertility are collectively called assisted reproductive techniques (ARTs).

Some cases of female infertility can be treated by administering hormones. For example, hormones that trigger ovulation may be given to women whose ovaries fail to release eggs properly. Women who tend to miscarry (spontaneously abort) may be given progesterone to enhance the receptivity of their uterine lining. However, some causes of infertility, such as scarred oviducts in women and low sperm counts in men, do not respond to hormone therapy. What can be done in these cases?

Artificial insemination is one option available to couples whose infertility is caused by a low sperm count. In this procedure, sperm that have been donated and stored at a sperm bank are deposited (usually with a syringe) in the woman's cervix or vagina at about the time of ovulation. Sperm from the male member of the couple may be concentrated and then used. Alternatively, couples may use semen from an anonymous donor. (Artificial insemination with donor sperm also is frequently used by lesbian couples seeking to have children.) Another possibility for couples in which the man has few sperm, or sperm that lack the strength or enzymes necessary to penetrate an egg, is intracytoplasmic sperm injection (ICSI). In this procedure, a tiny needle is used to inject a single sperm into an egg (Figure **18.A**) in a laboratory setting. If fertilization occurs, the embryo can be transferred to the uterus.

Some cases of infertility can be treated with in vitro fertilization. Literally meaning fertilization

FIGURE 18.A Intracytoplasmic sperm injection. An egg, held in place with a blunt-nosed pipette (right), is injected with a single sperm.

in glass, IVF involves placing eggs and sperm together in a dish in the laboratory. First, the woman is treated with hormones to trigger superovulation—the ovulation of several eggs, rather than the typical lone egg. (An abundance of eggs is the key to many infertility treatments. Large numbers of eggs can be fertilized to produce many zygotes, which in turn will develop into pre-embryos. Having several pre-embryos available allows selection of the healthiest ones for immediate use and freezing of other healthy ones for future use.) Next, the eggs are removed from the woman's ovaries with a suction device and placed into a dish that contains a sample of the man's sperm. If fertilization occurs, the zygotes are transferred to a solution that will support further development. A few days later, when the pre-embryos are at an early blastocyst stage (about 3 to 5 days after fertilization), one or more of them is transferred to the woman's uterus. The uterus has been primed with estrogen and progesterone, and it is hoped that the pre-embryos will implant and complete development there. Women with blocked oviducts may conceive with IVF because the technique bypasses the oviducts altogether. If the woman lacks a uterus, the couple can hire a surrogate mother to gestate their baby. The egg and sperm may come from the couple or from other individuals.

Failure of pre-embryos to implant is partially responsible for the relatively low success rate of IVF. (Implantation is also a major hurdle for fertile couples, who lose about one in three pregnancies through failed implantation.) The problem with IVF seems to be the rather violent squirt of the pre-embryo into a reproductive tract that is already traumatized from hormone treatments and retrieval of eggs. Two new procedures avoid the problem of the pre-embryo's abrupt arrival in the uterus. In gamete intrafallopian transfer (GIFT), eggs and sperm are collected from a couple and inserted into the woman's oviduct, where fertilization is then expected to occur. Afterward, any resulting pre-embryos drift naturally (and gently) into the uterus. The second procedure is zygote intrafallopian transfer (ZIFT). In this procedure, eggs

CONTINUED ON PAGE 380

Ethical Issue CONTINUED

and sperm are collected and brought together in a dish in the laboratory. If fertilization occurs, the resulting zygotes are inserted into the woman's oviducts, where they continue to develop and travel on their own to the uterus. Normal, healthy oviducts are needed for GIFT and ZIFT to work.

At the beginning of this essay we stated that about half of couples who seek treatment for infertility are eventually rewarded with the birth of a child. Success rates of ARTs range from about 20% to 28% live births per egg retrieved. Although costs of the techniques vary somewhat, each attempt typically costs between $8000 and $12,000, and multiple attempts often are needed. Many health insurance plans do not cover these expenses, because the procedures are considered experimental or elective. And sometimes assisted reproductive techniques result in exceptionally large families with exceptionally large demands and responsibilities (Figure **18.B**).

What about the couples who do not conceive with ARTs? Is there hope that some day they might also conceive? The answer is a

decided yes. Advances in reproductive research and technology are rapidly providing potential treatments for infertility. Someday, a uterine transplant may be an option. In March 2002, doctors in Saudi Arabia transplanted a uterus from a 46-year-old woman undergoing a hysterectomy into a 26-year-old woman. (The recipient's uterus had previously been removed because of excessive bleeding following a cesarean section.) The transplanted uterus had to be removed after 99 days because of blood clotting. Nevertheless, Saudi doctors viewed the transplant as a success and were hopeful of better outcomes in the future. Similar efforts are under way in the United States.

Scientists are also working on techniques with mice in which spermatogonia, the stem cells deep within the testes that produce sperm, are transferred from a fertile animal to a sterile one. The once sterile mouse can then sire offspring. Some day it might be possible to remove stem cells from a man with a low sperm count, encourage the cells to multiply under laboratory conditions, and then return them—now in much greater numbers—to their rightful owner, who might then father children.

What about research with eggs? Although sperm and pre-embryos are routinely frozen, eggs quickly become inviable when manipulated outside the body and are thus difficult to store. However, new techniques for freezing eggs are being developed. Research also is under way on ovarian tissue transplantation as a way to produce functioning ovaries. Tissue from ovaries rich in potential eggs could be removed from a young female, frozen, and then placed back in her body years later. It might also be possible, though more difficult, to transplant ovarian tissue between females. Perhaps the most controversial research focuses on using eggs from fetuses. Fetal ovaries are a rich source of eggs, containing about 2 million as compared with the estimated 400 eggs ovulated by most women over the course of their reproductive years. Scientists are investigating the possibility of transplanting into infertile women tissue from the ovaries of fetuses made available from elective or spontaneous abortions. Fetal eggs might one day be stored at an egg bank, where they could be used by infertile women. The babies produced from such eggs would be in the truly unusual position of having a biological mother who had been aborted. Indeed, the aborted fetus with her wealth of eggs could potentially become the biological mother of many children. Obviously, current and future reproductive technologies raise many ethical questions.

Questions to Consider

- If you donated eggs or sperm for use by infertile couples, should you have a claim (legal or otherwise) to any offspring produced?
- If you were charged with establishing policies at an infertility clinic, how would you decide what should happen to pre-embryos created at the clinic that turned out to be "extra"? Do they have a right to life? And who gets the pre-embryos when couples divorce or die?
- Do you think it is ethical to use ovarian tissue from fetuses as a source of eggs for infertile women?

FIGURE 18.B Some assisted reproductive techniques may result in multiple births. Shown here are the McCaughey septuplets, conceived as a result of fertility drugs.

implantation, the blastocyst digests its way inward until it is firmly embedded in the endometrium (Figure **18.6**). Implantation normally occurs high up on the back wall of the uterus. Sometimes, however, a blastocyst implants outside the uterus, and an *ectopic pregnancy* results. The vast majority of implantations outside the uterus occur in the oviducts, usually because passage of the dividing pre-embryo through the oviduct is impaired in some way. Factors that hinder passage of the pre-embryo through the oviduct include structural abnormalities and scar tissue from surgery or pelvic inflammatory disease (see Chapters 17 and 17a). In such instances, the embryo is surgically removed (and hence the pregnancy terminated) because the oviduct cannot support a pregnancy, and because rupture of the oviduct by a growing embryo and the resulting hemorrhage can be fatal to the mother. Some ectopic pregnancies reach the fetal stage.

An estimated one-third to one-half of all zygotes fail to become blastocysts and fail to implant. The failed zygotes and early pre-embryos are either reabsorbed by cells of the endometrium or expelled from the uterus in an early spontaneous abortion (such an end to a pregnancy is described as *spontaneous* because it was not medically induced). Causes of early spontaneous abortion include chromosomal abnormalities in the zygote and an inhospitable uterine environment for implantation. The latter might result from the presence of an intrauterine device (IUD) or inadequate production of the hormones estrogen and progesterone by the corpus luteum.

(Recall from Chapter 17 that the corpus luteum is a glandular structure that forms from the ovarian follicle after ovulation.) These early spontaneous abortions are included in the term *miscarriage,* which describes pregnancy loss occurring before 20 weeks gestation. (After 20 weeks, the fetus is considered potentially viable, with medical support, and such deliveries are described as preterm or premature births when they occur before 37 weeks gestation; see below).

When conditions are right, the blastocyst completes implantation by the end of the second week of the pre-embryonic period. During implantation, cells within the blastocyst produce **human chorionic gonadotropin (HCG)**, a hormone that enters the mother's bloodstream and is excreted in her urine. Many pregnancy tests screen for the presence of this hormone in the mother's urine. Enough HCG is produced by the end of the second week to be detected by the pregnancy test and yield a positive result. Its usefulness in pregnancy tests aside, the physiological function of HCG is to maintain the corpus luteum and stimulate it to continue producing the hormone progesterone. Progesterone is essential for maintenance of the endometrium; without an adequate supply of progesterone, the endometrium would be shed, as during menstruation.

Infertility is the inability of a female to conceive (become pregnant) or of a male to cause conception. Implantation is a major hurdle in the series of steps leading to a successful pregnancy. The Ethical Issue essay *Making Babies, but Not the Old-Fashioned Way* describes many of the options available to infertile couples who wish to have children.

Extraembryonic membranes

Toward the end of the pre-embryonic period, four membranes—the amnion, yolk sac, allantois, and chorion—begin to form around the pre-embryo (Figure **18.7**). Formation of these membranes extends into the embryonic period, when the developing human is called an embryo. The membranes lie outside the embryo and are called **extraembryonic membranes**. These membranes protect and nourish the embryo and later the fetus. The **amnion** surrounds the entire embryo, enclosing it in a fluid-filled space called the amniotic cavity. Amniotic fluid forms a protective cushion around the embryo that later can be examined as part of prenatal testing in a procedure known as amniocentesis (see Chapter 20). The **yolk sac** is the primary source of nourishment for embryos in many species of vertebrates. In embryonic humans, however, it remains quite small and

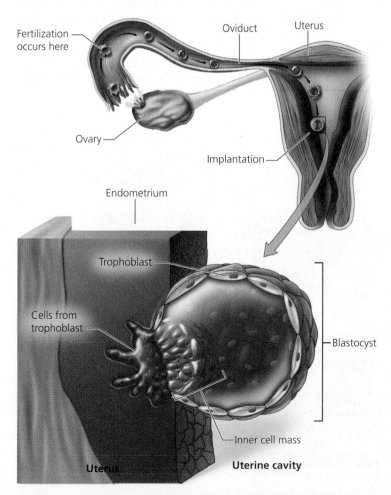

FIGURE 18.6 Implantation. About 6 days after fertilization, the blastocyst attaches to the endometrium of the uterus and begins to digest its way inward.

FIGURE 18.7 Extraembryonic membranes. The amnion, yolk sac, chorion, and allantois begin to form during the second to third week after fertilization.

does not provide nourishment. Human embryos receive nutrients from the placenta. The yolk sac in humans is a site of early blood cell formation. It also contains *primordial germ cells* that migrate to the embryo's gonads (testes or ovaries), where they differentiate into immature cells that will eventually become sperm or oocytes. The **allantois** is a small membrane whose blood vessels become part of the **umbilical cord**, the ropelike connection between the embryo and the placenta. The umbilical cord consists of blood vessels and supporting connective tissue. Finally, the **chorion** is the outermost membrane, which rests against the uterine cavity. The chorion develops largely from the trophoblast and becomes the embryo's major contribution to the placenta. The amnion, yolk sac, and allantois develop from the inner cell mass.

The placenta

The placenta orchestrates all interactions between the mother and the fetus. The placenta forms from the chorion of the embryo and a portion of the endometrium of the mother (specifically, the endometrium in the area where implantation occurred; Figure **18.8a**).

A major function of the placenta is to allow oxygen and nutrients to diffuse from maternal blood into embryonic blood. Wastes such as carbon dioxide and urea diffuse from embryonic blood into maternal blood. The placenta also produces hormones such as HCG, estrogen, and progesterone. Placental hormones, as mentioned earlier, are essential for the continued maintenance of pregnancy. High levels of HCG from the placenta may be responsible for *morning sickness,* the nausea and vomiting experienced by some women early in pregnancy. (Morning sickness is not restricted to the morning, by the way.)

Formation of the placenta begins shortly after implantation. During implantation, cells derived from the trophoblast rapidly divide and invade the endometrium. Cavities form that fill with blood from maternal capillaries severed by the invading cells. Soon, fingerlike processes of the chorion, called **chorionic villi,** grow into the endometrium (Figure 18.8b). These chorionic villi grow, divide, and continue their invasion of maternal tissue, causing ever larger cavities and pools of maternal blood to form. The placenta is fully developed by the third month of pregnancy. At this time, it weighs about 680 g (1.5 lb).

Chorionic villi contain blood vessels connected to the developing embryo. Oxygen and nutrients in the pools of maternal blood diffuse through the capillaries of the villi into the umbilical vein and travel to the embryo. Wastes leave the embryo by the umbilical arteries, move into capillaries within the chorionic villi, and diffuse into maternal blood. Thus, the chorionic villi provide exchange surfaces for diffusion of nutrients, oxygen, and wastes. Some chorionic villi also anchor the embryonic portion of the placenta to maternal tissue.

Under normal circumstances, there is no direct mixing of maternal and fetal blood; all exchanges occur across capillary walls. Nevertheless, the closeness of the maternal and fetal blood vessels within the placenta causes the fetus to share in maternal nutrition, habits, and lifestyle. In addition to beneficial nutrients and oxygen, harmful substances can cross the placenta from the mother to the fetus, including some drugs, alcohol, caffeine, toxins in cigarette smoke, and HIV (human immunodeficiency virus, the virus that causes AIDS).

Usually, implantation occurs high up on the back wall of the uterus, so the placenta forms in upper portions of the uterus. Sometimes, however, implantation occurs lower in the uterus, and the developing placenta grows to cover the cervix, the neck of the uterus that projects into the vagina; this condition is called *placenta previa*. Placenta previa may cause premature birth or maternal hemorrhage. Most women with diagnosed placenta previa have their baby delivered by cesarean section before labor begins.

Oxygen and nutrients diffuse from pools of maternal blood into capillaries within the chorionic villi and are carried to the fetus via vessels in the umbilical cord. Fetal wastes move in the opposite direction.

Maternal circulation

Endometrium of uterus

Maternal blood vessels

Fetal blood vessels

Fingerlike processes of the fetal chorion, called chorionic villi, extend into the endometrium of the mother.

Chorionic villus

Umbilical cord

Fetal circulation

Amniotic fluid

Placenta

2 weeks   4 weeks   8 weeks   12 weeks   38 weeks (full term)

(a) The placenta begins to form at about 2 weeks (shortly after implantation) and is fully developed by about 12 weeks.

(b) The internal structure of the placenta

FIGURE 18.8 The placenta is formed from the chorion of the embryo and the endometrium of the mother.

Cesarean section, often shortened to C-section, is the procedure by which the fetus and placenta are removed surgically from the uterus through an incision in the abdominal wall and uterus.

Embryonic Period

The embryonic period extends from the third to the eighth week of development. It is a time of great change, beginning with the formation of three distinct germ layers from which all tissues and organs develop. We first describe the general process by which germ layers form, and then we consider development of the central nervous system and reproductive system as examples of tissue and organ formation during the embryonic period. By the end of the embryonic period, all organs have formed, and the embryo has a distinctly human appearance. Three interrelated processes produce this tiny human: cell division (which continues from the pre-embryonic period); **cell differentiation** (the process by which cells become specialized with respect to structure and function); and **morphogenesis** (the development of overall body organization and shape).

Gastrulation

Morphogenesis begins during the third week after fertilization. Just before the start of morphogenesis, during implantation, the inner cell mass moves away from the surface of the blastocyst, and the amniotic cavity forms. The amniotic cavity is filled with amniotic fluid and lined by the amnion, one of the four extraembryonic membranes. The inner cell mass, which now becomes a flattened platelike structure called the *embryonic disk* (Figure **18.9**), is destined to become the embryo proper. But first, the cells within the embryonic disk must differentiate and migrate, forming three **primary germ layers** known as ectoderm, mesoderm, and endoderm. The cell movements that establish the primary germ layers are called **gastrulation**, and the embryo during this period is called a *gastrula* (Figure 18.9).

All tissues and organs develop from the primary germ layers. **Ectoderm** covers the surface of the embryo and forms the outer layer of skin and its derivatives such as hair, nails, oil glands, sweat glands, and mammary glands. Ectoderm also forms the nervous system. Another germ layer, the **endoderm**, turns inward to form the lining of the digestive tract. Endoderm also forms the lining of the urinary and respiratory tracts, as well as other organs and glands (for example, the pancreas, liver, thyroid gland, and parathyroid glands). **Mesoderm** fills some of the space between ectoderm and endoderm, and gives rise to muscle; bone and other connective tissue; and various organs, including the heart, kidneys, ovaries, and testes. Because gastrulation initiates the processes by which the developing embryo's body takes shape and becomes organized, it is considered a key part of morphogenesis.

As gastrulation proceeds, a flexible rod of mesoderm tissue called the **notochord** develops where the vertebral column will form. The notochord defines the long axis of the embryo and gives the embryo some rigidity. The notochord also prompts overlying ectoderm to begin formation of the central nervous system (CNS), as discussed shortly. Vertebrae eventually form around the notochord, and the notochord degenerates. The pulpy, elastic material in the center of intervertebral disks (pads that help cushion the bones of the vertebral column) is all that remains of our notochord.

Development of the central nervous system

A major milestone in embryonic development is the formation of the central nervous system (brain and spinal cord) from ectoderm, as shown in Figure **18.10**. The developing notochord induces the overlying ectoderm to thicken. This thickened region of ectoderm above the notochord is called the neural plate. The neural plate folds inward, forming a groove that extends the length of the embryo, along its back surface. The raised sides of the groove, known as neural folds, grow upward and eventually meet and fuse to form the **neural tube**, a fluid-filled tube that will become the central nervous system. The process by which the neural tube is

Gastrula: Embryo with three primary germ layers (ectoderm, mesoderm, and endoderm)

Day 16

Late blastocyst: Pre-embryo, with the embryonic disk, two layers of cells that become the embryo proper

Day 10

Early blastocyst: Hollow ball of cells with a fluid-filled cavity

Day 6

Morula: Solid ball of cells formed as the zygote undergoes cleavage

Day 4

Inner cell mass

Blastocyst cavity

Trophoblast

Amniotic cavity

Embryonic disk

Yolk sac

Ectoderm

Mesoderm

Endoderm

FIGURE 18.9 Early stages of development in cross section

Dorsal views of the embryo

Cross sections through the embryo

— Amnion —
— Amniotic cavity —
— Neural plate
— Ectoderm
— Mesoderm
— Endoderm
— Notochord
— Yolk sac

Step 1: The notochord induces overlying ectoderm to thicken and form the neural plate.

Day 17

— Neural groove —

Step 2: The neural plate folds inward, forming the neural groove.

Day 18

— Future brain
— Neural fold —
— Future spinal cord

Step 3: The raised sides of the neural groove, called neural folds, grow upward.

Day 21

— Surface ectoderm
— Somite —
— Neural tube
— Notochord —

Step 4: The neural folds fuse to form the neural tube, which will develop into the brain and spinal cord.

Day 23

FIGURE 18.10 Formation of the central nervous system from ectoderm. Dorsal views of a human embryo (left) and corresponding cross-sectional views or parts of such views (right) are shown at four different days during development of the brain and spinal cord.

formed is called **neurulation**, and the embryo during this period is called a *neurula*. The anterior portion of the neural tube develops into the brain, and the posterior portion forms the spinal cord. Alongside the neural tube, mesoderm cells organize into blocks called **somites**. Somites eventually form skeletal muscles of the neck and trunk, connective tissues, and vertebrae.

Failure of the neural tube to develop and close properly results in neural tube defects. *Spina bifida* ("split spine") is a type of neural tube defect in which part of the spinal cord develops abnormally, as does the adjacent area of the spine. The severity of spina bifida varies greatly, and some cases can be improved through surgery. *Anencephaly* is a neural tube defect that involves incomplete development of the brain and results in stillbirth or death shortly after birth.

Development of the reproductive system

Among the 23 chromosomes provided by the mother's egg is an X chromosome. Among the 23 chromosomes provided by the father's sperm is an X or a Y chromosome. The X and Y chromosomes are called sex chromosomes, and they determine the gender of human embryos. More specifically, the gender of an embryo is determined at fertilization by the type of sperm that fertilizes the egg. If an X-bearing sperm fertilizes the egg, then the zygote is XX and will normally develop as a female. If a Y-bearing sperm fertilizes the egg, then the zygote is XY and will normally develop as a male.

what would you do?

Methods are currently available to separate X-bearing sperm from Y-bearing sperm. During the procedure, sperm are treated with a fluorescent dye that binds to DNA. X-bearing and Y-bearing sperm glow differently because the X chromosomes have almost 3% more DNA than Y chromosomes have. Thus X- and Y-bearing sperm can be sorted by an automated machine. Such "sperm sorting" makes possible the selection of a child's gender. Couples could decide whether to use X-bearing sperm to produce a female baby or Y-bearing sperm to produce a male baby. Some couples want to select the gender of their child to avoid X-linked genetic disorders; others want to balance their families with respect to numbers of sons and daughters. The chosen sperm are deposited within the woman's vagina or cervix at a time when pregnancy is likely to occur. (The process of depositing semen within the female reproductive tract is called artificial insemination.) Should parents be allowed to choose the gender of their children? What implications would gender selection have for families and for society? If you were given the responsibility of deciding whether such technology should continue to be made available to parents, what would you do?

Male and female embryos have the same external and internal anatomy for the first few weeks of development; their reproductive organs have not yet differentiated. The embryos at this time are described as being "sexually indifferent." However, about 6 weeks after fertilization, a region of the Y chromosome—called SRY for sex-determining region of the Y chromosome—initiates development of testes in XY embryos. The testes soon begin producing testosterone, the sex hormone that directs development of male reproductive organs. Female embryos lack the Y chromosome; in its absence, ovaries develop. The development of female reproductive structures is not influenced by hormones, and female structures will develop even if ovaries do not fully develop. Thus, it is the absence of the Y chromosome and testosterone that leads to female development. We focus on development of the external

Undifferentiated stage at 6 weeks gestation

10 weeks gestation

14 weeks gestation

Female development

Bud between legs

Urogenital fold

Urogenital groove

Labioscrotal swelling

Anus

No Y chromosome

Development of reproductive structures does not require hormones.

Clitoris

Labia minora

Labia majora

Anus

Y chromosome

Male development

Development of reproductive structures requires testosterone from developing testes.

Glans penis

Shaft of penis

Scrotum

Anus

FIGURE 18.11 Development of external genitalia

genitalia, but keep in mind that internal reproductive organs also are undergoing differentiation.

Both male and female embryos of about 6 weeks of age have a small bud of tissue between their legs (Figure **18.11**). Just below this bud is a shallow depression called the urogenital groove. The urogenital groove is surrounded by urogenital folds, which in turn are surrounded by labioscrotal swellings. In the male embryo, testosterone produced by the newly differentiated testes causes the urogenital groove to elongate and completely close. The bud then becomes the glans penis; the urogenital folds develop into the shaft of the penis; and the labioscrotal swellings become the scrotum (into which the testes will later descend). In the female, the urogenital groove also elongates, but instead of closing, as in the male, it remains open. The bud becomes the clitoris in females, and the urogenital folds develop into the labia minora. The labioscrotal swellings of females become the labia majora. The formation of male and female reproductive structures is typically completed by the end of the third month of gestation (i.e., within the fetal period).

Fetal Period

The fetal period extends from the ninth week after fertilization until birth. Although tissues and organs continue to differentiate during this period, the most notable change in most body parts is rapid growth, made possible by the placenta. The placenta completes its development early in the fetal period. Through its efficient functioning, oxygen and nutrients are carried to cells of the fetus, and wastes such as carbon dioxide and urea are carried away.

Prenatal period **Postnatal period**

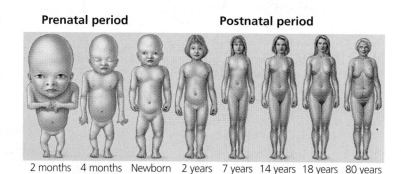

2 months 4 months Newborn 2 years 7 years 14 years 18 years 80 years

FIGURE 18.12 Allometric growth. Changes in body proportions occur throughout prenatal and postnatal development. For comparison, all stages are drawn to the same total height.

Growth

Growth during the fetal period is extremely rapid, as reflected in phenomenal increases in weight (from 8 g to 3400 g, or from about 0.3 oz to 120 oz) and substantial increases in length (the length as measured from the head to the rump changes from 50 to 360 mm, or from about 2 in. to 14 in.), when the pregnancy continues for the full 38 weeks. One striking change during the fetal stage is that the growth rate of the head slows relative to the growth rate of other regions of the body, altering the way the body is proportioned (Figure **18.12**). Difference in the relative rates of growth of various parts of the body is called **allometric growth**. Such growth continues after birth and helps to shape developing humans and other organisms.

Q *Which two structures in the fetus allow blood to bypass the pulmonary circulation?*

High oxygenation
Moderate oxygenation
Low oxygenation
Very low oxygenation

Ductus arteriosus becomes a ligament.

Foramen ovale closes and leaves a depression.

Ductus venosus becomes a ligament.

Umbilical vein becomes a ligament.

Umbilical arteries become ligaments.

Superior vena cava

Right atrium

Right ventricle

Inferior vena cava

Liver

Placenta

Umbilical cord

Aorta

Pulmonary trunk (divides into right and left pulmonary arteries)

Left atrium

Left ventricle

Lung

Abdominal aorta

Inferior vena cava

Hepatic portal vein

Navel (belly button)

Common iliac artery

(a) Fetal circulation is characterized by a connection to the placenta (the umbilical cord) and several bypasses around organs that do not yet perform their postnatal functions.

(b) At birth, the umbilical cord is tied off and cut, leaving the navel (belly button). The bypasses close, allowing more blood to reach the now functional organs of the newborn.

FIGURE 18.13 Fetal circulation and changes at birth

A *In the fetus, the foramen ovale (between the right and left atria) and the ductus arteriosus (on the pulmonary trunk) divert blood away from the lungs, which are not yet functional.*

Fetal circulation

The fetal circulatory system differs from circulation after birth because several organs—the lungs, kidneys, and liver, to name a few—do not perform their postnatal functions in the fetus (Figure **18.13**). Before birth, most blood is shunted past these organs through temporary vessels or openings. Recall that the fetus receives its oxygen and nutrients from maternal blood and gives up its carbon dioxide and wastes to maternal blood at the placenta.

Fetal blood must travel to the placenta to rid itself of carbon dioxide and wastes and to pick up oxygen and nutrients. It does so by flowing through umbilical arteries that branch off large arteries in the legs of the fetus. The two umbilical arteries run through the umbilical cord to the placenta. Once exchanges between fetal and maternal blood have occurred at the placenta, blood rich in oxygen and nutrients travels back to the fetus in the umbilical vein (within the umbilical cord; Figure 18.13a). Some of this blood flows to the fetal liver, which produces red blood cells but does not yet function in digestion. Most of the blood from the pla-

centa, however, bypasses the liver by means of a temporary vessel called the *ductus venosus* and heads to the heart.

Like the liver, fetal lungs are not yet functional and need only a small amount of blood for growth and removal of wastes from their cells. Once blood enters the right atrium of the heart, some of it passes to the right ventricle and on to the lungs, as it does in circulation after birth. Most of the blood, however, moves into the left atrium through a small hole in the wall between the atria, called the *foramen ovale*. The blood in the left atrium moves into the left ventricle and out to the body of the fetus. Another shunt, called the *ductus arteriosus*, connects the pulmonary trunk to the aorta and also functions to divert blood away from the lungs. Thus, blood flowing out of the right ventricle into the pulmonary trunk is shunted away from the lungs and into the aorta, where it travels to all areas of the fetus. Another glance at Figure 18.13a reveals that much of the blood traveling through the fetus is moderate to low in oxygen. Indeed, the umbilical vein is the only fetal vessel that carries fully oxygenated blood.

At birth—when the lungs, liver, and other organs begin their postnatal functions—fetal circulation converts to the postnatal pattern (Figure 18.13b). Blood flow to the placenta ceases when the umbilical cord is tied and cut off. The scar left by the cord becomes the baby's navel, or belly button. Within the infant, the umbilical arteries, umbilical vein, ductus venosus, and ductus arteriosus constrict, shrivel, and form ligaments. The foramen ovale normally closes shortly after birth, leaving a small depression in the wall between the two atria. In some newborns, the foramen ovale fails to close. Known as *blue babies,* these infants have a bluish appearance because much of their blood still bypasses the lungs and is low in oxygen. Fortunately, this defect can be corrected with surgery.

Birth

Birth, also called **parturition,** usually occurs about 38 weeks after fertilization. The process by which the fetus is expelled from the uterus and moved through the vagina to the outside world is called **labor.** Uterine contractions during true labor occur at regular intervals, are usually painful, and intensify with walking. Recall from Chapter 10 that the hormone oxytocin released from the posterior pituitary gland causes contractions of the smooth muscle of the uterus. These contractions, in turn, stimulate further release of oxytocin in a positive feedback loop. As true labor proceeds, contractions become more intense, and the interval between them decreases. In contrast, false labor consists of irregular contractions that fail to intensify or change with walking; these contractions are sometimes called Braxton Hicks contractions, after the doctor who first described them in 1872. These contractions routinely occur and are most common during the last few months of pregnancy.

Three Stages of True Labor

True labor can be divided into three stages (Figure **18.14**). The first stage, known as the *dilation stage,* begins with the onset of regular contractions and ends at the point when the cervix has fully dilated to 10 cm (4 in.). This stage usually lasts about 6 to 7 hours, although it can be shorter in women who previously have given birth. During the dilation stage, the amniotic sac usually ruptures,

releasing amniotic fluid. Known commonly as *breaking water,* rupture of the amniotic sac may be done deliberately by a doctor or midwife if it does not happen spontaneously. The second stage, the *expulsion stage,* begins with full dilation of the cervix and ends with delivery of the baby. This stage may last 1 or more hours. Some physicians make an incision to enlarge the vaginal opening, just before passage of the baby's head. This procedure, an *episiotomy,* facilitates delivery and avoids ragged tearing, which is generally slower to heal. Once delivery of the baby is complete, the umbilical cord is clamped and cut. The newborn takes his or her first breath, and the conversion of fetal circulation to the postnatal pattern begins. Labor, however, is not over. The third (and final) stage of true labor is the *placental stage,* which begins with delivery of the newborn and ends when the afterbirth, consisting of the placenta and fetal membranes, is expelled from the mother's body about 15 minutes after the baby. Continuing and powerful uterine contractions aid in expulsion of the placenta and constriction of maternal blood vessels torn during delivery. Any vaginal incision or tearing is sutured once labor has ended.

Most babies are born head first, facing the vertebral column of their mother. Some babies, however, are born buttocks first, and their delivery is called *breech birth.* Breech births are associated with difficult labors and umbilical cord accidents, such as compression or looping of the cord around the baby's neck. Thus, many physicians attempt to turn breech babies into the headfirst position before delivery. The baby may be delivered by cesarean section if turning is not successful.

Babies born at least 38 weeks after fertilization are called *full-term infants.* These babies weigh, on average, 3400 g (7.5 lb). Some babies are born 1 or more weeks late. Because the placenta begins to deteriorate with time, labor is typically induced if a pregnancy continues for 41 or more weeks. Babies born before 37 weeks of gestation are called *premature infants.* About 12% of babies born in the United States are born prematurely. Their chances for survival increase with length of time spent in the female reproductive tract. Doctors do not usually attempt to save infants born at 22 weeks gestation or less because, even with intensive medical care, major disabilities are almost inevitable. Such babies weigh about 630 g (1.4 lb). Amazingly, infants born at 25 weeks gestation and weighing

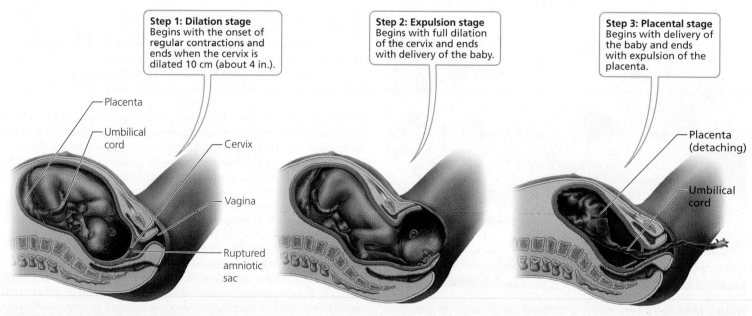

FIGURE 18.14 The stages of true labor

about 1 kg (2.2 lb) have a 50% to 80% chance of surviving, provided they receive intensive care. Intensive medical care is needed because the organ systems of these infants have not matured sufficiently to take over the functions normally performed by the mother's body. Care for premature infants often includes numerous blood transfusions, tube feeding, and maintenance on a respirator (Figure **18.15**). Even with excellent intensive care, health problems may persist well beyond infancy.

what would you do?

Babies born before 25 weeks gestation typically have a low chance of survival, even with excellent medical care. In addition, they have a very high probability of suffering from severe disabilities, if they do survive. Should efforts be made to save all such infants? Or should criteria be used to decide which infants the doctors should try to save and which they should let die? If you were given the responsibility of developing such criteria, what would you suggest? More to the point, if your infant were born before 25 weeks, what would you ask the doctor to do?

Role of the Placenta

In humans, the signal to initiate labor appears to come from the placenta in the form of *corticotropin-releasing hormone (CRH)*. Levels of CRH begin to rise in fetal and maternal bloodstreams beginning about 12 weeks into gestation. Sharp increases in CRH occur during the last few weeks of gestation. This placental hormone stimulates the anterior pituitary gland of the fetus to release adrenocorticotropic hormone, which, in turn, prompts the fetal adrenal glands to release a hormone that is converted by the placenta into estrogen. As a result of this conversion, levels of estrogen increase relative to progesterone, causing a cascade of events that initiate labor. These events include coordinated uterine contractions, dilation of the cervix, and release of oxytocin. Some recent studies support CRH as the initiating signal. In these studies, the level of CRH between weeks 16 and 20 of gestation predicted the timing of birth. Women with the highest levels of CRH were likely to deliver prematurely. Those with the lowest levels were likely to deliver late. The precise biological effects of CRH on the smooth muscle of the uterus are still being investigated; such information is critical to any future medical

FIGURE 18.15 Many premature infants require intensive care because their organs are not yet functional.

application involving the manipulation of CRH levels. Prevention of premature deliveries and the consequent health risks to infants is a major goal for understanding the events that initiate labor.

Drugs and Breathing Techniques

Most women experience pain during childbirth. The level of pain varies greatly and seems to depend on factors such as degree of fear and tension, the physical surroundings, and the support received. Typically, the more prepared and relaxed a woman is, the less intense pain she feels. Reduced stress is one reason health care workers encourage expectant mothers and their partners to enroll in childbirth classes. These classes provide information on the stages of labor and medical procedures associated with delivery. Childbirth classes also teach breathing and relaxation techniques.

Drugs may be administered to reduce the pain of childbirth. Analgesics—substances that relieve pain—may be administered intramuscularly or intravenously. Regional anesthetics, substances that produce loss of sensation in specific areas of the body, also may be used. For example, in epidural anesthesia, an anesthetic is injected in the lower back into the space between the dura mater (the outer membrane covering the spinal cord) and the vertebral canal. This injection blocks pain and motor impulses to the abdomen. Because motor impulses are blocked, epidural procedures are performed fairly early during labor so this effect will have worn off toward the end of labor, when pushing by the mother is critical for successful vaginal delivery. Epidural anesthesia is associated with slowing the fetal heartbeat. Thus, its use necessitates continuous fetal monitoring.

Many women rely on breathing or relaxation techniques rather than medications to relieve the pain of childbirth. Childbirth without the use of pain-killing drugs is often called *natural childbirth*. Whether to use medication during childbirth is a decision that is best made by weighing the costs and benefits to both mother and baby. Also, because it is impossible to predict with certainty what will occur during labor and delivery, all expectant mothers should keep an open mind.

Birth Defects

The development of a fertilized egg into a baby is an incredibly wondrous yet complex process. In view of its complexity, it is not difficult to imagine that things might go wrong along the way. Indeed, the potential for mistakes seems enormous. Thus, we should not be surprised to learn that not every zygote develops into a baby, and not all babies are born healthy. Developmental defects present at birth are called **birth defects.** They may involve structure, function, behavior, or metabolism. The study of birth defects is called teratology (*teratos,* monster), reflecting the unfortunate term used in earlier times to describe severely deformed infants.

The causes of birth defects may be genetic or environmental. Genetic causes include mutant genes or changes in the number or structure of chromosomes. Environmental causes include drugs, chemicals, radiation, deficiencies in maternal nutrition, and certain viruses, such as herpes simplex and rubella (the cause of German measles). Birth defects resulting from genetic causes will be discussed in Chapter 19. Some of the birth defects associated with psychoactive drugs were considered in Chapter 8a.

Environmental agents that disrupt development have their greatest effects during periods of rapid differentiation, when cells and tissues acquire specific functions and form organs. Recall that these events largely occur during the embryonic period (week 3

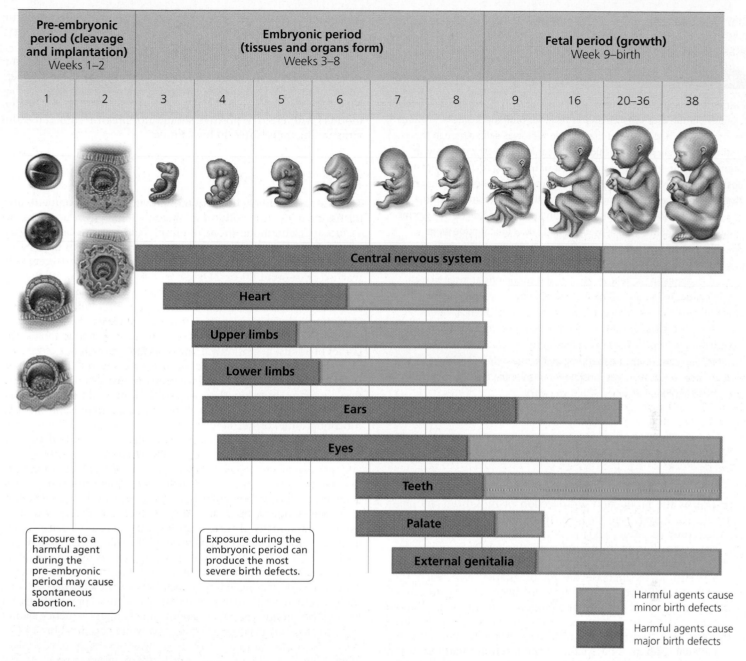

| Pre-embryonic period (cleavage and implantation) Weeks 1–2 | Embryonic period (tissues and organs form) Weeks 3–8 | Fetal period (growth) Week 9–birth |

Exposure to a harmful agent during the pre-embryonic period may cause spontaneous abortion.

Exposure during the embryonic period can produce the most severe birth defects.

Central nervous system

Heart

Upper limbs

Lower limbs

Ears

Eyes

Teeth

Palate

External genitalia

Harmful agents cause minor birth defects

Harmful agents cause major birth defects

FIGURE 18.16 Critical periods in development

through week 8). Exposure to disruptive agents during the embryonic period can cause major birth defects (Figure **18.16**). Such defects, characterized by major structural abnormalities, occur in 2% to 3% of newborns. Spina bifida is an example of a major birth defect. Disruptive agents produce more minor defects during the fetal period, when most organs are growing rather than differentiating. Minor birth defects such as having a single horizontal crease across the upper palm of the hand (instead of two creases) occur in about 4% to 5% of newborns.

We have said that all organs and organ systems develop primarily during the embryonic period. Nevertheless, different organs develop at somewhat different times and rates. Such variation results in each organ system having a critical period in which it is most susceptible to disruption by environmental agents. The CNS has a critical period extending from week 3 through week 16. During this time, the developing nervous system is highly sensitive, and disruptive agents can have major consequences. By compari-

son, exposure to such agents after week 16 tends to induce relatively minor defects. The CNS has the longest critical period. It extends beyond the embryonic period and into the fetal period. This long critical period may explain why the brain is the organ in which defects in structure and function are most commonly found. The critical period for development of the upper and lower limbs is relatively short, extending from about week 4 to week 6. It is during this short window of time that certain environmental agents cause major abnormalities such as tiny limbs or complete absence of limbs.

Another look at Figure 18.16 reveals that exposure to harmful agents during the first 2 weeks after fertilization is not known to cause birth defects. Development during this period (the pre-embryonic period) centers on formation of structures outside the embryo, such as the extraembryonic membranes described earlier. However, the developing pre-embryo is not immune to environmental influences. Disruptive agents in the pre-embryonic period may interfere with cleavage or implantation and cause a spontaneous abortion. Chromosomal abnormalities also account for a large proportion of spontaneous abortions at this time.

During the late 1950s and early 1960s, the drug thalidomide was widely used in Europe as a sedative and as relief for morning sickness. Previous animal testing had indicated that thalidomide was safe; although the testing reportedly did not include pregnant animals. Unfortunately, in humans, the drug caused major defects of the limbs such as complete absence of limbs or abnormally small limbs lacking elbows and knees. Thalidomide also caused abnormalities of the heart (some of which caused death shortly after birth), ears, and urinary and digestive systems. About 12,000 infants whose mothers had taken thalidomide were affected. In later years, thalidomide was found to be an effective treatment for conditions such as leprosy and cancer of the bone marrow as well as appearing to relieve some of the conditions associated with HIV infection. Today, thalidomide is available by prescription in the United States and is sold over the counter in South America, where "thalidomide babies" are still being born. Should a drug known to cause severe birth defects be made available for treatment of seriously ill adults? How can we ensure that pregnant women do not mistakenly take thalidomide? If you were responsible for developing a policy regarding the use of thalidomide, what would you do?

Milk Production by Mammary Glands

Lactation is the production and ejection of milk from the mammary glands. Recall from Chapter 10 that the hormone prolactin from the anterior pituitary gland promotes milk production. Recall also that oxytocin from the posterior pituitary gland stimulates milk ejection. The structure of the breast was described in Chapter 17.

Prolactin levels increase during pregnancy and reach their peak at birth. Milk production does not begin during pregnancy, because high levels of estrogen and progesterone inhibit the actions of prolactin. Thus, prolactin cannot initiate milk production until birth, when levels of estrogen and progesterone decline. Milk usually is available about 3 days later. In the interim, infants consume *colostrum*, a cloudy yellowish fluid produced by the breasts that has a different composition than milk. After birth, the infant's sucking on the breast stimulates the release of prolactin, promoting and maintaining the production of milk. At weaning, when sucking ends, so, too, does milk production.

Which is best—bottle or breast? Most people today believe that breast-feeding is best for infants. Advocates of breast-feeding point out that compared with commercial formulas—many of them based on cow's milk—breast milk is more digestible and much less likely to cause an allergic reaction, constipation, or obesity in infants. In addition, maternal milk and colostrum contain antibodies and special proteins that boost the immune system. Finally, obtaining milk from a breast requires more effort than sucking on a bottle. Health professionals think this greater effort promotes optimum development of the infant's jaws, teeth, and facial muscles.

Breast-feeding also is beneficial to the mother. Nursing helps the mother's uterus return toward its prepregnant size. When oxytocin is released in response to an infant's sucking, it helps the uterus shrink. Also, because milk production is energetically expensive, breast-feeding helps with maternal weight loss in the weeks and months after giving birth. Finally, breast-feeding offers some protection against breast cancer.

Despite its benefits, breast-feeding is not for everyone. Some women simply prefer bottle-feeding, while others have difficulty breast-feeding. Still others are warned against breast-feeding because the medications they take pass into breast milk. Finally, mothers who are HIV positive should not breast-feed because the virus can be transmitted in breast milk.

Postnatal Period

The postnatal period—the period of growth and development after birth—includes the following stages: infancy (from birth to 12 months), childhood (from 13 months to 12 or 13 years), puberty (from 12 to 15 years in girls and from 13 to 16 years in boys), adolescence (from puberty to late teens), and adulthood (generally reached by around 20 or 21 years of age). The start of adulthood is imprecise because of the many factors—physical, behavioral, societal—that influence how people define an adult. Growth and formation of bone usually are completed by age 25. **Aging**, the normal and progressive decline in the structure and function of the bodies of adults, begins only a few years after growth has ceased.

Observable characteristics of old age—graying and thinning hair, wrinkles and sagging skin, reduced muscle mass, and stooped posture—are familiar to us. However, we also grow old on the inside. For example, bones weaken and blood vessels stiffen. Nephrons, the functional units of the kidneys, decline in number and efficiency, ultimately challenging efforts by the kidneys to maintain the balance of fluids in our bodies. Aging also strikes our nervous system and sense organs, as evidenced by our deteriorating ability to remember, see, hear, taste, and smell. **Table 18.2** summarizes some of the changes to organ systems that typically occur with aging. Of course, we do not suddenly become "old." Changes to body systems occur gradually, and many of them begin to surface in middle age. For example, declines in basal metabolic rate will result in weight gain after about age 35 unless lifestyle changes are made to reduce caloric intake, increase activity, or both. Most people in their forties begin to experience a decreasing ability to focus on close objects, necessitating more frequent visits to the eye doctor and new prescriptions for lenses. Also, around age 50, our ability to hear high-frequency sounds starts to gradually decline, reflecting a slow but continual loss of hair cells in the inner ear that begins in our twenties! Even so, you might wonder why we discuss aging in a textbook geared toward college students. Our reasoning is simple; you can do a lot right now to ensure a high quality of life during old age (Figure **18.17**).

Possible Causes of Aging

Scientists do not agree about what causes our bodies to age. Some, with a "whole body" view, suggest that aging results from changes in critical body systems. For example, aging might be prompted by a decline in function of the immune system or by changing levels of certain hormones. Recall from Chapter 10 that the production of some hormones, such as growth hormone in both sexes and estrogen in females, declines as we age. Perhaps such declines induce the changes in bodily structure and function that characterize aging. Other scientists seek explanations for the causes of aging at the cellular and molecular levels.

Cessation of cell division

Ongoing cell division is necessary to replace cells that die. Without new cells, most tissues and organs could not continue to function

TABLE 18.2 Changes in Organ Systems as We Age

Organ System	Some Changes That Occur with Aging
Integumentary	Wrinkles appear as skin becomes thinner and less elastic. Sweat glands decrease in number, making regulation of body temperature more challenging. Hair thins owing to death of hair follicles and turns gray as pigment-producing cells die.
Skeletal	Bones become lighter and more brittle, especially in women after menopause. About 7.6 cm (3 in.) of height are lost as the intervertebral disks deteriorate and the vertebrae move closer together. Joints become stiff and painful due to decreased production of synovial fluid.
Muscular	Muscle mass decreases owing to loss of muscle cells and decreased size of remaining muscle cells.
Nervous	Brain mass decreases. Movements and reflexes slow as conduction velocity of nerve fibers decreases and release of neurotransmitters slows. Hearing becomes less acute as hair cells in the inner ear are lost. Ability of the eye to focus declines as the lens of the eye stiffens. Smell and taste become less acute.
Endocrine	In women, production of estrogen and progesterone decreases with menopause. In men, production of testosterone decreases. In both sexes, production of growth hormone decreases.
Cardiovascular	Cardiac output decreases as walls of the heart stiffen. Blood pressure rises as arteries become less elastic and clogged by fatty deposits.
Respiratory	Lung capacity decreases as alveoli break down and lung tissue becomes less elastic.
Digestive	Basal metabolic rate declines. Ability of the liver to detoxify substances declines.
Urinary	In both sexes, kidney mass declines, as does the rate of filtration of the blood by nephrons. Particularly in women, the external urethral sphincter weakens, causing incontinence. In men, the prostate gland (part of the reproductive system) enlarges, causing painful and frequent urination.
Reproductive	In men, fewer viable sperm are produced. In women, ovulation and menstruation cease at menopause.

FIGURE 18.17 Wise and informed lifestyle decisions made when young can lead to a healthy old age.

ter 21a). A tiny piece of each telomere is sliced off each time the DNA is copied before cell division. After a certain number of cell divisions, the telomere is gone, and the chromosome is no longer protected from the slicing. Chromosomes that sustain such damage can no longer participate in cell division. Cells grown in culture demonstrate this phenomenon, yet a clear link to human longevity has not been established.

Damage to DNA and other macromolecules

Other researchers postulate that highly reactive molecules known as free radicals disrupt cell processes and lead to aging. Free radicals are by-products of normal cellular activities. They have an unpaired electron and readily combine with and damage DNA, proteins, and lipids. Mitochondrial DNA seems particularly susceptible to such damage. Recall that mitochondria play a critical role in processing energy for cells (discussed in Chapter 3). Thus, damage to mitochondria threatens the supply of energy needed to sustain cellular activities. Aging also is associated with a decline in the ability of cells to repair damaged DNA. Such a decline might lead to an accumulation of gene mutations and ultimately to a decline in cell function.

Finally, some scientists have suggested that glucose—our main source of fuel—is the culprit. Glucose changes proteins such as collagen by causing cross-linkages to form between their molecules. This shackling of protein molecules may cause the stiffening of connective tissue and heart muscle associated with aging.

Is there a primary cause of aging? Most scientists believe that aging is not caused by a single factor, but rather by several processes that interact to produce our eventual deterioration and demise.

effectively. Yet cell division appears to slow in aging animals. Cells grown in culture in the laboratory do not divide indefinitely, supporting the idea that cessation of cell division is genetically programmed. In fact, they divide only a certain number of times. The number of divisions seems to be correlated with the age of the individual who donated the cells (whether the donor is a roundworm, mouse, or human) and the life span of the particular species. Telomeres, protective pieces of DNA at the tips of chromosomes, may help cells keep track of how many times they have divided (see Chap-

High-Quality Old Age

The news today is full of stories about antiaging products. For example, human growth hormone (HGH) is billed as being able to reverse many of the effects of aging. (Recall from Chapter 10 that growth hormone is secreted by the anterior pituitary gland.) Administration of HGH seems to increase lean body mass and the density of some bones. It also appears to reduce thinning of the skin and the amount of adipose (fat) tissue. However, the administration of HGH has side effects such as fluid accumulation, increased blood pressure, and diabetes. In addition, some animal studies have suggested that administering growth hormone might actually shorten life.

Aging is a normal biological process that, at present, cannot be slowed, stopped, or reversed. Today, the maximum documented life span for humans is 122 years, a record recently established by Madame Jeanne Calment of France (Figure **18.18**). Most of us will likely never reach her age. In fact, life expectancy for babies born in the United States today is about 77 years. While this news might depress you, especially after reading the long list of declines in organ systems outlined in Table 18.2, the good news is that we can stave off much of the disease and disability associated with aging. The human life span appears to be determined by genes, environment, and lifestyle. Physicians are now able to treat many conditions of old age. For example, worn-out hip or knee joints can be replaced with artificial joints. The clouding of vision caused by cataracts is now treated readily by replacing the old lens of the eye with an artificial lens. Drugs are being tested that may break the cross-links that glucose creates in proteins and thereby restore elasticity to our arteries. In addition, research is under way to determine if antioxidants (substances that inhibit the formation of free radicals) are effective in delaying certain aspects of aging.

Lifestyle is the factor over which we have the most personal control. Some components of a healthy lifestyle include proper nutrition, plenty of exercise and sleep, no smoking, and routine medical checkups. Indeed, the lifestyle choices we make when young can delay some aspects of aging. For example, we can delay wrinkling and aging of the skin by avoiding excessive exposure to the sun. The importance of a healthy lifestyle continues into our later years, when exercise, social and intellectual stimulation, and good nutrition can help to prevent the physical and mental declines associated with aging. Although it is never too late to change lifestyle

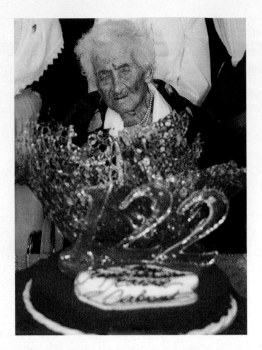

FIGURE 18.18 The longest documented human life span is 122 years; this record was established by Madame Jeanne Calment, shown here on her last birthday. She died in 1997.

habits, the earlier we begin to develop healthy habits, the better. Finally, aging is not only about declining organ systems; it has positive aspects as well. Not the least of these, as the years pass, are the gains we make in experience, perspective, and wisdom.

exploring further

In this chapter, we described the major milestones of human development, with a particular focus on the prenatal period. In the next chapter we consider the developmental milestones of early childhood and how careful monitoring of these milestones can be used to diagnose autism spectrum disorders. We also describe the symptoms and possible causes of these lifelong disorders as well as available treatments.

highlighting the concepts

Periods of Development in Human Life (p. 375)

- The period of development before birth is the prenatal period. The period of development after birth is the postnatal period.

Prenatal Period (pp. 375–387)

- The prenatal period can be subdivided into the pre-embryonic period, embryonic period, and fetal period. The pre-embryonic period runs from fertilization through the second week and is characterized by formation and implantation of the blastocyst. The extraembryonic membranes and placenta also begin to form at this time. The embryonic period extends from week 3 through week 8 and is characterized by gastrulation and the formation of organs and organ systems. The fetal period runs from the ninth week until birth and is a period of intense growth.
- Fertilization is the union of an egg and a sperm to form a single cell called the zygote.

- Cleavage is a rapid series of mitotic cell divisions that transforms the zygote into a morula (a solid ball of cells) and then a blastocyst (a hollow ball of cells with a fluid-filled cavity). Within the blastocyst are the inner cell mass, which will become the embryo and some of the extraembryonic membranes, and the trophoblast, which will form part of the placenta. Toward the end of the first week, the blastocyst begins implantation, the process by which the embryo becomes embedded in the endometrium of the uterus.
- Extraembryonic membranes—the amnion, yolk sac, chorion, and allantois—lie outside the embryo and begin to form during the second or third week after fertilization. The placenta, formed from the chorion of the embryo and the endometrium of the mother, is the organ that delivers nutrients and oxygen to the embryo (and later the fetus) and carries wastes away. The placenta also produces hormones such as estrogen, progesterone, human chorionic gonadotropin (HCG), and corticotropin-releasing hormone (CRH).

- Gastrulation includes the cell movements by which the primary germ layers—ectoderm, mesoderm, and endoderm—are established. Ectoderm forms the nervous system and the top layer of skin and its derivatives (hair, nails, oil glands, sweat glands, and mammary glands). Mesoderm forms muscle, bone, connective tissue, and organs such as the heart, ovaries, and testes. Endoderm forms organs such as the liver, some endocrine glands, and the lining of the urinary, respiratory, and digestive tracts.
- Neurulation is the process by which the neural tube forms from ectoderm. The anterior portion of the neural tube forms the brain, and the posterior portion forms the spinal cord. Somites, blocks of mesoderm organized alongside the neural tube, eventually form vertebrae, connective tissue, and skeletal muscles of the neck and trunk.
- The gender of a human embryo is determined at fertilization by the type of sperm (X-bearing or Y-bearing) that fertilizes the egg (which is X-bearing). An XX zygote will develop into a female, and an XY zygote into a male. Internal reproductive organs and external anatomy begin to differentiate about 6 weeks after fertilization, when a region on the Y chromosome initiates development of testes in male embryos. Absence of the Y chromosome results in female development.
- Growth during the fetal period is extremely rapid. The growth rate of the head slows relative to that of other parts of the body, producing changes in the way the body is proportioned. Such change in the relative growth rates of different parts of the body is called allometric growth.
- Fetal circulation differs from circulation after birth in that most blood is shunted through temporary vessels or openings past organs such as the lungs and liver, which do not yet perform their postnatal functions. At birth, when organs begin their postnatal functions, the bypasses of fetal circulation begin to close.

Birth (pp. 387–388)

- Labor is the process by which the fetus is expelled from the uterus and moved through the vagina into the outside world. Parturition (birth) usually occurs about 38 weeks after fertilization and marks the transition from the prenatal period of development to the postnatal period.

Birth Defects (pp. 388–390)

- Birth defects are developmental defects present at birth. Such defects may be caused by genetic factors (mutant genes or changes in the number or structure of chromosomes) or environmental agents such as drugs or radiation. Disruptive agents have their greatest effects on the developing embryo during periods of rapid differentiation, when organs and organ systems are forming.

Milk Production by Mammary Glands (p. 390)

- Lactation is the production and ejection of milk from the mammary glands. At birth, when levels of estrogen and progesterone drop, prolactin initiates milk production. Oxytocin causes milk ejection.

Postnatal Period (p. 390–392)

- Stages in postnatal development include infancy, childhood, puberty, adolescence, and adulthood. Growth stops in adulthood, and a few years later aging begins. Aging is the progressive decline in the structure and function of the body. Changes occur in all organ systems. Possible causes of aging include genetically programmed cessation of cell division; damage to DNA, protein, and lipids caused by free radicals; the inability of cells to repair damaged DNA; alteration of proteins by glucose such that cross-linkages form and produce a stiffening in tissues; and declines in the functioning of key organ systems.

recognizing key terms

fertilization *p. 375*
pre-embryonic period *p. 375*
pre-embryo *p. 375*
embryonic period *p. 375*
embryo *p. 375*
fetal period *p. 375*
fetus *p. 376*
zygote *p. 378*
cleavage *p. 378*
blastocyst *p. 378*
inner cell mass *p. 378*

trophoblast *p. 378*
placenta *p. 378*
implantation *p. 381*
human chorionic
  gonadotropin (HCG) *p. 381*
infertility *p. 381*
extraembryonic
  membranes *p. 381*
amnion *p. 381*
yolk sac *p. 381*
allantois *p. 382*

umbilical cord *p. 382*
chorion *p. 382*
chorionic villi *p. 382*
cesarean section *p. 383*
cell differentiation *p. 383*
morphogenesis *p. 383*
primary germ layers *p. 383*
gastrulation *p. 383*
ectoderm *p. 383*
endoderm *p. 383*
mesoderm *p. 383*

notochord *p. 383*
neural tube *p. 383*
neurulation *p. 384*
somite *p. 384*
allometric growth *p. 385*
parturition *p. 387*
labor *p. 387*
birth defect *p. 388*
lactation *p. 390*
aging *p. 390*

reviewing the concepts

1. List the three stages of prenatal development. What ages and major developmental milestones are associated with each stage? *pp. 375–387*
2. What prompts the destabilization of the acrosome on the head of a sperm? *p. 377*
3. How is fertilization of an oocyte by more than one sperm prevented? *p. 378*
4. Describe implantation. Where does it usually occur? What happens if it occurs elsewhere? *pp. 378, 381*
5. What are the functions of the four extraembryonic membranes? *pp. 381–382*
6. What is the placenta, and how does it form? Explain how nutrients, oxygen, and wastes are exchanged between fetal and maternal blood. *pp. 382–383*

7. What is gastrulation? What tissues and organs are formed from each of the three primary germ layers? *p. 383*
8. Describe formation of the central nervous system. *pp. 383–384*
9. How is the gender of a human embryo determined? *p. 384*
10. How does fetal circulation differ from circulation after birth? *pp. 386–387*
11. What are the three stages of labor? What initiates labor? *pp. 387–388*
12. Explain the relationship between the effects of environmental agents that disrupt development and embryonic age. *pp. 388–390*
13. When does milk production by a mother's breasts begin? What explains the timing? *p. 390*
14. What are some possible causes of aging? What can you do today to improve the quality of your old age? *pp. 390–392*
15. Fertilization
    a. typically occurs in the uterus.
    b. often involves more than one sperm uniting with an egg.
    c. is the process by which the zygote becomes embedded in the uterine lining.
    d. typically occurs in an oviduct.
16. The yolk sac
    a. is a primary source of nourishment for human embryos.
    b. is the embryo's major contribution to the placenta.
    c. contains primordial germ cells.
    d. encloses the embryo in a fluid-filled sac.
17. Which of the following does *not* characterize the placenta?
    a. Produces estrogen, progesterone, and human chorionic gonadotropin
    b. Is the site where fetal and maternal blood directly mix
    c. Appears to send the signal to initiate labor in humans
    d. Is expelled after birth

18. Neurulation
    a. is the process by which the neural tube forms.
    b. is the process by which the notochord forms.
    c. occurs just before gastrulation.
    d. involves endoderm.
19. The fetal period
    a. is the time when tissues and organs form.
    b. is characterized by rapid growth.
    c. runs from week 2 to week 8.
    d. is when exposure to harmful environmental agents is most likely to produce major birth defects.
20. Which of the following statements regarding childbirth is *true*?
    a. Most babies are born feet first.
    b. Delivery of the baby follows delivery of the placenta.
    c. Full-term babies are those born at 32 weeks gestation.
    d. Infants born prematurely at very low birth weight require intensive care after birth.
21. Within the blastocyst, the _____ becomes the embryo proper and some extraembryonic membranes, and the _____ becomes part of the placenta.
22. Soon after fertilization, the zygote undergoes _____, a series of rapid mitotic divisions without an increase in overall size.
23. The placenta forms from the _____ of the embryo and a portion of the _____ of the mother.
24. _____ is the process by which primary germ layers form.
25. The hormone _____ stimulates milk production, and the hormone _____ stimulates milk ejection.
26. _____ are highly reactive molecules, produced by normal cellular metabolism, that damage DNA and may lead to aging.

applying the concepts

1. Tanya is a few weeks pregnant and is experiencing severe abdominal pain on the right side. She wonders whether the pelvic inflammatory disease she had 2 years ago could have affected her pregnancy. What condition might Tanya have? What is typically done for women with this condition?
2. Juan was described as a "blue baby" at birth and underwent corrective surgery. What did the surgeons correct, and why?
3. Why might exposure to thalidomide, a drug known to disrupt development of the limbs, during weeks 4 to 6 of gestation produce more severe birth defects than would a similar level of exposure toward the end of gestation?

4. Dora is expecting her baby in about a month. She is deciding whether to breast-feed or bottle-feed. You are her physician. First describe how milk is produced and ejected from the mammary glands. Then, describe the advantages of breast-feeding and explain the circumstances in which you would recommend bottle-feeding to Dora instead.
5. Your grandmother is taking vitamin E and explains to you that it is a potential antioxidant. What is an antioxidant, and what "condition" is she hoping to treat? Is the vitamin E likely to work?

becoming information literate

Human growth hormone (HGH) is often touted as having antiaging effects. Prepare a position paper that recommends the use of HGH for this purpose. Use at least three reliable sources (books, journals, or websites). List each source you considered, and explain why you chose the three sources you used.

18a

SPECIAL TOPIC

Autism Spectrum Disorders

This boy has autism, a developmental disorder characterized by impaired communication, poor social skills, and unusual patterns of behavior.

Qingchen pulled his car into the driveway and sat for a minute, wondering what the young boy would be like. He had learned of the available childcare position in his developmental psychology program and was just about to go into the boy's home for an interview with his parents. He knew that Adam was diagnosed as having an autism spectrum disorder, but that could mean a lot of different things. Would he speak or make eye contact? Would he display the repetitive movements characteristic of some autistic kids? Would he be impulsive, hyperactive, aggressive? Regardless of Adam's situation, Qingchen knew he could rely on his training with special needs children. He relaxed a bit and got out of his car, eager to meet 10-year-old Adam and his parents.

When introduced to Qingchen, Adam did not speak; instead, he ran in circles around and around the room. Adam paused occasionally to stare at the ceiling fan, but soon he started running again. As he ran, Adam's parents described what they were looking for in a childcare provider—someone kind, responsible, and patient, who would work closely with Adam two afternoons a week when he got home from school. They explained that Adam did not cope well with change, and they had prior experience with caregivers who had been unable to deal with Adam's challenging condition. They wanted someone who could make at least a year-long commitment. Qingchen described in detail his training and previous positions. As they talked, Adam finally slowed down and eventually collapsed on the couch, and stared at the ceiling fan. By this time in the interview, Qingchen knew that he wanted the position. He could promise at least a year, and he was determined to engage Adam and to have fun with him. He began thinking of ways to work with Adam to help him develop better social and communication skills and to help Adam's parents, who clearly loved Adam and were working to build the best possible life for him.

In this chapter, we examine autism spectrum disorders. We look at their symptoms and possible causes. We also consider how these developmental disorders are diagnosed and treated. Finally, we explore the fear that childhood vaccines are linked to the onset of autism.

Characterization and Prevalence

Autism (also called autistic disorder) is a neurodevelopmental disorder characterized by impaired communication skills, poor social interactions, and unusual patterns of behavior. It has many of the same symptoms as pervasive developmental disorder not otherwise specified (PDD-NOS) and Asperger syndrome (sometimes called Asperger's disorder), so these three developmental disabilities are classified together as autism spectrum disorders (ASDs). Symptoms of ASDs begin in early childhood (for autism, the onset criterion is before the age of 3) and last a lifetime. The disorders are quite common: the Centers for Disease Control and Prevention (CDC) estimates that about 1 in 150 8-year-old children in the United States had an ASD in 2007. ASDs cross racial, ethnic, and socioeconomic lines, and they are four times more common in boys than girls. Estimates of the prevalence of ASDs have increased in recent decades, but the meaning of this increase is unclear. Some believe that the apparent increase in prevalence does not represent a true increase in number of cases, but rather increased awareness and recognition of the disorders as well as improved and expanding diagnostic criteria. ASDs are associated with other medical conditions, including Fragile X syndrome and untreated phenylketonuria (see Chapter 20). Autism is reported in 15% to 25% of individuals with genetically confirmed Fragile X syndrome; many of the remaining individuals show some symptoms of autism. About 6% to 20% of individuals with phenylketonuria meet the full criteria for autism. Nevertheless, less than 10% of ASD cases are associated with a diagnosed medical condition or known syndrome.

Autism was first described as a disorder in 1943 by Leo Kanner, an Austrian-born physician who immigrated to the United States. In 1944, Hans Asperger, an Austrian physician who remained in his country of birth, independently published his observations of children who were similar in many ways to those described by Kanner, except that they functioned at a higher cognitive level (Figure **18a.1**). Asperger was the first to describe the symptoms of the disorder that would later be named for him. Children with Asperger syndrome have impaired communication and poor social and motor skills, but they can be intellectually gifted. In fact, Asperger termed them "little professors" because of their ability to speak at length about their favorite topic, be it opera, astronomy,

(a) Leo Kanner described the symptoms of autism in 1943.

(b) Hans Asperger described in 1944 symptoms of the condition that would come to be known as Asperger syndrome.

FIGURE 18a.1 The symptoms of autism and Asperger syndrome were formally described by Austrian-born physicians in the 1940s.

or fossil fishes. Asperger's work was published in German, and it did not reach English-speaking audiences until the 1980s when English psychiatrist Lorna Wing, herself the mother of an autistic child, highlighted his work in one of her academic papers. PDD-NOS was formally defined in 1987 and describes individuals who have severe impairment in communication and social skills or who exhibit stereotyped behavior but do not meet the full criteria for autism, Asperger syndrome, or psychiatric disorders such as schizophrenia. Because some, but not all, of the features of another explicitly defined developmental or psychiatric condition are present, PDD-NOS is said to be a subthreshold condition. Current definitions of all three ASDs are based on the *Diagnostic and Statistical Manual of Mental Disorders,* Fourth Edition, Text Revision (*DSM-IV-TR*), a handbook that is widely used by psychologists and psychiatrists to classify mental disorders; the handbook is published and regularly updated by the American Psychiatric Association.

Symptoms

Symptoms of ASDs include marked deficits in communication and social skills and the performance of unusual and repetitive motor patterns (Figure **18a.2**). Although there is considerable overlap in diagnostic criteria for autism and Asperger syndrome, there are some differences (Table **18a.1**). At one end of the spectrum, some people with autism are profoundly challenged intellectually; at the other end, some with Asperger syndrome are intellectually gifted. Some people with autism never speak, while some with Asperger syndrome speak at length, but in one-sided conversations. In fact, whereas the diagnostic criteria for autism include having either a clinically significant delay in language or no speech at all, Asperger syndrome is defined as having no clinically significant general delay in language or cognitive development (cognitive development is not characterized in the diagnostic criteria for autism). Even *within* the three categories of ASDs set forth in the *DSM-IV-TR,* there is tremendous variation in the presence and intensity of symptoms.

Because autism, Asperger syndrome, and PDD-NOS share many symptoms and because there is continuing debate regarding their clinical boundaries, we provide a general description of symptoms for this group of disorders as a whole and note where symptoms are specific to autism or Asperger syndrome. Some ASD symptoms can be present in people with other medical conditions (for example, people with Fragile X syndrome may either meet the full criteria for autism or only show some symptoms of autism). Some of the symptoms can also be present in people who do not have an ASD or another medical condition. For example, some normally developing toddlers may go through a brief period during which they flap their hands when excited or frustrated—a behavior that is typical of some autistic children. Such flapping tends to occur when normally developing toddlers are incapable of fully expressing themselves through speech; when they become more fluent in speech, they stop flapping their hands. In contrast, the stereotyped behaviors characteristic of some individuals with ASDs (for example, hand flapping, rocking, and twirling) often extend well beyond the toddler years and can occur with such regularity and for such prolonged periods that they interfere with other activities. Similarly, tantrums, while not unusual in normally developing toddlers, are typically more severe and prolonged in children with ASDs and can extend beyond the toddler years. In general, the overall impairment experienced by those with an ASD makes every day of their life very challenging—and has consequences for their families and other people who care for them.

(a) Failure to make eye contact is an example of an impairment in nonverbal communication that may occur in someone with an ASD.

(b) Social withdrawal occurs in some people with ASDs.

(c) Restricted and repetitive behaviors also characterize those with ASDs. Here, an autistic teen continually touches his ears.

FIGURE 18a.2 Autism spectrum disorders (ASDs) are characterized by impaired communication (verbal and nonverbal), poor social skills, and the performance of unusual behaviors.

TABLE 18a.1 Diagnostic Criteria for Autism and Asperger Syndrome

Areas of Impairment (Number of Symptoms Required for Diagnosis*)	Symptoms	Autism	Asperger Syndrome
Communication (at least one symptom from list for autism)	No spoken language or delay in development of language	X	
	In those who speak, marked impairment in ability to converse with others	X	
	Use of stereotyped, repetitive, or idiosyncratic language	X	
	Lack of social imitative play or spontaneous imaginative play	X	
Social interaction (at least two symptoms from list for autism and Asperger syndrome)	Marked impairment in ability to regulate social interactions through nonverbal behaviors such as gestures, eye contact, and facial expressions	X	X
	Failure to develop age-appropriate relationships with peers	X	X
	Lack of spontaneous sharing of interests or experiences with others	X	X
	Lack of social or emotional reciprocity	X	X
Restricted, repetitive, and stereotyped patterns of behavior (at least one symptom from list for autism and Asperger syndrome)	Persistent preoccupation with stereotyped and restricted patterns	X	X
	Inflexible adherence to specific, nonfunctional rituals or routines	X	X
	Stereotyped or repetitive motor behavior, such as rocking or hand flapping	X	X
	Persistent preoccupation with parts of objects	X	X

Modified from the *Diagnostic and Statistical Manual of Mental Disorders, Fourth Edition, Text Revision* (DSM-IV-TR), American Psychiatric Association (2000).

*A diagnosis of autism requires a total of six (or more) items from the three areas of impairment, with the minimum required from each area of impairment shown in parentheses in the first column. A total number of required items is not part of the diagnostic criteria for Asperger syndrome.

Communication

Verbal communication skills of people with ASDs vary dramatically. About 40% do not speak at all; about 25% use some words and then lose them between 15 and 24 months of age. Other people with ASDs exhibit delays in speaking or develop speech at the appropriate time but speak with impaired use of language and poor social skills. Of those autistic children who speak, some may be unable to form meaningful sentences. Others may repeat words or phrases over and over, or echo what others have said rather than responding to them in conversation. Complete absence of speech, found in some autistic children, does not characterize children with Asperger syndrome. Children with Asperger syndrome may exhibit mild delays in speech, and their atypical language development (especially in the social use of language) may go unnoticed until preschool or somewhat later, when their inability to form friendships becomes apparent. People with ASDs may find the give-and-take of normal conversation difficult, and they may interrupt or continue talking too long on a subject of particular interest to them; some also use an odd tone of voice. Difficulties in conversation are very characteristic of individuals with Asperger syndrome, but may also occur in individuals with PDD-NOS or high-functioning autism.

Using and understanding nonverbal communication also pose problems for people with ASDs. In some cases, their facial expression is disconnected from their words; for example, they may smile when describing an extremely sad or frightening experience. Some have difficulty making eye contact, while others stand too close to the person they are speaking with. The ability to notice and understand the facial expressions and body language of others also may be poorly developed.

Social Skills

Impairments in communication are often associated with impairments in social skills. For example, an individual with an ASD who has trouble listening to others and engaging in the give-and-take of conversation will likely experience difficult social interactions. Inability to imitate the actions of others is characteristic of people with ASDs; this is a major disadvantage because imitation is an important way that young children learn how to speak and act in social situations. As a result, some individuals with ASDs say whatever comes to their mind, whether it is appropriate or not, their language seemingly unfiltered by social convention. Some people with ASDs may not want to interact with other people at all. Others may pursue social interactions but have difficulty forming and maintaining social relationships because of their impaired ability to communicate and to interact. Taking turns and sharing also can be particularly difficult for children with ASDs.

Adapting to changes in daily schedules can be challenging to those with ASDs; some may collapse in a severe and prolonged tantrum when a daily routine changes. These outbursts may frighten others or, at the very least, make them uncomfortable and less likely to engage in social interaction. Finally, other behavioral conditions frequently found in children with ASDs—such as impulsivity, hyperactivity, aggressiveness, self-injurious behavior, and atypical responses (over- or underreaction) to sensory stimuli such as touch, pain, smell, and sound—can further compromise social interactions.

Motor Patterns and Behavior

As noted earlier, repetitive movements, such as flapping the hands, rocking from side to side, and head banging can occur with ASDs. In children, the repeated actions may involve toys (for example, spinning the blades of a toy helicopter close to the eyes) or other objects (for example, repetitively turning lights on and off or opening and closing a door). These repetitive motor activities are called self-stimulatory activities, and they too make social interaction difficult. In addition to these repetitive movements, people with ASDs may exhibit poor motor coordination and atypical motor development. For example, motor clumsiness is viewed by many as a distinguishing feature of Asperger syndrome, although it is not currently listed as a defining characteristic by the *DSM-IV-TR*.

Some people with ASDs develop unusual rituals, such as touching several objects in succession and in precise order before leaving home. While these rituals may seem odd or unnecessary to observers, they can be very important to the person performing them. Indeed, disrupting or preventing these rituals can cause extreme frustration and tantrums. Preoccupation with parts of objects and all-consuming interests also characterize ASDs. For example, a young child with an ASD may be intensely interested in the wheels of a toy car and constantly spin them, but never play with the car as a whole. Some may be fixated on certain topics, such as train or tide timetables, that they talk about incessantly.

Timing of Symptom Development

Although symptoms of ASDs usually become apparent in the first few years after birth, the underlying neurological defects are thought to occur early in embryonic development. About 30% to 50% of parents of children with ASDs notice problems during the first year; 80% to 90% notice problems by 2 years of age. As mentioned previously, Asperger syndrome may be noticed later than autism because there are no clinically significant overall delays in speech and cognitive development. Nevertheless, most parents of a child with Asperger syndrome notice by the child's third birthday that there is something unusual about their child; some symptoms may be apparent in infancy.

In the case of a given child, different symptoms may appear at different ages. For example, at 2 years of age a child's communication skills may be delayed, but his or her motor skills may be age appropriate and lack any repetitive quality. Later, his or her motor skills may also show delays. It is worth noting that some children with autism develop certain communication, social, and motor skills on time and then subsequently lose them.

Diagnosis

Diagnostic criteria for ASDs have changed several times in recent decades. These changes are reflected, in part, in the multiple editions of the *DSM*, which provides guidelines for clinical diagnoses of mental health disorders. A key change occurred in *DSM-III*, issued in 1980, when autism was formally differentiated from schizophrenia as a developmental disorder rather than a psychiatric one, and specific criteria for autism were listed. Later editions of the *DSM* included modified criteria for autism and specifically listed as disorders PDD-NOS (*DSM-III Revised*, 1987) and Asperger syndrome (*DSM-IV*, 1994). Today, physicians begin to consider a diagnosis of ASD when a child fails to meet age-specific developmental milestones.

Children differ in the pace at which they develop. Nevertheless, there are age-specific developmental milestones to which their progress can be compared to identify delays (see Figure **18a.3** and Table **18a.2**). Identifying developmental delays is important because early diagnosis of an ASD can lead to early intervention, which can benefit the child. To this end, pediatricians and nurses routinely conduct developmental screening of infants and young

  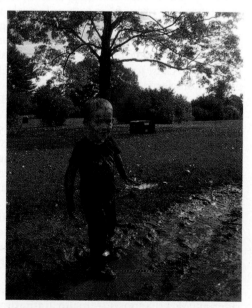

(a) One milestone, typically attained by the end of first year, is the ability to pull up to a standing position.

(b) The motor skills needed to build towers of blocks or other toys are usually attained after the first year.

(c) Some milestones concern social skills and behavior, and include showing independence and defiance.

FIGURE 18a.3 The pace at which a young child develops can be viewed in the context of age-specific developmental milestones. Shown here is the same child at 10 months, 20 months, and nearly 3 years of age.

TABLE 18a.2 Some Developmental Milestones Used to Assess a Young Child's Progress in the Areas of Communication, Social Behavior, and Motor Skills

Age	Developmental Milestones		
	Communication	Social Behavior	Motor Skills
By the end of the first year	Babbles with changes in tone Tries to imitate words Uses simple gestures and single words	Is shy with strangers Repeats gestures for attention Tests parental responses to behavior	Reaches sitting position without help Crawls forward on belly Pulls self to standing position
By the end of the second year	Uses simple phrases and several single words Points to named objects Repeats words heard in conversation	Imitates behavior of others Shows independence and defiance Shows some self-awareness	Walks independently and begins to run Kicks a ball Pulls or carries a toy while walking
By the end of the third year	Recognizes and identifies common objects Uses sentences with 4 or 5 words Speaks such that strangers can understand most words	Spontaneously shows affection Takes turns in games Separates from parents with relative ease	Runs with ease Pedals a tricycle Builds a tower of more than 6 blocks

More complete lists of developmental milestones can be found at www.cdc.gov/ncbddd/autism/actearly/screening.

children at their periodic physical examinations. In addition to asking the parents questions about their child's development, these health care professionals directly interact with the child to see how the child reacts, speaks, and moves (Figure **18a.4**). If delays are noted, then the parents may be advised to seek the opinion of a developmental pediatrician or psychologist, and additional screening may be performed. This screening typically involves several of the following diagnostic tools: extensive interviews of the parents regarding their child's developmental history; detailed records from the pediatrician of the child's developmental history; clinical observations of the child's behavior; psychological testing; speech, language, and hearing assessments; and physical and neurological examinations.

Several diagnostic checklists and rating scales for diagnosing ASDs are available. Some screening tools are used to differentiate children at risk of having an ASD from the general population. For example, the Checklist for Autism in Toddlers (CHAT) is designed for use with children aged 18 to 24 months, and a modification of CHAT (M-CHAT) is available for children aged 16 to 48 months (Note that despite their names, CHAT and M-CHAT are often used to screen for ASDs generally; they are not used exclusively to screen for autism.) The Childhood Asperger Screening Test (CAST) can be administered to children aged 4 to 11 years. Other screening tools are used to differentiate children at risk of having an ASD from a population of children with developmental disorders. For example, the Gilliam Autism Rating Scale (GARS) and the Gilliam Asperger's Disorder Scale (GADS) are designed to differentiate individuals with autism and Asperger syndrome, respectively, from those with other developmental disorders. GARS and GADS are used with individuals from 3 to 22 years of age, and they can be completed by a parent, teacher, or clinician.

The results from screening can then be used by a trained clinician, together with several other diagnostic tools, to consider an ASD diagnosis. A major limitation of current screening tools is that they have not been validated for use with children younger than 18 months old, although efforts are under way to do this. Also, screening tools have not proven particularly effective in distinguishing PDD-NOS from other developmental disorders.

Possible Causes

In the years following its formal description in 1943, autism was thought to be caused by aberrant parenting, an idea initially put forth by Leo Kanner and seized on by others. According to the "Refrigerator Mother" hypothesis, a cold, uncaring parent (usually the mother) caused the child to retreat into autism. It was not until the mid-1960s that this hypothesis was directly attacked. It was replaced with the view that autism is a neurodevelopmental disorder with a genetic basis and that it cannot be linked to any particular parenting style.

Although we now know that autism and other ASDs are not caused by aberrant parenting, we still do not know their precise causes. Most researchers agree that there are probably multiple causes and that genes as well as environment play a role.

Some research has focused on the neurobiological basis of ASDs. Neuroimaging studies and studies of brain tissue from people with ASDs indicate fundamental differences from controls in brain growth and organization, including increased brain volumes, reduced number of Purkinje cells (output neurons) in the cerebellum, and reduced size of neurons in the forebrain limbic system in people with ASDs. Many of these differences appear to originate during the prenatal period. For example, abnormal migration of cells during formation of the nervous system may affect brain structure and neural circuitry, and ultimately influence thinking and behavior. Functional neuroimaging techniques (imaging the brain during cognitive tasks or response to visual or auditory stimulation) suggest that people with ASDs use different cognitive strategies and may process certain types of information in different brain areas. A particularly consistent finding of neuroimaging studies is that people with ASDs display underactivation of the part of the temporal lobe involved in face recognition. Despite these advances in identifying structural and functional differences in the brains of those with ASDs, a reliable marker for these disorders has yet to be identified; for this reason, routine neuroimaging is not recommended as a diagnostic tool.

Two main types of studies indicate that autism has a strong genetic component. First, family studies show higher than expected

Q *Why does developmental screening play such an important role in diagnosing ASDs? Is there a medical test for these disorders?*

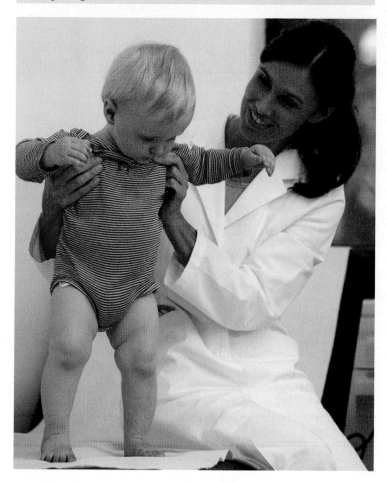

FIGURE 18a.4 Routine developmental screening at periodic visits to the pediatrician can help identify developmental delays or losses.

A *There is no medical test (e.g., blood test or scan of the brain) for ASDs; instead, doctors rely on several tools to assess behavioral symptoms. Typically, delays detected during routine developmental screening are further evaluated through parent interviews, psychological testing, and assessments of speech, language, and hearing.*

rates of autism among family members. For example, the rate of recurrence of autism in siblings of autistic individuals is 2% to 6%, which is 10 to 60 times greater than the prevalence of autism in the general population. Second, studies of twins demonstrate that autism has a genetic basis.

Recall from Chapter 18 that dizygotic (fraternal) twins occur when two secondary oocytes are fertilized by different sperm; these twins are no more genetically similar than siblings who are not twins. Monozygotic twins result from the splitting of a pre-embryo and are nearly genetically identical. (We say "nearly" here because new research has shown that while identical twins have very similar DNA, they do not have identical DNA. Identical twins may differ, for example, in the number of copies of a particular gene. It is not known exactly when these differences arise. Prior to this discovery, scientists knew that identical twins experience epigenetic changes, which are changes in gene expression induced by

environmental factors such as diet or exposure to alcohol or tobacco smoke. Although epigenetic changes affect the way genes "act," they do not involve changes in the underlying DNA sequence, so this new information about identical twins is very exciting.)

Researchers studying the genetics of autism have compared the incidence of autism in monozygotic and dizygotic twins. If one monozygotic twin has autism, then there is a 75% chance that the other twin will have autism as well. In contrast, if one dizygotic twin has autism, then there is a 3% chance that the other twin will have autism (note that this falls within the 2% to 6% rate of recurrence among non-twin siblings mentioned previously). These comparative findings indicate a genetic basis for autism because the incidence among twins is higher when they are nearly genetically identical. However, data for monozygotic twins also suggest an environmental component because despite being nearly genetically identical, both twins are not always autistic. These findings suggest that one twin was exposed to environmental factors during the prenatal and/or postnatal period that, in combination with a susceptible genetic background, led to the expression of autism. Although comparable twin studies are not yet available for Asperger syndrome, the disorder does run in families—indicating it, too, has a genetic basis.

It is unlikely that a single gene is responsible for the genetic component of an ASD. Indeed, current models suggest that several genes, perhaps as many as 15, are involved, and that when these genes are present in combination they lead to an increased vulnerability to autism that may be triggered by environmental factors. Research is under way to identify candidate genes and environmental triggers.

Very little is known about the environmental risk factors for ASDs. Some research focuses on maternal effects (specifically the intrauterine environment) and complications during pregnancy and birth. Prenatal exposure to the prescription drug thalidomide is linked to an increased risk of autism (recall from Chapter 18 that thalidomide also causes severe birth defects of the limbs), so in these cases, thalidomide served as an environmental trigger for autism. There is some evidence that maternal illness, such as rubella (German measles), during pregnancy is an environmental trigger for autism. Additional research is needed in these areas. One environmental variable that has been suspected—early childhood vaccines—is discussed later in the chapter.

Treatment and Therapy

There are no cures for ASDs, but educational interventions can help children with these developmental disorders reach their full potential. Successful educational programs provide structure, organization, and direction for the child. Such programs directly teach children with ASDs the social skills that other children learn by other means. Given the enormous individual variation in how ASDs are manifested, it is imperative that educational programs are designed for the individual child; to this end, school-age children typically have an Individualized Educational Plan (IEP). An IEP is developed and periodically reviewed by a team that includes the parents (or guardians), teachers, social workers, school psychologists, and representatives of the school district; depending on the services needed, other school personnel (for example, speech and occupational therapists) may participate. An IEP is federally guaranteed under the Individuals with Disabilities Education Act (IDEA), and ensures that a child with an ASD will receive the most appropriate education available. In addition to classroom accommodations, such plans may include speech therapy, occupational therapy (designed to improve social, fine motor, and self-help skills), and sensory integration therapy (designed to facilitate development of the nervous system's ability to process external stimuli such as touch, sound, and sight, in more typical ways).

Specific educational interventions may differ for children with different ASDs. For example, the typical difference in verbal abilities between children with autism and children with Asperger syndrome often necessitates different treatment approaches. Those autistic children with little or no verbal ability may be taught to communicate with picture cards, in an approach called the Picture Exchange Communication System (Figure **18a.5**). The better verbal abilities associated with Asperger syndrome mean that counseling and forms of talk therapy can be part of the treatment plan.

To date, no single therapeutic drug has been identified that produces major improvements in the core symptoms of ASDs—impairments in communication and social behavior and repetitive or unusual behaviors. However, certain drugs are used with limited to moderate success to treat some of the behavioral features that often accompany ASDs. For example, the Food and Drug Administration has approved the use of the antipsychotic drug risperidone in children with ASDs who display severe tantrums, aggression, and self-injurious behavior. Other drugs may be used to treat the hyperactivity, impulsivity, and anxiety that may be present in children with ASDs.

Some parents use practices and products outside of conventional medicine to relieve their child's ASD symptoms. Known as Complementary and Alternative Medicine (CAM), these treatments include dietary and nutritional therapies—such as removing from the child's diet the proteins gluten (found in wheat) and casein (found in dairy products)—and deep pressure therapy (for example, use of a nonscratching brush on the arms, hands, legs, feet, and back). These types of treatments are controversial and should always be discussed with the child's pediatrician before being used.

The prognosis for individuals with ASDs depends on many factors. In general, for children, better outcomes are associated with better verbal and cognitive abilities, less severe symptoms overall, and early identification of the disorder and appropriate intervention programs. The outcomes for adults with ASDs correlate best with cognitive abilities; those with at least normal intelligence have the best outcomes. For example, many adults with Asperger syndrome can earn a college degree and hold a mainstream job, although continued family and community support is often necessary to maintain a successful and independent life.

Fear That Vaccines Cause Autism

One of the major medical success stories has been the development of vaccines to prevent potentially deadly diseases, including measles, mumps, rubella, diphtheria, tetanus, and polio. Indeed, vaccine programs have reduced, and in some cases even eradicated, serious infectious diseases and have saved innumerable lives. These programs have been so successful that many people today may not know what these diseases even look like or how severe they can be. Despite the success of immunization programs, however, concerns about a possible link between certain vaccines and autism have been debated for at least a decade (Figure **18a.6**). The debate continues, even though there is no convincing scientific evidence of a causal relationship between childhood vaccines and autism.

(a) Here, a young autistic boy uses pictures to communicate with his teacher.

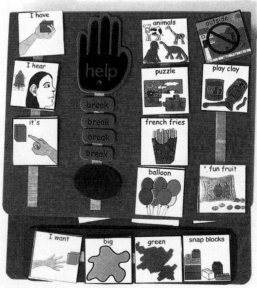

(b) A sample of cards used in the Picture Exchange Communication System

FIGURE 18a.5 The Picture Exchange Communication System is used to help autistic children with limited or no verbal abilities to communicate.

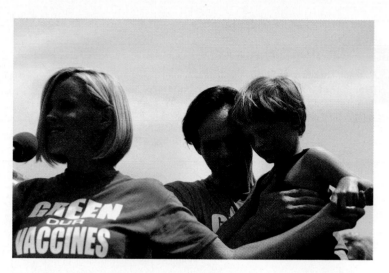

FIGURE 18a.6 Actress Jenny McCarthy speaking at a rally in Washington, D.C., in June 2008; also shown are her son Evan and actor Jim Carrey. McCarthy has been outspoken in her belief that vaccines are an environmental trigger for autism.

The first hypothesis that such a link existed arose out of a 1998 study of the records of 12 children who had both autism and irritable bowel disease. The latter was thought to be caused by a persistent measles-virus infection in the intestines. The parents or pediatricians of nine of the children suspected that the MMR (measles, mumps, and rubella) vaccine the children had received had caused the irritable bowel disease and contributed to the children's autism. The idea, which has not been supported by subsequent research, included the following suppositions: (1) The live virus in the MMR vaccine could cause a chronic measles infection in certain susceptible children; (2) this, in turn, could damage the bowels of these children; (3) the damaged bowels could allow certain peptides that are normally broken down by the gut to leak into the bloodstream before being completely broken down; and (4) once in the bloodstream, the peptides could damage the developing brain. Because there were too few cases in the study to establish a causal link between the MMR vaccine and autism, 10 of the 13 authors of the paper later retracted the interpretation of the data that had been presented in the paper. Other scientists criticized the study for lacking controls and using a biased sample of subjects.

Subsequent studies explored the possible link between the MMR vaccine and autism. The Institute of Medicine (IOM) of the National Academies reviewed all of these studies and issued a report in 2001 stating that evidence at the time did not support a link between the MMR vaccine and autism. The IOM recommended keeping the early childhood immunization schedule the same. In 2004, the IOM again reviewed studies of any causal relationship between the MMR vaccine and autism—and again concluded that there is no link between autism and the MMR vaccine. Studies published since 2004 have supported this conclusion. Indeed, a study published in 2008 found no evidence of an association between autism and persistent measles infection in the intestines or exposure to the MMR vaccine.

Another hypothesis linking autism to vaccines suggested that autism may be caused by a mercury-containing organic compound called thimerosal. Thimerosal had been used to prevent the growth of microorganisms in certain vaccines from the 1930s until the early 2000s. (Thimerosal was never used in the MMR vaccine, the other focus of contention.) Exposure to mercury is

harmful to the nervous system, so it is perhaps reasonable to think that thimerosal might cause problems in the developing nervous system that might result in autism. In 2004, an IOM report concluded that it is biologically plausible for the cumulative amount of mercury in the series of recommended vaccinations for infants and toddlers to exceed the maximum federal safety standards. However, the standards pertain to *methylmercury,* and thimerosal contains *ethylmercury,* which is handled differently in the body. Further, although the IOM did not dispute that mercury-containing compounds, such as thimerosal, might damage the nervous system, there was no evidence that such damage was associated with autism. Thus, the IOM concluded in 2004 that the bulk of evidence favored rejection of a causal relationship between thimerosal-containing vaccines and autism. To date, there is no convincing scientific evidence to refute the IOM's conclusion.

Despite the lack of convincing scientific evidence that thimerosal-containing vaccines cause autism, the Public Health Service agencies, the American Academy of Pediatrics, and vaccine manufacturers agreed in 1999 that, as a precautionary measure, thimerosal should be reduced or eliminated in vaccines. Although it took some time and effort to develop thimerosal-free vaccines, it was feasible to remove mercury from vaccines and thereby reduce an individual's total exposure to mercury. It is far more difficult to control an individual's exposure to other sources of environmental mercury (natural sources include volcanoes and forest fires, and other sources include landfills, incinerators, and certain industrial processes). Currently, vaccines routinely recommended for children under the age of 6 do not contain thimerosal, or they contain only trace amounts—except for the inactivated influenza (flu) vaccine (Table **18a.3**). Most supplies of this flu vaccine contain thimerosal, but manufacturing capabilities of thimerosal-free flu vaccines are increasing. Vaccines for adults and for children seven years of age and older are increasingly available in formulations without thimerosal or with only trace amounts.

Current scientific evidence does not support a causal association between either the MMR vaccine or thimerosal-containing vaccines and autism. Even so, a recent survey of parents of children with ASDs showed that 54% believe immunizations caused their child's ASD.

The case of Hannah Poling, a young child from Georgia, may further this perception. Hannah was born in 1998. According to her medical records, she was developing normally until she received 5 shots against 9 infectious diseases at the age of 19 months. Within two days of the vaccines, Hannah developed a high fever and cried continuously. Periods of high fever continued off and on; she became less responsive to verbal stimuli and began to exhibit unusual behaviors. The declines in her health continued; and in 2001 she was diagnosed with regressive encephalopathy, a disorder of the brain characterized by loss of previously acquired skills, such as language. The physician noted that her symptoms were consistent with an autism spectrum disorder and that she displayed features of mitochondrial disease (recall from Chapter 3 that mitochondria are the organelles that process energy for cells).

Because the brain requires a lot of energy to function properly, it is the organ most often affected when mitochondria do not function efficiently, and mitochondrial encephalopathy results. Upon further testing, Hannah was diagnosed with an inherited mitochondrial disorder. Children are usually not tested for mitochondrial diseases, so the connection—if there is one—between ASDs and mitochondrial diseases is unclear. Although it is not unusual for children with mitochondrial diseases to show behavioral and motor symptoms during their toddler years, Hannah's parents

TABLE 18a.3 Thimerosal Content of Early Childhood Vaccines

Vaccine	Age Administered (Months)*	Current Thimerosal Status (Number of Manufacturers)	Thimerosal History
Hepatitis B	Birth 1–2 6–18	Absent (2)	Approval for thimerosal-free formulations in August 1999 or January 2007
Diphtheria, tetanus, acellular pertussis (DTaP)*	2 4 6 15–18	Absent (2) or trace (1)	Approval for thimerosal-free formulation in September 2000; approval for trace thimerosal formulation in March 2001; formulation of one manufacturer never contained thimerosal
Haemophilus influenzae type b conjugate (Hib)	2 4 6 12–15	Absent (3)	Approval for thimerosal-free formulation in August 1999; formulations of two manufacturers never contained thimerosal
Inactivated poliovirus	2 4 6–18	Absent (1)	Never contained thimerosal
Pneumococcal conjugate (PCV7)	2 4 6 12–15	Absent (1)	Never contained thimerosal
Rotavirus	2 4 6	Absent (1)	Never contained thimerosal
Influenza, inactivated (flu shot)	At least 6 months, one dose yearly thereafter	Absent (1), trace (1), or present in greater than trace amounts (2)	Approval for trace thimerosal formulation in September 2001; approval for thimerosal-free formulation in December 2004
Influenza, live attenuated (nasal spray)	At least 24 months, one dose yearly thereafter	Absent (1)	Never contained thimerosal
Measles, mumps, rubella (MMR)	12–15	Absent (1)	Never contained thimerosal
Varicella (chicken pox)	12–18	Absent (1)	Never contained thimerosal

*Some of these vaccines have additional doses given at older ages; for example, DTaP, polio, MMR, and varicella are administered again at 4–6 years of age.

believed that the vaccines given at 19 months triggered her encephalopathy. The family brought their case to a federal program that compensates those injured by vaccines.

Created in 1988, the National Vaccine Injury Compensation Program (VICP) was established to ensure adequate supplies of vaccines, stabilize their costs, and provide a forum for individuals injured by vaccines. The 2007 decision by VICP to pay Hannah's family for her care was made public in spring 2008. Public health officials quickly stated that in settling this claim, the government made no statement that vaccines cause autism. Indeed, whereas certain illnesses, such as the flu, can exacerbate symptoms of encephalopathy in individuals with a mitochondrial disease, there is no convincing scientific evidence that vaccines cause or worsen mitochondrial diseases. In fact, because infections can be particularly harmful to children with mitochondrial diseases, it is recommended that they receive all vaccines according to the recommended schedule.

19

Chromosomes and Cell Division

Down syndrome, which results from an error in cell division, is the most frequent inherited cause of mild to moderate retardation.

405

As her younger brother walked across the stage to receive his high school diploma, Lynn had never been prouder. When Zach stopped the graduation procession, looked around, held up his diploma, and waved at her with that huge infectious smile of his, people in the auditorium cheered. Everyone in school knew Zach. He wore the mascot suit at home games and encouraged everyone to cheer for the teams.

He designed the huge Picasso-like murals used as a backdrop for the junior play and helped paint them and anchor them into place. It was the most original set *The Music Man* had ever had.

Zach's life hadn't been easy. He had Down syndrome, which means he was born with an extra chromosome 21. He had endured several heart surgeries as a young child and spent countless hours with speech therapists. People had not always

been kind to him either, partly because in some ways he was slower to learn than most people. Sometimes his feelings were hurt. Lynn nevertheless envied the people who would meet Zach for the first time next fall when he went to community college. He was going to study art, but Lynn knew that his most precious gift was his genius for teaching. He would teach other students to value and appreciate their own unique gifts.

In this chapter, we examine the role of two types of cell division, mitosis and meiosis in the human life cycle. We consider the physical basis of heredity—the chromosomes—and we consider how the chromosomes are parceled out during mitosis and meiosis. We finish the chapter by examining why it is important for each cell to have the correct number of chromosomes.

Two Types of Cell Division

We begin life as a single cell called a *zygote,* formed by the union of an egg and a sperm. By adulthood, our bodies consist of trillions of cells. What happened in the intervening years? How did we go from a single cell to the multitude of cells that make up the tissues of a fully functional adult? The answer is cell division, which happened over and over again as we grew. Even in adults, many cells continue to divide for growth and repair of body tissues. With very few exceptions, each of those cells carries the same genetic information as its ancestors. The type of nuclear division that results in identical body cells is called *mitosis.*

In Chapter 17 you learned that males and females produce specialized reproductive cells called gametes (eggs or sperm). You'll recall that *meiosis* is a special type of nuclear division that gives rise to gametes. In females, meiosis occurs in the ovaries and produces eggs. In males, meiosis occurs in the testes and produces sperm. Meiosis is important because through it the gametes end up with half the amount of genetic information (half the number of chromosomes) in the original cell. When the nuclei of an egg and sperm unite (fertilization), the chromosome number is restored to that of the original cell. As a result, the number of chromosomes in body cells remains constant from one generation to the next.

The roles of mitosis (which produces new body cells) and meiosis (which forms gametes) are summarized in the diagram of the human life cycle in Figure **19.1**. You will learn more about both mitosis and meiosis later in this chapter.

Form of Chromosomes

A **chromosome** is a combination of a DNA molecule (which contains genetic information for the organism) and specialized proteins called histones. Chromosomes are found in the cell nucleus. The information contained in the DNA molecules in chromosomes directs the development and maintenance of the body. The histones combined with the DNA are for support and control of gene activity. A **gene** is a specific segment of the DNA that directs

the synthesis of a protein, which in turn plays a structural or functional role within the cell. By coding for a specific protein, a gene determines the expression of a particular characteristic, or trait. Each chromosome in a human cell contains a specific assortment of genes. Like beads on a string, genes are arranged in a fixed sequence along the length of specific chromosomes.

In the human body, **somatic cells**—that is, all cells except for eggs or sperm—have 46 chromosomes. Those 46 chromosomes are actually 23 pairs of chromosomes. One member of each pair came from the mother's egg, and another member of each pair came from the father's sperm. Thus, each cell contains 23 **homologous chromosome pairs**, a pair being two chromosomes (one from the mother and one from the father) with genes for the same traits. Homologous pairs are called *homologues* for short. Any cell with two of each kind of chromosome is described as being **diploid** (annotated as $2n$, with n representing the number of each kind of chromosome). In diploid cells, then, genes also occur in pairs. The members of each gene pair are located at the same position on homologous chromosomes.

One of the 23 pairs of chromosomes consists of the **sex chromosomes** that determine whether a person is male or female. There are two types of sex chromosomes, X and Y. A person who has two X chromosomes is described as XX and is genetically female; a person who has an X and a Y chromosome is described as XY and is genetically male. The other 22 pairs of chromosomes are called the **autosomes.** The autosomes determine the expression of most of a person's inherited characteristics.

The Cell Cycle

In **mitosis**, one nucleus divides into two daughter nuclei containing the same number and kinds of chromosomes. But mitosis is only one phase during the life of a dividing cell. The entire sequence of events that a cell goes through from its origin in the division of its parent cell through its own division into two daughter cells is called the **cell cycle** (Figure **19.2**). The cell cycle consists of two major phases: interphase and cell division.

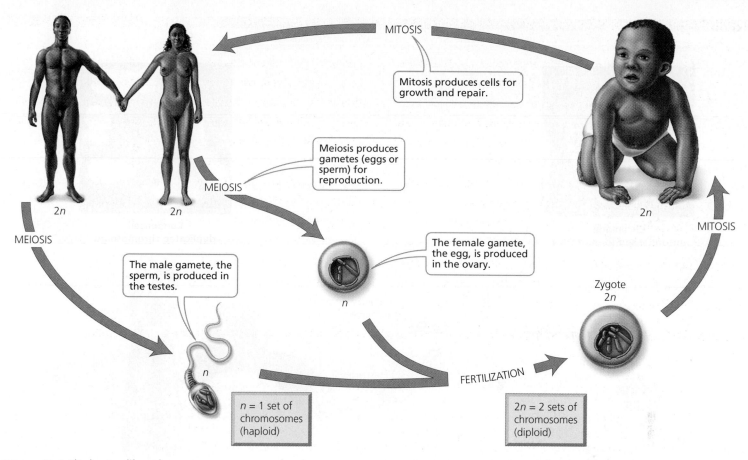

FIGURE 19.1 The human life cycle

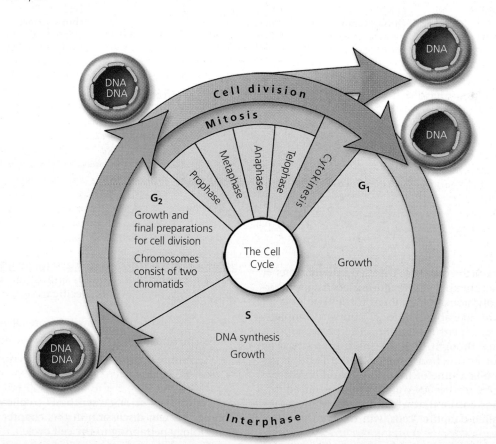

FIGURE 19.2 The cell cycle

Q *Describe the difference in the structure of a chromosome between the start of interphase and at the end of interphase.*

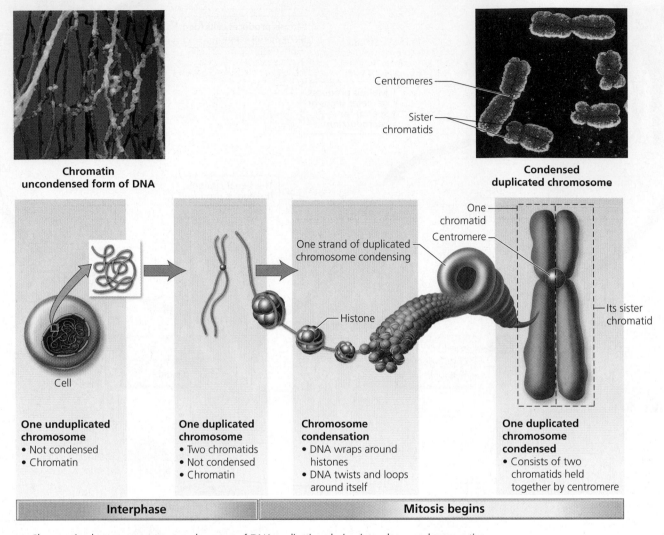

Chromatin
uncondensed form of DNA

Condensed
duplicated chromosome

Centromeres

Sister chromatids

One chromatid

Centromere

One strand of duplicated chromosome condensing

Histone

Its sister chromatid

Cell

One unduplicated chromosome
• Not condensed
• Chromatin

One duplicated chromosome
• Two chromatids
• Not condensed
• Chromatin

Chromosome condensation
• DNA wraps around histones
• DNA twists and loops around itself

One duplicated chromosome condensed
• Consists of two chromatids held together by centromere

Interphase

Mitosis begins

FIGURE 19.3 Changes in chromosome structure because of DNA replication during interphase and preparation for nuclear division in mitosis

A At the start of interphase, a chromosome is a single strand of DNA. At the end of interphase, a chromosome consists of two sister chromatids that are replicate copies of the original strand of DNA.

Interphase

Interphase is the period of the cell cycle between cell divisions. It accounts for most of the time that elapses during a cell cycle. During active growth and divisions (depending on the type of cell), an entire cell cycle might take about 16 to 24 hours to complete, and only 1 to 2 hours are spent in division. Interphase is not a "resting period," as once thought. Instead, interphase is a time when the cell carries out its functions and grows. If the cell is going to divide, interphase is a time of intense preparation for cell division. During interphase, the DNA and organelles are duplicated. These preparations ensure that when the cell divides, each of its resulting cells, called daughter cells, will receive the essentials for survival.

Interphase consists of three parts: G_1 (first "gap"), S (DNA synthesis), and G_2 (second "gap"). All three parts of interphase are

times of cell growth, characterized by the production of organelles and the synthesis of proteins and other macromolecules. There are, however, some events specific to certain parts of interphase

- G_1: A time of major growth before DNA synthesis begins
- S: The time during which DNA is synthesized (replicated)
- G_2: A time of growth after DNA is synthesized and before mitosis begins

The details of DNA synthesis (replication) are described in Chapter 21. Our discussion in this chapter introduces some basic terminology pertaining to the cell cycle.

Throughout interphase, chromosomes are long, thin threads that are often called *chromatin* (Figure **19.3**). They twist randomly

DNA replication during interphase forms two sister chromatids, which are banded together to form a chromosome.

During **mitosis**, sister chromatids separate and move to opposite ends of the cell.

During **cytokinesis**, the parent cell divides, forming two daughter cells. Each daughter cell has two copies of each chromosome (homologous pairs).

Centriole pair

FIGURE 19.4 An overview of mitosis

around one another like tangled strands of yarn. In this state, DNA can be synthesized (replicated) and genes can be active. At the start of interphase, during G_1, each chromosome consists of a DNA molecule and proteins. When the chromosomes are being replicated during the S phase, the chromosome copies remain attached. The two copies, each an exact replicate of the original chromosome, stay attached to one another at a region called the **centromere.** As long as the replicate copies remain attached, each copy is called a **chromatid.** The two attached chromatids are genetically identical and are called *sister chromatids.*

Division of the Nucleus and the Cytoplasm

Body cells divide continually in the developing embryo and fetus. Such division also plays an important role in the growth and repair of body tissues in children. In the adult, specialized cells, such as most nerve cells, lose their ability to divide. Late in G_1 of interphase, these cells enter what is called the G_0 stage; they are carrying out their normal cellular activities but do not divide. Other adult cells, such as liver cells, stop dividing but retain the ability to undergo cell division should the need for tissue repair and replacement arise. Still other cells actively divide throughout life. For example, the ongoing cell division in skin cells in adults serves to replace the enormous numbers of cells worn off each day.

The division of body cells (after interphase) consists of two processes that overlap somewhat in time. The first process, division of the nucleus, is called *mitosis.* The second process is *cytokinesis,* which is the division of the cytoplasm that occurs toward the end of mitosis (Figure **19.4**).

Mitosis: Creation of Genetically Identical Diploid Body Cells

For the purpose of discussion, mitosis is usually divided into four stages: prophase, metaphase, anaphase, and telophase. The major events of each stage are depicted in Figure **19.5**

- **Prophase** Mitosis begins with **prophase,** a time when changes occur in the nucleus as well as the cytoplasm. In the nucleus, the chromosomes condense as DNA wraps around histones. The DNA then loops and twists to form a tightly compacted structure (see Figure 19.3). When DNA is in this condensed state, it cannot be replicated, and gene activity is shut down. In this condensed state, the sister chromatids are easier to separate without breaking. At about this time, the nuclear membrane also begins to break down.

    Outside the nucleus, in the cytoplasm, the mitotic spindle forms. The mitotic spindle is made of microtubules associated with the centrioles (see Chapter 3). During prophase, the centrioles, duplicated during interphase, move away from each other toward opposite ends of the cell.

- **Metaphase** During the next stage of mitosis, **metaphase,** the chromosomes attach to the mitotic spindles, forming a line at what is called the equator (center) of the mitotic spindles. This alignment ensures each daughter cell receives one chromatid from each of the 46 chromosomes when the chromosomes separate at the centromere. Thus each daughter cell is a diploid cell that is genetically identical to the parent cell.

Nucleus

Interphase
• DNA duplicated
• Growth
• Preparation for cell division

Prophase
• Chromosomes condense

Metaphase
• Chromosomes (consisting of two chromatids) line up at equatorial plate

Interphase

Mitosis

Cell division

G_2 G_1

S

Interphase

FIGURE 19.5 The stages of cell division (mitosis and cytokinesis) captured in light micrographs and depicted in schematic drawings

• **Anaphase** **Anaphase** begins when the sister chromatids of each chromosome begin to separate, splitting at the centromere. Now separate entities, the sister chromatids are considered chromosomes in their own right. The spindle fibers pull the chromosomes toward opposite poles of the cell. By the end of anaphase, equivalent collections of chromosomes are located at the two poles of the cell.

• **Telophase** During **telophase**, a nuclear envelope forms around each group of chromosomes at each pole, and the mitotic spindle disassembles. The chromosomes also become more threadlike in appearance.

Cytokinesis

Cytokinesis—division of the cytoplasm—begins toward the end of mitosis, sometime during telophase. During this period, a band of microfilaments in the area where the chromosomes originally aligned contracts and forms a furrow, as shown in Figure **19.6**. The furrow deepens, eventually pinching the cell in two.

stop and think

Cancer cells divide rapidly and without end. One type of drug used in cancer chemotherapy inhibits the formation of spindle fibers. Why can this be an effective anticancer treatment?

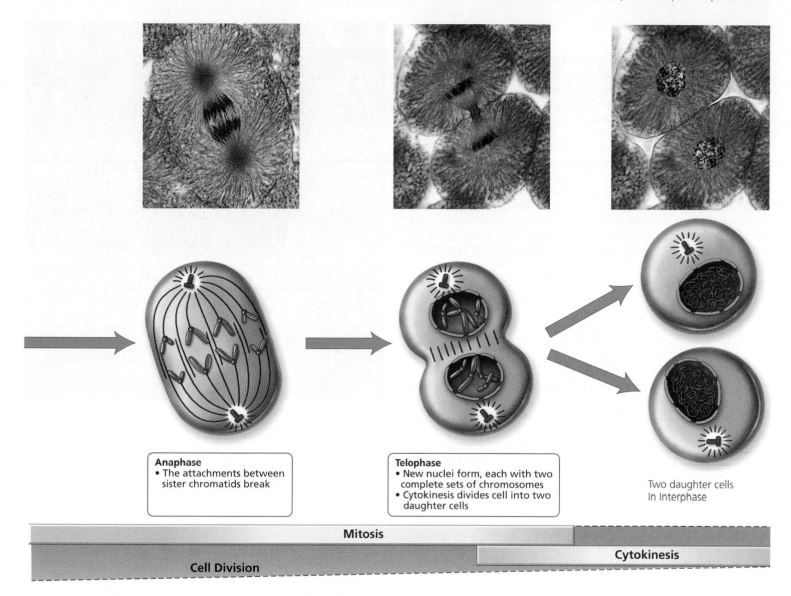

Anaphase
- The attachments between sister chromatids break

Telophase
- New nuclei form, each with two complete sets of chromosomes
- Cytokinesis divides cell into two daughter cells

Two daughter cells
In Interphase

Mitosis

Cytokinesis

Cell Division

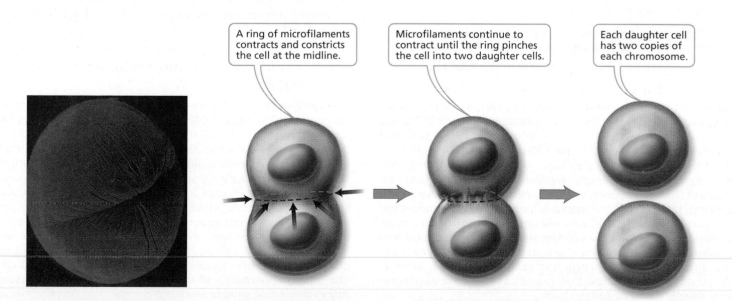

A ring of microfilaments contracts and constricts the cell at the midline.

Microfilaments continue to contract until the ring pinches the cell into two daughter cells.

Each daughter cell has two copies of each chromosome.

FIGURE 19.6 Cytokinesis is the division of the cytoplasm to form two daughter cells.

Karyotypes

As we have seen, a major feature of cell division is the shortening and thickening of the chromosomes. In this state, the chromosomes are visible with a light microscope and can be used for diagnostic purposes, such as when potential parents want to check their own chromosomal makeup for defects. One often-used method takes white blood cells from a blood sample and grows them for a while in a nourishing medium. The culture then is treated with a drug that destroys the mitotic spindle, thus preventing separation of the chromosomes and halting cell division at metaphase. Next the cells are fixed, stained, and photographed so that the images of the chromosomes can be arranged in pairs based on physical characteristics such as location of the centromere and overall length. The chromosomes are numbered from largest to smallest, in an arrangement called a **karyotype** (Figure **19.7**). Karyotypes can be checked for irregularities in number or structure of chromosomes.

Meiosis: Creation of Haploid Gametes

We have seen that the somatic cells contain a homologous pair of each type of chromosome, one member of each pair from the father and one member of each pair from the mother. Recall that a cell with homologous pairs of chromosomes is described as being diploid, 2*n*. The gametes—eggs or sperm—differ from somatic cells in that they are **haploid**, indicated by *n*, meaning that they have only one member of each homologous pair of chromosomes. As you read earlier in the chapter, gametes are produced by a type of cell division called **meiosis**, which is actually two divisions that result in up to four haploid daughter cells. When a sperm fertilizes an egg, a new cell—the zygote—is created. Because the egg and sperm both contribute a set of chromosomes to the zygote, it is diploid. After many mitotic cell divisions, a zygote can eventually develop into a new individual.

Functions of Meiosis

Meiosis serves two important functions:

- Meiosis keeps the number of chromosomes in a body cell constant from generation to generation.
- Meiosis increases genetic variability in the population.

Meiosis keeps the number of chromosomes in a body cell constant over generations because it creates haploid gametes (sperm and eggs) with only one member of each homologous pair of chromosomes. If gametes were produced by mitosis, they would be diploid; each sperm and egg would contain 46 chromosomes instead of 23. Then, if a sperm containing 46 chromosomes fertilized an egg with 46 chromosomes, the zygote would have 92 chromosomes. The zygote of the next generation would have 184 chromosomes, having been formed by an egg and sperm each containing 92 chromosomes. The next generation would have 368 chromosomes in each cell, and the next one 736—and so on. You can see that the chromosome number would quickly become unwieldy and, what is more important, alter the amount of genetic information in each cell. As we will see toward the chapter's end, even one extra copy of a single chromosome usually causes an embryo to die.

FIGURE 19.7 Chromosomes in dividing cells can be examined for defects in number or structure. A karyotype is constructed by arranging the chromosomes from photographs based on size and centromere location.

Meiosis also increases genetic variability in the population. Later in this chapter we consider the mechanisms by which it accomplishes this increase. Genetic variability is important because it provides the raw material through which natural selection can act, leading to the changes described collectively as evolution. The relationship between genetic variability and evolution is discussed in Chapter 22.

Two Meiotic Cell Divisions: Preparation for Sexual Reproduction

First, let's consider how meiosis keeps the chromosome number constant. The stages in meiosis are summarized in Figure **19.8**. Meiosis and mitosis begin the same way. Both are preceded by the same event—the replication of chromosomes. Unlike mitosis, however, meiosis involves *two* divisions. In the first division, the chromosome number is reduced, because the two homologues of each pair of chromosomes (each replicated into two chromatids attached by a centromere) are separated into two cells so that each cell has one member of each homologous pair of chromosomes. In the second division, the replicated chromatids of each chromosome are separated. We see, then, that meiosis begins with one diploid cell and, two divisions later, produces four haploid cells. The orderly movements of chromosomes during meiosis ensure that each haploid gamete produced contains one member of each

During **meiosis II**, sister chromatids separate and four haploid daughter cells are formed that will develop into gametes.

During **meiosis I**, homologous chromosomes separate into two haploid cells, each containing one member of each homologous pair.

DNA replication during interphase forms two copies of each chromosome, and the copies remain attached.

This **diploid parent** cell contains two homologous pairs of chromosomes.

$2n = 4$

Centromere

Homologous pair of chromosomes

$n = 2$

$n = 2$

FIGURE 19.8 Overview of meiosis. Meiosis reduces the chromosome number from the diploid number to the haploid number. Meiosis involves two cell divisions.

homologous pair of chromosomes. Although not shown in the summary figure, each of the two meiotic divisions has four stages similar to those in mitosis: prophase, metaphase, anaphase, and telophase.

Meiosis I

The first meiotic division—meiosis I—produces two cells, each with 23 chromosomes. Note that the daughter cells do not contain a random assortment of any 23 chromosomes. Instead, each daughter cell contains one member of each homologous pair, with each chromosome consisting of two sister chromatids.

It is important that each daughter cell receive one of each kind of chromosome during meiosis I. If one of the daughter cells had two of chromosome 3 and no chromosome 6, it would not survive. Although there would still be 23 chromosomes present, part of the instructions for the structure and function of the body (chromosome 6) would be missing. The separation of homologous chromosomes occurs reliably during meiosis I because, during prophase I (the *I* indicates this phase takes place during meiosis I), members of homologous pairs line up next to one an-

other by a phenomenon called **synapsis** ("bringing together"). For example, the chromosome 1 that was originally from your father would line up with the chromosome 1 originally from your mother. Paternal chromosome 2 would pair with maternal chromosome 2, and so on. During metaphase I, matched homologous pairs become positioned at the midline of the cell and attach to spindle fibers. The pairing of homologous chromosomes helps ensure that the daughter cells will receive one member of each homologous pair. Consider the following analogy. By pairing your socks before putting them in a drawer, you are more likely to put matching socks on your feet than if you randomly pulled out two socks.

Next, during anaphase I, the members of each homologous pair of chromosomes separate, and each homologue moves to opposite ends of the cell. During telophase I, cytokinesis begins, resulting in two daughter cells, each with one member of each chromosome pair. Each chromosome in each daughter cell still consists of two replicated sister chromatids. Telophase I is followed by *interkinesis,* a brief interphase-like period. Interkinesis differs from mitotic interphase in that there is no replication of DNA during interkinesis.

FIGURE 19.9 Stages of meiosis

Meiosis II

During the second meiotic division—meiosis II—each chromosome lines up in the center of the cell independently (as occurs in mitosis), and the sister chromatids (attached replicates) making up each chromosome separate. Separation of the sister chromatids occurs in both daughter cells that were produced in meiosis I. This event results in four cells, each containing one of each kind of chromosome. The events of meiosis II are similar to those of mitosis, except that only 23 chromosomes are lining up independently in meiosis II compared with the 46 chromosomes aligning independently in mitosis. Figure **19.9** depicts the events of meiosis. Table **19.1** and Figure **19.10** compare mitosis and meiosis.

Subsequent changes in the shape and functioning of the four haploid cells result in functional gametes. In males, one diploid cell can result in four functional sperm. In contrast, in females, meiotic divisions of one diploid cell result in only one functional egg and up to three nonfunctional cells called polar bodies. As a result, the egg contains most of the nutrients found in the original diploid cell, and these nutrients will nourish the early embryo (Figure **19.11**).

stop and think

If you were examining dividing cells under a microscope, how could you determine whether a particular cell was in metaphase of mitosis or metaphase I of meiosis?

Meiosis II: Separates Sister Chromatids

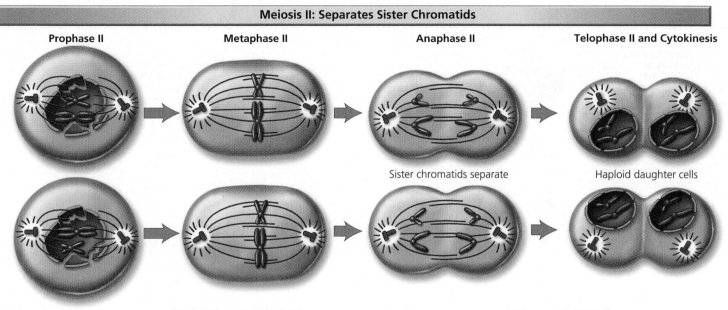

| **Prophase II** | **Metaphase II** | **Anaphase II** | **Telophase II and Cytokinesis** |

Sister chromatids separate

Haploid daughter cells

Prophase II
• Chromosomes condense again
• Occurs in both daughter cells

Metaphase II
• Chromosomes line up at the midline of the cell

Anaphase II
• Centromeres of sister chromatids separate
• Chromatids of each pair are now called chromosomes
• Chromosomes move to opposite poles

Telophase II
• One complete set of chromosomes is located at each pole
• Cytokinesis occurs in both daughter cells, forming four haploid daughter cells

---

TABLE 19.1 Mitosis and Meiosis Compared

Mitosis	**Meiosis**
Involves one cell division	Involves two cell divisions
Produces two diploid cells	Produces up to four haploid cells
Occurs in somatic cells	Occurs only in ovary and testes during the formation of gametes (egg and sperm)
Results in growth and repair	Results in gamete (egg and sperm) production
No exchange of genetic material	Parts of chromosomes are exchanged in crossing over
Daughter cells are genetically similar	Daughter cells are genetically dissimilar

FIGURE 19.10 A comparison of meiosis and mitosis

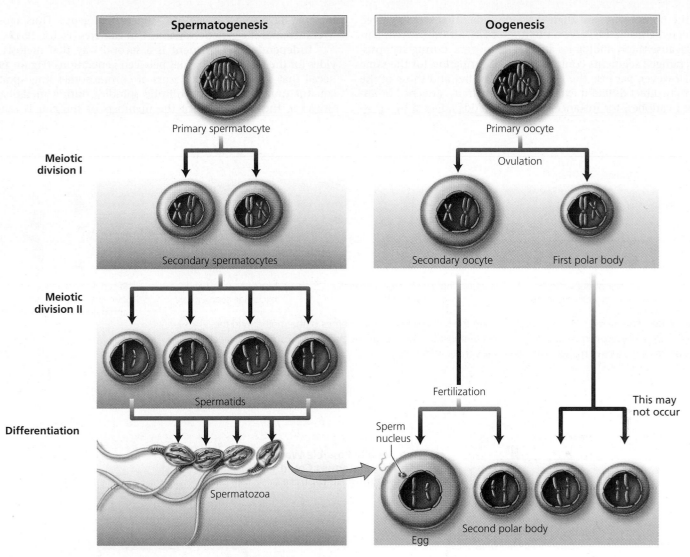

FIGURE 19.11 Comparison of spermatogenesis and oogenesis. Meiosis results in haploid cells that differentiate into mature gametes. Spermatogenesis produces four sperm cells that are specialized to transport the male's genetic information to the egg. Oogenesis produces up to three polar bodies and one ovum that is packed with nutrients to nourish the early embryo.

Genetic Variability: Crossing Over and Independent Assortment

At the moment of fertilization, when the nuclei of an egg and a sperm fuse, a new, *unique* individual is formed. Although certain family characteristics may be passed along, each child bears its own assortment of genetic characteristics (Figure **19.12**).

Genetic variation arises largely because of the shuffling of maternal and paternal forms of genes during meiosis. One way this mixing occurs is through a process called **crossing over**, in which corresponding pieces of chromatids of maternal and paternal homologues (nonsister chromatids) are exchanged during synapsis

FIGURE 19.12 Each child inherits a unique combination of maternal and paternal genetic characteristics due to the shuffling of chromosomes that occurs during meiosis. This photograph shows Eric and Mary Goodenough with their four sons: Derick, Stephen, David, and John.

when the homologues are aligned side by side. After crossing over, the affected chromatids have a mixture of DNA from the two parents. Because the homologues align gene by gene during synapsis, the exchanged segments contain genetic information for the same traits. However, because the genes of the mother and those of the father may direct different expressions of the trait—attached or unattached earlobes, for instance—the chromatids affected by cross-

ing over have a new, novel combination of genes. Thus, crossing over increases the genetic variability of gametes (Figure **19.13**).

Independent assortment is a second way that meiosis provides for the shuffling of genes between generations (Figure **19.14**). Recall that the homologous pairs of chromosomes line up at the equator (midpoint) of the mitotic spindles during metaphase I. However, the orientation of the members of the pair is random

FIGURE 19.13 Crossing over. During synapsis, when the homologous chromosomes of the mother and the father are closely aligned, corresponding segments of nonsister chromatids are exchanged. Each of the affected chromatids has a mixture of maternal and paternal genetic information.

FIGURE 19.14 Independent assortment. The relative positioning of homologous maternal and paternal chromosomes with respect to the poles of the cell is random. The members of each homologous pair orient independently of the other pairs. Notice that with only two homologous pairs, there are four possible combinations of chromosomes in the resulting gametes.

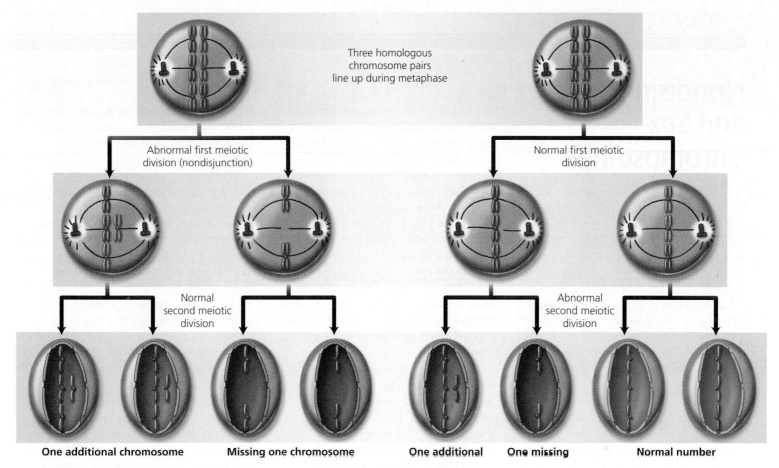

Three homologous chromosome pairs line up during metaphase

Abnormal first meiotic division (nondisjunction)

Normal first meiotic division

Normal second meiotic division

Abnormal second meiotic division

One additional chromosome **Missing one chromosome** **One additional** **One missing** **Normal number**

FIGURE 19.15 Nondisjunction is a mistake that occurs during cell division in which homologous chromosomes or sister chromatids fail to separate during anaphase. One of the resulting daughter cells will have three of one type of chromosome, and the other daughter cell will be missing that type of chromosome.

with respect to which member is closer to which pole. Thus, like the odds that a flipped coin will come up heads, there is a fifty-fifty chance that a given daughter cell will receive the maternal chromosome from a particular pair. Each of the 23 pairs of chromosomes orients independently during metaphase I. The orientations of all 23 pairs will determine the assortments of maternal and paternal chromosomes in the daughter cells. Thus, each child (other than identical siblings) of the same parents has a unique genetic makeup.

Extra or Missing Chromosomes

Most of the time, meiosis is a precise process that results in the chromosomes being distributed evenly to gametes. But meiosis is not foolproof. A pair of chromosomes or sister chromatids may adhere so tightly to one another that they do not separate during anaphase. As a result, both go to the same daughter cell, and the other daughter cell receives none of this type of chromosome (Figure **19.15**). The failure of homologous chromosomes to separate during meiosis I or of sister chromatids to separate during meiosis II is called **nondisjunction.**

What happens if nondisjunction creates a gamete with an extra or a missing chromosome and that gamete is then united

with a normal gamete during fertilization? The resulting zygote will have an excess or deficit of chromosomes. For instance, if the abnormal gamete has an extra chromosome, the resulting zygote will have three of one type of chromosome and two of the rest. This condition, in which there are three representatives of one chromosome, is called **trisomy.** If, on the other hand, a gamete that is missing a representative of one type of chromosome joins with a normal gamete during fertilization, the resulting zygote will have only one of that type of chromosome, rather than the normal two chromosomes. The condition in which there is only one representative of a particular chromosome in a cell is called **monosomy.** The imbalance of chromosome numbers usually causes abnormalities in development. Most of the time, the resulting malformations are severe enough to cause the death of the fetus, which will result in a miscarriage. Indeed, in about 70% of miscarriages, the fetus has an abnormal number of chromosomes.

When a fetus inherits an abnormal number of certain chromosomes—for instance, chromosome 21 or the sex chromosomes—the resulting condition is usually not fatal. The upset in chromosome balance does, however, cause a specific syndrome. (A *syndrome* is a group of symptoms that generally occur to-

Nondisjunction and Sex Chromosomes

Like autosomes, sex chromosomes may fail to separate during anaphase. This error can occur during either egg or sperm formation. A male is chromosomally XY, so when the X and Y separate during anaphase, equal numbers of X-bearing and Y-bearing sperm are produced. However, if nondisjunction of the sex chromosomes occurs during sperm formation, half of the resulting sperm will carry both X and Y chromosomes, whereas the other resulting sperm will not contain any sex chromosome. A female is chromosomally XX, so each of the eggs she produces should contain a single X chromosome. When nondisjunction of sex chromosomes occurs, however, an egg may contain two X chromosomes or none at all. When a gamete with an abnormal number of sex chromosomes is joined with a normal gamete during fertilization, the resulting zygote has an abnormal number of sex chromosomes (Figure **19.A**).

Turner syndrome occurs in individuals who have only a single X chromosome (XO). Approximately 1 in 2000 female infants is born with Turner syndrome, but this represents only a small percentage of the XO zygotes that are formed. Most of these XO zygotes are lost as miscarriages. A person with Turner syndrome has the external appearance of a female. The only hint of Turner syndrome may be a thick fold of skin on the neck. As she ages, however, she generally is noticeably shorter than her peers. Her chest is wide, and her breasts underdeveloped. In 90% of the women with Turner syndrome, the ovaries are also poorly developed, leading to infertility. Pregnancy may be possible through in vitro fertilization (see Chapter 18), in which a fertilized egg from a donor is implanted in her uterus.

Klinefelter syndrome is observed in males who are XXY. Although the extra X chromosome can be inherited as a result of nondisjunction during either egg or sperm formation, it is twice as likely to come from the egg. Increased maternal age may increase the risk slightly.

Klinefelter syndrome is fairly common. Approximately 1 in 500 to 1 in 1000 of all newborn males is XXY. However, not all XXY males display the symptoms of having an extra X chromosome. In fact, some of them live their lives without ever suspecting that they are XXY. When there are signs that a male has Klinefelter syndrome, they do not usually show up until puberty. During the teenage years, the testes of an XY male gradually increase in size. In contrast, the testes of many XXY males remain small and do not produce an adequate amount of the male sex hormone, testosterone. As a result of the testosterone insufficiency, these males may grow taller than average but remain less muscular. Secondary sex characteristics, such as facial and body hair, may fail to develop fully. The breasts may also develop slightly. The penis is usually of normal size, but the testes may not produce sperm; so men with Klinefelter syndrome may be sterile.

Nondisjunction can also result in a female with three X chromosomes (XXX, triple-X syndrome) or a male with two Y chromosomes (XYY, Jacob syndrome, produced when the chromatids of a replicated Y chromosome fail to separate). Most women with triple-X syndrome (XXX) have normal sexual development and are able to conceive children. Some triple-X females have learning disabilities and delayed language skills. Males with two Y chromosomes (XYY) are often taller than normal, and some have slightly lower than normal intelligence.

gether.) The Health Issue essay, *Turner Syndrome and Klinefelter Syndrome,* considers the consequences when sex chromosomes fail to separate.

Down syndrome

One in every 800 to 1000 infants is born with three copies of chromosome 21 (trisomy 21), a condition known as *Down syndrome.* Symptoms of Down syndrome include moderate to severe mental retardation, short stature or shortened body parts due to poor skeletal growth, and characteristic facial features (Figure **19.16**). Individuals with Down syndrome typically have a flattened nose, a forward-protruding tongue that forces the mouth open, upward-slanting eyes, and a fold of skin at the inner corner of each eye. Approximately 50% of all infants with Down syndrome have heart defects, and many of them die as a result of this defect. Blockage in the digestive system, especially in the esophagus or small intestine, is also common and may require surgery shortly after birth.

The risk of having a baby with Down syndrome increases with the mother's age. A 30-year-old woman is twice as likely to give birth to a child with Down syndrome as is a 20-year-old woman. After age 30, the risk rises dramatically. At age 45, a mother is 45 times as likely to give birth to a Down syndrome infant as is a 20-year-old woman.

It is possible to determine whether a 2-month-old fetus has Down syndrome. If you were a 30-year-old woman who became pregnant (or the father of the child), would you want to know whether the child would have Down syndrome? What criteria would you use to decide?

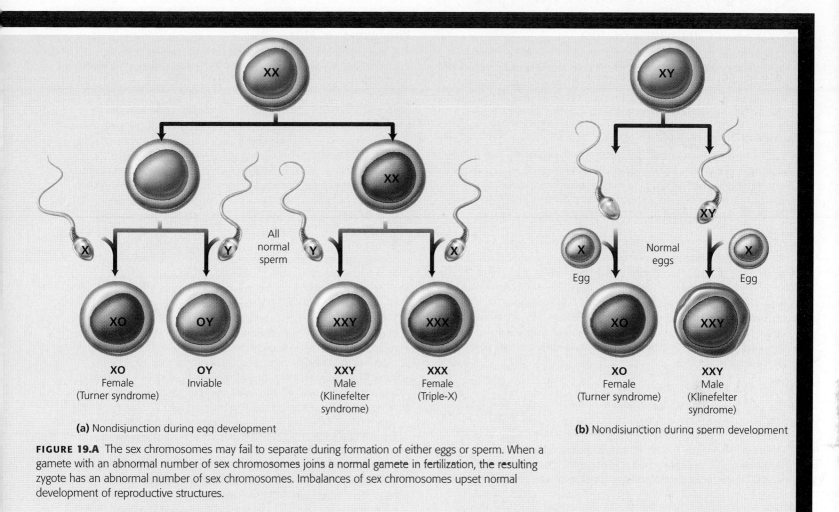

(a) Nondisjunction during egg development

(b) Nondisjunction during sperm development

FIGURE 19.A The sex chromosomes may fail to separate during formation of either eggs or sperm. When a gamete with an abnormal number of sex chromosomes joins a normal gamete in fertilization, the resulting zygote has an abnormal number of sex chromosomes. Imbalances of sex chromosomes upset normal development of reproductive structures.

exploring further

In this chapter we considered cell division: mitosis, which gives rise to new body cells for growth and repair, and meiosis, which gives rise to the gametes (eggs and sperm). In the next chapter, we consider mitosis further and explore stem cells, which are unspecialized cells that can divide continuously and develop into different tissue types.

FIGURE 19.16 A person with Down syndrome is moderately to severely mentally retarded and has a characteristic appearance.

highlighting the concepts

Two Types of Cell Division (p. 406)

- The human life cycle requires two types of nuclear division—mitosis and meiosis. Mitosis creates cells that are exact copies of the original cell. Mitosis occurs in growth and repair. Meiosis creates cells with half the number of chromosomes as were in the original cell. Gamete production requires meiosis.

Form of Chromosomes (p. 406)

- A chromosome contains DNA and proteins called histones. A gene is a segment of DNA that codes for a protein that plays a structural or functional role in the cell. Genes are arranged along a chromosome in a specific order. Each of the 23 different kinds of chromosomes in human cells contains a specific sequence of genes.
- Somatic cells (all cells except for eggs and sperm) are diploid; that is, they contain pairs of chromosomes, one member of each pair from each parent. Homologous chromosomes carry genes for the same traits. In humans, the diploid number of chromosomes is 46—23 homologous pairs. One pair of chromosomes, the sex chromosomes, determines gender. Males are XY, and females are XX. The other 22 pairs of chromosomes are called autosomes. Eggs and sperm are haploid; they contain only one set of chromosomes.

The Cell Cycle (pp. 406–409)

- The cell cycle consists of two major phases: interphase and cell division. Interphase is the period between cell divisions.
- During interphase, DNA and organelles become replicated in preparation for the cell to divide and produce two identical daughter cells. Somatic cell division consists of mitosis (division of the nucleus) and cytokinesis (division of the cytoplasm).

Mitosis: Creation of Genetically Identical Diploid Body Cells (pp. 409–411)

- In mitosis, the original cell, having replicated its genetic material, distributes it equally between its two daughter cells. There are four stages of mitosis: prophase, metaphase, anaphase, and telophase.
- Cytokinesis, division of the cytoplasm, usually begins sometime during telophase. A band of microfilaments at the midline of the cell contracts and forms a furrow. The furrow deepens and eventually pinches the cell in two.

Karyotypes (p. 412)

- A karyotype is an arrangement of chromosomes based on their physical characteristics, such as length and position of the centromere.

Meiosis: Creation of Haploid Gametes (pp. 412–422)

- Meiosis, a special type of nuclear division that occurs in the ovaries or testes, begins with a diploid cell and produces four haploid cells that will become gametes (eggs or sperm).
- Meiosis is important because it halves the number of chromosomes in gametes, thereby keeping the chromosome number constant between generations. When a sperm fertilizes an egg, a diploid cell called a zygote is created. After many successful mitotic divisions, the zygote may develop into a new individual.
- Before meiosis begins, the chromosomes are replicated, and the copies remain attached to one another by centromeres. The attached replicated copies are called sister chromatids.
- There are two cell divisions in meiosis. During the first meiotic division (meiosis I), members of homologous pairs are separated. Thus, the daughter cells contain only one member of each homologous pair (although each chromosome still consists of two replicated sister chromatids). During the second meiotic division (meiosis II), the sister chromatids are separated.
- Genetic recombination during meiosis results in variation among offspring from the same two parents. One cause of genetic recombination is crossing over, in which corresponding segments of DNA are exchanged between maternal and paternal homologues, creating new combinations of alleles in the resulting chromatids.
- A second cause of genetic recombination is the independent assortment of maternal and paternal homologues into daughter cells during meiosis I. The orientation of the members of the pair relative to the poles of the cell determines whether a daughter cell will receive the maternal or the paternal chromosome from a given pair. Each pair aligns independently of the others.
- Nondisjunction is the failure of homologous chromosomes or sister chromatids to separate during cell division. It results in an abnormal number of chromosomes in the resulting gametes, and in zygotes created by fertilization involving these gametes, which generally results in death of the fetus. Nondisjunction of chromosome 21 can result in Down syndrome.

recognizing key terms

chromosome *p. 406*
gene *p. 406*
somatic cells *p. 406*
homologous chromosome
  pair *p. 406*
diploid *p. 406*
sex chromosomes *p. 406*

autosomes *p. 406*
mitosis *p. 406*
cell cycle *p. 406*
interphase *p. 408*
centromere *p. 409*
chromatid *p. 409*
prophase *p. 409*

metaphase *p. 409*
anaphase *p. 410*
telophase *p. 410*
cytokinesis *p. 410*
karyotype *p. 412*
haploid *p. 412*
meiosis *p. 412*

synapsis *p. 413*
crossing over *p. 417*
independent assortment
  p. 418
nondisjunction *p. 419*
trisomy *p. 419*
monosomy *p. 419*

reviewing the concepts

1. Explain the relationship between genes and a chromosome. *p. 406*
2. Define mitosis and cytokinesis. *pp. 409–411*
3. Why is meiosis important? *p. 412*
4. Describe the alignment of chromosomes at the midline during meiosis I and meiosis II. Explain the importance of these alignments in creating haploid gametes from diploid cells. *pp. 412–415*
5. Explain how crossing over and independent assortment result in genetic recombination that causes variability among offspring (aside from identical twins) from the same two parents. *pp. 417–419*
6. Define nondisjunction. Explain how nondisjunction can result in abnormal numbers of chromosomes in a person. *pp. 419*
7. What causes Down syndrome? What are the usual characteristics of the condition? *p. 420–421*
8. The process of mitosis results in
   a. two haploid cells.
   b. two diploid cells.
   c. four haploid cells.
   d. four diploid cells.
9. DNA is synthesized (replicated) during
   a. interphase.
   b. prophase.
   c. metaphase.
   d. anaphase.
10. Crossing over occurs during which stage of meiosis?
    a. Prophase I
    b. Metaphase I
    c. Prophase II
    d. Metaphase II
11. During meiosis, the processes of _____ and _____ increase genetic diversity.
12. _____ chromosomes carry genes for the same traits.
13. _____ is the pairing of chromosomes during meiosis.
14. The stage of mitosis during which sister chromatids separate is _____.
15. The stage of meiosis during which sister chromatids separate is _____.

applying the concepts

1. Cathy is a 35-year-old woman who just finished graduate school. She and her husband, Bob, decided to start a family. When Cathy became pregnant, the doctor performed an amniocentesis to create a karyotype of the fetus's genes. The karyotype revealed that the fetus had three copies of chromosome 21. How could this condition occur? How will it affect the child?

2. A cell biologist is studying the cell cycle. She is growing the cells in culture, and they are actively dividing mitotically. One particular cell has half as much DNA as most of the other cells. Which stage of mitosis is this cell in? How do you know?

3. What would happen if the spindle fibers failed to form during mitosis?

becoming information literate

Several genetic disorders are caused by too many or too few chromosomes. Use at least three reliable sources (books, journals, websites) to describe at least one such disorder other than Down syndrome, Turner syndrome, and Klinefelter syndrome. Indicate which chromosomes are extra or missing in the disorder, and note the symptoms of the disorder. List each source you considered, and explain why you chose the three sources you used.

Additional questions can be found online at The Human Biology Place, www.humanbiology.com.

19a Special Topic

Stem Cells—A Repair Kit for the Body

Bone marrow contains stem cells that, when transplanted from a person who is a tissue match, can be used to treat leukemia.

Seamus was nervous and excited. The day for the bone marrow transplant had finally arrived. His younger brother Liam has leukemia, a type of cancer in which excessive numbers of white blood cells (leukocytes) are produced. Although the number of leukocytes is elevated, the cells are immature and are not effective in combating infection. Liam has lost a lot of weight and is frequently sick. He had chemotherapy and was in remission for a while, but the cancer returned.

Seamus is happy that he is a tissue match for his brother. In preparation for the bone marrow transplant, Liam's bone marrow, the source of the diseased blood cells, had to be destroyed. Today, doctors will remove some of the bone marrow from Seamus' pelvis and inject it into his brother. The bone marrow contains blood stem cells that can give rise to all types of blood cells. Healthy blood cells will soon repopulate Liam's blood.

In this chapter, we learn what stem cells are, where they are found, and the promises they may hold for the future.

Stem Cells: Unspecialized Cells

Imagine growing new heart cells to repair damage from a heart attack. Think about curing Parkinson's disease by restoring the dopamine-producing neurons that are lacking in such patients. What about generating insulin-producing pancreatic islet cells to cure diabetes? Can we find a cure for multiple sclerosis, Alzheimer's, Lou Gehrig's disease, and spinal cord injuries? How? These things may be possible by using a repair kit for the body, stem cells—cells that continually divide and retain the ability to develop into many types of cells—to produce the needed type of cell.

The common thread among these disorders is that they are caused by too little cell division or defective cell division. When there is too little cell division, the body cannot repair damaged tissue, such as neurons to repair spinal cord injury. Parkinson's disease, which is characterized by a lack of neurons that produce the neurotransmitter dopamine, and hemophilia, which is characterized by a lack of production of certain blood clotting factors by liver cells, are caused by defective cell function. If the damaged or defective cells could be replaced by healthy, functional cells, the disorders would be cured. Stem cells may be a source of functional cells to bring about those cures.

Most of the trillions of cells in your body have become specialized to perform a particular job. Muscle cells are specialized to contract, and neurons are specialized to conduct nerve impulses. The specialization of cells during embryonic development is directed by biological cues in each cell's immediate environment. The cues are usually provided by neighboring cells and include growth factors, surface proteins, salts, and contact with other cells. Because all cells within the same body have the same genetic makeup, the specialization of different cells to perform different functions means that particular genes in each type of cell have been turned on or off. Recall from the previous chapter that specialized cells usually do not divide again.

Stem cells, in contrast, are relatively unspecialized cells that divide continually, creating a pool of undifferentiated cells for possible use. If stem cells are given the correct signals—exposure to a particular growth factor or hormone, for example—they can be coaxed into differentiating into a particular specialized cell type. The specialized cell types can then be used to treat diseases or regenerate injured tissues. As we will see, stem cells from different sources differ in the variety of specialized cell types they can develop into.

Stem cells are categorized by the degree of flexibility in their developmental path (Figure **19a.1**). A fertilized egg can develop into all the types of cells in the body and is therefore considered to

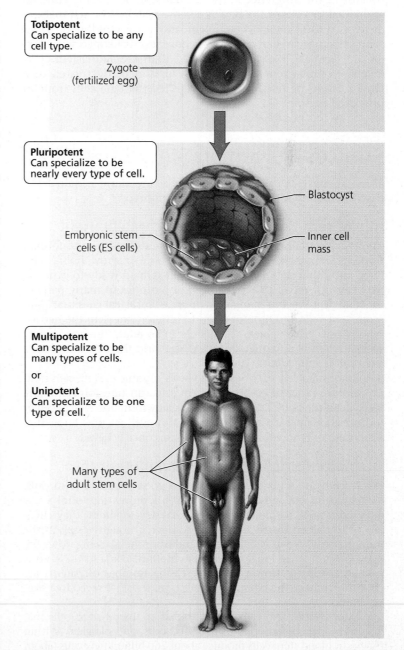

Totipotent
Can specialize to be any cell type.

Zygote (fertilized egg)

Pluripotent
Can specialize to be nearly every type of cell.

Blastocyst

Embryonic stem cells (ES cells)

Inner cell mass

Multipotent
Can specialize to be many types of cells.

or

Unipotent
Can specialize to be one type of cell.

Many types of adult stem cells

FIGURE 19a.1 Stem cells at different stages in human development be *totipotent*. After about a week of development, the embryo is a source of embryonic stem cells, which can develop into nearly every type of cell. Because the developmental path of embryonic stem cells is so flexible, they are described as being *pluripotent*. In an adult, some stem cells remain able to differentiate into several types of cells and are described as being *multipotent*. Still other adult stem cells are described as *unipotent*, because they can differentiate into only one type of cell. Thus, embryonic stem cells are more versatile than are adult stem cells.

The source of stem cells used for therapeutic purposes influences the kinds of cells they can become as well as the likelihood of the stem cells being rejected in the body of the person being treated. Each person's cells have self markers (MHC markers) identifying the cells as belonging in that body (see Chapter 13). These self markers are genetically determined, so the self markers of relative's cells will be more similar than those of unrelated individuals. Cells that are not recognized as belonging in the body, because of the difference in the self markers, are usually attacked and killed by cells of the body's defense system. The self markers develop during fetal development and early childhood. Thus, stem cells from an embryo or fetus have less developed self markers and are less likely to be rejected than are adult stem cells. Likewise, adult stem cells from the person being treated or a close relative are less likely to be rejected than are cells from an unrelated person.

Sources of Human Stem Cells

There are several sources of stem cells, including certain adult tissues, umbilical cord blood, and early embryos.

Adult Stem Cells: Unipotent and Multipotent

Adults have stem cells, but they are more difficult to locate than those in an embryo are. Waiting in the bone marrow, brain, skin, liver, and other organs, adult stem cells remain ready to generate new cells for repair or replacement of old ones in many parts of the body. Diseased or dying cells provide biological cues that summon stem cells and prompt them to differentiate into the needed type of cell. When a stem cell divides in an adult, one cell usually specializes to be a particular type of cell and the other remains a stem cell (Figure **19a.2**).

Adult stem cells do not seem to be as versatile as stem cells from an embryo. Whereas embryonic stem cells can transform into any cell type in the body, adult stem cells usually form one type of cell or form cells of a particular lineage only. However, we now know that adult stem cells are more versatile than was once believed.

Umbilical Cord Stem Cells: Multipotent

Blood from the umbilical cord is also a good source of stem cells. Stem cells do not settle into an infant's bone marrow until a few days after birth. Before that, during fetal development, they circulate in the bloodstream and therefore travel through vessels in the umbilical cord when circulating to and from the placenta. After the baby is born, it no longer needs its umbilical cord, so the cord is usually discarded. However, an increasing number of parents are choosing to have the blood stem cells from the cord saved in a storage bank.

Most of the stem cells in cord blood are blood stem cells that give rise to red blood cells, white blood cells, and platelets. Within the body, blood stem cells produce about 260 billion new cells (about an ounce of blood) every day. However, umbilical cord blood also

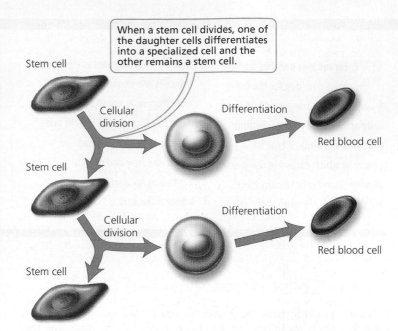

FIGURE 19a.2 Two important characteristics of stem cells are that they divide continually and that their daughter cells can differentiate into one or more specialized stem cells. Here, a blood stem cell divides, producing one daughter cell that becomes specialized to perform a function and another daughter cell that remains a stem cell to replenish the stem cell supply.

contains some stem cells that can turn into other kinds of cells—bone, cartilage, heart muscle, brain tissue, and liver tissue.

Stem cells from umbilical cord blood have some advantages over adult blood stem cells taken from bone marrow. Blood stem cells can be harvested from bone marrow, but the procedure is done in a hospital under general anesthesia. Stem cells are more easily extracted from umbilical cord blood because the cord is removed from the infant's body. Another advantage of taking stem cells from cord blood is that they are less likely to be rejected by the recipient than are adult stem cells from bone marrow. The self markers on the cord blood stem cells have not yet fully developed, so the match does not have to be as close as with adult stem cells from bone marrow. Finally, stem cells from cord blood are less likely to carry infections.

Because blood stem cells are able to produce an endless supply of blood cells, they hold promise for treating a host of blood conditions. For instance, some patients with the inherited disorders sickle-cell anemia and beta-thalassemia, in which abnormal forms of hemoglobin are produced, have already been treated successfully with stem cell therapy. Stem cells that produce normal hemoglobin can be transplanted into a person with the inherited anemia. Normal red blood cells then begin replacing the abnormal ones.

Most of the medical benefits that may be achieved using umbilical cord blood have yet to be realized. Nonetheless, there are already umbilical cord blood banks that store cord blood from newborn babies. Some parents pay a setup fee and an annual service fee to store their baby's cord blood just in case the child needs that blood or those stem cells some day. Government-owned banks collect and store thousands of samples of cord blood in hopes of having a tissue match for most individuals in the population. Researchers have developed ways to increase the number of umbilical cord blood stem cells by growing them in the laboratory.

The existence of umbilical cord blood banks raises certain social issues. Should blood stored in private blood banks be reserved only for the possible future need of the donor, or should it be made available for anyone in need whose tissue type matches? Should cord blood banks be privately owned or funded by the government? These are just a few of the many questions remaining to be addressed.

Embryonic Stem Cells: Pluripotent

Embryonic stem cells can divide continually and specialize into nearly any cell type. They come from several sources.

Unused embryos from fertility clinics

Most of the stem cells used for current research come from embryos that were created for reproductive purposes but were not used. Only a few days old, these embryos left in fertility clinics were destined for destruction. When the early embryo is about 6 to 7 days old, it is a rich source of stem cells because the cells it consists of are able to produce all the cells of the new individual. When stem cells are extracted from an early embryo, the embryo is about the size of the head of a pin and is called a blastocyst (see Chapter 18; see also Figure **19a.3**). It is a sphere of cells containing a cluster of about 20 to 30 cells, called the inner cell mass, adhering to one side of the sphere. The stem cells make up the inner cell mass. Embryonic stem cells are easy to harvest: the cells of the inner cell mass are extracted and cultured in the laboratory. They will continue to divide for years, creating a stem cell line.

Some people object to the use of embryonic stem cells because removing the stem cells destroys such an embryo, putting an end to its ability to become a fetus. The controversy has extended into the political realm. In August 2001, President George W. Bush announced that embryonic stem cell research would not receive federal funding under his administration unless the research was limited to using only previously existing stem cell lines. (Use of federal funds under President Bush was also prohibited for the creation of human embryos to be used in research or for reproductive cloning.) In mid-2006, the United States Congress voted to ease restrictions on stem cell research, but the decision was vetoed by President Bush. Today, there are only 21 embryonic stem cell lines approved for research, which means the genetic diversity of the allowed lines is limited. Furthermore, these cell lines are now old and don't grow well.

FIGURE 19a.3 Embryonic stem cells come from the inner cell mass, a cluster of 20 to 30 cells, from a 6- to 7-day old embryo. At this age, the embryo is about the size of a head of a pin.

When the embryo consists of just a few cells, it is possible to extract a single cell from an embryo without destroying the embryo. The cell removed from the embryo can be used to establish an embryonic stem cell line. The remaining embryonic cells continue development and can be implanted in a woman's uterus when it reaches the appropriate (blastocyst) stage. Thus, this technique has been used with some success to create "ethical" embryonic stem cell lines. Critics suggest that the procedure harms the embryo because compared with normal, intact embryos only 80% of those with a cell removed continue development. The success rate may be too low for government acceptance and funding of the technique.

Parthenotes

In a process called parthenogenesis, an egg develops without fertilization. Parthenogenesis occurs naturally in some animals, such as frogs. However, in most species, including humans, the egg must be artificially stimulated to develop in this way. If this stimulation occurs before the second polar body pinches off, the egg (secondary oocyte) contains the normal set of 46 chromosomes (23 pairs). The activated egg cell begins dividing as a fertilized egg would, but in mammals it is incapable of fully developing into offspring. Thus, using such an egg to create embryonic stem cell lines might trigger less controversy than would the use of a viable embryo.

Cells removed from the inner cell mass of an egg that has undergone parthenogenesis, called parthenotes, are pluripotent. Parthenotes might someday be used to develop cell lines that will develop into any type of cell needed for treatment. An advantage of using parthenotes is that these cells are a genetic tissue match to the woman who donated the egg and are not likely to be rejected if they are used to replace her damaged cells. Thus, a woman with a spinal cord injury could donate an egg to be stimulated to divide and specialize into nerve cells to treat her injury.

Though parthenogenesis does not occur naturally in humans, human parthenotes have been developed in the laboratory. Human parthenotes have not yet been used to treat diseases, but monkey parthenotes exist and provide a valuable research tool.

Reprogrammed adult cells

Suppose one could turn back the clock and stimulate an adult cell to revert to an embryonic stem cell. In 2006, researchers announced that they had done just that—they caused adult mouse skin cells to revert to pluripotent embryonic stem cells that could differentiate into any type of tissue. A short time later, in 2007, scientists created embryonic stem cells using human skin cells. Both groups of researchers used viruses to insert four genes into the skin cells. This is an exciting breakthrough—it creates embryonic stem cells without the need to destroy an embryo, and it could produce patient-specific cell lines without the possibility of rejection. Two concerns with embryonic stem cells created in this way are that two of the inserted genes are cancer-producing genes and that using viruses to deliver the genes carries a risk.

During the summer of 2008, researchers addressed these concerns. They created embryonic stem cells from adult skin cells using two genes that are not linked to cancer and then used a cocktail of drugs to revert the skin cells to embryonic stem cells. This research brings stem cells created from adult cells closer to clinical use. But, don't expect cures in the near future. Research on these stem cells will begin in the laboratory, and it will take years before it can be put to practical use in humans.

Somatic cell nuclear transfer

In *somatic cell nuclear transfer* (SCNT), the nucleus from a somatic body cell is transferred to an egg from which the egg nucleus has been removed. The newly created cell is then stimulated to begin embryonic development. All the cells of the embryo are genetically identical. Thus, somatic cell nuclear transfer is a form of *cloning*—producing genetically identical copies of a cell or organism.

Dolly, born on July 5, 1996, was the first sheep—indeed, the first mammal—to be cloned from an adult cell (Figure **19a.4**). She was created using somatic cell nuclear transfer, illustrated in Figure **19a.5**. In Dolly's case, the nucleus of a mammary cell from an adult sheep's udder was placed into an egg from which the nucleus had been removed. (Dolly was named after Dolly Parton, a country singer known for her mammary "cells" as well as for her voice.) The goal of Dr. Ian Wilmut, the Scotsman whose work resulted in Dolly, was to develop techniques that would eventually lead to the production of animals that could be used as factories for manufacturing proteins, such as hormones, that would be beneficial to humans. Cloning could make genetic engineering (discussed in Chapter 21) more efficient. The ability to clone an adult would mean a scientist would need to engineer an animal with a particular desired trait only once. Then, when the animal was old enough for scientists to be sure it had the desired trait, the animal could be reproduced exactly, in multiple copies. Cloning from an adult instead of from an embryo is advantageous because the scientist can be certain before cloning that the animal has the desired traits. In other words, "What you see is what you get." Since Dolly's birth, scientists have cloned several kinds of animals using the technique of somatic cell nuclear transfer.

Discussions about cloning often become heated when the possibility of human cloning is raised. In these discussions, a distinction is often drawn between reproductive cloning and therapeutic cloning. *Therapeutic cloning* would produce a clone of "replacement cells" having the same genetic makeup as a given patient so that they could be used in the patient's medical therapy without concern of being rejected by the immune system.

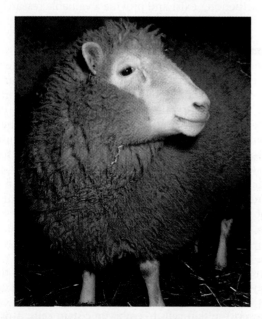

FIGURE 19a.4 Dolly, the first animal cloned from an adult cell, was created using a technique called somatic cell nuclear transfer.

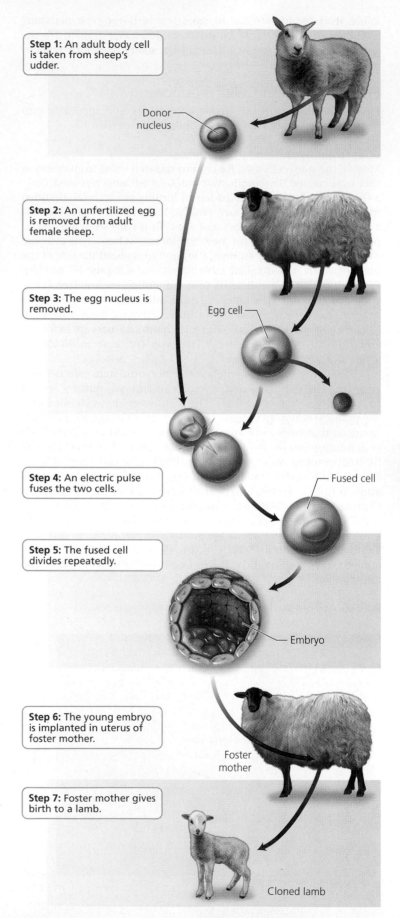

Step 1: An adult body cell is taken from sheep's udder.

Donor nucleus

Step 2: An unfertilized egg is removed from adult female sheep.

Step 3: The egg nucleus is removed.

Egg cell

Step 4: An electric pulse fuses the two cells.

Fused cell

Step 5: The fused cell divides repeatedly.

Embryo

Step 6: The young embryo is implanted in uterus of foster mother.

Foster mother

Step 7: Foster mother gives birth to a lamb.

Cloned lamb

FIGURE 19a.5 Somatic cell nuclear transfer used for reproductive cloning

The cells produced would be embryonic stem cells created using somatic cell nuclear transfer, the technique used to create Dolly. A cell would be taken from the patient, and its nucleus would be put into a donor egg cell from which the original nucleus had been removed. The newly created cell would then begin developing into an embryo (Figure **19a.6**). (If the patient's disease were genetic, a normal form of the relevant gene would be substituted for the defective gene before the nucleus was put in the enucleated egg. Replacement of a specific gene has been accomplished in mice but has not yet been done in humans.)

Once an embryo is created by somatic cell nuclear transfer, stem cells could be removed and treated with growth factors that make them develop into the type of cells needed for treatment. The stem cells could then be transplanted into the patient to replace faulty cells. For example, neurons might be transplanted to cure Parkinson's disease or to repair spinal cord damage, and insulin-producing cells might be transplanted to cure type 1 diabetes. Because the embryonic stem cells would have the same genetic makeup as the patient, they would not be attacked as foreign by the patient's body-defense responses.

The creation of a human embryo by somatic cell nuclear transfer has not yet been accomplished in humans. In 2004 and 2005, Hwang Woo-Suk, a South Korean scientist, claimed to have created a human embryo in this way and extracted embryonic stems cells. Later in 2005, the South Korean's work was declared fraudulent. He did not create an embryo by SCNT—but he did create the first human parthenotes (discussed earlier), a remarkable achievement in itself.

SCNT research has been hampered by a limited supply of human eggs. Some researchers have suggested using enucleated animal eggs instead of human eggs. The human nucleus transferred to the egg would direct development. Some people consider the idea of creating an animal human hybrid embryo to be immoral. The embryos are destroyed at the age of 14 days to ensure that such a hybrid would never fully develop. In 2008, the British Parliament voted not to ban the practice of creating animal human hybrid embryos for use in stem cell research.

In contrast to therapeutic cloning, *reproductive cloning* produces a new individual with a known genetic makeup. The cloning of nonhuman animals (like Dolly) is reproductive cloning. Currently, reproductive cloning is an extremely inefficient process. Hundreds of cloned embryos must be used to obtain one newborn mammal. When cloned embryos do proceed to develop into a new individual, they grow faster and larger than normal. There is also a suspicion that cloned mammals age prematurely. For example, there are indications that Dolly was genetically older than her birth age: one is that Dolly had arthritis, a painful joint condition usually found only in older animals. For reasons like these, experts agree that scientists are still far from being able to produce a cloned human baby.

If reproductive cloning of humans does become possible someday, what might this technology mean to our society? How would it affect human life? One thing it would *not* do is give us the power to create an exact copy of a specific person. Environment *and* genes (also often referred to as nurture and nature) determine personality characteristics. Although cloning could replicate the exact genetic makeup of a specific person, there would be no way to replicate all the experiences in the life of the person being cloned; so the clone would be a different person from the original one. Thus we could not replace a loved one who has died or achieve immortality of our own in the body of a clone. If such technology is ever successful, however, we could produce an identical twin of a person.

Q *Why is the nucleus removed from the donor egg?*

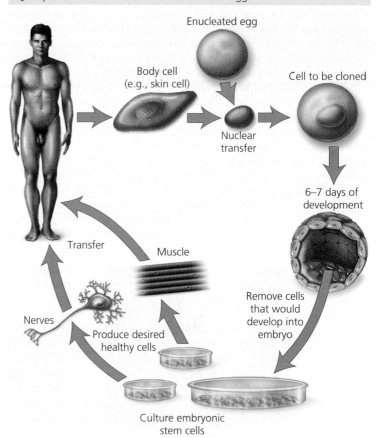

FIGURE 19a.6 Potential method for human therapeutic cloning using somatic cell nuclear transfer

A *The egg nucleus is removed so the only genetic information directing development is from the adult cell nucleus. The donor nucleus has genes for the desired trait.*

Potential Uses for Stem Cells

The use of stem cells is just beginning to blossom. Let's consider some of their potential uses.

Replacement for Damaged Cells

As of this writing, there are no established stem cell therapies in the United States—except for those that use cells extracted from bone marrow, circulating blood, or umbilical cord blood. There are, however, more than 2000 clinical trials in progress or looking for recruits. Certain other countries, China for example, are offering stem cell treatments. Although these treatments are unproven by U.S. scientific standards, some people are traveling abroad for treatment.

To date, most of the studies on stem cells as a source of replacement cells or as factories to produce proteins or hormones that the body is not making have been done on animals. Insulin-producing stem cells have eliminated symptoms of type 1 diabetes in mice. In rats, bone marrow stem cells move toward heart muscle with damage similar to that occurring in a heart attack. In the damaged heart muscle, stem cells promote heart muscle strength.

Growing New Organs

Adult stem cell therapy has had some success. In 2004, a German man had his jaw removed because of cancer. Doctors created a mesh mold in the shape of the jawbone that had been removed, and they implanted the mold into the muscle below the man's shoulder blade, along with some cow-derived bone mineral, a growth factor to stimulate bone growth, and blood extracted from the man's bone marrow, which contained stem cells (Figure **19a.7**). The mold was left in place on the man's shoulder until bone scans showed that new bone had formed around the mold. The new jaw then was removed, along with some muscle and blood vessels, and implanted in the correct location. Four weeks later, the man could chew solid food—a bratwurst sandwich! Two years later, doctors grew new urinary bladders for seven patients using the patients' own cells. In those cases, doctors extracted muscle and bladder cells from the patient and grew them in a petri dish. As the cells formed layers of tissue, the tissue was shaped into new bladders, which were then implanted into the patients. Within a few weeks, the bladders grew to normal size and performed the required functions.

Testing New Drugs

Before a new drug can go to clinical trials, it must be shown to be safe for animals and human cells cultured in petri dishes. The problem is that not all tissues will survive in tissue culture. For example, heart cells, brain cells, and liver cells do not. Stems cells may be a way to test new drugs for safety and effectiveness before testing them on humans.

Researchers are also using pluripotent stem cells to create cells that display the characteristics of cells with a particular disease. Cell cultures of these cells could then be used to study the nature of the disease or to develop drugs to treat the disease. Skin samples from Alzheimer's patients are being collected with an interest in converting them into pluripotent stem cells for such purposes.

(a)

(b)

(c)

FIGURE 19a.7 Adult stem cells from bone marrow were used to grow a new jaw to replace one that had been removed because of cancer. (a) A mold in the shape of the missing jaw was created out of mesh and seeded with bone marrow cells and bone growth factor. (b) The mold was placed in the muscle of the man's back until bone filled the mold. (c) The new jaw was then implanted to replace the missing jaw.

20

Genetics and Human Inheritance

Would you become a risk taker if you knew you had a genetic disease that causes death in middle age?

S teve's brother, Dan, is a risk taker. Two years ago, he hiked through the Andes in Chile. Four years ago, he learned to scuba dive. Recently, he took up sky diving.

Dan hasn't always been so daring. Six years ago, he was finishing law school and looking forward to a career in politics. Then their father was diagnosed with Huntington's disease, a disorder caused by the degeneration of brain cells. This devastating disease usually appears in middle age with symptoms of clumsiness and forgetfulness. Now

Dad is still able to work, but his handwriting has become illegible, and he cannot sit for long periods without twitching.

Huntington's disease is genetic. Dan and Steve were each told they had a 50% chance of carrying the gene. If they do carry it, they will surely develop the disease in middle age, because the gene for Huntington's disease is dominant. After Dad's diagnosis, Dan decided to have his genes analyzed to see if he carried the gene that affected their father. Unfortunately, he did. Dan then started to live the life of a risk

taker—what did he have to lose, he thought? Steve, on the other hand, elected not to have his genes tested but to continue to live the satisfying life he and his wife Jessica had always enjoyed. But now Jessica was pregnant. She wanted to have the child, but not if it would be born with the gene for Huntington's disease. She insisted that the baby's genes be tested. Fortunately for Steve, Jessica, and the baby, the test was negative for the Huntington's disease gene.

The genes we receive at the moment of conception influence all

the biochemical reactions taking place inside our cells, our susceptibility to disease, our behavior patterns, and even our life span. Our environment is also an important influence, but our genes provide the basic blueprint for our possibilities and limitations. In this chapter, you will learn more about the genetic foundation that has been so important in shaping who you are. You will learn how heritable traits are passed to new generations and how to predict the distribution of traits from one generation to the next.

Principles of Inheritance

The understanding of meiosis gained in Chapter 19 helps us answer important questions about inheritance: Why is your brother the only sibling with Mom's freckles and widow's peak (a hairline that comes to a point on the forehead)? How can you have blue eyes when both your parents are brown eyed? Will you be bald at 40, like Dad? Let's delve deeper into how chromosomes, meiosis, and heredity are related.

Before beginning, you may want to review some of the terms that were introduced in Chapter 19 and are summarized in Figure **20.1**. Recall that somatic (body) cells have a pair of every chromosome. Thus, human cells have 23 pairs of chromosomes. One member of each pair was inherited from the female parent and the other from the male parent. The chromosomes that carry genes for the same traits are a *homologous pair of chromosomes,* or homologues. Chromosomes are made of DNA and protein. Certain segments of the DNA of each chromosome function as genes. A **gene** directs the synthesis of a specific protein that can play either a structural or a functional role in the cell.[1] (In some cases, the gene directs the synthesis of a polypeptide that forms part of a protein.) In this way, the gene-determined protein can influence whether a certain **trait**, or characteristic, will develop. For instance, the formation of your brother's widow's peak was directed by a protein coded for by a gene that he inherited from Mom. Genes for the same trait are found at the same specific location on homologous chromosomes.

Different forms of a gene are called **alleles.** Alleles produce different versions of the trait they determine. For example, there is a gene that determines whether freckles will form. One allele of this

gene causes freckles to form; the other does not. Somatic cells carry two alleles for each gene, one allele on each homologous chromosome. If a person has at least one allele for freckles, melanin will be deposited, and freckles will form. If neither homologue bears the freckle allele that leads to melanin deposition, for example, the person will not have freckles.

Individuals with two copies of the same allele of a gene are said to be **homozygous** (*homo,* same; *zygo,* joined together) for

In a **homologous pair** of chromosomes, each member carries genes for the same traits. One member of each pair was inherited from the mother and the other from the father.

A **gene** is a segment of DNA located in a specific site on a specific chromosome that contains information for producing a particular protein (polypeptide).

A pair of **alleles**. An allele is an alternative form of a gene located on a specific site of a specific chromosome. One allele is inherited from the mother, and the other from the father.

[1]This is a simplified definition of a gene. As we will see in Chapter 21, some genes contain regulatory regions of DNA within their boundaries. Also, some genes code for RNA molecules that are needed for the production of a protein but are not part of it.

FIGURE 20.1 Important terms in genetics

that trait. Those with different alleles of a given gene are said to be **heterozygous** (*hetero,* different; *zygo,* joined together). When the effects of a certain allele can be detected, regardless of whether an alternative allele is also present, the allele is described as a **dominant allele**. Dimples and freckles are human traits dictated by dominant alleles. An allele whose effects are masked in the heterozygous condition is described a **recessive allele**. Because of this masking, only homozygous recessive alleles are expressed. Conditions such as cystic fibrosis, in which excessive mucus production impairs lung and pancreatic function; and albinism, in which the pigment melanin is missing in the hair, skin, and eyes, result from recessive alleles. It is customary to designate a dominant allele with a capital letter and a recessive allele with a lowercase letter—*A* and *a,* for example.

We observe the dominant form of the trait whether the individual is homozygous dominant (*AA*) or heterozygous (*Aa*) for that trait. As a consequence, we cannot always tell exactly which alleles are present. It is important to remember that an individual's genetic makeup is not always revealed by the individual's appearance. A **genotype** is the precise set of alleles a person possesses for a given trait or traits. It tells us whether the individual is homozygous or heterozygous for a given gene. A **phenotype**, on the other hand, is the *observable* physical trait or traits of an individual. Figure **20.2** shows the genotype or genotypes for several phenotypes in humans (for example, the freckled phenotype has two genotypes: *FF* and *Ff*). Table **20.1** summarizes terms commonly used in genetics as they apply to the inheritance of freckles, which is determined by a dominant allele.

Gamete Formation

Recall from Chapter 19 that the members of each homologous pair of chromosomes segregate during meiosis I, with each homologue going to a different daughter cell. Thus, an egg or a sperm has only one member of each homologous pair. Consider what this fact means for inheritance. Because the alleles for each gene segregate during gamete formation, half the gametes bear one allele, and half bear the other. This principle, known as the *law of segregation,* explains how, for every gene in our chromosomes, one of the alleles comes from our mother and one comes from our father.

Furthermore, each pair of homologous chromosomes lines up at the midline of the cell during meiosis I independently of the other pairs. The orientation of the paternal and maternal homologues relative to the poles of the cell (that is, with regard to which

Freckles: *FF* or *Ff*   No freckles: *ff*

Widow's peak: *WW* or *Ww*   Straight hairline: *ww*

Unattached earlobes: *EE* or *Ee*   Attached earlobes: *ee*

tt   *Tt*   *TT* or *Tt*
Tongue rolling

FIGURE 20.2 Genotypes for selected human phenotypes

TABLE 20.1 Review of Common Terms in Genetics

Genotypes: The Alleles That Are Present	Description	Phenotype: The Observable Trait (Examples)
FF	Homozygous dominant: • Two dominant alleles present. • Dominant phenotype expressed.	Freckles
Ff	Heterozygous: • Different alleles present. • Dominant phenotype expressed.	Freckles
ff	Homozygous recessive: • Two recessive alleles present. • Recessive phenotype expressed.	No freckles

homologue is closer to which pole) is entirely random. What this fact means for inheritance is that pairs of alleles for genes on different chromosomes segregate into gametes independently. This principle, known as the *law of independent assortment,* explains why the mixture of alleles that came from the mother and alleles that came from the father is different in every gamete.

Mendelian Genetics

During the nineteenth century, Gregor Mendel, a monk who grew up in a region of what was then Austria and is now part of the Czech Republic, worked out much of what we know today about the laws of heredity by performing specific crosses of pea plants. Although Mendel knew nothing about chromosomes, his ideas about the inheritance of traits are consistent with what we now know about the movement of chromosomes during meiosis. Mendel's ideas are used today to predict the outcome of hereditary crosses.

One-trait crosses

We begin our discussion by using Mendel's ideas to consider the inheritance of a single trait, using the example of freckles, a characteristic determined by a dominant allele. Suppose a freckled female who is homozygous dominant (*FF*) had a child with a homozygous recessive male with no freckles (*ff;* Figure **20.3**). The following sequence of steps allows us to predict the degree of likelihood that their child will have freckles.

1. **Identify the possible gametes that each parent can produce.** We know that alleles segregate during meiosis, but in this example, both parents are homozygous. Therefore, each can produce only one type of gamete (as far as freckles are concerned). The female produces gametes (eggs) with the dominant allele (*F*), and the male produces gametes (sperm) with the recessive allele (*f*).

2. **Use a Punnett square to determine the probable outcome of the genetic cross.** In a *Punnett square,* columns are set up and labeled to represent each of the possible gametes of one parent, let's say the father (Figure **20.4**). Remember, the alleles of each gene segregate during meiosis. In this case, then,

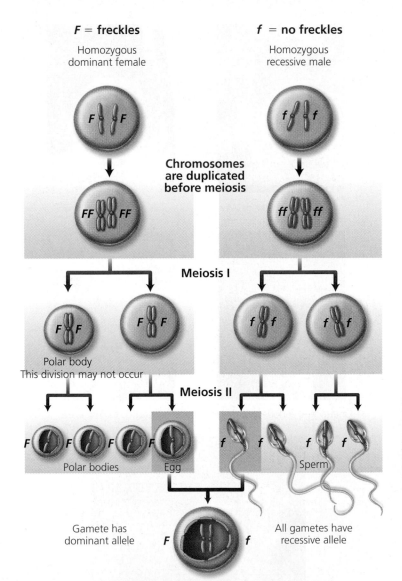

FIGURE 20.3 Gamete formation by a female who is homozygous dominant for freckles (*FF*), a male who is homozygous recessive for no freckles (*ff*), and the heterozygous (*Ff*) individual resulting from the union of these gametes.

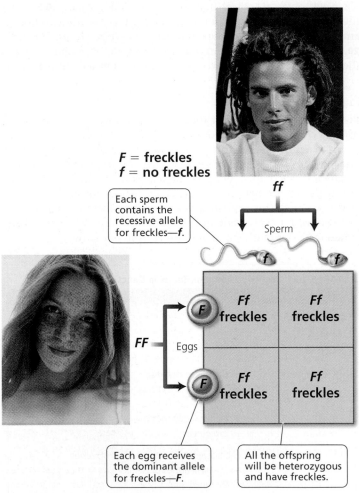

FIGURE 20.4 This Punnett square illustrates the probable offspring from a cross between a homozygous dominant female with freckles (*FF*) and a homozygous recessive male without freckles (*ff*). The columns are labeled with the possible gametes the male could produce (one gamete per column). The rows are labeled with the possible gametes the female could produce (one gamete per row). Combining the labels on the corresponding rows and columns yields the genotype of possible offspring.

there would be two columns to represent the gametes of the male without freckles, each labeled with a recessive allele, *f*. In a similar manner, rows are established across the columns and labeled to represent all the possible gametes formed by the other parent, in this case, the mother with freckles. There would be two rows in this Punnett square, each labeled *F*. Each square in the resulting table is then filled in by combining the labels of the corresponding rows and columns. The squares represent the possible offspring of these parents. In this first case, all the children would have freckles and would be heterozygous for the trait (*Ff*).

Now let's consider why it is possible for parents who are both heterozygous for the freckle trait (*Ff*) to have a child without freckles. The *F* and *f* alleles segregate during meiosis. So half the gametes bear the *F* allele, and half bear the *f* allele (Figure **20.5a**). This time the two rows in the Punnett square are labeled with *F* and *f*, and so are the two columns (Figure 20.5b). After filling the boxes according to the labels on rows and columns, we see that the probable genotypes of the children would be homozygous dominant (*FF*), heterozygous (*Ff*), and homozygous recessive (*ff*), in a genotypic ratio of 1 *FF* : 2 *Ff* : 1 *ff*. The ratio of phenotypes of children with freckles (*FF* and *Ff*) compared with children without freckles (*ff*) would be 3 : 1. This ratio means that each child born to this couple will have a 75% (3/4) chance of having freckles. But there is a 1 in 4, or 25%, chance that each child will not have freckles. A cross in which both parents are heterozygous for one trait of interest is called a *monohybrid cross*.

Two-trait crosses

We use the same steps to predict the probable outcome for inheritance of two traits of interest that we used for inheritance of a single trait—as long as the genes for the two traits are on different chromosomes.

1. **Identify the possible gametes that each parent can produce.** Like freckles, a widow's peak is controlled by a dominant allele. What would the children look like if the parents were a woman who is homozygous for both freckles and a widow's peak (*FFWW*) and a man with no freckles and a straight hairline (*ffww*)? To answer that question, we begin by determining the possible gametes each mate can produce. Since they are homozygous for both traits, the woman can produce only gametes bearing dominant alleles (*FW*), and the man can produce only gametes with the recessive alleles (*fw*).

2. **Use a Punnett square to determine the probable outcome of the genetic cross.** In this case, each parent can produce only one type of gamete, so all the children will have the same genotype and the same phenotype. All the children will be heterozygous for each trait (*FfWw*) and will have both freckles and a widow's peak.

Suppose one of these children mates with someone who is also heterozygous for freckles and a widow's peak. This would be a *dihybrid cross*, a mating of individuals who are both heterozygous

(a)

F = freckles
f = no freckles

(b)

There is a 3 in 4 chance (75%) that the child will have freckles (*FF* or *Ff*).

There is a 1 in 4 chance (25%) that the child will not have freckles (*ff*).

FIGURE 20.5 (a) Gamete formation by a person who is heterozygous for the freckle trait (*Ff*). (b) A Punnett square showing the probable outcome of a mating between two people who are heterozygous for the freckle trait (*Ff*).

for two traits of interest. Would it be possible for this couple to have a child who had neither freckles nor a widow's peak? It *would* be possible, but the chances are only 1 in 16. Let's see why.

First, determine the possible gametes that each parent could produce (Figure **20.6**). Keep in mind that alleles for a gene segregate and that genes for different traits that are located on different chromosomes will segregate independently of one another. There are, therefore, four possible allele combinations in gametes produced by a person who is heterozygous for these two different genes. The gametes are *FW*, *Fw*, *fW*, and *fw*. In this instance, we need to construct a Punnett square with *four* columns, because this time there are four possible male gametes, and four rows labeled with the possible female gametes. Each type of gamete has an equal chance of joining with any other type at fertilization. The squares are filled by combining the labels of the corresponding columns and rows, giving us the possible genotypes of the offspring. Notice in Figure **20.7** that the relative numbers of phenotypes possible for the next generation are 9 freckled, widow's peak; 3 freckled, straight hairline; 3 no freckles, widow's peak; 1 no freckles, straight hairline. We see, then, that the expected phenotypic ratio resulting from a dihybrid cross is always 9 : 3 : 3 : 1.

Pedigrees

It is sometimes important to find out the genotype of a human with a dominant phenotype for a particular trait. Since there are two possible genotypes for a dominant trait (homozygous dominant

and heterozygous dominant), we cannot know genotype based on phenotype alone. However, we can often deduce the unknown genotype by looking at the expression of the trait in the person's ancestors or descendants. A chart showing the genetic connections between individuals in a family is called a **pedigree.** Family or medical records are used to fill in the pattern of expression of the trait in question for as many family members as possible. Pedigrees are useful not just in determining an unknown genotype but also in predicting the chances that one's offspring will display the trait. Pedigrees for the inheritance of genetic disorders caused by a dominant allele on one of the non-sex chromosomes (called autosomal dominant) and of genetic disorders that are caused by recessive alleles on a pair of non-sex chromosomes (called autosomal recessive) are shown in Figure **20.8**. We will discuss genes on sex chromosomes later in the chapter.

Marfan syndrome is an autosomal dominant disorder (like the neurological disorder Huntington's disease, which was discussed in the chapter's opening scenario). Marfan syndrome is a connective tissue disorder in which a dominant allele for the production of an elastic connective tissue protein, fibrillin, produces a nonfunctional protein. Because connective tissue is widespread in the body, so are the symptoms of Marfan syndrome. Connective tissue is an important component in blood vessel walls, heart valves, tendons, ligaments, and cartilage. A serious problem caused by Marfan

Q *If a parent were homozygous recessive for freckles and heterozygous for widow's peak, how many types of gametes could form?*

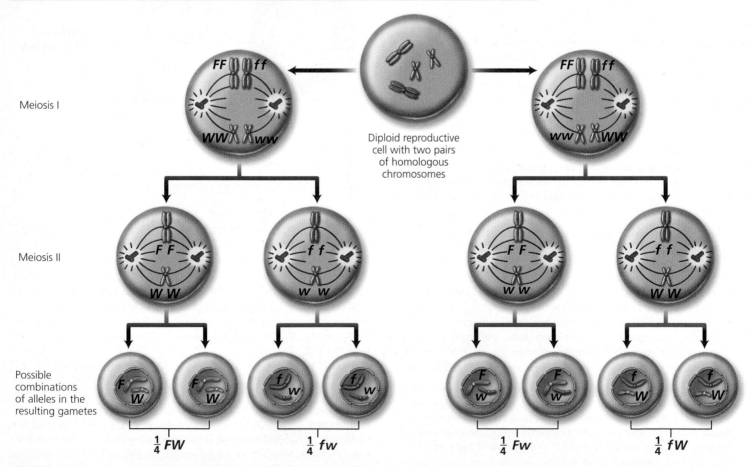

Meiosis I

Diploid reproductive cell with two pairs of homologous chromosomes

Meiosis II

Possible combinations of alleles in the resulting gametes

$\frac{1}{4}$ *FW* $\frac{1}{4}$ *fw* $\frac{1}{4}$ *Fw* $\frac{1}{4}$ *fW*

FIGURE 20.6 A person who is heterozygous for two genes that are located on different chromosomes can produce four different types of gametes.

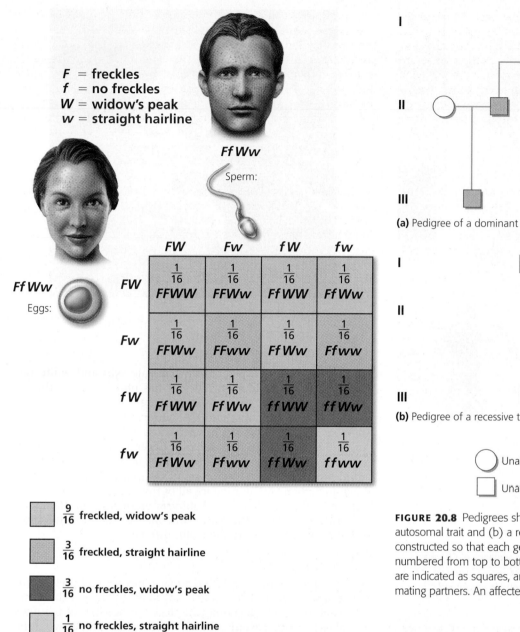

F = freckles
f = no freckles
W = widow's peak
w = straight hairline

FfWw

Sperm:

FfWw

Eggs:

	FW	Fw	fW	fw
FW	$\frac{1}{16}$ FFWW	$\frac{1}{16}$ FFWw	$\frac{1}{16}$ FfWW	$\frac{1}{16}$ FfWw
Fw	$\frac{1}{16}$ FFWw	$\frac{1}{16}$ FFww	$\frac{1}{16}$ FfWw	$\frac{1}{16}$ Ffww
fW	$\frac{1}{16}$ FfWW	$\frac{1}{16}$ FfWw	$\frac{1}{16}$ ffWW	$\frac{1}{16}$ ffWw
fw	$\frac{1}{16}$ FfWw	$\frac{1}{16}$ Ffww	$\frac{1}{16}$ ffWw	$\frac{1}{16}$ ffww

$\frac{9}{16}$ freckled, widow's peak

$\frac{3}{16}$ freckled, straight hairline

$\frac{3}{16}$ no freckles, widow's peak

$\frac{1}{16}$ no freckles, straight hairline

FIGURE 20.7 A dihybrid cross is a mating of individuals heterozygous for two traits, each governed by a gene on a different chromosome. Analyzed on a Punnett square, this cross illustrates the law of independent assortment—that is, each allele pair is inherited independently of others found on different chromosomes. The phenotypes of the offspring of a dihybrid cross would be expected to occur in a 9 : 3 : 3 : 1 ratio.

syndrome is weak walls of large blood vessels, because they can tear or burst.

If the pedigree in Figure 20.8a were depicting the inheritance of Marfan syndrome, what is the genotype of the males in the third generation who have Marfan syndrome? How do you know?

Genetic disorders are often caused by recessive alleles, so knowing whether the parents carry the allele will help predict both the possibility and the likelihood of that child being homozygous for

(a) Pedigree of a dominant trait

(b) Pedigree of a recessive trait

○ Unaffected female   ● Affected female

□ Unaffected male   ■ Affected male

FIGURE 20.8 Pedigrees showing the inheritance of (a) a dominant autosomal trait and (b) a recessive autosomal trait. A pedigree is constructed so that each generation occupies a different horizontal line, numbered from top to bottom, with the most ancestral at the top. Males are indicated as squares, and females as circles. A horizontal line connects mating partners. An affected individual is indicated with a colored symbol.

the trait and therefore born with the condition (Figure 20.8b). For example, cystic fibrosis (CF), a disorder in which abnormally thick mucus is produced, is controlled by a recessive allele. Approximately 1 in every 2000 infants in the United States is born with CF. It is a leading cause of childhood death; for children with the disorder, average length of life is 24 years. The three primary signs of CF are abnormally salty sweat, digestive problems, and respiratory problems. Many children with CF suffer from malnutrition because mucus clogs the pancreatic ducts, preventing pancreatic digestive enzymes from reaching the small intestine, where they would otherwise function in digestion. Thick mucus also plugs the respiratory passageways, making breathing difficult and increasing susceptibility to lung infections such as pneumonia (Figure **20.9**).

Because CF is inherited as a recessive allele, children with CF are usually born to normal, healthy parents who had no idea they carried the trait. A **carrier** is someone who displays the dominant phenotype but is heterozygous for a trait and can, therefore, pass the recessive allele to descendants. Approximately 1 in 22 Caucasians in the United States is a carrier for CF. (CF is less common among Asian Americans and rare among African Americans.)

FIGURE 20.9 Cystic fibrosis, controlled by a recessive gene, is a condition in which abnormally thick mucus is produced, causing serious digestive and respiratory problems. This child with cystic fibrosis is using a therapeutic toy to enhance airflow. When she exhales with enough force, the ribbons wave.

stop and think

If the pedigree in Figure 20.8b were depicting the inheritance of CF, what is the genotype of the male in the third generation who has CF? How do you know? Which individuals are carriers for the trait? How do you know?

The U.S. Surgeon General urges all Americans to create a pedigree of their family health history. The Surgeon General's Health Initiative website (www.hhs.gov/familyhistory) provides a computerized tool for creating a pedigree, but it can also be done without a computer. To create your own pedigree, collect information from your relatives about their own and their ancestors' health at your next family gathering. On the pedigree, indicate which individuals have experienced high blood pressure, a heart attack or stroke, cancer, diabetes, or any other disease common in your family. This health history may help predict your risk of developing certain diseases and encourage you to take preventive action before problems develop.

Dominant and Recessive Alleles

You may wonder what makes an allele dominant or recessive. In many cases, the dominant allele produces a normal, functional protein; but the recessive allele produces the protein in an altered form that does not function properly, or it does not produce any protein. Consider the inheritance of the most common form of albinism, the inability to produce the brown pigment melanin that normally gives color to the eyes, hair, and skin. Due to the lack of

FIGURE 20.10 A person with albinism lacks the brown pigment melanin in the skin, hair, and irises of the eyes.

melanin, a person with albinism has pale skin and white hair (Figure **20.10**). A child with the trait has pink eyes, but the eye color darkens to blue in an adult. Because there is no melanin in the skin to protect against sunlight's ultraviolet rays, a person with albinism is quite vulnerable to sunburn and skin cancer.

The ability to produce melanin depends on the enzyme tyrosinase. The dominant allele that results in normal skin pigmentation produces a functional form of tyrosinase. A single copy of the dominant allele can produce all of this enzyme that is needed. The recessive allele that causes albinism produces a nonfunctional form of tyrosinase. If there are two copies of the recessive allele, melanin cannot be formed, and albinism results.

Codominant Alleles

The examples we have described so far represent **complete dominance**, a situation in which a heterozygous individual exhibits the trait associated with the dominant allele but not that of the recessive allele. In other words, the dominant allele produces a functional protein, and the protein's effects are apparent; but the recessive allele produces a less functional protein or none at all, and its effects are not apparent. However, complete dominance is not the only possibility for a heterozygous genotype. In some cases, both alleles produce functional proteins. In this situation, described as **codominance**, the effects of *both* alleles are separately apparent in the heterozygous phenotype.

The inheritance of type AB blood is an example of codominance. Two alleles, I^A and I^B, result in the production of two different polysaccharides on the surface of red blood cells. In persons with type AB blood, both alleles are expressed, and their red blood cells have both A and B polysaccharides on their surface. (We return to the example of blood groups shortly.)

Incomplete Dominance

In **incomplete dominance**, the expression of a trait in a heterozygous individual is somewhere between the expression of the trait in a homozygous dominant individual and the expression of the trait in a homozygous recessive individual. The dominant allele produces a functional protein product. The recessive allele does not produce that product. As a result, a heterozygous person has only one "dose" of the protein product—half the amount in a homozygous dominant person.

Sickle-cell hemoglobin provides an example of incomplete dominance (Figure 20.11). Recall from Chapter 11 that hemoglobin is the pigment in red blood cells that carries oxygen. A red blood cell filled with normal hemoglobin (Hb^A) is a biconcave disk. The allele for sickling hemoglobin (Hb^S) produces an abnormal form of hemoglobin that is less efficient in binding oxygen. In the homozygous sickling condition (Hb^SHb^S), called sickle-cell anemia, the red blood cells contain only the abnormal form of hemoglobin. When the oxygen content of the blood drops below a certain level, as might occur during excessive exercise or respiratory difficulty, these red blood cells with abnormal hemoglobin become sickle-shaped and tend to clump together. The clumped cells can break open and clog capillaries, causing great pain. Vital organs may be damaged by lack of oxygen. People who are homozygous for sickle-cell anemia usually die at a young age.

The normal allele for the sickle-cell gene shows incomplete dominance, so people who are heterozygous Hb^AHb^S have the *sickle-cell trait.* They have only one "dose" of normal hemoglobin (Hb^A) instead of the normal two doses needed for healthy red blood cells. Thus, people with sickle-cell trait are generally healthy, but sickling and clumping of red cells may occur if there is a prolonged drop in the oxygen content of the blood, as might happen during travel at high elevations. (Sickle-cell anemia was discussed in more detail in Chapter 11.)

stop and think

Straight hair shows incomplete dominance over curly hair. A homozygous dominant person has straight hair; a heterozygous person has wavy hair; and a homozygous recessive person has curly hair. What is the probability that a curly-haired person and a wavy-haired person would have a child with wavy hair?

Hb^AHb^A normal red blood cell

Hb^AHb^S sickle-cell trait

Hb^SHb^S sickle-cell anemia

FIGURE 20.11 The inheritance of sickle-cell trait (Hb^AHb^S) is an example of incomplete dominance.

Pleiotropy

Besides providing an example of incomplete dominance, sickle-cell anemia is an example of **pleiotropy:** one gene leading to many effects. As you can see in Figure 20.12, the sickling of red blood cells caused by the abnormal hemoglobin has effects throughout the body. The sickled cells can break down, clog blood vessels, and accumulate in the spleen. These effects can affect the heart, brain, lungs, kidneys, and muscles and joints.

Multiple Alleles

Many genes have more than two alleles. When three or more forms of a given gene exist, they are referred to as **multiple alleles.** Keep in mind, however, that one individual has only two alleles for a given gene (one on each homologue), even if multiple alleles exist in the population.

The ABO blood types (discussed in Chapter 11) provide an example of multiple alleles. Blood type is determined by the presence of certain polysaccharides (sugars) on the surface of red blood cells. Type A blood has the A polysaccharide; type B has the B polysaccharide; type AB has both A and B polysaccharides; and type O has neither. The synthesis of each kind of polysaccharide is directed by a specific enzyme: one enzyme produces A; a different enzyme produces B. Each enzyme is specified by a different allele of the gene.

The gene controlling ABO blood types therefore has three alleles, I^A, I^B, and i. Alleles I^A and I^B specify the A and B polysaccharides, respectively. When both these alleles are present, both polysaccharides are produced. I^A and I^B are, therefore, codominant. Allele i, which produces no enzyme, is recessive to both I^A and I^B. The possible combinations of these alleles and the resulting blood types are shown in Table 20.2.

stop and think

A man who has blood type AB is named as fathering a child with blood type O. The mother has blood type B. Is it possible for the named man to be the father of this child? (*Hint:* What are the possible genotypes of the man, woman, and child? Given each possible genotype of this man and woman, what gametes could each produce? Use Punnett squares to determine whether any combination of these genotypes could produce a child with the same genotype as this child.)

Polygenic Inheritance

So far, we have discussed traits governed by single genes, although the genes may have multiple alleles. When a single gene controls a trait, the trait is usually either present or it is not, even though incomplete dominance or environmental factors may modify its expression. In the case of multiple alleles, there may be several distinct classes of phenotypes, as in A, B, AB, and O blood types.

TABLE 20.2 The Relationship between Genotype and ABO Blood Types

Genotype	Blood Type
I^AI^A, I^Ai	A
I^BI^B, I^Bi	B
I^AI^B	AB
ii	O

FIGURE 20.12 Sickle-cell anemia is an example of pleiotropy, a condition in which a single gene has many effects.

The expression of most traits is much more variable, however. Many traits, including height, skin color, and eye color, vary almost continuously from one extreme to another. Environment can play a role in creating such a smooth continuum. For instance, diet and disease influence adult height, and exposure to sunlight darkens skin color. But even when all environmental factors are equal, there is still considerable variation in the expression of certain traits. Such variation results from **polygenic inheritance**—that is, the involvement of two or more genes, often on different chromosomes, in producing a trait. The more genes involved, the smoother the gradations and the greater the extremes of trait expression.

Although human height is probably controlled by more than three genes, for our purposes we will imagine it is determined by only three, partly to simplify our discussion but also to show how much variation in expression is possible even with as few as three genes—A, B, and C—interacting to determine a trait.

Let's assume that the dominant alleles (A, B, C) of each gene add height, and the recessive alleles (a, b, c) do not. How tall would we expect the children to be if both parents were of medium height and heterozygous for all three genes? As you can see in Figure **20.13**, there would be seven genetic height classes, ranging from very short to very tall. The probability of the children having either extreme of stature is slim, 1/64. The most likely probability (a 20/64 chance) is that they will be of medium height, like their parents.

Skin color is also determined by several genes. The allele for the kind of albinism described above prevents melanin production, so if a person is homozygous recessive for this allele, no melanin can be deposited in the skin. In addition, there are probably at least four other genes involved in determining the amount of melanin deposited in the skin. Two alleles for each of four genes would create nine classes of skin color, ranging from pale to dark.

(a)

(b)

FIGURE 20.13 Human height varies along a continuum. (a) One reason is that height is determined by more than one gene (polygenic inheritance). This figure shows the distribution of alleles for tallness in children of two parents of medium height, assuming that three genes are involved in the determination of height. The top line of boxes shows the parental genotypes, and the second line of boxes indicates the possible genotypes of the offspring. Alleles for tallness are indicated with dark squares. (b) Students organized according to height.

Genes on the Same Chromosome

Scientists estimate that there are about 20,000 to 25,000 human genes distributed among the 23 pairs of chromosomes. Thus, each chromosome bears a great number of genes. Genes on the same chromosome tend to be inherited together because an entire chromosome moves into a gamete as a unit. Genes that tend to be inherited together are described as being *linked*. We see, then, that linked genes do not *usually* assort independently. *Usually* is emphasized here because there is a mechanism that can unlink genes on the same chromosome: crossing over (discussed in Chapter 19).

Sex-Linked Genes

Recall from Chapter 19 that one pair of chromosomes is called the sex chromosome. There are two kinds of sex chromosomes, X and Y. They are not truly homologous, because the Y chromosome is much smaller than the X chromosome, and they do not carry all of the same genes.[2] The Y chromosome carries very few genes, but it is important in determining gender. If a particular gene found only on the Y chromosome is present, an embryo will develop as a male. Without that gene (whether because there is no Y chromosome or because the gene is missing from the Y chromosome), an embryo will develop as a female. In contrast, most of the genes on an X chromosome have nothing to do with sex determination. For instance, genes for certain blood-clotting factors and for the pigments in cones (the photoreceptors responsible for color vision) are found on the X chromosome but not on the Y chromosome. Furthermore, the X chromosome has about as many genes as a typical autosome does, but the Y chromosome has relatively few. Thus, most genes on the X chromosome have no corresponding alleles on the Y chromosome and are known as **X-linked genes.**

Because most X-linked genes have no homologous allele on the Y chromosome, they have a different pattern of inheritance than do autosomes. A male is XY and therefore will express virtually all of the alleles on his single X chromosome, *even alleles that are recessive*. A female, on the other hand, is XX, so she does not always express recessive X alleles. As a result, the recessive phenotype of X-linked genes is much more common in males than in females (Figure **20.14**). Furthermore, a son cannot inherit an X-linked recessive allele from his father. To be male, a child must have inherited his father's Y chromosome, not his father's X chromosome. Consequently, a son can inherit an X-linked recessive allele only from his mother. A daughter, however, can inherit an X-linked recessive allele from either parent. She must be homozygous for the recessive allele to show the recessive phenotype. If she is heterozygous for the trait, she will have a normal phenotype but be a carrier for that trait. Among the disorders caused by X-linked recessive alleles are red-green color blindness, two forms of hemophilia, and Duchenne muscular dystrophy. Red-green color blindness, the inability to distinguish red and green, was discussed in Chapter 9. Hemophilia (discussed in Chapter 11) is a bleeding disorder caused by a lack of a blood-clotting factor: Hemophilia A is a lack of blood-clotting factor VIII, and hemophilia B is a lack of clotting factor IX. Duchenne muscular dystrophy is discussed in Chapter 6.

stop and think

Why is Duchenne muscular dystrophy inherited from one's mother but usually expressed only in sons? (*Hint:* Consider its mode of inheritance.)

[2]X and Y are considered to be a homologous pair because they each have a small region at one end that carries some of the same genes. During meiosis, the tiny homologous region on X and Y will pair in synapsis. As a result, they segregate into gametes in the same way that autosomes do.

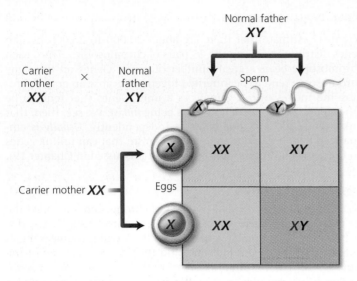

FIGURE 20.14 Genes that are X linked have a different pattern of inheritance than do genes on autosomes, as seen in this cross between a carrier mother and a father who is normal for the trait. The recessive allele is indicated in red. Notice that each son has a 50% chance of displaying the recessive phenotype. All daughters will appear normal, but each daughter has a 50% chance of being a carrier.

Autosomal Genes

The expression of certain autosomal genes, those that are not located on the sex chromosomes, is powerfully influenced by the presence of sex hormones, so their expression differs in males and females. These traits are described as *sex-influenced* traits.

Male pattern baldness, premature hair loss on the top of the head but not on the sides, is an example of a sex-influenced trait. Male pattern baldness is much more common in men than in women because its expression depends on both the presence of the allele for baldness and the presence of testosterone, the male sex hormone. The allele for baldness, then, acts as a dominant allele in males because of their high level of testosterone and as a recessive allele in females because females have a much lower testosterone level. A male with the allele will develop pattern baldness whether he is homozygous or heterozygous for the trait. However, only women who are homozygous for the trait will develop pattern baldness. When a woman does develop pattern baldness, it usually appears later in life than it does in a man. The allele is expressed in women because the adrenal glands produce a small amount of testosterone. After menopause, when the supply of estrogen declines, adrenal testosterone may cause the expression of the baldness gene. However, in many women, balding may be merely thinning of hair.

stop and think

Male pattern baldness was passed from father to son through at least four generations of the Adams family. John Adams (1735–1826), the second U.S. president, passed it to his son, John Quincy Adams (1767–1848), the sixth U.S. president. He, in turn, passed the gene to his son, Charles Frances Adams (1807–1886), a diplomat, who passed it to his son, Henry Adams (1838–1918), a historian. Why does father-to-son transmission of the trait rule out X-linked inheritance?

Breaks in Chromosomes

Chromosomes can break, which may lead to other alterations in structure. Breakage can be caused by certain chemicals, radiation, or viruses. Breakage also occurs as an essential part of crossing over. Although it does not happen often, chromosomes can be misaligned when crossing over occurs. Then, when the pieces reattach, one chromatid will have lost a segment, and the other will have gained a segment.

The loss of a piece of chromosome is called a **deletion**. The most common type of deletion occurs when the tip of a chromosome breaks off and then, during cell division, does not move into the same daughter cell as the rest of the chromosome. Deletion of more than a few genes on an autosome is usually lethal, and the loss of even small regions causes disorders.

In humans, the most common deletion, the loss of a small region near the tip of chromosome 5, causes cri-du-chat syndrome (meaning "cry of the cat"). An infant with this syndrome has a high-pitched cry that sounds like a kitten meowing. The unusual sound of the cry is caused by an improperly developed larynx (voice box). Infants with this syndrome have a round face; wide-set, downward-sloping eyes with a fold of skin at the corner of each eye; and misshapen ears (Figure **20.15**). Although the condition is not usually fatal, it does cause severe mental retardation.

The addition of a piece of chromosome is called a **duplication**. The effects of a duplication depend on its size and position. In general, however, a small duplication is less harmful than a deletion of comparable size. A small region of chromosome 9 is sometimes duplicated, resulting in cells containing three copies of this segment. The result is mental retardation, accompanied by facial characteristics that may include a bulbous nose; wide-set, squinting eyes; and a lopsided grin.

Genetic disorders also occur when certain sequences of DNA are duplicated multiple times. The Fragile X syndrome provides an example. The syndrome is so named because an abnormally long sequence of repeats caused by duplication makes the X chromosome fragile and easily broken. Besides making the chromosome fragile, the repeated DNA can shut down the activity of the entire chromosome. Fragile X syndrome is the most common form of inherited mental retardation, affecting roughly 1 in 1250 males and 1 in 2500 females. It is not known, however, exactly how Fragile X syndrome

A piece of chromosome 5 has been deleted.

FIGURE 20.15 Occurring in 1 out of every 50,000 live births, cri-du-chat syndrome is the most common genetic deletion found in humans. It is caused by the loss of a small region near the tip of chromosome 5.

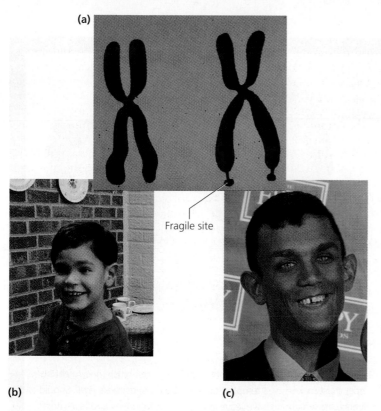

FIGURE 20.16 Fragile X syndrome. (a) Duplication of a region on the X chromosome makes the chromosome fragile and easily broken. (b) A child with Fragile X syndrome appears normal. (c) Characteristics of an adult with Fragile X syndrome include a long face and large ears. In addition, Fragile X syndrome causes mental retardation.

causes the retardation. Other characteristics may include attention deficit, hyperactivity, autistic symptoms, large ears, long face, and flat feet (Figure **20.16**).

what would you do?

The degree of mental retardation accompanying Fragile X syndrome is variable. Nearly all males who inherit a Fragile X chromosome exhibit retardation. About a quarter of the girls with Fragile X syndrome will develop mental retardation, although others will only have learning problems. Some cities screen children with mental retardation and children with learning difficulties for Fragile X chromosomes. People who endorse this practice argue that the children with Fragile X syndrome are then benefited because specialists such as speech therapists, counselors, and physicians can be called on to help. Others oppose the screening, arguing that there is no special treatment for children with Fragile X syndrome other than that available to all children with learning problems. After diagnosis, insurance companies may discriminate against the children and drop their health coverage. In your opinion, do the benefits of screening for Fragile X syndrome outweigh the disadvantages?

Detecting Genetic Disorders

More than 4000 disorders are known to have their roots in our genes. Tests are now available to look for predispositions to many of these genetic disorders. Some tests can even confirm the presence of a suspected disease-related allele in a particular person. Knowledge about the presence or absence of a faulty gene can be very helpful to couples who are planning a family. Normal, healthy parents can carry recessive alleles for disorders such as CF and Tay-Sachs disease (a disorder of lipid metabolism that causes death, usually between the ages of 1 and 5; discussed in Chapter 3), which they may pass on to their children. Testing is available for both of these recessive alleles. You can read more about the pros and cons of genetic testing in the Ethical Issue essay, *Gene Testing*.

When specific tests are unavailable, pedigree analysis can help prospective parents determine whether they *might* be carriers of recessive alleles. It cannot answer the question with certainty, but it does allow people to weigh the risks of passing a lethal allele to their children versus the possibility of having a child who is not affected.

Prenatal Genetic Testing

Prenatal testing of a fetus is usually recommended when a defective gene runs in the family or when the mother is older than 35 (because age increases the risk of problems due to failure of the homologous chromosomes to separate; see Chapter 19). There are two available procedures for diagnosing genetic problems in the fetus: amniocentesis and chorionic villi sampling (Figure **20.17**). Although it is possible to look for more than 100 disorders with these procedures, tests are run only for those disorders that are common as well as any that are of particular concern in that pregnancy. Reassuring results from either form of prenatal testing cannot guarantee a healthy baby, even though these tests are highly accurate in detecting genetic disorders.

In **amniocentesis**, a needle is inserted through the lower abdomen into the uterus, and a small amount of amniotic fluid—10 to 20 ml (about 2 to 4 tsp)—is withdrawn. (Ultrasound is performed first, to find the safest spot for insertion, away from the fetus, umbilical cord, and placenta.) Floating in the amniotic fluid are living cells that were sloughed off the fetus. These cells are grown in the laboratory for a week or two and then are examined for abnormalities in the number of chromosomes and for the presence of certain alleles that are likely to cause specific diseases. Biochemical tests are also done on the fluid to look for certain chemicals that indicate problems. For example, a high level of alpha-fetoprotein, a substance produced by the fetus, suggests a problem with the development of the central nervous system (a neural tube defect).

Amniocentesis is usually done between 15 and 20 weeks after the woman's last menstrual period, when there is enough amniotic fluid—about 250 ml (about 1 cup)—to minimize the risk of injuring the fetus. (A few medical centers are now able to perform amniocentesis at 12 weeks of pregnancy.) Amniocentesis is generally safe for both the mother and the fetus, but there is a small risk of triggering a miscarriage or of the needle injuring the mother and causing infection or bleeding.

Chorionic villi sampling (CVS) removes and analyzes a small amount of tissue containing chorionic villi, the small, fingerlike projections of the part of the placenta called the chorion (see Chapter 18). Cells of the chorion have the same genetic material as those of the fetus. With the help of ultrasound, a small tube is inserted through the vagina and cervix to where the villi are located. Gentle suction is then used to remove a small tissue sample, which can be analyzed for genetic abnormalities.

There are pros and cons to CVS. Advantages are that it can be performed several weeks earlier in the pregnancy than amniocentesis can, and the results are available within a few days. More than 95% of the high-risk women who opt for prenatal tests receive good news, and an early diagnosis saves weeks of worry over the health of the fetus. Also, if there is a genetic problem in the fetus

Gene Testing

Genetic screening is the practice of testing people who have no symptoms, to determine whether they carry genes that will influence their chances of developing certain genetic diseases. Genetic screening technologies are advancing rapidly, and their use is gaining popularity. However, genetic screening raises many ethical questions.

Among the advantages of genetic testing is that it enables people who discover they are at risk for a treatable or preventable condition to take steps to reduce their risk. By informing people that they carry a recessive allele they were unaware of or a dominant allele that is not expressed until late in life, it can also help reduce the incidence of serious genetic disorders in future generations. Consider Tay-Sachs disease, an autosomal recessive disorder that causes the death of children, usually by the age of 5. Tay-Sachs disease is especially prevalent in descendants of Jewish people from eastern Europe. As a result of voluntary screening programs, the number of children born with Tay-Sachs disease has decreased tenfold in many communities.

Genetic testing also has a dark side. The psychological consequences of test results can be devastating. Many genetic disorders cannot be prevented or treated. How does a person who may have one of these disorders prepare for the consequences of knowing *now* what will cause his or her death? Huntington's disease is caused by a dominant allele that provides no hints of its existence until relatively late in life, usually past child-bearing years. About 60% of the people with Huntington's disease are diagnosed between the ages of 35 and 50. The gene causes degeneration of the brain, leading to muscle spasms, personality disorders, and death, usually within 10 to 15 years. Because Huntington's disease is caused by a dominant allele, a bearer has a 50% chance of passing it to his or her children. Thus, a person whose parent died of Huntington's disease might well be tested

and receive the good news that the test did not detect the allele. But it is equally likely that the allele *will* show up in the test. Many persons at risk for Huntington's disease prefer to live without knowing their possible fate.

A predictive gene test confirming the risk of a serious disease can cause anxiety and depression in carriers and feelings of guilt in siblings who do not carry the allele. Yet many of these tests deal only in probabilities, not in certainties. Thus the carrier's worry will often prove unnecessary. A mutation in the *BRCA1* gene on chromosome 17, for example, has been found to increase a woman's risk of developing breast cancer and ovarian cancer. Carriers have an 85% chance of developing breast cancer by age 65. A woman who learns she is a carrier must make medical decisions that could influence the length of her life. One option would be to have frequent mammograms in the hope of discovering breast cancer, if it should develop, early enough for treatment. Of course, there is a chance that cancer would not be detected before it spread, making effective treatment difficult. A second option would be to have a preventative mastectomy immediately, even though there is a 15% chance that a person with the gene will *not* develop breast cancer.

There is also concern that the results of gene tests will not remain private information, but instead be used by employers as well as life and health insurers. If you were an employer who had genetic information about prospective employees, would you choose to invest time and money in training a person who carried an allele that increased the risk of cancer, heart disease, Alzheimer's disease, or alcoholism? As an insurer, would you knowingly cover such a carrier?

The results of gene testing can have both positive and negative consequences for those being tested and for their families. Who, then, should decide whether screening should be done, for which genes, on whom, and in

Gene testing can reveal whether someone has a treatable or preventable genetic disorder.

which communities? At first blush, one might be tempted to say, "There oughta be a law!" Should we leave ethical issues to judges and legislators? Should moral matters be decided by society or clergy? Or should they be personal decisions? These are not easy questions to answer, or even to think about—yet if we do not take part in the debate, we will be allowing others to decide these crucial issues for us.

Questions to Consider

- If gene testing *is* done, should the person being tested be told the results no matter what? If the affected person is an infant, should the parents always be told the results, even if the condition is poorly understood? How do we balance helping such children with the possibility of stigmatizing them?
- We live in a world of limited resources. In addition to deciding who should be tested, we must decide who should pay the bill. Both testing and treatment are expensive. Should testing be done only when treatment or preventive measures are available? How much say should the agent that pays for the procedure have in who is tested and who receives medical treatment?

and the couple wishes to terminate the pregnancy, the procedure can be performed earlier in the pregnancy, when it is safer for the mother. When abortion is not chosen, early diagnosis allows more time to plan the safest time, location, and method of delivery. A

disadvantage of CVS is that it has a slightly greater risk of triggering miscarriage than does amniocentesis.

If detected early enough, certain birth defects can be prevented. Congenital adrenal hyperplasia (an overgrowth of the adrenal glands), for instance, will cause a female fetus to develop abnormal genitalia, unless she is treated with hormones from week 10 to week 16 of gestation. Early diagnosis of this disorder through CVS can tell a physician whether hormone treatment is needed.

Newborn Genetic Testing

A simple blood test is now used routinely to screen newborns for phenylketonuria (PKU), an inherited metabolic disorder. People with PKU produce a defective enzyme that prevents them from converting phenylalanine (an amino acid in food) to tyrosine. As a result, they have too much phenylalanine in their bodies and too little tyrosine, an imbalance that somehow causes brain damage. Although nothing can be done to correct the enzyme, diagnosis of the genetic disorder allows doctors and parents to prevent brain damage by keeping the infant on a strict diet that excludes most phenylalanine. Nearly all proteins contain phenylalanine, so it is often necessary to substitute a specially prepared mixture of amino acids for most protein-containing foods, such as meat. It is also necessary to avoid foods containing the artificial sweetener NutraSweet, which contains aspartame, consisting of the amino acids phenylalanine and aspartic acid. When aspartame is digested, phenylalanine is separated from aspartic acid and can reach dangerous levels.

Adult Genetic Testing

Many predictive genetic tests for adults are now available or being developed. These tests identify people who are at risk of getting a disease but do not yet have symptoms. They are simple tests that can usually be done with a small blood sample. When steps can be taken to prevent the disease, predictive gene tests can be lifesaving. For instance, colon cancer will develop in nearly everyone who has the alleles for familial adenomatous polyposis, a condition in which thousands of benign polyps grow in the intestine. If the disorder is diagnosed, a person can be routinely inspected for colon polyps. Any polyps found can be removed, and cancer can be prevented. Genetic counselors help people understand their risks of developing inherited disorders and the medical consequences of such disorders.

Other predictive gene tests look for alleles that might predispose a person to a disorder. A protein that transports cholesterol in the blood, called ApoE, comes in three forms, each specified by a different allele. Having two alleles for ApoE-2, one form of the protein, causes catastrophically high blood cholesterol levels, which can lead to heart attack and stroke. Knowing that a person has this genetic makeup, a physician could prescribe medication to lower blood cholesterol.

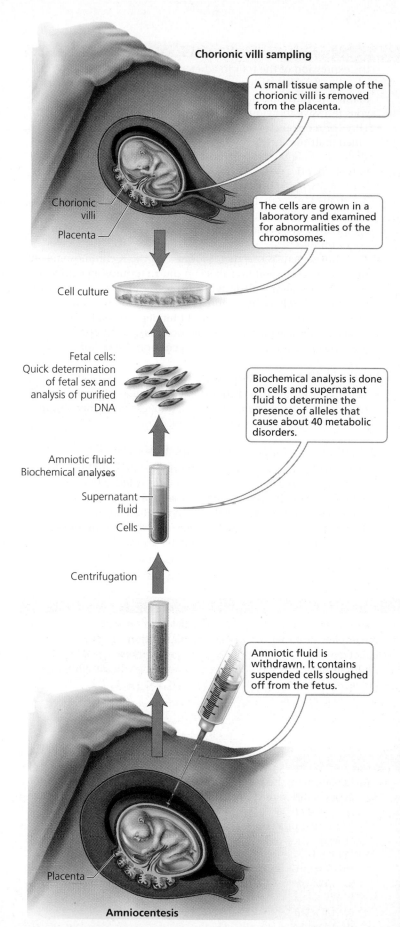

FIGURE 20.17 Amniocentesis and chorionic villi sampling (CVS) are procedures available for prenatal genetic testing.

what would you do?

Having two copies of another *ApoE* allele, *ApoE-4,* increases a person's risk of heart disease by 30% to 50%. It also nearly guarantees that the person will develop Alzheimer's disease by 80 years of age. Alzheimer's disease is an untreatable condition in which brain tissue degenerates (see Chapter 7), gradually robbing the person of memories, of the ability to function normally in society, and eventually of life itself. Suppose a gene test that is performed out of concern for a person's risk of heart disease reveals the presence of two copies of *ApoE-4*. In your opinion, is a physician with this knowledge morally obligated to tell the patient about the inevitability of Alzheimer's disease? If your genes were tested and found to have two copies of *ApoE-4*, would you want to be told? Why or why not?

highlighting the concepts

Principles of Inheritance (pp. 432–442)

- Different forms of a gene are called alleles. An individual who has two of the same alleles is said to be homozygous. An individual with two different alleles for a gene is said to be heterozygous. The allele that is expressed in the heterozygous condition is described as being dominant. The allele that is masked in the heterozygous condition is described as recessive.
- The genotype for one or more traits consists of the specific alleles present in an individual. The phenotype refers to the observable expression of the trait or traits.
- The alleles for each gene separate during gamete formation so that half the gametes receive one allele and the other half receive the other allele.
- Each pair of alleles located on one kind of chromosome separate into gametes independently of the alleles of a gene pair located on a different kind of chromosome.
- If a homozygous dominant individual (*AA*) mates with a homozygous recessive one (*aa*), the genotypes of all the offspring would be heterozygous (*Aa*) and the dominant phenotype. If heterozygous individuals (*Aa*) mate, the probable genotypes of children will be 1 in 4 (25%) homozygous dominant (*AA*) : 2 in 4 (50%) heterozygous dominant (*Aa*) : 1 in 4 (25%) homozygous recessive (*aa*). Their phenotypes will be 3 dominant : 1 recessive.
- Pedigrees, which are diagrams constructed to show the genetic relationships among individuals in an extended family, are often useful in determining the unknown genotypes of humans showing dominant phenotypes.
- In many cases, the dominant allele produces a functional protein, and the recessive allele produces a nonfunctional protein or no protein at all.
- In complete dominance, the dominant allele completely masks the recessive allele. When two alleles are codominant, both are separately apparent in the phenotype. In incomplete dominance, the expression of the trait in a heterozygous individual is somewhere in between the expression of the trait in a homozygous dominant individual and the expression of the trait in a homozygous recessive individual.
- Three or more alleles for a particular gene in a population are called multiple alleles. ABO blood types are determined by three alleles: I^A, I^B, and i. Blood type refers to the presence of certain polysaccharides on the surface of red blood cells.
- Many traits, including height, skin pigmentation, and eye color, are determined by more than one gene (polygenic inheritance). Such traits show a wide range of variation. Moreover, when many genes are involved in determining a trait, the variation in expression can be continuous.
- An X-linked gene is one that is located on the X chromosome and that has no corresponding allele on the Y chromosome. A recessive X-linked allele will always be expressed in a male, but it will be expressed only in the homozygous condition in a female.
- The expression of a sex-influenced trait depends on both the presence of the allele and the presence of sex hormones. Therefore, the expression of the allele depends on the person's sex.

Breaks in Chromosomes (pp. 442–443)

- The loss of a piece of a chromosome is called a deletion. The gain of a piece of chromosome is called a duplication. Either chromosome abnormality can cause a genetic disorder.

Detecting Genetic Disorders (pp. 443–445)

- Tests such as amniocentesis and chorionic villi sampling (CVS) are available to determine whether a fetus is likely to develop a genetic disease. In amniocentesis, a sample of amniotic fluid is taken. The fluid and the fetal cells in the fluid are analyzed for genetic problems. CVS samples cells from the chorion of the placenta and analyzes them for genetic disorders.

recognizing key terms

gene *p. 432*	recessive allele *p. 433*	codominance *p. 438*	deletion *p. 442*
trait *p. 432*	genotype *p. 433*	incomplete dominance *p. 438*	duplication *p. 442*
allele *p. 432*	phenotype *p. 433*	pleiotropy *p. 439*	amniocentesis *p. 443*
homozygous *p. 432*	pedigree *p. 436*	multiple alleles *p. 439*	chorionic villi sampling
heterozygous *p. 433*	carrier *p. 437*	polygenic inheritance *p. 440*	(CVS) *p. 443*
dominant allele *p. 433*	complete dominance *p. 438*	X-linked genes *p. 441*	

reviewing the concepts

1. What is the ratio of genotypes and phenotypes in the offspring resulting from a cross between a homozygous dominant individual and a homozygous recessive one? *pp. 434–435*
2. What is a pedigree? What can a family pedigree reveal about the inheritance of a trait? *pp. 436–438*
3. Explain what is meant by codominance by using an example. *p. 438*
4. Differentiate between multiple alleles and polygenic inheritance. *pp. 439–440*
5. What are linked genes? Why are they usually inherited together? What can cause such genes to become unlinked? *p. 441*

6. Explain why the pattern of inheritance for recessive X-linked genes is different from the pattern for recessive autosomal alleles. *p. 441*
7. What two procedures are used for prenatal genetic testing? How do they differ? *pp. 443–445*
8. Which of the following crosses could produce offspring with the recessive phenotype?
   a. *AA × aa*
   b. *Aa × Aa*
   c. *AA × Aa*
   d. *AA × AA*

9. All of the following crosses will have a 50% probability of producing 50% of the offspring with a heterozygous genotype *except*
   a. *AA × aa*
   b. *Aa × Aa*
   c. *AA × Aa*
   d. *Aa × aa*
10. A trait controlled by many genes is described as being _____.

11. The _____ of an individual is the physical expression of one or more genes of interest, and the _____ is the set of alleles the person possesses for the gene or genes of interest.
12. The genotype of a person with two copies of the same allele is _____, and the genotype of a person with two different alleles for a trait is _____.
13. Genes for different traits that are located on the same chromosome are described as being _____.

applying the concepts

1. Klaus has red-green color blindness, which is a sex-linked recessive trait. His wife, Helen, is homozygous for normal color vision. (Normal color vision is dominant to red-green color blindness.) What is the probability of their having a color-blind daughter? What is the probability of their having a color-blind son?
2. George and Sue have an infant, Sammy, who is lethargic, is vomiting, and has liver disease. Sammy is diagnosed with galactosemia, an autosomal recessive disorder in which the affected individuals are unable to metabolize the milk sugar galactose. Sammy is placed on a diet free of lactose and galactose and slowly recovers. George and Sue would like to have a second child. What are the chances that the second child will have galactosemia? (*Hint:* What are the genotypes of George and Sue? Use a Punnett square to determine the expected results of a cross with those genotypes.)
3. Explain why the offspring of first cousins are more likely to have harmful recessive traits than are offspring of unrelated individuals.
4. A woman with blood type AB names a man with blood type O as the father of her child. The child has blood type AB. Could the man be the father? Why or why not?
5. Straight hair shows incomplete dominance over curly hair. A homozygous dominant person has straight hair; a heterozygote has wavy hair; and a homozygous recessive person has curly hair. The first child of a curly-haired person and a wavy-haired person has wavy hair. What is the probability that a second child would have wavy hair?

becoming information literate

Use at least three reliable sources (books, journals, websites) to answer the following questions. Cite your sources, and explain why you choose them.

1. A "savior sibling" is a child born to save the life of a sibling. The older sibling's illness is usually a genetic blood disease, such as leukemia or Fanconi's anemia. It is hoped that the savior sibling will be a tissue match for the older sibling, so a bone marrow transplant from the younger sibling may save the older sibling's life. The embryos for a potential savior sibling are often created in a fertility clinic and tested for tissue compatibility before being implanted in the mother's uterus. If you were the parent of a child with leukemia and there were no family members who were tissue matches, would you consider conceiving a savior sibling? Identify the arguments on both sides of the issue, and defend your decision.
2. Identify at least two disorders that are caused by chromosome deletions and two that are caused by chromosome duplications. Which chromosomes are affected? What are the symptoms of the disorders?

Additional questions can be found online at The Human Biology Place, www.humanbiology.com.

21

DNA and Biotechnology

A DNA fingerprint is based on the sequence of bases in a person's DNA. Thus, a DNA fingerprint is unique to each person (except for those who happen to have identical siblings).

"Can DNA evidence really be used to solve crimes that occurred decades ago?" asked Sarah, a student in the college class that Detective Kim Young was speaking to.

"Yes, it's possible," Detective Young explained. "In the lab, DNA can be extracted from archived biological samples such as blood on clothing, saliva on a cigarette butt, or semen from a swab in a rape kit. Using methods that mimic natural DNA replication, we can multiply the sample and then characterize it. The tests focus on several sites in the DNA that are highly variable among individuals. If a suspect's DNA matches those sites, it is almost certain that he or she was the source of the original biological sample."

"But if a crime was committed years ago, who is considered a suspect?" asked Sean.

"Good question," Detective Young responded. "Each case is unique, but one approach is to compare DNA evidence to a database of DNA samples collected from convicted criminals. A number of "cold" cases have been solved because the guilty party was later convicted of a different crime and became a part of the database."

Another hand went up. "But I thought that DNA evidence was used to get people out of jail, not to put them in jail."

Detective Young explained, "Those are the cases we hear about. Many innocent people have been released from jail after serving years for crimes they didn't commit. Because it can help convict or to clear a person, DNA evidence can be the most powerful tool in the police's arsenal against crime."

In this chapter, we learn that DNA fingerprinting is possible because the DNA of each person (except for identical twins) is unique. We become familiar with the structure and function of DNA and discover how this molecule is able to serve as the basis of our genetic inheritance as well as the source for the diversity of life on Earth. We learn that the importance of DNA on a personal level is that it directs the synthesis of specific polypeptides (proteins) that play structural or functional roles in our bodies. We then consider the technology that our understanding of DNA has already made available and what possibilities such technology may hold for the future.

Form of DNA

DNA is sometimes referred to as the thread of life—and a very slender thread it is. When DNA is unwound, it measures a mere 50-trillionths of an inch in diameter. If all the DNA strands in a single cell were fastened together end to end, the thread would stretch more than 5 ft in length. DNA might also be considered the thread that ties all life together, because the DNA of organisms ranging from bacteria to humans is built from the same kinds of subunits. The order of these subunits encodes the information needed to make the proteins that build and maintain life.

Deoxyribonucleic acid, or **DNA**, is a double-stranded molecule resembling a ladder that is gently twisted to form a spiral called a double helix, as shown in Figure **21.1**. Each side of the ladder, including half of each rung, is made from a string of repeating subunits called nucleotides. You may recall from Chapter 2 that a nucleotide is composed of three subunits, including one sugar (deoxyribose, in DNA), one phosphate, and one nitrogenous base. DNA contains four types of nitrogenous bases: adenine (A), guanine (G), thymine (T), and cytosine (C). The sides of the ladder are composed of alternating sugars and phosphates; the rungs consist of paired nitrogenous bases. The bases attach to each other according to the rules of **complementary base pairing**: adenine pairs *only* with thymine (creating an A–T pair), and cytosine pairs *only* with guanine (creating a C–G pair). Each base pair is held together by weak hydrogen bonds. The pairing of complementary bases is specific due to the shapes of the bases and the number of hydrogen bonds that can form between them. You may also recall from Chapter 2 that a molecule formed by the joining of nucleotides is called a nucleic acid. Thus, DNA is a nucleic acid.

Because base pairing is so specific, the bases on one strand of DNA are *always* complementary to the bases on the other strand. Thus the order of bases on one strand determines the sequence of bases on the other strand. For instance, if the sequence of bases on one strand were CATATGAG, what would the complementary sequence be? Remember, cytosine (C) always pairs with guanine (G), and adenine (A) always pairs with thymine (T). As a result, the complementary sequence on the opposite strand would be GTATACTC.

The DNA within each human cell has an astounding 3 billion base pairs. Although the pairing of adenine with thymine and cytosine with guanine is specific and does not vary, the sequence of bases throughout the length of different DNA molecules can vary in myriad ways. As we will see, genetic information is encoded in the exact sequence of bases.

Replication of DNA

For DNA to be the basis of inheritance, its genetic instructions must be passed from one generation to the next. Moreover, for DNA to direct the activities of each cell, its instructions must be present in every cell. These requirements dictate that DNA be copied before both mitotic and meiotic cell division (see Chapter 19). It is important that the copies be exact. The key to the precision of the copying process is that the bases are complementary.

The copying process, or **DNA replication**, begins when an enzyme breaks the weak hydrogen bonds that hold together the paired bases that make up nucleotide strands of the double helix, thereby "unzipping" and unwinding the strands. As a result, the nitrogenous bases on the separated regions of each strand are temporarily exposed. Free nucleotide bases, which are always present within the nucleus, can then attach to complementary bases on the open DNA strands. Enzymes called *DNA polymerases* link the sugars and phosphates of the newly attached nucleotides to form a new strand. As each of the new double-stranded DNA molecules forms, it twists into a double helix.

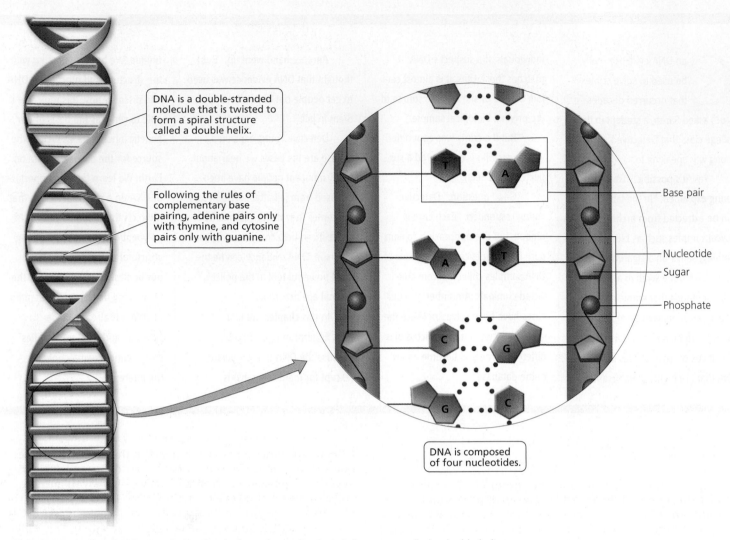

DNA is a double-stranded molecule that is twisted to form a spiral structure called a double helix.

Following the rules of complementary base pairing, adenine pairs only with thymine, and cytosine pairs only with guanine.

Base pair

Nucleotide

Sugar

Phosphate

DNA is composed of four nucleotides.

FIGURE 21.1 DNA is a double-stranded molecule that twists to form a spiral structure called a double helix.

Each strand of the original DNA molecule serves as a template for the formation of a new strand. This process is called **semiconservative replication,** because in each of the new double-stranded DNA molecules, one original (parent) strand is saved (conserved) and the other (daughter) strand is new. Look at Figure **21.2**. Notice the original (parental) strand of nucleotides in each new molecule of DNA. Complementary base pairing creates two new DNA molecules that are identical to the parent molecule.

Gene Expression

The process of replication ensures that genetic information is passed accurately from a parent cell to daughter cells and from generation to generation. The next obvious question is, "How does DNA issue commands that direct cellular activities?" The answer is that DNA directs the synthesis of another nucleic acid—**ribonucleic acid,** or **RNA.** RNA, in turn, directs the synthesis of a polypeptide (a part of a protein) or a protein. The protein may be a structural part of the cell or play a functional role, such as an enzyme that speeds up certain chemical reactions within the cell.

Recall from Chapter 20 that a **gene** is a segment of DNA that contains the instructions for producing a specific protein (or in some cases, a specific polypeptide).[1] The sequence of bases in DNA determines the sequence of bases in RNA, which in turn deter-

mines the sequence of amino acids of a protein. We say that the gene is expressed when the protein it codes for is produced. The resulting protein is the molecular basis of the inherited trait; it determines the phenotype.

Gene expression:

DNA → RNA → Protein

To more fully appreciate how gene expression works, we will consider each step in slightly greater detail.

RNA Synthesis

Just as the CEO of a major company issues commands from headquarters instead of from the factory floor, DNA issues instructions from the cell nucleus and not from the cytoplasm where the cell's work is done. RNA is the intermediary that carries the information encoded in DNA from the nucleus to the cytoplasm and directs the synthesis of the specified protein.

Like DNA, RNA is composed of nucleotides linked together, but there are some important differences between DNA and RNA, as shown in Table **21.1**. First, the nucleotides of RNA contain the

[1]We will develop this concept as the chapter proceeds. Some genes code for a polypeptide that is only part of a functional protein. A gene can also code for RNA that forms part of a ribosome or that transports amino acids during protein synthesis.

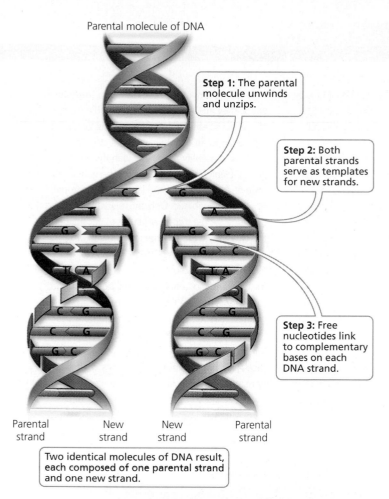

Parental molecule of DNA

Step 1: The parental molecule unwinds and unzips.

Step 2: Both parental strands serve as templates for new strands.

Step 3: Free nucleotides link to complementary bases on each DNA strand.

Parental strand | New strand | New strand | Parental strand

Two identical molecules of DNA result, each composed of one parental strand and one new strand.

FIGURE 21.2 DNA replication is called semiconservative because each daughter molecule consists of one "parental" strand and one "new" strand.

Step 1: The segment of DNA to be transcribed unwinds.

Step 2: RNA nucleotides pair with the complementary DNA bases and are linked together to form an RNA transcript.

DNA

RNA polymerase

DNA template

Step 3: The RNA transcript is released from the DNA.

RNA transcript

FIGURE 21.3 Transcription is the process of producing RNA from a DNA template.

The first step in converting the DNA message to a protein is to copy the message as RNA, by a process called **transcription.**

$$\text{DNA} \xrightarrow{\text{transcription}} \text{RNA} \longrightarrow \text{Protein}$$

Three types of RNA are produced in cells. Each plays a different role in protein synthesis (Table **21.2**). **Messenger RNA (mRNA)** carries DNA's instructions for synthesizing a particular protein from the nucleus to the cytoplasm. The order of bases in mRNA specifies the sequence of amino acids in the resulting protein, as we will see. Each **transfer RNA (tRNA)** molecule is specialized to bring a specific amino acid to where it can be added to a polypeptide that is under construction. **Ribosomal RNA (rRNA)** combines with proteins to form ribosomes, which are the structures on which protein synthesis occurs.

Transcription begins with the unwinding and unzipping of the specific region of DNA to be copied; these actions are performed by an enzyme. The DNA message is determined by the order of bases in the unzipped region of the DNA molecule. One of the unwound strands of the DNA molecule serves as the template during transcription. RNA nucleotides present in the nucleus pair with their complementary bases on the template—cytosine with guanine and uracil with adenine (Figure **21.3**). The signal to start transcription is given by a specific sequence of bases on DNA, called the **promoter.** An enzyme called **RNA polymerase** binds with the promoter on DNA and then moves along the DNA strand, opening up the DNA helix in front of it and then aligning the appropriate RNA nucleotides and linking them together; the region of DNA that has been transcribed zips again after RNA polymerase passes by. Another sequence of bases on the DNA signals RNA polymerase to stop transcription. After transcription ceases, the newly formed strand of RNA, called the *RNA transcript,* is released from the DNA.

TABLE 21.1 Comparisons of DNA and RNA

	DNA	RNA
Similarities	Are nucleic acids	
	Are composed of linked nucleotides	
	Have a sugar-phosphate backbone	
	Have four types of bases	
Differences	Is a double-stranded molecule	Is a single-stranded molecule
	Has a sugar deoxyribose	Has a sugar ribose
	Contains the bases adenine, guanine, cytosine, and thymine	Contains the bases adenine, guanine, cytosine, and uracil (instead of thymine)
	Functions primarily in the nucleus	Functions primarily in the cytoplasm

sugar ribose, instead of the deoxyribose found in DNA. Second, in RNA the nucleotide uracil (U) pairs with adenine, whereas in DNA thymine (T) pairs with adenine (A). Third, most RNA is single stranded. Recall that DNA is a double-stranded molecule.

Genetically Modified Food

From dinner tables to diplomatic circles, people are discussing genetically modified (GM) food. This relatively recent interest is somewhat ironic, considering that people in the United States have been eating GM food since the mid-1990s. More than 70% of processed foods sold in the United States contain genetically modified ingredients. Yet many people vehemently object to GM food.

Why is something as common as GM food controversial? The concerns about it can generally be divided into three categories: health issues, social issues, and environmental issues (Table **21.A**). Let's explore these categories one at a time.

Health Concerns

A panel of the National Academy of Sciences (NAS) has issued a report saying that genetically engineered crops do not pose health risks that cannot also be caused by crops created by conventional breeding. However, because genetic engineering could produce unintended harmful changes in food, the NAS panel recommends scrutiny of GM foods before they can be marketed. Currently, the U.S. Department of Agriculture, the Food and Drug Administration (FDA), and the Environmental Protection Agency regulate genetically modified foods. The NAS panel concluded that the GM foods already on the market are safe.

A common safety concern is that GM foods may contain allergens (substances that cause allergies). After a protein is produced, the cell modifies it in various ways. The protein may be modified in the genetically modified plant differently from the way it would in an unmodified cell, and the modification could produce an allergen. The likelihood that this may occur is reduced by rigorous testing. Most known allergens share certain properties. They are proteins, relatively small molecules, and resistant to heat, acid, and digestion in the stomach. If a protein produced by a GM plant has any of the properties typical of an allergen or is structurally similar to a known allergen, the FDA considers it to be a potential allergen and requires that the protein undergo additional allergy testing.

Bacterial resistance to antibiotics is likely to be a major threat to public health in this decade (see Chapter 13a). When bacteria are resistant to an antibiotic, the drug will not kill them and thus will no longer cure the human disease for which they are the cause. Some people worry about the scientific practice of putting genes for resistance to an antibiotic into GM crops as markers to identify the plants with the modified genes. Plant seedlings thought to be genetically modified are grown in the laboratory in the presence of an antibiotic. Only those seedlings with the gene for resistance will survive. Because of the way they were engineered, the surviving plants also contain the "useful" gene.

What worries some people is that the genes for resistance to antibiotics could be transferred to bacteria, making the bacteria resistant to antibiotics. The receiving bacteria might be those that normally live in the human digestive system, or they might be bacteria ingested with food. It is not known whether genes can be transferred from a plant to a bacterium. However, it is known that bacteria can easily and quickly transfer genes for antibiotic resistance to

TABLE 21.A Concerns about Genetically Modified Food

Health concerns	Is GM food safe for human consumption? Could GM crops increase bacterial resistance to antibiotics?
Environmental concerns	What effects will GM crops have on the level of use of pesticides? Can GM crops harm other organisms? Will GM crops become "superweeds"?
Social concerns	Are GM foods the proper approach to reducing world hunger?

TABLE 21.2 Review of the Functions of RNA

Molecule	Functions
Messenger RNA (mRNA)	Carries DNA's information in the sequence of its bases (codons) from the nucleus to the cytoplasm
Transfer RNA (tRNA)	Binds to a specific amino acid and transports it to be added, as appropriate, to a growing polypeptide chain
Ribosomal RNA (rRNA)	Combines with protein to form ribosomes (structures on which polypeptides are synthesized)

Messenger RNA usually undergoes certain modifications before it leaves the nucleus (Figure **21.4**). Most stretches of DNA between a promoter and the stop signal include regions that do not contain codes that will be translated into protein. These unexpressed regions of DNA are called *introns,* short for *intervening sequences.* The regions of mRNA corresponding to the introns are snipped out of the newly formed mRNA strand by enzymes before the strand leaves the nucleus. The remaining segments of DNA or mRNA, called *exons* for *expressed sequences,* splice together to form the sequence that directs the synthesis of a protein.

Protein Synthesis

The newly formed mRNA carries the genetic message (transcribed from DNA) from the nucleus to the cytoplasm, where it is translated into protein at the ribosomes. Just as we might translate a message written in Spanish into English, **translation** converts the one another. Thus, a harmless bacterium in the gut could transfer the gene for antibiotic resistance to a disease-causing bacterium.

The transfer of antibiotic-resistance genes from GM plants to bacteria could have serious consequences. For this reason, antibiotic-resistance marker genes are being phased out in favor of other marker genes, such as a green fluorescent protein. Scientists also have developed a way to inactivate the antibiotic-resistance gene if it were to be transferred to bacteria.

Environmental Concerns

Proponents of GM foods argue that herbicide-resistant and pesticide-resistant crops reduce the need for spraying with herbicides and pesticides. So far, experience has shown that the validity of this argument depends on the crop. Pest-resistant cotton has substantially reduced the use of pesticides, but pest-resistant corn probably has not. Farmers who grow herbicide-resistant crops still spray with herbicides, but they change the type of herbicide they use to a type that is less harmful to animals.

Unfortunately, engineered crops containing insecticides could have undesirable effects on insects. Genetically engineering insecticides into plants could hasten the development of insect resistance to that insecticide, making the insecticide ineffective—not just for the genetically modified crop, but for all crops.

Another concern is that genetically modified organisms could harm other organisms. For example, pollen from some pest-resistant corn has been shown to harm monarch butterfly caterpillars. Fortunately, monarch caterpillars rarely en-counter enough pollen to be harmed, and most of the pest-resistant corn grown in the United States today does not produce pollen that is harmful to monarch butterflies.

Critics of GM foods also fear that crops genetically engineered to resist herbicides could become "superweeds" that could not be controlled with existing chemicals. In Canada, canola crops in several areas have been genetically modified, each for resistance to a different herbicide. Because pollen from canola plants can spread about 8 km (5 mi.), neighboring crops have cross-pollinated, producing seeds that are resistant to many herbicides. Could seeds left behind after a harvest grow and begin to invade other areas? Indeed, in mid-2006, genetically engineered grass was found growing in the wild, near the location where a field test on the grass was performed a few years earlier.

Social Concerns

Proponents of GM food claim that GM food can assist in the battle against world hunger. We have seen that genetic engineering can produce crops that resist pests and disease. It can also produce crops with greater yields and crops that will grow in spite of drought, depleted soil, or excess salt, aluminum, or iron. Foods can also be genetically modified to contain higher amounts of specific nutrients. For example, cassava, a root that is grown for food in many poor regions of the world, has been genetically modified to provide the daily requirement of vitamins, minerals, and protein in a single meal. An additional benefit of the genetically modified cassava is that it is easier to prepare than normal cassava. The product will be tested in at least two African countries by 2010.

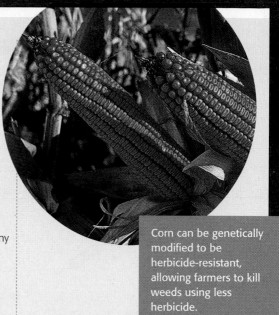

Corn can be genetically modified to be herbicide-resistant, allowing farmers to kill weeds using less herbicide.

Critics of using GM food to battle world hunger argue that the problem of hunger has nothing to do with an inability to produce enough food. The problem, they say, is a social one of distributing food so that it is available to the people who need it.

Questions to Consider

- Do you consider GM food to be a blessing or a danger to the world? What are your reasons?
- If a genetically modified organism that was created for food begins to cause environmental problems, who should be held accountable?
- Do you think that foods containing genetically modified components should be labeled?

---

nucleotide language of mRNA into the amino acid language of a protein.

$$\text{DNA} \xrightarrow{\text{transcription}} \text{RNA} \xrightarrow{\text{translation}} \text{Protein}$$

Before examining the process of translation, we should become more familiar with the language of mRNA.

The genetic code

To use any language, you must know what the words are and what they mean, as well as where sentences begin and end. The **genetic code** is the "language" of genes that translates the sequence of bases in DNA into the specific sequence of amino acids in a protein. We have seen that the sequence of bases in DNA determines the sequence of bases in mRNA through complementary base pairing. The "words" in the genetic code, called **codons**, are sequences of three bases on mRNA that specify 1 of the 20 amino acids or the beginning or end of the protein chain. All the codons of the genetic code are shown in Figure **21.5**. For instance, the codon UUC on mRNA specifies the amino acid phenylalanine. (The complementary sequence on DNA would be AAG.)

stop and think

Look at the strand of mRNA in Figure 21.3. Notice that the codon at the end of the mRNA strand is ACG. Which amino acid does this specify? (Use Figure 21.5.)

The four bases in RNA (A, U, C, and G) could form 64 combinations of three-base sequences. The number of possible codons, therefore, exceeds the number of amino acids. As Figure 21.5 indi-

Exon 1
Intron
Exon 2
Intron
Exon 3

Enzymes cut out introns

Enzymes

New mRNA molecule

Enzymes splice together exons

Exon 1

Exon 2

Modified mRNA molecule

Exon 3

FIGURE 21.4 Newly formed messenger RNA is modified before it leaves the nucleus. Noncoding regions of DNA called introns are snipped out of the corresponding regions of mRNA molecule. Segments of mRNA that code for protein are then spliced together.

cates, there are several sets of codons that code for the same amino acid. Note, too, that the codon AUG can either serve as a start signal to initiate translation or can specify the addition of the amino acid methionine to the growing protein chain, depending on where it occurs in the mRNA molecule. In addition, three codons (UAA, UAG, and UGA) are stop codons that signal the end of a protein and that do not code for an amino acid. If we think of the codons as genetic words, then a stop codon functions as the period at the end of the sentence.

Transfer RNA

A language interpreter translates a message from one language to another. Transfer RNA (tRNA) serves as an interpreter that converts the genetic message carried by mRNA into the language of protein, which is a particular sequence of amino acids. To accomplish this conversion, a tRNA molecule must be able to recognize both the codon on mRNA and the amino acid that the codon specifies—in other words, it must speak both languages.

There are many kinds of tRNA—at least one for each of the 20 amino acids. Each type of tRNA molecule binds to a particular amino acid. Enzymes ensure tRNA binds with the correct amino acid. The tRNA then ferries the amino acid to the correct location along a strand of mRNA (Figure **21.6**).

How does the tRNA know the correct location along mRNA? The location is determined by a sequence of three nucleotides on the tRNA called the **anticodon.** In a sense, the anticodon "reads" the language of mRNA by binding to a codon on the mRNA mole-

Q *If the sequence of bases following a start signal were AACUCAGCC, what amino acids would be specified?*

First base	Second base				Third base
	U	**C**	**A**	**G**	
U	UUU Phenylalanine	UCU Serine	UAU Tyrocine	UGU Cysteine	U
	UUC Phenylalanine	UCC Serine	UAC Tyrocine	UGC Cysteine	C
	UUA Leucine	UCA Serine	UAA *stop*	UGA *stop*	A
	UUG Leucine	UCG Serine	UAG *stop*	UGG Tryptophan	G
C	CUU Leucine	CCU Proline	CAU Histidine	CGU Arginine	U
	CUC Leucine	CCC Proline	CAC Histidine	CGC Arginine	C
	CUA Leucine	CCA Proline	CAA Glutamine	CGA Arginine	A
	CUG Leucine	CCG Proline	CAG Glutamine	CGG Arginine	G
A	AUU Isoleucine	ACU Threonine	AAU Asparagine	AGU Serine	U
	AUC Isoleucine	ACC Threonine	AAC Asparagine	AGC Serine	C
	AUA Isoleucine	ACA Threonine	AAA Lysine	AGA Arginine	A
	AUG *(start)* Methionine	ACG Threonine	AAG Lysine	AGG Arginine	G
G	GUU Valine	GCU Alanine	GAU Asparagine	GGU Glycine	U
	GUC Valine	GCC Alanine	GAC Asparagine	GGC Glycine	C
	GUA Valine	GCA Alanine	GAA Glutamic acid	GGA Glycine	A
	GUG Valine	GCG Alanine	GAG Glutamic acid	GGG Glycine	G

FIGURE 21.5 The genetic code. Each sequence of three bases on the mRNA molecules, called a codon, specifies a specific amino acid, a start signal, or a stop signal.

A *asparagine, serine, alanine*

cule according to the complementary base-pairing rules. When the tRNA's anticodon binds to the mRNA's codon, the specific amino acid attached to the tRNA is brought to the growing polypeptide chain. For example, a tRNA molecule with the anticodon AAA binds to the amino acid phenylalanine and ferries it to the mRNA molecule, where the codon UUC is presented for translation. Phenylalanine will then be added to the growing amino acid chain.

Amino acid attachment site: Binds to a specific amino acid.

Amino acid (phenylalanine)

Anticodon: Binds to codon on mRNA, following complementary base-pairing rules.

Anticodon

mRNA

FIGURE 21.6 A tRNA molecule is a short strand of RNA that twists and folds on itself. The job of tRNA is to ferry a specific amino acid to the ribosome and insert it in the appropriate position in the growing peptide chain.

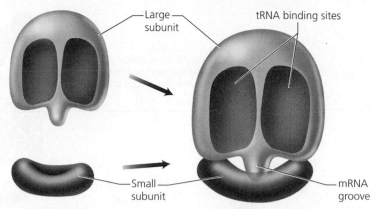

Large subunit

tRNA binding sites

Small subunit

mRNA groove

FIGURE 21.7 A ribosome consists of two subunits of different sizes. When the two subunits join together to form a functional ribosome, a groove for mRNA is formed. The ribosome has two binding sites for tRNA molecules. It also contains an enzyme that promotes the formation of a peptide bond between the amino acids that are attached to the tRNAs in the binding sites.

Large subunit

Second tRNA binding site

First tRNA binding site

Small subunit

mRNA

Step 1: The small ribosomal subunit joins to mRNA at the start codon, AUG.

Step 2: A tRNA with complementary anticodon pairs with the start codon. Ribosomal subunits join to form a functional ribosome.

FIGURE 21.8 Initiation of translation

Ribosomes

Ribosomes function as the workbenches on which proteins are built from amino acids. A ribosome consists of two subunits (small and large), each composed of ribosomal RNA (rRNA) and protein. The subunits form in the nucleus and are shipped to the cytoplasm. They remain separate except during protein synthesis. The role of the ribosome in protein synthesis is to bring the tRNA bearing an amino acid close enough to the mRNA to interact. As you can see in Figure **21.7**, when the two subunits fit together to form a functional ribosome, a groove for mRNA is formed. Two binding sites position tRNA molecules so that an enzyme in the ribosome can cause bonds to form between their amino acids.

Protein synthesis

Translation—essentially, protein synthesis—can be divided into three stages: initiation, elongation, and termination.

1. **During initiation, the major players in protein synthesis (mRNA, tRNA, and ribosomes) come together** (Figure **21.8**).

   • Step 1: The small ribosomal subunit attaches to the mRNA strand at the start codon.

   • Step 2: The tRNA with the complementary anticodon pairs with the start codon. The larger ribosomal subunit then joins the smaller one to form a functional, intact ribosome with mRNA positioned in a groove between the two subunits.

2. **Elongation of the protein occurs as additional amino acids are added to the chain** (Figure **21.9**).

   • Step 1: Codon recognition. With the start codon positioned in one binding site, the next codon is aligned in the other binding site.

   • Step 2: Peptide bond formation. The tRNA bearing an anticodon that will pair with the exposed codon slips into place at the binding site, and the amino acid it carries forms a peptide bond with the previous amino acid with the assistance of enzymes.

   • Step 3: Ribosome movement. The tRNA in the first binding site leaves the ribosome. The ribosome moves along the mRNA molecule, carrying the growing peptide chain and the remaining tRNA with its amino acid to the first binding site. This movement positions the next codon in the open site. An appropriate tRNA slips into the open site, and its

FIGURE 21.9 Elongation of the polypeptide during translation

Step 1:
- A tRNA with the appropriate anticodon pairs with the next codon on mRNA.
- Enzymes link the amino acids.

Polypeptide

Amino acid

Anticodon

mRNA

Codon Codon

Step 2:
- Enzymes link the amino acids.

New peptide bond

Step 3:
- The tRNA in the first binding site leaves the ribosome.
- The ribosome moves along the mRNA, exposing the next codon.
- Enzymes link the amino acids.
- The process is repeated many times.

Stop codon

mRNA movement

amino acid binds to the previous one. This process is repeated many times, adding one amino acid at a time to the growing polypeptide chain.

Many ribosomes may glide along a given mRNA strand at the same time, each producing its own copy of the protein directed by that mRNA (Figure **21.10**). As soon as one ribosome moves past the start codon, another ribosome can attach. A cluster of ribosomes simultaneously translating the same mRNA strand is called a **polysome.**

3. **Termination occurs when a stop codon moves into the ribosome** (Figure **21.11**).

- Step 1: Stop codon moves into ribosome. There are no tRNA anticodons that pair with the stop codons, so when a stop codon moves into the ribosome, protein synthesis is terminated.

- Step 2: Parts disassemble. The newly synthesized polypeptide, the mRNA strand, and the ribosomal subunits then separate from one another.

Large subunit

Polypeptide

Small subunit   Ribosome   mRNA

Direction of transcription

FIGURE 21.10 A polysome is a group of ribosomes reading the same mRNA molecule.

Step 1: The stop codon moves into the ribosome.

Step 2: Release factors cause the release of the newly formed polypeptide and the separation of the ribosomal subunits and the mRNA.

FIGURE 21.11 Termination of translation

Mutations

DNA is remarkably stable, and the processes of replication, transcription, and translation generally occur with amazing precision. However, sometimes DNA is altered, and the alterations can change its message. Changes in DNA are called **mutations.** One type of mutation occurs when whole sections of chromosomes become rearranged, duplicated, or deleted, as discussed in Chapter 20. Now that we are familiar with the chemical structure of DNA and how it directs the synthesis of proteins, we can consider another type of mutation—a gene mutation. A gene mutation results from changes in the order of nucleotides in DNA. Although a gene mutation can occur in any cell, the only way it can be passed on to offspring is if it is present in a cell that will become an egg or a sperm. A mutation that occurs in a body cell can affect the functioning of that cell and the subsequent cells produced by that cell, sometimes with disastrous effects; but it cannot be transmitted to a person's offspring.

One type of gene mutation is the replacement of one nucleotide pair by a different nucleotide pair in the DNA double helix. During DNA replication, bases may accidentally pair incorrectly. For example, adenine might mistakenly pair with cytosine instead of thymine. Repair enzymes normally replace the incorrect base with the correct one. However, sometimes the enzymes recognize that the bases are incorrectly paired but mistakenly replace the original base (the one on the old strand) rather than the new, incorrect one. The result is a complementary base pair consisting of the wrong nucleotides (Figure **21.12**).

Other types of gene mutations are caused by the insertion or deletion of one or more nucleotides. Generally, a mutation of this kind has more serious effects than does a mutation caused by substitution of one base pair for another. Recall that the mRNA is translated in units of three nucleotides (a unit called a codon). If one or two nucleotides are inserted or deleted, *all* the triplet codons that

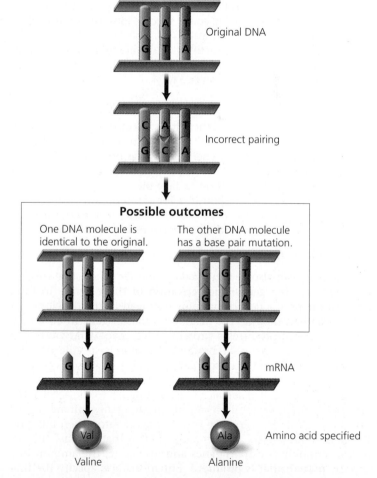

Possible outcomes

One DNA molecule is identical to the original.

The other DNA molecule has a base pair mutation.

Original DNA

Incorrect pairing

mRNA

Amino acid specified

Valine

Alanine

FIGURE 21.12 A base-pair substitution is a DNA mutation resulting when a base is paired incorrectly. This may change the amino acid specified by the mRNA and alter the structure of the protein.

follow the insertion or deletion are likely to change. Consequently, mutations due to the insertion or deletion of one or two nucleotides can greatly change the resulting protein. A sentence consisting of three-letter words (representing codons) illustrates what can happen.

Deleting a single letter from the sentence "The big fat dog ran" renders the sentence nonsensical:

Original:	THE BIG FAT DOG RAN
After deletion of the E in THE:	THB IGF ATD OGR AN

Turning Gene Activity On and Off

At the time of your conception, you received one set of chromosomes from your father and one set from your mother. The resulting zygote then began a remarkable series of cell divisions—some of which continue in many of your body cells to this day. With each division, the genetic information was faithfully replicated, and exact copies were parceled into the daughter cells. Thus, every nucleated cell you possess, except gametes, contains a complete set of identical genetic instructions for making every structure and performing every function in your body.

How, then, can liver, bone, blood, muscle, and nerve cells look and act so differently from one another? The answer is deceptively simple: Only certain genes are active in a certain type of cell; most genes are turned off in any given cell, which leads to specialization for specific jobs. The active genes produce specific proteins, which determine the structure and function of that particular cell. Indeed, as cells become specialized for specific jobs, the timing of the activity of specific genes is critical.

But what controls gene activity? How are genes turned on or off? The answers to those questions are a bit more complex, because gene activity is controlled in several ways.

Gene Activity at the Chromosome Level

At the chromosome level, gene activity is affected by the coiling and uncoiling of the DNA. When the DNA is tightly coiled, or condensed, the genes are not expressed. When a particular protein is needed in a cell, the region of the chromosome containing the necessary gene unwinds, allowing transcription to take place. Presumably, the uncoiling allows enzymes responsible for transcription to reach the DNA in that region of the chromosome. Other regions of the chromosome remain tightly coiled and therefore are not expressed.

Regulating the Activity of Genes

Gene activity can also be regulated by "master genes" that turn on a battery of other genes; the activation of those genes, in turn, leads to the production of proteins that lead to the development of a particular cell type. For instance, a master gene in an immature muscle cell produces a protein called myoD1. MyoD1 then turns on other genes that produce the muscle-specific proteins needed to transform the unspecialized cell into a muscle cell.

You can think of master genes like the ignition in a car. Other regions of DNA, called *enhancers,* are analogous to the accelerator. Like the ignition switch in a car, the master genes initiate the action in a cell. Enhancers, like the car's accelerator, then build on this action. Enhancers are segments of DNA that increase the *rate* of transcription of certain genes and, therefore, the amount of a specific protein that is produced. Enhancers also specify the timing of expression and a gene's response to external signals and developmental cues that affect gene expression.

Chemical Signals

Chemical signals can also regulate gene activity. You may recall from Chapter 10 that one of the ways certain hormones bring about their effects is by turning on specific genes. Steroid hormones, for instance, bind to receptors within a target cell. The hormone-receptor complex then finds its way to the nuclear chromatin and turns on specific genes. For example, one such complex turns on the genes in cells that produce facial hair—explaining why your father may have a beard but your mother probably does not, even though she has the necessary genes to grow one. In this case, the sex hormone testosterone binds to a receptor and turns on hair-producing genes. Facial hair follicle cells of both men and women have the necessary testosterone receptors. However, women usually do not produce enough testosterone to activate the hair-producing genes, so bearded women are rare.

stop and think

Why do female athletes who inject themselves with testosterone to stimulate muscle development sometimes develop increased facial hair?

In addition to hormones that turn on specific genes, regulatory proteins can activate a gene. An activator protein, for instance, can bind to DNA somewhere near the promoter for a gene. The activator protein then helps to position and activate RNA polymerase so that transcription begins.

Genetic Engineering

The manipulation of genetic material for human purposes, a practice called **genetic engineering**, began almost as soon as scientists started to understand the language of DNA. Genetic engineering is part of the broader endeavor of **biotechnology**, a field in which scientists make controlled use of living cells to perform specific tasks. Genetic engineering has been used to produce pharmaceuticals and hormones, improve diagnosis and treatment of human diseases, increase food production from plants and animals, and gain insight into the growth processes of cells.

Recombinant DNA

The basic idea behind genetic engineering is to put a gene of interest—in other words, one that produces a useful protein or trait—into another piece of DNA to create **recombinant DNA**, which is DNA combined from two or more sources. The recombinant DNA, carrying the gene of interest, is then placed into a rapidly multiplying cell that quickly produces many copies of the gene. The final harvest may consist of large amounts of the gene product or many copies of the gene itself. Let's take a closer look at the procedure one step at a time.

1. **The gene of interest is sliced out of its original organism and spliced into vector DNA.** Both the DNA originally containing the gene of interest and the **vector** DNA, which receives the transferred genes and transports it to a new cell, are cut at specific sequences that are recognized by a **restriction enzyme**. This is a type of enzyme that makes a staggered cut between specific base pairs in DNA, leaving several unpaired bases on each side of the cut. There are many kinds of restriction enzymes; each kind recognizes and cuts a different sequence of DNA. The stretch of unpaired bases produced on each side of the cut is called a *sticky end* because of its tendency to pair with the single-stranded stretches of complementary base sequences on the ends of other DNA molecules that were cut with the same restriction enzyme (Figure **21.13**).

   The sticky ends are the secret to splicing the gene of interest and the vector DNA. The sticky ends of DNA from different sources will be complementary and stick together as long as they have been cut with the same restriction enzyme.

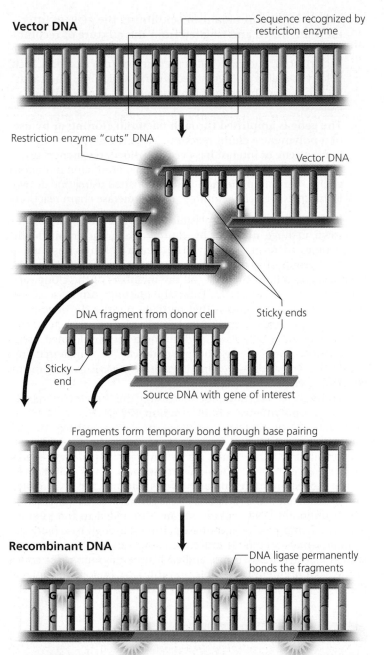

FIGURE 21.13 DNA from different sources can be spliced together using a restriction enzyme to make cuts in the DNA. A restriction enzyme makes a staggered cut at a specific sequence of DNA, leaving a region of unpaired bases on each cut end. The region of single-stranded DNA at the cut end is called a sticky end, because it tends to pair with the complementary sticky end of any other piece of DNA that has been cut with the same restriction enzyme, even if the pieces of DNA came from different sources.

The initial attachment between sticky ends is temporary, but the ends can be "pasted" together permanently by another enzyme, DNA ligase. The resulting recombinant DNA contains DNA from two sources.

2. **The recombinant DNA is transferred to a new host cell by the vector.** Biological carriers that ferry the recombinant DNA to a host cell are called vectors. For example, some bacteria have **plasmids**, small, circular pieces of self-replicating DNA that exist separately from the bacterial chromosome,[2] and they

FIGURE 21.14 An overview of genetic engineering using plasmids

are commonly used as vectors to carry a gene of interest into bacteria. The source DNA (that is, the source of the gene of interest) and the plasmid (vector) DNA are both treated with the same restriction enzyme. Afterward, fragments of source DNA, some of which will contain the gene of interest, will be incorporated into plasmids when their sticky ends join. The recombinant DNA is mixed with bacteria in a test tube. Under the right conditions, some of the bacterial cells will then take up the recombined plasmids (Figure **21.14**).

[2]Plasmids seem to have evolved as a means of moving genes between bacteria. A plasmid can replicate itself and pass, with its genes, into another bacterium.

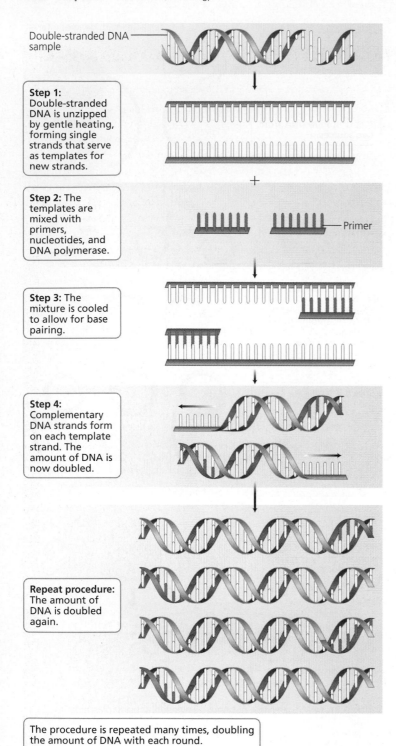

Double-stranded DNA sample

Step 1: Double-stranded DNA is unzipped by gentle heating, forming single strands that serve as templates for new strands.

Step 2: The templates are mixed with primers, nucleotides, and DNA polymerase.

Primer

Step 3: The mixture is cooled to allow for base pairing.

Step 4: Complementary DNA strands form on each template strand. The amount of DNA is now doubled.

Repeat procedure: The amount of DNA is doubled again.

The procedure is repeated many times, doubling the amount of DNA with each round.

FIGURE 21.15 The polymerase chain reaction (PCR) rapidly produces a multitude of copies of a single gene or of any desired segment of DNA. PCR amplifies DNA more quickly than does bacterial cloning. It has many uses besides genetic engineering, including DNA fingerprinting.

Although the basic strategy is usually the same, there are many variations on this theme of transporting a gene into a new host. For instance, the gene of interest is sometimes combined with viral DNA. The viruses are then used as vectors to insert the recombinant DNA into a host cell. Cells other than bacteria, including yeast or animal cells, can also be used as vectors.

3. **The recombinant organism containing the gene of interest is identified and isolated from the mixture of recombinants.** Each recombinant plasmid is introduced into a single bacterial cell, and each cell is then grown into a colony. Each colony contains a different recombinant plasmid. The bacteria containing the gene of interest must be identified and isolated.

4. **The gene is amplified through bacterial cloning or by use of a polymerase chain reaction.** After the colony containing the gene of interest has been identified, researchers usually amplify (that is, replicate) the gene, producing numerous copies. Gene amplification is accomplished using one of two techniques: bacterial cloning or a polymerase chain reaction.

Bacteria containing the plasmid with the gene of interest can be grown in huge numbers by cloning. Each bacterium divides many times to form a colony. Thus, each colony constitutes a clone—a group of genetically identical organisms all descended from a single cell. In this case, all the members of the clone carry the same recombinant DNA. Later, the plasmids can be separated from the bacteria, a process that partially purifies the gene of interest. The plasmids then can be taken up by other bacteria that will thus become capable of performing a service deemed useful by humans. Alternatively, the plasmids can be transferred into plants or animal cells—creating transgenic organisms—organisms containing genes from another species.

The second technique for increasing the amount of specific DNA is the **polymerase chain reaction (PCR)** (Figure **21.15**). In PCR, the DNA of interest is unzipped, by gentle heating, to break the hydrogen bonds and form single strands. The single strands, which will serve as templates, are then mixed with *primers*—special short pieces of nucleic acid—one primer with bases complementary to each strand. The primers serve as start tags for DNA replication. Nucleotides and a special heat-resistant DNA polymerase, which promotes DNA replication, are also added to the mixture, which is then cooled to allow base pairing. Through base pairing, a complementary strand forms for each single strand. The procedure is then repeated many times, and each time the number of copies of the DNA of interest is doubled. In this way, billions of copies of the DNA of interest can be produced in a short time.

what would you do?

Genetic engineering involves altering an organism's genes—adding new genes and traits to microbes, plants, or even animals. Do you think we have the right to "play God" and alter life-forms in this way? The U.S. Supreme Court has approved patenting of genetically engineered organisms, first of microbes and now of mammals such as pigs that are genetically modified for use in organ transplant. If you were asked to decide whether it is ethical to patent a new life-form, how would you respond?

Applications of Genetic Engineering

Genetic engineering has been used in two general ways.

- **Genetic engineering provides a way to produce large quantities of a particular gene product.** The useful gene is transferred to another cell, usually a bacterium or a yeast cell, that can be grown easily in large quantities. The cells are cultured under conditions that cause them to express the gene, after which the gene product is harvested. For example, genetically

Forensic Science, DNA, and Personal Privacy

So-called DNA fingerprints, like the more conventional prints left by fingers, can help identify the individuals they belong to out of a large population. DNA fingerprinting refers to techniques of identifying individuals on the basis of unique features of their DNA. DNA fingerprints are possible because many regions of DNA are composed of small, specific sequences of DNA that are repeated many times. Most commonly used are repeated units of 1 to 5 bases, which are called short tandem repeats (STRs). The number of times these sequences are repeated varies considerably from person to person, from a few to 100 repeats. Because of these differences, the segments can be used to match a sample of DNA to the person whose cells produced the sample.

The first step in preparing a DNA fingerprint is to extract DNA from a tissue sample. The type of tissue does not matter, and one type of tissue can be successfully compared to another type.

Commonly used sources include blood, semen, skin, and hair follicles, because they are not too painful to remove, they are readily available, or they are left at a crime scene.

First, the amount of DNA is greatly increased using PCR, as described in Figure 21.15. The primers used are sequence specific for the regions on either side of the repeating region. This produces many copies of the repeating region, which are then analyzed to determine the number of repeats present.

The FBI uses 13 STRs as a core set for forensic analysis. The resulting DNA fingerprint is unique to the person who produced the DNA. Moreover, any DNA sample taken from the same person would always be identical. *But* the fingerprint profiles resulting from the DNA of *different* people are always different (except perhaps for identical siblings), because the number and sizes of the fragments are determined by the unique sequence of bases in each person's DNA.

DNA fingerprinting has many applications, but the most familiar is probably its use in crime investigations. In these cases the DNA fingerprint is usually created from a sample of tissue, such as blood or hair follicles, collected at the crime scene. A fingerprint can be produced from tissue left at the scene years before. This fingerprint is then compared with the DNA fingerprints of various suspects. A match reveals, with a high degree of certainty, the person who was the source of the sample from the crime scene (Figure **21.A**).

Of course, the degree of certainty of a match between DNA fingerprints depends on how carefully the analysis was done. Because DNA fingerprints are being used as evidence in an increasing number of court cases each year, it is important that national standards be set to ensure the reliability of these molecular witnesses. It is generally easier to declare with certainty that two DNA fingerprints do *not* match than it is to be sure that they do. In the United States more than 200 convicts have been found innocent through DNA testing during the last decade.

Has DNA testing gone too far? All states in the United States collect DNA samples from people convicted of sex crimes and murder. Several other states also collect DNA samples from people convicted of other felonies, such as robbery. About 30 states collect DNA samples from people accused of misdemeanors, including loitering, shoplifting, or vandalism. In many cases, the DNA is stored in a database, even if the person is found innocent of the crime. People who are simply cooperating with the investigation may also provide DNA samples. These, too, are added to a national database.

Questions to Consider

- Do you think everyone arrested of a crime should have the right to DNA fingerprinting to prove his or her innocence? If so, who should pay for the process?
- Is this creation of a national database of DNA fingerprints an invasion of privacy? Is it any more so than a database of actual fingerprints or mug shots?
- Under what conditions do you think DNA samples should be obtained?

FIGURE 21.A The pattern of banding in a DNA fingerprint is determined by the sequence of bases in a person's DNA and is, therefore, unique to each person. A match between DNA fingerprints can identify the source of a tissue sample from a crime scene with a high degree of certainty. Which suspect's DNA fingerprint matches this specimen found at a crime scene?

FIGURE 21.16 Genetic engineering is used to produce large quantities of a desired protein or to create an organism with a desired trait. This girl has an underactive pituitary gland. Its undersecretion of growth hormone would have caused her to be very short, even as an adult. However, growth hormone from genetically engineered bacteria has helped her grow to an almost normal height.

engineered bacteria have been used to produce large quantities of human growth hormone (Figure **21.16**). Treatment with growth hormone allows children with an underactive pituitary gland to grow to nearly normal height.

- **Genetic engineering allows a gene for a trait considered useful by humans to be taken from one species and transferred to another species.** The transgenic organism then exhibits the desired trait. For example, scientists have endowed salmon with a gene from an eel-like fish. This gene causes the salmon to produce growth hormone year-round (something they do not normally do). As a result, the salmon grow faster than normal.

Environmental applications
Genetic engineering also has environmental applications. For example, in sewage treatment plants, genetically engineered microbes lessen the amount of phosphate and nitrate discharged into waterways. Phosphate and nitrate can cause excessive growth of aquatic plants, which could choke waterways and dams, and of algae, which can produce chemicals that are poisonous to fish and livestock. Microorganisms are also being genetically engineered to modify or destroy chemical wastes or contaminants so that they are no longer harmful to the environment. For instance, oil-eating microbes that can withstand the high salt concentrations and low temperatures of the oceans have proven useful in cleaning up after marine oil spills.

Livestock
Genetic engineering has also been used on livestock. Genetically engineered vaccines have been created to protect piglets against a form of dysentery called scours, sheep against foot rot and measles, and chickens against bursal disease (a viral disease that is often fatal). Genetically engineered bacteria produce bovine somatotropin (BST), a hormone naturally produced by a cow's pituitary gland that enhances milk production. Injections of BST can boost milk production by nearly 25%.

Transgenic animals have been created by injecting a fertilized egg with the gene of interest in a petri dish. The goals of creating transgenic animals include making animals with leaner meat, sheep with softer wool, cows that produce more milk, and animals that mature more quickly.

Pharmaceuticals
Genes have been put into a variety of cells, ranging from microbes to mammals, to produce proteins for treating allergies, cancer, heart attacks, blood disorders, autoimmune disease, and infections.

Genetically engineered bacteria have also been used to create vaccines for humans. You may recall from Chapter 13 that a vaccine typically uses an inactivated bacterium or virus to stimulate the body's immune response to the active form of the organism. The idea is that the body will learn to recognize proteins on the surface of the infectious organism and mount defenses against any organism bearing those proteins. Because the organism used in the vaccine was rendered harmless, the vaccine cannot trigger an infection. Scientists produce genetically engineered vaccines by putting the gene that codes for the surface protein of the infectious organism into bacteria. The bacteria then produce large quantities of that protein, which can be purified and used as a vaccine. The vaccine cannot cause infection, because only the surface protein is used instead of the infectious organism itself.

Plants have also been used to produce therapeutic proteins. Engineered bananas that produce an altered form of the hepatitis B virus surface protein are being developed as an edible vaccine against the liver disease hepatitis B. Someday, you may eat a banana in order to be vaccinated, instead of receiving an injection against hepatitis B. Plants are also being engineered to produce "plantibodies," antibodies made by plants. For example, soybeans are being cultivated that contain human antibodies to the herpes simplex virus that causes genital herpes. A human gene for an antibody that binds to tumor cells has been transplanted into corn. The antibodies can then deliver radioisotopes to cancer cells, selectively killing them.

Pharming is a word that comes from the combination of the words *farming* and *pharmaceuticals*. In gene pharming, transgenic animals are created that produce a protein with medicinal value in their milk, eggs, or blood. The protein is then collected and purified for use as a pharmaceutical. When the pharm animal is a mammal, the gene is expressed in mammary glands. The desired protein is then extracted and purified from milk (Figure **21.17**). For example, the gene for the protein alpha-1-antitrypsin (AAT) has been inserted into sheep that then secrete AAT in their milk. People with an inherited, potentially fatal form of emphysema (a lung disease) take AAT as a drug. It is also being tested as a drug to prevent lung damage in people with cystic fibrosis. The first drug made from the milk of a transgenetic goat was an anticlotting drug called ATryn. It is given to people with a blood-clotting deficiency when they must undergo surgery. Researchers have also created a transgenic goat to produce milk containing lysozyme, an antibacterial agent. Lysozyme can be used to treat intestinal infections that kill millions of children in underdeveloped countries.

Raw materials
Genetic engineering is also used to produce useful new raw materials. For example, spider silk is five times stronger than steel and still lightweight. Attempts have been made to farm spiders for their silk, but spiders are too aggressive to live close together. It is hoped that when goats that have been genetically engineered to possess the gene for spider silk reproduce, they will create a herd of goats that will secrete spider silk proteins in their milk (Figure **21.18**). The spider silk proteins could then be spun into a fine thread called BioSteel, which could be used for bulletproof clothing, thinner surgical thread, and stronger yet lighter racing cars and aircraft.

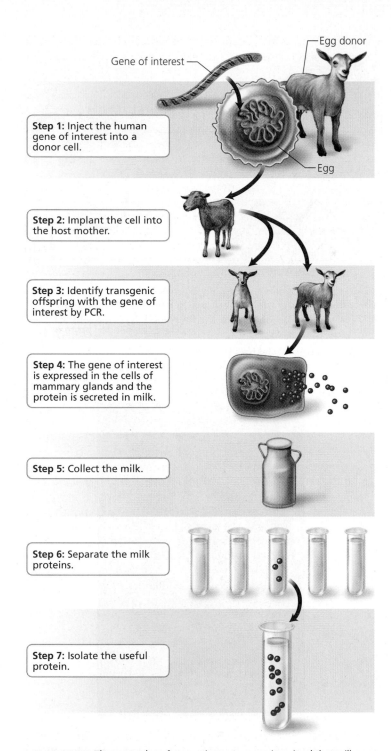

Step 1: Inject the human gene of interest into a donor cell.

Gene of interest

Egg donor

Egg

Step 2: Implant the cell into the host mother.

Step 3: Identify transgenic offspring with the gene of interest by PCR.

Step 4: The gene of interest is expressed in the cells of mammary glands and the protein is secreted in milk.

Step 5: Collect the milk.

Step 6: Separate the milk proteins.

Step 7: Isolate the useful protein.

FIGURE 21.17 The procedure for creating a transgenic animal that will produce a useful protein in its milk

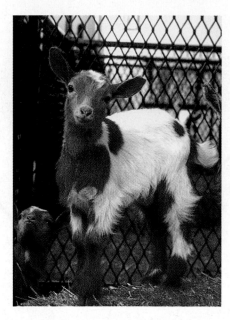

FIGURE 21.18 This transgenic goat has the gene for making spider silk, one of the strongest substances known. The spider silk protein can be extracted from the goat's milk and spun into threads that can be used for products in which strength and light weight are important qualities.

Agriculture

Most of us experience some of the results of genetic engineering at our dinner tables (see the Environmental Issue essay, *Genetically Modified Food*). The most common traits that have been genetically engineered into crops are resistance to pests and resistance to herbicides. Scientists also have developed two virus-resistant strains of papaya and distributed them to papaya growers in Hawaii, saving the industry from ruin. In addition, different strains of rice have been genetically engineered to resist disease-causing bacteria and to withstand flooding of the paddy. Other plants have been genetically engineered to be more nutritious. For example, golden rice is a strain of rice that has been genetically engineered to produce high levels of beta-carotene, a precursor of vitamin A, which is in short supply in certain parts of the world. More than 100 million children worldwide suffer from vitamin A deficiency, and 500,000 of them go blind every year because of that deficiency. Although golden rice cannot supply a complete recommended daily dose of vitamin A, the amount it contains could be helpful to a person whose diet is very low in vitamin A. Other crops have also been created that grow faster, produce greater yields, and have longer shelf lives.

Gene Therapy

The problems associated with many genetic diseases arise because a mutant gene fails to produce a normal protein product. The goal of **gene therapy** is to cure genetic diseases by putting normal, functional genes into the body cells that were affected by the mutant gene. The functional gene would then produce the needed protein.

Methods of delivering a healthy gene

One way a healthy gene can be transferred to a target cell is by means of viruses. Viruses generally attack only one type of cell. For instance, an adenovirus, which causes the common cold, typically attacks cells of the respiratory system. A virus consists largely of genetic material, commonly DNA, surrounded by a protein coat (see Chapter 13a). Once inside a cell, the viral DNA uses the cell's metabolic machinery to produce viral proteins. If a healthy gene is spliced into the DNA of a virus that has first been rendered harmless, the virus will deliver the healthy gene to the host cell and cause the desired gene product to be produced (Figure **21.19**).

Another type of virus used in gene therapy is a retrovirus, a virus whose genetic information is stored as RNA rather than DNA. Once inside the target cell, a retrovirus rewrites its genetic information as double-stranded DNA and inserts the viral DNA into a chromosome of the target cell.

Early gene therapy results

More than 4000 human diseases have been traced to defects in single genes. Although the Food and Drug Administration has not yet

Step 1: Incorporate a healthy form of the gene into the virus.

Step 2: Remove bone marrow stem cells from the patient.

Step 3: Infect the patient's stem cells with the virus that is carrying the healthy form of the gene.

Step 4: Return the genetically engineered stem cells to the patient. The gene is expressed to produce the needed protein.

FIGURE 21.19 Gene therapy using a virus. In gene therapy, a healthy gene is introduced into a patient who has a genetic disease caused by a faulty gene.

approved a gene therapy for any of these conditions, hundreds of clinical trials of gene therapies are currently under way, including trials of possible therapies for cystic fibrosis and cancer (discussed in Chapter 21a).

The first condition to be treated experimentally with gene therapy was a disorder referred to as severe combined immunodeficiency disease (SCID). The immune system of children with SCID is nonfunctional, leaving them vulnerable to infections. The cause of the problem is a mutant gene that prevents the production of an enzyme called adenosine deaminase (ADA). Without ADA, white blood cells never mature—they die while still developing in the bone marrow. The first gene therapy trial began in 1990, when white blood cells of a 4-year-old SCID patient, Ashanthi DeSilva, were genetically engineered to carry the ADA gene and then returned to her tiny body. Her own gene-altered white blood cells began producing ADA, and her body defense mechanisms were strengthened. Ashanthi's life began to change. She was not ill as often as she had been before. She could play with other children. However, the life span of white blood cells is measured in weeks, and when the number of gene-altered cells declined, new gene-altered cells had to be infused. Ashanthi is now in her twenties and has a reasonably healthy immune system. However, she still needs repeated treatments.

French scientists believe they have cured 10 children with X-SCID by using gene therapy (Figure **21.20**). X-SCID is a severe combined immunodeficiency syndrome caused by a mutant gene on the X chromosome. It is still too soon to know for certain whether all 10 children will require treatment in the future. However, four children in the French studies who had shown improvement in symptoms of X-SCID developed leukemia from the therapy.

Risks of gene therapy

Unfortunately, gene therapy using viruses has resulted in the death of an 18-year-old boy. Jessie Gelsinger died from a reaction to gene therapy treatment while participating in a clinical trial in 1999. Also, as mentioned above, four toddlers in France developed leukemia as a result of gene therapy that used retroviruses to treat X-SCID. Fortunately, the leukemia patients are now in remission.

FIGURE 21.20 Rhys Evans is the first person to be cured of X-linked severe combined immunodeficiency disease (X-SCID) by gene therapy. The immune system of a person with X-SCID is nonfunctional. Rhys Evans' immune system was strengthened, and he can now go to public places without fearing contact with people who might carry germs. He can play with other children.

what would you do?

Without treatment, children with SCID die at a young age. The gene therapy treatment for X-SCID that caused leukemia in four French boys does appear to have cured this deadly disorder in other patients. If you had a child with X-SCID, would you want him or her to have this gene therapy treatment? Why or why not? What factors would you consider in making your decision?

Genomics

A **genome** is the entire set of genes carried by one member of a species—in our case, one person. **Genomics** is the study of entire genomes and the interactions of the genes with one another and the environment.

Human Genome Project

One goal of genomics is to determine the location and sequences of genes. Researchers have developed supercomputers that automatically sequence (determine the order of bases in) DNA. The supercomputers were put to use on a massive scale in the Human Genome Project, a worldwide research effort, completed in 2003, to sequence the human genome. As a result, we now have some idea of the locations of genes along all 23 pairs of human chromosomes and the sequence of the estimated 3 billion base pairs that make up those chromosomes. Although the exact number of human genes is still not known for certain, scientists now estimate that the human genome consists of 20,000 to 25,000 genes, not 100,000 as originally thought. One reason for the smaller number of actual genes is that many gene families have related or redundant functions and therefore are able to share certain genes, so that fewer are needed to carry out all the body's functions. A second reason is that many genes are now known to code for parts of more than one protein.

In addition, researchers have identified and mapped to specific locations on specific chromosomes genes for more than 1400 genetic diseases. It is hoped that this information will give scientists a greater ability to diagnose, analyze, and eventually treat many of the 4000 diseases of humans that have a known genetic basis. Researchers have already cloned the genes responsible for many genetic diseases, including Duchenne muscular dystrophy, retinoblastoma, cystic fibrosis, and neurofibromatosis. These isolated genes can now be used to test for the presence of the same disease-causing genes in specific individuals. As we saw in Chapter 20, some gene tests can be used to identify people who are carriers for certain genetic diseases such as cystic fibrosis, allowing families to make choices based on known probabilities of bearing an affected child; similar tests can be used for prenatal diagnosis and for diagnosis before symptoms of the disease begin. After a disease-related gene has been identified, scientists can study it to learn more about the protein it codes for and perhaps discover ways to correct the problem.

We have also learned from the Human Genome Project that humans are identical in 99.9% of the sequences of their genes. As scientists gain greater understanding of the 0.1% of DNA that differs from person to person, they expect to learn more about why some people develop heart disease, cancer, or Alzheimer's disease and others do not.

Microarray Analysis

A second goal of genomics is to understand the mechanisms that control gene expression. More than 95% of human DNA does not code for protein; however, some of these noncoding DNA sequences function as regulatory regions that determine when, where, and how much of certain proteins are produced. Because gene activity plays a role in many diseases, the study of how these regions turn genes on or off may lead to advances in diagnosis and treatment.

One of the tools researchers use in this effort is the *microarray,* which consists of thousands of DNA sequences stamped onto a single glass slide called a *DNA chip*. Researchers use microarrays to monitor large numbers of DNA segments to discover which genes are active and which are turned off under different conditions, such as in different tissue types, different stages of development, or in health and disease. For example, they may use microarrays to identify genes that are active in cancerous cells but not in healthy cells (Figure **21.21**). Presumably, the genes that are active in cancerous cells play a role in the development of cancer.

Besides identifying gene activity in health and disease, microarray analysis is useful in identifying genetic variation in the members of a population. Some of these genetic differences are

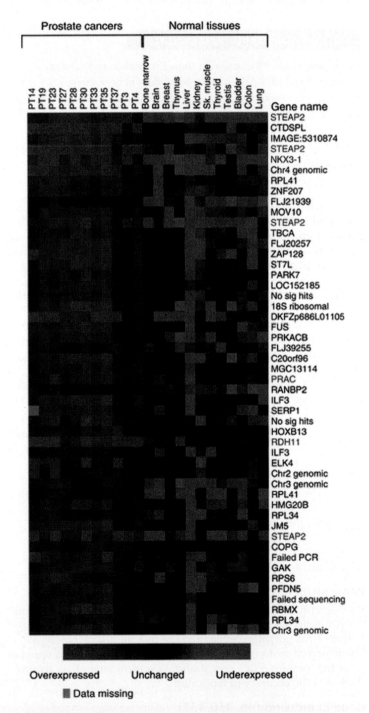

FIGURE 21.21 A comparison of microarrays showing the pattern of gene activity in prostate cancer and in normal tissue. The genes that are active in tissue with prostate cancer but not in normal tissue probably play a role in the development of cancer.

in the form of single-nucleotide polymorphisms (SNPs, or *snips*). These are DNA sequences that can vary by one nucleotide from person to person, and the differences in their protein products are thought to influence how we respond to stress and diseases, among other things. As researchers learn more about SNPs, they may be able to develop treatments tailored to the genetic makeup of each individual. These are the kinds of discoveries that can open the door for gene therapy. While individualized gene therapy may be useful in the future, we already use identification of individual differences in DNA on a regular basis in DNA fingerprinting (see the Ethical Issue essay, *Forensic Science, DNA, and Personal Privacy*).

what would you do?

Some people worry that once we know the location and function of every gene and have perfected the techniques of gene therapy, we will no longer limit gene manipulation to repairing faulty genes but will begin to modify genes to enhance human abilities. Should people be permitted to design their babies by choosing genes that they consider superior? What do you think? Where should the line be drawn? Who should draw that line? Who should decide which genes are "good?"

When SNPs are located near one another on a chromosome, they tend to be inherited together. A group of SNPs in a region of a chromosome is called a haplotype. The International HapMap Project is a scientific consortium whose purpose is to describe genetic variation between populations. Researchers collaborating on this project compare haplotype frequencies in groups of people who have a certain disease to those of a group without the disease, hoping to identify genes associated with the disease.

Comparison of Genomes of Different Species

The DNA of certain widely studied organisms, including the mouse, the fruit fly, a roundworm, yeast, slime mold, and honeybee have also been mapped. From these genomes, geneticists hope to gain some insight into basic biology, including basic principles of the organization of genes within the genome, gene regulation, and molecular evolution. Humans share many genes with other organisms. For example, we share 50% of our genes with the fruit fly and 90% of our genes with the mouse. These genetic similarities are evidence of our common evolutionary past. The genes and genetic mechanisms we share with other organisms are likely to be important in determining body plan as well as influencing development and aging.

exploring further

In Chapter 19, we learned about the cell cycle. In Chapters 20 and 21, we learned about genes, their inheritance, and their regulation, and we also considered how mutations affect gene functions. In Chapter 21a, we use this information to understand cancer, a family of diseases in which mutations in genes that regulate the cell cycle cause a loss of control over cell division.

highlighting the concepts

Form of DNA (p. 449)

- DNA consists of two strands of nucleotides linked by hydrogen bonds and twisted together to form a double helix. Each nucleotide consists of a phosphate, a sugar called deoxyribose, and one of four nitrogenous bases: adenine, thymine, cytosine, or guanine. The sugar and phosphate components of the nucleotides alternate along the two sides of the molecule. Pairs of bases meet and form hydrogen bonds in the interior of the double helix; these pairs resemble the rungs on a ladder.
- According to the rules of complementary base pairing, adenine binds only with thymine, and cytosine binds only with guanine.

Replication of DNA (pp. 449–450)

- DNA replication is semiconservative. Each new double-stranded DNA molecule consists of one old and one new strand. The enzyme DNA polymerase "unzips" the two strands of a molecule (the parent molecule), allowing each strand to serve as a template for the formation of a new strand. Complementary base pairing ensures the accuracy of replication.

Gene Expression (pp. 450–457)

- Genetic information is transcribed from DNA to RNA and then translated into a protein.
- Transcription is the synthesis of RNA by means of base pairing on a DNA template. RNA differs from DNA in that the sugar ribose

replaces deoxyribose, and the base uracil replaces thymine. Most RNA is single stranded.
- Messenger RNA (mRNA) carries the DNA genetic message to the cytoplasm, where it is translated into protein. The genetic code is read in sequences of three RNA nucleotides; each triplet is called a codon. Each of the 64 codons specifies a particular amino acid or indicates the point where translation should start or stop.
- Transfer RNA (tRNA) interprets the genetic code. At one end of the tRNA molecule is a sequence of three nucleotides called the anticodon that pairs with a codon on mRNA in accordance with base-pairing rules. The tail of the tRNA binds to a specific amino acid.
- Each of the two subunits of a ribosome consists of ribosomal RNA (rRNA) and protein. A ribosome brings tRNA and mRNA together for protein synthesis.
- Translation of the genetic code into protein begins when the two ribosomal subunits and an mRNA assemble, with the mRNA sitting in a groove between the ribosome's two subunits. The mRNA attaches to the ribosome at the mRNA's start codon. Then the ribosome slides along the mRNA molecule, reading one codon at a time. Molecules of tRNA ferry amino acids to the mRNA and add them to a growing protein chain. Translation stops when a stop codon is encountered. The protein chain then separates from the ribosome.

Mutations (pp. 457–458)

- A point mutation is a change in one or a few nucleotides in the sequence of a DNA molecule. When one nucleotide is mistakenly substituted for another, the function of the resulting protein may or may not affect the function of the protein. The insertion or deletion of a nucleotide always changes the resulting protein.

Turning Gene Activity On and Off (p. 458)

- Gene activity is regulated at several levels. Usually, most of the DNA is folded and coiled. For a gene to be active, the region of DNA in which it is located must be uncoiled. Gene activity can be affected by other segments of DNA. Master genes can turn other genes on. Regions of DNA called enhancers can increase the amount of RNA produced. Chemical signals such as regulatory proteins or hormones can also affect gene activity.

Genetic Engineering (pp. 458–464)

- Genetic engineering is the purposeful manipulation of genetic material by humans. It can be used to produce large quantities of a particular gene product or to transfer a desirable genetic trait from one species to another or to another member of the same species.
- Genetic engineering uses restriction enzymes to cut the source DNA, which contains the gene of interest, and the vector DNA at specific places, creating sticky ends composed of unpaired complementary bases that allow the cut segments to recombine. The recombinant vector is then used to transfer the recombinant DNA to a host cell. Common vectors include bacterial plasmids

and viruses. The host cell is often a type of cell that reproduces rapidly, such as a bacterium or yeast cell. Each time a host cell divides, both daughter cells receive a copy of the gene of interest. Introducing a gene from one species into a different species results in a transgenic plant or animal.

- Genetic engineering has had many applications in plant and animal agriculture, environmental science, and medicine.
- In gene therapy, a healthy form of a gene is introduced into body cells to correct problems caused by a defective gene.

Genomics (pp. 465–466)

- A genome consists of all the genes in a single organism. Genomics is the study of genomes and the interaction between genes and the environment. It is now believed that the human genome consists of 20,000 to 25,000 genes.
- Scientists use microarrays to analyze gene activity under different conditions. It uses DNA chips—glass slides with thousands of DNA segments stamped on them. The information may be helpful in treating genetic diseases. Microarray analysis also allows scientists to discover small differences in the gene sequences of people. Scientists hope to use this information to develop individualized treatments.
- Large portions of our DNA are the same as the DNA in other organisms. The closer the evolutionary relationship, the greater portion of DNA we have in common.

recognizing key terms

deoxyribonucleic acid (DNA) *p. 449*
complementary base pairing *p. 449*
DNA replication *p. 449*
semiconservative replication *p. 450*
ribonucleic acid (RNA) *p. 450*

gene *p. 450*
transcription *p. 451*
messenger RNA (mRNA) *p. 451*
transfer RNA (tRNA) *p. 451*
ribosomal RNA (rRNA) *p. 451*
promoter *p. 451*
RNA polymerase *p. 451*
translation *p. 452*

genetic code *p. 453*
codon *p. 453*
anticodon *p. 454*
polysome *p. 456*
mutation *p. 457*
genetic engineering *p. 458*
biotechnology *p. 458*
recombinant DNA *p. 458*

vector *p. 458*
restriction enzyme *p. 458*
plasmid *p. 459*
polymerase chain reaction (PCR) *p. 460*
gene therapy *p. 463*
genome *p. 465*
genomics *p. 465*

reviewing the concepts

1. Describe the structure of DNA. *p. 449*
2. Explain why complementary base pairing is crucial to exact replication of DNA. *pp. 449–450*
3. Why is DNA replication described as semiconservative? *p. 450*
4. Explain the roles of transcription and translation in converting the DNA message to a protein. *pp. 450–453*
5. In what ways does RNA differ from DNA? *p. 451*
6. What roles do mRNA, tRNA, and rRNA play in the synthesis of protein? *pp. 451–453*
7. Define *codon*. What role do codons play in protein synthesis? *pp. 453–454*
8. What is the role of an anticodon? *p. 454*
9. Describe the events that occur during the initiation of protein synthesis, the elongation of the protein chain, and the termination of synthesis. *pp. 455–456*
10. Why does a deletion have such a major effect on a cell? *pp. 457–458*
11. How is gene activity regulated? *p. 458*
12. Define *genetic engineering*. Explain the roles of restriction enzymes and vectors in genetic engineering. *pp. 458–459*

13. Describe some of the ways in which genetic engineering has been used in farming and medicine. *pp. 460, 462–463*
14. What is gene therapy? *pp. 463–464*
15. The complementary base for thymine is
    a. adenine.   b. cytosine.   c. guanine.   d. uracil.
16. Although the amount of any particular base in DNA will vary among individuals, the amount of guanine will always equal the amount of
    a. thymine.   b. adenine.   c. cytosine.   d. uracil.
17. A codon is located on
    a. DNA.   b. mRNA.   c. tRNA.   d. rRNA.
18. Translation produces
    a. a polypeptide chain.
    b. mRNA complementary to a template strand of DNA.
    c. tRNA complementary to mRNA.
    d. rRNA.
19. The anticodon is located on a molecule of _____.
20. In RNA, the nucleotide _____ binds with adenine.
21. In genetic engineering, the staggered cuts in DNA that allow genes to be spliced together are made by _____.

applying the concepts

Use the genetic code in Figure 21.5 (p. 254) to answer questions 1 and 2.

1. What would be the amino acid sequence in the polypeptide resulting from a strand of mRNA with the following bases equence?

    AUG ACA UAU GAG ACG ACU

2. The following are base sequences in four mRNA strands: one normal and three with mutations. (Keep in mind that translation begins with a start codon and ends with a stop codon.) Which of the mutated sequences is likely to have the most severe effects? Why? Which would have the least severe effects? Why?

    | Normal mRNA: | AUG ACA UAU GAG ACG ACU |
    | Mutation 1: | AUG ACC UAC GAA ACG ACC |
    | Mutation 2: | AUG ACU UAA GAG ACG ACA |
    | Mutation 3: | AUG ACG UAU GAG ACG ACG |

3. You are a crime scene investigator testifying at a murder trial. The DNA fingerprints shown on the right are those of a bloodstain at the murder scene (not the victim's blood) and those of seven suspects (numbered 1 through 7). Which suspect's blood matches the bloodstain from the crime scene?

becoming information literate

Describe some of the possible medical uses of information gained from the Human Genome Project. What ethical issues are raised by the project? Use at least three reliable sources (journals, books, websites) to answer these questions. Explain why you chose those sources.

Additional questions can be found online at The Human Biology Place, www.humanbiology.com.

21a SPECIAL TOPIC

Cancer

Exposure to the sun's ultraviolet light increases one's risk of skin cancer.

Johan has been a swimmer all his life, and he is helping pay for college by working as a lifeguard at Daytona Beach. He loves college life and his job, but for now he is happy to be home in Las Vegas for the summer. Johan's mother cooked him his favorite dinner to celebrate his first evening back at home. During the dinner conversation, Johan's mother commented on a dark spot on his ear.

"Has that always been there?" she asked. Johan looked in the mirror and admitted that he had never noticed it. They agreed he should have a doctor examine it.

When the doctor saw the spot, he immediately suggested that it be removed and sent to a laboratory for testing to determine whether it was skin cancer. Johan was fortunate; the region was only precancerous. But, he gained a new appreciation for the

association between sun exposure and skin cancer. He vowed to be more careful about using sunscreen and wearing a hat when out in the sun. After all, in North America someone dies of skin cancer every hour.

Cancer, the "Big C," is perhaps the disease that people in the industrialized world dread the most—and with good reason. Cancer touches the lives of nearly everyone. One of every three people in the United

States will develop cancer at some point in life, and the other two are likely to have a friend or relative with cancer.

In this chapter, we consider how cancer cells escape the normal controls over cell division. We then learn about some causes of cancer and how we can reduce our risk of developing the disease. Finally, we identify some means of diagnosing and treating cancer.

Uncontrolled Cell Division

All forms of cancer share one characteristic—uncontrolled cell division. Cancer cells may behave like aliens taking over our bodies, but they are actually traitorous cells from within our own bodies.

Benign or Malignant Tumors

An abnormal growth of cells can form a mass of tissue called a *tumor* or a *neoplasm* (meaning "new growth"). However, not all tumors are cancerous: tumors can be either benign or malignant. A *benign tumor* is an abnormal mass of tissue that is surrounded by a capsule of connective tissue and that usually remains at the site where it forms. Its cells do not invade surrounding tissue or spread to distant locations, although they can and do grow. In most cases, a benign tumor does not threaten life, because it can be removed completely by surgery. Benign tumors can be harmful when they press on nearby tissues enough to interfere with the functioning of those tissues. If a "benign" tumor of that type is also inoperable, as may occur with a tumor in the brain, it can be life threatening. Even so, only *malignant tumors,* tumors that can invade surrounding tissue and spread to multiple locations throughout the body, are properly called cancerous. The spread of cancer cells from one part of the body to another is called *metastasis.*

Stages of Cancer Development

Cells on their way to becoming cancerous are accumulating genetic damage. As a result, precancerous cells typically look different from normal cells. *Dysplasia* is the term used to describe the changes in shape, nuclei, and organization within tissues of precancerous cells (Figure **21a.1**). Their ragged edges give precancerous cells an abnormal shape. Their nuclei become unusually large and atypically shaped and may contain increased amounts of DNA. We can see the differences by comparing the chromosomes of a normal cell with those from a cancer cell. Notice in Figure **21a.2** that the cancer cell has extra copies of some chromosomes, is missing parts of some chromosomes, and has extra parts of other chromosomes. In a group, precancerous cells form a disorganized clump and, significantly, have an unusually high percentage of cells in the process of dividing.

Precancerous cell   Normal cell

FIGURE 21a.1 Cancer cells have an abnormal appearance. In dysplasia, precancerous cells have large, irregularly shaped nuclei that contain increased amounts of DNA.

Eventually, the tumor will reach a critical mass consisting of about a million cells. Although the tumor is still only a millimeter or two in diameter (smaller than a BB), the cells in the interior cannot get a sufficient supply of nutrients, and their own waste is poisoning them. This tiny mass is now called *carcinoma in situ,* which literally means "cancer in place."

If a tumor this size is to continue growing, it must attract a blood supply. Some of the tumor cells will start to secrete chemicals that cause blood vessels to invade the tumor. This process marks an ominous point of transition, because the tumor cells now have supply lines bringing in nutrients to support continued growth and carry away waste (Figure **21a.3**). Of equal importance, the tumor cells have an escape route; they can enter the blood or nearby lymphatic vessels and travel throughout the body. Like cancerous seeds, the cancer cells that spread, or metastasize, can begin to form tumors in their new locations.

Q *Which chromosomes have extra copies in the karyotype of the cancer cell? Which have extra pieces in the karyotype of the cancer cell? Which are missing pieces in the karyotype of the cancer cell?*

(a)

(b)

FIGURE 21a.2 A comparison of karyotypes from (a) a normal cell and (b) a cancerous cell shows that cancer cells contain extra chromosomes and chromosomes with extra pieces. (A karyotype is an arrangement of photographed chromosomes in their pairs, identified by physical features.)

A *Chromosomes 3, 5, 7, 8, 10, 11, 12, 13, 14, 16, 17, 20, and 22 have extra copies. Chromosomes 2, 4, 6, and 13 have extra pieces. Chromosomes 3, 4, 5, 6, 7, 8, 10, 13 14, and 18 are missing pieces.*

As long as a tumor stays in place, it can grow quite large and a surgeon would still be able to remove it (depending on the location). However, once cancer cells leave the original tumor, they usually spread to so many locations that a surgeon's scalpel is no longer an effective weapon. At this point, chemotherapy or radiation is generally used to kill the cancer cells wherever they are hiding (these treatments are discussed later in the chapter). The original tumor is rarely a cause of death. Instead, the tumors that form in distant sites in the body are responsible for 90% of the deaths of people with cancer.

Initial tumor cell: One cell acquires mutations, causing loss of control of cell division.

Cell divides more frequently than others.

Carcinoma in situ: Tumor remains at its site of origin.

Cells of malignant tumor:
• Attract a blood supply
• Gain the ability to leave the other cells
• Spread to distant sites (metastasize)

FIGURE 21a.3 The progression of cancer from the initial tumor cell to a malignant tumor

Once cancer cells have separated from the original tumor, they usually enter the cardiovascular or lymphatic system, which carries the renegade cells to distant sites. Thus, circulatory pathways in the body often explain the patterns of metastasis. For example, cancer cells escaping from tumors in most parts of the body, including the skin, encounter the next capillary bed in the lungs. Consequently, many cancers spread to the lungs. However, blood leaving the intestine travels directly to the liver, so colon cancer typically spreads to the liver.

The simplest explanation of how cancer causes death is that it interferes with the ability of body cells to function normally. For instance, cancer cells are greedy. They deprive normal cells of nutrients and thereby weaken the cells, sometimes to the point of death. Cancer cells can also prevent otherwise healthy cells from performing their usual functions. In addition, tumors can block blood vessels or air passageways in the respiratory system or press on vital nerve pathways in the brain.

Beginnings of Cancer

The 30 trillion to 50 trillion cells in the human body generally work cooperatively, much like the members of any organized society. There are "rules," or controls, that tell a cell when and how often to divide, when to self-destruct, and when to stay in place. However, cancer cells are outlaws. They evade the many controls that would normally maintain order in the body. Let's discuss some of the normal systems of checks and balances that regulate healthy cells and see how cancer cells are able to get around these safeguards to divide indefinitely and spread out of control.

Recall from Chapter 19 that the cell cycle is the life cycle of the cell. During the cell cycle, there are checkpoints at which the cell determines whether conditions are favorable for moving on to the next stage. This is the cell's system of damage control. If a healthy cell detects damage, such as a mutated gene, it stops the cell cycle, assesses the damage, and begins repair (Figure **21a.4**). If the repair is successful, the cell cycle resumes. If the damage is recognized as too severe to repair, a program of cell death is initiated, as will be

discussed shortly. Unfortunately, if the damage repair is unsuccessful or incomplete, genetic damage accumulates and can lead to cancer.

Tumor-suppressor genes are an important part of the cell's system of damage control. Some tumor-suppressor gene products detect damaged DNA.[1] When they do, other tumor-suppressor gene products serve as "managers of the cell's repair shop." These gene products assess the damage and coordinate the activities of other genes, whose products serve as "mechanics" and repair the damage. If the damage turns out to be too extensive, the manager activates still other genes whose products cause cell death. A particularly important tumor-suppressor gene is *p53*. We consider some of the activities of the p53 protein as we discuss the relationship between genes and cancer.

Lack of Restraint on Cell Division

When genes that regulate cell division are mutated, they usually do not function properly, and the cell loses control over cell division. Cancer is fundamentally a disease in which certain genes mutate and produce proteins that malfunction, or produce proteins in abnormal amounts or in inappropriate locations.

Two types of genes usually regulate cell division: proto-oncogenes and the tumor-suppressor genes mentioned earlier. Proto-oncogenes stimulate cell division in a variety of ways, including by producing growth factors or affecting their function or by producing proteins that affect the activity of certain genes. In contrast, tumor-suppressor genes inhibit or stop cell division. Thus, tumor-suppressor gene products act like brakes on cell division. The combined activities of these two types of genes allow

[1]Recall that genes exert their effect through the proteins they code for. Thus it is really the proteins that are acting.

A healthy cell dividing

DNA damage detected

Damage control
• Stop cell division
• Assess damage
• Repair damage

Repair is successful
• Cell returns to cell cycle

Repair fails
• Damage accumulates, leading to cancer

Damage too extensive for repair
• Programmed cell death

FIGURE 21a.4 Steps in controlling DNA damage during the cell cycle

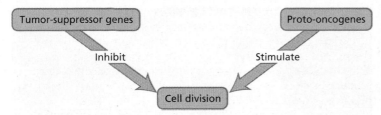

FIGURE 21a.5 Tumor-suppressor genes and proto-oncogenes normally control cell division so that it occurs only when needed. Mutations in these genes lead to loss of control over cell division and cancer.

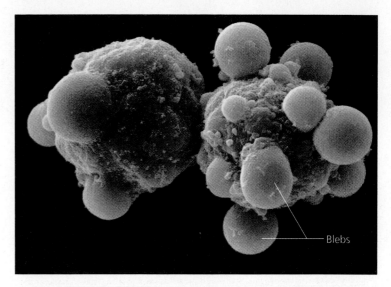

FIGURE 21a.6 Programmed cell death is a backup system that protects the body from a cell in which the genes regulating cell division have been damaged. DNA damage that is too extensive to repair normally triggers a genetic suicide program that causes the cell to self-destruct, as these cells are doing. As the cell goes through programmed cell death, its plasma membrane forms bulges called blebs. Cancer cells are able to evade this protective mechanism.

the body to control cell division to divide and develop normally, repair defective cells, and replace dead cells (Figure **21a.5**).

When mutations affect the functioning of these gene products, the normal system of checks and balances that regulates cell division goes awry, and the disruption can result in the unrestrained cell division that characterizes cancer. A mutation in a tumor-suppressor gene can promote cancer by taking the brakes off cell division. The tumor-suppressor gene *p53* produces a protein that regulates another gene whose job it is to produce a protein that keeps cells in a nondividing state. However, when *p53* mutates, cell division is no longer curbed. Mutant *p53* seems to be an important factor in more than half of all cancers. Mutation in another tumor-suppressor gene, called *RB*, causes retinoblastoma, which is a rare form of childhood eye cancer. The normal product of *RB* turns off a proto-oncogene that stimulates cell division. When *RB* mutates, the activity of the proto-oncogene is no longer inhibited, and cell division continues because the cell cannot exit the cell cycle. Two tumor-suppressor gene products that play a role in breast cancer—BRCA1 and BRCA2 proteins—initiate DNA repair. When these two genes mutate, damaged DNA is not repaired. Mutations then accumulate, which may set the cell on a course toward cancer.

A mutation in a proto-oncogene can also destroy the regulation of cell division. The mutated gene is called an oncogene, and it increases the stimulus for cell division or promotes cell division without a stimulus. An oncogene does to cell division what a stuck accelerator would do to the speed of a car. The proteins produced by many proto-oncogenes are growth factors or receptors for growth factors. When a proto-oncogene mutates and becomes an oncogene, the transformation often causes too much protein to be produced or makes the protein more active than usual. For example, the product of the *ras* gene normally signals the presence of a growth factor, which stimulates cell division. The *ras* oncogene protein is hyperactive and stimulates cell division even in the absence of growth factors. The *ras* oncogene is thought to be important in the development of most pancreatic and colon cancers, as well as some lung cancers. Other oncogenes play a role in leukemia and many of the most deadly forms of breast and ovarian cancer.

Most cells are anchored in place within tissues and organs and are in contact with appropriate neighboring cells. Normal cells have signaling systems that inform them of contact with other cells. As a result, when normal cells contact a neighbor, they stop dividing. This phenomenon is called *contact inhibition*. But cancer cells do not exhibit contact inhibition. Instead, they continue to divide, pile up on one another, and form a tumor.

DNA Damage and Cell Destruction

When the genes that regulate cell division are faulty, backup systems normally swing into play to protect the body from the renegade cell. One such system is programmed cell death, also called

apoptosis, in which cells activate a genetic suicide program in response to a biochemical or physiological signal. Activation of the so-called death genes prompts cells to manufacture proteins that then kill the cells. Often, the condemned cells go through a predictable series of physical changes that indicate the cell will die. During apoptosis, the outer membrane of the condemned cell produces bulges, called blebs, that are pinched off the cell (Figure **21a.6**). The blebs are an indication that cell will break down into membrane-enclosed fragments that are engulfed and removed by other cells.

Cancer cells often fail to trigger apoptosis. Although not the only way that cancer cells evade this safeguard, a faulty tumor-suppressor gene *p53* genes is often at least partly responsible. Besides producing a protein that inhibits cell division, the p53 protein normally prevents the replication of damaged DNA. If damage is detected, the p53 protein halts cell division until the DNA can be mended. If the damage is beyond repair, the p53 protein triggers the events that lead to programmed cell death.

In a cancer cell, however, a faulty p53 protein fails to initiate the events leading to cellular self-destruction, so the cells are free to divide in spite of genetic damage. Tumors containing cells with damaged *p53* genes grow aggressively and spread easily and quickly to new locations in the body. Cancer cells containing mutations in *p53* are difficult to kill with radiation or chemotherapy, because these techniques are intended to damage the DNA of the cancer cell and trigger programmed self-destruction. Because of mutations in *p53*, many cancer cells are simply unable to self-destruct in response to DNA damage.

Unlimited Cell Division

Healthy cells have yet another safeguard against unrestrained cell division: a mechanism that limits the number of times a cell can divide during its lifetime. When grown in the laboratory, most human cells divide only about 50 or 60 times before entering a nondividing state called senescence. Like sand running through an hourglass, cell division has a predetermined end.

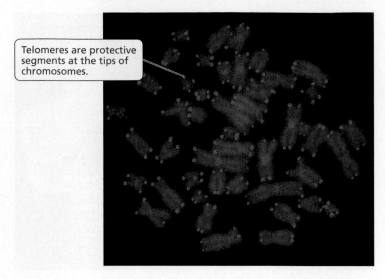

Telomeres are protective segments at the tips of chromosomes.

FIGURE 21a.7 Telomeres (shown here in yellow) may serve as molecular counting mechanisms that limit the number of times a cell can divide. Cancer cells retain the ability to construct new telomeres to replace the bits that are shaved off.

How does a cell "count" the number of times it has divided? The answer might lie in telomeres—pieces of DNA at the tips of chromosomes that protect the ends of the chromosomes much like the plastic pieces on the ends of shoelaces protect the shoelace—or in telomerase, the enzyme that constructs the telomeres (Figure **21a.7**). Soon after an embryo is fully developed, most cells stop producing telomerase, putting an end to the maintenance of telomere length. Each time DNA is copied in preparation for cell division, a tiny piece of every telomere in the cell is shaved off, shortening the chromosomes slightly. When the telomeres are completely gone, the chromosome tips can fuse together, disrupting the genetic message and causing the cell to die. Telomeres, then, may be the cell's way of limiting the number of times division can occur. When the telomeres are gone, time is up for that cell. Thus, telomere length may serve both as a gauge of a cell's age and as an indicator of how long that line of cells will continue to divide.

Some scientists currently suspect that the "fountain of youth" that bestows immortality on cancer cells, allowing them to divide indefinitely, may be their unceasing production of telomerase. This enzyme reconstructs the telomeres after each cell division, stabilizing telomere length and protecting the important genes at chromosome tips. Although most types of mature human cells can no longer produce telomerase, the genes for telomerase apparently become turned on in most cancer cells. Telomerase is present in nearly 90% of biopsies of human cancerous tumors.

Blood Supply to Cancer Cells

We have seen that cancer cells have escaped the normal cellular controls on cell division and are unable to issue the orders that would lead to their own death. Instead, they multiply and form a tumor.

As mentioned earlier, when a tumor reaches a critical size of about a million cells, its growth will stop unless it can attract a blood supply to deliver the nutrients it needs to support its growth and to remove waste. Cancer cells release special growth factors that cause capillaries to invade the tumor (Figure **21a.8**). These tiny blood vessels become the tumor's lifeline, removing wastes and delivering fresh nutrients and additional growth factors that will spur tumor growth. They also serve as pathways by which the cancer cells are able to leave the tumor and spread to other sites in the body.

New blood vessels   Tumor on spinal cord

FIGURE 21a.8 Tumor cells release growth factors that cause blood vessels to grow into the tumor mass. These vessels bring nutrients and additional growth factors and remove wastes. They also provide a pathway by which cancer cells can leave the tumor and spread to other locations in the body. Here, blood vessels have formed in a tumor on the spinal cord.

In a healthy person, blood vessel formation is uncommon and is usually limited to repairing cuts or other wounds. Abnormal invasion of blood vessels into tissues can cause damage. For instance, when blood vessels invade the eye's light-sensitive retina, blindness can result. When vessels invade joints, they can cause arthritis. To avoid such damage, cells produce a protein that prevents new blood vessels from forming in tissues. The gene that normally produces this protein is by now familiar—*p53*. Mutations in *p53* can block the production of the protein that prevents the attraction of blood vessels, allowing blood vessels to invade the tumor.

Adherence to Neighboring Cells

With access to blood vessels, the cancer cells can begin to spread. Their ability to travel through the body is yet another example of their freedom from normal cellular control mechanisms. Normal cells are "glued" in place by special molecules on their surfaces called cellular adhesion molecules (CAMs). When most normal cells become "unglued" from other cells, they stop dividing, and their genetic program for self-destruction is activated.

Cancer cells must become "unglued" from other cells to travel through the body. One way cancer cells break loose is by secreting enzymes that break down the CAMs that hold them and their neighbors in place. In this way, their anchors are broken, and mechanical barriers, such as basement membranes, that would prevent metastasis are breached. Unanchored cancer cells can continue dividing and evade self-destruction because their oncogenes send a false message to the nucleus saying that the cell is properly attached. Table **21a.1** presents a review of the control mechanisms that can fail, resulting in cancer.

Body Defense Cells

Despite all the safeguards that prevent cells from becoming cancerous, cancer cells develop in our bodies every day. Fortunately, certain body defense cells—natural killer cells and cytotoxic T cells (see Chapter 13)—usually kill those cancer cells. The processes that lead to the creation of cancer cells also produce new and slightly different proteins on cancer cell membranes. The defense cells recognize these proteins as nonself and destroy the cancer

TABLE 21a.1 Review of Control Mechanisms That Fail in Cancer

Mechanisms That Protect Cells from Cancer	Method of Evasion Used by Cancer Cells
Genetic controls on cell division	
Proto-oncogenes stimulate cell division through effects on growth factors and certain other cell-signaling mechanisms	Oncogenes promote cell division
Tumor-suppressor genes inhibit cell division	Mutations in tumor-suppressor genes take the "brakes" off cell division
Programmed cell death	
A genetic program that initiates events that lead to the death of the cell when damaged DNA is detected or another signal is received	Mutations in tumor-suppressor genes: Mutant gene *p53* no longer triggers cell death when damaged DNA is detected
Limitations on the number of times a cell can divide	
Telomeres protect the ends of chromosomes, but a fraction of each is shaved off each time the DNA is copied; when the telomeres are gone, the chromosome tips can stick together, causing the cell to die	Genes to produce telomerase, the enzyme that reconstructs telomeres, are turned on in cancer cells so telomere length is stabilized
Controls that prevent the formation of new blood vessels	
These controls are normally in effect except in a few instances such as wound healing	Cancer cells produce growth factors that attract new blood vessels and proteins that counter the normal proteins that inhibit blood vessel formation
Controls that keep normal cells in place	
Cellular adhesion molecules (CAMs) hold cells in place; unanchored cells' stop dividing and self-destruct	Cancer cells' oncogenes send a false message to the nucleus that the cell is properly anchored

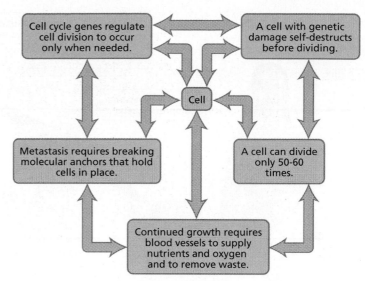

FIGURE 21a.9 Interacting control systems usually provide backup safeguards against cancer development.

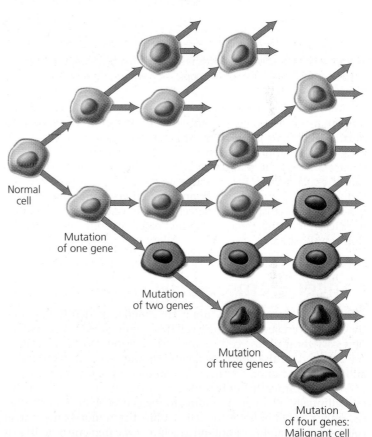

FIGURE 21a.10 Multiple mutations must occur and accumulate in a cell before the cell becomes cancerous.

cells. But sometimes cancer cells evade destruction. Some types of cancer cells actively inhibit the defense cells, and some simply multiply so quickly that the defense cells cannot destroy them all. In either case, the tumor is able to grow and spread.

Multiple Mutations

Healthy cells have interacting control systems that usually prevent cancer development (Figure **21a.9**). Normally, tumor-suppressor genes and proto-oncogenes regulate cell division so that it occurs only for growth and repair. If mutations occur, the cell will normally self-destruct before dividing and passing the genetic damage to its daughter cells. If those safeguards fail, the cell is usually prevented from dividing more than 50 to 60 times, because it lacks telomerase. If the telomerase gene is turned on, the cells will begin to starve due to lack of nutrients when the tumor consists of about a million cells. For a tumor to grow larger than this, the cells must attract a blood supply. To metastasize, cancer cells must break the molecules that anchor them in place.

With so many controls to circumvent, cancer development is a multistep process involving multiple mutations and changes in gene activity. The first mutation occurs and is passed on to all the descendant cells. Later—usually many years later—a second mutation occurs in one of the descendant cells containing the original mutation. Both mutations are passed to all the descendants of that cell. Many years later, a third mutation might occur in one of the daughter cells that already has two mutations. Each mutation brings the cell closer to becoming cancerous (Figure **21a.10**).

FIGURE 21a.11 Multiple mutations must occur in a single cell before it becomes cancerous. At least one proto-oncogene and three tumor-suppressor genes must mutate in colon cells before they become cancerous.

Damage must occur in *at least* two genes (and most commonly more than six genes) before cancer occurs. For instance, colon cells must accumulate damage in at least one proto-oncogene and three tumor-suppressor genes before they become cancerous (Figure **21a.11**). The number of damaged genes needed to produce cancer explains why it is possible to inherit a predisposition to a certain form of cancer. A person who inherits only one mutant gene may be predisposed to cancer. But a second event, a mutation in at least one other gene, is required before uncontrolled cell division is unleashed.

Cancer Stem Cell Hypothesis

All the cells of a cancerous tumor are genetically identical because they are descendants of a single cell that accumulated the mutations necessary for it to lose control over cell division. Do all the cells of the tumor have the ability to divide without restraint, metastasize, and form new tumors? Perhaps, but an increasing number of scientists are suggesting that only some cells within the tumor are capable of continually dividing. According to the cancer stem cell hypothesis, only a subpopulation of cells within the tumor—cancer stem cells—have the ability of unlimited self-renewal (replenishment) and give rise to the tumor.

Recall from Chapter 19a that stem cells are able to divide continually and to differentiate (specialize) into different types of cells. Embryonic stem cells taken from an early embryo can develop into all the cell types found in the body. In an adult, stem cells are sprinkled throughout tissues to give rise to new cells as needed for growth and repair. When an adult stem cell divides, one of the descendants remains a stem cell. The other daughter cell, sometimes called a *progenitor cell,* divides rapidly about 5 to 8 times, giving rise to a population of cells that will then specialize to form a particular type of cell.

We do know that not all cells in a tumor have the same capacity for unlimited self-renewal. Those cells with the capacity for unlimited self-renewal—cancer stem cells—have different protein markers on their surface than do other cells in the tumor. Populations of cancer stem cells have been isolated from bone marrow in the case of acute myeloid leukemia and from solid tumors in the breast or brain. Studies involving the injection of cancerous cells in mice have shown that far fewer cells are needed to initiate a tumor in a mouse when only cancer stem cells are used than if randomly selected cancerous cells are used. Some researchers suggest that the reason for the difference in the number of cells needed is that only cancer stem cells initiate tumor growth. Random samples of cells from a tumor may contain some cancer stem cells, but these represent only a fraction of the cells in a tumor. According to the cancer stem cell hypothesis, then, metastasis occurs when a cancer stem cell leaves the initial tumor and settles in a new location.

If the cancer stem cell hypothesis is correct, in which cells do the mutations occur? We don't know. Since stem cells are already able to divide continually, the simplest explanation is that the mutations leading to cancer occur in adult stem cells. However, it is also possible that cancer mutations occur in the progenitor cells that multiply several times before specializing. In this case, the mutations would cause the progenitor cells to become the cancer stem cells, which would give rise to most of the cells of the tumor.

The cancer stem cell hypothesis might also explain why traditional methods of treating cancer—radiation and chemotherapy (discussed shortly)—may shrink tumors, although the tumors often return. Such treatments are aimed at killing rapidly dividing cells such as progenitor cells. Death of progenitor cells would shrink the tumor. However, lingering cancer stem cells could replenish the population. Researchers are looking for ways to cure cancer by killing the cancer stem cells.

Known Causes of Cancer

We have seen that many of the tactics a cancer cell uses to evade normal cellular safeguards are consequences of changes in genes. Those genetic changes are often brought about by viruses or by mutations caused by exposure to certain chemicals or to radiation.

Viruses

It is estimated that viruses cause about 5% of the cancers in the United States (Table **21a.2**). Some of the viruses that cause cancer have oncogenes among their genes. Once inside the host cell, the viral oncogene behaves as a host oncogene would, taking the cell one step closer to becoming cancerous. A viral oncogene is partly why the human papilloma virus that causes genital warts can cause cervical and penile cancer. If the viral genetic information is in the form of RNA, the enzyme reverse transcriptase uses viral RNA to synthesize viral DNA, which then inserts into a host cell chromosome. Proteins produced by the viral DNA may then drive the cellular proto-oncogene to be expressed in abnormal levels or in the wrong place or time. RNA viruses can also pick up a proto-oncogene from one host cell and introduce it into a new host cell, thus promoting cell division. In other cases, a virus causes cancer because viral DNA becomes inserted into the host DNA in a location that disrupts the functioning of a gene that influences cell division. The viral DNA could, for example, be inserted into a regulatory gene that controls a proto-oncogene, breaking the switch that turns off the gene. Some viruses interfere with the function of the immune system, lessening its ability to find and destroy cancer cells as they arise.

Chemicals

A carcinogen is an environmental agent that fosters the development of cancer. Some chemicals, especially certain organic chemicals, cause cancer by causing mutations. As we saw in Chapter 21, a mutation in as few as one nucleotide in a DNA sequence can alter a gene's message. Thus, even a small alteration in DNA can wreak havoc with a cell's regulatory mechanisms and lead to cancer.

Chemical carcinogens are around us most of the time—in air, food, water, and other substances in our surroundings. We can attempt to avoid contact with some of them. For instance, tobacco smoke contains a host of chemical carcinogens. Among the carcinogens in tobacco smoke is one that specifically mutates the tumor-suppressor gene *p53* and another that specifically mu-

tates one of the *ras* oncogenes. Tobacco smoke is responsible for 30% of all cancer deaths and may contribute to as many as 60% of all cancer deaths in the United States. Excessive alcohol consumption is another cancer risk factor that can be avoided. Other chemical carcinogens are more difficult to avoid. These include benzene, formaldehyde, hydrocarbons, certain pesticides, and chemicals in some dyes and preservatives.

Some chemicals contribute to the development of cancer by stimulating cell division, which increases the chance of additional mutations arising. If a cancerous cell has already formed, this stimulation will cause the cancer to progress. Certain hormones can promote cancer in this way. For example, the female hormone estrogen stimulates cell division in the tissues of the breast and in the lining of the uterus (the endometrium). Sustained high levels of estrogen are linked with breast cancer;[2] and the incidence of endometrial cancer is elevated in postmenopausal women whose hormone replacement therapy consists entirely of estrogen. Estrogen does not seem to promote endometrial cancer when taken in combination with progesterone. However, since 2002, several studies have shown that estrogen taken in combination with progesterone does slightly increase a woman's risk of developing breast cancer. Furthermore, breast tumors in women taking combined hormone pills were larger and more likely to have spread than were tumors in women not taking hormone pills.

Radiation

Radiation, too, can lead to cancer by causing mutations in DNA. It is impossible to avoid exposure to radiation from natural sources, such as the ultraviolet light from the sun, cosmic rays, radon, and uranium. However, we can take reasonable precautions to minimize our risks. For example, sunlight's ultraviolet rays cause skin cancer. Although we probably would not choose to spend our lives entirely indoors to reduce the risk of skin cancer, it is wise to avoid sunbathing, as well as tanning lamps and tanning parlors. It is also a good idea to use a sunscreen whenever exposure to the sun is unavoidable.

Reducing the Risk of Cancer

Although we tend to think of cancer as one disease, it is in fact a family of more than 200 diseases, usually named for the organ in which the tumor arises. Cancers of the epithelial tissues are carcinomas. Leukemias are cancers of the bone marrow. Sarcomas are cancers of the muscle, bone, cartilage, or connective tissues. Lymphomas are cancers of the lymphatic tissues. Adenocarcinomas are cancers of the glandular epithelia. Figure **21a.12** shows the estimated number of cases of cancer and cancer deaths for various types of cancer, and Table **21a.3** indicates where in this textbook certain types of cancer are discussed.

Cancer is the second leading cause of death in industrialized countries, but the good news is that some lifestyle changes can greatly decrease your risk of developing cancer (Table **21a.4**). Tobacco use and unhealthy diet are responsible for two-thirds of all cancer deaths in the United States. Tobacco smoke is the leading carcinogen, and it is obvious how to modify that risk.

TABLE 21a.2 Some Viruses Linked to Human Cancer

Virus	Types of Cancer
Human papillomaviruses (HPVs)	Cervical, penile, and other anogenital cancers in men and women
Hepatitis B and C viruses	Liver cancer
Epstein-Barr virus	B cell lymphomas, especially Burkitt's lymphoma; nasopharyngeal carcinoma
Human T cell leukemia virus (HTLV-1)	Adult T cell leukemia
Cytomegalovirus (CMV)	Lymphomas and leukemias
Kaposi sarcoma-associated virus	Kaposi's sarcoma

[2]The link between estrogen and breast cancer is discussed in Chapter 17 and in the Chapter 10 Health Issue essay, *Is It Hot in Here, or Is It Me? Hormone Replacement Therapy and Menopause.*

Estimated New Cases

Male

Prostate
186,320 (25%)

Lung & bronchus
114,690 (15%)

Colon & rectum
77,250 (10%)

Urinary bladder
51,230 (7%)

Non-Hodgkin
lymphoma
35,450 (5%)

Melanoma
of the skin
34,950 (5%)

Kidney &
renal pelvis
33,130 (4%)

Oral cavity
& pharynx
25,310 (3%)

Leukemia
25,180 (3%)

Pancreas
18,770 (3%)

All sites
745,180 (100%)

Female

Breast
182,460 (26%)

Lung & bronchus
100,330 (14%)

Colon & rectum
71,560 (10%)

Uterine body
40,100 (6%)

Non-Hodgkin
lymphoma
30,670 (4%)

Thyroid
28,410 (4%)

Melanoma of
the skin
27,530 (4%)

Ovary
21,650 (3%)

Kidney &
renal pelvis
21,260 (3%)

Leukemia
19,090 (3%)

All sites
692,000 (100%)

Estimated Deaths

Male

Lung & bronchus
90,810 (31%)

Prostate
28,660 (10%)

Colon & rectum
24,260 (8%)

Pancreas
17,500 (6%)

Liver & intrahepatic
bile duct
12,570 (4%)

Leukemia
12,460 (4%)

Esophagus
11,250 (4%)

Urinary bladder
9,950 (3%)

Non-Hodgkin
lymphoma
9,790 (3%)

Kidney &
renal pelvis
8,100 (3%)

All sites
294,120 (100%)

Female

Lung & bronchus
71,030 (26%)

Breast
40,480 (15%)

Colon & rectum
25,700 (9%)

Pancreas
16,790 (6%)

Ovary
15,520 (6%)

Non-Hodgkin
lymphoma
9,370 (3%)

Leukemia
9,250 (3%)

Uterine body
7,470 (3%)

Liver & intrahepatic
bile duct
5,840 (2%)

Brain & other
nervous system
5,650 (2%)

All sites
271,530 (100%)

FIGURE 21a.12 The American Cancer Society's 2008 estimates for the leading types of cancer in terms of new cases and deaths. The figures do not include basal and squamous cell skin cancer or in situ carcinomas other than those of the urinary bladder. The percentages may not total 100% because of rounding.

Source: American Cancer Society, *Cancer Facts and Figures 2008* (Atlanta: American Cancer Society, 2008).

TABLE 21a.3 Some Discussions of Cancer in This Book

Cancer	Chapter
Skin	Chapter 4 (pp. 83–89)
Leukemia	Chapter 11 (p. 212)
Lung	Chapter 14 (pp. 290–291)
Colon, stomach, esophagus	Chapter 15 (pp. 304–307)
Testis, prostate	Chapter 17 (p. 347)
Breast	Chapter 17 (pp. 356–357)
Cervical	Chapter17a (p. 369)

TABLE 21a.4 Tips for Reducing Your Cancer Risk

1. Do not use tobacco. If you do, quit. Avoid exposure to secondhand smoke.

2. Reduce the amount of saturated fat in your diet, especially the fat from red meat.

3. Minimize your consumption of salt-cured, pickled, and smoked foods.

4. Eat at least five servings of fruit and vegetables every day.

5. Avoid excessive alcohol intake. If you consume alcohol, one or two drinks a day should be the maximum.

6. Watch your caloric intake, and maintain a healthy body weight.

7. Avoid excessive exposure to sunlight. Wear protective clothing. Use sunscreen.

8. Avoid unnecessary medical x-rays.

9. Have the appropriate screening exams on a regular basis. Women should have PAP tests and mammograms. Men should have prostate tests. All adults should have tests for colorectal cancer.

A few simple diet changes may reduce your risk of developing cancer. The best rules are to eat a well-balanced diet and to eat all foods in moderation. For instance, a high-fat diet is linked to colon and breast cancers. Most people in the United States consume far too much fat. Thus it is wise to reduce fat intake, especially saturated fat, which comes from animal sources such as red meat. Consuming large quantities of smoked, salt-cured, and nitrite-cured foods, such as ham, bologna, and salami, increases the risk of cancers of the esophagus and stomach.

A diet rich in fruits and vegetables can reduce your cancer risk because these foods are high in fiber, which can dilute the contents of the intestines, bind to carcinogens, and reduce the amount of time the carcinogens spend in the intestine by speeding passage of intestinal contents. The so-called colorful vegetables—vegetables having colors other than green—are usually high in antioxidant vitamins, and these vitamins may play a role in protecting against cancer. As their name implies, antioxidants interfere with oxidation, a process that can result in the formation of molecules called free radicals that can damage DNA and thereby lead to cancer. The three major antioxidants are beta-carotene, vitamin E, and vitamin C. The first two are common in red, yellow, and orange fruits and vegetables, and the last abounds in citrus fruits, among other sources.

Diagnosing Cancer

Early detection is critical to cancer survival because treatment is much more likely to be successful if the cancer has not yet spread. You know your own body better than anyone else does. The American Cancer Society suggests that you be alert for cancer's seven warning signs, the first letters of which spell the word CAUTION:

Change in bowel or bladder habit or function

A sore that does not heal

Unusual bleeding or bloody discharge

Thickening or lump in breast or elsewhere

Indigestion or difficulty swallowing

Obvious change in wart or mole

Nagging cough or hoarseness

But self-examination is not enough. There are additional ways to diagnose cancer—some more involved than others:

- **Routine screening.** Many routine tests can detect cancer in people who do not have symptoms. You can perform some of the tests on yourself; others require a visit to a medical professional (Table **21a.5**).
- **Imaging.** Many imaging techniques allow physicians to look inside the body and identify tumors. These include x-rays, computerized tomography (CT) scans, magnetic resonance imaging (MRI), and ultrasound (**Figure 21a.13**).

(a) Mammogram of a breast cancer tumor (white area)

(b) MRI of a cancerous brain tumor (bright purple area)

FIGURE 21a.13 Imaging techniques such as x-rays or MRIs can detect tumors.

TABLE 21a.5 Recommended Cancer Screening Tests

Guidelines suggested by the American Cancer Society for the early detection of cancer in people without symptoms, age 20 to 40

Cancer-related checkup every 3 years

Should include the procedures listed below plus health counseling (such as tips on quitting cigarette smoking) and examinations for cancers of the thyroid, testes, prostate, mouth, ovaries, skin, and lymph nodes. Some people are at higher than normal risk for certain cancers and may need to have tests more frequently.

Breast cancer	• Exam by doctor every 3 years • Self-exam every month • One baseline breast x-ray ages 35–40 Higher risk for breast cancer: Personal or family history of breast cancer; never had children; had first child after 30
Uterine cancer	• Pelvic exam every 3 years
Cervical cancer	• Yearly PAP test beginning at age 18 or when sexual activity begins Higher risk for cervical cancer: Early age at first intercourse; multiple sex partners

Guidelines suggested by the American Cancer Society for the early detection of cancer in people without symptoms, age 40 and over

Cancer-related checkup every year

Should include the procedures listed below plus health counseling (such as tips on quitting cigarette smoking) and examinations for cancers of the thyroid, testes, prostate, mouth, ovaries, skin, and lymph nodes. Some people are at higher than normal risk for certain cancers and may need to have tests more frequently.

Colon and rectal cancer	• Fecal occult blood test every year after age 50 • Flexible sigmoidoscopy beginning at age 50 and every 5 years thereafter Higher risk for colorectal cancer: Personal or family history of colon or rectal cancer; personal or family history of polyps in the colon or rectum; ulcerative colitis
Breast cancer	• Exam by doctor every 3 years • Self-exam every month • Breast x-ray every year after 40 Higher risk for breast cancer: Personal or family history of breast cancer; never had children; had first child after 30
Uterine cancer	• Pelvic exam every year
Cervical cancer	• Yearly PAP test Higher risk for cervical cancer: Early age at first intercourse; multiple sex partners
Endometrial cancer	• Endometrial tissue sample at menopause if at risk Higher risk of endometrial cancer: Infertility, obesity, failure of ovulation, abnormal uterine bleeding, estrogen therapy
Prostate cancer	• Yearly prostate-specific antigen (PSA) blood test and digital rectal exam after age 50

- **Biopsy.** Biopsy is the removal and analysis of a small piece of tissue suspected to be cancerous. A biopsy is often done using a needle instead of surgery. In either case, cells are then examined under a microscope to see whether they have the characteristic appearance of cancer cells.

- **Tumor marker tests.** When cancer is suspected, certain blood tests can be used to look for tumor markers, which are chemicals produced either by the cells of the tumor or by body cells in response to a tumor. Prostate cells, for example, produce prostate-specific antigen (PSA). Men normally have low levels of PSA in their blood; but abnormal proliferation of prostate cells, as would occur if a tumor were developing, can raise those levels. Thus elevated blood PSA levels suggest the presence of prostate cancer. Currently, PSA is the only tumor marker that is useful in the original diagnosis of a cancer, but other tumor markers may reveal whether certain cancers have spread or returned. For example, blood levels of a marker called TA–90 can help determine whether melanoma (a type of skin cancer) has spread. The tumor marker CA 125 can identify ovarian cancer. CA–15–3 indicates a recurrence of breast cancer, and CEA indicates a recurrence of colon cancer.

- **Genetic tests.** DNA analysis of cells found in certain bodily fluids or excretions can identify gene mutations associated with certain cancers: sputum is examined for signs of lung cancer, urine for signs of bladder cancer, and feces for signs of colon cancer. Other signs of cancer can be detected by still other tests. For instance, as noted earlier, the enzyme telomerase is produced by cancer cells but rarely by normal ones. A test for telomerase appears to be helpful in diagnosing certain cancers, but this test is still in an experimental stage.

Treating Cancer

The conventional cancer treatments—surgery, radiation therapy, and chemotherapy—are still the mainstays of cancer treatment. But many new treatments hold promise.

Surgery

When a cancerous tumor is accessible and can be removed without damaging vital surrounding tissue, surgery is usually performed to eradicate the cancer or remove as much as possible. If every cancer cell is removed, as can be done with early tumors (carcinoma in situ), a complete cure is possible. However, if cancer cells have begun to invade surrounding tissue or have spread to distant locations, surgery alone cannot "cure" the cancer. If the cancer has spread, surrounding tissue and perhaps even nearby lymph nodes may also be removed. Unfortunately, more than half of all tumors have already metastasized by the time of diagnosis, so further treatment is necessary.

Radiation

If cancer has spread from the initial site but is still localized, surgery is usually followed by radiation therapy (Figure **21a.14**). In some cases, such as cancer of the larynx (voice box), localized tumors that are difficult to remove surgically without damaging surrounding tissue may be treated with radiation alone.

As we have seen, radiation damages DNA, and extensive DNA damage triggers programmed cell death. The greatest damage caused by radiation is done to cells that are dividing rapidly. The

FIGURE 21a.14 Radiation therapy is often used to treat cancer that is localized.

intended targets of radiation, cancer cells, are dividing actively; but so are the cells of several types of tissues, called renewal tissues, whose cells normally continue dividing throughout life. These tissues include cells of the reproductive system, cells that replace layers of skin or the lining of the stomach, cells that give rise to blood cells, or cells that give rise to hair. Unfortunately, radiation cannot distinguish between cancer cells and renewal tissue, so good cells are sacrificed in killing the harmful ones. The destruction of renewal tissues leads to the side effects of radiation such as temporary sterility, nausea, anemia, and hair loss.

Chemotherapy

When cancer is thought to have spread by the time of diagnosis, chemotherapy is often used. In general, the drugs used in chemotherapy reach all parts of the body and kill all rapidly dividing cells, just as radiation does. Some of the drugs block DNA synthesis, others damage DNA, and a few others prevent cell division by interfering with other cellular processes. The side effects are similar to those that accompany radiation therapy.

As we have seen, the idea underlying radiation and chemotherapy is that the damage they do to DNA in rapidly dividing cells will cause the cells to self-destruct. However, *p53*, the gene that detects DNA damage and initiates programmed cell death, is mutant in more than half of all cancers. As a result, even though the treatment succeeds in damaging the DNA in cancer cells, the cells do not self-destruct, and treatment fails.

Immunotherapy

Cytotoxic T cells of the immune system continually search the body for abnormal cells, such as cancer cells, and kill any that they find (see Chapter 13). The goal of immunotherapy, then, is to boost the patient's immune system so that it becomes more effective in destroying cancer cells. One form of immunotherapy involves administering factors normally secreted by lymphocytes, including interleukin-2 (which stimulates lymphocytes that attack cancer cells), interferons (which stimulate the immune system and also directly affect the tumor cells), and tumor necrosis factor (which directly affects cancer cells, causing them to self-destruct).

Two types of vaccines can be used in the battle against cancer. One type is a vaccine against a virus that causes cancer. For example, a vaccine against four of the human papillomaviruses that cause cervical cancer was approved in the summer of 2006. Two of these viruses are HPV16 and HPV18, which cause 70% of the cases of cervical cancer. Federal health officials now recommend that all girls 10 to 12 years of age receive this vaccination.

The other type of vaccine is being tested in clinical trials with promising results. It is designed to work by stimulating T cells to attack and kill the cancer cells. Unlike most vaccines, these vaccines cannot *prevent* disease (cancer); they can only treat it. Cancer vaccines contain dead cancer cells, parts of cells, or proteins from cancer cells. Recall that vaccines cause the immune system to fight cells having the same characteristics as the cells in the vaccine. The vaccine strategy is now being tested against melanoma (a deadly form of skin cancer) and leukemia, as well as cancers of the kidney, prostate, colon, and lung.

Inhibition of Blood Vessel Formation

In recent years, there has been a major change in the way doctors and scientists think about cancer. Gone are the days when the only aim was to kill the cancer cells. As researchers have learned more about the molecular biology of cancer, new ways of slowing its progression or dealing with it as a genetic disease have been developed.

The formation of blood vessels is a critical step in the life of a tumor, because blood vessels bring nourishment and provide a pathway for cell migration. Researchers are working on ways to cut off these lifelines and starve the tumor. Many drugs have been developed for this purpose, and some are nearing the end of clinical trials. For example, when a certain drug that blocks blood vessel formation is combined with chemotherapy, the survival rate of patients with colorectal cancer has been shown to improve.

Gene Therapy

There are currently more than 400 clinical trials using gene therapy to treat cancer, but no means of gene therapy has been approved by the Food and Drug Administration (FDA) for cancer treatment. Nearly all these studies are in very early stages. One of the treatment strategies being tested is to insert normal tumor-suppressor genes into the cancerous cells. For instance, you may recall that gene *p53* normally triggers programmed cell death when DNA damage is detected but that this gene is often faulty in cancer cells. Researchers hope that inserting a healthy form of *p53* into cancer cells will lead to their death, causing the tumor to shrink.

Another strategy is to insert into a cancer cell a piece of DNA that will prevent an oncogene from exerting its effects. The inserted DNA is called antisense DNA because it is complementary to the mRNA produced by the oncogene. The antisense DNA would be expected to bind to the mRNA produced by the oncogene and prevent it from being translated into protein, thereby preventing the oncogene from exerting its effects. Currently, this method is being tried as a means of treating leukemia.

One of the most promising approaches using gene therapy is to insert a gene into tumor cells that makes the cells sensitive to a drug that will kill them. This method is now being evaluated as treatment for brain, ovarian, and prostate cancers. A viral gene for the enzyme thymidine kinase is inserted into the tumor cells, and when the gene is expressed, the resulting enzyme makes the cell sensitive to a drug called ganciclovir. The drug is inactive except inside the cells that produce the enzyme coded for by the inserted gene. Thus, only the tumor cells are killed.

In the fall of 2006, researchers announced that they had used gene therapy to cure two patients (out of 17 patients who were treated) of the aggressive skin cancer melanoma. The researchers used a virus to transfer a gene into body defense cells called T cells (discussed in Chapter 13). The inserted gene codes for a protein called T-cell receptor, or TCR. With this gene, the T cell can find tumor cells and destroy them.

22

Evolution and Our Heritage

The fossil record provides evidence of evolution by documenting that life on Earth has changed over time.

482

As Jorge and his classmates filed from the bus and gathered outside the main entrance to the natural history museum, he remembered how much he had enjoyed science museums as a child. Back then, he could name all the dinosaurs and most of the other animals in the exhibits. He could spout off, with considerable accuracy, the geological time periods when each creature lived. Then in high school and especially college, he had become interested in math and had moved away from biology courses. Now in the last semester of his undergraduate career, with his course requirements finally completed, he decided to return to his early interest in animal life and had enrolled in a Vertebrate Biology class. The first laboratory meeting for the course was a trip to the nearby natural history museum, where they were celebrating "Darwin Days," a series of exhibitions and events marking 200 years since the birth of Charles Darwin on February 12, 1809. Jorge recalled how Darwin had proposed that the incredible diversity of life on Earth was the product of evolution, and how this idea had its foundations in a 5-year voyage Darwin had taken as a young man along the coast of South America and nearby islands. Indeed, Darwin was 22 years old—about Jorge's age—when he began his voyage on the HMS *Beagle*.

As the students entered the building, Jorge wondered how much of his childhood knowledge about Darwin and past animal life would come back to him. He hoped that the panoramas, articulated skeletons, and fossils would jar his memory. He was especially eager to see the new exhibit on whale evolution that his instructor had described in lecture—how amazing that modern whales had evolved from terrestrial hoofed mammals and that fossils existed to chronicle this transition over time. Who knows, Jorge thought, maybe this course and its field trips would inspire him to get back into studying animals and evolution.

In this chapter, we focus on evolution. We address questions such as how did life arise and evolve on Earth? How does evolution work? How has evolution shaped species, including our own? What were our ancestors like?

Evolution of Life on Earth

Evolution can broadly be defined as descent with modification from a common ancestor. It is the process by which Earth's lifeforms have changed from their earliest beginnings to today. But how did life first arise on Earth?

Earth is estimated to be 4.5 billion years old. Evidence from physical and chemical changes in Earth's crust and atmosphere suggests that life has existed on Earth for about 3.8 billion years. The environment of the early Earth was very different from that of today and would have been an extremely hostile place for most organisms (Figure **22.1**). Earth's crust was hot and volcanic. Intense lightning and ultraviolet radiation struck Earth's surface, and there was almost no gaseous oxygen (O_2) in the atmosphere.

Scientists agree on the scarcity of oxygen, but debate the other components of the early atmosphere. Most models suggest that carbon dioxide (CO_2), nitrogen (N_2), and water (H_2O) were present. Other gases including carbon monoxide (CO), hydrogen (H_2), methane (CH_4), sulfur dioxide (SO_2), and hydrogen sulfide (H_2S) may have been present. Once the crust cooled, water vapor condensed as rain, and runoff collected in depressions to form early seas.

How might life have evolved under these conditions? In the following sections, we present a plausible sequence of events that most scientists believe explains the origin of life on Earth. The sequence, known as **chemical evolution**, suggests that life evolved from chemicals slowly increasing in complexity over a period of perhaps 300 million years.

FIGURE 22.1 Representation of the early Earth

Small Organic Molecules

Scientists hypothesize that conditions of the early Earth favored the synthesis of small organic molecules from inorganic molecules. Specifically, the low-oxygen atmosphere of the primitive Earth encouraged the joining of simple molecules to form complex molecules. The low-oxygen atmosphere was important because oxygen attacks chemical bonds. Scientists further hypothesize that the energy required for the joining of simple molecules could have come from the lightning and intense ultraviolet (UV) radiation striking the primitive Earth. (UV radiation was likely more intense during those times than it is now because young suns emit more UV radiation than do mature suns, and the early Earth lacked an ozone layer to shield it from much of the UV radiation.)

Stanley Miller and Harold Urey of the University of Chicago tested the hypothesis that organic molecules could be synthesized from inorganic ones in 1953. In their laboratory, these scientists re-created conditions presumed to be similar to those of the early Earth (Figure **22.2**). Miller and Urey discharged electric sparks (meant to simulate lightning) through an atmosphere that contained some of the gases thought to be present in the early atmosphere. They generated a variety of small organic molecules, supporting the hypothesis that organic molecules could be synthesized from inorganic ones.

The atmospheric composition used in the Miller–Urey experiment differed somewhat from the composition currently favored by scientists who study characteristics of the early Earth. Even so, many simulations conducted by other scientists using different gas mixtures (and energy sources) have produced organic compounds in varying amounts. Taken as a whole, these experiments demonstrate that organic molecules can be synthesized from inorganic molecules.

Macromolecules

Scientists hypothesize that these small organic molecules accumulated in the early oceans and over a long period formed a complex mixture. Somehow, perhaps by being washed onto clay or hot sand or lava, the small molecules joined to form macromolecules, such as proteins and nucleic acids. Some scientists suggest instead that deep-sea vents were important locations for the synthesis of small organic molecules and their joining to form larger molecules.

Which macromolecule led to the formation of the first cells? Some scientists suggest that RNA was the critical macromolecule, because it can act as an enzyme and because its self-replicating abilities allowed the transfer of information from one generation to the next. Cells today store their genetic information as DNA. Thus, if RNA was the first genetic material, then DNA is likely to have evolved later from an RNA template. Other scientists suggest that proteins were the macromolecules that led to the first cells. These scientists cite the greater chemical stability of amino acids, peptides, and proteins, as compared to nucleotides and nucleic acids, when exposed to salt (such as would occur in primordial seas) and intense UV radiation (such as that presumed to have struck the early Earth).

Early Cells

Scientists hypothesize that the newly formed organic macromolecules aggregated into droplet-like structures that were the precursors of cells. The early droplets displayed some of the same properties as living cells, such as the ability to maintain an internal environment different from surrounding conditions.

(a) Using this apparatus, Stanley Miller (shown) and Harold Urey demonstrated that simple organic molecules could be synthesized from inorganic ones in the low-oxygen environment of the primitive Earth.

The spark chamber contained gases similar to those in the primitive atmosphere, and the electrodes discharged sparks to simulate lightning.

Electrodes

Spark chamber

CH_4

NH_3 H_2

H_2O

To vacuum

Water in the boiling chamber simulated the primeval sea.

Condenser

Heat source

The trap at the bottom of the apparatus collected newly formed organic molecules.

(b) Diagram of the apparatus

FIGURE 22.2 Testing the hypothesis that organic molecules could be synthesized from inorganic ones

Fossil evidence indicates that the earliest cells were prokaryotes. Recall from Chapter 3 that prokaryotic cells lack membrane-enclosed organelles, such as the nucleus, and are typically smaller than eukaryotic cells. These early prokaryotic cells relied on anaerobic metabolism (metabolism in the absence of oxygen). Eventually, some of these cells captured energy from sunlight and made their own complex organic molecules from CO_2 and H_2O in their environment. This process, known as photosynthesis, produced oxygen as a by-product. Oxygen began to accumulate in the environment. Next came cells that could use the now abundant oxygen to harness energy from stored organic molecules; these cells used cellular respiration (aerobic metabolism; see Chapter 3).

So the question arises, "How did more complex cells arise from these early prokaryotic cells?" It's possible that some of the organelles within eukaryotic cells appeared when other, smaller organisms became incorporated into the early, primitive cells. Mitochondria, for example, may be descendants of once free-living bacteria. These bacteria either invaded or were engulfed by the ancient cells and formed a mutually beneficial relationship with them. This idea is called the **endosymbiont theory.** It is generally accepted by the biological community to explain the origin of some features of eukaryotic cells, including mitochondria. Scientists currently are not certain whether endosymbiosis was a factor in the origin of other eukaryotic features such as the membrane-bound nucleus. An additional possibility is that infolding of the plasma membrane of an ancient prokaryote produced some of the organelles (for example, the endoplasmic reticulum or Golgi complex) found in eukaryotic cells of today.

Fossils of prokaryotic cells have been dated at 3.5 billion years old, and scientists estimate that the first prokaryotic cells probably arose around 3.8 billion years ago. As we discuss later in the chapter, fossils are rarely formed and found, so the origin for a group of organisms is usually hypothesized to occur earlier than the oldest fossil evidence for that group. Eukaryotic cells evolved about 1.8 billion years ago. Multicellularity evolved in eukaryotes around 1.5 billion years ago and eventually led to organisms such as plants, fungi, and animals. Figure **22.3** summarizes the possible steps responsible for the origin of life on Earth.

Scale of Evolutionary Change

Evolution occurs on two levels. One level, microevolution, is small; and the other, macroevolution, is large. **Microevolution** occurs through changes in allele frequencies within a population over a few generations. **Macroevolution,** on the other hand, consists of larger-scale evolutionary change over longer periods of time, such as the origin of groups of species (for example, mammals) and mass extinctions (the catastrophic disappearance of large numbers of species). We begin with microevolution, examining genetic variation within populations and describing the causes of microevolution. We then turn to the larger-scale phenomena of macroevolution.

Microevolution

Look around, and you will see variation in almost any group of individuals belonging to the same species. Consider your classmates. They do not all look alike, and, unless you are an identical twin, you probably do not precisely resemble your brothers or sisters. Before looking at what makes individuals in such a group different, let's define some basic terminology. A **population** is a group of individuals of the same species living in a particular area. A population of

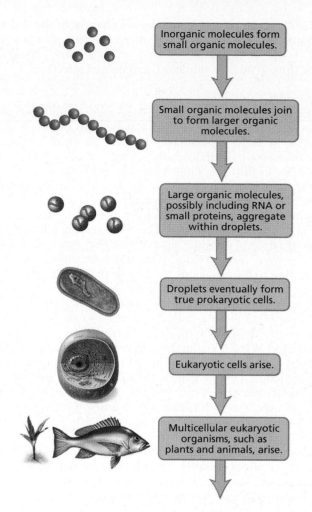

FIGURE 22.3 Possible steps in the origin of life on Earth

bluegill sunfish inhabits a pond, and a population of deer mice inhabits a small tract of forest. A **gene pool** consists of all the alleles of all the genes of all individuals in a population. (Recall from Chapter 20 that a *gene* is a segment of DNA on a chromosome that directs the synthesis of a specific protein, whereas *alleles* are different forms of a gene.) Now let's take a closer look at what makes individuals in a population different and examine some of the ways that variation can appear in populations.

Sexual reproduction and mutation produce variation in populations. Sexual reproduction shuffles alleles already present in the population. As discussed in Chapters 19 and 20, the gametes (eggs or sperm) of any one individual show substantial genetic variation due to crossing over and independent assortment during meiosis. Also, the combination of gametes that unite at fertilization is a chance event. Of the millions of sperm produced by a male, only one fertilizes the egg. This union produces a new individual with a new combination of alleles.

New genes and *new* alleles originate by **mutation,** a change in the nucleotide sequence of DNA. Mutations occur at a low rate in any set of genes. For example, the overall human mutation rate is estimated to be 1×10^{-6} per gene per generation. Because mutations occur at such a low rate, their contribution to genetic diversity in large populations is quite small. Mutations can appear spontaneously from mistakes in DNA replication, or they can be caused by outside sources such as radiation or chemical agents. Only mutations in cell lines that produce eggs or sperm can be passed to offspring.

The figure's step labels read:
- Inorganic molecules form small organic molecules.
- Small organic molecules join to form larger organic molecules.
- Large organic molecules, possibly including RNA or small proteins, aggregate within droplets.
- Droplets eventually form true prokaryotic cells.
- Eukaryotic cells arise.
- Multicellular eukaryotic organisms, such as plants and animals, arise.

Recall that microevolution involves changes in the frequency of certain alleles relative to others within the gene pool of a population. Some of the processes that produce those changes are genetic drift, gene flow, mutation, and natural selection.

Genetic drift

Genetic drift occurs when allele frequencies within a population change randomly because of chance alone. This process is usually negligible in large populations. However, in small populations (fewer than about 100 individuals), chance events can cause allele frequencies to drift randomly from one generation to the next. Two mechanisms that facilitate genetic drift in natural populations are the bottleneck effect and the founder effect.

Sometimes, dramatic reductions in population size occur because of disasters such as fires and earthquakes that kill many individuals at random. Consider a population that experiences a flood in which most members die. With fewer remaining individuals contributing to the gene pool, the genetic makeup of the survivors may not be representative of the original population. This change in the gene pool is the **bottleneck effect**, so named because the population experiences a dramatic decrease in size—much as the size of a bottle decreases at the neck. Certain alleles may be more or less common in the flood survivors than in the original population simply by chance. In fact, some alleles may be completely lost, resulting in reduced overall genetic variability among survivors.

Genetic drift also occurs when a few individuals leave their population and establish themselves in a new, somewhat isolated place. By chance alone, the genetic makeup of the colonizing individuals is probably not representative of the full gene pool of the population they left. Genetic drift in new, small colonies is called the **founder effect**. Because individuals mate within a group of reduced genetic diversity, this effect typically results in a relatively high frequency of inherited recessive disorders.

Gene flow

Another cause of microevolution is **gene flow**, which occurs when individuals move into and out of populations. As individuals come and go, they carry with them their unique sets of genes. Gene flow occurs if these individuals successfully interbreed (mate and produce offspring) with the resident population, adding to the gene pool.

The cessation of gene flow can be important to the formation of new species. A **species** is a population or group of populations whose members are capable of successful interbreeding. Such interbreeding must occur under natural conditions and produce fertile offspring. But consider what happens when a population becomes geographically isolated from other populations of the same species. For example, over the course of geologic time, sea level fluctuates. During periods when sea level decreases, a previously offshore island may reconnect with a continent. When sea level increases, the island will redevelop offshore. Suppose that during the period of low sea level a continuous population of frogs extends across the landscape. As sea level rises, however, and the island redevelops, the island population of frogs will be isolated from the one on the mainland. Frogs cannot cross saltwater, so the island population is effectively genetically isolated from the mainland population. The island population may take a separate evolutionary route as distinctly different sets of allele frequencies and mutations accumulate. Eventually, the isolated island population may become so different that it cannot successfully interbreed with the mainland population. At this point, there are two species of frogs instead of one. This process is called **speciation**.

Mutation

Mutations, you will recall, are rare changes in the DNA of genes; they are the third way that the frequencies of certain alleles can change relative to others within gene pools. Mutations produce new alleles that, when transmitted in gametes, cause an immediate change in the gene pool. Essentially the new (mutant) allele is substituted for another allele. Like gene flow, mutation can introduce new alleles to a population that are then acted upon by natural selection. If the frequency of the mutant allele increases in a population, it is not because mutations are suddenly occurring more frequently. Instead, possession of the mutant allele might confer some advantage that enables individuals with the mutant allele to produce more offspring than can those without it. In other words, the increased frequency in a population of the mutant allele relative to others results from natural selection, our next focus.

Natural selection

In his book *On the Origin of Species* (1859), Charles Darwin argued that species were not specially created, unchanging forms. He suggested that modern species are descendants of ancestral species. In other words, present-day species evolved from past species. Darwin also proposed that evolution occurred by the process of natural selection. His ideas can be summarized briefly as follows:

1. Individual variation exists within a species. Some of this variation is inherited.

2. Some individuals have more surviving offspring than do others because their particular inherited characteristics make them better suited to their local environment; this is the process of **natural selection.**

3. Evolutionary change occurs as the traits of individuals that survive and reproduce become more common in the population. Traits of less successful individuals become less common.

According to Darwin's ideas, an individual's evolutionary success can be measured by fitness (sometimes called Darwinian fitness). **Fitness** compares the number of reproductively viable offspring among individuals. Individuals with greater fitness—that is, producing more successful offspring—have more of their genes represented in future generations. To succeed in terms of evolution, one must reproduce (Figure **22.4**).

FIGURE 22.4 Fitness is the number of offspring left by an individual. These parents clearly have high fitness.

Conducting Research on Our Relatives

Chimpanzees look and behave somewhat differently than we do. Still, it is hard to look into their eyes and not see something of ourselves. Chimpanzees are our closest living relatives, sharing a remarkably high percentage of our DNA sequence. Is it ethical to keep chimpanzees in laboratory cages and use them for invasive scientific research that might benefit us? What about other primate species that we are more distantly related to?

In 2006 in the United States, 62,315 non-human primates were used in research; this represents the largest number since reporting began in 1973. Current predictions are that research with nonhuman primates will increase in the coming years, with one major effort directed at developing an HIV vaccine. At the same time, it is important to realize that nonhuman primates represent a fraction of the animals used in research; more than 90% of research animals are rodents, such as rats, mice, and guinea pigs.

Despite the controversy and cost of using nonhuman primates, they often are preferred as subjects in certain experiments precisely because they are so similar to humans. For example, human and nonhuman primates possess brains with similar organization, develop comparable plaques in their arteries, and experience many of the same changes in anatomy, physiology, and behavior with age. In some cases, Nobel Prize–winning research has resulted from the contributions of research with nonhuman primates, including development of vaccines for yellow fever (1951) and polio (1954) and insight into how visual information is processed in the brain (1981). Research with nonhuman primates has also led to significant advances in our understanding of Alzheimer's disease, AIDS, and severe acute respiratory syndrome (SARS).

The care and use of nonhuman primates (and other vertebrate animals) in research is regulated by federal agencies such as the Public Health Service and the U.S. Department of Agriculture. Animal research also is regulated at the local level. Each college, university, or research center has an Institutional Animal Care and Use Committee whose members include veterinarians, teachers, researchers, and members from the public. In addition to federal and local oversight, scientists and animal care personnel are making substantial efforts to provide appropriate housing for captive nonhuman primates and to consider their psychological well-being. Even with such efforts, however, controversy and questions remain.

Questions to Consider

- Should we ban the use of nonhuman primates in medical research? If we do, will progress in fighting diseases such as AIDS and Alzheimer's be slowed? If you or a loved one had one of these illnesses, would you feel differently about research using nonhuman primates?
- We use nonhuman primates in research precisely because they are similar to us.

The common chimpanzee (*Pan troglodytes*) is one of two living species in the genus *Pan*, the genus considered to include our closest living relatives. Chimpanzees normally inhabit tropical forests in central Africa, where they are now listed as endangered. When used in medical research, these highly social animals are often housed individually in cages.

At the same time, we morally justify our use of them by claiming they are different from us. Is there something fundamentally inconsistent with this line of thinking? Where would you draw the line when deciding which (if any) animals are acceptable for use as subjects in research that might benefit us?

Indeed, you could live more than 100 years, but your individual fitness would be zero if you did not reproduce. Some of the diseases or conditions discussed in earlier chapters are associated with zero fitness because they cause sterility (such as Turner's syndrome) or death before reproductive maturity (such as Tay-Sachs disease).

One result of natural selection is that populations become better suited to their particular environment. This transformation of the population toward better fitness in their environment is called **adaptation.** If the environment changes, however, the individuals who have become most finely attuned to the initial environment could lose their advantage, and other individuals with different alleles might be selected by nature to leave more offspring. If the environment once again stabilizes, the population reestablishes itself around a new set of allele frequencies that better meet the new environmental conditions.

The evolution of antibiotic resistance in bacteria provides an example of natural selection in action. Consider what can happen when you take an antibiotic to treat a bacterial infection. Many bacteria are killed by the treatment, but some may survive. Surviving bacteria have genes that confer resistance to the antibiotic. The survivors reproduce and pass on the trait for resistance to

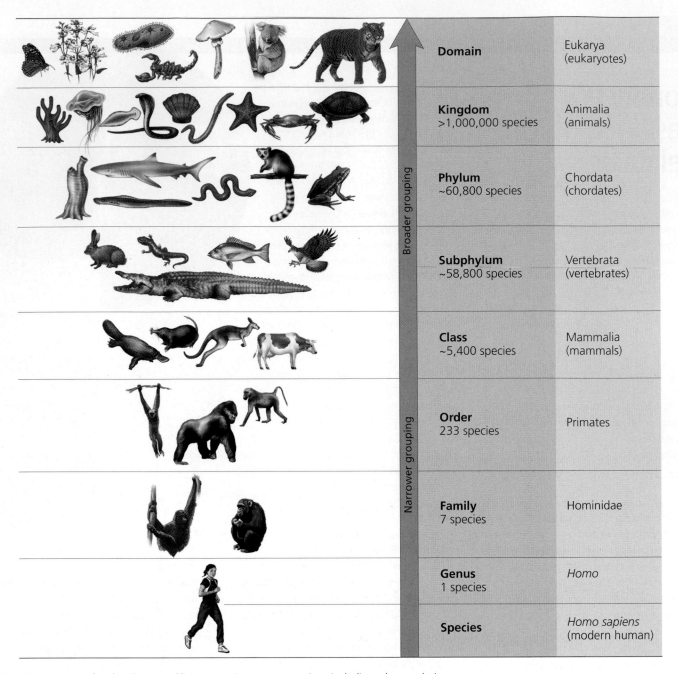

Domain		Eukarya (eukaryotes)
Kingdom >1,000,000 species		Animalia (animals)
Phylum ~60,800 species		Chordata (chordates)
Subphylum ~58,800 species		Vertebrata (vertebrates)
Class ~5,400 species		Mammalia (mammals)
Order 233 species		Primates
Family 7 species		Hominidae
Genus 1 species		*Homo*
Species		*Homo sapiens* (modern human)

Broader grouping → Narrower grouping

FIGURE 22.5 Categories in the classification of living organisms. Any organism, including a human being, can be classified using a hierarchy of increasingly general categories. Modern humans are called *Homo sapiens*. We are placed in the family Hominidae, along with gorillas (2 species), chimpanzees (2 species, common chimpanzee and bonobo), and orangutans (2 species). We are the only living species in our genus (*Homo*).

future generations of bacteria. Over time, antibiotic resistance becomes more common in bacterial populations than before. The evolution of drug-resistant strains can potentially become a serious threat to humankind (Chapter 13a).

Natural selection does not lead to perfect organisms. It can act on available variation only, and the available variation may not include the traits that would be ideal. Also, natural selection can only modify existing structures; it cannot produce completely new and different structures from scratch. Finally, organisms have to do many different things to survive and reproduce—such as escaping from predators and finding food, shelter, and mates—and it simply

is not possible to be perfect at everything. Indeed, adaptations often are compromises between the many competing demands the organism faces.

Macroevolution

Large-scale evolutionary change is macroevolution. Whereas microevolution involves changes in the frequencies of alleles within populations, macroevolution produces changes in groups of species, such as might occur with major changes in climate. Our discussion of macroevolution begins with a description of how species are named. We then consider how their evolutionary histories can be analyzed and diagrammed.

Scientific names

Systematic biology deals with the naming, classification, and evolutionary relationships of organisms. A universal system for naming and classifying organisms is essential for communicating information about them. Scientists use the naming system that Swedish naturalist Carl Linnaeus developed more than 200 years ago. Each organism is given a Latin binomial, or two-part name, consisting of the genus name followed by the specific epithet (the term *specific,* here, means relating to species). For example, humans are in the genus *Homo,* and our specific epithet is *sapiens,* so our binomial is *Homo sapiens.* By convention, the genus name and specific epithet are italicized, the first letter of the genus name is always capitalized, and the specific epithet is all lowercase. Sometimes, the genus name is abbreviated: *H. sapiens.*

Linnaeus also developed a system for classifying organisms using a series of increasingly broad categories: species, genus, family, order, class, phylum, and kingdom. Similar species were placed in the same genus; similar genera (the plural of *genus*) were placed in the same family; similar families in the same order, and so on. Above the kingdom level, scientists have added the category domain to Linnaeus's scheme (the three domains are Archaea, Bacteria, and Eukarya; see Chapter 1). Sometimes the Linnaean categories have subdivisions; for example, subfamilies within families, suborders within orders, and subphyla within phyla. Figure **22.5** presents the categories humans belong to.

Phylogenetic trees

Phylogenetic trees are branching diagrams used by scientists to depict hypotheses about evolutionary relationships among species or groups of species. Such trees can illustrate in simple graphic form concepts that are difficult to express in words.

Scientists developing hypotheses about these relationships may begin by creating a character matrix, such as the example in Figure **22.6a.** The character matrix can then be used to construct a phylogenetic tree. Typical matrices consist of vertical columns representing species or other groups, and horizontal rows representing "characters" that are either present or absent in those species or groups. Figure 22.6a shows a simple matrix with a shark (fish), frog (amphibian), and human (mammal) being compared regarding the presence or absence of three characters: two paired appendages (fins or limbs), individual digits, and hair. A phylogenetic tree based on the results from the matrix is shown in Figure 22.6b. This tree suggests that humans and frogs have more in common with one another (two paired appendages and individual digits) than either has with sharks (two paired appendages), and thus humans and frogs are likely to share a more recent common ancestor. The tree also shows that humans differ from frogs in having hair.

Evidence of Evolution

We know that evolution has occurred throughout Earth's history because the physical evidence of evolution surrounds us. Such evidence comes from many sources, including the fossil record, biogeography, the comparison of anatomical and embryological structures, and molecular biology.

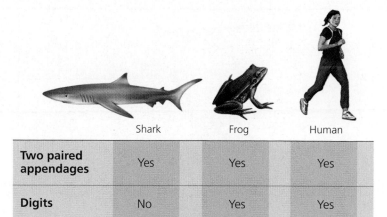

	Shark	Frog	Human
Two paired appendages	Yes	Yes	Yes
Digits	No	Yes	Yes
Hair	No	No	Yes

(a) A character matrix is used to construct a phylogenetic tree.

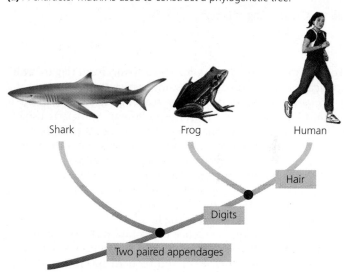

(b) A sample tree developed from the above character matrix

FIGURE 22.6 A phylogenetic tree depicts hypotheses about evolutionary relationships among organisms.

Fossil Record

Earth is littered with silent relics of organisms that lived long ago (Figure **22.7**). We find, for example, tiny spiders preserved in resin that dripped as sticky sap from some ancient tree. We find mineralized bones and teeth, hardened remains that tell us much about the ancestry of today's vertebrates (animals with a backbone). We also find impressions, such as footprints, of organisms that lived in the past. These preserved remnants and impressions of past organisms are **fossils.** Most fossils occur in sedimentary rocks, such as limestone, sandstone, shale, and chalk. These rocks form when sand and other particles settle to the bottoms of rivers, lakes, and oceans; accumulate in layers; and harden. Fossils also occur in volcanic ash, tar pits, and a few other specialized conditions.

(a) A spider preserved in amber

(b) An ancient act of predation preserved in sedimentary rocks

FIGURE 22.7 A sampling of past life in fossils

Fossilization is any process by which fossils form (Figure **22.8**). In a typical case, an organism dies and settles to the bottom of a body of water. If not destroyed by scavengers, the organism is buried under accumulating layers of sediment. Soft parts usually decay. Hard parts such as bones, teeth, and shells may be preserved if they become impregnated with minerals from surrounding water and sediments. As new layers of sediment are added, the older (lower) layers solidify under the pressure generated by overlying sediments. Eventually, if the sediments are uplifted by geological processes and the water disappears, weather may erode the surface of the rock formation and expose the fossil.

Fossils provide strong evidence of evolution. Fossils of extinct organisms show both similarities to and differences from living species. Similarities to other fossil and modern species are used to assess degrees of evolutionary relationships. Often, fossils reveal combinations of features not seen in any living forms. Such combinations help us understand how major new adaptations arose. Sometimes we are lucky enough to find transitional forms that closely link ancient organisms to modern species. Consider several fossil whales discovered in the last 30 or so years; these fossils document a progression from terrestrial forms with fore and hind limbs to more aquatic forms with reduced hind limbs to modern whales, which are fully aquatic and have no hind limbs (Figure **22.9a**). Additionally, some fossil whale remains have been discovered that have an ankle-bone with a diagnostic shape; the bone is the astragalus, and the shape is that of a double pulley (Figure 22.9b). The double pulley astragalus is characteristic of artiodactyls (an order of hoofed mammals that includes hippos, camels, deer, and cows). Discovery of this anklebone with a double pulley shape in fossil whales provides strong support for a close phylogenetic relationship between whales and artiodactyls.

Radiometric dating can be used to obtain estimates of the *absolute ages* of rocks and fossils. This technique relies on measuring the proportions of a radioactive isotope and its decay product. For example, radioactive potassium decays at a constant rate to form argon, so the ratio of radioactive potassium to argon in a fossil can be used to estimate the absolute age of the fossil. The *relative ages* of fossils can be determined because fossils found in deeper layers of rock are typically older than those found in layers closer to the surface. These kinds of observations enable scientists to

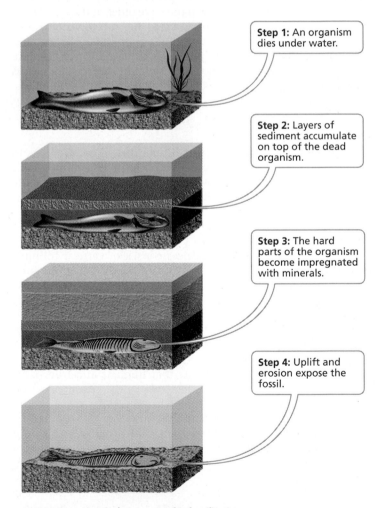

Step 1: An organism dies under water.

Step 2: Layers of sediment accumulate on top of the dead organism.

Step 3: The hard parts of the organism become impregnated with minerals.

Step 4: Uplift and erosion expose the fossil.

FIGURE 22.8 A typical sequence for fossilization

Bowhead whale,
Balaena mysticetus
- Extant
- 15–18 m long
- fully marine
- vestigial pelvis and hind limbs

Dorudon
- 40 million years ago
- 6 m long
- fully marine
- reduced hind limbs
- no connection of pelvis
  to vertebral column

Rodhocetus
- 46 million years ago
- 3 m long
- spent time on land and in water
- hind limbs
- pelvis connected to
  vertebral column

Pakicetus
- 52 million years ago
- 1.8 m long
- spent time on land and in water
- hind limbs
- pelvis connected to
  vertebral column

(a) Several fossils reveal that whales evolved from terrestrial mammals that returned to the water.

(b) Discovery in fossil whales of an ankle bone (astragalus) with a double pulley shape links whales and artiodactyls (an order of hoofed mammals that includes hippos, cows, deer, and pronghorn). In the left photograph, the astragalus on the left is from the fossil whale _Rodhocetus_ while that on the right is from a modern day pronghorn (shown in the right photograph).

FIGURE 22.9 The evolution of whales as revealed by transitional fossils

piece together the chronological emergence of different kinds of organisms. For example, fishes are the first fossil vertebrates to appear in deep (old) layers of rock. Above those layers, fossils of amphibians appear, then reptiles, then mammals, and finally birds. This chronological sequence for the appearance of the major groups of vertebrates has been supported by other lines of evidence, some of which we consider later in this section. Other large-scale evolutionary events revealed by the fossil record include changes in diversity over time and changes in faunas (animal life) and floras (plant life) as continents moved (geologists have mapped major changes in the sizes and locations of continents over time using the fossil record).

Although the fossil record tells us much about past life, it has limitations. First, fossils are relatively rare. When most animals or plants die, their remains are eaten by predators or scavengers or are broken down by microorganisms, chemicals, or mechanical processes. Even if a fossil should form, the chances are small that it will be exposed by erosion or other forces and not be destroyed by those same forces before it is discovered. Second, the fossil record represents a biased sampling of past life. Aquatic plants and animals have a much higher probability of being buried in deep sediment than do terrestrial organisms. Thus preservation of aquatic organisms is more likely. Large animals with a hard skeleton are far more likely to be preserved than are small animals with soft parts. Organisms from large, enduring populations are more likely to be represented in the fossil record than are those from small, quickly disappearing populations. Despite these limitations, fossils document that life on Earth has not always been the same as it is today. The simple fact of these changes is potent evidence of evolution.

Geographic Distributions

Biogeography is the study of the geographic distribution of organisms. Geographic distributions often reflect evolutionary history and relationships because related species are more likely than are unrelated species to be found in the same geographic area. A careful comparison of the animals in a given place with those occurring elsewhere can yield clues about the relationship of the groups. If groups of animals have been separated, biogeography can tell us how long ago the separation occurred.

For example, today we find many species of marsupials—mammal species such as opossums and kangaroos, in which the female often has a pouch—in Australia but only a few in North and South America. The presence of so many species of marsupials in Australia suggests that they arose from distant ancestors whose descendants were not replaced by animals arriving from other regions. New distributions of organisms occur by two basic mechanisms. In one mechanism, the organisms disperse to new areas. In the other mechanism, the areas occupied by the organisms move or are subdivided. Australia is an island, remote from other major continental landmasses. The evolutionary history of the Australian marsupials involves both dispersal and the movement of continents. Fossil evidence suggests that marsupials evolved in the Northern Hemisphere (probably North America) and that some dispersed southward into South America, then to Antarctica, and later to Australia, to which Antarctica was attached at the time (Figure **22.10**). As Australia and other landmasses slowly shifted to form the modern continental arrangement, the ancestors of today's marsupials were carried away from their place of origin to evolve in isolation in Australia. As the continental landmasses separated, they carried populations of other living things with them as well. Trees, freshwater fish, and even birds are quite different in Australia than in other parts of the world, reflecting Australia's long history of isolation and continental movement.

Comparative Anatomy and Embryology

Comparative anatomy, as its name suggests, is the comparison of the anatomies (physical structures) of different species. Common, or shared, traits among different species have long been considered a measure of relatedness. Put simply, two species with more shared traits are considered more closely related than are two species without shared traits (this principle underlies the use of character matrices to construct phylogenetic trees). For example, most vertebrates alive today have jaws and paired fins or limbs. All vertebrates with these features are likely to share a common ancestor. As another example, many very different vertebrates share similarities in the bones of their forelimbs, showing that they too have an ancestor in common (Figure **22.11**). Structures that are similar and that probably arose from a common ancestry are called **homologous structures**. The forelimbs that support bird wings and bat wings are homologous structures. Sometimes, however, similarities are not inherited from a common ancestor. For example, bird wings and insect wings

FIGURE 22.10 The story of marsupials and Australia involves both dispersal and movement of continents.

both permit flight, but they are made from entirely different structures. Whereas bird wings consist of forelimbs, insect wings are not true appendages; they are extensions of the insect's cuticle (exoskeleton). Thus, the wings of birds and insects do not reflect common ancestry. Instead, birds and insects independently evolved wings because of similar ecological roles and selection pressures, in a process known as **convergent evolution.** Structures that are similar because of convergent evolution are called **analogous structures.**

Homologous structures arise from the same kind of embryonic tissue. Hence, comparative embryology, the comparative study of early development, also can be a useful tool for studying evolution (Figure **22.12**). Common embryological origins can be considered evidence of common descent. For example, 4-week-old human embryos closely resemble embryos of other vertebrates, including fish. Indeed, human embryos at 4 weeks gestation come complete with a tail and gill pouches, as shown in Figure 22.12. As development proceeds, the gill pouches of fish develop into gills. The gill pouches of humans develop into other structures such as the auditory tubes connecting the middle ear and throat. Nevertheless, the fact that human, fish, and all other vertebrate embryos look very similar at early stages of development indicates common descent from an ancient ancestor.

FIGURE 22.11 Homologous structures. The similarity of the forelimb bones of humans, dolphins, bats, and birds suggests that these organisms share a common ancestry.

Comparative Molecular Biology

Just as visible traits such as forelimbs can be compared, so can the molecules that are the basic building blocks of life. For example, scientists can compare the sequences of amino acids in proteins or the nucleotide sequences in DNA. As described in Chapter 21, the Human Genome Project has provided information on the location of genes along our chromosomes and the order of the base pairs that make up our chromosomes. More recently, the chimpanzee's genome has been described and compared with that of humans. Such comparison reveals that the two genomes are strikingly similar; for example, the DNA sequence that can be directly compared between chimp and human genomes is about 99% identical.

Because of background radiation and errors in copying DNA, single-nucleotide changes in DNA, called point mutations, occur

Development

Fish

Gill pouches

Tail

Salamander

Gill pouches

Tail

Tortoise

Gill pouches

Tail

Chicken

Gill pouches

Tail

Human

Humans, like other vertebrates, have gill pouches and a tail early in development.

Gill pouches

Tail

FIGURE 22.12 Resemblance early in development indicates common descent. Embryos in the different representative vertebrates are not to scale; they have been drawn to the same approximate size to permit comparison.

constantly over evolutionary time with clocklike regularity. The rates of these changes vary from gene to gene. Once calibrated against the fossil record, these **molecular clocks** allow scientists to compare DNA sequences in two species as a way of estimating the amount of time that has passed since the two species diverged from a single common ancestor. The more different the sequences, the more time that has elapsed since their common ancestor. For example, comparison of DNA sequences tells us that humans and chimpanzees diverged from a common ancestor about 6 million years ago, making chimpanzees our closest living relatives. (See the Ethical Issue essay, *Conducting Research on Our Relatives.*)

We have learned about microevolution, macroevolution, and the evidence for evolution. Now let's look at our own past and see how humans evolved.

Human Evolution

We begin our discussion of human evolution with the primates, an order of mammals that includes humans, apes, monkeys, and related forms (such as lemurs). Scientists disagree about how long ago the first primates evolved. Paleontologists (scientists who study fossils) believe that primates evolved about 65 million years ago. This estimate takes into account that the oldest primate fossils are about 55 million years old, and as mentioned previously, organisms are assumed to evolve earlier than when they first appear in the fossil record. In contrast, molecular biologists have suggested that primates evolved about 90 million years ago. Their estimate is based on comparison of DNA sequences. Despite debate over when primates evolved, most scientists agree that the first primates probably arose from an insect-eating mammal that lived in trees. This ancestor to primates might have looked something like a modern tree shrew (Figure **22.13**).

FIGURE 22.13 A tree shrew. These modern animals resemble the arboreal, insect-eating mammals from which primates probably evolved more than 65 million years ago.

stop and think

In the following discussion of our ancestry, we describe the species that led to us. At some point the line *became* us. Before you start reading about our ancestry, what qualities would you now say are necessary for a species to qualify as human?

Primate Characteristics

Primates have several distinguishing characteristics (see Table **22.1**). Many of these characteristics reflect an arboreal lifestyle specialized for the visual hunting and manual capture of insects. For example, primates have flexible, rotating shoulder joints and exceptionally mobile digits with sensitive pads on their ends. Flattened nails replace claws. In many primate species, the big toe is separated from the other toes, and thumbs are opposable to other fingers. Thus, primates have grasping feet *and* hands, features that help in the pursuit and capture of insects along branches. In addition, a complex visual system (forward-facing eyes with stereoscopic vision) and a large brain relative to body size provide the well-developed depth perception, hand–eye coordination, and neuromuscular control needed by arboreal insectivores. The relatively large brain is also associated with complex social behavior (for example, members of social groups may form long-term alliances) and reliance on learned behavior (for example, tool use may be passed from one individual to the next through observation and imitation). Also, most primates give birth to only one infant at a time (even two is quite rare) and provide extensive parental care—these characteristics may reflect the difficulty of carrying and rearing multiple infants in trees.

Modern primates are divided into two main groups (suborders): Strepsirrhini and Haplorrhini. Suborder Strepsirrhini contains lemurs, lorises, and pottos (grouped together because they retain ancestral primate features such as small body size and nocturnal habits). Figure **22.14** shows representatives of this suborder. Suborder Haplorrhini contains monkeys, apes, and humans (Figure **22.15**).

TABLE 22.1 Review of Primate Characteristics

Flexible shoulder joints

Grasping forelimbs; some species with fully opposable thumbs

Grasping feet, with big toes separated from other toes (except humans)

Sensitive digits with flattened nails instead of claws

Forward-facing eyes with stereoscopic vision*

Small litter size

Large brain relative to body size

Complex social behavior, including extensive parental care

Reliance on learned behavior

* Vision that results from two forward-facing eyes with overlapping fields of view, producing an integrated, three-dimensional image; enables good depth perception.

In the past, the term *hominid* was used to describe members of the human lineage, such as species in the genera *Australopithecus* and *Homo* (discussed later in this chapter). At that time, human and prehuman species were the only members of the family Hominidae. Primate classification has changed, however, and apes now are included in the family Hominidae (refer, again to Figure 22.5). Thus, the term *hominid* now include apes and humans (members of the family Hominidae). The term **hominin** now is used for the human lineage and its immediate ancestors (members of the subfamily Homininae). As described earlier, molecular evidence suggests that the lines leading to modern humans and chimpanzees diverged about 6 million years ago. Molecular data further indicate that, after chimpanzees, gorillas are our next closest living relatives, followed by orangutans and then gibbons. Figure **22.16** shows these hypothesized relationships among living primates.

(a) Ring-tailed lemur (*Lemur catta*)

(b) Slender loris (*Loris tardigradus*)

(c) Potto (*Perodicticus potto*)

FIGURE 22.14 Examples of modern primates from suborder Strepsirrhini. The female loris with young in part (b) illustrates many of the features characteristic of all primates and associated with an arboreal lifestyle, including grasping hands and feet, forward-facing eyes, and small litter size.

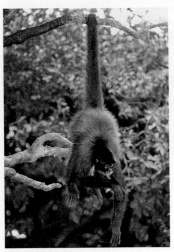

(a) Mexican spider monkey
(*Ateles geoffroyi vellerosus*)

(b) Olive baboons (*Papio anubis*)

(c) Bornean orangutans
(*Pongo pygmaeus*)

(d) Western gorilla (*Gorilla gorilla*)

FIGURE 22.15 Monkeys (such as spider monkeys and baboons) and apes (such as orangutans and gorillas) are placed with humans in the suborder Haplorrhini.

Lemurs   Pottos   New World monkeys   Old World monkeys   Gibbons   Orangutans   Gorillas   Chimpanzees   Humans

6 million years ago

at least 65 million years ago

Ancestral arboreal insectivore

FIGURE 22.16 Hypothesized relationships among extant primates. (Figures are not drawn to scale.)

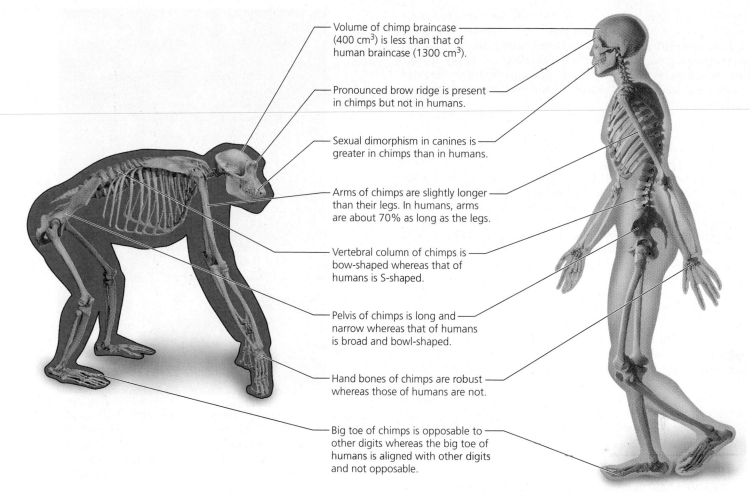

Volume of chimp braincase (400 cm³) is less than that of human braincase (1300 cm³).

Pronounced brow ridge is present in chimps but not in humans.

Sexual dimorphism in canines is greater in chimps than in humans.

Arms of chimps are slightly longer than their legs. In humans, arms are about 70% as long as the legs.

Vertebral column of chimps is bow-shaped whereas that of humans is S-shaped.

Pelvis of chimps is long and narrow whereas that of humans is broad and bowl-shaped.

Hand bones of chimps are robust whereas those of humans are not.

Big toe of chimps is opposable to other digits whereas the big toe of humans is aligned with other digits and not opposable.

FIGURE 22.17 Some major differences in skeletal anatomy and teeth between chimpanzees and humans. Many of these traits reflect differences in locomotion and stance. Whereas chimpanzees are quadrupedal knuckle-walkers, humans are bipedal with an upright stance.

Comparison of human and chimp skeletal anatomy

Humans are the most terrestrial of primates. Many aspects of our skeletal anatomy reflect this terrestrial lifestyle as well as our upright stance while walking. Walking on two feet is called **bipedalism.** Our S-shaped spine and relatively large patella (kneecap) reflect a bipedal gait. Although chimpanzees can walk on two feet, they typically use quadrupedal knuckle-walking when moving on the ground. Their hand bones are more robust than ours because they bear weight during terrestrial locomotion. Chimps also spend time in trees, where they use their arms in locomotion. Thus, the arms of chimps are long and exceptionally strong; the strength is reflected in the extensive areas on the scapula (shoulder blade) for the attachment of large arm muscles. Unlike humans, chimps have opposable big toes, another adaptation for climbing. Anatomical differences between chimpanzees and humans also are apparent in the skull and teeth. Chimps have a smaller braincase than humans, but more pronounced brow ridges and jutting jaws. The degree of *sexual dimorphism* (difference in appearance between the sexes) in canine teeth also is more pronounced in chimps than in humans; specifically, the canines are larger in males than in females in both species, but the sex difference is greater in chimps. Figure **22.17** shows some of the major differences between chimps and humans in hard anatomy (teeth and skeleton).

Paleoanthropology

Paleoanthropology is the scientific study of human origins and evolution. This field combines the disciplines of paleontology (the study of fossils) and anthropology (the study of humans). Paleoanthropology faces at least two major challenges: (1) the scarcity of hominin remains found to date; and (2) the difficulty of assessing whether observed variation in hominin remains represents variation between species or within species. Indeed, simply defining a species can be difficult when it comes to fossils. Recall that one definition of a species is that its members can successfully interbreed under natural conditions; this definition cannot be applied to fossils, so paleoanthropologists must rely on morphological differences (usually in skeletal anatomy) to define species.

Some of the difficulties associated with reconstructing past hominin diversity have arisen because of practices followed by early paleoanthropologists. In the past, paleoanthropologists tended to give each new fossil discovery a new name and to consider it an example of a separate line. In some cases, paleoanthropologists failed to consider the inevitability of variation in any given population. Two specimens that differed slightly in some traits were likely to be interpreted as belonging to different lines when in fact they simply may have been examples of variation within a species. (A look at the amount of variation in skeletal and dental anatomy among today's humans gives you an idea of wide variation that can occur within a species.) Also, it can be difficult to determine whether morphological differences between fossil hominins (or fossils of any taxonomic group) represent real differences or simply artifacts of the fossilization process. This is particularly true when few remains are available for examination and comparison, as they are for fossil hominins.

Misconceptions

Several popular misconceptions about human evolution exist among nonscientists. One misconception is the idea that we descended from chimpanzees or any of the other modern apes. Humans and chimpanzees represent separate phylogenetic branches that diverged about 6 million years ago. Thus the common ancestor of humans and chimpanzees was different from any modern species of ape.

Another misconception is that modern humans evolved in an orderly, stepwise fashion. We often see such a stepwise progression depicted in drawings, sometimes humorously, and its appeal lies in its simplicity. However, as is so often the case, the real story is less tidy and far more complex. The path to modern humans has been fraught with unsuccessful phenotypes leading to dead end after dead end. In fact, the path looks more like a family "bush" than an orderly progression from primitive to modern.

A final misconception is that, over the course of human evolution, the various bones and organ systems evolved simultaneously and at the same rate. They did not. There is no reason to believe that the human brain evolved at the same rate as, say, the appendix or the foot. Instead, different traits evolved at different times and rates, by a phenomenon known as **mosaic evolution.**

Bipedalism

Several evolutionary trends are apparent in the history of hominins. (Table **22.2** summarizes these major trends.) Bipedalism evolved early and probably set the stage for the evolution of other characteristics, such as increases in brain size. Cultural developments, such as tool use and language, are linked to increases in brain size. Once the hands were freed from the requirements of locomotion, they could be used for tasks such as making tools. Evidence that bipedalism preceded increases in brain size and cultural developments comes from fossilized hominin footprints found in Tanzania, Africa. These footprints, estimated to be about 3.6 million years old, were apparently made by two adults and a child (Figure **22.18**). The footprints clearly predate the oldest stone tools, from 2.6 million years ago. Other changes associated with upright posture include the S-shaped curvature of the vertebral column (the lumbar curve); modifications to the bones and muscles of the pelvis, legs, and feet; and positioning of the skull on top of the vertebral column (refer again to the human skeleton in Figure 22.17).

FIGURE 22.18 These hominin footprints from Laetoli, Tanzania, predate the oldest known tools and thus provide evidence that bipedalism preceded increases in brain size and cultural trends such as toolmaking. The larger prints were made by two individuals, one following in the other's footsteps. The smaller prints may have been made by a child walking with the two individuals.

The faces of hominins also changed. For example, the forehead changed from sloping to vertical, and sites of muscle attachment, such as the brow ridges and crests on the skull, became smaller. The jaws became shorter, and the nose and chin more prominent. The overall size difference between males and females decreased. Males of our early ancestors appear to have been 1.5 times as heavy as females. Modern human males weigh about 1.2 times as much as females.

In the following discussion of our ancestors, we focus on the hominins that we know the most about—those in the genus *Australopithecus* and the genus *Homo*. We also mention some recent finds of apparently older hominins. Keep in mind that as new hominin fossils are found and genetic studies conducted, the dates for the origin of some species may be pushed back.

Australopithecines

The first hominin remains discovered were given the genus name *Australopithecus,* meaning "southern ape." Species within *Australopithecus* are sometimes collectively termed australopithecines. *Australopithecus anamensis,* considered the earliest species of the australopithecine line, is known from a small number of fossils found in Kenya and Ethiopia and dated between 4.2 and 3.9 million years old. The most spectacular australopithecine fossil found to date is that of a young adult female of the species *Australopithecus afarensis* (because she was found in the Afar region of Ethiopia). She was named Lucy by the scientists who discovered her in 1974. More

TABLE 22.2 Review of Major Trends in Hominin Evolution
Bipedalism
Increasing brain size and associated cultural trends such as tool use, language, and behavioral complexity
Shortening of the jaw and flattening of the face
Reduced difference in size between males and females

than 60 pieces of Lucy's bones were found; when the bones were arranged, scientists estimated that, at death, she was about 1 m (3 ft) tall and weighed about 30 kg (66 lb; Figure **22.19**). Her bones were determined to be 3.2 million years old. As more remains were found, it became apparent that the males of Lucy's species were somewhat taller (about 1.5 m, or about 5 ft) and heavier (about 45 kg, or 99 lb). The brain of *A. afarensis* was similar in size to that of modern chimpanzees or gorillas—about 430 cm^3 (26 in.^{3}). Although many aspects of the anatomy of *A. afarensis* suggest adaptations for living in trees, the remains also indicate bipedalism. In *A. afarensis,* we see an example of mosaic evolution—bipedalism evolving before substantial increases in brain size.

Since the mid-1990s, researchers have found hominin remains older than those of *A. anamensis*. Some remains from Ethiopia were dated at 4.4 million years old and assigned to the species *Ardipithecus ramidus*. Some researchers think *A. ramidus* displayed bipedalism, although that point is debated. Another uncertainty is whether *A. ramidus* is the ancestor of *Australopithecus* or a separate line that became extinct.

(a) The remarkably complete skeleton of Lucy

(b) Reconstruction of Lucy on display at the St. Louis Zoo

FIGURE 22.19 Fossilized remains and reconstruction of Lucy, a young female of the hominin species *Australopithecus afarensis*. She was named Lucy because the Beatles' song "Lucy in the Sky with Diamonds" was playing the night Donald Johanson and his coworkers celebrated her discovery.

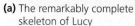

stop and think

Brain size and shape can be estimated by making an endocast, a model of the inside of the skull. Such reconstructions are possible even when only a few parts of the skull are discovered and reassembled. Endocasts reveal general brain anatomy and size, allowing scientists to draw tentative conclusions about the cognitive capabilities of the skull's owner. Endocasts do not, however, capture the folds or convolutions on the surface of a brain. Do you think endocasts and brain volumes make reliable indicators of intelligence? Why or why not?

About 3 million years ago, when *A. afarensis* had been in existence for nearly 1 million years, several new hominin species appeared in the fossil record. Scientists believe that *Australopithecus africanus*, one of these new species, was a hunting-and-gathering omnivore. *A. africanus,* like *A. afarensis,* was a gracile (or slender) hominin. Three more "robust" hominins (previously called *Australopithecus aethiopicus, A. robustus,* and *A. boisei,* but now considered by many researchers to represent a group deserving of placement in a separate genus, *Paranthropus*) also appeared and are thought to have been savanna-dwelling vegetarians. The robust hominins had a massive skull, heavy facial bones, a pronounced brow, and huge teeth. Whatever they ate, it required a lot of chewing. It is unclear whether Lucy's species, *A. afarensis,* gave rise to these other species or simply lived at the same time as they did. While the robust hominins appear to have been evolutionary dead ends, descendants of *A. afarensis* may have led to our genus, the genus *Homo*.

Homo habilis

Homo habilis ("handy man"), the first member of the modern genus of humans, appeared in the fossil record about 2.5 million years ago. The remains classified as *H. habilis* are highly variable, causing some researchers to question their classification. Some researchers believe the remains are varied enough to represent more than one species. *H. habilis* differed from *A. afarensis* primarily in brain size. The cranial capacity of *H. habilis* has been estimated at between 500 and 800 cm^3 (30 and 49 in.^{3}). Some scientists hypothesize that *H. habilis* was the first hominin to use stone tools.

Simple stone tools, dating from 2.5 million to 2.7 million years ago, have been found in Africa. Whether these tools were used by *H. habilis* or one of the species of robust hominins is unclear. *H. habilis* also may have been capable of rudimentary speech. Casts of one brain made from reassembled skull fragments indicate a bulge in Broca's area, the area of the brain important in speech (see Chapter 8).

Homo ergaster and Homo erectus

A new hominin, *Homo ergaster* ("working man"), appeared in the fossil record about 1.9 million years ago. The name reflects the many tools found with the remains. Traditionally, scientists had classified these remains as *Homo erectus* ("upright man"), but they now differentiate them from *H. erectus*. *H. ergaster* appears to have originated in East Africa and coexisted there for several thousand years with some of the robust hominins.

H. erectus is thought to have diverged from *H. ergaster* around 1.6 million years ago. *H. erectus* was a wanderer, believed by many to be the first hominin to migrate out of Africa, spreading to Asia. *H. erectus* differed from earlier hominins in being larger (up to 1.85 m, or 6 ft tall, and weighing at least 65 kg, or 143 lb) and less sexually dimorphic. *H. erectus* had a brain volume of about 1000 cm^3 (61 in.^{3}). Evidence indicates that *H. erectus* used sophisticated tools and weapons and in addition may have used fire. *H. erectus* disappeared from most locations about 400,000 years ago, but some remains from Java have been dated at only 50,000 years. The Java remains suggest that at least one population of *H. erectus* existed at the same time as modern humans (*Homo sapiens*).

Homo heidelbergensis, Homo sapiens, and Homo neanderthalensis

The origins of anatomically modern humans over the last 500,000 years are difficult to trace with certainty, and different interpretations exist. Traditionally, fossils that did not quite resemble modern humans were classified as Archaic *Homo sapiens*. Scientists now place these fossils in the species *Homo heidelbergensis;* the name refers to Heidelberg, Germany, where a fossil lower jaw intermediate to those of earlier forms and *H. sapiens* was found. Many scientists now believe that *H. heidelbergensis* evolved from *H. ergaster* and not *H. erectus. H. heidelbergensis* ranges from about 800,000 years ago to about 130,000 years ago, which is when the first anatomically modern human remains show up in the fossil record. Thus, scientists postulate that *H. sapiens* evolved from *H. heidelbergensis*.

The oldest fossil evidence for modern humans (*H. sapiens* or "thinking man") comes from Africa and is about 130,000 years old. *H. sapiens* differs from earlier humans in having a larger brain (1300 cm³, or 79 in.³), flat forehead, absent or very small brow ridges, prominent chin, and a very slender body form.

Neanderthals, close evolutionary relatives of ours, are known from Europe and Asia from about 200,000 years ago to 30,000 years ago. Neanderthals had distinct features apparently adapted for life in a cold climate. Some Neanderthals lived in caves ("the cave men"), and others made temporary camps (Figure **22.20a**). Neanderthal burial sites have been discovered, making them the first hominins known to have buried their dead. Also, the discovery of 50,000-year-old remains of sick, injured, and elderly individuals suggests that Neanderthals cared for the less fortunate among them.

Interestingly, Neanderthals had a larger braincase than do *H. sapiens* and a slightly larger brain volume (about 1450 cm³ or 88 in.³). However, these features may not correlate with intelligence but rather with the Neanderthals' more massive body. They had larger bones, suggesting heavier musculature, and rather short legs. They also had a thick brow ridge, large nose, broad face, and well-developed incisors and canines. Some anthropologists consider Neanderthals to be a subspecies of *H. sapiens* and call them *H. sapiens neanderthalensis* (according to this scheme, modern humans are known as *H. sapiens sapiens*). Most anthropologists, however, assign Neanderthals species status and call them *Homo neanderthalensis*.

Neanderthals vanished from the fossil record some 30,000 years ago for still mysterious reasons. Some scientists suggest they were outcompeted or simply killed outright by a form of *H. sapiens* called Cro-Magnons (Figure 22.20b). Other scientists suggest that interbreeding between anatomically modern humans and Neanderthals might have resulted in the loss of the Neanderthal phenotype. The extent and type of interactions between Neanderthals and Cro-Magnons are still debated. It is clear, however, that the Cro-Magnons had superior tools and weapons, including bows and arrows, knives, and stone-tipped spears. It is generally believed that Cro-Magnons were quite similar in appearance to humans of today and lived in small to moderate-sized groups. They also were accomplished hunters and artists.

About 12,000 years ago, *H. sapiens* changed from a nomadic lifestyle to a more sedentary one. Associated with this change were two major milestones in human history: the domestication of animals and the cultivation of crops. For example, mammals were domesticated for protection (dogs), food (cattle, pigs, and goats), transport (horses, camels, donkeys), wool (llamas and alpacas), and rodent control (cats and ferrets). Agriculture began with the cultivation of cereal grains about 9000 years ago.

Major milestones in human evolution are summarized in Table **22.3**, and the major hominin species are shown in Figure **22.21**.

(a) The Neanderthals had an appearance adapted for life in a cold climate. Some anthropologists consider Neanderthals to be a subspecies of our own species; others consider them a separate species.

(b) The Cro-Magnons were quite similar to us in appearance, and some anthropologists believe they were responsible for the disappearance of the Neanderthals.

FIGURE 22.20 Relatively recent representatives of the genus *Homo*. These photographs were taken at a museum display.

what would you do?

Human remains can tell scientists much about the diets, diseases, lifestyles, and genetic relationships of our ancestors. Such information can help piece together our evolutionary past. Sometimes, however, keeping human remains for scientific study conflicts with the wishes of modern-day descendants who wish to have their ancestors' remains returned to them for reburial. In the United States, for example, many museums and universities are developing policies for the treatment and disposition of Native American and Native Hawaiian remains. How should human remains be treated and, in the end, who should get them? If you were a museum director developing a policy for the treatment of human remains, what would you do?

TABLE 22.3 Review of Some Milestones in Human Evolution

Hominin	Years Ago	Milestone
Ardipithecus ramidus	4.4 million	Bipedalism?
Homo habilis	2.4–1.6 million	Tool use, speech
Homo erectus	1.6 million–50,000	Fire, migration
Homo neanderthalensis*	200,000–30,000	Buried their dead
Homo sapiens	130,000–present	Domestication of animals, agriculture

*Some scientists consider Neanderthals to be a subspecies of Homo sapiens *and call them* Homo sapiens neanderthalensis.

Did modern humans evolve several times in different regions? The idea that they did is known as the **multiregional hypothesis.** It suggests that modern humans evolved independently in locations such as Europe, Asia, and Africa from distinctive local populations of earlier humans. The alternative idea is known as the **Out of Africa hypothesis.** It suggests a single origin for all *H. sapiens*. According to the Out of Africa hypothesis, anatomically modern humans evolved from earlier humans in Africa and only later migrated to Europe, Asia, and other locations, where they replaced earlier human populations.

Q *Does this figure support or contradict the notion that humans evolved in an orderly, stepwise manner from primitive to modern? Explain your answer.*

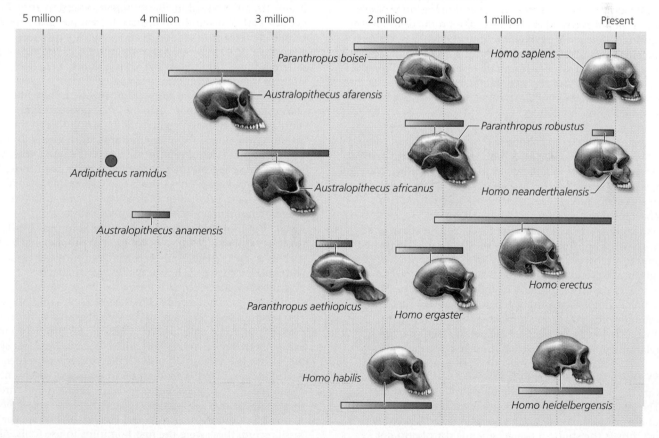

FIGURE 22.21 The major hominin species. Horizontal purple lines indicate the length of time each species existed. Fossil evidence for *Ardipithecus ramidus* is limited, so the dates when this species lived are not available; thus, we use a purple dot instead.

A *This figure contradicts the notion of an orderly progression from primitive to modern because it shows that more than one species of hominin existed simultaneously at some points in the past.*

highlighting the concepts

Evolution of Life on Earth (pp. 483–485)

- Earth is estimated to be 4.5 billion years old, and life is thought to have originated about 3.8 billion years ago. A plausible sequence of events known as chemical evolution suggests that life arose from small organic molecules, synthesized from inorganic molecules. The small organic molecules then grew increasingly complex over a long period of time. A critical step in this process was the origin of genetic material (possibly RNA and not DNA), which allowed the transfer of information from one generation to the next. Eventually, large organic molecules aggregated into droplets that became the precursors to cells.
- The earliest cells were prokaryotic. According to the endosymbiont theory, more complex cells formed as smaller organisms were incorporated into the cells, forming organelles such as mitochondria. Another possibility is that some organelles formed by infolding of the plasma membrane. Multicellularity evolved, leading to the appearance on Earth of organisms such as plants and animals.

Scale of Evolutionary Change (pp. 485–489)

- Microevolution involves change in the frequencies of alleles within populations over a few generations. Macroevolution is large-scale evolution such as the origin or extinction of groups of species over long periods of time. Speciation is the formation of new species.
- Populations are groups of individuals of the same species that live in a particular area. Sexual reproduction and mutation produce variation in populations. Regarding sexual reproduction, sources of variation include crossing over and independent assortment during meiosis. Also, fertilization produces a zygote with new combinations of alleles. Mutations, rare changes in the DNA of genes, produce new genes and new alleles.
- A gene pool is a collection of all the alleles of all the genes of all the individuals in a population.
- Causes of microevolution include genetic drift (random change in allele frequencies due to chance within a small population), gene flow (movement of alleles as individuals move into and out of populations), mutation (change in the DNA of genes), and natural selection (mechanism of evolutionary change by which traits of successful individuals—those that survive and reproduce—become more common in a population).
- Systematic biology deals with the naming, classification, and evolutionary relationships of organisms. Organisms are named according to a scheme developed by Carl Linnaeus: each organism is given a two-part name consisting of the genus name followed by the specific epithet. Organisms also may be classified using a hierarchy of increasingly general categories: species, genus, family, order, class, phylum, kingdom, and domain. A phylogenetic tree is a schematic diagram depicting hypothesized relationships among species or higher categories.

Evidence of Evolution (pp. 489–494)

- Fossils are the preserved remnants and impressions of past organisms. The fossil record provides evidence of evolution by documenting that life on Earth has not always been the same as it is today.
- Biogeography is the study of the geographic distribution of organisms. New distributions of organisms occur either when the organisms disperse to a new location or when the areas they occupy move or are subdivided. In general, related species are more likely than are unrelated species to be found in the same geographic area.
- Comparative anatomy and embryology also provide evidence of evolution. In general, species with more shared traits are considered more likely to be related. Structures that have arisen from common ancestry are called homologous structures and usually arise from the same embryonic tissue. Thus, common embryological origins can also be viewed as evidence of common descent.
- Molecules that are the basic building blocks of life can be compared for evidence of evolution. For example, scientists compare the sequences of amino acids in proteins or the nucleotide sequences in DNA of different species to gauge relatedness and to estimate the time of divergence from a most recent common ancestor.

Human Evolution (pp. 494–501)

- Humans are primates, an order of mammals that also includes lemurs, monkeys, and apes. Primates have forward-facing eyes with stereoscopic vision, flexible shoulder joints, and grasping forelimbs and feet. Flattened nails—rather than claws—cover their sensitive digits. Primates provide extensive parental care to a small number of offspring.
- There are two suborders of modern primates. Suborder Strepsirrhini includes lemurs, lorises, and pottos. Suborder Haplorrhini includes monkeys, apes, and humans. The term *hominin* refers to the human lineage and its immediate ancestors, such as species within the genera *Australopithecus* and *Homo*.
- Paleoanthropology is the study of human origins and evolution. Argument and confusion about human evolution arise, in part, because early paleoanthropologists did not recognize the variation likely to exist in any population. And so, mistakenly, they were inclined to interpret variation in traits as belonging to different lines. The scarcity of fossils is another challenge to the study of human evolution.
- Humans did *not* descend from chimpanzees; rather, humans and chimps represent separate branches that diverged from a common ancestor. Human evolution did *not* occur in an orderly progression from ancient to modern forms; during several periods two or more species of hominins lived at the same time, and some of those species lines were evolutionary dead ends. Traits of humans did *not* evolve at the same rate; instead, evidence indicates that traits of humans evolved at different rates, by a phenomenon known as mosaic evolution.
- Bipedalism probably evolved early on in hominins. Walking on two feet set the stage for the evolution of other characteristics such as an increase in brain size, which in turn was associated with cultural trends such as tool use and language.
- The oldest hominin remains found to date are those of *Ardipithecus ramidus*, estimated to be at least 4.4 million years old. Few fossils have been found of *Australopithecus anamensis*, the most primitive australopithecine; this species is believed to have existed between 4.2 and 3.9 million years ago. Excellent specimens have been found of *Australopithecus afarensis*, a species about 3.8 million years old. About 3 million years ago, several new hominin species appeared (*Australopithecus africanus* and three more robust species that are now placed in the genus *Paranthropus*).
- About 2.5 million years ago, *Homo habilis* remains appear in the fossil record; these were the first hominins to use tools. About 1.9 million years ago, *Homo ergaster* arose, and *Homo erectus* diverged from this species 1.6 million years ago. Fossils of *H. erectus* are not restricted to Africa, indicating that this was the first hominin to disperse from Africa; this species may also have used fire. The oldest remains of modern humans, *Homo sapiens*, are dated at 130,000 years old. *Homo neanderthalensis* was a cold-adapted species that coexisted with modern humans until about

30,000 years ago. Two major milestones of *H. sapiens* are the domestication of animals and the cultivation of crops.
- The multiregional hypothesis suggests that *H. sapiens* evolved independently in different regions from distinctive populations of

early humans. The Out of Africa hypothesis suggests that modern humans evolved from early humans in Africa and then dispersed to other regions, where they replaced existing hominin species.

recognizing key terms

evolution *p. 483*
chemical evolution *p. 483*
endosymbiont theory *p. 485*
microevolution *p. 485*
macroevolution *p. 485*
population *p. 485*
gene pool *p. 485*
mutation *p. 485*

genetic drift *p. 486*
bottleneck effect *p. 486*
founder effect *p. 486*
gene flow *p. 486*
species *p. 486*
speciation *p. 486*
natural selection *p. 486*
fitness *p. 486*

adaptation *p. 487*
phylogenetic trees *p. 489*
fossil *p. 489*
biogeography *p. 492*
homologous structure *p. 492*
convergent evolution *p. 492*
analogous structure *p. 492*
molecular clock *p. 494*

hominin *p. 495*
bipedalism *p. 497*
mosaic evolution *p. 498*
multiregional hypothesis *p. 501*
Out of Africa hypothesis *p. 501*

reviewing the concepts

1. How might life have evolved from inorganic molecules to complex cells? *pp. 483–485*
2. Distinguish between microevolution and macroevolution. *p. 485*
3. What are four sources of variation within populations? *p. 485*
4. How does genetic drift lead to microevolution? *p. 486*
5. Define speciation and relate it to gene flow. *p. 486*
6. Define natural selection. How can variation within populations be maintained in the face of natural selection? *p. 486*
7. Describe the binomial system by which organisms are named and the hierarchical system by which they are classified. *p. 489*
8. What is a phylogenetic tree? *p. 489*
9. What is a fossil? Describe the process of fossilization and relate it to limitations of the fossil record. *pp. 489–492*
10. How do new distributions of organisms arise? *p. 492*
11. Distinguish between homologous and analogous structures. *p. 492*
12. Describe how comparative embryology provides evidence of evolution. *p. 492*
13. What is a molecular clock? *pp. 493–494*
14. What characters set primates apart from other mammals? *p. 495*
15. Why do discussions of human evolution inspire controversy? *pp. 497–498*
16. What are three popular misconceptions about human evolution? *p. 498*
17. Describe the major species of hominins and trends in hominin evolution. *pp. 498–501*
18. Which of the following does *not* produce variation in populations?
   a. Bottleneck effect
   b. Mutation
   c. Crossing over
   d. Independent assortment
19. Which of the following occurs when fertile individuals move into and out of populations?
   a. Genetic drift
   b. Speciation
   c. Mutation
   d. Gene flow

20. Which of the following was in very short supply in the environment of the early Earth?
   a. Lightning
   b. Volcanoes
   c. Gaseous oxygen (O_2)
   d. UV radiation
21. The earliest cells
   a. were prokaryotic.
   b. were eukaryotic.
   c. evolved over 10 billion years ago.
   d. were part of multicellular organisms.
22. Which of the following primates is our closest living relative?
   a. Gorilla
   b. Orangutan
   c. Chimpanzee
   d. Gibbon
23. Which of the following features of an organism would promote fossilization?
   a. Terrestrial existence
   b. Member of a small population
   c. Soft body parts
   d. Aquatic existence
24. Which hominin was probably the first to migrate out of Africa?
   a. *Australopithecus afarensis*
   b. *Homo sapiens*
   c. *Homo erectus*
   d. *Australopithecus africanus*
25. The major events of human evolution occurred in
   a. Africa.
   b. South America.
   c. Europe.
   d. North America.
26. Which of the following hominin characters evolved the earliest?
   a. Bipedalism
   b. Large brain
   c. Language
   d. Use of fire
27. _____ is differential survival and reproduction.
28. _____ is when different traits evolve at different rates.
29. The _____ model of human evolution suggests that modern humans evolved independently in several places from local populations of earlier humans.

1. A friend of yours believes that all organisms were specially created. You believe in evolution and want to present your case to your friend. What would you say?
2. Can life arise on Earth from inorganic material today? Why or why not?
3. You are a biologist exploring the dense tropical rain forests of Brazil. You notice an unfamiliar medium-sized mammal moving above you in the trees. How would you determine whether this animal is a primate?
4. Tay-Sachs disease has zero fitness because it causes death before the individual reaches reproductive age. How does a trait with zero fitness persist in a population?

5. Did modern humans evolve from chimpanzees? Explain.
6. Apes have a fairly easy time giving birth, compared with humans. A female ape has a relatively large pelvis, and the small head of her infant passes easily through a roomy birth canal (the channel formed by the cervix, vagina, and vulva). Birth in humans is decidedly more difficult and risky. With its large head, the typical human fetus may spend hours making its way through a narrow birth canal. What trends in human evolution might have produced the tight squeeze of human birth?

Develop a presentation on tool use in extant vertebrates. Include the following in your presentation: a definition of tool use; the species in which tool use has been reported; the type of tool use described and the conditions under which it was observed; and any anatomical or behavioral traits associated with species that make and use tools. Use at least three sources; list these sources in your last slide, and briefly explain why you found them to be reliable.

Additional questions can be found online at The Human Biology Place, www.humanbiology.com.

23

Ecology, the Environment, and Us

The best legacy we can give our children is a world in ecological balance.

Jerome stopped the car next to the river. He knew that the eagles had started to arrive in Illinois a couple of days earlier. Bald eagles were once plentiful throughout North America. Three feet tall, with a majestic white head and impressive 7-foot wing span, they once nested and fished along most major waterways. Unfortunately, human settlers killed many eagles, and as the human population grew, wild places where the eagles could nest began to disappear. Moreover, when natural waters became polluted with industrial chemicals and pesticides, these substances eventually found their way into fish. Every time an eagle ate a contaminated fish, it was at risk. On July 4, 1976, the bald eagle, America's national bird, was officially listed as an Endangered Species. But now the eagles were coming back.

Jerome was eager to show them to his 3-year-old daughter, Alexis. "Look. There's a huge eagle up on the bluff!"

"Where?" asked Alexis, followed by "Wow! He's as tall as me!"

In this chapter, we see that humans are but one of a host of species that share our small planet. We have many of the same needs as other species, and we face many of the same threats. If we are ever to understand the world around us and our place in it, we must have some knowledge of its physical characteristics and understanding of our dependence on the other species we share it with.

Earth as an Ecosystem

Our focus in this chapter is ecology, a science whose name comes from the Greek words *oikos,* meaning "home," and *logos,* meaning "to study." Thus ecology is the study of our home—the Earth—encompassing both its living (biotic) components and nonliving (abiotic) components. More precisely, ecology is the study of the *interactions* between organisms and between organisms and the environment. Ecologists are the scientists who study these interactions.

If we could see the Earth (Figure **23.1**) from space, like an astronaut does, we would make two important observations about our home. First, we would see that Earth is isolated from other planets. So we could conclude that, aside from an occasional meteorite and other bits of debris from space, our planet has no source of new materials. In fact, many of the materials that came together to form it some 4.5 billion years ago cycle repeatedly from organism to organism and between the living and nonliving components of our world. A carbon atom in your body may once have been part of a dinosaur or part of Aristotle. Also, from our vantage point in space, we would be reminded by the light reflected from Earth's surface that this planet receives one very important contribution from without—energy, in the form of sunlight. As we will see, this energy is captured by green plants and transferred from organism to organism to sustain nearly all life on Earth.

FIGURE 23.1 A view of Earth from space shows us that the planet is isolated. Because there is no regular input of materials, important elements must be cycled from organism to organism and between Earth's living and nonliving components. The only input to the system is energy from the sun, which sustains nearly all life on Earth.

Biosphere

The part of the Earth where life exists is the **biosphere.** The biosphere includes many **ecosystems**, each made up of the organisms in a specific geographic area and their physical environment. All the living species in an ecosystem that can potentially interact form a **community.** A **population** is all the individuals of the *same species* that can potentially interact. Thus, populations of different species form a community.

When ecologists consider an individual species, they describe it according to its niche (sometimes called *ecological niche*). The **niche** is the organism's role in the ecosystem, defined by all the physical, chemical, and biological factors that keep the organism healthy and allow it to reproduce. Such factors include the nature of the organism's food and how it obtains this food; its predators; and its specific needs for shelter, as well as the temperature, light, water, and oxygen the organism requires to survive. Thus the organism's **habitat**—the physical place where it lives—is also a part of its niche. For example, the habitat of an African lion is semi-open plains. Its niche includes the habitat, when it is active (any time of day), how it obtains food (predation on large animals), how it relates to other animals (lives in social group called a pride; marks territory by roaring, urinating, and patrolling), and how it reproduces (gives birth to litters of 1 to 4 cubs after 110 days of pregnancy on average).

Ecological Succession

Ecosystems change over long periods (in fact, everything on Earth is constantly changing). The sequence of changes in the kinds of species making up a community is called ecological **succession**. There are two types of ecological succession: primary and secondary.

Primary succession occurs where no community previously existed. Such places may be found on rocky outcroppings, or where lava has solidified into a new surface, or where land appears as a glacier recedes or ice caps melt. At the start of primary succession, no soil exists.

The first living things to invade such an area are called *pioneer species*. Among the most prominent of these are lichens, which are actually two species—a fungus and a photosynthetic organism, usually an alga—combined in a mutually beneficial relationship. The fungus provides the attachment to the barren surface, retains water, and releases minerals from the rock to be used by the alga; the alga provides the food. Lichens secrete acid, which helps break down the rock, beginning soil formation (Figure **23.2**). In time, the lichens die and their remains mix with the rock particles, furthering soil formation in cracks and crevices.

Soil building is an extremely slow process, but once soil is in place, the rate of succession speeds up. Plants begin to appear. Their roots push into every crevice, and their leaves fall and decompose, accelerating the pace of soil building and new plant colonization. In some areas, trees eventually become the dominant plant form.

Each species that moves into the area changes the environmental conditions slightly, thus changing the available resources in ways that favor some species and hamper others. The community that eventually forms and remains, if no disturbances occur, is called the *climax community* (Figure **23.3**). The nature of a climax community is determined by many factors, including temperature, rainfall, nutrient availability, and exposure to sun and wind.

When an existing ecological community is cleared away—either by natural means or by human activity—and is then left alone by humans, it undergoes a sequence of changes in species composition known as *secondary succession*. Secondary succession occurs in areas where soil is already in place. Such areas include old, deserted fields and farms (originally cleared and planted by humans but later abandoned) or areas damaged by catastrophic fire, flood, wind, or overgrazing (Figure **23.4**). The initial invaders in secondary succession are likely to be grasses, weeds, and shrubs, but these are gradually outcompeted as other plants move in from the surrounding community. The area finally "heals," and the community that forms often resembles the one that existed before the disturbance.

Energy Flow

Virtually all the energy that propels life on this small planet comes from the sun. Only a small fraction of the sun's energy that reaches Earth's surface worldwide is captured and used by living organisms. Even so, the life that abounds on Earth owes its existence to that captured energy, which is shifted, shuffled, channeled, and scattered through various systems from one level to the next.

This thin mat of lichen is helping break down the bare rock, beginning soil formation.

After soil has begun to accumulate, plant species appear that often include shrubs and dwarf trees.

Trees often later become the dominant plant form, depending on elevation, annual rainfall, and average temperature.

FIGURE 23.2 Primary succession is the sequence of changes in the species composition of a community that begins where no life previously existed.

Temperate deciduous forest. These forests receive 75–125 cm (30–50 in.) of rainfall per year. Summers are hot, and winters are cold. Trees lose their leaves in the winter so as to avoid water loss when it is too cold to photosynthsize. Insects, mice, squirrels, and many species of birds are common in these forests.

Temperate grasslands. These grasslands receive 25–75 cm (10–30 in.) of rainfall per year. Long dry periods and fire are important factors in maintaining grasslands. Grazing animals such as antelope and burrowing animals such as prairie dogs are common.

Desert. Lack of water defines the desert community. Deserts receive less than 25 cm (10 in.) of rain each year. Most deserts are hot, but some are cold. Both plants and animals must be able to conserve water. Many desert plants are succulents with leaves that retain and store water. Animals may tend to avoid the sun by foraging at night.

Taiga. The taiga is composed of evergreen forests with variable rainfall of 50–100 cm (20–40 in.) per year. Winters are long and cold, and summers are short. The needles on evergreen trees help save water by providing little surface through which water can leave. Animals such as the grizzly bear, moose, wolf, and snowshoe hare are common.

Tropical rain forest. Tropical rain forests may receive 200–1000 cm (80–400 in.) of rain each year. It is hot throughout the year. Tropical rain forests have a tremendous diversity of life.

FIGURE 23.3 Selected climax communities of Earth. Environmental conditions, particularly the temperature and the availability of water, affect the distribution of organisms. Each species is adapted to certain conditions.

Food Chains and Food Webs

The flow of energy through the living world begins when light from the sun is absorbed by photosynthetic organisms, such as plants, algae, and cyanobacteria (a group of photosynthetic bacteria that usually live in water). *Photosynthesis* is a chemical process that essentially captures light energy and transforms it into the chemical energy of the sugar glucose, which is manufactured from carbon dioxide and water. The energy stored in the glucose molecules and oxygen released in the process of photosynthesis sustain nearly all life on Earth. The photosynthesizers themselves use some of the energy stored in these glucose molecules to fuel their own metabolic activities. Any remaining energy can be used for growth and reproduction. Once the photosynthesizer uses the energy in glucose to make new organic molecules, these molecules may become food for an animal.

The photosynthesizers, called the **producers**, form the lowest **trophic level** (*trophic* means "feeding"). All other organisms are **consumers** and use the energy that producers store (Figure **23.5**).

Consumers belong to higher trophic levels and are grouped on the basis of their food source.

- **Herbivores,** or **primary consumers,** eat plants.
- **Carnivores,** or **secondary consumers,** feed on herbivores. Some carnivores eat other carnivores, forming still higher trophic levels—tertiary and quaternary consumers.
- **Omnivores** eat both plants and animals.
- **Decomposers,** such as bacteria, fungi, and worms, consume dead organic material for energy and release inorganic material that can then be reused by producers.

Immediately after a fire there are no visible signs of life. Dead trees stand as ghostly reminders of the forest that had existed, and gray ash covers the forest floor.

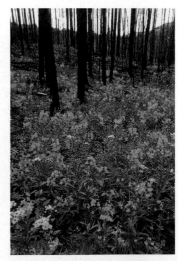

The following spring young plants, such as fireweed and heartleaf arnica, appear and begin the stages of secondary succession.

FIGURE 23.4 Secondary succession following the 1988 fires in Yellowstone National Park

FIGURE 23.6 Humans eat at several trophic levels. The width of the arrow indicates the relative amount of energy transferred.

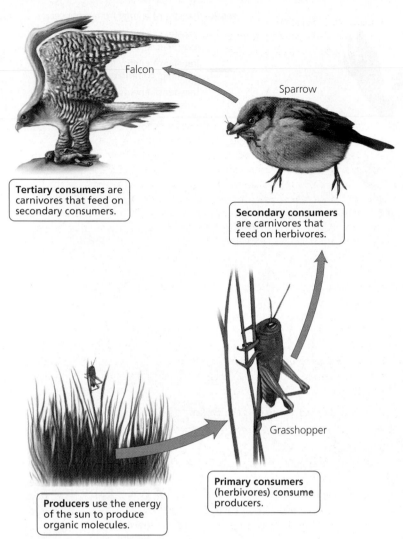

FIGURE 23.5 Trophic levels. The width of the arrow indicates the relative amount of energy transferred.

At one time, the pattern of feeding relationships responsible for the flow of energy through an ecological system was described as a **food chain**—a linear sequence in which A eats B, which then eats C, which then eats D, and so on. However, now we know that the chain analogy is too simplistic because many organisms eat at several trophic levels. To illustrate, consider the number of trophic levels on which humans feed. Whereas eating chickens—which are primary consumers—makes us secondary consumers, eating tuna (a predatory fish) makes us tertiary consumers (or quaternary consumers if the tuna has eaten another predatory fish). But we also can be considered primary consumers because we eat vegetables (Figure **23.6**). More realistic patterns of feeding relationships, consisting of many interconnected food chains, are described as **food webs**. Figure **23.7** describes part of a food web in a community where land meets water.

Energy Transfer through Trophic Levels

Energy is lost as it is transferred from one trophic level to the next. Although the efficiency of transfer can vary greatly depending on the organisms in the system, on average only 10% of the energy available at one trophic level is transferred to the next higher level. As a result, ecosystems rarely have more than four or five trophic levels.

As we consider why energy transfer between trophic levels is so inefficient, keep in mind that only the energy that is converted to **biomass** (the dry weight of the organism) is available to the next higher trophic level. One reason for energy loss between trophic levels is that roughly two-thirds of the energy in the food that is digested is used by the animal for cellular respiration. In addition, an animal must first expend energy to obtain its food, usually by grazing or hunting (the chicken in Figure **23.8** must do a lot of pecking). Furthermore, not all the food available at a given trophic level is captured and consumed. In addition, some of the food eaten cannot be digested and is lost as feces. The energy in the indigestible material is unavailable to the next higher trophic level. However, the remaining energy can be converted to biomass and will be available to the next higher trophic level. These losses become multiplied as the energy is transferred to successively higher trophic levels, until there simply is not enough food or energy left to feed another level. To put this another way, for every 100 calories of solar energy captured by producers, 10 calories are transferred to herbivores and only 1 calorie is transferred to carnivores (secondary consumers).

Ecological Pyramids

An **ecological pyramid** is a diagram that compares certain properties in a series of related trophic levels. The *pyramid of energy,* for example, in Figure **23.9** shows the amount of energy available at each trophic level. The base of the pyramid reflects *primary productivity*—the amount of light energy converted to chemical energy in organic molecules, primarily by photosynthetic organisms. The tiers representing successively higher trophic levels grow smaller, forming a pyramid, because only about 10% of the energy contained in one trophic level is transferred to the next. *Pyramids of biomass* describe the number of individuals at each trophic level multiplied by their biomass. Because the energy available at a trophic level determines the biomass that can be supported, a pyramid of energy and a pyramid of biomass generally have the same shape.

Q *On which trophic level would the hawk be feeding if it ate the duck?*

Transfer of energy from producer

Transfer of energy from primary consumer to secondary consumer

Transfer of energy from secondary consumer to tertiary consumer

Transfer of energy from tertiary consumer to quarternary consumer

Hawk (tertiary and quaternary consumer)

Red-winged blackbird (primary and secondary consumer)

Snake (tertiary consumer)

Duck (secondary consumer)

Heron (secondary, tertiary, and quarternary consumer)

Grasshopper (primary consumer)

Grass (producer)

Frog (secondary consumer)

Large fish (tertiary consumers)

Small fish (primary consumer)

Small fish (secondary consumers)

Zooplankton (primary consumers)

Algae (producer)

Snail (primary consumer)

Diatoms (producers)

Bacteria (decomposers)

Decomposing underwater plants

FIGURE 23.7 In this simplified food web, the arrows show the direction of flow of energy in the form of food. The width of the arrow indicates the relative amount of energy transferred.

FIGURE 23.8 As energy flows through a food web, only a small amount of it is stored as body mass and becomes available to the next higher trophic level. Some of the food energy is simply not captured; some is undigested and lost in fecal waste; and some is used for cellular respiration. Only the remaining energy becomes available to the next higher trophic level. The width of the arrow indicates the relative amount of energy transferred.

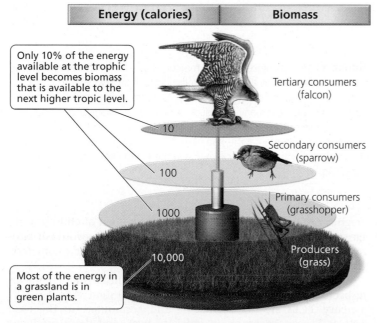

FIGURE 23.9 Ecological pyramids. Note that each trophic level contains less energy and less biomass than the level below it.

Health and Environmental Consequences of Ecological Pyramids

Ecological pyramids convey important lessons. Let's take look at two of these lessons: (1) nondegradable substances accumulate to higher concentrations in organisms living at higher trophic levels; and (2) more humans could be nourished on a vegetarian diet than on a diet containing meat.

Biological magnification

Chemicals that are essential to life—carbon, hydrogen, oxygen, nitrogen, and phosphorus—are passed from one trophic level to the next, thus being continuously recycled from organism to organism. Organic molecules are broken down and then either metabolized for energy or put together to form the biomass of another individual.

However, certain substances—including chlorinated hydrocarbon pesticides such as DDT, heavy metals such as mercury, and radioactive isotopes—are broken down or excreted very slowly. Substances like these tend to stay in the body, often stored in fatty tissues such as liver, kidneys, and the fat around the intestines.

The concentrations of such substances become magnified at each higher trophic level. Remember that, on average, only 10% of the energy available at one trophic level transfers to the next. Consequently, consumers at one trophic level must eat many organisms from the previous trophic level to obtain enough energy to support life. If the organisms that are eaten are contaminated, the pollutant will accumulate in the consumer. Consider a simplified example. Mercury, a nondegradable, potentially harmful substance, enters water through volcanic activity as well as through coal combustion and improper disposal of medical waste. Bacteria convert the mercury to a particularly toxic form, methyl mercury, which then works its way through the food web. If mercury pollutes the water in a certain aquatic ecosystem, phytoplankton (minute photosynthetic organisms that are abundant in aquatic environments) will absorb the mercury, and mercury levels in the phytoplankton will be in some dilute concentration that we will represent as 1. An herbivore such as a zooplankton (a minute nonphotosynthetic organism) feeds on large numbers of phytoplankton. The mercury ingested from the phytoplankton thus becomes more concentrated in the zooplankton's tissues than it was in the phytoplankton—let's say about 10 times more. Large numbers of zooplankton may in turn be eaten by a small fish. Once in the fish's body, the mercury stays there and accumulates, let's say another 10 times, to reach a relative concentration of 100. When these mercury-containing fish are eaten by a tuna, the mercury passes to the tuna's body and accumulates. Because many small fish must be consumed to keep a tuna alive, the mercury concentration in the tuna's body might be 1000 times greater than that in water. This tendency of a nondegradable chemical to become more concentrated in organisms as it passes along the food chain is known as **biological magnification** (Figure **23.10**).

Biological magnification is of more than theoretical concern for humans. We are often top carnivores, and we continue to pollute our environment with nondegradable, potentially harmful substances. If a human eats a long-lived predator—such as a tuna, swordfish, or shark—that has accumulated methyl mercury through biological magnification as described, that person could begin to accumulate dangerously high levels of mercury, too. High levels of mercury in humans affect the nervous system, causing muscle tremors, personality disorders, and birth defects. For this reason, the Food and Drug Administration now recommends that

Maintaining Our Remaining Biodiversity

Faced with powerful evidence of a marked reduction in Earth's biodiversity, some experts express guarded optimism that we may be able to slow or even stop this trend. Various measures are being suggested.

More developed (richer) and less developed (poorer) countries must take a careful census of their life-forms to produce inventories of the species they harbor. This need is especially acute in tropical countries, which, unfortunately, are often least able to afford such programs. Advocates thus argue that the effort must be worldwide, with developed countries subsidizing the research in less affluent areas.

Nations must cooperate in linking the economic development of impoverished regions, particularly the tropics, to conservation. Lending agencies must stipulate that certain areas be set aside and left undeveloped. Decisions about which locations are to remain undeveloped should be made with the advice of ecologists, so the effects on the world's biodiversity are minimized. (What effect do you think such rules would have had on the development of the United States if such restrictions were in place during the industrial revolution?)

Educating the people whose decisions have the most immediate effect on biodiversity should be a priority. For example, recent studies have shown that native people can make more money through sustainable use of a forest (as in gathering nuts and fruits) than they would if the forest were cleared for agriculture or ranching. Many people in developing countries are also learning that scientists worldwide are interested in the medicines and healing knowledge they have, so in a sense, the educational opportunities are reciprocal.

Biologists worldwide must work more closely with zoning and land-use personnel to maximize the use of areas being cleared or cultivated. Such multiple land-use planning includes, for example, rotating crops to maintain healthy soil and increase biodiversity or replacing single-species forests planted by paper companies with more diverse forests that could harbor more species of animals. Of course, the paper companies may ask why they should be required to reduce their profits to increase biodiversity. This is the type of issue that will have to be negotiated in the process of bringing people to an understanding that what is good for the environment is ultimately good for everyone.

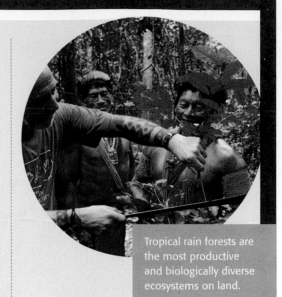

Tropical rain forests are the most productive and biologically diverse ecosystems on land.

Questions to Consider

- Many of the issues regarding preserving biodiversity involve trade-offs between activities that are valuable to society and activities that reduce the biodiversity that allows ecosystems to provide a stable food supply. How can these trade-offs be evaluated? Who should be responsible for making these decisions?
- Should agencies that work to maintain biodiversity receive governmental funding or rely on public funding?

FIGURE 23.10 Substances such as mercury that are broken down slowly or excreted slowly tend to accumulate in the body of an organism. The concentration becomes magnified at each successive trophic level, because a consumer must eat many individuals from a lower trophic level to stay alive. Because of this biomagnification, the mercury concentration in the tuna eaten by a human at the end of this food chain is about 1000 times greater than the mercury concentration in the phytoplankton at the beginning.

pregnant women, breast-feeding women, women of child-bearing age, and children stop eating shark, marlin, and swordfish altogether, and limit their intake of albacore (white) tuna to one 6-oz serving a week.

Polychlorinated biphenyls (PCBs) are industrial chemicals suspected of causing cancer and nervous system damage. Like mercury, PCBs are nondegradable and accumulate in the food web. PCBs can be found in chicken, beef, and dairy products. Some farm-raised Atlantic salmon also have PCB levels high enough to trigger health warnings from the Environmental

Feeds one human
(2,000 calories)

Herbivore
(2,000 calories)

Carnivore

Feeds 10 humans
(2,000 calories each)

Producers (grains)
(20,000 calories)

Producers (grains)
(20,000 calories)

Herbivores

FIGURE 23.11 Energy pyramids may hold an important lesson for humans. Because only about 10% of the energy available at one trophic level is available at the next higher level, approximately 10 times more people could be fed if they ate a vegetarian diet rather than a diet containing only animal protein.

Protection Agency. (Wild salmon have lower levels of PCBs.) In addition, PCBs have been called environmental estrogens because they mimic the effects of the sex hormone estrogen or enhance estrogen's effects. Scientists, recognizing that PCBs have had feminizing effects on certain male animals, are investigating the possibility that PCBs may be reducing human fertility (for example, by reducing human sperm count) and affecting the rates of cancer in certain reproductive structures (breasts, ovaries, prostate gland, and testes).

World hunger

The world's human population has grown at an alarming rate (a problem discussed in Chapter 24). The pyramid of energy suggests a way to feed the growing population more efficiently: persuade people to eat at lower trophic levels. Because only about 10% of the energy available on one trophic level is transferred to the next one, we see that

10,000 calories of corn energy ⟶ 1000 calories of
beef energy ⟶ 100 calories of human energy

However, if humans began to eat one level lower on the food chain, about 10 times more energy would be available to them:

10,000 calories of grain (corn, wheat, rice, and
so on) ⟶ 1000 calories of human energy

In short, more people could be fed and less land would have to be cultivated if we adopted a largely, or exclusively, vegetarian diet (Figure **23.11**). This is one reason that people in densely populated regions of the world, including China and India, are primarily vegetarians. As the human population continues to expand, meat is likely to become even more of a luxury throughout the world than it is today.

stop and think

The traditional diet of the Inuit, one of the native peoples of the North American coast, is part of a relatively long food chain:

Diatoms (producers) ⟶ Tiny marine animals ⟶
Fish ⟶ Seals ⟶ Inuits

How might the length of this food chain be one factor contributing to the small population size of Inuit groups?

Chemical Cycles

Earth's resources are limited. Life on Earth is demanding. Many of Earth's reserves would be depleted quickly if not for nature's cycling. Materials move through a series of transfers, from living to nonliving systems and back again (Figure **23.12**). Let's look at some of the more important of these **biogeochemical cycles**, the recurring pathways certain materials travel between living and nonliving systems.

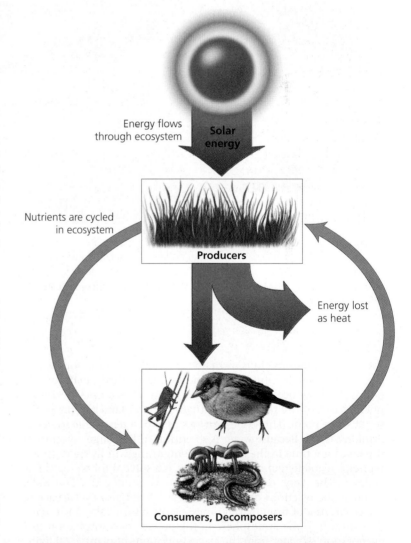

Energy flows
through ecosystem

Solar
energy

Nutrients are cycled
in ecosystem

Producers

Energy lost
as heat

Consumers, Decomposers

FIGURE 23.12 Through biogeochemical cycles, matter cycles between living organisms and the physical environment. This cycling of matter (gray arrows) is in contrast to the path of energy (yellow arrows), which flows through the ecosystem in one direction.

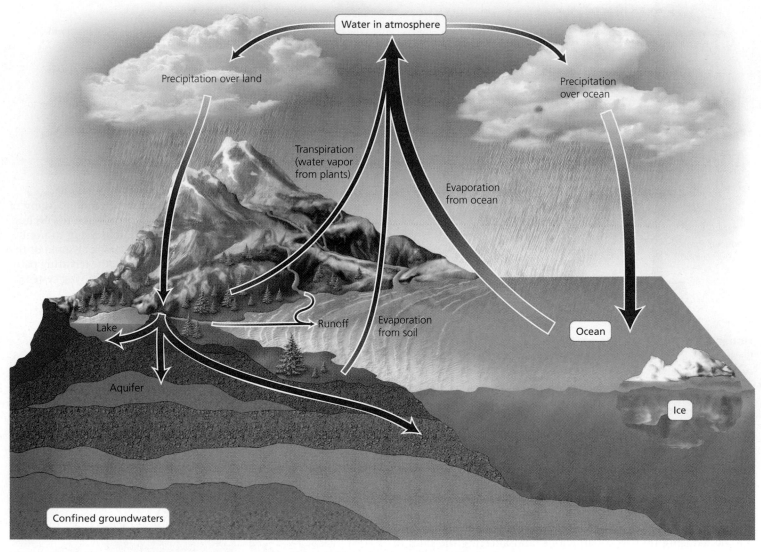

FIGURE 23.13 The water cycle. Water, which is essential to life, cycles from the atmosphere to the land as precipitation, collects in oceans and other bodies of water, and evaporates back to the atmosphere. Water also returns to the atmosphere in the form of vapor lost from the leaves of plants (transpiration). This cycling gives us a renewable source of drinking water. The width of the arrow indicates the relative contribution of the process to the cycle.

The Water Cycle

Each drop of rain reminds us that water recycles continuously, precipitating from the atmosphere and falling to Earth; collecting in ponds, lakes, or oceans; and then evaporating back into the atmosphere. Most of the rain or snow that falls over land returns to the sea at some point. This cycle provides us with a renewable source of drinking water. Because water is so critical to life, large amounts of it pause for a time in the bodies of living things. In living cells, water helps regulate temperature and acts as a solvent for biological reactions. The very oxygen we breathe is produced from water through the reactions of photosynthesis. Water also cycles back to the environment from living things; plants return 99% of the water they absorb to the atmosphere in the process of transpiration (the evaporation of water from the leaves and stems of plants). All living things carry out cell respiration, which generates water that is exhaled as water vapor. The water cycle is shown in Figure **23.13**.

Human activities and the water cycle

Humans have disrupted the water cycle in several ways. We have cut down all the trees in vast areas of forest. This deforestation has reduced the amount of transpiration and, therefore, the amount of water vapor returned to the atmosphere. Our urban areas have altered runoff patterns. When rain falls on land, some water seeps down to replenish groundwater. In cities, most rainwater flows into sewers and becomes part of waste water. The most significant way that humans disrupt the water cycle is by using more freshwater than is replenished (discussed in Chapter 24).

On a brighter side, we have developed some ways of recovering freshwater from the oceans and from wastewater. Some coastal cities are building desalination plants to remove salts from ocean water and make it suitable for human consumption. However, desalination is an expensive process that uses a lot of energy. The Tampa Bay Seawater Desalination Plant in Florida is the largest of its kind in North America. The plant produces about 95,000 cubic

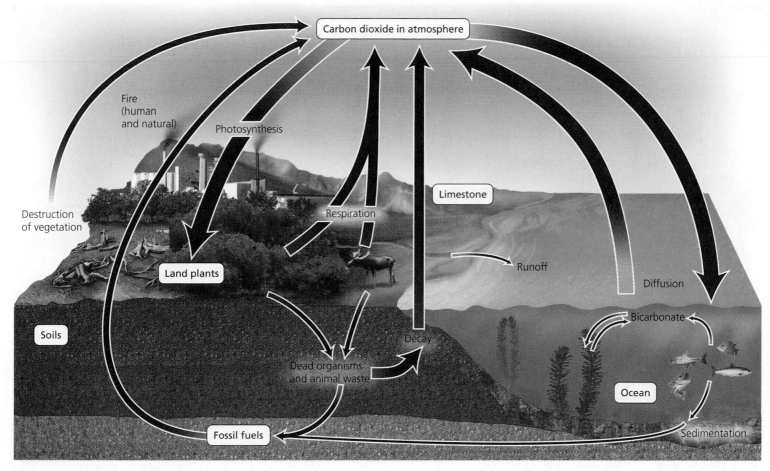

FIGURE 23.14 The carbon cycle. Carbon cycles between the environment and living organisms. Carbon dioxide (CO_2) is removed from the environment as producers use it to synthesize organic molecules by photosynthesis. The carbon in those organic molecules then moves through the food web, serving as a carbon source for herbivores, carnivores, and decomposers. Carbon is returned to the atmosphere as CO_2 when organisms use the organic compounds in cellular respiration. The width of the arrow indicates the relative contribution of the process to the cycle.

meters (25 million gallons) of freshwater a day, which accounts for 10% of the drinking water for the Tampa area. We have also developed technology to recover freshwater from waste water. This technology, often called "toilet-to-tap," is the subject of an Environmental Issue essay in Chapter 2.

The Carbon Cycle

In the carbon cycle, carbon moves from the environment, into the bodies of living things, and back to the environment (Figure **23.14**). Living organisms need carbon to build the molecules that give them life: proteins, carbohydrates, fats, and nucleic acids. Conversely, certain processes of living organisms—photosynthesis and respiration—are an integral part of the carbon cycle.

The primary movement of carbon from the environment into living organisms occurs during photosynthesis, as plants, algae, and cyanobacteria use carbon dioxide (CO_2) to produce sugars and other organic molecules. When photosynthesizers are eaten by herbivores, these organic molecules serve as a carbon source for the herbivores. The herbivores use that carbon to produce their own organic molecules, which then serve as a carbon source for carnivores. When an organism dies, the organic molecules in its body will serve as a carbon source for decomposers. However,

while alive, all organisms cycle carbon back to the environment through the reactions of cellular respiration, which breaks down organic molecules to CO_2.

Some carbon is significantly delayed before being cycled back into the environment. For example, carbon may remain tied up in the wood of some trees for hundreds of years. Most of the carbon that is currently not cycling is thought to be stored in limestone, a type of sedimentary rock formed from the shells of marine organisms that sank to the bottom of the ocean floor and were covered and compressed by newer sediments. Other vast carbon stores are the fossil fuels (oil, coal, and natural gas), so named because they formed from the remains of organisms that lived millions of years ago.

Three processes release carbon from long-term storage and return it to the environment: decomposition, erosion, and combustion. When trees die, for example, the natural process of decomposition will make the carbon available for new organisms, which will respire and release CO_2 to the atmosphere. The carbon in limestone is recycled through erosion. Millions of years after it forms, sedimentary rock containing limestone can be lifted to Earth's surface by movement of tectonic plates, where it is eroded by chemical and physical weathering. These changes make the

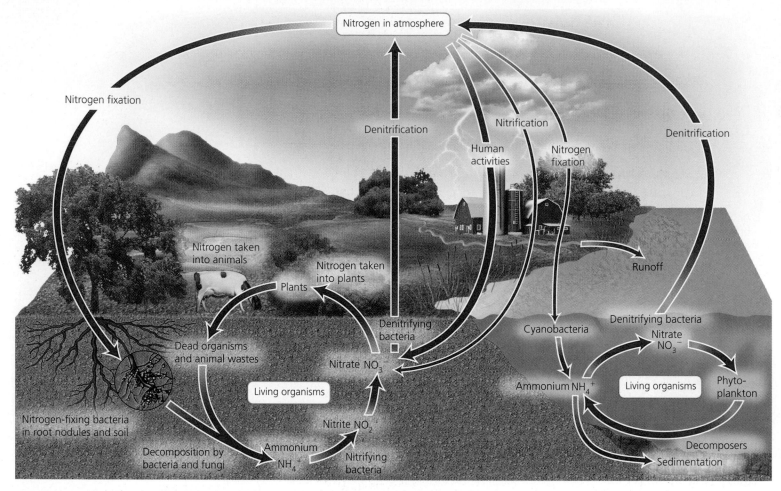

FIGURE 23.15 The nitrogen cycle. Atmospheric nitrogen can be converted to ammonium by nitrogen-fixing bacteria, which then convert the ammonium to nitrate, the main form of nitrogen absorbed by plants. Plants use nitrate to produce proteins and nucleic acids. Animals eat the plants and use the plant's nitrogen-containing chemicals to produce their own proteins and nucleic acids. When plants and animals die, their nitrogen-containing molecules are converted to ammonium by bacteria. Denitrifying bacteria return nitrogen to the atmosphere. The width of the arrow indicates the relative contribution of the process to the cycle.

carbon available to cycle through the food web once again. Combustion, or burning, returns the carbon in fossil fuels to the environment. Today, fossil fuels such as coal, oil, and natural gas are being burned in huge amounts, and the carbon they contain is being returned to the atmosphere as CO_2.

Carbon dioxide and global temperatures

Two human activities—burning fossil fuels and deforestation—are altering the carbon cycle and increasing the atmospheric carbon dioxide level. Recall that fossil fuels were formed from deposits of dead plants and animals that were buried in sediments and escaped decomposition between 345 million and 280 million years ago. High temperatures and pressure over millions of years converted the deposits to coal, oil, and natural gas. The burning of these fuels returns carbon to the environment in the form of CO_2. Deforestation—the removal of a forest without adequate replanting, as is occurring in areas of the Amazon rain forest and the U.S. Pacific Northwest—increases atmospheric CO_2 in two ways. First, it *reduces the removal* of CO_2 from the atmosphere by eliminating trees' photosynthesis. Second, the trees are often burned after cutting to clear the area, and burning *adds* CO_2 to the atmosphere.

The rise in atmospheric CO_2 raises concerns because CO_2 is one of the greenhouse gases that play a role in warming our atmosphere. Indeed, the scientific consensus is that the increase in atmospheric CO_2 is causing a rise in temperatures throughout the world—known popularly as global warming. Global climate change and its many consequences are discussed in the next chapter.

The Nitrogen Cycle

Nitrogen is a principal constituent of several molecules needed for life, including proteins and nucleic acids. Nitrogen is often in short supply to living systems, so its cycling is particularly important (Figure **23.15**).

The largest reservoir of nitrogen is the atmosphere, which is about 79% nitrogen gas (N_2). However, nitrogen gas cannot interact with life directly. (As you sit reading, you are bathed in nitrogen gas, but you do not interact with it.) Before it can be used, nitrogen gas must be converted to a form that living organisms can use—ammonium (NH_4^+). The process of converting nitrogen gas to ammonium is called **nitrogen fixation.** This is performed by nitrogen-fixing bacteria, many of which live in nodules on the

FIGURE 23.16 The phosphorus cycle. Phosphates dissolve from rocks in rainwater. They are then absorbed by producers and passed to other organisms in food webs. Decomposers return phosphates to the soil. Some phosphates are carried to the oceans and eventually deposited in marine sediments. The width of the arrow indicates the relative contribution of the process to the cycle.

roots of leguminous plants such as peas and alfalfa. Ammonium is then converted to nitrite (NO_2^-) and then to nitrate (NO_3^-) by nitrifying bacteria living in the soil, in a process called **nitrification.** The ammonium or nitrates are first absorbed by plants, which use the nitrogen to form plant proteins and nucleic acids. The nitrogen then passes through the food web and is incorporated into the nitrogen-containing compounds of animals.

When plants and animals die, decomposers such as bacteria break down the waste products and dead bodies of plants and animals, producing ammonium (NH_4^+). Much of the ammonium is converted to nitrate by nitrifying bacteria. Other bacteria balance the nitrogen cycle by performing a process called denitrification, in which the nitrates that are not assimilated into living organisms are converted to nitrogen gas. Denitrifying bacteria are found in wet soil, swamps, and estuaries.

Human activities and the nitrogen cycle

Human burning of fossil fuels has affected the nitrogen cycle by adding nitrogen dioxide (NO_2) gas (as well as sulfur dioxide—SO_2—gas) to the atmosphere, where they react with water vapor

to form acids. The acids eventually fall to Earth as acid rain, which is killing trees in northern forests and fish and amphibians in aquatic environments. (Acid rain is discussed in Chapter 2.) Sunlight can cause hydrocarbons and NO_2 to form photochemical smog that contains ozone, which is especially harmful to the respiratory system. (Photochemical smog is discussed in Chapter 24 in the Ethical Issue essay, *Air Pollution and Human Health.*)

The Phosphorus Cycle

Phosphorus is an important component of many biological molecules, including the genetic material DNA, energy-transfer molecules such as adenosine triphosphate (ATP), and phospholipids found in membranes. Phosphorus is also essential in vertebrate bones and teeth.

Unlike the water, carbon, and nitrogen cycles, the phosphorus cycle does not have an atmospheric component (Figure **23.16**). Instead, the reservoir for phosphorus is sedimentary rock, where it is found as phosphate ions. The cycle begins when erosion caused by rainfall or runoff from streams dissolves the phosphates in the rocks. The dissolved phosphate is readily absorbed by producers and incorporated into their biological molecules. When animals eat the plants, the phosphates are passed through food webs. Decomposers return the phosphates to the soil or water, where they become available to plants and animals once again. Much of the phosphate is lost to the sea. Although some of this phosphate may cycle through marine food webs, most of it becomes bound in sediment. The phosphates in sediment become unavailable to the biosphere unless geological forces bring the sediment to the surface.

Eutrophication

Human activity is also disturbing the phosphorus and nitrogen cycles. Inadequate nitrogen and phosphorus in the soil can slow plant growth. For this reason, many crops are fertilized with synthetic preparations containing both nitrogen (as ammonium) and phosphates. Phosphates from fertilizer can wash into nearby streams, rivers, ponds, or lakes in runoff. Fertilizer runoff is one cause of *eutrophication,* the enrichment of water in a lake or pond by nutrients. The nutrient boost can lead to an explosive growth of photosynthetic organisms, such as algae in deeper water and weeds in shallow areas. When these organisms die, their remains accumulate at the bottom of the lake. Decomposers then thrive, depleting the water of dissolved oxygen. Gradually, fish, such as pike, sturgeon, and whitefish, which require higher oxygen concentrations in the water, are replaced by species such as catfish and carp that can tolerate lower levels of dissolved oxygen. Eventually, the oxygen depletion can kill all fish and bottom-dwelling life.

Eutrophication is not just a problem in lakes and ponds; there are now more than 400 coastal regions of oceanic dead zones, regions where marine life can't survive. In the mid 1960s there were only 49 dead zones. The dead zones are caused by fertilizer runoff, which increases available nutrients for algae, and by global climate change, which increases the temperature of the top, well-oxygenated layer of the water, and prevents mixing with the lower, less-oxygenated layers. In 2008 the dead zone in the Gulf of Mexico was larger than its previous peak in 2002.

Biodiversity

In this chapter we see that organisms are not randomly scattered over the Earth. Instead, each is adapted to a particular niche, which allows it to remain healthy and to reproduce. Recall that an organism's niche includes physical, chemical, and biological factors. We also see in this chapter that the only input to nearly every ecosystem is solar energy, which producers use to manufacture organic molecules. Energy then flows through food webs. Resources, such as water, carbon, nitrogen, and phosphorus, cycle through living and nonliving systems. It's no surprise, then, that even small changes to an organism's niche can have ripple effects that disturb the entire ecosystem.

A current example of this ripple effect is damage being done to coral reefs. The damage begins with humans upsetting the carbon cycle by burning fossil fuels and cutting down forests. These human activities have raised the level of carbon dioxide in the atmosphere. Elevated atmospheric carbon dioxide causes more carbon dioxide to diffuse into the oceans, where it dissolves, forming carbonic acid. As a result, the oceans are becoming more acidic, causing damage to coral reef ecosystems.

As the human population grows, it consumes and pollutes more resources (discussed in the next chapter), which can have widespread effects on ecosystem Earth. Due to the interconnectedness of living and nonliving systems in an ecosystem, one effect of human disturbance may be changes in **biodiversity**—species richness. Biodiversity includes the number of species living in a given area and the abundance of each. Recently, scientists have raised an alarm worldwide in response to indications that globally, and especially in certain critical areas, biodiversity is decreasing. We are losing species, perhaps as many as 100 each day, largely because of human activity. *Mass extinctions,* the loss of many species from Earth, have occurred in previous eras, but never before because of humans. Today, many species are being forced to compete with us as we change the environment to suit ourselves, rendering it unsuitable for them.

How many species are there? No one knows. Scientific estimates range from 8 million to 30 million species now in existence, with about 90% of them living on land. However, only about 1.7 million of these species have been identified, and only 3% of those have been studied.

Most terrestrial species live in the tropics. Although tropical rain forests cover only 7% of Earth's surface, they are home to between 50% and 80%—estimated as 7 million to 8 million—of Earth's species (see the Ethical Issue essay, *Maintaining Our Remaining Biodiversity*).

Habitat destruction is largely responsible for the loss of biodiversity. The primary reasons habitats are destroyed are to create living space for humans and to provide room or resources for economic development. Calculations indicate that most of the original tropical rain forest will be destroyed by 2040. This means that in the next 35 years, we could lose a quarter of all the species on Earth. Evolutionary biologists tell us that, currently, we are losing species at the rate of 1000 to 10,000 times the average rate for the last 65 million years, since the extinction of the dinosaurs.

Rain forest is not the only type of habitat being destroyed. Lumbering and acid rain are destroying northern temperate forests. Also, marine ecosystems are being destroyed by pollution, overfishing, and coastal development. For example, shark populations have declined by more than 70% in the last 15 years. Commercial fishing is largely to blame for the reduction of shark populations. People eat shark meat and use the fins to make soup. Moreover, some sharks, hammerheads for example, are accidentally caught when they try to prey on the herring and squid being used as bait by people fishing for tuna or swordfish. The United States has federal regulations that restrict shark fishing; however, shark fishing is not regulated in Europe. If shark numbers continue to fall, we may not be able to save them from extinction. Sharks grow slowly, mature late in life, and have few young at a time; and females do not reproduce every year.

Perhaps you are wondering why we should care about the loss of species, especially those we never knew of. Several materialistic reasons immediately come to mind. The first direct benefit to humans of maintaining biodiversity is that biodiversity preserves the genetic diversity encoded in the chromosomes of species. This genetic diversity is useful for crossbreeding. The crossbreeding of two strains of a species, each possessing different desirable traits, can combine those desirable traits in a single new strain. For example, a new kind of corn was found on a Mexican hillside. (The farmer had to be persuaded not to plow it under to plant his usual corn crop.) The newly discovered corn was a perennial and proved to be resistant to a disease called corn smut, a fungal disease that causes the kernels to turn black and become oddly shaped. Plans were made to cross the perennial corn with common forms of agricultural corn, and these sorts of experiments continue.

Interestingly, the usefulness of genetic diversity as a reservoir of genetic stores has increased dramatically with modern technology. Owing to recent advances in genetic engineering, specific genes can be isolated from their source organisms and moved into other kinds of organisms. Thus the maintenance of genetic stores becomes even more important as we use genetic engineering to maximize crop yields or otherwise create new forms of organisms that might be useful to society (see Chapter 21).

The second direct benefit to humans of maintaining biodiversity lies in developing new kinds of medicines. About 25% of all known drugs come from plants. The rosy periwinkle from Madagascar, as discussed in Chapter 1, is a source of two anticancer drugs, vincristine and vinblastine; and the Mexican yam was once a source of oral contraceptives. Most of the plants with medicinal value have been found in the tropics, which as noted are being rapidly destroyed.

A third benefit is the many services that biodiversity provides in functioning ecosystems—cleansing water and air, enriching soil, cycling minerals, and pollinating crops, for example. Recall the important role of organisms in the biogeochemical cycles discussed earlier in this chapter. For example, as pollinators, bees contribute $15 billion a year to the productivity of agriculture in the United States each year. This is one reason for great concern over the decline in bee populations in recent years. Most of the organisms that could become crop pests are kept under control by their own predators.

We see, then, that there are many practical reasons to preserve biodiversity. Earth and the organisms inhabiting it are interconnected through energy flow through food webs and biogeochemical cycles. The health of ecosystem Earth depends on biodiversity.

highlighting the concepts

Earth as an Ecosystem (p. 506)

- Ecology is the study of the interactions between organisms and between organisms and their environment.
- Materials on Earth are recycled among living organisms and the environment. The only outside contributor to Earth is energy from the sun.

Biosphere (p. 506)

- The biosphere consists of all the ecosystems on Earth. An ecosystem consists of a community of organisms and their physical environment. An organism's niche is the specific role it plays in the community; its habitat is the place where it lives.

Ecological Succession (p. 507)

- Ecological succession is the sequence of changes in communities over long periods. Primary succession occurs where no community previously existed. The first settlers of a community are called pioneer species. A climax community eventually forms and remains as long as no disturbances occur. Secondary succession describes the sequences of changes that occur when an existing community is disturbed by human or natural means.

Energy Flow (pp. 507–513)

- Most of the energy in living systems comes from solar energy absorbed and stored in the molecules of photosynthetic organisms, called producers. The energy stored in producers' molecules enters the animal world through plant-eating herbivores (primary consumers), which may be eaten by carnivores (secondary consumers) or by animals that eat other carnivores (tertiary consumers). Decomposers consume dead organic material, releasing inorganic compounds that can be used by producers. The position of an organism in these feeding relationships is referred to as a trophic level.
- The feeding relationships that result in the one-way flow of energy through the ecosystem and in the cycling of materials among organisms are called food chains or food webs.
- Ecological pyramids depict the amount of energy or biomass at each trophic level. Pyramids of energy show the loss of energy from one trophic level to another. On average, only 10% of the energy available at one trophic level is available at the next higher level. Ecosystems generally have only four or five trophic levels. Pyramids of biomass have the same shape as pyramids of energy, because the available energy determines the biomass that can be formed.
- Biological magnification—the tendency for certain nondegradable substances to become more concentrated in organisms as it passes through a food web—is a consequence of the energy loss between trophic levels. Thus, top carnivores are most likely to be poisoned by nondegradable toxic substances in the environment.
- Because energy is lost with each transfer in the trophic scale, one way to feed more people would be for humans to adopt a largely vegetarian diet.

Chemical Cycles (pp. 513–518)

- In biogeochemical cycles, materials cycle between organisms and the environment.
- The water cycle is the pathway of water as it falls as precipitation; collects in ponds, lakes, and seas; and returns to the atmosphere through evaporation.
- The water cycle can be disturbed because of humans causing shortages through overuse of water supplies. Most water use is for agriculture, primarily irrigation. Irrigation can cause salts to accumulate in the soil (salinization), which can make the land unusable for agriculture.
- The carbon cycle is the worldwide circulation of carbon from the carbon dioxide in air to the carbon in organic molecules of living organisms and back to the air. Carbon enters living systems when photosynthetic organisms incorporate carbon dioxide into organic materials. Carbon dioxide is formed again when the organic molecules are used by the living organism for cellular respiration.
- Humans have disturbed the carbon cycle through activities that increase carbon dioxide levels in the atmosphere: burning fossil fuels, which directly adds carbon dioxide, and deforestation, which decreases the removal of carbon dioxide from the atmosphere. Carbon dioxide is a greenhouse gas that traps heat in Earth's atmosphere and causes global warming.
- The nitrogen cycle is the worldwide circulation of nitrogen from nonliving to living systems and back again. Atmospheric nitrogen (N_2) cannot enter living systems. Nitrogen-fixing bacteria living in nodules on the roots of leguminous plants convert N_2 to ammonium (NH_4^+), which is converted to nitrites (NO_2^-) and then to nitrates (NO_3^-) by nitrifying bacteria. The ammonium and nitrates are then available to plants to use in their proteins and nucleic

acids. Next, the nitrogen is transferred to organisms that consume the plants. Nitrates that are not assimilated into living organisms can be converted to nitrogen gas by denitrifying bacteria.

- Humans affect the nitrogen cycle by burning fossil fuels, which adds nitrogen dioxide to the atmosphere. Nitrogen dioxide reacts with water vapor in the atmosphere to form nitric oxide that falls to Earth as acid rain. Sunlight converts nitrogen dioxide and hydrocarbons to photochemical smog that damages the respiratory system.

- Phosphorus in the form of phosphates is washed from sedimentary rock by rainfall. The dissolved phosphates are used by producers to produce important biological molecules, including DNA and ATP. When animals eat producers or other animals, phosphates are passed through the food webs. Decomposers release phosphates into the soil or water from dead organisms.

- Humans have disrupted the nitrogen and phosphorus cycles through the industrial fixation of nitrogen to produce fertilizer and the addition of phosphates to fertilizer. Some of the phosphates wash into nearby waterways. Fertilizer runoff is one cause of eutrophication.

Biodiversity (pp. 518–519)

- Biodiversity, the number and variety of living things, is being reduced dramatically, largely because of human activity. Most of the loss is occurring in the tropics and is due to habitat destruction. Two practical reasons for concern over the loss of biodiversity are that the disappearing species could have genes that would someday prove useful or that they could be found to produce chemicals with medicinal qualities.

recognizing key terms

biosphere *p. 506*	producers *p. 508*	omnivore *p. 508*	biogeochemical cycle *p. 513*
ecosystem *p. 506*	trophic level *p. 508*	decomposers *p. 508*	nitrogen fixation *p. 516*
community *p. 506*	consumer *p. 508*	food chain *p. 509*	nitrification *p. 517*
population *p. 506*	herbivore *p. 508*	food web *p. 509*	biodiversity *p. 518*
niche *p. 506*	primary consumer *p. 508*	biomass *p. 509*	
habitat *p. 506*	carnivore *p. 508*	ecological pyramid *p. 509*	
succession *p. 507*	secondary consumer *p. 508*	biological magnification *p. 511*	

reviewing the concepts

1. What is ecological succession? How does primary succession differ from secondary succession? *p. 507*
2. Explain how energy flows through an ecosystem. *pp. 507–508*
3. Define the following terms: *producer, primary consumer, secondary consumer,* and *decomposer.* Explain the role each plays in cycling nutrients through an ecosystem. *p. 508*
4. Explain why the feeding relationships in a community are more realistically portrayed as a food web than as a food chain. *p. 509*
5. Explain the reasons for the inefficiency of energy transfer from one trophic level to the next higher one. Why does this loss of energy limit the number of possible trophic levels? *p. 509*
6. Define an energy pyramid. What causes the pyramidal shape? *p. 509*
7. What is meant by a biomass pyramid? How does it compare to an energy pyramid? *p. 509*
8. Define biological magnification. Explain how biological magnification is a consequence of the energy loss between trophic levels. Why should humans be concerned about biological magnification? *pp. 511–513*
9. Explain why more people could be fed on a vegetarian diet than on a diet in which meat provides most of the protein calories. *p. 513*

10. Describe the water cycle, the carbon cycle, the nitrogen cycle, and the phosphorus cycle. *pp. 514–518*
11. Explain some of the ways that humans are disturbing the water cycle. *pp. 514–515*
12. Which human activities are primarily responsible for the rising level of atmospheric carbon dioxide? *p. 516*
13. Define biodiversity. Where is it greatest? Why should we be concerned about the loss of biodiversity? *pp. 518–519*
14. Which of the following is *not* constantly recycled in the biosphere?
    a. Energy
    b. Water
    c. Carbon
    d. Nitrogen
15. Secondary succession is most likely to be found
    a. on rocky outcroppings.
    b. in areas that were clear-cut for timber.
    c. where an island has appeared.
    d. in areas where estuaries have filled in to form land.
16. An organism's role in a community is its _____.
17. An animal that eats an herbivore is called a _____.

applying the concepts

1. In a particular grassland ecosystem, energy flows in the following path:

   Grass $\longrightarrow$ Crickets $\longrightarrow$ Frogs $\longrightarrow$ Herons

   Assuming that the efficiency of energy transfer is typical, how many calories will the herons receive if there were 100,000 calories of grass?

2. Explain why the mercury levels in a lake may be low enough for the water to be safe to drink, yet fish from the same lake may be poisonous.

3. You are a crime scene investigator at a murder scene. Stuck to the bottom of the victim's shoe is a leaf unlike any others in the vicinity of the crime. What clues could you get from the leaf?

becoming information literate

Malaria is a disease transmitted by mosquitoes that infects 300 million people a year and kills about 200 million of them. DDT is a pesticide that is an affordable and effective way to kill mosquitoes. After being widely used in the 1950s, DDT was blamed for the alarming decline in certain species of birds during the 1960s and 1970s. The United States banned the use of DDT during the 1970s, and many other countries followed suit. Because of these bans, neither the United States nor the World Health Organization will fund the use of DDT to control malaria-causing mosquitoes. Some of the areas hit hardest by malaria—Africa, Asia, and Latin America—are too poor to afford other pesticides, which cost four to six times more than DDT.

Use at least three reliable sources (journals, newspapers, websites) to consider the social, health, economic, and political controversies regarding outside funding for the use of DDT to control mosquito populations in poor, malaria-stricken countries. Cite your sources, and explain why you chose the ones you used.

Additional questions can be found online at The Human Biology Place, www.humanbiology.com.

24

Human Population, Limited Resources, and Pollution

The demands of the growing human population, combined with the effectiveness of large-scale commercial fishing methods, have begun to deplete the rivers, lakes, and oceans of many species of fish.

Brad and Krista walked toward the boat, ready for their parasailing adventure. Dale, the driver, met them along the way. Krista asked nervously, "How long have you been taking people parasailing, Dale?"'

"About three years now," Dale explained, "ever since the fishing gave out around here and I had to give it up. The big trawlers have dangerously overexploited the waters. We would have had to stop fishing anyway, though. Some company dumped a load of electronic equipment—mostly cell phones—off the coast a while back, and now they've found lead and some other metals in the shellfish catches."

As they reached the boat, Krista said, "I love the ocean. I hate to see it misused. I know about water pollution and overfishing—but the ocean seems so huge! It's hard to imagine that anything this size could be so damaged."

Dale replied, "Overfishing and pollution have already cost many people their traditional livelihood. It will take a lot of countries working together to make conservation and cleanup a top priority before this part of the ocean can be a reliable fishery again."

In this chapter, we consider overfishing and other problems stemming from human population growth. We start by reviewing general principles governing population size. Then we consider how the rapid growth of the human population has led to pollution, depletion of Earth's resources, and global climate change. Last, we discuss how the choices we make today can affect the quality of life on Earth in the future.

Population Changes

There is no way to discuss human populations without arousing concern. The worries arise from two kinds of information. First, the increase in human numbers is startling, and we just do not know how long population growth can continue. Second, humans are using the world's natural resources much faster than they can be replaced (*if* they can be replaced). Although some resources are renewable, many are finite. We review the evidence for each of these trends and discuss possible consequences—and consider some solutions.

Population Growth Rate

Population dynamics describe how populations change in size. The human population, we can say, consists of all individuals alive at any time. This enormous population can be broken down into smaller groups. Thus we can speak of the population of the United States or Colombia or China. We can break it down further and consider, say, urban American populations versus rural ones.

Population size changes when individuals are added and removed at different rates. Usually, the rate is reported as the number of births or deaths per 1000 persons per year. Expressing a population's growth as a rate keeps the change in population size in perspective. For example, we would consider the addition of 1000 individuals to a population differently if it took place overnight than if it took place over a year. Furthermore, the addition of 1000 individuals would be more important if the initial population size were 100 than if it were 1000.

A population grows when more individuals are added than are subtracted. *Growth rate,* the difference between the birth rates and death rates of a population, is a measure of this event. Some individuals join a population or leave it by immigration or emigration, but most of a population's members are added by birth and removed by death. Most likely, your own family has added to the population growth over the last few generations. How many living descendants do your grandparents have (Figure **24.1**)?

In 2008, the estimated *birth rate* of the world's population was 20.2 births per 1000 individuals per year, and the *death rate* was 8.2 deaths per 1000 individuals per year. Thus the growth

FIGURE 24.1 Gladys Davis is surrounded by her six great-grandchildren. She and her husband had four children, two of whom had children of their own, producing three grandchildren. The three grandchildren produced these six great-grandchildren. By mid-2008, two of the children shown here had started their own families, producing six great-great-grandchildren. Although the size of each individual family was small, there are currently 15 living descendants of Jack and Gladys Davis. How much has your family grown in the last few generations?

rate of the world's population, an increase of 12 individuals per 1000, was 1.2%.

$$\frac{(\text{Births} - \text{Deaths})}{1000} = \frac{(20.2 - 8.2)}{1000} = \frac{12}{1000} = \frac{1.2}{100} = 1.2\%$$

However, knowing the growth rate is not enough to predict how quickly new individuals will be added to the population. We must also know the number of individuals in the starting population. Since added individuals also reproduce, population growth occurs much like compound interest accumulates in the bank—the more you start with, the more you end up with. At the same growth rate, then, the larger the size of the starting population, the more individuals are produced.

The age at which females have their first offspring dramatically affects the birth rate of a population. The younger women are when they begin to reproduce, the faster the population grows. In fact, the age when reproduction begins is the most important factor influencing a female's overall reproductive potential. For example, the increasing proportion of women who are postponing childbirth until their later reproductive years has been helping to slow the population growth rate of the United States. The birth rate in the United States is declining for women of all ages, but the largest drop in birth rate has occurred among women in their twenties. One reason may be that increasing numbers of women want to establish careers before beginning motherhood. Regardless of the reasons, this trend is contributing to slower U.S. population growth than in the past.

Besides birth rate, death rate is an important part of the equation that determines growth rate. Although the world birth rate has been steadily declining since 1970, the human population has continued to grow partly because the drop in death rate has been greater than the drop in birth rate. The discovery of antibiotics was certainly instrumental in the decline of death rates. However, even more important were improvements in sanitation, hygiene, and nutrition.

Although a growth rate of a few percent a year may not seem startling, its importance becomes clearer when it is expressed as **doubling time**—that is, the number of years it will take for a population to double at that rate of growth. To give you an idea of how important this measure is, if this page is 1/250 inch thick and were doubled (exponentially) only eight times, it would be an inch thick. At 12 more doublings, it would be as thick as a football field is long. At 42 times, it would reach to the moon; and at only 50 times, it would reach the 93 million miles to the sun. Obviously, knowing the doubling time of a population can yield some interesting predictions.

The simplest way to arrive at a doubling time is to divide the population's growth rate into 70 (a demographic constant value). Thus, if the world population continues to grow at the rate it did in 2008 (1.2%), the world population will double in just a little more than 58.8 years! This is how long it will be before we need two schools where there is now one and two roads, two dams, two telephone poles, two hospitals, two doctors, and two power plants where there is now one. With everything doubled, what happens to our quality of life in general? Doubling times vary widely in different countries, but in general, *less developed countries* (LDCs; poorer countries) have a doubling time of 50 years, *more developed countries* (MDCs; usually richer countries) have a doubling time of 304 years.

> ### stop and think
>
> A pair of cockroaches is placed on a small island. Assume that the doubling time for a population of cockroaches is 1 month. After 20 years the island contains half of the total number of roaches it could possibly hold. How much longer would it take until the island was completely filled with roaches? (*Hint:* What is the doubling time for the population?)

Age Structure

When we want to predict future growth, a population's **age structure**—the relative number of individuals of each age—can be helpful. The age structure of the population is important because only individuals within a certain age range reproduce. Among humans, for instance, toddlers and octogenarians are counted as members of the population, but they do not reproduce. The ages are often grouped into prereproductive, reproductive, and postreproductive categories. Generally, only individuals of reproductive age add to the population size. However, the prereproductive group (those who are currently too young to reproduce) usually get older; and when they enter the reproductive class, they have children, thus adding more members to the population. Even if the birth rate remains the same, the overall population size will grow more rapidly if the size of the reproductive class increases.

> ### stop and think
>
> Health care has improved greatly in the last century and has increased population growth. Why would measures that decrease child mortality (death) contribute more to population growth than would measures that increase life expectancy?

We see, then, that the relative size of the base of a population's age structure (the prereproductive age category) determines how quickly numbers will be added to the population in the future. A wide base to any age structure diagram reflects a growing population, whereas a narrow base characterizes a population that is getting smaller (Figure **24.2**). A large base to any such diagram, as exists in India, spells trouble regarding future demands on the country's commodities. Moderately stable nations, such as the United States, show a more consistent age distribution—with some fluctuation, but a small prereproductive population. The prereproductive base of Canada's age structure is smaller than the reproductive base. Canada's population will probably decline in the future.

Immigration and Emigration

If we consider the human population of the world as a whole, the effects of immigration and emigration on population size are eliminated. However, immigration and emigration can dramatically affect the population size of countries, cities, and regions. People tend to migrate out of LDCs; the migration rate is –0.4/1000. On the other hand, people tend to migrate into MDCs, where the average migration rate is 1.6/1000.

Patterns of Population Growth

Let's return to an idea we introduced earlier in this chapter—the importance of population size to the rate at which new individuals are added to a population. Recall that *when the growth rate remains constant,* the number of individuals added to the population increases more rapidly as the size of the population increases. This unrestricted growth at a constant rate is called *exponential growth.* When the size of a population growing in this fashion is shown graphically, we see a *J-shaped growth curve.*

Unrestrained growth occurs in environments that have plenty of resources and adequate waste removal. In the real world, however, these conditions rarely exist for long. What happens when the food supply begins to become depleted, when space runs out, or when wastes begin to accumulate? The answer to this question is more than theoretically interesting to humans.

The number of individuals of a given species that a particular environment can support for a prolonged period is called its **carrying capacity** (Figure **24.3**). It is determined by such factors as availability of resources, including food, water, and space; a means of cleaning away wastes; disease; and predation pressure.

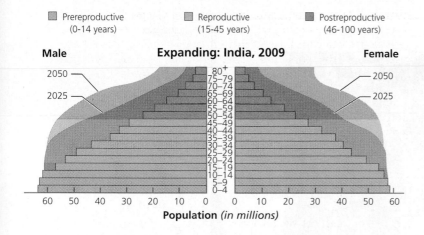

Male   **Expanding: India, 2009**   **Female**

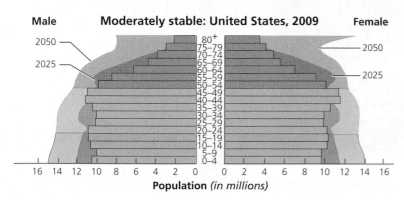

Male   **Moderately stable: United States, 2009**   **Female**

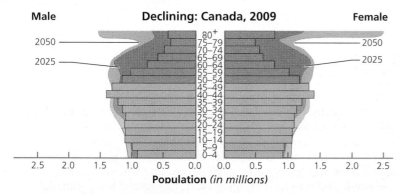

Male   **Declining: Canada, 2009**   **Female**

FIGURE 24.2 Age structures of India, the United States, and Canada. The age structures shown are estimates for 2009, 2025, and 2050.

Source: U.S. Census Bureau, International Data Base.

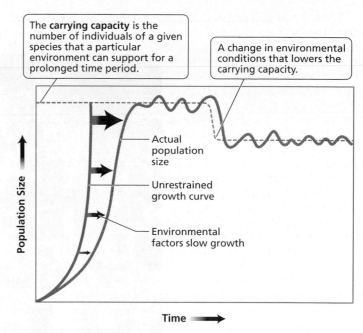

FIGURE 24.3 Population growth is often restrained by environmental factors, including the availability of food, water, and space and the accumulation of wastes. Environmental factors such as these determine the environment's carrying capacity. Eventually, growth levels off and the population size fluctuates around the carrying capacity. If a change in the environment lowers the carrying capacity, the population will stabilize at a smaller size.

If environmental limits are placed on population growth, we may wonder what might happen if a population overshoots the carrying capacity of the environment. One possibility is that environmental resources may become critically depleted, and the population may decline precipitously. More commonly, however, population growth is rapid while resources are plentiful. But as the population size approaches the carrying capacity of its environment, growth becomes slower and slower due to environmental pressures such as limited resources or accumulating wastes. Eventually, growth levels off and the population size fluctuates slightly around the carrying capacity—a pattern that forms an *S-shaped growth curve*. This pattern is called *logistic growth*.

How do these growth patterns apply to human population growth? For most of the period following the Stone Age, the human population grew steadily but relatively slowly. Around the time of the industrial revolution, the human population size began to increase rapidly, its growth pattern resembling a J-shaped curve. Now, however, the rapidity of its growth is disturbing (Figure **24.4**). Human population size did not reach 1 billion until 1804, but since then additional billions are being born at a much faster rate. In mid-2008, the world population was approximately 6.7 billion people. It is expected that, by 2018, our numbers will reach nearly 7.5 billion people.

The growth rate for human populations in some parts of the world is greater than in other parts. The growth rate in LDCs—where most people live in poverty—greatly exceeds the growth rate in MDCs, where people are usually wealthier. Even so, the growth rate of the world population has been slowing steadily over the past decade, suggesting that we may be reaching Earth's carrying capacity.

Environmental Factors and Population Size

The factors that reduce the size of populations can be described as density-dependent or density-independent. *Density-independent regulating factors* are causes of death that are not related to the density of individuals in a population (the number of individuals in a given area of habitat). These events include such natural disasters as floods, mudslides, earthquakes, hurricanes, and fires. For example, the earthquake that shook China in 2008 killed more than 69,000 people. Such events are density independent because adding or removing people from the population would not alter the mortality rate of the event itself.

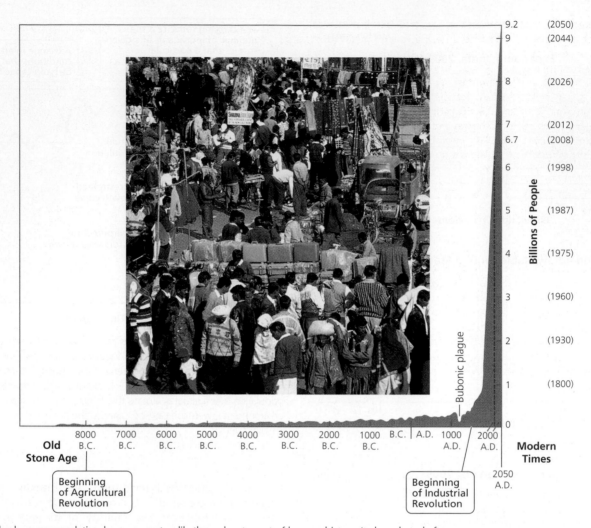

Billions of People

9.2 (2050)
9 (2044)
8 (2026)
7 (2012)
6.7 (2008)
6 (1998)
5 (1987)
4 (1975)
3 (1960)
2 (1930)
1 (1800)
0

Bubonic plague

Old Stone Age 8000 B.C. 7000 B.C. 6000 B.C. 5000 B.C. 4000 B.C. 3000 B.C. 2000 B.C. 1000 B.C. B.C. | A.D. 1000 A.D. 2000 A.D. **Modern Times**

2050 A.D.

Beginning of Agricultural Revolution

Beginning of Industrial Revolution

FIGURE 24.4 The human population has grown steadily throughout most of human history. It skyrocketed after the industrial revolution. The growth rate is now showing signs of slowing.

FIGURE 24.5 Food shortages may reflect density-dependent population controls, because they have a greater impact as population density increases.

Density-dependent regulating factors are events that have a greater impact on the population as conditions become more crowded. For example, famine can be a density-dependent factor. If only so much food is available, an increasing population would mean there was less food for each person until, finally, some people would begin to starve (Figure **24.5**). The greater the population density, the greater the effects of food scarcity on the population. Because disease-causing organisms and parasites spread more easily in crowded conditions than in uncrowded conditions, these too are density-dependent factors that regulate population sizes.

Earth's Carrying Capacity

Whatever your personal predictions for the future of humankind, one thing should be clear: the world is becoming an increasingly crowded place. You may recall from Chapter 23 that there is no input of new resources on Earth. Therefore, with our growing population, we run the risk of using up our resources and making our world unlivable because of our waste. In fact, human population size contributes to most of the problems we face today.

Earth's ability to support people depends on natural constraints, such as limited resource availability, as well as on human activities and choices. These, in turn, are influenced by economics, politics, technology, and values. Thus, Earth's carrying capacity for humans is uncertain and constantly changing. For instance, technological advances in agriculture and pollution control act to increase Earth's carrying capacity. At the same time, however, we have lowered the carrying capacity by consuming Earth's resources faster than they can be replaced—and, of course, some nonrenewable resources (such as fossil fuels) *cannot* be replaced.

Not surprisingly, estimates of Earth's carrying capacity vary widely, ranging from 5 billion to 20 billion people. Those who accept the lower values point to resource depletion and pollution as evidence that we have already exceeded Earth's carrying capacity with a world population of more than 6.7 billion.

Human Impacts on Earth's Carrying Capacity

An **ecological footprint** is a measure of the amount of productive land and water required to support a person or population based on its consumption levels. Everything a person uses—food, energy, water, housing space—comes from somewhere. Calculation of an ecological footprint includes everything that is consumed and the corresponding waste removal. Thus, ecological footprints describe the burden placed on Earth's carrying capacity.

Ecological footprints reflect lifestyle choices. Generally, more affluent people or populations have larger ecological footprints. Since wealth is not equally distributed around the globe, ecological footprint sizes vary among countries, with LDCs having smaller footprints than MDCs do (Figure **24.6**).

Agricultural Advances

Agricultural production has increased in many countries, largely due to the so-called *green revolution* of the 1970s and 1980s—the development of high-yield varieties of crops and the use of modern cultivation methods, including the use of farm machinery, fertilizers, pesticides, and irrigation. For example, Indonesia at one time imported more rice than any other country; but now it grows enough rice to feed its people, as well as some to export.

Nonetheless, the green revolution has a big price tag: high energy costs and environmental damage. Although crop yields may be four times greater than with more traditional methods, modern farming practices use up to 100 times more energy and mineral resources. It takes energy—usually obtained from fossil fuels—to produce fertilizers, power tractors and combines, and install and operate irrigation systems.

Depletion of Resources

An intact natural ecosystem usually retains soil and remains fertile. However, overuse and misuse of resources can decrease Earth's carrying capacity.

Soil erosion

As the human population grows, land is cultivated, grazed, and stripped of vegetation faster than it can recover. Wind and rain then carry away the topsoil, and the area's productivity declines. In this way, overfarming and overgrazing transform marginal farmland to desert, in a process called **desertification** (Figure **24.7**). According to the United Nations, a fifth of the world's population lives in areas currently threatened by desertification.

Deforestation

People often do not value what they have until it is gone. This may be true for forests. Some of us live in areas where trees are so common that we take them for granted. However, trees, especially

Q *What might account for the differences in the size of the ecological footprints of the nations shown here?*

FIGURE 24.6 An ecological footprint is a measurement that includes all the direct and indirect impacts of the use of resources by a person or population and is expressed as the amount of Earth's surface required for maintenance. It is usually expressed in hectares (ha). The citizens of some nations have much larger footprints than others.

A *More industrialized and affluent nations consume more of Earth's resources than poorer, less industrialized nations do.*

FIGURE 24.7 Desertification is the conversion of farmland, or in this case rangeland, to desert through overuse or other harmful practices.

when they are grouped together to form forests, are essential to global ecosystems. As we learned in Chapter 23, forests play an important role in water, carbon, and nitrogen cycles. Tree roots also reduce erosion by holding soil in place. If trees are cut down, rainwater runs off the land, carrying away soil and causing floods. In addition, ecosystems containing trees support an incredible variety of life. Trees also influence local and global climate, including temperature and rainfall.

Why are forests disappearing? The answer is simple: the human population is expanding. People need space in which to live, and they need wood for homes and furniture. Livestock cannot graze in forests, and crops cannot grow in forests, so trees are cut for pasture and farmland. Most trees are not replanted.

Deforestation is the removal of trees from an area without replacing them (Figure **24.8**). Deforestation is taking place in many regions of the world, including the United States. Before the colonization of North America, forests covered most of the eastern seacoast. Cities have now replaced many of those forests. In the U.S. Pacific Northwest, 80% of the forests are slated for logging.

Nonetheless, tropical forests—most of them located in less developed nations—are falling the fastest. Why? The first reason (based on impact) the land is being cleared is so that native families can feed themselves. The second reason is commercial logging. The third reason is cattle ranching. Cattle can graze for about 6 to 10 years after trees have been cleared from a tropical forest before shrubs take over and make the area unsuitable for rangeland. Foreign companies own most of these cattle ranches, and the beef is often exported to fast-food restaurant chains in other countries. Thus the decisions we make about what to eat for lunch may indirectly influence the rate of tropical deforestation. Other reasons include mining and the development of hydroelectric dams.

FIGURE 24.8 Deforestation damages soil quality.

Whatever the reason for tropical deforestation, soil fertility declines rapidly when these forests are cut. As a result, native people who depend on the soil for their living become poorer.

Overfishing

Overfishing is another practice that is lowering Earth's carrying capacity. Fishing has long provided humans with an abundant food supply, but now many fish populations are being depleted to such levels that some fish can no longer be caught in certain areas. Recent examples include Atlantic cod in New England and salmon in the northwestern United States. The problem is that we have not given the fish enough time to replace their numbers at their reduced population size. As numbers of fish have dwindled, the human response has been to fish harder, using more boats and new techniques, including electronic searches. Some species, the Atlantic bluefin tuna for instance, may already be so overfished that they will become extinct.

Water shortage

Earth has been called the Water Planet because water is so plentiful here. Still, relatively little is available for human use because 97% of Earth's water is in the oceans. You might think that at least all the freshwater would be available, but much of it is tied up in ice or clouds, hidden in underground rivers, or otherwise inaccessible for immediate human use. Indeed, freshwater scarcity is an emerging crisis.

In most regions, however, the underlying cause of water shortage is too many people drawing from a limited supply. Humans use water from two main sources: surface water, such as rivers and lakes, and groundwater, which is water found under Earth's surface in porous layers of rock, such as sand or gravel. When too much surface water is used in an area, ecosystems are affected. As much as 30% of a river's flow can usually be removed without affecting the natural ecosystem. However, in some parts of the southwestern United States, as much as 70% of the surface water has been removed.

Consider how population growth has affected the Colorado River. This once mighty river flowed with such force that it cut the Grand Canyon from the landscape. Today, just a trickle flows from the river's mouth because water is siphoned off along its course for irrigation, people's personal use, and recreational purposes. In 1922, seven states—Arizona, California, Colorado, Nevada, New Mexico, Utah and Wyoming—divided the rights to draw water from the Colorado River based on each state's needs. During the 1900s, California was permitted to take more than its agreed-upon share, because the other states did not use their full allotment. However, the population in all states has grown. For example, Nevada's population was so low in 1922 that it was allotted only 4% of the water from the Colorado River. Now, Las Vegas is the fastest-growing city in the nation, and some experts predict that it will run out of water by 2010. Lake Mead and Lake Powell, the two largest reservoirs in the southwestern United States, are fed by the Colorado River. The water level in these reservoirs in 2007 was half of what it was seven years earlier. Water rights were renegotiated in 2007. The upper states are permitted to draw more water when they need it, and the lower states are permitted to pump groundwater from other areas.

Human use of groundwater is also depleting the aquifers (porous layers of underground rock where groundwater is found). Water is added to aquifers by rainfall or melting snow that filters through the topsoil. In some areas, however, water is being removed from aquifers faster than it can be replenished. The

Ogallala Aquifer underlies eight states in the Great Plains region of the United States. Much of the water pumped up from the Ogallala Aquifer is used for irrigation and has made this region some of the most productive farmland in the country. However, the water level in the aquifer is dropping by 6 feet a year. The water tables beneath the highly populated northeastern United States are also dwindling dangerously.

In some places drought, or lack of rain, has compounded the problem of water scarcity caused by the growing human population. A drought has affected the western United States for more than a decade. In some regions, farming and ranching have been severely affected. For example, some ranchers in the West have sold off parts of their herds because there is no grass to feed them. Drought also increases the risk of wildfires that kill plants, wildlife, and humans as well as destroy property. (Climate change, discussed later in the chapter, can also be blamed for the increased numbers of wildfires in recent years—and for the extended average fire season in the western United States, which is now 2 months longer than it was in 1970.)

A **water footprint** is an indicator of direct and indirect water use by a person, locality, or nation. *Direct use* refers to water use at home; *indirect use* refers to water used to produce goods and services. Since not all goods used in a country are produced there, a nation's water footprint includes the water needed to produce that product inside and outside that country's border. North Americans have an exceptionally large water footprint. The global average yearly use of water per person is 1240 cubic meters. In the United States, each person uses of about 2500 cubic meters of water a year; in China, each person uses about 700 cubic meters of water a year.

These numbers are shocking, and you might be tempted to claim that *you* certainly do not use that much water. In one sense, you would be right. Personal use accounts for only a small percentage of total U.S. water use. Most of the water is used in agriculture. To feed its growing human population, our country increasingly relies on irrigation to make arid areas fruitful. The rest of the water is used primarily in industry for steam generation or the cooling of power plants.

Irrigation has pros and cons. It allows crops to grow in areas that would otherwise be barren. But it can also, in the long run, make the land unfit for agriculture. Irrigation water contains dissolved minerals. Whereas runoff from natural rainfall would carry these salts away, irrigation water soaks into the soil. Then, when the water evaporates from the soil, the salts are left behind. The resulting accumulation of salts in the soil is called *salinization*. Worldwide, salinization destroys the fertility of 5000 km^2 (1930 mi^2) of irrigated land each year.

stop and think

Conservationists sometimes buy wetlands, hoping to preserve the habitats of endangered plants and wildlife. Despite this conservation strategy, the wetlands sometimes dry up. Why is it also important to buy the rights to the water that feeds the wetland?

What steps can be taken to reduce water shortages?

1. **Reduce water use.** Each of us could help by individual efforts. However, because most water is used in agriculture, the biggest benefit would come from improved irrigation methods. Between 1950 and 1980, for example, Israel reduced its water wastage from 83% to a mere 5%, primarily by changing from spray irrigation to drip irrigation. In contrast,

more than half the water diverted for irrigation in California's Imperial Valley is wasted due to poorly designed irrigation systems.

2. **Raise the price of water.** The cost of water in the United States is substantially below its cost in European countries. Experience has shown that the consumer's interest in conserving water is directly related to its cost. Clearly, economic and legal incentives for conserving water are needed. Some experts suggest that water will be the most precious commodity in the twenty-first century, as oil was in the twentieth century.

Pollution

Another way we lower Earth's carrying capacity is by polluting resources, making the resource unfit for human use or damaging the environment in other ways.

Water pollution

Factories, refineries, and waste treatment plants release fluids of varying quality directly into our water supplies. Several contaminants responsible for surface water pollution are discussed in Chapter 23. For example, mercury and PCBs in water are examined as materials that become concentrated in organisms as these chemicals are passed up the food chain. We also considered how fertilizer runoff can lead to an overgrowth of algae and plants in bodies of water, which can deplete the oxygen content of the water so much that it no longer supports life.

The same materials that contaminate surface water can contaminate groundwater. Above- or belowground storage tanks can corrode and leak their contents, which may be oil, gasoline, or other hazardous liquids. Septic systems, which are designed to allow wastewater to slowly drain away from their sources, may leak bacteria, viruses, and household chemicals to groundwater. Hazardous waste sites and landfills can also leak harmful materials into groundwater.

Ozone depletion

Ozone, a gas whose molecules are composed of three atoms of oxygen (O_3), can be a good thing or a bad thing. At Earth's surface—say, anywhere in the first few miles of atmosphere—it is generally a bad thing. In fact, ozone is the primary component of photochemical smog, the noxious gas produced largely by sunlight interacting with air pollutants, such as hydrocarbons and nitrogen dioxide. Ozone irritates the eyes, skin, lungs, nose, and throat. (Effects of photochemical smog on the respiratory system are discussed in the Environmental Issue essay, *Air Pollution and Human Health*.) Ozone can also damage forests and crops and dissolve rubber.

In contrast, naturally produced ozone is an essential part of the stratosphere, a layer of the lower atmosphere that encircles the Earth about 10 to 45 km (6 to 28 mi) above its surface. The concentration of ozone in the stratosphere reaches levels of only about 1 molecule in 100,000. If all this ozone were compressed from top to bottom, its depth would equal only the diameter of a pencil lead. Still, the ozone is able to shield the Earth from excessive ultraviolet (UV) radiation from the sun; without it, most terrestrial life-forms could not exist. UV radiation causes cataracts, aging of the skin, sunburn, and snow blindness; and it is the primary cause of skin cancer that kills nearly 11,000 Americans each year. In addition, UV radiation inhibits the immune systems of animals and can interfere with plant growth.

In 1985, British scientists reported a sharp drop in the concentration of ozone over the Antarctic. This "hole" appears on a yearly cycle—at the beginning of the Antarctic spring (early September through mid-October; Figure **24.9**). The primary cause was discovered to be the action of chlorofluorocarbons (CFCs)—chemicals once important in cooling systems, as aerosol propellants, in the manufacture of plastic foam such as Styrofoam, and as solvents in the electronic industry. The CFCs drift up to the stratosphere, where UV radiation breaks them down into chlorine, fluorine, and carbon. Then, under the conditions found in the stratosphere, chlorine can react with ozone, converting it to oxygen. Because chlorine is not altered in this reaction, a single chlorine molecule can destroy thousands of ozone molecules.

Several laws are now in place to prevent the production or release of CFCs. In 1990 and 1992, industrialized countries signed agreements to reduce CFC production and have now phased out CFC production. It is expected that developing countries will phase out CFC production by 2010. Substitutes for CFCs have been found for aerosol cans, refrigerators, and air conditioners. There is evidence that the reduction in CFC production is paying off. In 1996, two years after CFC use peaked, chlorine levels in the lower atmosphere were slightly lower than before. By 1999, chlorine levels in the stratosphere were reduced. In 2008, scientists predicted that the ozone hole will recover by 2050–2070.

Global Climate Change

The word *climate* describes a region's average temperature, precipitation, humidity, barometric pressure, solar radiation, and other weather characteristics considered over a relatively long period of time. *Global climate change*, then, refers to changes in Earth's climate patterns—trends and variations. Although Earth's climate changes naturally over time, the rate of change today is extremely rapid.

The Intergovernmental Panel on Climate Change (IPCC), an international panel consisting of hundreds of scientists, was established by the United Nations Environmental Programme and the World Meteorological Organization to assess technical and scientific information regarding climate change as well as its social and economical implications. These groups scrutinized thousands of scientific papers and measurements of physical conditions on Earth. Here are two key conclusions of the IPCC's Fourth Assessment Report (2007).

1. The global climate is unquestionably getting warmer. The global temperature has increased 0.74°C in the last 100 years. Eleven out of 12 of the hottest years on record occurred between 1995 and 2006. During the last decades, the number of really hot days and heat waves increased, and the number of cold days decreased.

2. Most of the increase in global temperatures is due to human activity that releases greenhouse gases (carbon dioxide, methane, and nitrous oxide) into the atmosphere. The IPCC indicates that the "assessed likelihood, using expert judgment" that human activity is responsible for global warming is over 90%.

Nearly everyone agrees that the global climate is getting warmer, and all but a few skeptics agree that the elevated temperatures are due to human activities, primarily the burning of fossil fuels. We will look at the evidence supporting the link between greenhouse gases and global warming and climate change and then at the predicted consequences of global climate change.

Global Warming and Greenhouse Gases

Recall from Chapter 23 that humans are disrupting the natural carbon cycle by burning fossil fuels, which increases atmospheric carbon dioxide (CO_2), and by clear-cutting forests, which reduces the removal of CO_2 from the atmosphere. Because of these activities, the level of atmospheric carbon dioxide is rising. Carbon dioxide along with methane, nitrous oxides, and CFCs are considered greenhouse gases. Like the glass on a greenhouse, these gases allow the sunlight to pass through to Earth's surface, where it is absorbed and radiated back to the atmosphere as heat—long-wave infrared radiation. Greenhouse gases then absorb the infrared radiation, thus trapping the heat. (Figure **24.10**). Because of this effect, a growing concern is that the increase in atmospheric CO_2 due to human activities is leading to a rise in temperatures throughout the world—a situation known popularly as **global warming**.

Scientists rely on direct and indirect evidence of the link between global warming and greenhouse gases. Direct evidence comes from present-day measurement. Since 1958, atmospheric CO_2 has been measured at Mauna Loa Observatory in Hawaii. Indirect evidence comes from ice cores, long columns of ice taken from ice sheets, ice caps, or glaciers. The most recent ice is at the

A satellite image of the hole in the ozone layer over Antarctica. The ozone hole is depicted in blue.

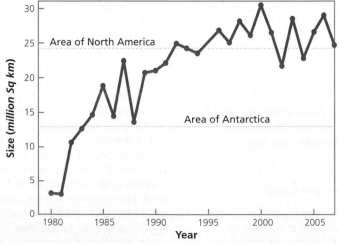

The recovery of the ozone layer is occuring more slowly than originally expected. Its recovery is expected by 2068.

The ozone layer absorbs ultraviolet (UV) radiation. A thinner ozone layer allows more UV radiation to reach the earth, increasing the cancer risk.

FIGURE 24.9 The thinning of the ozone layer

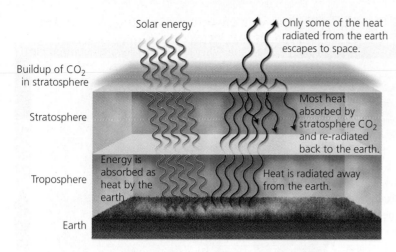

Solar energy

Only some of the heat radiated from the earth escapes to space.

Buildup of CO₂ in stratosphere

Stratosphere

Most heat absorbed by stratosphere CO₂ and re-radiated back to the earth.

Troposphere

Energy is absorbed as heat by the earth

Heat is radiated away from the earth.

Earth

FIGURE 24.10 Carbon dioxide and other greenhouse gases promote global warming by trapping heat (infrared radiation) in the atmosphere, much like a greenhouse glass traps heat. Thus, the global warming that is believed to be occurring due to the accumulation of these gases is known as the greenhouse effect.

top of the core; the oldest is at the bottom. Scientists can examine these ice cores and determine greenhouse gas concentrations, environmental temperature, and snowfall to understand the region's climate history. Notice the correlation between rising atmospheric CO_2 and global temperature in Figure **24.11**.

Some people do not believe that rising atmospheric CO_2 from human impacts is the cause of increasing global temperature. Some point out that rising temperatures could be the result of a natural climate cycle. Others suggest that domesticated animals, such as cattle, sheep, and goats, are to blame. Bacteria in the guts of these animals produce methane, a greenhouse gas whose heat-trapping ability is 20 times greater than that of carbon dioxide. The collective belches and flatulence of all the grazing animals on Earth accounts for 20% of the methane gas released into the atmosphere.

The IPCC predicts that Earth's surface temperatures will rise 1.8°C to 4.0°C (3.2°F to 7.2°F) during the twenty-first century. The range of the prediction for temperature increase is large due to uncertainties concerning the effects of many of the interacting factors, such as cloud cover due to evaporation, cooling effects of

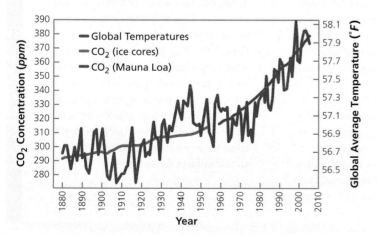

FIGURE 24.11 The concentration of carbon dioxide (CO_2) in the atmosphere has been increasing for many years. Two major causes are the burning of fossil fuels, which releases CO_2, and deforestation, which leaves fewer trees to remove CO_2 from the atmosphere. Global temperatures have also risen during this period.

atmospheric particulates such as sulfates, possible increased primary productivity due to the increase in CO_2, and ability of the ocean to absorb CO_2.

Why is there such commotion over global warming? Why should anyone care whether the atmosphere becomes a few degrees warmer? The answer is that global warming is closely related to global climate change, which has many social and economic consequences. Let's look at the current extent of global warming and possible consequences suggested in the 2007 IPCC report.

- **Melting ice caps, rising sea level, and warmer oceans.** Mountain glaciers and snow cover at both poles has declined. Land-based ice sheets in Greenland and Antarctica have been melting. When ice on land melts, sea level rises. In addition, the resulting reduction of white covering on Earth means less of the sun's energy is reflected back to space. Less reflection further increases warming, which leads to increased glacier melting. During the decade from 1993 to 2003, sea level rose about 31 mm (1.22 in.), and the temperature of the oceans increased. Ocean water expands as it warms, contributing further to the rise in sea level. According to the IPCC, the sea level could rise 18–59 cm (7–23 in.) during the twenty-first century.

  The temperature changes and, therefore, the melting of ice sheets is greatest in the Arctic, where it has adversely affected the food web. Because of the melted ice sheets, polar bears must swim long distances (instead of walking on the ice) to capture the seals they rely on for food. Swimming requires more energy than walking does, so polar bears are starving. As a result, polar bears are becoming an endangered species. The melting ice sheets also affect human populations. The Inuit, a native people of the North American coast, also rely on seals for food, and sea ice is dangerous to hunt on.

- **Coastal cities could flood.** The rising sea level would have the greatest effect on low-lying coastal countries such as Bangladesh, Egypt, Vietnam, and Mozambique. Seawater could cover significant areas in these densely populated lands. In the United States, major cities such as New York, Miami, Jacksonville, Boston, San Francisco, and Los Angeles could someday be largely underwater. Do you live near a coastline?

- **Changing weather patterns.** Global warming is causing changes in both temperature and rainfall patterns. This climate change is responsible for the drought-causing water shortage in the southwest United States. Most scientists agree that warmer oceans can fuel hurricanes. Hurricanes in the North Atlantic have intensified and will continue to intensify during the twenty-first century.

  Recall from Chapter 23 that the distribution of climax communities, each with its characteristic plant and animal life, is largely determined by temperature and rainfall. Because of global warming, some species will thrive and others may become extinct. There will be a shift in the location of agricultural regions, meaning food production in the central plains of the United States and Canada could drop. Areas that now produce enough food for export may not be able to produce enough for the local population. Meanwhile, other regions—parts of India and Russia, for instance—might receive increased rainfall that would benefit agriculture. These changes will alter the distribution of "haves" and "have-nots." How will the world community deal with the shifts in economic and political power?

Air Pollution and Human Health

Caution: The air you breathe may be hazardous to your health. It may even kill you—especially if you have heart or respiratory problems. In most major cities, poor air quality can be obvious, signaled by a brown haze. Even in remote national parks, air pollution is often significant enough to reduce visibility. Yet the consequences of air pollution can be subtle and slow to make themselves felt. They include damage to the environment as well as to human health.

Two major human sources of air pollution are motor vehicle exhaust and industrial emissions. The exhaust pipes on our cars and the smokestacks on factories spew oxides of sulfur, nitrogen, and carbon; a mixture of hydrocarbons; and many particulates (such as soot and smoke) into the air. In the atmosphere, sulfur dioxide and nitrogen dioxide dissolve in water vapor and form an aerosol of strong acids—sulfuric acid and nitric acid, respectively. Some of this aerosol may drift upward, forming acidic clouds that can be blown hundreds of miles by the winds and then fall as acid rain. On the other hand, the acidic aerosol may remain close to its source as a component of the haze created by air pollution. In addition, sunlight can cause hydrocarbons and nitrogen dioxide to react with one another and form a mix of hundreds of substances called photochemical smog. The most harmful component of photochemical smog is ozone, which attacks cells and tissues, irritates the respiratory system, damages plants, and even erodes rubber. Paradoxically, the ozone that is so damaging when it is found at ground level in photochemical smog is the same compound that is beneficial in the upper layers of the atmosphere, where it prevents much of the sun's ultraviolet radiation from reaching Earth's surface. Unfortunately, the ozone found in smog does not make its way to the ozone layer of the upper atmosphere, because it is converted to oxygen within a few days.

When we breathe polluted air, the respiratory system is, not surprisingly, the first to be affected. As air containing toxic substances fills the lungs, cells lining the airways and those within the lungs are injured. Damaged cells release histamine, which causes nearby capillaries to widen and become more permeable to fluid. As a result, fluid leaks from the capillaries and accumulates within the tissues. Even a brief exposure to oxides of sulfur (5 parts per million, or ppm, for a few minutes), the oxides of nitrogen (2 ppm for 10 minutes), or ozone leads to fluid accumulation, increased mucus production, and muscle spasms (intense involuntary contractions) in the bronchioles. These effects obstruct air flow and reduce gas exchange.

Long-term irritation of bronchi by pollutants is a cause of chronic bronchitis and emphysema. The process begins when irritation causes fluid accumulation that, in turn, stimulates mucus production and coughing. The cough and mucus, signs of chronic bronchitis, irritate the lungs even more. As the bronchitis continues, the air passageways become narrower, trapping air in the lungs. When the increased pressure accompanying a cough causes the overinflated alveoli to rupture, emphysema begins.

Some pollutants can cause cancer. They overload or in other ways damage the mechanisms that would normally cleanse the respiratory system, so that any cancer-causing chemicals in the inhaled air are no longer effectively removed. Within the airways these chemicals may then bring about changes in genetic material that can lead to cancer.

With so many documented health consequences of air pollution, you may wonder why the world's great minds haven't developed the technology to solve the problem. In fact, they have. But unfortunately, air pollution is not just a scientific problem; it is also a social, political, and economic problem. The technology to prevent

Air pollution has health, social, economic, and political consequences.

air pollution is available. For example, scrubbers can remove 90% of the particulate matter and sulfur dioxide from industrial smokestacks. However, the technology is costly.

Questions to Consider

- Are you willing to pay more for goods and services, such as food, clothing, and transportation, to offset the cost of air pollution reducing technology? How much more are you willing to pay for low-sulfur fuels, for instance?

- Some of the strategies for improving air quality are likely to impose a certain amount of inconvenience. Are you willing to carpool, take a bus, or better yet, walk instead of drive to improve the air quality in your community?

- Considering that the pollutants in air are often blown hundreds of miles from their source, are you willing to make the same sacrifices to improve a stranger's air quality?

- Who should make the laws for controlling pollution when the pollutants are likely to cross state or national borders? Who should enforce those laws?

- **Human health.** The IPCC predicts that global warming will have various negative effects on human health. The change in climate is likely to increase the number of deaths due to heat waves, flooding, and droughts leading to starvation. Climate change could also increase air pollution. In addition, because mosquitoes and ticks, as well as other vectors of disease, would thrive in a warmer climate, we may see increases in malaria, West Nile virus encephalitis (inflammation of the brain), Lyme disease, and the like.

stop and think

Scientists are working on a low-nitrogen diet for cattle and sheep to reduce the amount of methane these animals produce. How might such a diet affect global warming? On what factors might the outcome depend?

Carbon Footprint

A person's—or a nation's—**carbon footprint** is a measure of the amount of CO_2 entering the atmosphere due to that person's—or nation's—daily activities. It includes the carbon emissions directly from our activities as well as those from the whole life cycle—production through waste disposal—of the products we use.

Reduction of direct carbon footprint

We have the most control over carbon emissions from our own activities. How can you reduce the size of your carbon footprint? One way is to walk, ride a bicycle, or take public transportation instead of driving. When driving is necessary, carpool with others whenever possible. When you purchase appliances, choose energy-efficient ones. Minimize the use of heating or cooling systems in your home by programming your thermostat and wearing clothing suited to the season. Turn off the lights when you leave a room, and shut down your computer after using it. In short, conserve energy. The environment will benefit; the exercise will improve your health; and you will save money.

Reduction of global carbon footprint

To reduce future climate change, the leaders of 182 nations signed an agreement, the Kyoto Protocol, to reduce CO_2 emissions to pre-1990 levels through technology and reduced energy use. The Kyoto Protocol was ratified in early 2005. The United States has refused to ratify the agreement because it requires industrialized countries to reduce their emissions of greenhouse gases but does not require rapidly industrializing countries to reduce their emissions. Believing that technology can solve the problem of global warming, the United States and the European Union agreed to share information on technological advances.

Whether or not you believe energy usage and the burning of fossil fuels is affecting the global climate, one thing is certain: the supply of fossil fuels is limited. Oil, coal, and natural gas are *not* renewable resources. When they are gone, they are gone forever. Even if you are among the very few skeptics about the role of greenhouses gases in climate change, you should consider some of the possible social, political, economic, and environmental consequences of continued reliance on fossil fuels (Figure **24.12**). We will have to think through our choices carefully. For example, some

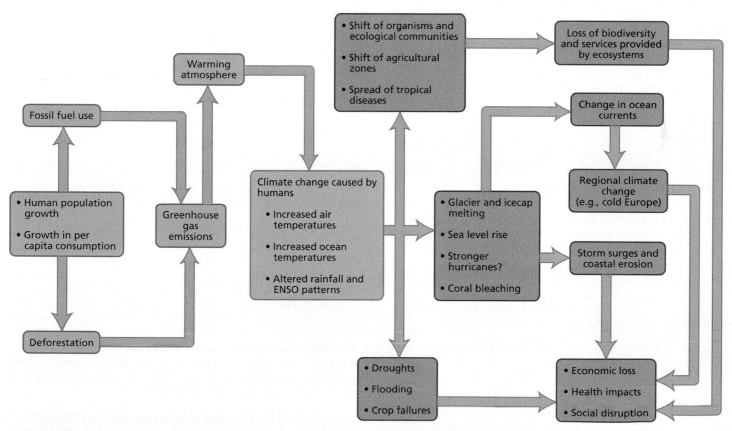

FIGURE 24.12 Global climate change (shown in the green box) is related to human use of fossil fuels, as shown in the boxes on the left. The social and economic consequences of global climate change are shown in the boxes on the right.

experts tout *biofuels*—fuels made from recently dead biological material—as the way to reduce our dependence on oil. Other experts argue that growing crops to make biofuel is driving up the cost of food. Sugarcane is sometimes used to make biofuel. Will increased use of biofuel speed deforestation of the Amazon rain forest to make room for growing sugarcane? How much stress will irrigating plants for biofuel place on our water supplies? Residents of several states in the Midwest are going to court to challenge the development of biofuel projects in their region.

Besides biofuel, what are our energy options to reduce reliance on fossil fuel? We have several choices, each best suited for different environments, each with costs and benefits.

Nuclear energy is the energy that holds protons and neutrons together in the nucleus of an atom. In nuclear power plants, we split atomic nuclei and convert the energy released to thermal energy, which we then use to create electricity. The process, called nuclear fission, does not produce greenhouse gases, and in that respect is good for environment. Mining uranium damages the environment less than mining for coal does. However, nuclear fission must be carefully controlled, and accidents have happened. In 1986, a nuclear disaster occurred at the Chernobyl Nuclear Power Plant in the Soviet Union. Approximately 600,000 people were exposed to radioactive fallout, and 57 people died as a direct result of the disaster. Another 9000 additional cancer deaths later occurred in people living within a wide radius. Accidents at nuclear power plants are extremely rare, but the results are disastrous. Another drawback to using nuclear power is the creation of radioactive waste and the problem of its disposal. Even so, today more than 400 nuclear power plants are operating in more than 30 countries.

Hydroelectric power plants use the energy of falling water to produce electricity. It does not produce greenhouse gases, it is efficient, and it is renewable (as long as it rains and snows). However, damming rivers damages affected habitats—both aquatic and terrestrial.

Other renewable energy technologies are not yet able to meet our electricity needs, but they show great promise. Solar power involves harnessing the sun's energy. In windy areas, giant windmills can convert wind power to electricity. Ocean currents can also be converted to electricity. Geothermal energy deep within the Earth can be used to heat water that can, in turn, be used to generate electricity.

Looking to the Future

In many ways, our grandparents were right: older ideas *were* better—at least, some were. Today's economy is wasteful. Many of us behave as if the world exists for humans alone.

In Chapter 23 and this chapter, we have seen that humans are a *small* part of the biosphere and that it must remain healthy if we are to remain healthy. We must realize that we are subject to the same principles that govern all other life—indeed, all of the Earth. Instead of trying to conquer nature, we must work with natural laws. Above all, we must recognize that Earth's resources are limited and must be shared with all living organisms as well as preserved for future generations.

This dramatic turnabout in thinking and behavior will not be easy to accomplish. It will require changing the way governments and businesses operate as well as modifying the ingrained habits of individuals. However, humans are by nature problem solvers. We now have the opportunity to approach with intelligence one of the greatest problems ever to confront humankind.

Jane Goodall, famed animal behavior researcher and founder of the Jane Goodall Institute, a center for environmental studies, is optimistic about our future. In her words, "My reasons for hope are fourfold: (1) the human brain; (2) the resilience of nature; (3) the energy and enthusiasm that is found or can be kindled among young people worldwide; and (4) the indomitable human spirit."[1] We have to be optimistic that a solution is possible and then work together to achieve it.

---

[1]Jane Goodall (with Phillip Berman), *Reasons for Hope: A Spiritual Journey* (New York: Warner Books, 1999), 233.

---

highlighting the concepts

Population Changes (pp. 523–524)

- Population dynamics describes how populations change in size. Population size changes when the number of individuals added differs from the number of individuals removed. Individuals are added through births and immigration. Individuals are removed through death and emigration.
- The change in population is usually expressed as a rate: the number of births or deaths for a certain number of individuals during a certain period (usually per 1000 individuals per year). If we rule out immigration and emigration, we can say a population's growth rate equals the birth rate minus the death rate.
- The age at which females have their first offspring is an important factor in determining a population's growth rate.
- The age structure of a population is an important determinant of future changes in population size. The age structure of a population consists of the relative numbers of individuals in each age category: prereproductive, reproductive, and postreproductive. A growing population has a large base of prereproductive individuals. A stable population has approximately equal numbers of individuals in each

age category. A population that is getting smaller has a large proportion of individuals who are past reproductive age.

Patterns of Population Growth (pp. 524–525)

- When it is not limited by finite resources, a population grows without restraint. This pattern is called exponential growth.
- The carrying capacity of the environment is the number of individuals (of a particular species) it can support over a long period of time. Carrying capacity is determined by the amount of available resources.
- Generally, as a population grows and its size approaches the carrying capacity of the environment, the growth rate slows and the population size levels off, fluctuating around the carrying capacity. This pattern is called logistic growth.

Environmental Factors and Population Size (pp. 525–526)

- Population size can be regulated by density-independent regulating factors, events such as natural disasters, whose effects are not influenced by the size of the population, and by density-dependent regulating factors, which are factors that have a greater impact as the population becomes more crowded. Density-dependent factors include food availability and disease.

Earth's Carrying Capacity (pp. 526–527)

- Humans have raised Earth's carrying capacity through technological advances, but they have also decreased it through resource depletion and pollution. The size of the human population contributes to many of the problems we face today.

Human Impacts on Earth's Carrying Capacity (pp. 527–530)

- An ecological footprint is a measure of the impact a person or population makes on the environment. It is expressed as the total amount of biological productive land and water needed to produce and dispose of the products that are consumed.
- Soil erosion due to overgrazing and overfarming is converting marginal farmlands to deserts, by a process called desertification.
- Deforestation—removing trees from an area without replacing them—is a growing problem throughout the world, especially in tropical rain forests.
- Overfishing is causing fish populations to fall below replacement levels.
- We are withdrawing more freshwater from available sources than can be replaced by precipitation.

- Pollution is making some freshwater sources unfit for human use.
- Air pollution in the form of chlorofluorocarbons (CFCs) has depleted the ozone layer in the lower atmosphere (the stratosphere). The ozone layer traps ultraviolet (UV) light, protecting life on Earth from the harmful effects of UV radiation.

Global Climate Change (pp. 530–534)

- Earth's surface temperature is getting warmer. This increase is more than 90% likely due to an increase in greenhouse gases resulting from human activities such as burning fossil fuels.
- Greenhouse gases (CO_2, methane, nitrous oxides, and CFCs) trap heat in Earth's atmosphere.
- As Earth's atmosphere gets warmer, we can expect continued melting of ice caps and glaciers, rising oceans that may flood coastal cities, climate change, and human health problems related to heat and vector-borne diseases.
- A carbon footprint is the amount of CO_2 entering the atmosphere due the daily activities of an individual or group of people. We can reduce our carbon footprint by reducing our reliance on fossil fuels. Alternative fuels each have their own costs and benefits.

Looking to the Future (p. 534)

- Humans are a small part of a large ecosystem. We must find ways to work within natural laws to preserve ecosystem Earth and its biodiversity.

recognizing key terms

population dynamics *p. 523*	carrying capacity *p. 524*	deforestation *p. 528*	global warming *p. 530*
doubling time *p. 524*	ecological footprint *p. 527*	water footprint *p. 529*	carbon footprint *p. 533*
age structure *p. 524*	desertification *p. 527*		

reviewing the concepts

1. Define the growth rate of a population. *p. 523*
2. What is meant by the age structure of a population? How is a population's age structure related to predictions of its future growth? *p. 524*
3. What is the carrying capacity of the environment? *pp. 524–525*
4. Differentiate between density-independent and density-dependent regulating factors. Give examples of each. *pp. 525–526*
5. What is an ecological footprint? *p. 527*
6. What determines whether ozone is helpful or harmful? What is causing the destruction of the ozone layer? *pp. 529–530*
7. What causes desertification? *p. 527*
8. Define deforestation. Where is it occurring most rapidly? What are the primary reasons for deforestation? *pp. 527–528*
9. What is meant by the greenhouse effect? Explain why there is concern that the rising level of atmospheric carbon dioxide could lead to global warming. *pp. 530–531*

10. Which of the following is an example of a density-dependent regulating factor?
    a. Earthquake
    b. Starvation
    c. Flood
    d. Drought
11. If a population reaches the carrying capacity of the environment,
    a. unrestrained growth will occur.
    b. the population will decline rapidly.
    c. food and other resources will increase.
    d. the population size will fluctuate around this level.
12. The ozone layer of the atmosphere absorbs
    a. carbon dioxide.
    b. chlorine.
    c. nitrogen dioxide.
    d. ultraviolet radiation.

1. The populations of Kenya and Italy (shown in the figure) have approximately the same number of people, and the growth rate of the two populations is the same. Assuming that the growth rate stays the same, will the populations have the same number of people in 50 years? Explain.

2. Around 1993, four species of Asian carp escaped from fish farms in Mississippi and Arkansas, and by 1997 they had spread from Arkansas to Louisiana. By 2003, the number of Asian carp in Louisiana had increased dramatically. Asian carp are very large fish that eat plankton, which many other freshwater fish also consume.
   a. Explain why the Asian carp population was able to increase extremely rapidly in a new environment (Louisiana).
   b. Explain why scientists are concerned that Asian carp will reduce the population size of other freshwater fish, even though the carp do not eat these other fish.

3. When soldiers returned home after World War II, many of them began having children who came to be called the baby boomers, the largest generation in United States history. Born between 1946 and 1964, the baby boomers began to turn 60 in 2006. Many will soon reach retirement age. How would you expect this change in population structure to affect how tax money will be spent?

4. Explain why population growth is usually expressed as a *rate*.

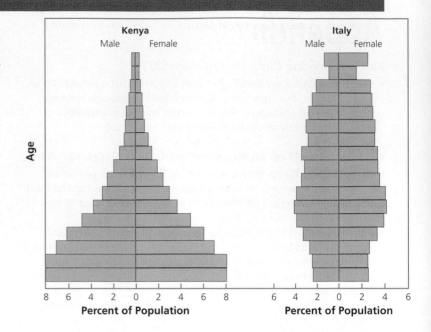

Use at least three reliable sources (journals, newspapers, books, websites) to answer the following questions. List each source you considered, and explain why you chose the three sources used.

1. Choose a body of water (river, lake, pond, or ocean) near your home. Is it polluted? If so, what are the main pollutants and their sources? If not, how has it been protected?

2. Use an online calculator to determine the size of your water footprint. Keeping your lifestyle in mind, what three steps could you take to reduce the size of your water footprint?

3. Use an online calculator to determine the size of your carbon footprint. Keeping your lifestyle in mind, what three steps could you take to reduce the size of your carbon footprint?

4. Some government leaders in the United States are advocating drilling for oil in the Arctic National Wildlife Refuge in Alaska. Some of the native people are in favor of this project. List the costs and benefits of this endeavor from economic, environmental, and social points of view.

Additional questions can be found online at The Human Biology Place, www. humanbiology.com.

Appendices

Appendix 1

Selected Answers to Reviewing the Concepts Questions

Chapter 1

10. c, 11. homeostasis, 12. hypothesis, 13. adaptive

Chapter 2

15. d, 16. b, 17. b, 18. a, 19. d, 20. denaturation, 21. nucleotides, 22. primary, 23. Phospholipids, 24. starch; glycogen, 25. pH

Chapter 3

12. c, 13. a, 14. d, 15. c, 16. b, 17. a, 18. a, 19. c, 20. Cytoplasm, 21. Pinocytosis, 22. nucleolus, 23. Oxygen, 24. lactic acid fermentation

Chapter 4

14. b, 15. a, 16. d, 17. calcium, 18. homeostasis

Chapter 5

10. c, 11. c, 12. axial, 13. calcium, 14. osteoblasts, 15. sprain

Chapter 6

12. c, 13. a, 14. actin, myosin, 15. sarcomere

Chapter 7

14. a, 15. c, 16. b, 17. b, 18. b, 19. myelin sheath, 20. sodium-potassium pump, 21. dopamine

Chapter 8

16. a, 17. a, 18. d, 19. hypothalamus, 20. medulla, 21. sympathetic nervous system, 22. cerebrum

Chapter 9

19. a, 20. b, 21. d, 22. a, 23. b, 24. cones, 25. lens, 26. cochlea, 27. sudden movement of the head, including acceleration and deceleration

Chapter 10

16. a, 17. d, 18. c, 19. c, 20. a, 21. Lipid-soluble; water-soluble, 22. gigantism; acromegaly, 23. calcitonin; parathormone, 24. adrenal cortex, 25. insulin; glucagon

Chapter 11

18. a, 19. c, 20. b, 21. transport oxygen, 22. hemoglobin, 23. fibrin

Chapter 12

20. a, 21. b, 22. b, 23. b, 24. sinoatrial node, 25. an aneurysm, 26. capillaries

Chapter 13

17. a, 18. d, 19. b, 20. a, 21. c, 22. natural killer cell, 23. histamine, 24. plasma cells, 25. macrophages

Chapter 14

15. a, 16. b, 17. b, 18. a, 19. a, 20. epiglottis, 21. carbonic anhydrase

Chapter 15

12. a, 13. b, 14. d, 15. d, 16. chyme, 17. liver, 18. starch, 19. cholecystokinin

Chapter 16

11. a, 12. c, 13. a, 14. c, 15. b, 16. The juxtaglomerular apparatus, 17. Hemodialysis, 18. internal; smooth; external; skeletal

Chapter 17

22. c, 23. b, 24. a, 25. b, 26. c, 27. epididymis, 28. oviduct

Chapter 18

15. d, 16. c, 17. b, 18. a, 19. b, 20. d, 21. inner cell mass; trophoblast, 22. cleavage, 23. chorion; endometrium, 24. Gastrulation, 25. prolactin; oxytocin, 26. Free radicals

Chapter 19

8. b, 9. a, 10. a, 11. crossing over and independent assortment, 12. homologous, 13. synapsis, 14. anaphase, 16. anaphase II

Chapter 20

8. b, 9. a, 10. polygenic, 11. phenotype, genotype, 12. homozygous, heterozygous, 13. linked

Chapter 21

15. a, 16. c, 17. b, 18. a, 19. tRNA, 20. uracil, 21. restriction enzymes

Chapter 22

18. a, 19. d, 20. c, 21. a, 22. c, 23. d, 24. c, 25. a, 26. a, 27. Natural selection, 28. Mosaic evolution, 29. multiregional

Chapter 23

14. a, 15. b, 16. niche, 17. secondary consumer, carnivore

Chapter 24

10. b, 11. d, 12. d

Appendix 2

Hints for Applying the Concepts Questions

Chapter 1

1. Each part of the question asks about a different group of Swedish children. Choose the correct group from the key and look at the line on the graph of the appropriate color.

2. Design an experiment with a control group and an experimental group.

3. What is an epidemiological study? What groups of children might you compare?

4. Consider the questions on pages 11–12.

Chapter 2

1. What functions do triglycerides perform in your body?

2. Cellulose is an important form of dietary fiber.

3. Consider the following qualities of water: polarity, heat of vaporization, and high heat capacity.

4. Consider the harmful effects of radiation on the body.

Chapter 3

1. Anesthetics need to cross the plasma membranes of nerve cells.

2. Mitochondria process energy for cells, and thus they occur in large numbers in cells with a high demand for energy.

3. Which element of the cytoskeleton is involved in cell division?

Chapter 4

1. Does cartilage have a blood supply?

2. What physiological mechanisms raise body temperature? What physiological mechanisms lower body temperature?

3. Where is connective tissue found?

Chapter 5

1. What happens to bone density if there is no stress placed on the bone?

2. What kind of activity builds bone density?

3. What structure would indicate that the bone was still capable of growth?

Chapter 6

1. What role does acetylcholine play in muscle contraction?

2. What causes tendinitis? How is it treated?

3. What role do calcium ions play in muscle contraction?

4. Are fast twitch or slow twitch fibers darker in color? How do the properties of fast twitch fibers differ from those of slow twitch fibers?

Chapter 7

1. What effect does an inhibitory neurotransmitter have on the postsynaptic neuron?

2. What would happen if a neurotransmitter were not removed from the synapse?

3. What factors cause ions to cross the membrane during an action potential? What role do potassium ions play in the action potential?

4. What role does the myelin sheath play in the conduction of an action potential?

5. Why is the resting potential important?

Chapter 8

1. What are the functions of the spinal cord? Would loss of any of the functions due to injury have varying effects depending on the location of injury?

2. What is the function of the sympathetic nervous system?

3. What structure of the brain is important in transferring short term memory to long term memory?

Chapter 9

1. In what type of vision are distant objects seen more clearly than nearby objects?

2. What part of the ear is responsible for equilibrium?

3. How would loud sounds affect the organ of hearing in the inner ear?

4. What changes when you change your focus from an object in the distance to a nearby object?

Chapter 10

1. Cortisone is a glucocorticoid.

2. Matt's age can be used to make an educated guess about his type of diabetes.

3. Theresa's symptoms and the timing of their onset suggest melatonin may be involved.

4. What hormones are produced by the adrenal cortex?

Chapter 11

1. Are the white blood cells that are produced in leukemia functional?

2. What regulates the circulating number of red blood cells?

3. What is the function of red blood cells? How is iron related to the ability of red blood cells to carry out their function?

4. Which antibodies against antigens on red blood cells does Raul have?

5. What could happen if either of Elizabeth's babies had Rh$^+$ blood?

6. What are the functions of platelets?

Chapter 12

1. What would be the result if a blood clot were lodged in a small blood vessel in the heart?

2. What happens in the lymph nodes when you get sick?

3. The pressure that propels blood through the arteries is equal to the pressure against the arterial walls. What force generates this pressure? What is the relationship between high blood pressure and atherosclerosis?

4. What happens if the valves do not close properly?

Chapter 13

1. Is a vaccine effective immediately?
2. How specific is the immune response?
3. What role do helper T cells play in the immune response?
4. How long does it take antibodies to form after the first exposure to an antigen?
5. In an organ transplant, what would happen to the transplanted cells if they had very different self MHC markers from the recipient's?

Chapter 14

1. What factors regulate breathing rate and tidal volume?
2. What is the function of the cilia in the respiratory tubules?
3. What happens to Juan's blood level of carbon dioxide when he holds his breath? How would this affect his breathing?
4. Does inhalation or expiration involve muscle contraction? Which is a passive process?

Chapter 15

1. What role does the pancreas play in digestion?
2. What is the relationship between diarrhea and water reabsorption?
3. What would cause skin to develop a yellow tone? What might the cause of the yellow skin tone have to do with a tattoo?
4. What substance is released into the small intestine when fatty food enters the small intestine?

Chapter 16

1. Consider the role of the external urethral sphincter in urination.
2. Coffee and beer are diuretics, but the mechanisms by which they produce their effects differ.
3. Consider the functions of the kidneys and the ways to replace these functions.
4. Which region of the nephron is involved in filtration?

Chapter 17

1. When making your recommendation for a means of contraception consider its effectiveness in preventing pregnancy, this couple's need for protection against STDs, and the health effects of the means of contraception.
2. What happens to the endometrium during menstruation?
3. What is the function of FSH?
4. What does warm temperature have to do with sperm count?

Chapter 18

1. What might pelvic inflammatory disease have done to Tanya's oviduct?
2. How does fetal circulation differ from circulation after birth?
3. Consider the concept of critical periods in development.
4. Consider the hormones involved in milk production and ejection.
5. Consider the potential role of free radicals in aging.

Chapter 19

1. What is nondisjunction?
2. Look at Figure 19.2.

Chapter 20

1. Colorblindness is a sex-linked trait.
2. What are the genotypes of George and Sue? Use a Punnett square to determine the expected results from a cross with those genotypes.
3. Recessive alleles are not expressed.
4. A recessive trait is only expressed in the homozygous condition.
5. Use a Punnett square to determine the outcome of the cross.

Chapter 21

1. What is the start codon? What is the stop codon? What amino acids do the other codons code for?
2. Translate each of the mRNA strands. Remember that more than one codon can code for the same amino acid.
3. Are any bands present in a father, but absent in both the mother and the child?

Chapter 22

1. Describe the evidence in support of evolution.
2. Consider chemical evolution and the conditions of the early Earth.
3. What characteristics distinguish primates from other mammals?
4. Tay-Sachs disease is caused by a recessive allele.
5. Consider misconceptions about human evolution.
6. Review major anatomical changes that occurred over the course of human evolution.

Chapter 23

1. On average, what percentage of the energy available at one trophic level is available to the next level?
2. What happens to mercury as it moves up the food chain?
3. Average rainfall and temperature largely determine the organisms found in a given location.

Chapter 24

1. What will happen to the size of each population as the prereproductive individuals reach reproductive age?
2a. What factors regulate population size?
2b. How might Asian carp affect factors regulating the population size of other species of fish?
3. How would spending differ between a young, growing population and an aging population?
4. The size of the population influences how quickly individuals are added to the population.

Appendix 3

The Human Body:
An Orientation

HOMEOSTATIC IMBALANCE

Homeostasis is so important that most disease can be regarded as a result of its disturbance, a condition called **homeostatic imbalance.** As we age, our body organs become less efficient, and our internal conditions become less and less stable. These events place us at an increasing risk for illness and produce the changes we associate with aging.

Examples of homeostatic imbalance will be provided throughout this book to enhance your understanding of normal physiological mechanisms. These homeostatic imbalance sections are preceded by the symbol ⚖ to alert you that an abnormal condition is being described. ▲

▶ DID YOU GET IT?

6. When we say that the body demonstrates homeostasis, do we mean that conditions in the body are unchanging? Explain your answer.

7. When we begin to become dehydrated, we usually get thirsty, which causes us to drink liquids. Is the thirst sensation part of a negative or a positive feedback control system? Defend your choice.

For answers, see Appendix D.

The Language of Anatomy

Learning about the body is exciting, but our interest sometimes dwindles when we are faced with the terminology of anatomy and physiology. Let's face it. You can't just pick up an anatomy and physiology book and read it as though it were a novel. Unfortunately, confusion is inevitable without specialized terminology. For example, if you are looking at a ball, "above" always means the area over the top of the ball. Other directional terms can also be used consistently because the ball is a sphere. All sides and surfaces are equal. The human body, of course, has many protrusions and bends. Thus, the question becomes: Above what? To prevent misunderstanding, anatomists use a set of terms that allow body structures to be located and identified clearly with just a few words. This language of anatomy is presented and explained next.

Anatomical Position

To accurately describe body parts and position, we must have an initial reference point and use directional terms. To avoid confusion, it is always assumed that the body is in a standard position called the **anatomical position.** It is important to understand this position because most body terminology used in this book refers to this body positioning *regardless* of the position the body happens to be in. The face-front diagrams in Figure 1.5 and Table 1.1 (on page 18) illustrate the anatomical position. As you can see, the body is erect with the feet parallel and the arms hanging at the sides with the palms facing forward.

- Stand up and assume the anatomical position. Notice that it is similar to "standing at attention" but is less comfortable because the palms are held unnaturally forward (with thumbs pointing away from the body) rather than hanging cupped toward the thighs.

Directional Terms

Directional terms allow medical personnel and anatomists to explain exactly where one body structure is in relation to another. For example, we can describe the relationship between the ears and the nose informally by saying, "The ears are located on each side of the head to the right and left of the nose." Using anatomical terminology, this condenses to, "The ears are lateral to the nose." Using anatomical terminology saves a good deal of description and, once learned, is much clearer. Commonly used directional terms are defined and illustrated in Table 1.1 (p. 18). Although most of these terms are also used in everyday conversation, keep in mind that their anatomical meanings are very precise.

Before continuing, take a minute to check your understanding of what you have read in Table 1.1. Give the relationship between the following body parts using the correct anatomical terms.

The wrist is _____ to the hand.

The breastbone is _____ to the spine.

The brain is _____ to the spinal cord.

The thumb is _____ to the fingers. (Be careful here. Remember the anatomical position.)

Study this figure for a moment to answer these two questions. Where would you hurt if you (1) pulled a groin muscle or (2) cracked a bone in your olecranal area?

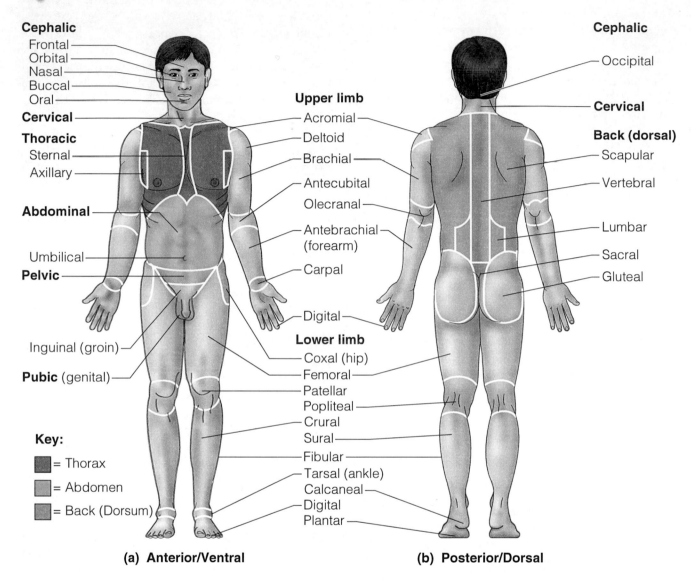

(a) Anterior/Ventral   **(b) Posterior/Dorsal**

FIGURE 1.5 **Regional terms: names of specific body areas.** In **(b)** the heels are raised slightly to show the inferior plantar surface (sole) of the foot.

Regional Terms

There are many visible landmarks on the surface of the body. Once you know their proper anatomical names, you can be specific in referring to different regions of the body.

Anterior Body Landmarks

Look at Figure 1.5a to find the following body regions. Once you have identified all the anterior body landmarks, cover the labels that describe what the structures are. Then go through the list again, pointing out these areas on your own body.

- **abdominal** (ab-dom′ĭ-nal): anterior body trunk inferior to ribs
- **acromial** (ah-kro′me-ul): point of shoulder
- **antebrachial** (an″te-bra′ke-ul): forearm
- **antecubital** (an″te-ku′bĭ-tal): anterior surface of elbow

- **axillary** (ak'sĭ-lar"e): armpit
- **brachial** (bra'ke-al): arm
- **buccal** (buk'al): cheek area
- **carpal** (kar'pal): wrist
- **cervical** (ser'vĭ-kal): neck region
- **coxal** (kox'al): hip
- **crural** (kroo'ral): leg
- **deltoid** (del'toyd): curve of shoulder formed by large deltoid muscle
- **digital** (dij'ĭ-tal): fingers, toes
- **femoral** (fem'or-al): thigh
- **fibular** (fib'u-lar): lateral part of leg
- **frontal** (frun'-tal): forehead
- **inguinal** (in'gwĭ-nal): area where thigh meets body trunk; groin
- **nasal** (na'zul): nose area
- **oral** (o'ral): mouth
- **orbital** (or'bĭ-tal): eye area
- **patellar** (pah-tel'er): anterior knee
- **pelvic** (pel'vik): area overlying the pelvis anteriorly
- **pubic** (pu'bik): genital region
- **sternal** (ster'nul): breastbone area
- **tarsal** (tar'sal): ankle region
- **thoracic** (tho-ras'ik): chest
- **umbilical** (um-bil'ĭ-kal): navel

Posterior Body Landmarks

Identify the following body regions in Figure 1.5b, and then locate them on yourself without referring to this book.

- **calcaneal** (kal-ka'neul): heel of foot
- **cephalic** (seh-fă'lik): head
- **femoral** (fem'or-al): thigh
- **gluteal** (gloo'te-al): buttock
- **lumbar** (lum'bar): area of back between ribs and hips
- **occipital** (ok-sip'ĭ-tal): posterior surface of head
- **olecranal** (ol-eh-cra'nel): posterior surface of elbow
- **popliteal** (pop-lit'e-al): posterior knee area
- **sacral** (sa'krul): area between hips
- **scapular** (skap'u-lar): shoulder blade region

- **sural** (soo'ral): the posterior surface of lower leg; the calf
- **vertebral** (ver'tĕ-bral): area of spine

The **plantar** region, or the sole of the foot, actually on the inferior body surface, is illlustrated along with the posterior body landmarks in Figure 1.5b.

Body Planes and Sections

When preparing to look at the internal structures of the body, medical students make a **section,** or cut. When the section is made through the body wall or through an organ, it is made along an imaginary line called a **plane.** Because the body is three-dimensional, we can refer to three types of planes or sections that lie at right angles to one another (Figure 1.6).

A **sagittal** (saj'ĭ-tal) **section** is a cut along the lengthwise, or longitudinal, plane of the body, dividing the body into right and left parts. If the cut is down the median plane of the body and the right and left parts are equal in size, it is called a **median,** or **midsagittal, section.**

A **frontal section** is a cut along a lengthwise plane that divides the body (or an organ) into anterior and posterior parts. It is also called a **coronal** (ko-ro'nal) **section.**

A **transverse section** is a cut along a horizontal plane, dividing the body or organ into superior and inferior parts. It is also called a **cross section.**

Sectioning a body or one of its organs along different planes often results in very different views. For example, a transverse section of the body trunk at the level of the kidneys would show kidney structure in cross section very nicely; a frontal section of the body trunk would show a different view of kidney anatomy; and a midsagittal section would miss the kidneys completely. Information on body organ positioning that can be gained by taking magnetic resonance imaging (MRI) scans along different body planes is illustrated in Figure 1.6. (MRI scans are described further in the "A Closer Look" box on pp. 8–9).

Body Cavities

Anatomy and physiology textbooks typically describe two sets of internal body cavities, called the dorsal and ventral body cavities, that provide different degrees of protection to the organs within them

(*Continues on page 20*)

TABLE 1.1   **Orientation and Directional Terms**

Term	Definition	Illustration	Example
Superior (cranial or cephalad)	Toward the head end or upper part of a structure or the body; above		The forehead is superior to the nose.
Inferior (caudal)*	Away from the head end or toward the lower part of a structure or the body; below		The navel is inferior to the breastbone.
Ventral (anterior)†	Toward or at the front of the body; in front of		The breastbone is anterior to the spine.
Dorsal (posterior)†	Toward or at the backside of the body; behind		The heart is posterior to the breastbone.
Medial	Toward or at the midline of the body; on the inner side of		The heart is medial to the arm.
Lateral	Away from the midline of the body; on the outer side of		The arms are lateral to the chest.
Proximal	Close to the origin of the body part or the point of attachment of a limb to the body trunk		The elbow is proximal to the wrist (meaning that the elbow is closer to the shoulder or attachment point of the arm than the wrist is).
Distal	Farther from the origin of a body part or the point of attachment of a limb to the body trunk		The knee is distal to the thigh.
Superficial (external)	Toward or at the body surface		The skin is superficial to the skeleton.
Deep (internal)	Away from the body surface; more internal		The lungs are deep to the rib cage.

*The term *caudal*, literally "toward the tail," is synonymous with *inferior* only to the inferior end of the spine.
†*Ventral* and *anterior* are synonymous in humans; this is not the case in four-legged animals. *Ventral* refers to the "belly" of an animal and thus is the inferior surface of four-legged animals. Likewise, although the dorsal and posterior surfaces are the same in humans, the term *dorsal* refers to an animal's back. Thus, the dorsal surface of four-legged animals is their superior surface.

Q *Which section type would separate the two eyes?*

(a) Median (midsagittal)   **(b)** Frontal (coronal) plane   **(c)** Transverse plane

Vertebral column

Intestines

Rectum

Right lung — Heart — Left lung

Liver — Stomach — Spleen

Spinal cord — Spleen

Aorta

Liver — Stomach

Subcutaneous fat layer

FIGURE 1.6 **The anatomical position and planes of the body—median, frontal, and transverse with corresponding MRI scans.** Diagrams identifying body organs seen in the MRI scans are at the bottom.

A *A midsagittal section would separate the two eyes.*

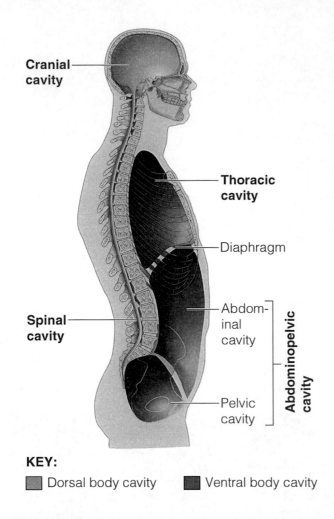

Cranial cavity

Thoracic cavity

Diaphragm

Abdominal cavity

Pelvic cavity

Abdominopelvic cavity

Spinal cavity

KEY:

Dorsal body cavity   Ventral body cavity

FIGURE 1.7   Body cavities. Notice the angular relationship between the abdominal and pelvic cavities.

(Figure 1.7). Because these cavities differ in their mode of embryological development and in their lining membranes, many anatomy reference books do not identify the dorsal, or neural, body cavity as an internal body cavity. However, the idea of two major sets of internal body cavities is a useful learning concept, so we will continue to use it here.

Dorsal Body Cavity

The **dorsal body cavity** has two subdivisions, which are continuous with each other. The **cranial cavity** is the space inside the bony skull. The brain is well protected because it occupies the cranial cavity. The **spinal cavity** extends from the cranial cavity nearly to the end of the vertebral column. The spinal cord, which is a continuation of the brain, is protected by the vertebrae, which surround the spinal cavity.

Ventral Body Cavity

The **ventral body cavity** is much larger than the dorsal cavity. It contains all the structures within the chest and abdomen, that is, the visceral organs in those regions. Like the dorsal cavity, the ventral body cavity is subdivided. The superior **thoracic cavity** is separated from the rest of the ventral cavity by a dome-shaped muscle, the **diaphragm** (di'ah-fram). The organs in the thoracic cavity (lungs, heart, and others) are somewhat protected by the rib cage. A central region called the **mediastinum** (me"de-as-ti'num) separates the lungs into right and left cavities in the thoracic cavity. The mediastinum itself houses the heart, trachea, and other visceral organs.

The cavity inferior to the diaphragm is the **abdominopelvic** (ab-dom"ĭ-no-pel'vik) **cavity.** Some prefer to subdivide it into a superior **abdominal cavity,** containing the stomach, liver, intestines, and other organs, and an inferior **pelvic cavity,** with the reproductive organs, bladder, and rectum. However, there is no actual physical structure dividing the abdominopelvic cavity. If you look carefully at Figure 1.7, you will see that the pelvic cavity is not continuous with the abdominal cavity in a straight plane, but that it tips away from the abdominal cavity in the posterior direction.

HOMEOSTATIC IMBALANCE

When the body is subjected to physical trauma (as often happens in an automobile accident, for example), the most vulnerable abdominopelvic organs are those within the abdominal cavity. The reason is that the abdominal cavity walls are formed only of trunk muscles and are not reinforced by bone. The pelvic organs receive a somewhat greater degree of protection from the bony pelvis in which they reside. ▲

Because the abdominopelvic cavity is quite large and contains many organs, it helps to divide it up into smaller areas for study. A scheme commonly used by medical personnel divides the abdominopelvic cavity into four more or less equal regions called *quadrants*. The quadrants are

(a)

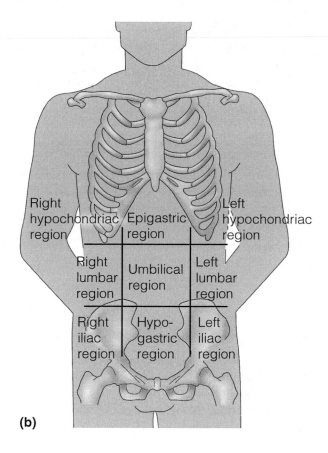

(b)

FIGURE 1.8 **Abdominopelvic surface and cavity. (a)** The four quadrants. **(b)** Nine regions delineated by four planes. The superior horizontal plane is at the inferior aspect of the ribs; the inferior horizontal plane is at the superior aspect of the hip bones, and the vertical planes are just medial to the nipples. **(c)** Anterior view of the ventral body cavity showing superficial organs.

then simply named according to their relative positions—that is, right upper quadrant (RUQ), right lower quadrant (RLQ), left upper quadrant (LUQ), and left lower quadrant (LLQ) (Figure 1.8a).

Another system, used mainly by anatomists, divides the abdominopelvic cavity into nine separate *regions* by four planes, as shown in Figure 1.8b. Although the names of the nine regions are unfamiliar to you now, with a little patience and study they will become easier to remember. As you locate these regions in the figure, notice the organs they contain by referring to Figure 1.8c.

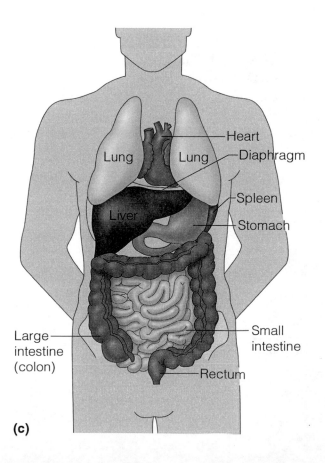

(c)

- The **umbilical region** is the centermost region, deep to and surrounding the umbilicus (navel).

- The **epigastric** (ep″ĭ-gas′trik) **region** is located superior to the umbilical region (*epi* = upon, above; *gastric* = stomach).

- The **hypogastric (pubic) region** is inferior to the umbilical region (*hypo* = below).

- The **right** and **left iliac**, or **inguinal**, **regions** are lateral to the hypogastric region (*iliac* = superior part of the hip bone).

- The **right** and **left lumbar regions** lie lateral to the umbilical region (*lumbus* = loin).

- The **right** and **left hypochondriac** (hi″po-kon′dre-ak) **regions** flank the epigastric region and contain the lower ribs (*chondro* = cartilage).

Open Body Cavities

In addition to the large closed body cavities, there are several smaller body cavities. Most of these are in the head and open to the body exterior. With the exception of the middle ear cavities, the body regions that house these cavities are all shown in Figure 1.5.

- **Oral and digestive cavities.** The oral cavity, commonly called the mouth, contains the teeth and tongue. This cavity is part of and continuous with the cavity of the digestive organs, which opens to the exterior at the anus.

- **Nasal cavity.** Located within and posterior to the nose, the nasal cavity is part of the respiratory system passageways.

- **Orbital cavities.** The orbital cavities (orbits) in the skull house the eyes and present them in an anterior position.

- **Middle ear cavities.** The middle ear cavities carved into the skull lie just medial to the eardrums. These cavities contain tiny bones that transmit sound vibrations to the hearing receptors in the inner ears.

▶ *DID YOU GET IT?*

8. Why is understanding the anatomical position important to an anatomy student?

9. The axillary and the acromial areas are both in the general area of the shoulder. To what specific body area does each of these terms apply?

10. Which kind of section would cut the brain into anterior and posterior parts?

11. If you wanted to separate the thoracic cavity from the abdominal cavity of a cadaver, which type of section would you make?

12. Of the spinal cord, small intestine, uterus, and heart, which are in the dorsal body cavity?

For answers, see Appendix D.

Glossary

A

Accommodation A change in the shape of the lens of the eye brought about by contraction of the smooth muscle of the ciliary body that changes the degree to which light rays are bent so that an image can be focused on the retina.

Acetylcholine A neurotransmitter found in both the central nervous system and the peripheral nervous system. It is the neurotransmitter released at neuromuscular junctions and causes muscle contraction.

Acetylcholinesterase An enzyme that breaks the neurotransmitter acetylcholine into its inactive component parts, acetate and choline. Acetylcholinesterase stops the action of acetylcholine at a synapse.

Acid Any substance that increases the concentration of hydrogen ions in solution.

Acinar cells Exocrine cells of the pancreas that secrete digestive enzymes into ducts that empty into the small intestine.

Acquired immune deficiency syndrome See AIDS.

Acromegaly A condition characterized by thickened bones and enlarged soft tissues caused by overproduction of growth hormone in adulthood.

Acrosome A membranous sac at the tip of a sperm cell that contains enzymes that facilitate sperm penetration into the egg during fertilization.

ACTH See adrenocorticotropic hormone.

Actin filaments The thin filaments in muscle cells composed primarily of the protein actin and essential to muscle contraction. In addition to actin, thin filaments contain two proteins important in the regulation of muscle contraction: tropomyosin and troponin.

Actin The contractile protein that makes up the major portion of the thin filaments in muscle cells. An actin (thin) filament is composed of actin, troponin, and tropomyosin. In muscle cells, contraction occurs when actin interacts with another protein called myosin.

Action potential A nerve impulse. An electrochemical signal conducted along an axon. A wave of depolarization caused by the inward flow of sodium ions followed by repolarization caused by the outward flow of potassium ions.

Active immunity Immune resistance in which the body actively participates by producing memory B cells and T cells after exposure to an antigen, either naturally or through vaccination.

Active site A specific location on an enzyme where the substrate binds.

Active transport The movement of molecules across the plasma membrane, usually against a concentration gradient (from a region of lower concentration to one of higher concentration) with the aid of a carrier protein and energy (usually in the form of adenosine triphosphate, or ATP) supplied by the cell.

Acute renal failure An abrupt, complete or nearly complete, cessation of kidney function.

Adaptation The process by which populations become better attuned to their particular environments as a result of natural selection.

Adaptive trait A characteristic (structure, function, or behavior) of an organism that makes an individual better able to survive and reproduce in its natural environment. Adaptive traits arise through natural selection.

Addison's disease An autoimmune disorder characterized by fatigue, loss of appetite, low blood pressure, and increased skin pigmentation resulting from undersecretion of glucocorticoids and aldosterone.

Adenosine triphosphate (ATP) A nucleotide that consists of the sugar ribose, the base adenine, and three phosphate groups. ATP is the energy currency of all living cells.

ADH See antidiuretic hormone.

Adhesion junction A specialized junction between cells in which the plasma membrane of adjacent cells is held together by protein filaments; a desmosome.

Adipose tissue A type of loose connective tissue that contains cells specialized for storing fat.

Adolescence The stage in postnatal development that begins with puberty and ends by about age 17. It is a period of rapid physical and sexual maturation during which the ability to reproduce is achieved.

Adrenal cortex The outer region of the adrenal gland that secretes glucocorticoids, mineralocorticoids, and gonadocorticoids.

Adrenal glands The body's two adrenal glands are located on top of the kidneys. The outer region of each adrenal gland secretes glucocorticoids, mineralocorticoids, and gonadocorticoids, and the inner region secretes epinephrine and norepinephrine.

Adrenal medulla The inner region of the adrenal gland that secretes epinephrine and norepinephrine.

Adrenaline See epinephrine.

Adrenocorticotropic hormone (ACTH) The anterior pituitary hormone that controls the synthesis and secretion of glucocorticoid hormones from the cortex of the adrenal glands.

Adulthood The stage in postnatal development that is generally reached somewhere between 18 and 21 years of age. Growth and formation of bone are usually completed by age 25, and thereafter developmental changes occur quite slowly.

Afferent (sensory) neuron A nerve cell specialized to conduct nerve impulses from the sensory receptors *toward* the central nervous system.

Age structure Of a population, the number of males and females of each age in a population. The ages are often grouped into prereproductive, reproductive, and postreproductive categories. Generally, only individuals of reproductive age add to the size of the population.

Agglutinate To clump together.

Aging The normal and progressive alteration in the structure and function of the body. Aging is possibly caused by declines in critical body systems, disruption of cell processes by free radicals, slowing or cessation of cell division, and decline in the ability to repair damaged DNA.

Agranulocytes The white blood cells without granules in their cytoplasm, including monocytes and lymphocytes.

AIDS Acquired immune deficiency syndrome. A diagnosis of AIDS is made when an HIV-positive person develops one of the following conditions: (1) a helper T cell count below 200/mm³ of blood; (2) one of 26 opportunistic infections, the most common of which are *Pneumocystis carinii* pneumonia and Kaposi's sarcoma, a cancer of connective tissue that affects primarily the skin; (3) a loss of more than 10% of body weight (wasting syndrome); or (4) dementia (mental incapacity such as forgetfulness or inability to concentrate).

Albinism A genetic inability to produce the brown pigment melanin that normally gives color to the eyes, hair, and skin.

Aldosterone A hormone (the primary mineralocorticoid) released by the adrenal cortex that stimulates the reabsorption of sodium within kidney nephrons.

Allantois The extraembryonic membrane that serves as a site of blood cell formation and later becomes part of the umbilical cord, the ropelike connection between the embryo and the placenta.

Allele An alternative form of a gene. One of two or more slightly different versions of a gene that code for different forms of the same trait.

Allergen An antigen that stimulates an allergic response.

Allergy A strong immune response to an antigen (an allergen) that is not usually harmful to the body.

Allometric growth The change in the relative rates of growth of various parts of the body. Such growth helps shape developing humans and other organisms.

Alveolus (plural, alveoli) A thin-walled rounded chamber. In the lungs, the alveoli are the surfaces for gas exchange. They form clusters at the end of each bronchiole that are surrounded by a vast network of capillaries. The alveoli greatly increase the surface area for gas exchange.

Amino acid The building blocks of proteins consisting of a central carbon atom bound to a hydrogen atom, an amino group (NH_2), a carboxyl group (COOH), and a side chain designated by the letter R. There are twenty amino acids important to human life; some can be synthesized by our bodies (nonessential amino acids), whereas others cannot be synthesized and must be obtained from the foods we eat (essential amino acids).

Amniocentesis A method of prenatal testing for genetic problems in a fetus in which amniotic fluid is withdrawn through a needle so that the fluid can be tested biochemically and the cells can be cultured and examined for genetic abnormalities.

Amnion The extraembryonic membrane that encloses the embryo in a fluid-filled space called the amniotic cavity. Amniotic fluid forms a protective cushion around the embryo that later can be examined as part of prenatal testing in a procedure known as amniocentesis.

Ampulla A wider region in a canal or duct. In the inner ear, the ampulla is found at the base of a semicircular canal in the inner ear.

Anabolic steroids Synthetic hormones that mimic testosterone and stimulate the body to build muscle and increase strength. Steroid abuse can have many dangerous side effects.

Anabolism The building (synthetic) chemical reactions within living cells, as when cells build complicated molecules from simple ones. Compare with catabolism.

Anal canal The canal between the rectum and the anus. Feces pass through the anal canal.

Analgesic A substance, such as Demerol, that relieves pain.

Analogous structure A structure of one organism that is similar to that of another organism because of convergent evolution and not because the organisms arose from a common ancestry. Compare with homologous structures.

Anaphase In mitosis, the phase when the chromatids of each chromosome begin to separate, splitting at the centromere. Now separate entities, the chromatids are considered chromosomes, and they move toward opposite poles of the cell.

Anaphylactic shock An extreme allergic reaction that occurs within minutes after exposure to a substance to which a person is allergic and that can cause pooling of blood in capillaries, which causes dizziness, nausea, and sometimes unconsciousness as well as extreme difficulty in breathing. Anaphylactic shock can lead to death.

Androgen A steroid sex hormone secreted by the testes in males and produced in small quantities by the adrenal cortex in both sexes.

Anemia A condition in which the blood's ability to carry oxygen is reduced. It can result from too little hemoglobin, too few red blood cells, or both.

Anencephaly A neural tube defect that involves incomplete formation of the brain and results in stillbirth or death shortly after birth.

Anesthesia The drug-induced loss of the sensation of pain. It may be general or regional.

Aneuploidy A general term describing the condition whereby gametes or cells contain too many or too few chromosomes compared with the normal number.

Aneurysm A blood-filled sac in the wall of an artery caused by a weak area in the artery wall.

Angina pectoris Choking or strangling chest pain, usually experienced in the center of the chest or slightly to the left, that is caused by a temporary insufficiency of blood flow to the heart. It begins during physical exertion or emotional stress, when the demands on the heart are increased and the blood flow to the heart muscle can no longer meet the needs.

Angioplasty A procedure that widens the channel of an artery obstructed because of atherosclerosis. It involves inflating a tough, plastic balloon inside the artery.

Angiotensin I Renin converts angiotensinogen into this protein.

Angiotensin II A protein that stimulates the adrenal gland to release aldosterone.

Anorexia nervosa An eating disorder characterized by deliberate self-starvation, a distorted body image, and low body weight.

ANP See atrial natriuretic peptide.

Antagonistic pairs Muscles arranged in pairs so that the actions of the members of the pair are opposite to one another. This arrangement is characteristic of most skeletal muscles.

Antibody A Y-shaped protein produced by plasma cells during an immune response that recognizes and binds to a specific antigen because of the shape of the molecule. Antibodies defend against invaders in a variety of ways, including neutralization, agglutination and precipitation, or activation of the complement system.

Antibody-mediated immune responses Immune system responses conducted by B cells that produce antibodies and that defend primarily against enemies that are free in body fluids, including toxins or extracellular pathogens, such as bacteria or free viruses.

Anticodon A three-base sequence on transfer RNA (tRNA) that binds to the complementary base pairs of a codon on the mRNA.

Antidiuretic hormone (ADH) A hormone manufactured by the hypothalamus but stored in and released from the posterior pituitary. It regulates the amount of water reabsorbed by the distal convoluted tubules and collecting ducts of nephrons. ADH causes water retention at the kidneys and elevates blood pressure. It is also called vasopressin.

Antigen A substance that is recognized as foreign by the immune system. Antigens trigger an immune response.

Antigen-presenting cell (APC) A cell that presents an antigen to a helper T cell, initiating an immune response toward that antigen. The most important type of antigen-presenting cell is a macrophage.

Aorta The body's main artery that conducts blood from the left ventricle toward the cells of the body. The aorta arches over the top of the heart and gives rise to the smaller arteries that feed the capillary beds of the body tissues.

Apoptosis A series of predictable physical changes in a cell that is undergoing programmed cell death. Apoptosis is sometimes used as a synonym for programmed cell death.

Appendicular skeleton The part of the skeleton comprising the pectoral girdle (shoulders), the pelvic girdle (pelvis), and the limbs (arms and legs).

Appendix A slender closed pouch that extends from the large intestine near the juncture with the small intestine.

Aqueous humor The fluid within the anterior chamber of the eye. It supplies nutrients and oxygen to the cornea and lens and carries away their metabolic wastes.

Arachnoid The middle layer of the meninges (the connective tissue layers that protect the central nervous system).

Areolar connective tissue A type of loose connective tissue composed of cells in a gelatinous matrix. It serves as a universal packing material between organs and anchors skin to underlying tissues and organs.

Arrector pili The tiny, smooth muscles attached to the hair follicles in the dermis.

Arteriole A small blood vessel located between an artery and a capillary. Arterioles serve to regulate blood flow through capillary beds to various regions of the body. They also regulate blood pressure. Arterioles are barely visible to the naked eye.

Artery A large-diameter muscular tube (blood vessel) that transports blood away from the heart toward the cells of body tissues. Arteries conduct blood low in oxygen to the lungs and blood high in oxygen to the body tissues. Arteries typically have thick muscular and elastic walls that dampen the blood pressure pulsations caused by heart contractions.

Arthritis An inflammation of a joint.

Artificial insemination A treatment for infertility in which sperm are deposited in the woman's cervix or vagina at about the time of ovulation.

ASDs See autism spectrum disorders.

Asperger syndrome A neurodevelopmental disorder characterized by impaired social interaction and unusual patterns of behavior, including restricted, repetitive, and stereotyped motor patterns; also called Asperger's disorder. Asperger syndrome differs from autism in having no clinically significant general delay in language.

Association neuron An interneuron. These neurons are located within the central nervous system between sensory and motor neurons and serve to integrate information.

Asthma A condition marked by spasms of the muscles of bronchioles, making air flow difficult. It is often triggered by allergy.

Astigmatism Irregularities in the curvature of the cornea or lens that cause distortions of a visual image because the irregularities cause light rays to converge unevenly.

Atherosclerosis A narrowing of the arteries caused by thickening of the arterial walls and a buildup of lipid (primarily cholesterol) deposits. Atherosclerosis reduces blood flow through the vessel, choking off the vital supply of oxygen and nutrients to the tissues served by that vessel.

Atom A unit of matter that cannot be further broken down by chemical means; it is composed of subatomic particles, which include protons (positively charged particles), neutrons (with no charge), and electrons (with negative charges).

Atomic number The number of protons in the nucleus of an atom.

ATP See adenosine triphosphate.

Atrial fibrillation Rapid, ineffective contractions of the atria of the heart.

Atrial natriuretic peptide (ANP) The hormone released by cells in the right atrium of the heart in response to stretching of the heart caused by increased blood volume and pressure. ANP decreases water and solute reabsorption by the kidneys, resulting in the production of large amounts of urine.

Atrioventricular (AV) node A region of specialized cardiac muscle cells located in the partition between the two atria. It receives an electrical signal that spreads through the atrial walls from the sinoatrial node and relays the stimulus to the ventricles by means of a bundle of specialized muscle fibers, called the atrioventricular bundle, that runs along the wall between the ventricles.

Atrioventricular (AV) valves Heart valves located between the atria and the ventricles that keep blood flowing in only one direction, from the atria to the ventricles. The right AV valve consists of three flaps of tissue and is also called the tricuspid valve. The left AV valve consists of two flaps of tissue and is also called the bicuspid or the mitral valve.

Atrioventricular bundle A tract of specialized cardiac muscle cells that runs along the wall between the ventricles of the heart and conducts an electrical impulse that originated in the sinoatrial (SA) node and was conducted to the AV node to the ventricles. The bundle forks into right and left branches and then divides into many other specialized cardiac muscle cells, called Purkinje fibers, that penetrate the walls of the ventricles.

Atrium (plural, atria) An upper chamber of the heart that receives blood from veins and pumps it to a ventricle.

Auditory tubes Small tubes that join the upper region of the pharynx (throat) with the middle ear. They help to equalize the air pressure between the middle ear and the atmosphere. Also called eustachian tubes.

Autism A neurodevelopmental disorder characterized by impaired communication and social interaction, and the presence of unusual patterns of behavior, including restricted, repetitive, and stereotyped motor patterns; also called autistic disorder.

Autism spectrum disorders (ASDs) A group of neurodevelopmental disorders that includes autism, Asperger syndrome, and pervasive developmental disorder not otherwise specified.

Autoimmune disorder An immune response misdirected against the body's own tissues.

Autonomic nervous system The part of the peripheral nervous system that governs the involuntary, unconscious activities that maintain a relatively stable internal environment. The autonomic nervous system has two branches: the sympathetic and the parasympathetic.

Autosomes The 22 pairs of chromosomes (excluding the pair of sex chromosomes) that determine the expression of most of the inherited characteristics of a person.

Autotroph An organism that makes its own food (organic compounds) from inorganic substances. The autotrophs include photoautotrophs, which use the energy of light, and chemoautotrophs, which use the energy in chemicals.

Axial skeleton The part of the skeleton comprising the skull, the vertebral column, the breastbone (sternum), and the rib cage.

Axon terminal The tip of a branch of an axon that releases a chemical (neurotransmitter) that alters the activity of the target cell. A synaptic knob.

Axon A long extension from the cell body of a neuron that carries an electrochemical message away from the cell body toward another neuron or effector (muscle or gland). The tips of the axon release a chemical called a neurotransmitter that can affect the activity of the receiving cell. Typically, there is one long axon on a neuron.

B

B cell See B lymphocyte.

B lymphocyte B cell. A type of white blood cell important in antibody-mediated immune responses that can transform into a plasma cell and produce antibodies.

Balanced polymorphism A phenomenon in which natural selection maintains two or more alleles for a trait in a population from one generation to the next. It occurs when the environment changes frequently or when the heterozygous condition is favored over either homozygous condition.

Ball-and-socket joint A joint that allows motion in all directions, such as the shoulder and hip joints.

Barr body A structure formed by a condensed, inactivated X chromosome in the body cells of female mammals.

Basal body The structure that anchors the microtubules of a cilium or flagellum to a cell. It contains nine triplets of microtubules arranged in a ring.

Basal cell carcinoma The most common type of skin cancer, occurring in the rapidly dividing cells of the basal layer of the epidermis.

Basal ganglia A region of the cerebrum consisting of collections of cell bodies located deep within it called the white matter. They are important in coordinating movement and may also play a role in cognition and memory of learned skills.

Basal metabolic rate (BMR) A measure of the minimum energy required to keep an awake, resting body alive. It generally represents between 60% and 75% of the body's energy needs.

Base Any substance that reduces the concentration of hydrogen ions in solution.

Basement membrane A noncellular layer beneath epithelial tissue that binds the epithelial cells to underlying connective tissue. It helps epithelial tissue resist stretching and forms a boundary.

Basilar membrane The floor of the central canal in the cochlea of the inner ear that supports the spiral organ (of Corti), which is the true site of hearing; when the basilar membrane vibrates in response to sound, hair cells on the spiral organ are bent, generating electrochemical messages that are interpreted as sound.

Basophil A white blood cell that releases histamine, a chemical that both attracts other white blood cells to the site and causes blood vessels to widen during an inflammatory response.

Benign tumor An abnormal mass of tissue that usually remains at the site where it forms.

Bicuspid valve A heart valve located between the left atrium and ventricle. It is also called the mitral valve or the left atrioventricular (AV) valve.

Bile A mixture of water, ions, cholesterol, bile pigments, and bile salts that emulsifies fat (keeps fat as small globules), facilitating digestion. Bile is produced by the liver, stored in the gallbladder, and acts in the small intestine.

Bilirubin A red pigment produced from the breakdown of the heme portion of hemoglobin by liver cells. It is excreted by the liver in bile.

Binary fission A type of asexual reproduction in which the genetic information is replicated and then a cell, a bacterium for example, or organism divides into two equal parts.

Biodiversity The number and variety of all living things in a given area. It includes genetic diversity, species diversity, and ecological diversity.

Biofeedback The use of artificial signals to provide feedback about unconscious visceral and motor activity, particularly that associated with stress.

Biogeochemical cycle The recurring process by which materials (for example, carbon, water, nitrogen, and phosphorus) cycle between living and nonliving systems and back again.

Biogeography The study of the geographic distribution of organisms. New distributions of organisms occur when organisms move to new areas (dispersal) and when areas occupied by the organisms move or are subdivided.

Biological magnification The tendency of a nondegradable chemical to become more concentrated in organisms as it passes along a food chain.

Biomass In ecosystems, the dry weight of the body mass of a group of organisms in a particular habitat.

Biopsy The removal and examination, usually microscopic, of a piece of tissue to diagnose a disease, usually cancer.

Biosphere The part of the earth in which life is found. It encompasses all of the earth's living organisms.

Biotechnology The industrial or commercial use or alteration of living organisms, cells, or molecules to achieve specific useful goals.

Bioterrorism The use of biological agents, such as viruses, parasites, bacteria and their toxins, to intimidate or attack societies or governments. There is concern that biological agents could be intentionally introduced to food or water supplies.

Bipedalism Walking on two feet. The trait that evolved early in hominin evolution and set the stage for the evolution of other characteristics, such as increases in brain size.

Bipolar neuron A neuron that has only two processes. The axon and the dendrite extend from opposite sides of the cell body. Bipolar neurons are receptor cells found only in some of the special sensory organs, such as in the retina of the eye and in the olfactory membrane of the nose.

Birth defects Developmental defects present at birth. Such defects involve structure, function, behavior, or metabolism and may or may not be hereditary.

Birth rate The number of births per a specified number of individuals in the population during a specific time.

Bladder A muscular saclike organ that receives urine from the two ureters and temporarily stores it until release into the urethra.

Blastocyst The stage of development consisting of a hollow ball of cells. It contains the inner cell mass, a group of cells that will become the embryo, and the trophoblast, a thin layer of cells that will give rise to part of the placenta.

Blind spot The region of the retina where the optic nerve leaves the eye and on which there are no photoreceptors. Objects focused on the blind spot cannot be seen.

Blood pressure The force exerted by the blood against the walls of the blood vessels. It is caused by the contraction of the ventricles and is influenced by vasoconstriction.

Blood type A characteristic of a person's red blood cells determined on the basis of large molecules, primarily proteins, on the surface of the plasma membrane.

Blood Connective tissue that consists of cells and platelets suspended in plasma, a liquid matrix.

Blood-brain barrier A mechanism that protects the central nervous system by selecting the substances permitted to enter the cerebrospinal fluid from the blood. The barrier results from the relative impermeability of the capillaries in the brain and spinal cord.

Blue babies Newborns whose foramen ovale, the fetal opening between the right and left atria of the heart, fails to close. As a result, much of their blood still bypasses the lungs and is low in oxygen. The condition can be corrected with surgery.

BMR See basal metabolic rate.

Bolus A small, soft ball of food mixed with saliva.

Bone marrow The soft material filling the cavities in bones. Yellow bone marrow serves as a fat-storage site. Red bone marrow is the site where blood cells are produced.

Bone remodeling The ongoing process of bone deposition and absorption in response to hormonal and mechanical factors.

Bone Strong connective tissue with specialized cells in a hard matrix composed of collagen fibers and mineral salts.

Bottleneck effect The genetic drift associated with dramatic, unselective reductions in population size so that by chance alone the genetic makeup of survivors is not representative of the original population.

Brain waves The patterns recorded in an EEG (electroencephalogram) that reflect the electrical activity of the brain and are correlated with the person's state of alertness.

Brain The organ composed of neurons and glial cells that receives sensory input and integrates, stores, and retrieves information.

Breast The front of the chest, especially either of the two protuberant glandular organs (mammary glands) that in human females and other female mammals produce milk to nourish newborns.

Breathing center A region in the medulla of the brain that controls the basic breathing rhythm.

Breech birth Delivery in which the baby is born buttocks first rather than head first. It is associated with difficult labors and umbilical cord accidents.

Bronchi (singular, bronchus) The respiratory passageways between the trachea and the bronchioles that conduct air into the lungs.

Bronchial tree The term given to the air tubules in the respiratory system because their repeated branching resembles the branches of a tree.

Bronchioles A series of small tubules branching from the smallest bronchi inside each lung.

Bronchitis Inflammation of the mucous membranes of the bronchi, causing excess mucus and a deep cough.

Brush border A fuzzy border of microvilli on the surface of absorptive epithelial cells of the small intestine.

Buffer A substance that prevents dramatic changes in pH by removing excess hydrogen ions from solution when concentrations increase and adding hydrogen ions when concentrations decrease.

Bulbourethral glands Cowper's glands. Male accessory reproductive glands that release a clear slippery liquid immediately before ejaculation.

Bulimia nervosa An eating disorder characterized by binge eating followed by purging by means of self-induced vomiting, enemas, laxatives, or diuretics.

Bursa (plural, bursae) A flattened sac containing a thin film of synovial fluid that surrounds and cushions certain synovial joints. Bursae are common in locations where ligaments, muscles, skin, or tendons rub against bone.

Bursitis Inflammation of a bursa (a sac in a synovial joint that acts as a cushion). Bursitis causes fluid to build up within the bursa, resulting in intense pain that becomes worse when the joint is moved and cannot be relieved by resting in any position.

C

C-section See cesarean section.

Calcitonin (CT) A hormone secreted by the thyroid gland when blood calcium levels are high. It stimulates the removal of calcium from the blood and inhibits the breakdown of bone.

Callus A mass of repair tissue formed by collagen fibers secreted from fibroblasts or woven bone that forms around and links the ends of a broken bone.

Capillary A microscopic blood vessel between arterioles and venules with walls only one cell layer thick. It is the site where the exchange of materials between the blood and the tissues occurs.

Capillary bed A network of true capillaries servicing a particular area. Precapillary sphincters regulate blood flow through the capillary bed. When the sphincters relax, blood fills the capillary bed and materials can be exchanged between the blood and the tissues. When the sphincters contract, blood flows directly from an arteriole to a venule, bypassing the capillaries.

Carbaminohemoglobin The compound formed when carbon dioxide binds to hemoglobin.

Carbohydrate An organic molecule that provides fuel for the human body. Carbohydrates, which we know as sugars and starches, can be classified by size into the monosaccharides, disaccharides, and polysaccharides.

Carbon footprint A measure of the amount of carbon dioxide that enters the atmosphere due to the activities of a person or population; it includes personal activities and the activities needed for production and waste removal of the products consumed.

Carbonic anhydrase An enzyme in the red blood cells that catalyzes the conversion of unbound carbon dioxide to carbonic acid.

Carcinogen A substance that causes cancer.

Carcinoma in situ A tumor that has not spread; "cancer in place."

Cardiac cycle The events associated with the flow of blood through the heart during a single heartbeat. It consists of systole (contraction) and diastole (relaxation) of the atria and then of the ventricles of the heart.

Cardiac muscle A contractile tissue that makes up the bulk of the walls of the heart. Cardiac muscle cells are cylindrical and have branching interconnections between cells. Cardiac muscle cells are striped (striated) and have a single nucleus. Contraction of cardiac muscle is involuntary.

Cardiovascular Pertaining to the heart and blood vessels.

Cardiovascular system The organ system composed of the heart and blood vessels. The cardiovascular system distributes blood, delivers nutrients, and removes wastes.

Carnivore An animal that obtains energy by eating other animals. A secondary consumer.

Carpal tunnel syndrome A condition of the wrist and hand whose symptoms may include numbness or tingling in the affected hand, along with pain in the wrist, hand, and fingers that is caused by repeated motion in the hand or wrist, causing the tendons to become inflamed and press against the nerve.

Carrier An individual who displays the dominant phenotype but is heterozygous for a trait and can therefore pass the recessive allele to descendants.

Carrying capacity The number of individuals of a given species that a particular environment can support for a prolonged time period. The carrying capacity of the environment is determined by such factors as availability of resources, including food, water, and space; ability to clean away wastes; and predation pressure.

Cartilage A type of specialized connective tissue with a firm gelatinous matrix containing protein fibers for strength. The cartilage cells (chondrocytes) lie in small spaces (lacunae) within the matrix.

Catabolism Chemical reactions within living cells that break down complex molecules into simpler ones, releasing energy from chemical bonds. Compare with anabolism.

Cataract A cloudy or opaque lens. Cataracts reduce visual acuity and may be caused by glucose accumulation associated with Type I diabetes, excessive exposure to sunlight, and exposure to cigarette smoke.

CD4 cell See helper T cell.

Cecum A pouch that hangs below the junction of the small and large intestines; the appendix extends from the cecum.

Cell The smallest structure that shows all the characteristics of life.

Cell adhesion molecule (CAM) A molecule that pokes through the plasma membranes of most cells and helps hold cells together to form tissues and organs.

Cell body The part of a neuron that contains the organelles and nucleus needed to maintain the cells.

Cell cycle The entire sequence of events that a cell goes through from its origin in the division of a parent cell through its own division into two daughter cells. The cell cycle consists of two major phases: interphase and cell division.

Cell differentiation The process by which cells become specialized with respect to structure and function.

Cell theory This fundamental organizing principle of biology states that (1) a cell is the smallest unit of life; (2) cells make up all living things, from unicellular to multicellular organisms; and (3) new cells arise from pre-existing cells.

Cell-mediated immune responses Immune system responses conducted by T cells that protect against cellular threats, including body cells that have become infected with viruses or other pathogens and cancer cells.

Cellular respiration The oxygen-requiring pathway by which glucose is broken down by cells to yield carbon dioxide, water, and energy.

Cellulose A structural polysaccharide found in the cell walls of plants. Humans lack the enzymes necessary to digest cellulose, and thus it passes unchanged through our digestive tract. Although cellulose has no value as a nutrient, it is an important form of dietary fiber known to facilitate the passage of feces through the large intestines.

Cementum A calcified but sensitive part of a tooth that covers the root.

Central nervous system (CNS) The brain and the spinal cord.

Centriole A structure, found in pairs, within a centrosome. Each centriole is composed of nine sets of triplet microtubules arranged in a ring.

Centromere The region of a replicated chromosome at which sister chromatids are held together until they separate during cell division.

Centrosome The region near the nucleus that contains centrioles. It forms the mitotic spindle during prophase.

Cerebellum A region of the brain important in sensory–motor coordination. It is largely responsible for posture and smooth body movements.

Cerebral cortex The extensive area of gray matter covering the surfaces of the cerebrum. It is often referred to as the conscious part of the brain. The cerebral cortex has sensory, motor, and association areas.

Cerebral white matter A region of the cerebrum beneath the cortex consisting primarily of myelinated axons that are grouped into tracts that allow various regions of the brain to communicate with one another.

Cerebrospinal fluid The fluid bathing the internal and external surfaces of the central nervous system. It serves as a shock absorber, supports the brain, nourishes the brain, delivers chemical messengers, and removes waste products.

Cerebrovascular accident See stroke.

Cerebrum The largest and most prominent part of the brain, composed of the cerebral hemispheres. It is responsible for thinking, sensory perception, originating most conscious motor activity, personality, and memory.

Cervical cap A barrier means of contraception consisting of a small rubber dome that fits snugly over the cervix and is held in place partly by suction. It prevents sperm from reaching the egg.

Cervix The narrow neck of the uterus that projects into the vagina whose opening provides a passageway for materials moving between the vagina and the body of the uterus.

Cesarean section A procedure by which the baby and placenta are removed from the uterus through an incision in the abdominal wall and uterus. The term is often shortened to C-section.

Chancre A painless bump that forms during the first stage of syphilis at the site of contact, usually within 2 to 8 weeks of the initial contact.

Chemical digestion A part of the digestive process that involves breaking chemical bonds so that complex molecules are broken into their component subunits. Chemical digestion produces molecules that can be absorbed into the bloodstream and used by the cells.

Chemical evolution The sequence of events by which life evolved from chemicals slowly increasing in complexity over perhaps 300 million years.

Chemistry The branch of science concerned with the composition and properties of material substances, including their abilities to change into other substances.

Chemoreceptor A sensory receptor specialized to respond to chemicals. We describe the input from the chemoreceptors of the mouth as taste (gustation) and from those of the nose as smell (olfaction). Other chemoreceptors monitor levels of chemicals in body fluids, such as carbon dioxide, oxygen, and glucose.

Childhood The stage in postnatal development that runs from about 13 months to 12 or 13 years of age. Growth during this period is initially rapid and then slows. Toward the end of childhood there is a dramatic increase in growth known as a growth spurt.

Chitin A structural polysaccharide found in the exoskeletons (hard outer coverings) of animals such as insects, spiders, and crustaceans.

Chlamydia A genus of bacteria. In this text, it is an infection (usually sexually transmitted) caused by *Chlamydia trachomatus*, commonly causing urethritis and pelvic inflammatory disease.

Cholecystokinin A hormone secreted by the small intestine that stimulates the pancreas to release its digestive enzymes and the gallbladder to contract and release bile.

Chordae tendineae Strings of connective tissue that anchor the atrioventricular valves to the wall of the heart, preventing the backflow of blood.

Chorion The extraembryonic membrane that becomes the embryo's major contribution to the placenta.

Chorionic villi Fingerlike projections of the chorion that grow into the uterine lining of the mother during formation of the placenta and become part of the placenta.

Chorionic villi sampling (CVS) A procedure for screening for genetic defects of a fetus by removing a piece of chorionic villi and examining the cells for genetic abnormalities.

Choroid The pigmented middle layer of the eyeball that contains blood vessels.

Chromatid One of the two identical replicates of a duplicated chromosome. The two chromatids that make up a chromosome are held together by a centromere and are referred to as sister chromatids. During cell division, the two strands separate and each becomes a chromosome in one of the two daughter cells.

Chromatin DNA and associated proteins in a dispersed, rather than condensed, state.

Chromosomal mutation A change in DNA in which a section of a chromosome becomes rearranged, duplicated, or deleted.

Chromosome DNA (which contains the genetic information of a cell) and specialized proteins, primarily histones.

Chronic renal failure A progressive and often irreversible decline in the rate of glomerular filtration.

Chylomicron A particle formed when proteins coat the surface of the products of lipid digestion, making lipids soluble in water and allowing them to be transported throughout the body.

Chyme The semifluid, creamy mass created during digestion once the food has been churned and mixed with the gastric juices of the stomach.

Cilia Extensions of the plasma membrane found on some cells, such as those lining the respiratory tract, that move in a back-and-forth motion. They are usually shorter and much more numerous than flagella but have the same 9 + 2 arrangement of microtubules at their core.

Ciliary body A portion of the middle coat of the eyeball near the lens that consists of smooth muscle and ligaments. Contractions of the smooth muscle of the ciliary body change the shape of the lens, which then focuses images on the retina.

Circulatory system An organ system composed of the cardiovascular system (heart and blood vessels) and the lymphatic system (lymphatic vessels and lymphoid tissues and organs).

Circumcision The surgical removal of the foreskin of the penis, usually performed when the male is an infant.

Cirrhosis A chronic disease of the liver in which the liver becomes fatty and the liver cells are gradually replaced with scar tissue.

Citric acid cycle The cyclic series of chemical reactions that follows the transition reaction and yields two molecules of adenosine triphosphate (one from each acetyl CoA that enters the cycle) and several molecules of nicotine adenine dinucleotide (NADH) and flavin adenine dinucleotide (FADH$_2$), carriers of high-energy electrons that enter the electron transport chain. This phase of cellular respiration occurs inside the mitochondrion and is sometimes called the Krebs cycle.

Cleavage A rapid series of mitotic cell divisions in which the zygote first divides into two cells, and then four cells, and then eight cells, and so on. Cleavage usually begins about one day after fertilization as the zygote moves along the oviduct toward the uterus.

Climax community The relatively stable community that eventually forms at the end of ecological succession and remains if no disturbances occur.

Clitoris A small, erectile body in the female that plays a role in sexual stimulation. It develops from the same embryological structure from which the penis develops in the male.

Clonal selection The hypothesis that, by binding to a receptor on a lymphocyte surface, an antigen selectively activates only those lymphocytes able to recognize that antigen and programs that lymphocyte to divide, forming an army of cells specialized to attack the stimulating antigen.

Clone A population of identical cells descended from a single ancestor.

CNS See central nervous system.

Cochlea The snail-shaped portion of the inner ear that contains the actual organ of hearing, the spiral organ (of Corti).

Codominance The condition in which the effects of both alleles are separately expressed in a heterozygote.

Codon A three-base sequence on messenger RNA (mRNA) that specifies one of the 20 common amino acids or the beginning or end of the protein chain.

Coenzyme An organic molecule such as a vitamin that functions as a cofactor and helps enzymes convert substrate to product.

Cofactor A nonprotein substance such as zinc, iron, and vitamins that helps enzymes convert substrate to product. It may permanently reside at the active site of the enzyme or may bind to the active site at the same time as the substrate.

Collagen fibers Strong insoluble protein fibers common in many connective tissues.

Collecting ducts Within the kidneys, the tubes that receive filtrate from the distal convoluted tubules of many nephrons and that eventually drain into the renal pelvis. Some tubular secretion occurs along collecting ducts.

Colon The division of the large intestine composed of the ascending colon, the transverse colon, and the descending colon.

Colostrum A cloudy yellowish fluid produced by the breasts in the interval after birth when milk is not yet available. Its composition is different from that of milk.

Columnar epithelium A type of epithelial tissue composed of tall, rectangular cells that are specialized for secretion and absorption.

Coma An unconscious state caused by trauma to neurons in regions of the brain responsible for stimulating the cerebrum, particularly those in the reticular activating system or thalamus. Coma can be caused by mechanical shock, such as might be caused by a blow to the head, tumors, infections, drug overdose (from barbiturates, alcohol, opiates, or aspirin), or failure of the liver or kidney.

Combination birth control pill A means of hormonal contraception that consists of a series of pills with synthetic forms of estrogen and progesterone. The hormones in the pills mimic the effects of natural hormones ordinarily produced by the ovaries and inhibit FSH and LH secretion by the anterior pituitary gland and, therefore, prevent the development of an egg and ovulation.

Common cold An upper respiratory infection caused by one of the adenoviruses.

Community An assortment of organisms of various species interacting in a defined habitat.

Compact bone Very dense, hard bone, containing internal spaces of microscopic size and narrow channels that contain blood vessels and nerves. It makes up the shafts of long bones and the outer surfaces of all bones.

Complement system A group of about 20 proteins that enhances the body's defense mechanisms. The complement system destroys cellular pathogens by creating holes in the plasma membrane, making the cell leaky, enhancing phagocytosis, and stimulating inflammation.

Complementary base pairing The process by which specific bases are matched: adenine with thymine (in DNA) or with uracil (in RNA) and cytosine with guanine. Each base pair is held together by weak hydrogen bonds.

Complementary proteins A combination of foods each containing incomplete proteins that provide ample amounts of all essential amino acids when combined.

Complete dominance In genetic inheritance, the dominant allele in a heterozygote completely masks the effect of the recessive allele. Complete dominance often occurs because the dominant allele produces a functional protein and the recessive allele produces a less functional protein or none at all.

Complete protein A protein that contains ample amounts of all the essential amino acids. Animal sources of protein are generally complete proteins.

Compound A molecule that contains two or more different elements.

Computed tomography (CT scanning) A method of visualizing body structures, including the brain, using an x-ray source that moves in an arc around the body part to be imaged, thereby providing different views of the structure.

Concentration gradient A difference in the number of molecules or ions between two adjacent regions. Molecules or ions tend to move away from an area where they are more concentrated to an area where they are less concentrated. Each type of molecule or ion moves in response to its own concentration gradient.

Conclusion An interpretation of the data collected in an experiment.

Condom, female A barrier means of contraception used by a female that consists of a loose sac of polyurethane held in place by flexible rings (one at each end). It is used to prevent sperm from entering the female tract, and it also reduces the risk of spreading sexually transmitted infections.

Condom, male A barrier means of contraception consisting of a thin sheath of latex or animal intestines that is rolled onto an erect penis, where it prevents sperm from entering the vagina. A latex condom also helps prevent the spread of sexually transmitted diseases.

Cone One of the three types of photoreceptors responsible for color vision.

Confounding variable In a controlled experiment, it is a second variable between the control group and the experimental group.

Conjoined twins Individuals that develop from a single fertilized ovum that fails to completely split in two at an early stage of cleavage. Such twins have identical genetic material and thus are always the same gender. They may be surgically separated after birth.

Connective tissue Tissue that binds together and supports other tissues of the body. All connective tissues contain cells in an extracellular matrix, which consists of protein fibers and a noncellular ground substance.

Constipation Infrequent, difficult bowel movements of hard feces. Constipation occurs when feces move through the large intestine too slowly and too much water is reabsorbed.

Consumer In ecosystems, an organism that obtains energy and raw materials by eating the tissues of other organisms.

Contact inhibition The phenomenon whereby cells placed in a dish in the presence of growth factors stop dividing once they have formed a monolayer. This may result from competition among the cells for growth factors and nutrients. Cancer cells do not display density-dependent contact inhibition and continue to divide, piling up on one another until nutrients run out.

Continuous ambulatory peritoneal dialysis (CAPD) A method of hemodialysis whereby the peritoneum, one of the body's own selectively permeable membranes, is used as the dialyzing membrane. It is an alternative to the artificial kidney machine during kidney failure.

Contraceptive sponge A barrier means of contraception consisting of a sponge containing spermicide.

Control group In a controlled scientific experiment, the control group is the one in which the variable is unaltered for comparison to the experimental group.

Controlled experiment An experiment in which the subjects are divided into two groups, usually called the control group and the experimental group. Ideally, the groups differ in only the factor(s) of interest.

Convergence In vision, the process by which the eyes are directed toward the midline of the body as an object moves closer. Convergence is necessary to keep the image focused on the fovea of the retina.

Convergent evolution The process by which two species become more alike because they have similar ecological roles and selection pressures. For example, birds and insects independently evolved wings.

Core temperature The temperature in body structures below the skin and subcutaneous layers.

Cornea A clear, transparent dome located in the front and center of the eye that both provides the window through which light enters the eye and helps bend light rays so that they focus on the retina.

Coronary arteries The arteries that deliver blood to cardiac muscle.

Coronary artery bypass A technique for bypassing a blocked coronary blood vessel to restore blood flow to the heart muscle. Typically, a segment of a leg vein is removed and grafted so that it provides a shunt between the aorta and a coronary artery past the point of obstruction.

Coronary artery disease (CAD) A condition in which fatty deposits associated with atherosclerosis form on the inside of coronary arteries, obstructing the flow of blood. It is the underlying cause of the vast majority of heart attacks.

Coronary circulation The system of blood vessels that services the tissues of the heart itself.

Coronary sinus A vessel that returns deoxygenated blood collected from the heart muscle to the right atrium of the heart. The coronary sinus is formed from the merger of cardiac veins.

Corpus callosum A band of myelinated axons (white matter) that connects the two cerebral hemispheres so they can communicate with one another.

Corpus luteum A structure in the ovary that forms from the follicle cells remaining in the ovary after ovulation. The corpus luteum functions as an endocrine structure that secretes estrogen and progesterone.

Corticotropin-releasing hormone (CRH) A hormone released from the placenta that seems to initiate labor.

Covalent bond A chemical bond formed when outer shell electrons are shared between atoms.

Cowper's glands See bulbourethral glands.

Cranial nerves Twelve pairs of nerves that arise from the brain and service the structures of the head and certain body parts such as the heart and diaphragm. Cranial nerves can be sensory, motor, or mixed.

Cranium The skeletal portion of the skull that forms the cranial case. It is formed from eight (sometimes more) flattened bones including the frontal bone, two parietal bones, the occipital bone, two temporal bones, the sphenoid bone, and the ethmoid bone.

Creatine phosphate A compound stored in muscle tissue that serves as an alternative energy source for muscle contraction.

Cretinism A condition characterized by dwarfism, mental retardation, and slowed sexual development. It is caused by undersecretion of thyroid hormone during fetal development or infancy.

CRH See corticotropin-releasing hormone.

Cristae Infoldings of the inner membrane of a mitochondrion.

Cross-bridges Myosin heads. Club-shaped ends of a myosin molecule that bind to actin filaments and can swivel, causing actin filaments to slide past the myosin filaments, which causes muscle contraction.

Cross-tolerance The development of tolerance for a drug that is not used, caused by the development of tolerance to another, usually similar, drug.

Crossing over The breaking and rejoining of nonsister chromatids of homologous pairs of chromosomes during meiosis (specifically at prophase I when homologous chromosomes pair up side by side). Crossing over results in the exchange of corresponding segments of chromatids and increases genetic variability in populations.

Crown The part of a tooth that is visible above the gum line. It is covered with enamel, a nonliving material that is hardened with calcium salts.

CT scanning See computed tomography.

Cuboidal epithelium A type of epithelial tissue composed of cube-shaped cells that are specialized for secretion and absorption.

Culture Social influences that produce an integrated pattern of knowledge, belief, and behavior.

Cupula A pliable gelatinous mass covering the hair cells within the ampulla of the semicircular canals of the inner ear and whose movement bends hair cells, triggering the generation of nerve impulses that are interpreted by the brain as movement of the head.

Cushing's syndrome A condition characterized by accumulation of fluid in the face and redistribution of body fat caused by prolonged exposure to cortisol.

Cutaneous membrane The skin. It is thick, relatively waterproof, and dry.

Cystitis Inflammation of the urinary bladder caused by bacteria.

Cytokinesis The division of the cytoplasm and organelles into two daughter cells during cell division. Cytokinesis usually occurs during telophase.

Cytomegalovirus Any of a group of highly host-specific herpes viruses that produce an infection characterized by unique large cells with nuclear inclusions. Cytomegalovirus infects many people in childhood but can be reactivated in people with an HIV infection.

Cytoplasm The part of a cell that includes the aqueous fluid within the cell and all the organelles with the exception of the nucleus.

Cytoskeleton A complex network of protein filaments within the cytoplasm that gives the cell its shape, anchors organelles in place, and functions in the movement of entire cells or certain organelles or vesicles within cells. The cytoskeleton includes microtubules, microfilaments, and intermediate filaments.

Cytotoxic T cell A type of T lymphocyte that directly attacks infected body cells and tumor cells by releasing chemicals called perforins that cause the target cells to burst.

D

Darwinian fitness See fitness.

Decomposer An organism that obtains energy by consuming the remains or wastes of other organisms. Decomposers release inorganic materials that can then be used by producers. Bacteria and fungi are important decomposers.

Deductive reasoning A logical progression of thought proceeding from the general to the specific. It involves making specific deductions based on a larger generalization or premise. The statement is usually in the form of an "if … then" premise.

Deforestation Removing trees from an area without replacing them.

Dehydration synthesis The process by which polymers are formed. Monomers are linked together through the removal of a water molecule.

Deletion Pertaining to chromosomes, the loss of a nucleotide or segment of a chromosome.

Denaturation The process by which changes in the environment of a protein, such as increased heat or changes in pH, cause it to unravel and lose its three-dimensional shape. Change in the shape of a protein results in loss of function.

Dendrite A process of a neuron specialized to pick up messages and transmit them toward the cell body. There are typically many short branching dendrites on a neuron.

Dense connective tissue Connective tissue that contains many tightly woven fibers and is found in ligaments, tendons, and the dermis.

Density-dependent regulating factor One of many factors that have a greater impact on the population size as conditions become more crowded. Such factors include disease and starvation.

Density-independent regulating factor One of many factors that regulate population size by causing deaths that are not related to the density of individuals in a population. Such factors include natural disasters.

Dentin A hard, bonelike substance that forms the main substance of teeth. It is covered by enamel on the crown and by cementum on the root.

Deoxyribonucleic acid (DNA) The molecular basis of genetic inheritance in all cells and some viruses. A category of nucleic acids that usually consists of a double helix of two nucleotide strands. The sequence of nucleotides carries the instructions for assembling proteins.

Depolarization A change in the difference in electrical charge across a membrane that moves it from a negative value toward 0 mV. During a nerve impulse (action potential), depolarization is caused by the inward flow of positively charged sodium ions.

Dermis The layer of the skin that lies just below the epidermis and is composed of connective tissue. The dermis contains blood vessels, oil glands, sensory structures, and nerve endings. The dermis does not wear away.

Desertification The process by which overfarming and overgrazing transform marginal farmlands and rangelands to deserts.

Desmosome A type of junction between cells that anchors adjacent cells together.

Detrital food web Energy flow begins with detritus (organic material from the remains of dead organisms) that is eaten by a primary consumer.

Detritivore An organism that obtains energy by consuming the remains or wastes of other organisms. Detritivores release inorganic materials that can then be used by producers.

Detrusor muscle A layer of smooth muscle within the walls of the urinary bladder. It plays a role in urination.

Diabetes insipidus A condition characterized by excessive urine production caused by inadequate ADH production.

Diabetes mellitus A condition characterized by excessive urine production, an bnormally high blood glucose level, and the presence of glucose in the urine. Caused by deficient production of insulin (type 1) or decreased sensitivity to insulin (type 2).

Diaphragm A broad sheet of muscle that separates the abdominal and thoracic cavities. When the diaphragm contracts, inhalation occurs.

Diaphragm, contraceptive A barrier means of contraception that consists of a dome-shaped soft rubber cup on a flexible ring. A diaphragm is used in conjunction with a spermicide to prevent sperm from reaching the egg.

Diarrhea Abnormally frequent, loose bowel movements. Diarrhea occurs when feces pass through the large intestine too quickly and too little water is reabsorbed. Diarrhea sometimes leads to dehydration.

Diastole Relaxation of the heart. Atrial diastole is the relaxation of the atria. Ventricular diastole is the relaxation of the ventricles.

Diastolic pressure The lowest blood pressure in an artery during the relaxation of the heart. In a typical, healthy adult, the diastolic pressure is about 80 mm Hg.

Digestive system The organ system that breaks down and absorbs food. The digestive system includes the mouth, esophagus, stomach, small intestine, and large intestine. Associated structures include the teeth, tongue, salivary glands, liver, gallbladder, and pancreas.

Dilation stage The first stage of true labor. It begins with the onset of contractions and ends when the cervix has fully dilated to 10 cm (4 in.).

Diploid The condition of having two sets of chromosomes in each cell. Somatic (body) cells are diploid.

Disaccharide A molecule formed when two monosaccharides covalently bond to each other through dehydration synthesis. It is known as a double sugar.

Distal convoluted tubule The section of the renal tubule where reabsorption and secretion occur.

Diuretic A substance that promotes urine production. Alcohol is a diuretic.

DNA (deoxyribonucleic acid) The molecular basis of genetic inheritance in all cells and some viruses. A category of nucleic acids that usually consists of a double helix of two nucleotide strands. The sequence of nucleotides carries the instructions for assembling proteins.

DNA fingerprint The pattern of DNA fragments that have been cut by a restriction enzyme and sorted by size. Each person has a characteristic, individual DNA fingerprint.

DNA library A large collection of cloned recombinant DNA fragments containing the entire genome of an organism.

DNA ligase An enzyme that catalyzes the formation of bonds between the sugar and the phosphate molecules that form the sides of the DNA ladder during replication, repair, or the creation of recombinant DNA.

DNA polymerase Any one of the enzymes that catalyze the synthesis of DNA from free nucleotides using one strand of DNA as a template.

Dominant allele The allele that is fully expressed in the phenotype of an individual who is heterozygous for that gene. The dominant allele usually produces a functional protein, whereas the recessive allele does not.

Dopamine A neurotransmitter in the central nervous system thought to be involved in regulating emotions and in the brain pathways that control complex movements.

Dorsal nerve root The portion of a spinal nerve that arises from the back (posterior) side of the spinal cord and contains axons of sensory neurons. It joins with the ventral nerve root to form a single spinal nerve, which passes through the opening between the vertebrae.

Doubling time The number of years required for a population to double in size at a given, constant growth rate.

Down syndrome A collection of characteristics that tend to occur when an individual has three copies of chromosome 21. It is also known as trisomy 21.

Drug cocktail A combination of drugs used to treat people who are HIV positive. The combination usually includes a drug that blocks reverse transcription and a protease inhibitor.

Ductus arteriosus A small vessel in the fetus that connects the pulmonary artery to the aorta. It diverts blood away from the lungs.

Ductus venosus A small vessel in the fetus through which most blood from the placenta flows, bypassing the liver.

Duodenum The first region of the small intestine. The duodenum receives chyme from the stomach and digestive juices from the pancreas and liver.

Duplication Pertaining to chromosomes, the duplication of a region of a chromosome that often results from fusion of a fragment from a homologous chromosome.

Dura mater The tough, leathery outer layer of the meninges that protects the central nervous system. Around the brain, the dura mater has two layers that are separated by a fluid-filled space containing blood vessels.

Dysplasia The changes in shape, nuclei, and organization of adult cells. It is typical of precancerous cells.

E

Eardrum See tympanic membrane.

ECG See electrocardiogram.

Ecological footprint A measure of the amount of productive land and water used by a person or population to produce products consumed and to remove the waste of products consumed.

Ecological pyramid A diagram in which blocks represent each tropic (feeding) level.

Ecological succession The sequence of changes in the species making up a community over time.

Ecology The study of the interactions among organisms and between organisms and their environment.

Ecosystem All the organisms living in a certain area that can potentially interact, together with their physical environment.

Ectoderm The primary germ layer that forms the nervous system, epidermis, and epidermal derivatives such as hair, nails, and mammary glands.

Ectopic pregnancy A pregnancy in which the embryo (blastocyst) implants and begins development in a location other than the uterus, most commonly in an oviduct (a tubal pregnancy).

Edema Swelling caused by the accumulation of interstitial fluid.

EEG See electroencephalogram.

Effector A muscle or a gland that brings about a response to a stimulus.

Effector cells Lymphocytes that are responsible for the attack on cells or substances not recognized as belonging in the body.

Efferent (motor) neuron A neuron specialized to carry information *away from* the central nervous system to an effector, either a muscle or a gland.

Egg A mature female gamete. An ovum. The egg contains nutrients and the mother's genetic contribution to the next generation.

EKG See electrocardiogram.

Elastic cartilage The most flexible type of cartilage because of an abundance of wavy elastic fibers in its matrix.

Elastic fibers Coiled proteins found in connective tissues that allow the connective tissue to be stretched and recoil. Elastic fibers are common in tissues that require elasticity.

Electrocardiogram (ECG or EKG) A graphical record of the electrical activities of the heart.

Electroencephalogram (EEG) A graphical record of the electrical activity of the brain.

Electron transport chain A series of carrier proteins embedded in the inner membrane of the mitochondrion that receives electrons from the molecules of nicotine adenine dinucleotide (NADH) and flavin adenine dinucleotide ($FADH_2$) produced by glycolysis and the citric acid cycle. During the transfer of electrons from one molecule to the next, energy is released and this energy is then used to make adenosine triphosphate (ATP). Oxygen is the final electron acceptor in the chain.

Element Any substance that cannot be broken down into simpler substances by ordinary chemical means.

Embolus A blood clot that drifts through the circulatory system and can lodge in a small blood vessel and block blood flow.

Embryo The developing human from week 3 through week 8 of gestation (the embryonic period).

Embryonic disk The flattened platelike structure that will become the embryo proper. It develops from the inner cell mass.

Embryonic period The period of prenatal development that extends from week 3 through week 8 of gestation. It is when tissues and organs form.

Emigration The departure of individuals from a population for some other area.

Emphysema A condition in which the alveolar walls break down, thicken, and form larger air spaces, making gas exchange difficult. This change results in less surface area for gas exchange and an increase in the volume of residual air in the lungs.

Enamel A nonliving material that is hardened with calcium salts and covers the crown of a tooth.

Encephalitis An inflammation of the meninges around the brain.

Endocardium A thin layer that lines the cavities of the heart.

Endocrine gland A gland that lacks ducts and releases its products (hormones) into the fluid just outside the cells.

Endocrine system The organ system that, along with the nervous system, functions in internal communication. It consists of endocrine glands, such as the pituitary gland and thyroid gland, and of organs, such as the kidneys and pancreas, that contain some endocrine tissue but have functions in addition to hormone secretion.

Endocytosis The process by which large molecules and single-celled organisms such as bacteria enter cells. It occurs when a region of the plasma membrane surrounds the substance to be ingested, then pinches off from the rest of the membrane, enclosing the substance in a saclike structure called a vesicle that is released into the cell. Two types of endocytosis are phagocytosis ("cell eating") and pinocytosis ("cell drinking").

Endoderm The primary germ layer that forms some organs and glands (for example, the pancreas, liver, thyroid gland, and parathyroid glands) and the epithelial lining of the urinary, respiratory, and gastrointestinal tracts.

Endometriosis A painful condition in which tissue from the lining of the uterus (the endometrium) is found outside the uterine cavity.

Endometrium The inner layer of the uterus consisting of connective tissue, glands, and blood vessels. The endometrium thickens and develops with each menstrual cycle and is then lost as menstrual flow. It is the site of embryo implantation during pregnancy.

Endoplasmic reticulum The network of internal membranes within eukaryotic cells. Whereas rough endoplasmic reticulum (RER) has ribosomes attached to its surface, smooth endoplasmic reticulum (SER) lacks ribosomes and functions in the production of phospholipids for incorporation into cell membranes.

Endorphin A chemical released by nerve cells that binds to the so-called opiate receptors on the pain-transmitting neurons and quells the pain. The term is short for *endo*genous mor*phine*-like substance.

Endosymbiont hypothesis The hypothesis that organelles such as mitochondria were once free-living prokaryotic organisms that either invaded or were engulfed by primitive eukaryotic cells with which they established a symbiotic (mutually beneficial) relationship.

Endothelium The lining of the heart, blood vessels, and lymphatic vessels. It is composed of flattened, tight-fitting cells. The endothelium forms a smooth surface that minimizes friction and allows the blood or lymph to flow over it easily.

Enkephalin A chemical released by nerve cells that binds to the so-called opiate receptors on the pain-transmitting neurons and quells the pain.

Enzyme A substance (usually a protein, but sometimes an RNA molecule) that speeds up chemical reactions without being consumed in the process.

Enzyme–substrate complex Complex formed when a substrate binds to an enzyme at the active site.

Eosinophil The type of white blood cell important in the body's de-fense against parasitic worms. It releases chemicals that help coun-teract certain inflammatory chemicals released during an allergic response.

Epidermis The outermost layer of the skin, composed of epithelial cells.

Epididymis A long tube coiled on the surface of each testis that serves as the site of sperm cell maturation and storage.

Epiglottis A part of the larynx that forms a movable lid of cartilage covering the opening into the trachea (the glottis).

Epinephrine Adrenaline. A hormone secreted by the adrenal medulla, along with norepinephrine, in response to stress. They initiate the physiological "fight-or-flight" reaction.

Epiphyseal plate A plate of cartilage that separates the head of the bone from the shaft, permitting the bone to grow. In late adolescence, the epiphyseal plate is replaced by bone, and growth stops. The epiphyseal plate is commonly called the growth plate.

Episiotomy An incision made to enlarge the vaginal opening, just before passage of the baby's head at the end of the second stage of labor.

Epithelial tissue One of the four primary tissue types. The tissue that covers body surfaces, lines body cavities and organs, and forms glands.

Equatorial plate A plane at the midline of a cell where chromosomes line up during mitosis or meiosis.

Erythrocyte A red blood cell. A nucleus-free biconcave cell in the blood that is specialized for transporting oxygen to cells and assists in transporting carbon dioxide away from cells.

Erythropoietin A hormone released by the kidneys when the oxygen content of the blood declines that stimulates red blood cell production.

Esophagus A muscular tube that conducts food from the pharynx to the stomach using peristalsis.

Essential amino acid Any of the eight amino acids that the body cannot synthesize and, therefore, must be supplied in the diet.

Estrogen A steroid sex hormone produced by the follicle cells and the corpus luteum in the ovary. Estrogen helps oocytes mature, stimulates cell division in the endometrium and the breast with each uterine cycle, and maintains secondary sex characteristics. The adrenal cortex also secretes estrogen.

Eukaryotic cell A cell with a nucleus and extensive internal membranes that divide it into many compartments and enclose organelles. Eukaryotes include cells in plants, animals, and all other organisms except bacteria and archaea.

Eustachian tubes Auditory tubes. Small tubes that join the upper region of the pharynx (throat) with the middle ear. They help to equalize the air pressure between the middle ear and the atmosphere.

Eutrophication The enrichment of water in a lake or pond by nutrients. Eutrophication is often caused by nitrogen or phosphate that washes into bodies of water.

Evolution Descent with modification from a common ancestor. It is the process by which life forms on the earth have changed over time.

Excitatory synapse A synapse in which the response of the receptors for that neurotransmitter on the postsynaptic membrane increases the likelihood that an action potential will be generated in the postsynaptic neuron. The postsynaptic cell is excited because it becomes less negative than usual (slightly depolarized), usually because of the inflow of sodium ions.

Excretion The elimination of wastes and excess substances from the body.

Exhalation Breathing out (expiration) involves the movement of air out of the respiratory system into the atmosphere.

Exhaustion phase The final phase of the general adaptation syndrome that occurs in response to extreme and prolonged stress. During the exhaustion phase, the heart, blood vessels, and adrenal glands begin to fail after the taxing metabolic and endocrine demands of the resistance phase.

Exocrine glands Glands that secrete their product through ducts onto body surfaces, into the spaces within organs, or into a body cavity. Examples include the salivary glands of the mouth and the oil and sweat glands of the skin.

Exocytosis The process by which large molecules leave cells. It occurs when products packaged by cells in membrane-bound vesicles move toward the plasma membrane. Upon reaching the plasma membrane, the membrane of the vesicle fuses with it, spilling its contents outside the cell.

Exon The nucleotide sequences of a newly synthesized messenger RNA (mRNA) that are spliced together to form the mature mRNA that is ultimately translated into protein.

Exophthalmos A condition characterized by protruding eyes that is caused by the accumulation of interstitial fluid due to oversecretion of thyroid hormone.

Experimental group In a controlled scientific experiment, the experimental group is the one in which the variable is altered.

Expiration The process by which air is moved out of the respiratory system into the atmosphere. It is also called exhalation.

Expiratory reserve volume The additional volume of air that can be forcefully expelled from the lungs after normal exhalation.

Expulsion stage The second stage of true labor. It begins with full dilation of the cervix and ends with delivery of the baby.

External auditory canal The canal leading from the pinna of the ear to the eardrum (tympanic membrane).

External respiration The exchange of oxygen and carbon dioxide between the lungs and the blood.

External urethral sphincter A sphincter made of skeletal muscle that surrounds the urethra. This voluntary sphincter helps stop the flow of urine down the urethra when we wish to postpone urination.

Exteroceptor A sensory receptor that is located near the surface of the body and that responds to changes in the environment.

Extracellular fluid The watery solution outside cells. It is also called interstitial fluid.

Extraembryonic membranes Membranes that lie outside the embryo, where they protect and nourish the embryo and later the fetus. They include the amnion, yolk sac, chorion, and allantois.

F

Facial bones The bones that form the face. They are composed of 14 bones that support several sensory structures and serve as attachments for most muscles of the face.

Facilitated diffusion The movement of a substance from a region of higher concentration to a region of lower concentration with the aid of a membrane protein that either transports the substance from one side of the membrane to the other or forms a channel through which it can move.

Farsightedness A condition in which distant objects are seen more clearly than near ones. Farsightedness occurs either because the eyeball is too short or the lens is too thin, causing the image to be focused behind the retina.

Fascicle A bundle of skeletal muscle fibers (cells) that forms a part of a muscle. Each fascicle is wrapped in its own connective tissue sheath.

Fast-twitch muscle cells Muscle fibers that contract rapidly and powerfully, with little endurance. They have few mitochondria and large glycogen reserves. They depend on anaerobic pathways to generate adenosine triphosphate (ATP) during muscle contraction.

Fatigue A state in which a muscle is physiologically unable to contract despite continued stimulation. Muscle fatigue results from a relative deficit of adenosine triphosphate (ATP).

Fat-soluble vitamin A vitamin that does not dissolve in water and is stored in fat. This group includes vitamins A, D, E, and K.

Fatty acid Chains of carbon atoms bonded to hydrogens with an acidic group (COOH) at one end. Three fatty acids bond to a molecule of glycerol to form a triglyceride (fat).

Feces Waste material discharged from the large intestine during defecation. Feces consist primarily of undigested food, sloughed-off epithelial cells, water, and millions of bacteria.

Fermentation A pathway by which cells can harvest energy in the absence of oxygen. It nets only 2 molecules of ATP as compared with the approximately 36 molecules produced by cellular respiration.

Fertilization The union between an egg (technically a secondary oocyte) and a sperm. It takes about 24 hours from start to finish and usually occurs in a widened portion of the oviduct, not far from the ovary.

Fetal alcohol syndrome A group of characteristics in children born to mothers who consumed alcohol during pregnancy. It can include certain facial features including an eye fold near the bridge of the nose, mental retardation, and slow growth.

Fetal period The period of prenatal development that extends from week 9 of gestation until birth. It is when rapid growth occurs.

Fetus The developing human from week 9 of gestation until birth (the fetal period).

Fever An abnormally elevated body temperature. Fever helps the body fight disease-causing invaders in a number of ways.

Fibrillation Rapid, ineffective contraction of the heart.

Fibrin A protein formed from fibrinogen by thrombin that forms a web that traps blood cells, forming a blood clot.

Fibrinogen A plasma protein produced by the liver that is important in blood clotting. It is converted to fibrin by thrombin.

Fibroblasts Cells in connective tissue that secrete the protein fibers that are found in the matrix of the connective tissue. Fibroblasts also secrete collagen fibers for the repair of body tissues.

Fibrocartilage Cartilage with a matrix containing many collagen fibers. Fibrocartilage is found around the edges of joints and the intervertebral disks.

Fibrous joints Joints that are held together by connective tissue and lack a joint cavity. Most fibrous joints do not permit movement.

Fight-or-flight response The body's reaction to stress or threatening situations by the stimulation of the sympathetic division of the autonomic nervous system.

First messenger A water-soluble hormone that binds to a receptor on the plasma membrane of a target cell. This binding activates a molecule within the cell, called the second messenger, which influences enzyme activity there.

Fitness The average number of reproductively viable offspring left by an individual. It is sometimes called Darwinian fitness.

Flagellum A whiplike appendage of a cell that moves in an undulating manner. It is composed of an extension of the plasma membrane containing microtubules in a 9 + 2 array. It is found on some cells, such as sperm cells.

Floating ribs The last two ribs that do not attach directly to the sternum (breastbone).

Fluid mosaic A term used to describe the structure of the plasma membrane. Proteins interspersed throughout the lipid molecules give the membrane its mosaic quality. The ability of some proteins to move sideways gives the membrane its fluid quality.

Follicle A spherical structure in the ovary that contains an oocyte and is surrounded by follicle cells.

Follicle-stimulating hormone (FSH) A hormone secreted by the anterior pituitary gland that in females stimulates the development of the follicles in the ovaries, resulting in the development of ova (eggs) and the production of estrogen, and in males stimulates sperm production.

Fontanels The "soft spots" in the skull of a newborn. The membranous areas in the skull of a newborn that hold the skull bones together before and shortly after birth. The fontanels are gradually replaced by bone.

Food chain The successive series of organisms through which energy (in the form of food) flows in an ecosystem. Each organism in the series eats or decomposes the preceding one. It begins with the photosynthesizers and flows to herbivores and then to carnivores.

Food web The interconnection of all the feeding relationships (food chains) in an ecosystem.

Foodborne illness An illness that results from ingesting contaminated food or water. Those caused by pathogens (bacteria, viruses, parasites) are considered infections while those caused by chemicals or toxins are considered poisonings. Symptoms first appear in the gastrointestinal tract and include diarrhea and vomiting. Treatment usually involves giving fluids to prevent dehydration; antibiotics may be prescribed if the illness is caused by bacteria. Many go unreported.

Foramen magnum The opening at the base of the skull (in the occipital bone) through which the spinal cord passes.

Foramen ovale In the fetus, a small hole in the wall between the right atrium and left atrium of the heart that allows most blood to bypass the lungs.

Formed elements Cells or cell fragments found in the blood. They include platelets, white blood cells, and red blood cells.

Fossilization The process by which fossils form. Typically an organism dies in water and is buried under accumulating layers of sediments. Hard parts become impregnated with minerals from surrounding water and sediments. Eventually the fossil may be exposed when sediments are uplifted and wind erodes the rock formation.

Fossils The preserved remnants or impressions of past organisms. Most fossils occur in sedimentary rocks.

Founder effect Genetic drift associated with the colonization of a new place by a few individuals so that by chance alone the genetic makeup of the colonizing individuals is not representative of the population they left.

Fovea A small region on the retina that contains a high density of cones but no rods. Objects are focused on the fovea for sharp vision.

Frameshift mutation A mutation that occurs when the number of nucleotides inserted or deleted is not a multiple of three, causing a change in the codon sequence on the mRNA molecule as well as a change in the resulting protein.

Fraternal twins Individuals that develop when two oocytes are released from the ovaries and fertilized by different sperm. Such twins may or may not be the same gender and are as similar genetically as any siblings. They are also called dizygotic twins.

Free radicals Molecular fragments that contain an unpaired electron.

FSH See follicle-stimulating hormone.

Full-term infant Baby born at least 38 weeks after fertilization.

G

Gallbladder A muscular pea-sized sac that stores, modifies, and then concentrates bile. Bile is released from the gallbladder into the small intestine.

Gamete intrafallopian transfer (GIFT) A procedure in which eggs and sperm are collected from a couple and then inserted into the woman's oviduct, where fertilization may occur. If fertilization occurs, resulting embryos drift naturally into the uterus.

Gamete A reproductive cell (sperm or egg) that contains only one copy of each chromosome. A sperm and egg fuse at fertilization, producing a zygote.

Ganglion (plural, ganglia) A collection of nerve cell bodies outside the central nervous system.

Gap junction A type of junction between cells that links the cytoplasm of adjacent cells through small holes, allowing physical and electrical continuity between cells.

GAS See general adaptation syndrome.

Gastric glands Any one of several glands in the stomach mucosa that contribute to the gastric juice (hydrochloric acid and pepsin).

Gastric juice The mixture of hydrochloric acid (HCl) and pepsin released into the stomach.

Gastrin A hormone released from the stomach lining in response to the presence of partially digested proteins. Gastrin triggers the production of gastric juice by the stomach.

Gastrointestinal (GI) tract A long tubular system specialized for the processing and absorption of food that begins at the mouth and continues to the esophagus, stomach, intestines, and anus. Several accessory glands empty their secretions into the GI tract to assist digestion.

Gastrula The embryo during gastrulation, when cells move to establish primary germ layers.

Gastrulation Cell movements that establish the primary germ layers of the embryo. The embryo during this period is called a gastrula.

Gated ion channel An ion channel that is opened to allow ions to pass through or closed to prevent passage by changes in the shape of a protein that functions as a gate.

Gene A segment of DNA on a chromosome that directs the synthesis of a specific polypeptide that will play a structural or functional role in the cell. Some genes have regulatory regions of DNA within their boundaries. Also, some genes code for RNA

molecules that are needed for the production of the polypeptide but are not part of it.

Gene flow Movement of alleles between populations as a result of the movement of individuals. It is a cause of microevolution.

Gene pool All of the alleles of all of the genes of all individuals in a population.

Gene therapy Treating a genetic disease by inserting healthy functional genes into the body cells that are affected by the faulty gene.

General adaptation syndrome (GAS) A series of physiological adjustments made by our bodies in response to prolonged, extreme stress.

General senses The sensations that arise from receptors in the skin, muscles, joints, bones, and internal organs and include touch, pressure, vibration, temperature, a sense of body and limb position, and pain.

Genetic code The base triplets in DNA that specify the amino acids that go into proteins or that function as start or stop signals in protein synthesis. It is used to convert the linear sequence of bases in DNA to the sequence of amino acids in proteins.

Genetic drift The random change in allele frequencies within a population due to chance alone. It is a cause of microevolution that is usually negligible in large populations.

Genetic engineering The manipulation of genetic material for human practical purposes.

Genital herpes A sexually transmitted disease caused by the herpes simplex virus (HSV) that is usually characterized by painful blisters on the genitals. It is usually caused by HSV-2 but can be caused by HSV-1.

Genital warts Warts that form in the genital area caused by the human papillomaviruses (HPV). These viruses also cause cervical cancer and penile cancer.

Genome The complete set of DNA of an organism, including all of its genes.

Genotype The genetic makeup of an individual. It refers to precise alleles that are present.

Gigantism A condition characterized by rapid growth and unusual height caused by abnormally high levels of growth hormone in childhood; also called giantism.

GIFT See gamete intrafallopian transfer.

Gingivitis An inflammation of the gums.

Gland Epithelial tissue that secretes a product.

Glaucoma A condition in which the pressure within the anterior chamber of the eye increases as a result of the buildup of aqueous humor. It can cause blindness.

Glial cells Nonexcitable cells in the nervous system that are specialized to support, protect, and insulate neurons. Also called neuroglial cells or neuroglia.

Global warming A long-term increase in atmospheric temperatures caused by a buildup of carbon dioxide (CO_2) and other greenhouse gases in the atmosphere. Greenhouse gases trap heat in the atmosphere.

Glomerular (Bowman's) capsule A cuplike structure surrounding the glomerulus of a nephron.

Glomerular filtration The process by which water and dissolved substances move from the blood in the glomerulus to the inside of Bowman's capsule.

Glomerulus A tuft of capillaries within the renal corpuscle of a nephron.

Glottis The opening to the airways of the respiratory system from the pharynx into the larynx.

Glucagon The hormone secreted by the pancreas that elevates glucose levels in the blood.

Glucocorticoids Hormones secreted by the adrenal cortex that affect glucose homeostasis, thereby influencing metabolism and resistance to stress.

Gluconeogenesis The conversion of noncarbohydrate molecules to glucose.

Glycogen The storage polysaccharide of animals. This complex carbohydrate is stored in the liver and muscles where it serves as a short-term energy source that can be broken down to release energy-packed glucose molecules.

Glycolysis The splitting of glucose, a six-carbon sugar, into two three-carbon molecules called pyruvate. Glycolysis takes place in the cytoplasm of a cell and is the starting point for cellular respiration and fermentation.

GnRH See gonadotropin-releasing hormone.

Goiter, simple An enlarged thyroid gland caused by iodine deficiency.

Golgi complex An organelle consisting of flattened membranous disks that functions in protein processing and packaging.

Golgi tendon organs The highly branched nerve fibers located in the tendons that sense the degree of muscle tension.

Gonad An ovary in a female or a testis in a male. The gonads produce gametes (eggs or sperm) and sex hormones.

Gonadocorticoids The male and female sex hormones, androgens and estrogens, secreted by the adrenal cortex.

Gonadotropin-releasing hormone (GnRH) A hormone produced by the hypothalamus that causes the secretion of luteinizing hormone and follicle-stimulating hormone from the anterior pituitary gland.

Gonorrhea A sexually transmitted disease caused by the bacterium *Neisseria gonorrhoeae* that commonly causes urethritis and pelvic inflammatory disease. It may not cause symptoms, especially in women.

Graafian follicle A mature follicle in the ovary.

Graded potential A temporary local change in the membrane potential that varies directly with the strength of the stimulus.

Granulocytes White blood cells with granules in their cytoplasm, including neutrophils, eosinophils, and basophils.

Graves' disease An autoimmune disorder caused by oversecretion of thyroid hormone. It is characterized by increased heart and metabolic rates, sweating, nervousness, and exophthalmos.

Gray matter Regions of the central nervous system that contain neuron cell bodies and unmyelinated axons. These regions are gray because they lack myelin. Gray matter is important in neural integration.

Greenhouse effect An increase in atmospheric carbon dioxide (CO_2) that could lead to a rise in temperatures throughout the world. Greenhouse gases trap heat in the atmosphere.

Ground substance In connective tissue the ground substance forms the extracellular matrix that the cells are embedded in. It is composed of protein fibers and noncellular material.

Growth factor A type of signaling molecule that stimulates growth by stimulating cell division in target cells.

Growth hormone (GH) An anterior pituitary hormone with the primary function of stimulating growth through increases in protein synthesis, cell size, and rates of cell division. GH stimulates growth in general, especially bone growth.

Growth plate (Epiphyseal plate) A plate of cartilage that separates each end of a bone from its shaft that permits bone to grow.

Gumma A large sore that forms during the third stage of syphilis.

H

Habitat The natural environment or place where an organism, population, or species lives.

Hair cells A type of mechanoreceptor that generates nerve impulses when bent or tilted. Hair cells in the inner ear are responsible for hearing and equilibrium.

Hair root plexus The nerve endings that surround the hair follicle and are sensitive to touch.

Haploid The condition of having one set of chromosomes, as in eggs and sperm.

HCG See human chorionic gonadotropin.

Heart attack The death of heart muscle cells caused by an insufficient blood supply; a myocardial infarction.

Heart murmur Heart sounds other than "lub dup" that are created by turbulent blood flow. Heart murmurs can indicate a heart problem, such as a malfunctioning valve.

Heart A muscular pump that keeps blood flowing through an animal's body. The human heart has four chambers: two atria and two ventricles.

Heartburn A burning sensation behind the breastbone that occurs when acidic gastric juice backs up into the esophagus.

Heimlich maneuver A procedure intended to force a large burst of air out of the lungs to dislodge material lodged in the trachea.

Helper T cell The kind of T lymphocyte that serves as the main switch for the entire immune response by presenting the antigen to B cells and by secreting chemicals that stimulate other cells of the immune system. It is also known as a T4 cell or a CD4 cell, after the receptors on its surface.

Hematocrit The percentage of red blood cells in blood by volume. It is a measure of the oxygen-carrying ability of the blood.

Hemodialysis The use of artificial devices, such as the artificial kidney machine, to cleanse the blood during kidney failure.

Hemoglobin The oxygen-binding pigment in red blood cells. It consists of four subunits, each made up of an iron-containing heme group and a protein chain.

Hemolytic disease of the newborn A condition in which the red blood cells of an Rh-positive fetus or newborn are destroyed by anti-Rh antibodies previously produced in the bloodstream of an Rh-negative mother.

Hemophilia An inherited blood disorder in which there is insufficient production of blood-clotting factors. Hemophilia results in excessive bleeding in joints, deep tissues, and elsewhere. Hemophilia usually occurs in males.

Hepatitis An inflammation of the liver. Hepatitis is usually caused by one of six viruses.

Herbivore An animal that eats primary producers (green plants or algae). A primary consumer.

Herpes simplex virus See HSV-1 and HSV-2.

Heterotroph An organism that cannot make its own food from inorganic substances and instead consumes other organisms or decaying material.

Heterozygote advantage The phenomenon in which the heterozygous condition is favored over either homozygous condition. It maintains genetic variation within a population in the face of natural selection.

Heterozygous The condition of having two different alleles for a particular gene.

Hinge joint A joint that permits motion in only one plane, such as the knee joint or the elbow.

Hippocampus The part of the limbic system of the brain that plays a role in converting short-term memory into long-term memory.

Histamine A substance released by basophils and mast cells during an inflammatory response that causes blood vessels to widen (dilate) and become more permeable.

Homeostasis The ability of living things to maintain a relatively constant internal environment in all levels of body organization.

Hominid A member of the family Hominidae, which now includes apes and humans. In the past, only humans and their immediate ancestors, such as species within the genus *Australopithecus*, were placed in Hominidae.

Hominin A member of the subfamily Homininae, which includes the human lineage and its immediate ancestors.

Homologous chromosomes A pair of chromosomes that bear genes for the same traits. One member of each pair came from each parent. Homologous chromosomes are the same size and shape and line up with one another during meiosis I.

Homologous structures Structures that have arisen from a common ancestry. Compare with analogous structure.

Homozygous The condition of having two identical alleles for a particular gene.

Hormonal implants A means of hormonal contraception consisting of silicon rods containing progesterone that are implanted under the skin in the upper arm and prevent pregnancy for up to 5 years.

Hormone A chemical messenger released by cells of the endocrine system that travels through the circulatory system to affect receptive target cells.

Host (vector) DNA The DNA that is recombined with pieces of DNA from another source (that might contain a desirable gene) in the formation of recombinant DNA.

HPV See human papillomavirus.

HSV-1 Herpes simplex virus 1. HSV-1 usually infects the upper half of the body and causes cold sores (fever blisters), but it can cause genital herpes if contact is made with the genital area.

HSV-2 Herpes simplex virus 2. HSV-2 causes genital herpes, but it can cause cold sores if contact is made with the mouth.

Human chorionic gonadotropin (HCG) A hormone produced by the cells of the early embryo (blastocyst) and the placenta that maintains the corpus luteum for approximately the first 3 months of pregnancy. HCG enters the bloodstream of the mother and is excreted in her urine. HCG forms the basis for many pregnancy tests.

Human papillomavirus (HPV) One of the group of viruses that commonly cause genital warts.

Hyaline cartilage A type of cartilage with a gel-like matrix that provides flexibility and support. It is found at the end of long bones as well as parts of the nose, ribs, larynx, and trachea.

Hydrocephalus A condition resulting from the excessive production or inadequate drainage of cerebrospinal fluid.

Hydrogen bond A weak chemical bond formed between a partially positively charged hydrogen atom in a molecule and a partially negatively charged atom in another molecule or in another region of the same molecule.

Hydrolysis The process by which polymers are broken apart by the addition of water.

Hydrophilic Water-loving. The heads of phospholipids (components of the plasma membrane) are hydrophilic.

Hydrophobic Water-fearing. The tails of phospholipids (components of the plasma membrane) are hydrophobic.

Hyperglycemia An elevated blood glucose level.

Hypertension High blood pressure. A high upper (systolic) value usually suggests that the person's arteries have become hardened and are no longer able to dampen the high pressure of each heartbeat. The lower (diastolic) value is generally considered more important because it indicates the pressure when the heart is relaxing.

Hyperthermia Abnormally elevated body temperature.

Hypertonic solution A solution with a higher concentration of solutes than plasma, for example.

Hypodermis The layer of loose connective tissue below the epidermis and dermis that anchors the skin to underlying tissues and organs.

Hypoglycemia Depressed levels of blood glucose often resulting from excess insulin.

Hypophysis See pituitary gland.

Hypothalamus A small brain region located below the thalamus that is essential to maintaining a stable environment within the body. The hypothalamus influences blood pressure, heart rate, digestive activity, breathing rate, and many other vital physiological processes. It acts as the body's "thermostat"; regulates food intake, hunger, and thirst; coordinates the activities of the nervous system and the endocrine (hormonal) system; is part of the circuitry for emotions; and functions as a master biological clock.

Hypothermia Abnormally low body temperature.

Hypothesis A testable explanation for a specific set of observations that serves as the basis for experimentation.

Hypotonic solution A solution with a lower concentration of solutes than plasma, for example.

I

ICSI See intracytoplasmic sperm injection.

Identical twins Individuals that develop from a single fertilized ovum that splits in two at an early stage of cleavage. Such twins have nearly identical genetic material and are always the same gender. They are also called monozygotic twins.

Immigration Movement of new individuals from other populations into an area.

Immune response The body's response to specific targets not recognized as belonging in the body.

Immune system The system of the body directly involved with body defenses against specific targets—pathogens, cells, or chemicals not recognized as belonging in the body.

Immunoglobulin (Ig) Any of the five classes of proteins that constitute the antibodies.

Implantation The process by which a blastocyst (pre-embryo) becomes embedded in the lining of the uterus. It normally occurs high up on the back wall of the uterus.

Impotence The inability to achieve or maintain an erection long enough for sexual intercourse.

In vitro fertilization (IVF) A procedure in which eggs and sperm are placed together in a dish in the laboratory. If fertilization occurs, early-stage embryos are then transferred to the woman's uterus, where it is hoped they will implant and complete development. It is a common treatment for infertility resulting from blocked oviducts.

Incomplete dominance In genetic inheritance, expression of the trait in a heterozygous individual is somewhere in between expression of the trait in a homozygous dominant individual and homozygous recessive individual.

Incomplete proteins Proteins that are deficient in one or more of the essential amino acids. Plant sources of protein are generally incomplete proteins.

Incontinence A condition characterized by the escape of small amounts of urine when sudden increases in abdominal pressure, perhaps caused by laughing, sneezing, or coughing, force urine past the external sphincter. This condition is common in women, particularly after childbirth, an event that may stretch or damage the external sphincter, making it less effective in controlling the flow of urine.

Incus The middle of three small bones in the middle ear that transmit information about sound from the eardrum to the inner ear. The incus is also known as the anvil.

Independent assortment Of chromosomes, the process by which homologous chromosomes and the alleles they carry segregate randomly during meiosis, creating mixes of maternal and paternal chromosomes in gametes. This is an important source of genetic variation in populations.

Independent assortment, law of In genetic inheritance, a principle that states that the alleles of unlinked genes (those that are located on different chromosomes) are randomly distributed to gametes.

Inductive reasoning A logical progression of thought proceeding from the specific to the general. It involves the accumulation of facts through observation until the sheer weight of the evidence forces some general statement about the phenomenon. A conclusion is reached on the basis of a number of observations.

Infancy The stage in postnatal development that roughly corresponds to the first year of life. It is a time of rapid growth when total body length usually increases by one-half and weight may triple.

Infertility The inability to conceive (become pregnant) or to cause conception (in the case of males).

Inflammatory response A nonspecific body response to injury or invasion by foreign organisms. It is characterized by redness, swelling, heat, and pain.

Influenza The flu. Influenza is a viral infection caused by any of the variants of influenza A or influenza B viruses.

Informed consent A document that a person must sign before participating in an experiment that lists all possible harmful consequences that might result from participation.

Inguinal canal A passage through the abdominal wall through which the testes pass in their descent to the scrotum and that contains the testicular artery and vein and the vas deferens. In females, contains the round ligament, which attaches to the uterus.

Inhalation Breathing in. Inhalation (inspiration) involves the movement of air into the respiratory system.

Inhibin A hormone produced in the testes that increases with sperm count and inhibits follicle-stimulating hormone secretion and, therefore, inhibits sperm production.

Inhibiting hormone A hormone that inhibits secretion of another hormone.

Inhibitory synapse A synapse in which the response of the receptors for that neurotransmitter on the postsynaptic membrane decreases the likelihood that an action potential will be generated in the postsynaptic neuron. The postsynaptic cell is inhibited because its resting potential becomes more negative than usual.

Inner cell mass A group of cells within the blastocyst that will become the embryo proper and some extraembryonic membranes.

Inner ear A series of passageways in the temporal bone that houses the organs for hearing (cochlea) and the sense of equilibrium (vestibular apparatus).

Insertion The end of the muscle that is attached to the bone that moves when the muscle contracts.

Insoluble fiber A fiber that does not easily dissolve in water. These fibers include cellulose, hemicellulose, and lignin.

Inspiration Inhalation. The movement of air into the respiratory system.

Inspiratory reserve volume The volume of air that can be forcefully brought into the lungs after normal inhalation.

Insulin shock A condition that results from severely depressed glucose levels in which brain cells fail to function properly, causing convulsions and unconsciousness.

Insulin The hormone secreted by the pancreas that reduces glucose levels in the blood.

Integral proteins Proteins embedded in the plasma membrane, either completely or incompletely spanning the bilayer.

Integumentary system The skin.

Intercalated disks Thickenings of the plasma membranes of cardiac muscle cells that strengthen cardiac tissue and promote rapid conduction of impulses throughout the heart.

Intercostal muscles The layers of muscles between the ribs that raise and lower the rib cage during breathing.

Interferon A type of defensive protein produced by T lymphocytes that slows the spread of viruses already in the body by interfering with viral replication. Interferons also attract macrophages and natural killer cells, which kill the viral-infected cell.

Interleukin 1 A chemical secreted by a macrophage that activates helper T cells in an immune response.

Interleukin 2 A chemical released by a helper T cell that activates both B cells and T cells.

Intermediate filament A component of the cytoskeleton made from fibrous proteins. It functions in the maintenance of cell shape and anchoring organelles such as the nucleus.

Internal respiration Movement of oxygen from the blood to the tissues, and movement of carbon dioxide from the tissues to the blood.

Internal urethral sphincter A thickening of smooth muscle at the junction of the bladder and the urethra. The action of this sphincter is involuntary and keeps urine from flowing into the urethra while the bladder is filling.

Interneuron An association neuron. Neurons located within the central nervous system between sensory and motor neurons that serve to integrate information.

Interoceptor A sensory receptor located inside the body, where it monitors conditions. Interoceptors play a vital role in maintaining homeostasis. They are an important part of the feedback loops that regulate blood pressure, blood chemistry, and breathing rate. Interoceptors may also cause us to feel pain, hunger, or thirst, thereby prompting us to take appropriate action.

Interphase The period between cell divisions when the DNA, cytoplasm, and organelles are duplicated and the cell grows in size. Interphase is also the time in the cell's life cycle when the cell carries out its functions in the body.

Interstitial cells Cells located between the seminiferous tubules in the testes that produce the male steroid sex hormones, collectively called androgens.

Intervertebral disks Pads of cartilage that help cushion the bones of the vertebral column.

Intracytoplasmic sperm injection (ICSI) A procedure in which a tiny needle is used to inject a single sperm cell into an egg. It is an option for treating infertility when the man has few sperm or sperm that lack the strength or enzymes necessary to penetrate the egg.

Intrauterine device (IUD) A means of contraception consisting of a small plastic device that either is wrapped with copper wire or contains progesterone. It is inserted into the uterus to prevent pregnancy.

Intrinsic factor A protein secreted by the stomach necessary for the absorption of vitamin B_{12} from the small intestine.

Intron A portion of a newly formed mRNA that is cut out of the mature mRNA molecule and is not expressed (used to form a protein).

Ion channel A protein-lined pore or channel through a plasma membrane through which one type or a few types of ions can pass. Nerve cell ion channels are important in the generation and propagation of nerve impulses.

Ion An atom or group of atoms that carries an electric charge resulting from the loss or gain of electrons.

Ionic bond A chemical bond that results from the mutual attraction of oppositely charged ions.

Iris The colored portion of the eye. The iris regulates the amount of light that enters the eye.

Iron-deficiency anemia A reduction in the ability of the blood to carry oxygen due to an insufficient amount of iron in the diet, an inability to absorb iron from the digestive system, or blood loss.

Ischemia A temporary reduction in blood supply caused by obstructed blood flow. It causes reversible damage to heart muscle.

Islets of Langerhans See pancreatic islets.

Isotonic solution A solution with the same concentration of solutes as plasma, for example.

Isotopes Atoms that have the same number of protons but different numbers of neutrons.

IUD See intrauterine device.

IVF See in vitro fertilization.

J

Jaundice A condition in which the skin develops a yellow tone caused by the buildup of bilirubin in the blood and its deposition in certain tissues such as the skin. It is an indication that the liver is not handling bilirubin adequately.

Joint A point of contact between two bones; an articulation.

Junctional complexes Membrane specializations that attach adjacent cells to each other to form a contiguous sheet. There are three kinds of junctions between cells: tight junctions, desmosomes, and gap junctions.

Juxtaglomerular apparatus The region of the kidney nephron where the distal convoluted tubule contacts the afferent arteriole bringing blood into the glomerulus. Cells in this area secrete renin, an enzyme that triggers events eventually leading to increased reabsorption of sodium and water by the distal convoluted tubules and collecting ducts of nephrons.

K

Kaposi's sarcoma A cancer that forms tumors in connective tissue and manifests as pink or purple marks on the skin. It is common in people with a suppressed immune system, such as people living with HIV/AIDS, and is thought to be associated with a new virus in the herpes family, HHV-8.

Karyotype The arrangement of chromosomes based on physical characteristics such as length and location of the centromere. Karyotypes can be checked for defects in number or structure of chromosomes.

Keratinocytes Cells of the epidermis that undergo keratinization, the process in which keratin gradually replaces the contents of maturing cells.

Ketoacidosis A lowering of blood pH resulting from the accumulation of breakdown by-products of fats.

Kidney stones Small, hard crystals formed in the urinary tract when substances such as calcium (the most common constituent), uric acid, or magnesium ammonium phosphate precipitate from urine as a result of higher than normal concentrations. They are also called renal calculi.

Kidneys Reddish, kidney bean–shaped organs responsible for filtering wastes and excess materials from the blood, assisting the respiratory system in the regulation of blood pH, and maintaining fluid balance by regulating the volume and composition of blood and urine.

Klinefelter syndrome A genetic condition resulting from nondisjunction of the sex chromosomes in which a person inherits an extra X chromosome that results in an XXY genotype. The person has a male appearance.

Krebs cyclee See citric acid cycle.

L

Labia majora Two elongated skin folds lateral to the labia minora. They are part of the female external genitalia.

Labia minora Two small skin folds on either side of the vagina and interior to the labia majora. They are part of the external genitalia of a female.

Labor The process by which the fetus is expelled from the uterus and moved through the vagina and into the outside world. During true labor, uterine contractions occur at regular intervals, are often painful, and intensify with walking. Labor is usually divided into the dilation stage, expulsion stage, and placental stage. False labor is characterized by irregular contractions that fail to intensify or change with walking.

Lactation The production and ejection of milk from the mammary glands. The hormone prolactin from the anterior pituitary gland promotes milk production, and the hormone oxytocin released from the posterior pituitary gland makes milk available to the suckling infant by stimulating milk ejection, or let-down.

Lacteal A lymphatic vessel in an intestinal villus that aids in the absorption of lipids.

Lactic acid fermentation The process by which glucose is broken down by muscle cells when oxygen is low during strenuous exercise.

Lacuna (plural, lacunae) A tiny cavity. It contains osteocytes (bone cells) in the matrix of bone and cartilage cells in the matrix of cartilage.

Lanugo Soft, fine hair that covers the fetus beginning about the third or fourth month after conception.

Large intestine The final segment of the gastrointestinal tract, consisting of the cecum, colon, rectum, and anal canal. The large intestine helps absorb water, forms feces, and plays a role in defecation.

Laryngitis An inflammation of the larynx in which the vocal cords become swollen and can no longer vibrate and produce sound.

Larynx The voice box or Adam's apple. A boxlike cartilaginous structure between the pharynx and the trachea held together by muscles and elastic tissue.

Latent period Pertaining to muscle contraction, the interval between the reception of the stimulus and the beginning of muscle contraction.

Latin binomial The two-part scientific name that consists of the genus name followed by the specific epithet.

Lens A transparent, semispherical body of tissue behind the iris and pupil that focuses light on the retina.

Leukemia A cancer of the blood-forming organs that causes white blood cell numbers to increase. The white blood cells are abnormal and do not effectively defend the body against infectious agents.

Leukocytes White blood cells. They are cells of the blood including neutrophils, eosinophils, basophils, monocytes, B lymphocytes, and T lymphocytes. Leukocytes are involved in body defense mechanisms and the removal of wastes, toxins, or damaged, abnormal cells.

LH See luteinizing hormone.

Life expectancy The average number of years a newborn is expected to live.

Ligament A strong band of connective tissue that holds the bones together, supports the joint, and directs the movement of the bones.

Limbic system A collective term for several structures involved in emotions and memory.

Linkage The tendency for a group of genes located on the same chromosome to be inherited together.

Lipid A compound, such as a triglyceride, phospholipid, or steroid, that does not dissolve in water.

Lipid-soluble hormone A hormone that moves easily through the plasma membrane of cells and combines with receptors inside target cells to activate certain genes and stimulate protein synthesis. Steroid hormones are lipid-soluble hormones. Steroids are derived from cholesterol and secreted by the ovaries, testes, and adrenal glands.

Liver A large organ that functions mainly in the production of plasma proteins, the excretion of bile, the storage of energy reserves, the detoxification of poisons, and the interconversion of nutrients.

Local signaling molecules Chemical messengers, such as neurotransmitters, prostaglandins, growth factors, and nitric oxide, that act locally rather than traveling to distant sites within the body.

Locus The point on a chromosome where a particular gene is found.

Longitudinal fissure A deep groove that separates the cerebrum into two hemispheres.

Long-term memory Memory that stores a large amount of information for hours, days, or years.

Loop of the nephron (Loop of Henle) A section of the renal tubule that resembles a hairpin turn. Reabsorption occurs here.

Loose connective tissue Connective tissue, such as areolar and adipose tissue, that contains many cells in which the fibers of the matrix are fewer in number and more loosely woven than those found in dense connective tissue.

Lower esophageal sphincter A ring of muscle at the juncture of the esophagus and the stomach that controls the flow of materials between the esophagus and the stomach. It relaxes to allow food into the stomach and contracts to prevent too much food from moving back into the esophagus.

Lumen The hollow cavity or channel of a tubule through which transported material flows.

Luteinizing hormone (LH) A hormone secreted by the anterior pituitary gland that in females stimulates ovulation and the formation of the corpus luteum (which produces estrogen and progesterone) and prepares the mammary glands for milk production. In males, it stimulates testosterone production by the interstitial cells within the testes.

Lymph nodes Small nodular organs found along lymph vessels that filter lymph. The lymph nodes contain macrophages and lymphocytes, cells that play an essential role in the body's defense system.

Lymph The fluid within the vessels of the lymphatic system. It is derived from the fluid that bathes the cells of the body (interstitial fluid).

Lymphatic system A body system consisting of lymph, lymphatic vessels, and lymphatic tissue and organs. The lymphatic system helps return interstitial fluid to the blood, transports the products of fat digestion from the digestive system to the blood, and assists in body defenses.

Lymphatic vessels The vessels through which lymph flows. A network of vessels that drains interstitial fluid and returns it to the blood supply and transports the products of fat digestion from the digestive system to the blood supply.

Lymphocyte A type of white blood cell important in nonspecific and specific (immune) body defenses. The lymphocytes include B lymphocytes (B cells) that transform into plasma cells and produce antibodies and T lymphocytes (T cells) that are important in defense against foreign or infected cells.

Lymphoid organs Various organs that belong to the lymphatic system, including the tonsils, spleen, thymus, and Peyer's patches.

Lymphoid tissue The type of tissue that predominates in the lymphoid organs except the thymus. The organs in which lymphoid tissue is found are the lymph nodes, tonsils, and spleen. Lymphoid tissue is an important component of the immune system.

Lymphoma Cancer of the lymphoid tissues. In people with AIDS, it commonly affects the B cells.

Lysosomal storage diseases Disorders such as Tay-Sachs disease caused by the absence of lysosomal enzymes. In these disorders, molecules that would normally be degraded by the missing enzymes accumulate in the lysosomes and interfere with cell functioning.

Lysosome An organelle that serves as the principal site of digestion within the cell.

Lysozyme An enzyme present in tears, saliva, and certain other body fluids that kills bacteria by disrupting their cell walls.

M

Macroevolution Large-scale evolutionary changes such as those that might result from long-term changes in the climate or position of the continents. Examples include mass extinctions and the evolution of mammals.

Macromolecule A giant molecule of life such as a nucleic acid, protein, or polysaccharide. A macromolecule is formed by the joining together of smaller molecules.

Macrophage A large phagocytic cell derived from a monocyte that lives in loose connective tissue and engulfs anything detected as foreign.

Magnetic resonance imaging (MRI) A means of visualizing a region of the body, including the brain, in which the picture results from differences in the way the hydrogen nuclei in the water molecules within the tissues vibrate in response to a magnetic field created around the area to be pictured.

Malignant tumor A cancerous tumor. An abnormal mass of tissue that can invade surrounding tissue and spread to multiple locations throughout the body.

Malleus The first of three small bones in the middle ear that transmit information about sound from the eardrum to the inner ear. The malleus is also known as the hammer.

Malnourishment A form of hunger that occurs when the diet is not balanced and the right foods are not eaten.

Mammary glands The milk-producing glands in the breasts.

Mass The measure of how much matter is in an object.

Mast cells Small, mobile connective tissue cells often found near blood vessels. In response to injury, mast cells release histamine, which dilates blood vessels and increases blood flow to an area, and heparin, which prevents blood clotting.

Matrix In connective tissue the matrix is the material that the cells are embedded in. The matrix consists of ground substance, which is made up of protein fibers and noncellular material.

Matter Anything that takes up space and has mass. Matter is made up of atoms.

Mechanical digestion A part of the digestive process that involves physically breaking food into smaller pieces.

Mechanoreceptor A sensory receptor that is specialized to respond to distortions in the receptor itself or in nearby cells. Mechanoreceptors are responsible for the sensations we describe as touch, pressure, hearing, and equilibrium.

Medulla oblongata The part of the brain stem containing reflex centers for some of life's most vital physiological functions: the pace of the basic breathing rhythm, the force and rate of heart contraction, and blood pressure. It connects the spinal cord to the rest of the brain.

Medullary cavity The cavity in the shaft of long bones that is filled with yellow marrow.

Medullary rhythmicity center The region of the brain stem controlling the basic rhythm of breathing.

Meiosis A type of cell division that occurs in the gonads and gives rise to gametes. As a result of two divisions (meiosis I and meiosis II), haploid gametes are produced from diploid germ cells.

Meissner's corpuscles Encapsulated nerve cell endings that are common on the hairless, sensitive areas of the skin, such as the lips, nipples, and fingertips, and tell us exactly where we have been touched.

Melanin A pigment produced by the melanocytes of the skin. There are two forms of melanin: black-to-brown and yellow-to-red.

Melanocytes Spider-shaped cells located at the base of the epidermis that manufacture and store melanin, a pigment involved in skin color and absorption of ultraviolet radiation.

Melanocyte-stimulating hormone (MSH) The anterior pituitary hormone that stimulates melanin production.

Melanoma The least common and most dangerous form of skin cancer. It arises in the melanocytes, the pigment-producing cells of the skin.

Melatonin A hormone secreted by the pineal gland that may influence daily rhythms, fertility, and aging.

Membranous epithelium A type of epithelial tissue that forms linings and coverings. Depending on its location, it may be specialized to either protect, secrete, or absorb.

Memory cell A lymphocyte (B cell or T cell) of the immune system that forms in response to an antigen and that circulates for a long period of time; such cells are able to mount a quick immune response to a subsequent exposure to the same antigen.

Meninges Three protective connective tissue membranes that surround the central nervous system: the dura mater, the pia mater, and the arachnoid.

Meningitis An inflammation of the meninges (protective coverings of the brain and spinal cord).

Menopause The end of a female's reproductive potential when ovulation and menstruation cease.

Menstrual (uterine) cycle The sequence of events that occurs on an approximately 28-day cycle in the uterine lining (endometrium) that involves the thickening of and increased blood supply to the endometrium and the loss of the endometrium as menstrual flow.

Merkel cells Cells of the epidermis found in association with sensory neurons where the epidermis meets the dermis.

Merkel disk The Merkel cell–neuron combination that functions as a sensory receptor for light touch, providing information about objects contacting the skin. It is found on both the hairy and the hairless parts of the skin.

Mesoderm The primary germ layer that gives rise to muscle, bone, connective tissue, and organs such as the heart, kidneys, ovaries, and testes.

Messenger RNA (mRNA) A type of RNA synthesized from and complementary to a region of DNA that attaches to ribosomes in the cytoplasm and specifies the amino acid order in the protein. It carries the DNA instructions for synthesizing a particular protein.

Metabolism The sum of all chemical reactions within the living cells.

Metaphase In mitosis, the phase when the chromosomes, guided by the fibers of the mitotic spindle, form a line at the center of the cell. As a result of this alignment, when the chromosomes split at the centromere, each daughter cell receives one chromatid from each chromosome and thus a complete set of the parent cell's chromosomes.

Metastasize To spread from one part of the body to another part not directly connected to the first part. Cancerous tumors metastasize and form new tumors in distant parts of the body.

MHC markers Molecules on the surface of body cells that label the cell as "self."

Microevolution Changes in populations at the genetic level. The causes include genetic drift, gene flow, natural selection, and mutation.

Microfilament A component of the cytoskeleton made from the globular protein actin. Microfilaments form contractile units in muscle cells and are responsible for amoeboid movement.

Microtubule A component of the cytoskeleton made from the globular protein tubulin. Microtubules are responsible for the movement of cilia and flagella and serve as tracks for the movement of organelles and vesicles.

Microvilli Microscopic cytoplasm-filled extensions of the cell membrane that serve to increase the absorptive surface area of the cell.

Midbrain A region of the brain stem that coordinates reflex responses to auditory and visual stimuli.

Middle ear An air-filled space in the temporal bone that includes the tympanic membrane (eardrum) and three small bones (the malleus, incus, and stapes; sometimes called the hammer, anvil, and stirrup). It serves as an amplifier of sound pressure waves.

Mineralocorticoids Hormones secreted by the adrenal cortex that affect mineral homeostasis and water balance.

Minipill A birth control pill that contains only progesterone.

Mitochondrion (plural, mitochondria) An organelle within which most of cellular respiration occurs in a eukaryotic cell. Cellular respiration is the process by which oxygen and an organic fuel such as glucose are consumed and energy is released and used to form ATP.

Mitosis A type of cell division occurring in somatic cells in which two identical cells, called daughter cells, are generated from a single cell. The original cell first replicates its genetic material and then distributes a complete set of genetic information to each of its daughter cells. Mitosis is usually divided into prophase, metaphase, anaphase, and telophase.

Mitral valve A heart valve located between the left atrium and left ventricle that prevents the backflow of blood from the ventricle to the atrium. It is also called the bicuspid valve or the left atrioventricular (AV) valve.

Molecular clock The idea that there is a constant rate of divergence of macromolecules (such as proteins) from one another. It is based on the notion that single nucleotide changes in DNA (point mutations) and the amino acid changes in proteins that can be produced by some point mutations occur with steady, clocklike regularity. It permits comparison of molecular sequences to estimate the time of separation between species (the more differences in sequence, the more time that has elapsed since the common ancestor).

Molecule A chemical structure composed of atoms held together by covalent bonds.

Monoclonal antibodies Defensive proteins specific for a particular antigen secreted by a clone of genetically identical cells descended from a single cell.

Monocyte The largest white blood cell. Monocytes are active in fighting chronic infections, viruses, and intracellular bacterial infections. A monocyte can transform into a phagocytic macrophage.

Monohybrid cross A genetic cross that considers the inheritance of a single trait from individuals differing in the expression of that trait.

Monomer A small molecule that joins with identical molecules to form a polymer.

Mononucleosis A viral disease caused by the Epstein-Barr virus that results in an elevated level of monocytes in the blood. It causes fatigue and swollen glands, and there is no available treatment.

Monosaccharide The smallest molecular unit of a carbohydrate. Monosaccharides are known as simple sugars.

Monosomy A condition in which there is only one representative of a chromosome instead of two representatives.

Mons veneris A round fleshy prominence over the pubic bone in a female. Part of the female external genitalia.

Morning sickness The nausea and vomiting experienced by some women early in pregnancy. It is not restricted to the morning and may be caused, in part, by high levels of the hormone human chorionic gonadotropin (HCG).

Morphogenesis The development of body form that begins during the third week after fertilization.

Morula A solid ball of 12 or more cells produced by successive divisions of the zygote. The name reflects its resemblance to the fruit of the mulberry tree.

Mosaic evolution The phenomenon whereby various traits evolve at their own rates.

Motor (efferent) neuron A neuron specialized to carry information *away from* the central nervous system to an effector, either a muscle or a gland.

Motor unit A motor neuron and all the muscle fibers (cells) it stimulates.

MRI See magnetic resonance imaging.

mRNA See messenger RNA.

MSH See melanocyte-stimulating hormone.

Mucosa The innermost layer of the gastrointestinal tract. It secretes mucus that helps lubricate the tube, allowing food to slide through easily.

Mucous membranes Sheets of epithelial tissue that line many passageways in the body that open to the exterior. Mucous membranes are specialized to secrete and absorb.

Mucus A sticky secretion that serves to lubricate body parts and trap particles of dirt and other secretions. It also helps protect the stomach from the action of gastric juice.

Multiple alleles Three or more alleles of a particular gene existing in a population. The alleles governing the ABO blood types provide an example.

Multiple sclerosis An autoimmune disease in which the body's own defense mechanisms attack myelin sheaths in the nervous system. As a patch of myelin is repaired, a hardened region called a sclerosis forms.

Multipolar neuron A neuron that has at least three processes, including an axon and a minimum of two dendrites. Most motor neurons and association neurons are multipolar.

Multiregional hypothesis The idea that modern humans evolved independently in several different areas from distinctive local populations of *Homo erectus*. Compare with Out of Africa hypothesis.

Muscle fiber A muscle cell.

Muscle spindles Specialized muscle fibers with sensory nerve cell endings wrapped around them that report to the brain whenever a muscle is stretched.

Muscle tissue Tissue composed of muscle cells that contract when stimulated and passively lengthen to the resting state. There are three types of muscle tissue: skeletal, smooth, and cardiac.

Muscle twitch Contraction of a muscle in response to a single stimulus.

Muscularis The muscular layers of the gastrointestinal tract. These layers help move food through the gastrointestinal system and mix food with digestive secretions.

Mutation A change in the base sequence of the DNA of a gene. A mutation may occur spontaneously or be caused by outside sources, such as radiation or chemical agents.

Myelin sheath An insulating layer around axons that carry nerve impulses over relatively long distances that is composed of multiple wrappings of the plasma membrane of certain glial cells. Outside the brain and spinal cord, Schwann cells form the myelin sheath. The myelin sheath greatly increases the speed at which impulses travel and assists in the repair of damaged axons. The Schwann cells that form the myelin sheath are separated from one another by short regions of exposed axon called nodes of Ranvier.

Myocardial infarction A heart attack. A condition in which a part of the heart muscle dies because of an insufficient blood supply.

Myocardium Cardiac muscle tissue that makes up the bulk of the heart. The contractility of the myocardium is responsible for the heart's pumping action.

Myofibril A rodlike bundle of contractile proteins (myofilaments) found in skeletal and cardiac muscle cells essential to muscle contraction.

Myofilament A contractile protein within muscle cells. There are two types: myosin (thick) filaments and actin (thin) filaments.

Myoglobin An oxygen-binding pigment in muscle fibers.

Myometrium The smooth muscle layer in the wall of the uterus.

Myosin filaments The thick filaments in muscle cells composed of the protein myosin and essential to muscle contraction. A myosin molecule is shaped like a golf club with two heads.

Myosin heads Club-shaped ends of a myosin molecule that bind to actin filaments and can swivel, causing actin filaments to slide past the myosin filaments, which causes muscle contraction. They are also called cross-bridges.

Myxedema A condition characterized by swelling of the facial tissues because of the accumulation of interstitial fluids caused by undersecretion of thyroid hormone.

N

Nasal cavities Two chambers in the nose, separated by the septum.

Nasal conchae The three convoluted bones within each nasal cavity that increase surface area and direct airflow.

Nasal septum A thin partition of cartilage and bone that divides the inside of the nose into two nasal cavities.

Natural childbirth Childbirth without the use of pain-killing drugs.

Natural killer (NK) cells A type of cell in the immune system. These cells, probably lymphocytes, roam the body in search of abnormal cells and quickly kill them.

Natural selection The process by which some individuals live longer and produce more offspring than other individuals because their particular inherited characteristics make them better suited to their local environment.

Nearsightedness Myopia. Nearsightedness is a visual condition in which nearby objects can be seen more clearly than distant objects. Nearsightedness occurs because either the eyeball is elongated or the lens is too thick, causing the image to be focused in front of the retina.

Negative feedback mechanism The homeostatic mechanism in which the outcome of a process feeds back on the system, shutting down the process.

Nephrons Functional units of the kidneys responsible for the formation of urine. These microscopic tubules number 1 million to 2 million per kidney and perform filtration (only certain substances are allowed to pass out of the blood and into the nephron), reabsorption (some useful substances are returned from the nephron to the blood), and secretion (the nephron directly removes wastes and excess materials in the blood and adds them to the filtered fluid that becomes urine).

Nerve A bundle of parallel axons, dendrites, or both from many neurons. A nerve is usually covered with tough connective tissue.

Nervous tissue Tissue consisting of two types of cells, neurons and neuroglia, that make up the brain, spinal cord, and nerves.

Neural tube The embryonic structure that gives rise to the brain and spinal cord.

Neuroglia (neuroglial cells) Cells of the nervous system that support, insulate, and protect nerve cells; also called glial cells.

Neuromuscular junction The area of contact between the terminal end of a motor neuron and the sarcolemma of a skeletal muscle fiber. When an action potential reaches the terminal end of the motor neuron, acetylcholine is released, triggering events that can lead to muscle contraction.

Neurons Nerve cells involved in intercellular communication. A neuron consists of a cell body, dendrites, and an axon. Neurons are excitable cells in the nervous system specialized to generate and transmit electrochemical signals called action potentials or nerve impulses.

Neurotransmitter A chemical released from the axon tip of a neuron that affects the activity of another cell (usually a nerve, muscle, or gland cell) by altering the electrical potential difference across the membrane of the receiving cell.

Neurula The embryo during neurulation, formation of the brain and spinal cord from ectoderm.

Neurulation A series of events during embryonic development when the central nervous system (brain and spinal cord) forms from ectoderm. During this period, the embryo is called a neurula.

Neutrophil A phagocytic white blood cell important in defense against bacteria and removal of cellular debris. Most abundant of white blood cells.

New World monkeys A group of monkeys whose members are arboreal, have nostrils that open to the side, and have a grasping (prehensile) tail. They occur in South and Central America and include spider monkeys, capuchins, and squirrel monkeys.

Niche The role of a species in an ecosystem. The niche includes the habitat, food, nest sites, and so on. It describes how a member of a particular species uses materials in the environment and how it interacts with other organisms.

Nitric oxide A local signaling molecule that dilates blood vessels; also functions as a neurotransmitter.

Nitrification The conversion of ammonia to nitrate (NO_3^-) by nitrifying bacteria living in the soil.

Nitrogen fixation The process of converting nitrogen gas to ammonium (a nitrogen-containing molecule that can be used by living organisms). The process of nitrogen fixation is carried out by nitrogen-fixing bacteria living in nodules on the roots of leguminous plants such as peas and alfalfa.

Node of Ranvier A region of exposed axon between Schwann cells forming a myelin sheath. In myelinated nerves, the impulse jumps from one node of Ranvier to the next, greatly increasing the speed of conduction. This type of transmission is called saltatory conduction.

Nondisjunction Failure of the members of a pair of homologous chromosomes or the sister chromatids to separate during mitosis or meiosis. Nondisjunction results in cells with an abnormal number of chromosomes.

Norepinephrine Noradrenaline. A hormone secreted by the adrenal medulla, along with epinephrine, in response to stress. They initiate the physiological "fight-or-flight" reaction. Norepinephrine is also a neurotransmitter found in both the central and peripheral nervous systems. In the central nervous system, it is important in the regulation of mood, in the pleasure system of the brain, arousal, and dreaming sleep. Norepinephrine is thought to produce an energizing "good" feeling. It is also thought to be essential in hunger, thirst, and sex drive.

Notochord The flexible rod of tissue that develops during gastrulation and signals where the vertebral column will form. The notochord defines the axis of the embryo, gives the embryo some rigidity, and prompts overlying ectoderm to begin formation of the central nervous system. During development, vertebrae form around the notochord. The notochord eventually degenerates, existing only as the pulpy, elastic material in the center of intervertebral disks.

Nuclear envelope The double membrane that surrounds the nucleus.

Nuclear pore An opening in the nuclear envelope that permits communication between the nucleus and the cytoplasm.

Nucleolus A specialized region within the nucleus that forms and disassembles during the course of the cell cycle. It plays a role in the generation of ribosomes, organelles involved in protein synthesis.

Nucleoplasm The chromatin and the aqueous environment within the nucleus.

Nucleotide A subunit of DNA composed of one five-carbon sugar (either ribose or deoxyribose), one phosphate group, and one of five nitrogen-containing bases. Nucleotides are the building blocks of nucleic acids (DNA and RNA).

Nucleus The command center of the cell containing almost all the genetic information.

O

Oil glands Glands associated with the hair follicles that produce sebum. They are also called sebaceous glands.

Old World monkeys A group of monkeys whose members lack a prehensile tail, often having a short tail or none at all, and have nostrils that open downward. Some Old World monkeys are arboreal and some are terrestrial. Examples include baboons and rhesus monkeys.

Olfactory receptor Sensory receptors that respond to odorous molecules; sensory receptors for the sense of smell.

Oligosaccharide A chain of a few monosaccharides (simple sugars) joined together by dehydration synthesis. Disaccharides, formed by the joining of two monosaccharides, are an example.

Omnivore An organism that feeds on a variety of food types, such as plants and animals.

Oocyte A cell whose meiotic divisions will produce an ovum and up to three polar bodies.

Oogenesis The production of ova (eggs), including meiosis and maturation.

Oogonium (plural, oogonia) A germ cell in an ovary that divides, giving rise to oocytes.

Opsin One of several proteins that can be bound to retinal to form the visual pigments in rods and cones.

Optic nerve One of two nerves, one from each eye, responsible for bringing processed electrochemical messages from the retina to the brain for interpretation.

Organ of Corti The spiral organ. The portion of the cochlea in the inner ear that contains receptor cells that sense vibrations caused by sound. It is most directly responsible for the sense of hearing.

Organ A structure composed of two or more different tissues with a specific function.

Organ system A group of organs with a common function.

Organelle A component within a cell that carries out specific functions. Some organelles, such as the nucleus and mitochondria, have membranes while others, such as ribosomes and microtubules, do not.

Origin In reference to a muscle, the end of the muscle that is attached to the bone that remains relatively stationary during a movement.

Osmosis A special case of diffusion in which water moves across the plasma membrane or any other selectively permeable membrane from a region of lower concentration of solute to a region of higher concentration of solute.

Osteoarthritis An inflammation in a joint that is caused by degeneration of the surfaces of the joint caused by wear and tear.

Osteoblast A bone-forming cell.

Osteoclast A large cell responsible for the breakdown and absorption of bone.

Osteocytes Mature bone cells found in lacunae that are arranged in concentric rings around the central canal. Cytoplasmic projections from osteocytes extend tiny channels that connect with other osteocytes.

Osteon The structural unit of compact bone that appears as a series of concentric circles of lacunae. The lacunae contain bone cells around a central canal containing blood vessels and nerves.

Osteoporosis A decrease in bone density that occurs when the destruction of bone outpaces the formation of new bone, causing bone to become thin, brittle, and susceptible to fracture.

OT See oxytocin.

Otoliths Granules of calcium carbonate embedded in gelatinous material in the utricle and saccule of the ear. Otoliths cause the gelatin to slide over and bend sensory hair cells when the head is moved. The bending generates nerve impulses that are sent to the brain for interpretation as the position of the head.

Out of Africa hypothesis The idea that modern humans evolved from *Homo erectus* in Africa and later migrated to Europe, Asia, and Australia. It suggests a single origin for *Homo sapiens*. Compare with multiregional hypothesis.

Outer ear The external appendage on the outside of the head (pinna) and the canal (the external auditory canal) that extends to the eardrum. It functions as the receiver for sound vibrations.

Oval window A membrane-covered opening in the inner ear (cochlea) through which vibrations from the stirrup (stapes) are transmitted to fluid within the cochlea.

Ovarian cycle The sequence of events in the ovary that lead to ovulation. The cycle is approximately 28 days long and is closely coordinated with the menstrual cycle.

Ovary One of the female gonads. The female gonads produce the ova (eggs) and the hormones estrogen and progesterone.

Oviduct One of two tubes that conduct the ova from the ovary to the uterus in the female reproductive system. It is also called a uterine tube or a fallopian tube.

Ovulation The release of the secondary oocyte from the ovary.

Ovum (plural, ova) A mature egg; a large haploid cell that is the female gamete.

Oxygen debt The amount of oxygen required after exercise to oxidize the lactic acid formed during exercise.

Oxyhemoglobin Hemoglobin bound to oxygen.

Oxytocin (OT) The hormone released at the posterior pituitary that stimulates uterine contractions and milk ejection.

P

Pacemaker See sinoatrial (SA) node.

Pacinian corpuscle A large encapsulated nerve cell ending that is located deep within the skin and near body organs that responds when pressure is first applied. It is important in sensing vibration.

Pain receptor A sensory receptor that is specialized to detect the physical or chemical damage to tissues that we sense as pain. Pain receptors are sometimes classified as chemoreceptors, because they often respond to chemicals liberated by damaged tissue, and occasionally as mechanoreceptors, because they are stimulated by physical changes, such as swelling, in the damaged tissue.

Palate The roof of the mouth. The front region of the palate, the hard palate, is reinforced with bone. The tongue pushes against the hard palate while mixing food with saliva. The soft palate is farther to the back of the mouth and consists of only muscle. The soft palate prevents food from entering the nose during swallowing.

Paleoanthropology The scientific study of human origins and evolution.

Pancreas An accessory organ behind the stomach that secretes digestive enzymes, bicarbonate ions to neutralize the acid in chyme, and hormones that regulate blood sugar.

Pancreatic islets Small clusters of endocrine cells in the pancreas; also called islets of Langerhans.

Parasympathetic nervous system The branch of the autonomic nervous system that is active during restful conditions. Its effects generally oppose those of the sympathetic nervous system. The parasympathetic nervous system adjusts bodily functions so that energy is conserved during nonstressful times.

Parathormone See parathyroid hormone.

Parathyroid glands Four small, round masses at the back of the thyroid gland that secrete parathyroid hormone (parathormone).

Parathyroid hormone (PTH) A hormone released from the parathyroid glands that regulates blood calcium levels by stimulating osteoclasts to break down bone. PTH, also called parathormone, is secreted when blood calcium levels are too low.

Parental generation The parents—the individuals in the earliest generation under consideration.

Parkinson's disease A progressive disorder that results from the death of dopamine-producing neurons that lie in the heart of the brain's movement control center, the substantia nigra. Parkinson's disease is characterized by slowed movements, tremors, and muscle rigidity.

Parturition Birth, which usually occurs about 38 weeks after fertilization.

Passive immunity Temporary immune resistance that develops when a person receives antibodies that were produced by another person or animal.

Pathogen A disease-causing organism.

PCR See polymerase chain reaction.

PDD-NOS See pervasive developmental disorder not otherwise specified.

Pectoral girdle The bones that connect the arms to the rib cage. The pectoral girdle is composed of the shoulder blades (scapulae) and the collarbones (clavicles).

Pedigree A chart showing the genetic connections among individuals in an extended family that is often used to trace the expression of a particular trait in that family.

Pelvic girdle The bones that connect the legs to the vertebral column. The pelvic girdle is composed of the paired hipbones.

Pelvic inflammatory disease (PID) A general term for any bacterial infection of a woman's pelvic organs. PID is usually caused by sexually transmitted bacteria, especially those that cause chlamydia and gonorrhea.

Penis The cylindrical external reproductive organ of a male through which most of the urethra extends and that serves to deliver sperm into the female tract during sexual intercourse.

Pepsin A protein-splitting enzyme initially secreted in the stomach in the inactive form of pepsinogen that is activated into pepsin by hydrochloric acid.

Peptic ulcer A local defect in the surface of the stomach or small intestine characterized by dead tissue and inflammation.

Peptide A chain containing only a few amino acids.

Perforin A type of protein released by a natural killer cell that creates numerous pores (holes) in the target cell, making it leaky. Fluid is then drawn into the leaky cell because of the high salt concentration within, and the cell bursts.

Pericardium The fibrous sac enclosing the heart that holds the heart in the center of the chest without hampering its movements.

Perichondrium The layer of dense connective tissue surrounding cartilage that contains blood vessels, which supply the cartilage with nutrients.

Periodontitis An inflammation of the gums and the tissues around the teeth.

Periosteum The membranous covering that nourishes bone.

Peripheral nervous system The part of the nervous system outside the brain and spinal cord. It keeps the central nervous system in continuous contact with almost every part of the body. It is composed of nerves and ganglia. The two branches are the somatic and the autonomic nervous systems.

Peripheral proteins Proteins attached to the inner or outer surface of the plasma membrane.

Peristalsis Rhythmic waves of muscular contraction and relaxation in the walls of hollow tubular organs, such as the digestive organs, that serve to push contents through the tubes.

Peroxisome An enzyme-containing organelle within which chemical reactions occur that generate hydrogen peroxide. Such reactions have diverse functions ranging from the breakdown of fats to the detoxification of poisons and alcohol.

Pervasive developmental disorder not otherwise specified (PDD-NOS) A subthreshold condition used to describe individuals with impaired communication and social interaction or who exhibit stereotyped behavior, but who do not meet the full criteria for autism, Asperger syndrome, or certain psychiatric disorders.

PET scan See positron emission tomography.

pH A measure of hydrogen ion concentration of a solution; values range from 1 to 14 on the pH scale.

pH scale A scale for measuring the concentration of hydrogen ions. The scale ranges from 0 to 14, with a pH of 7 being neutral, a pH of less than 7 being acidic, and a pH of greater than 7, basic.

Phagocytes Scavenger cells specialized to engulf and destroy particulate matter, such as pathogens, damaged tissue, or dead cells.

Phagocytosis The process by which cells such as white blood cells ingest foreign cells or substances by surrounding the foreign material with cell membrane. It is a type of endocytosis.

Pharynx The space shared by the respiratory and digestive systems that is commonly called the throat. The pharynx is a passageway for air, food, and liquid.

Phenotype The observable physical and physiological traits of an individual. Phenotype results from the inherited alleles and their interactions with the environment.

Phospholipid An important component of cell membranes. It has a nonpolar "water-fearing" tail (made up of fatty acids) and a polar "water-loving" head (containing an R group, glycerol, and phosphate).

Photoreceptor A sensory receptor specialized to detect changes in light intensity. Photoreceptors are responsible for the sensation we describe as vision.

Phylogenetic trees Generalized descriptions of the history of life. They depict hypotheses about evolutionary relationships among species or higher taxa.

Physical dependence A condition in which continued use of a drug is needed to maintain normal cell functioning.

Pia mater The innermost layer of the meninges (the connective tissue layers that protect the central nervous system).

PID See pelvic inflammatory disease.

Piloerection Contraction of the arrector pili muscles causing hairs to stand on end and form a layer of insulation.

Pineal gland The gland that produces the hormone melatonin and is located at the center of the brain.

Pinealocyte A cell of the pineal gland that secretes melatonin.

Pinna The visible part of the ear on each side of the head that gathers sound and channels it to the external auditory canal.

Pinocytosis A type of endocytosis in which droplets of fluid and the dissolved substances therein are engulfed by cells.

Pituitary dwarfism A condition caused by insufficient growth hormone during childhood.

Pituitary gland The endocrine organ connected to the hypothalamus by a short stalk. It consists of the anterior and posterior lobes and is also called the hypophysis.

Pituitary portal system The system in which a capillary bed in the hypothalamus connects to veins that lead into a capillary bed in the anterior lobe of the pituitary gland. It allows hormones of the hypothalamus to control the secretion of hormones from the anterior pituitary gland.

Placebo In a controlled experiment to test the effectiveness of a drug, it is a substance that appears to be identical to a drug but has no known effect on the condition for which it is taken.

Placenta previa The condition in which the placenta forms in the lower half of the uterus, entirely or partially covering the cervix. It may cause premature birth or maternal hemorrhage and usually makes vaginal delivery impossible.

Placenta The organ that delivers oxygen and nutrients to the embryo and carries carbon dioxide and wastes away from it. The placenta is also called the afterbirth.

Placental stage The third (and final) stage of true labor. It begins with delivery of the baby and ends when the placenta detaches from the wall of the uterus and is expelled from the mother's body.

Plaque A bumpy layer consisting of smooth muscle cells filled with lipid material, especially cholesterol, that bulges into the channel of an artery and reduces blood flow. Another type of plaque is a buildup of food material and bacteria on teeth that leads to tooth decay.

Plasma A straw-colored liquid that makes up about 55% of blood. It serves as the medium for transporting materials within the blood. Plasma consists of water (91%–93%) with substances dissolved in it (7%–9%).

Plasma cell The effector cell, produced from a B lymphocyte, that secretes antibodies.

Plasma membrane The thin outer boundary of a cell that controls the movement of substances into and out of the cell.

Plasma proteins Proteins dissolved in plasma, including albumins, which are important in water balance between cells and the blood; globulins, which are important in transporting various substances in the blood; and antibodies, which are important in the immune response.

Plasmid A small, circular piece of self-replicating DNA that is separate from the chromosome and found in bacteria. Plasmids are often used as vectors in recombinant DNA research.

Plasmin An enzyme that breaks down fibrin and dissolves blood clots. Plasmin is formed from plasminogen.

Plasminogen A plasma protein. It is the inactive precursor of plasmin.

Platelet A cell fragment of a megakaryocyte that releases substances necessary for blood clotting. It is formed in the red bone marrow from a precursor cell called a megakaryocyte. It is sometimes called a thrombocyte.

Platelet plug A mass of platelets clinging to the protein fiber collagen at a damaged blood vessel to prevent blood loss.

Pleiotropy One gene having many effects.

PMS See premenstrual syndrome.

Point mutation A mutation that involves changes in one or a few nucleotides in DNA.

Polar body Any of three small nonfunctional cells produced during the meiotic divisions of an oocyte. The divisions also produce a mature ovum (egg).

Polygenic inheritance Inheritance in which several independently assorting or loosely linked genes determine the expression of a trait.

Polymer A large molecule formed by the joining together of many smaller molecules of the same general type (monomers).

Polymerase chain reaction (PCR) A technique used to amplify (increase) the quantity of DNA in vitro using primers, DNA polymerase, and nucleotides.

Polypeptide A chain containing 10 or more amino acids.

Polysaccharide A complex carbohydrate formed when large numbers of monosaccharides (most commonly glucose) join together to form a long chain through dehydration synthesis. Most polysaccharides store energy or provide structure.

Polysome A cluster of ribosomes simultaneously translating the same messenger RNA (mRNA) strand.

Pons A part of the brain that connects upper and lower levels of the brain.

Population A group of potentially interacting individuals of the same species living in a distinct geographic area.

Population dynamics Changes in population size over time.

Portal system A system whereby a capillary bed drains to veins that drain to another capillary bed.

Positive feedback mechanism The mechanism by which the outcome of a process feeds back on the system, further stimulating the process.

Positron emission tomography (PET) A method that can be used to measure the activity of various brain regions. The person being scanned is injected with a radioactively labeled nutrient, usually glucose, that is tracked as it flows through the brain. The radioisotope emits positively charged particles, called positrons. When the positrons collide with electrons in the body, gamma rays are released. The gamma rays can be detected and recorded by PET receptors. Computers then use the information to construct a PET scan that shows where the radioisotope is being used in the brain.

Postnatal period The period of development after birth. It includes the stages of infancy, childhood, puberty, adolescence, and adulthood.

Postsynaptic neuron The neuron located after the synapse. The receiving neuron in a synapse. The membrane of the postsynaptic neuron has receptors specific for certain neurotransmitters.

Precapillary sphincter A ringlike muscle that acts as a valve that opens and closes a capillary bed. Contraction of the precapillary sphincter squeezes the capillary shut and directs blood through a thoroughfare channel to the venule. Relaxation of the precapillary sphincter allows blood to flow through the capillary bed.

Pre-embryo The developing human from fertilization through the second week of gestation (the pre-embryonic period).

Pre-embryonic period The period during prenatal development that extends from fertilization through the second week. Cleavage and implantation follow fertilization.

Prefrontal cortex An association area of the cerebral cortex that is important in decision making.

Premature infant A baby born before 37 weeks of gestation.

Premenstrual syndrome (PMS) A collection of uncomfortable symptoms, including irritability, stress, and bloating, that appears 7 to 10 days before a woman's menstrual period and is associated with hormonal cycling.

Prenatal period The period of development before birth. It is further subdivided into the pre-embryonic period (from fertilization through the second week), the embryonic period (from the third through the eighth weeks), and the fetal period (from the ninth week until birth).

Presynaptic neuron The neuron located before the synapse. The sending neuron in a synapse. The neuron in a synapse that releases neurotransmitter from its synaptic knobs into the synaptic cleft.

Primary consumer An herbivore. An animal that eats primary producers (green plants or algae).

Primary germ layers The layers produced by gastrulation from which all tissues and organs form. They are ectoderm, mesoderm, and endoderm.

Primary motor area A band of the frontal lobe of the cerebral cortex that initiates messages that direct voluntary movements.

Primary productivity In ecosystems, the gross primary productivity is the amount of light energy that is converted to chemical energy in the bonds of organic molecules during a given period. The net primary productivity is the amount of productivity left after the photosynthesizers have used some of the energy stored in organic molecules for their own metabolic activities.

Primary response The immune response that occurs during the body's first encounter with a particular antigen.

Primary somatosensory area A band of the parietal lobe of the cerebral cortex to which information is sent from receptors in the skin regarding touch, temperature, and pain and from receptors in the joints and skeletal muscles.

Primary spermatocyte The original large cell that develops from a spermatogonium during sperm development in the seminiferous tubules. It undergoes meiosis and gives rise to secondary spermatocytes.

Primary structure The precise sequence of amino acids of a protein. This sequence, determined by the genes, dictates a protein's structure and function.

Primary succession The sequence of changes in the species making up a community over time that begins in an area where no community previously existed and ends with a climax community.

Primordial germ cells Cells that migrate from the yolk sac of the developing human to the ovaries or testes, where they differentiate into immature cells that will eventually become sperm or oocytes.

PRL See prolactin.

Probe A single-stranded molecule of radioactive DNA or RNA with a sequence of bases complementary to the sequence in the gene of interest that is used to locate the desirable gene.

Prodrome The symptoms that precede recurring outbreaks of a disease such as genital herpes.

Producers In ecosystems, the producers are the organisms that convert energy from the physical environment into chemical energy in the bonds of organic molecules through photosynthesis or chemosynthesis. The producers form the first trophic level.

Product A material at the end of a chemical reaction.

Progesterone A female sex hormone produced by the corpus luteum in the ovary. Progesterone helps prepare the endometrium (lining) of the uterus for pregnancy and maintains the endometrium.

Programmed cell death A genetically programmed series of events that causes a cell to self-destruct.

Prokaryotic cell A cell that lacks a nucleus and other membrane-enclosed organelles. The prokaryotes include bacteria and archaea.

Prolactin (PRL) An anterior pituitary hormone that stimulates the mammary glands to produce milk.

Promoter A specific region on DNA next to the "start" gene that controls the expression of the gene.

Prophase In mitosis, the phase when the chromosomes begin to thicken and shorten, the nucleolus disappears, the nuclear envelope begins to break down, and the mitotic spindle forms in the cytoplasm.

Prostaglandins The lipid molecules found in and released by the plasma membranes of most cells. They are often called local hormones because they exert their effects on the secreting cells themselves or on nearby cells.

Prostate gland An accessory reproductive gland in males that surrounds the urethra as it passes from the bladder. Its secretions contribute to semen and serve to activate the sperm and to counteract the acidity of the female reproductive tract.

Proteins The macromolecules composed of amino acids linked by peptide bonds. The functions of proteins include structural support, transport, movement, and regulation of chemical reactions.

Prothrombin A plasma protein synthesized by the liver that is important in blood clotting. It is converted to an active form (thrombin) by thromboplastin that is released from platelets.

Prothrombin activator A blood protein that converts prothrombin to thrombin as part of the blood-clotting process.

Protozoans A group of single-celled organisms with a well-defined eukaryotic nucleus. Protozoans can cause disease by producing toxins or by releasing enzymes that prevent host cells from functioning normally.

Proximal convoluted tubule The section of the renal tubule where reabsorption and secretion occur.

Pseudopodia The temporary extensions of a cell formed by microfilaments and used when feeding and moving. The name means "false foot."

PTH See parathyroid hormone.

Puberty The stage in postnatal development when secondary sexual characteristics such as pubic and underarm hair develop. This stage usually occurs slightly earlier in girls (from 12 to 15 years of age) than in boys (from 13 to 16 years of age).

Pulmonary arteries Blood vessels that carry blood low in oxygen from the right ventricle to the lungs, where it is oxygenated.

Pulmonary circuit (or circulation) The pathway that transports blood from the right ventricle of the heart to the lungs and back to the left atrium of the heart.

Pulmonary veins Blood vessels that carry oxygenated blood from the lungs to the left atrium of the heart.

Pulp The center of a tooth that contains the tooth's life-support systems.

Pulse The rhythmic expansion of an artery created by the surge of blood pushed along the artery by each contraction of the ventricles of the heart. With each beat of the heart, the wave of expansion begins, moving along the artery at the rate of 6 to 9 meters per second.

Punnett square A diagrammatic method used to determine the probable outcome of a genetic cross. The possible allele combinations in the gametes of one parent are used to label the columns and the possible allele combinations of the other parent are used to label the rows. The alleles of each column and each row are then paired to determine the possible genotypes of the offspring.

Pupil The small hole through the center of the iris through which light passes to enter the eye. The size of the pupil is altered to regulate the amount of light entering the eye.

Purkinje fibers The specialized cardiac muscle cells that deliver an electrical signal from the atrioventricular bundle to the individual heart muscle cells in the ventricles.

Pyelonephritis An infection of the kidneys caused by bacteria.

Pyloric sphincter A ring of muscle between the stomach and small intestine that regulates the emptying of the stomach into the small intestine.

Pyramid of biomass A diagram in which blocks represent the amount of biomass (dry body mass of organisms) available at each trophic (feeding) level.

Pyramid of energy A graphical representation in which blocks represent the decreasing amount of energy available at each trophic (feeding) level.

Pyramid of numbers A graphical representation of the number of individuals at each trophic level.

Pyrogen A fever-producing substance.

Pyruvate The three-carbon compound produced by glycolysis, which is the first phase of cellular respiration.

Q

Quaternary structure The shape of an aggregate protein. It is determined by the mutually attractive forces between the protein's subunits.

R

Radioisotopes Isotopes that are unstable and spontaneously decay, emitting radiation in the form of gamma rays and alpha and beta particles.

RAS See reticular activating system.

RDS See respiratory distress syndrome.

Receptor potential An electrochemical message (a change in the degree of polarization of the membrane) generated in a sensory receptor in response to a stimulus. Receptor potentials vary in magnitude with the strength of the stimulus.

Receptor A protein molecule located in the cytoplasm and on the plasma membrane of cells that is sensitive to chemical messengers.

Recessive allele The allele whose effects are masked in the heterozygous condition. The recessive allele usually produces a nonfunctional protein.

Recombinant DNA Segments of DNA from two sources that have been combined in vitro and transferred to cells in which their information can be expressed.

Recruitment A process of increasing the strength of muscle contraction by increasing the number of motor units being stimulated.

Rectum The final section of the gastrointestinal tract. The rectum receives and temporarily stores the feces.

Red blood cell See erythrocyte.

Red marrow Blood cell–forming connective tissue found in the marrow cavity of certain bones.

Reduction division The first meiotic division (meiosis I) that produces two cells, each of which contains one member of each homologous pair (23 chromosomes with replicates attached in humans).

Referred pain Pain felt at a site other than the area of origin.

Reflex arc A neural pathway consisting of a sensory receptor, a sensory neuron, usually at least one interneuron, a motor neuron, and an effector.

Reflex A simple, stereotyped reaction to a stimulus.

Refractory period The interval following an action potential during which a neuron cannot be stimulated to generate another action potential.

Relaxin The hormone released from the placenta and the ovaries. It initiates labor and facilitates delivery by dilating the cervix and relaxing the ligaments and cartilage of the pubic bones.

Releasing hormone A hormone that stimulates hormone secretion by another gland.

Renal corpuscle The portion of the nephron where fluid is filtered. It consists of a tuft of capillaries, the glomerulus, and a surrounding cuplike structure called Bowman's (glomerular) capsule.

Renal cortex The outer region of the kidney, containing renal columns.

Renal failure A decrease or complete cessation of glomerular filtration.

Renal medulla The inner region of the kidney. It contains cone-shaped structures called renal pyramids.

Renal pelvis The innermost region of the kidney; the chamber within the kidney.

Renal tubule The site of reabsorption and secretion by the nephron. It consists of the proximal convoluted tubule, the loop of Henle, and the distal convoluted tubule.

Renin An enzyme released by cells of the juxtaglomerular apparatus of nephrons. Renin converts angiotensinogen, a protein produced by the liver and found in the plasma, into another protein, angiotensin I. These actions of renin initiate a series of hormonal events that leads to increased reabsorption of sodium and water by the distal convoluted tubules and collecting ducts of nephrons.

Rennin The gastric enzyme that breaks down milk proteins.

Replication Copying from a template, as occurs during the synthesis of new DNA from preexisting DNA.

Repolarization The return of the membrane potential to approximately its resting value. Repolarization of the nerve cell membrane during an action potential occurs because of the outflow of potassium ions.

RER See rough endoplasmic reticulum.

Residual volume The amount of air that remains in the lungs after a maximal exhalation.

Resistance phase The phase of the general adaptation syndrome that follows the alarm reaction. It is characterized by anterior pituitary release of adrenocorticotropic hormone (ACTH), thyroid-stimulating hormone (TSH), and growth hormone (GH) and the sustainment of metabolic demands by the body's fat reserves.

Respiratory distress syndrome (RDS) A condition in newborns caused by an insufficient amount of surfactant, causing the alveoli of the lungs to collapse and thereby making breathing difficult.

Respiratory system The organ system that carries out gas exchange. The respiratory system includes the nose, pharynx, larynx, trachea, bronchi, and lungs.

Resting potential The separation of charge across the plasma membrane of a neuron when the neuron is not transmitting an action potential. It is primarily caused by the unequal distributions of sodium ions, potassium ions, and large negatively charged proteins on either side of the plasma membrane. The resting potential of a neuron is about -70 mV.

Restriction enzyme An enzyme that recognizes a specific sequence of bases in DNA and cuts the DNA into two strands at that sequence. Restriction enzymes are used to prepare DNA containing "sticky ends" during the creation of recombinant DNA. Their natural function in bacteria is to control the replication of viruses that infect the bacteria.

Reticular activating system (RAS) An extensive network of neurons that runs through the medulla and projects to the cerebral cortex. It filters out unimportant sensory information before it reaches the brain and controls changing levels of consciousness.

Reticular fibers Interconnected strands of collagen in certain connective tissues that branch extensively. Networks of reticular fibers support soft tissues, including the liver and spleen.

Retina The light-sensitive innermost layer of the eye containing numerous photoreceptors (rods and cones).

Retinal The light-absorbing portion of pigment molecules in the photoreceptors. Retinal combines with one of four opsins (proteins) to form the light-absorbing pigments in rods and cones.

Retrovirus Any one of the viruses that contain only RNA and carry out transcription from RNA to DNA (reverse transcription).

Rh factor A group of antigens found on the surface of the red blood cells of most people. A person who has these antigens is said to be Rh$^+$. A person who lacks these antigens is Rh$^-$.

Rheumatoid arthritis An inflammation of a joint caused by an autoimmune response. It is marked by inflammation of the synovial membrane and excess synovial fluid accumulation in the joints, causing swelling, pain, and stiffness.

Rhodopsin The light-absorbing pigment in the photoreceptors called rods. Rhodopsin is responsible for black and white vision.

Rhythm method of birth control A method of reducing the risk of pregnancy by avoiding intercourse on all days that might result in sperm and egg meeting.

Ribonucleic acid (RNA) A single-stranded nucleic acid that contains ribose (a five-carbon sugar), phosphate, adenine, uracil, cytosine, or guanine. RNA plays a variety of roles in protein synthesis.

Ribosomal RNA (rRNA) A type of RNA that combines with proteins to form the ribosomes, structures on which protein synthesis occurs. The most abundant form of RNA.

Ribosome The site where protein synthesis begins in a cell. It consists of two subunits, each containing ribosomal RNA and proteins.

RNA (ribonucleic acid) A single-stranded nucleic acid that contains ribose (a five-carbon sugar), phosphate, adenine, uracil, cytosine, or guanine. RNA plays a variety of roles in protein synthesis.

RNA polymerase One of the group of enzymes necessary for the synthesis of RNA from a DNA template. It binds with the promoter on DNA that aligns the appropriate RNA nucleotides and links them together.

Rod One of the photoreceptors containing rhodopsin and responsible for black and white vision. Rods are extremely sensitive to light.

Root The part of a tooth that is below the gum line. It is covered with a calcified, yet living and sensitive, connective tissue called cementum.

Root canal A channel through the root of a tooth that contains the blood vessels and nerves.

Rough endoplasmic reticulum (RER) Endoplasmic reticulum that is studded with ribosomes. It produces membrane.

Round window A membrane-covered opening in the cochlea that serves to relieve the pressure caused by the movements of the oval window.

rRNA See ribosomal RNA.

Rugae Folds in the mucosa of the lining of the empty stomach's walls that can unfold, allowing the stomach to expand as it fills.

S

SAD See seasonal affective disorder.

Salinization An accumulation of salts in soil caused by irrigation over a long period of time that makes the land unusable.

Saliva The secretion from the salivary glands that helps moisten and dissolve food particles in the mouth, facilitating taste and digestion. An enzyme in saliva (salivary amylase) begins the chemical digestion of starch.

Salivary amylase An enzyme in saliva that begins the chemical digestion of starches, breaking them into shorter chains of sugars.

Salivary glands Exocrine glands in the facial region that secrete saliva into the mouth to begin the digestion process.

Saltatory conduction The type of nerve transmission along a myelinated axon in which the nerve impulse jumps from one node of Ranvier to the next. Saltatory conduction greatly increases the speed of nerve conduction.

Sarcomere The smallest contractile unit of a striated or cardiac muscle cell.

Sarcoplasmic reticulum An elaborate form of smooth endoplasmic reticulum found in muscle fibers. The sarcoplasmic reticulum takes up, stores, and releases calcium ions as needed in muscle contraction.

Schizophrenia A mental illness characterized by hallucinations and disordered thoughts and emotions that is caused by excessive activity at dopamine synapses in one part of the brain (the midbrain). As a result, dopamine is no longer in the proper balance with glutamate, a neurotransmitter released by neurons in another brain region (the cerebral cortex).

Schwann cell A type of glial cell in the peripheral nervous system that forms the myelin sheath by wrapping around the axon many times. The myelin sheath insulates axons, increases the speed at which impulses are conducted, and assists in the repair of damaged neurons.

Science A systematic approach to acquiring knowledge through carefully documented investigation and experimentation.

Scientific method A procedure underlying most scientific investigations that involves observation, formulating a hypothesis, making predictions, experimenting to test the predictions, and drawing conclusions. Experimentation usually involves a control group and an experimental group that differ in one or very few factors (variables). New hypotheses may be generated from the results of experimentation.

Sclera The white part of the eye that protects and shapes the eyeball and serves as a site of attachment for muscles that move the eye.

SCN See suprachiasmatic nucleus.

Scrotum A loose fleshy sac containing the testes.

Seasonal affective disorder (SAD) A form of depression associated with winter months when overproduction of melatonin is triggered by short day length.

Sebaceous glands See oil glands.

Sebum An oily substance made of fats, cholesterol, proteins, and salts secreted by the oil glands.

Second messenger A molecule in the cytoplasm of a cell that is activated when a water-soluble hormone binds to a receptor on the surface of the cell. Second messengers influence the activity of enzymes and ultimately the activity of the cell to produce the effect of the hormone.

Secondary consumer A carnivore. An animal that obtains energy by eating other animals.

Secondary oocyte A haploid cell formed by meiotic division of a primary oocyte. It is released from an ovary at ovulation.

Secondary response The immune response during the body's second or subsequent exposures to a particular antigen. The secondary immune response is much quicker than is the primary response because memory cells specific for the antigen are present.

Secondary spermatocyte A haploid cell formed by meiotic division of a primary spermatocyte during sperm development in the seminiferous tubules.

Secondary structure The bending and folding of the chain of amino acids of a protein to produce shapes such as coils, spirals, and pleated sheets. These shapes form as a result of hydrogen bonding between different parts of the polypeptide chain.

Secondary succession The sequence of changes in the species making up a community over time that takes place after some disturbance destroys the existing life. Soil is already present.

Secretin A hormone released by the small intestine that inhibits the secretion of gastric juice and stimulates the release of bicarbonate ions from the pancreas and the production of bile in the liver.

Segregation, law of A genetic principle that states that the alleles for each gene separate (segregate) during meiosis and gamete formation, so half of the gametes bear one allele and the other half bear the other allele.

Selectively permeable A characteristic of the plasma membrane because it permits some substances to move across and denies access to others.

Semen The fluid expelled from the penis during male orgasm. Semen consists of sperm and the secretions of the accessory glands.

Semicircular canals Three canals in each ear that are oriented at right angles to one another and contain sensory receptors that precisely monitor any sudden movement of the head. They detect body position and movement.

Semiconservative replication Replication of DNA in which the two strands of a DNA molecule become separated and each serves as a template for a new double-stranded DNA. Each new double-stranded molecule consists of one new strand and one old strand.

Semilunar valves Heart valves located between each ventricle and its connecting artery that prevent the backflow of blood from the artery to the ventricle. Whereas the cusps of the atrioventricular (AV) valves are flaps of connective tissue, those of the semilunar valves are small pockets of tissue attached to the inner wall of their respective arteries.

Seminal vesicles A pair of male accessory reproductive glands located posterior to the urinary bladder. Their secretions contribute to semen and serve to nourish the sperm cells, reduce the acidity in the vagina, and coagulate sperm.

Seminiferous tubules Coiled tubules within the testes where sperm are produced.

Sensory adaptation A gradual decline in the responsiveness of a sensory receptor that results in a decrease in awareness of the stimulus.

Sensory (afferent) neuron A nerve cell specialized to conduct nerve impulses from the sensory receptors *toward* the central nervous system.

Sensory receptors The structures specialized to respond to changes in their environment (stimuli) by generating electrochemical messages that are eventually converted to nerve impulses if the stimulus is strong enough. The nerve impulses are then conducted to the brain, where they are interpreted to build our perception of the world.

Septum (of heart) A wall that separates the right and left sides of the heart.

SER See smooth endoplasmic reticulum.

Serosa A thin layer of connective tissue that forms the outer layer of the gastrointestinal tract. It secretes a fluid that reduces friction with contacting surfaces.

Serotonin A neurotransmitter in the central nervous system thought to promote a generalized feeling of well-being.

Serous membranes Sheets of epithelial tissue that line the thoracic and abdominal cavities and the organs within them. Serous membranes secrete a fluid that lubricates the organs within these cavities.

Sex chromosomes The X and Y chromosomes. The pair of chromosomes involved in determining gender.

Sex-influenced inheritance An autosomal genetic trait that is expressed differently in males and females, usually because of the presence of sex hormones.

Sex-linked gene A gene located on the X chromosome.

Sexual dimorphism A difference in appearance between males and females within a species.

Short-term memory Memory of new information that lasts for a few seconds or minutes.

Sickle-cell anemia A type of anemia caused by a mutation that results in a change in one amino acid in a globin chain of hemoglobin (the iron-containing protein in red blood cells that transports oxygen). Such a change causes the red blood cell to assume a crescent (sickle) shape when oxygen levels are low. The sickle-shaped cells clog small blood vessels, leading to pain and tissue damage from insufficient oxygen.

Simple diffusion The spontaneous movement of a substance from a region of higher concentration to a region of lower concentration.

Simple epithelial tissue Epithelial tissue with only a single layer of cells.

Simple goiter An enlarged thyroid gland caused by iodine deficiency.

Sinoatrial (SA) node A region of specialized cardiac muscle cells located in the right atrium near the junction of the superior vena cava that sets the pace of the heart rate at about 70 to 80 beats a minute. It is also known as the pacemaker. The SA node sends out an electrical signal that spreads through the muscle cells of the atria, causing them to contract.

Sinuses Large, air-filled spaces in the bones of the face.

Sinusitis Inflammation of the mucous membranes of the sinuses making it difficult for the sinuses to drain their mucous fluid.

Skeletal muscle A contractile tissue. One of three types of muscle in the body. Skeletal muscle cells are cylindrical, have many nuclei, and have stripes (striations). Skeletal muscle provides for conscious, voluntary control over contraction. It attaches to bones and forms the muscles of the body. It is also called striated muscle.

Skeleton A framework of bones and cartilage that functions to support and protect internal organs and to permit body movement.

Sliding filament model A model of the mechanism of muscle contraction in which the myofilaments actin and myosin slide across one another, causing the sarcomere to shorten. When enough sarcomeres shorten, the muscle contracts.

Slow-twitch muscle cells Muscle fibers that are specialized to contract slowly but with incredible endurance when stimulated. They contain an abundant supply of myoglobin and mitochondria and are richly supplied with capillaries. They depend on aerobic pathways to generate adenosine triphosphate (ATP) during muscle contraction.

Small intestine The organ located between the stomach and large intestine responsible for the final digestion and absorption of nutrients.

Smooth endoplasmic reticulum (SER) Endoplasmic reticulum without ribosomes. It produces membrane and detoxifies drugs.

Smooth muscle A contractile tissue characterized by the lack of visible striations and by unconscious control over its contraction. It is found in the walls of blood vessels and airways and in organs such as the stomach, intestines, and bladder.

Sodium-potassium pump A molecular mechanism in a plasma membrane that uses cellular energy in the form of adenosine triphosphate (ATP) to pump ions against their concentration gradients. Typically, each pump ejects three sodium ions from the cell while bringing in two potassium ions.

Soluble fiber A type of dietary fiber that either dissolves or swells in water. It includes the pectins, gums, mucilages, and some hemicelluloses. Soluble fiber has a gummy consistency.

Somatic cells All body cells except for gametes (egg and sperm). Somatic cells contain the diploid number of chromosomes, which in humans is 46.

Somatic nervous system The part of the peripheral nervous system that carries information to and from the central nervous system, resulting in voluntary movement and sensations.

Somites Blocks formed from mesoderm cells of the developing embryo that eventually form skeletal muscles of the neck and trunk, connective tissues, and vertebrae.

Source (donor) DNA DNA containing the "gene of interest" that will be combined with host DNA to form recombinant DNA.

Special senses The sensations of smell, taste, vision, hearing, and the sense of balance or equilibrium.

Speciation The formation of a new species.

Species A population or group of populations whose members are capable of successful interbreeding under natural conditions. Such interbreeding must produce fertile offspring.

Sperm A mature male gamete. A spermatozoon.

Spermatid A haploid cell that is formed by mitotic division of a haploid secondary spermatocyte and that develops into a spermatozoon.

Spermatocyte A cell developed from a spermatogonium during sperm development in the seminiferous tubules.

Spermatogenesis The series of events within the seminiferous tubules that gives rise to physically mature sperm from germ cells. It involves meiosis and maturation.

Spermatogonium (plural, spermatogonia) The undifferentiated male germ cells in the seminiferous tubules that give rise to spermatocytes.

Spermicides A means of contraception that consists of sperm-killing chemicals in some form of a carrier, such as foam, cream, jelly, film, or tablet.

Sphincter A ring of muscle between regions of a system of tubes that controls the flow of materials from one region to another past the sphincter.

Sphygmomanometer A device for measuring blood pressure. A sphygmomanometer consists of an inflatable cuff that wraps around the upper arm attached to a device that can measure the pressure within the cuff.

Spina bifida A birth defect in which the neural tube fails to develop and close properly. The mother's taking vitamins and folic acid before conception appears to reduce the chance of having a baby with spina bifida. Some cases can be improved with surgery.

Spinal cord A tube of neural tissue that is continuous with the medulla at the base of the brain and extends about 45 cm (17 in.) to just below the last rib. It conducts messages between the brain and the rest of the body and serves as a reflex center.

Spinal nerves Thirty-one pairs of nerves that arise from the spinal cord. Each spinal nerve services a specific region of the body. Spinal nerves carry both sensory and motor information.

Spiral organ (of Corti) The portion of the cochlea in the inner ear that contains receptor cells that sense vibrations caused by sound. It is most directly responsible for the sense of hearing.

Spleen The largest lymphoid organ; it contains a reservoir of lymphocytes and removes old or damaged red blood cells from the blood.

Spongy bone The bone formed from a latticework of thin struts of bone with marrow-filled areas between the struts. It is found in the ends of long bones and within the breastbone, pelvis, and bones of the skull. Spongy bone is less dense than compact bone and is made of an irregular network of collagen fibers surrounded by a calcium matrix.

Sprain Damage to a ligament (a strap of connective tissue that holds bones together).

Squamous cell carcinoma The second most common form of skin cancer that arises in the newly formed skin cells as they flatten and move toward the skin surface.

Squamous epithelium A type of epithelial tissue composed of flattened cells. It forms linings and coverings.

Stapes The last of three small bones in the middle ear that transmit information about sound from the eardrum to the inner ear. The stapes is also known as the stirrup.

Starch The storage polysaccharide in plants.

Statistical significance In a scientific experiment, statistical significance is a measure of the probability that the results are due to chance.

Stem cell A type of cell that can give rise to other types of cells.

Steroid A lipid, such as cholesterol, consisting of four carbon rings with functional groups attached.

Steroid hormones A group of closely related hormones chemically derived from cholesterol and secreted primarily by the ovaries, testes, and adrenal glands.

Stimulus Changes in the internal or external environment that a sensory receptor can detect and respond to by generating electrochemical messages.

Stomach A muscular sac that is well designed for the storage of food, the liquefaction of food, and the initial chemical digestion of proteins.

Stratified epithelial tissue Epithelial tissue with several layers of cells.

Strep throat A sore throat that is caused by *Streptococcus* bacteria.

Stress incontinence A mild form of incontinence characterized by the escape of small amounts of urine when sudden increases in abdominal pressure force urine past the external urethral sphincter.

Striated muscle See skeletal muscle.

Stroke A cerebrovascular accident. A condition in which nerve cells die because the blood supply to a region of the brain is shut off, usually because of hemorrhage or atherosclerosis. The extent and location of the mental or physical impairment caused by a stroke depend on the region of the brain involved.

Submucosa The layer of the digestive tract between the mucosa and the muscularis; the submucosa contains blood vessels, lymph vessels, and nerves.

Substrate The material on which an enzyme works.

Succession, ecological The sequence of changes in the species making up a community over time.

Summation (of muscle contraction) A phenomenon that results when a muscle is stimulated to contract before it has time to completely relax from a previous contraction. The response to each stimulation builds on the previous one.

Superovulation The ovulation of several oocytes. It is usually prompted by administration of hormones.

Suppressor T cell A type of T lymphocyte that turns off the immune response when the level of antigen falls by releasing chemicals that dampen the activity of both B cells and T cells.

Suprachiasmatic nucleus (SCN) The region of the brain in the hypothalamus where the "master clock" controlling biological rhythms is believed to reside.

Surface-to-volume ratio The physical relationship that dictates that increases in the volume of a cell occur faster than increases in its surface area. This relationship explains why most cells are small.

Surfactant Phospholipid molecules coating the alveolar surfaces that prevent the alveoli from collapsing.

Survivorship The number of individuals of a group born in the same year that is expected to be alive at any given age. It is one way to represent age-specific mortality.

Suture An immovable joint between the bones of the skull.

Sweat glands The sweat glands of the skin. One type of sweat gland is functional throughout life and releases sweat onto the surface of the skin. Another type releases its secretions into hair follicles and becomes functional at puberty.

Sympathetic nervous system The branch of the autonomic nervous system responsible for the "fight-or-flight" responses that occur during stressful or emergency situations. Its effects are generally opposite to those of the parasympathetic nervous system.

Synapse The site of communication between a neuron and another cell, such as another neuron or a muscle cell.

Synapsis The physical association of homologous pairs of chromosomes that occurs during prophase I of meiosis. The term literally means "bringing together."

Synaptic cleft The gap between two cells forming a synapse, for example, two communicating nerve cells.

Synaptic knob A small bulblike swelling of an axon terminal that releases neurotransmitter. An axon terminal.

Synaptic vesicle A tiny membranous sac containing molecules of a neurotransmitter. Synaptic vesicles are located in the synaptic knobs of axon endings, and they release their contents when an action potential reaches the synaptic knob.

Synergistic muscles Two or more muscles that work together to cause movement in the same direction.

Synovial cavity A fluid-filled space surrounding a synovial joint formed by a double-layered capsule. The fluid within the cavity is called synovial fluid.

Synovial fluid A viscous, clear fluid within a synovial cavity that acts as both a shock absorber and a lubricant between the bones.

Synovial joint A freely movable joint. A synovial joint is surrounded by a fluid-filled cavity. This is the most abundant type of joint in the body.

Synovial membranes Membranes that line the cavities of freely movable joints and secrete a fluid that lubricates the joint.

Syphilis A sexually transmitted disease caused by the bacterium *Treponema pallidum*. If untreated, it can progress through three stages and cause death. The first stage is characterized by a painless craterlike bump called a chancre that forms at the site where the bacterium entered the body.

Systematic biology The discipline that deals with the naming, classification, and evolutionary relationships of organisms. It is also called systematics.

Systemic circuit (or circulation) The pathway of blood from the left ventricle of the heart to the cells of the body and back to the right atrium.

Systole Contraction of the heart. Atrial systole is contraction of the atria. Ventricular systole is contraction of the ventricles.

Systolic pressure The highest pressure in an artery during each heartbeat. The higher of the two numbers in a blood pressure reading. In a typical, healthy adult, the systolic pressure is about 120 mm Hg.

T

T cell See T lymphocyte.

T lymphocyte T cell. A type of white blood cell. Some T lymphocytes attack and destroy cells that are not recognized as belonging in the body, such as an infected cell or a cancerous cell.

T4 cell A helper T cell. The kind of T lymphocyte that serves as the main switch for the entire immune response by presenting the antigen to B cells and by secreting chemicals that stimulate other cells of the immune system.

Tanning The buildup of melanin in the skin in response to ultraviolet (UV) exposure.

Target cell A cell with receptors that recognize and bind a specific hormone.

Taste bud A structure consisting of receptors responsible for the sense of taste surrounded by supporting cells. Taste buds are located primarily on the surface epithelium and certain papillae of the tongue.

Taste hairs Microvilli that project into a pore at the tip of the taste bud that bear the receptors for certain chemicals found in food.

Taxon (plural, taxa) A group under consideration, such as a genus, family, or order.

TB See tuberculosis.

Tectorial membrane A membrane that forms the roof of the organ of Corti (the actual organ of hearing). It projects over and is in contact with the sensory hair cells. Pressure waves caused by sound cause the sensory cells to push against the tectorial membrane and bend, resulting in nerve impulses that are carried to the brain by the auditory nerve.

Telomerase The enzyme that synthesizes telomeres.

Telomere A piece of DNA at the tips of chromosomes that protects the ends of the chromosomes.

Telophase In mitosis, the phase when nuclear envelopes form around the group of chromosomes at each pole, the mitotic spindle is disassembled, and nucleoli reappear. The chromosomes also become less condensed and more threadlike in appearance.

Temporomandibular joint (TMJ) syndrome A group of symptoms including headaches, toothaches, and earaches caused by physical stress on the mandibular joint.

Tendinitis Inflammation of a tendon caused by excessive stress on the tendon.

Tendon A band of connective tissue that connects muscle to bone.

Terminal hair Thick, strong hair found on the scalp, eyebrows, eyelashes, and after puberty, the underarms and pubic area.

Tertiary structure The three-dimensional shape of proteins formed by hydrogen, ionic, and covalent bonds between different side chains.

Testes The male gonads. The male reproductive organs that produce sperm and the hormone testosterone.

Testosterone A sex hormone needed for sperm production and the maintenance of male reproductive structures.

Testosterone is produced primarily by the interstitial cells of the testes.

Tetanus A smooth, sustained contraction of muscle caused when stimuli are delivered in such rapid succession that there is no time for muscle relaxation.

TH See thyroid hormone.

Thalamus A brain structure located below the cerebral hemispheres that is important in sensory experience, motor activity, stimulation of the cerebral cortex, and memory.

Theory A broad-ranging explanation for some aspect of the universe that is consistent with many observations and experiments.

Thermoreceptor A sensory receptor specialized to detect changes in temperature.

Threshold The degree to which the voltage difference across the plasma membrane of a neuron or other excitable cell must change to trigger an action potential.

Thrombin A plasma protein formed from prothrombin by thromboplastin that is important in blood clotting. It converts fibrinogen to fibrin, which forms a web that traps blood cells and forms the clot.

Thrombocyte See platelet.

Thrombus A stationary blood clot that forms in the blood vessels. A thrombus can block blood flow.

Thymopoietin A hormone produced by the thymus gland involved in the maturation of T lymphocytes.

Thymosin A hormone produced by the thymus gland involved in the maturation of T lymphocytes.

Thymus gland A gland located on the top of the heart that secretes the hormones thymopoietin and thymosin. It decreases in size as we age.

Thyroid gland The shield-shaped structure at the front of the neck that synthesizes and secretes thyroid hormone and calcitonin.

Thyroid hormone (TH) A hormone released by the thyroid gland that regulates blood pressure and the body's metabolic rate and production of heat. It also promotes normal development of several organ systems.

Thyroid-stimulating hormone (TSH) The anterior pituitary hormone that acts on the thyroid gland to stimulate the synthesis and release of thyroid hormones.

Tidal volume The amount of air inhaled or exhaled during a normal breath.

Tight junction A type of junction between cells in which the membranes of neighboring cells are attached, forming a seal to prevent fluid from flowing across the epithelium through the minute spaces between adjacent cells.

Tissue A group of cells that work together to perform a common function.

Tolerance A progressive decrease in the effectiveness of a drug with continued use.

Tongue The large skeletal muscle studded with taste buds that aids in speech and eating.

Total lung capacity The total volume of air contained in the lungs after the deepest possible breath. It is calculated by adding the residual volume to the vital capacity.

Trabecula (plural, trabeculae) A supporting bar or strand of spongy bone that forms an internal strut that braces the bone from within.

Trachea The tube that conducts air into the thoracic cavity toward the lungs. The trachea is reinforced with C-shaped rings of cartilage to prevent it from collapsing during inhalation and exhalation.

Trait A phenotypically expressed characteristic.

Transcription The process by which a complementary single-stranded messenger RNA (mRNA) molecule is formed from a single-stranded DNA template. As a result, the information in DNA is transferred to RNA.

Transfer RNA (tRNA) A type of RNA that binds to a specific amino acid and transports it to the appropriate region of messenger RNA (mRNA). Transfer RNA acts as an interpreter between the nucleic acid language of mRNA and the amino acid language of proteins.

Transgenic organism An organism that contains certain genes from another species that code for a desired trait. It can be created, for example, by injecting foreign DNA into an egg cell or an early embryo.

Transition reaction The phase of cellular respiration that follows glycolysis and involves pyruvate reacting with coenzyme A (CoA) in the matrix of the mitochondrion to form acetyl CoA. The acetyl CoA then enters the citric acid cycle.

Translation Protein synthesis. The process of converting the nucleotide language of messenger RNA (mRNA) into the amino acid language of a protein.

Transverse tubules T tubules. The tiny, cylindrical inpocketings of the muscle fiber's plasma membrane that carry nerve impulses to almost every sarcomere.

Tricuspid valve A heart valve located between the right atrium and right ventricle that prevents the backflow of blood from the ventricle to the atrium. It is also called the right atrioventricular (AV) valve.

Triglycerides The lipids composed of one molecule of glycerol and three fatty acids. They are known as fats when solid and oils when liquid.

Trisomy A condition in which there are three representatives of a chromosome instead of only two representatives.

tRNA See transfer RNA.

Trophic level The feeding level of one or more populations in a food web. The producers form the first trophic level. Herbivores, which eat the producers, form the second trophic level. Carnivores that eat herbivores form the third trophic level. Carnivores that eat other carnivores form the fourth trophic level.

Trophoblast A group of cells within the blastocyst that gives rise to the chorion, the extraembryonic membrane that will become part of the placenta.

Tropic hormone A hormone that influences another endocrine gland.

Tropomyosin A protein on the thin (actin) filaments in muscle cells that works with troponin to prevent actin and myosin from binding in the absence of calcium ions.

Troponin A protein on the thin (actin) filaments in muscle cells that works with tropomyosin to prevent actin and myosin from binding in the absence of calcium ions.

TSH See thyroid-stimulating hormone.

Tubal ligation A sterilization procedure in females in which each oviduct is cut and sealed to prevent sperm from reaching the eggs.

Tubal pregnancy An ectopic pregnancy in which the embryo implants in an oviduct. This is the most common type of ectopic pregnancy.

Tuberculosis (TB) A highly contagious disease caused by a rod-shaped bacterium, *Mycobacterium tuberculosis*. TB is spread by coughing.

Tubular reabsorption The process by which useful materials are removed from the filtrate within the renal tubule and returned to the blood.

Tubular secretion The process by which wastes and excess ions that escaped glomerular filtration are removed from the blood and added to the filtrate within the renal tubule.

Tumor A neoplasm. An abnormal growth of cells. A tumor forms from the new growth of tissue in which cell division is uncontrolled and progressive.

Turner syndrome A genetic condition resulting from nondisjunction of the sex chromosomes in which a person has 22 pairs of autosomes and a single, unmatched X chromosome (XO). The person has a female appearance.

Tympanic membrane The eardrum. A membrane that forms the outer boundary of the middle ear and that vibrates in response to sound waves. Vibrations of the tympanic membrane are transferred through the middle ear by three small bones (malleus, incus, and stapes; also known as the hammer, anvil, and stirrup) to the inner ear, where hearing occurs when neural messages are generated in response to the pressure waves caused by the vibrations.

Type 1 diabetes mellitus An autoimmune disorder characterized by abnormally high glucose in the blood due to insufficient production of insulin by cells in the pancreas.

Type 2 diabetes mellitus A condition characterized by a decreased sensitivity to insulin caused by decreased numbers of insulin receptors on target cells.

U

Umbilical cord The ropelike connection between the embryo (and later the fetus) and the placenta. It consists of blood vessels (two umbilical arteries and one umbilical vein) and supporting connective tissue.

Undernourishment Starvation. A form of hunger that occurs when inadequate amounts of food are eaten.

Ureters Tubular organs that carry urine from the kidneys to the urinary bladder.

Urethra The muscular tube that transports urine from the floor of the urinary bladder to the outside of the body. In males, it also conducts sperm from the vas deferens out of the body through the penis.

Urethritis Inflammation of the urethra caused by bacteria.

Urinalysis An analysis of the volume, microorganism content, and physical and chemical properties of urine.

Urinary bladder The muscular organ that temporarily stores urine until it is excreted from the body.

Urinary incontinence Lack of voluntary control over urination. Incontinence is the norm for infants and children younger than 2 or 3 years old, because nervous connections to the external urethral sphincter are incompletely developed. In adults, incontinence may result from damage to the external sphincter (often caused, in men, by surgery on the prostate gland), disease of the urinary bladder, and spinal cord injuries that disrupt the pathways along which travel impulses related to conscious control of urination. In any age group, urinary tract infection can result in incontinence.

Urinary retention The failure to completely or normally expel urine from the bladder. This condition may result from lack of the sensation to urinate, as might occur temporarily after general anesthesia, or from contraction or obstruction of the urethra, a condition caused, in men, by enlargement of the prostate gland. Immediate treatment for retention usually involves use of a urinary catheter to drain urine from the bladder.

Urinary system The system that consists of two kidneys, two ureters, one urinary bladder, and one urethra. Its main function is to regulate the volume, pressure, and composition of the blood.

Urinary tract infection (UTI) An infection caused by bacteria in the urinary system. Most bacteria enter the urinary system by moving up the urethra from outside the body.

Urination The process, involving both involuntary and voluntary actions, by which the urinary bladder is emptied. It is also called voiding or micturition.

Urine The yellowish fluid produced by the kidneys. It contains wastes and excess materials removed from the blood. Urine produced by the kidneys travels down the ureters to the urinary bladder, where it is stored until being excreted from the body through the urethra.

Uterine (menstrual) cycle The sequence of events that occurs on an approximately 28-day cycle in the uterine lining (endometrium) that involves the thickening of and increased blood supply to the endometrium and the loss of the endometrium as menstrual flow.

Uterus A hollow muscular organ in the female reproductive system in which the embryo implants and develops during pregnancy.

UTI See urinary tract infection.

V

Vaccination A procedure that introduces a harmless form of the disease-causing organism into the body to stimulate immune responses against that antigen.

Vagina A muscular tube in the female reproductive system that extends from the uterus to the vulva and serves to receive the penis during sexual intercourse and as the birth canal.

Vaginitis An inflammation of the vagina.

Variable In a controlled experiment, the factor that differs between the control group and experimental groups.

Varicose veins Veins that have become stretched and distended because blood is prevented from flowing freely and so accumulates, or "pools," in the vein. A common cause of varicose veins is weak valves within the veins.

Vas deferens A tubule that conducts sperm from the epididymis to the urethra.

Vasectomy A sterilization procedure in men in which the vas deferens on each side is cut and sealed to prevent sperm from leaving the man's body.

Vasoactive intestinal peptide (VIP) A hormone released by the small intestine into the bloodstream that triggers the small intestine to release intestinal juices.

Vasoconstriction A decrease in the diameter of blood vessels, commonly of the arterioles. Blood flow through the vessel is reduced, and blood pressure rises as a result of vasoconstriction.

Vasodilation An increase in the diameter of blood vessels, commonly of the arterioles. Blood flow through the vessels increases, and blood pressure decreases as a result of vasodilation.

Vasopressin See antidiuretic hormone.

Vector A biological carrier, usually a plasmid or a virus, that ferries the recombinant DNA to the host cell.

Vein A blood vessel formed by the merger of venules that transports blood back toward the heart. Veins have walls that are easily stretched, so they serve as blood reservoirs, holding up to 65% of the body's total blood supply.

Vellus hair Soft, fine hair that persists throughout life covering most of the body surface.

Vena cava One of two large veins that empty oxygen-depleted blood from the body to the right atrium of the heart. The superior vena cava delivers blood from regions above the heart. The inferior vena cava delivers blood from regions below the heart.

Ventilation In respiration, breathing.

Ventral nerve root The portion of a spinal nerve that arises from the front (anterior) side of the spinal cord and contains axons of motor neurons. It joins with the dorsal nerve root to form a single spinal nerve, which passes through the opening between the vertebrae.

Ventricle One of the two lower chambers of the heart that receive blood from the atria. The ventricles function as the main pumps of the heart. The right ventricle pumps blood to the lungs. The left ventricle pumps blood to body tissues.

Ventricular fibrillation Rapid, ineffective contractions of the ventricles of the heart, which render the ventricles useless as pumps and stop circulation.

Venule A small blood vessel that receives blood from the capillaries. Venules merge into larger vessels called veins. The exchange of materials between the blood and tissues across the walls of a venule is minimal.

Vertebra One of a series of joined bones that forms the vertebral column.

Vertebral column The "backbone." It is composed of 26 vertebrae (7 cervical, 12 thoracic, 5 lumbar, 1 sacrum, and 1 coccyx) and associated tissues. The spinal cord passes through a central canal within the vertebrae.

Vesicle A membrane-bound sac formed during endocytosis.

Vestibular apparatus A closed fluid-filled maze of chambers and canals within the inner ear that monitors the movement and position of the head and functions in the sense of balance.

Vestibule A space or cavity at the entrance to a canal. In the inner ear, the vestibule is a structure consisting of the utricle and saccule.

Villi (singular, villus) Small fingerlike projections on the small intestine wall that increase surface area for absorption.

VIP See vasoactive intestinal peptide.

Virus A minute infectious agent that consists of a nucleic acid encased in protein. A virus cannot replicate outside a living host cell.

Vital capacity The maximal amount of air that can be moved into and out of the lungs during forceful breathing.

Vitiligo A condition in which melanocytes disappear from areas of the skin, leaving white patches in their wake.

Vitreous humor The jellylike fluid filling the posterior cavity of the eye between the lens and the retina that helps to keep the eyeball from collapsing and holds the thin retina against the wall of the eye.

Vocal cords Folds of tissue in the larynx that vibrate when air passes through them, producing sound.

Vulva External genitalia of a female that surround the opening of the vagina and urethra.

W

Water footprint A measure of the amount of water used by a person or population for personal use and for the production of and waste removal of products consumed.

Water-soluble hormone A hormone that cannot pass through the plasma membrane on its own, so it influences target cells indirectly, through second messenger systems. Second messenger systems initiate enzyme cascades within the cell that ultimately activate certain enzymes. Water-soluble hormones include protein and peptide hormones, such as those secreted by the pancreas and pituitary gland.

Water-soluble vitamin A vitamin that dissolves in water. Water-soluble vitamins include vitamin C and the various B vitamins.

Werner's syndrome A rare inherited disease characterized by premature aging.

White blood cells See leukocytes.

White matter Regions of the central nervous system that are white owing to the presence of myelinated nerve fibers. White matter is important in neural communication over distances.

X

X-linked genes Genes located on the X chromosome. Most X-linked genes have no corresponding allele on the Y chromosome and will be expressed in a male, and in a female if she is homozygous.

Y

Yellow marrow A connective tissue found in the shaft of long bones that stores fat. It forms from red marrow, and, if the need arises, it can convert back to red marrow and form blood cells.

Yolk sac The extraembryonic membrane that is the primary source of nourishment for embryos in many species of vertebrates. In embryonic humans, however, the yolk sac does not provide nourishment and remains quite small (human embryos receive nutrients from the placenta). In humans, the yolk sac is a site of blood cell formation and contains cells, called primordial germ cells, that migrate to the gonads, where they differentiate into immature cells that will eventually become sperm or oocytes.

Z

Zygote The diploid cell resulting from the joining of an egg nucleus and a sperm nucleus. The first cell of a new individual.

Zygote intrafallopian transfer (ZIFT) A procedure in which zygotes created by the union of egg and sperm in a dish in the laboratory are inserted into the woman's oviducts. Zygotes travel on their own from the oviducts to the uterus.

Credits

Chapter 15 CO15 Getty Images. 15.4 Chris Bjornberg/Photo Researchers. 15.8c WG/SPL/Photo Researchers. 15.9a ISM/Phototake. 15.9b Eye of Science/Photo Researchers. 15.9e Richard Kessel and Randy Kardon/Visuals Unlimited. 15.A E. Walker/SPL/Photo Researchers. 15.13 Martin Rotker/Phototake. 15.15 Lester V. Bergman/Corbis.

Chapter 15a CO15a Superstock. 15a.2bc Rachel Epstein/PhotoEdit. 15a.2bl Felicia Martinez/PhotoEdit. 15a.2br Tom Main/Getty Images. 15a.2tl Dorling Kindersly. 15a.2tr Charles D. Winters/Photo Researchers. 15a.3l Peggy Greb/USDA/Agricultural Research Service. 15a.3r Tony Craddock/Getty Images. 15a.4l Susan C. Bourgoin/Jupiter Images. 15a.4r n/a. 15a.05 center John Heseltine/SPL/Photo Researchers. 15a.05 left Dorling Kindersly. 15a.05 right Maximilian Stock/SPL/Photo Researchers. 15a.09a Associated Press. 15a.09b Associated Press. 15a.09c Jason Merritt/Getty Images. 15a.11 SIPA Press.

Chapter 16 CO16 Erik Isakson/Getty Images. 16.UO1 Ian Hooton/Photo Researchers. 16.05e Randy Kardon & Richard Kessel/Visuals Unlimited. 16.06a Dr. David Furness/Wellcome Trust Medical Photographic Library. 16.Aa Courtesy of Leonard Berlin, Rush North Shore Medical Center Radiology Department, Skokie, IL. 16.Ab Phototake. 16.11 Getty Images. 16.12 Phanie/PictureQuest. 16.14 Will & Deni McIntyre/Photo Researchers. 16.15 Chris Preist/SPL/Photo Researchers. 16.17 Ryan McVay/Getty Images.

Chapter 17 CO17 Judy Goodenough. 17.2 P.M. Motta, K.R. Porrer, and P.M. Andrews/Photo Researchers. 17.3 Ed Reschke/Peter Arnold. 17.4 Juergen Berger, Max Planck Institute/Photo Researchers. 17.8 bottom Gary Martin/Visuals Unlimited. 17.8 top P. Bagavandoss/Photo Researchers. 17.10a Reuters/Corbis. 17.10b Reuters/Corbis. 17.10c Gary Parker/Photo Researchers. 17.10d SUI/Photo Researchers. 17.10e Michael Newman/PhotoEdit. 17.10f Joel Gordon/Joel Gordon Photography.

Chapter 17a CO17a Corbis. 17a.1 bottom Alfred Pasieka/Photo Researchers. 17a.1 center Terry Beveridge/Getty Images. 17a.1 top David M Phillips/Visuals Unlimited. 17a.2 CDC. 17a.4 bottom Science VU/Visuals Unlimited. 17a.4 center Lester V. Bergman/Corbis. 17a.4 top Photo Researchers. 17a.5a National Archives and Records Administration. 17a.5b Mediscan/Visuals Unlimited. 17a.5c Photo Researchers. 17a.6 Photo Researchers. 17a.8 Chris Bjornberg/Photo Researchers.

Chapter 18 CO18 Andersen Ross/Getty Images. 18.1 SPL/Photo Researchers. 18.2a Yorgos Nikas/SPL/Photo Researchers. 18.2b Photo Lennart Nilsson/Albert Bonnier Forlag. 18.2c Claude Edelmann/Photo Researchers. 18.2d Photo Lennart Nilsson/Albert Bonnier Forlag/A CHILD IS BORN, Dell Publishing Company. 18.5a Getty Images. 18.5b Mei-Chuan Jau/Dallas Morning News/Corbis. 18.5c Getty Images. 18.A Hank Morgan/SPL/Photo Researchers. 18.B Brooks Craft/Corbis. 18.15 Knut Mueller/Das Photoarchiv/Peter Arnold. 18.17 Fabio Cardoso/zefa/Corbis. 18.18 George Gobet/Associated Press.

Chapter 18a CO18a Michael Macor/San Francisco Chronicle/Corbis. 18a.1a National Library of Medicine. 18a.1b Universitat Wein. 18a.2a Adalberto Roque/AFP/Getty Images. 18a.2b Karen Pulfer Focht/The Commercial Appeal. 18a.2c Pete Jenkins/Alamy. 18a.3a Mary Pato. 18a.3b Mary Pato. 18a.3c Mary Pato. 18a.4 Wolfgang Flamisch/zefa/Corbis. 18a.5a Pyramid Educational Consultants. 18a.5b Pyramid Educational Consultants. 18a.6 Jose Luis Magana/Associated Press.

Chapter 19 CO19 Gregory Bull/Associated Press. 19.3 left Biophoto Associates / Photo Researchers. 19.3 right Biophoto Associates/Photo Researchers. 19.5 all Ed Reshke/Peter Arnold. 19.6 bottom Centers for Disease Control. 19.7 CNRI/Photo Researchers. 19.12 Judy Goodenough. 19.16 Bernd Wittich/Visuals Unlimited.

Chapter 19a CO19a Masterfile. 19a.3 Pascal Goetgheluck/Photo Researchers. 19a.4 Roslin Institute/Phototake. 19a.7a–c The Lancet, Vol. 364, August 28, 2004, pp 735–736 and 766–770, PH Warnke et al.

Chapter 20 CO20 Darryl Leniuk. 20.2 bottom Bert Krages/Visuals Unlimited. 20.2 bottom left Ali Goldstein/Associated Press. 20.2 bottom right Jeff Scheid/Getty Images. 20.2 center left Superstock. 20.2 center right Getty Images. 20.2 top left Holger Scheibe/Corbis. 20.2 top right Gio Barto/Getty Images. 20.4 left Holger Scheibe/Corbis. 20.4 right Getty Images. 20.9 Hattie Young/SPL/Photo Researchers. 20.10 Radhu Sighet/Landov. 20.12a&b Stanley Flegler/Visuals Unlimited. 20.13 University of Florida. 20.15 left Five P Minus Society. 20.15 right Courtesy of University of Washington Medical Center. 20.16a Visuals Unlimited. 20.16b Wellcome Trust Medical Photographic Library. 20.16c Vince Bucci/Getty Images. 20.UO1 vario images GmbH & Co.KG/Alamy.

Chapter 21 CO21 Andrew Brookes/Corbis. 21.UO2. 21.6 Alfred Pasieka/Photo Researchers. 21.A Orchid Biosciences. 21.16 Science VU/Visuals Unlimited. 21.18 Sean O'Neil/Alamy. 21.20 Michael Stephens/Empics. 21.21 Louis M. Staudt, Molecular Diagnosis of Burkitt's Lymphoma, New England Journal of Medicine, June 8, 2006, Vol. 354 (23), 2431–2442. Page 468 Orchid Cellmark.

Chapter 21a CO21a Ruddy Gold/age footstock. 21a.1 Photo Researchers. 21a.2a Photo Researchers. 21a.2b Dept. of Clinical Cytogenics,Addenbrookes/Photo Researchers. 21a.6 David McCarthy/Photo Researchers. 21a.7 right SUI/Visuals Unlimited. 21a.7right Peter Landsdorp/Visuals Unlimited. 21a.13a ISM/Phototake. 21a.13b BSIP/Photo Researchers. 21a.14 Photolibrary.

Chapter 22 CO22 PCL/Alamy. 22.2 Roger Ressmeyer/Corbis. 22.4 Don Mason/Getty Images. 22.UO1 Kristen Mosher/Danita Delimont. 22.7a Colin Keathes/Dorling Kindersly. 22.7b Ken Lucas/Visuals Unlimited. 22.9a Dr. Philip D. Gingerich. 22.9b Robert Shantz/Alamy. 22.13 Frans Lanting/Minden Pictures. 22.14a Kevin Schafer/Gett Images. 22.14b Mistuaki Iwago/Minden Pictures. 22.14c Fulvio Ambrosi/Bruce Coleman. 22.15a Tom McHugh/Photo Researchers. 22.15b Kennan Ward/Corbis. 22.15c Cyril Ruoso/Peter Arnold. 22.15d Frans Lanting/Minden Pictures. 22.18 John Reader/Photo Researchers. 22.19a Natural History Museum of London. 22.19b Univ. of New Mexico, Albuqurque, Maxwell Museum of Anthropology. 22.20a Natural History Museum of London. 22.20b Volker Steger/Photo Researchers.

Chapter 23 CO23 Michael Quinton/Getty Images. 23.1 NASA. 23.3 bottom Michael Melford/Getty Images. 23.3 center Kim Heacox/Getty Images. 23.3 top Stephen J. Krasemann/DRK Photo. 23.4 Renee Lynn/Corbis. 23.4 third row Doug Sokell/Visuals Unlimited. 23.4 fifth row Michael Schneider/Peter Arnold. 23.4 fourth row Frans Lanting/Minden Pictures. 23.4 left Tom Stack & Associates. 23.4 second row Jake Rajs/Getty Images. 23.4 top Michael Busselle/Getty Images. 23.UO1 Amazon Conservation Team.

Chapter 24 CO24 Jeff Foott/Getty Images. 24.1 Dr. Judy Goodenough. 24.4 Harald Sund/Getty Images. 24.5 Associated Press. 24.7 Mark Boulton/Photo Researchers. 24.8 Paul Edmondson/Getty Images. 24.9a NASA. 24.9b Christopher Pillitz/Getty Images. 24.UO2 Joel W. Rogers/Corbis.

Index

Note: "f" indicates a figure and "t" indicates a table.

A

Abdominal cavity, 79f
ABO blood types, 212–213f
Abstinence, 358
Accommodation, 166
Acetylcholine, 110, 125, 130, 146
Acetylcholinesterase, 125, 130
Acid, 23
Acid rain, 25
Acne, 85
Acquired immunodeficiency disease (AIDS), 370–373
Acromegaly, 189
Acrosome, 348–349, 349f
ACTH, *see* adrenocorticotropic hormone
Actin, 75, 109f–110f
Action potential, 126f–127f
Active immunity, 255–256t
Active site, 32
Active transport, 52, 53f, 54t, 302
Adaptation
    evolutionary, 487
    sensory, 162
Adaptive trait, 4
Addison's disease, 194
Adenosine triphosphate, *see* ATP
ADH, *see* antidiuretic hormone
Adhesion junction, 77f
Adipose tissue, 74f, 75
Adrenal gland, 146, 185f, 194–196, 198
    cortex, 194–196, 198
    medulla, 196, 198
Adrenaline, *see* epinephrine
Adrenocorticotropic hormone (ACTH), 188f, 190
Adult stem cells, 426
Aerobic exercise, 234
Age structure, 524, 525f
Aging, 200, 390–392
Agranulocytes, 207t, 208
AIDS, 370–373
Air pollution, 532
Albinism, 82f, 433, 438
Alcohol, 152–156
Aldosterone, 194, 333–334
Allantois, 381–382
Allele, 432f
Allergies, 258t, 259f
Allometric growth, 385
Alveoli, 277f, 279t, 281f–282
Alzheimer's disease, 130
Amino acid, 29, 31
Amniocentesis, 443, 445f

Amnion, 381
Amphetamine, 158
Ampulla, 176, 177f
Amygdala, 142f
Amyotropic lateral sclerosis (ALS), 122
Anabolic pathway, 63
Anabolic steroid abuse, 117
Anal canal, 295t, 296f, 306
Analogous structure, 492
Anaphase 410
Anaphylactic shock, 259
Androgen, 194, 347
Anemia, 210, 212
Anencephaly, 384
Aneurysm, 222–223
Angina, 235
Angiography, 235, 236f
Angiotensin, 334
Anorexia nervosa, 322
Antagonistic muscles, 107f
Anterior pituitary gland, *see* pituitary gland
Antibiotic resistance, 266, 452–453
Antibiotics, 266
Antibodies, 253f–254t
Antibody-mediated responses, 250–251, 253f–254
Anticodon, 454f
Antidiuretic hormone (ADH), 188f, 190–191, 333
Antigen, 249f, 253f–254
Antihistamines, 259
Anus, 295t, 296f
Aorta, 221f
Aortic bodies, 285f
Apoptosis, 473f
Appendicular skeleton, 96f–97, 99, 101
Aqueous chamber, 165, 166t
Archaea, 4, 47
Areolar connective tissue, 73t, 74f, 75
Arteries, 220–223
Arteriole, 222f, 223, 224f
Arthritis, 103
Artificial insemination, 379
Asbestos, 61–62
Ascaris, 269
Asperger syndrome, *see* autism spectrum disorders
Assisted reproductive techniques (ARTs), 379–380
Association neuron, *see* interneuron
Asthma, 282, 283
Astigmatism, 167t–168f
Atherosclerosis, 227, 234–235f, 314–315
Atom, 15
Atomic number, 16

Atomic weight, 16
ATP (adenosine triphosphate), 34
Atrial natriuretic peptide, 333t, 334
Atrioventricular bundle, 231
Atrioventricular node, 231f
Atrioventricular valves, 226f, 228f
Atrium, 226f
Auditory
    canal, 172f, 174t
    nerve, 173
    tube, 172f–173, 174t
Australopithecus, 495, 498–499, 501f
Autism spectrum disorders
    causes, 400–401
    characterization, 396–397
    diagnosis, 399–400
    prevalence, 396
    prognosis, 402
    symptoms, 397–399
    treatment, 401–402
Autoimmune disorders, 257–258
Autonomic nervous system, 135, 136f, 144–146
Autosomal genes, 442
Autosome, 406
AV node, *see* atrioventricular node
Avian flu, 272, 273
Axial skeleton, 96f–98
Axon, 76, 122f

B

B cells (B lymphocytes), 249, 251t, 252
Bacteria, 4, 244, 264f–266
Balance, 176, 177f
Baldness, 442
Basal body, 62
Basal cell carcinoma, 83f
Basal metabolic rate, 320
Base, 23
Basement membrane, 71
Basilar membrane, 173f
Basophils, 207t
Benign tumor, 470
Bicarbonate ion, 284–285
Bicuspid valve, 228
Bile, 210, 301–302
Bilirubin, 210
Binary fission, 265f
Biodiversity, 512, 518–519
Biofeedback, 198
Biogeochemical cycles, 513f–518
Biogeography, 492
Biological clock, 141
Biological magnification, 511–513
Biomass, 509
Biosphere, 5, 6f, 506